Your Free

Visitor  Discount Card

CARD PICTURE: NATIONAL SEAL SANCTUARY HELSTON CORNWALL

GW00336450

saving you £££'s at Top Attractions around Britain

To use your card simply remove from the page along the perforations and sign your name on the reverse. Your card is now valid to be used at 100's of attractions around Britain. Keep it safe in your purse or wallet.

Look out for the 99/00 symbol under the entries, this means these attractions are offering discounts to holders of the Visitor Discount Card. The discount offer is shown in the entry listing text for example:

Discount Card Offer: Two for the price of one.

To claim your discount* simply show the card when purchasing your entrance tickets.

*Some attractions also require a voucher, these attractions are clearly marked in the guide, in these instances cut out a voucher from the voucher page at the back of the guide, and surrender it at the attraction concerned. Further vouchers are available by sending a s.a.e. to Best Guides. We would always suggest that you take your guide book with you when visiting.

In the unlikely event that you encounter any problems using your card please telephone Best Guides on 0800 316 8900 or write to P O Box 427 Northampton NN2 7YJ or e-mail cards@bestguides.demon.co.uk and we will help

g
BEST GUIDES

Don't lose your place... use our handy page marker ▥▶

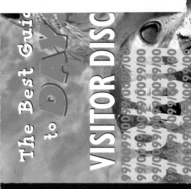

The Best Guide to DAYS OUT

VISITOR DISCOUNT

guide to
attraction
symbols

🚼	Suitable for pushchairs
👶	Mother & baby facilities
♿	Disabled facilities
DISCOUNT 99/00	Visitor Discount Card offer
🐕	No dogs: except guide dogs
🚗	Parking on site
🚗	Parking nearby
£	Charged parking
🧺	Picnic areas
☕	Light refreshments
🍴	Cafè-restaurant
🍷	Licensed cafè-restaurant
🎂	Special events held
�֎	National Trust property
✿	National Trust for Scotland

TO VALIDATE THE CARD PLEASE SIGN YOUR NAME ON THE SIGNATURE PANEL BELOW

Visitor Discount Card
saving you £££'s at Top Attractions around Britain

Below is a selection, from over 350 top attractions around Britain* that appear in our guides at which you can obtain discounts using Best Guides Visitor Discount Card. The full details on all 350+ attractions and the offers they are making can be found in the guides. *If you have purchased a regional guide the details of some of the attractions listed below may not appear in your edition. Your card, however, is still valid at these attractions.*

 English Heritage property

 CADW Welsh Historic

 Historic Scotland

 Guided tours available

 Photography allowed

 Beach / coastal area

 Visa accepted

 Mastercard accepted

 All major cards accepted

 Corporate facilities

 Wedding ceremonies

 Educational packs

 Celebration catering

 Gift shop

 Good weather attraction

 All weather attraction

BEST GUiDES 1999/2000

American Adventure World	Hedingham Castle
Anglesey Sea Zoo	Hergest Croft Gardens
Appuldurombe House	Highland Wildlife Park
Arley Hall & Gardens	Hutton in the Forest
Athelhampton House	Land's End Visitor Centre
Attingham Park	Leighton Buzzard Railway
Bekonscot Model Village	Liverpool FC Tours
Bentley Wildfowl & Museum	London Zoo
Blair Drummond Safari Park	National Maritime Museum
Blickling Hall	National Museum Cardiff
Bramham Park	National Tramway Museum
Brantwood	Peckforton Castle
Brewers Quay	RHS Garden Hyde Hall
Castle Coole	RAF Museum Hendon
Chedder Caves & Gorge	Romney Hythe Railway
Chislehurst Caves	Royal Doulton
Chester Zoo	Ryton Organic Gardens
Cobham Hall	Sainsbury Centre
Cotswold Wildlife Park	Samares Manor
Dalemain House & Gdn	Sherwood Forest Farm Park
Dartington Crystal	Southport Zoo
Dean Forest Railway	Shuttleworth Collection
Deep Sea World	Squerryes Court
Design Museum	Stapeley Water Gardens
Didcot Railway Centre	Staunton Country Park
Drayton Manor Park	Sulgrave Manor
Dreamland Fun Park	The Canterbury Tales
Druidstone Wildlife Park	The Heights of Abraham
Eyam Hall	The Helicopter Museum
Flamingo Land	The Oxford Story
Ford Green Hall	Traquair House
Frontier Land	UK Bungee Club
Granada Studios	WWT Martin Mere

The Best Guide to **DAYS OUT** ever!

Special Events Around Britain 99/2000

This edition published February 1999
Printed and bound in Italy by LegoPrint
Distributed in the UK by Biblios Star Road Partridge Green
West Sussex RH13 8LD T01403 710971
Sales by Best Guides Ltd P O Box 427 Northampton NN2 7YJ England
T 01604 711994 F 01604 722446 e-mail info@bestguides.demon.co.uk
Cover photo credits: Getty Images - National Trust,
English Heritage photographic libraries & various attractions whose
pictures and details are published in the guide
www.bestguides.demon.co.uk www.ukplus.co.uk www.thisislondon.com

BEST GUIDES

GOING OUT Guides for **OUTGOING** People

BEST GU*i*DES CREDITS

Edited by: Alyson Spark
Database Researchers: Debora Stone, Leisa Griggs
Database Programming: David White
Administration: Jayne Moore
Publisher: Martin Spark

INTRODUCTION

Welcome to the 99/2000 Millennium edition of our Special Events guide. We list over 6,000 events for you to choose from. Please remember that many events are dependent on the weather for their success and all dates are subject to change. Please check with the attractions concerned *before* visiting to make sure the event is still on or that the date has not been changed.

Best Guides event listings appear on Internet sites operated in partnership with Associated Newspapers, publishers of the London Evening Standard and the Mail on Sunday, they have been a great success with the **www.thisislondon.com** site being voted Top UK Internet Site 1998. Best Guides listings can now be accessed on the Internet @ www.thisislondon.com under the section London Guide and at **www.ukplus.co.uk** where our complete UK wide information is available. Updated every week they provide an unrivalled source of UK wide 'Days Out' information. We recommend a visit, they are some of the best on the net!

Please mention 'The Best Guide to Days Out ever!' when calling or visiting

MEDIEVAL ARCHER AT WARWICK CASTLE ON ONE OF THEIR POPULAR EVENT DAYS

Regional Breakdown

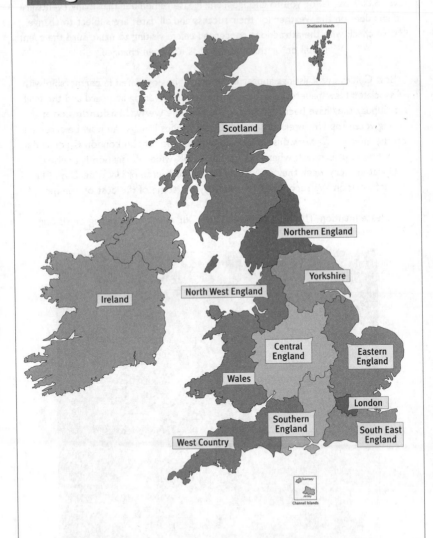

CONTENTS

BEST GUiDES

GOING OUT Guides for **OUTGOING** People

Central England

Including:
- *Derbyshire*
- *Nottinghamshire*
- *Leicestershire*
- *Staffordshire*
- *Shropshire*
- *Hereford*
- *Worcester*
- *West Midlands*
- *Warwickshire*
- *Gloucestershire*
- *Northamptonshire*

Music For All Seasons - Spring
1/3/99
1/3/99
RYTON ORGANIC GARDENS
Tel: 01203 303517
A sequence of music workshops themed on the seasons. Join us for one or more of the days. Open to everyone, including complete beginners! If you play an instrument please bring it along. Listen to seasonal works by the great composers and, using the melodies of the countryside, create your own music. Time: 10.00-16.00.
Gardens

St. David's Day
1/3/99
1/3/99
RYTON ORGANIC GARDENS
Tel: 01203 303517
A celebration of the best of Welsh home cooking in our Restaurant accompanied by lilting music from Wales. Information and bookings on 01203 307142.
Gardens

Free State Room Tours
1/3/99
31/3/99
WARWICK CASTLE
Tel: 01926 406600
Discover the secrets of the Great Hall and State Rooms on the FREE tours every weekday during March
Castles

Jenner Postage Stamp Issue
2/3/99
2/3/99
JENNER MUSEUM
Tel: 01453 810631
Post Office to issue "Jenner" Postage Stamp (First Day Covers from Museum)
Museum- Science

Enabled Day
3/3/99
3/3/99
WOLVERHAMPTON RACECOURSE
Tel: 01902 421421
Racing from Dunstall Park
Racecourses

The Principles of Hedge Laying
4/3/99
4/3/99
RYTON ORGANIC GARDENS
Tel: 01203 303517
A practical course for people with an interest in maintaining hedges. Time: 09.30-dusk. Cost: £38.00.
Gardens

Countdown to the Millennium
5/3/99
6/3/99
ROYAL DOULTON VISITOR CENTRE
Tel: 01782 292434
The first opportunity to see the new Royal Doulton products created to celebrate the new millennium, and the chance to meet the designers and artists
Factory Tours and Shopping

Small Woodland Management of Native Trees

5/3/99
7/3/99
RYTON ORGANIC GARDENS
Tel: 01203 303517
A practical course for people with an interest in maintaining trees, from a small garden to a small woodland. Each day beings at 09.30 and finishes at dusk. Cost: £38.00 per day (attendance on all days is NOT necessary).
Gardens

Staines Crucifixion
6/3/99
COVENTRY CATHEDRAL AND VISITORS CENTRE
Tel: 01203 227597
A performance of this great work by the world-famous Cathedral Choir, to be recorded by BBC Radio 2, call for further information
Cathedrals

BRDC Marshalls's Club Raceday
6/3/99
6/3/99
SILVERSTONE CIRCUIT
Tel: 01327 857271
Circuit: National. Feature: Club Races. Please call for further information
Motor Racing Circuit

Chamber Music Concert: Aurora Wind Ensemble
6/3/99
6/3/99
SULGRAVE MANOR
Tel: 01295 760205
In the Grand Hall. The Aurora Wind Ensemble perform a variety of enjoyable music. Light buffet supper with wine will follow the concert. Commences 19.30. Tickets: £15.00 inclusive of Supper
Historic Houses

National Hunt Racing
6/3/99
6/3/99
WARWICK RACECOURSE
Tel: 01926 491553
Racing from 14.05 with the last race at 17.15
Racecourses

Bavarian Night
6/3/99
6/3/99
WOLVERHAMPTON RACECOURSE
Tel: 01902 421421
Racing on all weather track with Bavarian themed entertainment. Packages available to include racecourse entrance, three course meal, racecard, and dancing to either a live band or disco. Racing from 19.00
Racecourses

Snowdrop Spectacular
6/3/99
7/3/99
HODSOCK PRIORY GARDENS
Tel: 01909 591204
Annual event for early gardeners.
Gardens

Friends of Thomas the Tank Engine

6/3/99 7/3/99	**MIDLAND RAILWAYS CENTRE** Tel: 01773 747674/749788 Featuring "Thomas," the "Fat Controller," "Diesel" and Oswald the talking engine.

Railways Steam/Light

Memorabilia

6/3/99 7/3/99	**NATIONAL EXHIBITION CENTRE** Tel: 0121 780 4141 x2604 Halls 7 & 8. Europe's largest science fiction, film, cult TV, pop and comic collectors' fair. 10.00-17.00. Please telephone Made In Heaven, tel 01899 221622 for further information. Ticket sales NEC Box Office 0121 767 4555

Exhibition Centres

Dance and Music Weekend

6/3/99 7/3/99	**THE COMMANDERY** Tel: 01905 355071 Carolus Terpsichore, a seventeenth century group from Essex invite you to see period dancing and plays. The normal admission charge applies and access is from 10.00-17.00 on Saturday and from 13.30 on Sunday

Historic Buildings

3 of a Kind & 1 Other

6/3/99 28/3/99	**CORINIUM MUSEUM** Tel: 01285 655611 Photography exhibition by local cameramen/women

Museum- Roman

Rosalind Bliss and Tim Clarice

6/3/99 3/4/99	**DERBY MUSEUM AND ART GALLERY** Tel: 01332 716659 An exciting exhibition showing work of two regional artists depicting panoramas on free-standing screens and landscapes paintings on paper.

Museums

World of the Sea Dragons

6/3/99 4/9/99	**DUDLEY MUSEUM AND ART GALLERY** Tel: 01384 815571/815575 Stuning fossils of Jurassic sea monsters and other amazing creatures from prehistoric oceans

Museums

Fabulous Frocks

6/3/99 1/1/00	**PICKFORD'S HOUSE SOCIAL HISTORY MUSEUM** Tel: 01332 255363 Stunning evening dresses and accessories

Historic Houses

Drayton Croft Mallory Trophy

7/3/99 7/3/99	**MALLORY PARK** Tel: 01455 842931/2/3 Roadstocks, solo and sidecar, 125-1300cc. £7.00. Please telephone 0930 55 59 60 for further information.

Motor Racing Circuit

MATHS

8/3/99 12/3/99	**NATIONAL WATERWAYS MUSEUM** Tel: 01452 318054 An education special for schools only, please call for details

Museum- Waterways

Schools' Wildlife Week

8/3/99 12/3/99	**RYTON ORGANIC GARDENS** Tel: 01203 303517 A chance for schools within travelling distance to find out about: bio-diversity; life in the soil; mini-beasts, etc. Activities linked to the National Curriculum. Cost: £2.50 per child.

Gardens

Women's Health Course

10/3/99 10/3/99	**RYTON ORGANIC GARDENS** Tel: 01203 303517 The course covers three main areas - helping to prevent breast cancer and osteoporosis plus the natural menopause. Time: 10.00-16.00.

Gardens

National Hunt Racing

11/3/99 11/3/99	**TOWCESTER RACECOURSE** Tel: 01327 353414 Come and enjoy a day at Towcester Races and experience the true atmosphere of Jump Racing with birch flying, jockeys urging and hooves pounding

Racecourses

Crufts '99

11/3/99 14/3/99	**NATIONAL EXHIBITION CENTRE** Tel: 0121 780 4141 x2604 Halls 1-5. Please telephone The Kennel Club, tel 0171 493 7838 for further information. Ticket sales NEC Box Office 0121 767 4850. For Main Ring Tickets contact The Kennel Club 0171 518 1012

Exhibition Centres

Sewing For Pleasure

11/3/99 14/3/99	**NATIONAL EXHIBITION CENTRE** Tel: 0121 780 4141 x2604 Hall 12. Learn, buy and be inspired by over 200 stands covering a wide variety of fabrics, embroidery, quilting and other textile crafts. Please telephone International Craft & Hobby Fair Ltd, tel 01425 272711 for further information

Exhibition Centres

Hobbycrafts

Further more detailed information on the attractions listed can be found in Best Guides *Visitor Attractions* Guide under the classifications shown

11/3/99 14/3/99	**NATIONAL EXHIBITION CENTRE** Tel: 0121 780 4141 x2604 Hall 11. Whatever your craft come and see over 100 exhibitors demonstrating, teaching and selling supplies for over 30 different hobbies. Please telephone International Craft & Hobby Fair Exhibitors, tel 01425 272711. Ticket sales NEC Box Office 0121 767 4552 *Exhibition Centres*

SET '99 Water - Always on Tap

12/3/99 21/3/99	**LICHFIELD HERITAGE CENTRE** Tel: 01543 256611 A hands on exhibition jointly presented by the Environment Agency, Seven Trent and South Staffordshire Water for National Science Week *Exhibition Centres*

Mystery Day

13/3/99 13/3/99	**MANOR HOUSE MUSEUM** Tel: 01536 534219 What will be happening? Call in and find out. *Museum- Local History*

Goods Gala

13/3/99 13/3/99	**MIDLAND RAILWAYS CENTRE** Tel: 01773 747674/749788 Demonstrating goods trains with shunting - pick-up goods trains, a 1920's goods train and a 1950's train. *Railways Steam/Light*

Smoking Fish/Meat/Cheese

13/3/99 13/3/99	**RYTON ORGANIC GARDENS** Tel: 01203 303517 Introducing the traditional skills and knowledge of preserving food by smoking. Time: 09.30-17.00. Cost: £48.00 includes all materials and ingredients. *Gardens*

Parapsychology with Kathy Stranks

13/3/99 13/3/99	**RYTON ORGANIC GARDENS** Tel: 01203 303517 An introductory course about psychic events and how to recognise them. Learn about the processes involved when a psychic event occurs, from coincidence to premonition. Time: 10.00-16.00. *Gardens*

SUNBAC Raceday

13/3/99 13/3/99	**SILVERSTONE CIRCUIT** Tel: 01327 857271 Circuit: National. Feature: Club Races. Please call for further information *Motor Racing Circuit*

Lincoln Trial

13/3/99 13/3/99	**WOLVERHAMPTON RACECOURSE** Tel: 01902 421421 One of the major meetings of the racing calendar at Dunstall Park. Racing from 14.00 *Racecourses*

Miniatura - International Dolls' House Show

13/3/99 14/3/99	**NATIONAL EXHIBITION CENTRE** Tel: 0121 780 4141 x2604 Halls 10 & 10/11 Link. Sat: advance booking only, Sun: open to all. Please telephone Miniatura, tel 0121 749 7330 for further information. Ticket sales NEC Box Office 0121 767 4800 *Exhibition Centres*

Craft Fair

13/3/99 14/3/99	**RAGLEY HALL** Tel: 01789 762090 Wonderful variety of handcrafted goods direct from the artist/craftsmen who have made them *Historic Houses & Gardens*

Activity Weekend

13/3/99 14/3/99	**WALSALL LEATHER MUSEUM** Tel: 01922 721153 There will be something for everyone this weekend as we offer you the opportunity to try your hand at a whole host of leathercraft activities. Whether it be carving, braiding, stitching or skiving, we guarantee it'll be lots of fun. 10.30-15.00. Admission Free *Museum- Industrial*

States of Matter: Solids, Liquids and Gases

13/3/99 21/3/99	**JODRELL BANK SCIENCE CENTRE, PLANETARIUM AND ARBORETUM** Tel: 01477 571339 The Williams Science teams popular demonstrations and activities which explore molecules, temperature and gases. There are lots of pops and bangs as well as clouds of vapour! Two sessions per day. Please ring 01477 571339 ext 221 for timings *Science Centres*

Science Week

13/3/99 21/3/99	**QUARRY BANK MILL AND STYAL COUNTRY PARK** Tel: 01625 527468 'Waterforce' Schools Competition 15th-19th, Family Drop-ins 13th/14th & 20th/21st. Further information including times, prices and bookings available by calling Quarry bank Mill *Heritage Centres*

Pleasure Learning
13/3/99 NATIONAL WATERWAYS MUSEUM
18/12/99 Tel: 01452 318054
Tugs course, have you ever wanted to pilot a tug on the canal, here's your opportunity to learn. One day course available each month, call for course details
Museum- Waterways

Mothers' Day Special
14/3/99 BLACK COUNTRY LIVING MUSEUM
14/3/99 Tel: 0121 557 9643 info
Bring your mum for a day out, she'll come in free! Mums can discover how Victorian mothers coped without modern conveniences such as washing machines and microwaves. Lunches available in the Stables Restaurant - pre-book by phoning 0121 557 4341
Industrial Heritage

Mothering Sunday Lunches
14/3/99 CALKE ABBEY
14/3/99 Tel: 01332 863822
Bring your Mother along for a special lunch, pre-booking only, call to book
Historic Houses & Gardens

Mother's Day
14/3/99 CLUMBER PARK
14/3/99 Tel: 01909 476592
Bring your Mother along for a slap-up lunch at Clumber Restaurant. Two sittings. Book early, Catering Manager: 01909 484122
Historic Houses & Gardens

Spring Cup
14/3/99 MALLORY PARK
14/3/99 Tel: 01455 842931/2/3
Club motorcycle racing with races for solo and sidecar machinery. £7.00. Please telephone 0930 55 59 60 for further information.
Motor Racing Circuit

Mothers Day Sunday
14/3/99 MIDLAND RAILWAYS CENTRE
14/3/99 Tel: 01773 747674/749788
Lunch on a steam train.
Railways Steam/Light

Mothering Sunday
14/3/99 NATIONAL WATERWAYS MUSEUM
14/3/99 Tel: 01452 318054
OK Dads, if you have forgotten Mothering Sunday, why not bring here along for a special treat! Call for details
Museum- Waterways

Mother's Day Special

NORTHAMPTON AND LAMPORT RAILWAY
14/3/99 Tel: 01604 847318
14/3/99 All day long, Mother's, Grandmother's & if you have one Great Grandmother's can travel for free, so long as your a mum it's no charge
Railways Steam/Light

Mothers Day
14/3/99 RYTON ORGANIC GARDENS
14/3/99 Tel: 01203 303517
Bring Mum for a special lunch in our Restaurant this Mothering Sunday. Booking essential on 01203 307142.
Gardens

Gardeners Day
14/3/99 SULGRAVE MANOR
14/3/99 Tel: 01295 760205
Demonstrations, plant sleas, exhibitions and displays. Usual opening times. A£4.50 C£2.25
Historic Houses

Mothers Day
14/3/99 THE BASS MUSEUM
14/3/99 Tel: 01283 511000
Treat mother on her special day. £9.95 inc., 4 course meal, entertainment and a gift for Mum. Bookings only, contact Hospitality Manager on 01283 513514
Breweries

Steeplechase Meeting
15/3/99 STRATFORD-ON-AVON RACECOURSE
15/3/99 Tel: 01789 267949/269411
Enjoy a day at the races
Racecourses

VIKINGS
15/3/99 NATIONAL WATERWAYS MUSEUM
19/3/99 Tel: 01452 318054
An education special for schools only, please call for details
Museum- Waterways

Careers Live 1999
16/3/99 NATIONAL EXHIBITION CENTRE
17/3/99 Tel: 0121 780 4141 x2604
Hall 18. Please telephone Jarvis Exhibitions Ltd, tel 0181 464 4129 for further information
Exhibition Centres

The National Hunt Festival
16/3/99 CHELTENHAM RACECOURSE
18/3/99 Tel: 01242 513014
The 20 races offer well in excess of £1million prize money and attract the finest horses from all over Britain, Ireland and France. For these 3 dramatic days, the elegant Spa town of Cheltenham plays host to visitors from all over the world, drawn to celebrate

Further more detailed information on the attractions listed can be found in Best Guides *Visitor Attractions* Guide under the classifications shown

the annual Olympics of steeplechasing. Gates open 10.30, first race 14.00. There is plenty to see and do before the racing with trade stands, bands and paddock interviews. Crowd levels for each of the 3 days will be strictly limited with Thursday - Cheltenham God Cup Day being "all ticket" therefore early booking is advised

Racecourses

St. Patrick's Day
17/3/99 RYTON ORGANIC GARDENS
17/3/99 Tel: 01203 303517
Join in the crack! A celebration of Irish cuisine in our Restaurant. Information and bookings on 01203 307142.

Gardens

Volpon (or The Fox)
17/3/99 ROYAL SHAKESPEARE COMPANY
9/10/99 Tel: 01789 296655
Performed at the Swan Theatre. Director: Lindsay Posner, Designer: Joanna Parker, Lighting: Peter Mumford. Arguably the greatest satire on man's lust for wealth. Prices vary from: £5.00-£36.00. Booking from 30th Jan 99

Arts & Entertainment

The Individual Homes, Home Building & Renovating Show
18/3/99 NATIONAL EXHIBITION CENTRE
21/3/99 Tel: 0121 780 4141 x2604
Hall 10 & 10/11 Link. Please telephone Centaur Communications Ltd, tel 01527 834438 for further information

Exhibition Centres

Mail Order Live 1999
19/3/99 NATIONAL EXHIBITION CENTRE
21/3/99 Tel: 0121 780 4141 x2604
Hall 12. This is a new show. Please telephone Berber Events Ltd, tel 0181 871 9977 for further information

Exhibition Centres

Murder Mystery
20/3/99 BADDESLEY CLINTON HOUSE
20/3/99 Tel: 01564 783294
Marmion's Moated Manor Murder Mystery, commences 19.30, tickets £30.00 call for booking details

Historic Houses & Gardens

Greeting Cards
20/3/99 BILSTON CRAFT GALLERY AND MUSEUM
20/3/99 Tel: 01902 409143
Children's art workshop making greeting cards. Time: 10.30-12.00. Cost: Free. Booking essential

Art Galleries

Tales in the Woods

20/3/99 CLUMBER PARK
20/3/99 Tel: 01909 476592
A family walk with stories, led by Warden Nigel Dorrington. Meet: 10.00, Conservation Centre. A£1.50 C£0.75. Cost: A£1.50 C£0.75. Booking essential

Historic Houses & Gardens

Mamod Model Day
20/3/99 NATIONAL WATERWAYS MUSEUM
20/3/99 Tel: 01452 318054
Perfect pieces of engineering in miniature with rod's and pistons turning. Fun for all the family

Museum- Waterways

Peterborough Motor Club Raceday
20/3/99 SILVERSTONE CIRCUIT
20/3/99 Tel: 01327 857271
Circuit: National. Feature: Club Races. Please call for further information

Motor Racing Circuit

Diesel & Steam Weekend
20/3/99 MIDLAND RAILWAYS CENTRE
21/3/99 Tel: 01773 747674/749788
With both steam and diesel locomotives and passenger trains.

Railways Steam/Light

Record & CD Collectors' Fair
20/3/99 NATIONAL EXHIBITION CENTRE
21/3/99 Tel: 0121 780 4141 x2604
Pavilion. Please telephone P & J Promotions, tel 01273 463017 for further information

Exhibition Centres

Exhibition - A Big Hand For
20/3/99 NOTTINGHAM CASTLE MUSEUM AND ART GALLERY
11/4/99 Tel: 0115 915 3700
Paintings, photography and 3-D work by regional artists

Castles

Lambing
20/3/99 COTSWOLD FARM PARK
25/4/99 Tel: 01451 850307
Newborn lambs, maybe even watch one being born. Experienced shepherds on hand to answer your questions

Farm Parks

Arturo Di Stafano: Strands
20/3/99 DJANOGLY ART GALLERY
2/5/99 Tel: 0115 951 3192
Scenes from the artist's own life - real or imagined - are played out against a series of London settings in oil paintings which combine intensely personal imagery with a belief in the values of craftsmanship and tradition.

Art Galleries

John Lill

21/3/99   CASTLE THEATRE

21/3/99   Tel: 01933 270007 Box Office

John Lill, internationally renowned piano virtuoso, returns giving a master's touch to Beethoven's most famous piano concerto, The Emperor. Also included is Strong on Oaks, Strong on the Causes of Oaks by Michael Nyman (composer of the film soundtrack to The Piano), a very approachable suite of lively music and Mendelssohn's Scottish Symphony, composed after a holiday in the Highlands. Performance Time: 19.30

Arts & Entertainment

British Formula 3

21/3/99   DONINGTON PARK

21/3/99   Tel: 01332 810048

Bridgestone Ginetta, Porsche Classic Touring Cars, BMW Four Plus, Formula Europa.

Motor Racing Circuit

Super Coupes

21/3/99   MALLORY PARK

21/3/99   Tel: 01455 842931/2/3

ARP F3, Ford S, Ford Si, Tomcat/Vento, Mighty Minis, Radical Sportscars, SoM. £8.00. Please telephone 0930 55 59 60 for further information.

Motor Racing Circuit

SCIENCE

22/3/99   NATIONAL WATERWAYS MUSEUM

26/3/99   Tel: 01452 318054

An education special for schools only, please call for details

Museum- Waterways

National Hunt Racing

24/3/99   TOWCESTER RACECOURSE

24/3/99   Tel: 01327 353414

Come and enjoy a day at Towcester Races and experience the true atmosphere of Jump Racing with birch flying, jockeys urging and hooves pounding

Racecourses

SET Week '99

24/3/99   ALTON TOWERS

26/3/99   Tel: 0990 204060 24hr

Available for school parties only. Gareth Jones, the children's TV presenter, hosts three days of science fun and lectures on the park. School children can take part in testing out scientific theories such as gravity and speeds by riding and viewing rides - and it's all part of the National Curriculum! Call for details

Theme Parks

A Midsummer Night's Dream

25/3/99   ROYAL SHAKESPEARE COMPANY

9/10/99   Tel: 01789 296655

Performed at the Royal Shakespeare Theatre. Director: Michael Boyd, Designer: Tom Piper, Lighting: Chris Davey. A dream wood outside Athens - for lovers, fairies and mechanicals. Prices vary from: £5.00-£39.00. Booking from 30th Jan 99

Arts & Entertainment

Making Real Bread

26/3/99   RYTON ORGANIC GARDENS

26/3/99   Tel: 01203 303517

Make a wide range of interesting and wholesome breads, and understand the principles of doughs, ensuring consistent and high quality results. Time: 09.30-17.00. Cost: £38.00 includes all materials and ingredients.

Gardens

Adult Rag Rug Workshop

27/3/99   BILSTON CRAFT GALLERY AND MUSEUM

27/3/99   Tel: 01902 409143

Learn how to make traditional rag rugs. time: 10.00-16.00. Cost: £10.00. Booking essential

Art Galleries

Demonstration

27/3/99   BILSTON CRAFT GALLERY AND MUSEUM

27/3/99   Tel: 01902 409143

Sugar craft and Easter decoration demonstration. Time: 14.00. Cost: Free

Art Galleries

Music Recital

27/3/99   SUDBURY HALL AND THE MUSEUM OF CHILDHOOD, THE NATIONAL TRUST

27/3/99   Tel: 01283 585305

Baroque music recital and supper featuring Equinox Strings. Time: 19.30. Tickets: £17.00

Country Estates

Mixed Meeting

27/3/99   WARWICK RACECOURSE

27/3/99   Tel: 01926 491553

Irish Theme Day with Flat and Jump racing. First race 14.10, last race 17.20

Racecourses

Spring Diesel Gala

27/3/99   MIDLAND RAILWAYS CENTRE

28/3/99   Tel: 01773 747674/749788

Featuring as many our fleet of 25 mainline diesel locos in action as possible.

Railways Steam/Light

Memorabilia

27/3/99   NATIONAL EXHIBITION CENTRE

28/3/99   Tel: 0121 780 4141 x2604

Hall 17. Europe's largest science fiction,

Further more detailed information on the attractions listed can be found in Best Guides *Visitor Attractions* Guide under the classifications shown

film, cult TV, pop and comic collectors fair. Times: 10.00-17.00. Please telephone: Made in Heaven, 01899 221622 for further information

Exhibition Centres

New Artists and Crafts Exhibition

27/3/99
28/3/99

RAGLEY HALL

Tel: 01789 762090

Please telephone for further information

Historic Houses & Gardens

Spring Lambs

27/3/99
28/3/99

SHUGBOROUGH ESTATE

Tel: 01889 881388

Meet all the new arrivals and take time to cuddle the baby lambs down at Shugborough Park Farm. A£4.00 Reduced £3.00 Family Ticket £10.00

Historic Houses & Gardens

Microprose Silverstone Spring Trophy

27/3/99
28/3/99

SILVERSTONE CIRCUIT

Tel: 01327 857271

Circuit: International. Feature: British F3, GT etc. Please call for further information

Motor Racing Circuit

Easter Eggstravaganza

27/3/99
11/4/99

BLACK COUNTRY LIVING MUSEUM

Tel: 0121 557 9643 info

A fortnight of activities including egg painting, traditional street games and the Mystery Objects Trail

Industrial Heritage

Cromwell's Times, 400 Years On

27/3/99
15/5/99

GLOUCESTER FOLK MUSEUM

Tel: 01452 526467

Celebrates quartercentenary of Cromwell's birth. Includes blackjacks, bottles, wassail cups and bowls, embroidery, slipware, Bellamurè jugs, Charles I letters and arms and armour

Museum- Local History

Exhibition - Travelling Companions

27/3/99
23/5/99

NOTTINGHAM CASTLE MUSEUM AND ART GALLERY

Tel: 0115 915 3700

Two impressionist paintings by Seurat and Monet from the National Gallery shown alongside works from the museum's own collection including Bonington and Braque

Castles

W. J. Bassett-Lowkw A Model World

27/3/99
6/6/99

NORTHAMPTON CENTRAL MUSEUM AND ART GALLERY

Tel: 01604 238548

Design, architecture and model engineering - featuring 78 Derngate

Art Galleries

Pleasure Learning Course

27/3/99
26/6/99

NATIONAL WATERWAYS MUSEUM

Tel: 01452 318054

Learn the trade of the Blacksmith. One day courses for all would be Blacksmiths, call for details

Museum- Waterways

On Your Bike

28/3/99
28/3/99

CLUMBER PARK

Tel: 01909 476592

A guided cycle ride - exploring Clumber's cycle trails - 13 miles. Cycle hire available. Time: 14.30-16.30. Cost: £1.50 - own bike, £3.00 with cycle hire. Booking essential

Historic Houses & Gardens

Great Club Motorsport

28/3/99
28/3/99

MALLORY PARK

Tel: 01455 842931/2/3

Sports 2000, FV. RoS, Stock Hatch, Caterham. £8.00. Please telephone 0930 55 59 60 for further information.

Motor Racing Circuit

Gloucester Boat and Watersports Jumble

28/3/99
28/3/99

NATIONAL WATERWAYS MUSEUM

Tel: 01452 318054

1000's of new and used bargains!! 200 stalls. Boats, dinghies, canoes, sailboards, engines, outboards, chandlery, fishing tackle, tools, electrics, clothing, diving equipment, trailers, accessories, rope, paint and miscellany. Everything the professional or beginner needs for offshore, river, canal or lake at prices and discounts that defy competition. Admission A£2.50 (including free admission to the museum), accompanied C£Free. Stalls: covered £26.00 uncovered £22.00

Museum- Waterways

Holy Week

28/3/99
4/4/99

LICHFIELD CATHEDRAL

Tel: 01543 306240

Special services throughout the week leading up to Easter Day

Cathedrals

Children's Activity Days

30/3/99
31/3/99

CLUMBER PARK

Tel: 01909 476592

Are you wild about wildlife and crazy about Clumber? Two days of workshops, games and outdoor activities for children between 8-11 years. Cost: £10.00 per day. Family rates available. Booking essential

Historic Houses & Gardens

Easter Eggstravaganza
30/3/99 MIDLAND RAILWAYS CENTRE
11/4/99 Tel: 01773 747674/749788
All our usual attractions and a children's treasure hunt.

Railways Steam/Light

Fun Art Workshops
1/4/99 MANSFIELD MUSEUM AND ART GALLERY
13/4/99 Tel: 01623 463088
Dates: 1st, 8th & 13th April. Art workshops for 5-15 year old. Please contact the museum for further information

Museum- Local History

Gloucestershire Society of Botanical Illustrator's Annual Exhibition
1/4/99 CORINIUM MUSEUM
18/4/99 Tel: 01285 655611
This exhibition features the work of amateur and professional botanical illustrators. The GSBI actively seeks to encourage people to take up the art of Botanical Illustration and members of the society will be present during the exhibition. This exhibition will have works for sale

Museum- Roman

Spokes, Spanners and Sparkplugs
1/4/99 COTSWOLD HERITAGE CENTRE
25/4/99 Tel: 01451 860715
In the Cell Block Gallery. An exhibition by the Cotswold Section of the Vintage Motorcycle Club of motorbikes and associated objects

Heritage Centres

Sculpture in the Wilderness
1/4/99 THE FERRERS CENTRE FOR ARTS AND
30/4/99 CRAFTS
Tel: 01332 865408
Students of Loughborough University of Art & Design will build sculptural pieces within the woods here at Staunton Harold. Around 25 students will each build a sculptural work from wind blown and found organic material which over several months will decompose. For further information please call Jeremy Gossington on 01332 865408

Craft Galleries

Easter Egg Hunt
2/4/99 ILAM PARK
2/4/99 Tel: 01335 350245/350503
Easter Egg Hunt with a difference - family fun finding hidden eggs. Other activities during the day also. C£1.50. Time: 11.00-14.00

Country Parks

Bunnykins Celebration
2/4/99 ROYAL DOULTON VISITOR CENTRE
3/4/99 Tel: 01782 292434
A celebration of the 65th anniversary of Royal Doulton Bunnykins, the world's favourite nurseryware, and now a collectable figure range

Factory Tours and Shopping

Easter in the Forest
2/4/99 DEAN HERITAGE CENTRE
5/4/99 Tel: 01594 822170
Celebrate Spring with 'Signs of Spring' woodland walks, children's activities, Easter Egg Hunt, spinning demonstrations and an animal corner.

Heritage Centres

Easter Egg Hunt
2/4/99 HAWKSTONE PARK
5/4/99 Tel: 01939 200300
Search for the clues to find an egg, great fun for all the family

Parks

Easter Fair and Living Van Rally
2/4/99 IRONBRIDGE GORGE MUSEUMS
5/4/99 Tel: 01952 432166
The Gypsy Caravans will be clustered around the Fun Fair whilst the occupants demonstrate flower making and tell fortunes or simply show off the interior of their van. Children will enjoy following the animal trail and meeting donkeys, goats, Easter chicks, pigs, horses etc. and listening to a story teller who will tell stores that hold you spell bound. Normal admission price

Museum- Industrial

Ross-on-Wye Real Ale Festival 1999
2/4/99 ROSS-ON-WYE REAL ALE FESTIVAL 1999
5/4/99 Tel: 01989 562765
Excellent ales, great food, live music every evening.

Festivals

Easter Customs and Traditions
2/4/99 SULGRAVE MANOR
5/4/99 Tel: 01295 760205
The Tudor Lord of the Manor and his Cook tell of the Easter customs through the ages. The house is beautifully decorated with spring flowers. Usual opening times A£4.50 C£2.25

Historic Houses

Easter Steam Weekend
2/4/99 THE BASS MUSEUM
5/4/99 Tel: 01283 511000
A three day festival of nostalgia and steam with working engines from all over the country, with side stalls and

Further more detailed information on the attractions listed can be found in Best Guides *Visitor Attractions* Guide under the classifications shown

demonstrations

Breweries

Easter Encampment
2/4/99 THE COMMANDERY
5/4/99 Tel: 01905 355071
The Commandery's fearsome fighting force, the Worcester Militia will be establishing a seventeenth century camp in the grounds and recreating period life in the Commandery House. The normal admission charge applies and access is from 10.00-17.00 on Fri, Sat & Mon and from 13.30-17.30 on Sun

Historic Buildings

The Easter Siege
2/4/99 WARWICK CASTLE
5/4/99 Tel: 01926 406600
The Castle is under siege - mediaeval style. With a stunning display of falconry, there is plenty to celebrate this Easter Weekend.

Castles

Drawn to the Park
2/4/99 CLUMBER PARK
7/4/99 Tel: 01909 476592
Enjoy expert tuition from artist Duncan Wood of the New English School of Drawing. Come for one day or receive a discount by booking all six days. Beginners and experienced artists welcome. Cost: £27.00 per day. Booking essential. Time: 10.00-16.30. To book call Lynn Mowbray 01909 486411

Historic Houses & Gardens

The Marsh Mallow/Pasta Experience
2/4/99 JODRELL BANK SCIENCE CENTRE, PLANETARIUM AND ARBORETUM
7/4/99 Tel: 01477 571339
The Williams Science teams popular demonstrations and activities which explore the structure of matter return to challenge, fascinate and delight visitors. No extra charge but numbers are limited by the space available for each session

Science Centres

House Opens
3/4/99 RAGLEY HALL
3/4/99 Tel: 01789 762090
Please telephone for further information

Historic Houses & Gardens

Easter Eggstravaganza
3/4/99 LYME PARK
4/4/99 Tel: 01663 766492
Family fun. Easter egg hunt, decorate the Easter egg, Easter bonnet and bonnet making etc.

Historic Houses

Avoncroft Easter Fair
3/4/99 AVONCROFT MUSEUM OF HISTORIC BUILDINGS
5/4/99 Tel: 01527 831363
Avoncroft comes alive with steam engines, rides craft fair and fun for all

Museum- Local History

Craft Fair
3/4/99 GAWSWORTH HALL
5/4/99 Tel: 01260 223456
Exhibitors from all over the country, displaying the finest examples of British craftmanship

Historic Houses

Easter Egg Weekend
3/4/99 NORTHAMPTON AND LAMPORT RAILWAY
5/4/99 Tel: 01604 847318
Steam ride through the countryside. Fun for all the family. Children receive a creme egg. 11.30-16.45, 20min journey

Railways Steam/Light

Thunderball
3/4/99 SANTA POD RACEWAY
5/4/99 Tel: 01234 782828
Drag racing action from some of the wildest cars and bikes including Top Alcohol and 200mph Pro Modified Doorslammers

Motor Sports

Easter Races
3/4/99 TOWCESTER RACECOURSE
5/4/99 Tel: 01327 353414
To celebrate the anniversary of the Empress of Austria's first visit to Easton Neston in 1876 the 'Knights of Arkley' will provide a feast of medieval pageantry with spectacular jousting displays, skill at arms, tilting at rings and fighting on foot with swords and battleaxes. This extremely colourful and entertaining spectacle together with a traditional hand turned Fun Fair is great fun for all the family

Racecourses

Easter Holiday Activities
3/4/99 NATIONAL WATERWAYS MUSEUM
11/4/99 Tel: 01452 318054
Oooh, there's so much to do we just do not have the space to fit it all in, but it will be great for all the family

Museum- Waterways

Cheltenham Schools Art
3/4/99 CHELTENHAM ART GALLERY AND MUSEUM
24/4/99 Tel: 01242 237431
Annual blast of energy and colour from the young artists who attend Cheltenham schools

Museum- Art

Easter Egg Hunt
4/4/99 BADDESLEY CLINTON HOUSE
4/4/99 Tel: 01564 783294
Children's Easter Egg Hunt with quiz around the grounds offering a chocolate reward. 12.00 onwards, £1.50 per child (tickets on gate)
Historic Houses & Gardens

Vintage Motorcycle Racing & Displays
4/4/99 MALLORY PARK
4/4/99 Tel: 01455 842931/2/3
Sidecars and three-wheelers. £8.00. Please telephone 0930 55 59 60 for further information.
Motor Racing Circuit

Easter Egg Hunt
4/4/99 SNIBSTON DISCOVERY PARK
4/4/99 Tel: 01530 510851
Hunt for the clues hidden around the museum, solve the riddle and win a Cadbury's Creme Egg! Free gallery paying visitors. 11.00-17.00. Suitable for all ages
Industrial Heritage

Medieval Music
4/4/99 BOLSOVER CASTLE
5/4/99 Tel: 01246 823349
Come and listen to the lovely music with Trevor James. A£3.10 C£1.60 Concessions£2.30
Castles

Civil War Encampment
4/4/99 BOSCOBEL HOUSE
5/4/99 Tel: 01902 850244
17th-century re-enactment by The Siege Group. A£4.00 C£2.00 Concessions£3.00
Historic Houses

Easter Bunny Hunt
4/4/99 BROADFIELD HOUSE GLASS MUSEUM
5/4/99 Tel: 01384 812745
Two family fun days with things to make, quizzes, demonstrations and our ever-popular bunny hunt
Museum- Glass

Auto Trader British Touring Cars
4/4/99 DONINGTON PARK
5/4/99 Tel: 01332 810048
Formula Vauxhall Junior, Vauxhall Vectra SRi V6, Slick 50 Formula Ford, Ford Credit Fiesta, Formula Renault Sport, Renault Spider Cup.
Motor Racing Circuit

Medieval Entertainers & Music - Heuristics & Hautbois

4/4/99 GOODRICH CASTLE
5/4/99 Tel: 01600 890538
Lively medieval music played by a costumed duo. From 12.00. A£3.50 C£1.80 Concessions£2.60. EH Members Free
Castles

Victorian Easter Bank Holiday
4/4/99 HOLDENBY HOUSE, GARDENS AND FALCONRY CENTRE
5/4/99 Tel: 01604 770074
Celebrate Easter the Victorian way with Carriage rides; House tours (Monday only), Victorian games; Teas in the Victorian tearoom; Crafts; Easter Egg Hunt; Easter Bunny and much more
Historic Houses & Gardens

Looking Up
4/4/99 JODRELL BANK SCIENCE CENTRE, PLANETARIUM AND ARBORETUM
5/4/99 Tel: 01477 571339
Members of Macclesfield Astronomical Society will be enthusing visitors with their interest in astronomy through a display of telescopes, live observations of sunspots (weather permitting) and computer programmes
Science Centres

Saxon / Viking Battle
4/4/99 KENILWORTH CASTLE
5/4/99 Tel: 01926 852078
Come and watch a re-enactment battle performed by Regia Anglorium. A£4.00 C£2.00 Concessions£3.00
Castles

Easter Re-Opening Extravaganza
4/4/99 MIDDLETON HALL
5/4/99 Tel: 01827 283095
Easter time celebrations and seasonal entertainment for all the family. Sun: 14.00-17.00, Mon: 11.00-17.00. A£2.50 C£1.50
Historic Houses & Gardens

Easter Egg Hunt
4/4/99 OLD DAIRY FARM CENTRE
5/4/99 Tel: 01327 340525
A fun time for the children finding the eggs which are hidden around the farm. 11.00-17.00
Farms

Restaurant Open for Easter Lunch
4/4/99 RYTON ORGANIC GARDENS
5/4/99 Tel: 01203 303517
Special celebration lunches available in the Restaurant. Booking essential on 01203 307142.
Gardens

Family Entertainers - Labyrinth

Further more detailed information on the attractions listed can be found in Best Guides *Visitor Attractions* Guide under the classifications shown

Productions
STOKESAY CASTLE
4/4/99
5/4/99
Tel: 01588 672544
Games, have-a-go archery, costumes for children to try on and talks on weaponry. From 12.00. A£3.50 C£1.80 Concessions£2.60. EH Members Free
Castles

Easter Sunday and Monday Egg Hunts
SUDELEY CASTLE AND GARDENS
4/4/99
5/4/99
Tel: 01242 602308
Easter Sunday: Chocolate Easter Egg Hunt for children, Easter Monday: Sarah Faberge Egg Treasure Hunt for adults
Castles

Midlands Festival Of Transport
WESTON PARK
4/4/99
5/4/99
Tel: 01952 850207
A fine collection of vintage and classic vehicles. Arena displays, good all round Family Entertainment
Historic Houses & Gardens

Lambing Time
BENTLEY FIELDS OPEN FARM
4/4/99
9/4/99
Tel: 01335 330240
Rare and commercial sheep lambing
Farms

Easter Treasure Hunt
SHERWOOD FOREST FARM PARK
4/4/99
4/5/99
Tel: 01623 823558
Family fun looking for answers among the many animal friends
Farm Parks

Cruise Season
NATIONAL WATERWAYS MUSEUM
4/4/99
3/10/99
Tel: 01452 318054
Call us for a list of the: All Day Cruises, Lunchtime Cruises (11.00-14.00), Tea Cruises (15.00-17.00), Sunset Cruises (19.00-22.00), BBQ Cruises (19.30-23.30) and Disco Cruises (20.00-Midnight)
Museum- Waterways

Easter Monday
BLACK COUNTRY LIVING MUSEUM
5/4/99
5/4/99
Tel: 0121 557 9643 info
Bring a painted egg and join in the egg rolling competition, or a bonnet for the Easter Bonnet Parade. Spectators welcome! Visitors who wear a bonnet they have decorated and children who bring painted eggs will have free entry to the Museum on the day
Industrial Heritage

Basketmaking Demonstration

COTSWOLD HERITAGE CENTRE
5/4/99
5/4/99
Tel: 01451 860715
In the Cell Block Gallery. Norah Kennedy will be demonstrating this traditional craft
Heritage Centres

Eurocar Raceday
MALLORY PARK
5/4/99
5/4/99
Tel: 01455 842931/2/3
Opening round of the 1999 championship, plus Super Classic FF, Honda SC. £10.00. Please telephone 0930 55 59 60 for further information.
Motor Racing Circuit

Easter Egg Treasure Hunt
ROCKINGHAM CASTLE
5/4/99
5/4/99
Tel: 01536 770240
A treasure hunt for Easter Eggs around the extensive gardens and grounds of Rockingham Castle, designed to offer a suitably themed activity for the younger members of the family - both in age or attitude! No extra charge
Castles

Clowning Capers
SNIBSTON DISCOVERY PARK
5/4/99
5/4/99
Tel: 01530 510851
Displays of clowning with activities, clown film shows in the Century Theatre and a magic car! No additional charge to museum paying visitors. Time: 11.00-17.00. Family fun for all ages
Industrial Heritage

Easter Family Fun Day
WALSALL LEATHER MUSEUM
5/4/99
5/4/99
Tel: 01922 721153
Positively an extravaganza of fun and mayhem for all the family. Come and help us celebrate with quizzes, competitions and entertainers galore. And what's more, it's all free! 10.30-16.00
Museum- Industrial

Bank Holiday Meeting
WARWICK RACECOURSE
5/4/99
5/4/99
Tel: 01926 491553
A family fun day with children's entertainment and a creche available. First Flat race at 14.30, last race 17.20
Racecourses

Traditional Activities
QUARRY BANK MILL AND STYAL COUNTRY PARK
6/4/99
11/4/99
Tel: 01625 527468
Traditional activites at the Apprentice House. Further information including times, prices and bookings available by calling Quarry bank Mill

Heritage Centres

Children's Half Term Workshop: Mad Hatters

7/4/99
8/4/99 · WALSALL LEATHER MUSEUM

Tel: 01922 721153

Make yourself an extraordinary Easter hat that's sure to turn a few heads. All you need to bring with you is your imagination - the wilder the better! 10.00-12.30 & 13.30-16.00. £1.00 per session (payable in advance). Suitable for ages 8-12. Booking essential (from 9 Mar)

Museum- Industrial

Don Carlos

7/4/99
7/10/99 · ROYAL SHAKESPEARE COMPANY

Tel: 01789 296655

Performed at The Other Place. Cast Includes: Marquis of Posa: Ray Fearnon, Don Carlos: Rupert Penry-Jones, The Inquisitor: John Rogan, King Philip: John Woodvine. Spain 1568. A passionate high tragedy. Power, freedom, idealism, betrayal and ultimately murder. Prices vary from: £10.00-£20.00. Booking from 30th Jan 99

Arts & Entertainment

Fruity Pictures

8/4/99
8/4/99 · BILSTON CRAFT GALLERY AND MUSEUM

Tel: 01902 409143

Children's art workshop making pictures from real fruit and vegetables. Time: 10.30-12.00 & 13.30-15.00. Cost: £2.00. Booking essential

Art Galleries

BBC Match Of The Day Live

8/4/99
11/4/99 · NATIONAL EXHIBITION CENTRE

Tel: 0121 780 4141 x2604

Halls 6-8 & 20. Please telephone BBC Haymarket Exhibitions Ltd, tel 0121 780 4141 for further information. Ticket sales NEC Box Office 0121 767 4144

Exhibition Centres

The NEC Antiques For Everyone Fair

8/4/99
11/4/99 · NATIONAL EXHIBITION CENTRE

Tel: 0121 780 4141 x2604

Hall 5. A major event featuring 600 dealers exhibiting in a two-section event based on the highly successful NEC August Fair. 200 dealers offer antiques and fine art datelined to 1914 in plush, stand-fitted Section One; 400 dealers occupy unit-displays in Section Two, showing all things antique and collectable made prior to 1940. An enormous range of very fine quality antiques and collectibles for every pocket with prices from less than £10 to over £100,000.

Please telephone BBC Haymarket Exhibitions Ltd, tel 0171 402 2555 for further information. Ticket sales NEC Box Office 0121 767 4789

Exhibition Centres

Cheltenham International Jazz Festival 1999

9/4/99 · CHELTENHAM INTERNATIONAL JAZZ FESTIVAL 1999

11/4/99 · Tel: 01242 227979 Box Office

Jazz of all kinds from around the world including blues, R'N'B, contemporary, Be Bop and Avant Garde. Good eating and many free events. Big headliners and lots of new bands.. Prices: A£5.00-£18.00, C&Concessions (25% discount on standby). Tickets available from Box Office: 01242 227979

Festivals

Bike 1999

9/4/99 · NATIONAL EXHIBITION CENTRE

11/4/99 · Tel: 0121 780 4141 x2604

Halls to be confirmed. Please telephone Future Publishing Ltd, tel 01225 442244 for further information

Exhibition Centres

Angling

9/4/99 · NATIONAL EXHIBITION CENTRE

11/4/99 · Tel: 0121 780 4141 x2604

Hall 1. Please telephone Consumer Exhibitions Ltd, tel 0181 948 1666 for further information. Ticket sales NEC Box Office 0121 767 4030

Exhibition Centres

Othello

9/4/99 · ROYAL SHAKESPEARE COMPANY

7/10/99 · Tel: 01789 296655

Performed at the Royal Shakespeare Theatre. Director: Michael Attenborough, Designer: Robert Jones, Lighting: Peter Mumford. Festering sexual jealousy and racial conflict. Playing in the RST for the first time since 1985. Prices vary from: £5.00-£39.00. Booking from 30th Jan 99

Arts & Entertainment

The Family Reunion

9/4/99 · ROYAL SHAKESPEARE COMPANY

7/10/99 · Tel: 01789 296655

Performed at the Swan Theatre. Cast Includes: Dr Warburton: Richard Cordery, Ivy: Cherry Morris, Violet: Bridget Turner, Amy: Margaret Tyzack, Mary: Zoe Waites. A Country house murder mystery. A drama of sin, redemption and the burden of responsibility written by the 20th century's greatest verse playwright and inspired by The Oresteia. Prices vary from: £5.00-£36.00. Booking from 30th Jan 99

Arts & Entertainment

Step into Spring
10/4/99 CLUMBER PARK
10/4/99 Tel: 01909 476592
Meet a tree, create smelly potions, unlock the magic of the woods on a family walk with a difference. Cost: A£1.50 C£0.75. Booking essential

Historic Houses & Gardens

Let's Go Make a Kite!
10/4/99 MANOR HOUSE MUSEUM
10/4/99 Tel: 01536 534219
Kite making for all, visiting children are welcome to join us in a kite making session. 10.00-16.00

Museum- Local History

Chamber Music Concert: Western Wynde
10/4/99 SULGRAVE MANOR
10/4/99 Tel: 01295 760205
In the Grand Hall. Western Wynde in a dazzling programme of instrumental and vocal music from Mediaeval times to present day. Light buffet supper with wine will follow the concert. Commences 19.30. Tickets: £15.00 inclusive of Supper

Historic Houses

Sporting Heroes
10/4/99 WOLVERHAMPTON RACECOURSE
10/4/99 Tel: 01902 421421
Evening Racing from Dunstall Park

Racecourses

Chronicles of Narnia Weekend
10/4/99 HAWKSTONE PARK
11/4/99 Tel: 01939 200300
For all fans of the C S Lewis books. Why not relive the BBC television series, as filmed in the park. Call for further details

Parks

Toy & Train Collectors Fair
10/4/99 NATIONAL EXHIBITION CENTRE
11/4/99 Tel: 0121 780 4141 x2604
Hall 17. Please telephone John Webb of D & J Fairs, tel 01526 398198 for further information

Exhibition Centres

Gamkeepers Fair
10/4/99 SHUGBOROUGH ESTATE
11/4/99 Tel: 01889 881388
Official BASC Annual Country Fair. Competitions, falconry, displays and clay shoots. Over 100 stalls with something for all the family. Separate charge for the

event

Historic Houses & Gardens

Tudor Life
10/4/99 THE COMMANDERY
11/4/99 Tel: 01905 355071
The Tudor and Stuart Society re-create life in a Tudor household. Highlights will include cookery techniques and what the Tudors did on those long television free evenings

Historic Buildings

Spring Craft Fair
10/4/99 WALSALL LEATHER MUSEUM
11/4/99 Tel: 01922 721153
Don't worry if you missed our spectacular Christmas Craft Emporium, because we'll be ready to offer you a fresh selection of hand-crafted goodies to welcome in the Spring. Don't miss this opportunity for a browse and to catch up with what local craftspeople are up to in 1999! 10.00-17.00. Admission Free

Museum- Industrial

Adult Workshop
11/4/99 BILSTON CRAFT GALLERY AND MUSEUM
11/4/99 Tel: 01902 409143
Creative textile and embroidery. Time: 10.00-16.00. Cost: £5.00. Booking essential

Art Galleries

Orienteering
11/4/99 DUDMASTON HALL
11/4/99 Tel: 01746 780866
Harlequins Orienteering Club. Starts at 10.00

Historic Houses & Gardens

First National Finance Race of the Year
11/4/99 MALLORY PARK
11/4/99 Tel: 01455 842931/2/3
Open solos, BSP, Ap 125/250, Ho 500/600 800. £12.00/£10.00. Please telephone 0930 55 59 60 for further information

Motor Racing Circuit

Walking Stick Workshop
11/4/99 SNIBSTON DISCOVERY PARK
11/4/99 Tel: 01530 510851
Join the rangers to learn about the traditional art of walking stick making and make your own stick to take home. Time: 11.00-13.00. A charge of £10.00 per stick will be made. Limited places. Advance booking essential from 1/3/99

Industrial Heritage

Quiz Night

12/4/99	**MR STRAW'S HOUSE**
12/4/99	Tel: 01909 482380

Quiz night at Regancy Hotel, Carlton Road, Worksop at 20.30. Cost: £1.00 per person, including pie and peas supper

Lived Here

Little Five Jelly Challenge

12/4/99	**ALTON TOWERS**
14/4/99	Tel: 0990 204060 24hr

Look out all you wobblers! Alton Towers is throwing a jelly packed challenge to all aspiring pink-knuckle riders during the Little Five Jelly week in association with Rowntree's Jelly. Under 8's are invited to ride five designated kids' rides around the park, and if they succeed, they can claim a free wobbler t-shirt.

Theme Parks

Shakespeare in the Park

14/4/99	**HAWKSTONE PARK**
14/4/99	Tel: 01939 200300

Enjoy one of William Shakespeare's plays, acted out in the glorious grounds of Hawkstone Park. Bring a rug and a picnic, call for further details, prices and times

Parks

Race Days

14/4/99	**CHELTENHAM RACECOURSE**
15/4/99	Tel: 01242 513014

Wednesday features the Faucets Silver Trophy Chase and Thursday offers Pony Club Members a very special occasion with pre-race tours and all-inclusive package. Admission £12.00

Racecourses

Square Foot Gardening

15/4/99	**RYTON ORGANIC GARDENS**
15/4/99	Tel: 01203 303517

Learn how easy it is to grow an impressive crop of vegetables in the smallest of spaces. Based on the book by Mel Bartholomew available in the Ryton Shop. Time: 10.00-12.30.

Gardens

Birds and Breakfast

16/4/99	**SUDBURY HALL AND THE MUSEUM OF CHILDHOOD, THE NATIONAL TRUST**
16/4/99	Tel: 01283 585305

Guided tour around the grounds followed by breakfast in the Coach House. Meet: 07.00. Cost: £7.50, limited availability

Country Estates

Granada MKII Collection

16/4/99	**BILLING AQUADROME LIMITED**
18/4/99	Tel: 01604 408181

Please telephone 0116 225 8598 for further information

Country Leisure Parks

Behind The Scenes Days

17/4/99	**CHATSWORTH**
17/4/99	Tel: 01246 582204/565300

Spend a day backstage at Chatsworth and meet the people who look after the House and its collections, the Garden and Park. Book on 01246 582204 contact Mrs Sue Gregory

Historic Houses & Gardens

Craft Fair

17/4/99	**QUARRY BANK MILL AND STYAL COUNTRY PARK**
17/4/99	Tel: 01625 527468

Sale of quality crafts produced by skilled crafts people for all over the UK. Further information including times, prices and bookings available by calling Quarry bank Mill

Heritage Centres

Steeplechase Racing

17/4/99	**STRATFORD-ON-AVON RACECOURSE**
17/4/99	Tel: 01789 267949/269411

Enjoy a day at the races

Racecourses

Belton Horse Trials

17/4/99	**BELTON HOUSE**
18/4/99	Tel: 01476 566116

The annual horse trials. Entry via Belton Village entrance. £8.00 per car. Further details on 01775 680333 - Charles Harrison

Historic Houses

Gardeners Weekend

17/4/99	**RAGLEY HALL**
18/4/99	Tel: 01789 762090

The weekend features specialist plant growers/nurseries, gardening equipment, gardening roadshow, craft fair, country crafts and family entertainment

Historic Houses & Gardens

Model Engineering Weekend

17/4/99	**SEVERN VALLEY RAILWAY**
18/4/99	Tel: 01299 403816

Engineering in miniature complementing the real thing. Many displays at various stations, call for further details

Railways

Silverstone International Raceday

17/4/99	**SILVERSTONE CIRCUIT**
18/4/99	Tel: 01327 857271

Circuit: International. Feature: BTCC. Please call for further information

Further more detailed information on the attractions listed can be found in Best Guides *Visitor Attractions* Guide under the classifications shown

Motor Racing Circuit

Exhibition - Light Sensitive
17/4/99 NOTTINGHAM CASTLE MUSEUM AND ART
16/5/99 GALLERY
Tel: 0115 915 3700
Five contemporary European artists who
use the photographic medium silver
gelatin

Castles

Its Transparent!
17/4/99 BROADFIELD HOUSE GLASS MUSEUM
27/6/99 Tel: 01384 812745
Crafts Council touring exhibition featuring current work by contemporary British
artists

Museum- Glass

Spring Plant Sale
18/4/99 CALKE ABBEY
18/4/99 Tel: 01332 863822
11.00-17.00. Property open as usual.
Free parking, entry to sale £1.00

Historic Houses & Gardens

"Writing From The Past"
18/4/99 ILAM PARK
18/4/99 Tel: 01335 350245/350503
Workshop with local calligraphy expert
Derek Harley. Cost: £2.50/person. Time:
10.30-12.30

Country Parks

Drayton Croft Mallory Trophy
18/4/99 MALLORY PARK
18/4/99 Tel: 01455 842931/2/3
Roadstocks, solo and sidecar 125-
1300cc. £7.00. Please telephone 0930
55 59 60 for further information.

Motor Racing Circuit

Colour Your Life with Maya Rose
18/4/99 RYTON ORGANIC GARDENS
18/4/99 Tel: 01203 303517
Colour healer, Maya Rose, will introduce
you to the power of colour in influencing
your life. Time: 15.00-16.30. Cost:
£10.00.

Gardens

LITERACY
19/4/99 NATIONAL WATERWAYS MUSEUM
23/4/99 Tel: 01452 318054
An education special for schools only,
please call for details

Museum- Waterways

Pests and Diseases
21/4/99 RYTON ORGANIC GARDENS
21/4/99 Tel: 01203 303517
How to identify and deal with pests and
diseases in the organic garden. Time:
14.00-16.30.

Gardens

Making Compost (RHS)
21/4/99 RYTON ORGANIC GARDENS
21/4/99 Tel: 01203 303517
Find out how to recycle garden rubbish
and up to 60% of household rubbish
organically. Time: 10.00-12.00. Why not
stay on for the afternoon session of
pests and diseases?

Gardens

Race Meeting
21/4/99 TOWCESTER RACECOURSE
21/4/99 Tel: 01327 353414
Enjoy a day at Towcester Races and
experience the true atmosphere of Jump
Racing with birch flying, jockeys urging
and hooves pounding

Racecourses

BBC Good Homes Show
21/4/99 NATIONAL EXHIBITION CENTRE
25/4/99 Tel: 0121 780 4141 x2604
Halls 4 & 5. Please telephone Consumer
Exhibitions Ltd, tel 0181 948 1666 for further information. Ticket sales NEC Box
Office 0121 767 4000

Exhibition Centres

Making Real Bread
23/4/99 RYTON ORGANIC GARDENS
23/4/99 Tel: 01203 303517
Make a wide range of interesting and
wholesome breads, and understand the
principles of doughs, ensuring consistent and high quality results. Time:
09.30-17.00. Cost: £38.00 includes all
materials and ingredients.

Gardens

Exhibition
23/4/99 THE COMMANDERY
23/4/99 Tel: 01905 355071
Oliver Cromwell exhibition opens

Historic Buildings

St George's Day
23/4/99 WARWICK CASTLE
23/4/99 Tel: 01926 406600
See the St George's Knight, listen to his
legends and find out about our St
George-Guy of Warwick.

Castles

National Hunt Racing
23/4/99 WARWICK RACECOURSE
23/4/99 Tel: 01926 491553
Evening meeting with first race at 17.30,
last race 20.00

Racecourses

A.A.C. Spring Nationals
23/4/99 BILLING AQUADROME LIMITED
25/4/99 Tel: 01604 408181
Tel 01604 408181 for more details

Country Leisure Parks

Spring Horse Trials

23/4/99 WESTON PARK
25/4/99 Tel: 01952 850207
Three day event of all classes, includes
Dressage, Show Jumping and Cross
Country

Historic Houses & Gardens

Gardeners Day

24/4/99 BIDDULPH GRANGE GARDEN
24/4/99 Tel: 01782 517999
Garden staff will be one hand to demonstrate Turf and Machinery maintenance.
There will also be Children's seed sowing
and demonstrations on taking cuttings,
pruning and Dahlia production

Gardens

BARC Sprint Meeting

24/4/99 SILVERSTONE CIRCUIT
24/4/99 Tel: 01327 857271
Circuit: Stowe. Feature: Club Races.
Please call for further information

Motor Racing Circuit

VSCC Vintage Raceday

24/4/99 SILVERSTONE CIRCUIT
24/4/99 Tel: 01327 857271
Circuit: National. Feature: Club Races.
Please call for further information

Motor Racing Circuit

Equestrian Extravaganza

24/4/99 WOLVERHAMPTON RACECOURSE
24/4/99 Tel: 01902 421421
Racing from Dunstall Park

Racecourses

A Medieval Garrison

24/4/99 KENILWORTH CASTLE
25/4/99 Tel: 01926 852078
Livery and maintenance. A£4.00 C£2.00
Concessions£3.00

Castles

Nostalgia Weekend

24/4/99 MIDLAND RAILWAYS CENTRE
25/4/99 Tel: 01773 747674/749788
Half price fares for senior citizens.

Railways Steam/Light

Diesel & Steam Weekend

24/4/99 MIDLAND RAILWAYS CENTRE
25/4/99 Tel: 01773 747674/749788
With both steam and diesel locomotives
hauling pasenger trains.

Railways Steam/Light

Spring Steam Gala

24/4/99 SEVERN VALLEY RAILWAY
25/4/99 Tel: 01299 403816
An intensive service of trains and your
Rover Tickets will give you admission to
other attractions, call now for further

details

Railways

The History Man

24/4/99 STOKESAY CASTLE
25/4/99 Tel: 01588 672544
Enjoy unusual guided tours with Brian
McNerney, presenter of the BBC's popular History Man programmes. But be
warned, his enthusiasm is notoriously
contagious... and there is no antidote!
Performing without costumes, props or
even a safety net, he brings the past to
life before your very eyes! A£3.50 C£1.80
Concessions£2.60

Castles

South Cerney Millennium

24/4/99 CORINIUM MUSEUM
1/6/99 Tel: 01285 655611
An exhibition looking at the history of
this Gloucestershire village over the
1000 years since the award of its charter

Museum- Roman

Robert Ball - Prints 1936-1996

24/4/99 CHELTENHAM ART GALLERY AND MUSEUM
3/7/99 Tel: 01242 237431
60 years of etchings and wood engravings by Painswick artist Robert Ball,
including illustrations of Cotswold
Ballads

Museum- Art

Big Breakfast Dawn Walk

25/4/99 BADDESLEY CLINTON HOUSE
25/4/99 Tel: 01564 783294
Meet at the car park (at 05.50) 06.00
start for a 3 hour gentle stroll around
the estate, and wider countryside to see
and hear the sights and sounds of the
morning shift. Then relax and enjoy
breakfast in the Baddesley Clinton
restaurant. Advanced booking required:
£10.50 English Breakfast, £7.50
Continental Breakfast. Max. 30 persons,
sorry No Dogs

Historic Houses & Gardens

BMW Drivers Club

25/4/99 BILLING AQUADROME LIMITED
25/4/99 Tel: 01604 408181
Tel 01362 691144 for more details

Country Leisure Parks

The Birds of Clumber

25/4/99 CLUMBER PARK
25/4/99 Tel: 01909 476592
Discover the birds of late Spring on a
guided walk with Clumber Volunteer,
Ron Overton. Binoculars advisable.
Start: 10.00. Cost: £1.50 per person.
Booking essential

Further more detailed information on the attractions listed can be found
in Best Guides *Visitor Attractions* Guide under the classifications shown

Historic Houses & Gardens

Adult Dayschool - Basketmaking
25/4/99 COTSWOLD HERITAGE CENTRE
25/4/99 Tel: 01451 860715
In the Cell Block Gallery. Make a basket in a day using traditional basketmaking techniques, 10.00-17.00, £22.00 (10% discount with Cotswold Museums Card)
Heritage Centres

NCCPG (Lincolnshire)
25/4/99 HARLAXTON MANOR GARDENS
25/4/99 Tel: 01476 592101
Rare and unusual plant fair. Please call for further details
Historic Houses & Gardens

Race Day
25/4/99 MALLORY PARK
25/4/99 Tel: 01455 842931/2/3
Formula Renault, Mini Se7en, Mini Miglia, Westfield sportscars, FF2000, SoM. £8.00. Please telephone 0930 55 59 60 for further information.
Motor Racing Circuit

Bears and Dolls
25/4/99 NATIONAL EXHIBITION CENTRE
25/4/99 Tel: 0121 780 4141 x2604
Pavilion. Time: 10.30-16.30. Please telephone: Miniatura, 0121 749 7330 for further information
Exhibition Centres

An Introduction to Watercolour Painting
25/4/99 RYTON ORGANIC GARDENS
25/4/99 Tel: 01203 303517
One-day beginners' painting and drawing workshop. Techniques, tips and tricks of the professional artist. Using perspective and composition to improve your skills. Time: 09.30-16.30. Cost: £20.00.
Gardens

Fishing Match
25/4/99 SNIBSTON DISCOVERY PARK
25/4/99 Tel: 01530 510851
An opportunity to join the rangers at the end of the fishing season on the ponds at Snibston Grange Nature Reserve. The match will last from 09.00-13.00. For further details and booking contact the rangers on 01530 510851 or 0973 194829. Tickets available from Monday 5/4/99
Industrial Heritage

Riders Asssociation of Triumph Rally
25/4/99 STANFORD HALL
25/4/99 Tel: 01788 860250
The second Spring rally of the Riders Association of Triumph for all modern Hinckley built Triumph motorcycles. Demonstrations, displays, band, barbecue. 11.00 - 16.00. Gates open by 10.00
Historic Houses

National Gardens Scheme Open Day
25/4/99 SUDELEY CASTLE AND GARDENS
25/4/99 Tel: 01242 602308
All proceeds are donated to the National Gardens Scheme
Castles

VICTORIANS
25/4/99 NATIONAL WATERWAYS MUSEUM
30/4/99 Tel: 01452 318054
An education special for schools only, please call for details
Museum- Waterways

Greek Night
27/4/99 WOLVERHAMPTON RACECOURSE
27/4/99 Tel: 01902 421421
Racing on all weather track with Greek themed entertainment. Packages available to include racecourse entrance, three course meal, racecard, and dancing to either a live band or disco. Racing from 19.00
Racecourses

Garden Tour
28/4/99 BELTON HOUSE
28/4/99 Tel: 01476 566116
Guided tour with Head Gardener followed by glass of wine and nibbles. Meet: 18.30. Cost: £6.00, booking essential
Historic Houses

Behind The Scenes Days
28/4/99 CHATSWORTH
28/4/99 Tel: 01246 582204/565300
Spend a day backstage at Chatsworth and meet the people who look after the House and its collections, the Garden and Park. Book on 01246 582204 contact Mrs Sue Gregory
Historic Houses & Gardens

Hunter Chase Evening
28/4/99 CHELTENHAM RACECOURSE
28/4/99 Tel: 01242 513014
Hunter Chasers from all over the country converge on Cheltenham for this most popular occasion when the amateur riders take on the same fences that were jumped in the Gold Cup. A great family, end of season event with entertainments and boxes available at £528 plus VAT including dinner for 12. Admission £12.00. First race at 17.25 (please call to confirm)

Racecourses

Oroonoko
28/4/99
6/10/99
ROYAL SHAKESPEARE COMPANY
Tel: 01789 296655
Performed at The Other Place. Director: Gregory Doran, Designer: Niki Turner, Lighting: Tim Mitchell. Aphra Behn's famous Restoration novel is dramatised in its entirity for the first time. Biyi Bandele's bold and comic retelling of the life of Oroonoko, the Royal slave, is set in both the West Indies and West Africa of the 1650s. Prices vary from: £10.00-£20.00. Booking from 30th Jan 99
Arts & Entertainment

Homes & Gardens Show
29/4/99
1/5/99
SUDELEY CASTLE AND GARDENS
Tel: 01242 602308
What's in for the home and garden for 1999, plenty to see and do and to give you ideas
Castles

Ely & District C.C.C.
30/4/99
2/5/99
BILLING AQUADROME LIMITED
Tel: 01604 408181
Tel 01353 624033 for more details
Country Leisure Parks

Ampthill under 11's
30/4/99
3/5/99
BILLING AQUADROME LIMITED
Tel: 01604 408181
Tel 01604 408181 for more details
Country Leisure Parks

Knutsford Royal May Day
1/5/99
1/5/99
KNUTSFORD ROYAL MAY DAY 1999
Tel: 01565 633143
Procession including horse drawn vehicles, approximately 500 children in costume, bands, vintage bicycles including Penny Farthings, morris dancing, May Queen crowning, country dancing, maypole dancing and the largest travelling fun fair in the North West. Procession: 14.00. Admission Free
Festivals

Silverstone RallySprint
1/5/99
1/5/99
SILVERSTONE CIRCUIT
Tel: 01327 857271
Circuit: Roger Clark. Feature: One Make Challenge. Please call for further information
Motor Racing Circuit

Albrighton Point to Point
1/5/99
1/5/99
WESTON PARK
Tel: 01952 850207
An enjoyable family day out with plenty of action
Historic Houses & Gardens

The International Classic Motor Show
1/5/99
2/5/99
NATIONAL EXHIBITION CENTRE
Tel: 0121 780 4141 x2604
Halls 4 & 5. Please telephone Centre Exhibitions, tel 0121 780 4141 for further information. Ticket sales NEC Box Office 0121 767 4767
Exhibition Centres

HSCC Historic Race Meeting
1/5/99
2/5/99
SILVERSTONE CIRCUIT
Tel: 01327 857271
Circuit: Stowe. Feature: Club Races. Please call for further information
Motor Racing Circuit

Medieval Life
1/5/99
2/5/99
THE COMMANDERY
Tel: 01905 355071
The Companions of the Black Bear will be re-creating life from 14.50-15.00. Amongst the activities to see will be weaving, basketmaking, cookery, fighting, archery and puppeteering
Historic Buildings

Calke Abbey Craft Show
1/5/99
3/5/99
CALKE ABBEY
Tel: 01332 863822
Craft sale and demonstrations, with examples of fine crafts ranging from jewellery to furniture, entry charge including National Trust members, parking free, call for further details
Historic Houses & Gardens

An Anglo Saxon Experience
1/5/99
3/5/99
COTSWOLD HERITAGE CENTRE
Tel: 01451 860715
In the Cell Block Gallery. Meet Angelcynn, the Anglo-Saxon re-enactors, as seen on Time Team
Heritage Centres

Vintage Train Weekend
1/5/99
3/5/99
MIDLAND RAILWAYS CENTRE
Tel: 01773 747674/749788
Featuring our museum train in public service and staff in period costume.
Railways Steam/Light

Friends of Thomas Weekend
1/5/99
3/5/99
NORTHAMPTON AND LAMPORT RAILWAY
Tel: 01604 847318
Meet Thomas, his friends Sir Topham Hatt, the Fat Controller and Percy and many more
Railways Steam/Light

The Siege of Sulgrave
1/5/99
3/5/99
SULGRAVE MANOR
Tel: 01295 760205
Witness a re-enactment of an actual event that took place at Sulgrave in 1644

Further more detailed information on the attractions listed can be found in Best Guides *Visitor Attractions* Guide under the classifications shown

during the English Civil War. Usual opening times. A£4.50 C£2.25

Historic Houses

May Day Festival
1/5/99 WARWICK CASTLE
3/5/99 Tel: 01926 406600
The May Day festival gathering takes place at the Castle. Birds of Prey can also be seen circling the ramparts.

Castles

Exhibition
1/5/99 COTSWOLD HERITAGE CENTRE
23/5/99 Tel: 01451 860715
In the Cafe Gallery. Ann Blockley's prints of animals and landscapes

Heritage Centres

Annual Cider and Perry Competiton
1/5/99 CIDER MUSEUM AND KING OFFA DISTILLERY
30/5/99 Tel: 01432 354207
Organised by the friends of the Cider Museum, dates to be arranged, but it will be in May, call for further details

Museum- Food & Drink

Help in the Home
1/5/99 COTSWOLD HERITAGE CENTRE
31/5/99 Tel: 01451 860715
In the Cell Block Gallery. A look at the changes in home life during the 20th-century through the changes in fashion and gadgets! Featuring a collection of Shelagh Lovett Turner

Heritage Centres

2nd Art Mix
1/5/99 BILSTON CRAFT GALLERY AND MUSEUM
13/6/99 Tel: 01902 409143
A celebration of the wealth of talent in the B.C. Anyone can enter their work for display

Art Galleries

Home Makers
1/5/99 BILSTON CRAFT GALLERY AND MUSEUM
3/7/99 Tel: 01902 409143
A selling exhibition of craft objects designed for the home

Art Galleries

"Piggy Days"
2/5/99 SHERWOOD FOREST FARM PARK
3/5/98 Tel: 01623 823558
An in depth look at the many different rare breeds of pig who live at the farm park

Farm Parks

Land Rover Marque Day
2/5/99 HERITAGE MOTOR CENTRE
2/5/99 Tel: 01926 641188
Land Rovers galore, call for further infor-

mation

Museum- Motor

The Honda £25,000 SuperClub Championship
2/5/99 MALLORY PARK
2/5/99 Tel: 01455 842931/2/3
125, 250, F600, F400, SoT, PBO, F11 s/c, MuZ. £7.00. Please telephone 0930 55 59 60 for further information.

Motor Racing Circuit

Volkswagen Owners Club Rally
2/5/99 STANFORD HALL
2/5/99 Tel: 01788 860250
Warwickshire & Leicestershire branch. Telephone 01788 860250 for more details, admission price charged. Gates open by 10.00. Special admission price for this event

Historic Houses

The Slighting of Ashby Castle
2/5/99 ASHBY-DE-LA-ZOUCH CASTLE
3/5/99 Tel: 01530 413343
Living history weapons, drill and musket firing. A£3.50 C£1.80 Concessions£2.50

Castles

Bank Holiday Miniature Steamers
2/5/99 BLACK COUNTRY LIVING MUSEUM
3/5/99 Tel: 0121 557 9643 info
Come and marvel at the workings of the miniature steam engines

Industrial Heritage

Ballads and Bayonets
2/5/99 BOLSOVER CASTLE
3/5/99 Tel: 01246 823349
With the 47th & Hautbois group re-enacting the 18th-century. A£3.50 C£1.80 Concessions£2.60

Castles

Medieval Monastic Entertainers
2/5/99 BUILDWAS ABBEY
3/5/99 Tel: 01952 433274
Try your hand at calligraphy or authentic period games as this popular duo take a light-hearted look at monastic customs, crafts and lifestyles. Learn about food preparation, herbs and spice in cooking and medicine, the mechanics of building and lifting and may other skills. From 12.00. A£3.00 c£1.50 Concessions£2.30 EH Members Free

Historical Remains

Spring Country Craft Fair
2/5/99 EASTNOR CASTLE
3/5/99 Tel: 01531 633160
Now in its fifth year this successful craft event brings together many of the countries best craftsmen and women. The

craft village is dramatically situated in the Courtyard in front of the Castle and on the beautiful Valley Lawn. Visitors have the chance to try their hand at various traditional crafts and there will be entertainment for all ages throughout the weekend

Castles

Medieval Living History
2/5/99 GOODRICH CASTLE
3/5/99 Tel: 01600 890538
15th century military and domestic life, with crafts, men-at-arms and period games. From 12.00. A£4.00 C£2.00 Concessions£3.00. EH Members Free

Castles

The Lion, the Witch and the Wardrobe
2/5/99 KENILWORTH CASTLE
3/5/99 Tel: 01926 852078
Come and see Labyrinth Productions perform this wonderful children's classic. A£4.00 C£2.00 Concessions£3.00

Castles

May Day Entertainment
2/5/99 MIDDLETON HALL
3/5/99 Tel: 01827 283095
Continuous entertainment both days of singers, dancers and children's attractions. May Day Pole. Sun: 14.00-17.00, Mon: 11.00-17.00. A£2.50 C£1.50

Historic Houses & Gardens

9th Staffordshire Classic Car Event
2/5/99 SHUGBOROUGH ESTATE
3/5/99 Tel: 01889 881388
Displays of over 750 cars, bikes, buses and agricultural vehicles from 1905 to the present day. Separate charge for this event

Historic Houses & Gardens

Tudor Players - Diabolus in Musica
2/5/99 STOKESAY CASTLE
3/5/99 Tel: 01588 672544
Elizabethan travelling players. A£3.50 C£1.80 Concessions£2.60. EH Members Free

Castles

Flower Fair
3/5/99 HERGEST CROFT GARDENS
3/5/99 Tel: 01544 230160
With specialist plant and craft stalls, charity auction, garden walks and other attractions, £5.00 entry, call for further details

Gardens

Race Day

MALLORY PARK
3/5/99 Tel: 01455 842931/2/3
3/5/99 Porsche 924, Open Sportscar series, Ford XR, F600, Road saloons, SoM. £8.00. Please telephone 0930 55 59 60 for further information.

Motor Racing Circuit

Burton Classic Car Rally
3/5/99 THE BASS MUSEUM
3/5/99 Tel: 01283 511000
This very popular event attracts classic vehicles from all over the British Isles

Breweries

May Day Bank Holiday Race Meeting
3/5/99 TOWCESTER RACECOURSE
3/5/99 Tel: 01327 353414
The highly acclaimed 1st Dragoons Victorian Cavalry will be topping the bill for entertainment. Visitors will be able to enjoy this magnificent colourful regiment as they demonstrate their skill between races. Victorian Fun Fair rides for the children

Racecourses

Bank Holiday Meeting
3/5/99 WARWICK RACECOURSE
3/5/99 Tel: 01926 491553
A family fun day with children's entertainment and a creche available. First Flat race at 14.15, last race 17.25

Racecourses

Animal Sense-ations
3/5/99 JODRELL BANK SCIENCE CENTRE, PLANETARIUM AND ARBORETUM
4/5/99 Tel: 01477 571339
How do animals find out about the world about them. These workshops seek to show you how. Demonstrations in the Environmental Discovery Centre. No extra charge but capacity will be limited by available space at each session. Also held on 30-31 May 1999

Science Centres

Evening Race Meeting
7/5/99 STRATFORD-ON-AVON RACECOURSE
7/5/99 Tel: 01789 267949/269411
Evening Steeplechase Meeting

Racecourses

British Empire Trophy
7/5/99 SILVERSTONE CIRCUIT
8/5/99 Tel: 01327 857271
Circuit: Grand Prix. Feature: FIA GT. Please call for further information

Motor Racing Circuit

Galloway Antiques Fair

Further more detailed information on the attractions listed can be found in Best Guides *Visitor Attractions* Guide under the classifications shown

7/5/99 9/5/99	**SUDELEY CASTLE AND GARDENS** Tel: 01242 602308 Quality antiques for sale, call for further details *Castles*

Bat Walk

8/5/99 8/5/99	CANONS ASHBY HOUSE Tel: 01327 860044 Meet: 20.00 in the car park. Booking essential *Historic Houses*

The Trees of Clumber

8/5/99 8/5/99	CLUMBER PARK Tel: 01909 476592 Guided walk with Mary Jones, book author and Clumber Volunteer. Time: 10.00. Cost: £1.50 per person. Booking essential *Historic Houses & Gardens*

Lichfield Cathedral Special Choir

8/5/99 8/5/99	LICHFIELD CATHEDRAL Tel: 01543 306240 with St Chad's Camerata sing Rossini's Stabat Mater and Schubert's Mass in G, Tickets: £12.00, £10.00, £8.00, unreserved £6.00, call to book *Cathedrals*

WWI

8/5/99 8/5/99	MANOR HOUSE MUSEUM Tel: 01536 534219 Experience World War I with the Pershings Dughboys, call for details *Museum- Local History*

New Solihull Festival 1999

8/5/99 8/5/99	NEW SOLIHULL FESTIVAL 1999 Tel: 01676 535818 Smiths Wood Steel Band, 11.00, Birminghams Bach Choir, St Alphege Church, 19.30, call for booking and prices *Festivals*

Randwick WAP

8/5/99 8/5/99	RANDWICK WAP 1999 Tel: 01453 766782 Colourful procession around village lanes and playing field with Mayor and Queen carried shoulder high. Cheese rolling, mayor ducking, morris dancing, traditional music, varied entertainment, dog show and display and stalls. 13.00-17.00. Admission Free, Car Park £1.50 *Festivals*

Dawn Chorus Walk

8/5/99 8/5/99	ROCKINGHAM CASTLE Tel: 01536 770240 Definitely one for the dedicated! Led by an expert, no more than 30 people will

have the opportunity to tour some of the remoter parts of the estate and enjoy the awakening of nature, particularly the birdsong. At 07.00 the party returns to the Castle for a traditional English breakfast before going home to get on with the DIY. Time: 04.00. Tickets: £6.50 each from the Estate Office. Early booking is advised

Castles

National Hunt Racing

8/5/99 8/5/99	WARWICK RACECOURSE Tel: 01926 491553 First race at 17.45 , last race at 20.15 *Racecourses*

Red Devils Night

8/5/99 8/5/99	WOLVERHAMPTON RACECOURSE Tel: 01902 421421 Racing on all weather track with themed entertainment. Packages available to include racecourse entrance, three course meal, racecard, and dancing to either a live band or disco. Racing from 19.00 *Racecourses*

Sterling C.C.

8/5/99 9/5/99	BILLING AQUADROME LIMITED Tel: 01604 408181 Tel: 01604 624033 for details *Country Leisure Parks*

A.S.C.M.

8/5/99 9/5/99	BILLING AQUADROME LIMITED Tel: 01604 408181 Tel 01604 408181 for more details *Country Leisure Parks*

Angling Fair

8/5/99 9/5/99	CHATSWORTH Tel: 01246 582204/565300 One of the only specialist Angling Fairs in the country catering for games, coarse and sea-fishing enthusiasts, with added attractions for families *Historic Houses & Gardens*

Standard Tank Weekend

8/5/99 9/5/99	MIDLAND RAILWAYS CENTRE Tel: 01773 747674/749788 Featuring two British Rail standard Four tank locomotives on passenger trains. *Railways Steam/Light*

The Bard's Best Bits - Oddsocks Theatre

8/5/99 9/5/99	STOKESAY CASTLE Tel: 01588 672544 Once again this hugely entertaining group comprehensively demolish Shakespeare! See the best bits from Julius Caesar, Romeo and Juliet and A

Midsummer Night's Dream. Don't miss it! A£4.00 C£2.00 Concessions£3.00. EH Members Free

Castles

Physical Evidence

8/5/99 DJANOGLY ART GALLERY
20/6/99 Tel: 0115 951 3192
Call venue for further details, no information available at this stage

Art Galleries

Specialist Plant Fair

9/5/99 BELTON HOUSE
9/5/99 Tel: 01476 566116
Gardens are open today in aid of the National Gardens Scheme - proceeds will be given to the Scheme which helps to preserve and restore some of the finest gardens in the country

Historic Houses

Plant Market

9/5/99 BIRMINGHAM BOTANICAL GARDENS AND GLASSHOUSES
9/5/99 Tel: 0121 454 1860
Thousands of plants from dozens of specialist growers

Gardens- Botanical

John Newbold Trophy for Solos

9/5/99 MALLORY PARK
9/5/99 Tel: 01455 842931/2/3
Plus solos 125-1300cc, Open & F11 sidecars. £7.00. Please telephone 0930 55 59 60 for further information.

Motor Racing Circuit

Car Treasure Hunt

9/5/99 MR STRAW'S HOUSE
9/5/99 Tel: 01909 482380
From car park at 14.00. Cost: £3.00 per car

Lived Here

National Vintage Communications Fair

9/5/99 NATIONAL EXHIBITION CENTRE
9/5/99 Tel: 0121 780 4141 x2604
Hall 11. Please telephone Sunrise Press, tel 01392 411565 for further information

Exhibition Centres

Stationary Engine Display

9/5/99 NATIONAL WATERWAYS MUSEUM
9/5/99 Tel: 01452 318054
Full-sized engines of all makes pumping and emptying, showing many aspects of work performed by them

Museum- Waterways

New Solihull Festival 1999

9/5/99 NEW SOLIHULL FESTIVAL 1999
9/5/99 Tel: 01676 535818
Festival Services, St Alphege Church, 11.00 & 18.30. Meridian Wind Orchestre,

Library Theatre, 15.00. Call for prices and booking details

Festivals

Kites Sunday

9/5/99 ROCKINGHAM CASTLE
9/5/99 Tel: 01536 770240
An al fresco day for kite-fliers of all ages. Because of its hill-side location the Castle can enjoy good conditions for kites. There will be an element of organisation on the day but it is intended to be mainly a day for free expression and a family picnic - possibly combining both. Bring your own kite to fly and you will quality for free entry, otherwise normal charges apply. Time: 13.00-16.30

Castles

Rare and Unusual Plant Fair

9/5/99 RYTON ORGANIC GARDENS
9/5/99 Tel: 01203 303517
Primrose Plant Fairs will be holding their annual plant selling extravaganza at Ryton Organic Gardens. A wide range of garden plants for the enthusiast, general gardener and collector. Time: 10.00-16.00. Restaurant booking essential on 01203 307142. Admission to the Fair: A£2.00 C£Free Concessions £1.50. Admission to Ryton Organic Gardens is at normal rates.

Gardens

National Mills Day

9/5/99 STAINSBY MILL
9/5/99 Tel: 01246 850430
An opportunity to see a water powered mill in working order - normal admission prices apply. Time: 11.00-16.00

Watermill

Rover P4 Drivers Guild National Rally

9/5/99 STANFORD HALL
9/5/99 Tel: 01788 860250
Telephone 01788 860250 for more details. Gates open by 10.00

Historic Houses

Dawn Chorus

9/5/99 SUDBURY HALL AND THE MUSEUM OF CHILDHOOD, THE NATIONAL TRUST
9/5/99 Tel: 01283 585305
Guided tour around the grounds followed by breakfast in the Coach House. Meet: 04.00. Cost: £7.50, limited availability

Country Estates

New Solihull Festival 1999

10/5/99 NEW SOLIHULL FESTIVAL 1999
10/5/99 Tel: 01676 535818
Orgain Recital, Jonathan Rees Williams

(from St. George's Chapel Windsor Castle) 13.00, then Choral Concert 'Mosaic' St Alphege Church 19.30, call for prices and booking details

Festivals

Evening Race Meeting

| 10/5/99 | TOWCESTER RACECOURSE |
| 10/5/99 | Tel: 01327 353414 |

Following an exciting evening of racing Towcester Racecourse will give you a 'Ticket to Ride' back to the sixties with the unmistakable sounds of the 'Fab Four'. 'The Cavern Beatles' will perform live on stage with memorable hits of yesteryear

Racecourses

New Solihull Festival 1999

| 11/5/99 | NEW SOLIHULL FESTIVAL 1999 |
| 11/5/99 | Tel: 01676 535818 |

Music by Students of Solihull Sixth Form College, at the College, Widney Manor Road at 13.00. Piano Recital, Neil Crosland, at the Library Theatre at 19.30, call for prices and booking details

Festivals

New Solihull Festival 1999

| 12/5/99 | NEW SOLIHULL FESTIVAL 1999 |
| 12/5/99 | Tel: 01676 535818 |

Organ Recital, David Briggs (from Gloucester Cathedral), St Alphege CHurch at 13.00. Fine Arts Brass Ensemble 19.30, call for prices and booking details

Festivals

New Solihull Festival 1999

| 13/5/99 | NEW SOLIHULL FESTIVAL 1999 |
| 13/5/99 | Tel: 01676 535818 |

Piano Recital, Jack Gibbons, Library Theatre 13.00

Festivals

Birminghaam National Dog Show

| 13/5/99 | ARBURY HALL |
| 16/5/99 | Tel: 01203 382804 |

Biggest national dog show of the year, call for further information

Historic Houses

New Solihull Festival 1999

| 14/5/99 | NEW SOLIHULL FESTIVAL 1999 |
| 14/5/99 | Tel: 01676 535818 |

'Thé Dansant', Jeremy Ballard Exhibition Room, 14.00-16.00. 'Best of British Jazz', Library Theatre 19.30, call for prices and booking details

Festivals

Evening Race Meeting

| 14/5/99 | STRATFORD-ON-AVON RACECOURSE |
| 14/5/99 | Tel: 01789 267949/269411 |

Evening Steeplechase Meeting

Racecourses

Maytime Musical Evening

| 14/5/99 | KEDLESTON HALL AND PARK (NATIONAL TRUST) |
| 15/5/99 | Tel: 01332 842191 |

Period pieces of gossip in the sumptuous Saloon at Kedleston Hall. A costumed entertainment presented by Musical Miscellany, to include a light buffet supper and glass of wine. Tickets: £25.00, strictly limited for each evening

Historic Houses

Dawn Chorus Walk

| 15/5/99 | CALKE ABBEY |
| 15/5/99 | Tel: 01332 863822 |

Meet: 04.30. Followed by breakfast. Booking essential

Historic Houses & Gardens

Behind The Scenes Days

| 15/5/99 | CHATSWORTH |
| 15/5/99 | Tel: 01246 582204/565300 |

Spend a day backstage at Chatsworth and meet the people who look after the House and its collections, the Garden and Park. Book on 01246 582204 contact Mrs Sue Gregory

Historic Houses & Gardens

The History Man

| 15/5/99 | HAUGHMOND ABBEY |
| 15/5/99 | Tel: 01743 709661 |

Enjoy unusual guided tours with Brian McNerney, presenter of the BBC's popular History Man programmes. But be warned, his enthusiasm is notoriously contagious... and there is no antidote! Performing without costumes, props or even a safety net, he brings the past to life before your very eyes! A£2.50 C£1.30 Concessions£1.90

Historic Buildings

New Solihull Festival 1999

| 15/5/99 | NEW SOLIHULL FESTIVAL 1999 |
| 15/5/99 | Tel: 01676 535818 |

Orchestral Concert, Orchestra of St John's, Smith Square At Alphege Church 19.30, call for prices and booking details

Festivals

Aeroboot '99

| 15/5/99 | NEWARK AIR MUSEUM |
| 15/5/99 | Tel: 01636 707170 |

The museum's well known aviation and avionics sale to raise money for the museum's Building Appeal. Come along one and all and enjoy a good rummage

Museum- Aviation

Homeopathic First Aid

15/5/99 RYTON ORGANIC GARDENS

15/5/99 Tel: 01203 303517

Discover how to treat toothache, sprains, bites and stings, etc. using homeopathy. Time: 10.00-16.00. Cost: £22.00 (£20.00 HDRA members)

Gardens

Making Hanging Baskets

15/5/99 RYTON ORGANIC GARDENS

15/5/99 Tel: 01203 303517

Find out how to plant up attractive hanging baskets, tubs and pots with ease. Time: 10.00-12.00 or alternatively 13.00-15.00. Cost includes basket liner, growing medium and 3 plants. Extra plants will be on sale or bring your own.

Gardens

Museum Time Machine!

15/5/99 AVONCROFT MUSEUM OF HISTORIC BUILDINGS

16/5/99 Tel: 01527 831363

History comes alive with re enactments of over 600 years of English Life

Museum- Local History

Artillery Firing

15/5/99 BOSCOBEL HOUSE

16/5/99 Tel: 01902 850244

The firing of various artillery pieces by the English Civil War Society. A£4.00 C£2.00 Concessions£3.00

Historic Houses

Narrow Gauge "Simplex Weekend"

15/5/99 MIDLAND RAILWAYS CENTRE

16/5/99 Tel: 01773 747674/749788

4 Simplex locomotives in action on Golden Valley Light Railway and new diesel locomotive traffic.

Railways Steam/Light

Tribute to the Canberra - 1949-1999

15/5/99 NEWARK AIR MUSEUM

16/5/99 Tel: 01636 707170

Two days of open cockpits, flypasts and displays to celebrate 50 years since Canberra Jet Bombers first flight in 1949. A great weekend for all the family

Museum- Aviation

Friends of Thomas the Tank Engine

15/5/99 SEVERN VALLEY RAILWAY

16/5/99 Tel: 01299 403816

The first of TWO weekends of Thomas and his many friends who are up to all sorts of tricks on the railway. The Fat Controller is in charge or his he? Next weekend 22 May-23 May.

Railways

Medieval Fighting Techniques

15/5/99 THE COMMANDERY

16/5/99 Tel: 01905 355071

The Medieval Combat Society will be demonstrating fighting techniques from the Medieval period. There will be several 45 minute slots run throughout the day

Historic Buildings

Museum's Week: Georgian Junket

15/5/99 PICKFORD'S HOUSE SOCIAL HISTORY MUSEUM

22/5/99 Tel: 01332 255363

Feast your eyes on the cooking demonstration in the Georgian Kitchen. 1820s-1830s recipes cooked on the Kitchen Range

Historic Houses

Museums Week 1998

15/5/99 CORINIUM MUSEUM

23/5/99 Tel: 01285 655611

Please telephone for further information

Museum- Roman

Lichfield's Treasures

15/5/99 LICHFIELD HERITAGE CENTRE

23/5/99 Tel: 01543 256611

National Museum' Week - exhibiting valuable silver / gold plate held within the Treasury, Civic / Regimental / Church

Exhibition Centres

National Museum's Week

15/5/99 NATIONAL WATERWAYS MUSEUM

23/5/99 Tel: 01452 318054

A nationwide celebration of the educational wealth stored in the UK's Museums, what are we doing, come along a find out!

Museum- Waterways

Museums Week

15/5/99 QUARRY BANK MILL AND STYAL COUNTRY PARK

23/5/99 Tel: 01625 527468

Quarry Bank Mill is celebrating Museums Week with activities based of the theme of FOOD, come and join us. Further information including times, prices and bookings available by calling Quarry bank Mill

Heritage Centres

Spring Plant Fair

16/5/99 ATTINGHAM PARK

16/5/99 Tel: 01743 708123

Opportunity to buy local homegrown plants at reasonable prices. Time: 11.00. Cost: A£1.80 C£0.90

Historic Houses & Gardens

Family Fun Day

Further more detailed information on the attractions listed can be found in Best Guides *Visitor Attractions* Guide under the classifications shown

| 16/5/99 | **BELTON HOUSE** |
| 16/5/99 | Tel: 01476 566116 |

It's all planned and ready, all you have to do is turn up. Plenty for the whole family. Usual opening times and NO additional charges

Historic Houses

Plant Sale

| 16/5/99 | **BIDDULPH GRANGE GARDEN** |
| 16/5/99 | Tel: 01782 517999 |

Up to 20 nurseries will be represented with an excellent choice of plants from trees to annuals and everything in between. Many rare and unusual plants will also be for sale

Gardens

The History Man

| 16/5/99 | **BUILDWAS ABBEY** |
| 16/5/99 | Tel: 01952 433274 |

Enjoy unusual guided tours with Brian McNerney, presenter of the BBC's popular History Man programmes. But be warned, his enthusiasm is notoriously contagious... and there is no antidote! Performing without costumes, props or even a safety net, he brings the past to life before your very eyes! A£2.50 C£1.30 Concessions£1.90

Historical Remains

Kite Flying Day

| 16/5/99 | **CALKE ABBEY** |
| 16/5/99 | Tel: 01332 863822 |

With kite making workshop from 10.00. Bring your own kite. Admission Free. Vehicle charge £2.50

Historic Houses & Gardens

Spring Plant Fair

| 16/5/99 | **CANONS ASHBY HOUSE** |
| 16/5/99 | Tel: 01327 860044 |

Third successful year. A wide selection of plants for sale, refreshments, parking, toilets all set in the beautiful grounds of Canon's Ashby House, 11.00-16.00. All proceeds from plants sold at National Trust Plant Fairs go towards helping NT gardens nationwide

Historic Houses

Spring Plant Fair

| 16/5/99 | **CLUMBER PARK** |
| 16/5/99 | Tel: 01909 476592 |

For all those budding garden enthusiasts. Time: 11.00-16.00. Please call for further information

Historic Houses & Gardens

Partake Elizabethan Dancers

| 16/5/99 | **HADDON HALL** |
| 16/5/99 | Tel: 01629 812855 |

Performances of 16th century dances accompanied by the lute will be held throughout the day. Informal talks on dress, music and social etiquette

Historic Houses

Airbourne Forces Parade

| 16/5/99 | **HARDWICK HALL** |
| 16/5/99 | Tel: 01246 850430 |

Time: 10.00-12.00. Please telephone for further information

Historic Houses

Formula Saloons

| 16/5/99 | **MALLORY PARK** |
| 16/5/99 | Tel: 01455 842931/2/3 |

Gin, AH, 2CV, Caterham, Sports Saloons, 250cc Kats. £8.00. Please telephone 0930 55 59 60 for further information.

Motor Racing Circuit

Tram-jam-Boree

| 16/5/99 | **NATIONAL TRAMWAY MUSEUM** |
| 16/5/99 | Tel: 01773 852565 |

Busy and bustling streets, always a Vintage Tram in sight to get a taste of rush-hour, yet still far more relaxed than today's! Call for further details

Museum- Transport

Silk Printing

| 16/5/99 | **QUARRY BANK MILL AND STYAL COUNTRY PARK** |
| 16/5/99 | Tel: 01625 527468 |

A delightful exhibition of art work produced on silk. Further information including times, prices and bookings available by calling Quarry bank Mill

Heritage Centres

'Days Gone By' - A Hundred Years of Industry in Leicestershire

| 16/5/99 | **SNIBSTON DISCOVERY PARK** |
| 16/5/99 | Tel: 01530 510851 |

Snibston's contribution to 'Museum Week' will look at the industries of Leicestershire during the 20th-century. Come and look round the galleries at Snibston and see a demonstration of railway shunting. Make bricks, see colliery films in the theatre, join in reminiscing about the 'old days' and see how much things have changes, identify some of our hidden industrial treasures and listen to an expert talk about 'snap' (food). Time: 11.00-17.00. No additional charge to museum paying visitors

Industrial Heritage

Leicestershire Ford RS Owners Club Rally

16/5/99
16/5/99
STANFORD HALL
Tel: 01788 860250
Telephone 01788 860250 for more
details. Gates open by 10.00. Special
admission price for this event
Historic Houses

Spring Plant Fair
16/5/99
16/5/99
**SUDBURY HALL AND THE MUSEUM OF
CHILDHOOD, THE NATIONAL TRUST**
Tel: 01283 585305
For all those budding garden enthusi-
asts. There will be rare plants on sale.
Time: 12.00
Country Estates

Winchcombe Horse Show
16/5/99
16/5/99
SUDELEY CASTLE AND GARDENS
Tel: 01242 602308
The ideal day out for all horse lovers,
call for further details
Castles

Birthday Celebrations
17/5/99
17/5/99
JENNER MUSEUM
Tel: 01453 810631
Edward Jenner's 250th Birthday celebra-
tions
Museum- Science

18th-Century Redcoats
17/5/99
18/5/99
THE COMMANDERY
Tel: 01905 355071
The 36th Regiment of Foote re-creates
the lives of eighteenth century Redcoats
Historic Buildings

Living Art
17/5/99
22/5/99
MANSFIELD MUSEUM AND ART GALLERY
Tel: 01623 463088
An opportunity to see local artists at
work in the Gallery
Museum- Local History

Gardens Walk
18/5/99
18/5/99
CLUMBER PARK
Tel: 01909 476592
Enjoy an evening walk through the gar-
dens with Brian Wilde, who has retired
this year from the post of Gardener-in-
Charge at Clumber. Meet: 18.30,
Conservation Centre. Cost: £1.50 per
person, booking essential
Historic Houses & Gardens

Dressage Festival
18/5/99
18/5/99
SHUGBOROUGH ESTATE
Tel: 01889 881388
Staffordshire's only national dressage
competition, attracting horses and riders
from all over the U.K. £2.00 per vehicle
Historic Houses & Gardens

A Walk in South Wood

20/5/99
20/5/99
CALKE ABBEY
Tel: 01332 863822
Meet at 19.00 at Saracen's Head car
park. No booking required. £Free
Historic Houses & Gardens

Horse & Hound Meeting
21/5/99
22/5/99
STRATFORD-ON-AVON RACECOURSE
Tel: 01789 267949/269411
Friday is an evening meeting
Racecourses

Family Fun Day
22/5/99
22/5/99
ATTINGHAM PARK
Tel: 01743 708123
Sponsored by Midlands Electricity
Board. Admission Cost to be advised
Historic Houses & Gardens

**Horse Drawn Vehicle and Welsh Cob
Show**
22/5/99
22/5/99
BILLING AQUADROME LIMITED
Tel: 01604 408181
Tel 01708 340848 / 0171 473 1454 for
more details
Country Leisure Parks

Family Fun Day
22/5/99
22/5/99
CALKE ABBEY
Tel: 01332 863822
A great day out for the whole family
from 11.00-16.00. Normal admission
charges apply, plus additional £0.50 per
child
Historic Houses & Gardens

Focus on Wildlife
22/5/99
22/5/99
CLUMBER PARK
Tel: 01909 476592
A practical workshop to help you
improve your wildlife photographs.
Please bring a camera. Time: 14.00-
17.00. Cost: A£5.00 C£2.50, booking
essential
Historic Houses & Gardens

Spiders Walk
22/5/99
22/5/99
CLUMBER PARK
Tel: 01909 476592
Discover some of Clumber's 200 species
of spider with expert Tom Faulds. Time:
10.00-12.00. Cost: £1.50 per person,
booking essential
Historic Houses & Gardens

Silverstone Rally Sprint
22/5/99
22/5/99
SILVERSTONE CIRCUIT
Tel: 01327 857271
Circuit: Roger Clark. Feature: Stars &
Cars of British Rally. Please call for fur-
ther information
Motor Racing Circuit

Bat Evening

Further more detailed information on the attractions listed can be found
in Best Guides *Visitor Attractions* Guide under the classifications shown

SNIBSTON DISCOVERY PARK
22/5/99
22/5/99
Tel: 01530 510851
Join the Rangers and the Leicestershire Bat Group to learn about the fascinating life of bats. There will be a talk and a slide show followed by a walk in the Grange Nature Reserve. Please meet in the museum foyer at 20.00 wearing suitable clothing and footwear. Suitable for all ages. £1.00 per person from 1/5/99. Advance booking is essential
Industrial Heritage

Music in the Garden
22/5/99
22/5/99
SUDELEY CASTLE AND GARDENS
Tel: 01242 602308
Enjoy the music provided by Lydbrook Band, call for further details
Castles

The History Man
22/5/99
22/5/99
WITLEY COURT
Tel: 01299 896636
Enjoy unusual guided tours with Brian McNerney, presenter of the BBC's popular History Man programmes. But be warned, his enthusiasm is notoriously contagious... and there is no antidote! Performing without costumes, props or even a safety net, he brings the past to life before your very eyes! A£3.50 C£1.80 Concessions£2.60
Historic Houses & Gardens

Parisian Night
22/5/99
22/5/99
WOLVERHAMPTON RACECOURSE
Tel: 01902 421421
Racing on all weather track with Parisian themed entertainment. Packages available to include racecourse entrance, three course meal, racecard, and dancing to either a live band or disco. Racing from 19.00
Racecourses

Living History Weekend
22/5/99
23/5/99
BLACK COUNTRY LIVING MUSEUM
Tel: 0121 557 9643 info
The Friends of the Museum spend the weekend living in 1920's conditions in the many cottages and houses. Witness their attempts to wash, cook, clean and entertain themselves without all the modern conveniences which we take for granted!
Industrial Heritage

Military Vehicle Rally
22/5/99
23/5/99
BOLSOVER CASTLE
Tel: 01246 823349
Various performers in a military vehicle display

Castles

Chatsworth Horse Trials
22/5/99
23/5/99
CHATSWORTH
Tel: 01246 582204/565300
Including dressage, show-jumping and cross country
Historic Houses & Gardens

Diesel & Steam Weeekend
22/5/99
23/5/99
MIDLAND RAILWAYS CENTRE
Tel: 01773 747674/749788
With both steam and diesel power on passenger trains.
Railways Steam/Light

Seni 1999
22/5/99
23/5/99
NATIONAL EXHIBITION CENTRE
Tel: 0121 780 4141 x2604
Pavilion. Please telephone Premiere Management & Marketing, 01277 264696 for further information
Exhibition Centres

Friends of Thomas the Tank Engine Weekend
22/5/99
23/5/99
SEVERN VALLEY RAILWAY
Tel: 01299 403816
The second of TWO weekends of Thomas and his many friends who are up to all sorts of tricks on the railway. The Fat Controller is in charge or his he? Previous weekend 15 May-16 May.
Railways

Meet a Roman Soldier
22/5/99
23/5/99
WALL ROMAN SITE (LETOCETUM)
Tel: 01543 480768
A Roman Centurion talking about Roman armour and military skills. Plus guided tours. From 13.00. A£2.50 C£1.25 Concessions£1.90. EH Members Free
Roman Sites

Poets at Wroxeter
22/5/99
23/5/99
WROXETER ROMAN CITY
Tel: 01743 761330
Poets in the ruins, together with guided tours. Normal admission prices apply
Roman Remains

Gloucester History Festival
22/5/99
4/7/99
GLOUCESTER FOLK MUSEUM
Tel: 01452 526467
Exhibitions and events throughout the City, including Life and Work in Victorian Gloucester exhibition at the Folk Museum
Museum- Local History

Life and Work in Victorian Gloucester
22/5/99
4/7/99
GLOUCESTER FOLK MUSEUM
Tel: 01452 526467
Domestic and trade items, costume, old photographs, maps and paintings on

Victorian Gloucester (part of the History Festival)

Museum- Local History

Exhibition - Urban

22/5/99 NOTTINGHAM CASTLE MUSEUM AND ART GALLERY

18/7/99 Tel: 0115 915 3700

Twentieth century works from the Tate Gallery Liverpool on a city theme including artists such as Lowry and Mondrian

Castles

Paint the Garden (Free)

23/5/99 CANONS ASHBY HOUSE

23/5/99 Tel: 01327 860044

Have a go at painting or drawing the beautiful gardens of Canon's Ashby House. Experts on hand, materials supplied. 12.00-17.00

Historic Houses

Birds before Breakfast

23/5/99 HARDWICK HALL

23/5/99 Tel: 01246 850430

A two-hour walking listening to dawn chorus followed by full english breakfast in Great Kitchen. Meet: 04.30 at Information Centre. Limited numbers - booking essential. Cost: £8.00 per person. Tel: 01246 851787

Historic Houses

The History Man

23/5/99 KENILWORTH CASTLE

23/5/99 Tel: 01926 852078

Enjoy unusual guided tours with Brian McNerney, presenter of the BBC's popular History Man programmes. But be warned, his enthusiasm is notoriously contagious... and there is no antidote! Performing without costumes, props or even a safety net, he brings the past to life before your very eyes! A£3.50 C£1.80 Concessions£2.60

Castles

Historic Racing

23/5/99 MALLORY PARK

23/5/99 Tel: 01455 842931/2/3

Saloon & sportscars including the Derek Bell Trophy, Jaguar XK Trophy. £10.00. Please telephone 0930 55 59 60 for further information.

Motor Racing Circuit

Medieval Archery

23/5/99 PEVERIL CASTLE

23/5/99 Tel: 01433 620613

15th century archery and combat-at-arms. From 12.00. A£3.00 C£1.50 Concessions£2.30

Castles

Butterfly Walks

23/5/99 RYTON ORGANIC GARDENS

23/5/99 Tel: 01203 303517

Join the Butterfly Conservation Society on one of three butterfly tours at Ryton Organic Gardens. See the many different varieties of butterflies that grace the gardens and find out which plants will attract them into your own garden. From Ryton Organic Gardens Shop at 14.00, 15.15 & 16.15. No extra charge for tours on top of normal admission rates.

Gardens

Cactus Show

23/5/99 RYTON ORGANIC GARDENS

23/5/99 Tel: 01203 303517

Lots of varieties of Cacti and Succulents to see. Expert advice available. Time: 10.00-16.00. Free admission to the Show, normal admission rates apply for the gardens.

Gardens

Northants and Rutland C.C

25/5/99 BILLING AQUADROME LIMITED

5/6/99 Tel: 01604 408181

Tel 01604 408181 for more details

Country Leisure Parks

Cricket Match

26/5/99 GLOUCESTER CRICKET FESTIVAL 1999

29/5/99 Tel: 01242 514420

Gloucestershire versus Essex.

Festivals

BARC Raceday

27/5/99 SILVERSTONE CIRCUIT

27/5/99 Tel: 01327 857271

Circuit: National. Feature: Club Races. Please call for further information

Motor Racing Circuit

Craft Fair

28/5/99 BIRMINGHAM BOTANICAL GARDENS AND GLASSHOUSES

28/5/99 Tel: 0121 454 1860

The best Craft Fair in town! Over 50 stalls showing the best the country can offer

Gardens- Botanical

Making Bread

28/5/99 RYTON ORGANIC GARDENS

28/5/99 Tel: 01203 303517

Make a wide range of interesting and wholesome breads, and understand the principles of doughs, ensuring consistent and high quality results. Time: 09.30-17.00. Cost: £38.00 includes all materials and ingredients.

Gardens

Pop into Wonderland

| 28/5/99 28/5/99 | **SUDBURY HALL AND THE MUSEUM OF CHILDHOOD, THE NATIONAL TRUST** Tel: 01283 585305 Craft activities in Harness Room. Time: 13.00-16.00. Cost: £1.00 |
| | *Country Estates* |

Last Race Meeting Celebrations

| 28/5/99 28/5/99 | **TOWCESTER RACECOURSE** Tel: 01327 353414 To celebrate the last meeting of the Season 'The Royal Family' the ultimate tribute to Queen will recreate the musical story of Freddie Mercury and the Glam Rock era |
| | *Racecourses* |

Alice in Wonderland Quest

| 29/5/99 29/5/99 | **SUDBURY HALL AND THE MUSEUM OF CHILDHOOD, THE NATIONAL TRUST** Tel: 01283 585305 Mad Hatter's Tea Party. Cost: £0.50 per child |
| | *Country Estates* |

Barn Dance - RBB Band

| 29/5/99 | **SUDBURY HALL AND THE MUSEUM OF CHILDHOOD, THE NATIONAL TRUST** Tel: 01283 585305 A Family Barn Dance to be held in the Stableyard with licensed bar. Time: 18.30. Cost: A£4.00 C£1.50 Family Ticket £9.50. Tickets available by pre-booking only, please apply to the property for booking |
| | *Country Estates* |

Flat Meeting

| 29/5/99 29/5/99 | **WARWICK RACECOURSE** Tel: 01926 491553 First meeting 18.20, last race 20.50 |
| | *Racecourses* |

Willow Structures

| 29/5/99 30/5/99 | **RYTON ORGANIC GARDENS** Tel: 01203 303517 A two day course in creating living willow structures, covering selection of material, harvesting, design and practical construction work. Times: 09.30 on 29th to 16.00 on 30th. Cost: £115.00 (£95.00 HDRA members). Accommodation is not included in the cost, but we can supply a list of local places where you can stay. |
| | *Gardens* |

Craft Fair

| 29/5/99 31/5/99 | **CLUMBER PARK** Tel: 01909 476592 Three-day craft fair in partnership with the Kidney Foundation. Entry £1.00 |
| | *Historic Houses & Gardens* |

Craft Fair

| 29/5/99 31/5/99 | **GAWSWORTH HALL** Tel: 01260 223456 Exhibitors from all over the country, displaying the finest examples of British craftmanship |
| | *Historic Houses* |

Hay Childrens Festival of the Arts 1999

| 29/5/99 31/5/99 | **HAY CHILDRENS FESTIVAL OF THE ARTS 1999** Tel: 0113 230 4661 An annual festival, held in Hay-on-Wye, for primary school-age children of 6-12 years with a programme of educational hands-on workshops, readings by best-selling childrens authors and poets: including Roger McGough, Jo Rowling, Kay Umansky and Colin Hawkins. Theatre performances for 6-12 years and the under 6's are welcome to come along with their parents. The 1999 programme includes Wayne Sleep Dance workshops, journalism and cartooning with The Funday Times and Warner Brothers, computer animation, movemation, photography, digital camera work, wood carving, Dorling Kindersley arts workshops, cookery, mucis and much more. |
| | *Festivals* |

Womble Weekend

| 29/5/99 31/5/99 | **LYME PARK** Tel: 01663 766492 Join us on this eco-friendly family event and meet your favourite Womble! |
| | *Historic Houses* |

Steam Up Weekend

| 29/5/99 31/5/99 | **NORTHAMPTON AND LAMPORT RAILWAY** Tel: 01604 847318 All running steam locomotives will have a showing throughout each day, with a special guest loco |
| | *Railways Steam/Light* |

FIA Professional European Championships 1999

| 29/5/99 31/5/99 | **SANTA POD RACEWAY** Tel: 01234 782828 Round 1 of Europe's most prestigious Drag Racing Championships with Top Fuel Dragsters, Funny Cars, Drag Bikes and night racing . |
| | *Motor Sports* |

Spring Craft Show

| 29/5/99 31/5/99 | **SHUGBOROUGH ESTATE** Tel: 01889 881388 A fascinating range of traditional craft skills. See skilled craft people at work. |

Fun for all the family. Separate charge for this event

Historic Houses & Gardens

The American Frontier

29/5/99
31/5/99
SULGRAVE MANOR
Tel: 01295 760205
See the America that controlled Col. John Washington when he emigrated from England in 1656. Indians, Traders, Backwoodsmen. Usual opening times A£4.50 C£2.25

Historic Houses

Oak Apple Festival

29/5/99
31/5/99
THE COMMANDERY
Tel: 01905 355071
The Worcester Militia re-creates the celebration commemorating the Restoration to the throne of Charles II. Join the Merrie Monarch and his entourage at the Commandery

Historic Buildings

Jousting Weekend

29/5/99
31/5/99
WARWICK CASTLE
Tel: 01926 406600
In mediaeval times, pride - and a 12ft lance - usually came before a fall! Also another chance to see the falconer in action

Castles

Traditional Charcoal Burning

29/5/99
2/6/99
DEAN HERITAGE CENTRE
Tel: 01594 822170
Witness the ancient craft of charcoal burning using traditional wood and turf stack. This method is rarely practiced elsewhere in Britain, call for booking details

Heritage Centres

Spring Celebration Week

29/5/99
6/6/99
BLACK COUNTRY LIVING MUSEUM
Tel: 0121 557 9643 info
A week of Spring celebrations, traditional sports and old-fashioned games such as egg and spoon races, skipping, marbles, jacks and hopscotch. Come and relive your youth and show your children and grandchildren how it's done!

Industrial Heritage

Friends of Thomas the Tank Engine

29/5/99
6/6/99
MIDLAND RAILWAYS CENTRE
Tel: 01773 747674/749788
With Thomas and his many friends including Oswald the talking enging at the Midland Railway Centre.

Railways Steam/Light

Shearing

29/5/99
20/6/99
COTSWOLD FARM PARK
Tel: 01451 850307
Watch the experts relieve our 950 sheep of their winter woollies. See the spinning demonstrations, the rare breeds. Coloured fleeces for sale

Farm Parks

If you want to get ahead, Get a Hat!

29/5/99
10/7/99
PICKFORD'S HOUSE SOCIAL HISTORY MUSEUM
Tel: 01332 255363
Exhibition of hats and bonnets

Historic Houses

Warwick Mayfest Celebrations

30/5/99
5/5/99
WARWICK MAYFEST CELEBRATIONS 1999
Tel: 01926 410747
Warwick Arts Society celebrates its twentieth anniversary during 1999. Celebrations will be the keynote of the year, rather than specific themes. There will be Purcell's King Arthur by the Gabrieli Consort & Players, a concert with the St Mary's Choirs and Fine Arts Brass with a commissioned work from Jonathan Girling, The Burning Bush, The Pirasti Trio and friends, celebrating their 10th anniversary and the final concert will be given by the London Mozart Players, celebrating their fiftieth birthday, under Matthias Bamert with Kevin Bowyer playing the Poulenc Organ Concerto. Please call for venue and ticket information

Festivals

Novice Racers Day

30/5/99
30/5/99
MALLORY PARK
Tel: 01455 842931/2/3
See the stars of tomorrow. Roadstocks, Juniors, sdo & sidecar, 125-1300cc. £7.00. Please telephone 0930 55 59 60 for further information.

Motor Racing Circuit

Magic Show

30/5/99
30/5/99
SNIBSTON DISCOVERY PARK
Tel: 01530 510851
By popular demand, Terry Boxx Children's entertainment will present his fun packed magic shows. Shows at 12.00, 14.00 & 16.00. Tickets £1.00 per person or free to museum paying visitors

Industrial Heritage

Sheep Shearing

30/5/99
31/5/99
ASH END HOUSE CHILDREN'S FARM
Tel: 0121 329 3240
Sheep Shearing and Wool Spinning Demonstration

Farms

The Lion, the Witch & the Wardrobe

30/5/99 BOSCOBEL HOUSE
31/5/99 Tel: 01902 850244
Come along to see this magical children's classic performed by Labyrinth Productions. A£5.00 C£2.50 Concessions£3.80

Historic Houses

Athurian Battle

30/5/99 HAWKSTONE PARK
31/5/99 Tel: 01939 200300
Witness a live Athurian Battle recreating the Dark Ages - Britain's most turbulent era, call for further details

Parks

Civil War Weekend

30/5/99 HOLDENBY HOUSE, GARDENS AND FALCONRY CENTRE
31/5/99 Tel: 01604 770074
Living History Camp with combat demonstrations, Dressing the Knight, Cooking and Clothing with much more.

Historic Houses & Gardens

Medieval Entertainments

30/5/99 KENILWORTH CASTLE
31/5/99 Tel: 01926 852078
Fighting knights, dancing, stories, children's games and juggling. A£4.00 C£2.00 Concessions£3.00

Castles

Tudor Players

30/5/99 LYDDINGTON BEDE HOUSE
31/5/99 Tel: 01572 822438
Performed by the Melford Hys Companie a Tudor re-enactment. A£3.00 C£1.50 Concessions£2.30

Historic Houses

Tudor Roadshow

30/5/99 MIDDLETON HALL
31/5/99 Tel: 01827 283095
Entertainment for all the family including: displays, music and games. Sun: 14.00-17.00, Mon 11.00-17.00 A£2.50 C£1.50

Historic Houses & Gardens

Transport Show

30/5/99 RAGLEY HALL
31/5/99 Tel: 01789 762090
Please telephone for further information

Historic Houses & Gardens

Antique Event and Fair

30/5/99 ROCKINGHAM CASTLE
31/5/99 Tel: 01536 770240
Laid on by Field Dog Fairs, this will be their second year at Rockingham. More than just another Antiques Fair, with lec-

tures, demonstrations, outside attractions to back up the large marquee where the antiques dealers are located. There is also a 'fringe' clement on stalls outside the marquee - something for everyone! Charges will be marginally adjusted to allow for this popular event. Time: 10.30-17.00 daily

Castles

"Woolly Sheep" Days

30/5/99 SHERWOOD FOREST FARM PARK
31/5/99 Tel: 01623 823558
A lighthearted look at traditional shearing skills and sheep management, spinning and knitting

Farm Parks

Sealed Knot

30/5/99 SUDELEY CASTLE AND GARDENS
31/5/99 Tel: 01242 602308
Bank Holiday entertainment for all the family including battle re-enactments

Castles

The Imperial Roman Army

30/5/99 WROXETER ROMAN CITY
31/5/99 Tel: 01743 761330
Find out about the life of a Roman soldier, his armour and his weaponry. Ermine Street Guard. A£4.00 C£2.00 Concessions£3.00

Roman Remains

Holiday Activities

30/5/99 NATIONAL WATERWAYS MUSEUM
6/6/99 Tel: 01452 318054
Help it's the holidays! Do not dispair, bring those little darlings to us, we've plenty in store to keep them busy, call for details

Museum- Waterways

Sheep Shearing

31/5/99 BENTLEY FIELDS OPEN FARM
31/5/99 Tel: 01335 330240
Rare and commercial sheep sheared all day, 11.00-18.00

Farms

Steam Fair and Country Show with Fred Dibnah

31/5/99 EASTNOR CASTLE
31/5/99 Tel: 01531 633160
Fred is returning to Eastnor once again aboard the mighty steam engine Atlas which he helped to restore for the Castle owner Mr James Hervey-Bathurst. As well as a full line up of working engines and models in the Castle Courtyard there will be displays of Falconry, Gun Dogs, Morris Dancing and local traditional crafts

Castles

Cricket Match
31/5/99 GLOUCESTER CRICKET FESTIVAL 1999
31/5/99 Tel: 01242 514420
Gloucestershire versus Worcestershire.

Festivals

Proton Challenge
31/5/99 MALLORY PARK
31/5/99 Tel: 01455 842931/2/3
A1, AR, Fiats, Mighty Minis, Super Road
S, MG Midgets, SoM. £8.00. Please telephone 0930 55 59 60 for further information.

Motor Racing Circuit

Coopering Demonstration
1/6/99 CIDER MUSEUM AND KING OFFA
DISTILLERY
30/6/99 Tel: 01432 354207
By Mr Ray Cotterell. Date to be
arranged, call for further details

Museum- Food & Drink

Weekday Entertainment
1/6/99 WARWICK CASTLE
31/8/99 Tel: 01926 406600
Each weekday come and watch the
medieval craftsmen demonstrate their
skills; learn about the battle tatics of the
Archer; hear the Jailer's tales of his prisoners; the Red Knight will tell you of the
Glory of War; watch the Knights engage
in hand-to-hand combat

Castles

Flat Meeting
2/6/99 WARWICK RACECOURSE
2/6/99 Tel: 01926 491553
First meeting at 14.00, last race at 17.00

Racecourses

Guided Walks
2/6/99 KEDLESTON HALL AND PARK (NATIONAL
TRUST)
11/8/99 Tel: 01332 842191
Every Wednesday. Join us for an evening
walk in the beautiful park at Kedleston,
the setting for Kedleston Hall. Start off in
the Gardens, walking up the Long Walk
to visit the Hermitage. Next out on to
Harepit Hill, then down to see the boat
house. Follow the water upstream and
cross the brook into Haywood, see the
National Trust's work to restore the
ancient woodland naturally. The next
stop is the Woodyard where all the
estate's timber was brough years ago.
Finish off the walk back on the car park
with a glass of wine. No charge is made
for the walk but donations are most welcome. All walks start at 19.00, all

Wednesdays

Historic Houses

National Gardens Scheme Open Day
3/6/99 KEDLESTON HALL AND PARK (NATIONAL
TRUST)
3/6/99 Tel: 01332 842191
Please call the venue for further information

Historic Houses

The Summer Country Style Fair
3/6/99 NATIONAL EXHIBITION CENTRE
6/6/99 Tel: 0121 780 4141 x2604
Halls 10, 10/11 Link & 11. Please telephone Orchard Events Ltd, tel 0181 742
2020 for further information. Ticket
sales NEC Box Office 0121 767 4151

Exhibition Centres

MG Car Club Race Meeting
4/6/99 SILVERSTONE CIRCUIT
5/6/99 Tel: 01327 857271
Circuit: International. Feature: Club
Races. Please call for further information

Motor Racing Circuit

National Street Rod Association
4/6/99 BILLING AQUADROME LIMITED
6/6/99 Tel: 01604 408181
Hundreds of 'Rods,' advice, displays,
trade hall, entertainment. Please call for
more details

Country Leisure Parks

Open Day
5/6/99 THE BARBER INSTITUTE OF FINE ARTS
5/6/99 Tel: 0121 414 7333
Art and music events and activities for
all the family

Art Galleries

Mardi Gras
5/6/99 WOLVERHAMPTON RACECOURSE
5/6/99 Tel: 01902 421421
Racing on all weather track with themed
entertainment. Packages available to
include racecourse entrance, three
course meal, racecard, and dancing to
either a live band or disco. Racing from
19.00

Racecourses

Bee-Keeping Weekend
5/6/99 CIDER MUSEUM AND KING OFFA
DISTILLERY
6/6/99 Tel: 01432 354207
Herefordshire Bee-Keepers Association
visit the Museum with their observation
chamber of live bees

Museum- Food & Drink

Flowers and Garden Show

Further more detailed information on the attractions listed can be found
in Best Guides *Visitor Attractions* Guide under the classifications shown

5/6/99 6/6/99	**EASTNOR CASTLE** Tel: 01531 633160 A new gardening event at Eastnor Castle giving visitors the opportunity to buy all they need for their gardens from specialist plant exhibitors. There will also be free advice from television and radio experts, demonstrations, talks, family entertainment and refreshments *Castles*

The 7th Etruria Canal Festival

5/6/99 6/6/99	ETRURIA INDUSTRIAL MUSEUM Tel: 01782 233114 Gathering of historic boats, traditional crafts, jazz, steam rally, children's events and much more! *Museum- Industrial*

The Bards Best Bits - Oddsocks Productions

5/6/99 6/6/99	HARDWICK OLD HALL Tel: 01246 850431 Once again this hugely entertaining group comprehensively demolish Shakespeare! See the best bits from Julius Caesar, Romeo and Juliet and A Midsummer Night's Dream. Don't miss it! A£3.50 C£1.80 Concessions£2.60 *Historic Houses*

Sheepdog Demonstrations

5/6/99 6/6/99	KENILWORTH CASTLE Tel: 01926 852078 Enjoyable demonstrations of sheepdogs, sheep and geese. From 12.00. A£4.00 C£2.00 Concessions£3.00 *Castles*

Record & CD Collectors' Fair

5/6/99 6/6/99	NATIONAL EXHIBITION CENTRE Tel: 0121 780 4141 x2604 Pavilion. Please telephone P & J Promotions, tel 01273 463017 for further information *Exhibition Centres*

Tudor Life

5/6/99 6/6/99	THE COMMANDERY Tel: 01905 355071 The Tudor and Stuart Society will be demonstrating life in a Tudor household *Historic Buildings*

Tudor Mercenaries

5/6/99 6/6/99	WARWICK CASTLE Tel: 01926 406600 Let the Castle echo to the sounds of battle as you witness the clash of Tudor Mercenaries. See the colour and splendor of a 16th century mercenary camp from this unique chapter in history. *Castles*

Cheltenham Art Club

5/6/99 26/6/99	CHELTENHAM ART GALLERY AND MUSEUM Tel: 01242 237431 A range of works in various media from active and enthusiastic club members *Museum- Art*

Shakespeare and the Written Word

5/6/99 4/7/99	COTSWOLD HERITAGE CENTRE Tel: 01451 860715 In the Cell Block Gallery. An exhibition of calligraphy by the Oxford Scribes. There will be items for sale *Heritage Centres*

Motor Transport Spectacular

6/6/99 6/6/99	ARBURY HALL Tel: 01203 382804 Vintage Car Rally with displays of cars, bikes, buses and agricultural vehicles *Historic Houses*

Victorian Day

6/6/99 6/6/99	DEAN HERITAGE CENTRE Tel: 01594 822170 A celebration of Victorian life in the Forest of Dean. Includes children's games, traditional crafts, competitions and much, much more, call for further information *Heritage Centres*

Scottish Dancing Display

6/6/99 6/6/99	DUDMASTON HALL Tel: 01746 780866 Swinging sporrens and high kicks to delight the eye! *Historic Houses & Gardens*

Period Garden Plant Sale

6/6/99 6/6/99	FORD GREEN HALL Tel: 01782 233195 Lots of unusual plants and herbs for sale, many at bargain prices. *Historic Houses*

750 Formula

6/6/99 6/6/99	MALLORY PARK Tel: 01455 842931/2/3 F4, Austin 7, KC, Hot Hatch. £8.00. Please telephone 0930 55 59 60 for further information. *Motor Racing Circuit*

Storytelling

6/6/99 6/6/99	PEVERIL CASTLE Tel: 01433 620613 Traditional folk tales, myths and legends. A£2.00 C£1.00 Concessions£1.50 *Castles*

Acorns Hospice Day

6/6/99 6/6/99	RAGLEY HALL Tel: 01789 762090 To be confirmed

Historic Houses & Gardens

Jaguar XK Rally
6/6/99 ROCKINGHAM CASTLE
6/6/99 Tel: 01536 770240
The Jaguar XK Register's National event. If you have an affection for these handsome mechanical beasts you are unlikely to see a better selection anywhere else in the country. Normal charges apply. Time: 11.30-16.00
Castles

Donkey Day
6/6/99 SHUGBOROUGH ESTATE
6/6/99 Tel: 01889 881388
Incorporating a lively day of rides, including a Donkey Grand National at championship status. A£4.00, reduced £3.00
Historic Houses & Gardens

Lea-Francis Owners Club Rally & Jaguar Enthusiasts Club - Midlands Day
6/6/99 STANFORD HALL
6/6/99 Tel: 01788 860250
Telephone 01788 860250 for more details as this event may be held on a second date 4th July 99. Gates open by 10.00
Historic Houses

Tank and Pond Dipping
6/6/99 SUDBURY HALL AND THE MUSEUM OF CHILDHOOD, THE NATIONAL TRUST
6/6/99 Tel: 01283 585305
Exploring creatures that live in the deep. Cost: £5.00 per family group
Country Estates

Family Fun Day
6/6/99 WORCESTER RACECOURSE
6/6/99 Tel: 01905 25364
Enjoy a day at the races with children's entertainment available. Admission prices from £5.50-£13.50, C£Free. Discount available for advance group bookings
Racecourses

Music For All Seasons - Summer
7/6/99 RYTON ORGANIC GARDENS
7/6/99 Tel: 01203 303517
A sequence of music workshops themed on the seasons. Join us for one or more of the days. Open to everyone, including complete beginners! If you play an instrument please bring it along. Listen to seasonal works by the great composers and, using the melodies of the countryside, create your own music. Time: 10.00-16.00.

Gardens

Flat Meeting
7/6/99 WARWICK RACECOURSE
7/6/99 Tel: 01926 491553
First race at 18.45, last race 21.15. A£9.00 C£Free
Racecourses

Fearsome Five Challenge
7/6/99 ALTON TOWERS
11/6/99 Tel: 0990 204060 24hr
Approach with cautin! Only the brave should take on the Fearsome Five Challenge in association with Nestle's Lion Bar. Ride the fave scariest white knuckle rides in Britain - Oblivion, Nemesis, Corkscrew, Black Hole and Ripsaw to claim a free limited edition t-shirt!
Theme Parks

Margaret Murton Needlepoint Design Workshop
7/6/99 CALKE ABBEY
12/6/99 Tel: 01332 863822
Booking essential. Cost: £80.00 (£75.00 for NT members). NOT on 8th, 10th or 11th June
Historic Houses & Gardens

Buttonhook Society
7/6/99 CORINIUM MUSEUM
18/7/99 Tel: 01285 655611
An exhibition by the Buttonhook Society
Museum- Roman

EGYPTIANS
8/6/99 NATIONAL WATERWAYS MUSEUM
9/6/99 Tel: 01452 318054
An education special for schools only, please call for details
Museum- Waterways

Backstairs Tour
9/6/99 BELTON HOUSE
9/6/99 Tel: 01476 566116
Two hour historical tour of the functional parts of the house, starting at 19.30. Complete with a glass of wine in the Butler's Pantry. Cost: £10.00, booking essential
Historic Houses

Behind The Scenes Days
9/6/99 CHATSWORTH
9/6/99 Tel: 01246 582204/565300
Spend a day backstage at Chatsworth and meet the people who look after the House and its collections, the Garden and Park. Book on 01246 582204 contact Mrs Sue Gregory
Historic Houses & Gardens

Taming of the Shrew

Further more detailed information on the attractions listed can be found in Best Guides *Visitor Attractions* Guide under the classifications shown

9/6/99 10/6/99	**PAINSWICK ROCOCO GARDEN** Tel: 01452 813204 Outdoor Shakespeare with covered seating, picnic first in the gardens. Please telephone for further information *Gardens*
11/6/99 11/6/99	**Bat & Moth Walk** **CALKE ABBEY** Tel: 01332 863822 Meet 09.00 in the main car park. No booking required. £Free *Historic Houses & Gardens*
11/6/99 13/6/99	**Bargain Weekend Two and Fireworks** **BILLING AQUADROME LIMITED** Tel: 01604 408181 Tel 01604 408181 for more details *Country Leisure Parks*
11/6/99 13/6/99	**Landrover Workers C.C.C** **BILLING AQUADROME LIMITED** Tel: 01604 408181 Tel 01203 385747 for more details *Country Leisure Parks*
11/6/99 13/6/99	**Peugeot Talbot C.C.C** **BILLING AQUADROME LIMITED** Tel: 01604 408181 Tel 01604 408181 for more details *Country Leisure Parks*
11/6/99 13/6/99	**Ironbridge Bluegrass and Roots Festival '99** **IRONBRIDGE BLUEGRASS AND ROOTS FESTIVAL '99** Tel: 01952 505565 A three day festival of music and dance. Bluegrass, Cajun, Folk, Blues and Gospel. Two stages, Workshops, Working Crafts, Children's Events, Real Ale, Good Food and Camping. Acts for 1999 so far are: Daisey Belle, Alan Munde and Joe Carr, Si Khan, Wrekin Havoc and Cuckoo Oak. Times: from 19.30 Fri - 20.00 Sun. Prices: A36.00 C(12-16)£18.00 Family Ticket (Sat only A2+C2)£25.00 OAPs£33.00. Group rates available *Festivals*
11/6/99 7/10/99	**Anthony and Cleopatra** **ROYAL SHAKESPEARE COMPANY** Tel: 01789 296655 Performed at the Royal Shakespeare Theatre. Cast Includes: Cleopatra: Francis de la Tour, Antony: Alan Bates. A private, passionate love affair played out on the public and political stages of ancient Rome and exotic Egypt. Prices vary from: £5.00-£39.00. Booking from 30th Jan 99 *Arts & Entertainment*
12/6/99 12/6/99	**Heathland Walk** **CLUMBER PARK** Tel: 01909 476592 Find out why Clumber is recognised nationally for the importance of its wildlife in this event for National Heathland Week with Head Warden Stuart Chappell. Time: 10.00-12.00. Cost: £1.50 per person, booking essential *Historic Houses & Gardens*
12/6/99 12/6/99	**Music Day** **MANOR HOUSE MUSEUM** Tel: 01536 534219 As part of National Music Week, the Museum is hosting a visit from period musicians and a collector of musical autometa to entertain visitors. 10.00-16.00 *Museum- Local History*
12/6/99 12/6/99	**Orchard Refreshments** **MR STRAW'S HOUSE** Tel: 01909 482380 Tea and cakes in the orchard, plus plant stall. Time: 11.00-16.00 *Lived Here*
12/6/99 12/6/99	**Afternoon of Scottish Country Dance** **SHUGBOROUGH ESTATE** Tel: 01889 881388 A flavour of Scotland performed by the Royal Scottish Country Dance Society. Admission - £2.00 per vehicle *Historic Houses & Gardens*
12/6/99 12/6/99	**VSCC Vintage Raceday** **SILVERSTONE CIRCUIT** Tel: 01327 857271 Circuit: National. Feature: Club Races. Please call for further information *Motor Racing Circuit*
12/6/99 12/6/99	**Medieval Fun Day** **SUDELEY CASTLE AND GARDENS** Tel: 01242 602308 Travel back the 1400s and discover how people of the 12th and 13th centuries lived and entertained themselves *Castles*
12/6/99 13/6/99	**Redcoats of George III** **BOSCOBEL HOUSE** Tel: 01902 850244 The 47th Foot. Living history encampment, drill, musket firing and a fascinating comparison between the uniform, weaponry and conditions of a British Soldier from 1778 and 1998, presented by this award-winning small group. A£4.00 C£2.00 Concessions£3.00 *Historic Houses*
	Antiques Fair

12/6/99 13/6/99	**HERITAGE MOTOR CENTRE** Tel: 01926 641188 Top class antiques, from top class dealers, call for details *Museum- Motor*

Gunpowder, Treason & Plot

12/6/99 13/6/99	**LYDDINGTON BEDE HOUSE** Tel: 01572 822438 Performed by Bills & Bows. A£3.00 C£1.50 Concessions£2.30 *Historic Houses*

Model Railway Exhibition

12/6/99 13/6/99	**MIDLAND RAILWAYS CENTRE** Tel: 01773 747674/749788 Models and suppliers display in our museum building. *Railways Steam/Light*

Diesels Galore

12/6/99 13/6/99	**NORTHAMPTON AND LAMPORT RAILWAY** Tel: 01604 847318 All running Diesel locomotives will have a showing throughout each day *Railways Steam/Light*

Heavey Horse

12/6/99 13/6/99	**SEVERN VALLEY RAILWAY** Tel: 01299 403816 Santa Specials: Santa and his Helpers visit the railway with presents for the children advanced booking required *Railways*

The Warwick Guard

12/6/99 13/6/99	**WARWICK CASTLE** Tel: 01926 406600 See the foot soldiers being put through their paces within the Castle grounds *Castles*

Johnny Reb and Billy Yank

12/6/99 13/6/99	**WITLEY COURT** Tel: 01299 896636 Performed by the 55th Virginia. A£5.00 C£2.50 Concessions£3.80 *Historic Houses & Gardens*

Tudor Living History

12/6/99 20/6/99	**SULGRAVE MANOR** Tel: 01295 760205 For 9 days the Manor will be run exactly as it was in the time of Washington's of the Tudor period. Usual opening times. A£4.50 C£2.25 *Historic Houses*

Cycle Orienteering Event

13/6/99 13/6/99	**CLUMBER PARK** Tel: 01909 476592 Combine the skills of route planning and cycling on Clumber's new cycle orienteering course. No experience necessary. Cycle hire available. Time: 14.00-17.00.

Cost: £1.50 with own bike, £3.00 with cycle hire, booking essential. Full list of events for National Bike Week available on 01909 476592

Historic Houses & Gardens

Teddy Bear's Picnic

13/6/99 13/6/99	**LYME PARK** Tel: 01663 766492 Meet Rupert the Bear. Fun and games for all the family. Don't forget to bring your teddy. *Historic Houses*

Post TT Bike Fest with General Guarantee

13/6/99 13/6/99	**MALLORY PARK** Tel: 01455 842931/2/3 Classic and modern racing, displays, parades, Aj, Co. £12.00/£10.00. Please telephone 0930 55 59 60 for further information. *Motor Racing Circuit*

RAF Cosford Open Day

13/6/99 13/6/99	**ROYAL AIRFORCE MUSEUM, COSFORD** Tel: 01902 376200 Call for further information *Museum- Aviation*

Alfa-Romeo Owners Club National Rally

13/6/99 13/6/99	**STANFORD HALL** Tel: 01788 860250 Telephone 01788 860250 for more details. Admission charged. Gates open by 10.00. Special admission price for this event *Historic Houses*

Alice in Wonderland

13/6/99 13/6/99	**SUDBURY HALL AND THE MUSEUM OF CHILDHOOD, THE NATIONAL TRUST** Tel: 01283 585305 Lewis Carroll's Alice in Wonderland presented by the Troubadour Theatre Company performed outside. Time: 16.30. Pre-booking only. Please bring rugs and picnics. *Country Estates*

Champagne and Strawberries

16/6/99 16/6/99	**WOLVERHAMPTON RACECOURSE** Tel: 01902 421421 Afternoon Racing from Dunstall Park *Racecourses*

BBC Gardeners' World Live

16/6/99 20/6/99	**NATIONAL EXHIBITION CENTRE** Tel: 0121 780 4141 x2604 Halls 5 & 9. Gardening showbiz meets the very best in horticulture at this fun and energetic show. As well as enjoying the imaginative Show Gardens, beautiful

Further more detailed information on the attractions listed can be found in Best Guides *Visitor Attractions* Guide under the classifications shown

displays in the RHS Floral Marquee, and countless garden accessory stands, visitors have the opportunity to learn from their favourite gardening celebrities at BBC Gardeners' World Live. The BBC Gardeners' World Magazine Theatre is an exceptionally popular feature giving visitors a rare opportunity to hear from gardeners such as Alan Titchmarsh and Pippa Greenwood at first hand. Plants and gardening sundries are for sale and RHS members can relax in a exclusive refreshment area. Please telephone the Royal Horticultural Society, tel 0171 630 7422 for further information. Ticket sales NEC Booking Office 0121 767 4111

Exhibition Centres

Tales from Ovid

| 16/6/99 | ROYAL SHAKESPEARE COMPANY |
| 7/10/99 | Tel: 01789 296655 |

Performed at the Swan Theatre. Director: Tim Supple, Designer & Co-Director: Melly Still, Music: Adrian Lee. Erotic, terrifying, sublime. Tales from Greek myth and Roman folklore, spun by Ovid in The Metamorphoses 2000 years ago and retold by the late Poet Laureate Ted Hughes. Prices vary from: £5.00-£36.00. Booking from 30th Jan 99

Arts & Entertainment

Gilbert and Sullivan

| 18/6/99 | KEDLESTON HALL AND PARK (NATIONAL TRUST) |
| 18/6/99 | Tel: 01332 842191 |

An evening concert of Gilbert and Sullivan in the Marble Hall with singers from the D'Oyly Carte Opera Company. Commences at 19.30. Tickets: £12.00, include view of state rooms from 18.45 and glass of wine. Please apply to the the regional booking office on 01909 511061

Historic Houses

10th Middlewich Folk and Boat Festival

| 18/6/99 | 10TH MIDDLEWICH FOLK AND BOAT FESTIVAL 1999 |
| 20/6/99 | Tel: 01606 836896 |

This unique event celebrates 'the first 10 years' with this entire historic salt town coming to life. Concerts, workshops, displays and a craft market take place in the town centre. International artists include Cherish The Ladies (USA), Black Umfolosi (Zimbabwe) and Tanglefoot (Canada). Our traditional narrowboat rally on the Trent and Mersey canal stretches from one end of town to the other, where canalside venues combine with the main site to provide a weekend of entertainment for all the family. Weekend tickets prices before 1 June A£25.00 C(12-16)£15.00 C(accompanied under 12)£Free. Tickets available from Box Office, 6 Southway, Middlewich, Cheshire CW10 9BL. Tel 01606 832850

Festivals

Mid Anglian Section C.C.

| 18/6/99 | BILLING AQUADROME LIMITED |
| 20/6/99 | Tel: 01604 408181 |

Please telephone 01553 766005 for further information

Country Leisure Parks

American Auto Club

| 18/6/99 | BILLING AQUADROME LIMITED |
| 20/6/99 | Tel: 01604 408181 |

Thousands of American Cars and lots of American entertainment. You will not believe your eyes - guaranteed!!

Country Leisure Parks

Silverstone SuperBike International

| 18/6/99 | SILVERSTONE CIRCUIT |
| 20/6/99 | Tel: 01327 857271 |

Circuit: International. Feature: British Superbike Championship. Please call for further information

Motor Racing Circuit

Tutbury Arts Festival 1999

| 18/6/99 | TUTBURY ARTS FESTIVAL 1999 |
| 20/6/99 | Tel: 01530 564414 |

Various venues at various times. After a highly successful launch in 1998, The Tutbury Arts Festival this year will be offering a three-day visual arts exhibition of paintings, sculpture, calligraphy and photography, a full-scale performance of Handel's "Messiah" in Tutbury's 11th century Priory Church with the Vivaldi Concertante orchestra from London and the Derby Bach Choir, plus jazz, puppetry and other events. Brochure giving full details published in May 1999. Price: No single charge - varies with event

Festivals

Cookies Couch of Confessions

| 19/6/99 | BADDESLEY CLINTON HOUSE |
| 19/6/99 | Tel: 01564 783294 |

A cabaret whodunnit entertainment. Commences 19.30. Tickets £30.00 (for tickets please send a cheque payable to 'National Trust (Enterprises)' and s.a.e. to the property

Historic Houses & Gardens

The Woodlands of Clumber
19/6/99 CLUMBER PARK
19/6/99 Tel: 01909 476592
Discover how Clumber's woodlands are managed with Head Forester, Frank Rhodes. Meet: 10.00, Hardwick village car park. Cost: £1.50 per person, booking essential
Historic Houses & Gardens

Annual Plant Fair
19/6/99 HANBURY HALL
19/6/99 Tel: 01527 821214
Usual admission prices apply. Garden tickets: A£2.50 C£1.00. Time: 11.00-17.30
Historic Houses & Gardens

Guided Walk: Ilam Tops and Valley Bottoms
19/6/99 ILAM PARK
19/6/99 Tel: 01335 350245/350503
See Dovedale and Ilam from a new perspective. Cost: £2.50 per person inclusive NT parking. This walk will also take place on: Sunday 18 September
Country Parks

Much Ado About Nothing
19/6/99 KENILWORTH CASTLE
19/6/99 Tel: 01926 852078
Classic theatre. Normal admission prices apply
Castles

Music from the Movies
19/6/99 SHUGBOROUGH ESTATE
19/6/99 Tel: 01889 881388
A superb open air evening concert with classic film music and glorious technicoloured fireworks as the grand climax. Gates open from 17.00. A£17.00 C£10.00
Historic Houses & Gardens

Open First Aid Competition
19/6/99 SNIBSTON DISCOVERY PARK
19/6/99 Tel: 01530 510851
Another opportunity to watch first aid teams from across the country using the setting of Snibston to solve first aid scenarios. Come and watch the teams race against the clock in a search for the best team. See local press for further details after early May
Industrial Heritage

Billies' Holiday playing Blues in the Night
19/6/99 SUDBURY HALL AND THE MUSEUM OF CHILDHOOD, THE NATIONAL TRUST
19/6/99 Tel: 01283 585305
An outdoor event to be held in the Stableyard. Licensed bar. Time: 19.30.

Cost: £8.00. Tickets by pre-booking only, please apply to the property for booking
Country Estates

National Deaf Children's Society and Caribbean Night
19/6/99 WOLVERHAMPTON RACECOURSE
19/6/99 Tel: 01902 421421
Charity Evening from Dunstall Park
Racecourses

Medieval Entertainment
19/6/99 ASHBY-DE-LA-ZOUCH CASTLE
20/6/99 Tel: 01530 413343
The pageantry of the medieval world recreated with fighting knights, dances, music and drama. The Lion Rampant. A£4.00 C£2.00 Concessions£3.00
Castles

Auto Trader British Touring Cars
19/6/99 DONINGTON PARK
20/6/99 Tel: 01332 810048
Formula Vauxhall Junior, Vauxhall Vectra SRi V6, Slick 50 Formula Ford, Ford Credit Fiesta, Formula Renault Sport, Renault Spider Cup.
Motor Racing Circuit

Diesel and Steam Weekend
19/6/99 MIDLAND RAILWAYS CENTRE
20/6/99 Tel: 01773 747674/749788
Featuring both steam and diesel power hauling passenger trains.
Railways Steam/Light

Gardner Engine Rally
19/6/99 NATIONAL WATERWAYS MUSEUM
20/6/99 Tel: 01452 318054
Lorries, buses, cars and boats. Demonstrating the many vehicles using Gardner Diesel Engines
Museum- Waterways

Rainbow Craft Fair
19/6/99 ROCKINGHAM CASTLE
20/6/99 Tel: 01536 770240
Rainbow Craft Fairs are synonymous with quality and good design. More than one hundred exhibitors are located in two spacious marquees, offering a wide range of attractive items for sale, with some live displays for good measure. Rainbow Fairs are now in their fourth year at Rockingham and are deservedly popular. Admission charges adjusted for the event but compare favourably with normal charges. Time: 10.30-17.00
Castles

An Introduction to Permaculture
19/6/99 RYTON ORGANIC GARDENS
20/6/99 Tel: 01203 303517
Weekend course to cover principles and

Further more detailed information on the attractions listed can be found in Best Guides *Visitor Attractions* Guide under the classifications shown

practice from good gardening to good community building. Times: 09.30-17.00 each day. Cost for the weekend: £80.00 (£70.00 HDRA members).

Gardens

Organic Gardening Weekend
19/6/99 RYTON ORGANIC GARDENS
20/6/99 Tel: 01203 303517
Organic gardeners throughout the country will be opening their gardens to the general public over this weekend. Ask for a free directory.

Gardens

Medieval Family Entertainers
19/6/99 STOKESAY CASTLE
20/6/99 Tel: 01588 672544
Games, squire-training and talks on weaponry and armour. Also, try your hand at spinning, weaving and calligraphy and learn about herbal medicine. A£3.50 C£1.80 Concessions£2.60. EH Members Free

Castles

Feather Perfect
19/6/99 SUDELEY CASTLE AND GARDENS
20/6/99 Tel: 01242 602308
A stunning display of the art of Falconry, call for further details

Castles

Military Manouvres
19/6/99 THE COMMANDERY
20/6/99 Tel: 01905 355071
The 36th Regiment of Foote return for more eighteenth century military manouvres

Historic Buildings

Birds of Prey
19/6/99 WARWICK CASTLE
20/6/99 Tel: 01926 406600
Magnificent birds of prey return to circle the ramparts and swoop over your heads

Castles

Telford Model Air Show
19/6/99 WESTON PARK
20/6/99 Tel: 01952 850207
Model aircraft displays at their best plus family and children's entertainment

Historic Houses & Gardens

Legends of King Arthur
19/6/99 WROXETER ROMAN CITY
20/6/99 Tel: 01743 761330
Performed by Labyrinth Productions. A£4.00 C£2.00 Concessions£3.00

Roman Remains

Young Images 1999
19/6/99 NORTHAMPTON CENTRAL MUSEUM AND

ART GALLERY
18/7/99 Tel: 01604 238548
Work by contemporary young local artists

Art Galleries

Fathers Day Special
20/6/99 BLACK COUNTRY LIVING MUSEUM
20/6/99 Tel: 0121 557 9643 info
Bring your dad for a day out and discover what life was like in days gone by. See metal-working and glass-cutting demonstrations, go underground on a coal mine tour, or ride on a vintage vehicle. Dads will have the chance to enjoy a portion of fish and chips cooked on the range in the 1930's Fried Fish Shop and a pint of real ale in the Bottle and Glass Inn on the house!

Industrial Heritage

Herbs, Hives and History Day
20/6/99 CANONS ASHBY HOUSE
20/6/99 Tel: 01327 860044
Family activities from 13.00. Normal admission

Historic Houses

Cycle Sunday
20/6/99 HANBURY HALL
20/6/99 Tel: 01527 821214
Arrive at Hanbury by bicycle and receive admission for half price

Historic Houses & Gardens

Austin Marque Day
20/6/99 HERITAGE MOTOR CENTRE
20/6/99 Tel: 01926 641188
Call for more information.

Museum- Motor

Drayton Croft Mallory Trophy
20/6/99 MALLORY PARK
20/6/99 Tel: 01455 842931/2/3
ACU F1/F11 sidecar and single cylinders, sdo and sidecar 125-1300cc. £7.00. Please telephone 0930 55 59 60 for further information.

Motor Racing Circuit

Fathers Day Sunday
20/6/99 MIDLAND RAILWAYS CENTRE
20/6/99 Tel: 01773 747674/749788
Lunnch on board our mid-day Midland dinner train.

Railways Steam/Light

A Mane Event!
20/6/99 NATIONAL TRAMWAY MUSEUM
20/6/99 Tel: 01773 852565
The only chance this year to trot the tracks in a very venerable horse tram

Museum- Transport

Father's Day

20/6/99 20/6/99	NORTHAMPTON AND LAMPORT RAILWAY Tel: 01604 847318 A special treat for all father's, no matter what the generation you can travel free *Railways Steam/Light*

Concert

20/6/99
20/6/99   RAGLEY HALL
Tel: 01789 762090
Please telephone for further information
Historic Houses & Gardens

All About Pigs

20/6/99
20/6/99   SHUGBOROUGH ESTATE
Tel: 01889 881388
Celebrate Father's Day and join in the fun...oiling, scrubbing and handling. Definitely an 'oink' of a day for all pig lovers. Licensed bar. A£4.00 Reduced £3.00
Historic Houses & Gardens

Ford AVO Owners Club Rally & Morris Register (Midlands Region) Rally

20/6/99
20/6/99   STANFORD HALL
Tel: 01788 860250
Telephone 01788 860250 for more details. Gates open by 10.00
Historic Houses

Fathers Day

20/6/99
20/6/99   THE BASS MUSEUM
Tel: 01283 511000
Now it's Dad's turn to be spoiled. £9.95 inc. 4 course meal, entertainment and a gift for Dad. Bookings only, contact Hospitality Manager on 01283 513514
Breweries

Banbury Run

20/6/99
20/6/99   TOWCESTER RACECOURSE
Tel: 01327 353414
The Banbury Run, now in it 51st year, is still the highest goal in the Vintage Motorcycling Calendar. Vintage motorcycles dating back to the late nineteenth centry will compete for these coveted awards
Racecourses

Historic & Commerical Vehicles Rally

20/6/99   WEST MIDLAND SAFARI AND LEISURE PARK
20/6/99   Tel: 01299 402114
Buses, lorries, engines, all working and in top class condition
Safari Parks

Summer Diesel Gala

20/6/99
27/6/99   MIDLAND RAILWAYS CENTRE
Tel: 01773 747674/749788
Featuring as many of our fleet of 25 main line diesel locomotives in action as possible.

Railways Steam/Light

Romeo and Juliet

22/6/99
27/6/99   GAWSWORTH HALL
Tel: 01260 223456
Enjoy the spectacle and romance of this classic love story, set in the splendour of the renaissance. Presented by the Wilmslow Gren Room Society, and directed by Garth Jones this production promises colour costumes and beautiful music and will inspire all who love and have loved! 22nd & 23rd A£10.50 C£5.00, 24th & 27th A£10.50 C£7.50, 25th A£12.50 C£8.50 & 26th A£14.00 C£9.50. Ticket prices include admission to the Hall from 14.00 onwards. Group bookings of 25+ 10% discount. Seating is a fully covered grandstand, bring and rug and a picnic. Booking via Gawsworth Hall direct.
Historic Houses

Summer Care of Soft Fruit

23/6/99
23/6/99   RYTON ORGANIC GARDENS
Tel: 01203 303517
This course will cover early and mid-summer management of strawberries, raspberries, gooseberries, redcurrants, etc. Time: 10.00-12.30.
Gardens

Flat Racing

23/6/99
23/6/99   WARWICK RACECOURSE
Tel: 01926 491553
Racing at Warwick first race at 14.20, last race 16.50
Racecourses

Twelfth Night

24/6/99
24/6/99   ASHBY-DE-LA-ZOUCH CASTLE
Tel: 01530 413343
Come and enjoy a Shakespeare classic performed by Heartbreak Productions. A£8.00 C£4.00 Concessions£6.00
Castles

Evening Meeting

25/6/99
25/6/99   STRATFORD-ON-AVON RACECOURSE
Tel: 01789 267949/269411
Evening Steeplechase Meeting
Racecourses

The Jungle Book

25/6/99
26/6/99   CLUMBER PARK
Tel: 01909 476592
Adaptation by the English Playtour Theatre. Performance starts: 19.00. Tickets: A£8.00 C£4.00 Concessions£7.00. Please book on 01909 476592 or 01302 751169
Historic Houses & Gardens

Barclays bank C.C.

Further more detailed information on the attractions listed can be found in Best Guides *Visitor Attractions* Guide under the classifications shown

25/6/99
27/6/99
BILLING AQUADROME LIMITED
Tel: 01604 408181
Wide part of field please. Please telephone 01455 553356 for further information

Country Leisure Parks

The Foresters C.C.C.
25/6/99
27/6/99
BILLING AQUADROME LIMITED
Tel: 01604 408181
Please telephone 01530 832265 for further information

Country Leisure Parks

Ford Corsair O.C.
25/6/99
27/6/99
BILLING AQUADROME LIMITED
Tel: 01604 408181
Tel 0181 395 4089 for more details

Country Leisure Parks

Royal Doulton Symposium
25/6/99
28/6/99
ROYAL DOULTON VISITOR CENTRE
Tel: 01782 292434
Scheduled to coincide with the annual Doulton Collectors' Fair in Stafford, this event will cater for Royal Doulton enthusiasts with special displays and presentations

Factory Tours and Shopping

Opera Brava
26/6/99
26/6/99
BADDESLEY CLINTON HOUSE
Tel: 01564 783294
Presents: Mozart's Don Giovanni al fresco. Gates open 18.00, performance 19.30, A£14.00 C(5-16)£7.00 in advance, A£16.00 C(5-16)£8.00 at the door (for tickets please send a cheque payable to 'National Trust (Enterprises)' and s.a.e. to the property. Bring seating and a picnic

Historic Houses & Gardens

Family Fun Day
26/6/99
26/6/99
CALKE ABBEY
Tel: 01332 863822
A great day out for the whole family from 11.00-16.00. Normal admission charges apply, plus additional £0.50 per child

Historic Houses & Gardens

Organic Vegetable Growing Day
26/6/99
26/6/99
RYTON ORGANIC GARDENS
Tel: 01203 303517
A day devoted to vegetable growing. Talks, demos and activities for everyone - including special beginner sessions 'Vegetable growing for the terrified'. Time: 10.00-16.00. Cost: A£2.50 C£1.25 Concessions £2.00. HDRA/RHS/North Hort. Soc members FREE.

Gardens

National Gardens Scheme (Ryton Organic Gardens)
26/6/99
26/6/99
RYTON ORGANIC GARDENS
Tel: 01203 303517
In support of the National Garden Scheme Charity. Time: 10.00-17.00. Cost: A£2.50 C£1.25 Concessions £2.00. HDRA/RHS/North Hort. Soc members FREE.

Gardens

Appellation Clog Dance Workshop
26/6/99
SUDBURY HALL AND THE MUSEUM OF CHILDHOOD, THE NATIONAL TRUST
26/6/99
Tel: 01283 585305
Time: 10.00-12.00. Booking essential

Country Estates

Fertility Dancing
26/6/99
THE COMMANDERY
26/6/99
Tel: 01905 355071
The anicent art of fertility dancing will be given a more modern perspective when the Nancy Butterfly dancers will entertain at 14.30 and 15.45

Historic Buildings

Rainbow Craft Fair
26/6/99
ARBURY HALL
27/6/99
Tel: 01203 382804
The infamous Rainbow Craft Fair held over the weeked at Arbury Hall, please call for further information

Historic Houses

The History Man
26/6/99
ASHBY-DE-LA-ZOUCH CASTLE
27/6/99
Tel: 01530 413343
Enjoy unusual guided tours with Brian McNerney, presenter of the BBC's popular History Man programmes. But be warned, his enthusiasm is notoriously contagious... and there is no antidote! Performing without costumes, props or even a safety net, he brings the past to life before your very eyes! A£3.00 C£1.50 Concessions£2.30

Castles

Rushden Mini Steam Enthusiasts
26/6/99
BILLING AQUADROME LIMITED
27/6/99
Tel: 01604 408181
Tel 01933 663222 for more details

Country Leisure Parks

Jacobites and Redcoats
26/6/99
BOLSOVER CASTLE
27/6/99
Tel: 01246 823349
18th-century performance by the New France and Old England Groups. A£4.00 C£2.00 Concessions£3.00.

Castles

Craft Fair

26/6/99 27/6/99	**HADDON HALL** Tel: 01629 812855 Held in the Hall grounds. Traditional rural crafts. Admission extra *Historic Houses*
26/6/99 27/6/99	**Outdoor Play: A Man for all Seasons** **HANBURY HALL** Tel: 01527 821214 New Pilgrim Players. Performance starts: 19.00. Bring picnics, rugs and chairs *Historic Houses & Gardens*
26/6/99 27/6/99	**Falcons & Gundogs** **KENILWORTH CASTLE** Tel: 01926 852078 Come and enjoy the feather perfect falconry. A£4.00 C£2.00 Concessions£3.00 *Castles*
26/6/99 27/6/99	**Leamington Jazz Weekend** **LEAMINGTON JAZZ WEEKEND 1999** Tel: 01926 410747 Two days of jazz featuring a range of performers. Concerts include Stan Tracey Big Band - a Tribute to Duke Ellington and Benny Goodman Evening - Big Band featuring Alan Barnes. Please call for venues and ticket information *Festivals*
26/6/99 27/6/99	**Earth & Fire V** **RUFFORD CRAFT CENTRE** Tel: 01623 822944 Seventy potters from this country and abroad selling their work in the beautiful surroundings of Rufford Country Park with plenty of children's activities and fun events to please all the family *Craft Galleries*
26/6/99 27/6/99	**Bonsai Festival** **SHUGBOROUGH ESTATE** Tel: 01889 881388 Courtesy of the South Staffordshire Bonsai Society *Historic Houses & Gardens*
26/6/99 27/6/99	**Civil War Surgeon** **STOKESAY CASTLE** Tel: 01588 672544 Listen to presentations about gruesome 17th century surgery, see the implements used and meet the leeches who were used as an important medical aid. A£3.50 C£1.80 Concessions£2.50 *Castles*
26/6/99 27/6/99	**Medieval Jousting Tournament** **SUDELEY CASTLE AND GARDENS** Tel: 01242 602308 Hear the thunder of hooves, the cheer of the crowd and the clashing of swords as the knights so bold fight for the fair

	lady's colours *Castles*
26/6/99 27/6/99	**Civil War** **WARWICK CASTLE** Tel: 01926 406600 The Castle is gripped by Civil War, see the soldiers preparing for battle *Castles*
26/6/99 27/6/99	**The National Hovercraft Championships** **WESTON PARK** Tel: 01952 850207 A spectator sport event with plenty of action for the whole family to enjoy *Historic Houses & Gardens*
26/6/99 15/7/99	**Exhibition** **COTSWOLD HERITAGE CENTRE** Tel: 01451 860715 In the Cafe Gallery. Landscape in wool by Mary Frame *Heritage Centres*
26/6/99 18/7/99	**University Summer Exhibition** **DJANOGLY ART GALLERY** Tel: 0115 951 3192 This annual Summer Exhibition promises to be as diverse as ever. Drawings, paintings and sculpture will be shown alongside jewellery, ceramics and textiles in a show with something for everyone *Art Galleries*
26/6/99 28/8/99	**The Pet Show** **BILSTON CRAFT GALLERY AND MUSEUM** Tel: 01902 409143 Exhibition featuring and exploring our love of pets and animals. Plenty of activities for families *Art Galleries*
26/6/99 4/9/99	**Queen Mary to Ark Royal** **DERBY INDUSTRIAL MUSEUM** Tel: One Man's Ships. Exhibition of model ships and memoribilia by a Derby model maker. Admission Free
27/6/99 27/6/99	**Opera Brava: Barber of Seville** **BADDESLEY CLINTON HOUSE** Tel: 01564 783294 Rossini's best-loved comic opera performed al fresco. Gates open 18.00, peformance 19.30, A£14.00 C(5-16)£7.00 in advance, A£16.00 C(5-16)£8.00 at the door (for tickets please send a cheque payable to 'National Trust (Enterprises)' and s.a.e. to the property. Bring seating and a picnic *Historic Houses & Gardens*

Further more detailed information on the attractions listed can be found in Best Guides *Visitor Attractions* Guide under the classifications shown

M.G.O.C.
27/6/99 BILLING AQUADROME LIMITED
27/6/99 Tel: 01604 408181
Please telephone 01954 232106 for further information
Country Leisure Parks

Eurocar Raceday
27/6/99 MALLORY PARK
27/6/99 Tel: 01455 842931/2/3
Close racing on the Mallory Mile, plus Honda SC, SoM. £10.00. Please telephone 0930 55 59 60 for further information.
Motor Racing Circuit

Medieval Entertainments
27/6/99 PEVERIL CASTLE
27/6/99 Tel: 01433 620613
Archery, dance and children's activities from 12.00 with mini 13th century tournament at 15.00. A£3.00 C£1.50 Concessions£2.30. EH Members Free
Castles

Concert: Music from the Movies
27/6/99 RAGLEY HALL
27/6/99 Tel: 01789 762090
Outdoor concert featuring classic music, film music. Bring your own picnic and re-live treasured moments from films past and present, culminating with glorious technicoloured fireworks
Historic Houses & Gardens

American Civil War Society & Rover SD1 Club Rally
27/6/99 STANFORD HALL
27/6/99 Tel: 01788 860250
Battle 15.00. Telephone 01788 860250 for more details on the Rover SD1 Car Club. Gates open by 10.00
Historic Houses

Lancashire Clog Dance Workshop
27/6/99 SUDBURY HALL AND THE MUSEUM OF CHILDHOOD, THE NATIONAL TRUST
27/6/99 Tel: 01283 585305
Time: 10.00-12.00. Booking essential
Country Estates

Shakespeare in the Paddock
27/6/99 TOWCESTER RACECOURSE
27/6/99 Tel: 01327 353414
Enjoy one of Shakespeare's best loved comedies 'Twelfth Night' performed in the beautiful surroundings of this picturesque racecourse. Bring a rug or chair and relax with a picnic whilst Heartbreak Productions stage their unique interpretation of a classic tale
Racecourses

Marching Bands Competition

27/6/99 WEST MIDLAND SAFARI AND LEISURE PARK
27/6/99 Tel: 01299 402114
Bands from all over the country compete for this National award
Safari Parks

Ladies Day
27/6/99 WORCESTER RACECOURSE
27/6/99 Tel: 01905 25364
Enjoy a day at the races with racing from 14.25. Admission prices from £5.50-£13.50, C£Free. Discount available for advance group bookings
Racecourses

Elizabethan Dance Workshop
30/6/99 SUDBURY HALL AND THE MUSEUM OF CHILDHOOD, THE NATIONAL TRUST
30/6/99 Tel: 01283 585305
Time: 19.00-21.00. Booking essential
Country Estates

Music Festival
30/6/99 QUARRY BANK MILL AND STYAL COUNTRY PARK
4/7/99 Tel: 01625 527468
A celebration of all types of music, with concerts to suit all tastes. Further information including times, prices and bookings available by calling Quarry bank Mill
Heritage Centres

Warwick and Leamington Festival
30/6/99 WARWICK AND LEAMINGTON FESTIVAL 1999
10/7/99 Tel: 01926 496277
The opening concert with the European community Chamber Orchestra will feature local girls Juliette Bausor (BBC Young Musician of the Year finalist) and Emma Bell (Kathleen Ferrier winner) and other large scale concerts in St Mary's Warwick will include The Hanover Band with Catherine Bott, The King's Consort with Crispian Steele-Perkins and the Leamington Bach Choir. The Fireworks concerts will be on 3 & 4 July given by the CBSO under Sakari Oramo and Twelfth Night and Henry V will also be given in the Castle grounds. Please call for venue and ticket information
Festivals

Camelot
1/7/99 GAWSWORTH HALL
3/7/99 Tel: 01260 223456
Lerner and Loewe's passionate and moving story, presented by the stars of tomorrow. The Arden School of Theatre presents this energetic new production

full of magic, spectacle and pagentry. Accompanied by a full orchestra. 1st & 2nd A£11.00 C£f5.00, 3rd A£18.00 C£8.50. Ticket prices include admission to the Hall from 14.00 onwards. Group bookings of 25+ 10% discount. Seating is a fully covered grandstand, bring and rug and a picnic. Booking via Gawsworth Hall direct.

Historic Houses

Ledbury Poetry Festival 1999
1/7/99
11/7/99
LEDBURY POETRY FESTIVAL 1999
Tel: 01531 634156
A lively clutch of readings and workshops, jazz, exhibitions and open reading contests at various venues around Ledbury. Cost: varied from £2.00-£25.00. Please call for further information.

Festivals

Diana's Final Resting Place
1/7/99
30/8/99
ALTHORP HOUSE AND PARK
Tel: 01604 592020 tickets
Open only from Diana, Princess of Wales' birthday to the eve of the anniversary of her death for those wishing to pay their respects and view the £2 million project by the Earl Spencer to commemorate his sister's life

Historic Houses & Gardens

Milk!
1/7/99
31/10/99
COTSWOLD FARM PARK
Tel: 01451 850307
Discover the origin of the milk you pour on your cereal and find out how WE get it for you

Farm Parks

Flat Meeting
2/7/99
2/7/99
WARWICK RACECOURSE
Tel: 01926 491553
Racing at Warwick first race at 14.00, last race 17.05

Racecourses

Ford Capri
2/7/99
4/7/99
BILLING AQUADROME LIMITED
Tel: 01604 408181
Please telephone for further information. Contact: Mr P Blundel

Country Leisure Parks

TR Drivers Club
2/7/99
4/7/99
BILLING AQUADROME LIMITED
Tel: 01604 408181
Please telephone 01452 614234 for further information

Country Leisure Parks

Ford Cortina 1600E O.C.

2/7/99
4/7/99
BILLING AQUADROME LIMITED
Tel: 01604 408181
Tel 01604 408181 for more details

Country Leisure Parks

Birmingham International Jazz Festival 1999
2/7/99
11/7/99
BIRMINGHAM INTERNATIONAL JAZZ FESTIVAL 1999
Tel: 0121 454 7020
Over 200 events, 90% of which are free to the public. The Festival encompasses every type of Jazz from trad to mainstream and modern to contemporary.

Festivals

Shakespeare in the Garden
3/7/99
3/7/99
ARBURY HALL
Tel: 01203 382804
A truly wonderful performance of Shakespeare's 'Comedy of Errors' please call for times and prices

Historic Houses

Parapsychology with Kathy Stranks
3/7/99
3/7/99
RYTON ORGANIC GARDENS
Tel: 01203 303517
An introductory course about psychic events and how to recognise them. Learn about the processes involved when a psychic event occurs, from coincidence to premonition. Time: 10.00-16.00.

Gardens

Day of Dance
3/7/99
3/7/99
SUDBURY HALL AND THE MUSEUM OF CHILDHOOD, THE NATIONAL TRUST
Tel: 01283 585305
Cultural and historic dances from schools, professional and amateur groups. Admission Free. Grounds open: 12.00

Country Estates

Opera Evening
3/7/99
3/7/99
WESTON PARK
Tel: 01952 850207
An outdoor Opera evening with the English Symphony Orchestra, call for further details

Historic Houses & Gardens

Sporting Heroes
3/7/99
3/7/99
WOLVERHAMPTON RACECOURSE
Tel: 01902 421421
National Hunt Evening Race Meeting

Racecourses

Living History Weekend
3/7/99
4/7/99
BLACK COUNTRY LIVING MUSEUM
Tel: 0121 557 9643 info
The Friends of the Museum spend the weekend living in 1920's conditions in

Further more detailed information on the attractions listed can be found in Best Guides *Visitor Attractions* Guide under the classifications shown

the many cottages and houses. Witness their attempts to wash, cook, clean and entertain themselves without all the modern conveniences which we take for granted!

Industrial Heritage

Medieval Combat
3/7/99
4/7/99
KENILWORTH CASTLE
Tel: 01926 852078
The Harlech Medieval Society. 13th century knights in combat, archery contest, have-a-go archery and games. From 11.00. A£4.00 C£2.00 Concessions£3.00

Castles

Birdwathcers' Summer Fair
3/7/99
4/7/99
MIDDLETON HALL
Tel: 01827 283095
And Wildlife Photo Fair. Sat 10.00-18.00, Sun 10.00-17.00. A£3.50

Historic Houses & Gardens

Tedy Bears Picnic
3/7/99
4/7/99
MIDLAND RAILWAYS CENTRE
Tel: 01773 747674/749788
Free train rides for any child bringing a teddy bear.

Railways Steam/Light

Civil War Re-enactment: Lord Robartes Regiment of Foote
3/7/99
4/7/99
ROCKINGHAM CASTLE
Tel: 01536 770240
Re-enactments can be lack-lustre, but not this one! A combination of the ancient Castle and a group of people dedicated to authenticity will provide two memorable days of entertainment as history is brough alive at Rockingham. No extra charge. Rockingham Castle's associations with the Civil Ware are a strong part of its history. In more modern times the Castle served as the location for the BBC epic 'By the Sword Divided'. Thus it provides a highly realistic setting for a Civil War re-enactment which, this year, is being staged for the first time at Rockingham by Lord Robarte's Regiment of Foote. Time: 12.30-16.30

Castles

Gardeners Weekend
3/7/99
4/7/99
SHUGBOROUGH ESTATE
Tel: 01889 881388
Shugborough hosts this fascinating insight into the gardening world. Floral displays, gardening exhibits, over 60 supportive craft stalls and experts on hand to answer any horticultural queries. 10.00-18.00. Separate charge for show

Historic Houses & Gardens

American War of Independence
3/7/99
4/7/99
SULGRAVE MANOR
Tel: 01295 760205
Meet George Washington and experience the life and times of the soldiers during this major period of World History. Usual opening times. A£4.50 C£2.25

Historic Houses

Grand Fireworks Concert
3/7/99
4/7/99
WARWICK CASTLE
Tel: 01926 406600
An evening of music performed by the world famous City of Birmingham Symphony Orchestra, set in grounds with a spectacular fireworks finale. Evenings only and tickets must be purchased in advance.

Castles

Birds of Prey
3/7/99
4/7/99
WARWICK CASTLE
Tel: 01926 406600
The majestic bird of prey return once again for another spectacular display

Castles

Sheepdog Demonstrations
3/7/99
4/7/99
WITLEY COURT
Tel: 01299 896636
Enjoyable demonstrations of sheepdogs, sheep and geese. A£4.00 C£2.00 Concessions£3.00

Historic Houses & Gardens

Mystery Plays
3/7/99
11/7/99
LICHFIELD HERITAGE CENTRE
Tel: 01543 256611
Special event held during Lichfield Festival Week showing the costumes and production of the Lichfield Mystery Plays

Exhibition Centres

Dave McKean - Journey
3/7/99
28/8/99
CHELTENHAM ART GALLERY AND MUSEUM
Tel: 01242 237431
An exhibition of comic artwork, photography, illustration and design by one of the most innovative and influential illustrators working in the field today

Museum- Art

Balusters & Beilbys
3/7/99
14/11/99
BROADFIELD HOUSE GLASS MUSEUM
Tel: 01384 812745
Stunning exhibition of rare 18th-century glass from a private collection never before displayed to the public

Museum- Glass

Children's Festival
4/7/99 BOLSOVER CASTLE
4/7/99 Tel: 01246 823349
A wonderful and unique day out for children of all ages. Theatre and puppet shows, storytelling, arts and crafts workshops and themed activities. Under 5's area. From 12.00. Free to children accompanied by an adult (one adult, max 5 children). A£3.00 Concessions£2.50

Castles

Standard Triumph Marque Day
4/7/99 HERITAGE MOTOR CENTRE
4/7/99 Tel: 01926 641188
What a way to celebrate the 4th July but with a Triumph!! Call for details

Museum- Motor

Guided Walk: Glory of Grassland
4/7/99 ILAM PARK
4/7/99 Tel: 01335 350245/350503
Spend an afternoon with warden and discover how we monitor our species rich grassland, then have a go yourself. Meet at Wetton Mill Trackside carpark at 13.45. £2.00 per person. Sorry no dogs. Fairly strenuous

Country Parks

Classic Sports Cars
4/7/99 MALLORY PARK
4/7/99 Tel: 01455 842931/2/3
Aston Martin and other classic sports cars including Tr, MG, Mor, Jag, F Junior, Anglo-American. £10.00. Please telephone 0930 55 59 60 for further information.

Motor Racing Circuit

Medieval Archery
4/7/99 PEVERIL CASTLE
4/7/99 Tel: 01433 620613
15th century archery and combat-at-arms. From 12.00. A£3.00 C£1.50 Concessions£2.30

Castles

An Introduction to Watercolour Painting
4/7/99 RYTON ORGANIC GARDENS
4/7/99 Tel: 01203 303517
One-day beginners' painting and drawing workshop. Techniques, tips and tricks of the professional artist. Using perspective and composition to improve your skills. Time: 09.30-16.30. Cost: £20.00.

Gardens

Junior Fishing Match

4/7/99 SNIBSTON DISCOVERY PARK
4/7/99 Tel: 01530 510851
An opportunity for under 16's to join the rangers in a fishing match at the start of the new season in the attractive setting of the Grange Nature Reserve. The match will last from 09.00-13.00. For further details and booking contact the Rangers on 01530 510851 or 0973 194829

Industrial Heritage

Velocette Motorcycle Owners Club Rally
4/7/99 STANFORD HALL
4/7/99 Tel: 01788 860250
Telephone 01788 860250 for more details. Also possibly the Jaguar Enthusiasts Club Rally although it could be held on an earlier date 6th June 99, call for further details. Gates open by 10.00

Historic Houses

Children's Folk Dance Day
4/7/99 SUDBURY HALL AND THE MUSEUM OF CHILDHOOD, THE NATIONAL TRUST
4/7/99 Tel: 01283 585305
Local schools participation. Time: 12.00. Admission Free

Country Estates

Graduates from L.C.A.D
4/7/99 THE FERRERS CENTRE FOR ARTS AND CRAFTS
2/8/99 Tel: 01332 865408
Selected ceramics and sculptural pieces within the exhibition room and courtyard

Craft Galleries

Evening Event
6/7/99 HARDWICK HALL
6/7/99 Tel: 01246 850430
Evening for teachers and families to see the Mill and Park. Light refreshments. Time: 18.45-21.45. Admission Free

Historic Houses

Shakespeare - The Tempest
6/7/99 CHAVENAGE
10/7/99 Tel: 01666 502329
Open-air production by Chavenage Productions. Covered stands

Historic Houses

Designing With Plants
7/7/99 RYTON ORGANIC GARDENS
7/7/99 Tel: 01203 303517
A few well chosen plants can transform your garden without the expense and mess associated with hard-landscaping - we can show you how. Time: 10.00-16.00.

Gardens

A Midsummer Night's Dream

7/7/99
10/7/99
CLUMBER PARK
Tel: 01909 476592
By William Shakespeare. Open-air the-atre from the Clumber Players, call for further details

Historic Houses & Gardens

The Mikado

7/7/99
11/7/99
GAWSWORTH HALL
Tel: 01260 223456
The return of the Pheonix Opera, direct-ed by Geoffrey Shovelton, with this hilar-ious, sparkling look at Victorian England pretending to be Japanese! 20 piece orchestra under the musical direction of John Brophy. 7th, 8th and 9th A£14.00 C£10.00, 10th & 11th A£18.00 C£13.00. Ticket prices include admission to the Hall from 14.00 onwards. Group book-ings of 25+ 10% discount. Seating is a fully covered grandstand, bring and rug and a picnic. Booking via Gawsworth Hall direct.

Historic Houses

Jazz and Barbeque Evening

8/7/99
8/7/99
WORCESTER RACECOURSE
Tel: 01905 25364
Enjoy a day at the races with racing from 14.25. Admission prices from £5.50-£13.50, C£Free. Discount available for advance group bookings

Racecourses

RAC British Grand Prix

8/7/99
11/7/99
SILVERSTONE CIRCUIT
Tel: 01327 857271
Circuit: Grand Prix. Feature: FIA Formula 1 & Formula 3000. Please call for further information

Motor Racing Circuit

Ghost Tour

9/7/99
9/7/99
BELTON HOUSE
Tel: 01476 566116
Tale of Belton's other side as you move through its darkened rooms and corri-dors. Bring a torch. Time: 19.30. Cost: £7.50, limited numbers so booking essential

Historic Houses

Professional Services Day

9/7/99
9/7/99
WOLVERHAMPTON RACECOURSE
Tel: 01902 421421
Afternoon Racing from Dunstall Park

Racecourses

Art of Living: Decorative Arts Fair

9/7/99
11/7/99
EASTNOR CASTLE
Tel: 01531 633160
For those who desire the best and unusual in their homes, their gardens and their lifestyle... Art, furniture, tex-tiles, fashion, jewellery, food, wine and unusual plants can all be found at this fascinating show. If you feel that the enrichment of your senses and the beau-ty of your surroundings are important to the enjoyment of life - this fair is a must for you. (Provisional)

Castles

The Lichfield International Festival 1999

9/7/99
18/7/99
LICHFIELD CATHEDRAL
Tel: 01543 306240
A simply superb Festival of Music and the Arts - held in the Cathedral, catering for all, from classical to jazz, from Mediaeval Market to films, call for fur-ther details

Cathedrals

Open-air Band Concert

10/7/99
10/7/99
DUDMASTON HALL
Tel: 01746 780866
Alveley Village Band perform at 18.30. Bring your own picnic and rug. Cost: A£4.00 C£2.00

Historic Houses & Gardens

The 1999 Derbyshire Prom

10/7/99
KEDLESTON HALL AND PARK (NATIONAL TRUST)
Tel: 01332 842191
Open-air concert featuring the Midland Symphony Orchestra with conductor Iain Sutherland. Firework finale. Gates open 17.00 for concert at 20.00. Tickets A£15.00 C£(5-16)£7.50 in advance, A£17.00 C£8.50 on the gate. Please apply to the the regional booking office on 01909 511061

Historic Houses

Countryside Day

10/7/99
10/7/99
MANOR HOUSE MUSEUM
Tel: 01536 534219
All things countryside, plenty to keep you entertained

Museum- Local History

Shakespeare at Ryton - Love, Lust and Loyalty

10/7/99
10/7/99
RYTON ORGANIC GARDENS
Tel: 01203 303517
A fast moving production of diverse excerpts from some of Shakespeare's best loved plays. Woven together by original music and song. Set in the gar-

den or inside if wet. Time: 19.00. Ticket Price: from £6.00. Optional buffet or you may picnic in the gardens.

Gardens

Cookery

10/7/99 ASHBY-DE-LA-ZOUCH CASTLE
11/7/99 Tel: 01530 413343

Come and sample the Historic Haute Cuisine at Ashby-de-la-Zouch Castle

Castles

Zephyr MK JV O.C.

10/7/99 BILLING AQUADROME LIMITED
11/7/99 Tel: 01604 408181

Please telephone 0181 330 2159 for further information

Country Leisure Parks

Opel Manta OC

10/7/99 BILLING AQUADROME LIMITED
11/7/99 Tel: 01604 408181

Please telephone 01827 894904 for further information

Country Leisure Parks

Medieval Surgeon

10/7/99 KENILWORTH CASTLE
11/7/99 Tel: 01926 852078

A fascinating and gruesome insight into 13th century medical care with presentations about cause, effect and treatment of wounds and everyday ailments. A£3.50 C£1.80 Concessions£2.60

Castles

Victorian Weekend

10/7/99 WARWICK CASTLE
11/7/99 Tel: 01926 406600

Learn about costume, etiquette and lifestyle during a weekend of Victoriana

Castles

Drawn to the Park

10/7/99 CLUMBER PARK
15/7/99 Tel: 01909 476592

Another chance to improve your artistic skills with Duncan Wood, a member of the New English School of Drawing. Come for one day or all 6. Cost: £27.00 per day, booking essential

Historic Houses & Gardens

Tony de Saulles - Cartoonist (provisional)

10/7/99 CHELTENHAM ART GALLERY AND MUSEUM
4/9/99 Tel: 01242 237431

An exhibition by local illustrator of 'Horrible Science' books

Museum- Art

Doll's Tea Party

10/7/99 PICKFORD'S HOUSE SOCIAL HISTORY

MUSEUM

11/9/99 Tel: 01332 255363

A visiting collection of dolls

Historic Houses

Insects of Clumber

11/7/99 CLUMBER PARK
11/7/99 Tel: 01909 476592

Meet butterflies, beetles and shield bugs with invertebrate enthusiasts Allan and Annette Binding. Meet: 10.00, Conservation Centre. Cost: £1.50 per person, booking essential

Historic Houses & Gardens

Gary Walker Memorial Meeting

11/7/99 MALLORY PARK
11/7/99 Tel: 01455 842931/2/3

With races for solos only, including juniors. £7.00. Please telephone 0930 55 59 60 for further information.

Motor Racing Circuit

Road Rally

11/7/99 MIDLAND RAILWAYS CENTRE
11/7/99 Tel: 01773 747674/749788

A gathering of historic road vehicles at the Midland Railway Centre.

Railways Steam/Light

Toy & Train Collectors Fair

11/7/99 NATIONAL EXHIBITION CENTRE
11/7/99 Tel: 0121 780 4141 x2604

Hall 17. Please telephone John Webb of D & J Fairs, tel 01526 398198 for further information

Exhibition Centres

Band Music

11/7/99 PEVERIL CASTLE
11/7/99 Tel: 01433 620613

Performed by the Silver Band. A£3.00 C£1.50 Concessions£2.30

Castles

Sporting Escort Owners Club National Rally

11/7/99 STANFORD HALL
11/7/99 Tel: 01788 860250

Telephone 01788 860250 for more details. Admission charged. Gates open by 10.00. Special admission price for this event

Historic Houses

Music at Stokesay

11/7/99 STOKESAY CASTLE
11/7/99 Tel: 01588 672544

Performed by the Ensemble Musica Salopia. Normal admission prices apply

Castles

Steeplechase Meeting

11/7/99 11/7/99	**STRATFORD-ON-AVON RACECOURSE** Tel: 01789 267949/269411 Steeplechase Meeting *Racecourses*

Warwick Courtiers

11/7/99 11/7/99	**SUDELEY CASTLE AND GARDENS** Tel: 01242 602308 Elegantly clothed of the Court of Warwick visit the Castle, call for further details *Castles*

Landrover Safari

12/7/99 12/7/99	**ILAM PARK** Tel: 01335 350245/350503 Join a National Trust Warden as he patrols Dovedale, seeing it as you have never done before. Cost: £2.00 per per- son. Time: 09.30. Other dates for this event are: Thursdays, 15th, 26th & 29th *Country Parks*

Great Value Night

12/7/99 12/7/99	**WOLVERHAMPTON RACECOURSE** Tel: 01902 421421 National Hunt Evening Meeting *Racecourses*

Art and Architecture

12/7/99 14/7/99	**CALKE ABBEY** Tel: 01332 863822 Drawing and painting workshops led by American artist, Ken Cooper. Booking essential *Historic Houses & Gardens*

Cricket Match

14/7/99 17/7/99	**CHELTENHAM CRICKET FESTIVAL 1999** Tel: 01242 514420 Gloucestershire versus Worcestershire. *Festivals*

Thw Wind in the Willows

14/7/99 17/7/99	**GAWSWORTH HALL** Tel: 01260 223456 By Kenneth Graham, adapted by Alan Bennett. This version first performed at the Royal National Theatre Dec 90. Ratty, Mole, Badger and Mt Road plus the Riverbankers, the Wild Wooders and a host of other characters come to life in a setting as real as the riverbank itself! Directed by Alan Clements. 14th, 15th & 16th A£11.00 C£8.00, 17th A£14.00 C£10.00. Ticket prices include admission to the Hall from 14.00 onwards. Group bookings of 25+ 10% discount. Seating is a fully covered grandstand, bring and rug and a picnic. Booking via Gawsworth Hall direct. *Historic Houses*

Buxton Festival 1999

15/7/99 25/7/99	**BUXTON FESTIVAL 1999** Tel: 01298 72190 (Box Office) Nightly performances at the Opera House, lunchtime recitals, afternoon concerts, masses and a programme of walks. Visit Chatsworth House, Lyme Park (Pemberley in the BBC's Pride and Prejudice), Pooles Cavern, Buxton Museum and Art Gallery. *Festivals*

Stockport Open Exhibition

15/7/99 30/8/99	**STOCKPORT ART GALLERY** Tel: 0161 474 4453 A selected exhibition of paintings, draw- ings, prints and sculpture from work submitted by artists resident in the North West. Submission dates: 2-3 July 1999 *Art Galleries*

Folk at the Park

16/7/99 16/7/99	**CLUMBER PARK** Tel: 01909 476592 An open-air folk rock concert featuring The Old Rope String Band, Edward II and Lindisfarne. Radio roadshow before the main performance. Firework finale. Gates open at 16.00, concert starts 19.00. Tickets A£15.00 C£(5-16)£7.50 in advance, A£17.00 C£8.50 on the gate. Please apply to the the regional booking office on 01909 511061 *Historic Houses & Gardens*

International Dance and Music Festival

16/7/99 18/7/99	**BELTON HOUSE** Tel: 01476 566116 Organised in conjunction with South Kesteven District Council. Please call property for further information *Historic Houses*

Land Rover Off Road Events

16/7/99 18/7/99	**BILLING AQUADROME LIMITED** Tel: 01604 408181 Largest 4 x 4 show in Great Britain. Everything for the 4 x 4'er and his family. Tel 01379 890056 for more details *Country Leisure Parks*

International Sports Racing Series

16/7/99 18/7/99	**DONINGTON PARK** Tel: 01332 810048 Formula Palmer Audi, Ferrari 355, Porsche Cup, European Formula Europa, Renault Clio V5, Ferrari/Porsche. *Motor Racing Circuit*

Malvern Classic Mountain Bike Rally (Deer Park)

| 16/7/99 | EASTNOR CASTLE |
| 18/7/99 | Tel: 01531 633160 |

Castles

Stainsby Folk Festival 1999

| 16/7/99 | STAINSBY FOLK FESTIVAL 1999 |
| 18/7/99 | Tel: 01246 559036 |

Concerts, dancing, crafts, children's entertainment, workshops, singing competition, informal music and song sessions. Pre-booking Before 1 July - 3 days: A£30.00 for weekend, after 1 July: A£35.00 for weekend AccompaniedC£Free. Individual Concert tickets: A£10.00. Caravans: £10.00 for weekend, space limited.

Festivals

Alice in Wonderland

| 17/7/99 | CALKE ABBEY |
| 17/7/99 | Tel: 01332 863822 |

English Playtour Theatre present open-air evening performances. Time: 18.30. Please bring a rug and picnic. Enquiries on 01302 751169

Historic Houses & Gardens

Swinging 60s

| 17/7/99 | CLUMBER PARK |
| 17/7/99 | Tel: 01909 476592 |

An open-air concert with firework finale. Featuring Gerry & the Pacemakers, Marmalade and The Swinging Blue Jeans. Gates open 16.00 for 19.00 start. Tickets A£15.00 C£(5-16)£7.50 in advance, A£17.00 C£8.50 on the gate. Please apply to the the regional booking office on 01909 511061

Historic Houses & Gardens

Teddy Bears' Picnic

| 17/7/99 | DUDMASTON HALL |
| 17/7/99 | Tel: 01746 780866 |

Bring your own picnic. Variety of entertainment. 14.00-17.00. Tickets: A£2.50 C£Free

Historic Houses & Gardens

Orchard Refreshments

| 17/7/99 | MR STRAW'S HOUSE |
| 17/7/99 | Tel: 01909 482380 |

Tea and cakes in the orchard. Time: 11.00-16.00

Lived Here

Stroud International Brick and Rolling Pin Throwers

| 17/7/99 | STROUD INTERNATIONAL BRICK AND ROLLING PIN THROWERS 1999 |
| 17/7/99 | Tel: 01453 882039 |

One of the more, unusual Festivals where teams of 6 Brick Throwers and 6 Rolling Pin Throwers representing 4 countries: Australia / Canada / USA and England. All competitors throw in their own country on the same day, you could say this is a world-wide event!

Festivals

Shakespeare

| 17/7/99 | SUDELEY CASTLE AND GARDENS |
| 17/7/99 | Tel: 01242 602308 |

The Rain or Shine Theatre Company present an outdoor performance of William Shakespeare's A Comedy of Errors, call for full booking information

Castles

Evening Flat Racing

| 17/7/99 | WARWICK RACECOURSE |
| 17/7/99 | Tel: 01926 491553 |

Organise a party outing for a night at the races. Group rates available. First race at 18.35, last race 21.05

Racecourses

Much Ado About Nothing

| 17/7/99 | WITLEY COURT |
| 17/7/99 | Tel: 01299 896636 |

Classical theatre performance. Normal admission prices apply

Historic Houses & Gardens

Medieval Surgeon

| 17/7/99 | BOLSOVER CASTLE |
| 18/7/99 | Tel: 01246 823349 |

A fascinating and gruesome insight into 13th century medical care with presentations about cause, effect and treatment of wounds and everyday ailments. A£3.50 C£1.80 Concessions£2.50

Castles

Traditional Song

| 17/7/99 | GOODRICH CASTLE |
| 18/7/99 | Tel: 01600 890538 |

Historical music performed by The Dunns. A£3.50 C£1.80 Concessions£2.60

Castles

Diesel & Steam Weekend

| 17/7/99 | MIDLAND RAILWAYS CENTRE |
| 18/7/99 | Tel: 01773 747674/749788 |

Featuring both steam and diesel power on passenger trains.

Railways Steam/Light

Light Model Aircraft Show

| 17/7/99 | ROYAL AIRFORCE MUSEUM, COSFORD |
| 18/7/99 | Tel: 01902 376200 |

Call for further details

Museum- Aviation

Sweet Pea Festival

Further more detailed information on the attractions listed can be found in Best Guides *Visitor Attractions* Guide under the classifications shown

17/7/99 18/7/99	**SHUGBOROUGH ESTATE** Tel: 01889 881388 Floral displays decorate the Mansion House courtesy of the Sweet Pea Society

Historic Houses & Gardens

Restoration

17/7/99 18/7/99	**STOKESAY CASTLE** Tel: 01588 672544 Historical music performed by Hogarth's Heroes. A£4.00 C£2.00 Concessions£3.00

Castles

The Warwick Guard

17/7/99 18/7/99	**WARWICK CASTLE** Tel: 01926 406600 The Warwick Guard foot soldiers perform a drill in the Courtyard

Castles

Balloon Festival and Nightfire Spectacular

17/7/99 18/7/99	**WESTON PARK** Tel: 01952 850207 Skydiving arena displays, aerobatics, hot air balloon displays. A full day of superb entertainment. A wonderful display of glowing hot air balloons set to music with a firework finale

Historic Houses & Gardens

Hinterland Project Tours

17/7/99 18/7/99	**WROXETER ROMAN CITY** Tel: 01743 761330 With Roger White. Normal admission prices apply

Roman Remains

Exhibition - Picture, Picture on the Wall

17/7/99 1/9/99	**NOTTINGHAM CASTLE MUSEUM AND ART GALLERY** Tel: 0115 915 3700 Paintings and activities to develop new ways of enjoying art for the very young

Castles

Cricket Match

18/7/99 18/7/99	**CHELTENHAM CRICKET FESTIVAL 1999** Tel: 01242 514420 Gloucestershire versus Yorkshire.

Festivals

Supercar Sunday

18/7/99 18/7/99	**HERITAGE MOTOR CENTRE** Tel: 01926 641188 It's a Summer Sunday Afternoon, go out, come here, it'll be great

Museum- Motor

Alice in Wonderland

18/7/99 18/7/99	**ILAM PARK** Tel: 01335 350245/350503 Troubadour Theatre perform this family classic. Time: 15.00 (gates open 14.00). Cost: A£4.50 C£2.00

Country Parks

Children's Day

18/7/99 18/7/99	**KIRBY HALL** Tel: 01536 203230 A wonderful fun-packed day for Children put on by Labyrinth Productions. A£4.00 C£2.00 Concessions£3.00

Historic Houses

Vintage Racing and Sportscars

18/7/99 18/7/99	**MALLORY PARK** Tel: 01455 842931/2/3 Pre and Post-War. The most evocative cars seen and heard all season! £10.00. Please telephone 0930 55 59 60 for further information.

Motor Racing Circuit

In Living Memory

18/7/99 18/7/99	**NATIONAL TRAMWAY MUSEUM** Tel: 01773 852565 We dare you! Visit wearing full Edwardian and Victorian period costume and we'll reward you with free admission!

Museum- Transport

Member's Day

18/7/99 18/7/99	**NORTHAMPTON AND LAMPORT RAILWAY** Tel: 01604 847318 Members of the Northampton and Lamport Preservation Society enjoy a free ride, so if you are a Member, remember a free ride today

Railways Steam/Light

Triumph Car Rally

18/7/99 18/7/99	**RAGLEY HALL** Tel: 01789 762090 Please telephone for further information

Historic Houses & Gardens

Twelfth Night

18/7/99 18/7/99	**ROCKINGHAM CASTLE** Tel: 01536 770240 Shakespeare is sometimes said to be to England what Burns is to Scotland. Combine the Bard with the tranquil outdoor setting of the Terrace at Rockingham Castle on a summer's evening, perhaps with a well-prepared picnic hamper to hand, and you have the sort of event which will keep a reflective smile on your face for the rest of the week. Heartbreak Productions, old friends of the Castle, stage the 1999 curricular choice of Shakespeare's works at

what must be one of the most spectacular settings of its kind. Time: 19.30. Tickets from the Estate office £8.00 & £5.00. Make up a party!

Castles

Goose Fair
18/7/99 SHUGBOROUGH ESTATE
18/7/99 Tel: 01889 881388
Witness a haphazard medley of riotous characters, entertainers and colourful market sellers, all the fun of the 1820 village fair at Shugborough Park Farm. Licensed bar and market stalls

Historic Houses & Gardens

Honda Motorcycle Classic Gathering
18/7/99 STANFORD HALL
18/7/99 Tel: 01788 860250
Telephone 01788 860250 for more details. Gates open by 10.00

Historic Houses

Cricket Match
19/7/99 CHELTENHAM CRICKET FESTIVAL 1999
19/7/99 Tel: 01242 514420
Gloucestershire versus Sri Lanka.

Festivals

Midsummer Night's Dream
20/7/99 PAINSWICK ROCOCO GARDEN
24/7/99 Tel: 01452 813204
Outdoor Shakespeare with covered seating, picnic before in the grounds. Please telephone for further information

Gardens

The Cotton Club Review
21/7/99 GAWSWORTH HALL
21/7/99 Tel: 01260 223456
Featuring: Joe Chisholm. The Jiving Lindy Hoppers and Harry Strutters Hot Rhythm Orchestra. Reviving the 1920s Harlem atmosphere of the great Cotton Club, prohibition, Al Capone set against the great music of Duke Ellington, Cab Callaway etc!! A music and dance spectacular. A£15.50 C£11.50. Ticket prices include admission to the Hall from 14.00 onwards. Group bookings of 25+ 10% discount. Seating is a fully covered grandstand, bring and rug and a picnic. Booking via Gawsworth Hall direct.

Historic Houses

Behind the Scenes Day
21/7/99 WORCESTER RACECOURSE
21/7/99 Tel: 01905 25364
Enjoy a day at the races with racing from 14.15. Admission prices from £5.50-£13.50, C£Free. Discount available for advance group bookings

Racecourses

Cricket Match
21/7/99 CHELTENHAM CRICKET FESTIVAL 1999
24/7/99 Tel: 01242 514420
Gloucestershire versus Durham.

Festivals

Finbar Furey in Concert
22/7/99 GAWSWORTH HALL
22/7/99 Tel: 01260 223456
(subject to confirmation) Hailed as Ireland Prince of Pipers Finbar is a musical legend. Enjoy the passionate and haunting sound of the Irish pipes - one not to be missed. A£15.50 C£11.50. Ticket prices include admission to the Hall from 14.00 onwards. Group bookings of 25+ 10% discount. Seating is a fully covered grandstand, bring and rug and a picnic. Booking via Gawsworth Hall direct.

Historic Houses

Twelfth Night
23/7/99 CALKE ABBEY
23/7/99 Tel: 01332 863822
An open-air performance given by Heartbreak Productions. Commences 19.30. Gates open 18.30. Cost: A£7.00 C£3.00. Bring rugs and picnics

Historic Houses & Gardens

Victorian Concert of Words and Music
23/7/99 CANONS ASHBY HOUSE
23/7/99 Tel: 01327 860044
Performance time: 19.30. Booking essential. Further information from property

Historic Houses

Kenny Ball and Laurie Chescoe
23/7/99 GAWSWORTH HALL
23/7/99 Tel: 01260 223456
Great Jazz music from the master himself, with the added attractions of Laurie Chescoe to start the evening off. A£16.50 C£11.50. Ticket prices include admission to the Hall from 14.00 onwards. Group bookings of 25+ 10% discount. Seating is a fully covered grandstand, bring and rug and a picnic. Booking via Gawsworth Hall direct.

Historic Houses

Bug Jam '99
23/7/99 SANTA POD RACEWAY
25/7/99 Tel: 01234 782828
Europe's largest Voltswagen Beetle event with Drag Racing, Jet Cars, Static Shows, Side-Shows. Live bands and DJs playing indie, dance, drum'n'bass and other styles

Motor Sports

Further more detailed information on the attractions listed can be found in Best Guides *Visitor Attractions* Guide under the classifications shown

23/7/99 31/7/99	**Wolkswagen Type 2 O.C.** BILLING AQUADROME LIMITED Tel: 01604 408181 Please telephone for further information. Contact: Mr Miners *Country Leisure Parks*

Sun Power!

23/7/99 JODRELL BANK SCIENCE CENTRE, PLANETARIUM AND ARBORETUM

1/6/00 Tel: 01477 571339

This new planetarium show is the first of the Science Centre's activities focussed on the Sun and light prior to the total eclipse of the Sun in August and the new Millennium

Science Centres

A Lincolnshire Prom

24/7/99 BELTON HOUSE

24/7/99 Tel: 01476 566116

Open-air concert featuring all the promenade favourites. The English National Orchestra conducted by Jae Alexander, accompanied by soloist Janet Mooney, Spitfire aerial display and choreographed firework finale. Gates open 17.00, performance starts 20.00. Ticket Prices: A£15.00 in advance, A£17.00 on the day C(5-16)£7.50 in advance £8.50 on the day. This programme is very popular so please book early. Please apply the regional booking office on 01909 511061

Historic Houses

Fireworks Concert 20.00

24/7/99 COUGHTON COURT

24/7/99 Tel: 01789 762435

Gates open at 17.30 for picnics, top class fireworks display, call for further details

Historic Houses & Gardens

The Magic of Frank Sinatra

24/7/99 GAWSWORTH HALL

24/7/99 Tel: 01260 223456

A tribute to the big band era awaits the first part of the evening. The second half forms a medley of Frank Sinatra's best loved songs, performed by Andy Prior and accompanied by his big band! A£16.05 C£12.00. Ticket prices include admission to the Hall from 14.00 onwards. Group bookings of 25+ 10% discount. Seating is a fully covered grandstand, bring and rug and a picnic. Booking via Gawsworth Hall direct.

Historic Houses

Fireworks and Laser Symphony Concert

SHUGBOROUGH ESTATE

24/7/99
24/7/99 Tel: 01889 881388

A spectacular evening of live music and magnificent fireworks, brilliant lasers and dancing water fountains. A£19.00 C£10.00. Book early to avoid disappointment

Historic Houses & Gardens

Steeplechase Meeting

24/7/99 STRATFORD-ON-AVON RACECOURSE

24/7/99 Tel: 01789 267949/269411

Enjoy a day at the races

Racecourses

Ford Cortina Owners Club Rally

24/7/99 BILLING AQUADROME LIMITED

25/7/99 Tel: 01604 408181

Please telephone Val Law on 0116 289 7029 for further information

Country Leisure Parks

V.B.O.A

24/7/99 BILLING AQUADROME LIMITED

25/7/99 Tel: 01604 408181

Please telephone for further information. Contact: Mandy Sanderson

Country Leisure Parks

Living History Weekend

24/7/99 BLACK COUNTRY LIVING MUSEUM

25/7/99 Tel: 0121 557 9643 info

The Friends of the Museum spend the weekend living in 1920's conditions in the many cottages and houses. Witness their attempts to wash, cook, clean and entertain themselves without all the modern conveniences which we take for granted!

Industrial Heritage

Sir Henry Dryden Festival

24/7/99 CANONS ASHBY HOUSE

25/7/99 Tel: 01327 860044

Celebrating the life of Sir Henry Dryden, antiquarian, on the 100th anniversary of his death. Saturday: Dryden Society and students day. Sunday: Exhibitions, talks, guided tours, book signing, commemorative church service, garden fayre and organ recitals

Historic Houses

Medieval Monastic Entertainers

24/7/99 HAILES ABBEY

25/7/99 Tel: 01242 602398

Try your hand at calligrapy or authentic period games as this popular duo take a light-hearted look at monastic customs, crafts and lifestyles. Learn about food preparation, herbs and spice in cooking and medicine, the mechanics of building, lifting and many other skills. Part of

Cistercian 900. From 12.00. A£3.00 C£1.50 Concessions£2.30 English Heritage members Free

Abbeys

Heart Link Leicester, Street Organ Festival 1999

24/7/99
25/7/99

HEART LINK LEICESTER, STREET ORGAN FESTIVAL 1999

Tel: 01509 880803

The largest of all British Organ Festival's in England with around 35 street fair organs coming from all over England and Wales to support "Heart Link, the East Midlands Children's Heart Care Association for which there is a street collection. The streets of Leicester are filled with music played on instruments recalling the music of yesteryear. The organ grinders will be delighted to explain how their instruments work and allow you to "Have a Grind"! Time: 09.30-16.30. Admission Free.

Festivals

Heart Link Steam and Vintage Festival 1999

24/7/99
25/7/99

HEART LINK STEAM AND VINTAGE FESTIVAL 1999

Tel: 01509 880803

Over 300 exhibits including steam engines, mini steam, vintage commercials, cars, motorbikes, tractors, barn engines, fair organs, trade area, bar, refreshments, children's funfair. A fun packed two day show with something for everyone. All proceeds are donated to Heart Link Children's Charity of Glenfield Hospital, Leicester. Cost: A£2.50 C&OAPs£1.50. Car Park by donation. Time: 11.00-17.00.

Festivals

History Fair

24/7/99
25/7/99

KENILWORTH CASTLE

Tel: 01926 852078

A history fair showing a multi-period. With various performers. A£4.00 C£2.00 Concessions£3.00

Castles

Restoration Household

24/7/99
25/7/99

LYDDINGTON BEDE HOUSE

Tel: 01572 822438

Performed by The Siege Group, a 17th-century re-enactment. A£3.50 C£1.80 Concessions£2.50

Historic Houses

Disabled Weekend

24/7/99
25/7/99

MIDLAND RAILWAYS CENTRE

Tel: 01773 747674/749788

Free train rides for registered disabled.

Railways Steam/Light

Medieval Life

24/7/99
25/7/99

THE COMMANDERY

Tel: 01905 355071

The Companions of the Black Bear will be re-creating Medieval Life

Historic Buildings

The Eckford Sweet Pea Society of Wem 1999

24/7/99
25/7/99

THE ECKFORD SWEET PEA SOCIETY OF WEM 1999

Tel: 01948 840779

To celebrate the Ter-Centenary of the Sweet Pea coming to this country from Sicily. With Wem having enjoyed a connection with Sweet Peas for well over a hundred years due to the sterling work of Henry Eckford it is fitting the town should be chosen to host such a prestigious event. The show will be held on the edge of Town at the Adams School, in the Stanier Hall and a large marquee. Times: Sat 10.00-17.00, Sun 10.00-16.00. Prices: A&OAPs£0.50 C£Free

Festivals

Jousting Weekend

24/7/99
25/7/99

WARWICK CASTLE

Tel: 01926 406600

Imagine how is must feel to face nearly a ton of flesh and armour charging at you, full tilt! An experience not to be missed.

Castles

Hands on in the Mill

24/7/99
31/8/99

QUARRY BANK MILL AND STYAL COUNTRY PARK

Tel: 01625 527468

A chance to see how the Quarry bank Mill operates, and what it is capable of producing. Further information including times, prices and bookings available by calling Quarry bank Mill

Heritage Centres

Summer Holidays Special

24/7/99
5/9/99

BLACK COUNTRY LIVING MUSEUM

Tel: 0121 557 9643 info

Enjoy all the Museum's best features along with traditional children's street games, crafts and a quizzical trail. The daily changing programme includes working horses, Charabang Tours, canal art painting and baking

Industrial Heritage

Exhibition: Picasso and Printmaking in Paris

Further more detailed information on the attractions listed can be found in Best Guides *Visitor Attractions* Guide under the classifications shown

24/7/99	**NOTTINGHAM CASTLE MUSEUM AND ART GALLERY**
19/9/99	Tel: 0115 915 3700

Prints by Picasso and his contemporaries

Castles

Sarah Lawrence Feltworks

24/7/99	**PICKFORD'S HOUSE SOCIAL HISTORY MUSEUM**
19/9/99	Tel: 01332 255363

Specialist exhibition for feltwork

Historic Houses

Ford Granada MK1 & MKII Drivers

25/7/99	**BILLING AQUADROME LIMITED**
25/7/99	Tel: 01604 408181

Tel 0860 759504 for more details

Country Leisure Parks

Cricket Match

25/7/99	**CHELTENHAM CRICKET FESTIVAL 1999**
25/7/99	Tel: 01242 514420

Gloucestershire versus Warwickshire.

Festivals

History Walk

25/7/99	**CLUMBER PARK**
25/7/99	Tel: 01909 476592

Although Clumber House was demolished in the 1930s, many fascinating features of the Estate remain. Guided walk with Visitor Services Manager, Trevor Pressley. Meet: 14.00, Information Point. Cost: £1.50 per person, booking essential

Historic Houses & Gardens

Performing Arts Concert (Deer Park)

25/7/99	**EASTNOR CASTLE**
25/7/99	Tel: 01531 633160

Castles

National Archaeology Day

25/7/99	**FORGE MILL NEEDLE MUSEUM AND BORDESLEY ABBEY VISITOR CENTRE**
25/7/99	Tel: 01527 62509

Archaeological activities at the museum in the Archaeological Activity Centre

Museum- Mill

Light Summer Classics

25/7/99	**GAWSWORTH HALL**
25/7/99	Tel: 01260 223456

Relax with a glass of wine, soak in the sumpteous setting and listen to the strains of Bach, Elgar, Grainger, Handel, Lehar and Strauss drifting on the summer breeze. Presented by the 25 piece L'Orchestre de la Reigne, musical director Lee Longdon. A£16.50 C£12.00. Ticket prices include admission to the Hall from 14.00 onwards. Group bookings of 25+ 10% discount. Seating is a fully covered grandstand, bring and rug and a picnic. Booking via Gawsworth Hall direct.

Historic Houses

Partake Elizabethan Dancers

25/7/99	**HADDON HALL**
25/7/99	Tel: 01629 812855

Performances of 16th century dances accompanied by the lute will be held throughout the day. Informal talks on dress, music and social etiquette

Historic Houses

Classic Motorcycle Racing

25/7/99	**MALLORY PARK**
25/7/99	Tel: 01455 842931/2/3

Racing and parades, solo and sidecar. £8.00. Please telephone 0930 55 59 60 for further information.

Motor Racing Circuit

Conservation Day

25/7/99	**SNIBSTON DISCOVERY PARK**
25/7/99	Tel: 01530 510851

Join the Rangers for an informative and entertaining day which focuses on nature and rural crafts. There will be a large variety of displays by nature and conservation groups and demonstrations by crafts people. Attractions include falconry, Shire horses and ferret racing - a great day out for all the family. 10.00-16.00 in the Grange Nature Reserve. Free

Industrial Heritage

Vintage Motorcycle Club Founders Day Rally

25/7/99	**STANFORD HALL**
25/7/99	Tel: 01788 860250

Telephone 01788 860250 for more details. Gates open by 10.00. Special admission price for this event

Historic Houses

Mini Beast Hunt and Art Workshop

25/7/99	**SUDBURY HALL AND THE MUSEUM OF CHILDHOOD, THE NATIONAL TRUST**
25/7/99	Tel: 01283 585305

Children to draw the beasties. Cost: £5.00 per family group

Country Estates

Music in the Gardens

25/7/99	**SUDELEY CASTLE AND GARDENS**
25/7/99	Tel: 01242 602308

Enjoy the music whafting through the gardens presented by Lydbrook Band

Castles

Open-air Theatre - 'The Waterbabies'

27/7/99 **DUDMASTON HALL**
27/7/99 Tel: 01746 780866
Presented by Illyria., 19.00, garden
opens 18.00. Seating is not provided,
bring rugs or chairs and your own picnic.
A£8.00 C£5.00
Historic Houses & Gardens

**The Good Old Days, Old Tyme Music
Hall**
28/7/99 **GAWSWORTH HALL**
28/7/99 Tel: 01260 223456
Featuring the talents of Duggie
Chapman, CLive Webb (ITV's Mad
Magician from Tiz Waz) Beryl Johnson
(international singing sensation) Steve
Barclay (from The Comedians) the 5 Roly
Polys (The Dancing Amazons!) and John
Stokes (Bachelors). A£15.50 C£11.50.
Ticket prices include admission to the
Hall from 14.00 onwards. Group book-
ings of 25+ 10% discount. Seating is a
fully covered grandstand, bring and rug
and a picnic. Booking via Gawsworth
Hall direct.
Historic Houses

Medieval Coin Making
28/7/99 **THE COMMANDERY**
29/7/99 Tel: 01905 355071
Experience Medieval coin making with
Grunal Moneta. The coins are all produced by hand and you can even have a
go at making your own coins
Historic Buildings

Twelfth Night
28/7/99 **WITLEY COURT**
29/7/99 Tel: 01299 896636
Presented by Heartbreak Productions, a
sparkling comedy laced with a soupcon
of romance, a touch of poetry, and huge
great dollops of seething lust! A£8.00
C£4.00 Concessions£6.00
Historic Houses & Gardens

Molecules on the Move
28/7/99 **JODRELL BANK SCIENCE CENTRE,
PLANETARIUM AND ARBORETUM**
2/9/99 Tel: 01477 571339
Return of the Williams Science Team and
their popular science 'join in ' demonstrations for families on space travel
from rocket launches to parachute drag.
No extra charge but numbers are limited
at each session
Science Centres

Grimesthrope Colliery Brass Band
29/7/99 **GAWSWORTH HALL**
31/7/99 Tel: 01260 223456
The real stars of Brassed Off return for

more evenings of Heroisim and Valour -
bring a Union Jack! 29th & 30th A£13.00
C£8.00. 31st A£17.50 C£14.50. Ticket
prices include admission to the Hall from
14.00 onwards. Group bookings of 25+
10% discount. Seating is a fully covered
grandstand, bring and rug and a picnic.
Booking via Gawsworth Hall direct.
Historic Houses

Opera in the Park
30/7/99 **CANONS ASHBY HOUSE**
30/7/99 Tel: 01327 860044
Opera Brava perform Barber of Seville.
Performance time: 19.30
Historic Houses

Twelfth Night
30/7/99 **KENILWORTH CASTLE**
31/7/99 Tel: 01926 852078
Presented by Heartbreak Productions, a
sparkling comedy laced with a soupcon
of romance, a touch of poetry, and huge
great dollops of seething lust! A£8.00
C£4.00 Concessions£6.00
Castles

Coys International Historic Festival
30/7/99 **SILVERSTONE CIRCUIT**
1/8/99 Tel: 01327 857271
Presented by Chrysler. Circuit: Hist.
Grand Prix. Feature: Historic Races &
Rallysprint. Please call for further infor-
mation
Motor Racing Circuit

Battle Proms Concert
31/7/99 **ATTINGHAM PARK**
31/7/99 Tel: 01743 708123
Music with Cavalry, cannon and fireworks. Cost to be advised
Historic Houses & Gardens

Butterfly Walks
31/7/99 **RYTON ORGANIC GARDENS**
31/7/99 Tel: 01203 303517
Join the Butterfly Conservation Society
on one of three butterfly tours at Ryton
Organic Gardens. See the many different
varieties of butterflies that grace the
gardens and find out which plants will
attract them into your own garden. From
Ryton Organic Gardens Shop at 14.00,
15.15 & 16.15. No extra charge for tours
on top of normal admission rates.
Gardens

Welsh Day
31/7/99 **WORCESTER RACECOURSE**
31/7/99 Tel: 01905 25364
Experience a day at the races with racing
from 13.50. Admission prices from
£5.50-£13.50, C£Free. Discount available

Further more detailed information on the attractions listed can be found
in Best Guides *Visitor Attractions* Guide under the classifications shown

for advance group bookings

Racecourses

Toyota Enthusiasts Club
31/7/99 BILLING AQUADROME LIMITED
1/8/99   Tel: 01604 408181
Tel 01604 408181 for more details

Country Leisure Parks

Granada MKI and MKII Drivers
31/7/99 BILLING AQUADROME LIMITED
1/8/99   Tel: 01604 408181
Tel 0860 759504 for more details

Country Leisure Parks

Hot Air Balloon Meet (Deer Park)
31/7/99 EASTNOR CASTLE
1/8/99   Tel: 01531 633160
The West Midlands Balloon Club are coming to Eastnor Deer Park this year for their annual meet. This is the first event of its kind at Eastnor and it promises to be a wonderful spectacle. There will be entertainment and refreshments available throughout the afternoon and at the end of the day, a mass of Hot Air Balloons will rise majestically over the Malvern Hills

Castles

Medieval Combat
31/7/99 GOODRICH CASTLE
1/8/99   Tel: 01600 890538
13th century knights in combat, archery contest, have-a-go archery and games. From 11.00. A£3.50 C£1.80 Concessions£2.60. EH Members Free

Castles

Newfoundland Dog Trials
31/7/99 RAGLEY HALL
1/8/99   Tel: 01789 762090
Newfoundland dog water trials and show

Historic Houses & Gardens

Medieval Weekend
31/7/99 ROCKINGHAM CASTLE
1/8/99   Tel: 01536 770240
Rockingham Castle is the only Castle left in England where the Norman ground plan can still be clearly seen. This new event takes advantage of that distinction to offer a weekend of medieval activities where the emphasis is on participation and authenticity. See local advertising for detailed programme

Castles

Traditional Song
31/7/99 STOKESAY CASTLE
1/8/99   Tel: 01588 672544
A family of musicians performing delightful unaccompanied song. A£3.50

C£1.80 Concessions£2.60. EH Members Free

Castles

The Warwick Guard
31/7/99 WARWICK CASTLE
1/8/99   Tel: 01926 406600
They're back again, going through their paces

Castles

Friends of Thomas the Tank Engine
31/7/99 MIDLAND RAILWAYS CENTRE
8/8/99   Tel: 01773 747674/749788
With Thomas and his Midland Railway Centre friends including Oswald the talking engine.

Railways Steam/Light

Stars, Stripes and Stitchhes
31/7/99 SULGRAVE MANOR
8/8/99   Tel: 01295 760205
The Manor's Annual Needlework Festival. Demonstrations, displays, exhibitions. Daily changing series of events. Send for full programme

Historic Houses

Teddy Bear's Picnic
1/8/99 CLUMBER PARK
1/8/99   Tel: 01909 476592
If you go down to the woods today...... Stories and music. Time: 14.00-16.00. Cost: C£1.00, accompanying adults and Teddy Bears £Free

Historic Houses & Gardens

Die Fledermaus
1/8/99 GAWSWORTH HALL
1/8/99   Tel: 01260 223456
By Johann Strauss, presented by London City Orchestra with a 12 piece orchestra. Featuring, amongst others, Naomi Harvey, Andrew Forbes Lane and Julian Jensen. Strauss's much loved story of mistaken identity, misunderstandings and champagne! A£18.50 C£14.00. Ticket prices include admission to the Hall from 14.00 onwards. Group bookings of 25+ 10% discount. Seating is a fully covered grandstand, bring and rug and a picnic. Booking via Gawsworth Hall direct.

Historic Houses

Guided Walk: Woodland Wonders
1/8/99 ILAM PARK
1/8/99   Tel: 01335 350245/350503
Discover more about how the National Trust manages it woodlands. Meet at Wetton Mill Trackside carpark at 13.45. £2.00 per person. Sorry no dogs. Fairly strenuous

Country Parks

Leicester Caribbean Carnival

1/8/99 LEICESTER CARIBBEAN CARNIVAL '99

1/8/99 Tel: 0116 253 0491

This is a great family day out, an event not to be missed. The Leicester Carnival has developed into the most successful festival in the East Midlands attracting over ninety thousand people from all walks of life, for one glorious day. The fun starts at 10.00 when the park is open to the public. At 12.00 the park is blessed by the Bishop of Leicester and the Carnival declared open by the Lord Mayor of Leicester. The bright and colourful procession leaves Victoria Park at approximately 13.00 led by Leicester's Carnival Queen, Mama, Prince and Princess, and followed by all the floats/troupes and Steelbands.

Carnivals

Drayton Croft Mallory Trophy

1/8/99 MALLORY PARK

1/8/99 Tel: 01455 842931/2/3

Roadstocks, solo and sidecar 125-1300cc. £7.00. Please telephone 0930 55 59 60 for further information.

Motor Racing Circuit

Victorian Circus & Street Market

1/8/99 SHUGBOROUGH ESTATE

1/8/99 Tel: 01889 881388

All the colour and bustle of a traditional market as costumed merchants and street entertainers invite visitors to enjoy this most Victorian spectacle. Admission includes car parking and entry to the Country Museum

Historic Houses & Gardens

Jaguar Enthusiasts Club Rally

1/8/99 STANFORD HALL

1/8/99 Tel: 01788 860250

Telephone 01788 860250 for more details. Gates open by 10.00. Special admission price for this event

Historic Houses

Holiday Activities

1/8/99 NATIONAL WATERWAYS MUSEUM

31/8/99 Tel: 01452 318054

Plenty to keep the children amused and entertained during the Holidays, call for details

Museum- Waterways

Shackleton 50th Anniversary

1/8/99 NEWARK AIR MUSEUM

31/8/99 Tel: 01636 707170

A fabulous event organised to celebrate the 50th anniversary of the first flight of the Avro Shackleton, final dates to be agreed call venue for further details

Museum- Aviation

15th Annual Robin Hood Festival

2/8/99 SHERWOOD FOREST COUNTRY PARK AND VISITOR CENTRE

8/8/99 Tel: 01623 823202/824490

A week of medieval merriment in the home of the world's most famous outlaw; includes so much for all the family you'll have to come back each day

Forest Visitor Centres

Children's Nature Day

3/8/99 ILAM PARK

3/8/99 Tel: 01335 350245/350503

Fun environmental activities. Ages 5-10. Cost: C£1.50. Time: 11.00

Country Parks

Baddesley Bug Hunt

4/8/99 BADDESLEY CLINTON HOUSE

4/8/99 Tel: 01564 783294

Meet at the car park (13.50) for 14.00 start for a 2 hour hunt. Come face to face with the creepy crawlies of the waterworld and land. Bring wellies and a net if you have one. Afterwards the children can enjoy a glass of squash and a biscuit from the restaurant. Advanced booking required. C£1.50 - all children must be accompanied by a parent/adult. Max. 50 persons, Sorry No Dogs

Historic Houses & Gardens

Wardens Walks

4/8/99 CLUMBER PARK

4/8/99 Tel: 01909 476592

Two chances to enjoy a guided walk with Warden Roy Turner. Meet at 14.00 and again at 18.30, Conservation Centre. Cost: £1.50 per person, booking essential

Historic Houses & Gardens

Twelfth Night

4/8/99 GOODRICH CASTLE

5/8/99 Tel: 01600 890538

A Shakespeare classic performed by Heartbreak Productions. A£8.00 C£4.00 Concessions£6.00

Castles

A Woman of No Importance

4/8/99 GAWSWORTH HALL

7/8/99 Tel: 01260 223456

Classic period drama by Oscar Wilde, directed by Alan Clements. 4th, 5th & 6th A£11.00 C£8.00, 7th A£14.00 C£10.00. Ticket prices include admission to the Hall from 14.00 onwards. Group bookings of 25+ 10% discount. Seating is a fully covered grandstand, bring and rug and a picnic. Booking via Gawsworth Hall direct.

Historic Houses

Children's Activity Afternoons
4/8/99 FORD GREEN HALL
25/8/99 Tel: 01782 233195
A series of four creative 'drop-in' afternoons on Wednesday 4th, 11th, 18th & 25th August. Activities for children with an historical theme.

Historic Houses

"Simple Medieval Crafts"
5/8/99 ILAM PARK
5/8/99 Tel: 01335 350245/350503
Another chance to join Derek Harley. Cost: £2.50 per person. Time: 10.30-12.00 & 14.00-15.30

Country Parks

The NEC Antiques For Everyone Fair
5/8/99 NATIONAL EXHIBITION CENTRE
8/8/99 Tel: 0121 780 4141 x2604
Hall 5. A major event featuring 600 dealers exhibiting in a two-section event. 200 dealers offer antiques and fine art datelined to 1914 in plush, stand-fitted Section One; 400 dealers occupy unit-displays in Section Two, showing all things antique and collectable made prior to 1940. An enormous range of very fine quality antiques and collectibles for every pocket with prices from less than £10 to over £100,000. 25,000 visitors anticipated. Open Thur & Fri 11.00-20.00, Sat & Sun 11.00-18.00

Exhibition Centres

Timon of Athens
5/8/99 ROYAL SHAKESPEARE COMPANY
9/10/99 Tel: 01789 296655
Performed at the Royal Shakespeare Theatre. Cast Includes: Timon: Alan Bates, Alcibiades: Rupert Penry-Jones, Apemantus: Richard McCabe & Flavius: John Woodvine. Deserted by his friends as a victim of his own generosity, Timon retreats to a cave to rail against all mankind. Last performed by the RSC in 1980 at The Other Place, Timon of Athens is staged in the RST for the first time since 1965. Prices vary from: £5.00-£39.00. Booking from 30th Jan 99

Arts & Entertainment

Gala Opera by Opera Brava
6/8/99 ROCKINGHAM CASTLE
6/8/99 Tel: 01536 770240
Another new event for Rockingham. Some of our thespian supporters wondered why we did not stage open-air opera in the same setting. Opera Brava will provide the response with an evening devoted to highlights from a variety of operas. Another opportunity for the hamper experts to achieve new heights of creativity, but don't forget the candles! See local advertising for further information

Castles

Picnic in the Park
6/8/99 WOLVERHAMPTON RACECOURSE
6/8/99 Tel: 01902 421421
Racing from Dunstall

Racecourses

Lads Night
6/8/99 WORCESTER RACECOURSE
6/8/99 Tel: 01905 25364
Theme night with racing from 17.50. Admission prices from £5.50-£13.50, discount available for advance group bookings, 2 complimentary badges for groups of 12-39 or 4 complimentary badges for 40+

Racecourses

Leather Festival
6/8/99 WALSALL LEATHER MUSEUM
8/8/99 Tel: 01922 721153
Three days of fun, celebrating Walsall's historic craft with lashings of events and activities for all the family

Museum- Industrial

Conflict at the Castle - Wargaming
7/8/99 BOLSOVER CASTLE
7/8/99 Tel: 01246 823349
Performed by the Dragoon Militaria Group. Normal admission prices apply.

Castles

Bat Walk
7/8/99 CLUMBER PARK
7/8/99 Tel: 01909 476592
Clumber is home to 7 species of bat, bring a torch and discover more about this hi-tech hunter. Meet: 19.00, Conservation Centre. Cost: £1.50 per person, booking essential

Historic Houses & Gardens

Open-air Theatre - 'Twelfth Night'
7/8/99 DUDMASTON HALL
7/8/99 Tel: 01746 780866
Presented by Illyria., 19.30, garden opens 18.00. Seating is not provided, bring rugs or chairs and your own picnic. A£8.00 C£5.00

Historic Houses & Gardens

Cotton Motorcycle Rally

7/8/99
7/8/99
GLOUCESTER FOLK MUSEUM
Tel: 01452 526467
Rally featuring approximately 30 Cotton motorcycles made in Gloucester from 1920s to late 1970s. Many are ridden to the Rally
Museum- Local History

The National Gundogs Association Championships 1999
7/8/99
7/8/99
NATIONAL EXHIBITION CENTRE
Tel: 0121 780 4141 x2604
Halls 3 & 3A. Please telephone The National Gundog Association, 01773 812326 for further information
Exhibition Centres

Outdoor 'Fireworks and Laser Symphony Concert'
7/8/99
7/8/99
RAGLEY HALL
Tel: 01789 762090
Please telephone for further information
Historic Houses & Gardens

Fireworks & Laser Symphony Concert
7/8/99
7/8/99
RAGLEY HALL
Tel: 01789 762090
Fireworks & Laser concerts are an irresistible summer cocktail. The piquant mixture is a blend of some of the best classical music ever written spiced with your mouth-watering picnics in the park and the whole topped by a liberal sprinkling of spectacle. It is delectable, exciting, satisfying and fun. Included in the programme this year are 'Light Cavalry Overtures' 'Skaters' Waltz' and Borodin's breathtaking 'Polovtsian Dances'...all with magnificent fireworks, brilliant lasers and whirling water fountains. Book early. Group bookings, with a discount of up to 20% for all concerts, can be made by reserving now and confirming final numbers at a later date. Ticket Hotline: 01625 56 00 00
Historic Houses & Gardens

Bentley Drivers Club Raceday
7/8/99
7/8/99
SILVERSTONE CIRCUIT
Tel: 01327 857271
Circuit: National. Feature: Club Races. Please call for further information
Motor Racing Circuit

Summer Murder Night - HMS Titanic
7/8/99
7/8/99
SNIBSTON DISCOVERY PARK
Tel: 01530 510851
By popular demand Pavanne return with another acclaimed murder night. Join Captain Smith and his guests on Sunday 14/4/99 in the a la carte restaurant on B deck. Doors open 19.30. The perfor-

mance starts at 20.00. A meal will be included in the ticket price. Telephone 01530 510851 after May. Advance booking essential
Industrial Heritage

Steeplechase Meeting
7/8/99
7/8/99
STRATFORD-ON-AVON RACECOURSE
Tel: 01789 267949/269411
Enjoy a day at the races
Racecourses

Jazz Concert
7/8/99
7/8/99
SUDELEY CASTLE AND GARDENS
Tel: 01242 602308
Gloucestershire Youth Jazz Orchestra present and evening of open air Jazz music, call for booking information
Castles

Alice in wonderland
7/8/99
8/8/99
ASHBY-DE-LA-ZOUCH CASTLE
Tel: 01530 413343
Labyrinth Productions. Follow Alice and White Rabbit as they go through Wonderland, meeting all manner of weird, wonderful and totally mad characters. A£3.50 C£1.80 Concessions£2.60
Castles

International Koi
7/8/99
8/8/99
BILLING AQUADROME LIMITED
Tel: 01604 408181
Please telephone for further information. Contact: John Woodall
Country Leisure Parks

Medieval Music, Calligraphy and Spinning
7/8/99
8/8/99
BUILDWAS ABBEY
Tel: 01952 433274
Fascinating medieval crafts and lively medieval music, as part of Cistercian 900. From 12.00. A£2.50 C£1.30 Concessions£1.90 EH Members Free
Historical Remains

Focus on Wildlife Weekend
7/8/99
8/8/99
KEDLESTON HALL AND PARK (NATIONAL TRUST)
Tel: 01332 842191
Demonstrations, hands-on learning, walks, slide shows
Historic Houses

The Soprano in Pink
7/8/99
8/8/99
LYDDINGTON BEDE HOUSE
Tel: 01572 822438
Rhiannon Gayle. Delightful 17th and 18th century song and spinet music, with gossip and talks about Georgian fashions. A£3.00 C£1.50 Concessions£2.30
Historic Houses

Riverside Fstival 1999

Further more detailed information on the attractions listed can be found in Best Guides *Visitor Attractions* Guide under the classifications shown

7/8/99 8/8/99	**RIVERSIDE FESTIVAL 1999** Tel: 0115 915 3595 A huge, two day jamboree of free family entertainment. Spread down the length of the Victoria Embankment there's a thousand and one things for people of all ages to do, whether it's enjoying the riotous street entertainers, braving the latest hair-raising fairground rides, browsing round the craft stalls, tuning into the roadshows or choosing which mouth-watering foods to eat, you'll soon be lost in the colourful, vibrant atmosphere that makes the Riverside Festival a favourite. DON'T forget, on Sunday the kids will love the Red Hot Lobster Tour featuring the Rug Rats. For those who enjoy the outdoor music festival atmosphere there is a melding of musical and cultural styles from the Pacific, via the Americas, Africa and Europe. *Festivals*

Organic Gardening Weekend

7/8/99 8/8/99	RYTON ORGANIC GARDENS Tel: 01203 303517 Organic gardeners throughout the country will be opening their gardens to the general public over this weekend. Ask for a free directory. *Gardens*

Fuchsia Festival

7/8/99 8/8/99	SHUGBOROUGH ESTATE Tel: 01889 881388 Courtesy of the Stafford & District Fuchsia Society decorating the ground floor of the Mansion House. A£4.00, reduced £3.00 *Historic Houses & Gardens*

Medieval Entertainment - Merrie England

7/8/99 8/8/99	STOKESAY CASTLE Tel: 01588 672544 Fighting knights, dancing, stories, children's games and juggling. From 12.00. A£3.50 C£1.80 Concessions£2.50. EH Members Free *Castles*

Winning the Spurs

7/8/99 8/8/99	WARWICK CASTLE Tel: 01926 406600 Knights in battle fight to win their spurs, and the falconer returns to the Castle *Castles*

American Civil War

7/8/99 8/8/99	WESTON PARK Tel: 01952 850207 A battle re-inactment authentically per-

formed in the woodland grounds
Historic Houses & Gardens

Chocolate

7/8/99 25/9/99	MANSFIELD MUSEUM AND ART GALLERY Tel: 01623 463088 An innovative exhibition focusing on new art made with and about chocolate *Museum- Local History*

Herefordshire Country Fair (Deer Park)

8/8/99 8/8/99	EASTNOR CASTLE Tel: 01531 633160 *Castles*

Race Day

8/8/99 8/8/99	MALLORY PARK Tel: 01455 842931/2/3 Formula Renault, Westfield Sportscars, Classic and historic touring cars, BMW, sports 1600. £8.00. Please telephone 0930 55 59 60 for further information. *Motor Racing Circuit*

Butterfly Walks

8/8/99 8/8/99	RYTON ORGANIC GARDENS Tel: 01203 303517 Join the Butterfly Conservation Society on one of three butterfly tours at Ryton Organic Gardens. See the many different varieties of butterflies that grace the gardens and find out which plants will attract them into your own garden. From Ryton Organic Gardens Shop at 14.00, 15.15 & 16.15. No extra charge for tours on top of normal admission rates. *Gardens*

Aston Martin Owners Club Raceday

8/8/99 8/8/99	SILVERSTONE CIRCUIT Tel: 01327 857271 Circuit: National. Feature: Club Races. Please call for further information *Motor Racing Circuit*

Francis Barnett Motorcycle Owners Club Rally

8/8/99 8/8/99	STANFORD HALL Tel: 01788 860250 Telephone 01788 860250 for more details. Gates open by 10.00. Special admission price for this event *Historic Houses*

MG 75th Anniversay

9/8/99 9/8/99	HERITAGE MOTOR CENTRE Tel: 01926 641188 Bring along your MG to join 100's of others, and help us blow out the candles on this historical day *Museum- Motor*

Elgar Day

9/8/99	**WORCESTER RACECOURSE**
9/8/99	Tel: 01905 25364

Racing from 14.15. Admission prices from £5.50-£13.50, discount available for advance group bookings, 2 complimentary badges for groups of 12-39 or 4 complimentary badges for 40+

Racecourses

Caring for Wildlife Week

9/8/99	**HARDWICK HALL**
13/8/99	Tel: 01246 850430

A week of activities in the park looking at the wildlife that live on and visit the estate. Activities open to all, but aimed at children between the ages of 4-14. Children must be accompanied by an adult. Limited numbers - booking essential. Tel. 01246 851787 for further details

Historic Houses

Summer Pruning of Top Fruit

10/8/99	**RYTON ORGANIC GARDENS**
10/8/99	Tel: 01203 303517

This course will cover the annual pruning of plums and cherries and summer work on restricted forms of apples and pears. Time: 10.00-12.30.

Gardens

Music from the Movies

11/8/99	**GAWSWORTH HALL**
11/8/99	Tel: 01260 223456

A stunning collection of favourite themes, taken from the greatest movies of all time - Star Wars; Titanic; Gone with the Wind; The Deer Hunter and Out of Africa to name a few. Presented b the 25 piece L'Orchestre de la Reigne, musical director Lee Langdon. A£16.50 C£12.00. Ticket prices include admission to the Hall from 14.00 onwards. Group bookings of 25+ 10% discount. Seating is a fully covered grandstand, bring and rug and a picnic. Booking via Gawsworth Hall direct.

Historic Houses

Observations

11/8/99	**JODRELL BANK SCIENCE CENTRE, PLANETARIUM AND ARBORETUM**
11/8/99	Tel: 01477 571339

Observations and activities centred around the total eclipse of the Sun

Science Centres

Children's Activities

11/8/99	**SUDBURY HALL AND THE MUSEUM OF CHILDHOOD, THE NATIONAL TRUST**
15/8/99	Tel: 01283 585305

11th: Pond/Tank dipping; 12th: Mini Beast Hunt; 13th: Tree Trail plus; 14th:

Environmental Games; 15th: Wildlife Crafts. Sessions: 12.00-14.00 & 14.00-16.00. Cost: £1.00

Country Estates

A Box at the Opera

12/8/99	**GAWSWORTH HALL**
12/8/99	Tel: 01260 223456

A varied programme with excerpts from Marriage of Figaro, Carmen, Cosi Fan Tuti, La Boheme and La Traviata. Presented by Martina McEvoy, our soloists are Naomi Harvey, Andrew Forbes Lane, Mark Oldfield and Valery Reid, accompanied by a 12 piece orchestra under the musical direction of Richard Balcome. A£16.00 C£12.00. Ticket prices include admission to the Hall from 14.00 onwards. Group bookings of 25+ 10% discount. Seating is a fully covered grandstand, bring and rug and a picnic. Booking via Gawsworth Hall direct.

Historic Houses

Music Festival

12/8/99	**WESTON PARK**
15/8/99	Tel: 01952 850207

A selection of classical musical evenings performed in the magnificent house with Gourmet Dinner. An outdoor 'Proms' concert in traditional style with a spectacular firework finale. Outdoor Pop Concert - artiste to be announced, call for further information call for times and prices

Historic Houses & Gardens

A Warwickshire Testimony - World Premiere

12/8/99	**ROYAL SHAKESPEARE COMPANY**
23/9/99	Tel: 01789 296655

Performed at The Other Place. A new play by April de Angelis. Director: Alison Sutcliffe, Designer: Paul Farnsworth. Funny, fresh, disarming - these simple snapshots of a century of change show how village life transforms the lives of Aunty Edie and her niece Dorothy. Prices vary from: £10.00-£20.00. Booking from 30th Jan 99

Arts & Entertainment

The Best of the West End

13/8/99	**CALKE ABBEY**
13/8/99	Tel: 01332 863822

Open air concert with a performance of songs form the most popular West End Musicals and a brilliant firework finale. Gates open 17.00. Performance starts 20.00. Tickets A£15.00 C£(5-16)£7.50 in

Further more detailed information on the attractions listed can be found in Best Guides *Visitor Attractions* Guide under the classifications shown

advance, A£17.00 C£8.50 on the gate,
£22.20 if both concerts booked together. Booking office 01909 511061

Historic Houses & Gardens

Marion Montgomery
13/8/99 GAWSWORTH HALL
13/8/99 Tel: 01260 223456
A highlight of the 1998 season, Marion
and her stunning jazz trio return for
anouth smooth, sophisticated evening
of unforgettable jazz. A£16.00 C£12.00.
Ticket prices include admission to the
Hall from 14.00 onwards. Group bookings of 25+ 10% discount. Seating is a
fully covered grandstand, bring and rug
and a picnic. Booking via Gawsworth
Hall direct.

Historic Houses

Alice in Wonderland
13/8/99 KEDLESTON HALL AND PARK (NATIONAL
TRUST)
13/8/99 Tel: 01332 842191
Open-air evening theatre performed by
Troubadour Theatre. Performance starts:
19.00. Please bring a rug and a picnic

Historic Houses

Evening Flat Racing
13/8/99 WARWICK RACECOURSE
13/8/99 Tel: 01926 491553
Organise a party outing for a night at the
races. Group rates available. First race at
17.50, last race 20.20

Racecourses

All Seasons Caravan Club
13/8/99 BILLING AQUADROME LIMITED
15/8/99 Tel: 01604 408181
Please telephone Sue Stewart, 0116 230
1351 for further information

Country Leisure Parks

Granada MKII Collection
13/8/99 BILLING AQUADROME LIMITED
15/8/99 Tel: 01604 408181
Please telephone for further information. Contact: Rod Bamford, 0116 225
8598

Country Leisure Parks

**The Rivals - Outdoor Theatre
Production**
13/8/99 SULGRAVE MANOR
15/8/99 Tel: 01295 760205
The Motley Crew Theatre Company
return to perform in the gardens of the
Manor. 19.00 on Friday and Saturday,
15.00 matinee on Sunday. Why not bring
a bottle, a full picnic, or even just a
friend and enjoy the play. Whatever the
weather the show will go on! A£7.50

C&OAPs£5.00. Please write or phone to
book 01295 760205

Historic Houses

Victorian Day
14/8/99 BIDDULPH GRANGE GARDEN
14/8/99 Tel: 01782 517999
Staff and volunteers will be dressed in
costume abd traditional Victorian dishes
will be available in the tea room

Gardens

Classical Spectacular
14/8/99 CALKE ABBEY
14/8/99 Tel: 01332 863822
Open air concert featuring The English
National Orchestra with a grand firework
finale. Gates open 17.00. Performance
starts 20.00. Tickets A£15.00 C£(5-
16)£7.50 in advance, A£17.00 C£8.50 on
the gate, £22.50 if both concerts booked
together. Booking office 01909 511061.
House and gardens closed all day

Historic Houses & Gardens

Wild about Wildlife
14/8/99 CLUMBER PARK
14/8/99 Tel: 01909 476592
A wildlife open day with talks, walks and
fun activities to help explain the work
that goes into managing Clumber's
wildlife. Time: 10.00-16.00. Suitable for
adults and children. No additional
charge

Historic Houses & Gardens

Alice in Wonderland
14/8/99 CLUMBER PARK
14/8/99 Tel: 01909 476592
Dramatisation by Troubadour Theatre.
Performance Times: 14.00 & 18.00.
Please bring rugs and picnics

Historic Houses & Gardens

Fivepenny Piece
14/8/99 GAWSWORTH HALL
14/8/99 Tel: 01260 223456
They just keep getting better and better!
Laugh at their jokes and sing along to all
the old favourites. A£14.00 C£10.00.
Ticket prices include admission to the
Hall from 14.00 onwards. Group bookings of 25+ 10% discount. Seating is a
fully covered grandstand, bring and rug
and a picnic. Booking via Gawsworth
Hall direct.

Historic Houses

Cartoon Making
14/8/99 MANOR HOUSE MUSEUM
14/8/99 Tel: 01536 534219
Visitng cartoonist Steve Marchant welcome visiting children to a session of

cartooning, call for details

Museum- Local History

The 1999 Music & Fireworks Spectacular

14/8/99
14/8/99
STANFORD HALL
Tel: 01788 860250
Telephone 01788 860250 for more details. Gates open 10.00. Special admission price for this event

Historic Houses

Fashion Festival/Weatherby Dash

14/8/99
14/8/99
WOLVERHAMPTON RACECOURSE
Tel: 01902 421421
Racing from Dunstall

Racecourses

Avoncroft Arts Festival

14/8/99
15/8/99
AVONCROFT MUSEUM OF HISTORIC BUILDINGS
Tel: 01527 831363
Music, dancing, exhibitions, huge art and more. Part of the Three Choirs Festival Fringe, call for fuller details

Museum- Local History

Cobra National Weekend & Other Replica Owners Club

14/8/99
15/8/99
BILLING AQUADROME LIMITED
Tel: 01604 408181
Please telephone either Doug Waller, 01376 514416 or Paul Mobbs, 01933 227788 for further information

Country Leisure Parks

Model Spectacular (Deer Park)

14/8/99
15/8/99
EASTNOR CASTLE
Tel: 01531 633160

Castles

International Mini Meeting

14/8/99
15/8/99
HERITAGE MOTOR CENTRE
Tel: 01926 641188
The first Mini meeting this year, don't forget the Minis 40th Birthday celebrations held here on 3rd October 99

Museum- Motor

History in Action IV

14/8/99
15/8/99
KIRBY HALL
Tel: 01536 203230
Enjoy the world's largest and best festival of multi-period living history and re-enactment. Bigger and better than ever, with an action-packed two-day programme featuring around 2000 participants from over 50 top societies including from Europe. Gates open 09.30, with major displays from 10.30-17.30. Includes historical craft market with over 50 stalls, children's activities, catering areas and ample free parking. A£9.50

C£5.00 Concessions£7.50

Historic Houses

MCN British Superbike Championship

14/8/99
15/8/99
MALLORY PARK
Tel: 01455 842931/2/3
The country's biggest and best motorcycle race series. 125, 250 & 600 British Champs, 600 Shootout. Saturday qualifying, Sunday Raceday. £5.00-£16.00. Please telephone 0930 55 59 60 for further information.

Motor Racing Circuit

Garden Railway Festival & Narrow Gauge Railway Gala

14/8/99
15/8/99
MIDLAND RAILWAYS CENTRE
Tel: 01773 747674/749788
Models and full size narrow gauge railways.

Railways Steam/Light

750 Motor Club Race Meeting

14/8/99
15/8/99
SILVERSTONE CIRCUIT
Tel: 01327 857271
Circuit: National. Feature: Club Races. Please call for further information

Motor Racing Circuit

Medieval Music - Trevor James

14/8/99
15/8/99
STOKESAY CASTLE
Tel: 01588 672544
Enjoy melodies and dance tunes dating back to the 12th century. A£3.50 C£1.80 Concessions£2.50

Castles

Shakespeare

14/8/99
15/8/99
SUDELEY CASTLE AND GARDENS
Tel: 01242 602308
The Festival Players present an outdoor performance of William Shakespeare's Taming of The Shrew, call for full booking information

Castles

Medieval Life

14/8/99
15/8/99
THE COMMANDERY
Tel: 01905 355071
The Companions of the Black Bear will be re-creating Medieval life

Historic Buildings

Jousting Weekend

14/8/99
15/8/99
WARWICK CASTLE
Tel: 01926 406600
Let the Jousting commence! Hear the clash of steel and the crash of knights being hurled from their steeds

Castles

Miller Magic

15/8/99
15/8/99
GAWSWORTH HALL
Tel: 01260 223456
The welcome return of John Miller and

his big band, with his own tribute to his Uncle Glenn! With special guest Fiona Paige. A£15.50 C£11.50. Ticket prices include admission to the Hall from 14.00 onwards. Group bookings of 25+ 10% discount. Seating is a fully covered grandstand, bring and rug and a picnic. Booking via Gawsworth Hall direct.

Historic Houses

Guided Walk: Butterflies on Bardbury's Bank

15/8/99
15/8/99   ILAM PARK
Tel: 01335 350245/350503
Join a warden as he undertakes his butterfly survey, while learning how to identify these fast flying insects. Meet at Ilam Hall School Room at 10.30. *Booking important due to weather dependancy. £2.00 per person. Sorry no dogs. Fairly strenuous

Country Parks

Medieval Archery

15/8/99
15/8/99   PEVERIL CASTLE
Tel: 01433 620613
15th century archery and combat-at-arms. From 12.00. A£3.00 C£1.50 Concessions£2.30

Castles

Animal Magic

15/8/99
15/8/99   SHUGBOROUGH ESTATE
Tel: 01889 881388
Meet all creatures great and small... from rare and endangered species. In association with WWF. Also supported by Staffordshire Bee Keepers' Association. Fun activities throughout the day. Suitable for all ages. A£4.00, reduced £3.00

Historic Houses & Gardens

Mid-Summer Stroll

15/8/99
15/8/99   SNIBSTON DISCOVERY PARK
Tel: 01530 510851
Enjoy a guided walk around the Snibston site looking at the interesting wildlife and plants of the local area. The day can be finished off with a refreshing cup of tea at Snibston's cafe. Please wear suitable clothing and footwear. Time: 15.00-17.00. Suitable for all ages. Limited places. For ticket details contact 01530 510851 after 1/7/99. Advance booking essential

Industrial Heritage

Zundapp-Bella Enthusiasts' Club Rally

15/8/99
15/8/99   STANFORD HALL
Tel: 01788 860250
Telephone 01788 860250 for more

details. Gates open by 10.00

Historic Houses

Children's Fun Week

16/8/99
20/8/99   EASTNOR CASTLE
Tel: 01531 633160
Last year nearly 5000 visitors enjoyed an amazing range of activities for children of all ages and this year we are offering even more great value entertainment. There will be Bouncy Castles, Velcro Olympics, Bunjee and Gladiator Challenges, Punch and Judy Shows, Magicians, Painting Competitions, Bertie and fun-filled Double Decker Bus, Arms and Armour Demonstrations, Circus Skill Workshops and much, much more!

Castles

Trusty's Treasure Trail

17/8/99
17/8/99   ILAM PARK
Tel: 01335 350245/350503
Follow Trusty's trail to find the hidden treasure. Cost: £1.00 per child

Country Parks

Bat Night

18/8/99
18/8/99   RYTON ORGANIC GARDENS
Tel: 01203 303517
Bat expert, Chris Brook-Harris, will be talking about this delightful, flying mammal at 20.00 and then taking visitors on a bat tour of Ryton Organic Gardens. Time: 20.00-22.00. Cost: £5.00 (£4.00 HDRA members) includes tea/coffee.

Gardens

Prestige Figures Days

18/8/99
19/8/99   ROYAL DOULTON VISITOR CENTRE
Tel: 01782 292434
A rare opportunity to see Royal Doulton's prestige figure range. These exquisite pieces take several weeks to create and are available to special order only

Factory Tours and Shopping

A Murder is Announced

18/8/99
21/8/99   GAWSWORTH HALL
Tel: 01260 223456
by Agatha Christie, adapted by Leslie Darbon. The announcement is in the local paper, stating the time and place of a murder, to occur in Miss Blacklocks country house. The victim is an unknown and unsuspecting visitor, and Miss Marple is called to unravel the ensuing puzzle! See if you can beat her to the dramatic confrontation before the final curtain! 18th, 19th & 20th A£11.00 C£8.00, 21st A£14.00 C£10.00. Ticket prices include admission to the Hall from

14.00 onwards. Group bookings of 25+ 10% discount. Seating is a fully covered grandstand, bring and rug and a picnic. Booking via Gawsworth Hall direct.

Historic Houses

Ross-on-Wye International Festival 1999

19/8/99 ROSS-ON-WYE INTERNATIONAL FESTIVAL 1999

30/8/99 Tel: 01594 562768 TIC

The Festival consists of tweleve days of the very best in music, theatre, dance, opera and comedy from the UK and abroad. Once again, this year Ross-on-Wye will take on a truly international flavour, as performers, acts and companies from as far-a-field as Israel and Japan come together to take part in this fantastic event. The Festival site is situated on the banks of the River Wye looking up at this historic town of Ross. Additional events include International Dance and a full programme of free fringe and street activities taking place in and around the Festival site and Ross-on-Wye town centre. The Festival brochure will be available from mid June 1999, brochure Hotline: 01594 541070.

Festivals

Narthampton Balloon Festival

20/8/99 NORTHAMPTON BALLOON FESTIVAL 1999

22/8/99 Tel: 01604 238791

Over 200,000 people visited the 1998 festival making it one of the most successful ever held. Three days of Balloon glows, flights, fireworks and festival fun.

Balloon Festivals

Sounds of the 70s

21/8/99 CLUMBER PARK

21/8/99 Tel: 01909 476592

An open-air concert with firework finale. Featuring Edwin Starr, Bjorn Again and Hot Chocolate. Gates open 16.00 for 19.00 start. Tickets A£15.00 C£(5-16)£7.50 in advance, A£17.00 C£8.50 on the gate. Please apply to the the regional booking office on 01909 511061

Historic Houses & Gardens

Bat, Wine and Cheese Evening

21/8/99 HARDWICK HALL

21/8/99 Tel: 01246 850430

An evening looking at the world of bats on the estate followed by wine and cheese in the Great Kitchen or, weather permitting, outside. Limited numbers - booking essential. Meet: 19.00 at the Hall car park. Cost: £15.00 per person

Historic Houses

Silverstone RallySprint

21/8/99 SILVERSTONE CIRCUIT

21/8/99 Tel: 01327 857271

Circuit: Roger Clark. Feature: Stars & Cars of National Rally. Please call for further information

Motor Racing Circuit

Mini 40th Celebration

21/8/99 SILVERSTONE CIRCUIT

21/8/99 Tel: 01327 857271

Circuit: International. Feature: Mini Festival & National Racing. Please call for further information

Motor Racing Circuit

Horticultural Show

21/8/99 THE BASS MUSEUM

21/8/99 Tel: 01283 511000

Bass Gardening Club will hold their 33rd Annual Vegetable & Flower Show in the Dray Shed. 10.00-17.00

Breweries

The Age of Progress

21/8/99 BOLSOVER CASTLE

22/8/99 Tel: 01246 823349

History Matters Group. A£3.50 C£1.80 Concessions£2.60

Castles

Re-enactment of Battle of Bosworth Field (1485)

21/8/99 BOSWORTH BATTLEFIELD VISITOR CENTRE AND COUNTRY PARK

22/8/99 Tel: 01455 290429

A medieval weekend with living history displays, medieval market and battle re-enactment

Battlefields

Craft Fair

21/8/99 COUGHTON COURT

22/8/99 Tel: 01789 762435

Summer craft show in marquees in front park and refeshments and entertainment

Historic Houses & Gardens

Meet the Mad Hatter!

21/8/99 GOODRICH CASTLE

22/8/99 Tel: 01600 890538

Performed by the Inner State Theatre Company. A£3.10 C£1.60 Concessions£2.30

Castles

Medieval Calligraphy & Spinning

21/8/99 HAILES ABBEY

22/8/99 Tel: 01242 602398

Step back in time to the 15th century and see how a 'clerk of minor orders' went about his business! Authentic calligraphy, illuminating book making skills are demonstrated, plus the use of an unusual spindle wheel. A£3.00 C£1.50 Concessions£2.30

Abbeys

Medieval Life
21/8/99 KENILWORTH CASTLE
22/8/99 Tel: 01926 852078
The Medieval Free Company. 15th century military and domestic life, with crafts, children's games, archery, squire training and combat. From 12.00. A£4.00 C£2.00 Concessions£3.00

Castles

Enid Blyton Weekend
21/8/99 MIDLAND RAILWAYS CENTRE
22/8/99 Tel: 01773 747674/749788
Featuring Noddy, the Famous Five and much more.

Railways Steam/Light

Diesel & Steam Weekend
21/8/99 MIDLAND RAILWAYS CENTRE
22/8/99 Tel: 01773 747674/749788
Featuring steam and diesel locomotives on passenger trains.

Railways Steam/Light

Warwickshire and West Midlands Game Fair
21/8/99 RAGLEY HALL
22/8/99 Tel: 01789 762090
Includes continuous main arena events with sheepdog demonstrations, basic gun dog events, military bands, sidesaddle riding displays and many other exhibitions, demonstrations and displays

Historic Houses & Gardens

Birds of Prey
21/8/99 WARWICK CASTLE
22/8/99 Tel: 01926 406600
Wonderful birds of prey return once again to the Castle for another spectacular display

Castles

The Victorian Love Story
21/8/99 IRONBRIDGE GORGE MUSEUMS
23/8/99 Tel: 01952 432166
A day long peripatetic drama in which members of the public may take part if they wish to - for example, attend a wedding, join in the bachelor party etc. Normal admission prices apply

Museum- Industrial

Three Choirs Festival
21/8/99 WORCESTER CATHEDRAL
27/8/99 Tel: 01905 28854/21004
The oldest annual festival in Europe featuring choirs from Gloucester, Hereford

and Worcester Cathedrals

Cathedrals

Paint the Landscape
22/8/99 ILAM PARK
22/8/99 Tel: 01335 350245/350503
Anytime from 11.00-16.00. Small donation for materials

Country Parks

Championship Club Racing
22/8/99 MALLORY PARK
22/8/99 Tel: 01455 842931/2/3
With solos and sidecars 125-1300cc. £7.00. Please telephone 0930 55 59 60 for further information.

Motor Racing Circuit

Last Night of the Proms
22/8/99 SHUGBOROUGH ESTATE
22/8/99 Tel: 01889 881388
A superb musical evening with rousing singing, waving flags, terrific atmosphere and stunning fireworks. All add up to a breathtaking finale, as the orchestra play Land of Hope and Glory. A£16.50 C£10.00. Please telephone 01625 560000 for details and bookings. Gates open 17.00. Book early to avoid disappointment

Historic Houses & Gardens

Computacenter Silverstone Summer Fest '99
22/8/99 SILVERSTONE CIRCUIT
22/8/99 Tel: 01327 857271
Circuit: International. Feature: Race & Music Festival. Please call for further information

Motor Racing Circuit

Midlands Austin 7 Car Club Rally
22/8/99 STANFORD HALL
22/8/99 Tel: 01788 860250
Also, Salmons Tickford Enthusiasts' Club Rally. Telephone 01788 860250 for more details. Gates open by 10.00

Historic Houses

Pony Club Championshhios
24/8/99 WESTON PARK
26/8/99 Tel: 01952 850207
Three days of Dressage, Showjumping and Cross Country for youngsters. A must for Equestrian lovers

Historic Houses & Gardens

Family Fun Day
25/8/99 WORCESTER RACECOURSE
25/8/99 Tel: 01905 25364
Entertainment for all the family, with children's entertainment available. Racing from 14.00. Admission prices from £5.50-£13.50, C£Free, discount

available for advance group bookings
Racecourses

Medieval Coin Making
25/8/99 THE COMMANDERY
26/8/99 Tel: 01905 355071
Experience Medieval coin making with
Grunal Moneta. The coins are all produced by hand and you can even have a
go at making your own coins
Historic Buildings

Exhibition
25/8/99 COTSWOLD HERITAGE CENTRE
12/9/99 Tel: 01451 860715
In the Cell Block Gallery. An exhibition by
the Area of Outstanding Natural Beauty
Team
Heritage Centres

Basketmaking Demonstration
26/8/99 COTSWOLD HERITAGE CENTRE
26/8/99 Tel: 01451 860715
In the Cell Block Gallery. With Norah
Kennedy. Please call for further information
Heritage Centres

Opera Classics
27/8/99 TOWCESTER RACECOURSE
27/8/99 Tel: 01327 353414
Opera Exclusive! Have put together a
special programme of opera classics to
be performed in the Grace Stand with
the Racecourse as a spectacular backdrop. Guests will be shown to their
tables and prior to dinner will enjoy an
hour of opera favourites
Racecourses

Ampthil Under 11's
27/8/99 BILLING AQUADROME LIMITED
30/8/99 Tel: 01604 408181
Please telephone for further information. Contact: Julie Cooper
Country Leisure Parks

Last Night of the Proms
28/8/99 TOWCESTER RACECOURSE
28/8/99 Tel: 01327 353414
This outdoor picnic prom will re-create
the atmosphere of The Royal Albert Hall.
To culminate the evening a spectacular
firework display will fill the skies to the
chorus of Land of Hope and Glory
Racecourses

PBFA Book Fair
28/8/99 HERITAGE MOTOR CENTRE
29/8/99 Tel: 01926 641188
Please call for more details
Museum- Motor

Craft Fair

GAWSWORTH HALL
28/8/99 GAWSWORTH HALL
30/8/99 Tel: 01260 223456
Exhibitors from all over the country, displaying the finest examples of British
craftmanship
Historic Houses

Working Craft Show
28/8/99 KEDLESTON HALL AND PARK (NATIONAL
TRUST)
30/8/99 Tel: 01332 842191
Family workshops and entertainment.
No charge for park/garden over week-
end. Time: 10.30-18.00. Entry to show:
A£3.00 C£Free
Historic Houses

Vintage Train Weekend
28/8/99 MIDLAND RAILWAYS CENTRE
30/8/99 Tel: 01773 747674/749788
Featuring our museum train in public
use and staff in period costume.
Railways Steam/Light

Teddy Bear Weekend
28/8/99 NORTHAMPTON AND LAMPORT RAILWAY
30/8/99 Tel: 01604 847318
Any child under 16 accompanied by a
teddy bear will get to enjoy a free ride.
Also the famous Hunt the Teddy
Competition will excite and delight visitors over the weekend
Railways Steam/Light

Shugborough Summer Craft Fair
28/8/99 SHUGBOROUGH ESTATE
30/8/99 Tel: 01889 881388
A major craft show with something of
interest for all the family. An excellent
selection of contemporary crafts, with
interesting demonstrations and skills on
display. Separate charge for this event
Historic Houses & Gardens

Seven Years War - 1756-1763
28/8/99 SULGRAVE MANOR
30/8/99 Tel: 01295 760205
George Washington's first experience as
a soldier fighting for the King as a
Redcoat against the French and the
Indians. Usual opening times. A£4.50
C£2.25
Historic Houses

Town & Country Festival
28/8/99 TOWN AND COUNTRY FESTIVAL 1999
30/8/99 Tel: 01203 696969
The Town and Country Festival is the
Midlands biggest family fun day
out.1999 Grand Ring attractions include
The Devil's Horseman, The Kangaroo Kid
and the White Helmets Motorcycle Team.
A£7.00 C(5-15)£4.00 Family Ticket

Further more detailed information on the attractions listed can be found
in Best Guides *Visitor Attractions* Guide under the classifications shown

£17.50 OAPs£4.00

Festivals

Medieaval Festival
28/8/99 WARWICK CASTLE
30/8/99 Tel: 01926 406600
Jousting and Birds of Prey feature over this Bank Holiday weekend. Come and join us in our Medieaval Festival with a host of side shows and costumed characters.

Castles

Summer Festival
28/8/99 BLACK COUNTRY LIVING MUSEUM
1/9/99 Tel: 0121 557 9643 info
Five days of lively activities in and around the streets of the old-fashioned canal-side village. Enjoy celebrations typical of a traditional Wake Week, including street entertainment, hurdy gurdys, and an old-fashioned street market

Industrial Heritage

Art, Trade or Mystery
28/8/99 NORTHAMPTON CENTRAL MUSEUM AND ART GALLERY
26/9/99 Tel: 01604 238548
Lace and lace making in Northamptonshire

Art Galleries

Betafoods Dog Agility
29/8/99 BILLING AQUADROME LIMITED
29/8/99 Tel: 01604 408181
Please telephone for further information. Contact: Jim Davidson

Country Leisure Parks

European Motorcycle Stunt Championships
29/8/99 MALLORY PARK
29/8/99 Tel: 01455 842931/2/3
A full day of non-stop stunt riding action, plus fun fair. £10.00. Please telephone 0930 55 59 60 for further information.

Motor Racing Circuit

Medieval Tournament
29/8/99 ASHBY-DE-LA-ZOUCH CASTLE
30/8/99 Tel: 01530 413343
Plantagenet Medieval Society. Armoured knights fight for supremacy in a colourful tourney. A£3.00 C£1.50 Concessions£2.30

Castles

Medieval Combat
29/8/99 BOLSOVER CASTLE
30/8/99 Tel: 01246 823349
The Harlech Medieval Society. 13th century knights in combat, archery contest, have-a-go archery and games. From

11.00. A£4.00 C£2.00 Concessions£3.00

Castles

Family Fun Days
29/8/99 BROADFIELD HOUSE GLASS MUSEUM
30/8/99 Tel: 01384 812745
Lots to do and see in and around the museum with traditional games and stalls, craft workshops and demonstrations

Museum- Glass

FIA European Trucks
29/8/99 DONINGTON PARK
30/8/99 Tel: 01332 810048
British Truck Racing Association, 250cc Gearbox Karts, Thoroughbred Grand Prix, Sport Palmer Honda, Gilera Scooters.

Motor Racing Circuit

The Berkeley Household: Living History in the Wars of the Roses
29/8/99 EASTNOR CASTLE
30/8/99 Tel: 01531 633160
Medieval history comes alive at Eastnor Castle when over fifty members of the renowned history group, The White Company set up camp in the Castle grounds. Visitors will see arrows speeding from archers' longbows, swords will clash as soldiers meet in combat and at the forge armourers will be making authentic arms and armour. Succulent medieval dishes will be prepared over an open fire while other women will demonstrate the techniques used to make their shoes and clothing

Castles

The Siege of Goodrich Castle, 1646
29/8/99 GOODRICH CASTLE
30/8/99 Tel: 01600 890538
A 17th century production performed by The English Civil War Society. A£4.00 C£2.00 Concessions£3.00

Castles

Medieval Weekend
29/8/99 HOLDENBY HOUSE, GARDENS AND FALCONRY CENTRE
30/8/99 Tel: 01604 770074
Medieval times at Holdenby House. Living History Camp with combat demonstrations, Dressing the Knight, Cooking and Clothing with much more. Along with our resident pine workshop and bodger, children's farm, tearoom, shop and play area to fill at day at Holdenby.

Historic Houses & Gardens

Gunpowder, Treason & Plot

29/8/99	**KENILWORTH CASTLE**
30/8/99	Tel: 01926 852078
	Tudor re-enactment performed by Bills & Bows. A£4.00 C£2.00 Concessions£3.00
	Castles

Victorian Weekend

29/8/99	**MIDDLETON HALL**
30/8/99	Tel: 01827 283095
	Costume, period entertainment and games for the family. Sun 14.00-17.00, Mon 11.00-17.00
	Historic Houses & Gardens

A National Festival of Transport

29/8/99	**NATIONAL TRAMWAY MUSEUM**
30/8/99	Tel: 01773 852565
	A wheel-deep weekend that never stays still. Vintage vehicles of all types drive and jostle for street space with Vintage trams. Sparkling little cameos all weekend - anything from fire-fighting the old-fashioned way to the arrest of a dangerous 'spy'!
	Museum- Transport

Vikings! Middle England

29/8/99	**ROCKINGHAM CASTLE**
30/8/99	Tel: 01536 770240
	Last year the Normans returned to Rockingham Castle and provided one of the most popular programmes offered. So it really is by popular demand that they are back once again, this time wearing their true Viking colours. Once again Rockingham's ancient walls and towers effortlessly turn the clock back over the centuries to provide a stunning setting for this exciting event. Time: 12.30-16.30. No extra charges
	Castles

Soldiers of George III

29/8/99	**STOKESAY CASTLE**
30/8/99	Tel: 01588 672544
	Re-enactment of 18th-century by the Association of Crown Forces. A£3.20 C£1.60 Concessions£2.40
	Castles

Town & Country Fayre

29/8/99	**WESTON PARK**
30/8/99	Tel: 01952 850207
	Two days of arena demonstrations and family entertainment including: Monstor Trucks, Shire Horses and Traction. Fun Fair
	Historic Houses & Gardens

Roman Festival

29/8/99	**WROXETER ROMAN CITY**
30/8/99	Tel: 01743 761330
	Learn how to cook or make a pot Roman

Style, or find out about herbs and make-up. Meet 1st century legionaries, watch 5th century soldiers at drill and in combat against barbarian raiders, plus cooking, mosaic making and a down trodden slave bemoaning his lot! From 12.00. A£4.00 C£2.00 Concessions£3.00. EH Members Free

Roman Remains

Medieval Fun Days

29/8/99	**SUDELEY CASTLE AND GARDENS**
30/9/99	Tel: 01242 602308
	Why not spend your August Bank Holiday Travel discovering the way we lived and entertained ourselves during the 12th & 13th centuries. Plenty to see and do all weekend
	Castles

Eurocar Raceday

30/8/99	**MALLORY PARK**
30/8/99	Tel: 01455 842931/2/3
	The closest racing you will see!! Plus SoM, fun fair. £10.00. Please telephone 0930 55 59 60 for further information.
	Motor Racing Circuit

Medieval Jousting by the Lake

30/8/99	**RAGLEY HALL**
30/8/99	Tel: 01789 762090
	A recreated 14th century tournament, complete with all its pomp, pageantry and knights testing each others skills in the art of combat
	Historic Houses & Gardens

Bank Holiday Racing

30/8/99	**WARWICK RACECOURSE**
30/8/99	Tel: 01926 491553
	A family fun day with children's entertainment and a creche available. First Flat race at 14.00, last race 16.30
	Racecourses

Castle Characters

1/9/99	**WARWICK CASTLE**
30/9/99	Tel: 01926 406600
	Weekends through September, come and meet our colour Castle characters such as the Archer, the Jailer, the Red Knight or the Wandering Minstrels
	Castles

Herefordshire Photography Festival 1999

1/9/99	**HEREFORDSHIRE PHOTOGRAPHY FESTIVAL 1999**
31/10/99	Tel: 01432 351964
	The Herefordshire Photography Festival is an annual celebration of photography. Food in the theme for this year's festival. Dates yet to be confirmed, details are

available in a newsletter, call venue for details

Festivals

Outdoor Concert. 'Last Night of the Proms'

3/9/99 RAGLEY HALL
3/9/99 Tel: 01789 762090

Proms concerts have now established themselves firmly in the outdoor concert calendar, with rousing singing, flag waving, terrific atmosphere with a breathtaking firework finale

Historic Houses & Gardens

Friends of Thomas the Tank Engine

3/9/99 DEAN FOREST RAILWAY
5/9/99 Tel: 01594 843423 info line

Come along and meet Thomas and Wilbert the Forest Engine

Railways

FIA Historic Grand Touring Cars Cup

3/9/99 DONINGTON PARK
5/9/99 Tel: 01332 810048

FIA GT, FIA European for Historic Touring Cars, FIA Lurani Trophy for Formula Junior Cars, European BOSS Formula, Porsche Cup, BARC Formula Renault, Open Fortuna by Nissan.

Motor Racing Circuit

Murder Mystery

4/9/99 BADDESLEY CLINTON HOUSE
4/9/99 Tel: 01564 783294

Marmion's Moated Manor Murder Mystery, commences 19.30, tickets £30.00 call for booking details

Historic Houses & Gardens

50th Moreton & District Agricultural Show

4/9/99 COTSWOLD HERITAGE CENTRE
4/9/99 Tel: 01451 860715

In the Cell Block Gallery. Visit the crafts tent, meet local crafts people and members of the museum staff

Heritage Centres

Festival of Fireworks

4/9/99 SHUGBOROUGH ESTATE
4/9/99 Tel: 01889 881388

A unique opportunity to savour 5 breathtaking displays, staged by some of Britain's best fireworks companies - all in one evening. A spectacular "show of shows" not to be missed in the beautiful grounds of Shugborough. Separate charge for show

Historic Houses & Gardens

Steeplechase Meeting

4/9/99 STRATFORD-ON-AVON RACECOURSE
4/9/99 Tel: 01789 267949/269411

Enjoy a day at the races

Racecourses

Mediaeval Night

4/9/99 WOLVERHAMPTON RACECOURSE
4/9/99 Tel: 01902 421421

Racing on all weather track with Mediaeval themed entertainment. Packages available to include racecourse entrance, three course meal, racecard, and dancing to either a live band or disco. Racing from 19.00

Racecourses

Living History Weekend

4/9/99 BLACK COUNTRY LIVING MUSEUM
5/9/99 Tel: 0121 557 9643 info

The last of the Friends' Live-in weekends heralds the end of the Summer Holidays. The Friends of the Museum spend the weekend living in 1920's conditions in the many cottages and houses. Witness their attempts to wash, cook, clean and entertain themselves without all the modern conveniences which we take for granted!

Industrial Heritage

Country Fair

4/9/99 CHATSWORTH
5/9/99 Tel: 01246 582204/565300

Two day event for all the family, including massed pipe and military bans, hot-air balloons, free-fall parachuting and over 100 trades stands, House and Garden open to Country Fair visitors only

Historic Houses & Gardens

Medieval Music

4/9/99 GOODRICH CASTLE
5/9/99 Tel: 01600 890538

Enjoy melodies and dance tunes dating back to the 12th century. From 12.00. A£3.10 C£1.60 Concessions£2.30

Castles

Autumn Garden Festival

4/9/99 SUDELEY CASTLE AND GARDENS
5/9/99 Tel: 01242 602308

Delight in the abundance of the beautiful displays as we celebrate Autumn in style, call for further details

Castles

Civil War Re-enactment

4/9/99 THE COMMANDERY
5/9/99 Tel: 01905 355071

The Worcester Militia prepare and carry out a faithful recreation of Worcester's involvement in the final conflict of the Civil War. Events will be staged at the

Commandery and on the outskirts of the city

Historic Buildings

The International 4x4 & Military Show
4/9/99 WESTON PARK
5/9/99 Tel: 01952 850207
For all 4x4 and Military vehicle enthusiasts. Mud Run, Public Off Road Course. Trade stands

Historic Houses & Gardens

Remembered by Association
4/9/99 CHELTENHAM ART GALLERY AND MUSEUM
6/11/99 Tel: 01242 237431
Divers Memory project which draws on reserve collections and connected narratives in a surreal and thought-provoking way

Museum- Art

Plant Sale
5/9/99 BIDDULPH GRANGE GARDEN
5/9/99 Tel: 01782 517999
Up to 20 nurseries will be represented with an excellent choice of plants from trees to annuals and everything in between. Many rare and unusual plants will also be for sale

Gardens

Fete & Country Music Festival
5/9/99 BIRMINGHAM BOTANICAL GARDENS AND GLASSHOUSES
5/9/99 Tel: 0121 454 1860
Charity stalls, craft fair and Country Music with line dancing displays

Gardens- Botanical

Partake Elizabethan Dancers
5/9/99 HADDON HALL
5/9/99 Tel: 01629 812855
Performances of 16th century dances accompanied by the lute will be held throughout the day. Informal talks on dress, music and social etiquette

Historic Houses

Drayton Croft Mallory Trophy
5/9/99 MALLORY PARK
5/9/99 Tel: 01455 842931/2/3
Roadstocks, solo and sidecar. £7.00. Please telephone 0930 55 59 60 for further information.

Motor Racing Circuit

Nature Activity Day
5/9/99 SNIBSTON DISCOVERY PARK
5/9/99 Tel: 01530 510851
Join the Rangers and explore aspects of nature at Snibston. Between 08.30-10.00 take a stroll round the site to identify birds and learn more about how and where they live. Admission Free, no

booking required. A bird table workshop will be held from 11.00-13.00 and a charge of £10.00 will be made for each table. Advance booking is essential for each session and suitable clothing and footwear should be worn for the walk. For further information please call 01530 510851 after 26 July

Industrial Heritage

Music at Stokesay
5/9/99 STOKESAY CASTLE
5/9/99 Tel: 01588 672544
Performed by the Ensemble Musica Salopia. Normal admission prices apply

Castles

The Garden Nature Reserve City and Guilds
6/9/99 RYTON ORGANIC GARDENS
6/9/99 Tel: 01203 303517
First of 5 sessions. Find out how to take better care of and encourage more wildlife into your garden. Two hours of classroom-based theory, combined with visits to relevant areas of the gardens. This session is "An Introduction to ecological principles and wildlife habitats". It is hoped that by the end of the course participants will want to sit for the City and Guilds examination in this subject. However, you may just opt for one or two of the sessions, the choice is yours! Time: 14.00-16.15.

Gardens

Organic Gardening City and Guilds
6/9/99 RYTON ORGANIC GARDENS
6/9/99 Tel: 01203 303517
First of 5 sessions which will introduce the basics of good gardening practice (with an emphasis on organics). This session is "characteristic of Soil and how to look after it". Time: 10.00-12.30.

Gardens

Save Your Own Seed (RHS)
8/9/99 RYTON ORGANIC GARDENS
8/9/99 Tel: 01203 303517
Behind the scenes of the Heritage Seed Library, saving and storing seeds. Time: 10.00-13.00. Optional tour of HSL in the afternoon.

Gardens

Oak Antique Festival
9/9/99 CHAVENAGE
12/9/99 Tel: 01666 502329
Country oak furniture pre-1830. Country and Fruitwood pre-1870. Twenty stands. Additional entrance fee

Historic Houses

Making Real Bread
10/9/99 RYTON ORGANIC GARDENS
10/9/99 Tel: 01203 303517
Make a wide range of interesting and wholesome breads, and understand the principles of doughs, ensuring consistent and high quality results. Time: 09.30-17.00. Cost: £38.00 includes all materials and ingredients.

Gardens

Weekend Special
10/9/99 WORCESTER RACECOURSE
11/9/99 Tel: 01905 25364
Racing from 14.00. Admission prices from £5.50-£13.50, discount available for advance group bookings, 2 complimentary badges for groups of 12-39 or 4 complimentary badges for 40+

Racecourses

Artsfest 1999
10/9/99 ARTSFEST 1999
12/9/99 Tel: 0121 622 1234
A weekend of free arts and entertainment events encompasing a wide range of music, comedy, cabaret, dance, drama and visual arts. Highlights include performances by the City Of Birmingham Symphony Orchestra, Birmingham Royal Ballet, Royal Shakespeare Company and Kokuma Dance Theatre.

Festivals

FIA Professional European Championships 1999
10/9/99 SANTA POD RACEWAY
12/9/99 Tel: 01234 782828
Final Round of Europe's most prestigious Drag Racing Championships with Top Fuel Dragsters, Funny Cars, Drag Bikes and night racing

Motor Sports

Galloway Antiques Fair
10/9/99 SUDELEY CASTLE AND GARDENS
12/9/99 Tel: 01242 602308
Quality antiques for sale, call for further information

Castles

Behind The Scenes Days
11/9/99 CHATSWORTH
11/9/99 Tel: 01246 582204/565300
Spend a day backstage at Chatsworth and meet the people who look after the House and its collections, the Garden and Park. Book on 01246 582204 contact Mrs Sue Gregory

Historic Houses & Gardens

Mediaeval Day

Manor House Museum
11/9/99 MANOR HOUSE MUSEUM
11/9/99 Tel: 01536 534219
12th and 13th century visitors meet 21st century vistors!

Museum- Local History

Eight Clubs 50th Anniversary Raceday
11/9/99 SILVERSTONE CIRCUIT
11/9/99 Tel: 01327 857271
Circuit: National. Feature: Club Races. Please call for further information

Motor Racing Circuit

National Heritage Open Day
11/9/99 WORCESTER CATHEDRAL
11/9/99 Tel: 01905 28854/21004
Special tours and access to parts of the Cathedral. Admission Free

Cathedrals

General Lee's Infantry
11/9/99 BOSCOBEL HOUSE
12/9/99 Tel: 01902 850244
American Civil War re-enacted by the 55th/18th Virginia. A£4.00 C£2.00 Concessions£3.00

Historic Houses

National Heritage Days
11/9/99 GLOUCESTER FOLK MUSEUM
12/9/99 Tel: 01452 526467
Folk Museum and Transport Museum open free of charge to all visitors

Museum- Local History

The History Man
11/9/99 GOODRICH CASTLE
12/9/99 Tel: 01600 890538
Enjoy unusual guided tours by the presenter of the BBC's every popular History Man programmes, Brian McNerney. But be warned, his enthusiasm is notoriously contagious and there is no antidote! Performing without costumes, props or even a safety net, he brings the past to life before your very eyes! From 12.00. A£3.50 C£1.80 Concessions£2.60. EH Members Free

Castles

Levellers, 1649
11/9/99 KENILWORTH CASTLE
12/9/99 Tel: 01926 852078
17th century re-enactment by The English Civil War Society. A£4.00 C£2.00 Concessions£3.00

Castles

Standard Tank Weekend
11/9/99 MIDLAND RAILWAYS CENTRE
12/9/99 Tel: 01773 747674/749788
Featuring 2 British Railways standard tank locomotives on passenger trains.

Railways Steam/Light

Business Expo 1999
11/9/99 NATIONAL EXHIBITION CENTRE
12/9/99 Tel: 0121 780 4141 x2604
Hall 11. Please telephone Business Expo
Exhibitions Ltd, 0117 973 5333 for further information
Exhibition Centres

Autumn Steam Up
11/9/99 NORTHAMPTON AND LAMPORT RAILWAY
12/9/99 Tel: 01604 847318
All running steam locomotives will have
a showing throughout each day, with a
special guest loco
Railways Steam/Light

Garden Fair
11/9/99 RAGLEY HALL
12/9/99 Tel: 01789 762090
The weekend features specialist plant
growers/nurseries, gardening equipment, gardening roadshow, craft fair and
family entertainment. Includes admission to grounds, gardens and adventure
playground
Historic Houses & Gardens

Losing the Thread
11/9/99 CORINIUM MUSEUM
17/10/99 Tel: 01285 655611
Modern tapestries and textile art. There
will be items for sale
Museum- Roman

Objects from a Life Time
11/9/99 BILSTON CRAFT GALLERY AND MUSEUM
30/10/99 Tel: 01902 409143
Beautiful craft objects which have been
specially commissioned to mark important occasions in peoples lives
Art Galleries

Dorothy Anne Clark
11/9/99 THE FERRERS CENTRE FOR ARTS AND
CRAFTS
8/11/99 Tel: 01332 865408
Solo exhibition of Dorothy's mixed
media work
Craft Galleries

Veteran, Vintage & Classic Car Show
12/9/99 HERITAGE MOTOR CENTRE
12/9/99 Tel: 01926 641188
All cars, all ages, for all the family. Call
for further details
Museum- Motor

Race Day
12/9/99 MALLORY PARK
12/9/99 Tel: 01455 842931/2/3
ARP F3, Global Lights, Classic FF &
FF2000, MG Midgets, Monoposto,
Scooters, SoM. £8.00. Please telephone
0930 55 59 60 for further information.

Motor Racing Circuit
Toy Train and Collectors Fair
12/9/99 NATIONAL EXHIBITION CENTRE
12/9/99 Tel: 0121 780 4141 x2604
Hall 17. Please telephone D & J Fairs,
01526 398198 for further information
Exhibition Centres

Medieval Entertainments
12/9/99 PEVERIL CASTLE
12/9/99 Tel: 01433 620613
Archery, dance and children's activities
from 12.00 with mini 13th century tournament at 15.00. A£3.00 C£1.50
Concessions£2.30. EH Members Free
Castles

Heavy Horse and Harvest
12/9/99 SHUGBOROUGH ESTATE
12/9/99 Tel: 01889 881388
A unique opportunity to see over 20
gentle giants at work at Shugborough
Park Farm. Demonstrations and traditional harvest methods from field to
farmhouse. In conjunction with Midlands
Association of Heavy Horses. Licensed
bar. A£4.00 Reduced £3.00
Historic Houses & Gardens

Wedding Fair
12/9/99 SHUGBOROUGH ESTATE
12/9/99 Tel: 01889 881388
Here's your chance to meet the experts.
From the trade stands and fashion
shows to the icing on the cake. Separate
charge for this event
Historic Houses & Gardens

Mini Owners Club National Rally
12/9/99 STANFORD HALL
12/9/99 Tel: 01788 860250
Telephone 01788 860250 for more
details. Gates open by 10.00. Special
admission price for this event
Historic Houses

National Garden Scheme Open Day
12/9/99 SUDELEY CASTLE AND GARDENS
12/9/99 Tel: 01242 602308
All proceeds are donated to the National
Gardens Scheme
Castles

National Model Boat Championships
12/9/99 BILLING AQUADROME LIMITED
13/9/99 Tel: 01604 408181
Please telephone for further information. Contact: Mick Fields
Country Leisure Parks

Stately Sculpture
12/9/99 THE FERRERS CENTRE FOR ARTS AND

Further more detailed information on the attractions listed can be found
in Best Guides *Visitor Attractions* Guide under the classifications shown

CRAFTS
28/3/00   Tel: 01332 865408
An exhibition by Loughborough
Sculpture Group
Craft Galleries

The Garden Nature Reserve City and Guilds
13/9/99   RYTON ORGANIC GARDENS
13/9/99   Tel: 01203 303517
Session 2. Ideas for woodland and
meadow-type areas within the garden. It
is hoped that by the end of the course
participants will want to sit for the City
and Guilds examination in this subject.
However, you may just opt for one or
two of the sessions, the choice is yours!
Gardens

Organic Gardening City and Guilds
13/9/99   RYTON ORGANIC GARDENS
13/9/99   Tel: 01203 303517
Session 2 - Soil and fertility and plant
nutrition. It is hoped that by the end of
the course participants will want to sit
for the City and Guilds examination in
this subject. However, you may just opt
for one or two of the sessions, the
choice is yours!
Gardens

Exhibition
14/9/99   COTSWOLD HERITAGE CENTRE
10/10/99   Tel: 01451 860715
In the Cell Block Gallery. An exhibition by
local artists and crafts people including
felt makers and papermakers such as
the artist Lyn Griffiths
Heritage Centres

Making Something Special for Christmas
17/9/99   RYTON ORGANIC GARDENS
17/9/99   Tel: 01203 303517
Jam and other preserves. Herbs, vine-
gars, chutneys, etc. Time: 09.30-17.00.
Cost: £38.00.
Gardens

Umpah Evening
18/9/99   THE BASS MUSEUM
18/9/99   Tel: 01283 511000
Join the Heinz Miller Umpah Band for a
swingalong, singalong evening with a
traditional Beer Kellar atmosphere
Breweries

Spanish Night
18/9/99   WOLVERHAMPTON RACECOURSE
18/9/99   Tel: 01902 421421
Racing on all weather track with Spanish
themed entertainment. Packages available to include racecourse entrance,

three course meal, racecard, and dancing to either a live band or disco. Racing
from 19.00
Racecourses

Medieval Entertainers
18/9/99   BOLSOVER CASTLE
19/9/99   Tel: 01246 823349
Games, squire-training and talks on
weaponry and armour. Also, try your
hand at spinning, weaving and calligraphy and learn about herbal medicine.
A£3.50 C£1.80 Concessions£2.60
Castles

Medieval Living History
18/9/99   KENILWORTH CASTLE
19/9/99   Tel: 01926 852078
15th century military and domestic life,
with crafts, men-at-arms and period
games. A£4.00 C£2.00
Concessions£3.00
Castles

Autumn Diesel Gala
18/9/99   MIDLAND RAILWAYS CENTRE
19/9/99   Tel: 01773 747674/749788
As many of our fleet of 25 main line
diesel locomotives in action as possible.
Railways Steam/Light

Antiques Event and Fair
18/9/99   ROCKINGHAM CASTLE
19/9/99   Tel: 01536 770240
So well-received was this event in 1998
that we asked Field Dog Fairs to stage
two in 1999. The programme is as for the
May event, except that there may be
some more exhibitors at this one. Time:
10.30-16.30
Castles

Silverstone International Raceday
18/9/99   SILVERSTONE CIRCUIT
19/9/99   Tel: 01327 857271
Circuit: International. Feature: BTCC
(Finals). Please call for further information
Motor Racing Circuit

Harvest Home
18/9/99   SULGRAVE MANOR
19/9/99   Tel: 01295 760205
Discover and enjoy all about the traditional ways harvest has been celebrated
through the ages. Mummers, Morris
Men, Music, Dancing, a great weekend
for all the family. Usual opening times.
A£4.50 C£2.25
Historic Houses

The Midland Game & Country Sports Fair

18/9/99 19/9/99	**WESTON PARK** Tel: 01952 850207 A true Country Sports Fair with a large collection of trade stands *Historic Houses & Gardens*

MX5 Owners Club

19/9/99 19/9/99	**BILLING AQUADROME LIMITED** Tel: 01604 408181 Please telephone Tony Jennings, 01293 447228, for further information *Country Leisure Parks*

Morris Marque Day

19/9/99 19/9/99	**HERITAGE MOTOR CENTRE** Tel: 01926 641188 Bring yours, if you've got one, or come anyway and join in the fun. *Museum- Motor*

The Mellano Trophy Race

19/9/99 19/9/99	**MALLORY PARK** Tel: 01455 842931/2/3 Solos 125-1300cc, F1 & F11 sidecars, powerbikes. £7.00. Please telephone 0930 55 59 60 for further information. *Motor Racing Circuit*

The History Man

19/9/99 19/9/99	**PEVERIL CASTLE** Tel: 01433 620613 Enjoy unusual guided tours with Brian McNerney, presenter of the BBC's popular History Man programmes. But be warned, his enthusiasm is notoriously contagious... and there is no antidote! Performing without costumes, props or even a safety net, he brings the past to life before your very eyes! A£2.50 C£1.30 Concessions£1.90 *Castles*

National Gardens Scheme (Ryton Organic Gardens)

19/9/99 19/9/99	**RYTON ORGANIC GARDENS** Tel: 01203 303517 In support of the National Garden Scheme Charity. Time: 10.00-17.00. Cost: A£2.50 C£1.25 Concessions £2.00. HDRA/RHS/North Hort. Soc members FREE. *Gardens*

Colour Your Life with Maya Rose

19/9/99 19/9/99	**RYTON ORGANIC GARDENS** Tel: 01203 303517 Colour healer, Maya Rose, will introduce you to the power of colour in influencing your life. Time: 15.00-16.30. Cost: £10.00. *Gardens*

Scott Moytorcycle Owners Club Rally

19/9/99 19/9/99	**STANFORD HALL** Tel: 01788 860250 Also, L.E. Velo Motorcycle Owners Club Rally. Telephone 01788 860250 for more details. Gates open by 10.00 *Historic Houses*

World Barrel Rolling Championships

19/9/99 19/9/99	**THE BASS MUSEUM** Tel: 01283 511000 Join contestantsfrom home and abroad competing for the coveted Perpetual Trophy, teams of two welcome *Breweries*

The Garden Nature Reserve City and Guilds

20/9/99 20/9/99	**RYTON ORGANIC GARDENS** Tel: 01203 303517 Session 3. Planting and providing for birds, bees and butterflies. It is hoped that by the end of the course participants will want to sit for the City and Guilds examination in this subject. However, you may just opt for one or two of the sessions, the choice is yours! *Gardens*

Organic Gardening City and Guilds

20/9/99 20/9/99	**RYTON ORGANIC GARDENS** Tel: 01203 303517 Session 3. Compost making. It is hoped that by the end of the course participants will want to sit for the City and Guilds examination in this subject. However, you may just opt for one or two of the sessions, the choice is yours! *Gardens*

Flat Race Meeting

21/9/99 21/9/99	**WARWICK RACECOURSE** Tel: 01926 491553 Flat racing from 14.00, last race 17.00 *Racecourses*

Vegetarian Indian Cookery with Holly Jones

25/9/99 25/9/99	**RYTON ORGANIC GARDENS** Tel: 01203 303517 How to create mouth-watering, vegetarian Indian dishes. There will be plenty of opportunity to ask questions and to try the dishes afterwards. Time: 10.00-13.30. *Gardens*

Tote Day

25/9/99 25/9/99	**WORCESTER RACECOURSE** Tel: 01905 25364 Tote Day with racing from 14.45. Admission prices from £5.50-£13.50, discount available for advance group bookings

Further more detailed information on the attractions listed can be found in Best Guides *Visitor Attractions* Guide under the classifications shown

Racecourses

Boaters Gathering

25/9/99
26/9/99

BLACK COUNTRY LIVING MUSEUM

Tel: 0121 557 9643 info

A weekend of traditional narrow boating activities on and around the Museum's canal basin and old-fashioned working Boat Dock

Industrial Heritage

The King's Shilling

25/9/99
26/9/99

BOSCOBEL HOUSE

Tel: 01902 850244

18th-century. British Marines, 1777. A£4.00 C£2.00 Concessions£3.00

Historic Houses

Western Branchline Festival

25/9/99
26/9/99

DEAN FOREST RAILWAY

Tel: 01594 843423 info line

Intensive passenger and demonstration freight trains - four tank engines in steam - excellent photographic opportunities

Railways

Restoration

25/9/99
26/9/99

HARDWICK OLD HALL

Tel: 01246 850431

Hogarth's Heroes. 17th-century. A£3.10 C£1.60 Concessions£2.30

Historic Houses

Diesel & Steam Weekend

25/9/99
26/9/99

MIDLAND RAILWAYS CENTRE

Tel: 01773 747674/749788

Featuring steam and diesel locomotives on passenger trains.

Railways Steam/Light

Miniatura - International Dolls' House Show

25/9/99
26/9/99

NATIONAL EXHIBITION CENTRE

Tel: 0121 780 4141 x2604

Hall 11 & 10/11 Link. Please telephone Miniatura, 0121 749 7330 for further information

Exhibition Centres

Record & CD Collectors' Fair

25/9/99
26/9/99

NATIONAL EXHIBITION CENTRE

Tel: 0121 780 4141 x2604

Pavilion. Please telephone P & J Promotions, 01273 463017 for further information

Exhibition Centres

Modellers Weekend

25/9/99
26/9/99

NATIONAL WATERWAYS MUSEUM

Tel: 01452 318054

Traction engines, sailing boats and remote controlled vessels go hand in glove with the different skilled, accurate scale models demonstrating their capa-

bilities

Museum- Waterways

Friends of Thomas Weekend

25/9/99
26/9/99

NORTHAMPTON AND LAMPORT RAILWAY

Tel: 01604 847318

Meet Thomas, his friends Sir Topham Hatt, the Fat Controller and Percy and many more

Railways Steam/Light

Dahlia Festival

25/9/99
26/9/99

SHUGBOROUGH ESTATE

Tel: 01889 881388

Courtesy of the Birmingham Dahlia Society decorating the ground floor of the Mansion House. A£4.00 Reduced £3.00

Historic Houses & Gardens

BRSCC Race Meeting

25/9/99
26/9/99

SILVERSTONE CIRCUIT

Tel: 01327 857271

Circuit: National. Feature: Club Races. Please call for further information

Motor Racing Circuit

Exhibition - Satellites of Fashion

25/9/99

21/11/99

NOTTINGHAM CASTLE MUSEUM AND ART GALLERY

Tel: 0115 915 3700

Shoes, hats and bags by leading contemporary designers

Castles

Box of Delights

25/9/99

1/1/00

PICKFORD'S HOUSE SOCIAL HISTORY MUSEUM

Tel: 01332 255363

A selection of historic toys chosen with Christmas in mind

Historic Houses

Fungi and the Bogeymen

26/9/99
26/9/99

ILAM PARK

Tel: 01335 350245/350503

Meet the bogeymen on Stanton Moor to explore some of the fact and myths about fungi. Parking limited. TBA 10.30. £2.00 per person. Sorry no dogs. Fairly strenuous

Country Parks

Race Day

26/9/99
26/9/99

MALLORY PARK

Tel: 01455 842931/2/3

Supersports 200, BMW, MG, Classic and historic saloons, classic thunder, production saloons. £8.00. Please telephone 0930 55 59 60 for further information.

Motor Racing Circuit

Funtasia

26/9/99	**NATIONAL TRAMWAY MUSEUM**
26/9/99	Tel: 01773 852565

Children! Grab a grown-up, bring them with you, and you only get in FREE, you can enjoy all kinds of extra attractions

Museum- Transport

An Introduction to Watercolour Painting

26/9/99	**RYTON ORGANIC GARDENS**
26/9/99	Tel: 01203 303517

One-day beginners' painting and drawing workshop. Techniques, tips and tricks of the professional artist. Using perspective and composition to improve your skills. Time: 09.30-16.30. Cost: £20.00.

Gardens

Heavy Horse Parade

26/9/99	**THE BASS MUSEUM**
26/9/99	Tel: 01283 511000

Come along to see these amazing beautiful heavy horses on parade, not to be missed!

Breweries

Dudley Glass Festival '99

26/9/99	**BROADFIELD HOUSE GLASS MUSEUM**
3/10/99	Tel: 01384 812745

Eight days of demonstrations, workshops, talks and exhibitions celebrating the best of British Contemporary glass

Museum- Glass

The Garden Nature Reserve City and Guilds

27/9/99	**RYTON ORGANIC GARDENS**
27/9/99	Tel: 01203 303517

Session 4. Dark, damp and wet places for wildlife, including establishing a garden pond. It is hoped that by the end of the course participants will want to sit for the City and Guilds examination in this subject. However, you may just opt for one or two of the sessions, the choice is yours!

Gardens

Organic Gardening City and Guilds

27/9/99	**RYTON ORGANIC GARDENS**
27/9/99	Tel: 01203 303517

Session 4. Crop rotation and crop protection. It is hoped that by the end of the course participants will want to sit for the City and Guilds examination in this subject. However, you may just opt for one or two of the sessions, the choice is yours!

Gardens

Behind The Scenes Days

29/9/99	**CHATSWORTH**
29/9/99	Tel: 01246 582204/565300

Spend a day backstage at Chatsworth and meet the people who look after the House and its collections, the Garden and Park. Book on 01246 582204 contact Mrs Sue Gregory

Historic Houses & Gardens

The 16th National Knitting and Needlecraft Exhibition

30/9/99	**NATIONAL EXHIBITION CENTRE**
3/10/99	Tel: 0121 780 4141 x2604

Hall 12. Sewing, cross stitch, hand and machine knitting, patchwork and quilting, fashion displays, workshops, demonstrations, talks and many other attractions. On the door A£6.50 OAPs£5.00. £1.00 off if ordered in advance Ticket Hotline: 0117 970 1370

Exhibition Centres

Inland Waterways Exhibition

1/10/99	**NATIONAL WATERWAYS MUSEUM**
31/1/99	Tel: 01452 318054

Dates have not been confirmed, proposed exhibition detailing 4000 years of Inland Waterways, call for details

Museum- Waterways

National Franchise Exhibition

1/10/99	**NATIONAL EXHIBITION CENTRE**
3/10/99	Tel: 0121 780 4141 x2604

Hall 9 & 8/9 Link. Fri-Sat: 10.00-17.00, Sun: 10.00-16.00. Please telephone Miller Freeman Exhibitions & Conferenceess Ltd, tel 0181 742 2828 for further information

Exhibition Centres

National Wedding Show 1999

1/10/99	**NATIONAL EXHIBITION CENTRE**
3/10/99	Tel: 0121 780 4141 x2604

Hall 1. Fri 13.00-18.00, Sat & Sun 10.00-18.00. Please telephone Wedding Shows (UK) Ltd, tel 01462 485881 for further information. Ticket sales from NEC Box Office, tel 0121 767 4717

Exhibition Centres

The Midlands Homebuyer Show 1999

1/10/99	**NATIONAL EXHIBITION CENTRE**
3/10/99	Tel: 0121 780 4141 x2604

Hall 10. Fri 11.00-18.00, Sat & Sun 10.00-18.00. Please telephone Homebuyer Events Ltd, tel 0181 877 3636 for further information

Exhibition Centres

LIVING HISTORY

1/10/99	**NATIONAL WATERWAYS MUSEUM**
15/10/99	Tel: 01452 318054

An education special for schools only,

Further more detailed information on the attractions listed can be found in Best Guides *Visitor Attractions* Guide under the classifications shown

please call for details

Museum- Waterways

Cider Making Demonstration

1/10/99
31/10/99

CIDER MUSEUM AND KING OFFA DISTILLERY

Tel: 01432 354207

Dates to be arranged, call venue for further details. See how cider apples are milled and pressed

Museum- Food & Drink

Family Day at Ryton

2/10/99
2/10/99

RYTON ORGANIC GARDENS

Tel: 01203 303517

As part of the 'Campaign for Learning's National Family Weekend' (1-3 October), we are offering free entry to the gardens for children on Saturday 9th October and the chance to win a year's family membership of HDRA. For more details of the national campaign please phone Geraldine Murphy on 0121 643 0774.

Gardens

Harvest Supper in the Restaurant

2/10/99
2/10/99

RYTON ORGANIC GARDENS

Tel: 01203 303517

Bookings and information on 01203 307142

Gardens

Pests and Diseases

2/10/99
2/10/99

RYTON ORGANIC GARDENS

Tel: 01203 303517

How to identify and deal with pests and diseases in the organic garden. Time: 14.00-16.30.

Gardens

Making Compost

2/10/99
2/10/99

RYTON ORGANIC GARDENS

Tel: 01203 303517

Find out how to recycle garden rubbish and up to 60% of household rubbish organically. Time: 10.00-12.00. Why not stay on for the afternoon session of pests and diseases?

Gardens

750 Motor Club Raceday

2/10/99
2/10/99

SILVERSTONE CIRCUIT

Tel: 01327 857271

Circuit: National. Feature: Club Races. Please call for further information

Motor Racing Circuit

Chamber Music Concert

2/10/99
2/10/99

SULGRAVE MANOR

Tel: 01295 760205

In the Grand Hall. A variety of enjoyable music. Light buffet supper with wine will follow the concert. Commences 19.30. Tickets: £15.00 inclusive of Supper

Historic Houses

Stockmarket Stagger

2/10/99
2/10/99

WOLVERHAMPTON RACECOURSE

Tel: 01902 421421

A fun night out combined with Flat Racing from 19.00. Hospitality packages available to include racecourse entrance, three course meal, racecard, and dancing to either a live band or disco.

Racecourses

Christmas Craft Fair

2/10/99
3/10/99

EASTNOR CASTLE

Tel: 01531 633160

Start your Christmas shopping early this year by visiting our very popular Christmas Craft Fair. Choose from a wide range of handmade items made by accomplished craftspeople who will be demonstrating their various skills in the Craft Marquees

Castles

WI Market

2/10/99
3/10/99

MIDDLETON HALL

Tel: 01827 283095

Stalls selling and demonstrating crafts. Sat 14.00-17.00, Sun 11.00-17.00

Historic Houses & Gardens

Standard Power Display

2/10/99
3/10/99

MIDLAND RAILWAYS CENTRE

Tel: 01773 747674/749788

Display of agricultural and industrial machinery.

Railways Steam/Light

Crafts at Stanford Hall (Lady Fayre)

2/10/99
3/10/99

STANFORD HALL

Tel: 01788 860250

Telephone 01788 860250 for more details. Admission charged. Gates open by 10.00. Special admission price for this event

Historic Houses

Tudor Living History

2/10/99
10/10/99

SULGRAVE MANOR

Tel: 01295 760205

See the cook, the alchemist, the smith, the brewer and a host of other characters in this Tudor re-enactment with a difference - the added attraction of some fine song, dance and theatre staged in the garden. Commences 14.00-17.00 weekdays and 10.30-17.00 Sat & Sun

Historic Houses

Exhibition - Autumn Glory

2/10/99
31/10/99

COTSWOLD HERITAGE CENTRE

Tel: 01451 860715

In the Cafe Gallery. An exhibition of

quilts and ragrugs by Esther Barrett
Heritage Centres

Ken East Retrospective 1949-1999
2/10/99 NORTHAMPTON CENTRAL MUSEUM AND
ART GALLERY
14/11/99 Tel: 01604 238548
From sketchbook to studio; 50 years of
study in visual arts
Art Galleries

The End of an Era?
2/10/99 PICKFORD'S HOUSE SOCIAL HISTORY
MUSEUM
1/1/00 Tel: 01332 255363
Exhibition of objects given to the museum in the last year
Historic Houses

Drayton Croft Mallory Trophy
3/10/99 MALLORY PARK
3/10/09 Tel: 01455 842931/2/3
Roadstocks, solos and sidecars. Club
finals day. £7.00. Please telephone 0930
55 59 60 for further information
Motor Racing Circuit

Plant Sale
3/10/99 HERGEST CROFT GARDENS
3/10/99 Tel: 01544 230160
All garden enthusiasts come along to
our plant fair. Please call for further
information
Gardens

40th Mini Anniversary
3/10/99 HERITAGE MOTOR CENTRE
3/10/99 Tel: 01926 641188
Minis here, Minis there, little Minis
everywhere. Happy 40th Birthday!
Museum- Motor

House Closes
3/10/99 RAGLEY HALL
3/10/99 Tel: 01789 762090
Please telephone for further information
Historic Houses & Gardens

Harvest Praise for All
3/10/99 RYTON ORGANIC GARDENS
3/10/99 Tel: 01203 303517
Open air church service organised by
Queens Road Baptist Church, Coventry.
Time: 15.00-16.30. Entry to the service is
free. A collection will be taken in support of HDRA's overseas work. Everyone
welcome.
Gardens

**The Garden Nature Reserve City and
Guilds**
4/10/99 RYTON ORGANIC GARDENS
4/10/99 Tel: 01203 303517
Session 5. Management problems and
solutions. It is hoped that by the end of

the course participants will want to sit
for the City and Guilds examination in
this subject. However, you may just opt
for one or two of the sessions, the
choice is yours!
Gardens

Organic Gardening City and Guilds
4/10/99 RYTON ORGANIC GARDENS
4/10/99 Tel: 01203 303517
Session 5. Weed control and irrigation. It
is hoped that by the end of the course
participants will want to sit for the City
and Guilds examination in this subject.
However, you may just opt for one or
two of the sessions, the choice is yours!
Gardens

Sotherby's Antiques Valuation Day
4/10/99 SUDBURY HALL AND THE MUSEUM OF
CHILDHOOD, THE NATIONAL TRUST
4/10/99 Tel: 01283 585305
Ever wondered what the dusty old thing
in the corner was worth, bring it along
today and find out (portable items only).
10.00-15.00. Pre-booking only. Tickets
£5.00, please apply to the property for
booking
Country Estates

The Woodworking & Turning Show
8/10/99 NATIONAL EXHIBITION CENTRE
10/10/99 Tel: 0121 780 4141 x2604
Hall 10. 09.30-17.30. Please telephone
Nexus Special Interests, tel 01442
266551 for further information
Exhibition Centres

Autumn Horse Trials
8/10/99 WESTON PARK
10/10/99 Tel: 01952 850207
One of the most popular Equestrian
events in the calendar
Historic Houses & Gardens

Cheltenham Festival of Literature
8/10/99 50TH CHELTENHAM FESTIVAL OF
LITERATURE 1999
24/10/99 Tel: 01242 521621
venues: Cheltenham Town Hall and
Everyman Theatre. 1999 marks the 50th
anniversary of one of the world's first
Literature Festivals. Founded in the cul-
ture-hungry post-war years, the Festival
continues to bring readers and writers
together for a unique annual celebration
of the written word. From Dylan Thomas
and John Betjeman to Anthony Burgess
and Allen Ginsburg, writers worldwide
have come to perform in Cheltenham's
very special atmosphere and brought
books alive to generations of readers.

Further more detailed information on the attractions listed can be found
in Best Guides *Visitor Attractions* Guide under the classifications shown

While the 50th Festival will celebrate this illustrious past, it will also explore the breadth and richness of contemporary writing and look ahead to the next fifty years. To celebrate a remarkable half century, the 1999 Festival will double in length, offering Festival-goers a two-week opportunity to see some of the world's greatest authors.

Festivals

Cookies Couch of Confessions

9/10/99	BADDESLEY CLINTON HOUSE
9/10/99	Tel: 01564 783294

A cabaret whodunnit entertainment. Commences 19.30. Tickets £30.00 (for tickets please send a cheque payable to 'National Trust (Enterprises)' and s.a.e. to the property

Historic Houses & Gardens

Behind The Scenes Days

9/10/99	CHATSWORTH
9/10/99	Tel: 01246 582204/565300

Spend a day backstage at Chatsworth and meet the people who look after the House and its collections, the Garden and Park. Book on 01246 582204 contact Mrs Sue Gregory

Historic Houses & Gardens

Meet the Romans!

9/10/99	MANOR HOUSE MUSEUM
9/10/99	Tel: 01536 534219

The Romans are coming to Kettering, but we are promised they are a friendly bunch!

Museum- Local History

Parapsychology with Kathy Stranks

9/10/99	RYTON ORGANIC GARDENS
9/10/99	Tel: 01203 303517

An introductory course about psychic events and how to recognise them. Learn about the processes involved when a psychic event occurs, from coincidence to premonition. Time: 10.00-16.00.

Gardens

Students Day

9/10/99	WORCESTER RACECOURSE
9/10/99	Tel: 01905 25364

Racing from 14.20. Admission prices from £5.50-£13.50, discount available for advance group bookings, 2 complimentary badges for groups of 12-39 or 4 complimentary badges for 40+

Racecourses

Eliminators (Model Boats)

9/10/99	BILLING AQUADROME LIMITED
10/10/99	Tel: 01604 408181

Please telephone for further information. Contact: Mick Fields

Country Leisure Parks

Diesel & Steam Weekend

9/10/99	MIDLAND RAILWAYS CENTRE
10/10/99	Tel: 01773 747674/749788

Featuring steam and diesel locomotives on passenger trains.

Railways Steam/Light

Warley National Model Railway Show 1999

9/10/99	NATIONAL EXHIBITION CENTRE
10/10/99	Tel: 0121 780 4141 x2604

Hall 9. Sat 10.00-18.00, Sun 10.00-17.00. Please telephone Warley MRC Exhibitions Ltd, tel 0121 558 8851 for further information. Ticket sales NEC Box Office 0121 767 4499

Exhibition Centres

Craft Fair

9/10/99	RAGLEY HALL
10/10/99	Tel: 01789 762090

Wonderful variety of handcrafted goods direct from the artist/craftsmen who have made them

Historic Houses & Gardens

Christmas Craft Fair

9/10/99	SHUGBOROUGH ESTATE
10/10/99	Tel: 01889 881388

A special selection of crafts for those early Christmas shoppers. Separate charge for this event

Historic Houses & Gardens

Silverstone Autumn Gold Cup

9/10/99	SILVERSTONE CIRCUIT
10/10/99	Tel: 01327 857271

Circuit: International. Feature: British F3, GT etc. Please call for further information

Motor Racing Circuit

Far Cotton W.M.C. Fishing Match

10/10/99	BILLING AQUADROME LIMITED
10/10/99	Tel: 01604 408181

Please telephone for further information. Contact: Kevin David

Country Leisure Parks

Eurocar Raceday

10/10/99	MALLORY PARK
10/10/99	Tel: 01455 842931/2/3

Getting closer at the season end!! Plus Honda SC. £10.00. Please telephone 0930 55 59 60 for further information.

Motor Racing Circuit

Music for all Seasons - Autumn

| 11/10/99 | **RYTON ORGANIC GARDENS** |
| 11/10/99 | Tel: 01203 303517 |

A sequence of music workshops themed on the seasons. Join us for one or more of the days. Open to everyone, including complete beginners! If you play an instrument please bring it along. Listen to seasonal works by the great composers and, using the melodies of the countryside, create your own music. Time: 10.00-16.00.

Gardens

Dive '99 - The International Sub-Aqua & Watersports Show

| 15/10/99 | **NATIONAL EXHIBITION CENTRE** |
| 17/10/99 | Tel: 0121 780 4141 x2604 |

Hall 20. Sat 09.30-18.00, Sun 09.00-17.30. Please telephone Dive Show Ltd, tel 0181 943 4288 for further information

Exhibition Centres

The Birmingham Ski & Snowboard Show 1999

| 15/10/99 | **NATIONAL EXHIBITION CENTRE** |
| 17/10/99 | Tel: 0121 780 4141 x2604 |

Hall 9. Fri 12.00-21.30, Sat-Sun 10.00-19.00. Please telephone DMG Pinnacle Ltd, tel 0181 515 2000 for further information. Ticket sales NEC Box Office 0121 767 4433

Exhibition Centres

Your Health Show

| 15/10/99 | **NATIONAL EXHIBITION CENTRE** |
| 17/10/99 | Tel: 0121 780 4141 x2604 |

Hall 19. The UK's largest health and fitness exhibition for consumers, covering health products, treatments and services. Learn more about what's new, innovative and ground-breaking in the health arena this Autumn. Find out: How to fight flu and stay cold free this winter; Which foods to eat to keep you warm and healthy; How to keep the energy levels high when winter gets you down; All you need to know about supplements and vitamins, feng shui, hormone imbalances, back-pain, acupuncture, stress, allergies, aromatherapy, dental-care and Viagra. Hundreds of ways to keep you fighting fit all season long! Special show features include free lectures and seminars from top health experts, writers and broadcasters such as Hazel Courteney, Jan de Vries, and Patrick Holford; Healthy Cookery Theatre featuring organic food and celebrity chefs; Live Stage presenting non-stop demonstrations of yoga, pilates, keep-fit, music

and dance. New features for this autumn include Dental Care Focus - the UK's first ever dental exhibition feature for consumers; Allergy Zone - a low allergen area of the show, focused on the fight against allergies and beating the sneezes; Fitness Zone - take those first steps to fitness with market leading fitness companies, health clubs and experts; Alternative Therapies Village - try out an Indian Head Massage, consult a Shaman, have your aura photographed, or discover the ancient art of feng shui. Admission £8.00 on the door or £6.00 booked in advance. For further information and timetable call the ticket hotline on 0121 767 4040

Exhibition Centres

HSCC Historic Race Day

| 16/10/99 | **SILVERSTONE CIRCUIT** |
| 16/10/99 | Tel: 01327 857271 |

Circuit: National. Feature: Club Races. Please call for further information

Motor Racing Circuit

Steeplechase Meeting

| 16/10/99 | **STRATFORD-ON-AVON RACECOURSE** |
| 16/10/99 | Tel: 01789 267949/269411 |

Enjoy a day at the races

Racecourses

Italian Themed Evening

| 16/10/99 | **WOLVERHAMPTON RACECOURSE** |
| 16/10/99 | Tel: 01902 421421 |

A fun night out combined with Flat Racing from 19.00. Hospitality packages available to include racecourse entrance, three course meal, racecard, and dancing to either a live band or disco.

Racecourses

Harvest Home

16/10/99	**AVONCROFT MUSEUM OF HISTORIC**
	BUILDINGS
17/10/99	Tel: 01527 831363

Demonstrations of ancient harvesting, traditional games, song and dance celebrating Autumn

Museum- Local History

The King's Shilling

| 16/10/99 | **BOLSOVER CASTLE** |
| 17/10/99 | Tel: 01246 823349 |

British Marines, 1777. A£3.10 C£1.60 Concessions£2.30 EH Members Free

Castles

Antiques Fair

| 16/10/99 | **HERITAGE MOTOR CENTRE** |
| 17/10/99 | Tel: 01926 641188 |

The last one of the year, call for more

information
Museum- Motor

Branch Line Weekend
16/10/99 MIDLAND RAILWAYS CENTRE
17/10/99 Tel: 01773 747674/749788
Featuring the line being used to demonstrate services on a typical Midland Branch Line in the 1950's.
Railways Steam/Light

Cake Decoration & Sugarcraft Show 1999
16/10/99 NATIONAL EXHIBITION CENTRE
17/10/99 Tel: 0121 780 4141 x2604
Hall 8. 09.30-17.30. Please telephone Future Publishing Ltd, tel 01225 442244 for further information
Exhibition Centres

Rainbow Christmas Craft Fair
16/10/99 ROCKINGHAM CASTLE
17/10/99 Tel: 01536 770240
For those who believe in getting ahead with their Christmas shopping this event can be a real boost - but even if you aren't that well organised the same degrees of quality and design that applied at the June event, of which this weekend is a virtual repeat, also prevail here. If you missed it the first time round now's your chance! And a Happy Christmas to you and yours. Time: 10.30-17.00
Castles

Apple Day Celebrations
16/10/99 CIDER MUSEUM AND KING OFFA DISTILLERY
31/10/99 Tel: 01432 354207
Annual Festival fo the Apple including display of cider apple varities
Museum- Food & Drink

Hallowe'en Happenings
16/10/99 THE WHITE POST MODERN FARM CENTRE
7/11/99 Tel: 01623 882977
Haunted Barn with moving floors and exhibits - where you soon find you are not alone! Witches trail and fun with the pumpkin people!
Animal Farms

The Black Country at War
16/10/99 DUDLEY MUSEUM AND ART GALLERY
19/3/00 Tel: 01384 815571/815575
Dramatic and evocative reconstructions of life in the Black Country during WWII
Museums

Lydney Road & Rail Show
17/10/99 DEAN FOREST RAILWAY
17/10/99 Tel: 01594 843423 info line
Preservation rally of road vehicles, in its

18th year, at Norchard car park
Railways

Festival of Sidecars
17/10/99 MALLORY PARK
17/10/99 Tel: 01455 842931/2/3
Lots of three wheel action, racing and displays, F1, F11, classic and vintage, plus solos. £7.00. Please telephone 0930 55 59 60 for further information.
Motor Racing Circuit

Apple Day
17/10/99 RYTON ORGANIC GARDENS
17/10/99 Tel: 01203 303517
Many varieties of apples on display for both tasting and buying. Competitions, demonstrations and talks. Cost: A£2.50 C£1.25 Concessions £2.00. HDRA/RHS/North Hort. Soc members FREE.
Gardens

Apple Day
17/10/99 RYTON ORGANIC GARDENS
17/10/99 Tel: 01203 303517
A feast of apples with tastings, identification, tales, cookery demonstrations, competitions and garden tours.
Gardens

FRENCH
18/10/99 NATIONAL WATERWAYS MUSEUM
22/10/99 Tel: 01452 318054
An education special for schools only, please call for details
Museum- Waterways

Behind The Scenes Days
20/10/99 CHATSWORTH
20/10/99 Tel: 01246 582204/565300
Spend a day backstage at Chatsworth and meet the people who look after the House and its collections, the Garden and Park. Book on 01246 582204 contact Mrs Sue Gregory
Historic Houses & Gardens

Planning a Fruit Garden
20/10/99 RYTON ORGANIC GARDENS
20/10/99 Tel: 01203 303517
An indoor course, looking at the planning and planting of new soft and top fruit. Time: 10.00-12.30.
Gardens

Making Real Bread
23/10/99 RYTON ORGANIC GARDENS
23/10/99 Tel: 01203 303517
Make a wide range of interesting and wholesome breads, and understand the principles of doughs, ensuring consistent and high quality results. Time: 09.30-17.00. Cost: £38.00 includes all

materials and ingredients.
Gardens

MCC Motorcycle Club Raceday
23/10/99 SILVERSTONE CIRCUIT
23/10/99 Tel: 01327 857271
Circuit: National. Feature: Club Races.
Please call for further information
Motor Racing Circuit

Beer Festival
23/10/99 WORCESTER RACECOURSE
23/10/99 Tel: 01905 25364
Experience a day at the races with all the
fun starting at 14.35
Racecourses

Medieval Entertainers
23/10/99 STOKESAY CASTLE
24/10/99 Tel: 01588 672544
Games, squire-training and talks on
weaponry and armour. Also, try your
hand at spinning, weaving and calligraphy and learn about herbal medicine.
A£3.50 C£1.80 Concessions£2.60
Castles

Apple Day
23/10/99 SULGRAVE MANOR
24/10/99 Tel: 01295 760205
The annual celebration of the apple and
its local distinctiveness. Apple cookery,
apple identification, ciders to try and
buy, a host of stalls and crafts throughout the house and in marquees in the
grounds. Spend a whole day at the
Manor to see it all. Commences 10.00-
17.00
Historic Houses

Treasure Trail Half-Term
23/10/99 NATIONAL TRAMWAY MUSEUM
30/10/99 Tel: 01773 852565
A really rewarding half-term for Junior
Sherlocks! Clues for all ages (and some
for Senior Sherlocks) give the thrill of
the case and the chance of a prize
Museum- Transport

Firework & Special Effects Spectacular
23/10/99 ALTON TOWERS
31/10/99 Tel: 0990 204060 24hr
The last two weekends in October. Finish
the year with a bang at the UK's largest
and most exciting fireworks and special
effects event. World record breaking fireworks, lasers, lights, special effects,
music and stunning scenery all combine
to make a show nothing short of mind-
blowing! Enjoy the Park and stay on for
the Fireworks for FREE!
Theme Parks

Half Term Holiday Activities

Black Country Living Museum
23/10/99 BLACK COUNTRY LIVING MUSEUM
31/10/99 Tel: 0121 557 9643 info
Please telephone for further information
Industrial Heritage

Oswald the Talking Engine's Week
23/10/99 MIDLAND RAILWAYS CENTRE
31/10/99 Tel: 01773 747674/749788
All our usual attractions and Oswald the
talking engine.
Railways Steam/Light

All Hallows Week
23/10/99 WARWICK CASTLE
31/10/99 Tel: 01926 406600
Learn about the many ghostly goings-on
at Warwick Castle, and hear of the
famous witch-trials of olde Warwickshire
Castles

Women in Art
23/10/99 CORINIUM MUSEUM
7/11/99 Tel: 01285 655611
The biennial exhibition of art by members of the WI. There will be items for
sale
Museum- Roman

The Artist's Model
23/10/99 DJANOGLY ART GALLERY
12/12/99 Tel: 0115 951 3192
Its role in British Art ffrom Wilkie to
Spencer, call for further details
Art Galleries

Christmas Selling Exhibition
23/10/99 BILSTON CRAFT GALLERY AND MUSEUM
8/1/00 Tel: 01902 409143
A unique Christmas decoration & gift
exhibition
Art Galleries

Autumn Ramble
24/10/99 BADDESLEY CLINTON HOUSE
24/10/99 Tel: 01564 783294
Meet is the car park (09.50) for 10.00
start for a 2 hour ramble around the
estate parkland. Advanced booking
required. £2.50 per person, Max. 40,
Dogs welcome of leads
Historic Houses & Gardens

Family Fun Day
24/10/99 BIRMINGHAM BOTANICAL GARDENS AND
GLASSHOUSES
24/10/99 Tel: 0121 454 1860
Lots of free entertainment and art exhibition - children admitted free
Gardens- Botanical

Eurocar
24/10/99 DONINGTON PARK
24/10/99 Tel: 01332 810048
Eurocar V8, Eurocar V6, Pickup Trucks,
Legends, Formula First, VW Beetles,

Caterham Graduates.

Motor Racing Circuit

Club Motorcycle Racing

24/10/99 MALLORY PARK

24/10/99 Tel: 01455 842931/2/3

Solos and sidecars. £7.00. Please telephone 0930 55 59 60 for further information.

Motor Racing Circuit

National Vintage Communications Fair

24/10/99 NATIONAL EXHIBITION CENTRE

24/10/99 Tel: 0121 780 4141 x2604

Hall 11. 10.30-16.00. Please telephone Sunrise Press, tel 01392 411565 for further information

Exhibition Centres

BMCRC Motorcycle Club Raceday

24/10/99 SILVERSTONE CIRCUIT

24/10/99 Tel: 01327 857271

Circuit: National. Feature: Club Races. Please call for further information

Motor Racing Circuit

Halloween Spooktacular

25/10/99 ALTON TOWERS

28/10/99 Tel: 0990 204060 24hr

You just can't keep a good ghost down, and children's favourite Caspter will be at the 1999 spooktacular to prove it! The live stage show featuring a variety of undead signers and dancers, plus spectacular cabaret performers is a huge hit with visitors, and a spine chilling selection of rides will run in the dark.

Theme Parks

Matthais Stomer: Isaac Blessing Jacob

26/10/99 THE BARBER INSTITUTE OF FINE ARTS

16/1/00 Tel: 0121 414 7333

Exhibition to explore the biblical theme of Isaac Blessing Jacob

Art Galleries

Our House, Central's Ideal Home Show 1999

27/10/99 NATIONAL EXHIBITION CENTRE

31/10/99 Tel: 0121 780 4141 x2604

Halls 3 & 3a. 09.00-18.00. Please telephone DMG Angex Ltd, tel 0181 515 2000 for further information. Ticket sales NEC Box Office 0121 767 4114

Exhibition Centres

Steeplechase Meeting

28/10/99 STRATFORD-ON-AVON RACECOURSE

28/10/99 Tel: 01789 267949/269411

Race Meeting

Racecourses

Lady Alice's Ghostly Tour

THE COMMANDERY

28/10/99 THE COMMANDERY

28/10/99 Tel: 01905 355071

Presented by The Commandery Civil War Centre. Pre-booked tickets only, mulled wine and cookies included commences 20.00. Adults only. Tickets: A£7.00 OAPs£6.00

Historic Buildings

Spooky Tours

29/10/99 QUARRY BANK MILL AND STYAL COUNTRY PARK

30/10/99 Tel: 01625 527468

Dare you take the Spooky Tour? Watch out, someone's watching you. Further information including times, prices and bookings available by calling Quarry bank Mill

Heritage Centres

Photo Action '98

29/10/99 NATIONAL EXHIBITION CENTRE

31/10/99 Tel: 0121 780 4141 x2604

Pavilion & Hall 1. 10.00-17.00. Please telephone Centre Exhibitions, tel 0121 780 4141 for further information. Ticket sales NEC Box Office 0121 767 4909

Exhibition Centres

Behind The Scenes Days

30/10/99 CHATSWORTH

30/10/99 Tel: 01246 582204/565300

Spend a day backstage at Chatsworth and meet the people who look after the House and its collections, the Garden and Park. Book on 01246 582204 contact Mrs Sue Gregory

Historic Houses & Gardens

Fantastic Fireworks

30/10/99 HERITAGE MOTOR CENTRE

30/10/99 Tel: 01926 641188

You can never see enough of those colourful sparks lighting up the night sky, call us now for further information

Museum- Motor

Ghostly Gaslight

30/10/99 IRONBRIDGE GORGE MUSEUMS

30/10/99 Tel: 01952 432166

A traditional Halloween celebration, with witches, ghouls and ghosts around every corner

Museum- Industrial

Halloween Fireworks Party

30/10/99 MIDLAND RAILWAYS CENTRE

30/10/99 Tel: 01773 747674/749788

Travel by train to our fireworks display.

Railways Steam/Light

Spooky Tours

30/10/99 QUARRY BANK MILL AND STYAL COUNTRY

30/10/99	PARK Tel: 01625 527468 A Drop-in for younger children. Further information including times, prices and bookings available by calling Quarry bank Mill <div align=right>*Heritage Centres*</div>

Halloween

30/10/99 RYTON ORGANIC GARDENS
30/10/99 Tel: 01203 303517

Ghouls, ghosts, monsters and fiends await your arrival for an extra-special evening meal on this All Hallows eve. Polish up those teeth and come 'dressed to impress' to possibly win yourself a free meal for two with wine. Booking essential on 01203 307142.

Gardens

Halloween at Dunstall Park

30/10/99 WOLVERHAMPTON RACECOURSE
30/10/99 Tel: 01902 421421

A fun night out combined with Flat Racing from 19.00. Hospitality packages available to include racecourse entrance, three course meal, racecard, and dancing to either a live band or disco.

Racecourses

Newton Day

30/10/99 WOOLSTHORPE MANOR
30/10/99 Tel: 01476 860338

Family gathering of Newtons - following research of the Newton Family Tree to find descendants of Sir Isaac Newton

Historic Houses

Woodland Weekend

30/10/99 DEAN HERITAGE CENTRE
31/10/99 Tel: 01594 822170

Discover the wonders of woodland with modern forestry displays and traditional woodland crafts. Activities for children include pumpkin lanterns & mask making with a little apple bobbing thrown in for fun

Heritage Centres

BARC Westfield Sportscars

31/10/99 DONINGTON PARK
31/10/99 Tel: 01332 810048

Firestone MG Owners Club, CSCC/BARC Classic Saloon and Historic Touring Cars, CSCC/BARC Post Historic Touring Cars, CSCC/BARC Group One Touring Cars, Ace Vehicle Deliveries Sports and Saloons Cars, Bell Security Guarding Formula Saloon Cars.

Motor Racing Circuit

Hallowe'en Spooktacular Event

31/10/99 GLADSTONE WORKING POTTERY MUSEUM
31/10/99 Tel: 01782 319232

Take a guided tours of the museum with a costumed character who will tell you spooky stories of days gone by. A very popular event - book early to avoid disappointment. Tickets pre-booking only (1998 prices as guide only) A£3.75 C£2.25

Museum- Pottery

Club Motorsport at its Best!

31/10/99 MALLORY PARK
31/10/99 Tel: 01455 842931/2/3

F4, 750 Trophy, RoS, Stock Hatch, Cat, KC. £8.00. Please telephone 0930 55 59 60 for further information.

Motor Racing Circuit

Starlight Special

31/10/99 NATIONAL TRAMWAY MUSEUM
31/10/99 Tel: 01773 852565

Feel cobbles underfoot, linger beneath old-fashioned street lights, hear the clatter of hooves and the rumble of trams. A very special experience indeed. Until 19.30

Museum- Transport

Free State Room Tours

1/11/99 WARWICK CASTLE
30/11/99 Tel: 01926 406600

Every weekday except Christmas Day. Join our guides on a free tour of the State Rooms and Great Hall and discover some of the secrets of Christmas past

Castles

Behind The Scenes Days

2/11/99 CHATSWORTH
2/11/99 Tel: 01246 582204/565300

Spend a day backstage at Chatsworth and meet the people who look after the House and its collections, the Garden and Park. Book on 01246 582204 contact Mrs Sue Gregory

Historic Houses & Gardens

National Hunt Racing

2/11/99 WARWICK RACECOURSE
2/11/99 Tel: 01926 491553

National Hunt racing at its best with the first race at 13.40, last race 16.10

Racecourses

Behind the Scenes Days

4/11/99 CHATSWORTH
4/11/99 Tel: 01246 582204/565300

Spend a day backstage at Chatsworth and meet the people who look after the House and its collections, the Garden and Park. Book on 01246 582204 contact Mrs Sue Gregory

Historic Houses & Gardens

Lynton C.C.
4/11/99
7/11/99
BILLING AQUADROME LIMITED
Tel: 01604 408181
Please telephone for further information. Contact: Mr Norris. No charge at gate

Country Leisure Parks

Traditional Bonfire Night
5/11/99
5/11/99
BLACK COUNTRY LIVING MUSEUM
Tel: 0121 557 9643 info
The most memorable bonfire night around with the added safety of no fireworks. Enjoy two bonfires and the unique atmosphere of the old-fashioned village lit by candle and gaslight

Industrial Heritage

Fireworks Display
5/11/99
5/11/99
CLUMBER PARK
Tel: 01909 476592
Choreographed to music. Time: 18.00. A£5.00

Historic Houses & Gardens

Coventry Morris Engines
5/11/99
7/11/99
BILLING AQUADROME LIMITED
Tel: 01604 408181
Please telephone John Watts, 01455 448386 for further information

Country Leisure Parks

Welcome Deaf Campers
5/11/99
7/11/99
BILLING AQUADROME LIMITED
Tel: 01604 408181
Please telephone Robert Rawley, 0181 868 1324 for further information

Country Leisure Parks

Trailer Caravan Club
5/11/99
7/11/99
BILLING AQUADROME LIMITED
Tel: 01604 408181
Please telephoneMr R Brown, 01604 717470, for further information

Country Leisure Parks

Land Rover C.C.C.
5/11/99
7/11/99
BILLING AQUADROME LIMITED
Tel: 01604 408181
Please telephone Sharon Salter, 01203 385747 for further information

Country Leisure Parks

West Midlands C.C.C.
5/11/99
7/11/99
BILLING AQUADROME LIMITED
Tel: 01604 408181
Please telephone Paul Morris, 0121 706 5423 for further information

Country Leisure Parks

Wild Rose C.C.
5/11/99
7/11/99
BILLING AQUADROME LIMITED
Tel: 01604 408181
Please telephone for further information. Contact: Faith Walker

Country Leisure Parks

Bargain weekend Four and Fireworks
5/11/99
7/11/99
BILLING AQUADROME LIMITED
Tel: 01604 408181
Tel 01604 408181 for more details

Country Leisure Parks

Traditional Bonfire Night
6/11/99
6/11/99
IRONBRIDGE GORGE MUSEUMS
Tel: 01952 432166
On Bonfire Night the Victorian Town is a very special place with the craftsmen working in the flickering gaslight as the Guy is paraded through the streets to the huge bonfire. Fantastic fireworks display follows. Separate ticket required

Museum- Industrial

Fireworks Night
6/11/99
6/11/99
MIDLAND RAILWAYS CENTRE
Tel: 01773 747674/749788
Travel by train to our fireworks display.

Railways Steam/Light

Homeopathic First Aid
6/11/99
6/11/99
RYTON ORGANIC GARDENS
Tel: 01203 303517
Discover how to treat toothache, sprains, bites and stings, etc. using homeopathy. Time: 10.00-16.00. Cost: £22.00 (£20.00 HDRA members)

Gardens

Smoking Fish/Meat/Cheese
6/11/99
6/11/99
RYTON ORGANIC GARDENS
Tel: 01203 303517
Introducing the traditional skills and knowledge of preserving food by smoking. Time: 09.30-17.00. Cost: £48.00 includes all materials and ingredients.

Gardens

Bonfire Night
6/11/99
6/11/99
SHUGBOROUGH ESTATE
Tel: 01889 881388
Annual firework display organised by Stafford Round Table. Separate charge for this event

Historic Houses & Gardens

BRRDC Winter Warmer Raceday
6/11/99
6/11/99
SILVERSTONE CIRCUIT
Tel: 01327 857271
Circuit: National. Feature: Club Races. Please call for further information

Motor Racing Circuit

Chamber Music Concert
6/11/99
6/11/99
SULGRAVE MANOR
Tel: 01295 760205
In the Grand Hall. A variety of enjoyable music. Light buffet supper with wine will follow the concert. Commences 19.30.

Tickets: £15.00 inclusive of Supper
Historic Houses

The International Classic Motor Show

6/11/99 NATIONAL EXHIBITION CENTRE
7/11/99 Tel: 0121 780 4141 x2604
Halls 4 & 5. 09.30-17.30. Please telephone Centre Exhibitions, tel 0121 780 4141 for further information. Ticket sales NEC Box Office 0121 767 4767
Exhibition Centres

International Motorcycle Show

6/11/99 NATIONAL EXHIBITION CENTRE
14/11/99 Tel: 0121 780 4141 x2604
Halls 8-12. 10.00-18.00. Please telephone MCI Exhibitions Ltd, tel 01203 559955 for further information
Exhibition Centres

Bonfire and Firework Spectacular

7/11/99 TOWCESTER RACECOURSE
7/11/99 Tel: 01327 353414
Guy Fawkes night will be celebrated in true spectacular style. This bonfire and firework display is organised with safety in mind, providing family entertainment with an impressive firework display by the famous Kimbolton Firework Company
Racecourses

Bonfire & Firework Spectacular

7/11/99 WESTON PARK
7/11/99 Tel: 01952 850207
Complete with a Petticoat Lane style market and two stunning firework displays, call for times and prices
Historic Houses & Gardens

Schools' Recycling Week

8/11/99 RYTON ORGANIC GARDENS
12/11/99 Tel: 01203 303517
A chance for schools within travelling distance to find out about the importance of recycling and composting, etc. Activities linked to the National Curriculum. Cost: £2.50 per child
Gardens

Grade 2 Worcester Novices Chase

10/11/99 WORCESTER RACECOURSE
10/11/99 Tel: 01905 25364
Racing from 13.00. Admission prices from £5.50-£13.50, discount available for advance group bookings, 2 complimentary badges for groups of 12-39 or 4 complimentary badges for 40+
Racecourses

Principles of Hedge Laying

11/11/99 RYTON ORGANIC GARDENS
11/11/99 Tel: 01203 303517
A practical course for people with an interest in maintaining hedges. Time: 09.30-dusk. Cost: £38.00.
Gardens

Crafts Alive At Christmas

11/11/99 NATIONAL EXHIBITION CENTRE
14/11/99 Tel: 0121 780 4141 x2604
Hall 6. Over 150 top quality traditional and modern craftsmen demonstrating and selling hand made British Crafts. 09.30-17.30 17.00 on Sun. A£6.50 C(0-16)£1.00 or Free if accompanied by an Adult OAPs£5.50
Exhibition Centres

Hobbycrafts

11/11/99 NATIONAL EXHIBITION CENTRE
14/11/99 Tel: 0121 780 4141 x2604
Hall 7. Whatever your craft come and see over 100 exhibitors demonstrating, teaching and selling supplies for over 30 different hobbies. 09.30-17.30 17.00 on Sun. A£6.50 C(0-16)£1.00 or Free if accompanied by an Adult OAPs£5.50
Exhibition Centres

Small Woodland Management of Native Trees

12/11/99 RYTON ORGANIC GARDENS
14/11/99 Tel: 01203 303517
A practical course for people with an interest in maintaining trees, from a small garden to a small woodland. Each day beings at 09.30 and finishes at dusk. Cost: £38.00 per day (attendance on all days is NOT necessary).
Gardens

Viking Invasion!

13/11/99 MANOR HOUSE MUSEUM
13/11/99 Tel: 01536 534219
If you see Long Boats parked in Kettering you know the Vikings are in Town, so pop along and meet them!
Museum- Local History

Jazz and Blues Night

13/11/99 WOLVERHAMPTON RACECOURSE
13/11/99 Tel: 01902 421421
A fun night out combined with Flat Racing from 19.00. Hospitality packages available to include racecourse entrance, three course meal, racecard, and dancing to either a live band or disco.
Racecourses

Memorabilia

13/11/99 NATIONAL EXHIBITION CENTRE
14/11/99 Tel: 0121 780 4141 x2604
Hall 17. Europe's largest science fiction, film, cult TV, pop and comic collectors' fair. 10.00-17.00. Please telephone Made

Further more detailed information on the attractions listed can be found in Best Guides *Visitor Attractions* Guide under the classifications shown

In Heaven, tel 01899 221622 for further information. Ticket sales NEC Box Office 0121 767 4555

Exhibition Centres

Fairyland Fantasy

13/11/99 THE WHITE POST MODERN FARM CENTRE
24/12/99 Tel: 01623 882977

Real Nativity in real stable - join in - costumes provided - daily performances! Walk through Fairyland, Santa - daily. Free gifts and free mince pies for adults!

Animal Farms

Made in the Middle

13/11/99 BILSTON CRAFT GALLERY AND MUSEUM
8/1/00 Tel: 01902 409143

Furniture, jewellery, textiles, ceramics etc. made by craftspeople living and working in the Midlands

Art Galleries

Ray Hedger - Don Cordrey: The Cotswold Landscape in Paintings

13/11/99 CORINIUM MUSEUM
30/1/00 Tel: 01285 655611

Two artists from the Cotswolds exhibit their work and the inspirations behind the art on display. There will be items for sale

Museum- Roman

Embroiders Casket

14/11/99 SULGRAVE MANOR
14/11/99 Tel: 01295 760205

A day of delights for all those with an interest in historic needlework. Inspired by the Manor's important on-going project, "The New Elizabethan Embroideries", this day will feature a fascinating assortment of artefacts throughout the house - from samplers to stumpwork, some to just gaze at and some to buy. Plus, demonstrations and stands. Commences 10.30-16.30

Historic Houses

MATHS

14/11/99 NATIONAL WATERWAYS MUSEUM
19/11/99 Tel: 01452 318054

An education special for schools only, please call for details

Museum- Waterways

Gloucester Christmas Celebration 1999

14/11/99 GLOUCESTER CHRISTMAS CELEBRATION 1999
25/12/99 Tel: 01452 396620

Christmas celebrations in the town centre. Cartoon celebrities launch the event. There will be clowns, music and street entertainment every Thursday and Sunday evenings until Christmas. Time: Christmas Launch event: 14th 12.00-18.00. Thur Eve: 17.00-21.00. Sat 09.00-18.00. Sun 10.00-16.30. Admission Free.

Festivals

Animal Kingdom

14/11/99 THE FERRERS CENTRE FOR ARTS AND CRAFTS
11/1/00 Tel: 01332 865408

Christmas exhibition, mixed media, ceramics, wood, sculpture

Craft Galleries

National Hunt Racing

18/11/99 WARWICK RACECOURSE
18/11/99 Tel: 01926 491553

National Hunt racing from 13.20, with the last race at 15.50

Racecourses

CBBC's Big Bash & CBBC's Little Bash

18/11/99 NATIONAL EXHIBITION CENTRE
21/11/99 Tel: 0121 780 4141 x2604

Halls 4 & 5, 19 & 20. 09.00-18.00. Please telephone BBC Haymarket Exhibitions Ltd, tel 0171 402 2555 for further information. Ticket sales NEC Box Office 0121 767 4477

Exhibition Centres

Music Show

19/11/99 NATIONAL EXHIBITION CENTRE
21/11/99 Tel: 0121 780 4141 x2604

Hall 9 & 8/9 Link. Please telephone Mammoth Events Ltd, 01353 665577 for further information

Exhibition Centres

Derbyshire Caravan Club Rally

19/11/99 THE BASS MUSEUM
21/11/99 Tel: 01283 511000

Please telephone for further information

Breweries

Supreme Cat Show

20/11/99 NATIONAL EXHIBITION CENTRE
20/11/99 Tel: 0121 780 4141 x2604

Halls 10-12. 10.30-17.00. Please telephone the Governing Council of the Cat Fancy, tel 01278 427575 for further information

Exhibition Centres

Smoking Fish/Meat/Cheese

20/11/99 RYTON ORGANIC GARDENS
20/11/99 Tel: 01203 303517

Introducing the traditional skills and knowledge of preserving food by smoking. Time: 09.30-17.00. Cost: £48.00 includes all materials and ingredients.

Gardens

Wulfrun Stakes

| 20/11/99 | **WOLVERHAMPTON RACECOURSE** |
| 20/11/99 | Tel: 01902 421421 |

Afternoon televised Flat Race Meeting from 14.00

Racecourses

Record & CD Collectors' Fair

| 20/11/99 | **NATIONAL EXHIBITION CENTRE** |
| 21/11/99 | Tel: 0121 780 4141 x2604 |

Pavilion. 10.00-17.00. Please telephone P & J Promotions, tel 01273 463017 for further information

Exhibition Centres

Network Q RAC Rally of Great Britain

| 20/11/99 | **SILVERSTONE CIRCUIT** |
| 21/11/99 | Tel: 01327 857271 |

Circuit: All. Feature: FIA World Rally Championship. Please call for further information

Motor Racing Circuit

Santa Specials

| 20/11/99 | **MIDLAND RAILWAYS CENTRE** |
| 24/12/99 | Tel: 01773 747674/749788 |

Santa on the train, presents for the children, mince pie and drink for the adults.

Railways Steam/Light

Lo-co Glass

| 20/11/99 | **BROADFIELD HOUSE GLASS MUSEUM** |
| 16/1/00 | Tel: 01384 812745 |

Work by Louise Hawkins and Colin Edwards - this year's residents in the museum's scholarship studio

Museum- Glass

Vegetarian Christmas Cooking with Holly Jones

| 21/11/99 | **RYTON ORGANIC GARDENS** |
| 21/11/99 | Tel: 01203 303517 |

Colour and flavour for festive catering. Time: 10.00-13.30

Gardens

Stir Up Sunday

| 21/11/99 | **SHUGBOROUGH ESTATE** |
| 21/11/99 | Tel: 01889 881388 |

Traditional Christmas Pudding making day in the Victorian kitchens and laundry. See the servants at work preparing for the festive celebrations. A£4.00 Reduced £3.00

Historic Houses & Gardens

BRITAIN SINCE 1930s

| 22/11/99 | **NATIONAL WATERWAYS MUSEUM** |
| 26/11/99 | Tel: 01452 318054 |

An education special for schools only, please call for details

Museum- Waterways

Winter Fruit Pruning

| 23/11/99 | **RYTON ORGANIC GARDENS** |
| 23/11/99 | Tel: 01203 303517 |

This course will cover all types of top and soft fruits. Time: 10.00-12.30

Gardens

BBC Good Food Show '99

| 24/11/99 | **NATIONAL EXHIBITION CENTRE** |
| 28/11/99 | Tel: 0121 780 4141 x2604 |

Halls 17-20. 10.00-18.00. Please telephone consumer Exhibitions Ltd, tel 0181 948 1666 for further information. Ticket sales NEC Box Office 0121 767 4000

Exhibition Centres

Dickensian Christmas Craft & Gift Fayre

| 26/11/99 | **ALTON TOWERS** |
| 28/11/99 | Tel: 0990 204060 24hr |

Up to 255 skilled crafts people with quality seasonal crafts to suit every pocket. Commences 10.00-18.00. Tickets: A£3.00-£5.00 C(5-15)£1.00 OAPs£2.00-£3.00. Commences 10.00-18.00

Theme Parks

BBC Network East Live - Mega Mela '99

| 26/11/99 | **NATIONAL EXHIBITION CENTRE** |
| 28/11/99 | Tel: 0121 780 4141 x2604 |

Halls 9-12. 09.00-18.00. Please telephone BBC Haymarket Exhibitions Ltd, tel 0171 402 2555 for further information. Ticket sales NEC Box Office 0121 767 4545

Exhibition Centres

Designing with Plants (RHS)

| 27/11/99 | **RYTON ORGANIC GARDENS** |
| 27/11/99 | Tel: 01203 303517 |

A few well chosen plants can transform your garden without the expense and mess associated with hard-landscaping - we show you how. Time: 10.00-16.00

Gardens

National Hunt Racing

| 27/11/99 | **WARWICK RACECOURSE** |
| 27/11/99 | Tel: 01926 491553 |

National Hunt racing from 12.30, last race 15.35

Racecourses

Country and Western Night

| 27/11/99 | **WOLVERHAMPTON RACECOURSE** |
| 27/11/99 | Tel: 01902 421421 |

Enjoy a Country and Western themed evening combined with Flat Racing. Packages available to include racecourse entrance, three course meal, racecard, and dancing to either a live

Further more detailed information on the attractions listed can be found in Best Guides *Visitor Attractions* Guide under the classifications shown

band or disco.

Racecourses

National Christmas Lacemakers' Fair

27/11/99 NATIONAL EXHIBITION CENTRE
28/11/99 Tel: 0121 780 4141 x2604
Pavilion. 10.00-17.00. Please telephone J & J Ford, tel 01543 491000 for further information

Exhibition Centres

Yule Tide Craft Fair

27/11/99 RAGLEY HALL
28/11/99 Tel: 01789 762090
Beautiful british crafts selected to solve all your Christmas gift problems

Historic Houses & Gardens

Contemporary Art Auction

27/11/99 NOTTINGHAM CASTLE MUSEUM AND ART GALLERY
11/12/99 Tel: 0115 915 3700
Works for sale by regional makers and artists. Auction date: Saturday 11 December

Castles

Christmas Fantasy

27/11/99 CLEARWELL CAVES ANCIENT IRON MINES
24/12/99 Tel: 01594 832535
The caverns are transformed into a Christmas wonderland where children meet Santa and receive a present. A great festive event for all ages

Caves

The Pullman Cars of the Midland Railway

27/11/99 DERBY INDUSTRIAL MUSEUM
22/1/00 Tel:
Exhibition based on Midland Railway Pullman Cars and their pioneering role in Britain's railway history

Satellites of Fashion

27/11/99 NORTHAMPTON CENTRAL MUSEUM AND ART GALLERY
23/1/00 Tel: 01604 238548
An avant-garde fashion display of hats, bags and shoes. A touring exhibition from the Crafts Council

Art Galleries

From Darkness to Light

28/11/99 LICHFIELD CATHEDRAL
28/11/99 Tel: 01543 306240
Advent Carol Service by candlelight, call for times

Cathedrals

Christmas Lunch

28/11/99 WARWICK CASTLE
24/12/99 Tel: 01926 406600
Thursday to Sunday (subject to availabil-

ity) served at 12.30. Availability for larger groups (min 40 people) also being offered Monday-Wednesday. Traditional four-course lunch in the 14th century Undercroft Restaurant. Pre-booking essential, book early to avoid disappointment. 1998 prices for guidance only: A£22.50 C(4-16inc)£14.50, includes admission to the Castle and Grounds. Vegetarian option available

Castles

Victorian Entertainment Weekends

28/11/99 WARWICK CASTLE
27/12/99 Tel: 01926 406600
Every Sunday. Take a ride in a Victorian horse and carriage or be entertained by our Victorian policeman. Listen to popular festive music from our Victorian musicians

Castles

Christmas Shopping Day

29/11/99 WORCESTER RACECOURSE
29/11/99 Tel: 01905 25364
Racing from 12.45. Admission prices from £5.50-£13.50, discount available for advance group bookings, 2 complimentary badges for groups of 12-39 or 4 complimentary badges for 40+

Racecourses

Planning a Vegetable Garden

1/12/99 RYTON ORGANIC GARDENS
1/12/99 Tel: 01203 303517
Methods of growing vegetables plus lots of advice on crop rotation, clearing weeds and feeding the soil. Time: 10.00-16.00.

Gardens

Market Day

1/12/99 WOLVERHAMPTON RACECOURSE
1/12/99 Tel: 01902 421421
Afternoon racing with a chance to shop for a few Christmas gifts from Dunstall Park

Racecourses

The Great Black Country Santa Hunt

1/12/99 BLACK COUNTRY LIVING MUSEUM
5/12/99 Tel: 0121 557 9643 info
Santa and his helpers are hard at work making gifts for delivery on Christmas Eve. Join the hunt, explore the Museum and see if you can find Santa and receive a gift. Pre-booking only by phoning 0121 520 8054. Also on: 11-12 & 18-19 December

Industrial Heritage

Kingmaker's Feast

1/12/99	**WARWICK CASTLE**
23/12/99	Tel: 01926 406600

Served at 19.30 in the 14th Century Undercroft. 1998 prices for guidance only: A£40.00. Your evening begins as you are lead through the Castle's premier mediaeval attraction - Kingmaker - a preparation for battle. Beneath the vaulted ceiling of the 14th century Undercroft, your five course feast is served. The revelry begins with wine flowing as freely as the gossip and tale that surround the impending battle, an historic moment in the Castle's past. This is intermingled with lively music throughout the evening.

Castles

Christmas Nativity

1/12/99	**ASH END HOUSE CHILDREN'S FARM**
24/12/99	Tel: 0121 329 3240

The nativity story and Father Christmas sing-along, help with the story of the very first Christmas, call for times and further details

Farms

Extended Opening Hours for Christmas

1/12/99	**CIDER MUSEUM AND KING OFFA DISTILLERY**
31/12/99	Tel: 01432 354207

Christmas shopping at the museum's exclusive gift shop. Dates to be confirmed, call for further details

Museum- Food & Drink

The NEC Antiques For Everyone Fair

2/12/99	**NATIONAL EXHIBITION CENTRE**
5/12/99	Tel: 0121 780 4141 x2604

Hall 5. 400+ antiques dealers offer antiques and fine art. Exhibits datelined to 1914 in plush, stand-fitted Section One; to 1940 for all things collectable in Section Two. An enormous range of very fine quality antiques and collectibles for every pocket with prices from less than £10 to over £100,000. 20,000 visitors anticipated. Open Thur & Fri 11.00-20.00, Sat & Sun 11.00-18.00

Exhibition Centres

Carols in the COurtyard

3/12/99	**CANONS ASHBY HOUSE**
3/12/99	Tel: 01327 860044

Set in the splendid Courtyard of Canon's Ashby House, further details available on 01327 860044

Historic Houses

Making Real Bread

3/12/99	**RYTON ORGANIC GARDENS**
3/12/99	Tel: 01203 303517

Make a wide range of interesting and wholesome breads, and understand the principles of doughs, ensuring consistent and high quality results. Time: 09.30-17.00. Cost: £38.00 includes all materials and ingredients.

Gardens

Dickens' Evening

3/12/99	**SUDBURY HALL AND THE MUSEUM OF CHILDHOOD, THE NATIONAL TRUST**
3/12/99	Tel: 01283 585305

A delightful evening to bring in the Christmas season. Join with other in the Saloon for supper. Limited availability, pre-booking only

Country Estates

Dickensian Christmas Fayre

3/12/99	**HERITAGE MOTOR CENTRE**
5/12/99	Tel: 01926 641188

Celebrate Christmas in style, the Victorian way, plenty of traditional present ideas to help out with the last minute shopping. Commences 10.00-18.00. Tickets: A£3.00-£5.00 C(5-15)£1.00 OAPs£2.00-£3.00

Museum- Motor

The Clothes Show Live '99

3/12/99	**NATIONAL EXHIBITION CENTRE**
8/12/99	Tel: 0121 780 4141 x2604

Halls 6-12 & 17-20. 09.00-18.30. Please telephone Barker Brown Ltd, tel 0171 637 3313 for further information. Ticket sales NEC Box Office 0121 767 4444

Exhibition Centres

Chamber Music Concert

4/12/99	**SULGRAVE MANOR**
4/12/99	Tel: 01295 760205

In the Grand Hall. A variety of enjoyable music. Light buffet supper with wine will follow the concert. Commences 19.30. Tickets: £15.00 inclusive of Supper

Historic Houses

Soul and Motown Night

4/12/99	**WOLVERHAMPTON RACECOURSE**
4/12/99	Tel: 01902 421421

Enjoy a Soul and Motown Night combined with Flat Racing. Packages available to include racecourse entrance, three course meal, racecard, and dancing to either a live band or disco.

Racecourses

British National Racing Pigeon Show '99

Further more detailed information on the attractions listed can be found in Best Guides *Visitor Attractions* Guide under the classifications shown

| 4/12/99 | NATIONAL EXHIBITION CENTRE |
| 5/12/99 | Tel: 0121 780 4141 x2604 |

Hall 3a. 10.00-17.00. Please telephone The Racing Pigeon Publishing Company Ltd, tel 0171 831 4050 for further information

Exhibition Centres

National Cage & Aviary Birds Exhibition

| 4/12/99 | NATIONAL EXHIBITION CENTRE |
| 5/12/99 | Tel: 0121 780 4141 x2604 |

Hall 1. Sat 09.30-18.00, Sun 09.30-17.00. Please telephone Sovereign Exhibition Management, tel 01460 66616 for further information

Exhibition Centres

Santa Specials, Sat & Sun during Dec & Christmas Eve

| 4/12/99 | NORTHAMPTON AND LAMPORT RAILWAY |
| 24/12/99 | Tel: 01604 847318 |

A Steam hauled service. Take a Steam Train ride along the Northampton & Lamport Railway from Pitsford & Brampton station. As there are a large number of children (and adults) who want to meet Santa, he has asked us to make appointments for your visit. These start at 10.45 then at 30min intervals with 16.15 being the last appointment. We have arranged for the trains to run a very frequent service, so having seen Santa there will be minimum delay before you can then board the Steam Train, enjoy the ride and your refreshments. Every child will receive a present from Santa, a soft drink and biscuits. Every adult will receive a glass of sherry and a mince pie. The fare for adults and children, inclusive of present, refreshments on the train, and steam journey is £5.50. Children's fares are for those aged 2-15 years. Infants (under 2 years) pay a special fare of £3.00 and will receive a present from Santa. Owing to the popularity of our Santa Specials, advance booking is essential in order to guarantee a ride. In the event of cancellation or exchange of pre-booked tickets, there will be an administration charge of £3.00 per booking. (Prices based on 98 details and are for guidance only)

Railways Steam/Light

A Tudor Christmas

| 4/12/99 | SULGRAVE MANOR |
| 31/12/99 | Tel: 01295 760205 |

The Great Hall of the Manor is splendidly bedecked with seasonal greenery, with the log fire burning and beeswax candles glowing. Meet the Lord of the Manor and his Cook to hear of the customs and traditions of our early Christmasses. Enjoy a warming wassail and sweetmeats, and, on some days, be amazed by the Mummers plays. Each weekend during Dec except 25 & 26 AND again from Mon 27-31 Dec. Commences: 10.30-13.00 & 14.00-16.30.

Historic Houses

Christmas Craft Fair

| 5/12/99 | FORGE MILL NEEDLE MUSEUM AND BORDESLEY ABBEY VISITOR CENTRE |
| 5/12/99 | Tel: 01527 62509 |

Please call for further information

Museum- Mill

Santa Specials

| 5/12/99 | DEAN FOREST RAILWAY |
| 24/12/99 | Tel: 01594 843423 info line |

Santa Special commence on 5th Dec and every Saturday and Sunday until the 24 Dec. With midweek Specials running call for further details. Trains leave Norchard Station 5 times during each Santa Special day. Prices: (approx) A&C£6.00 to include seasonal refreshments and a present for each child given by Santa on the train. There are limited disabled and wheelchair access and pre-booking is advisable for midweek trains. Call the Norchard Gift Shop to make Credit Card bookings on 01594 845840

Railways

Music for All Seasons - Winter

| 6/12/99 | RYTON ORGANIC GARDENS |
| 6/12/99 | Tel: 01203 303517 |

A sequence of music workshops themed on the seasons. Join us for one or more of the days. Open to everyone, including complete beginners! If you play an instrument please bring it along. Listen to seasonal works by the great composers and, using the melodies of the countryside, create your own music. Time: 10.00-16.00.

Gardens

Christmas at Shugborough

| 7/12/99 | SHUGBOROUGH ESTATE |
| 9/12/99 | Tel: 01889 881388 |

Victorian evenings with festive decorations, candle lit Mansion House, Christmas market and a host of seasonal entertainment

Historic Houses & Gardens

Christmas by Candlelight

10/12/99 RUDDINGTON FRAMEWORK KNITTERS' MUSEUM

10/12/99 Tel: 0115 984 6914

Seasonal music and poetry evening. Traditional carol singing with choir. Museum candlelit, hot and cold refreshments with brazier and hot chestnuts, shop

Museums

Ladies Kennel Association Championship Dog Show

10/12/99 NATIONAL EXHIBITION CENTRE

11/12/99 Tel: 0121 780 4141 x2604

Halls 2-4. 08.00-18.00. Please telephone Ladies Kennel Association, tel 01453 832944 for further information

Exhibition Centres

A Victorian Christmas

11/12/99 MANOR HOUSE MUSEUM

11/12/99 Tel: 01536 534219

Christmas started with the Victorians, we have Prince Albert to thank for the Christmas Tree! But what else did they do over the Christmas season, with not a telly in sight? Come along a find out

Museum- Local History

Hands on in the Mill and Christmas Trail Quiz

11/12/99 QUARRY BANK MILL AND STYAL COUNTRY PARK

11/12/99 Tel: 01625 527468

Find out how the Mill works and enter our fun Christmas Quiz. Further information including times, prices and bookings available by calling Quarry bank Mill

Heritage Centres

Christmas Concert

11/12/99 SUDBURY HALL AND THE MUSEUM OF CHILDHOOD, THE NATIONAL TRUST

11/12/99 Tel: 01283 585305

Beautiful music, beautiful surrounds at a beautiful time of the year. Limited availability, pre-booking only

Country Estates

Christmas Party Night

11/12/99 WOLVERHAMPTON RACECOURSE

11/12/99 Tel: 01902 421421

Plenty of festive cheer together with Flat Racing. Packages available to include racecourse entrance, three course meal, racecard, and dancing to either a live band or disco. Racing from 19.00

Racecourses

Willow Structures

11/12/99 RYTON ORGANIC GARDENS

12/12/99 Tel: 01203 303517

A two day course in creating living willow structures, covering selection of material, harvesting, design and practical construction work. Time: 09.30 on 29th to 16.00 on 30th. Cost: £115.00 (£95.00 HDRA members). Accommodation is not included in the cost, but we can supply a list of local places where you can stay.

Gardens

Toy and Train Collectors' Fair

12/12/99 NATIONAL EXHIBITION CENTRE

12/12/99 Tel: 0121 780 4141 x2604

Hall 17. 10.30-16.30. Please telephone John Webb of D & J Fairs, tel 01526 398198 for further information

Exhibition Centres

Victorian Christmas Parties

12/12/99 QUARRY BANK MILL AND STYAL COUNTRY PARK

19/12/99 Tel: 01625 527468

Celebrate Christmas the traditional way with our Victorian Christmas Parties on 12 & 19 December. Further information including times, prices and bookings available by calling Quarry Bank Mill

Heritage Centres

Victorian Christmas Festival

16/12/99 GLADSTONE WORKING POTTERY MUSEUM

17/12/99 Tel: 01782 319232

Lots of things to see and so at our ever popular Christmas event. Brass Band and Children's Choir, traditional festive decorations, children's rides, Victorian stalls, free entertainment. A wonderfully festive Victorian spectacle! Book well in advance (1998 prices as guide only) A£3.75 C£2.25, commences 18.30

Museum- Pottery

Christmas Evening

17/12/99 BLACK COUNTRY LIVING MUSEUM

18/12/99 Tel: 0121 557 9643 info

Enjoy a special evening in the unique, nostalgic atmosphere of the old-fashioned village lit by candle and gaslight. Carol singers, hot chestnuts and mulled wine in the Bottle and Glass Inn. Pre-booking only by phoning 0121 520 8054

Industrial Heritage

National Hunt Racing

18/12/99 WARWICK RACECOURSE

18/12/99 Tel: 01926 491553

National Hunt Racing at its best with the first race at 12.20, last race 15.35. A£9.00 C(0-16)£Free. Group rates avail-

able
Racecourses

Santa Specials
18/12/99 NORTHAMPTON AND LAMPORT RAILWAY
19/12/99 Tel: 01604 847318
Meet Santa, get a present, have a ride on our steam train with sherry and mince pies for the adults
Railways Steam/Light

Santa Specials
24/12/99 NORTHAMPTON AND LAMPORT RAILWAY
24/12/99 Tel: 01604 847318
Meet Santa, get a present, have a ride on our steam train with sherry and mince pies for the adults
Railways Steam/Light

Cathedral Carol Service
26/12/99 LICHFIELD CATHEDRAL
26/12/99 Tel: 01543 306240
The only Cathderal to hold a Carol Service on Boxing Day, call for times
Cathedrals

Plum Pudding Meeting
26/12/99 MALLORY PARK
26/12/99 Tel: 01455 842931/2/3
Winter racing, mostly 'bikes', with single seater and SuperMoto. £8.00. Please telephone 0930 55 59 60 for further information.
Motor Racing Circuit

Mince Pie Specials
26/12/99 NORTHAMPTON AND LAMPORT RAILWAY
1/1/00 Tel: 01604 847318
A Steam hauled service. Admission price includes a ride on the train. Children must be accompanied by an Adult. Includes refreshments on the train.
A£3.20 OAPs£2.10 C(3 -15)£2.10
C(Under 3)£Free Platform Ticket £0.50
(prices are for guidance only)
Railways Steam/Light

Post Christmas Special
26/12/99 BLACK COUNTRY LIVING MUSEUM
2/1/00 Tel: 0121 557 9643 info
Take a break from the Christmas television and turkey and enjoy the special Christmas atmosphere of the old-fashioned village with fish and chips from the Fried Fish Shop
Industrial Heritage

Mince Pie Specials
26/12/99 MIDLAND RAILWAYS CENTRE
3/1/00 Tel: 01773 747674/749788
Steam trains and mince pies, museum, country park and farm park.
Railways Steam/Light

Boxing Day Meeting

27/12/99 WOLVERHAMPTON RACECOURSE
27/12/99 Tel: 01902 421421
Escape the turkey and tinsel and come racing!
Racecourses

Last Race of the Century!
30/12/99 STRATFORD-ON-AVON RACECOURSE
30/12/99 Tel: 01789 267949/269411

Racecourses

National Hunt Racing
31/12/99 WARWICK RACECOURSE
31/12/99 Tel: 01926 491553
Racing from 12.15, last race at 15.40
Racecourses

The 8th Etruria Canal Festival and IWA
4/6/00 ETRURIA INDUSTRIAL MUSEUM
5/6/00 Tel: 01782 233114
Millennium boat festival, steam rally, jazz bands, crafts and more
Museum- Industrial

Mystery Plays
5/6/00 COVENTRY CATHEDRAL AND VISITORS CENTRE
18/6/00 Tel: 01203 227597
The tradition of Mystery Plays lives on in the ruins of Coventry Cathedral
Cathedrals

International Church Music Festival
21/6/00 COVENTRY CATHEDRAL AND VISITORS CENTRE
24/6/00 Tel: 01203 227597
A festival of Church musicians from all over the world presenting concerts of traditional church music
Cathedrals

Benjamin Britten's War Requiem
14/11/00 COVENTRY CATHEDRAL AND VISITORS CENTRE
14/11/00 Tel: 01203 227597
A performance of this piece, commissioned to celebrate the Consecration of Coventry Cathedral on the 60th Anniversary of Coventry's bombing
Cathedrals

Eastern England

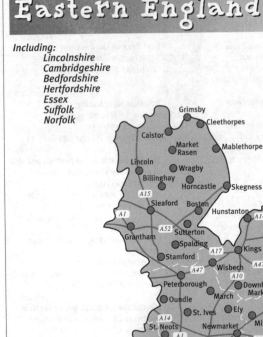

Exhibition: The Pleasures of Peace
1/3/99
1/4/99
SAINSBURY CENTRE FOR VISUAL ARTS
Tel: 01603 456060/593199
Mid-Century craft and art in Britian. In the Upper and Lower Galleries.

Art Galleries

The Art of Dunwich Heath
1/3/99
18/12/99
DUNWICH HEATH AND MINSMERE BEACH
Tel: 01728 648505
Every Saturday. A practical course for all, involving drawing, water colours and oils, run by a local artist. Ongoing course - join for a day or several sessions. Time: 10.00-16.00. Tickets: £10.00 per session

Conservation Parks

Special Party Rates Racing Day
6/3/99
6/3/99
HUNTINGDON STEEPLECHASES LTD
Tel: 01480 453373
See competitive racing and all the thrills and spills of National Hunt Racing with special rates for groups and coach parties. For further details about private facilities for your party call 01480 453373

Racecourses

Pudding Weekend
6/3/99
7/3/99
ICKWORTH HOUSE PARK AND GARDENS
Tel: 01284 735270
Sheer indulgence for those who love traditional puddings. Time: 12.00-16.00. Tickets: £8.50, booking essential, call 01284 735270.

Historic Houses & Gardens

Thomas' Branchline Weekend
6/3/99
7/3/99
NENE VALLEY RAILWAY
Tel: 01780 784444
Meet the children's favourite little blue engine at Wansford Station

Railways Steam/Light

National Trust Volunteers Work Party
7/3/99
7/3/99
DUNWICH HEATH AND MINSMERE BEACH
Tel: 01728 648505
Help the Warden and Ipswich National Trust Volunteers in a conservation task on the property, bring either packed lunch or food available in the Restaurant. Hot drinks provided. Start: 10.30. Admission Free, no booking required

Conservation Parks

UK Computer Fair
7/3/99
7/3/99
EAST OF ENGLAND SHOWGROUND
Tel: 01733 234451
One of the largest Computer Fairs in the country

Showgrounds

What Tree Is It?
7/3/99
7/3/99
HATFIELD FOREST
Tel: 01279 870678
An opportunity to learn about the great variety of trees in the Forest, thie similarities and differences and how to identify them. Commences: 11.00-13.00. Tickets: £2.00 C£1.00 Family Ticket (A2+C2)£5.00. Please note that you must book for all events except where stated otherwise. Please send a cheque payable to National Trust, along with an s.a.e. for your tickets.

Forests

Up with the Larks
7/3/99
7/3/99
HIGH LODGE FOREST CENTRE
Tel: 01842 810271/815434
An early morning walk in search of one of Britain's rarest birds - the woodlark - and a chance to hear its magical song. Meet: 07.00 at the Forest District Office, Santon Downham. Cost: A£2.00 C£1.00. Please book in advance - tickets available from 15 Feb 1999

Forest Visitor Centres

East Midlands Doll Fair
7/3/99
7/3/99
WOBURN ABBEY
Tel: 01525 290666
Located in the Sculpture Gallery, the opportunity to buy dolls and toys, antique and new from the 54 exhibitors. Parking and grounds free for Doll Fair. House open but extra charge

Stately Homes

Annual Lecture: Capital of Essex: The Development of Chelmsford by David Jones
12/3/99
12/3/99
CHELMSFORD AND ESSEX REGIMENT MUSEUM
Tel: 01245 353066
The county town's progress down the years focusing on its people and culture and institutions like the Local board of Health and the Borough Council. Venue: Cramphorn Theatre. Time: 20.00. Tickets: A£3.50 Concessions£2.50 - book from Civic Theatres Box Office: 01245 606505

Museum- Local History

Waking Up Ickworth House
12/3/99
12/3/99
ICKWORTH HOUSE PARK AND GARDENS
Tel: 01284 735270
Guided tour of Ickworth House and its preparations for the new season. Conservation in action. Time: 10.00-12.00. Tickets: £10.00 includes coffee on arrival. Booking essential, maximum of

50. Call 01284 735270.

Historic Houses & Gardens

Cook's Tours of Norfolk's Culinary Heritage

12/3/99 BRANCASTER
24/4/99 Tel: 01485 210719

Held in the Brancaster Millennium Activity Centre, and given by Alison Sloane, the Catering Manager at Oxburgh Hall and Peckover House. Call for fuller details. DATES: 12-14 Mar & 23-24 Apr 1999.

Nature Reserves

Magical Metals

13/3/99 CAMBRIDGE AND COUNTY FOLK MUSEUM
13/3/99 Tel: 01223 355159

A children's Saturday activity where your children can take part in a matealwork workshop, 14.30-15.45

Museum- Folk

Vintage and Commercial Vehicle Auction

13/3/99 EAST OF ENGLAND SHOWGROUND
13/3/99 Tel: 01733 234451

Large auction of vintage and commercial vehicles

Showgrounds

Pudding Weekend

13/3/99 ICKWORTH HOUSE PARK AND GARDENS
14/3/99 Tel: 01284 735270

Sheer indulgence for those who love traditional puddings. Time: 12.00-16.00. Tickets: £8.50, booking essential, call 01284 735270.

Historic Houses & Gardens

Legion XIIII On Guard

13/3/99 VERULAMIUM MUSEUM AND PARK
14/3/99 Tel: 01727 819339

Roman soldiers are in the museum describing the tactics of Roman warfare

Museums

The Life and Times of Oliver Cromwell

13/3/99 STAMFORD MUSEUM
3/7/99 Tel: 01780 766317

An exhibition to celebrate the 400th anniversary of Oliver Cromwell's birth

Museum- Local History

Clubmans Bikes (RETFORD)

14/3/99 CADWELL PARK CIRCUIT
14/3/99 Tel: 01507 343248

All classes of national solo motorcycles and sidecars. Full Circuit, Grade-E. On the Gate: £10.00-£28.00. In Advance: Non £8.00-£25.00, Club £7.00-£22.00. Two Day Pass: Non £11.00-£30.00, Club £10.00-£27.00. Three Day Pass: Non £32.00, Club £29.00. Qualifying: £5.00-

£14.00. C£Free. Programme £Free-£5.00. Seating (BH): £Free-£8.00. Group Tickets: Non £90.00-£95.00, Club £80.00-£85.00. Season Ticket Inc. of Club Membership: £135.00. You can buy your tickets for any of the 1999 events in advance any time up to 4 days before an event and make a saving, Tel: 0870 60 60 611

Motor Racing Circuit

Mothering Sunday at Felbrigg Hall

14/3/99 FELBRIGG HALL
14/3/99 Tel: 01263 837444

Special Mother's Day lunch in the Park Restaurant. Price: £11.95 (three courses with a special gift for Mum). Please book direct with the restaurant 01263 838237. Craft exhibition in the stable block.

Historic Houses & Gardens

Mothering Sunday

14/3/99 LEIGHTON BUZZARD RAILWAY
14/3/99 Tel: 01525 373888 (24hours)

Free chocolate cake for mums and grans travelling on the train

Railways Steam/Light

Mothering Sunday Walk

14/3/99 OXBURGH HALL, GARDEN AND ESTATE
14/3/99 Tel: 01366 328258

A guided woodland walk by Graham Donachie, Head Gardener. Meet in the orchard. Bring Mum along for a special treat, special menu in the restaurant. Normal admission by garden ticket only

Historic Buildings

Huntingdon's Traditional Raceday

17/3/99 HUNTINGDON STEEPLECHASES LTD
17/3/99 Tel: 01480 453373

Entrance to all enclosures today is £5.00 and Cheltenham's National Hunt Festival will be shown live on all the closed circuit television screens. Racing from 13.50

Racecourses

Wicken Wildlife Watch

18/3/99 WICKEN FEN (NT) NATURE RESERVE
18/3/99 Tel: 01353 720274

Find out some weird and wonderful facts about animals - the biggest, the smallest, the most poisonous, the most colourful, the laziest and the fastest! £0.25 for Watch members £1.00 for non-members but please phone to book your place (8-12 year olds) 16.30-18.00

Nature Reserves

Watercolour Painting

19/3/99 11/4/99	**BRANCASTER** Tel: 01485 210719 Held in the Brancaster Millennium Activity Centre, and given by Ken Tidd. Suitable for participants with some experience. DATES: 19-21 Mar & 9-11 Apr 1999. Call for further details. *Nature Reserves*

A Stour Valley Saunter In Constable Country

20/3/99 20/3/99	**BRIDGE COTTAGE** Tel: 01206 298260 A sizzling brunch followed by John Constable's views of the vale and visiting one of his favourite villages, Dedham. Time: 10.45. Tickets: £8.50. *Historic Buildings*

A Taste of Felbrigg

20/3/99 20/3/99	**FELBRIGG HALL** Tel: 01263 837444 A special food tasting in the Park Restaurant today. Demonstrations and tasting from a local Norfolk butcher, baker and brewer with a home made Felbrigg dessert to complete your lunch. £8.50 includes a glass of Norfolk wine. Numbers are limited early booking is advisable. Call 01263 838237 to book your table. *Historic Houses & Gardens*

Market Rasen Fixture - Farmers' Day

20/3/99 20/3/99	**MARKET RASEN RACECOURSE** Tel: 01673 843434 First Race: 14.10. Please call for further information *Racecourses*

Science Day

20/3/99 20/3/99	**WICKEN FEN (NT) NATURE RESERVE** Tel: 01353 720274 An exciting family event all about renewable energy. Lots of exhibits and experiments. Tickets A£3.75 C£2.50. 11.00-15.00 *Nature Reserves*

Festival of Discovery SET 99

20/3/99 21/3/99	**CLEETHORPES HUMBER ESTUARY DISCOVERY CENTRE** Tel: 01472 323232 Celebrate the Science, Engineering and Technology of the Humber & discover the science in your life - from your daily bread to the chemistry of colour *Exhibition Centres*

National Shire Horse Show

20/3/99 21/3/99	**EAST OF ENGLAND SHOWGROUND** Tel: 01733 234451 Internationally recognised breed event

for the biggest of all horses
Showgrounds

Spring Plant Sale

20/3/99 21/3/99	**HATFIELD HOUSE** Tel: 01707 262823 In aid of charity. Shop and restaurant open. A£3.50 C£2.80. 11.00-18.00. Tel: 01707 262823 for further information *Historic Houses & Gardens*

Suffolk Art Society Biennial Members' Exhibition

20/3/99 9/5/99	**GAINSBOROUGH'S HOUSE** Tel: 01787 372958 Exhibition in the Lower Gallery, with Gainsborough Drawings from the permanent collection in the Weaving Room *Birth Places*

Sea Dreams: Art Salutes the Boat

20/3/99 9/5/99	**USHER GALLERY** Tel: 01522 527980 This fun and colourful exhibition celebrates the boat as a vehicle for dreams, imaginings and stories, and features the work of six 20th century artists *Art Galleries*

Children's Poetry Competition

20/3/99 17/9/99	**ICKWORTH HOUSE PARK AND GARDENS** Tel: 01284 735270 A special competition to celebrate the National Year of Reading 1999. Children and young people aged 5-7, 8-11, and 12-16 are invited to write a poem on the theme of "Special Things About Ickworth". Entries will be judged by an independent panel of judges. Winners will be announced and presented with prizes at Ickworth on 8 October, National Poetry Day. Poems will be used to help prepare Ickworth's Statement of Significance. Entry Free. Details on 01284 735270. *Historic Houses & Gardens*

British Championship Bikes (MCRCB)

21/3/99 21/3/99	**CADWELL PARK CIRCUIT** Tel: 01507 343248 Honda CB500-Stars of Tomorrow, Honda Hornets 600 Cup, Aprillia RS125 Challenge, Aprillia RS 250 Challenge, British Sports Championship and National 600 Championship. Full Circuit, Grade-D. On the Gate: £10.00-£28.00. In Advance: Non £8.00-£25.00, Club £7.00-£22.00. Two Day Pass: Non £11.00-£30.00, Club £10.00-£27.00. Three Day Pass: Non £32.00, Club £29.00. Qualifying: £5.00-£14.00. C£Free. Programme £Free-£5.00. Seating (BH):

£Free-£8.00. Group Tickets: Non £90.00-£95.00, Club £80.00-£85.00. Season Ticket Inc. of Club Membership: £135.00. You can buy your tickets for any of the 1999 events in advance any time up to 4 days before an event and make a saving, Tel: 0870 60 60 611

Motor Racing Circuit

Wake up Trust the Hedgehog Trail!

21/3/99   HATFIELD FOREST
21/3/99   Tel: 01279 870678

Find the secret clues and discover the first signs of Spring and meet Trusty the Hedgehog, 10.00-14.30, A£Free C£3.00. Please note that you must book for all events except where stated otherwise. Please send a cheque payable to National Trust, along with an s.a.e. for your tickets

Forests

Spring Saunter

21/3/99   HIGH LODGE FOREST CENTRE
21/3/99   Tel: 01842 810271/815434

A guided walk to put the spring in your step. Find out what's sprung, what's springing and what's about to spring into place. Meet: 11.00 at Lynford Arboretum. Cost: A£2.00 C£1.00 - please book in advance - tickets available from 1 Mar

Forest Visitor Centres

Clubmans Motorcycles (NEW ERA)

21/3/99   SNETTERTON CIRCUIT
21/3/99   Tel: 01953 887303

All classes of national solo motorcycles and sidecars. Full Circuit, Grade-E. On the Gate: £10.00-£28.00. In Advance: Non £8.00-£25.00, Club £7.00-£22.00. Two Day Pass: Non £11.00-£30.00, Club £10.00-£27.00. Three Day Pass: Non £32.00, Club £29.00. Qualifying: £5.00-£14.00. C£Free. Programme £Free-£5.00. Seating (BH): £Free-£8.00. Group Tickets: Non £90.00-£95.00, Club £80.00-£85.00. Season Ticket Inc. of Club Membership: £150.00. You can buy your tickets for any of the 1999 events in advance any time up to 4 days before an event and make a saving, Tel: 0870 60 60 611

Motor Racing Circuit

100 Years At Wicken Fen

26/3/99   WICKEN FEN (NT) NATURE RESERVE
26/3/99   Tel: 01353 720274

A talk on the changes that have taken place over the past 100 years and of the plans for the Fen's future. A£2.50. Talk

starts at 19.30

Nature Reserves

Antiques Fair

26/3/99   EAST OF ENGLAND SHOWGROUND
27/3/99   Tel: 01733 234451

Large antiques fair displaying antiques and collectibles

Showgrounds

The Quilt Fair

26/3/99   CHILFORD HALL VINEYARD
28/3/99   Tel: 01223 892641

Three day exhibition with a huge quilt display, demonstrations and related items on sale. A£5.00 Concessions£4.00 (98 prices for guidance only)

Vineyards

Craft Weekends

26/3/99   BRANCASTER
18/4/99   Tel: 01485 210719

Held in the Brancaster Millennium Activity Centre. Craft course suitable for beginners and intermediate interest groups. Call for further details.

Nature Reserves

Bird Walk

27/3/99   HATFIELD FOREST
27/3/99   Tel: 01279 870678

Take the opportunity to walk around the Forest and hear the great variety of birds that make their home in Hatfield Forest. Commences 10.00-12.00. Tickets: A£2.00 C£1.00 Family Ticket (A2+C2)£5.00. Please note that you must book for all events except where stated otherwise. Please send a cheque payable to National Trust, along with an s.a.e. for your tickets

Forests

Easter Fayre

27/3/99   SOUTHEND ON SEA BOROUGH COUNCIL
27/3/99   Tel: 01702 215166

Be entertained by musicians, jugglers, jesters, clowns, balloon modelling, dancing and much more. An Easter Fayre Market will stretch along much of the High Street, with all proceeds to Fairhavens South East Christian Hospice. 11.00-16.00

Festivals

Theatre Organ Concert

27/3/99   ST. ALBAN'S ORGAN MUSEUM
27/3/99   Tel: 01727 851557/869693

Donald MacKenzie. Commences 19.45, tickets £3.50, call to book

Museum- Music

Cinema 100

27/3/99
23/5/99
MILL GREEN MUSEUM AND MILL
Tel: 01707 271362
An exhibition looking at the history of cinema and film-making locally
Watermill

Peterborough in Cromwell's time
27/3/99
27/11/99
PETERBOROUGH MUSEUM AND ART GALLERY
Tel: 01733 343329
An exhibition held to celebrate the 400th anniversary of Oliver Cromwell. What was it like under his rule? Come along and find out more
Museum- Local History

MG Mania (MGCC)
28/3/99
28/3/99
CADWELL PARK CIRCUIT
Tel: 01507 343248
Thoroughbred Sports Cars, International BCV8, Midget Challenge, Metro Challenge, MG Phoenix, ACE MG Cockshoot, MGF Trophy. Full Circuit, Grade-D. On the Gate: £10.00-£28.00. In Advance: Non £8.00-£25.00, Club £7.00-£22.00. Two Day Pass: Non £11.00-£30.00, Club £10.00-£27.00. Three Day Pass: Non £32.00, Club £29.00. Qualifying: £5.00-£14.00. C£Free. Programme £Free-£5.00. Seating (BH): £Free-£8.00. Group Tickets: Non £90.00-£95.00, Club £80.00-£85.00. Season Ticket Inc. of Club Membership: £135.00. You can buy your tickets for any of the 1999 events in advance any time up to 4 days before an event and make a saving, Tel: 0870 60 60 611
Motor Racing Circuit

Easter Egg Hunt
28/3/99
28/3/99
HEDINGHAM CASTLE
Tel: 01787 460261
Come and hunt for Easter eggs around the Castle grounds with Taro the Jester
Castles

Welcome to Rye House Marsh
28/3/99
28/3/99
RYE HOUSE MARSH AND RYE MEADS MEADOWS
Tel: 01992 460031
Another opportunity for new birdwatchers and visitors to Rye House to explore the bird life and improve your birdwatching skills. 10.00-12.00
Nature Reserves

Industry Trains Display Days
28/3/99
10/10/99
LEIGHTON BUZZARD RAILWAY
Tel: 01525 373888 (24hours)
Award-winning recreation of freight trains from the past, bringing to life our unique collection of working locomotives and wagon. To be held on: 28 March, 25 April, 23 May, 11 July, 8 August, 5th September & 10 October
Railways Steam/Light

Roman Cooking
29/3/99
2/4/99
COLCHESTER CASTLE MUSEUM
Tel: 01206 282931/282932
Find out what delicacies the Romans enjoyed eating and try your hand at making them. Roman cooking begins at 11.00-13.00 and again from 14.00-16.00. Free (after admission to the Castle)
Museum- Local History

Managing Reedbeds for Wildlife
30/3/99
20/3/99
WICKEN FEN (NT) NATURE RESERVE
Tel: 01353 720274
An interesting course led by Property Manager Adrian Colston and Head Warden Martin Lester based on their experiences of managing reedbeds to encourage the wildlife of Wicken Fen. A£25.00 includes lunch, 10.00-17.00
Nature Reserves

Art Attack
30/3/99
30/3/99
WICKEN FEN (NT) NATURE RESERVE
Tel: 01353 720274
Recycle old rubbish into beautiful butterfly wings and dragonflies. A&C(over 3)£2.50. 14.00-16.00
Nature Reserves

Holiday Club
31/3/99
31/3/99
DUNWICH HEATH AND MINSMERE BEACH
Tel: 01728 648505
Children's environmental activities for those aged 6-12 years. Bring packed lunch or lunch money, 10.00-14.00, C£4.00 A£Free, booking essential, please apply direct to the property for booking by telephone 01728 648505 or by post to with a sae to: Dunwich Heath & Minsmere Beach, Saxmundham, Suffolk IP17 3DJ with a cheque made payable to The National Trust (Enterprises)
Conservation Parks

Easter Eggstravaganza
1/4/99
1/4/99
WICKEN FEN (NT) NATURE RESERVE
Tel: 01353 720274
Come and play games and have fun with Trusty the Hedgehog. A&C(over 3)£2.50. 10.00-12.00 or 14.00-16.00
Nature Reserves

Good Friday Car Races (BRSCC)
2/4/99
2/4/99
SNETTERTON CIRCUIT
Tel: 01953 887303
Tomcat/Vento Challenge, Alfas, Auto Italia, Formula Saloons. Full Circuit,

Grade-E. On the Gate: £10.00-£28.00. In Advance: Non £8.00-£25.00, Club £7.00-£22.00. Two Day Pass: Non £11.00-£30.00, Club £10.00-£27.00. Three Day Pass: Non £32.00, Club £29.00. Qualifying: £5.00-£14.00. C£Free. Programme £Free-£5.00. Seating (BH): £Free-£8.00. Group Tickets: Non £90.00-£95.00, Club £80.00-£85.00. Season Ticket Inc. of Club Membership: £150.00. You can buy your tickets for any of the 1999 events in advance up time up to 4 days before an event and make a saving, Tel: 0870 60 60 611

Motor Racing Circuit

Championship Bikes (NEW ERA)

2/4/99
3/4/99

CADWELL PARK CIRCUIT

Tel: 01507 343248

All classes of national solo motorcycles and sidecars. Full Circuit, Grade-D. On the Gate: £10.00-£28.00. In Advance: Non £8.00-£25.00, Club £7.00-£22.00. Two Day Pass: Non £11.00-£30.00, Club £10.00-£27.00. Three Day Pass: Non £32.00, Club £29.00. Qualifying: £5.00-£14.00. C£Free. Programme £Free-£5.00. Seating (BH): £Free-£8.00. Group Tickets: Non £90.00-£95.00, Club £80.00-£85.00. Season Ticket Inc. of Club Membership: £135.00. You can buy your tickets for any of the 1999 events in advance any time up to 4 days before an event and make a saving, Tel: 0870 60 60 611

Motor Racing Circuit

Englisc Drohtnung - Anglo-Saxon Life

2/4/99
3/4/99

WEST STOW ANGLO SAXON VILLAGE

Tel: 01284 728718

A family of Anglo-Saxons in costume come to live in one of the houses and demonstrate what keeps them busy. 10.00-17.00. Last entry 16.00. A£5.00 C&Concessions£4.00 Family Ticket £15.00

Archaeological Interest

Country Skills and Working Craft Fair

2/4/99
5/4/99

BLICKLING HALL

Tel: 01263 738030

Held in the Walled Garden. Whatever your preferred craft, you will find plenty to see and do here. Commences 10.00-17.00. Tickets: £2.50 on the door

Historic Houses & Gardens

Great Easter Egg Quiz & Re-creation of Tudor Life at Eastertide

2/4/99
5/4/99

KENTWELL HALL

Tel: 01787 310207

Fun Quizz for all the family and Tudor baking, dairy work and Easter celebrations. Time: 11.00-17.00. Prices: A£7.75 C£5.20 OAPs£6.70. Pre-booked groups 20+ 20% discount

Historic Houses & Gardens

Easter Fun

2/4/99
5/4/99

LEIGHTON BUZZARD RAILWAY

Tel: 01525 373888 (24hours)

Meet the Leighton Buzzard Easter Bunny, and join in our prize competition. Demonstration freight train on Saturday, Chocolate eggs for the children on Sunday. Extra steam locos on Monday

Railways Steam/Light

Easter Egg Hunt

2/4/99
5/4/99

WHIPSNADE WILD ANIMAL PARK

Tel: 01582 872171

An Easter egg hunt around the park, with clowns and Big Rabbit and a colouring competition with prizes. See the new born animals and Whipsnade in its full glory. Easter egg tokens are hidden around the Park for children to find. They can be exchanged for an Easter egg at the Egg Control Centre. Also the chance to meet all the Spring Babes in the Park

Wildlife Parks

Hunt The White Rabbit

2/4/99
5/4/99

WOBURN SAFARI PARK

Tel: 01525 290407

Easter trail for children

Safari Parks

Easter Egg Hunt

2/4/99
7/4/99

COLCHESTER ZOO

Tel: 01206 331292

Join in the hunt for 100 golden eggs hidden around the Zoo and trade them for a real Easter Egg (one prize per person)

Zoos

Exhibition: Michelle Perry

2/4/99
1/5/99

NATIONAL HORSERACING MUSEUM AND TOURS

Tel: 01638 667333

A selling exhibition of racing paintings by Michelle Perry, whose work has been commissioned by Richard Dunwoody, Lester Piggott, Stanley Clarke, Adrian Maguire and others. Michelle's work, which is surprisingly diverse in style, will also be available for purchase in the form of fine art prints. Admission Free. On the 8th April at 14.00, Michelle will give a practical demonstration and short

talk about her work.

Museum- Horse racing

Behind the Scene Tour (Daily)

2/4/99   NATIONAL HORSERACING MUSEUM AND TOURS

31/10/99 Tel: 01638 667333

Take a look at the fascinating Horseracing Industry with an expert guide steeped in racing history. The tour takes in the Equine Swimming Pool, a Trainer's Yard, the world famous Gallops, and the National Stud. The afternoon is passed learning about the history past and present of the Horseracing Industry in the Museum

Museum- Horse racing

All Day Introduction to Horseracing Tour (Daily)

2/4/99   NATIONAL HORSERACING MUSEUM AND TOURS

31/10/99 Tel: 01638 667333

Spend a day at the races in the Members Enclosure. Includes a tour of the Equine Swimming Pool, a Trainer's Yard and the world famous Gallops. Your guide will teach you how to place a bet and spot the racing celebrities. Contact the Musuem for further details

Museum- Horse racing

Easter Egg Trail

3/4/99   OXBURGH HALL, GARDEN AND ESTATE

3/4/99   Tel: 01366 328258

Easter Egg trail around the grounds. Commences 11.00. Normal opening times and admission charges apply. £1.00 entry fee for trail

Historic Buildings

Clubmans Motorcycles (BMCRC)

3/4/99   SNETTERTON CIRCUIT

4/4/99   Tel: 01953 887303

All classes of national solo motorcycles and sidecars. Full Circuit, Grade-D. On the Gate: £10.00-£28.00. In Advance: Non £8.00-£25.00, Club £7.00-£22.00. Two Day Pass: Non £11.00-£30.00, Club £10.00-£27.00. Three Day Pass: Non £32.00, Club £29.00. Qualifying: £5.00-£14.00. C£Free. Programme £Free-£5.00. Seating (BH): £Free-£8.00. Group Tickets: Non £90.00-£95.00, Club £80.00-£85.00. Season Ticket Inc. of Club Membership: £150.00. You can buy your tickets for any of the 1999 events in advance any time up to 4 days before an event and make a saving, Tel: 0870 60 60 611

Motor Racing Circuit

Easter Patchwork Quilt and Quilting Exhibition

3/4/99   FELBRIGG HALL

5/4/99   Tel: 01263 837444

Free exhibition in the stable block all weekend

Historic Houses & Gardens

The Art of the Garden

3/4/99   CHELMSFORD AND ESSEX REGIMENT MUSEUM

23/5/99 Tel: 01245 353066

Looking at the artistry and craft of Essex gardens from the earliest examples to those from a modern designer. We get a glimpse of Roman and Medieval gardens as uncovered by archaeologists and visit the great Essex houses and parks. A Museums in Essex touring exhibition with contributions from the Essex Gardens Trust and Writtle College

Museum- Local History

Demonstration Freight Train Days

3/4/99   LEIGHTON BUZZARD RAILWAY

12/9/99 Tel: 01525 373888 (24hours)

More railway history relived, as a freight train shares the line with the passenger service. To be held on: 3rd April, 29th May & 12th September

Railways Steam/Light

Sunrise, Cliff Top Celebration

4/4/99   DUNWICH HEATH AND MINSMERE BEACH

4/4/99   Tel: 01728 648505

St James. Easter Day Service at 06.00. Donations, no booking required.

Conservation Parks

Easter Egg Hunt

4/4/99   DUNWICH HEATH AND MINSMERE BEACH

4/4/99   Tel: 01728 648505

Easter egg trails from the shop, activities from the Field Study Centre. Time: 11.00-16.00. Tickets: £1.50

Conservation Parks

Easter Egg Hunt

4/4/99   HATFIELD FOREST

4/4/99   Tel: 01279 870678

Follow the trail to find the Easter Eggs - suitable for all ages who like chocolate! No booking necessary. Normal car park charge of £3.00 applies. NT members £Free

Forests

Eggcentric Easter Activities

4/4/99   ICKWORTH HOUSE PARK AND GARDENS

4/4/99   Tel: 01284 735270

Easter fun for families at Ickworth. Includes Easter Egg Hunt and Wildlife Trail. Time: 14.00-16.00. Standard Park

Admission plus £0.50 for trail sheet.

Historic Houses & Gardens

Craft Fair

4/4/99
5/4/99

AUDLEY END HOUSE

Tel: 01799 522399

Where you will be able to purchase unusual gifts for family and friends. With various performers. Normal admission prices apply.

Historical Remains

Barleylands Easter Steam Up

4/4/99

BARLEYLANDS FARM MUSEUM AND VISITORS CENTRE

5/4/99

Tel: 01268 282090/532253

Vintage tractors and steam engines, miniature steam railway, glassblowing demonstrations, rural craft demonstrations, donkey rides, bouncy castle, tractor and trailer rides, 10.00-17.00

Museum- Farms

Easter Egg Trail

4/4/99
5/4/99

BLICKLING HALL

Tel: 01263 738030

Hidden around the Gardens is a trail, what's at the end of it! £1.00 additional charge

Historic Houses & Gardens

Easter Classic Motorcycles (CRMC)

4/4/99
5/4/99

CADWELL PARK CIRCUIT

Tel: 01507 343248

All classes of national solo motorcycles and sidecars. Full Circuit, Grade-D. On the Gate: £10.00-£28.00. In Advance: Non £8.00-£25.00, Club £7.00-£22.00. Two Day Pass: Non £11.00-£30.00, Club £10.00-£27.00. Three Day Pass: Non £32.00, Club £29.00. Qualifying: £5.00-£14.00. C£Free. Programme £Free-£5.00. Seating (BH): £Free-£8.00. Group Tickets: Non £90.00-£95.00, Club £80.00-£85.00. Season Ticket Inc. of Club Membership: £135.00. You can buy your tickets for any of the 1999 events in advance any time up to 4 days before an event and make a saving, Tel: 0870 60 60 611

Motor Racing Circuit

Hatching Weekend

4/4/99

ELSHAM HALL COUNTRY AND WILDLIFE PARK

5/4/99

Tel: 01652 688698

A chance to hold a real easter egg and chicks. Please call 01652 688698

Wildlife Parks

Garden Show

4/4/99
5/4/99

ELTON HALL

Tel: 01832 280468

This event offers the keen gardener an opportunity to browse amongst a selection of plants and sundry stalls. Get free advice from radio and TV experts. Refreshments. 10.00-17.00

Historic Houses & Gardens

Opening of the Victorian Prison

4/4/99
5/4/99

LINCOLN CASTLE

Tel: 01522 511068

A chance to experience life inside the spectacular Victorian Prison at Lincoln Castle. Meet the Governor, Matron, Surgeon, cChaplain and the Wardens together with a selection of felons. Normal admission charges will apply

Castles

Raptor Foundation

4/4/99
5/4/99

LINTON ZOOLOGICAL GARDENS

Tel: 01223 891308

Meet Gordon Robertson from the Raptor Foundation and hear all about their work with injured birds of prey and meet some of their tame owls

Zoos- Conservation

Anglo-Saxon Activity Days

4/4/99
5/4/99

WEST STOW ANGLO SAXON VILLAGE

Tel: 01284 728718

Activities of all kinds for all ages, and the opportunity to talk to knowledgeable 'Anglo-Saxons' about life 1500 years ago. A family of Anglo-Saxons in costume come to live in one of the houses and demonstrate what keeps them busy. 10.00-17.00. Last entry 16.00. A£5.00 C&Concessions£4.00 Family Ticket £15.00

Archaeological Interest

Easter Monday Family Fun Day

5/4/99
5/4/99

HUNTINGDON STEEPLECHASES LTD

Tel: 01480 453373

Bring the family to Huntingdon where a large crowd and great atmosphere promises to make it a wonderful day out. All children under 16 can enter free of charge and with a fully supervised creche, bouncy castle, tubeslide and face-painting, there is lots to do for all the family. Racing from 14.00

Racecourses

Easter Monday Fixture

5/4/99
5/4/99

MARKET RASEN RACECOURSE

Tel: 01673 843434

First Race: 14.15. Very popular Spring meeting - National Hunt Jump Racing combined with family entertainments for children

Racecourses

750 M/C Race Day (750 M/C)
SNETTERTON CIRCUIT
5/4/99
5/4/99
Tel: 01953 887303
Formula 4, Kit Cars, 750 Formula, Radicals, Hot Hatch, 750 Trophy x2. Full Circuit, Grade-D. On the Gate: £10.00-£28.00. In Advance: Non £8.00-£25.00, Club £7.00-£22.00. Two Day Pass: Non £11.00-£30.00, Club £10.00-£27.00. Three Day Pass: Non £32.00, Club £29.00. Qualifying: £5.00-£14.00. C£Free. Programme £Free-£5.00. Seating (BH): £Free-£8.00. Group Tickets: Non £90.00-£95.00, Club £80.00-£85.00. Season Ticket Inc. of Club Membership: £150.00. You can buy your tickets for any of the 1999 events in advance any time up to 4 days before an event and make a saving, Tel: 0870 60 60 611

Motor Racing Circuit

"The Southend Shake Down" Ace Cafe - Motorcycle Run
SOUTHEND ON SEA BOROUGH COUNCIL
5/4/99
5/4/99
Tel: 01702 215166
A number of motorcyclists will leave Ace Cafe, London, at approximately 10.30 and are due to arrive along the seafront at 13.30 to be on display to the public

Festivals

Wandering Musician
TATTERSHALL CASTLE
5/4/99
5/4/99
Tel: 01526 342543
Peter Bull entertains whilst wandering around Tattershall

Castles

Gilbert de Grondement
COLCHESTER CASTLE MUSEUM
5/4/99
9/4/99
Tel: 01206 282931/282932
Gilbert, the Norman monk gives an insight into Colchester's new beginnings after the battle of Hastings. Also try creating your own manuscript. Free (after admission to the Castle)

Museum- Local History

Children's Fun Day
WIMPOLE HALL
5/4/99
31/5/99
Tel: 01223 207257
Something special for the younger members of the family, normal admission applies. DATES: 5 Apr, 3 & 31 May & 29 Aug

Country Parks

Easter Fun at the Castle

LINCOLN CASTLE
6/4/99
8/4/99
Tel: 01522 511068
Fun, games and live entertainment for kids during the Easter Holidays. Face painting, clowns, bouncy castle, and storytelling will keep everyone entertained from 10.00-14.00 each day, while the adults can relax in the Castle Cafe or wander the Castle's walls and grounds. Normal admission charges will apply

Castles

Easter Holiday Activities
VERULAMIUM MUSEUM AND PARK
6/4/99
9/4/99
Tel: 01727 819339
The industrial revolution - how machines and factories began - construct your own inventions

Museums

Holiday Club
DUNWICH HEATH AND MINSMERE BEACH
7/4/99
7/4/99
Tel: 01728 648505
Children's environmental activities for those aged 6-12 years. Bring packed lunch or lunch money, 10.00-14.00, C£4.00 A£Free, booking essential, please apply direct to the property for booking by telephone 01728 648505 or by post to with a sae to: Dunwich Heath & Minsmere Beach, Saxmundham, Suffolk IP17 3DJ with a cheque made payable to The National Trust (Enterprises)

Conservation Parks

Trailer Trips
ORFORD NESS
7/4/99
6/10/99
Tel: 01394 450900
First Wednesday in the month. These trips follow most of the visitor route and are designed for those unable to walk more than short distances. Places are limited in number and on a strictly first come first served basis, however, to guarantee a place it is possible to book on 01394 450057. Time: 10.00-13.00 & 14.00-17.00 only. Cost: Members £6.00, Non-members £8.00, price inclusive of ferry.

Nature Reserves

Garden Tour - Spring
ANGLESEY ABBEY, GARDENS AND LODE MILL
8/4/99
8/4/99
Tel: 01223 811200
Discussion on the maintenance and practical care of a herbaceous border, with the division of plants and a chance for visitors to have a go. Also included will be a look at the wonderful Hyacinth

display (conditions allowing), led by
Richard Ayres. Time: 18.30. Tickets £5.00
(including National Trust members), all
ticket applications should be addressed
to The Property Manager and include
sae to: Anglesey Abbey, Gardens and
Lode Mill, Quy Road, Lode, Cambridge
CB5 9EJ

Historic Houses & Gardens

Expedition to the Bottom of the Deep

8/4/99   WICKEN FEN (NT) NATURE RESERVE
8/4/99   Tel: 01353 720274
Boatman, pond skaters, cyclops and diving beetles, come and see them all during our expedition. A&C(8-13)£2.50.
10.00-12.00 or 14.00-16.00

Nature Reserves

Lunch with Trusty the Hedgehog

9/4/99   FELBRIGG HALL
9/4/99   Tel: 01263 837444
Meet Trusty the Hedgehog at his lunch
party today, face-painting and special
hedgehog trail too. Commences: 11.00-
14.00. Tickets: C£5.00 no unaccompanied children. Light lunch for Mums and
Dads for £2.50. Call 01263 832237 for
booking with the Restaurant

Historic Houses & Gardens

Friends of Thomas The Tank Engine

9/4/99   NORTH NORFOLK RAILWAY
11/4/99   Tel: 01263 822045
See the Friends of Thomas the Tank
Engine on the North Norfolk Railway

Railways Steam/Light

Winslow Jazz Festival

9/4/99   WINSLOW JAZZ FESTIVAL 1999
11/4/99   Tel: 01296 730575 Box Office
Venue: Streets of Winslow, Winslow
Parish Church and Bell Hotel. Jazz and
dine at the Bell Hotel, Jazz Parade in
Winslow Streets and a Jazz service at
Winslow Parish Church. Times: at vari-
ous times over the weekend. Ticket
Prices: Various, please telephone Box
Office: 01296 730575 for further infor-
mation and tickets

Festivals

Lincolnshire Kart Races (LCKC)

11/4/99   CADWELL PARK CIRCUIT
11/4/99   Tel: 01507 343248
All classes of International 125cc, 210cc
& 250cc Karts and all National Classes.
Club Circuit, Grade-E. On the Gate:
£10.00-£28.00. In Advance: Non £8.00-
£25.00, Club £7.00-£22.00. Two Day
Pass: Non £11.00-£30.00, Club £10.00-
£27.00. Three Day Pass: Non £32.00,

Club £29.00. Qualifying: £5.00-£14.00.
C£Free. Programme £Free-£5.00.
Seating (BH): £Free-£8.00. Group
Tickets: Non £90.00-£95.00, Club
£80.00-£85.00. Season Ticket Inc. of
Club Membership: £135.00. You can buy
your tickets for any of the 1999 events in
advance any time up to 4 days before an
event and make a saving, Tel: 0870 60
60 611

Motor Racing Circuit

Wildlife Walk: Birds of the Heath

11/4/99   DUNWICH HEATH AND MINSMERE BEACH
11/4/99   Tel: 01728 648505
A guided walk with the Warden to discover the varied bird life of the property.
Time: 09.00. Tickets: £3.00.

Conservation Parks

CD/Record Fair

11/4/99   EAST OF ENGLAND SHOWGROUND
11/4/99   Tel: 01733 234451
Large fair displaying a whole range of
cd's and records

Showgrounds

Spring Walk

11/4/99   LYVEDEN NEW BIELD
11/4/99   Tel: 01832 205358
A Spring walk to discover the remains of
the Elizabethan garden. Time: 14.00.
Cost: £2.00 per person, booking essential

Historic Houses

Spring Trophy Meeting (BARC)

11/4/99   SNETTERTON CIRCUIT
11/4/99   Tel: 01953 887303
Formula Renaults, Westfields, Porsche
Classics, Classic 1600s, MGs. Full Circuit,
Grade-D. On the Gate: £10.00-£28.00. In
Advance: Non £8.00-£25.00, Club £7.00-
£22.00. Two Day Pass: Non £11.00-
£30.00, Club £10.00-£27.00. Three Day
Pass: Non £32.00, Club £29.00.
Qualifying: £5.00-£14.00. C£Free.
Programme £Free-£5.00. Seating (BH):
£Free-£8.00. Group Tickets: Non £90.00-
£95.00, Club £80.00-£85.00. Season
Ticket Inc. of Club Membership: £150.00.
You can buy your tickets for any of the
1999 events in advance any time up to 4
days before an event and make a saving,
Tel: 0870 60 60 611

Motor Racing Circuit

Spring Kite Festival

11/4/99   THE SHUTTLEWORTH COLLECTION
11/4/99   Tel: 0891 323310
A chance to enjoy the wonderful colours
and spectacular designs of the kite.

Further more detailed information on the attractions listed can be found
in Best Guides *Visitor Attractions* Guide under the classifications shown

Bring your family. A small number of trade stands are available for you to buy your own and have a go.

Museum- Aviation

'A Policeman's Lot'
CHURCH FARM MUSEUM
Tel: 01754 766658
11/4/99
8/8/99
An exhibition tracing the history of the police force

Museum- Farms

Red Cross Day
WOBURN ABBEY
Tel: 01525 290666
13/4/99
13/4/99
Gardens open for Red Cross only

Stately Homes

Garden Open Day - Meet the Gardener
OXBURGH HALL, GARDEN AND ESTATE
Tel: 01366 328258
14/4/99
14/4/99
Tours of the Workshop and Greenhouse area, 11.30-14.30. Normal opening times and admission charges apply

Historic Buildings

Heathland Hanging Course
DUNWICH HEATH AND MINSMERE BEACH
Tel: 01728 648505
14/4/99
5/5/99
A four-week course in which you will learn to spin with a drop spindle; Dye with natural dyes; Felt with wool from the sheep that graze on the Heath; All joined together with weaving and stitches to make your very own Heathland hanging. There will be a complimentary fifth day in which the hangings will be completed, photographed and hung. Time: 10.00-13.00, 14, 21 & 28 April & 5 May 1999. Price: £45.00 Course Fees

Conservation Parks

Exhibition: Churchill and Horseracing
NATIONAL HORSERACING MUSEUM AND TOURS
Tel: 01638 667333
14/4/99
30/7/99
Lord Randolph Churchill was a keen racing man who won the 1889 Oaks with L'Abbesse de Jouarre, but his son Sir Winston did not register his own colours until he was 75. Shortly thereafter he was elected to the Jockey Club. His first horse, Colonist II, won 13 races for him, thus encouraging him to become an enthusiastic owner-breeder. This display, drawn from the Churchill Archives Centre, includes a wealth of letters and photographs. Admission Free. On the 12th May at 14.30, Dr Brendon will give a lecture on the Churchill Archives and the Churchill's interests in racing.

Museum- Horse racing

Wicken Wildlife Watch
WICKEN FEN (NT) NATURE RESERVE
Tel: 01353 720274
15/4/99
15/4/99
Find out what lurks beneath the water at Wicken Fen in this session all about pond life. £0.25 for Watch members £1.00 for non-members. Please phone to book your place (8-12 years). 16.30-18.00

Nature Reserves

Ponies (UK) Spring Show
EAST OF ENGLAND SHOWGROUND
Tel: 01733 234451
16/4/99
16/4/99
British Show Pony Society Spring Championship Show

Showgrounds

Patchwork and Quilting Workshop
FELBRIGG HALL
Tel: 01263 837444
16/4/99
16/4/99
A day long workshop with local expert Sally Holman. The workshop includes coffee, lunch and expert tuition and a tour of some of the most textile rich rooms of the hall. Commences: 10.00-16.00. Tickets: £20.00 please bring your own materials. Pre-booking essential. Bookings can be made by telephone, to the address, or in person.

Historic Houses & Gardens

Angelica, Florence & Rosemary Host an Evening at Oxburgh
OXBURGH HALL, GARDEN AND ESTATE
Tel: 01366 328258
16/4/99
16/4/99
These three very herbal ladies will be appearing as part of a cast of several delivering themselves in different roles, in pies, pâtes and puddings. Come and learn about growing herbs from Graham Donachie then taste some dishes illustrating the versatility of these herbs. Time: 19.00. Tickets: £12.50, booking essential

Historic Buildings

National Folk Music Festival
NATIONAL FOLK MUSIC FESTIVAL 1999
Tel: 01296 415333 Box Office
16/4/99
18/4/99
Venue: Sutton Bonington Campus. Concerts, lectures, workshops, informal sessions. There are participatory informal sessions where anyone who wishes to can take part either in a long session or in a music session. Times: Start Fri 20.00, Finish Sun 17.00. Ticket Prices: TBC. Tickets available from Box Office: 01296 415333

Festivals

Manningtree Meander

| 17/4/99 | **BRIDGE COTTAGE** |
| 17/4/99 | Tel: 01206 298260 |

After a delicious brunch, commence your guided walk along the River Stour Estuary to Manningtree. Enjoy its local history, buildings and tales of the Witch Finder General! Time: 10.45. Tickets: £8.50.

Historic Buildings

Storytelling
| 17/4/99 | **TATTERSHALL CASTLE** |
| 17/4/99 | Tel: 01526 342543 |

Storytelling for adults and children by Polly Howat from 14.00

Castles

Craft Fair
| 17/4/99 | **ELTON HALL** |
| 18/4/99 | Tel: 01832 280468 |

50 stands of lovely handmade goods. All under cover in the picturesque Stable Block. Home-made refreshments. 10.00-17.00

Historic Houses & Gardens

Wood Sale
| 17/4/99 | **ICKWORTH HOUSE PARK AND GARDENS** |
| 18/4/99 | Tel: 01284 735270 |

Buy exotic and native woods at Ickworth's famous Wood Sale. Time: 10.00-16.00. Standard Park Admission.

Historic Houses & Gardens

Living History Encampment
| 17/4/99 | **LINCOLN CASTLE** |
| 18/4/99 | Tel: 01522 511068 |

The Lincoln Castle Garrison will be setting up camp within the Castle grounds, to test equipment and train for forthcoming battles. Normal admission charges will apply

Castles

Medieval Entertainers
| 17/4/99 | **ORFORD CASTLE** |
| 18/4/99 | Tel: 01394 450472 |

Games, squire-training and talks on weaponry and armour. Also, try your hand at spinning, weaving and calligraphy and learn about herbal medicine. From 12.00. A£3.00 C£1.50 Concessions£2.30

Castles

Private Stud Tours
| 17/4/99 | **NATIONAL HORSERACING MUSEUM AND TOURS** |
| 18/9/99 | Tel: 01638 667333 |

17th April, 22nd May, 19th June, 24th July, 21st August & 18th September only. All-morning tour which includes a personal tour of a world-famous PRIVATE stud near Newmarket as well as the gallops, a yard and the equine swimming pool. Several top stallions will be paraded in front of you and you will have the opportunity to talk to stable staff. Departs 09.00 sharp each day. Price: £15.00.

Museum- Horse racing

Dawn Chorus Walk
| 18/4/99 | **BLICKLING HALL** |
| 18/4/99 | Tel: 01263 738030 |

Take a tour of the Gardens to hear the sound of the waking birds. An early start of 05.30 argh! But the cooked breakfast that follows will make it worth it. A£9.50, booking essential. Bookings can be made by telephone, to the address, or in person.

Historic Houses & Gardens

Clubmans Motorcycles (PEGASUS)
| 18/4/99 | **CADWELL PARK CIRCUIT** |
| 18/4/99 | Tel: 01507 343248 |

All classes of national solo motorcycles and sidecars. Club Circuit, Grade-E. On the Gate: £10.00-£28.00. In Advance: Non £8.00-£25.00, Club £7.00-£22.00. Two Day Pass: Non £11.00-£30.00, Club £10.00-£27.00. Three Day Pass: Non £32.00, Club £29.00. Qualifying: £5.00-£14.00. C£Free. Programme £Free-£5.00. Seating (BH): £Free-£8.00. Group Tickets: Non £90.00-£95.00, Club £80.00-£85.00. Season Ticket Inc. of Club Membership: £135.00. You can buy your tickets for any of the 1999 events in advance any time up to 4 days before an event and make a saving, Tel: 0870 60 60 611

Motor Racing Circuit

Auto Jumble
| 18/4/99 | **EAST OF ENGLAND SHOWGROUND** |
| 18/4/99 | Tel: 01733 234451 |

An event for car enthusiasts looking for 'that part'

Showgrounds

Spring Flowers
| 18/4/99 | **HATFIELD FOREST** |
| 18/4/99 | Tel: 01279 870678 |

Come along for a walk around the Forest looking for a wide variety of spring flowers and learn how our management ensures their continued survival. Commences 14.00-16.00. Tickets: A£2.00 C£1.00 Family Ticket (A2+C2)£5.00. Car Park £3.00, NT memebers Free. Please note that you must book for all events except where stated otherwise. Please

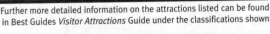

Further more detailed information on the attractions listed can be found in Best Guides *Visitor Attractions* Guide under the classifications shown

send a cheque payable to National Trust, along with an s.a.e. for your tickets.

Forests

Wood Fair and Wood Craft Skills Day
18/4/99 ICKWORTH HOUSE PARK AND GARDENS
18/4/99 Tel: 01284 735270
Demonstrations, exhibitions and family activities on Woodland themes. Runs concurrent with second day of wood sale. Time: 11.00-16.00. Standard Park Admission.

Historic Houses & Gardens

Teddy Bears' Outing
18/4/99 LEIGHTON BUZZARD RAILWAY
18/4/99 Tel: 01525 373888 (24hours)
Accompanied children with teddies travel free. Meet our own giant teddy, and join in the family entertainment

Railways Steam/Light

Migrant Melange
18/4/99 RYE HOUSE MARSH AND RYE MEADS MEADOWS
18/4/99 Tel: 01992 460031
Meet the first migrants to return from the south and try identifying some warblers

Nature Reserves

Endurance Motorcycles (KRC)
18/4/99 SNETTERTON CIRCUIT
18/4/99 Tel: 01953 887303
6 Hour endurance race including 400cc, 600cc, 1100cc and Single, Twins and Triples. Full Circuit, Grade-E. On the Gate: £10.00-£28.00. In Advance: Non £8.00-£25.00, Club £7.00-£22.00. Two Day Pass: Non £11.00-£30.00, Club £10.00-£27.00. Three Day Pass: Non £32.00, Club £29.00. Qualifying: £5.00-£14.00. C£Free. Programme £Free-£5.00. Seating (BH): £Free-£8.00. Group Tickets: Non £90.00-£95.00, Club £80.00-£85.00. Season Ticket Inc. of Club Membership: £150.00. You can buy your tickets for any of the 1999 events in advance any time up to 4 days before an event and make a saving, Tel: 0870 60 60 611

Motor Racing Circuit

Private Gardens Open
18/4/99 WOBURN ABBEY
18/4/99 Tel: 01525 290666
National Garden Scheme. There are over 100 species of daffodil and narcissi at Woburn, a splendid Spring display. There are also many types of primula. Extra charge applies. Also on: 27 June

Stately Homes

Dawn Chorus
18/4/99 WICKEN FEN (NT) NATURE RESERVE
25/4/99 Tel: 01353 720274
Hear and see the birds and animals of Wicken Fen at the best time of day. Meet at 4.45 on 18 & 25 Apr, A£4.50 C£2.50 includes hot croissants and coffee

Nature Reserves

National Motorhomes and Tourer Rally
23/4/99 EAST OF ENGLAND SHOWGROUND
25/4/99 Tel: 01733 234451
A camp for mobile and motorhome enthusiasts

Showgrounds

Alice in WonderlandDawn Chorus
24/4/99 HATFIELD FOREST
24/4/99 Tel: 01279 870678
Be up with the larks to see and hear the huge range of birdlife. Commences 07.30 (yes, am!) Tickets: A£2.00 C£1.00 Family Ticket (A2+C2)£5.00. Please note that you must book for all events except where stated otherwise. Please send a cheque payable to National Trust, along with an s.a.e. for your tickets.

Forests

Market Rasen Fixture - Spring Meeting
24/4/99 MARKET RASEN RACECOURSE
24/4/99 Tel: 01673 843434
First Race: 14.10. Please call for further information

Racecourses

Stowe Kite Festival
24/4/99 STOWE LANDSCAPE GARDENS
25/4/99 Tel: 01280 822850
Following on last year's success, this event is now two days and will attract professionals and amateurs alike. An exciting family weekend where you can make and learn about kites, or just watch the experts. Refreshments available, 10.00-16.00.

Gardens

St. Georges Day Festival
24/4/99 WREST PARK GARDENS
25/5/99 Tel: 01525 860152
Enjoy a traditionally English event, with music, medieval craft market, morris dancing and demonstrations of sheepdog techniques, have-a-go archery, medieval tournament and Elizabethan travelling players performing St. George and the Dragon plays. Plus children's entertainments. A great family day out! From 12.00. A£5.00 C£2.50 Concessions£3.80 EH Members Free

Gardens

Porsche Power (BRSCC)

25/4/99
25/4/99

CADWELL PARK CIRCUIT
Tel: 01507 343248
Porsche Classics x4, Alfas, Auto Italia
plus support. Full Circuit, Grade-D. On
the Gate: £10.00-£28.00. In Advance:
Non £8.00-£25.00, Club £7.00-£22.00.
Two Day Pass: Non £11.00-£30.00, Club
£10.00-£27.00. Three Day Pass: Non
£32.00, Club £29.00. Qualifying: £5.00-
£14.00. C£Free. Programme £Free-£5.00.
Seating (BH): £Free-£8.00. Group
Tickets: Non £90.00-£95.00, Club
£80.00-£85.00. Season Ticket Inc. of
Club Membership: £135.00. You can buy
your tickets for any of the 1999 events in
advance any time up to 4 days before an
event and make a saving, Tel: 0870 60
60 611

Motor Racing Circuit

Flint Knapping

25/4/99
25/4/99

GRIME'S GRAVES
Tel: 01842 810656
Stone age man returns to demonstrate
how he made tools, axes and arrow-
heads from flint. From 12.00. A£2.50
C£1.30 Concessions£1.90. EH Members
Free

Museum- Mining

A Migration Meander

25/4/99
25/4/99

ORFORD NESS
Tel: 01394 450900
A look at passage migrants on this
important coastal site. No experience
necessary. For an early start meet at
07.00 at the Martello Tower at
Slaughden. Bring suitable clothing and
footwear for the weather. Bring binoculars or telescope. Bring own food and
drink. Cost: £10.00 for all.

Nature Reserves

Topcats (JCC)

25/4/99
25/4/99

SNETTERTON CIRCUIT
Tel: 01953 887303
Jaguar XK Saloon Challenge x 2, TR
Register, Sports Racing & GT Morgan
Challenge, Jaguar Challenge, MG
Cockshoot, Sports Car Race, Allcomers
Race, JCC Centurion Challenge. Full
Circuit, Grade-D. On the Gate: £10.00-
£28.00. In Advance: Non £8.00-£25.00,
Club £7.00-£22.00. Two Day Pass: Non
£11.00-£30.00, Club £10.00-£27.00.
Three Day Pass: Non £32.00, Club
£29.00. Qualifying: £5.00-£14.00.
C£Free. Programme £Free-£5.00.

Seating (BH): £Free-£8.00. Group
Tickets: Non £90.00-£95.00, Club
£80.00-£85.00. Season Ticket Inc. of
Club Membership: £150.00. You can buy
your tickets for any of the 1999 events in
advance any time up to 4 days before an
event and make a saving, Tel: 0870 60
60 611

Motor Racing Circuit

Hunter Chase Evening

27/4/99
27/4/99

HUNTINGDON STEEPLECHASES LTD
Tel: 01480 453373
An evening meeting of competitive rac-
ing beginning at17.15

Racecourses

Postgraduate Study Days at Ickworth

27/4/99
29/4/99

ICKWORTH HOUSE PARK AND GARDENS
Tel: 01284 735270
Lectures and seminars on the management, conservation and interpretation of
an English Country House, Park and
Gardens. Time: 10.00-16.00 each day.
Tickets: £10.00 per student per day,
£5.00 reduction if all 3 days booked
(£25.00), booking essential. Programme
available call 01284 735270.

Historic Houses & Gardens

Theatre Organ Concert

1/5/99
1/5/99

ST. ALBAN'S ORGAN MUSEUM
Tel: 01727 851557/869693
David Peckham (USA) commences 19.45
tickets £3.50, call to book

Museum- Music

Children's Festival

1/5/99
2/5/99

ELSHAM HALL COUNTRY AND WILDLIFE
PARK
Tel: 01652 688698
Entertainment for children in the Barn
Theatre. Free with Park admission

Wildlife Parks

Clubmans Bikes (BMCRC)

1/5/99
2/5/99

SNETTERTON CIRCUIT
Tel: 01953 887303
All classes of national solo motorcycles
and sidecars. Full Circuit, Grade-D. On
the Gate: £10.00-£28.00. In Advance:
Non £8.00-£25.00, Club £7.00-£22.00.
Two Day Pass: Non £11.00-£30.00, Club
£10.00-£27.00. Three Day Pass: Non
£32.00, Club £29.00. Qualifying: £5.00-
£14.00. C£Free. Programme £Free-£5.00.
Seating (BH): £Free-£8.00. Group
Tickets: Non £90.00-£95.00, Club
£80.00-£85.00. Season Ticket Inc. of
Club Membership: £150.00. You can buy
your tickets for any of the 1999 events in
advance any time up to 4 days before an

Further more detailed information on the attractions listed can be found
in Best Guides *Visitor Attractions* Guide under the classifications shown

event and make a saving, Tel: 0870 60 60 611

Motor Racing Circuit

Recreation of Tudor Life at May Day
KENTWELL HALL
1/5/99
3/5/99 Tel: 01787 310207
With May Queen, Jack O'Green and Tudor Maypole dancing and other May Day celebrations. Time: 11.00-18.00. Prices: A£7.75 C£5.20 OAPs£6.70. Pre-booked groups 20+ 20% discount

Historic Houses & Gardens

Model Engineers Festival
NORMANBY HALL COUNTRY PARK
1/5/99
3/5/99 Tel: 01724 720588
Models, boat pool, miniature steam vehicles and railway running. Time: 10.00-16.30.

Country Parks

Steam Weekend
WHIPSNADE WILD ANIMAL PARK
1/5/99
3/5/99 Tel: 01582 872171
Traction engines, trains and vintage vehicles to make a hot and steamy experience

Wildlife Parks

Adventure Weekend
WOBURN SAFARI PARK
1/5/99
3/5/99 Tel: 01525 290407
Adventure weekend, including activities: abseiling and canoeing

Safari Parks

Exhibition: Roger Ackling
SAINSBURY CENTRE FOR VISUAL ARTS
1/5/99
1/7/99 Tel: 01603 456060/593199
In the Upper Gallery. Provisional Dates, please call for confirmation.

Art Galleries

Minibus tours - An Insiders Introduction to Racing
NATIONAL HORSERACING MUSEUM AND TOURS
1/5/99
16/10/99 Tel: 01638 667333
1st May, 15th May, 26th June, 7th July, 14th August, 2nd October & 16th October only. All day minibus tours, starting with visits to the equine swimming pool, a yard and the gallops to see how trainers, lads and horses prepare for the race. During the afternoon your expert guide will take you to the races and explain how to judge form, betting and much more. Includes entry to Members' Enclosure. Departs 09.20 sharp each day. Price: A£40.00 C(under 12)£16.00.

Museum- Horse racing

Championship Bikes (RETFORD)
CADWELL PARK CIRCUIT
2/5/99
2/5/99 Tel: 01507 343248
All classes of national solo motorcycles and sidecars. Full Circuit, Grade-D. On the Gate: £10.00-£28.00. In Advance: Non £8.00-£25.00, Club £7.00-£22.00. Two Day Pass: Non £11.00-£30.00, Club £10.00-£27.00. Three Day Pass: Non £32.00, Club £29.00. Qualifying: £5.00-£14.00. C£Free. Programme £Free-£5.00. Seating (BH): £Free-£8.00. Group Tickets: Non £90.00-£95.00, Club £80.00-£85.00. Season Ticket Inc. of Club Membership: £135.00. You can buy your tickets for any of the 1999 events in advance any time up to 4 days before an event and make a saving, Tel: 0870 60 60 611

Motor Racing Circuit

The Eighteenth Heritage Coast Walk/Run
DUNWICH HEATH AND MINSMERE BEACH
2/5/99
2/5/99 Tel: 01728 648505
Three Routes will be open 26 miles, 14 miles & 6 miles. Please contact Mrs D Clarke, 27 Meadowside, Wickham Market, IP13 0UD, Tel. 01728 747636 for further information

Conservation Parks

Truckfest
EAST OF ENGLAND SHOWGROUND
2/5/99
2/5/99 Tel: 01733 234451
A festival for truck enthusiasts

Showgrounds

British Driving Society Meet
ICKWORTH HOUSE PARK AND GARDENS
2/5/99
2/5/99 Tel: 01284 735270
Horses and Carriages parade and drive in beautiful Ickworth Park. Time: 14.30-16.00. Standard Park Admission.

Historic Houses & Gardens

May Air Display
IMPERIAL WAR MUSEUM, DUXFORD
2/5/99
2/5/99 Tel: 0891 516816 premium line
Britain's first major Air Show of the year, this event will not only commemorate the 75th Anniversary of the Royal Naval Fleet Air Arm, but also the 55th Anniversary of D-Day. A£12.00 Concessions£6.00 OAPs£10.00. Advance Tickets: A£10.50 Concessions£5.00 OAPs£8.00. Advance Coach Rate: £360.00 closing date for coach bookings 19.4.99. Advance tickets for this event maybe purchased by credit card through TicketMaster 24hrs, daily on 0990 344

4444, from Jan 1999

Museum- Aviation

Dawn Chorus I

2/5/99 RYE HOUSE MARSH AND RYE MEADS
2/5/99 MEADOWS

Tel: 01992 460031

Hear the reserve waking up, and learn a few birdsongs. Coffee and croissants (50p extra) after. 04.00-06.00

Nature Reserves

Spring Air Display

2/5/99 THE SHUTTLEWORTH COLLECTION
2/5/99 Tel: 0891 323310

A light-hearted start to the flying display season typically featuring aerobatics and stunt flying plus a chance to step back in time to the pre-war air display era. The Shuttle Mansion House will be open 14.00-17.00 for visitors to se the splendour of this home.

Museum- Aviation

Wicken Fen's Birthday Bash

2/5/99 WICKEN FEN (NT) NATURE RESERVE
2/5/99 Tel: 01353 720274

Join us in celebrating Wicken Fen's 100th birthday. A day packed with activities and fun for all the family. A£4.50 C£2.50, 11.00-17.00

Nature Reserves

Gardeners Weekend

2/5/99 AUDLEY END HOUSE
3/5/99 Tel: 01799 522399

Our annual show with many exhibitors, craft stalls, music and children's entertainment. Plants and produce to buy. Demonstrators and farm animals. A£4.00 Concessions£3.00 C£2.00 (House extra, subject to capacity). EH Members Free

Historical Remains

Barleylands May Madness

2/5/99 BARLEYLANDS FARM MUSEUM AND
VISITORS CENTRE

3/5/99 Tel: 01268 282090/532253

Vintage tractors and steam engines, animal centre, craft studios, miniature steam railway, glassblowing demonstrations, rural craft demonstrations, donkey rides, bouncy castle, tractor and trailer rides, 10.00-17.00

Museum- Farms

Family Walk

2/5/99 BLICKLING HALL
3/5/99 Tel: 01263 738030

Wildlife Waking Up. Come and see the sleepy eyed inhabitants of the grounds at Blickling, look who's rubbing their

eyes - with a 07.00 start it could be you! A£2.50 C(under 12)£1.50. Bookings can be made by telephone, to the address, or in person.

Historic Houses & Gardens

Norfolk Birdwatching Festival

2/5/99 BLICKLING HALL
3/5/99 Tel: 01263 738030

Held in the Walled Garden, who to spot, where to spot and how to recognise BIRDS! Commences: 09.30-17.00. Separate admission ever: A£3.00 C£1.00.

Historic Houses & Gardens

Jousting Tournament

2/5/99 HEDINGHAM CASTLE
3/5/99 Tel: 01787 460261

Presented by The Knights of Royal England. Two lively days of entertainment, full regalia, flashing steel, lots of colourful Charging Knights, and sword fighting by those honourable and no doubt some dishonourable. Plus Taro the Jester. Call for admission prices

Castles

Medieval Living History

2/5/99 ORFORD CASTLE
3/5/99 Tel: 01394 450472

15th century military encampment, drill, archery, mumming plays and dancing. From 12.00. A£3.00 C£1.50 Concessions£2.30. EH Members Free

Castles

Classic Car Show

2/5/99 THE SHUTTLEWORTH COLLECTION
3/5/99 Tel: 0891 323310

A two day meeting of Classics held in the beautiful grounds of Old Warden Park in the heart of rural Bedfordshire. A real mecca for all car lovers, is a must. The mansion house will be open on these days.

Museum- Aviation

Eurocar Bank Holiday Bonanza (BRSCC)

3/5/99 SNETTERTON CIRCUIT
3/5/99 Tel: 01953 887303

Eurocar V6 and V8 Championships debut at Snetterton, Pick-Ups, Legends. Full Circuit, Grade-C. On the Gate: £10.00-£28.00. In Advance: Non £8.00-£25.00, Club £7.00-£22.00. Two Day Pass: Non £11.00-£30.00, Club £10.00-£27.00. Three Day Pass: Non £32.00, Club £29.00. Qualifying: £5.00-£14.00. C£Free. Programme £Free-£5.00. Seating (BH): £Free-£8.00. Group

Tickets: Non £90.00-£95.00, Club £80.00-£85.00. Season Ticket Inc. of Club Membership: £150.00. You can buy your tickets for any of the 1999 events in advance any time up to 4 days before an event and make a saving, Tel: 0870 60 60 611

Motor Racing Circuit

Stilton Cheese Rolling
3/5/99 STILTON CHEESE ROLLING 1999
3/5/99 Tel: 01780 434201
Venue: Stilton Village Centre. Mayday celebrations, processions, street entertainment, stilton cheese rolling competitions, stalls, sideshows, fairground, music, fancy dress. Times: 10.00-14.30. Admission Free

Festivals

Archaeology Day
3/5/99 WEST STOW ANGLO SAXON VILLAGE
3/5/99 Tel: 01284 728718
A fun day for all the family, packed with activities to help you find out more about the archaeology of this fascinating site. Activities of all kinds for all ages, and the opportunity to talk to knowledgeable 'Anglo-Saxons' about life 1500 years ago. A family of Anglo-Saxons in costume come to live in one of the houses and demonstrate what keeps them busy. 10.00-17.00. Last entry 16.00. A£5.00 C&Concessions£4.00 Family Ticket £15.00

Archaeological Interest

Market Rasen Fixture
5/5/99 MARKET RASEN RACECOURSE
5/5/99 Tel: 01673 843434
First race: 14.00. Please call for further information

Racecourses

Living Crafts
6/5/99 HATFIELD HOUSE
9/5/99 Tel: 01707 262823
Hundreds of crafts, 25th year. Time: 10.00-18.00. Cost: A£6.50 C£3.00 Group £5.50. Tel: 01705 426523 for further information

Historic Houses & Gardens

First Friday
7/5/99 ANGLESEY ABBEY, GARDENS AND LODE MILL
7/5/99 Tel: 01223 811200
Take a closer look at The Lower Gallery. Time: 13.00-16.00. Normal admission charges apply.

Historic Houses & Gardens

Stour Valley Picnic Ramble

8/5/99 BRIDGE COTTAGE
8/5/99 Tel: 01206 298260
An extended 8 mile ramble to the more distant parts of the Stour Valley. Visiting Langham church and the villages of East Bergholt, Stratford St Mary and Dedham. Traditional picnic fare provided to be enjoyed alfresco. Bring a small rucksack. Time: 10.00. Tickets: £9.95.

Historic Buildings

Ermine Street Guard
8/5/99 VERULAMIUM MUSEUM AND PARK
8/5/99 Tel: 01727 819339
An encampment in the Verulamium Park, displays include soldiers training and firing of artillery pieces

Museums

Aquatic Invertebrates
8/5/99 WICKEN FEN (NT) NATURE RESERVE
8/5/99 Tel: 01353 720274
Expert Dr Laurie Friday of Cambridge University will introduce students to the diversity of the Aquatic Invertebrates of Wicken Fen. A£25.00 includes lunch

Nature Reserves

Fenland Walk
8/5/99 WICKEN FEN (NT) NATURE RESERVE
8/5/99 Tel: 01353 720274
An informative but gentle stroll around the Fen. A£3.75 C£2.50 14.00-16.00

Nature Reserves

National Mills Day
8/5/99 ANGLESEY ABBEY, GARDENS AND LODE MILL
9/5/99 Tel: 01223 811200
See Lode Watermill in action. Time: 11.00-16.00. Normal admission charges apply.

Historic Houses & Gardens

Coastguard Special: World War II Rationing
8/5/99 DUNWICH HEATH AND MINSMERE BEACH
9/5/99 Tel: 01728 648505
A weekend of sample food from during the war and displays, information in the Restaurant.

Conservation Parks

Festival of Norfolk Food and Drink 1999
8/5/99 FESTIVAL OF NORFOLK FOOD AND DRINK 1999
9/5/99 Tel: 01692 403069
An event to promote Norfolk produced food and drink. Over 50 trade stands exhibiting, Norfolk scouts and guides campfire cooking competition. Celebrity TV cooks: Lesley Waters, James Martin

stars of Ready, Steady Cook and Food and Drink prgrammes, Patrick Anthony and Mary Berry returning by popular request to delight you with their knowledge and expertise together with other excellent local hotel ad restaurant chefs. Walking around the covered Exhibition you will be able to sample the real taste of Norfolk and talk to Farmers and Growers. Inspect an Army Field Kitchen and try their cooking!

Festivals

Living History Festival

8/5/99 OXBURGH HALL, GARDEN AND ESTATE
9/5/99 Tel: 01366 328258
Meet costumed characters of the Tudor Times. Commences: 13.00-16.00. Normal opening times and admission prices apply

Historic Buildings

MCN British Superbike Championships (MCRCB)

8/5/99 SNETTERTON CIRCUIT
9/5/99 Tel: 01953 887303
British Superbike x 2, British 125cc, British 250cc, British 600cc plus support. Full Circuit, Grade-B. On the Gate: £10.00-£28.00. In Advance: Non £8.00-£25.00, Club £7.00-£22.00. Two Day Pass: Non £11.00-£30.00, Club £10.00-£27.00. Three Day Pass: Non £32.00, Club £29.00. Qualifying: £5.00-£14.00. C£Free. Programme £Free-£5.00. Seating (BH): £Free-£8.00. Group Tickets: Non £90.00-£95.00, Club £80.00-£85.00. Season Ticket Inc. of Club Membership: £150.00. You can buy your tickets for any of the 1999 events in advance any time up to 4 days before an event and make a saving, Tel: 0870 60 60 611

Motor Racing Circuit

Historic Touring Cars (BARC)

9/5/99 CADWELL PARK CIRCUIT
9/5/99 Tel: 01507 343248
Post Historic Group 1 Touring Cars, Classic Touring Cars, Classic Formula Ford 2000s, Classic 1600s, Monopostos, ModProd Saloons. Full Circuit, Grade-D. On the Gate: £10.00-£28.00. In Advance: Non £8.00-£25.00, Club £7.00-£22.00. Two Day Pass: Non £11.00-£30.00, Club £10.00-£27.00. Three Day Pass: Non £32.00, Club £29.00. Qualifying: £5.00-£14.00. C£Free. Programme £Free-£5.00. Seating (BH): £Free-£8.00. Group Tickets: Non £90.00-£95.00, Club

£80.00-£85.00. Season Ticket Inc. of Club Membership: £135.00. You can buy your tickets for any of the 1999 events in advance any time up to 4 days before an event and make a saving, Tel: 0870 60 60 611

Motor Racing Circuit

National Mill Day

9/5/99 CROMER WINDMILL
9/5/99 Tel: 01279 843301
Please call for further information

Windmills

Guided Walk: War on the Heath

9/5/99 DUNWICH HEATH AND MINSMERE BEACH
9/5/99 Tel: 01728 648505
A walk with the Warden talking about World War II on Dunwich Heath and Minsmere Beach. Time: 10.00. Tickets: £3.00

Conservation Parks

Dawn Chorus II

9/5/99 RYE HOUSE MARSH AND RYE MEADS MEADOWS
9/5/99 Tel: 01992 460031
Hear the reserve waking up, and learn a few birdsongs. Coffee and croissants (50p extra) after. 04.00-06.00

Nature Reserves

Nightingale Walk

11/5/99 HATFIELD FOREST
11/5/99 Tel: 01279 870678
An opportunity to hear the wonderful song of the nightingale, with a visit to the Hop Poles public house. Dinner available if required - cost approx £5.00 per head to be paid on the night. Commences 21.30 ish. Tickets: A£2.00 C£1.00 Family Ticket (A2+C2)£5.00. Please note that you must book for all events except where stated otherwise. Please send a cheque payable to National Trust, along with an s.a.e. for your tickets.

Forests

Behind the Scenes at Orford Ness

11/5/99 ORFORD NESS
11/5/99 Tel: 01394 450900
A chance to hear and see about management of a National Trust Property. Do Wardens just sit and watch birds all day? Come and see for yourself. Bring suitable clothing for the weather. Tea and coffee provided but bring your own lunch. Binoculars may be useful. Meet: 10.00 prompt at Orford Quay. Depart: approx. 16.00. Cost: £15.00 for all.

Nature Reserves

The Benfleet Beer Festival
11/5/99 THE BENFLEET BEER FESTIVAL 1999
11/5/99 Tel: 01268 882473
Over 41 British real ales and bottled
beers from around the world to try.
Experts from CAMRA will be on hand to
advise and discuss the merits of each
beer. Special entertainment evenings on
Thursday and Saturday. Time: 11.00-
15.00 & 18.00-11.00/11.30. Price: A£1.00
entry fee, £5.00 entertainment (to
include price of commemorative glass).
Over 18 years only
Festivals

Evening Meeting
12/5/99 HUNTINGDON STEEPLECHASES LTD
12/5/99 Tel: 01480 453373
An evening meeting of competitive racing from 18.05
Racecourses

Garden Open Day
12/5/99 OXBURGH HALL, GARDEN AND ESTATE
12/5/99 Tel: 01366 328258
Meet the Gardener, tours of the workshop and greenhouse area, 11.30
&14.30, normal opening times and
admission charges apply
Historic Buildings

Chelmsford Cathedral Festival
12/5/99 CHELMSFORD CATHEDRAL FESTIVAL 1999
22/5/99 Tel: 01245 359890
Classical and jazz concerts, film, poetry,
talks, dance, street music and theatre,
lectures, midday music box, organ
recitals, fringe lectures and performances, exhibitions and much more.
Time: 20.00 daily. Prices: Various
Festivals

Verulamium Museum Diamond Jubilee
12/5/99 VERULAMIUM MUSEUM AND PARK
26/5/99 Tel: 01727 819339
A Lecture Series (dates: 12, 19 & 26 May)
on recent research into Roman
Verulamium call for details
Museums

Wicken Wildlife Watch
13/5/99 WICKEN FEN (NT) NATURE RESERVE
13/5/99 Tel: 01353 720274
Find out what lurks beneath the water at
Wicken Fen in this session all about
pond life. £0.25 for Watch members
£1.00 for non-members. Please phone to
book your place (8-12 years). 16.30-
18.00
Nature Reserves

Volunteer Open Day

15/5/99 NORTH NORFOLK RAILWAY
15/5/99 Tel: 01263 822045
Visit our railway and join our friendly
volunteer workforce
Railways Steam/Light

From RFC to AWRE
15/5/99 ORFORD NESS
15/5/99 Tel: 01394 450900
A look at the 20th century military histo-
ry of Orford Ness. Meet: 10.00 prompt at
Orford Quay. Depart: approx. 16.00.
Bring suitable clothing for the weather.
Bring own food and drink. Cost: £12.50
for all. Maximum 24 people.
Nature Reserves

Sunset Display 1
15/5/99 THE SHUTTLEWORTH COLLECTION
15/5/99 Tel: 0891 323310
The first of several Sunset Displays to be
held at Old Warden Aerodrome this year
Museum- Aviation

History Fair
15/5/99 AUDLEY END HOUSE
16/5/99 Tel: 01799 522399
A history fair showing a multi-period.
With various performers. A£5.00 C£2.50
Concessions£3.80
Historical Remains

Championship Bikes (NEW ERA)
15/5/99 CADWELL PARK CIRCUIT
16/5/99 Tel: 01507 343248
All classes of national solo motorcycles
and sidecars. Full Circuit, Grade-D. On
the Gate: £10.00-£28.00. In Advance:
Non £8.00-£25.00. Club £7.00-£22.00.
Two Day Pass: Non £11.00-£30.00, Club
£10.00-£27.00. Three Day Pass: Non
£32.00, Club £29.00. Qualifying: £5.00-
£14.00. C£Free. Programme £Free-£5.00.
Seating (BH): £Free-£8.00. Group
Tickets: Non £90.00-£95.00, Club
£80.00-£85.00. Season Ticket Inc. of
Club Membership: £135.00. You can buy
your tickets for any of the 1999 events in
advance any time up to 4 days before an
event and make a saving, Tel: 0870 60
60 611
Motor Racing Circuit

The French & Indian Wars
15/5/99 WREST PARK GARDENS
16/5/99 Tel: 01525 860152
New France and Old England of the 18th-
century. A£4.00 C£2.00
Concessions£3.00
Gardens

Museums Week
15/5/99 CHELMSFORD AND ESSEX REGIMENT

23/5/99	MUSEUM Tel: 01245 353066 Activities to be announced on the theme of Food, Herbs, Medicine *Museum- Local History*

A MAC Touring Exhibition

15/5/99 27/6/99	GAINSBOROUGH'S HOUSE Tel: 01787 372958 Kate Malone: The Allotment in the Lower Gallery with Essex Landscapes by Collin Wilkin in the Weaving Room *Birth Places*

Spring Plant Fair

16/5/99 16/5/99	ANGLESEY ABBEY, GARDENS AND LODE MILL Tel: 01223 811200 11.00-17.30. A plant fair for all gardening enthusiasts. *Historic Houses & Gardens*

Evening Walk

16/5/99 16/5/99	BLICKLING HALL Tel: 01263 738030 Gentle escorted evening walk through peaceful countryside, hear the birds, smell the countryside as it settles for the night. Commences: 19.30. A£2.50 C£1.50. Bookings can be made by telephone, to the address, or in person. *Historic Houses & Gardens*

The Stour Marshes Circular

16/5/99 16/5/99	BRIDGE COTTAGE Tel: 01206 298260 Once brunch has been enjoyed you will be guided through the lower Dedham Vale which is infrequently visited. A circular tour of the valley which takes in Cattawade and returns by the river all the way. Time: 10.45. Tickets: £8.50. *Historic Buildings*

Exotic Pets Day

16/5/99 16/5/99	BUTTERFLY AND WILDLIFE PARK Tel: 01406 363833 Informative and fun packed day for children of all ages. Have you ever held a tarantula, a scorpion, a 15 foot Python or a Giant Hissing Cockroach. Now is your chance! This is a day with a difference! *Wildlife Parks*

Farming Models and Model Traction Engine

16/5/99 16/5/99	CHURCH FARM MUSEUM Tel: 01754 766658 An exciting opportunity to view a variety of working models and talk with their owners *Museum- Farms*

Plant Fair

16/5/99 16/5/99	DUNWICH HEATH AND MINSMERE BEACH Tel: 01728 648505 To support Education at Dunwich Heath. Time: 11.00-16.00. Admission Free *Conservation Parks*

Giant 75th Birthday Ramble

16/5/99 16/5/99	HATFIELD FOREST Tel: 01279 870678 Join us to celebrate 75 years of the Trust's ownership of Hatfield Forest. Lots to see and do, including the announcement of the winners of our competiton. Costumed characters through the ages. Commences 11.00-16.00. Tickets: A£3.00 C£1.50 Family Ticket (A2+C2)£6.00. Car parking £3.00 NT members £Free. Please note that you must book for all events except where stated otherwise. Please send a cheque payable to National Trust, along with an s.a.e. for your tickets. *Forests*

Three Gardens Walk

16/5/99 16/5/99	ICKWORTH HOUSE PARK AND GARDENS Tel: 01284 735270 Join Head Gardener Jan Michalak on a guided walk around three of Ickworth's gardens; the Albana Plantation (Woodland Garden), the Italian Garden, and a garden in progress - the restoration of the East Wind Flower Garden. Tour price includes finger buffet in East Wing Conservatory, served at 12.15. Time: 10.30-12.15. Tickets: £12.50, booking essential call 01284 735270. *Historic Houses & Gardens*

Museums Week Open Day

16/5/99 16/5/99	LEIGHTON BUZZARD RAILWAY Tel: 01525 373888 (24hours) Behind the scenes tours. Quarry digger at work. Small steam locos double-heading passenger trains *Railways Steam/Light*

Spring Plant Fair

16/5/99 16/5/99	OXBURGH HALL, GARDEN AND ESTATE Tel: 01366 328258 Garden enthusiasts come along for our Spring Plant Fair, also various stalls and home made cakes, jam/marmalade, piccalilli and chutney from the restaurant. Normal opening times *Historic Buildings*

MG Car Races (MGCC)

16/5/99 16/5/99	SNETTERTON CIRCUIT Tel: 01953 887303 Thoroughbred Sports Cars, International BCV8, Midget Challenge, Metro

Further more detailed information on the attractions listed can be found in Best Guides *Visitor Attractions* Guide under the classifications shown

Challenge, MG Phoenix, ACE MG Cockshoot, MGF Trophy. Full Circuit, Grade-D. On the Gate: £10.00-£28.00. In Advance: Non £8.00-£25.00, Club £7.00-£22.00. Two Day Pass: Non £11.00-£30.00, Club £10.00-£27.00. Three Day Pass: Non £32.00, Club £29.00. Qualifying: £5.00-£14.00. C£Free. Programme £Free-£5.00. Seating (BH): £Free-£8.00. Group Tickets: Non £90.00-£95.00, Club £80.00-£85.00. Season Ticket Inc. of Club Membership: £150.00. You can buy your tickets for any of the 1999 events in advance any time up to 4 days before an event and make a saving. Tel: 0870 60 60 611

Motor Racing Circuit

Quarry Machinery Display Days

16/5/99
4/9/99

LEIGHTON BUZZARD RAILWAY
Tel: 01525 373888 (24hours)
Experience the classic RB-10 digger at work loading sand wagons, just like it used to do for a living. To be held on: 16 May, 1st August & 4th September

Railways Steam/Light

Vineyard Tour and Supper

17/5/99
17/5/99

ICKWORTH HOUSE PARK AND GARDENS
Tel: 01284 735270
Tour Ickworth's own vineyard with the creators of Ickworth's vineyard, Jillian Simms and Charles Macready, then enjoy supper in the Servants' Hall Restaurant. Bring waterproofs and walking shoes. Time: 18.00-21.00. Cost: £18.50, includes wine tasting.

Historic Houses & Gardens

Adult Learners Week / Museums Week

17/5/99
23/5/99

ICKWORTH HOUSE PARK AND GARDENS
Tel: 01284 735270
Events and activities to mark Adult Learners Week / Museums Week. Details, times and prices on 01284 735270.

Historic Houses & Gardens

Weatherbys

18/5/99
18/5/99

NATIONAL HORSERACING MUSEUM AND TOURS
Tel: 01638 667333
Weatherbys have been administering racing since 1770, publishing the General Stud Book, registering owners' colours and horses' names, processing race day information and publishing racecards. A full-day excursion to their fascinating office in Northamptonshire - you really can't understand racing unless you've been here! Departs 09.00.

Price: £25.00 including transport and buffet lunch.

Museum- Horse racing

Team Challenge

19/5/99
19/5/99

HATFIELD FOREST
Tel: 01279 870678
An opportunity to take part in a variety of team navigational, physical and mental challenges in Hatfield Forest - why not test yourself and have fun! Commences 19.00-21.00. A£3.00 Team Ticket (Ax4)£6.00. Please note that you must book for all events except where stated otherwise. Please send a cheque payable to National Trust, along with an s.a.e. for your tickets

Forests

A Fan-tastic Evening at Ickworth

19/5/99
19/5/99

ICKWORTH HOUSE PARK AND GARDENS
Tel: 01284 735270
A delicious supper in Ickworth's Servants' Hall Restaurant followed by a lively talk on the use and history of fans. Time: 20.00-22.30. Cost: £15.00, booking essential on 01284 735270.

Historic Houses & Gardens

Painting and Drawing - Beginners

19/5/99
19/5/99

ORFORD NESS
Tel: 01394 450900
As part of Adult Learners Week there is a chance to come to learn the basics of painting and drawing in this unusual landscape. Tuition will be provided. Bring suitable clothing for the weather. Bring own food and drink. Some basic equipment can be provided, check for details. Meet: 09.30 prompt at Orford Quay. Depart: approx. 17.00. Cost: £17.50 for all. Maximum 20 people.

Nature Reserves

Tallington Beer Festival 1999

19/5/99
22/5/99

TALLINGTON BEER FESTIVAL 1999
Tel: 01780 763036
Real Ale Beer Festival with over 60 real ales. Live bands every night; Wed 19 - James Joyce Band (Irish/American). Thur 20 - March to the Grave (Punk/Rock). Fri 21 - That's That! (Pop/Rock covers). Sat 22 - Band From County Hell (Folk). ALSO in No. 2 Beer Tent Fri & Sat - Dr Busker, the last Victorian Pianist/ Accordian (Hilarious (blue!) Alternative).

Festivals

Chandelier Tour and Supper

20/5/99
20/5/99

ICKWORTH HOUSE PARK AND GARDENS
Tel: 01284 735270
A private view of Ickworth House as

dusk falls. The magnificent state rooms will be lit by the exquisitely beautiful chandeliers, creating a memorable setting for a guided tour led by the House Manager. Ickworth's collection of Regency furniture, silver, and Old Master paintings will all be featured. The tour is preceded by a two course supper in the Servants' Hall Restaurant. Time: 19.00-22.30. Cost: £18.00, booking essential, call 01284 735270.

Historic Houses & Gardens

International League for the Protection of Horses

20/5/99 NATIONAL HORSERACING MUSEUM AND TOURS

24/8/99 Tel: 01638 667333

20th May & 24th August only. All-day visit to the home of rescued and retired horses and ponies, situated on the Norfolk/Suffolk borders. Visit the exhibition area and the stableyard and hear about rehabilitation and vetinary care. You may see the lunging and backing of unbroken youngsters. Picnic area, shop and cafe. Departs 09.30 both days. Price: £15.00.

Museum- Horse racing

Norfolk Supper

21/5/99 FELBRIGG HALL

21/5/99 Tel: 01263 837444

An evening of Norfolk tales and local fare. Four course supper of traditional Norfolk dishes interspersed with an evening of entertainment provided by Norfolk's very own Keith Skipper. Tickets: £17.95, please book direct with the Restaurant on 01263 832237

Historic Houses & Gardens

Around the Park with the Archaeologist

22/5/99 ICKWORTH HOUSE PARK AND GARDENS

22/5/99 Tel: 01284 735270

Discover the secrets of Ickworth's historic landscape. Bring walking shoes and waterproofs. Time: 10.30-12.00 & 14.30-16.00. Booking essential, 01284 735270.

Historic Houses & Gardens

The Bard's Best Bits - Oddsocks Productions

22/5/99 CASTLE ACRE PRIORY

23/5/99 Tel: 01760 755394

Once again this hugely entertaining group comprehensively demolish Shakespeare! See the best bits from Julius Caesar, Romeo and Juliet and A Midsummer Night's Dream. Don't miss it! A£3.50 C£1.80 Concessions£2.60

Priory

Clubmans Bikes (NEW ERA)

22/5/99 SNETTERTON CIRCUIT

23/5/99 Tel: 01953 887303

All classes of national solo motorcycles and sidecars. Full Circuit, Grade-E. On the Gate: £10.00-£28.00. In Advance: Non £8.00-£25.00, Club £7.00-£22.00. Two Day Pass: Non £11.00-£30.00, Club £10.00-£27.00. Three Day Pass: Non £32.00, Club £29.00. Qualifying: £5.00-£14.00. C£Free. Programme £Free-£5.00. Seating (BH): £Free-£8.00. Group Tickets: Non £90.00-£95.00, Club £80.00-£85.00. Season Ticket Inc. of Club Membership: £150.00. You can buy your tickets for any of the 1999 events in advance any time up to 4 days before an event and make a saving, Tel: 0870 60 60 611

Motor Racing Circuit

Tallington Steam and Country Festival 1999

22/5/99 TALLINGTON STEAM AND COUNTRY FESTIVAL 1999

23/5/99 Tel: 01780 763063

A full programme of family entertainment, including sky diving, motorcycle display team, dog handling display. Also 1st round of Power Pulling Grand Prix. Over 80 steam engines + over 800 other vintage vehicles and exhibits. Rural crafts, market, auction, heavy horses, rare breeds, beer festival, fairground, live bands, sheep shearing, helicopter rides etc.

Festivals

Nexus Flying Displays

22/5/99 THE SHUTTLEWORTH COLLECTION

8/8/99 Tel: 0891 323310

Mostly two day, weekend events for the aeromodeller. Something of interest for all ages. Small scale, Large scale and a good range of trade stands. You will be made most welcome. Dates: 22 & 23 May; 12 & 13 June; 24 & 25 July; 7 & 8 August; and the Festival of Flight on the 11 & 12 September

Museum- Aviation

Championship Cars (BRSCC)

23/5/99 CADWELL PARK CIRCUIT

23/5/99 Tel: 01507 343248

Porsche 924S, XR2 Challenge, XR3 Challenge plus support. Full Circuit,

Grade-D. On the Gate: £10.00-£28.00. In Advance: Non £8.00-£25.00, Club £7.00-£22.00. Two Day Pass: Non £11.00-£30.00, Club £10.00-£27.00. Three Day Pass: Non £32.00, Club £29.00. Qualifying: £5.00-£14.00. C£Free. Programme £Free-£5.00. Seating (BH): £Free-£8.00. Group Tickets: Non £90.00-£95.00, Club £80.00-£85.00. Season Ticket Inc. of Club Membership: £135.00. You can buy your tickets for any of the 1999 events in advance any time up to 4 days before an event and make a saving, Tel: 0870 60 60 611

Motor Racing Circuit

British Motorcycle Show
23/5/99 EAST OF ENGLAND SHOWGROUND
23/5/99 Tel: 01733 234451
Europe's largest Motorcycle Show

Showgrounds

Guided Walk
23/5/99 ORFORD NESS
23/5/99 Tel: 01394 450900
Walk with the Warden looking at the many varied aspects of this unique site. Meet: 10.00 prompt at Orford Quay. Depart approx. 16.00. Cost: £12.50 for all. Maximum 24 people. Bring suitable clothing for the weather. Bring own food and drink.

Nature Reserves

Sunset Stroll
23/5/99 RYE HOUSE MARSH AND RYE MEADS MEADOWS
23/5/99 Tel: 01992 460031
The most peaceful time of day, and a good time to see cuckoos, if we're lucky, plus a bat or two. 19.00-21.00

Nature Reserves

Willow Sculpture Course
23/5/99 WEST STOW ANGLO SAXON VILLAGE
23/5/99 Tel: 01284 728718
Learn from an expert how to make willow sculptures and fencing which may even continue growing! Plenty of practical work involved. A£15.00 Concessions£10.00. Please book by 8 May

Archaeological Interest

Chandelier Tour and Supper
24/5/99 ICKWORTH HOUSE PARK AND GARDENS
24/5/99 Tel: 01284 735270
A private view of Ickworth House as dusk falls. The magnificent state rooms will be lit by the exquisitely beautiful chandeliers, creating a memorable setting for a guided tour led by the House

Manager. Ickworth's collection of Regency furniture, silver, and Old Master Paintings will all be featured. The tour is preceded by a two course supper in the Servants' Hall Restaurant. Time: 19.00-22.30. Cost: £18.00, booking essential, 01284 735270.

Historic Houses & Gardens

Mid-Summer, Mid-Week, Mystery Meander
27/5/99 BRIDGE COTTAGE
27/5/99 Tel: 01206 298260
After a delicious cream tea at Bridge Cottage tea rooms set off for a glorious guided walk on a mid-summer's evening into Constable Country. Time: 16.00. Tickets: £6.50.

Historic Buildings

Vineyard Tour and Supper
27/5/99 ICKWORTH HOUSE PARK AND GARDENS
27/5/99 Tel: 01284 735270
Tour Ickworth's own vineyard with the creators of Ickworth's vineyard, Jillian Simms and Charles Macready, then enjoy supper in the Servants' Hall Restaurant. Bring waterproofs and walking shoes. Time: 18.00-21.00. Cost: £18.50, includes wine tasting.

Historic Houses & Gardens

Sir Michael Stoute's Freemason Lodge
28/5/99 NATIONAL HORSERACING MUSEUM AND TOURS
22/7/99 Tel: 01638 667333
28th May & 22nd July only. Visit the gallops and the horses' swimming pool, followed by a visit to Sir Michael Stoute's Freemason Lodge yard. You are very likely to meet some of his staff, as well as his horses. Departs 09.20 sharp. Price: £15.00.

Museum- Horse racing

Afternoon Cream Tea Stroll
29/5/99 BRIDGE COTTAGE
29/5/99 Tel: 01206 298260
Idle away an afternoon in the spectacular Lawford Dale, visit its pretty and unique church. Finishing back at Bridge Cottage for a traditional home made cream tea. Time: 13.00. Tickets: £6.50.

Historic Buildings

Market Rasen Evening Fixture
29/5/99 MARKET RASEN RACECOURSE
29/5/99 Tel: 01673 843434
First Race: 18.30. Call venue for full details

Racecourses

Introduction to the National

Vegatation Classification
29/5/99 WICKEN FEN (NT) NATURE RESERVE
29/5/99 Tel: 01353 720274
A one day course designed to train participants how to conduct the survey work and interpret the results. This course is particularly related to fen habitats. A£25.00 includes lunch. 10.00-17.00
Nature Reserves

Championship Bikes (RETFORD)
29/5/99 CADWELL PARK CIRCUIT
30/5/99 Tel: 01507 343248
All classes of national solo motorcycles and sidecars. Full Circuit, Grade-E. On the Gate: £10.00-£28.00. In Advance: Non £8.00-£25.00, Club £7.00-£22.00. Two Day Pass: Non £11.00-£30.00, Club £10.00-£27.00. Three Day Pass: Non £32.00, Club £29.00. Qualifying: £5.00-£14.00. C£Free. Programme £Free-£5.00. Seating (BH): £Free-£8.00. Group Tickets: Non £90.00-£95.00, Club £80.00-£85.00. Season Ticket Inc. of Club Membership: £135.00. You can buy your tickets for any of the 1999 events in advance any time up to 4 days before an event and make a saving, Tel: 0870 60 60 611
Motor Racing Circuit

Scunthorpe Horse Trials
29/5/99 NORMANBY HALL COUNTRY PARK
30/5/99 Tel: 01724 720588
Horse trials including dressage, show jumping and cross country eventing. Time: 09.00-17.00. Tel: 01724 720588 for further information
Country Parks

Craft and Country Skills Fair
29/5/99 FELBRIGG HALL
31/5/99 Tel: 01263 837444
Presented by Eastern Events. High quality crafts from selected designer craftspeople and demonstrations of traditional country skills against the backdrop of one of the finest 17th century houses in Norfolk. Admission: A£3.00 C(under 14)£Free OAPs£2.50
Historic Houses & Gardens

Recreation of Tudor Life at Whitsuntide
29/5/99 KENTWELL HALL
31/5/99 Tel: 01787 310207
Life at Kentwell in the 16th century. Time: 11.00-18.00. Prices: A£7.75 C£5.20 OAPs£6.70. Pre-booked groups 20+ 20% discount

Historic Houses & Gardens
Exhibition & Countryside Day
29/5/99 MANNINGTON GARDENS AND COUNTRYSIDE
31/5/99 Tel: 01263 584175
Tent exhibition/sale and Countryside Day
Gardens

Englisc Ham - At home with an Anglo-Saxon Family
29/5/99 WEST STOW ANGLO SAXON VILLAGE
31/5/99 Tel: 01284 728718
Nothing to do with meat, but everything to do with being at home in the Anglo-Saxon village. A costumed family invite you to investigate their home. A£5.00 C&Concessions£4.00 Family Ticket 15.00. 10.00-17.00 Last entry 16.00
Archaeological Interest

Befordshire Spring Craft Show
29/5/99 WOBURN ABBEY
31/5/99 Tel: 01525 290666
Popular craft fair with a variety of exhibitors and entertainments for all the family. 10.00-18.00. Admission charge not set until 6 weeks before event. Call 01283 820548
Stately Homes

Radio Controlled Grand Prix
29/5/99 WOBURN SAFARI PARK
31/5/99 Tel: 01525 290407
Come and have some fast fun
Safari Parks

Garden Show
29/5/99 WREST PARK GARDENS
31/5/99 Tel: 01525 860152
Everything for the garden, with specialist talks and entertainment too!
Gardens

Chelmsford Life and Loves Remembered
29/5/99 CHELMSFORD AND ESSEX REGIMENT MUSEUM
8/8/99 Tel: 01245 353066
Reminiscences, art and craft from Admirals Reach Nursing Home
Museum- Local History

Barbie's Party
29/5/99 VERULAMIUM MUSEUM AND PARK
12/9/99 Tel: 01727 819339
Now 40! We are honouring the event with an exhibition of her life!
Museums

The Ice Age in Peterborough
29/5/99 PETERBOROUGH MUSEUM AND ART

GALLERY

27/11/99 Tel: 01733 343329

Exhibition based around the recent spectacular finds, call for further details

Museum- Local History

Boom Time

29/5/99 MILL GREEN MUSEUM AND MILL

28/11/99 Tel: 01707 271362

Hatfield in the 1950s and 1960s. An exhibition researched by Hatfield residents who moved into the New Town in the 1950s.

Watermill

Cromwell's Army

30/5/99 AUDLEY END HOUSE

31/5/99 Tel: 01799 522399

Performed by the English Civil War Society. A£5.00 C£3.00 Concessions£4.50

Historical Remains

Barleylands May Family Weekend

30/5/99 BARLEYLANDS FARM MUSEUM AND VISITORS CENTRE

31/5/99 Tel: 01268 282090/532253

Vintage tractors and steam engines, animal centre, craft studios, miniature steam railway, glassblowing demonstrations, rural craft demonstrations, donkey rides, bouncy castle, tractor and trailer rides, 10.00-17.00

Museum- Farms

Gala Weekend and Vehicle Rally

30/5/99 COLNE VALLEY RAILWAY AND MUSEUM

31/5/99 Tel: 01787 461174

Every available steam and diesel locomotive ooperates plus displays of vintage vehicles

Railways

The Peterborough Classic Car Show

30/5/99 ELTON HALL

31/5/99 Tel: 01832 280468

Hundreds of classic vehicles including pre/post war saloons, sports, American, commercial, military, classic motorcycles, plus kit, custom, replica etc. Refreshments. 10.00-17.00

Historic Houses & Gardens

Hedingham Castle Under Siege

30/5/99 HEDINGHAM CASTLE

31/5/99 Tel: 01787 460261

Authentic encampment with various displays, longbow archery competition and afternoon sieges of the keep

Castles

It's a Knockout

30/5/99 LINCOLN CASTLE

31/5/99 Tel: 01522 511068

A weekend of fun and festivities, with teams battling it out to raise funds for the LEPRA Association. Admission charges to be advised

Castles

British GT Championship Meeting (BRDC)

30/5/99 SNETTERTON CIRCUIT

31/5/99 Tel: 01953 887303

British GT Championship, National Saloon Car, MGF Cup, Supersports 200, Marcos mantis, Ginetta G27, Mini Miglia & Se7en. Full Circuit, Grade-C. On the Gate: £10.00-£28.00. In Advance: Non £8.00-£25.00, Club £7.00-£22.00. Two Day Pass: Non £11.00-£30.00, Club £10.00-£27.00. Three Day Pass: Non £32.00, Club £29.00. Qualifying: £5.00-£14.00. C£Free. Programme £Free-£5.00. Seating (BH): £Free-£8.00. Group Tickets: Non £90.00-£95.00, Club £80.00-£85.00. Season Ticket Inc. of Club Membership: £150.00. You can buy your tickets for any of the 1999 events in advance any time up to 4 days before an event and make a saving, Tel: 0870 60 60 611

Motor Racing Circuit

LTS Rail Southend Airshow

30/5/99 SOUTHEND ON SEA BOROUGH COUNCIL

31/5/99 Tel: 01702 215166

Europe's largest free Airshow, staged against the backdrop of the Thames Estuary, on the Western Esplanade, Southend Seafront, has an action packed two days. Incorporating a full flying programme, arena events, exhibitions, ground entertainment, market and craft stalls, classic cars, Army, Navy and Royal Marines Town Show and much more

Festivals

Medieval Living History Weekend

30/5/99 TATTERSHALL CASTLE

31/5/99 Tel: 01526 342543

With Lincoln Castle Garrison, and other events. Time: 10.30-17.00. Normal admission

Castles

Wendover Canal Festival at Tring

30/5/99 WENDOVER CANAL FESTIVAL AT TRING 1999

31/5/99 Tel: 01296 748036 Box Office

Large craft fair, arena events, boat trips, canal boats, novelty dog event, clowns, live music, trade stands, military vehicle rides, children's rides, classic cars. Something for all the family.

Festivals

Championship Bikes (NEW ERA)
31/5/99 CADWELL PARK CIRCUIT
31/5/99 Tel: 01507 343248
All classes of national solo motorcycles and sidecars. Full Circuit, Grade-D. On the Gate: £10.00-£28.00. In Advance: Non £8.00-£25.00, Club £7.00-£22.00. Two Day Pass: Non £11.00-£30.00, Club £10.00-£27.00. Three Day Pass: Non £32.00, Club £29.00. Qualifying: £5.00-£14.00. C£Free. Programme £Free-£5.00. Seating (BH): £Free-£8.00. Group Tickets: Non £90.00-£95.00, Club £80.00-£85.00. Season Ticket Inc. of Club Membership: £135.00. You can buy your tickets for any of the 1999 events in advance any time up to 4 days before an event and make a saving, Tel: 0870 60 60 611

Motor Racing Circuit

Family Fun Day
31/5/99 HUNTINGDON STEEPLECHASES LTD
31/5/99 Tel: 01480 453373
Bring the family to Huntingdon where a large crowd and great atmosphere promises to make it a wonderful day out. All children under 16 can enter free of charge and with a fully supervised creche, bouncy castle, tubeslide and face-painting, there is lots to do for all the family. Racing from 14.00

Racecourses

Half-term Activities for Families
31/5/99 ICKWORTH HOUSE PARK AND GARDENS
31/5/99 Tel: 01284 735270
Includes Scavenger Hunts, Mini-beast Safaris and Wild Flower Spotting (self-guided activities). Standard Park Admission.

Historic Houses & Gardens

Family Woodland Ramble
31/5/99 ICKWORTH HOUSE PARK AND GARDENS
31/5/99 Tel: 01284 735270
A gentle walk in Ickworth's beautiful woods with the Head Forester, discover the beauties of summer woodland and wildlife. 1.5km flat surfaced route, suitable for pushchairs and toddlers as well as the rest of the family. Wear waterproofs. Time: 14.00-15.30. Cost: A£5.00 C(5+)£1.00 Family Ticket (A2+C2)£10.00, includes Park Admission. Booking essential on 01284 735270.

Historic Houses & Gardens

Luton Carnival 1999
31/5/99 LUTON CARNIVAL 1999
31/5/99 Tel: 01582 876083
Entertainment, carnival procession, stalls, refreshments, associated events. Admission Free

Carnivals

Roman Pottery
31/5/99 COLCHESTER CASTLE MUSEUM
4/6/99 Tel: 01206 282931/282932
Make Roman oil lamps with the potter, Sally Whelton. Free (after admission to the Castle)

Museum- Local History

The Victorian Age
31/5/99 THE MANOR HOUSE MUSEUM
5/7/99 Tel: 01284 757076/757072
Please call for further informationCostumes and artifacts of the Victorians as used at the Manor

Museum- Costume

Oddities at Oxburgh
1/6/99 OXBURGH HALL, GARDEN AND ESTATE
1/6/99 Tel: 01366 328258
Competition - Can you find the items at odds with the House, Garden and Tea Room?! From 13.00. Normal opening times and admission charges apply

Historic Buildings

Spring Activity Days
1/6/99 WEST STOW ANGLO SAXON VILLAGE
3/6/99 Tel: 01284 728718
Have fun in the Country Park, please call for 01284 728718 for details of activities planned

Archaeological Interest

Going Dippy with Trusty
1/6/99 WICKEN FEN (NT) NATURE RESERVE
3/6/99 Tel: 01353 720274
A chance to help Trusty the Hedgehog discover what lurks beneath the water at the Fen. A&C(3-12) Tues & Thur10.00-12.00 or 14.00-16.00, £2.50

Nature Reserves

Exhibition: Annual Museology MA
1/6/99 SAINSBURY CENTRE FOR VISUAL ARTS
30/6/99 Tel: 01603 456060/593199
In the Lower Gallery. Provisional Dates, please call for confirmation.

Art Galleries

Holiday Club
2/6/99 DUNWICH HEATH AND MINSMERE BEACH
2/6/99 Tel: 01728 648505
Children's environmental activities for those aged 6-12 years. Bring packed lunch or lunch money, 10.00-14.00,

C£4.00 A£Free, booking essential, please apply direct to the property for booking by telephone 01728 648505 or by post to with a sae to: Dunwich Heath & Minsmere Beach, Saxmundham, Suffolk IP17 3DJ with a cheque made payable to The National Trust (Enterprises)

Conservation Parks

Pond Dip Day

2/6/99   HATFIELD FOREST

2/6/99   Tel: 01279 870678

Have a go at finding and identifying the huge variety of wildlife that lives in our ponds at Hatfield Forest. Commences 11.00-15.00. Tickets: A£Free C£2.00. Car Park £3.00 NT members £Free. Please note that you must book for all events except where stated otherwise. Please send a cheque payable to National Trust, along with an s.a.e. for your tickets.

Forests

Children's Garden Tour with Trusy the Hedgehog

3/6/99   ANGLESEY ABBEY, GARDENS AND LODE MILL

3/6/99   Tel: 01223 811200

14.00. Children 5-17, and adults get a tour around the garden with Trusty the Hedgehog, tickets £3.00, all ticket applications should be addressed to The Property Manager and include sae to: Anglesey Abbey, Gardens and Lode Mill, Quay Road, Lode, Cambridge CB5 9EJ.

Historic Houses & Gardens

Sole Bay Literature Festival

3/6/99   SOLE BAY LITERATURE FESTIVAL 1999

3/6/99   Tel: 01803 867373

About 20 writers giving talks and running workshops. Novelists, biographers, poets, politicians, anyone who has written an interesting book could be there. Accommodation can be arranged through the festival in the hotels in the town

Festivals

First Friday

4/6/99   ANGLESEY ABBEY, GARDENS AND LODE MILL

4/6/99   Tel: 01223 811200

Take a closer look at The Library. Time: 13.00-16.00. Normal admission charges apply.

Historic Houses & Gardens

The Secrets Behind the Park

5/6/99   BLICKLING HALL

5/6/99   Tel: 01263 738030

Escorted walk when the park is quiet: myths, legends and nightfliers. Commences: 19.30. A£2.50 C£1.50. Bookings can be made by telephone, to the address, or in person.

Historic Houses & Gardens

Constable's Candlelight Supper

5/6/99   BRIDGE COTTAGE

5/6/99   Tel: 01206 298260

After a gentle guided stroll around Flatford visiting the famous locations immortalised by John Constable, return to a candle lit cottage to indulge in an 18th century supper. Time: 19.00. Tickets: £14.95.

Historic Buildings

Flint Knapping

5/6/99   GRIME'S GRAVES

5/6/99   Tel: 01842 810656

Stone age man returns to demonstrate how he made tools, axes and arrowheads from flint. From 12.00. A£2.50 C£1.30 Concessions£1.90. EH Members Free

Museum- Mining

Carnival Night Fixture

5/6/99   MARKET RASEN RACECOURSE

5/6/99   Tel: 01673 843434

First race: 18.40. Please call for further information

Racecourses

Anglo-Saxon Language Couse

5/6/99   WEST STOW ANGLO SAXON VILLAGE

5/6/99   Tel: 01284 728718

An introductory course looking at Old English, where and how to read it and how to spot it in modern English. A£15.00 Concessions£10.00. 10.30-16.30. Please book by 22 May

Archaeological Interest

An Introduction to Ground Beetles

5/6/99   WICKEN FEN (NT) NATURE RESERVE

5/6/99   Tel: 01353 720274

An introductory one day course on how to identify these interesting beetles. Led by National expert Brian Emersham. A£25.00 includes lunch 10.00-17.00

Nature Reserves

Jazz in the Stables

5/6/99   WIMPOLE HALL

5/6/99   Tel: 01223 207257

The Ken Colyer Trust New Orleans Jazz Band, 19.30, tickets £8.00. Please apply to the property for booking, either by post with an s.a.e. or call: 01223

207001/207257

Country Parks

Victorian

5/6/99 AUDLEY END HOUSE
6/6/99 Tel: 01799 522399

Beaux Stratagems. A£6.00 C£3.00 Concessions£4.50

Historical Remains

World Oceans Weekend

5/6/99 CLEETHORPES HUMBER ESTUARY
DISCOVERY CENTRE
6/6/99 Tel: 01472 323232

Join our celebration of the seas with activities, workshops, talks and exhibitions for all the family

Exhibition Centres

Model Railway Exhibition

5/6/99 NORTH NORFOLK RAILWAY
6/6/99 Tel: 01263 822045

Please call for further information

Railways Steam/Light

Woburn Garden Show and Maze

5/6/99 WOBURN ABBEY
6/6/99 Tel: 01525 290666

Extra charge applies. One of the finest Hornbeam mazes in the country. Only open twice during the year. Maze also open on: 22 August

Stately Homes

Falcons and Gundogs

5/6/99 WREST PARK GARDENS
6/6/99 Tel: 01525 860152

Come and enjoy the feather perfect falconry. A£3.50 C£1.80 Concessions£2.60

Gardens

Walpole St Peter's Church Flower Festival 1999

5/6/99 WALPOLE ST PETERS'S CHURCH FLOWER
FESTIVAL 1999
9/6/99 Tel: 01945 780235

Perhaps the finest village church in England and especially famous for its Annual Flower Festival. One of the oldest and grandest of its kind attracting coach parties and family outings from far and wide, all enjoying the huge displays of choice blooms inside the church and the many stalls and popular catering outside the building. Sat 5th June: RAF Honington Station (voluntary) Band Concert commences 18.30. Sunday 6th June: Festival Eucharist at 10.30 and Popular Songs of Praise with Kings Lynn Town Band commences 18.30. Facilities are available for the disabled. Booking form for Luncheons and Set Teas for Group Bookings available on application

to the above telephone number.

Festivals

The Homes of Football

5/6/99 USHER GALLERY
31/7/99 Tel: 01522 527980

This popular exhibition is the work of Stuart Clarke, the official photographer to the football trust. His spectacular photography will be accompanied by memorabilia and sculpture. "An excellent collection of outstanding photographs which truly capture the passion of the game" - Tony Blair

Art Galleries

Wildlife Walk: Wild Flowers of the Heath

6/6/99 DUNWICH HEATH AND MINSMERE BEACH
6/6/99 Tel: 01728 648505

Enjoy the summer flowers of Dunwich guided by a local botanist. Time: 11.00. Cost: 3.00

Conservation Parks

Hatfield Forest Treasure Hunt

6/6/99 HATFIELD FOREST
6/6/99 Tel: 01279 870678

Have fun and take part in our treasure hunt. Try your hand at solving clues, take part in various challenges and find the hidden treasure!. Commences 11.00-15.00. Tickets: A£3.00 C£1.50 Family/Team Tickets (A2+C2or team of 4)£6.00. Car Park £3.00 NT members £Free. Please note that you must book for all events except where stated otherwise. Please send a cheque payable to National Trust, along with an s.a.e. for your tickets.

Forests

Raptor Foundation

6/6/99 LINTON ZOOLOGICAL GARDENS
6/6/99 Tel: 01223 891308

Meet Gordon Robertson from the Raptor Foundation and hear all about their work with injured birds of prey and meet some of their tame owls

Zoos- Conservation

Evening Telegraph Motor Show

6/6/99 NORMANBY HALL COUNTRY PARK
6/6/99 Tel: 01724 720588

Latest cars in one beautiful outdoor showroom. Time: 10.00-17.00.

Country Parks

Bird Safari

6/6/99 ORFORD NESS
6/6/99 Tel: 01394 450900

A tour around the site to get a closer look at the summer residents on the

Further more detailed information on the attractions listed can be found in Best Guides *Visitor Attractions* Guide under the classifications shown

Ness. Bring suitable clothing for the weather. Bring own food and drink. Bring binoculars. Meet: 07.30 prompt at Orford Quay. Depart: approx. 12.30. Cost: £15.00 for all. Maximum 24 people.

Nature Reserves

Flora Foray
6/6/99 RYE HOUSE MARSH AND RYE MEADS MEADOWS
6/6/99 Tel: 01992 460031
See the reserve at the best time of day, and enjoy an introduction to our wild flowers. 19.00-21.00

Nature Reserves

Vintage Motorcycle Day (VMCC)
6/6/99 SNETTERTON CIRCUIT
6/6/99 Tel: 01953 887303
Classic and Vintage motorcycle action. Full Circuit, Grade-D. On the Gate: £10.00-£28.00. In Advance: Non £8.00-£25.00, Club £7.00-£22.00. Two Day Pass: Non £11.00-£30.00, Club £10.00-£27.00. Three Day Pass: Non £32.00, Club £29.00. Qualifying: £5.00-£14.00. C£Free. Programme £Free-£5.00. Seating (BH): £Free-£8.00. Group Tickets: Non £90.00-£95.00, Club £80.00-£85.00. Season Ticket Inc. of Club Membership: £150.00. You can buy your tickets for any of the 1999 events in advance any time up to 4 days before an event and make a saving, Tel: 0870 60 60 611

Motor Racing Circuit

Southend Brass Band Competition
6/6/99 SOUTHEND ON SEA BOROUGH COUNCIL
6/6/99 Tel: 01702 215166
Leading Brass Bands from the South East Region will each play their chosen programme for up to 40 minutes. Six solid silver trophies to be won. Held at the Cliffs Bandstand 11.00-19.00. Restaurant and bar facilities available. Box office/credit card bookings: 01702 343605

Festivals

Southend Half Marathon
6/6/99 SOUTHEND ON SEA BOROUGH COUNCIL
6/6/99 Tel: 01702 215166
This annual event starting at the Leisure & Tennis Centre, Garon's Park at 10.00 is an aid of Fairhaven's and Little Haven Children's Hospice. For entry forms and further information please call 01702 220350

Festivals

Great British Picnic Flying Day
6/6/99 THE SHUTTLEWORTH COLLECTION
6/6/99 Tel: 0891 323310
The Shuttleworth Veteran Aeroplane Society are the organisers of the 14th Great British Picnic which is open to anyone who arrives in or on any form of road transport manufactured before 1 January 1960. Flying display usually features a demonstration race round a short course near Old Warden Airfield and recaptures some of the atmosphere of pre-war air racing. The Shuttle Mansion House will be open 14.00-17.00 for visitors to se the splendour of this home.

Museum- Aviation

Open Air Theatre
9/6/99 ANGLESEY ABBEY, GARDENS AND LODE MILL
9/6/99 Tel: 01223 811200
Illyria present Twelfth Night by William Shakespeare. Performance starts: 19.30, gates open: 18.30. Seating is not provided, please bring rugs or chairs. Picnics welcome. Tickets to be confirmed.

Historic Houses & Gardens

Schools Day
9/6/99 THE SHUTTLEWORTH COLLECTION
9/6/99 Tel: 0891 323310
A great day out for the younger child at school. Come and see a short airdisplay put on especially for the children. There is a small display of aeromodel flying, a commentator and a chance to meet the Pilots. A very education day out.

Museum- Aviation

A Walk with the Warden
10/6/99 HATFIELD FOREST
10/6/99 Tel: 01279 870678
A chance to wander through the more remote areas of the Forest learning how we manage the woodlands and why Hatfield Forest is of National importance. Commences 14.00-16.00. Tickets: A£2.00 C£1.00 Family Ticket (A2+C2)£5.00. Car park £3.00 NT members £Free. Please note that you must book for all events except where stated otherwise. Please send a cheque payable to National Trust, along with an s.a.e. for your tickets.

Forests

Luca Cumani's Bedford House Stables
10/6/99 NATIONAL HORSERACING MUSEUM AND

TOURS

10/6/99 Tel: 01638 667333

A tour visiting Luca Cumani's large public stable. The yard has a fascinating history, and is now one of the largest in Newmarket, with a 'Who's Who' of owners and a series of modern barns complementing the Victorian architecture. Departs 09.20 sharp. Price: £15.00.

Museum- Horse racing

Aldebriugh Festival of Music and the Arts 1999

11/6/99 ALDEBURGH FESTIVAL OF MUSIC AND THE ARTS 1999

27/6/99 Tel: 01728 452935

Held at Snape Maltings Concert Hall and other venues in and around Aldeburgh. Founded in 1948 by Benjamin Britten, Peter Pears and Eric Crozier, the festival combines international performers, living composers, new commissions, operas and exhibitions.

Festivals

Cycle Day

12/6/99 CHURCH FARM MUSEUM

12/6/99 Tel: 01754 766658

Join in the fun at Church, whilst being 'green' and getting fit

Museum- Farms

Fish Supper and a Talk

12/6/99 DUNWICH HEATH AND MINSMERE BEACH

12/6/99 Tel: 01728 648505

A chance to taste fish dishes and learn how to cook fish with a talk on local sea fishing. Time: 18.00. Tickets: £12.95

Conservation Parks

Market Rasen Fixture

12/6/99 MARKET RASEN RACECOURSE

12/6/99 Tel: 01673 843434

First race: 14.15. Please call for further information

Racecourses

Jousting

12/6/99 AUDLEY END HOUSE

13/6/99 Tel: 01799 522399

Medieval jousting by various performers. A£5.00 C£2.50 Concessions£3.80

Historical Remains

Model Engineering Exhibition

12/6/99 COLNE VALLEY RAILWAY AND MUSEUM

13/6/99 Tel: 01787 461174

Varied collection of model engineering including model trains

Railways

Monks on the Run

12/6/99 DENNY ABBEY AND THE FARMLAND

MUSEUM

13/6/99 Tel: 01223 860489

Regia Anglorum Group of the Saxon/Viking period. A£3.00 C£1.50 Concessions£2.30

Abbeys

Fishy Weekend

12/6/99 DUNWICH HEATH AND MINSMERE BEACH

13/6/99 Tel: 01728 648505

A weekend of fish dishes served in the Restaurant.

Conservation Parks

Alice in Wonderland

12/6/99 FRAMLINGHAM CASTLE

13/6/99 Tel: 01728 724189

Labyrinth Productions. Follow Alice and White Rabbit as they go through Wonderland, meeting all manner of weird, wonderful and totally mad characters. A£4.00 C£2.00 Concessions£3.00

Castles

Transport Festival

12/6/99 NENE VALLEY RAILWAY

13/6/99 Tel: 01780 784444

Full steam ahead for a fascinating day out

Railways Steam/Light

Diesel Gala

12/6/99 NORTH NORFOLK RAILWAY

13/6/99 Tel: 01263 822045

Everything for the diesel enthusiast including an increased service of trains

Railways Steam/Light

Herbaeceous Borders with Daphne Ledward

13/6/99 BUTTERFLY AND WILDLIFE PARK

13/6/99 Tel: 01406 363833

TV & Radio personality Daphne Ledward at the Park all day with questions and answers sessions

Wildlife Parks

Clubmans Bikes (DPMC)

13/6/99 CADWELL PARK CIRCUIT

13/6/99 Tel: 01507 343248

All classes of national solo motorcycles and sidecars. Club Circuit, Grade-E. On the Gate: £10.00-£28.00. In Advance: Non £8.00-£25.00, Club £7.00-£22.00. Two Day Pass: Non £11.00-£30.00, Club £10.00-£27.00. Three Day Pass: Non £32.00, Club £29.00. Qualifying: £5.00-£14.00. C£Free. Programme £Free-£5.00. Seating (BH): £Free-£8.00. Group Tickets: Non £90.00-£95.00, Club £80.00-£85.00. Season Ticket Inc. of Club Membership: £135.00. You can buy your tickets for any of the 1999 events in

Further more detailed information on the attractions listed can be found in Best Guides *Visitor Attractions* Guide under the classifications shown

advance any time up to 4 days before an event and make a saving, Tel: 0870 60 60 611

Motor Racing Circuit

Botanical Sandlings
13/6/99 DUNWICH HEATH AND MINSMERE BEACH
13/6/99 Tel: 01728 648505
Secret sandlings walk. Please call for further information.

Conservation Parks

Rural Pastimes
13/6/99 EUSTON HALL
13/6/99 Tel: 01842 766366
Country Fair in Euston Park, many attractions to suit all tastes

Historic Houses & Gardens

National Garden Scheme Day
13/6/99 FELBRIGG HALL
13/6/99 Tel: 01263 837444
Your visit to the gardens at Felbrigg Hall will contribute to the upkeep of local charities through the national fund raising scheme. Please find time to visit us today. Usual admission

Historic Houses & Gardens

Bugs and Beasties
13/6/99 HATFIELD FOREST
13/6/99 Tel: 01279 870678
Come along and discover the secret world of the bugs and beasties of Hatfield Forest. Commences 14.00-16.00. Tickets: A£2.00 C£1.00 Family Ticket (A2+C2)£5.00. Car Park £3.00 NT members £Free. Please note that you must book for all events except where stated otherwise. Please send a cheque payable to National Trust, along with an s.a.e. for your tickets.

Forests

'Much Ado About Nothing'
13/6/99 HATFIELD HOUSE
13/6/99 Tel: 01707 262823
Shakespeare in the park. Theatre set-up perform in the afternoon. Tel: 01707 262823 for further information

Historic Houses & Gardens

Vintage Vehicle Rally
13/6/99 LINCOLN CASTLE
13/6/99 Tel: 01522 511068
The Lincolnshire Vintage Vehicle Society's summer rally, now a regular feature of the Castle's event programme. Normal admission applies

Castles

Luton Festival of Transport 1999

13/6/99 **Luton Festival of Transport 1999**
13/6/99 Tel: 01582 876083
Veteran, vintage and classic cars, plus other transport: buses, commercials, fire engines etc. Time: 10.00-17.00. Heritage Centre: open all day. Cost: Admission charge. Car Park £Free. Tickets available on the day.

Festivals

Championship Race Day (BRSCC)
13/6/99 SNETTERTON CIRCUIT
13/6/99 Tel: 01953 887303
Programme to be confirmed. Full Circuit, Grade-D. On the Gate: £10.00-£28.00. In Advance: Non £8.00-£25.00, Club £7.00-£22.00. Two Day Pass: Non £11.00-£30.00, Club £10.00-£27.00. Three Day Pass: Non £32.00, Club £29.00. Qualifying: £5.00-£14.00. C£Free. Programme £Free-£5.00. Seating (BH): £Free-£8.00. Group Tickets: Non £90.00-£95.00, Club £80.00-£85.00. Season Ticket Inc. of Club Membership: £150.00. You can buy your tickets for any of the 1999 events in advance any time up to 4 days before an event and make a saving, Tel: 0870 60 60 611

Motor Racing Circuit

Afternoon Stroll
14/6/99 BLICKLING HALL
14/6/99 Tel: 01263 738030
Take a leisurely stroll through the countryside. An escorted walk for the less agile. Commences: 15.00. A£2.50 C£1.50. Bookings can be made by telephone, to the address, or in person.

Historic Houses & Gardens

Friends of Thomas The Tank Engine
14/6/99 COLNE VALLEY RAILWAY AND MUSEUM
27/6/99 Tel: 01787 461174
Thomas and around a dozen other Friends of Thomas visit the Railway. Many other games and activities available. Pre-booking essential

Railways

Beautiful Country Homes Day
15/6/99 WOLTERTON PARK
15/6/99 Tel: 01263 584175
Interior design, trade stalls and demonstrations

Historic Houses & Gardens

Garden Open Day
16/6/99 OXBURGH HALL, GARDEN AND ESTATE
16/6/99 Tel: 01366 328258
Meet the Gardener, tours of the workshop and greenhouse area, 11.30 &14.30, normal opening times and

admission charges apply

Historic Buildings

Mid-Summer, Mid-Week, Mystery Meander

17/6/99 ᴮʀɪᴅɢᴇ ᴄᴏᴛᴛᴀɢᴇ
17/6/99 Tel: 01206 298260

After a delicious cream tea at Bridge Cottage tea rooms set off for a glorious guided walk on a mid-summer's evening into Constable Country. Time: 16.00. Tickets: £6.50.

Historic Buildings

A Lady's Flower Basket At Ickworth

17/6/99 ɪᴄᴋᴡᴏʀᴛʜ ʜᴏᴜꜱᴇ ᴘᴀʀᴋ ᴀɴᴅ ɢᴀʀᴅᴇɴꜱ
17/6/99 Tel: 01284 735270

Ickworth celebrates summer with a demonstration of summer flower arranging and a country-house tea served in the conservatory of the East Wing Flower Garden. Time: 14.00-16.00. Cost: £8.50, booking essential, 01284 735270.

Historic Houses & Gardens

Wicken Wildlife Watch

17/6/99 ᴡɪᴄᴋᴇɴ ꜰᴇɴ (ɴᴛ) ɴᴀᴛᴜʀᴇ ʀᴇꜱᴇʀᴠᴇ
17/6/99 Tel: 01353 720274

Find out what lurks beneath the water at Wicken Fen in this session all about pond life. £0.25 for Watch members £1.00 for non-members. Please phone to book your place (8-12 years). 16.30-18.00

Nature Reserves

East of England Show

18/6/99 ᴇᴀꜱᴛ ᴏꜰ ᴇɴɢʟᴀɴᴅ ꜱʜᴏᴡɢʀᴏᴜɴᴅ
20/6/99 Tel: 01733 234451

Regional Agricultural event with a national reputation for excellence

Showgrounds

Thaxted Festival

18/6/99 ᴛʜᴀxᴛᴇᴅ ꜰᴇꜱᴛɪᴠᴀʟ 1999
11/7/99 Tel: 01371 831421

Concerts, recitals, and a wide variety of classical music and jazz. Weekends 19.30 / 20.00

Festivals

Lakeside Open Air Concert

19/6/99 ʙʟɪᴄᴋʟɪɴɢ ʜᴀʟʟ
19/6/99 Tel: 01263 738030

Last Night of the Proms by the Norfolk Symphony Orchestra. Bring picnics and seating. Commences: 18.30. Tickets A£11.00 C£5.00 in advance, £12.50 C£6.00 on the door. Bookings can be made by telephone, to the address, or in person.

Historic Houses & Gardens

Clubman Bikes (PEGASUS)

19/6/99 ᴄᴀᴅᴡᴇʟʟ ᴘᴀʀᴋ ᴄɪʀᴄᴜɪᴛ
19/6/99 Tel: 01507 343248

All classes of national solo motorcycles and sidecars. Club Circuit, Grade-E. On the Gate: £10.00-£28.00. In Advance: Non £8.00-£25.00, Club £7.00-£22.00. Two Day Pass: Non £11.00-£30.00, Club £10.00-£27.00. Three Day Pass: Non £32.00, Club £29.00. Qualifying: £5.00-£14.00. C£Free. Programme £Free-£5.00. Seating (BH): £Free-£8.00. Group Tickets: Non £90.00-£95.00, Club £80.00-£85.00. Season Ticket Inc. of Club Membership: £135.00. You can buy your tickets for any of the 1999 events in advance any time up to 4 days before an event and make a saving, Tel: 0870 60 60 611

Motor Racing Circuit

Sunset Display 2

19/6/99 ᴛʜᴇ ꜱʜᴜᴛᴛʟᴇᴡᴏʀᴛʜ ᴄᴏʟʟᴇᴄᴛɪᴏɴ
19/6/99 Tel: 0891 323310

The second of the Sunset Display series will feature the oldest of the aeroplanes from the Collection depicting the pioneering age of flight

Museum- Aviation

An Introduction to Dragonflies

19/6/99 ᴡɪᴄᴋᴇɴ ꜰᴇɴ (ɴᴛ) ɴᴀᴛᴜʀᴇ ʀᴇꜱᴇʀᴠᴇ
19/6/99 Tel: 01353 720274

A one day course learning about these fascinating creatures, their ecology and identification and the various species found at Wicken Fen. A£25.00 includes lunch, 10.00-17.00

Nature Reserves

Festival of Gardening

19/6/99 ʜᴀᴛꜰɪᴇʟᴅ ʜᴏᴜꜱᴇ
20/6/99 Tel: 01707 262823

17th annual garden spectacular. Time: 10.00-18.00. Cost: A£6.50 C£3.00 Group £5.50. Tel: 01707 262823 for further information

Historic Houses & Gardens

Search for Adventure

19/6/99 ʟɪɴᴄᴏʟɴ ᴄᴀꜱᴛʟᴇ
20/6/99 Tel: 01522 511068

A showcase for outdoor activities that can be found in Lincolnshire, for all ages. A chance to try canoeing, scuba diving, mountaineering, skiing, walking, and a host of other pastimes and activities all to be found within the borders of Lincolnshire. Admission A£3.00 C£1.00 Family Ticket £7.00

Castles

The History Man

19/6/99
20/6/99 ORFORD CASTLE   *Railways Steam/Light*

Tel: 01394 450472

Enjoy unusual guided tours with Brian McNerney, presenter of the BBC's popular History Man programmes. But be warned, his enthusiasm is notoriously contagious... and there is no antidote! Performing without costumes, props or even a safety net, he brings the past to life before your very eyes! A£3.00 C£1.50 Concessions£2.30

Castles

Lakeside Jazz Brunch

20/6/99
20/6/99 BLICKLING HALL

Tel: 01263 738030

A perfect combination of a summer afternoon, Jazz music and a great setting, bring a picnic and seating. Commences: 11.00-15.00. Tickets £6.00 in advance, £7.50 on the door. Bookings can be made by telephone, to the address, or in person.

Historic Houses & Gardens

Vintage Motorcycles (VMCC)

20/6/99
20/6/99 CADWELL PARK CIRCUIT

Tel: 01507 343248

All classes of vintage motorcycles. Full Circuit, Grade-D. On the Gate: £10.00-£28.00. In Advance: Non £8.00-£25.00, Club £7.00-£22.00. Two Day Pass: Non £11.00-£30.00, Club £10.00-£27.00. Three Day Pass: Non £32.00, Club £29.00. Qualifying: £5.00-£14.00. C£Free. Programme £Free-£5.00. Seating (BH): £Free-£8.00. Group Tickets: Non £90.00-£95.00, Club £80.00-£85.00. Season Ticket Inc. of Club Membership: £135.00. You can buy your tickets for any of the 1999 events in advance any time up to 4 days before an event and make a saving, Tel: 0870 60 60 611

Motor Racing Circuit

Father's Day Lunch

20/6/99
20/6/99 FELBRIGG HALL

Tel: 01263 837444

Special Father's Day lunch in the Park Restaurant. Price: £11.95 (three courses with a special gift for Dad). Please book direct with the restaurant 01263 838237.

Historic Houses & Gardens

Fathers' Day

20/6/99
20/6/99 LEIGHTON BUZZARD RAILWAY

Tel: 01525 373888 (24hours)

Treat Dad to a train ride and free loco ride (subject to availability). Small steam locos double-heading passenger trains

My Lady's Amble

20/6/99
20/6/99 OXBURGH HALL, GARDEN AND ESTATE

Tel: 01366 328258

Meet in the orchard for an amble through the Garden and My Lady's Wood with Head Gardener Graham Donachie, followed by "brunch" of sausage, bacon and mushrooms on cheese bread. Tea or coffee. Time: 10.00. Ticket: £6.50, booking essential

Historic Buildings

Summer Solstice Sunset Stroll

20/6/99 RYE HOUSE MARSH AND RYE MEADS MEADOWS

20/6/99 Tel: 01992 460031

Make the most of one of the longest days of the year; your last opportunity for a visit to the reserve in the quiet of the evening. 19.00-21.00

Nature Reserves

Aston Martin Race Day (AMOC)

20/6/99
20/6/99 SNETTERTON CIRCUIT

Tel: 01953 887303

Ferrari Maranello, Intermarque, Pre War / Felthams / 50's sports, Anglo-American, Formula Junior, Flemings, Austin Healeys, Post War Astons, MGCC Anglia Phoenix, Porsche v Ferrari Challenge. Full Circuit, Grade-D. On the Gate: £10.00-£28.00. In Advance: Non £8.00-£25.00, Club £7.00-£22.00. Two Day Pass: Non £11.00-£30.00, Club £10.00-£27.00. Three Day Pass: Non £32.00, Club £29.00. Qualifying: £5.00-£14.00. C£Free. Programme £Free-£5.00. Seating (BH): £Free-£8.00. Group Tickets: Non £90.00-£95.00, Club £80.00-£85.00. Season Ticket Inc. of Club Membership: £150.00. You can buy your tickets for any of the 1999 events in advance any time up to 4 days before an event and make a saving, Tel: 0870 60 60 611

Motor Racing Circuit

Clifftop Classics

20/6/99 SOUTHEND ON SEA BOROUGH COUNCIL

20/6/99 Tel: 01702 215166

'Classic Brass' The Southend Band and a Guest Band will be performing at the Cliffs Bandstand at 19.00. Ticket prices to be confirmed. Box Office and credit card bookings: 01702 343605/215120. Restaurant and bar facilities available

Festivals

Storytelling

| 20/6/99 | TATTERSHALL CASTLE |
| 20/6/99 | Tel: 01526 342543 |

Storytelling for adults and children by
Polly Howat from 14.00

Castles

Great Annual Recreation of Tudor Life

| 20/6/99 | KENTWELL HALL |
| 11/7/99 | Tel: 01787 310207 |

Life at Kentwell in the year 1600. Other
weekdays during these three weeks are
for school parties only - please call for
Schools booking pack. Sat, Sun & Fri 3
July. Other weekdays during these three
weeks are for school parties only -
please phone for Schools Booking Pack.
Time: 11.00-17.00, Fri, Sat & Sun only 2
& 9 July. Prices: A£11.25 C£8.00
OAPs£9.75. Pre-booked groups 20+ 20%
discount

Historic Houses & Gardens

Longest Day Celebration

| 21/6/99 | HATFIELD FOREST |
| 21/6/99 | Tel: 01279 870678 |

Join us on a walk to experience the
Forest at its most beautiful, at the start
of our summertime!. Commences: 06.00-
08.00. Tickets: £2.00 C£1.00 Family
Ticket (A2+C2)£5.00. Please note that
you must book for all events except
where stated otherwise. Please send a
cheque payable to National Trust, along
with an s.a.e. for your tickets.

Forests

Arab Horse Race Meeting

| 21/6/99 | HUNTINGDON STEEPLECHASES LTD |
| 21/6/99 | Tel: 01480 453373 |

Members £13.00 Paddock £10.00 Course
£5.00 C(0-16)£Free

Racecourses

Garden Tour - Summer

| 24/6/99 | ANGLESEY ABBEY, GARDENS AND LODE MILL |
| 24/6/99 | Tel: 01223 811200 |

Demonstrations of the wide range of
machingery used on Anglesey Abbey's
35 acres of lawns, and the application of
fertiliser. Tour of garden included led by
Richard Ayres. Time: 18.30. Tickets £5.00
(including National Trust members), all
ticket applications should be addressed
to The Property Manager and include
sae to: Anglesey Abbey, Gardens and
Lode Mill, Quy Road, Lode, Cambridge
CB5 9EJ

Historic Houses & Gardens

Comedy of Errors

| 25/6/99 | MANNINGTON GARDENS AND |

| 25/6/99 | COUNTRYSIDE |
| | Tel: 01263 584175 |

Outdoor Shakespeare by the Rain or
Shine Theatre

Gardens

Thomas' Birthday Party Weekend

| 25/6/99 | NENE VALLEY RAILWAY |
| 27/6/99 | Tel: 01780 784444 |

Help Thomas celebrate his Birthday in
style, advance booking necessary

Railways Steam/Light

Pudding Sampling

| 26/6/99 | DUNWICH HEATH AND MINSMERE BEACH |
| 26/6/99 | Tel: 01728 648505 |

A light meal followed by many pudding
tastings with an introduction and
demonstration. Time: 18.00. Tickets:
£12.95

Conservation Parks

Snake Encounter

| 26/6/99 | LINTON ZOOLOGICAL GARDENS |
| 26/6/99 | Tel: 01223 891308 |

Meet 'Emily' or 'Kaa,' one of our South
American Boa constrictors at 15.30. You
will discover that they are not cold and
slimy but really quite nice creatures after
all!

Zoos- Conservation

Introduction to Grasses

| 26/6/99 | WICKEN FEN (NT) NATURE RESERVE |
| 26/6/99 | Tel: 01353 720274 |

A one day course learning about what is
often perceived to be a difficult group of
plants. A one day course learning about
these fascinating creatures, their ecology and identification and the various
species found at Wicken Fen. A£25.00
includes lunch, 10.00-17.00

Nature Reserves

The Lion, the Witch and the Wardrobe

| 26/6/99 | AUDLEY END HOUSE |
| 27/6/99 | Tel: 01799 522399 |

An old classic performed by Labyrinth
Productions. A£4.00 C£2.00
Concessions£3.00

Historical Remains

750 M/C Race Day (750 M/C)

| 26/6/99 | CADWELL PARK CIRCUIT |
| 27/6/99 | Tel: 01507 343248 |

Hot Hatch, Formula 4, Kit Cars, 750
Trophy, Formula Vee x2, 750 Formula.
Club Circuit, Grade-D. On the Gate:
£10.00-£28.00. In Advance: Non £8.00-
£25.00, Club £7.00-£22.00. Two Day
Pass: Non £11.00-£30.00, Club £10.00-
£27.00. Three Day Pass: Non £32.00,
Club £29.00. Qualifying: £5.00-£14.00.

C£Free. Programme £Free-£5.00.
Seating (BH): £Free-£8.00. Group
Tickets: Non £90.00-£95.00, Club
£80.00-£85.00. Season Ticket Inc. of
Club Membership: £135.00. You can buy
your tickets for any of the 1999 events in
advance any time up to 4 days before an
event and make a saving, Tel: 0870 60
60 611

Motor Racing Circuit

Pudding Weekend

26/6/99　DUNWICH HEATH AND MINSMERE BEACH
27/6/99　Tel: 01728 648505
A weekend of puddings in the
Restaurant

Conservation Parks

Tudor Rebellion and Repression

26/6/99　FRAMLINGHAM CASTLE
27/6/99　Tel: 01728 724189
Tudor re-enactment performed by Bills &
Bows. A£4.00 C£2.00 Concessions£3.00

Castles

Family Entertainment

26/6/99　HEDINGHAM CASTLE
27/6/99　Tel: 01787 460261
Entertainment with Brouhaha, plus falconry displays. Essex Yeomanry Brass
Band play Sunday afternoon with
Strawberries and Cream down by the
lake

Castles

Championship Bikes (NEW ERA)

26/6/99　SNETTERTON CIRCUIT
27/6/99　Tel: 01953 887303
All classes of national solo motorcycles
and sidecars. Full Circuit, Grade-D. On
the Gate: £10.00-£28.00. In Advance:
Non £8.00-£25.00, Club £7.00-£22.00.
Two Day Pass: Non £11.00-£30.00, Club
£10.00-£27.00. Three Day Pass: Non
£32.00, Club £29.00. Qualifying: £5.00-
£14.00. C£Free. Programme £Free-£5.00.
Seating (BH): £Free-£8.00. Group
Tickets: Non £90.00-£95.00, Club
£80.00-£85.00. Season Ticket Inc. of
Club Membership: £150.00. You can buy
your tickets for any of the 1999 events in
advance any time up to 4 days before an
event and make a saving, Tel: 0870 60
60 611

Motor Racing Circuit

National Southern Rose Show

26/6/99　THE GARDENS OF THE ROSE (ROYAL
　　　　　NATIONAL ROSE SOCIETY)
27/6/99　Tel: 01727 850461
The first national show of this year held
in the South of England

Gardens- Roses

Moth Club Charity Flying Days

26/6/99　THE SHUTTLEWORTH COLLECTION
27/6/99　Tel: 0891 323310
Not a flying display this weekend, but a
chance to buy a flight in a Tiger Moth,
Puss Moth, Hornet Moth or Leopard
Moth for all those fascinated by these
aircraft from the '20s and '30s

Museum- Aviation

National Gardens Scheme Day

27/6/99　ANGLESEY ABBEY, GARDENS AND LODE
　　　　　MILL
27/6/99　Tel: 01223 811200
Al proceeds for the National Gardens
Scheme fund. Normal admission charges
apply.

Historic Houses & Gardens

Wild Walk at Flatford

27/6/99　BRIDGE COTTAGE
27/6/99　Tel: 01206 298260
A walk with the warden looking at the
wildlife in this famous area. There will be
a pond dip in the millstream by Willy
Lott's House, its your chance to find out
what exactly is under the water in The
Haywain view! The afternoon will finish
with a cream tea in the tea rooms. Time:
14.00 at the Dry Dock at Flatford.
Tickets: A£5.00 C£4.00.

Historic Buildings

Euston Hall and Garden Open

27/6/99　EUSTON HALL
27/6/99　Tel: 01842 766366
Garden and Hall Open Day 14.30-17.00

Historic Houses & Gardens

Guided Walk

27/6/99　ORFORD NESS
27/6/99　Tel: 01394 450900
Walk with the Warden looking at the
many varied aspects of this unique site.
Meet: 10.00 prompt at Orford Quay.
Depart approx: 16.00. Cost: £12.50 for
all. Maximum 24 people. Bring suitable
clothing for the weather. Bring own food
and drink.

Nature Reserves

National Garden Scheme Day

27/6/99　OXBURGH HALL, GARDEN AND ESTATE
27/6/99　Tel: 01366 328258
Proceeds go to the Natioanl Gardens
Scheme. Time: 11.00. Normal opening
times and admission charges for entry to
the House and Garden. Garden only
admission: A£2.00 C£0.50

Historic Buildings

Concert in the Park

27/6/99
27/6/99 **SOUTHEND ON SEA BOROUGH COUNCIL**
Tel: 01702 215166
Concert in Priory Park featuring the
Royal Philharmonic Orchestra and Grand
Fireworks Finale. Gates open at 16.00,
entertainment from 18.00, main concert
at 20.00. Tickets £15.00 in advance
C(under 12)Half price. Ticket Hotline:
01702 207409. Catering and bar facilities available

Festivals

Wildflower Walk
27/6/99 **WICKEN FEN (NT) NATURE RESERVE**
27/6/99 Tel: 01353 720274
Experience the wildflowers of the Fen at
their best. 14.00-16.00. A£3.75 C£2.50

Nature Reserves

Cotswold Morris Dancing
27/6/99 **WREST PARK GARDENS**
27/6/99 Tel: 01525 860152
Traditional style Cotswold morris dancing to enjoy. A£3.20 C£1.60
Concessions£2.40

Gardens

Leighton Buzzard Railway 80th Birthday
27/6/99 **LEIGHTON BUZZARD RAILWAY**
28/6/99 Tel: 01525 373888 (24hours)
Come along to the year's big party!
Visiting loco, and lots of trains on the
move. Historical cavalcade on Saturday
evening. Classic vehicles rally on Sunday

Railways Steam/Light

Vineyard Open Days
27/6/99 **ICKWORTH HOUSE PARK AND GARDENS**
26/9/99 Tel: 01284 735270
On the last Sunday of each month the
creators of Ickworth's vineyard, Jillian
Simms and Charles Macready open the
vineyard to visitors. Explore the vineyard
trail and meet Jillian and Charles over a
tasting of Ickworth Walled Garden
wines. Time: 10.00-16.00, 27 June, 25
July, 22 August & 26 September.
Standard Park Admission. Self-guided
trail sheet provided on arrival in park,
plus £2.50 for wine tasting at Vineyard,
C£0.50 for non-alcoholic grape juice.

Historic Houses & Gardens

Camfest
28/6/99 **CAMFEST 1999**
24/7/99 Tel: 01223 503333
Focus on as many different art forms as
possible. Art Galleries, Musicals, Opera,
Drama, Poetry Reading, Story Telling,
Children's workshops and much more.
Tickets available from Box Office: 01223

359547

Festivals

Royal Norfolk Show
30/6/99 **NORFOLK SHOW GROUND**
1/7/99 Tel: 01603 748931
Entertainment for all the family. Grand
Ring Programme which offers all day
long entertainment with majestic heavy
horses to tiny chicks. Dog show - judging takes place on both days of the
show. Fabulous Flower Show with stunning floral displays. Craft Fair and Trade
Stands including probably the largest
motor show in East Anglia. Superb Art
Exhibition with pictures and sculptures
for sale.

Showgrounds

Wisbech Rose Fair
30/6/99 **WISBECH ROSE FAIR 1999**
3/7/99 Tel: 01945 461393
One of the largest flower festivals in East
Anglia. See exotic blooms and traditional English blooms brought together in a
themed display set against the backdrop
of St Peter and St Pauls Church. Visit the
gardens and browse among stalls.
09.30-20.30 daily. Admission Free

Festivals

Vikings in Lincolnshire
1/7/99 **TATTERSHALL CASTLE**
31/8/99 Tel: 01526 342543
An exhibition from Lincolnshire County
Council. Dates to be confirmed

Castles

Market Rasen Fixture
2/7/99 **MARKET RASEN RACECOURSE**
2/7/99 Tel: 01673 843434
First race: 14.10. Please call for further
information

Racecourses

VHF and UHF Radio Competition
2/7/99 **DUNWICH HEATH AND MINSMERE BEACH**
4/7/99 Tel: 01728 648505
Co-ordinated between all the national
radio societies of Europe. Represented
by The De Montfort University Amateur
Radio Society, Leicester. 01455 552648

Conservation Parks

Festival Fortnight
2/7/99 **FESTIVAL FORTNIGHT 1999**
18/7/99 Tel: 01908 610526
Concerts: classical, big band, jazz,
drama, dance and morris dancers, procession of floats, displays, stalls, workshops, children's entertainment, funfair,
exhibitions, barbecue and history walks.
Held at various venues within Newport

Further more detailed information on the attractions listed can be found
in Best Guides *Visitor Attractions* Guide under the classifications shown

Pagnell: Swan Hotel, Lovat Hall, Tickford Abbey and others.

Festivals

Cromwell's Head and its Curious History

2/7/99 CROMWELL MUSEUM
26/9/99 Tel: 01480 425830

Oliver Cromwell Exhibition Tue-Fri 11.00-13.00, &14.00-17.00, Sat & Sun 11.00-13.00 & 14.00-16.00

Museum- Local History

Concert in the Park with Fireworks

3/7/99 WIMPOLE HALL
3/7/99 Tel: 01223 207257

Open Air Concert in the Park with Buddy Holly and the Cricketers, bring picnic and rugs. Tickets £14.00 in advance. Please apply to the property for booking, either by post with an s.a.e. or call: 01223 207001/207257

Country Parks

Stud Tour

3/7/99 WOBURN ABBEY
3/7/99 Tel: 01525 290666

Stately Homes

Wildflower Weekend

3/7/99 BUTTERFLY AND WILDLIFE PARK
4/7/99 Tel: 01406 363833

The Butterfly Park is one of the largest growers of wildflowers - see then all at close quarters

Wildlife Parks

Surgeons Through the Ages

3/7/99 CASTLE ACRE PRIORY
4/7/99 Tel: 01760 755394

Fascinating yet gruesome insight into medical care, cause, effect and treatments! Visitors are advised to check with the venue closer to the event. A£4.00 C£2.00 Concessions£3.00

Priory

The History Man

3/7/99 DENNY ABBEY AND THE FARMLAND MUSEUM
4/7/99 Tel: 01223 860489

Enjoy unusual guided tours with Brian McNerney, presenter of the BBC's popular History Man programmes. But be warned, his enthusiasm is notoriously contagious... and there is no antidote! Performing without costumes, props or even a safety net, he brings the past to life before your very eyes!

Abbeys

Wildflower Walk

4/7/99 HATFIELD FOREST
4/7/99 Tel: 01279 870678

A chance to discover the secret properties, folklore and ecology of the wildflowers of the Forest. Commences 14.00-16.00. Tickets: £2.00 C£1.00 Family Ticket (A2+C2)£5.00. Car park £3.00 NT members £Free. Please note that you must book for all events except where stated otherwise. Please send a cheque payable to National Trust, along with an s.a.e. for your tickets.

Forests

Access Day for Visitors with Disabilities

4/7/99 ORFORD NESS
4/7/99 Tel: 01394 450900

Special arrangements to enable visits to Orford Ness. Time: 10.00-17.00. Cost: £Free.

Nature Reserves

Marshland and Minibeasts

4/7/99 RYE HOUSE MARSH AND RYE MEADS MEADOWS
4/7/99 Tel: 01992 460031

Meet and learn about our many creepy-crawlies. Search under stones and logs, in bushes and in the mud and water! Pre-booking essential. 10.00-12.00.

Nature Reserves

Clifftop Classics

4/7/99 SOUTHEND ON SEA BOROUGH COUNCIL
4/7/99 Tel: 01702 215166

Strauss and Viennese Concert with Southend Festival Orchestra. Ticket price £10.00. Held at the Cliffs Bandstand at 19.00. Box Office and credit card bookings: 01702 343605/215120. Restaurant and bar facilities available

Festivals

Stowe Model Yacht Regatta

4/7/99 STOWE LANDSCAPE GARDENS
4/7/99 Tel: 01280 822850

A delightful day of yachting (miniature size), call venue for further details

Gardens

Summer Air Show

4/7/99 THE SHUTTLEWORTH COLLECTION
4/7/99 Tel: 0891 323310

There is usually a large gathering of specialist car clubs at this event to add interest to the varied flying display. The Shuttle Mansion House will be open 14.00-17.00 for visitors to se the splendour of this home.

Museum- Aviation

Butterfly Walk

4/7/99	**WICKEN FEN (NT) NATURE RESERVE**
4/7/99	Tel: 01353 720274

A tour of the Fen with Warden Ralph
Sargeant, looking at the different
species of butterflies and their habitat.
A£3.75 C£2.50. 14.00-16.00

Nature Reserves

Concert in the Park with Fireworks

4/7/99	**WIMPOLE HALL**
4/7/99	Tel: 01223 207257

The Chris Barber Jazz and Blues Band
with Paul Jones, bring a picnic and a rug.
Tickets £14.00 in advance. Please apply
to the property for booking, either by
post with an s.a.e. or call: 01223
207001/207257

Country Parks

The British Rose Festival

6/7/99	**THE GARDENS OF THE ROSE (ROYAL NATIONAL ROSE SOCIETY)**
11/7/99	Tel: 01727 850461

The principal British Rose event of the
year

Gardens- Roses

Wildlife in the Garden

7/7/99	**FELBRIGG HALL**
7/7/99	Tel: 01263 837444

A special walk and talk with one of the
National Trust's gardening team at
Felbrigg Hall. The evening includes a
glass of wine and a tour of the walled
garden. Commences: 18.00. Tickets:
£6.00. Bookings can be made by telephone, to the address, or in person.

Historic Houses & Gardens

Ely Folk Festival

9/7/99	**ELY FOLK FESTIVAL 1999**
9/7/99	Tel: 01353 741032

Various bands, Morris dancers, real ale
bar, concerts, sessions, workshops and
children's workshops. Fri Eve £8.00 Sat
All day £14.00 Sun All day £12.00

Festivals

International Organ Festival

9/7/99	**ST. ALBANS CATHEDRAL**
17/7/99	Tel: 01727 860780

Please telephone 01727 846126 for further information

Cathedrals

**Wildlife Walk and Supper: Summer
Barbeque and Nightjar Walk**

10/7/99	**DUNWICH HEATH AND MINSMERE BEACH**
10/7/99	Tel: 01728 648505

An open air supper with a selection of
meat and vegetarian meals with the
opportunity to enjoy a guided walk and
encounter the mystical Nightjar bird.

Time: 19.30. Tickets: £3.00 for walk,
food individually priced

Conservation Parks

**The Comedy of Errors by William
Shakespeare**

10/7/99	**ICKWORTH HOUSE PARK AND GARDENS**
10/7/99	Tel: 01284 735270

Open air performance in Ickworth's stunning Italian Garden by Mad Dogs and
Englishmen Theatre Company. Bring
Picnics, waterproofs and cushions (seating not provided). No barbeques. Prices
to be advised. Booking essential on
01284 735270.

Historic Houses & Gardens

**Transatlantic Challenge (TRANS CHAL-
LENGE)**

10/7/99	**CADWELL PARK CIRCUIT**
11/7/99	Tel: 01507 343248

Programme to be confirmed. Full Circuit,
Grade-D. On the Gate: £10.00-£28.00. In
Advance: Non £8.00-£25.00, Club £7.00-
£22.00. Two Day Pass: Non £11.00-
£30.00, Club £10.00-£27.00. Three Day
Pass: Non £32.00, Club £29.00.
Qualifying: £5.00-£14.00. C£Free.
Programme £Free-£5.00. Seating (BH):
£Free-£8.00. Group Tickets: Non £90.00-
£95.00, Club £80.00-£85.00. Season
Ticket Inc. of Club Membership: £135.00.
You can buy your tickets for any of the
1999 events in advance any time up to 4
days before an event and make a saving,
Tel: 0870 60 60 611

Motor Racing Circuit

Bikes

10/7/99	**DUNWICH HEATH AND MINSMERE BEACH**
11/7/99	Tel: 01728 648505

Mosquito Bikes, London Cycle Ride.
Possible Bike Fair and events on Sunday
11th.

Conservation Parks

Sheepdog Demonstrations

10/7/99	**FRAMLINGHAM CASTLE**
11/7/99	Tel: 01728 724189

Enjoyable demonstrations of sheepdogs,
sheep and geese. From 12.00. A£3.50
C£1.80 Concessions£2.50

Castles

Grimsthrope Antiques Fair

10/7/99	**GRIMSTHORPE CASTLE**
11/7/99	Tel: 01778 591205

Please call venue for further information

Historic Houses & Gardens

Flying Legends

10/7/99
11/7/99
IMPERIAL WAR MUSEUM, DUXFORD
Tel: 0891 516816 premium line
Europe's premier Warbirds Air Show, featuring some of the century's finest combat aircraft, is unique weekend of aviation legends. A£15.00 Concessions£7.50 OAPs£12.00. Advanced Tickets: A12.50 Concessions£6.25 OAPs£10.00. Advanced Coach Rates: £450.00 closing date 28.6.99. Advance tickets for this event maybe purchased by credit card through TicketMaster 24hrs, daily on 0990 344 4444, from Jan 1999
Museum- Aviation

SAM35 Vintage Gala
10/7/99
11/7/99
THE SHUTTLEWORTH COLLECTION
Tel: 0891 323310
Antique models and small scale flying make this a fascinating day for the model enthusiast. Usually some trade stands.
Museum- Aviation

Butterfly Flutterings
11/7/99
11/7/99
HATFIELD FOREST
Tel: 01279 870678
A chance to see and learn about the ecology of the many different butterflies you can find in the Forest and in your Garden. Tickets: £2.00 C£1.00 Family Ticket (A2+C2)£5.00.Car Park £3.00 NT members £Free. Please note that you must book for all events except where stated otherwise. Please send a cheque payable to National Trust, along with an s.a.e. for your tickets.
Forests

Bringing Together Archaeology and Conservation
11/7/99
11/7/99
LYVEDEN NEW BIELD
Tel: 01832 205358
A Summer walk including the Elizabethan water garden. Time: 14.00. Cost: £2.00, booking essential
Historic Houses

Clubmans Bikes (RETFORD)
11/7/99
11/7/99
SNETTERTON CIRCUIT
Tel: 01953 887303
All classes of national solo motorcycles and sidecars. Full Circuit, Grade-E. On the Gate: £10.00-£25.00. In Advance: Non £8.00-£25.00. Club £7.00-£22.00. Two Day Pass: Non £11.00-£30.00, Club £10.00-£27.00. Three Day Pass: Non £32.00, Club £29.00. Qualifying: £5.00-£14.00. Programme £Free-£5.00. Seating (BH): £Free-£8.00. Group Tickets: Non £90.00-£95.00, Club

£80.00-£85.00. Season Ticket Inc. of Club Membership: £150.00. You can buy your tickets for any of the 1999 events in advance any time up to 4 days before an event and make a saving, Tel: 0870 60 60 611
Motor Racing Circuit

Southend Sprint Triathlon
11/7/99
11/7/99
SOUTHEND ON SEA BOROUGH COUNCIL
Tel: 01702 215166
More than 300 entrants competing in a gruelling 750m sea swim, 20km cycle ride and a 5km run. For entry forms and further information please call 01702 610142. Held at Shoebury East Beach
Festivals

Identifying Sedges
11/7/99
11/7/99
WICKEN FEN (NT) NATURE RESERVE
Tel: 01353 720274
A one day course learning about what is often perceived to be a difficult group of plants A£25.00 includes lunch. 10.00-17.00
Nature Reserves

Bygones Day
11/7/99
11/7/99
WOLTERTON PARK
Tel: 01263 584175
Display and demonstrations. Historic vehicles and crafts
Historic Houses & Gardens

Behind the Scenes at Orford Ness
12/7/99
12/7/99
ORFORD NESS
Tel: 01394 450900
A chance to hear and see about management of a National Trust Property. Do Wardens just sit and watch birds all day? Come and see for yourself. Bring suitable clothing for the weather. Tea and coffee provided but bring your own lunch. Binoculars may be useful. Meet: 10.00 prompt at Orford Quay. Depart: approx. 16.00. Cost: £15.00 for all.
Nature Reserves

Scandal! Racing Frauds and Betting Coups
12/7/99
29/8/99
NATIONAL HORSERACING MUSEUM AND TOURS
Tel: 01638 667333
An exploration of frauds, doping, ringers, poisioning and much more - and how racing tries to prevent such scandals today.
Museum- Horse racing

Wildlife in the Woods
14/7/99
14/7/99
FELBRIGG HALL
Tel: 01263 837444
A special walk and talk with one of the

National Trust's forestry team at Felbrigg Hall. The evening includes a glass of wine and a tour of the Felbrigg Great Wood. Commences: 18.00. Tickets: £6.00. Bookings can be made by telephone, to the address, or in person.

Historic Houses & Gardens

Focus on Bats

14/7/99 HATFIELD FOREST

14/7/99 Tel: 01279 870678

Come along to see and hear some of the batty inhabitants of the Forest. Bring a torch if you have one. Commences 20.30-22.30. Tickets: £2.00 C£1.00 Family Ticket (A2+C2)£5.00. Please note that you must book for all events except where stated otherwise. Please send a cheque payable to National Trust, along with an s.a.e. for your tickets.

Forests

Garden Open Day

14/7/99 OXBURGH HALL, GARDEN AND ESTATE

14/7/99 Tel: 01366 328258

Meet the Gardener, tours of the workshop and greenhouse area, 11.30 &14.30, normal opening times and admission charges apply

Historic Buildings

Southend Cricket Festival

14/7/99 SOUTHEND ON SEA BOROUGH COUNCIL

18/7/99 Tel: 01702 215166

14-17 July Essex V Middlesex, 18 July Essex V Hampshire. Held at Southchurch Park. Catering and bar facilities available. For further information please telephone 01245 252420

Festivals

Wicken Wildlife Watch

15/7/99 WICKEN FEN (NT) NATURE RESERVE

15/7/99 Tel: 01353 720274

Find out what lurks beneath the water at Wicken Fen in this session all about pond life. £0.25 for Watch members £1.00 for non-members. Please phone to book your place (8-12 years). 16.30-18.00

Nature Reserves

Open Air Music - Roses & Heart Strings

16/7/99 ANGLESEY ABBEY, GARDENS AND LODE MILL

16/7/99 Tel: 01223 811200

The music of Rogers and Hart perform 19.30, tickets available from Jane Gaskell, The Animal Health Trust, PO Box 5, Newmarket, Suffolk CB8 8JH, Tel: 01638 751000

Historic Houses & Gardens

Autotrader British Touring Car Championships - Night Races (TOCA)

16/7/99 SNETTERTON CIRCUIT

17/7/99 Tel: 01953 887303

Touring Cars x 2, including a floodlit night time race, Formula Ford, Ford Fiestas, Formula Renault, Renault Spiders, Formula Vauxhall Junior, Vauxhall Vectras. Full Circuit, Grade-A. On the Gate: £10.00-£28.00. In Advance: Non £8.00-£25.00, Club £7.00-£22.00. Two Day Pass: Non £11.00-£30.00, Club £10.00-£27.00. Three Day Pass: Non £32.00, Club £29.00. Qualifying: £5.00-£14.00. C£Free. Programme £Free-£5.00. Seating (BH): £Free-£8.00. Group Tickets: Non £90.00-£95.00, Club £80.00-£85.00. Season Ticket Inc. of Club Membership: £150.00. You can buy your tickets for any of the 1999 events in advance any time up to 4 days before an event and make a saving, Tel: 0870 60 60 611

Motor Racing Circuit

Hacheston Rose Festival 1999

16/7/99 HACHESTON ROSE FESTIVAL 1999

18/7/99 Tel: 01473 622807

A well-established local festival. Each year a different flower club decorates the church bringing their own ideas and individuality to the overall design. This year the Orwell Flower Club from Ipswich is doing the honours. As well as the Church, there will be a craft fair to visit, housed in a marquee close by. A number of different events are taking place over the weekend. On the Friday evening, there is a concert in the church given by pupils from Thomas Mills High School in Framlingham. Alternatively, there is a Line Dance taking place in the marquee. On Saturday evening there is an organ recital given by Christopher Manners at 19.30. Rounding off the weekend, the Gyppeswyck Garland, a ladies' clog dancing side, will be dancing in the churchyard on Sunday afternoon and after the Grand Draw there will be a Songs of Praise at 18.00.

Festivals

International Dance and Music Festival 1999

16/7/99 INTERNATIONAL DANCE AND MUSIC FESTIVAL 1999

18/7/99 Tel: 01476 406155

After six successful years at Grimsthorpe

Castle we are moving to Belton House, Nr Grantham. A weekend packed full of concerts, ceilidhs, performances and workshops from some of the best known folk musicians and dance companies plus international artists. We also have a children's tent, craft and stalls, great food and drink plus free camping in the delightful setting of Belton House.

Festivals

Open Air Music
17/7/99 ANGLESEY ABBEY, GARDENS AND LODE
17/7/99 MILL
Tel: 01223 811200
The Carnival Band return from the spirit of carnival to 'turn the world upside down.' Performance starts: 20.00, gates open: 18.30. Seating is not provided, please bring rugs or chairs, picnics welcome, early booking discount of 20% available for postal bookings received by 31 May, tickets £8.50, in advance £10.50 on the day, all ticket applications should be addressed to The Property Manager and include sae to: Anglesey Abbey, Gardens and Lode Mill, Quy Road, Lode, Cambridge CB5 9EJ

Historic Houses & Gardens

Secret Sandlinngs Walk: Moths
17/7/99 DUNWICH HEATH AND MINSMERE BEACH
17/7/99 Tel: 01728 648505
For more details please contact 'The Sandling Project'. Tickets: £Free

Conservation Parks

Jazz Concert
17/7/99 FRAMLINGHAM CASTLE
17/7/99 Tel: 01728 724189
Performed by Wingfield Arts. Normal admission prices apply

Castles

Sunset Display 3
17/7/99 THE SHUTTLEWORTH COLLECTION
17/7/99 Tel: 0891 323310
During the evening, Shuttleworth Collection aeroplanes on view will range from World War II examples to the pioneers of flight and include one or two sole survivors from World War I

Museum- Aviation

Wildlife for Kids
17/7/99 WICKEN FEN (NT) NATURE RESERVE
17/7/99 Tel: 01353 720274
Learn all about the wildlife at Wicken Fen. A day packed with activities and fun for all the family. C£3.50. Bring an adult for Free! 11.00-17.00

Nature Reserves

Medieval Archery
17/7/99 CASTLE ACRE PRIORY
18/7/99 Tel: 01760 755394
Displays of skilled archery, weaponry and combat, plus shooting of a 14th century ballista. Mounted archer, knight and have-a-go archery. A£3.50 C£1.80 Concessions£2.50

Priory

Craft Fair
17/7/99 ELTON HALL
18/7/99 Tel: 01832 280468
50 stands of lovely handmade goods. All under cover in the picturesque Stable Block. Home-made refreshments. 10.00-17.00

Historic Houses & Gardens

A Tudor Revel
17/7/99 HATFIELD HOUSE
18/7/99 Tel: 01707 262823
Jousting, archery, craftsmen, jesters - a great day out! Cost: A£6.50 C£3.00 Group £5.50. Tel: 01707 262823 for further information

Historic Houses & Gardens

Englisc Ham
17/7/99 WEST STOW ANGLO SAXON VILLAGE
18/7/99 Tel: 01284 728718
Nothing to do with meat, but everything to do with being at home in the Anglo-Saxon village. A costumed family invite you to investigate their home. A£5.00 C&Concessions£4.00 Family Ticket 15.00. 10.00-17.00 Last entry 16.00

Archaeological Interest

Tech Team - Anglo-Saxon Boat Building Course
17/7/99 WEST STOW ANGLO SAXON VILLAGE
18/7/99 Tel: 01284 728718
A two day course with a leading expert in Anglo-Saxon woodwork. Help to make a replica of an Anglo-Saxon dugout boat! Numbers are limited, book early to avoid disappointment, closing date 3 July. A£50.00 Concessions£35.00. 10.30-16.30

Archaeological Interest

Village Spotlight: West Deeping
17/7/99 STAMFORD MUSEUM
2/10/99 Tel: 01780 766317
An exhibition looking at the life and history of the village of West Deeping

Museum- Local History

Open Air Music
18/7/99 ANGLESEY ABBEY, GARDENS AND LODE

MILL

18/7/99 Tel: 01223 811200

Amadeus Boldwicket's Red Hot Peppers Jazz Band perform 19.30, gates open 18.30, seating is not provided, please bring rugs or chairs, picnics welcome, tickets £8.50 in advance, £10.50 on the day, early booking discount of 20% available for postal bookings received by 31 May, all ticket applications should be addressed to The Property Manager and include sae to: Anglesey Abbey, Gardens and Lode Mill, Quy Road, Lode, Cambridge CB5 9EJ

Historic Houses & Gardens

Classic Car Show

18/7/99 **AUDLEY END HOUSE**

18/7/99 Tel: 01799 522399

Hundreds of classic vehicles on display, of all ages and marques. Automart, Autoglym, Concours, Autojumble. A£5.00 Concessions£4.00 C£2.00. (House extra, subject to capacity) EH Members Free

Historical Remains

Cadwell Super Cats (BRSCC)

18/7/99 **CADWELL PARK CIRCUIT**

18/7/99 Tel: 01507 343248

Caterham Superlights, Caterham Roadsports, Tomcat/Vento Challenge, Mighty Minis, Formula Ford 1600s, MGs. Full Circuit, Grade-D. On the Gate: £10.00-£28.00. In Advance: Non £8.00-£25.00, Club £7.00-£22.00. Two Day Pass: Non £11.00-£30.00, Club £10.00-£27.00. Three Day Pass: Non £32.00, Club £29.00. Qualifying: £5.00-£14.00. C£Free. Programme £Free-£5.00. Seating (BH): £Free-£8.00. Group Tickets: Non £90.00-£95.00, Club £80.00-£85.00. Season Ticket Inc. of Club Membership: £135.00. You can buy your tickets for any of the 1999 events in advance any time up to 4 days before an event and make a saving, Tel: 0870 60 60 611

Motor Racing Circuit

Songs of Praise on the Heath

18/7/99 **DUNWICH HEATH AND MINSMERE BEACH**

18/7/99 Tel: 01728 648505

An outside service surrounded by heath and sea. Time: 18.30. £Free, no booking required.

Conservation Parks

Classic Car Rally

18/7/99 **ICKWORTH HOUSE PARK AND GARDENS**

18/7/99 Tel: 01284 735270

Admire the sleek lines of Italian Classic cars displayed against the Italiante splendour of Ickworth's Rotunda. Time: 12.00-16.00. Standard Park Admission.

Historic Houses & Gardens

Symphony Concert Laser spectacular

18/7/99 **LINCOLN CASTLE**

18/7/99 Tel: 01522 511068

The Performing Arts Symphony Orchestra returns to Lincoln castle with a dynamic programme of music from outer space and a spectacular laser display finale. Tickets A£17.00 C(5-16)£10.00

Castles

Clifftop Classics

18/7/99 **SOUTHEND ON SEA BOROUGH COUNCIL**

18/7/99 Tel: 01702 215166

'Opera Gala and Proms finale' - Concert Southend Festival Orchestra and Chorus. Ticket price £10.00. Held at Cliffs Bandstand at 19.00. Box Office and credit card bookings: 01702 343605/215120. Restaurant and bar facilities available

Festivals

Wandering Musician

18/7/99 **TATTERSHALL CASTLE**

18/7/99 Tel: 01526 342543

Peter Bull entertains whilst wandering around Tattershall

Castles

Sedge Harvest Tour

18/7/99 **WICKEN FEN (NT) NATURE RESERVE**

18/7/99 Tel: 01353 720274

Sedge has been harvested at Wicken Fen since 1414. Learn all about it and have a go at harvesting it yourself with Warden Mark Cornel. Please bring gloves. A£3.75 C£2.50 14.00-16.00

Nature Reserves

Jaguar National Rally

18/7/99 **WOBURN ABBEY**

18/7/99 Tel: 01525 290666

Jaguar car enthusiasts National Rally day

Stately Homes

Barn Owl Sunday

18/7/99 **BUTTERFLY AND WILDLIFE PARK**

19/7/99 Tel: 01406 363833

This special day gives everyone the chance to handle a Barn owl. Two special 20 minute Barn owl talks will be given during the day by our resident falconer. Visit the Hawk and Owl Trust Stand, also an exhibition by the "World Owl Trust." Birds of Prey flying display at

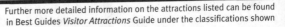

Further more detailed information on the attractions listed can be found in Best Guides *Visitor Attractions* Guide under the classifications shown

12.00 & 15.00

Wildlife Parks

Dick Francis Minibus Tour

20/7/99 NATIONAL HORSERACING MUSEUM AND TOURS

20/7/99 Tel: 01638 667333

Explore parts of Newmarket which are featured in the famous crime-writer's novels and learn more of his career. Lasts about 2 hours. Time: 14.00. Price: £5.00.

Museum- Horse racing

East of England Championship Dog Show

20/7/99 EAST OF ENGLAND SHOWGROUND

22/7/99 Tel: 01733 234451

Championship Dog Show event with the Peterborough Royal Foxhound Show on 21 July, and Harriers & Beagles Show on 22 July

Showgrounds

Wildlife in the House

21/7/99 FELBRIGG HALL

21/7/99 Tel: 01263 837444

A special walk and talk with one of the National Trust's housekeeping team at Felbrigg Hall. The evening includes a glass of wine and a tour of the house. Commences: 18.00. Tickets: £6.00. Bookings can be made by telephone, to the address, or in person.

Historic Houses & Gardens

Guided Walk

21/7/99 ORFORD NESS

21/7/99 Tel: 01394 450900

Walk with the Warden looking at the many varied aspects of this unique site. Meet: 10.00 prompt at Orford Quay. Depart approx. 16.00. Cost: £12.50 for all. Maximum 24 people. Bring suitable clothing for the weather. Bring own food and drink.

Nature Reserves

Theatre & Concert Week

21/7/99 KENTWELL HALL

25/7/99 Tel: 01787 310207

Please enquire for full programme

Historic Houses & Gardens

Royal National Rose Show

22/7/99 THE GARDENS OF THE ROSE (ROYAL NATIONAL ROSE SOCIETY)

25/7/99 Tel: 01727 850461

A completely new rose show to be held in Cheshire

Gardens- Roses

Twelfth Night

23/7/99 LINCOLN CASTLE

3/8/99 Tel: 01522 511068

The Lincoln Shakespeare Company celebrates its 20th Shakespearean production in their inimitable style, with an open-air performance of 'Twelfth Night,' one of the Bard's best loved plays. Admission by ticket only, price to be advised

Castles

School's Out - Summer Fun

23/7/99 CLEETHORPES HUMBER ESTUARY DISCOVERY CENTRE

8/9/99 Tel: 01472 323232

Ask for our special summer events leaflet for details of environmental games, plays, workshops and guided walks

Exhibition Centres

Derby Phoenix Bikes (DPMC)

24/7/99 CADWELL PARK CIRCUIT

24/7/99 Tel: 01507 343248

All classes of National solo motorcycles. Full Circuit, Grade-D. On the Gate: £10.00-£28.00. In Advance: Non £8.00-£25.00, Club £7.00-£22.00. Two Day Pass: Non £11.00-£30.00, Club £10.00-£27.00. Three Day Pass: Non £32.00, Club £29.00. Qualifying: £5.00-£14.00. C£Free. Programme £Free-£5.00. Seating (BH): £Free-£8.00. Group Tickets: Non £90.00-£95.00, Club £80.00-£85.00. Season Ticket Inc. of Club Membership: £135.00. You can buy your tickets for any of the 1999 events in advance any time up to 4 days before an event and make a saving, Tel: 0870 60 60 611

Motor Racing Circuit

National Archaeology Day

24/7/99 CHELMSFORD AND ESSEX REGIMENT MUSEUM

24/7/99 Tel: 01245 353066

Family activities on an archaeological theme. Admission Free

Museum- Local History

Countryside Fun Day

24/7/99 HATFIELD FOREST

24/7/99 Tel: 01279 870678

A wide variety of activities from pond dipping to woodland exploration, with many opportunities for you all to join in the fun! Commences 10.00-16.00. Small fee for some of the activities. No booking necessary. Car Park £3.00 NT members £Free.

Forests

Channel 4 Summer Special
24/7/99 MARKET RASEN RACECOURSE
24/7/99 Tel: 01673 843434
First race: 14.05. Please call for further
information
Racecourses

Concert
24/7/99 AUDLEY END HOUSE
25/7/99 Tel: 01799 522399
A musical concert with various performers. Normal admission prices apply.
Historical Remains

Norfolk Formula 3 (BARC)
24/7/99 SNETTERTON CIRCUIT
25/7/99 Tel: 01953 887303
British Formula 3 Championship,
Formula Europa Opel, Ginettas,
Westfields, BMWs, Gilera Scotters,
Celebrity Race. Full Circuit, Grade-C. On
the Gate: £10.00-£28.00. In Advance:
Non £8.00-£25.00, Club £7.00-£22.00.
Two Day Pass: Non £11.00-£30.00, Club
£10.00-£27.00. Three Day Pass: Non
£32.00, Club £29.00. Qualifying: £5.00-
£14.00. C£Free. Programme £Free-£5.00.
Seating (BH): £Free-£8.00. Group
Tickets: Non £90.00-£95.00, Club
£80.00-£85.00. Season Ticket Inc. of
Club Membership: £150.00. You can buy
your tickets for any of the 1999 events in
advance any time up to 4 days before an
event and make a saving, Tel: 0870 60
60 611
Motor Racing Circuit

Summer Festival
24/7/99 COLCHESTER ZOO
31/8/99 Tel: 01206 331292
Come along a join us at the Zoo for a
wonderful week of special activites
planned to keep all the family amused.
Zoos

**A Stour Valley Saunter In Constable
Country**
25/7/99 BRIDGE COTTAGE
25/7/99 Tel: 01206 298260
A sizzling brunch followed by John
Constable's views of the vale and visiting
one of his favourite villages, Dedham.
Time: 10.45. Tickets: £8.50.
Historic Buildings

Pegasus Clubmans Bikes (PEGASUS)
25/7/99 CADWELL PARK CIRCUIT
25/7/99 Tel: 01507 343248
All classes of national solo motorcycles
and sidecars. Full Circuit, Grade-E. On
the Gate: £10.00-£28.00. In Advance:
Non £8.00-£25.00, Club £7.00-£22.00.

Two Day Pass: Non £11.00-£30.00, Club
£10.00-£27.00. Three Day Pass: Non
£32.00, Club £29.00. Qualifying: £5.00-
£14.00. C£Free. Programme £Free-£5.00.
Seating (BH): £Free-£8.00. Group
Tickets: Non £90.00-£95.00, Club
£80.00-£85.00. Season Ticket Inc. of
Club Membership: £135.00. You can buy
your tickets for any of the 1999 events in
advance any time up to 4 days before an
event and make a saving, Tel: 0870 60
60 611
Motor Racing Circuit

Sandford Mill Open Day
25/7/99 CHELMSFORD AND ESSEX REGIMENT
MUSEUM
25/7/99 Tel: 01245 353066
Hands-on science exhibits and visiting
displays for all the family. Admission
Free; tel 01245 475498 for details.
Venue: Sandford Mill, Sandford Mill
Road, Chelmer Village
Museum- Local History

MD Foods Teddy Bears' Picnic
25/7/99 COLCHESTER ZOO
25/7/99 Tel: 01206 331292
Free entry for all under 5s who are
accompanied by their favourite teddy
bear. Best dressed teddy competition for
the bears plus a giant picnic with costumed characters
Zoos

St James' Traditional Fayre
25/7/99 DUNWICH HEATH AND MINSMERE BEACH
25/7/99 Tel: 01728 648505
Outside Cottages. Time: 10.00-16.00.
A£3.00 C£1.00.
Conservation Parks

Flint Knapping
25/7/99 GRIME'S GRAVES
25/7/99 Tel: 01842 810656
Stone age man returns to demonstrate
how he made tools, axes and arrowheads from flint. From 12.00. A£2.50
C£1.30 Concessions£1.90. EH Members
Free
Museum- Mining

National Garden Scheme Day
25/7/99 OXBURGH HALL, GARDEN AND ESTATE
25/7/99 Tel: 01366 328258
Proceeds go to the Natioanl Gardens
Scheme. Time: 11.00. Normal opening
times and admission charges for entry to
the House and Garden. Garden only
admission: A£2.00 C£0.50
Historic Buildings

Classic Car Run

Further more detailed information on the attractions listed can be found
in Best Guides *Visitor Attractions* Guide under the classifications shown

25/7/99 25/7/99	**SOUTHEND ON SEA BOROUGH COUNCIL** Tel: 01702 215166 Approximately 200 pre-1970 vehicles will set off from London and follow a route to Southend Seafront when they will be on display, bringing a touch of nostalgia with them. Display from 12.30 *Festivals*

Summer Activity Days

27/7/99 29/7/99	**WEST STOW ANGLO SAXON VILLAGE** Tel: 01284 728718 Have fun in the Country Park, please call for 01284 728718 for details of activities planned *Archaeological Interest*

Moonlight Madness

28/7/99 28/7/99	**HATFIELD FOREST** Tel: 01279 870678 Join us to experience the Forest at night, hear the calls and screeches. Bring a torch. Commences: 22.00-Midnight. Tickets: £2.00 C£1.00 Family Ticket (A2+C2)£5.00. Please note that you must book for all events except where stated otherwise. Please send a cheque payable to National Trust, along with an s.a.e. for your tickets. *Forests*

Marriage of Figaro

28/7/99	**MANNINGTON GARDENS AND COUNTRYSIDE** Tel: 01263 584175 Opera in the garden setting *Gardens*

Mysteries and Histories

29/7/99 29/7/99	**ICKWORTH HOUSE PARK AND GARDENS** Tel: 01284 735270 Explore the history of Ickworth House through objects of Ickworth House and discover the stories of who used them. Suitable for children up to age 12 and carers. Family teas available in restaurant. Time: 13.00-16.30. Standard House Admission. £5.00 deposit (returnable) on Mysteries and Histories Handling Box. No booking but timed tickets on Handling Boxes. *Historic Houses & Gardens*

Trusty Gets Arty

29/7/99 29/7/99	**WICKEN FEN (NT) NATURE RESERVE** Tel: 01353 720274 Come and get arty with Trusty the Hedgehog. Please wear old clothes. A&C£2.50 (3-7 years). 10.00-12.00 or 14.00-16.00 *Nature Reserves*

Seafood Supper

30/7/99 30/7/99	**FELBRIGG HALL** Tel: 01263 837444 Provisional. An evening in the Felbrigg Park Restaurant inspired by the North Norfolk Coast. A four course supper of local seafood with musical accompaniment provided by popular folk and shanty group The Castaways. Tickets: £17.95. Bookings can be made by telephone to the Restaurant on 01263 832237 *Historic Houses & Gardens*

Last Night of the Proms

30/7/99 30/7/99	**ICKWORTH HOUSE PARK AND GARDENS** Tel: 01284 735270 Proms Concerts have now established themselves firmly in the outdoor concert calendar, giving many of the audience a chance to return to a favourite venue for one final concert before the end of the summer. Rousing, singing, waving flags and terrific atmosphere with Firework Finale, all add up to a breathtaking finale, as the orchestra , conducted by Nicholas Smith, plays 'Land of Hope and Glory'. Proms concerts tend to sell out early: please reserve tickets in good time, especially group bookings. Tickets A£17.00 C(5-18)£10.00. Ticket Hotline: 01625 56 00 00 or call 01284 735270. *Historic Houses & Gardens*

Verulamium Exposed

31/7/99 2/9/99	**VERULAMIUM MUSEUM AND PARK** Tel: 01727 819339 An exhibition of Verulamium in photographs from the past eighty years *Museums*

A Stour Valley Saunter In Constable Country

31/7/99 31/7/99	**BRIDGE COTTAGE** Tel: 01206 298260 A sizzling brunch followed by John Constable's views of the vale and visiting one of his favourite villages, Dedham. Time: 10.45. Tickets: £8.50. *Historic Buildings*

World Music Concert

31/7/99 31/7/99	**FRAMLINGHAM CASTLE** Tel: 01728 724189 Music of the world performed by Wingfield Arts. Normal admission prices apply *Castles*

Open-Air Musical Evening

31/7/99 31/7/99	**GRIMSTHORPE CASTLE** Tel: 01778 591205 Please call venue for further information *Historic Houses & Gardens*

Snake Encounter

31/7/99 LINTON ZOOLOGICAL GARDENS
31/7/99 Tel: 01223 891308
Meet 'Emily' or 'Kaa,' one of our South
American Boa constrictors at 15.30. You
will discover that they are not cold and
slimy but really quite nice creatures after
all!

Zoos- Conservation

Ladies' Night Fixture

31/7/99 MARKET RASEN RACECOURSE
31/7/99 Tel: 01673 843434
First race: 18.15. Please call for further
information

Racecourses

Concert

31/7/99 AUDLEY END HOUSE
1/8/99 Tel: 01799 522399
A musical concert with various performers. Normal admission prices apply.

Historical Remains

Sheepdog Demonstrations

31/7/99 CASTLE ACRE PRIORY
1/8/99 Tel: 01760 755394
Enjoyable demonstrations of sheepdogs,
sheep and geese. From 12.00. A£3.50
C£1.80 Concessions£2.50. EH Members
Free

Priory

Medieval Days

31/7/99 HEDINGHAM CASTLE
1/8/99 Tel: 01787 460261
Dancing, minstrels, jugglers, archery,
drama and knights in combat; presented
by The Lion Rampant

Castles

Thomas's Big Weekend

31/7/99 NENE VALLEY RAILWAY
1/8/99 Tel: 01780 784444
Thomas and his old pals are set to have
a great time this weekend!

Railways Steam/Light

750 Weekend Festival (750 M/C)

31/7/99 SNETTERTON CIRCUIT
1/8/99 Tel: 01953 887303
Formula 4, Roadsports, Formula Vee x2,
Formel V, Sports 2000, Radicals,
Caterhams x2, Lowcost Sports. Full
Circuit, Grade-D. On the Gate: £10.00-
£28.00. In Advance: Non £8.00-£25.00,
Club £7.00-£22.00. Two Day Pass: Non
£11.00-£30.00, Club £10.00-£27.00.
Three Day Pass: Non £32.00, Club
£29.00. Qualifying: £5.00-£14.00.
C£Free. Programme £Free-£5.00.
Seating (BH): £Free-£8.00. Group
Tickets: Non £90.00-£95.00, Club

£80.00-£85.00. Season Ticket Inc. of
Club Membership: £150.00. You can buy
your tickets for any of the 1999 events in
advance any time up to 4 days before an
event and make a saving, Tel: 0870 60
60 611

Motor Racing Circuit

Faith '99

31/7/99 EAST OF ENGLAND SHOWGROUND
7/8/99 Tel: 01733 234451
Kingdom Faith Ministries organise Faith
'99, please call 01403 211505 for further
information

Showgrounds

Family Fly-A-Kite Day

1/8/99 BLICKLING HALL
1/8/99 Tel: 01263 738030
Up-up and awayyyyyy, bring your kites
and we'll decorate the skies over
Blickling Hall Gardens. Commences:
10.00-16.00. Admission and parking Free

Historic Houses & Gardens

Big Cat Car Races (JCC)

1/8/99 CADWELL PARK CIRCUIT
1/8/99 Tel: 01507 343248
Jaguar XK Saloon x 2, TR Register
Championship, Sports Racing and GT,
Morgan Challenge, Jaguar Challenge,
Phoenix MG, Sportscar Race, MG Metro,
JCC Centurian Challenge. Full Circuit,
Grade-D. On the Gate: £10.00-£28.00. In
Advance: Non £8.00-£25.00, Club £7.00-
£22.00. Two Day Pass: Non £11.00-
£30.00, Club £10.00-£27.00. Three Day
Pass: Non £32.00, Club £29.00.
Qualifying: £5.00-£14.00. C£Free.
Programme £Free-£5.00. Seating (BH):
£Free-£8.00. Group Tickets: Non £90.00-
£95.00, Club £80.00-£85.00. Season
Ticket Inc. of Club Membership: £135.00.
You can buy your tickets for any of the
1999 events in advance any time up to 4
days before an event and make a saving,
Tel: 0870 60 60 611

Motor Racing Circuit

Summer Garden Party

1/8/99 CHURCH FARM MUSEUM
1/8/99 Tel: 01754 766658
Fun, food and festivities for all the family
arranged by the friends of the museum

Museum- Farms

Model Mania

1/8/99 LEIGHTON BUZZARD RAILWAY
1/8/99 Tel: 01525 373888 (24hours)
Our famous annual display of working
transport models. Also quarry digger at
work

Jousting Tournament

1/8/99
1/8/99

LINCOLN CASTLE
Tel: 01522 511068

Lincoln Castle's annual Jousting Tournament featuring the mounted knights and foot soldiers of the Nottingham Jousting Association. An exciting and spectacular afternoons entertainment. Admission A£3.00 C£1.00 Family Ticket £7.00

Castles

Victorian Day

1/8/99
1/8/99

NORMANBY HALL COUNTRY PARK
Tel: 01724 720588

See the servants prepare for the return of the family from London in 1891. Time: 13.00-16.30.

Country Parks

East Anglian Croquet Federation Tournament

1/8/99
1/8/99

OXBURGH HALL, GARDEN AND ESTATE
Tel: 01366 328258

Including "have-a-go" lawn for the public. Normal opening times and admission charges

Historic Buildings

Military Pageant

1/8/99
1/8/99

THE SHUTTLEWORTH COLLECTION
Tel: 0891 323310

The flying display which features the machines which saw service in both World War I and World War II and hopefully some currently in RAF, Navy or Army Service. The Shuttle Mansion House will be open 14.00-17.00 for visitors to se the splendour of this home.

Museum- Aviation

Snape Proms 1999

1/8/99
31/8/99

SNAPE PROMS 1999
Tel: 01728 452935

Snape Proms is the longest running concert series outside of London with a mixture of jazz, folk, music theatre, opera: anything and everything!

Festivals

Free Open Air Summer Concerts

1/8/99
5/9/99

FELBRIGG HALL
Tel: 01263 837444

On the five Sunday afternoons from 1 Aug to the 5 Sept the National Trust at Felbrigg will be providing you with FREE Summer entertainment. Open Air performances from five local musical groups; ranging from choral to jazz. Why not enjoy lunch in the restaurant beforehand or order yourself an afternoon tea to

enjoy during the performance? Further details available on 01263 838297.

Historic Houses & Gardens

Ickworth Challenge Day

2/8/99
2/8/99

ICKWORTH HOUSE PARK AND GARDENS
Tel: 01284 735270

Environmental activities for children and young people (10-14) and 14+. Serious fun involved! Booking essential call 01284 735270 for details. Prices to be advised.

Historic Houses & Gardens

Exhibition: Five Equestrian Artists

2/8/99
29/8/99

NATIONAL HORSERACING MUSEUM AND TOURS
Tel: 01638 667333

Selling exhibition of paintings by local equine artists, including Neil Cawthorne. Admission Free.

Museum- Horse racing

Painters Exhibition

3/8/99
29/8/99

GAINSBOROUGH'S HOUSE
Tel: 01787 372958

Exhibition of the work of Andrew Vass, Hugh Webster and Christopher Northall in the Lower Gallery. Contemporary Lettercutting in Stone exhibition held in the Garden

Birth Places

Summer Fun at Lincoln Castle

3/8/99
31/8/99

LINCOLN CASTLE
Tel: 01522 511068

Fun, games and live entertainment in the grounds of Lincoln Castle every Tuesday and Thursday in August, 10.00-14.00, for children up to the age of 12 years. Adults can relax in the grounds or take advantage of the facilities in the Castle's Tea Rooms. Normal admission charges will apply

Castles

Holiday Club

4/8/99
4/8/99

DUNWICH HEATH AND MINSMERE BEACH
Tel: 01728 648505

Children's environmental activities for those aged 6-12 years. Bring packed lunch or lunch money, 10.00-14.00, C£4.00 A£Free, booking essential, please apply direct to the property for booking by telephone 01728 648505 or by post to with a sae to: Dunwich Heath & Minsmere Beach, Saxmundham, Suffolk IP17 3DJ with a cheque made payable to The National Trust (Enterprises)

Conservation Parks

Have a Go

| 5/8/99 | DUNWICH HEATH AND MINSMERE BEACH |
| 5/8/99 | Tel: 01728 648505 |

Family event, try your hand at pond dipping, Heathland trails and minibeast hunts. Time: 14.00-16.00. Tickets: £1.00 per person per one hour session. No booking required.

Conservation Parks

Lunch Time Barbeque

| 5/8/99 | DUNWICH HEATH AND MINSMERE BEACH |
| 5/8/99 | Tel: 01728 648505 |

Family meals served in the open-air. Time: 12.00-14.00. Tickets: Individual prices, no booking required.

Conservation Parks

Ickworth Challenge Day

| 5/8/99 | ICKWORTH HOUSE PARK AND GARDENS |
| 5/8/99 | Tel: 01284 735270 |

Environmental activities for children and young people (10-14) and 14+. Serious fun involved! Booking essential call 01284 735270 for details. Prices to be advised.

Historic Houses & Gardens

Wild Art

| 5/8/99 | WICKEN FEN (NT) NATURE RESERVE |
| 5/8/99 | Tel: 01353 720274 |

Try your hand at designing something wild and wacky with clay, paint or have a go at screen-printing. Please wear old clothes. A&C£2.50 (7-12 years). 10.00-12.00 or 14.00-16.00.

Nature Reserves

Children's Extravaganza in the Garden

| 5/8/99 | OXBURGH HALL, GARDEN AND ESTATE |
| 6/8/99 | Tel: 01366 328258 |

Organised in association with Eastern Events. Supported by Eastern Daily Press. Tom-Tom Circus Troupe, Fun Bus, Face Painting, Wagon Rides, Treasure Hunt plus many other stalls and attractions, 10.00-17.00. Admission : A£1.00 C£4.00 Group rate 12+ Children £3.00 each. Please note no reductions on above charges for NT members, bookings on 01366 328258

Historic Buildings

First Friday

| 6/8/99 | ANGLESEY ABBEY, GARDENS AND LODE MILL |
| 6/8/99 | Tel: 01223 811200 |

Take a closer look at the History of Anglesey Abbey. Normal admission charges apply.

Historic Houses & Gardens

War of the Worlds

| 6/8/99 | BLICKLING HALL |
| 6/8/99 | Tel: 01263 738030 |

A spectacular family Sci-Fi, Firework and Laser Show held in the Park. Bring picnics and seating. Commences: 20.45. Tickets: £7.50 C£2.50 in advance, A£9.00 C£4.00 on the door. Bookings can be made by telephone, to the address, or in person.

Historic Houses & Gardens

Arts in Clay

| 6/8/99 | HATFIELD HOUSE |
| 8/8/99 | Tel: 01707 262823 |

5th National pottery and ceramics fair, sales, demonstrations, hands-on. Time: 10.00-18.00. Cost: A£5.00. Tel: 01494 450504 for further information

Historic Houses & Gardens

Medieval Weekend

| 7/8/99 | LINCOLN CASTLE |
| 8/8/98 | Tel: 01522 511068 |

Lincoln Castle returns to the 15th century with a major gathering of medieval soldiers and their followers. The Castle will be stormed and defended to the last. Normal admission charges will apply

Castles

Comedy of Errors - Shakespeare

| 7/8/99 | DUNWICH HEATH AND MINSMERE BEACH |
| 7/8/99 | Tel: 01728 648505 |

Performed by the Mad Dogs Theatre Company. Time: 19.00-21.30 approx. Tickets: A£7.50 in advance, A£9.00 on the day, C(0-12)£Free.

Conservation Parks

Folk Concert

| 7/8/99 | FRAMLINGHAM CASTLE |
| 7/8/99 | Tel: 01728 724189 |

Performed by Wingfield Arts. Normal admission prices apply

Castles

Alice in Wonderland

| 7/8/99 | TATTERSHALL CASTLE |
| 7/8/99 | Tel: 01526 342543 |

Outdoor theatre performed by Troubador Theatre. Performance starts: 18.00. Please bring rugs and picnics

Castles

Victorian

| 7/8/99 | AUDLEY END HOUSE |
| 8/8/99 | Tel: 01799 522399 |

Beaux Stratagems. A£6.00 C£3.00 Concessions£4.50

Historical Remains

Championship Bikes (BMCRC)

Further more detailed information on the attractions listed can be found in Best Guides *Visitor Attractions* Guide under the classifications shown

7/8/99
8/8/99
Cadwell Park Circuit
Tel: 01507 343248
All classes of national solo motorcycles and sidecars. Full Circuit, Grade-D. On the Gate: £10.00-£28.00. In Advance: Non £8.00-£25.00, Club £7.00-£22.00. Two Day Pass: Non £11.00-£30.00, Club £10.00-£27.00. Three Day Pass: Non £32.00, Club £29.00. Qualifying: £5.00-£14.00. C£Free. Programme £Free-£5.00. Seating (BH): £Free-£8.00. Group Tickets: Non £90.00-£95.00, Club £80.00-£85.00. Season Ticket Inc. of Club Membership: £135.00. You can buy your tickets for any of the 1999 events in advance any time up to 4 days before an event and make a saving. Tel: 0870 60 60 611

Motor Racing Circuit

7/8/99
8/8/99
Medieval Surgeon
Denny Abbey and the Farmland Museum
Tel: 01223 860489
A fascinating and gruesome insight into 13th century medical care with presentations about cause, effect and treatment of wounds and everyday ailments. A£2.00 C£1.00 Concessions£1.75.

Abbeys

7/8/99
8/8/99
Craft Fair
Grimsthorpe Castle
Tel: 01778 591205
Please call venue for further information

Historic Houses & Gardens

7/8/99
8/8/99
Brouhaha
Hedingham Castle
Tel: 01787 460261
Family entertainment with Brouhaha plus falconry displays. Children's workshop with drama roleplay

Castles

7/8/99
8/8/99
Radio Ickworth
Ickworth House Park and Gardens
Tel: 01284 735270
Bury St Edmunds' Amateur Radio Society's annual weekend at Ickworth House. Exhibition of Vintage radios, and Radio Ickworth radio station received calls from all over the world. Time: 10.00-16.30. Standard Park Admission.

Historic Houses & Gardens

Recreation of Tudor Life at Lammastide and Tudor Longbow Archery Shoot
7/8/99
8/8/99
Kentwell Hall
Tel: 01787 310207
Life at Kentwell in the year 1600. Time:

11.00-18.00. Prices: A£6.50 C£4.40 OAPs£5.60. Pre-booked groups 20+ 20% discount

Historic Houses & Gardens

Teddy Weekend
7/8/99
8/8/99
Whipsnade Wild Animal Park
Tel: 01582 872171
A splendid time for teddy bears with competitions and lots of fun for the whole family too!

Wildlife Parks

The Living House
7/8/99
9/8/99
West Stow Anglo Saxon Village
Tel: 01284 728718
A costumed family living in the Anglo-Saxon village will be happy to spare some time to show and explain the many things they need to do to survive the changing seasons. A£5.00 C&Concessions£4.00 Family Ticket £15.00

Archaeological Interest

Open-air Theatre - The Water babies
8/8/99
8/8/99
Blickling Hall
Tel: 01263 738030
Presented by Illyria. Seating is not provided, please bring rugs or chairs. Commences: 18.30. A£4.00 in advance £4.00 on the door, C(under 12)£Free. Bookings can be made by telephone, to the address, or in person.

Historic Houses & Gardens

Essex Yeomanry Brass Band
8/8/99
8/8/99
Hedingham Castle
Tel: 01787 460261
Come and listen the brass in the afternoon with Strawberries and Cream down by the lake

Castles

Family Fun Day
8/8/99
8/8/99
Market Rasen Racecourse
Tel: 01673 843434
First race: 14.10. Please call for further information

Racecourses

Saltmarsh Explorer
8/8/99
8/8/99
Orford Ness
Tel: 01394 450900
An important habitat but also nature's own sea defence. Come and explore this fascinating structure with an expert. Bring suitable clothing for weather including wellingtons. Bring own food and drink. Binoculars may be useful. Meet: 10.00 prompt at Orford Quay. Depart: approx. 16.00. Cost: £17.50 for all. Maximum 24 people.

Nature Reserves

Dragons, damsels and nymphs

8/8/99 RYE HOUSE MARSH AND RYE MEADS
MEADOWS

8/8/99 Tel: 01992 460031

See the variety of dragonflies and butterflies active at this time of year. 10.00-12.00

Nature Reserves

Championship Cars (BRSCC)

8/8/99 SNETTERTON CIRCUIT

8/8/99 Tel: 01953 887303

Programme to be confirmed. Full Circuit, Grade-D. On the Gate: £10.00-£28.00. In Advance: Non £8.00-£25.00, Club £7.00-£22.00. Two Day Pass: Non £11.00-£30.00, Club £10.00-£27.00. Three Day Pass: Non £32.00, Club £29.00. Qualifying: £5.00-£14.00. C£Free. Programme £Free-£5.00. Seating (BH): £Free-£8.00. Group Tickets: Non £90.00-£95.00, Club £80.00-£85.00. Season Ticket Inc. of Club Membership: £150.00. You can buy your tickets for any of the 1999 events in advance any time up to 4 days before an event and make a saving, Tel: 0870 60 60 611

Motor Racing Circuit

Wildflower Walk

8/8/99 WICKEN FEN (NT) NATURE RESERVE

8/8/99 Tel: 01353 720274

Experience the wildflowers of the Fen at their best. 14.00-16.00. A£3.75 C£2.50

Nature Reserves

Ickworth Challenge Day

9/8/99 ICKWORTH HOUSE PARK AND GARDENS

9/8/99 Tel: 01284 735270

Environmental activities for children and young people (10-14) and 14+. Serious fun involved! Booking essential call 01284 735270 for details. Prices to be advised.

Historic Houses & Gardens

The Water Babies by Illyria

10/8/99 OXBURGH HALL, GARDEN AND ESTATE

10/8/99 Tel: 01366 328258

Please bring rugs or chairs. Ticket prices to be confirmed. Time: 18.30

Historic Buildings

Children's Activity Day

10/8/99 TATTERSHALL CASTLE

10/8/99 Tel: 01526 342543

Run by Lincolnshire County Council, linked to the Vikings in Lincolnshire exhibition on show. Time: 10.30-17.00. Small charge to cover materials

Castles

Holiday Club

11/8/99 DUNWICH HEATH AND MINSMERE BEACH

11/8/99 Tel: 01728 648505

Children's environmental activities for those aged 6-12 years. Bring packed lunch or lunch money, 10.00-14.00, C£4.00 A£Free, booking essential, please apply direct to the property for booking by telephone 01728 648505 or by post to with a sae to: Dunwich Heath & Minsmere Beach, Saxmundham, Suffolk IP17 3DJ with a cheque made payable to The National Trust (Enterprises)

Conservation Parks

Focus on Bats

11/8/99 HATFIELD FOREST

11/8/99 Tel: 01279 870678

Come along to see and hear some of the batty inhabitants of the Forest. Bring a torch if you have one. Commences 20.00-22.00. Tickets: £2.00 C£1.00 Family Ticket (A2+C2)£5.00. Please note that you must book for all events except where stated otherwise. Please send a cheque payable to National Trust, along with an s.a.e. for your tickets.

Forests

Painting and Drawing Day

11/8/99 ORFORD NESS

11/8/99 Tel: 01394 450900

A chance for artists to spend a day and 'do their own thing' at this unique site. Some walking may be involved. Bring suitable clothing for the weather. Bring own food and drink. Some basic equipment can be provided, check for details. Meet: 09.30 prompt at Orford Quay. Depart: approx. 17.00. Cost: £17.50 for all. Maximum 20 people.

Nature Reserves

Shingle Explorer

11/8/99 ORFORD NESS

11/8/99 Tel: 01394 450900

Come and see what lives on the largest vegetated shingle split in Europe. A look at the ecology of this rare and hostile habitat. Bring suitable clothing for the weather. Bring own food and drink. Binoculars may be useful. Meet: 10.00 prompt at Orford Quay. Depart: approx. 16.00. Cost: £17.50 for all. Maximum 24 people.

Nature Reserves

Twelfth Night by Illyria

Further more detailed information on the attractions listed can be found in Best Guides *Visitor Attractions* Guide under the classifications shown

11/8/99 11/8/99	**OXBURGH HALL, GARDEN AND ESTATE** Tel: 01366 328258 Please bring rugs or chairs. Ticket prices to be confirmed. Time: 19.00 *Historic Buildings*

Garden Open Day

11/8/99 11/8/99	**OXBURGH HALL, GARDEN AND ESTATE** Tel: 01366 328258 Meet the Gardener, tours of the workshop and greenhouse area, 11.30 &14.30, normal opening times and admission charges apply *Historic Buildings*

Solar Eclipse Day

11/8/99 11/8/99	**WICKEN FEN (NT) NATURE RESERVE** Tel: 01353 720274 Test your senses by touch, taste, smell and sound. Follow a trail blind-folded, learn to use a compass and solve the treasure trail. A&C£2.50 (7-12 years). 10.00-12.00 or 14.00-16.00 *Nature Reserves*

Taro the Jester

11/8/99 12/8/99	**HEDINGHAM CASTLE** Tel: 01787 460261 Bring the children for lots of fun with Taro the Jester *Castles*

Have a Go

12/8/99 12/8/99	**DUNWICH HEATH AND MINSMERE BEACH** Tel: 01728 648505 Family event, try your hand at pond dipping, Heathland trails and minibeast hunts. Time: 14.00-16.00. Tickets: £1.00 per person per one hour session. No booking required. *Conservation Parks*

Lunch Time Barbeque

12/8/99 12/8/99	**DUNWICH HEATH AND MINSMERE BEACH** Tel: 01728 648505 Family meals served in the open-air. Time: 12.00-14.00. Tickets: Individual prices, no booking required. *Conservation Parks*

Twelfth Night

12/8/99 12/8/99	**HATFIELD FOREST** Tel: 01279 870678 Performed by Illyria at 19.00 an outdoor performance for children, call for pricing details. Please note that you must book for all events except where stated otherwise. Please send a cheque payable to National Trust, along with an s.a.e. for your tickets. *Forests*

Ickworth's Great Eccentrics Day

12/8/99 12/8/99	**ICKWORTH HOUSE PARK AND GARDENS** Tel: 01284 735270 Strange and unusual family fun at Ickworth Park, plus special events in Ickworth House. Shop and restaurant open. Time: 10.00-16.00. Standard Park Admission. Reduced House Admission: A£1.50 C£Free. *Historic Houses & Gardens*

Southend Carnival Week

13/8/99 21/8/99	**SOUTHEND ON SEA BOROUGH COUNCIL** Tel: 01702 215166 Many carnival events throughout the week around the town including Children's Fancy Dress competition, Beautiful Toddlers Parade, Dog Show, Bouncy Castle Fun Day, to name but a few. All week the Carnival Fair will be in Chalkwell Park, with rides and games for all the family. For further information please call 01702 713849 *Festivals*

Comedy of Errors and Mad Dogs and Englishmen

14/8/99 14/8/99	**FELBRIGG HALL** Tel: 01263 837444 Open Air Shakespeare returns to Felbrigg this summer with a presentation of one of the bard's most famous comedies. Performed in the grass courtyard, please bring your own rug or chair (no tables please). Commences: 19.30 (with Gates opening at 18.30 for picnics) performance is 2 hours long with an interval. Tickets: A£8.00 Concessions£6.00. Book your tickets at the box office on 01263 731660. *Historic Houses & Gardens*

Identifying Grasshoppers

14/8/99 14/8/99	**WICKEN FEN (NT) NATURE RESERVE** Tel: 01353 720274 A one day course learning about these fascinating creatures, their ecology and identification and the various species found at Wicken Fen. A£25.00 includes lunch. 10.00-17.00 *Nature Reserves*

Concert in the Gardens with Fireworks

14/8/99 14/8/99	**WIMPOLE HALL** Tel: 01223 207257 John Slaughter Blues Band, bring a picnic and a rug. Tickets £14.00 in advance. Please apply to the property for booking, either by post with an s.a.e. or call: 01223 207001/207257 *Country Parks*

Brouhaha

| 14/8/99 | **HEDINGHAM CASTLE** |
| 15/8/99 | Tel: 01787 460261 |

Family entertainment with Brouhaha plus falconry displays. Children's workshop with drama roleplay

Castles

Anglo-Saxon Family

| 14/8/99 | **WEST STOW ANGLO SAXON VILLAGE** |
| 15/8/99 | Tel: 01284 728718 |

Bring the whole family along to compare the way they live with the lives of the costumed Anglo-Saxon family who are living in the village. A£5.00 C&Concessions£4.00 Family Ticket 15.00

Archaeological Interest

Flatford's Family Evening Extravaganza

| 15/8/99 | **BRIDGE COTTAGE** |
| 15/8/99 | Tel: 01206 298260 |

Enjoy an evening of fun and games at Bridge Cottage with Trusty the Hedgehog! A Summer Supper will be served. Time: 17.30. Tickets: A£5.00 C£4.00.

Historic Buildings

Championship Cars (BRSCC)

| 15/8/99 | **CADWELL PARK CIRCUIT** |
| 15/8/99 | Tel: 01507 343248 |

Porsche 924s, Formula 600s, XR2 Challenge, XR3 Challenge, Mini Miglias, Mini se7ens. Full Circuit, Grade-D. On the Gate: £10.00-£28.00. In Advance: Non £8.00-£25.00, Club £7.00-£22.00. Two Day Pass: Non £11.00-£30.00, Club £10.00-£27.00. Three Day Pass: Non £32.00, Club £29.00. Qualifying: £5.00-£14.00. C£Free. Programme £Free-£5.00. Seating (BH): £Free-£8.00. Group Tickets: Non £90.00-£95.00, Club £80.00-£85.00. Season Ticket Inc. of Club Membership: £135.00. You can buy your tickets for any of the 1999 events in advance any time up to 4 days before an event and make a saving, Tel: 0870 60 60 611

Motor Racing Circuit

Family Fun Day

| 15/8/99 | **LEIGHTON BUZZARD RAILWAY** |
| 15/8/99 | Tel: 01525 373888 (24hours) |

Helping you survive the long summer holidays! Family entertainment and fun rides (extra charges apply)

Railways Steam/Light

Wandering Musician

| 15/8/99 | **TATTERSHALL CASTLE** |
| 15/8/99 | Tel: 01526 342543 |

Peter Bull entertains whilst wandering around Tattershall

Castles

Vintage Transport Day

| 15/8/99 | **THE SHUTTLEWORTH COLLECTION** |
| 15/8/99 | Tel: 0891 323310 |

A unique combination of veteran and vintage vehicles and aircraft, recreating transport from the Edwardian period to the thirties. The Shuttle Mansion House will be open 14.00-17.00 for visitors to se the splendour of this home.

Museum- Aviation

Frank Bramley RA

| 15/8/99 | **USHER GALLERY** |
| 24/10/99 | Tel: 01522 527980 |

A major exhibition focusing on the work of this significant Victorian Lincolnshire Artist. Including key loans from national and private collections it forms a unique opportunity to enjoy Bramley's remarkable paintings

Art Galleries

Blooming Marvellous

| 15/8/99 | **CHURCH FARM MUSEUM** |
| 31/10/99 | Tel: 01754 766658 |

A colourful exhibition looking at gardens and gardeners through the ages

Museum- Farms

Childrens Activity Week

| 16/8/99 | **CHELMSFORD AND ESSEX REGIMENT MUSEUM** |
| 20/8/99 | Tel: 01245 353066 |

For 8-year olds and over, on a Medical theme. Half-day sessions, 10.00-12.30 & 13.30-16.00 (afternoons repeat morning activities). Admission Free but BOOKING ESSENTIAL from start of July

Museum- Local History

Water Babies

| 17/8/99 | **HATFIELD FOREST** |
| 17/8/99 | Tel: 01279 870678 |

An outdoor theatre performance by the Illyria Theatre Company, times and prices to be confirmed. Please note that you must book for all events except where stated otherwise. Please send a cheque payable to National Trust, along with an s.a.e. for your tickets.

Forests

Holiday Club

| 18/8/99 | **DUNWICH HEATH AND MINSMERE BEACH** |
| 18/8/99 | Tel: 01728 648505 |

Children's environmental activities for those aged 6-12 years. Bring packed lunch or lunch money, 10.00-14.00, C£4.00 A£Free, booking essential, please apply direct to the property for booking by telephone 01728 648505 or by post to with a sae to: Dunwich Heath & Minsmere Beach, Saxmundham, Suffolk IP17 3DJ with a cheque made payable to The National Trust (Enterprises)

Conservation Parks

Horseracing Forensic Laboratory
18/8/99 NATIONAL HORSERACING MUSEUM AND TOURS
18/8/99 Tel: 01638 667333
A rare opportunity to visit the laboratory (transport included) and learn how horses are dope-tested. Lasts about 1-1.5 hours. Time: 14.30. Price: £10.00.

Museum- Horse racing

Guided Walk
18/8/99 ORFORD NESS
18/8/99 Tel: 01394 450900
Walk with the Warden looking at the many varied aspects of this unique site. Meet: 10.00 prompt at Orford Quay. Depart approx: 16.00. Cost: £12.50 for all. Maximum 24 people. Bring suitable clothing for the weather. Bring own food and drink.

Nature Reserves

Open Air Theatre
18/8/99 ANGLESEY ABBEY, GARDENS AND LODE MILL
19/8/99 Tel: 01223 811200
Illyria present The Water Babies. Don't forget your picnics and seating for this performance. Time: 17.30. Tickets: A£7.00 C(3-12)£5.00.

Historic Houses & Gardens

Taro the Jester
18/8/99 HEDINGHAM CASTLE
19/8/99 Tel: 01787 460261
Bring the children for lots of fun with Taro the Jester

Castles

Ponies (UK) Summer Championships
18/8/99 EAST OF ENGLAND SHOWGROUND
22/8/99 Tel: 01733 234451
British Show Pony Society Summer Championship Show

Showgrounds

Family Fun Day
19/8/99 BLICKLING HALL
19/8/99 Tel: 01263 738030
Wild about Wildlife, plenty to entertain and education the whole family. Commences: 11.00-16.00. Usual admission charge.

Historic Houses & Gardens

Lunch Time Barbeque

19/8/99 DUNWICH HEATH AND MINSMERE BEACH
19/8/99 Tel: 01728 648505
Family meals served in the open-air. Time: 12.00-14.00. Tickets: Individual prices, no booking required.

Conservation Parks

Have A Go!
19/8/99 DUNWICH HEATH AND MINSMERE BEACH
19/8/99 Tel: 01728 648505
Family event, try your hand at pond-dipping, heath land trails and minibeast hunts. £1.00 per person for one hour session. 14.00-16.00

Conservation Parks

Bugs and Beasties
19/8/99 HATFIELD FOREST
19/8/99 Tel: 01279 870678
Come along and discover the secret world of the bugs and beasties of Hatfield Forest. Commences 14.00-16.00. Tickets: A£2.00 C£1.00 Family Ticket (A2+C2)£5.00. Car Park £3.00 NT members £Free. Please note that you must book for all events except where stated otherwise. Please send a cheque payable to National Trust, along with an s.a.e. for your tickets.

Forests

Fun at the Fen with Trusty
19/8/99 WICKEN FEN (NT) NATURE RESERVE
19/8/99 Tel: 01353 720274
Come and have fun and games on the fen with Trusty the Hedgehog. A&C£2.50 (3-7 years) 10.00-12.00 or 14.00-16.00

Nature Reserves

Lunch with Trusty the Hedgehog
20/8/99 FELBRIGG HALL
20/8/99 Tel: 01263 837444
Meet Trusty the Hedgehog at his lunch party today, face-painting and special hedgehog trail too. Commences: 12.00-14.00. Tickets: C£5.00 no unaccompanied children. Light lunch for Mums and Dads for £2.50. Call 01263 832237 for booking with the Restaurant

Historic Houses & Gardens

Firework and Laser Symphony Concert
20/8/99 BLICKLING HALL
21/8/99 Tel: 01263 738030
An evening concert with spectacular firework display and Water Dancing Display-they just keep on getting better, bring picnics and seating. Commences: 18.30. Tickets A£19.00 C£10.00. Early booking advised: bookings can be made by telephone, to the address, or in person.

Historic Houses & Gardens

A weekly updated selection of UK wide special events can be found on the award winning sites @ www.thisislondon.com *and* www.ukplus.co.uk

An Opera Gala with Fireworks
21/8/99 HATFIELD HOUSE
21/8/99 Tel: 01707 262823
Opera in the park, picnic under the stars.
Time: 19.00. Cost: A£15.00. Court Opera
Productions Tickets: 01707 332880 /
0171 957 4041
Historic Houses & Gardens

Wildlife Day
21/8/99 LINCOLN CASTLE
21/8/99 Tel: 01522 511068
A day of fun and entertainment for all
the family to support Weirfield Wildlife
Hospital. Grooming displays; pets; reptiles; activities; stalls and arena displays, a great day out. Admission
A£3.00 C£1.00 Family Ticket £7.00
Castles

Illuminated Carnival Procession
21/8/99 SOUTHEND ON SEA BOROUGH COUNCIL
21/8/99 Tel: 01702 215166
Grand illuminated Carnival Procession
leaving Chalkwell Shelter at 20.00. The
Procession will travel along Western
Esplanade, Marine Parade arriving at
Eastern Esplanade at around 22.00.
Switching on of the Southend
Illuminations by a celebrity guest
approximately 20.30. Grand Fireworks
Display from Southend Pier at approxi-
mately 21.30
Festivals

Flying Proms 1999
21/8/99 THE SHUTTLEWORTH COLLECTION
21/8/99 Tel: 0891 323310
An evening of flying accompanied by live
orchestral music. An evening full of
atmosphere, bring a picnic is you wish,
although catering is provided
Museum- Aviation

Georgian
21/8/99 AUDLEY END HOUSE
22/8/99 Tel: 01799 522399
Beaux Stratagems & Rhiannon. A£6.00
C£3.00 Concessions£4.50
Historical Remains

Alice in Wonderland
21/8/99 CASTLE ACRE PRIORY
22/8/99 Tel: 01760 755394
Labyrinth Productions. Follow Alice and
White Rabbit as they go through
Wonderland, meeting all manner of
weird, wonderful and totally mad characters. A£3.50 C£1.80 Concessions£2.60
Priory

Antiques Fair

21/8/99 ELTON HALL
22/8/99 Tel: 01832 280468
This show attracts both local and national dealers with a very good selection of
furniture and general antiques. 10.00-
17.00
Historic Houses & Gardens

Brouhaha
21/8/99 HEDINGHAM CASTLE
22/8/99 Tel: 01787 460261
Family entertainment with Brouhaha
plus falconry displays. Children's workshop with drama roleplay
Castles

De Havilland Moth Club Annual Fly In
21/8/99 WOBURN ABBEY
22/8/99 Tel: 01525 290666
Enjoy the atmosphere as over 100 de
Havilland planes fly to Woburn for two
days of aerobatics and competition. The
event is included in the Park entry
charge £5.00 per car
Stately Homes

Meet the Saxons
21/8/99 WEST STOW ANGLO SAXON VILLAGE
29/8/99 Tel: 01284 728718
Another family of Anglo-Saxons in costume takes over the village and invites
you into their homes. You may be sur-
prised at some of the objects they can
make and the things they tell you
Archaeological Interest

**Shuttleworth & Nuffield Trophies
(VSCC)**
22/8/99 CADWELL PARK CIRCUIT
22/8/99 Tel: 01507 343248
Vintage, Pre and Post War Racing and
Sports Cars. Full Circuit, Grade-D. On the
Gate: £10.00-£28.00. In Advance: Non
£8.00-£25.00, Club £7.00-£22.00. Two
Day Pass: Non £11.00-£30.00, Club
£10.00-£27.00. Three Day Pass: Non
£32.00, Club £29.00. Qualifying: £5.00-
£14.00. C£Free. Programme £Free-£5.00.
Seating (BH): £Free-£8.00. Group
Tickets: Non £90.00-£95.00, Club
£80.00-£85.00. Season Ticket Inc. of
Club Membership: £135.00. You can buy
your tickets for any of the 1999 events in
advance any time up to 4 days before an
event and make a saving, Tel: 0870 60
60 611
Motor Racing Circuit

Dixieland to Swing
22/8/99 HATFIELD HOUSE
22/8/99 Tel: 01707 262823
A night of jazz and fireworks with Sid

Further more detailed information on the attractions listed can be found
in Best Guides *Visitor Attractions* Guide under the classifications shown

Lawrence and Kenny Ball. Time: 19.00.
Cost: A£15.00. Tickets: 01707 332880 /
0171 957 4041

Historic Houses & Gardens

Essex Yeomanry Brass Band
22/8/99　HEDINGHAM CASTLE
22/8/99　Tel: 01787 460261
Come and listen the brass in the afternoon with Strawberries and Cream down
by the lake

Castles

Wildlife Day
22/8/99　OXBURGH HALL, GARDEN AND ESTATE
22/8/99　Tel: 01366 328258
Trusty the Hedgehog and The Hedgehog
Society will be at Oxburgh Hall. There
will also be a conservation game,
wildlife trail and story-telling. Normal
opening times and admission charges

Historic Buildings

Rolling Thunder (BARC)
22/8/99　SNETTERTON CIRCUIT
22/8/99　Tel: 01953 887303
Classic Thunder, Classic Saloons, Classic
& Historic Saloons, Post-Historic Touring
Cars, Group 1 Touring Cars, Sports 1600,
ModProd Saloons, Caterham Graduates,
MonoPosto. Full Circuit, Grade-D. On the
Gate: £10.00-£28.00. In Advance: Non
£8.00-£25.00. Club £7.00-£22.00. Two
Day Pass: Non £11.00-£30.00, Club
£10.00-£27.00. Three Day Pass: Non
£32.00, Club £29.00. Qualifying: £5.00-
£14.00. C£Free. Programme £Free-£5.00.
Seating (BH): £Free-£8.00. Group
Tickets: Non £90.00-£95.00, Club
£80.00-£85.00. Season Ticket Inc. of
Club Membership: £150.00. You can buy
your tickets for any of the 1999 events in
advance any time up to 4 days before an
event and make a saving, Tel: 0870 60
60 611

Motor Racing Circuit

Commercial Vehicles Road Run
22/8/99　WOBURN ABBEY
22/8/99　Tel: 01525 290666
More vehicles than the Chelsea run - displays and competitions by category of
vehicle

Stately Homes

Dizzy Spells and Wicked Wheelies
22/8/99　ICKWORTH HOUSE PARK AND GARDENS
28/8/99　Tel: 01284 735270
The Young National Trust Theatre erupt
into Ickworth Park with its new
Environmental Show. Family
Entertainment each afternoon. NOT 23rd

or 26th August. Booking essential call
01284 735270 for details. Prices to be
advised.

Historic Houses & Gardens

Holiday Club
25/8/99　DUNWICH HEATH AND MINSMERE BEACH
25/8/99　Tel: 01728 648505
Children's environmental activities for
those aged 6-12 years. Bring packed
lunch or lunch money, 10.00-14.00,
C£4.00 A£Free, booking essential,
please apply direct to the property for
booking by telephone 01728 648505 or
by post to with a sae to: Dunwich Heath
& Minsmere Beach, Saxmundham,
Suffolk IP17 3DJ with a cheque made
payable to The National Trust
(Enterprises)

Conservation Parks

Bright Eyes and Bushy Tails
25/8/99　HATFIELD FOREST
25/8/99　Tel: 01279 870678
Come and search for signs and tracks of
the wide variety of mammals that live in
the Forest. Tickets: £2.00 C£1.00 Family
Ticket (A2+C2)£5.00. Car Park £3.00 NT
members £Free. Please note that you
must book for all events except where
stated otherwise. Please send a cheque
payable to National Trust, along with an
s.a.e. for your tickets.

Forests

From RFC to AWRE
25/8/99　ORFORD NESS
25/8/99　Tel: 01394 450900
A look at the 20th century military history of Orford Ness. Meet: 10.00 prompt at
Orford Quay. Depart: approx. 16.00.
Bring suitable clothing for the weather.
Bring own food and drink. Cost: £12.50
for all. Maximum 24 people.

Nature Reserves

Taro the Jester
25/8/99　HEDINGHAM CASTLE
26/8/99　Tel: 01787 460261
Bring the children for lots of fun with
Taro the Jester

Castles

Lunch Time Barbeque
26/8/99　DUNWICH HEATH AND MINSMERE BEACH
26/8/99　Tel: 01728 648505
Family meals served in the open-air.
Time: 12.00-14.00. Tickets: Individual
prices, no booking required.

Conservation Parks

Have A Go!

A weekly updated selection of UK wide special events can be found on
the award winning sites @ www.thisislondon.com *and* www.ukplus.co.uk

26/8/99
26/8/99

DUNWICH HEATH AND MINSMERE BEACH
Tel: 01728 648505

Family event, try your hand at pond-dipping, heath land trails and minibeast hunts. £1.00 per person for one hour session. 14.00-16.00

Conservation Parks

Minibeast Magic and Mayhem
26/8/99
26/8/99
WICKEN FEN (NT) NATURE RESERVE
Tel: 01353 720274

Meet some monster mini-beasts from other countries! A&C£2.50 (7-13 years) 10.00-12.00 or 14.00-16.00

Nature Reserves

High Summer Recreation of Tudor Life
27/8/99
30/8/99
KENTWELL HALL
Tel: 01787 310207

Life at Kentwell in the year 1600. Time: 11.00-18.00. Prices: A£7.75 C£5.20 OAPs£6.70. Pre-booked groups 20+ 20% discount

Historic Houses & Gardens

A Medieval Summer's Evening
28/8/99
28/8/99
FRAMLINGHAM CASTLE
Tel: 01728 724189

Come and listen to The Lion Rampant on this hot summer's evening. A£5.00 C£2.50 Concessions£3.80

Castles

Flint Knapping
28/8/99
28/8/99
GRIME'S GRAVES
Tel: 01842 810656

Stone age man returns to demonstrate how he made tools, axes and arrowheads from flint. From 12.00. A£2.50 C£1.30 Concessions£1.90. EH Members Free

Museum- Mining

Brouhaha
28/8/99
28/8/99
HEDINGHAM CASTLE
Tel: 01787 460261

Family entertainment with Brouhaha plus falconry displays. Children's workshop with drama roleplay

Castles

Snake Encounter
28/8/99
28/8/99
LINTON ZOOLOGICAL GARDENS
Tel: 01223 891308

Meet 'Emily' or 'Kaa,' one of our South American Boa constrictors at 15.30. You will discover that they are not cold and slimy but really quite nice creatures after all!

Zoos- Conservation

Championship Bikes (NEW ERA)

28/8/99
29/8/99

SNETTERTON CIRCUIT
Tel: 01953 887303

All classes of national solo motorcycles and sidecars. Full Circuit, Grade-D. On the Gate: £10.00-£28.00. In Advance: Non £8.00-£25.00, Club £7.00-£22.00. Two Day Pass: Non £11.00-£30.00, Club £10.00-£27.00. Three Day Pass: Non £32.00, Club £29.00. Qualifying: £5.00-£14.00. C£Free. Programme £Free-£5.00. Seating (BH): £Free-£8.00. Group Tickets: Non £90.00-£95.00, Club £80.00-£85.00. Season Ticket Inc. of Club Membership: £150.00. You can buy your tickets for any of the 1999 events in advance any time up to 4 days before an event and make a saving, Tel: 0870 60 60 611

Motor Racing Circuit

Bedfordshire Millennium Festival
28/8/99
30/8/99
THE SHUTTLEWORTH COLLECTION
Tel: 0891 323310

A large scale outdoor event to celebrate the millennium. A whole range of exciting experiences, both past and present and the future. The event is held in Old Warden Park.

Museum- Aviation

Millennium Festival
28/8/99
30/8/99
THE SWISS GARDEN
Tel: 01767 627666

A simply wonderful 3 day festival being held to celebrate the coming Millennium. Set in the beautiful surroundings of the Shuttleworth Mansion, Old Warden Park. Not to be missed. Call for further information

Gardens

Craft Fayre
28/8/99
30/8/99
WREST PARK GARDENS
Tel: 01525 860152

Large scale show with a selection of crafts and entertainment.

Gardens

Park Life
28/8/99
3/10/99
CHELMSFORD AND ESSEX REGIMENT MUSEUM
Tel: 01245 353066

Prodigy, puppetworks, heatwaves, torrential rain, Les Miserables, queueing for toilets, fireworks, brilliant music, re-enactments, dashing ladies, walks and talks! What do you remember about events in Hylands Park in recent years? Come and have your memory jolted in this exhibition of photographs and objects about Hylands Park life in recent

years

Museum- Local History

Raptor Foundation
29/8/99   LINTON ZOOLOGICAL GARDENS
29/8/99   Tel: 01223 891308
Meet Gordon Robertson from the Raptor Foundation and hear all about their work with injured birds of prey and meet some of their tame owls

Zoos- Conservation

Open-Air Worship
29/8/99   LYVEDEN NEW BIELD
29/8/99   Tel: 01832 205358
An open-air service of worship with brass band. Time: 17.30. Further details from property

Historic Houses

Gardener's Weekend
29/8/99   AUDLEY END HOUSE
30/8/99   Tel: 01799 522399
Our annual summer show with many exhibitors, craft stalls, music and children's entertainment. Plants and produce to buy. Demonstrators and farm animals. A£4.00 Concessions£3.00 C£2.00 (House extra, subject to capacity). EH Members Free

Historical Remains

MCN British Superbike Championship (MCRCB)
29/8/99   CADWELL PARK CIRCUIT
30/8/99   Tel: 01507 343248
British Superbike x 2, British 125cc, British 250cc, British 600cc, plus support. Full Circuit, Grade-B. On the Gate: £10.00-£28.00. In Advance: Non £8.00-£25.00, Club £7.00-£22.00. Two Day Pass: Non £11.00-£30.00, Club £10.00-£27.00. Three Day Pass: Non £32.00, Club £29.00. Qualifying: £5.00-£14.00. C£Free. Programme £Free-£5.00. Seating (BH): £Free-£8.00. Group Tickets: Non £90.00-£95.00, Club £80.00-£85.00. Season Ticket Inc. of Club Membership: £135.00. You can buy your tickets for any of the 1999 events in advance any time up to 4 days before an event and make a saving, Tel: 0870 60 60 611

Motor Racing Circuit

Medieval Living History
29/8/99   CASTLE ACRE PRIORY
30/8/99   Tel: 01760 755394
15th century military and domestic life, with crafts, men-at-arms and period games. A£3.50 C£1.80 Concessions£2.60

Priory

Medieval Entertainment
29/8/99   FRAMLINGHAM CASTLE
30/8/99   Tel: 01728 724189
Games, squire-training and talks on weaponry and armour. Also, try your hand at spinning, weaving and calligraphy and learn about herbal medicine. A£4.00 C£2.00 Concessions£3.00

Castles

Jousting Tournament
29/8/99   HEDINGHAM CASTLE
30/8/99   Tel: 01787 460261
Presented by The Knights of Royal England. Two lively days of entertainment, full regalia, flashing steel, lots of colourful Charging Knights, and sword fighting by those honourable and no doubt some dishonourable. Plus family fun with Brouhaha. Call for admission prices

Castles

Opening of Victorian Prison
29/8/99   LINCOLN CASTLE
30/8/99   Tel: 01522 511068
A final chance to experience life behind the bars of Lincoln Castle's Victorian Prison. Visit the condemned cell, meet the Governor and Matron, the Felons and Wardens. Normal admission charges will apply

Castles

Traditional Song
29/8/99   ORFORD CASTLE
30/8/99   Tel: 01394 450472
Come and listen to this family group perform some wonderful historical music. A£3.00 C£1.50 Concessions£2.30

Castles

Teddy's Bear Picnic
30/8/99   CHURCH FARM MUSEUM
30/8/99   Tel: 01754 766658
Treat your teddy to a special day out, plenty of fun for all with games and prizes galore

Museum- Farms

St. John's Ambulance Fun Day
30/8/99   GRIMSTHORPE CASTLE
30/8/99   Tel: 01778 591205
Please call venue for further information

Historic Houses & Gardens

Family Fun Day
30/8/99   HUNTINGDON STEEPLECHASES LTD
30/8/99   Tel: 01480 453373
Bring the family to Huntingdon where a large crowd and great atmosphere promises to make it a wonderful day

out. All children under 16 can enter free of charge and with a fully supervised creche, bouncy castle, tubeslide and face-painting, there is lots to do for all the family. Racing from 14.00

Racecourses

Archie Scott-Brown Trophy (BRSCC)
30/8/99   SNETTERTON CIRCUIT
30/8/99   Tel: 01953 887303
TVR Tuscans, Alfas, Auto Italia. Full Circuit, Grade-C. On the Gate: £10.00-£28.00. In Advance: Non £8.00-£25.00, Club £7.00-£22.00. Two Day Pass: Non £11.00-£30.00, Club £10.00-£27.00. Three Day Pass: Non £32.00, Club £29.00. Qualifying: £5.00-£14.00. C£Free. Programme £Free-£5.00. Seating (BH): £Free-£8.00. Group Tickets: Non £90.00-£95.00, Club £80.00-£85.00. Season Ticket Inc. of Club Membership: £150.00. You can buy your tickets for any of the 1999 events in advance any time up to 4 days before an event and make a saving, Tel: 0870 60 60 611

Motor Racing Circuit

Anglo-Saxon Activity Day
30/8/99   WEST STOW ANGLO SAXON VILLAGE
30/8/99   Tel: 01284 728718
Activities of all kinds for all ages and the opportunity to talk to knowledgeable 'Anglo-Saxons' about life 1500 years ago. A£5.00 C&Concessions£4.00 Family Ticket £15.00

Archaeological Interest

Mid-Summer, Mid-Week, Mystery Meander
2/9/99   BRIDGE COTTAGE
2/9/99   Tel: 01206 298260
After a delicious cream tea at Bridge Cottage tea rooms set off for a glorious guided walk on a mid-summer's evening into Constable Country. Time: 16.00. Tickets: £6.50.

Historic Buildings

Mask and Mobile Makking
2/9/99   WICKEN FEN (NT) NATURE RESERVE
2/9/99   Tel: 01353 720274
Make masks, mobiles and collages out of natural objects with Trusty the Hegehog. A&C£2.50 (3-7 years). 10.00-12.00 or 14.00-16.00

Nature Reserves

First Firday
3/9/99   ANGLESEY ABBEY, GARDENS AND LODE

MILL
3/9/99   Tel: 01223 811200
Take a closer look at The Upper Gallery. Time: 13.00-16.00. Normal admission charges apply.

Historic Houses & Gardens

Fen Wildlife Day
4/9/99   WICKEN FEN (NT) NATURE RESERVE
4/9/99   Tel: 01353 720274
Learn all about the wildlife at Wicken Fen. Exhibitions, demonstrations, guided walks, children activities, and refreshments. 11.00-17.00. Tickets: A£4.50 C£2.50

Nature Reserves

Hatfield Forest Wood Fair
4/9/99   HATFIELD FOREST
5/9/99   Tel: 01279 870678
Wood sale together wigh a display of traditional wood crafts. Admission normal, commences 10.00-17.00, car parking charge of £3.00 per car applies. National Trust members free

Forests

September Steam-Up
4/9/99   LEIGHTON BUZZARD RAILWAY
5/9/99   Tel: 01525 373888 (24hours)
Our annual steamy weekend. Everything that can move will move, including a visiting loco. Quarry digger at work on Saturday. Industry Trains Display on Sunday

Railways Steam/Light

Steam Gala
4/9/99   NORTH NORFOLK RAILWAY
5/9/99   Tel: 01263 822045
Enjoy the thrill of steam with our specialised weekend

Railways Steam/Light

Clubmans Bikes (BMCRC)
4/9/99   SNETTERTON CIRCUIT
5/9/99   Tel: 01953 887303
All classes of national solo motorcycles and sidecars. Full Circuit, Grade-E. On the Gate: £10.00-£28.00. In Advance: Non £8.00-£25.00, Club £7.00-£22.00. Two Day Pass: Non £11.00-£30.00, Club £10.00-£27.00. Three Day Pass: Non £32.00, Club £29.00. Qualifying: £5.00-£14.00. C£Free. Programme £Free-£5.00. Seating (BH): £Free-£8.00. Group Tickets: Non £90.00-£95.00, Club £80.00-£85.00. Season Ticket Inc. of Club Membership: £150.00. You can buy your tickets for any of the 1999 events in advance any time up to 4 days before an event and make a saving, Tel: 0870 60

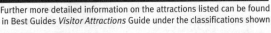

Further more detailed information on the attractions listed can be found in Best Guides *Visitor Attractions* Guide under the classifications shown

60 611

Motor Racing Circuit

Heavy Horse Show and Country Show

4/9/99
5/9/99

WIMPOLE HALL

Tel: 01223 207257

See the beautiful Shire Horses 10.30-17.00, standard admission

Country Parks

Bedfordshire Autumn Craft Fair

4/9/99
5/9/99

WOBURN ABBEY

Tel: 01525 290666

Popular craft fair with a variety of exhibitors and entertainments for all the family. 10.00-18.00. Admission charge not set until 6 weeks before event. Call 01283 820548

Stately Homes

Relief Printing Today

4/9/99
31/10/99

GAINSBOROUGH'S HOUSE

Tel: 01787 372958

Relief Printing Exhibition held in the Lower Gallery. Collection of Platinum and Silver Photographs by Noel Myles in the Weaving Room

Birth Places

750 M/C Autumn Race Day (750 M/C)

5/9/99
5/9/99

CADWELL PARK CIRCUIT

Tel: 01507 343248

Stock Hatch, 750 Formula, Sport 2000, Formula 4, Kit Cars x2, Roadsports, Formula Vee x2, Radicals x2. Full Circuit, Grade-D. On the Gate: £10.00-£28.00. In Advance: Non £8.00-£25.00, Club £7.00-£22.00. Two Day Pass: Non £11.00-£30.00, Club £10.00-£27.00. Three Day Pass: Non £32.00, Club £29.00. Qualifying: £5.00-£14.00. C£Free. Programme £Free-£5.00. Seating (BH): £Free-£8.00. Group Tickets: Non £90.00-£95.00, Club £80.00-£85.00. Season Ticket Inc. of Club Membership: £135.00. You can buy your tickets for any of the 1999 events in advance any time up to 4 days before an event and make a saving, Tel: 0870 60 60 611

Motor Racing Circuit

Sponsored Walk: Aldeburgh to Dunwich Heath

5/9/99
5/9/99

DUNWICH HEATH AND MINSMERE BEACH

Tel: 01728 648505

Support the National Trust and Victim Support. Please send S.A.E. for details marked 'Sponsored Walk'.

Conservation Parks

Euston Hall and Gardens Open

5/9/99
5/9/99

EUSTON HALL

Tel: 01842 766366

Garden and Hall Open Day 14.30-17.00

Historic Houses & Gardens

Ace Owners' Club Concours D'elegance

5/9/99
5/9/99

ICKWORTH HOUSE PARK AND GARDENS

Tel: 01284 735270

Vintage and Classic cars displayed against the Italiante splendours of Ickworth House. Time: 12.00-16.00. Standard Park Admission.

Historic Houses & Gardens

East Anglian Croquet Federation Finals

5/9/99
5/9/99

ICKWORTH HOUSE PARK AND GARDENS

Tel: 01284 735270

Demon croquet on the velvet lawns of Ickworth House, also, Golf Croquet for all to try. Time: 10.00-16.00. Standard Park Admission.

Historic Houses & Gardens

Charities Day

5/9/99

MANNINGTON GARDENS AND COUNTRYSIDE

5/9/99

Tel: 01263 584175

Hall open. Entertainment, stalls, in aid of Chatter Box Charity

Gardens

Shuttleworth Pageant

5/9/99
5/9/99

THE SHUTTLEWORTH COLLECTION

Tel: 0891 323310

This is the display at which we try to fly as many Shuttleworth Collection aeroplanes as possible, to the accompaniment of examples from our vintage motor car and motor cycle collections, with suitably attired drivers and passengers from the Shuttleworth Veteran Aeroplane Society. The Shuttle Mansion House will be open 14.00-17.00 for visitors to se the splendour of this home.

Museum- Aviation

Exhibition: Trevor Jones, Photographer in Residence

7/9/99
31/10/99

NATIONAL HORSERACING MUSEUM AND TOURS

Tel: 01638 667333

Selling exhibition of photographs by Trevor Jones, the Museum's Photographer in Residence for 1999. Trevor has covered all the major sporting events during his career, but now concentrates on the horse racing and blood stock industry. He is well-known and respected world-wide for the vibrancy and range of his work. Admission Free. Prints available to order from £27.00. On 28th September & 29th October at 13.30

spend a day at the races with Trevor. Booking essential. £40.00 (includes members' badge and transport).

Museum- Horse racing

Garden History & Design Course

8/9/99 ANGLESEY ABBEY, GARDENS AND LODE MILL

8/9/99 Tel: 01223 811200

Please enquire for separate leaflet on this course, which will run on four separate days in Sept, Oct, Jan and Feb. Time: 10.30-16.00.

Historic Houses & Gardens

Ickworth's Autumn Colours

10/9/99 ICKWORTH HOUSE PARK AND GARDENS

10/9/99 Tel: 01284 735270

An autumnal walk in Ickworth's glowing woods led by the Head Forester. Bring walking shoes and waterproofs. Time: 10.00-12.00. Cost: £5.00, booking essential, call 01284 735270.

Historic Houses & Gardens

Bat Walk

10/9/99 WICKEN FEN (NT) NATURE RESERVE

10/9/99 Tel: 01353 720274

Learn all about these often misunderstood creatures and of the different species at Wicken Fen with Property Manager Adrian Colston. Starts at 19.30, A£3.75 C£2.50

Nature Reserves

Country Lifestyle Fair

10/9/99 HATFIELD HOUSE

12/9/99 Tel: 01707 262823

Everything under one roof for country folk. Time: 10.00-17.00. Cost: A£5.00. For further information please tel: 01494 450504

Historic Houses & Gardens

Essex Steam Rally and Country Fair

11/9/99 BARLEYLANDS FARM MUSEUM AND VISITORS CENTRE

12/9/99 Tel: 01268 282090/532253

Country show for all the family, 80 steam engines, vintage tractors, cars, motorbikes and commercials. Many rural demonstrations, working heavy horses, full arena programmes, 150 craft stands, trade stands and food hall, 10.00-17.00, (98 prices, for guideline only) A£5.00 C&OAPs&Students£2.00

Museum- Farms

VW Action

11/9/99 EAST OF ENGLAND SHOWGROUND

12/9/99 Tel: 01733 234451

Live bands, top DJs, concourse/show cars, trade stands, mega movie screen

(all night), speedway, autojumble, club displays, stunt displays, marching bands, "Miss VW" competition, charity auction

Showgrounds

Classic Bikes (CRMC)

11/9/99 SNETTERTON CIRCUIT

12/9/99 Tel: 01953 887303

All classes of national solo motorcycles and sidecars. Full Circuit, Grade-D. On the Gate: £10.00-£28.00. In Advance: Non £8.00-£25.00, Club £7.00-£22.00. Two Day Pass: Non £11.00-£30.00, Club £10.00-£27.00. Three Day Pass: Non £32.00, Club £29.00. Qualifying: £5.00-£14.00. C£Free. Programme £Free-£5.00. Seating (BH): £Free-£8.00. Group Tickets: Non £90.00-£95.00, Club £80.00-£85.00. Season Ticket Inc. of Club Membership: £150.00. You can buy your tickets for any of the 1999 events in advance any time up to 4 days before an event and make a saving, Tel: 0870 60 60 611

Motor Racing Circuit

Old Leigh Regatta

11/9/99 SOUTHEND ON SEA BOROUGH COUNCIL

12/9/99 Tel: 01702 215166

The annual weekend of fun and frivolity held in a traditional old fishing town atmosphere. The unique combination of sailing races and novelty water events, together with the unusual sights of cockle and banana eating contests and football on the mud, have made this an eagerly awaited event. For further information please call 01702 710851

Festivals

Jazz Prints

11/9/99 PETERBOROUGH MUSEUM AND ART GALLERY

10/10/99 Tel: 01733 343329

An exhibition of prints inspired the magical charms of jazz

Museum- Local History

Sports Saloon Challenge (BARC)

12/9/99 CADWELL PARK CIRCUIT

12/9/99 Tel: 01507 343248

Caterham Superlights, Caterham Roadsports, Austin Healeys, BMWs, Ginettas, 2CVs, Sports 1600s, Westfields. Full Circuit, Grade-D. On the Gate: £10.00-£28.00. In Advance: Non £8.00-£25.00, Club £7.00-£22.00. Two Day Pass: Non £11.00-£30.00, Club £10.00-£27.00. Three Day Pass: Non £32.00, Club £29.00. Qualifying: £5.00-

Further more detailed information on the attractions listed can be found in Best Guides *Visitor Attractions* Guide under the classifications shown

£14.00. C£Free. Programme £Free-£5.00. Seating (BH): £Free-£8.00. Group Tickets: Non £90.00-£95.00, Club £80.00-£85.00. Season Ticket Inc. of Club Membership: £135.00. You can buy your tickets for any of the 1999 events in advance any time up to 4 days before an event and make a saving, Tel: 0870 60 60 611

Motor Racing Circuit

Wildlife Walk: Marmalade, Muffins and Moths

12/9/99 DUNWICH HEATH AND MINSMERE BEACH
12/9/99 Tel: 01728 648505
A chance to lift the lid on the moths of Dunwich Heath followed by marmalade and muffins. Time: 08.00. Tickets: £5.50.

Conservation Parks

Pond Dip Day

12/9/99 HATFIELD FOREST
12/9/99 Tel: 01279 870678
Have a go at finding and identifying the huge variety of wildlife that lives in our ponds at Hatfield Forest. Commences 11.00-14.00. Tickets: A£Free C£2.00. Car Park £3.00 NT members £Free. Please note that you must book for all events except where stated otherwise. Please send a cheque payable to National Trust, along with an s.a.e. for your tickets.

Forests

National Garden Scheme Open Day

12/9/99 ICKWORTH HOUSE PARK AND GARDENS
12/9/99 Tel: 01284 735270
Gardens open and all proceeds go to local charities. Time: 10.00-15.00.

Historic Houses & Gardens

Duxford 1999 Air Show

12/9/99 IMPERIAL WAR MUSEUM, DUXFORD
12/9/99 Tel: 0891 516816 premium line
Duxford's September Air Show will be celebrating a century of air power, and will feature aircraft from the earliest days of military aviation, up to the supersonic combat aircraft of today. A£15.00 Concessions£7.50 C£Free* OAPs£12.00. Advance Tickets: A£12/50 Concessions£6.25 OAPs£10.00. *Children must be accompanied by an adult to qualify for FREE entry. Advance Coach Rates: £450.00 closing date 31.8.99. Advance tickets for this event maybe purchased by credit card through TicketMaster 24hrs, daily on 0990 344 4444, from Jan 1999

Museum- Aviation

Free Entry Day

15/9/99 OXBURGH HALL, GARDEN AND ESTATE
15/9/99 Tel: 01366 328258
The House will be open from 11.00 for free entry.

Historic Buildings

Free Entry Day

15/9/99 WICKEN FEN (NT) NATURE RESERVE
15/9/99 Tel: 01353 720274
Come and explore the Fen for free! Guided walks at 11.00 and 14.00

Nature Reserves

Wicken Wildlife Watch

16/9/99 WICKEN FEN (NT) NATURE RESERVE
16/9/99 Tel: 01353 720274
Learn all about wildlife at our monthly Watch group meeting for kids. £0.25 for Watch members £1.00 for non-members but please phone to book your place (8-12 years) 16.30-18.00

Nature Reserves

National Hunt Racing

17/9/99 HUNTINGDON STEEPLECHASES LTD
17/9/99 Tel: 01480 453373
A day of competitive racing from 14.20. For information on group bookings or private facilities for your party please contact 01480 453373

Racecourses

Behind the Scenes at Huntingdon Racecourse

17/9/99 NATIONAL HORSERACING MUSEUM AND TOURS
17/9/99 Tel: 01638 667333
Minibus tour which will take you on a tour of the racecourse, including the weighing room and jockey's sauna. There will be time for lunch (not included) before indulging in a feast of National Hunt racing in the afternoon, with your guide on hand to advise you. Departs 09.30. Price: £25.00 includes bade for members' enclosure.

Museum- Horse racing

Great Autumn Rose Show

17/9/99 THE GARDENS OF THE ROSE (ROYAL NATIONAL ROSE SOCIETY)
19/9/99 Tel: 01727 850461
The lovely colours of autumn roses can be seen at their best at this show

Gardens- Roses

Murder Mystery Supper

18/9/99 DUNWICH HEATH AND MINSMERE BEACH
18/9/99 Tel: 01728 648505
A murder has been committed. Can you spot the clues. Join in with a sizzling supper and evening of detection and fun. Time: 18.00. Tickets: £18.95.

Conservation Parks

Market Rasen Fixture

18/9/99 MARKET RASEN RACECOURSE
18/9/99 Tel: 01673 843434
First race: 14.15. Please call for further information

Racecourses

Identifying Mammals

18/9/99 WICKEN FEN (NT) NATURE RESERVE
18/9/99 Tel: 01353 720274
A one day course learning about the various species of mammals found at Wicken Fen, their ecology and identification. A£25.00 includes lunch, 10.00-17.00

Nature Reserves

Tail End Event

18/9/99 EAST OF ENGLAND SHOWGROUND
19/9/99 Tel: 01733 234451
Motorcycling Festival

Showgrounds

Craft Fair

18/9/99 ELTON HALL
19/9/99 Tel: 01832 280468
50 stands of lovely handmade goods. All under cover in the picturesque Stable Block. Home-made refreshments. 10.00-17.00

Historic Houses & Gardens

Recreation of Tudor Life at Michaelmas

18/9/99 KENTWELL HALL
19/9/99 Tel: 01787 310207
Life at Kentwell in the year 1600. Time: 11.00-17.00. Prices: A£6.50 C£4.40 OAPs£5.60. Pre-booked groups 20+ 20% discount

Historic Houses & Gardens

Marine Conservation Society Beachwatch '99

18/9/99 ORFORD NESS
19/9/99 Tel: 01394 450900
Join other volunteers to survey and clean the beach as part of an International Coastal Clean-up. Details available later.

Nature Reserves

750 M/C Autumn Weekender (750 M/C)

18/9/99 SNETTERTON CIRCUIT
19/9/99 Tel: 01953 887303
Programme to be confirmed. Full Circuit, Grade-E. On the Gate: £10.00-£28.00. In Advance: Non £8.00-£25.00, Club £7.00-£22.00. Two Day Pass: Non £11.00-£30.00, Club £10.00-£27.00. Three Day Pass: Non £32.00, Club £29.00. Qualifying: £5.00-£14.00. C£Free.

Programme £Free-£5.00. Seating (BH): £Free-£8.00. Group Tickets: Non £90.00-£95.00, Club £80.00-£85.00. Season Ticket Inc. of Club Membership: £150.00. You can buy your tickets for any of the 1999 events in advance any time up to 4 days before an event and make a saving, Tel: 0870 60 60 611

Motor Racing Circuit

Steam Fayre

18/9/99 THE SHUTTLEWORTH COLLECTION
19/9/99 Tel: 0891 323310
Vintage steam vehicles from near and far, ideal for steam enthusiasts, held in Old Warden Park.

Museum- Aviation

Nature for Adults

19/9/99 BLICKLING HALL
19/9/99 Tel: 01263 738030
Back to your childhood - exploring nature for grown-ups! Commences: 15.00. Tickets: A£2.50. Bookings can be made by telephone, to the address, or in person.

Historic Houses & Gardens

MG Masters (MGCC)

19/9/99 CADWELL PARK CIRCUIT
19/9/99 Tel: 01507 343248
Thoroughbred Sports Cars, International BCV8, Midget Challenge, Metro Challenge, MG Phoenix, ACE MG Cockshoot, MGF Trophy. Full Circuit, Grade-D. On the Gate: £10.00-£28.00. In Advance: Non £8.00-£25.00, Club £7.00-£22.00. Two Day Pass: Non £11.00-£30.00, Club £10.00-£27.00. Three Day Pass: Non £32.00, Club £29.00. Qualifying: £5.00-£14.00. C£Free. Programme £Free-£5.00. Seating (BH): £Free-£8.00. Group Tickets: Non £90.00-£95.00, Club £80.00-£85.00. Season Ticket Inc. of Club Membership: £135.00. You can buy your tickets for any of the 1999 events in advance any time up to 4 days before an event and make a saving, Tel: 0870 60 60 611

Motor Racing Circuit

National Garden Scheme Day

19/9/99 FELBRIGG HALL
19/9/99 Tel: 01263 837444
Your visit to the gardens at Felbrigg Hall will contribute to the upkeep of local charities through the national fund raising scheme. Please find time to visit us today. Usual admission

Historic Houses & Gardens

Ickworth Plant Fair

19/9/99 19/9/99	**ICKWORTH HOUSE PARK AND GARDENS** Tel: 01284 735270 Ickworth's annual Autumn Plant Fair featuring the best of specialist nurseries. Time: 10.00-17.00. Standard Park Admission. *Historic Houses & Gardens*

Mad Hatter's Extravaganza

19/9/99 19/9/99	**LEIGHTON BUZZARD RAILWAY** Tel: 01525 373888 (24hours) Accompanied children with mad hats travel free. Enjoy the family entertainment, and enter our prize competition *Railways Steam/Light*

Donkey Show

19/9/99 19/9/99	**WIMPOLE HALL** Tel: 01223 207257 10.30-17.00, standard admission *Country Parks*

Folklore of Trees

22/9/99 22/9/99	**HATFIELD FOREST** Tel: 01279 870678 Myths , legends and medicinal usage ancient and modern will be discussed whilst enjoying a leisurely stroll through the Forest. Commences 14.00-16.00. Tickets: £2.00 C£1.00 Family Ticket (A2+C2)£5.00. Car Park £3.00 NT members £Free. Please note that you must book for all events except where stated otherwise. Please send a cheque payable to National Trust, along with an s.a.e. for your tickets. *Forests*

Photography Day

22/9/99 22/9/99	**ORFORD NESS** Tel: 01394 450900 A chance to develop your techniques in black and white using the unique back this 'secret site'. Tuition will be provided by Nick Catling. Bring own equipment. Bring suitable clothing for the weather. Bring own food and drink. Meet: 09.30 prompt at Orford Quay. Depart: approx. 17.00. Cost: £25.00 for all, includes a free film. Maximum 20 people. *Nature Reserves*

Garden Open Day

22/9/99 22/9/99	**OXBURGH HALL, GARDEN AND ESTATE** Tel: 01366 328258 Meet the Gardener, tours of the workshop and greenhouse area, 11.30 &14.30, normal opening times and admission charges apply *Historic Buildings*

Abbey Event - Flower Festival

22/9/99	**ANGLESEY ABBEY, GARDENS AND LODE MILL**

26/9/99	Tel: 01223 811200 13.00-16.30. Glorious nature. Normal admission charges apply. *Historic Houses & Gardens*

Garden Skills Day

23/9/99 23/9/99	**ANGLESEY ABBEY, GARDENS AND LODE MILL** Tel: 01223 811200 Find out how the gardeners at Anglesey Abbey Gardens manage the hedging, tree surgery and lawn care. *Historic Houses & Gardens*

Eastern Events Craft Fair

24/9/99 26/9/99	**CHILFORD HALL VINEYARD** Tel: 01223 892641 Three days filled with craft and craft related exhibitors, with demonstrations and displays/ A£2.50 Concessions£2.00 (98 prices for guidance only) *Vineyards*

Poetry Festival 1999

24/9/99 26/9/99	**POETRY FESTIVAL 1999** Tel: 01553 691661/761919 Eight leading UK or International poets will be invited to stay the weekend and will give a reading and join in discussions. *Festivals*

ON SHOW 12

24/9/99 28/11/99	**USHER GALLERY** Tel: 01522 527980 Annual open-submission exhibition which provides a show case for the work of younger, less-established artists from the Eastern Arts Board Region *Art Galleries*

Clubmans Bikes (PEGASUS)

25/9/99 25/9/99	**CADWELL PARK CIRCUIT** Tel: 01507 343248 All classes of national solo motorcycles and sidecars. Club Circuit, Grade-E. On the Gate: £10.00-£28.00. In Advance: Non £8.00-£25.00, Club £7.00-£22.00. Two Day Pass: Non £11.00-£30.00, Club £10.00-£27.00. Three Day Pass: Non £32.00, Club £29.00. Qualifying: £5.00-£14.00. C£Free. Programme £Free-£5.00. Seating (BH): £Free-£8.00. Group Tickets: Non £90.00-£95.00, Club £80.00-£85.00. Season Ticket Inc. of Club Membership: £135.00. You can buy your tickets for any of the 1999 events in advance any time up to 4 days before an event and make a saving, Tel: 0870 60 60 611 *Motor Racing Circuit*

Native American Day

25/9/99
25/9/99
WICKEN FEN (NT) NATURE RESERVE
Tel: 01353 720274
Event starts at 11.00-15.00, Tickets
A&C£3.50. Details to be confirmed,
please telephone for further information
Nature Reserves

Identifying Snails

25/9/99
25/9/99
WICKEN FEN (NT) NATURE RESERVE
Tel: 01353 720274
A one day course learning about these
strange little creatures, their ecology
and identification and the various
species found at Wicken Fen. A£25.00
includes lunch, 10.00-17.00
Nature Reserves

Medieval Monastic Entertainers

25/9/99
26/9/99
DENNY ABBEY AND THE FARMLAND
MUSEUM
Tel: 01223 860489
Try your hand at calligraphy or authentic
period games as this popular duo take a
light-hearted look at monastic customs,
crafts and lifestyles. Learn about food
preparation, herbs and spice in cooking
and medicine, the mechanics of buildid-
ng and lifting and many other skills.
A£3.00 C£1.50 Concessions£2.30
Abbeys

Chocoholics Heavenly Weekend

25/9/99
26/9/99
DUNWICH HEATH AND MINSMERE BEACH
Tel: 01728 648505
Chocolate is served in many different
ways in the Restaurant. No booking
required.
Conservation Parks

1940's Weekend

25/9/99
26/9/99
NORTH NORFOLK RAILWAY
Tel: 01263 822045
Travel back with us to wartime Norfolk
Railways Steam/Light

Smugglers & Revenue Men

25/9/99
26/9/99
ORFORD CASTLE
Tel: 01394 450472
1678: Can the revenue men stop local
people in their lucrative trade of smuggling wool abroad? Plots abound! From
12.00. A£3.50 C£1.80 Concessions£2.50.
EH Members Free
Castles

Clubmans Bikes (RETFORD)

26/9/99
26/9/99
CADWELL PARK CIRCUIT
Tel: 01507 343248
All classes of national solo motorcycles
and sidecars. Club Circuit, Grade-E. On
the Gate: £10.00-£28.00. In Advance:
Non £8.00-£25.00, Club £7.00-£22.00.

Two Day Pass: Non £11.00-£30.00, Club
£10.00-£27.00. Three Day Pass: Non
£32.00, Club £29.00. Qualifying: £5.00-
£14.00. C£Free. Programme £Free-£5.00.
Seating (BH): £Free-£8.00. Group
Tickets: Non £90.00-£95.00, Club
£80.00-£85.00. Season Ticket Inc. of
Club Membership: £135.00. You can buy
your tickets for any of the 1999 events in
advance any time up to 4 days before an
event and make a saving, Tel: 0870 60
60 611
Motor Racing Circuit

Nature Arts and Crafts Day

26/9/99
26/9/99
HATFIELD FOREST
Tel: 01279 870678
Come along and make an animal box for
your garden, and take part in various
other craft activities for all the family.
Commences: 13.00-16.00. Tickets:
C£3.00. Car Park £3.00 NT members
£Free. Please note that you must book
for all events except where stated other-
wise. Please send a cheque payable to
National Trust, along with an s.a.e. for
your tickets.
Forests

Family Fun Day

26/9/99
26/9/99
HUNTINGDON STEEPLECHASES LTD
Tel: 01480 453373
Bring the family to Huntingdon where a
large crowd and great atmosphere
promises to make it a wonderful day
out. All children under 16 can enter free
of charge and with a fully supervised
creche, bouncy castle, tubeslide and
face-painting, there is lots to do for all
the family. Racing from 14.30
Racecourses

Guided Walk

26/9/99
26/9/99
ORFORD NESS
Tel: 01394 450900
Walk with the Warden looking at the
many varied aspects of this unique site.
Meet: 10.00 prompt at Orford Quay.
Depart approx: 16.00. Cost: £12.50 for
all. Maximum 24 people. Bring suitable
clothing for the weather. Bring own food
and drink.
Nature Reserves

Historic Race Day (HSCC)

26/9/99
26/9/99
SNETTERTON CIRCUIT
Tel: 01953 887303
All classes of historic racing and sports
cars. Full Circuit, Grade-D. On the Gate:
£10.00-£28.00. In Advance: Non £8.00-
£25.00, Club £7.00-£22.00. Two Day

Further more detailed information on the attractions listed can be found
in Best Guides *Visitor Attractions* Guide under the classifications shown

Pass: Non £11.00-£30.00, Club £10.00-£27.00. Three Day Pass: Non £32.00, Club £29.00. Qualifying: £5.00-£14.00. C£Free. Programme £Free-£5.00. Seating (BH): £Free-£8.00. Group Tickets: Non £90.00-£95.00, Club £80.00-£85.00. Season Ticket Inc. of Club Membership: £150.00. You can buy your tickets for any of the 1999 events in advance any time up to 4 days before an event and make a saving, Tel: 0870 60 60 611

Motor Racing Circuit

Kite Society Autumn Display

26/9/99   THE SHUTTLEWORTH COLLECTION
26/9/99   Tel: 0891 323310
Another chance to take part in this colourful spectacle. Fly your kite all day on the airfield at Old Warden in lovely scenery.

Museum- Aviation

Behind the Scenes at Orford Ness

29/9/99   ORFORD NESS
29/9/99   Tel: 01394 450900
A chance to hear and see about management of a National Trust Property. Do Wardens just sit and watch birds all day? Come and see for yourself. Bring suitable clothing for the weather. Tea and coffee provided but bring your own lunch. Binoculars may be useful. Meet: 10.00 prompt at Orford Quay. Depart: approx. 16.00. Cost: £15.00 for all.

Nature Reserves

Vendange Supper

30/9/99   ICKWORTH HOUSE PARK AND GARDENS
30/9/99   Tel: 01284 735270
Celebrate the White Grape harvest at Ickworth with a tour of Ickworth's vineyard led by its creators, Jillian Simms and Charles Macready, followed by a Vendange Supper. Bring walking shoes and waterproofs. Time: 18.00-21.00. Cost: £18.50, includes wine tasting. Booking essential call 01284 735270.

Historic Houses & Gardens

First Firday

1/10/99   ANGLESEY ABBEY, GARDENS AND LODE MILL
1/10/99   Tel: 01223 811200
Take a closer look at The Living Room. Time: 13.00-16.00. Normal admission charges apply.

Historic Houses & Gardens

Remembering Cromwell

1/10/99   CROMWELL MUSEUM
1/12/99   Tel: 01480 425830
An exhibition of Cromwell in Popular Culture. Tue-Fri 13.00-16.00, Sat 11.00-13.00 & 14.00-16.00, Sun 14.00-16.00

Museum- Local History

Autumn Leaves

2/10/99   BRIDGE COTTAGE
2/10/99   Tel: 01206 298260
After a heart warming brunch, enjoy John Constable's views of the vale in all its glorious autumnal colours. Time: 10.45. Tickets: £8.50.

Historic Buildings

Autumn Extra

2/10/99   LEIGHTON BUZZARD RAILWAY
2/10/99   Tel: 01525 373888 (24hours)
Small locos double-heading passenger trains, plus Steam Glow floodlit photography event in the evening (extra charge applies)

Railways Steam/Light

Clubmans Bikes (NEW ERA)

2/10/99   CADWELL PARK CIRCUIT
3/10/99   Tel: 01507 343248
All classes of national solo motorcycles and sidecars. Full Circuit, Grade-E. On the Gate: £10.00-£28.00. In Advance: Non £8.00-£25.00, Club £7.00-£22.00. Two Day Pass: Non £11.00-£30.00, Club £10.00-£27.00. Three Day Pass: Non £32.00, Club £29.00. Qualifying: £5.00-£14.00. C£Free. Programme £Free-£5.00. Seating (BH): £Free-£8.00. Group Tickets: Non £90.00-£95.00, Club £80.00-£85.00. Season Ticket Inc. of Club Membership: £135.00. You can buy your tickets for any of the 1999 events in advance any time up to 4 days before an event and make a saving, Tel: 0870 60 60 611

Motor Racing Circuit

Living History Festival

2/10/99   OXBURGH HALL, GARDEN AND ESTATE
3/10/99   Tel: 01366 328258
Meet costumed Characters from the Tudor Times. Commences 13.00-16.00. Normal opening times and admission charges apply

Historic Buildings

Five Hours Walking!

3/10/99   BLICKLING HALL
3/10/99   Tel: 01263 738030
A long distance walk, for those who would like to see parts of the estate that the others walks miss. Commences: 11.00 for about 5 hours, bring a picnic.

A£5.00. Bookings can be made by telephone, to the address, or in person.

Historic Houses & Gardens

Championship Car Races (BRSCC)

3/10/99 SNETTERTON CIRCUIT
3/10/99 Tel: 01953 887303
Formula 600s, Porsche 924s plus support. Full Circuit, Grade-D. On the Gate: £10.00-£28.00. In Advance: Non £8.00-£25.00, Club £7.00-£22.00. Two Day Pass: Non £11.00-£30.00, Club £10.00-£27.00. Three Day Pass: Non £32.00, Club £29.00. Qualifying: £5.00-£14.00. C£Free. Programme £Free-£5.00. Seating (BH): £Free-£8.00. Group Tickets: Non £90.00-£95.00, Club £80.00-£85.00. Season Ticket Inc. of Club Membership: £150.00. You can buy your tickets for any of the 1999 events in advance any time up to 4 days before an event and make a saving, Tel: 0870 60 60 611

Motor Racing Circuit

Autumn Air Day

3/10/99 THE SHUTTLEWORTH COLLECTION
3/10/99 Tel: 0891 323310
This is the last of 1998's flying display days and with the possible onset of autumnal weather, the programme will include the more robust aircraft from the Collection. The Shuttle Mansion House will be open 14.00-17.00 for visitors to se the splendour of this home.

Museum- Aviation

Steam Threshing

3/10/99 CHURCH FARM MUSEUM
10/10/99 Tel: 01754 766658
Step back in time and experience the sights and sounds of harvest as it once was

Museum- Farms

Inspired by the Past

3/10/99 VERULAMIUM MUSEUM AND PARK
27/11/99 Tel: 01727 819339
A celebration of stitching showing current trends in textiles and embroidery

Museums

Bedford Beer Festival

6/10/99 BEDFORD BEER FESTIVAL 1999
9/10/99 Tel: 0171 438 7600
Venue: Corn Exchange, St Pauls Square, Bedford. Sample Real Ales from all over the UK. Also sample Belgian Beer. Saturday evening listen to live music. Times: 7-10 Oct 1998. 7th: 17.00-22.45; 8th: 11.30-14.30 & 17.00-22.45; 9th & 10th: 11.30-22.45. Prices: A£2.00 per

head after 18.00, except Fri A£2.50 per head. C£Free (not allowed after 18.00). Special discounts to CAMRA members. Tickets available from the door

Festivals

Talk: Galleywood Common Success Story by Tony Walentowicz

8/10/99 CHELMSFORD AND ESSEX REGIMENT MUSEUM
8/10/99 Tel: 01245 353066
Describing the restoration of parts of the common to its former glory as a lowland heath. Time: 20.00. Cost: £1.00, Friends of the Museum £0.50. Booking essential on 01245 353066

Museum- Local History

Windham Supper

8/10/99 FELBRIGG HALL
8/10/99 Tel: 01263 837444
Provisional. Enjoy a four course Victorian Supper in the Park Restaurant with musical interludes. Enjoy an evening of 19th century food and song much as the Windham family at the Hall would have exprienced more than a 100 years ago. Commences: 19.00 for 17.30. Tickets: £17.95, limited numbers, please book direct with the Restaurant on 01263 838237

Historic Houses & Gardens

National Hunt Racing

8/10/99 HUNTINGDON STEEPLECHASES LTD
8/10/99 Tel: 01480 453373
See competitive racing with all the thrills and spills of National Hunt Racing. First race at 14.10

Racecourses

Autumn Leaves

10/10/99 BRIDGE COTTAGE
10/10/99 Tel: 01206 298260
After a heart warming brunch, enjoy John Constable's views of the vale in all its glorious autumnal colours. Time: 10.45. Tickets: £8.50.

Historic Buildings

Autumn Saloon Spectacular (BRSCC)

10/10/99 CADWELL PARK CIRCUIT
10/10/99 Tel: 01507 343248
ModProd Saloons, Fiats, Alfas and Auto Italia plus support. Full Circuit, Grade-D. On the Gate: £10.00-£28.00. In Advance: Non £8.00-£25.00, Club £7.00-£22.00. Two Day Pass: Non £11.00-£30.00, Club £10.00-£27.00. Three Day Pass: Non £32.00, Club £29.00. Qualifying: £5.00-£14.00. C£Free. Programme £Free-£5.00. Seating (BH): £Free-£8.00. Group

Tickets: Non £90.00-£95.00, Club £80.00-£85.00. Season Ticket Inc. of Club Membership: £135.00. You can buy your tickets for any of the 1999 events in advance any time up to 4 days before an event and make a saving, Tel: 0870 60 60 611

Motor Racing Circuit

Wildlife Walk: Fungi Foray
10/10/99 DUNWICH HEATH AND MINSMERE BEACH
10/10/99 Tel: 01728 648505
Guided by an expert. Join us for our annual fungi hunt, what's safe and what's not. Time: 10.30 & 14.00. Tickets: £4.00.

Conservation Parks

Autumn Exhibition
10/10/99 EAST OF ENGLAND SHOWGROUND
10/10/99 Tel: 01733 234451
Small livestock and rare breeds

Showgrounds

Trusty the Hedgehog Hibernation Trail
10/10/99 HATFIELD FOREST
10/10/99 Tel: 01279 870678
Find the secret clues, and discover the different types of food Trusty needs to eat before going to sleep for the winter. Tickets: C£3.00. Car Park £3.00 NT members £Free. Please note that you must book for all events except where stated otherwise. Please send a cheque payable to National Trust, along with an s.a.e. for your tickets.

Forests

Formula Palmer Audi Race Day (BARC)
10/10/99 SNETTERTON CIRCUIT
10/10/99 Tel: 01953 887303
Formula Palmer Audi, K Sport, 1600, BMW Challenge, Caterham Sport Scholarship, Post Historic Touring Cars, Group 1 Touring Cars, Modified Production Saloon, Austin Healey Club Race. Full Circuit, Grade-D. On the Gate: £10.00-£28.00. In Advance: Non £8.00-£25.00, Club £7.00-£22.00. Two Day Pass: Non £11.00-£30.00, Club £10.00-£27.00. Three Day Pass: Non £32.00, Club £29.00. Qualifying: £5.00-£14.00. C£Free. Programme £Free-£5.00. Seating (BH): £Free-£8.00. Group Tickets: Non £90.00-£95.00, Club £80.00-£85.00. Season Ticket Inc. of Club Membership: £150.00. You can buy your tickets for any of the 1999 events in advance any time up to 4 days before an event and make a saving, Tel: 0870 60 60 611

Motor Racing Circuit

Southend Classic 10K Road Race
10/10/99 SOUTHEND ON SEA BOROUGH COUNCIL
10/10/99 Tel: 01702 215166
Enjoy the scenic route along Southend's picturesque Seafront providing a fast flat course for both experienced runners and beginners. Race starts at 11.00. For an entry form or further information please write to: 101 Kenilworth Avenue, Westcliff-on-Sea, Essex SS0 0BA

Festivals

Mushroom Mania
11/10/99 DUNWICH HEATH AND MINSMERE BEACH
11/10/99 Tel: 01728 648505
They will be served all day in the Restaurant. No booking required.

Conservation Parks

Vendange Supper
14/10/99 ICKWORTH HOUSE PARK AND GARDENS
14/10/99 Tel: 01284 735270
Celebrate the Red Grape harvest at Ickworth with a tour of Ickworth's vineyard led by its creators, Jillian Simms and Charles Macready, followed by a Vendange Supper. Bring walking shoes and waterproofs. Time: 18.00-21.00. Cost: £18.50, includes wine tasting. Booking essential call 01284 735270.

Historic Houses & Gardens

Wicken Wildlife Watch
14/10/99 WICKEN FEN (NT) NATURE RESERVE
14/10/99 Tel: 01353 720274
Learn all about wildlife at our monthly Watch group meeting for kids. £0.25 for Watch members £1.00 for non-members but please phone to book your place (8-12 years) 16.30-18.00

Nature Reserves

The Quintessential Quince
15/10/99 OXBURGH HALL, GARDEN AND ESTATE
15/10/99 Tel: 01366 328258
An evening looking at this old fashioned fruit grown in Oxburgh's orchard. Graham Donachie will talk about growing Quince and Alison Sloan will prepare some delicious savoury and sweet dishes for tasting. Recipes will be available. Time: 19.00. Tickets: £12.50, booking essential

Historic Buildings

Water Voles
15/10/99 WICKEN FEN (NT) NATURE RESERVE
15/10/99 Tel: 01353 720274
A talk by leading expert Adrian Colston on the decline of one of the country's favourite mammals - Ratty from Wind in

the Willows. A£2.50, starts at 19.30

Nature Reserves

Vintage Motorcycles (VMCC)

16/10/99 CADWELL PARK CIRCUIT

16/10/99 Tel: 01507 343248

All classes of Vintage motorcycles. Club Circuit, Grade-E. On the Gate: £10.00-£28.00. In Advance: Non £8.00-£25.00, Club £7.00-£22.00. Two Day Pass: Non £11.00-£30.00, Club £10.00-£27.00. Three Day Pass: Non £32.00, Club £29.00. Qualifying: £5.00-£14.00. C£Free. Programme £Free-£5.00. Seating (BH): £Free-£8.00. Group Tickets: Non £90.00-£95.00, Club £80.00-£85.00. Season Ticket Inc. of Club Membership: £135.00. You can buy your tickets for any of the 1999 events in advance any time up to 4 days before an event and make a saving, Tel: 0870 60 60 611

Motor Racing Circuit

Mushroom Mania

16/10/99 HATFIELD FOREST

16/10/99 Tel: 01279 870678

Walk with the experts to identify the many species of fungi present in the Forest. Tickets: £2.00 C£1.00 Family Ticket (A2+C2)£5.00. Car Park £3.00 NT members £Free. Please note that you must book for all events except where stated otherwise. Please send a cheque payable to National Trust, along with an s.a.e. for your tickets.

Forests

Guided Walk

16/10/99 ORFORD NESS

16/10/99 Tel: 01394 450900

Walk with the Warden looking at the many varied aspects of this unique site. Meet: 10.00 prompt at Orford Quay. Depart approx: 16.00. Cost: £12.50 for all. Maximum 24 people. Bring suitable clothing for the weather. Bring own food and drink.

Nature Reserves

Christmas Fair

16/10/99 AUDLEY END HOUSE

17/10/99 Tel: 01799 522399

Our third annual Christmas Craft Fair where you will be able to purchase unusual gifts for family and friends. A£4.00 Concessions£3.00 C£2.00 (House extra, subject to capacity) EH Members Free

Historical Remains

Apple Weekend

16/10/99 DUNWICH HEATH AND MINSMERE BEACH

17/10/99 Tel: 01728 648505

Apples will be served all day in the Restaurant. No booking required.

Conservation Parks

Deer Safari

16/10/99 DUNWICH HEATH AND MINSMERE BEACH

17/10/99 Tel: 01728 648505

A joint event with RSPB, Forest Enterprise & National Trust. Booking Office, 01728 648281 - RSPB. Time: 06.00 both days at Dunwich Heath. Tickets: £18.50.

Conservation Parks

Cats

16/10/99 STAMFORD MUSEUM

1/1/00 Tel: 01780 766317

An exhibition all about cats, their health, behaviour and history. Includes a display of cats in art

Museum- Local History

Pastimes in Times Past: Fun and Games in Chelmsford

16/10/99 CHELMSFORD AND ESSEX REGIMENT MUSEUM

23/1/00 Tel: 01245 353066

Athletics, bowls, cockfights, crafts, football, golf and horse-racing are just some of the subjects covered in this exhibition about leisure pursuits in Chelmsford over the past two centuries. Find out about 'Cook's World', the Young Peoples' Progressive Party and the Odde Volumes Society. Spot someone you remember from the Fantasy Football team, in an exhibition researched by the Friends of Chelmsford Museum

Museum- Local History

Crafts and Hobbies

17/10/99 CHURCH FARM MUSEUM

17/10/99 Tel: 01754 766658

Special chance to see a large variety of crafts and hobbies both old and new

Museum- Farms

Auto Jumble

17/10/99 EAST OF ENGLAND SHOWGROUND

17/10/99 Tel: 01733 234451

An event for car enthusiasts looking for 'that part'

Showgrounds

Roundtable Children's Hobble

17/10/99 HATFIELD FOREST

17/10/99 Tel: 01279 870678

Details to be announced. Car Park £3.00 NT members £Free

Forests

Further more detailed information on the attractions listed can be found in Best Guides *Visitor Attractions* Guide under the classifications shown

Autumn Air Show

17/10/99 IMPERIAL WAR MUSEUM, DUXFORD

17/10/99 Tel: 0891 516816 premium line

The country's last major air show of the Millennium, this event will feature an outstanding array of Duxford-based historic aircraft. Your last chance to see these rare and historic aircraft this century. A£12.00 Concessions£6.00 OAPs£10.00. Advance Tickets: A£10.50 Concessions£5.00 OAPs£8.00. Advance Coach Rates: £360.00 closing date 4.10.99. Advance tickets for this event maybe purchased by credit card through TicketMaster 24hrs, daily on 0990 344 4444, from Jan 1999

Museum- Aviation

A Migration Meander

17/10/99 ORFORD NESS

17/10/99 Tel: 01394 450900

A look at passage migrants on this important coastal site. No experience necessary. For an early start meet at 07.00 at the Martello Tower at Slaughden. Bring suitable clothing and footwear for the weather. Bring binoculars or telescope. Bring own food and drink. Cost: £10.00 for all.

Nature Reserves

East Midlands Doll Fair

17/10/99 WOBURN ABBEY

17/10/99 Tel: 01525 290666

Located in the Sculpture Gallery, the opportunity to buy dolls and toys, antique and new from the 54 exhibitors. 10.30-16.30

Stately Homes

Chandelier Tour and Supper

21/10/99 ICKWORTH HOUSE PARK AND GARDENS

21/10/99 Tel: 01284 735270

A private view of Ickworth House as dusk falls. The magnificent state rooms will be lit by the exquisitely beautiful chandeliers, creating a memorable setting for a guided tour led by the House Manager. Ickworth's collection of Regency furniture, silver, and Old Master paintings will all be featured. The tour is preceded by a two course supper in the Servants' Hall Restaurant. Time: 19.00-22.30. Cost: £18.00, booking essential, call 01284 735270.

Historic Houses & Gardens

Garden Tour - Autumn

23/10/99 ANGLESEY ABBEY, GARDENS AND LODE

MILL

23/10/99 Tel: 01223 811200

A tour of the entire garden to view the wonderful colours, led by Richard Ayres. Time: 14.00. Tickets £5.00 (including National Trust members), all ticket applications should be addressed to The Property Manager and include sae to: Anglesey Abbey, Gardens and Lode Mill, Quy Road, Lode, Cambridge CB5 9EJ

Historic Houses & Gardens

Autumn Leaves

23/10/99 BRIDGE COTTAGE

23/10/99 Tel: 01206 298260

After a heart warming brunch, enjoy John Constable's views of the vale in all its glorious autumnal colours. Time: 10.45. Tickets: £8.50.

Historic Buildings

Fun Day

23/10/99 CHELMSFORD AND ESSEX REGIMENT MUSEUM

23/10/99 Tel: 01245 353066

Activities for families with games and sport. Admission Free

Museum- Local History

Autumn Meeting

23/10/99 MARKET RASEN RACECOURSE

23/10/99 Tel: 01673 843434

First race: 14.15. Please call for further information

Racecourses

Anglo-Saxon Weaving Course

23/10/99 WEST STOW ANGLO SAXON VILLAGE

23/10/99 Tel: 01284 728718

Find out the basic techniques used the Anglo-Saxons to make cloth. Led by a professional weaver, this course will allow you to try out the methods for yourself. 10.30-16.30. A£15.00 Concessions£10.00. Places are limited, please book by 9 Oct

Archaeological Interest

Mananging Wet Grasslands for Birds

23/10/99 WICKEN FEN (NT) NATURE RESERVE

23/10/99 Tel: 01353 720274

An interesting course led by Property Manager Adrian Colston and Head Warden Martin Lester based on their experiences of managing grasslands to encourage the birdlife of Wicken Fen. A£25.00 includes lunch. 10.00-17.00

Nature Reserves

Halloween

23/10/99 AUDLEY END HOUSE

24/10/99 Tel: 01799 522399

Beaux Stratagems. Halloween the

Victorian way. A£6.00 C£3.00
Concessions£4.50

Historical Remains

750 M/C Birkett 6 Hour (750 M/C)
23/10/99 SNETTERTON CIRCUIT
24/10/99 Tel: 01953 887303
23 October: Race prepared cars, 24
October: Road going cars. Full Circuit,
Grade-E. On the Gate: £10.00-£28.00. In
Advance: Non £8.00-£25.00, Club £7.00-
£22.00. Two Day Pass: Non £11.00-
£30.00, Club £10.00-£27.00. Three Day
Pass: Non £32.00, Club £29.00.
Qualifying: £5.00-£14.00. C£Free.
Programme £Free-£5.00. Seating (BH):
£Free-£8.00. Group Tickets: Non £90.00-
£95.00, Club £80.00-£85.00. Season
Ticket Inc. of Club Membership: £150.00.
You can buy your tickets for any of the
1999 events in advance any time up to 4
days before an event and make a saving,
Tel: 0870 60 60 611

Motor Racing Circuit

Children's Toy Town Weekend
23/10/99 NORTH NORFOLK RAILWAY
25/10/99 Tel: 01263 822045
Please call for further information

Railways Steam/Light

October Half Term Fun
23/10/99 COLCHESTER ZOO
30/10/99 Tel: 01206 331292
Beastly Bugs, Creepy Crawly Week.
Enjoy the activity hour with a whole host
of creepy crawly Halloween activities,
including Halloween face painting and
story time. Check times before you visit.

Zoos

Secret Sandlings Walk: Fungi
24/10/99 DUNWICH HEATH AND MINSMERE BEACH
24/10/99 Tel: 01728 648505
Meet at the Phoenix Trail Car Park,
Rendlesham Forest Centre, Forest
Enterprise at 14.00. No booking
required. Enquiries, 01394 450164.

Conservation Parks

Autumn Colours
24/10/99 HATFIELD FOREST
24/10/99 Tel: 01279 870678
One of the most beautiful times of the
year in the Forest. Join a warden to visit
some of the most special areas to experience the colours. Commences: 14.00-
16.00. Tickets: £2.00 C£1.00 Family
Ticket (A2+C2)£5.00. Car Park £3.00 NT
members £Free. Please note that you
must book for all events except where
stated otherwise. Please send a cheque

payable to National Trust, along with an
s.a.e. for your tickets.

Forests

Creepy Crawlies and Scary Stories
25/10/99 ICKWORTH HOUSE PARK AND GARDENS
29/10/99 Tel: 01284 735270
Half-term fun for families. Self-guided
activities. Time: 13.00-16.00. Standard
Park Admission.

Historic Houses & Gardens

Autumn Activity Days
26/10/99 WEST STOW ANGLO SAXON VILLAGE
28/10/99 Tel: 01284 728718
Have fun in the Country Park, please call
for 01284 728718 for details of activities
planned

Archaeological Interest

Holiday Club
27/10/99 DUNWICH HEATH AND MINSMERE BEACH
27/10/99 Tel: 01728 648505
Children's environmental activities for
those aged 6-12 years. Bring packed
lunch or lunch money, 10.00-14.00,
C£4.00 A£Free, booking essential,
please apply direct to the property for
booking by telephone 01728 648505 or
by post to with a sae to: Dunwich Heath
& Minsmere Beach, Saxmundham,
Suffolk IP17 3DJ with a cheque made
payable to The National Trust
(Enterprises)

Conservation Parks

Hibernating Hedgehogs
27/10/99 WICKEN FEN (NT) NATURE RESERVE
27/10/99 Tel: 01353 720274
Come and learn all about hedgehogs
and why they hibernate. 10.00-12.00 or
14.00-16.00. Tickets: A&C (7-12 years)
£2.50

Nature Reserves

Spooky Ghosts and Batty Bats
29/10/99 WICKEN FEN (NT) NATURE RESERVE
29/10/99 Tel: 01353 720274
Find out about bats and vampires. Bring
a pumpkin and carve it up. Come
dressed up in your spookiest outfit and
you may win a prize. A&C£2.50 (7-12
years). 10.00-12.00 or 14.00-16.00

Nature Reserves

Children's Garden Tour
30/10/99 ANGLESEY ABBEY, GARDENS AND LODE
MILL
30/10/99 Tel: 01223 811200
With Trusty the hedgehog. Time: 14.00.
Tickets (including full access for the gardens) A&C(5-17)£3.00.

Historic Houses & Gardens

Halloween
30/10/99 BRIDGE COTTAGE
30/10/99 Tel: 01206 298260
A spooky stroll followed by a sizzling supper.......... of course only for those who dare!! Time: 19.00. Tickets: £14.95.

Historic Buildings

Spooky Supper
30/10/99 DUNWICH HEATH AND MINSMERE BEACH
30/10/99 Tel: 01728 648505
A tantalising and terrifying supper served by ghouls and ghosts, followed by a lantern walk onto the Heath for stories to send shivers down your spine. Time: 18.00. Tickets: £13.50.

Conservation Parks

Witches, Pumpkins & Fireworks
30/10/99 HATFIELD HOUSE
30/10/99 Tel: 01707 262823
A celebration of Halloween. Gates open 17.00, Fireworks 18.30. Bonfire and barbeque A£5.00 C£2.50

Historic Houses & Gardens

Hallowe'en Evening
30/10/99 OXBURGH HALL, GARDEN AND ESTATE
30/10/99 Tel: 01366 328258
Come if you dare for a spoooooooooky evening. Time: 19.00. Tickets: £10.00, booking essential

Historic Buildings

Ghost Walk
30/10/99 WICKEN FEN (NT) NATURE RESERVE
30/10/99 Tel: 01353 720274
Wicken's infamous ghost walk. Story telling and ghostly happenings around the boardwalk. Dress warmly. Not suitable for under 10's. A£4.50 C£2.50. Starts at 19.30

Nature Reserves

Natural Healing Exhibition
30/10/99 CHILFORD HALL VINEYARD
31/10/99 Tel: 01223 892641
From Herbal Remedies to Homeopathic practices we've got the lot, call for further details

Vineyards

Hallowe'en Mask Making
30/10/99 THE MANOR HOUSE MUSEUM
31/10/99 Tel: 01284 757076/757072
A workshop suitable for 10-14 years olds. Two sesions at 14.00-16.00 each day. £2.00 per child

Museum- Costume

Essex Salon of Photography
30/10/99 SOUTHEND ON SEA BOROUGH COUNCIL
11/12/99 Tel: 01702 215166
This annual photographic competition and exhibition is now in its 39th year, with entries from professional and amateur photographers from around the country. For further information please call 01702 215640

Festivals

Hallowe'en Celebrations
31/10/99 BLICKLING HALL
31/10/99 Tel: 01263 738030
Blickling Hall invites you to join them in celebrating Hallowe'en. Walks in the garden and park after dark what's stirring, have you got the nerve? Commences: 17.00-18.30. ALSO Spooktacular Tours at: 18.00, 20.00 & 23.00 Boo! Bookings can be made by telephone, to the address, or in person.

Historic Houses & Gardens

Spooky Walk
31/10/99 HATFIELD FOREST
31/10/99 Tel: 01279 870678
Ghosts, goblins, witches and warlocks - do they exist? Come and find out - if you dare... Bring a torch and some strong nerves. Commences: 20.00-22.00. Tickets: £2.00 C£1.00 Family Ticket (A2+C2)£5.00. Please note that you must book for all events except where stated otherwise. Please send a cheque payable to National Trust, along with an s.a.e. for your tickets.

Forests

Spirits of the Past
31/10/99 ICKWORTH HOUSE PARK AND GARDENS
31/10/99 Tel: 01284 735270
A special Halloween Event in Ickworth House. Meet the shades of Ickworth past and learn about Ickworth House and its history. Time: 18.00-20.00. Cost: A£5.00 C(5+)£1.00 Family Ticket A2+C2)£10.00. Booking essential 01284 735270.

Historic Houses & Gardens

Winter Championship Series (BRSCC)
31/10/99 SNETTERTON CIRCUIT
31/10/99 Tel: 01953 887303
Winter GT, Winter Saloons, Winter Formula Ford, Winter Formula First, Winter Minis, Winter Fiestas. Full Circuit, Grade-D. On the Gate: £10.00-£28.00. In Advance: Non £8.00-£25.00, Club £7.00-£22.00. Two Day Pass: Non £11.00-£30.00, Club £10.00-£27.00. Three Day Pass: Non £32.00, Club £29.00.

Qualifying: £5.00-£14.00. C£Free.
Programme £Free-£5.00. Seating (BH):
£Free-£8.00. Group Tickets: Non £90.00-
£95.00, Club £80.00-£85.00. Season
Ticket Inc. of Club Membership: £150.00.
You can buy your tickets for any of the
1999 events in advance any time up to 4
days before an event and make a saving,
Tel: 0870 60 60 611

Motor Racing Circuit

Hallowe'en Ghost Hunt
31/10/99 THE MANOR HOUSE MUSEUM
31/10/99 Tel: 01284 757076/757072
A ghostly tour of the Manor for both
adults and childen. Childrens' Tour:
18.00 £2.00; Adult Tour: 19.00 £5.00

Museum- Costume

Dunwich Heath Lunchtime Lecture
3/11/99 DUNWICH HEATH AND MINSMERE BEACH
3/11/99 Tel: 01728 648505
Please send an SAE marked 'Lectures'
for further details. A light lunch followed
by a lecture in the Field Study Centre.
Time: 12.30. Tickets: £9.95.

Conservation Parks

First Friday
5/11/99 ANGLESEY ABBEY, GARDENS AND LODE
MILL
5/11/99 Tel: 01223 811200
Take a Closer look at The Wiildlife inside
the House. Time: 14.00 at the
Restaurant.

Historic Houses & Gardens

Pudding Weekend
6/11/99 ICKWORTH HOUSE PARK AND GARDENS
7/11/99 Tel: 01284 735270
Sheer indulgence for those who love traditional puddings. Time: 12.00-16.00.
Tickets: £8.50, booking essential, call
01284 735270.

Historic Houses & Gardens

Bedfordshire Christmas Craft Fair
6/11/99 WOBURN ABBEY
7/11/99 Tel: 01525 290666
Popular craft fair with a variety of
exhibitors and entertainments for all the
family. 10.00-18.00. Admission charge
not set until 6 weeks before event. Call
01283 820548

Stately Homes

Craft Fair
6/11/99 WOBURN SAFARI PARK
7/11/99 Tel: 01525 290407
A beautiful Christmas craft fair to buy
those unusual gifts

Safari Parks

Sudbury's Choice

6/11/99 GAINSBOROUGH'S HOUSE
16/1/00 Tel: 01787 372958
The people of Sudbury's selection from
the Collection held in the Lower Gallery.
Christmas Crafts in the Weaving Room

Birth Places

Autumn Colours
7/11/99 HATFIELD HOUSE
7/11/99 Tel: 01707 262823
Special opening of the gardens and
park, 11.00-17.00, shop and restaurant
open. A£3.50 C£2.80

Historic Houses & Gardens

Lynn Stages Rally (KLDMC)
7/11/99 SNETTERTON CIRCUIT
7/11/99 Tel: 01953 887303
Sideways action from Rally Saloons. Full
Circuit, Grade-E. On the Gate: £10.00-
£28.00. In Advance: Non £8.00-£25.00,
Club £7.00-£22.00. Two Day Pass: Non
£11.00-£30.00, Club £10.00-£27.00.
Three Day Pass: Non £32.00, Club
£29.00. Qualifying: £5.00-£14.00.
C£Free. Programme £Free-£5.00.
Seating (BH): £Free-£8.00. Group
Tickets: Non £90.00-£95.00, Club
£80.00-£85.00. Season Ticket Inc. of
Club Membership: £150.00. You can buy
your tickets for any of the 1999 events in
advance any time up to 4 days before an
event and make a saving, Tel: 0870 60
60 611

Motor Racing Circuit

National Hunt Racing
9/11/99 HUNTINGDON STEEPLECHASES LTD
9/11/99 Tel: 01480 453373
See competitive racing with all the thrills
and spills of National Hunt Racing. First
race at 13.10

Racecourses

Ickworth House Putting to Bed Tour
9/11/99 ICKWORTH HOUSE PARK AND GARDENS
9/11/99 Tel: 01284 735270
Go behind the scenes at Ickworth House
to discover how the House and its collections are prepared for winter conservation and re-decoration programmes.
Time: 10.00-12.00. Cost: A£10.00
C(5+)£2.00, price includes coffee/soft
drink. Booking essential call 01284
735270.

Historic Houses & Gardens

**High Street Christmas Celebrity
Switch-On and Gala Night**
11/11/99 SOUTHEND ON SEA BOROUGH COUNCIL
11/11/99 Tel: 01702 215166
Come and join our celebrities as we

throw the switch to light up the Christmas tree and illuminations that run the full length of the High Street, followed by a Christmas Parade with Father Christmas and his sleigh pulled by live reindeer. Fun starts at 17.00

Festivals

St Martin's Day
11/11/99 ST MARTIN'S DAY
11/11/99 Tel: 01908 372825
St Martin's church, firing of Fenny Poppers (mini cannons packed with gunpowder and paper resembling cast iron beer mugs), in Leon recreation ground. Visit Bletchley Park (scene of WWII code breaking activity). Times: 12.00, 14.00 & 16.00 in Leon Recreation Ground, 19.00 in the Church. Admission Free

Festivals

Spooky Supper
13/11/99 DUNWICH HEATH AND MINSMERE BEACH
13/11/99 Tel: 01728 648505
A repeat of a tantalising and terrifying supper served by ghouls and ghosts, followed by a lantern walk onto the Heath for stories to send shivers down your spine. Time: 18.00. Tickets: £13.50.

Conservation Parks

Market Rasen Fixture
13/11/99 MARKET RASEN RACECOURSE
13/11/99 Tel: 01673 843434
First race: 13.00. Please call for further information

Racecourses

Wildfowl Walk
13/11/99 WICKEN FEN (NT) NATURE RESERVE
13/11/99 Tel: 01353 720274
A Guided walk around the Mere on Adventurers' Fen with Head Warden Martin Lester looking at the different species that visit Wicken Fen at this time of year. A£3.75 C£2.50. 10.00-11.30

Nature Reserves

Pudding Weekend
13/11/99 ICKWORTH HOUSE PARK AND GARDENS
14/11/99 Tel: 01284 735270
Sheer indulgence for those who love traditional puddings. Time: 12.00-16.00. Tickets: £8.50, booking essential, call 01284 735270.

Historic Houses & Gardens

CD/Record Fair
14/11/99 EAST OF ENGLAND SHOWGROUND
14/11/99 Tel: 01733 234451
Large collection of CD's and records

Showgrounds

Winter Championships (BRSCC)
14/11/99 SNETTERTON CIRCUIT
14/11/99 Tel: 01953 887303
Winter GT, Winter Saloons, Winter Formula Ford, Winter Formula First, Winter Minis, Winter Fiestas. Full Circuit, Grade-E. On the Gate: £10.00-£28.00. In Advance: Non £8.00-£25.00, Club £7.00-£22.00. Two Day Pass: Non £11.00-£30.00, Club £10.00-£27.00. Three Day Pass: Non £32.00, Club £29.00. Qualifying: £5.00-£14.00. C£Free. Programme £Free-£5.00. Seating (BH): £Free-£8.00. Group Tickets: Non £90.00-£95.00, Club £80.00-£85.00. Season Ticket Inc. of Club Membership: £150.00. You can buy your tickets for any of the 1999 events in advance any time up to 4 days before an event and make a saving, Tel: 0870 60 60 611

Motor Racing Circuit

Lincolnshire Artists' Society
14/11/99 USHER GALLERY
19/12/99 Tel: 01522 527980
The Annual Exhibition of members of the Society provides an opportunity to view and purchase works of art in a broad range of styles and media

Art Galleries

Dunwich Heath Lunchtime Lecture
17/11/99 DUNWICH HEATH AND MINSMERE BEACH
17/11/99 Tel: 01728 648505
Please send an SAE marked 'Lectures' for further details. A light lunch followed by a lecture in the Field Study Centre. Time: 12.30. Tickets: £9.95.

Conservation Parks

Wicken Widlife Watch
18/11/99 WICKEN FEN (NT) NATURE RESERVE
18/11/99 Tel: 01353 720274
Learn all about wildlife at our monthly Watch group meeting for kids. £0.25 for Watch members £1.00 for non-members but please phone to book your place (8-12 years) 16.30-18.00

Nature Reserves

The Birds of Wicken Fen
19/11/99 WICKEN FEN (NT) NATURE RESERVE
19/11/99 Tel: 01353 720274
A talk all about the resident birds and the many feathered visitors to Wicken Fen. A£2.50, starts at 19.30

Nature Reserves

The Quilt Fair
19/11/99 CHILFORD HALL VINEYARD
21/11/99 Tel: 01223 892641
Three day exhibition with a huge quilt display, demonstrations and related

items on sale. A£5.00 Concessions£4.00
(98 prices for guidance only)

Vineyards

Peterborough Steeplechase

20/11/99 HUNTINGDON STEEPLECHASES LTD
20/11/99 Tel: 01480 453373
Huntingdon's premier race of the year, a
Grade 2 Chase which always attracts the
very best horses in training. Racing from
12.50

Racecourses

Pudding Weekend

20/11/99 ICKWORTH HOUSE PARK AND GARDENS
21/11/99 Tel: 01284 735270
Sheer indulgence for those who love traditional puddings. Time: 12.00-16.00.
Tickets: £8.50, booking essential, call
01284 735270.

Historic Houses & Gardens

Christmas Craft Fair

20/11/99 WIMPOLE HALL
21/11/99 Tel: 01223 207257
Come and find those unusual gifts for
Christmas at our Christmas Craft Fair,
10.30-17.00, Admission £2.00

Country Parks

Pacesetters

20/11/99 PETERBOROUGH MUSEUM AND ART
GALLERY
1/1/00 Tel: 01733 343329
An event to take us into the year 2000
with an exhibition of cutting edge British
painting

Museum- Local History

Students' Day

23/11/99 MARKET RASEN RACECOURSE
23/11/99 Tel: 01673 843434
First race: 12.50. Please call for further
information

Racecourses

Light Up A Life

25/11/99 SOUTHEND ON SEA BOROUGH COUNCIL
25/11/99 Tel: 01702 215166
Help to illuminate the Fair Havens'
Christmas tree in the High Street by
sponsoring a light in memory of a loved
one, telephone 01702 220350. The tree
will be illuminated at 17.30 following a
Service and Blessing of the Book of
Remembrance. The names of each loved
one honoured will be entered into a
Book of Remembrance, which will be
displayed at Southend Crematorium,
Sutton Road

Festivals

Christmas Fayre

27/11/99 SOUTHEND ON SEA BOROUGH COUNCIL
28/11/99 Tel: 01702 215166
Enjoy Christmas shopping whilst being
entertained by clowns, jugglers, stilt
walkers, music and much more. A christmas market will stretch through much of
the high Street, with all proceeds to
Fairhavens South East Christian Hospice.
Held 11.00-16.00

Festivals

Santa's Enchanted Grotto

27/11/99 COLCHESTER ZOO
24/12/99 Tel: 01206 331292
Meet Father Christmas and his real
Reindeer! Take a trip through the
Enchanted Grotto to receive a present.
Festive face painting and Animal Petting
Area. DATES: 27 & 28 Nov, 4 & 5, 11-24
Dec

Zoos

Advent Christmas Lunch

28/11/99 ICKWORTH HOUSE PARK AND GARDENS
28/11/99 Tel: 01284 735270
Start your Christmas celebrations early
with a special luncheon in the Servants'
Hall Restaurant to mark the season of
Advent. Time: 12.00-14.00. Cost: £13.00,
booking essential call 01284 735270.

Historic Houses & Gardens

Santa Specials

28/11/99 NENE VALLEY RAILWAY
24/12/99 Tel: 01780 784444
Join Santa on board his steam train specials every Sat, Sun and Wed plus
Christmas Eve!

Railways Steam/Light

Dunwich Heath Lunchtime Lecture

1/12/99 DUNWICH HEATH AND MINSMERE BEACH
1/12/99 Tel: 01728 648505
Please send an SAE marked 'Lectures'
for further details. A light lunch followed
by a lecture in the Field Study Centre.
Time: 12.30. Tickets: £9.95.

Conservation Parks

Wind in the Willows

1/12/99 ICKWORTH HOUSE PARK AND GARDENS
17/12/99 Tel: 01284 735270
Enter the magical world of Ratty, Mole,
Toad and Badger. A special exhibition for
Christmas. Time: 10.00-16.00 (weekends
only, plus each day 12-19 December).
Cost: £A£1.00 C(3+)£0.50.

Historic Houses & Gardens

Annual Members' Guest Day

2/12/99 MARKET RASEN RACECOURSE
2/12/99 Tel: 01673 843434
First race: 12.50. Please call for further

Further more detailed information on the attractions listed can be found
in Best Guides *Visitor Attractions* Guide under the classifications shown

information
Racecourses

Wildfowl Walk
2/12/99 WICKEN FEN (NT) NATURE RESERVE
2/12/99 Tel: 01353 720274
A Guided walk around the Mere on Adventurers' Fen with Head Warden Martin Lester looking at the different species that visit Wicken Fen at this time of year. A£3.75 C£2.50. 10.00-11.30
Nature Reserves

Garden Tour - Winter
4/12/99 ANGLESEY ABBEY, GARDENS AND LODE MILL
4/12/99 Tel: 01223 811200
A tour of the garden led by Richard Ayres, followed by a Winter Warmer lunch in the Restaurant. Time: 11.00. Tickets: £8.00 to be confirmed (including National Trust Members).
Historic Houses & Gardens

Rally Stages (SMBC)
4/12/99 CADWELL PARK CIRCUIT
5/12/99 Tel: 01507 343248
Sideways action from Rally Saloons. Club Circuit, Grade-E. On the Gate: £10.00-£28.00. In Advance: Non £8.00-£25.00, Club £7.00-£22.00. Two Day Pass: Non £11.00-£30.00, Club £10.00-£27.00. Three Day Pass: Non £32.00, Club £29.00. Qualifying: £5.00-£14.00. C£Free. Programme £Free-£5.00. Seating (BH): £Free-£8.00. Group Tickets: Non £90.00-£95.00, Club £80.00-£85.00. Season Ticket Inc. of Club Membership: £135.00. You can buy your tickets for any of the 1999 events in advance any time up to 4 days before an event and make a saving, Tel: 0870 60 60 611
Motor Racing Circuit

Elizabethan Yuletide
4/12/99 HEDINGHAM CASTLE
5/12/99 Tel: 01787 460261
Festivities of Music and Dance, with unique and unusual gifts for Christmas
Castles

Santa Specials
4/12/99 NORTH NORFOLK RAILWAY
5/12/99 Tel: 01263 822045
Meet Santa at his winter wonderland on the North Norfolk Railway. Also held on 11-12 & 18-24 Dec
Railways Steam/Light

Christmas Luncheon

5/12/99 ICKWORTH HOUSE PARK AND GARDENS
5/12/99 Tel: 01284 735270
Enjoy a traditional Christmas Luncheon in Ickworth's Servants' Hall Restaurant. Time: 12.00-14.00. Cost: £15.50, booking essential call 01284 735270.
Historic Houses & Gardens

Christmas Extravaganza
6/12/99 DUNWICH HEATH AND MINSMERE BEACH
6/12/99 Tel: 01728 648505
A family day to ease you into the festive season. Charges for some activities. No booking required. Time: 10.00 onwards.
Conservation Parks

Pensioners Christmas Lunch
8/12/99 DUNWICH HEATH AND MINSMERE BEACH
9/12/99 Tel: 01728 648505
Time: 12.00 for 12.30 both days. Tickets: £11.50. Please call for further information.
Conservation Parks

Christmas Party Day at the Races
9/12/99 HUNTINGDON STEEPLECHASES LTD
9/12/99 Tel: 01480 453373
Huntingdon offers a top class days entertainment and great value for money. For further details about private facilities and special rates for your Christmas party call 01480 453373
Racecourses

The Magic of Christmas
10/12/99 BLICKLING HALL
11/12/99 Tel: 01263 738030
Craft Fair, Carol Singing and Tours of the Hall, see Blickling Hall in all its glory bedecked with the Christmas trimmings. Booking essential. Bookings can be made by telephone, to the address, or in person.
Historic Houses & Gardens

Traditional Christmas Lunch
11/12/99 DUNWICH HEATH AND MINSMERE BEACH
11/12/99 Tel: 01728 648505
Time: 12.00 for 12.30. Tickets: £16.50. Please call for further information.
Conservation Parks

Get Crafty with Trusty
11/12/99 WICKEN FEN (NT) NATURE RESERVE
11/12/99 Tel: 01353 720274
Come and help Trusty the Hedgehog make presents for Christmas - try your hand at making candles, cards, pomanders, painting on glass and screen-printing. A&C£2.50 (3-8 years). 10.00-12.00 or 14.00-16.00
Nature Reserves

Auto Jumble

12/12/99 EAST OF ENGLAND SHOWGROUND
12/12/99 Tel: 01733 234451
A fair for all car enthusiasts
Showgrounds

Christmas Music and Poetry
12/12/99 ICKWORTH HOUSE PARK AND GARDENS
12/12/99 Tel: 01284 735270
A celebration of Christmas in the grand
Entrance Hall of Ickworth House. Time:
13.30-15.00. Cost: A£3.00 C(5+)£1.00.
Booking essential call 01284 735270.
Historic Houses & Gardens

Christmas Luncheon
12/12/99 ICKWORTH HOUSE PARK AND GARDENS
12/12/99 Tel: 01284 735270
Enjoy a traditional Christmas Luncheon
in Ickworth's Servants' Hall Restaurant.
Time: 12.00-14.00. Cost: £15.50, booking
essential call 01284 735270.
Historic Houses & Gardens

Ickworth's Christmas Cracker
12/12/99 ICKWORTH HOUSE PARK AND GARDENS
19/12/99 Tel: 01284 735270
8 days of celebrations and Christmas
activities for all the family in the House,
Park and Gardens. The Shop and
Restaurant will be open each day from
12.00-17.00 for Christmas Shopping,
meals and refreshments.
Historic Houses & Gardens

Santa Specials
12/12/99 COLNE VALLEY RAILWAY AND MUSEUM
23/12/99 Tel: 01787 461174
Bring the family along to experience a
traditional Christmas atmosphere. Santa
will be riding on the steam train, hand-
ing out presents to children in their
reserved seats. Please call for ticket
prices, booking essential. Trains operating 12, 18-19, 22-23 Dec
Railways

Christmas Card Workshop
13/12/99 ICKWORTH HOUSE PARK AND GARDENS
13/12/99 Tel: 01284 735270
Learn how to make unique and beautiful
Christmas cards. Time: 13.30-15.00.
Cost: A£5.00 C£1.00, booking essential
call 01284 735270.
Historic Houses & Gardens

Lantern Making Workshop
14/12/99 ICKWORTH HOUSE PARK AND GARDENS
14/12/99 Tel: 01284 735270
Make spectacular Christmas lanterns.
Workshop ends with lantern procession,
mince pies and carols in Ickworth
House. Time: 13.30-16.00. Cost: A£7.50
C£2.00, booking essential call 01284

735270.
Historic Houses & Gardens

Evergreen Walk
15/12/99 ICKWORTH HOUSE PARK AND GARDENS
15/12/99 Tel: 01284 735270
Join the Head Gardener, Jan Michalak on
a Winter Walk in Ickworth's gardens.
Bring walking shoes and waterproofs.
Time: 10.30-12.00. Cost: £5.00, booking
essential call 01284 735270.
Historic Houses & Gardens

Cambridgeshire's Mammals
15/12/99 WICKEN FEN (NT) NATURE RESERVE
15/12/99 Tel: 01353 720274
A talk about the diverse range of mammals found in Cambridgeshire, including
the measures being taken to conserve
them. A£2.50. Starts at 19.30
Nature Reserves

In the Bleak Mid-winter
16/12/99 ICKWORTH HOUSE PARK AND GARDENS
16/12/99 Tel: 01284 735270
Discover the Ickworth's Woodlands in
Winter with Head Forester Nigel
Mackinnon. Bring walking shoes and
waterproofs. Time: 10.30-12.00. Cost:
£5.00, booking essential call 01284
735270
Historic Houses & Gardens

Wicken Wildlife Watch
16/12/99 WICKEN FEN (NT) NATURE RESERVE
16/12/99 Tel: 01353 720274
Learn all about wildlife at our monthly
Watch group meeting for kids. £0.25 for
Watch members £1.00 for non-members
but please phone to book your place (8-
12 years) 16.30-18.00
Nature Reserves

Flowers for Winter / Christmas
17/12/99 ICKWORTH HOUSE PARK AND GARDENS
17/12/99 Tel: 01284 735270
A demonstration of flower arranging for
the Christmas period. Time: 14.00-16.00.
Cost: £8.50, ticket price includes a
mince pie and mulled wine. Booking
essential call 01284 735270.
Historic Houses & Gardens

Christmas Luncheon
18/12/99 ICKWORTH HOUSE PARK AND GARDENS
18/12/99 Tel: 01284 735270
Enjoy a traditional Christmas Luncheon
in Ickworth's Servants' Hall Restaurant.
Time: 12.00-14.00. Cost: £15.50, booking
essential call 01284 735270.
Historic Houses & Gardens

Victorian Father Christmas

Further more detailed information on the attractions listed can be found
in Best Guides *Visitor Attractions* Guide under the classifications shown

18/12/99
19/12/99

ICKWORTH HOUSE PARK AND GARDENS

Tel: 01284 735270

Ickworth's traditional Father Christmas visits Ratty, Mole, Toad and Badger in the "Wind in the Willows" exhibition. Time: 10.00-16.00 each day. Cost: C£3.00 (includes gift).

Historic Houses & Gardens

Mince Pie Specials

26/12/99
2/1/00

NORTH NORFOLK RAILWAY

Tel: 01263 822045

Receive a mince pie and sherry whilst travelling with us

Railways Steam/Light

Boxing Day Meeting

27/12/99
27/12/99

HUNTINGDON STEEPLECHASES LTD

Tel: 01480 453373

Join Huntingdon's Family Fun Day where all children under 16 can enter free of charge and with a fully supervised creche, bouncy castle, tubeslide and face-painting, there is lots to do for all the family. Racing from 13.00

Racecourses

Boxing Day Meeting

27/12/99
27/12/99

MARKET RASEN RACECOURSE

Tel: 01673 843434

First race: 12.30. Please call for further information

Racecourses

What Does Santa Get Up To After Christmas

27/12/99
30/12/99

COLCHESTER ZOO

Tel: 01206 331292

Come and meet Santa as he puts his feet up after the Christmas rush and help him to feed his hard-working reindeer! A free goody bag is included for every full paying child.

Zoos

Ickworth's Millennium Hug!!

1/1/00
1/1/00

ICKWORTH HOUSE PARK AND GARDENS

Tel: 01284 735270

A fund raising event to mark the Millennium. Ickworth needs 2,000 people to join hands around its famous Rotunda. Join this unique celebration of the New Year. Time: 12.00-15.00. Cost: £2.00 (includes Ickworth Millennium Hug Certificate).

Historic Houses & Gardens

Primetime Exhibition

1/1/00

CLEETHORPES HUMBER ESTUARY DISCOVERY CENTRE

31/12/00

Tel: 01472 323232

Exhibition to be confirmed, call venue nearer to the time. Celebrate

Cleethorpes position on the Prime Meridian with an exhibition of time and change on the Humber Estuary from Log boats to Harrison's sea clocks

Exhibition Centres

New Year Ramble

9/1/00
9/1/00

DUNWICH HEATH AND MINSMERE BEACH

Tel: 01728 648505

A 5 mile walk followed by soup and a roll with the option of a further afternoon walk. Time: 10.00. Tickets: £5.50.

Conservation Parks

Dunwich Heath Lunchtime Lecture

12/1/00
12/1/00

DUNWICH HEATH AND MINSMERE BEACH

Tel: 01728 648505

Please send an SAE marked 'Lectures' for details. A light lunch followed by a lecture in the Field Study Centre. Time: 12.30. Tickets: £9.95.

Conservation Parks

Ivy Smith: Paintings and Prints

22/1/00
19/3/00

GAINSBOROUGH'S HOUSE

Tel: 01787 372958

Exhibition of paintings and prints in the Lower Gallery

Birth Places

Dunwich Heath Lunchtime Lecture

26/1/00
26/1/00

DUNWICH HEATH AND MINSMERE BEACH

Tel: 01728 648505

Please send an SAE marked 'Lectures' for further details. A light lunch followed by a lecture in the Field Study Centre. Time: 12.30. Tickets: £9.95.

Conservation Parks

Royal Norfolk Show

28/6/00
29/6/00

NORFOLK SHOW GROUND

Tel: 01603 748931

Entertainment for all the family. Grand Ring Programme which offers all day long entertainment with majestic heavy horses to tiny chicks. Dog show - judging takes place on both days of the show. Fabulous Flower Show with stunning floral displays. Craft Fair and Trade Stands including probably the largest motor show in East Anglia. Superb Art Exhibition with pictures and sculptures for sale.

Showgrounds

Ireland

Music in Ireland
2/3/99
26/3/99
NORTH DOWN HERITAGE CENTRE
Tel: 01247 270371
Travelling exhibition on contemporary
Irish composers
Museum- Local History

Talking and Listening Week
8/3/99
12/3/99
PALACE STABLES HERITAGE CENTRE
Tel: 01861 529629
School event: National Year of Reading.
For more information contact Rachel or
Phillipine in the Education Department
on 01861 529629 or email
cooperr@armagh.gov.uk
Heritage Centres

Mum-A-Thon
14/3/99
14/3/99
COLIN GLEN COUNTRY PARK
Tel: 01232 614115
Bring your Mum and a sticky bun! A
quick walking race for Mothers followed
by tea and buns. While your Mum walks
you can make a great Mother's Day card
using stencils and collage, then present
it to your Mum with a lovely cup of tea.
Prizes for fastest Mums and best cards.
Commences 14.00, Admission £1.00
Country Parks

SET Week
15/3/99
19/3/99
PALACE STABLES HERITAGE CENTRE
Tel: 01861 529629
School event: Key Stage 1-4. For more
information contact Rachel or Phillipine
in the Education Department on 01861
529629 or email
cooperr@armagh.gov.uk
Heritage Centres

Music at Castle Coole
17/3/99
17/3/99
CASTLE COOLE
Tel: 01365 322690
In the Grand Hall. Courtney Kenny performs 'A Boy for Life', a celebration of
Percy French. Tickets £12.00 (book 2 or
more recitals at discount rate £10.00,
excludes 'A Night at the Opera' evening).
Price includes a wine reception in the
Breakfast Room where guests can meet
the performers. 100 seats only so book
early! Starts: 20.00. Please telephone
01365 322690 for further information
Historic Houses

Hey You, What's That?
28/3/99
28/3/99
COLIN GLEN COUNTRY PARK
Tel: 01232 614115
Pick up some hints on outdoor photography and photographing wildlife. This
event will launch the start of the 'Colin
Glen in Focus' photgraphic competition.

Commences 14.00, Admission £1.00.
Country Parks

Opening of the Flat Season
28/3/99
28/3/99
CURRAGH RACECOURSE
Tel: 00 353 45 441205
Irish Lincolnshire. Please call for further
information
Racecourses

Children's Easter Egg Hunt
4/4/99
4/4/99
CASTLE WARD
Tel: 01396 881204
Come and find those craftily hidden eggs
in Catle Ward. Please telephone 01396
881204 for further information
Historic Houses

Guided Walk
4/4/99
4/4/99
CROM ESTATE
Tel: 013657 38118/174
A guided walk listening to the history of
Crom Estate. Meet: 15.00 at the Visitor
Centre. Please telephone 013657 38118
for further information
Woods

Easter Egg Trail
4/4/99
4/4/99
FLORENCE COURT
Tel: 01365 348249
15.00-17.00. Normal admission prices
apply. Please telephone 01365 348249
for further information
Historic Houses & Gardens

Easter Eggcentricities
4/4/99
4/4/99
SPRINGHILL
Tel: 016487 48210
Make an Easter Bonnet, paint and roll an
egg 14.00-18.00, sponsored by BT
Northern Ireland, please telephone
01648 748210 for further information
Historic Houses

Easter Egg Hunt
5/4/99
5/4/99
CASTLE COOLE
Tel: 01365 322690
Come and look for these craftily hidden
Easter eggs at Castle Coole. Time: 14.00.
Please telephone 01365 322690 for fur-
ther information
Historic Houses

Easter Eggspedition
5/4/99
5/4/99
COLIN GLEN COUNTRY PARK
Tel: 01232 614115
Follow the clues through the forest to
win Easter prizes, and keep alert for
other hidden treasurers en-route.
Commences 14.00, Admission £1.00
Country Parks

Easter Eggstravaganza & Craft Fair

5/4/99	THE ARGORY
5/4/99	Tel: 018687 84753

Easter fun and unusual gifts for sale.
Time: 13.00-18.00. Please telephone
01868 784753 for further information

Historic Houses & Gardens

Easter Country Market & Craft Fair

5/4/99	WELLBROOK BEETLING MILL
5/4/99	Tel: 016487 51735

Come and buy those unusual gifts. Time:
14.00-18.00. Please telephone 016487
51735 for further information

Museum- Waterworks

Jameson Irish Grand National Grade 1

5/4/99	FAIRYHOUSE RACECOURSE
7/4/99	Tel: 00 353 1 825 6167

Great racing over Easter Bank Holiday
with Irish Grand National on 5 Apr,
Power Gold Cup Grade 1 on 6 Apr and
Dan Moore Handicap Chase on 7 Apr

Racecourses

Garden Walk

7/4/99	MOUNT STEWART HOUSE, GARDEN AND TEMPLE OF THE WINDS
1/9/99	Tel: 012477 88387/88487

Every Wednesday with Professor Tony
Wright. Normal admission rates apply

Historic Houses & Gardens

Lake Walk

8/4/99	MOUNT STEWART HOUSE, GARDEN AND TEMPLE OF THE WINDS
2/9/99	Tel: 012477 88387/88487

Every Thursday. With Professor Tony
Wright. Normal admission rates apply

Historic Houses & Gardens

Mediaeval Banquets

10/4/99	DUNGUAIRE CASTLE
31/10/99	Tel: 00353 61 360788

Food from the rich earth, music made in
heaven. Your host, the Earl, will speedily
take you back through history as he
proudly oversees your comfort and
entertainment. Twice nightly all year,
17.30 and 20.45 (subject to demand).
Seats 140 each sitting. Prices: A£30.00
C£(10-12)£22.75 C(6-9)£15.50 C(0-
5)£Free, Groups 20+ pax 10% discount
£27.00 each, call to book

Castles

Gladness Stakes

11/4/99	CURRAGH RACECOURSE
11/4/99	Tel: 00 353 45 441205

Home of the Classics. Please call for further information

Racecourses

Vintage & Classic Vehicle Rally

24/4/99	THE ARGORY
24/4/99	Tel: 018687 84753

From 12.00 onwards. Please telephone
01868 784753 for further information

Historic Houses & Gardens

Gardening Demonstrations

24/4/99	ROWALLANE GARDEN
25/9/99	Tel: 01238 510131

Last Saturday of each month. Art of the
Gardener technique demonstrations,
14.30

Gardens

Tetrarch Stakes

25/4/99	CURRAGH RACECOURSE
25/4/99	Tel: 00 353 45 441205

Home of the Classics. Please call for further information

Racecourses

Jazz Band in the Garden

25/4/99	MOUNT STEWART HOUSE, GARDEN AND TEMPLE OF THE WINDS
25/4/99	Tel: 012477 88387/88487

The Ulster Jazz Band entertain you in the
garden from 15.00-17.00. Normal admission rates apply

Historic Houses & Gardens

Jazz in the Garden

25/4/99	MOUNT STEWART HOUSE, GARDEN AND TEMPLE OF THE WINDS
26/9/99	Tel: 012477 88387/88487

Held on the last Sunday of each month.
Relax to the sounds of the Ulster Jazz
Band, performing in the Sunken Garden,
15.00-17.00

Historic Houses & Gardens

'The Spring Garden Walk'

27/4/99	MOUNT STEWART HOUSE, GARDEN AND TEMPLE OF THE WINDS
27/4/99	Tel: 012477 88387/88487

Guests to meet in the Ticket Office and
are invited to light refreshments. Tour of
the Garden conducted by Head
Gardener, Nigel Marshall followed by
light supper in Tea Room. Time: 19.30.
By ticket only £6.00

Historic Houses & Gardens

Music at Castle Coole

29/4/99	CASTLE COOLE
29/4/99	Tel: 01365 322690

In the Grand Hall. The Katona Twins, guitar duo from Hungary. Tickets £12.00
(book 2 or more recitals at discount rate
£10.00, excludes 'A Night at the Opera'
evening). Price includes a wine reception
in the Breakfast Room where guests can
meet the performers. 100 seats only so
book early! Starts: 20.00

Further more detailed information on the attractions listed can be found
in Best Guides *Visitor Attractions* Guide under the classifications shown

Historic Houses

Georgian May Day Festivities
1/5/99
1/5/99
PALACE STABLES HERITAGE CENTRE
Tel: 01861 529629
Archbishop Richard Robinson 'ere since his arrival in Armagh in the year of our Lord 1765, hath endeavoured to advance the town as a place of learning and culture. In his efforts to achieve the latter he thinks it a goodly notion to hold a Ball for the local gentry. Although undoubtedly not comparable in size with the Balls of London, Dublin or bath, 'twill certainly be a grand occassion which no one can afford to miss if they wish themselves to be considered members of polite society. Call for further details

Heritage Centres

Wicklow Gardens Festival 1999
1/5/99
30/6/99
WICKLOW GARDENS FESTIVAL 1999
Tel: 00 353 404 66058/9
A series of garden openings and related events takes place annually in May/June with many smaller private gardens participating. There will be over 50 gardens and events to choose from including heritage houses and gardens, flower arranging and gardening day schools, private gardens, special events and floral cuisine.

Festivals

Traditional Song, Food and Dance
1/5/99
31/10/99
BUNRATTY CASTLE AND FOLK PARK
Tel: 00353 61 360788
Held in the barn in the Folk Park twice nightly subject to demand at 17.30 and 20.45 hours, call for details

Castles

Mediaeval Banquets
1/5/99
31/10/99
KNAPPOGUE CASTLE
Tel: 00353 61 360788
Food from the rich earth, music made in heaven. Your host, the Earl, will speedily take you back through history as he proudly oversees your comfort and entertainment. Twice nightly all year, 17.30 and 20.45 (subject to demand). Seats 140 each sitting. Prices: A£32.00 C£(10-12)£24.25 C(6-9)£16.50 C(0-5)£Free, Groups 20+ pax 10% discount £28.80 each, call to book

Castles

Percy French Collection
1/5/99
31/12/99
NORTH DOWN HERITAGE CENTRE
Tel: 01247 270371
New permanent display devoted to Irish Songwriter and Artist

Museum- Local History

Bluebell Walk
2/5/99
2/5/99
CASTLE WARD
Tel: 01396 881204
A walk with a difference with Dr Valerie Hall at 14.00, please telephone 01396 881204 for further information

Historic Houses

Guided Walk
2/5/99
2/5/99
CROM ESTATE
Tel: 013657 38118/174
A guided walk listening to the history of Crom Estate. Meet: 15.00 at the Visitor Centre. Please telephone 013657 38118 for further information

Woods

Percy French - Irish Entertainer
3/5/99
3/5/99
NORTH DOWN HERITAGE CENTRE
Tel: 01247 270371
Opening of new permanent gallery devoted to Percy French

Museum- Local History

Farming in the Forties & Steam Working Day
3/5/99
3/5/99
PATTERSON'S SPADE MILL
Tel: 01849 433619
Family fun with machinery displays and competitions, live circus acts with Streetwise Theatre. Time: 12.00-18.00

Museum- Mill

Easter Georgian Festival
4/5/99
5/4/99
PALACE STABLES HERITAGE CENTRE
Tel: 01861 529629
How did the guests and servants of the Church of Ireland Archbishop celebrate Easter in Georgian times? Discover for yourself by visiting the Palace Stables and travelling back in time over 200 years to 1786.

Heritage Centres

Special Needs Week
4/5/99
7/5/99
PALACE STABLES HERITAGE CENTRE
Tel: 01861 529629
School event. For more information contact Rachel or Phillipone in the Education Department on 01861 529629 or email cooperr@armagh.gov.uk

Heritage Centres

Percy French Evening
7/5/99
MOUNT STEWART HOUSE, GARDEN AND TEMPLE OF THE WINDS
Tel: 012477 88387/88487
By Ticket only. Time to be confirmed. Please call for further information

Historic Houses & Gardens

National Hunt Racing

8/5/99	**FAIRYHOUSE RACECOURSE**
3/11/99	Tel: 00 353 1 825 6167
	Race days: 8 May, 2 June, 4 & 21 Aug, 15
	Sept, 6 & 17 Oct, 3 Nov
	Racecourses

	Apple Blossom Day
9/5/99	**ARDRESS HOUSE**
9/5/99	Tel: 01762 851236
	Time: 14.00-18.00. Please telephone
	01762 851236 for further information
	Historic Houses

	Walk in the Woods
9/5/99	**COLIN GLEN COUNTRY PARK**
9/5/99	Tel: 01232 614115
	Join in this family day out, and learn the
	fascinating history of trees and wood-
	lands, examine the forest floor for a
	wide variety of flora. Commences 14.00,
	Admission £0.50
	Country Parks

	Orienteering Day
12/5/99	**PALACE STABLES HERITAGE CENTRE**
12/5/99	Tel: 01861 529629
	School event. For more information con-
	tact Rachel or Phillipine in the Education
	Department on 01861 529629 or email
	cooperr@armagh.gov.uk
	Heritage Centres

	Gronigen Guitar Duo
13/5/99	**NORTH DOWN HERITAGE CENTRE**
13/5/99	Tel: 01247 270371
	Classical guitar recital at 20.00
	Museum- Local History

	Mount Stewart Gardening
	Extravaganza
15/5/99	**MOUNT STEWART HOUSE, GARDEN AND**
	TEMPLE OF THE WINDS
16/5/99	Tel: 012477 88387/88487
	A-Z of gardening. Admission £2.50 which
	includes entrance to House and
	Gardens. National Trust members admis-
	sion to show only £1.00. Time: 11.00-
	18.00
	Historic Houses & Gardens

	Spring Plant Fair
16/5/99	**CASTLE COOLE**
16/5/99	Tel: 01365 322690
	Lots of beautiful Spring plants and bulbs
	on sale for all those garden enthusiasts.
	Time: 14.00
	Historic Houses

	Plant & Craft Fair
16/5/99	**CASTLE WARD**
16/5/99	Tel: 01396 881204
	Come along for those unusual gifts and
	beautiful plants, please telephone 01396
	881204 for further information

Historic Houses

	Spring Plant Fair
16/5/99	**SPRINGHILL**
16/5/99	Tel: 016487 48210
	Beautiful spring flowers and bulbs for
	the budding garden enthusiast. Time:
	14.00-17.00. Please telephone 01648
	748210 for further information
	Historic Houses

	Spring Plant Fair
16/5/99	**THE ARGORY**
16/5/99	Tel: 018687 84753
	A must for all gardening enthusiasts,
	12.00-17.00, please telephone 01868
	784753 for further information
	Historic Houses & Gardens

	Hunt Self Portrait Exhibition
19/5/99	**THE HUNT MUSEUM**
9/6/99	Tel: 00353 61 312833
	By students of Limerick Institute of
	Technology's School of Art and Design.
	Museums

	Three Islands Trek & Picnic -
	Strangford Lough Wildlife Centre
22/5/99	**CASTLE WARD**
22/5/99	Tel: 01396 881204
	Trek to Chapel, Mid and South Islands to
	examine the flora, fauna and historical
	aspects of the area. Bring a picnic lunch!
	Meet Greyabbey 11.00
	Historic Houses

	Hibernia Foods Irish 2000 Guineas and
	Airlie/Coolmore Irish 1000 Guineas
22/5/99	**CURRAGH RACECOURSE**
23/5/99	Tel: 00 353 45 441205
	Please call for further information
	Racecourses

	Fossil Foray (with Andrew Jeram)
23/5/99	**COLIN GLEN COUNTRY PARK**
23/5/99	Tel: 01232 614115
	Come along and discover a hidden
	Jurassic Park in Colin Glen. If you are
	lucky enough to find a fossil you may
	keep it! Commences 14.00, Admission
	£1.00
	Country Parks

	Woodland Walk
23/5/99	**FLORENCE COURT**
23/5/99	Tel: 01365 348249
	Led by Jo Whetmough, 15.00-17.00,
	please telephone 01365 348249 for fur-
	ther information
	Historic Houses & Gardens

	Strand Racing
25/5/99	**LAYTOWN RACECOURSE**
25/5/99	Tel: 00 353 41 42111
	Laytown Races holds its annual after-

noon Strand Race which has taken place since 1901. Please call 041 42111 for further information

Racecourses

Music at Castle Coole
27/5/99 CASTLE COOLE
27/5/99 Tel: 01365 322690
In the Grand Hall. Pianist Phillip Dyson, performs music by Chopin, Lizst, Debussy, Billy Mayerl and Scott Joplin. Tickets £12.00 (book 2 or more recitals at discount rate £10.00, excludes 'A Night at the Opera' evening). Price includes a wine reception in the Breakfast Room where guests can meet the performers. 100 seats only so book early! Starts: 20.00. Please telephone 01365 322690 for further information

Historic Houses

Teddy Bears' Picnic
29/5/99 CASTLE WARD
29/5/99 Tel: 01396 881204
When you go down to the woods today be sure of a big surprise! Please telephone 01396 881204 for further information

Historic Houses

NI Stationary Engine Club Display
29/5/99 PATTERSON'S SPADE MILL
29/5/99 Tel: 01849 433619
Stationary Engines on display from 14.00-18.00. Please call 01849 433619 for further information

Museum- Mill

Seals around Strangford Lough
30/5/99 CASTLE WARD
30/5/99 Tel: 01396 881204
Come and watch these beautiful creatures do what comes naturally. Please telephone 01396 881204 for further information

Historic Houses

Guided Walk
30/5/99 CROM ESTATE
30/5/99 Tel: 013657 38118/174
A guided walk listening to the history of Crom Estate. Meet: 15.00 at the Visitor Centre. Please telephone 013657 38118 for further information

Woods

BT Country Fair
30/5/99 FLORENCE COURT
30/5/99 Tel: 01365 348249
13.00-18.00, please telephone 01365 348249 for further information

Historic Houses & Gardens

Musical House Tours

The Argory
30/5/99 Tel: 01868 784753
30/5/99 14.00-18.00, please telephone 01868 784753 for further information

Historic Houses & Gardens

Bat Evening
4/6/99 ARDRESS HOUSE
4/6/99 Tel: 01762 851236
An illustrated talk followed by a 'Bat Hunt' walk. Time: 20.00

Historic Houses

Gallinule Stakes
4/6/99 CURRAGH RACECOURSE
4/6/99 Tel: 00 353 45 441205
Evening meetings. Please call for further information

Racecourses

Castle Ward Opera
4/6/99 CASTLE WARD
26/6/99 Tel: 01396 881204
Nightly except Mon & Wed. Please telephone 01396 881204 for further information

Historic Houses

Mid-Ulster Vintage Rally
5/6/99 SPRINGHILL
5/6/99 Tel: 016487 48210
13.00-17.00, please telephone 01648 748210 for further information

Historic Houses

Coffee on the Colonnade
5/6/99 CASTLE COOLE
28/8/99 Tel: 01365 322690
Every Saturday from 11.00-13.00

Historic Houses

Candle Making
6/6/99 COLIN GLEN COUNTRY PARK
6/6/99 Tel: 01232 614115
Try your hand at candle making using natural materials gathered from the forest such as bark, sand, leaves, stones and flowers! Commences 14.00, Admission £1.00

Country Parks

Guided Walk: World Oceans Day 'Seal Watch'
6/6/99 MURLOUGH NATURE RESERVE
6/6/99 Tel: 013967 51467/24362
Meet at Keel Point which is the last road in Dundrum on your left when travelling towards Newcastle, 14.30

Nature Reserves

Teddy Bears's Picnic
12/6/99 SPRINGHILL
12/6/99 Tel: 016487 48210
If you go down to the woods today be sure of a big surprise! Time: 14.00-18.00.

Please telephone 01648 748210 for further information

Historic Houses

Guided Woodland Walk

13/6/99 CASTLE COOLE
13/6/99 Tel: 01365 322690
Fresh air and exercise walking through the magical woodland of Castle Coole. Start: 15.00

Historic Houses

Music at Castle Coole

17/6/99 CASTLE COOLE
17/6/99 Tel: 01365 322690
In the Grand Hall. A Night at the Opera - an evening of operatic arias, duets etc. Tickets £15.00. Price includes a wine reception in the Breakfast Room where guests can meet the performers. 100 seats only so book early! Please telephone 01365 322690 for further information

Historic Houses

Mid Summer Treasure Hunt

18/6/99 THE ARGORY
18/6/99 Tel: 018687 84753
With Barbeque and dancing, 18.30-late, please telephone 01868 784753 for further information and tickets

Historic Houses & Gardens

Seals and Seabirds Boat Trips - Strangford Lough Wildlife Centre

19/6/99 CASTLE WARD
19/6/99 Tel: 01396 881204
Enjoy the views, seals and seabirds of the Strangford Narrows and the Angus Rock. See the Kittiwakes nesting on the cliff face of Gunn's Island off Ballyhoman. Boat leaves Portaferry / Strangford at 14.00

Historic Houses

Teddy Bears' Picnic

19/6/99 FLORENCE COURT
19/6/99 Tel: 01365 348249
Bring your teddies and picnics for a great day out, 14.00-17.00, please telephone 01365 348249 for further information

Historic Houses & Gardens

Hot Jazz

19/6/99 ROWALLANE GARDEN
19/6/99 Tel: 01238 510131
Sit back and listen to jazz in the evening at the bandstand at 20.00

Gardens

Band Concert in the Garden

20/6/99 MOUNT STEWART HOUSE, GARDEN AND

TEMPLE OF THE WINDS

20/6/99 Tel: 012477 88387/88487
Music by the Dave Glover Band. Time: from 18.00. Ticket price to be confirmed

Historic Houses & Gardens

Guided Walk: Launch of the New Murlough Nature Trail

20/6/99 MURLOUGH NATURE RESERVE
20/6/99 Tel: 013967 51467/24362
Meet at Murlough Information Centre which is located at the Trust's car park on the main Dundrum to Newcastle road, beside Lazy BJ Caravan Park, 14.30

Nature Reserves

Horse Drive

20/6/99 ROWALLANE GARDEN
20/6/99 Tel: 01238 510131
Meet in the car park at 14.30

Gardens

Goffs £100,000 Challenge Race

25/6/99 CURRAGH RACECOURSE
26/6/99 Tel: 00 353 45 441205
Evening Meeting on 25 June. 26 June Independent Newspapers, Pretty Polly Stakes. Please call for further information

Racecourses

Seals and Seabirds Boat Trips - Strangford Lough Wildlife Centre

26/6/99 CASTLE WARD
26/6/99 Tel: 01396 881204
Enjoy the views, seals and seabirds of the Strangford Narrows and the Angus Rock. See the Kittiwakes nesting on the cliff face of Gunn's Island off Ballyhoman. Boat leaves Portaferry / Strangford at 15.00

Historic Houses

Moth Morning - Strangford Lough Wildlife Centre

26/6/99 CASTLE WARD
26/6/99 Tel: 01396 881204
Investigate a moth trap, identify and discover the beauty of the moths found there and then release. Completely moth friendly! Time: 10.00

Historic Houses

Musical Evening

26/6/99 FLORENCE COURT
26/6/99 Tel: 01365 348249
With 'Gaslight'. Time: 20.00. Tickets: £9.00, includes wine and light supper. Please telephone 01365 348249 for further information

Historic Houses & Gardens

Children's Nature Ramble

27/6/99	**CASTLE WARD**
27/6/99	Tel: 01396 881204
	Lorna Tinman takes the children on a ramble to remember, please telephone 01396 881204 for further information
	Historic Houses

Ferns, Foxgloves and Fairies

27/6/99	**COLIN GLEN COUNTRY PARK**
27/6/99	Tel: 01232 614115
	Find out about the legends and folklore surrounding Colin Glen Forest Park, everything from the Black bull of Colin Glen to the fairies associated with the foxglove. Commences 14.00, Admission £0.50
	Country Parks

Budweiser Irish Derby

27/6/99	**CURRAGH RACECOURSE**
27/6/99	Tel: 00 353 45 441205
	Please call for further details
	Racecourses

Band Concert

27/6/99	**FLORENCE COURT**
27/6/99	Tel: 01365 348249
	Concert in the Stable Yard at 15.00. Normal admission prices apply. Please telephone 01365 348249 for further information
	Historic Houses & Gardens

Jazz Band in the Garden

27/6/99	**MOUNT STEWART HOUSE, GARDEN AND TEMPLE OF THE WINDS**
27/6/99	Tel: 012477 88387/88487
	The Ulster Jazz Band entertain you in the Garden from 15.00-17.00. Normal admission rates apply
	Historic Houses & Gardens

Courtyard Attractions

27/6/99	**THE ARGORY**
27/6/99	Tel: 018687 84753
	14.00-18.00, please telephone 01868 784753 for further information
	Historic Houses & Gardens

Annual Three Day Meeting

30/6/99	**BELLEWSTOWN RACECOURSE**
2/7/99	Tel: 00 353 41 42111
	Bellewtown Races holds its annual three day meeting with a wonderful local and carnival like atmosphere. All evening races
	Racecourses

Summer Barbeque & Hot Jazz

3/7/99	**CASTLE COOLE**
3/7/99	Tel: 01365 322690
	Great food and wonderful music on this hot July evening. Start: 20.00
	Historic Houses

Guided Walk: Caring for Countryside, Caring for Wildlife

7/7/99	**MURLOUGH NATURE RESERVE**
7/7/99	Tel: 013967 51467/24362
	What the National Trust are doing to conserve the wildlife of Murlough Nature Reserve. Meet at Murlough Information Centre which is located at the Trust's car park on the main Dundrum to Newcastle road, beside Lazy BJ Caravan Park, 14.30
	Nature Reserves

Kildangan Stud Irish Oaks

11/7/99	**CURRAGH RACECOURSE**
11/7/99	Tel: 00 353 45 441205
	Please call for further information
	Racecourses

Intertidal Archaeology - Strangford Lough Wildlife Centre

18/7/99	**CASTLE WARD**
18/7/99	Tel: 01396 881204
	Visit Chapel Island, view the historical site, fish and traps recently discovered archaeological remains, Greyabbey 10.30
	Historic Houses

Circus Show

18/7/99	**CROM ESTATE**
18/7/99	Tel: 013657 38118/174
	Learn circus skills and watch the show. Time: 15.00
	Woods

Guided Walk

18/7/99	**CROM ESTATE**
18/7/99	Tel: 013657 38118/174
	A guided walk listening to the history of Crom Estate. Meet: 15.00 at the Visitor Centre. Please telephone 013657 38118 for further information
	Woods

Summer Garden Walk

20/7/99	**MOUNT STEWART HOUSE, GARDEN AND TEMPLE OF THE WINDS**
20/7/99	Tel: 012477 88387/88487
	Guests to meet in the Ticket Office and are invited to light refreshments. Tour of the Garden conducted by Head Gardener, Nigel Marshall followed by a light supper in the Tea Room. Time: 19.30. By ticket only £6.00
	Historic Houses & Gardens

Meld Stakes

23/7/99	**CURRAGH RACECOURSE**
23/7/99	Tel: 00 353 45 441205
	Please call for further information
	Racecourses

Woodland Walk

25/7/99	**CASTLE WARD**
25/7/99	Tel: 01396 881204

Ann McComb will take you on a peaceful woodland walk at 14.00, please telephone 01396 881204 for further information

Historic Houses

	Nature's Way
25/7/99	**COLIN GLEN COUNTRY PARK**
25/7/99	Tel: 01232 614115

A workshop focusing on art, learn to use the natural materials gathered from the forest to make sculptures and collages. Commences 14.00, Admission £0.50

Country Parks

	Guided Walk
25/7/99	**CROM ESTATE**
25/7/99	Tel: 013657 38118/174

A guided walk listening to the history of Crom Estate. Meet: 15.00 at the Visitor Centre. Please telephone 013657 38118 for further information

Woods

	Jazz Band in the Garden
25/7/99	**MOUNT STEWART HOUSE, GARDEN AND TEMPLE OF THE WINDS**
25/7/99	Tel: 012477 88387/88487

The Ulster Jazz Band entertain you in the Garden from 15.00-17.00. Normal admission rates apply

Historic Houses & Gardens

	BT Children's Fun Day
25/7/99	**THE ARGORY**
25/7/99	Tel: 018687 84753

13.00-18.00, please telephone 01868 784753 for further information

Historic Houses & Gardens

	Guided Walk: Bloody Bridge, Mourn Coastal Footpath & William's Harbour
28/7/99	**MURLOUGH NATURE RESERVE**
28/7/99	Tel: 013967 51467/24362

A tale of murder, smuggling and wrack harvests. Meet at Bloody Bridge car park which is a few miles south of Newcastle on the Newcastle to Kilkell road, 14.30

Nature Reserves

	Small Pets Competition
1/8/99	**CROM ESTATE**
1/8/99	Tel: 013657 38118/174

Come and see these gorgeous little animals prance around for all to see and admire. Time: 15.00

Woods

	Guided Walk
1/8/99	**CROM ESTATE**
1/8/99	Tel: 013657 38118/174

A guided walk listening to the history of Crom Estate. Meet: 15.00 at the Visitor Centre. Please telephone 013657 38118 for further information

Woods

	Guided Walk: Conies and Ponies the Chompers and Munchers
1/8/99	**MURLOUGH NATURE RESERVE**
1/8/99	Tel: 013967 51467/24362

A chance to see the exmoor ponies and learn the history of the warren. Meet at Murlough Information Centre which is located at the Trust's car park on the main Dundrum to Newcastle road, beside Lazy BJ Caravan Park, 14.30

Nature Reserves

	Musical House Tours
1/8/99	**THE ARGORY**
1/8/99	Tel: 018687 84753

14.00-18.00, please telephone 01868 784753 for further information

Historic Houses & Gardens

	Gala Picnic Concert with Fireworks
7/8/99	**CASTLE WARD**
7/8/99	Tel: 01396 881204

Music and good food under the sun with fantastic firework finale. Please telephone 01396 881204 for further information

Historic Houses

	Victorian Fashion Show
7/8/99	**FLORENCE COURT**
7/8/99	Tel: 01365 348249

Advance booking - tickets £6.00, includes glass of wine. Show starts: 20.00. Please telephone 01365 348249 for further information

Historic Houses & Gardens

	Heavy Horse Show & Judging
7/8/99	**PATTERSON'S SPADE MILL**
7/8/99	Tel: 01849 433619

Watch these beautiful creatures parade in all their glory. Time: 10.30-18.00

Museum- Mill

	A Turning
7/8/99	**ROWALLANE GARDEN**
8/8/99	Tel: 01238 510131

Guild of Wood Turners demonstration and sale in the stableyard at 14.30

Gardens

	Country Capers
8/8/99	**ARDRESS HOUSE**
8/8/99	Tel: 01762 851236

Try your hand at throwing the horseshoe, beat the goalie, or race for glory in the egg and spoon race and a host of other fun events, 14.00-16.00

Historic Houses

Further more detailed information on the attractions listed can be found in Best Guides *Visitor Attractions* Guide under the classifications shown

Mad Hatter's Tea Party
8/8/99 COLIN GLEN COUNTRY PARK
8/8/99 Tel: 01232 614115
Children's Summer Tea Party as part of
the West Belfast Festival, with fancy
dress, nature walks, face painting and
games. Prizes for best fancy dress costume. Commences 14.00, Admission
£1.00
Country Parks

Guided Walk
8/8/99 CROM ESTATE
8/8/99 Tel: 013657 38118/174
A guided walk listening to the history of
Crom Estate. Meet: 15.00 at the Visitor
Centre. Please telephone 013657 38118
for further information
Woods

Family Sports Day
8/8/99 CROM ESTATE
8/8/99 Tel: 013657 38118/174
Come on, don't be lazy, have a go!. Time:
15.00
Woods

**Guided Walk: Glen River, Thomas's
Quarry and Millstone Mountain**
8/8/99 MURLOUGH NATURE RESERVE
8/8/99 Tel: 013967 51467/24362
A chance to see Lindsay's Leap, an ice
house, a magalith and Black Stairs.
Meet Donard Car Park, 14.30
Nature Reserves

**Bat Walk - Strangford Lough Wildlife
Centre**
13/8/99 CASTLE WARD
13/8/99 Tel: 01396 881204
An insight into the mysteries of the bat -
see them live, watch them leaving their
roosts and listen to them using a bat
detector. Time: 20.30
Historic Houses

Ridgewood Pearl Desmond Stakes
14/8/99 CURRAGH RACECOURSE
14/8/99 Tel: 00 353 45 441205
Please call for further information
Racecourses

County Down Traction Engine Rally
14/8/99 MOUNT STEWART HOUSE, GARDEN AND
TEMPLE OF THE WINDS
14/8/99 Tel: 012477 88387/88487
In the Paddock Fields from 10.00.
Admission rates to be confirmed. Please
telephone 012477 88387 for further
information
Historic Houses & Gardens

**Shore Foray & Picnic - Strangford
Lough Wildlife Centre**
15/8/99 CASTLE WARD
15/8/99 Tel: 01396 881204
Visit an island and explore the shore at
low tide. Discover the marine creatures
hidden from view under stones and sea-
weed. Finishes with a picnic on the
island, begins at 10.00
Historic Houses

Guided Walk
15/8/99 CROM ESTATE
15/8/99 Tel: 013657 38118/174
A guided walk listening to the history of
Crom Estate. Meet: 15.00 at the Visitor
Centre. Please telephone 013657 38118
for further information
Woods

Punch & Judy
15/8/99 CROM ESTATE
15/8/99 Tel: 013657 38118/174
Traditional shows all afternoon from
15.00 onwards
Woods

Guided Walk: The Secret Ring Reserve
15/8/99 MURLOUGH NATURE RESERVE
15/8/99 Tel: 013967 51467/24362
Its Wildlife and glorious heathland heritage. Meet at Murlough Information
Centre which is located at the Trust's car
park on the main Dundrum to Newcastle
road, beside Lazy BJ Caravan Park, 14.30
Nature Reserves

Courtyard Attractions
15/8/99 THE ARGORY
15/8/99 Tel: 018687 84753
14.00-18.00, please telephone 01868
784753 for further information
Historic Houses & Gardens

**Wildlife Walk - Strangford Lough
Wildlife Centre**
18/8/99 CASTLE WARD
18/8/99 Tel: 01396 881204
View the Wildlife at ballymacormick
Point, meet Groomsport 14.00
Historic Houses

Vintage Vehicle Rally
21/8/99 CASTLE COOLE
21/8/99 Tel: 01365 322690
Lots of vintage vehicles on display from
14.00
Historic Houses

**Historical Boat Trip - Strangford Lough
Wildlife Centre**
21/8/99 CASTLE WARD
21/8/99 Tel: 01396 881204
Enjoy the scenery and view of many of
the castles and historical sites of
Strangford Lough. Boat leaves Portaferry

/ Strangford at 14.00

Historic Houses

Go Latin At Colin Grove Forest Park

22/8/99 COLIN GLEN COUNTRY PARK
22/8/99 Tel: 01232 614115
A percussion workshop learning about the rhythms of Samba and other Latin American music. Commences 14.00, Admission £0.50

Country Parks

Guided Walk

22/8/99 CROM ESTATE
22/8/99 Tel: 013657 38118/174
A guided walk listening to the history of Crom Estate. Meet: 15.00 at the Visitor Centre. Please telephone 013657 38118 for further information

Woods

Treasure Hunt

22/8/99 CROM ESTATE
22/8/99 Tel: 013657 38118/174
Hunt the mysterious treasure which is carefully hidden in the Crom Estate. Time: 15.00

Woods

Summer Craft Fair & Children's Fun Day

22/8/99 FLORENCE COURT
22/8/99 Tel: 01365 348249
13.00-18.00, please telephone 01365 348249 for further information

Historic Houses & Gardens

Bog Walk

22/8/99 THE ARGORY
22/8/99 Tel: 018687 84753
A fascinating look at the plants, creatures and landscape of the ???? bog at 14.00. Please telephone 01868 784753 for further information

Historic Houses & Gardens

Wildlife Walk - Strangford Lough Wildlife Centre

25/8/99 CASTLE WARD
25/8/99 Tel: 01396 881204
View the flora and fauna of Orlock Point, meet Groomsport 14.00

Historic Houses

Music at Castle Coole

26/8/99 CASTLE COOLE
26/8/99 Tel: 01365 322690
In the Grand Hall. Korean pianist Young Choon-Park performs music by Mozart, Schubert, Chopin. Tickets £12.00 (book 2 or more recitals at discount rate £10.00, excludes 'A Night at the Opera' evening). Price includes a wine reception in the Breakfast Room where guests can meet the performers. 100 seats only so book early!

Historic Houses

Georgian Weekend

27/8/99 PALACE STABLES HERITAGE CENTRE
30/8/99 Tel: 01861 529629
Georgian musical evening Fri 27 August, New Murder Mystery 28 August and Georgian Festival with calendar theme Sun 29 and Mon 30 August, call for further details

Heritage Centres

Guided Walk

28/8/99 CROM ESTATE
28/8/99 Tel: 013657 38118/174
A guided walk listening to the history of Crom Estate. Meet: 15.00 at the Visitor Centre. Please telephone 013657 38118 for further information

Woods

The Hare in Northern Ireland

29/8/99 CASTLE WARD
29/8/99 Tel: 01396 881204
Illustrated lecture and walk with Carina Dinger-Kerser at 14.00, please telephone 01396 881204 for further information

Historic Houses

Magic Show

29/8/99 CROM ESTATE
29/8/99 Tel: 013657 38118/174
Marvel at the magic of Paul Gomac at 15.00

Woods

Tattersalls Breeders Stakes

29/8/99 CURRAGH RACECOURSE
29/8/99 Tel: 00 353 45 441205
Please call for further information

Racecourses

Family Day - Craft Fair & Great Balloon Race

30/8/99 THE ARGORY
30/8/99 Tel: 018687 84753
A fun-filled day for the whole family with a craft fair where you can purchase those unusual gifts and a spectacular balloon race. Time: 13.00-18.00, please telephone 01868 784753 for further information

Historic Houses & Gardens

Festival of Family Fun

5/9/99 CASTLE COOLE
5/9/99 Tel: 01365 322690
A brilliant day out for the whole family with lots of entertainments and competitions. Starts: 14.00

Historic Houses

Moyglare Stud Stakes

5/9/99	**Curragh Racecourse**
5/9/99	Tel: 00 353 45 441205
	Please call for further information
	Racecourses

Musical House Tours

5/9/99	**The Argory**
5/9/99	Tel: 018687 84753
	14.00-18.00, please telephone 01868 784753 for further information
	Historic Houses & Gardens

Jefferson Smurfit Memorial Irish St. Leger

18/9/99	**Curragh Racecourse**
19/9/99	Tel: 00 353 45 441205
	Classic Racing with Aga Khan Studs National Stakes on Sunday
	Racecourses

Guided Woodland Walk

19/9/99	**The Argory**
19/9/99	Tel: 018687 84753
	Come out for a breath of fresh air and exercise to see the beautiful woodland around the Argory. Meet: 14.00. Please telephone 01868 784753 for further information
	Historic Houses & Gardens

Fungi Foray

26/9/99	**Castle Ward**
26/9/99	Tel: 01396 881204
	A walk with Dr Roy Anderson at 14.00. He will advise you on what's safe and what's not in the Fungi world, please telephone 01396 881204 for further information
	Historic Houses

Musical House Tours

26/9/99	**The Argory**
26/9/99	Tel: 018687 84753
	14.00-18.00, please telephone 01868 784753 for further information
	Historic Houses & Gardens

Irish Cesarewitch

2/10/99	**Curragh Racecourse**
2/10/99	Tel: 00 353 45 441205
	Please call for further information
	Racecourses

Juddmonte Beresford Stakes/Blandford Stakes

16/10/99	**Curragh Racecourse**
16/10/99	Tel: 00 353 45 441205
	Please call for further information
	Racecourses

Guided Walk: Caring for the Countryside

17/10/99	**Murlough Nature Reserve**
17/10/99	Tel: 013967 51467/24362
	An update on the National Trust's man-

agement to conserve the wildlife of Murlough dunes. Meet at Murlough Information Centre which is located at the Trust's car park on the main Dundrum to Newcastle road, beside Lazy BJ Caravan Park, 14.30

Nature Reserves

Autumn Craft Fair

24/10/99	**Florence Court**
24/10/99	Tel: 01365 348249
	13.00-17.00, please telephone 01365 348249 for further information
	Historic Houses & Gardens

Racing from Thurles

28/10/99	**Thurles Racecourse**
28/10/99	Tel: 00 353 504 22253
	The Best of Premier County Racing. Please call for further information
	Racecourses

Curragh Carpets Raceday

29/10/99	**Curragh Racecourse**
29/10/99	Tel: 00 353 45 441205
	Evening meeting, please call for further information
	Racecourses

Hallowe'en Murder Mystery

29/10/99	**Palace Stables Heritage Centre**
30/10/99	Tel: 01861 529629
	...... a foul and heinous murder has been committed which you are cordiannly invited to help solve. Who is the culprit? What was the motive? How and when was the nefarious deed committed? An alternative evening's entertainment with a unique historical slant for would-be sleuths. Call for further details
	Heritage Centres

Putting the House to Bed

6/11/99	**Florence Court**
6/11/99	Tel: 01365 348249
	Tour at 14.00, tickets £5.00 (includes tea), advanced booking essential, please telephone 01365 348249 for further information
	Historic Houses & Gardens

Racing from Thurles

11/11/99	**Thurles Racecourse**
25/11/99	Tel: 00 353 504 22253
	The Best of Premier County Racing. Meetings on 11 & 25 Nov. Please call for further information
	Racecourses

Hattons Grace Hurdle Grade 1

27/11/99	**Fairyhouse Racecourse**
28/11/99	Tel: 00 353 1 825 6167
	Premier racing from Thurles with Drinmore Chase Grade 1 and Royal Bond

Hurdle Grade 1

Racecourses

Christmas Country Market

27/11/99 WELLBROOK BEETLING MILL

28/11/99 Tel: 016487 51735

Come and buy those unusual Christmas gifts. Please telephone 016487 51735 for further information

Museum- Waterworks

Christmas Georgian Festival

1/12/99 PALACE STABLES HERITAGE CENTRE

31/12/99 Tel: 01861 529629

'Tis December 1786 and the household of the Arcbishop prepares for the season's festivities. Doubtless His Grace, being a bountiful and generous host, will entertain lavishly. His servents - despite the burden of their duties - look forward to bedecking the household with greenery, singing Christmas carols and making, and indeed partaking of a little mulled wine. Dates are to be set, please call venue nearer the time. Also available for Evening Events for Groups, call for details

Heritage Centres

Racing from Thurles

2/12/99 THURLES RACECOURSE

19/12/99 Tel: 00 353 504 22253

The Best of Premier County Racing. Meetings on 2 & 19 Dec. Please call for further information

Racecourses

Further more detailed information on the attractions listed can be found in Best Guides *Visitor Attractions* Guide under the classifications shown

London

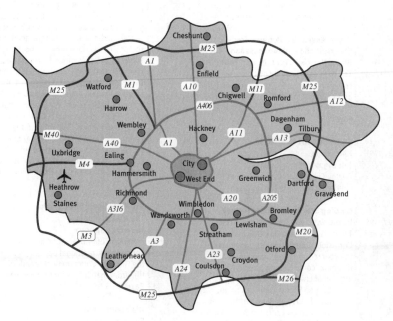

Platform: Night Must Fall
1/3/99 ROYAL NATIONAL THEATRE AND TOURS
1/3/99 Tel: 0171 452 3000 Box Office
Cottesloe. Start at 18.00 and last for
approximately 45 minutes. Tickets:
A£4.00 Concessions£3.00. Tickets for 10
or more Platorms are £3.50 each (£2.50
Concessions). Please telephone 0171
452 3020 for further information
Theatres

**Foyer Music: The Poulenc Trio -
Classical oboe, piano, bassoon**
1/3/99 ROYAL NATIONAL THEATRE AND TOURS
1/3/99 Tel: 0171 452 3000 Box Office
Free Concert evening (pre-performance)
and at lunchtime on Saturdays, in the
'Djanogly Concert Pitch' in the Lyttleton
Foyer
Theatres

Children's Art Exhibition
1/3/99 HALL PLACE
13/3/99 Tel: 01322 526574 x204
Bexley Civic Society annual event for
children who live in the Borough.
Historic Houses & Gardens

Guiding Star by Jonathan Harvey
1/3/99 ROYAL NATIONAL THEATRE AND TOURS
5/4/99 Tel: 0171 452 3000 Box Office
Cottesloe: One of the best new plays of
the year, a scorching, searching domestic drama conceived on an epic scale
and full of Liverpool wit and waggery.
Performance Times: Evenings 19.30: 1, 2,
11, 18, 19, 20, 22, 23 & 31 Mar & 1, 3 & 5
Apr; Matinees 14.30: 11, 20 & 23 Mar & 1
& 3 Apr. The majority of seats costs
£18.00, with some seats (restricted
view) at £12.00. Under18s£8.00,
OAPs£10.50, NT Education student
groups £7.50, Registered disabled and
one companion per person, Visually
Impaired & Wheelchair users (one Free
companion) £16.00
Theatres

The Forest by Alexander Ostrovsky
1/3/99 ROYAL NATIONAL THEATRE AND TOURS
10/4/99 Tel: 0171 452 3000 Box Office
Lyttleton. Ostrovsky, considered by many
to be the father of Russian drama, created blisteringly real and sardonically
funny accounts of Russian life, and in
doing so paved the way for Chekhov and
others. His tragi-comedy, The Forest -
one of Russia's most celebrated plays,
but almost unknown in Britain - has
been adapted by Alan Ayckbourn: another master of black comedy. Gennadiy, an

impoverished actor and romantic inno-
cent, arrives at the country estate of his
aunt, pretending to be rich and hoping
for peace and comfort. Instead, he finds
himself caught up in a network of
intrigue where forbidden love, spying,
treachery, lust, rapacious greed and
financial double-dealings are rife.
Performance Times: Evenings 19.30: 1, 2,
3, 4, 11, 12, 13, 29, 30 & 31 Mar & 8, 9 &
10 Apr; Matinee 14.15: 2, 13 & 30 Mar &
10 Apr. Tickets: Evenings £10.00-£27.00,
Previews & Sat Matinee £8.00-£22.00,
Weekday Matinee £9.00-£15.00. Under
18s£8.00, OAPs£10.50, Registered disabled & Visually-Impaired £7.00-£17.00,
Wheelchair Users £15.00-£17.00, Adult
groups £12.00-£21.00, NT Education
group members & Student standby
£7.50, School groups (under 19) ££8.00-
£9.00, College groups (aged 19-25)
£10.50-£12.50, Day Seats £8.00-£12.50,
Standby £10.00-£14.00, Standing £4.50-
£5.00
Theatres

Six Days Shalt Thou Labour
1/3/99 THE JEWISH MUSEUM
2/5/99 Tel: 0171 284 1997
Exhibition of photographs by Elaine
Kennedy on traditional occupants among
the Hassidic Community of Stamford
Hill, from match-making to the Matzah-
Baking
Museum- Religious

It's About Time
1/3/99 SCIENCE MUSEUM
1/3/00 Tel: 0171 938 8000
The incredible precision of atomic time
is vital to our everyday ives. Digital communication, navigation in space and on
earth and many everyday technologies
depend on the research of the time sci-
entists. This new exhibition situated on
the Ground Floor offers an intriguing
look at atomic clocks today and in the
future and their impact on the way we
live.
Museum- Science

**Sally Brown - The Original Alice: from
manuscript to Wonderland**
2/3/99 BRITISH LIBRARY
2/3/99 Tel: 0171 412 7332
The manuscript book originally entitled
'Alice's Adventures Underground,' a gift
from Charles Lutwidge Dodgson to the
'dear child' Alice Liddell, is one of the
Library's greatest treasures. Curator

Further more detailed information on the attractions listed can be found
in Best Guides *Visitor Attractions* Guide under the classifications shown

Sally Brown traces the history of the 'Alice' manuscript from its beginnings as a tale told on a summer boat trip in Oxford to its publication in book form.
Time: 13.30. Admission Free

Museum- Library

Ian Kershaw - Hitler and the 'Final Solution'

2/3/99
2/3/99
BRITISH LIBRARY
Tel: 0171 412 7332

Professor Kershaw begins by considering the possible roots of Hitler's pathological anti-semitism, then assesses Hitler's role in the radicalisation of Nazi anti-Jewish policy, focusing particularly on the emergence of the Nuremberg Laws of 1935, on the November pogrom of 1938 (Reichskristallnacht) and its aftermath, and on the intensified barbarisation in Poland between 1939-1941. He then addresses the complex issue of the emergence of the 'Final Solution' between the German invasion of the Soviet Union in June 1941 and the Wannsee Conference of January 1942, concentrating on Hitler's precise rôle and evaluating the latest research, including the implications of the desk-diary of Himmler, recently discovered in Moscow. Ian Kershaw is Professor of Modern History at the University of Sheffield and the author of Hitler 1889-1936: Hubris. He was historical adviser to the TV series 'The Nazis: A Warning From History', winner of a BAFTA award.
Time: 18.15. Tickets: £5.00
Concessions£3.50

Museum- Library

Foyer Music: The Phil Hopkins Trio - Jazz

2/3/99
2/3/99
ROYAL NATIONAL THEATRE AND TOURS
Tel: 0171 452 3000 Box Office

Free Concert evening (pre-performance) and at lunchtime on Saturdays, in the 'Djanogly Concert Pitch' in the Lyttleton Foyer

Theatres

Confex 1999 / Incentive 1999

2/3/99
4/3/99
EARLS COURT OLYMPIA
Tel: 0171 385 1200

Earls Court 1. Organiser: Miller Freeman UK Ltd.

Exhibition Centres

Lord of the Dance

2/3/99   WEMBLEY CONFERENCE AND EXHIBITION

CENTRE

4/3/99
Tel: 0181 902 8833
In Theatre Format at 20.00. Tickets: £17.50-£20.00.

Exhibition Centres

Foyer Music: The De Visee Ensemble - 16th/17th century music

3/3/99
3/3/99
ROYAL NATIONAL THEATRE AND TOURS
Tel: 0171 452 3000 Box Office

Free Concert evening (pre-performance) and at lunchtime on Saturdays, in the 'Djanogly Concert Pitch' in the Lyttleton Foyer

Theatres

London International Stamp and Cover Show

3/3/99
6/3/99
RHS ROYAL HORTICULTURAL HALLS
Tel: 0171 834 4333

A consumer show with a wide range of dealers selling stamps and postal history. Call for further details

Exhibition Centres

126th Annual Exhibition

3/3/99
26/3/99
AGNEW'S
Tel: 0171 629 6176

Annual exhibition of English watercolours and drawings

Art Galleries

The Riot by Nick Darke

3/3/99
10/4/99
ROYAL NATIONAL THEATRE AND TOURS
Tel: 0171 452 3000 Box Office

Cottesloe. The 20th century's just around the corner and the natives of Newlyn are restless. When a dispute amongst fishermen over Sunday observance turns into a battle between rival towns, the army is called to quell the riot. Caught in the crossfire is Thomas Bolitho - merchant, magistrate, mine owner and mayor - who respects the fishermen's beliefs, but knows that riots are bad for business. When he tries to play each end against the other, both ends turn on him. Performance Times: Evenings 19.30: 3, 4, 5, 6, 8, 9, 12, 13, 15, 16 & 17 Mar; Matinees 14.30: 4, 6, 13 & 16 Mar. The majority of seats costs £18.00, with some seats (restricted view) at £12.00. Under18s£8.00, OAPs£10.50, NT Education student groups £7.50, Registered disabled and one companion per person, Visually Impaired & Wheelchair users (one Free companion) £16.00

Theatres

Orazio Gentileschi at the Court of Charles I

3/3/99 NATIONAL GALLERY
23/5/99 Tel: 0171 839 3321
Sunley Room. Admission Free. Further
information will appear when available
Art Galleries

Platform: Waiting for Lefty
4/3/99 ROYAL NATIONAL THEATRE AND TOURS
4/3/99 Tel: 0171 452 3000 Box Office
Lyttleton. Start at 18.00 and last for
approximately 45 minutes. Tickets:
A£4.00 Concessions£3.00. Tickets for 10
or more Platorms are £3.50 each (£2.50
Concessions). Please telephone 0171
452 3020 for further information
Theatres

Foyer Music: Katari - Bolivian quartet
4/3/99 ROYAL NATIONAL THEATRE AND TOURS
4/3/99 Tel: 0171 452 3000 Box Office
Free Concert evening (pre-performance)
and at lunchtime on Saturdays, in the
'Djanogly Concert Pitch' in the Lyttleton
Foyer
Theatres

Thames Barrier Operation Scheme
4/3/99 THAMES BARRIER VISITORS CENTRE
4/3/99 Tel: 0181 305 4188
See the Thames Barrier in operation this
Tuesday approximate closure times
08.30-11.00
The Unusual

The National Wedding Show
4/3/99 EARLS COURT OLYMPIA
7/3/99 Tel: 0171 385 1200
Olympia Grand Hall. The ultimate one
stop wedding experience. Everything
you need for planning a wedding under
one roof, live fashion show six times per
day, show guide included in price of
admission. Ticket Prices: £9.00 in
advance, £10.00 on the door. Wedding
Party, admits 5, £30.00 in advance only.
Pre-booking is advisable. Advance Ticket
Hotline: 01462 485896. For further information please telephone Wedding
Shows (UK) Ltd, tel: 01462 485881
Exhibition Centres

Exhibition
4/3/99 BURGH HOUSE
21/3/99 Tel: 0171 431 0144
Gerard Mansell Still Lifes and
Landscapes of rural France - Brittany, the
Limousin and the Pyrénées
Historic Houses

Platform: Our Town
5/3/99 ROYAL NATIONAL THEATRE AND TOURS
5/3/99 Tel: 0171 452 3000 Box Office
Cottesloe. Start at 18.00 and last for

approximately 45 minutes. Tickets:
A£4.00 Concessions£3.00. Tickets for 10
or more Platorms are £3.50 each (£2.50
Concessions). Please telephone 0171
452 3020 for further information
Theatres

Lifetime Careers Ltd
5/3/99 WEMBLEY CONFERENCE AND EXHIBITION
CENTRE
5/3/99 Tel: 0181 902 8833
A careers open day for the 1st year A-
level students who wish to obtain fur-
ther information about Oxford and
Cambridge Universities. Admission is
Free, registration from 09.00
Exhibition Centres

**Foyer Music: Al Pinches - ragtime gui-
tar**
5/3/99 ROYAL NATIONAL THEATRE AND TOURS
6/3/99 Tel: 0171 452 3000 Box Office
Free Concert evening (pre-performance)
and at lunchtime on Saturdays, in the
'Djanogly Concert Pitch' in the Lyttleton
Foyer
Theatres

The Oddysey
5/3/99 WAREHOUSE THEATRE
4/4/99 Tel: 0181 680 4060 Box Office
Following their sell-out performance last
Easter of 'Three Men In A Boat,' and in
the tradition of 'Pirates' and 'Ben Hur',
Performance Theatre Company return
with the world premiere of their version
of 'The Odyssey'. High energy and mad-
cap family fun guaranteed! Times and
prices to be confirmed.
Theatres

Betrayal by Harold Pinter
5/3/99 ROYAL NATIONAL THEATRE AND TOURS
7/4/99 Tel: 0171 452 3000 Box Office
Lyttleton. As we approach the end of the
century, and twenty years after it was
given its world premiere in the Lyttleton,
Harold Pinter's ultimate 'triangular relationship' play can be seen as one of the
defining works of our time. 'Beytrayal' is
a new departure and a bold one....
Pinter has found a way of making memory active and dramatic, giving an audience the experience of the mind's accel-
erating momentum as it pieces together
the past with a combination of curiosity
and regret. He shows man betrayed not
only by man, but by time... a master
craftsman honouring his talent by setting it new, difficult tasks' New Society.
Performance Times: Evenings 19.30: 5,

6, 8, 9 & 10 Mar & 1, 3, 5, 6 & 7 Apr;
Matinees 14.15: 6 & 9 Mar, 3 & 7 Apr.
Tickets: Evenings £10.00-£27.00,
Previews & Sat Matinee £8.00-£22.00,
Weekday Matinee £9.00-£15.00. Under
18s£8.00, OAPs£10.50, Registered disabled & Visually-Impaired £7.00-£17.00,
Wheelchair Users £15.00-£17.00, Adult
groups £12.00-£21.00, NT Education
group members & Student standby
£7.50, School groups (under 19) ££8.00-
£9.00, College groups (aged 19-25)
£10.50-£12.50, Day Seats £8.00-£12.50,
Standby £10.00-£14.00, Standing £4.50-
£5.00

Theatres

Mrs Bettons Dressing

6/3/99	GUNNERSBURY PARK MUSEUM
6/3/99	Tel: 0181 992 1612

A lecture and demonstration followed by
a private viewing of the 'Mrs Beeton'
exhibition. Starts at 15.00. Ticket Prices:
A£6.00 Concessions £4, available from
the museum

Museum- Social History

The Sailboat & Windsurf Show

6/3/99	ALEXANDRA PALACE
7/3/99	Tel: 0181 365 2121

Great & West Hall. A spectacular show
for the committed and novice sailor
wind-surfer alike. Exhibitors include
chandlers, sail makers, sailing schools,
club and class associations, dinghies
and boards. Times: Sat 10.00-18.00, Sun
10.00-17.00. Admission: A£7.50 C£2.50.
For tickets in advance tel: 01703 650885
A£6.50 C£2.00. Organiser: Royal
Yachting Association 01703 627425

Historic Buildings

Soldiers Lives Through the Ages

6/3/99	NATIONAL ARMY MUSEUM
7/3/99	Tel: 0171 730 0717

A weekend of special events during
which visitors will be able to discover
what life has been like for soldiers fighting in Britain's armies since Tudor times.
Re-enactors from different periods will
bring the Museum's Galleries vividly to
life. A series of illustrated talks will
examine issues like pay, fighting conditions and social life for the soldier
through the ages

Museum- Military

Troilus and Cressida by William Shakespeare

6/3/99	ROYAL NATIONAL THEATRE AND TOURS
27/3/99	Tel: 0171 452 3000 Box Office

Olivier. Shakespeare's Troilus and
Cressida is one of the most philosophical works of the 17th century. Its central
idea - a study of human values - is pow-
erfully focused in its central event: the
war between the Greeks and the Trojans
over the abduction of the beautiful, legendary Helen. The Greek camp is by
turns wily, cynical, stupid and profound.
Within the walls of Troy, the culture is
defined by codes of honour and romantic chivalry. These two views of life are
pitted against each other in a series of
brilliantly argued scenes, throughout
which the central character of Troilus is
wrenched and divided, culminating in
his bitter loss of Cressida to the Greeks.
Performance times: Evenings 19.00: 8, 9,
10, 11, 12, 13, 15 (Press Night), 16, 17, 18,
19, 20 Mar; Matinees 13.30: 13 & 20 Mar.
Tickets: Evenings £10.00-£27.00,
Previews & Sat Matinee £8.00-£22.00,
Weekday Matinee £9.00-£15.00. Under
18s£8.00, OAPs£10.50, Registered disabled & Visually-Impaired £7.00-£17.00,
Wheelchair Users £15.00-£17.00, Adult
groups £12.00-£21.00, NT Education
group members & Student standby
£7.50, School groups (under 19) ££8.00-
£9.00, College groups (aged 19-25)
£10.50-£12.50, Day Seats £9.00-£12.50,
Standby £10.00-£14.00, Standing £4.50-
£5.00

Theatres

Exhibition

6/3/99	BURGH HOUSE
27/6/99	Tel: 0171 431 0144

Musicians in Hampstead. Composers,
conductors and performers living in
Hampstead between 1880 & 1960

Historic Houses

Walk from Burgh House

7/3/99	BURGH HOUSE
7/3/99	Tel: 0171 431 0144

Springett's Wood and other secret
places, led by Brian Seddon, naturalist,
commences 14.30, tickets: £1.00

Historic Houses

Make Me a Match

7/3/99	THE JEWISH MUSEUM
7/3/99	Tel: 0171 284 1997

A husband and wife's view of matchmak-
ing with Ian and Bella Sharer.
Admission: £4.00 or £6.50 including
beigel lunch and admission to Museum

galleries. (£1.00 discount for Museum Friends). Please book in advance. Time: 11.00.

Museum- Religious

Platform: Gaslight

8/3/99
8/3/99

ROYAL NATIONAL THEATRE AND TOURS

Tel: 0171 452 3000 Box Office

Cottesloe. Start at 18.00 and last for approximately 45 minutes. Tickets: A£4.00 Concessions£3.00. Tickets for 10 or more Platorms are £3.50 each (£2.50 Concessions). Please telephone 0171 452 3020 for further information

Theatres

Foyer Music: Valentin & Dai-Chi - piano duo

8/3/99
8/3/99

ROYAL NATIONAL THEATRE AND TOURS

Tel: 0171 452 3000 Box Office

Free Concert evening (pre-performance) and at lunchtime on Saturdays, in the 'Djanogly Concert Pitch' in the Lyttleton Foyer

Theatres

Neil Diamond in the Round

8/3/99

WEMBLEY CONFERENCE AND EXHIBITION CENTRE

14/3/99

Tel: 0181 902 8833

Performances: 8 & 9 then 11, 13 & 14 March at 20.00. Tickets: £27.50 & £30.00

Exhibition Centres

Anthony Minghella - Literature and the Cinema

9/3/99
9/3/99

BRITISH LIBRARY

Tel: 0171 412 7332

Anthony Minghella, Oscar-winning director of 'The English Patient,' is one of the brightest talents in contemporary cinema, and largely responsible for thrusting Herodotus into the bestseller lists! Here he talks about literature as a source for film. As well as adapting Michael Ondaatje's Booker-winning novel for the screen, Anthony Minghella has recently been working on a film version of Patricia Highsmith's 'The Talented Mr Ripley.' A further project, based on Charles Frazier's 'Cold Mountain,' will follow. Presented by the Centre for the Book in the Crossovers series. Time: 18.15. Tickets: £5.00 Concessions£3.50

Museum- Library

Timothy Day - Music in Performance

9/3/99
9/3/99

BRITISH LIBRARY

Tel: 0171 412 7332

Performers frequently claim to be carrying out the composer's instructions. But

from recordings, we now know how Elgar performed Elgar, how Strauss conducted Strauss, how Prokofiev played Prokofiev - and their playing styles are not followed by performers today. Why do performing styles of classical music change? And why have music historians been so reluctant to study music in performance? Time: 13.30. Admission Free

Museum- Library

Foyer Music: David Gordon - jazz piano

9/3/99
9/3/99

ROYAL NATIONAL THEATRE AND TOURS

Tel: 0171 452 3000 Box Office

Free Concert evening (pre-performance) and at lunchtime on Saturdays, in the 'Djanogly Concert Pitch' in the Lyttleton Foyer

Theatres

Platform: An Inspector Calls

10/3/99
10/3/99

ROYAL NATIONAL THEATRE AND TOURS

Tel: 0171 452 3000 Box Office

Lyttleton. Start at 18.00 and last for approximately 45 minutes. Tickets: A£4.00 Concessions£3.00. Tickets for 10 or more Platorms are £3.50 each (£2.50 Concessions). Please telephone 0171 452 3020 for further information

Theatres

Foyer Music: Yash Bash - Bulgarian folk duo

10/3/99
10/3/99

ROYAL NATIONAL THEATRE AND TOURS

Tel: 0171 452 3000 Box Office

Free Concert evening (pre-performance) and at lunchtime on Saturdays, in the 'Djanogly Concert Pitch' in the Lyttleton Foyer

Theatres

Pastel Society Annual Exhibition

10/3/99
21/3/99

MALL GALLERIES

Tel: 0171 930 6844

Vibrant and exciting exhibition of contemporary works in pastels

Art Galleries

Foyer Music: Pipe Dreams - classical flutes and piano

11/3/99
11/3/99

ROYAL NATIONAL THEATRE AND TOURS

Tel: 0171 452 3000 Box Office

Free Concert evening (pre-performance) and at lunchtime on Saturdays, in the 'Djanogly Concert Pitch' in the Lyttleton Foyer

Theatres

"Railway and Canal Interchange in London" by Malcolm Tucker

11/3/99
11/3/99

THE LONDON CANAL MUSEUM

Tel: 0171 713 0836

Commences 19.30, call for details

Further more detailed information on the attractions listed can be found in Best Guides *Visitor Attractions* Guide under the classifications shown

Museum- Canal

Groundwork For Gardeners

11/3/99 MUSEUM OF GARDEN HISTORY
12/3/99 Tel: 0171 401 8865
A two day practical Gardening Course
with Anne Jennings. Tickets £120.00 to
include materials, coffee, lunch and an
information folder. Commences 11.00-
16.00

Museum- Gardening

**Royal Watercolour Society Spring
Exhibition**

11/3/99 BANKSIDE GALLERY
18/4/99 Tel: 0171 928 7521
Featured artist: William Selby RWS. The
first opportunity to see fresh work from
the Members of the Royal Watercolour
Society. William is a Yorkshireman and a
son of a coalminer, he loves to paint the
open and wild countryside of the moor-
lands which he renders in breathtaking
colour

Art Galleries

Jackson Pollock

11/3/99 TATE GALLERY
6/9/99 Tel: 0171 887 8000
The Tate Gallery is to host the first retrospective exhibition of the work of
Jackson Pollock held in Britain for more
then 40 years. Widely considered to be
the most challenging and influential
American painter of the 20th century,
Pollock was one of the primary creators
of modern art after the Second World
War. It will offer a remarkable opportunity to see in full the work of this extraordinary and controversial artist. A£7.50
Concessions£5.00 Family Ticket £19.00.
Advance booking: First Call 0870 842
2233 (£1.60 booking fee). Daily 10.00-
17.40, last admission 17.00

Art Galleries

Platform: A Streetcar Named Desire

12/3/99 ROYAL NATIONAL THEATRE AND TOURS
12/3/99 Tel: 0171 452 3000 Box Office
Lyttleton. Start at 18.00 and last for
approximately 45 minutes. Tickets:
A£4.00 Concessions£3.00. Tickets for 10
or more Platorms are £3.50 each (£2.50
Concessions). Please telephone 0171
452 3020 for further information

Theatres

**The Evening Standard Homebuyer
Show**

12/3/99 EARLS COURT OLYMPIA
14/3/99 Tel: 0171 385 1200
Olympia 2. Homebuyers will find hundreds of homes under one roof from
starter flats to retirement cottages. In
fact everything one needs to know about
property, brought together inside a huge
one stop property shop. Ticket Prices:
£5.00. For more information please telephone Homebuyer Events Ltd, tel: 0181
877 3636

Exhibition Centres

National Science Week SET '99

12/3/99 GRANT MUSEUM OF ZOOLOGY AND
COMPARATIVE ANATOMY
21/3/99 Tel: 0171 504 2647
Exploring the Skeleton. This event is still
in the planning stages and therefore
details cannot be confirmed. Further
information will be available from mid
February, call 0171 504 2647

Museums

Science Week at the Science Museum

12/3/99 SCIENCE MUSEUM
23/3/99 Tel: 0171 938 8000
We invite you to join in the national celebration of science, engineering and technology at the Science Museum fro SET
'99. There will be special events all week
including a giant camera obscura -
where you walk in and become part of
the exhibit and see images from around
the Museum projected within. The
Museum will also be opening its doors
outside normal hours to offer a special
programme fro adults; enjoy a glass of
wine, relax to jazz music and explore the
Museum at your own leisure.

Museum- Science

Fit For Human Use?

12/3/99 SCIENCE MUSEUM
1/8/99 Tel: 0171 938 8000
Have you ever wondered how to make a
medicine bottle that can be opened by
an arthritic 80-year-old but not by a
child? Or why your dentist's chair is
more like a bad than a chair? This
revealing exhibition situated on the third
floor examines all aspects of ergonomics
- the study of relationship between the
workers and their environment focusing
especially on the equipment they use.

Museum- Science

**Foyer Music: The Gill Morley Duo - vio-
lin / piano**

13/3/99 ROYAL NATIONAL THEATRE AND TOURS
13/3/99 Tel: 0171 452 3000 Box Office
Free Concert evening (pre-performance)
and at lunchtime on Saturdays, in the
'Djanogly Concert Pitch' in the Lyttleton

Foyer

Theatres

Foyer Music: The Theo Travis Trio - jazz

13/3/99 ROYAL NATIONAL THEATRE AND TOURS
13/3/99 Tel: 0171 452 3000 Box Office
Free Concert evening (pre-performance) and at lunchtime on Saturdays, in the 'Djanogly Concert Pitch' in the Lyttleton Foyer

Theatres

Rock & Pop Fair

13/3/99 EARLS COURT OLYMPIA
14/3/99 Tel: 0171 385 1200
Olympia 2. The world's greatest selection of Cds/Records plus Memorabilia, Books, Videos, Tapes, Programmes, etc. Bargains, Rarities and recollections on sale by exhibitors from every continent. Buy / Sell / Trade. Opening Times: 10.00-17.00. For further information please telephone VIP Events, tel: 0116 2711977

Exhibition Centres

Millions of Years in the Building for SET 99

13/3/99 BRITISH LIBRARY
20/3/99 Tel: 0171 412 7332
Hard white limestone from the Jura, red granite from Norway and deep red sandstone from Burns Country: these are the contribution that the stones used in building the British Library at St Pancras make to the geology of Camden. Inside the Entrance Hall more types of stone can be seen. Come and find out on a walk around the Library during Science Engineering and Technology Week (SET 99). The tour will be led by Eric Robinson, Senior Lecturer in Geology at University College London. Admission Free but please book with Maureen Heath on 0171 412 7470

Museum- Library

3-Dimensional Art Exhibition

13/3/99 HALL PLACE
11/4/99 Tel: 01322 526574 x204
An Arts Council of Bexley's open 3-Dimensional art exhibition.

Historic Houses & Gardens

18th Century Fine Art - Pallas Unveil'd

13/3/99 ORLEANS HOUSE GALLERY
3/5/99 Tel: 0181 892 0221
Life and Art of Lady Dorothy Savile, Countess of Burlington (1699-1758). This study of Countess Burlington's own artwork and her patronage of figures such

as Alexander Pope and David Garrick, is staged to celebrate the tercentenary of her birth

Art Galleries

Antique and Collectors Fair

14/3/99 ALEXANDRA PALACE
14/3/99 Tel: 0181 365 2121
Great Hall. London's largest Antiques Fair with over 700 stands plus furniture selling wide range of quality items from 18th century onwards. Established for over 25 years. Times: Public 11.30-17.00 Trade 10.00. Admission: A£3.00, (Accompanied)C£Free, Trade£5.00 (with business card). Organiser: Pig & Whistle Promotions 0181 883 7061

Historic Buildings

A Scribe in the Gallery

14/3/99 THE JEWISH MUSEUM
14/3/99 Tel: 0171 284 1997
Aryeh Freedman, a sofer (Hebrew scribe), demonstrates the art of Hebrew calligraphy. Children welcome. No extra charge on admission. Booking not required. Time: 14.00-15.30.

Museum- Religious

Foyer Music: The Kelvin Christiane Trio - jazz

15/3/99 ROYAL NATIONAL THEATRE AND TOURS
15/3/99 Tel: 0171 452 3000 Box Office
Free Concert evening (pre-performance) and at lunchtime on Saturdays, in the 'Djanogly Concert Pitch' in the Lyttleton Foyer

Theatres

Workshop - 45 mins: Mind Games

15/3/99 TWO10 GALLERY
15/3/99 Tel: 0171 611 7211
Reverse the world with inverting goggles. Make your world expand and shrink. Improve your memory. Fool your brain, learn some psychology and generally enjoy yourself at Mind Games - a hands-on, brains-on experience. Times: 14.00 & 15.30. Suitable for ages 16+.

Art Galleries

The Georgian Garden

16/3/99 MUSEUM OF GARDEN HISTORY
16/3/99 Tel: 0171 401 8865
Chronology of Gardening Day with Caroline Holmes. Tickets £40.00 commences 11.00-16.00

Museum- Gardening

Foyer Music: H Palmer & R Hubbert - oboe / piano

Further more detailed information on the attractions listed can be found in Best Guides *Visitor Attractions* Guide under the classifications shown

16/3/99 16/3/99	**ROYAL NATIONAL THEATRE AND TOURS** Tel: 0171 452 3000 Box Office Free Concert evening (pre-performance) and at lunchtime on Saturdays, in the 'Djanogly Concert Pitch' in the Lyttleton Foyer

Theatres

Health Talk - 30 mins: Messing Around With Genes

16/3/99 16/3/99	**TWO10 GALLERY** Tel: 0171 611 7211 What is genetic engineering? Why do it? Where is it leading? Developmental biologist domic Delaney discusses these important questions. Time: 14.30. Suitable for ages 16+.

Art Galleries

RHS Early Spring Show

16/3/99 17/3/99	**RHS ROYAL HORTICULTURAL HALLS** Tel: 0171 834 4333 Open 1st day 10.30-19.00, 2nd day 10.00-17.00, 24 hour information line: 0171 649 1885

Exhibition Centres

Happy Days

16/3/99 16/4/99	**JILL GEORGE GALLERY LTD** Tel: 0171 439 7319 Exhibition of paintings and prints by Chris Orr

Art Galleries

Turner's Papers II

16/3/99 13/6/99	**TATE GALLERY** Tel: 0171 887 8000 'First of all respect your paper' was Turner's response to a request for advice on watercolour painting. Throughout his life Turner carefully matched his materials to his vision, and his choice of paper for watercolours was often unorthodox. This exhibition explores the papers Turner used in the later part of his career, and follows on from a previous display which showed the results of research into the early papers. It includes frame works and sketchbooks from the Tuner Bequest, together with loans which illustrate the developments in paper-making which produced the papers Turner used. Admission Free

Art Galleries

Anne Harvey & Ann Thwaite - Emily Tennyson talks to her Biographer

17/3/99 17/3/99	**BRITISH LIBRARY** Tel: 0171 412 7332 In 1823 a small girl looked out of a house in Horncastle and observed 13-year-old Alfred Tennyson, waiting while

the two fathers discussed business. Twenty-seven years later, when he became Poet Laureate, Emily Selwood married Alfred Tennyson. What kept them apart and what eventually brought them together has never before been fully explored. A hundred years after her death, Anne Harvey speaks as the poet's wife in an interview with Ann Thwaite, her biographer. The dramatised dialogue casts new light not only on a neglected Victorian woman, but on Tennyson himself. Ann Thwaite won the Duff Cooper Prize in 1985 for her biography of Edmund Gosse. She is now working on a life of Philip Henry Gosse (the 'father' of Father and Son). Presented by the Centre for the Book. Time: 18.15. Tickets: £5.00 Concessions£3.50

Museum- Library

Platform: Men Should Weep

17/3/99 17/3/99	**ROYAL NATIONAL THEATRE AND TOURS** Tel: 0171 452 3000 Box Office Cottesloe. Start at 18.00 and last for approximately 45 minutes. Tickets: A£4.00 Concessions£3.00. Tickets for 10 or more Platorms are £3.50 each (£2.50 Concessions). Please telephone 0171 452 3020 for further information

Theatres

Foyer Music: The Piano Plus Ensemble - piano / clarinet / viola

17/3/99 17/3/99	**ROYAL NATIONAL THEATRE AND TOURS** Tel: 0171 452 3000 Box Office Free Concert evening (pre-performance) and at lunchtime on Saturdays, in the 'Djanogly Concert Pitch' in the Lyttleton Foyer

Theatres

BBC Good Food Show London

17/3/99 21/3/99	**EARLS COURT OLYMPIA** Tel: 0171 385 1200 Olympia Grand Hall. The capital's premier food and drink event, bringing together talented celebrity chefs and TV personalities offering hundreds of new recipe ideas - plus the latest kitchen gadgets, new food products and delicious wines. Pre-booking is advisable. For further information please telephone Consumer Exhibitions Ltd, tel: 0181 948 1666

Exhibition Centres

The Colleen Bawn by Dion Boucicault

17/3/99 27/3/99	**ROYAL NATIONAL THEATRE AND TOURS** Tel: 0171 452 3000 Box Office Lyttleton. The clandestine marriage of

Eily O'Connor 'the Colleen Bawn,' brings together a gallery of pettifogging attorneys, landed gentry and roguish peasantry in this classic tale of love and intrigue across the classes in 19th-century Ireland. Crammed with action, spectacle and high emotion, this production was first staged at The Abbey Theatre, Dublin where it received wide critical acclaim. Performance Times: Evenings 19.30: 17, 18 (Press Night 19.00), 19, 20, 22, 23, 24, 25, 26 & 27 Mar; Matinee 14.15: 20, 25 & 27 Mar. Tickets: Evenings £10.00-£27.00, Previews & Sat Matinee £8.00-£22.00, Weekday Matinee £9.00-£15.00, Under 18s£8.00, OAPs£10.50, Registered disabled & Visually-Impaired £7.00-£17.00, Wheelchair Users £15.00-£17.00, Adult groups £12.00-£21.00, NT Education group members & Student standby £7.50, School groups (under 19) £8.00-£9.00, College groups (aged 19-25) £10.50-£12.50, Day Seats £8.00-£12.50, Standby £10.00-£14.00, Standing £4.50-£5.00

Theatres

The Sparkler Of Albion
17/3/99   DICKENS HOUSE MUSEUM
29/9/99   Tel: 0171 405 2127
One-man Dickens Show performed by Geoffrey Harris on Wednesday Evenings, 19.30

Historic Houses

Foyer Music: Gabriel Keen - classical piano
18/3/99   ROYAL NATIONAL THEATRE AND TOURS
18/3/99   Tel: 0171 452 3000 Box Office
Free Concert evening (pre-performance) and at lunchtime on Saturdays, in the 'Djanogly Concert Pitch' in the Lyttleton Foyer

Theatres

Health Talk - 30 mins: The Pig Issue
18/3/99   TWO10 GALLERY
18/3/99   Tel: 0171 611 7211
Kate Burrell explores the science and ethical issues surrounding xenotransplantation - the use of genetically modified animal organs for human transplant. Time: 14.30. Suitable for ages 16+.

Art Galleries

The Daily Mail Ideal Home Exhibition in Partnership With Barclays Mortgages
18/3/99   EARLS COURT OLYMPIA
11/4/99   Tel: 0171 385 1200
Earls Court 1&2. The world famous Daily

Mail Ideal Home Exhibition gives visitors ideas for the home and garden and plenty of opportunities for shopping. Press & Preview day only 17 March. For further information please contact DMG Exhibition Group Ltd, tel: 0181 515 2000

Exhibition Centres

The Lady's Not For Burning
19/3/99   ROYAL NATIONAL THEATRE AND TOURS
19/3/99   Tel: 0171 452 3000 Box Office
Cottesloe. Tickets: A£4.00 Concessions£3.00. Tickets for 10 or more Platorms are £3.50 each (£2.50 Concessions). Please telephone 0171 452 3020 for further information

Theatres

Foyer Music: Global Connection - world music
19/3/99   ROYAL NATIONAL THEATRE AND TOURS
19/3/99   Tel: 0171 452 3000 Box Office
Free Concert evening (pre-performance) and at lunchtime on Saturdays, in the 'Djanogly Concert Pitch' in the Lyttleton Foyer

Theatres

Boola Bear
20/3/99   PITSHANGER MANOR AND GALLERY
20/3/99   Tel: 0181 567 1227
Presented by Fo-Fum Puppet Productions, 14.00-15.00 for 3-6 year olds. Tickets: £3.00. A delightful story abour a Polar Bear who does not like the cold. Boola Bear is visited by the walrus doctor who tells him to move somewhere hot, so he builds himself a boat made of ice and sets off inc search of the sun. He thinks he has discovered the island of his dreams, only to find it is the back of a sleeping whale called Bigmouth, who wakes up feeling very hungry... A rod and glove puppet show

Historic Houses

Craic Galore - A Festival of Irish Arts
20/3/99   ROYAL NATIONAL THEATRE AND TOURS
20/3/99   Tel: 0171 452 3000 Box Office
To welcome The Abbey Theatre from Dublin with their production of 'The Colleen Bawn,' on the Saturday following Saint Patrick's Day the National Theatre will present a special one-day Irish Festival with music, dance, poetry, book-stalls, food and drink. Time: 11.30-23.30. Admission Free

Theatres

The London Classic Motor Show

Further more detailed information on the attractions listed can be found in Best Guides *Visitor Attractions* Guide under the classifications shown

20/3/99	**ALEXANDRA PALACE**
21/3/99	Tel: 0181 365 2121

Great Hall, West Hall, North West Hall, Panorama Site. Hundreds of gleaming classic vehicles set in the magnificent Alexandra Palace. Concours and club displays, special features, autojumble, trade, classic cars for sale etc, etc. Times: 10.00-18.00 both days. Admission: A£7.50 C£3.00 OAPs£6.50. Advance tickets available 01296 631181/632040. Organiser: Greenwood's Exhibitions

Historic Buildings

London Orchid Show 1999

20/3/99	**RHS ROYAL HORTICULTURAL HALLS**
21/3/99	Tel: 0171 834 4333

Amongst London's best-kept secrets are the RHS two-day Flower Shows at Westminster. Each month, Britain's top nurseries transform the enormous Horticultural Halls, all chasing the coveted RHS Gold Medal. The passing seasons are reflected in their exhibits, from the delicate snowdrops and hellebores of winter, to autumn's showy displays of dahlias and chrysanthemums. Exhibitors are always keen to give advice, and plants are available to purchase. Open 1st day 10.30-18.00, 2nd day 10.30-17.00, 24 hour information line: 0171 649 1885

Exhibition Centres

The Incisive Eye Exhibition

20/3/99	**HALL PLACE**
18/4/99	Tel: 01322 526574 x204

The wood engravings of Colin See-Paynton RE - a comprehensive survey of his work.

Historic Houses & Gardens

Craftsman Day

21/3/99	**SPENCER HOUSE**
21/3/99	Tel: 0171 499 8620

The methods and techniques employed in bringing Spencer House back to its original splendour will be explained and demonstrated by the skilled people involved in the 10 year restoration of this important building. Commences 11.00-17.00

Historic Houses

SBC Mozart Festival

22/3/99	**ROYAL FESTIVAL HALL AND HAYWARD GALLERY**
22/3/99	Tel: 0171 960 4242

Mozart's concertos are all uniquely characterised by their own special moods and orchestral colourings, and Murray Perahia's many recordings and performances have long been recognised for their legitimacy (Perahia directs from the keyboard) and for their sheer beauty and sparkle. This concert features two of the later works: the sunny C major with its celebrated slow movement (familiar from the film Elvira Madigan), and the almost unbearably optimistic B-flat, composed in the last year of the composer's life. In both works the craftsmanship and lyricism are breathtaking, a faint glimmer of something darker beneath the surface adding a sublime pathos in both cases. The concert also includes a performance, conducted by Laszlo Heltay, of Mozart's beautiful Vespers, which features the celebrated soprano aria Laudate Dominum. Performance Time: 19.30. Ticket Prices: £30.00 (dest), £24.00 (cfg), £18.00 (blu), £14.50 (hv), £10.00 (jm), £5.00 (aknor). Concessions: Westminster Rescard 10% discount on single tickets. Standby concessions available (£6.00) for students, OAPs and the unemployed. All concessions are subject to availability. Telephone credit card booking: £1.00 handling charge applies when booking through the RFH Box Office

Arts & Entertainment

Foyer Music: J Spotswood & M Smith - clarinet / piano

22/3/99	**ROYAL NATIONAL THEATRE AND TOURS**
22/3/99	Tel: 0171 452 3000 Box Office

Free Concert evening (pre-performance) and at lunchtime on Saturdays, in the 'Djanogly Concert Pitch' in the Lyttleton Foyer

Theatres

Exhibition: Orpington Photographic Society

22/3/99	**BROMLEY MUSEUM AND PRIORY GARDENS**
27/3/99	Tel: 01689 873826

Contact Miss Pettigrew on 01689 857313 for further information

Museums

Platform: Death of a Salesman

23/3/99	**ROYAL NATIONAL THEATRE AND TOURS**
23/3/99	Tel: 0171 452 3000 Box Office

Lyttleton. Start at 18.00 and last for approximately 45 minutes. Tickets: A£4.00 Concessions£3.00. Tickets for 10 or more Platorms are £3.50 each (£2.50 Concessions). Please telephone 0171 452 3020 for further information

Theatres

Foyer Music: Helen Crayford - Rags to Riches piano

23/3/99 ROYAL NATIONAL THEATRE AND TOURS
23/3/99 Tel: 0171 452 3000 Box Office
Free Concert evening (pre-performance) and at lunchtime on Saturdays, in the 'Djanogly Concert Pitch' in the Lyttleton Foyer

Theatres

Weather Gallery

23/3/99 SCIENCE MUSEUM
23/3/99 Tel: 0171 938 8000
The newly refurbished Weather gallery opens today - supported by the Meteorological Office. Why do meteorologists drill holes in trees? What does is mean when the swallows fly low? What is a lightening strike and where does it go? Find the answers to these questions and more in the new refurbishment of the Weather Gallery.

Museum- Science

Lessons in LIfe

23/3/99 PITSHANGER MANOR AND GALLERY
28/3/99 Tel: 0181 567 1227
An installation of drawings from Ealing Schools with the Royal Academy of Arts and the Yakult Outreach Programme

Historic Houses

The Flora of the Falkland Islands

24/3/99 MUSEUM OF GARDEN HISTORY
24/3/99 Tel: 0171 401 8865
An evening lecture by Geoffrey Moir, held in The Ark, tickets £6.00 available in advance from the Museum. Commences 19.00

Museum- Gardening

Platform: The Pink Room (Absolute Hell)

24/3/99 ROYAL NATIONAL THEATRE AND TOURS
24/3/99 Tel: 0171 452 3000 Box Office
Lyttleton. Start at 18.00 and last for approximately 45 minutes. Tickets: A£4.00 Concessions£3.00. Tickets for 10 or more Platorms are £3.50 each (£2.50 Concessions). Please telephone 0171 452 3020 for further information

Theatres

Foyer Music: The David Gordon Trio - jazz

24/3/99 ROYAL NATIONAL THEATRE AND TOURS
24/3/99 Tel: 0171 452 3000 Box Office
Free Concert evening (pre-performance) and at lunchtime on Saturdays, in the 'Djanogly Concert Pitch' in the Lyttleton Foyer

Theatres

Knowledge Management

24/3/99 EARLS COURT OLYMPIA
25/3/99 Tel: 0171 385 1200
Olympia 2. Building on the huge success of the 1998 event, the 1999 Knowledge Management Conference and Exhibition is predicted to be a key date for Company Directors, Information Managers, IT Managers, HR Managers etc. Ticket Prices: Free if booked in advance, £15.00 on door. Pre-registration is advisable. For further information please contact Learned Information (Europe) Ltd, tel: 01865 388000

Exhibition Centres

Survivors Poetry

25/3/99 PITSHANGER MANOR AND GALLERY
25/3/99 Tel: 0181 567 1227
A unique literature organisation which promotes poetry by survivors of mental distress. It organises workshops and performances across the country and has produced a number of well-reviewed anthologies including, the acclaimed Beyond Bedlam. A Workshop commences 17.00-19.00 Fee £3.00 Concessions£2.00 (includes entry to performance). Performance commences: 19.30

Historic Houses

Foyer Music: Bandoska - gypsy trio

25/3/99 ROYAL NATIONAL THEATRE AND TOURS
25/3/99 Tel: 0171 452 3000 Box Office
Free Concert evening (pre-performance) and at lunchtime on Saturdays, in the 'Djanogly Concert Pitch' in the Lyttleton Foyer

Theatres

Knot Gardens

25/3/99 MUSEUM OF GARDEN HISTORY
26/3/99 Tel: 0171 401 8865
Design and Maintence. A Two day practical course with Anne Jennings. Commences 11.00-16.00 each day. A£120.00 includes coffee, lunch, materials and an information folder. Please book places in advance from the Museum

Museum- Gardening

Royal Institute of Painters in Watercolour

25/3/99 MALL GALLERIES
18/4/99 Tel: 0171 930 6844
British contemporary watercolours by Members and non-members showing a wide variety of styles and techniques in

Further more detailed information on the attractions listed can be found in Best Guides *Visitor Attractions* Guide under the classifications shown

the use of watercolour and water soluble mediums.

Art Galleries

From the Bomb to the Beatles
25/3/99 IMPERIAL WAR MUSEUM
29/5/99 Tel: 0171 416 5000
Social and cultural change in the post war years

Museum- Military

The Arts of the Sikh Kingdoms
25/3/99 VICTORIA AND ALBERT MUSEUM
25/7/99 Tel: 0171 938 8441
An intriguing exhibition celebrating the artistic heritage of the Sikhs

Museum- Art

Lectures
26/3/99 BURGH HOUSE
26/3/99 Tel: 0171 431 0144
Lectures from the Heath, David Sullivan gicing the first of the series. Commences 19.00, tickets £6.00 including wine

Historic Houses

Music Open Workshop
26/3/99 PITSHANGER MANOR AND GALLERY
26/3/99 Tel: 0181 567 1227
14.00-15.30. Admission Free. Come and join members of the Soundscape Project, and have a go playing and making musical instruments, recording music and see what the group have been doing over the past year.

Historic Houses

Platform: The Deep Blue Sea
26/3/99 ROYAL NATIONAL THEATRE AND TOURS
26/3/99 Tel: 0171 452 3000 Box Office
Lyttleton. Start at 18.00 and last for approximately 45 minutes. Tickets: A£4.00 Concessions£3.00. Tickets for 10 or more Platorms are £3.50 each (£2.50 Concessions). Please telephone 0171 452 3020 for further information

Theatres

Computing Careers
26/3/99 RHS ROYAL HORTICULTURAL HALLS
27/3/99 Tel: 0171 834 4333
A consumer event for all those interested in furthering or pursuing a careers in Information Technology, call for further details

Exhibition Centres

Foyer Music: Jonathan Gee - jazz piano / vocals
26/3/99 ROYAL NATIONAL THEATRE AND TOURS
27/3/99 Tel: 0171 452 3000 Box Office
Free Concert evening (pre-performance) and at lunchtime on Saturdays, in the 'Djanogly Concert Pitch' in the Lyttleton Foyer

Theatres

The Head of the River Race
27/3/99 LONDON TOURIST BOARD
27/3/99 Tel: 0171 932 2000
This is a professional race for eights and is rowed over the 4.25m Thames Championship course from Mortlake to Putney (the boat race in reverse). The best way to see the race is to stand on the towpath above Chiswick Bridge half an hour or so before the Race and watch the crews being marshalled into their start order, and then to walk along the bank towards Putney. Programmes on sale from vendors along the towpath

Tourist Information Centres

Drawing for Art? Drawing for Life?
27/3/99 PITSHANGER MANOR AND GALLERY
27/3/99 Tel: 0181 567 1227
Artists, Paul Brandford and Charlette Steel have taught life drawing workshops in primary and secondary schools as part of the Royal Academy of Art and Yakult Outreach Programme over the last 10 years. They will lead an informal gallery talk around the Lessons in Life installation, looking at the way in which drawing can play a key role in the development of young people's self-awareness, imagination and creativity. Commences 15.00, admission Free

Historic Houses

Open Day
27/3/99 TWO10 GALLERY
27/3/99 Tel: 0171 611 7211
Sure to be a fun-packed day! The final Saturday you can visit the 'Science for Life' exhibition in London. Now is your last chance to enjoy some of the exciting events that 'Science for Life' has to offer. Shrink down to a fraction of your normal size by entering our million times magnified human cell in the 'Discover the Cell' tour, ages 16+, 11.00 & 14.00; reverse the world with inverting goggles in the 'Mind Games' workshop, 16+, 11.00-17.00; assist Detective Inspector Mike O'Chondria to discover who, out of three main suspects, murdered prize-winning scientist Dr Lisa Somes in the 'DNA Detective' Workshop, 12+, 13.00 & 15.00; and the 'DNA Your Onions' Workshop, 10+, 11.30 & 14.15.

Art Galleries

Courage Trophy

27/3/99 28/3/99	**HORSE GUARDS** *Theatres*

HORSE GUARDS
27/3/99
28/3/99
Tel: 0891 505452
The annual competitive military skills competition for units of the Territorial Army on Longmoor training area
Historic Buildings

Easter Holidays
27/3/99
20/4/99
SCIENCE MUSEUM
Tel: 0171 938 8000
Easter Holiday events explore then theme of transport - past, present and future. Science is brough to life through demonstrations, workshops, storytelling and galley drama. Whatever your age and interest, you will find something to enjoy
Museum- Science

London International Bookfair
28/3/99
30/3/99
EARLS COURT OLYMPIA
Tel: 0171 385 1200
Olympia Grand and National Halls. The London International Bookfair is the most important Spring event in the European publishing calendar. Opening Times: Public admission after 14.00 each day. Ticket Prices: £10.00 pre-registered, £15.00 on the door. For further information please contact Reed Exhibition Companies (UK) Ltd, tel: 0181 910 7815
Exhibition Centres

Meat Loaf
28/3/99
30/3/99
WEMBLEY CONFERENCE AND EXHIBITION CENTRE
Tel: 0181 902 8833
Performances: 28 & 30 at 19.30. Tickets £17.50 & £23.50
Exhibition Centres

1-2-3-4-5 Page Book
29/3/99
ESTORICK COLLECTION OF MODERN ITALIAN ART
29/3/99
Tel: 0171 704 9522
Age: 7-12 years, explore the possibilities of the bookmaking with artist Karly Allen and produce your own limited edition counting book. 10.30-12.30, C£6.00, booking is essential call Roberta Cremoncini 0171 704 9522
Art Galleries

Platform: Dry Rot
29/3/99
ROYAL NATIONAL THEATRE AND TOURS
29/3/99
Tel: 0171 452 3000 Box Office
Cottesloe. Start at 18.00 and last for approximately 45 minutes. Tickets: A£4.00 Concessions£3.00. Tickets for 10 or more Platorms are £3.50 each (£2.50 Concessions). Please telephone 0171 452 3020 for further information

Theatres
Foyer Music: The Mark Ambler Trio - jazz
29/3/99
ROYAL NATIONAL THEATRE AND TOURS
29/3/99
Tel: 0171 452 3000 Box Office
Free Concert evening (pre-performance) and at lunchtime on Saturdays, in the 'Djanogly Concert Pitch' in the Lyttleton Foyer

Theatres
Exhibition: Vincent New, local artist
29/3/99
BROMLEY MUSEUM AND PRIORY GARDENS
5/5/99
Tel: 01689 873826
In association with Sevenoaks Museum. For further information please contact Dr Alan Tyler, Curator or Melanie Parker, Assistant Curator, at the Museum on 01689 873826

Museums
Platform: The Mousetrap
30/3/99
ROYAL NATIONAL THEATRE AND TOURS
30/3/99
Tel: 0171 452 3000 Box Office
Cottesloe. Start at 18.00 and last for approximately 45 minutes. Tickets: A£4.00 Concessions£3.00. Tickets for 10 or more Platorms are £3.50 each (£2.50 Concessions). Please telephone 0171 452 3020 for further information

Theatres
Foyer Music: J Stein & T Gardner - flute / cello
30/3/99
ROYAL NATIONAL THEATRE AND TOURS
30/3/99
Tel: 0171 452 3000 Box Office
Free Concert evening (pre-performance) and at lunchtime on Saturdays, in the 'Djanogly Concert Pitch' in the Lyttleton Foyer

Theatres
Gardens and Landscapes Engraved
30/3/99
MUSEUM OF GARDEN HISTORY
18/4/99
Tel: 0171 401 8865
Exhibition by Hilary Paynter
Museum- Gardening

Sylvia Wright - The Bedford Psalter-Hours
31/3/99
BRITISH LIBRARY
31/3/99
Tel: 0171 412 7332
John, Duke of Bedford commissioned a most unusual prayer book in London in or around 1417. The illumination of his Psalter-Hours is based upon the royal entry of Henry V after the victory at Agincourt. The book also contains some of the most advanced portraiture in Europe. Family members, friends and enemies appear with carefully selected biblical texts associated with dynastic

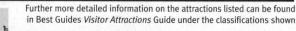

Further more detailed information on the attractions listed can be found in Best Guides *Visitor Attractions* Guide under the classifications shown

legends, the authors of which also appear in the illumination. The identification of these images sheds new light on royal patronage of the arts at a critical time in cultural history. Dr Sylvia Wright was recently a Centre for the Book Fellow at the British Library. Presented by the Centre for the Book. Time: 18.15. Tickets: £5.00 Concessions£3.50

Museum- Library

Foyer Music: The Branco Stoysin Duo - Brazillian jazz guitars

31/3/99 ROYAL NATIONAL THEATRE AND TOURS
31/3/99 Tel: 0171 452 3000 Box Office
Free Concert evening (pre-performance) and at lunchtime on Saturdays, in the 'Djanogly Concert Pitch' in the Lyttleton Foyer

Theatres

Moscow State Circus

31/3/99 ALEXANDRA PALACE
11/4/99 Tel: 0181 365 2121
In the Park - Upper Football Pitch. The world's finest circus brings an all-new group of Russian artistes from the circuses of the former U.S.S.R. in a brand new 'state of the art' big top. Times: Weekdays 17.00-20.00, Sat, Sun, Good Fri & Easter Mon 14.00 & 17.00. Admission: A£8.00, £12.00, £16.00 & £20.00, C&OAPs&Students&UB40's £6.00, £9.00, £15.00 & £12.00. Organiser: Moscow State Circus 01932 83000 from 25 February 0421 565557

Historic Buildings

Foyer Music: David Perkins - classical piano

1/4/99 ROYAL NATIONAL THEATRE AND TOURS
1/4/99 Tel: 0171 452 3000 Box Office
Free Concert evening (pre-performance) and at lunchtime on Saturdays, in the 'Djanogly Concert Pitch' in the Lyttleton Foyer

Theatres

Easter Bank Holiday Fun Fair

1/4/99 ALEXANDRA PALACE
11/4/99 Tel: 0181 365 2121
Traditional family fun fair held on the Boating Lake car park. Dodgems, waltzers and many other rides, stalls, sideshows, kiddies rides, candy floss etc. Weekends & Bank Holiday 12.00-22.00. Weekdays 12.00-20.00 (special reduced price on all rides for Tuesday). Organiser: Fun Fair Amusements, Mobile No: 0860 310970

Historic Buildings

Easter Egg Hunt

1/4/99 IMPERIAL WAR MUSEUM
11/4/99 Tel: 0171 416 5000
Children's T.V. favourites feature in the hunt. Free chocolate mini eggs

Museum- Military

Hippeastrum Celebration

1/4/99 KEW GARDENS ROYAL BOTANIC GARDENS
30/4/99 Tel: 0181 940 1171
Have you ever celebrated Hippeastrum? Find out what, why, where and when, call for details.

Gardens- Botanical

Ruskin Pottery

1/4/99 GEFFRYE MUSEUM
1/6/99 Tel: 0171 739 9893
This special exhibition will examine the work of the world renowned Ruskin Pottery, call for further details

Museum- Interiors

Cuthbert Broderick Exhibition

1/4/99 ROYAL INSTITUTE OF BRITISH ARCHITECTS HEINZ GALLERY
1/6/99 Tel: 0171 307 3628
Exhibition of the works of the Architect of Leeds Town Hall

Art Galleries

Indian Folk Bronzes

1/4/99 BRITISH MUSEUM
30/6/99 Tel: 0171 636 1555
From the Polsky Collection on room 33b

Museums

Turner & Whistler

1/4/99 THE LONDON CANAL MUSEUM
31/7/99 Tel: 0171 713 0836
Images of the Thames, call for further details

Museum- Canal

Horse Drawn Wagonette Rides

1/4/99 OSTERLEY PARK
31/10/99 Tel: 0181 568 7714
Fridays and Saturdays during open season. Enjoy a leisurely ride around the park with our Head Gardener and her horse Puzzle in an 18th century style wagonette. Rides last approximately 30mins. Spaces are limited and must be pre-booked by telephoning 0181 568 7714. Tickets £3.00 per person

Historic Houses

Glimpses of Housekeeping

1/4/99 OSTERLEY PARK
31/10/99 Tel: 0181 568 7714
See and talk to our House Steward while she undertakes an example of day-to-day conservation housekeeping. Free

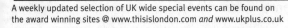

with every house entry. Twice monthly during April-October, call 0181 568 7714 for details

Historic Houses

Changing of the Guard
1/4/99 HORSE GUARDS
31/12/99 Tel: 0891 505452
Horse-Guards Mon-Sat 11.00, Sun 10.00. Ceremony takes place at the Tilt Yard which is the forecourt of Horse Guards building. Details on 0891 505 452

Historic Buildings

Racing from Kempton
3/4/99 KEMPTON PARK RACECOURSE
3/4/99 Tel: 01932 782292
Saturday is Milcars Easter Stakes and Milcars Masaka Stakes. Bank Holiday Monday is Coral Rosebery Handicap. For further details including race times and ticket prices please contact venue direct

Racecourses

Foyer Music: The Kevin Street Duo - accordion / violin
3/4/99 ROYAL NATIONAL THEATRE AND TOURS
3/4/99 Tel: 0171 452 3000 Box Office
Free Concert evening (pre-performance) and at lunchtime on Saturdays, in the 'Djanogly Concert Pitch' in the Lyttleton Foyer

Theatres

Modelex '99
3/4/99 ROYAL AIR FORCE MUSEUM ,
4/4/99 Tel: 0181 205 2266
A model exhibition featuring plane, trains, cars, dolls houses, hundreds of exciting models

Museum- Aviation

Creative '99
3/4/99 ALEXANDRA PALACE
5/4/99 Tel: 0181 365 2121
Great Hall. High quality finished craft products from 150 UK craftmakers together with fine art, craft and hobby supplies plus free workshop sessions. Times: Sat 10.30-17.30, Sun & Mon 10.00-17.30. Admission: A£7.00 C(12-16)£3.00 C(0-12)£Free OAPs£5.00. Organiser: Marathon Event Management 01273 833884

Historic Buildings

The Three Little Pigs and Captain Grimey
3/4/99 PUPPET THEATRE BARGE
30/5/99 Tel: 0171 249 6876 Box Office
Whitty rendering of this popular tale to delight the youngest audience members. Daily performances duing Easter &

School Holidays, then Sat & Sun at 15.00. A£6.00 C&Concessions£5.50

Boat Trips

Easter 1740s
4/4/99 CHISWICK HOUSE
5/4/99 Tel: 0181 995 0508
Beaux Stratagems perform an 18th-century Easter setting. Normal admission prices apply

Historic Houses & Gardens

Past Pleasures
4/4/99 MARBLE HILL HOUSE
5/4/99 Tel: 0181 892 5115
Pleasures of the 18th-century. Normal admission prices apply

Historic Houses

18th Century Dance
4/4/99 RANGER'S HOUSE
5/4/99 Tel: 0181 853 0035
18th century revelries with costumed dancers. From 12.00. Normal admission price

Historic Houses & Gardens

1940's Children's Easter
4/4/99 TILBURY FORT
5/4/99 Tel: 01375 858489
Come and experience how children celebrated Easter in the 1940's. Normal admission prices apply.

Forts

London Harness Horse Parade
5/4/99 LONDON TOURIST BOARD
5/4/99 Tel: 0171 932 2000
Venue: Battersea Park, London SW11. Please telephone 01733 234451 for further information

Tourist Information Centres

Foyer Music: Carol Wells - Screen Gems - piano
5/4/99 ROYAL NATIONAL THEATRE AND TOURS
5/4/99 Tel: 0171 452 3000 Box Office
Free Concert evening (pre-performance) and at lunchtime on Saturdays, in the 'Djanogly Concert Pitch' in the Lyttleton Foyer

Theatres

Wembley Antiques and Collectors Antique Fair
5/4/99 WEMBLEY CONFERENCE AND EXHIBITION CENTRE
5/4/99 Tel: 0181 902 8833
Antiques fair open to the trade and the public displaying antiques, collectibles plus an area specifically for antique furniture. Hall 3. Admission £2.75 on the door

Exhibition Centres

Further more detailed information on the attractions listed can be found in Best Guides *Visitor Attractions* Guide under the classifications shown

Candide by Voltaire

5/4/99
10/4/99
Royal National Theatre and Tours
Tel: 0171 452 3000 Box Office
Olivier. Voltaire's towering work of comic and philosophical genius is one of the glories of 18th century satire and is as relevant today as when it was first written. Candide explores a world that is dominated by violence, greed, war, hatred and a series of catastrophic events seemingly unmitigated by goodness, truth, beauty or God. Voltaire's great achievement is to temper his merciless analysis of human cruelty, and the apparent emptiness of heaven, with extraordinary wit and good humour. While disturbed by his story, we also find ourselves laughing uproariously at it. Performance Times Evenings 19.15: 5, 6, 7, 8, 9 & 10, 12, 13 (Press Night 19.00), 14, 15, 16 Apr; Matinee 14.00: 10 & 17 Apr. Tickets: Evenings £12.00-£30.00, Previews & Sat Matinee £9.00-£25.00, Weekday Matinee £10.00-£17.00. Under 18s£10.00, OAPs£12.00, Registered disabled & Visually-Impaired £8.00-£19.00, Wheelchair Users £17.00-£19.00, Adult groups £14.00-£24.00, NT Education group members & Student standby £10.00, School groups (under 19) ££9.00-£10.00, College groups (aged 19-25) £11.00-£13.50, Day Seats £9.00-£14.00, Standby £11.00-£15.00, Standing £5.00-£6.00

Theatres

Platform: Waiting For Godot

6/4/99
6/4/99
Royal National Theatre and Tours
Tel: 0171 452 3000 Box Office
Lyttleton. Start at 18.00 and last for approximately 45 minutes. Tickets: A£4.00 Concessions£3.00. Tickets for 10 or more Platorms are £3.50 each (£2.50 Concessions). Please telephone 0171 452 3020 for further information

Theatres

Foyer Music: the Frances Knight Trio - Jazz

6/4/99
6/4/99
Royal National Theatre and Tours
Tel: 0171 452 3000 Box Office
Free Concert evening (pre-performance) and at lunchtime on Saturdays, in the 'Djanogly Concert Pitch' in the Lyttleton Foyer

Theatres

Belsay, Burgundy and Beyond

7/4/99
7/4/99
Museum of Garden History
Tel: 0171 401 8865
Archaeology in Historic Gardens. An evening lecture by Brian Dix held in The Ark, tickets £6.00 available in advance from the Museum. Commences 19.00

Museum- Gardening

Foyer Music: The Helios Duo - classical flute / guitar

7/4/99
7/4/99
Royal National Theatre and Tours
Tel: 0171 452 3000 Box Office
Free Concert evening (pre-performance) and at lunchtime on Saturdays, in the 'Djanogly Concert Pitch' in the Lyttleton Foyer

Theatres

Family Day at The National

8/4/99
8/4/99
Royal National Theatre and Tours
Tel: 0171 452 3000 Box Office
A day of free activities and performances for all the family throughout the National's foyers, terraces and in Theatre Square. Street entertainment, storytelling, theatre, music to listen to and play and face painting will be provided to ensure that there is something for all the family. Time: 10.00-18.00. Admission Free

Theatres

"Measham Pottery" by Mike Beech

8/4/99
8/4/99
The London Canal Museum
Tel: 0171 713 0836
Mike Beech, Curator, Foxton Canal Museum, call for details

Museum- Canal

Spring Needlecraft

8/4/99
11/4/99
Earls Court Olympia
Tel: 0171 385 1200
Olympia 2. Organiser: Future Events Ltd.

Exhibition Centres

Foyer Music: the Michael Garrick Trio - Jazz

9/4/99
9/4/99
Royal National Theatre and Tours
Tel: 0171 452 3000 Box Office
Free Concert evening (pre-performance) and at lunchtime on Saturdays, in the 'Djanogly Concert Pitch' in the Lyttleton Foyer

Theatres

Platform: Long Day's Journey Into Night

9/4/99
9/4/99
Royal National Theatre and Tours
Tel: 0171 452 3000 Box Office
Lyttleton. Start at 18.00 and last for approximately 45 minutes. Tickets: A£4.00 Concessions£3.00. Tickets for 10 or more Platorms are £3.50 each (£2.50

Concessions). Please telephone 0171 452 3020 for further information

Theatres

Foyer Music: John Human - classical piano

10/4/99   ROYAL NATIONAL THEATRE AND TOURS
10/4/99   Tel: 0171 452 3000 Box Office

Free Concert evening (pre-performance) and at lunchtime on Saturdays, in the 'Djanogly Concert Pitch' in the Lyttleton Foyer

Theatres

Medieval Monastic Entertainers

10/4/99   CHAPTER HOUSE AND PYX CHAMBER OF WESTMINSTER ABBEY
11/4/99   Tel: 0171 222 5897

Try your hand at calligraphy or authentic period games as this popular duo take a light-hearted look at monastic customs, crafts and lifestyles. Learn about food preparation, herbs and spices in cooking and medicine, the mechanics of building and lifting and many other skills. From 12.00. A£2.50 C£1.30 Concessions£1.90. EH Members £Free

Abbeys

Kitchen Keepers

11/4/99   GUNNERSBURY PARK MUSEUM
11/4/99   Tel: 0181 992 1612

Meet the servants of Gunnersbury Mansion and help them spring clean our original Victorian kitchens. Children can dress up and learn about life in domestic service. 13.30-18.00

Museum- Social History

Major General's Inspection

12/4/99   HORSE GUARDS
12/4/99   Tel: 0891 505452

Inspection of The King's Troop Royal Horse Artillery in Regents Park on Cumberland Green at 10.00

Historic Buildings

Duchamp and Brancusi

12/4/99   TATE GALLERY
23/8/99   Tel: 0171 887 8000

Examines the work of two pioneers of modern art who in different ways radically reshaped the language of art in the early decades of this century. Among key works, the display includes Duchamp's The Bride Stripped Bare by her Batchelors, Even (The Large Glass) 1965-6 and Brancusi's Fish 1926. Admission Free

Art Galleries

Fun with Pots

13/4/99   CROFTON ROMAN VILLA
13/4/99   Tel: 01689 873826

Meet a Potter and make your very own Roman pot and oil lamp. Suitable for ages 7-12. Time: 10.00-12.00 & 14.00-16.00. Cost: £4.00 per child. Book through 01869 873826

Roman Villas

RHS Flower Show

13/4/99   RHS ROYAL HORTICULTURAL HALLS
14/4/99   Tel: 0171 834 4333

Open 1st day 10.30-19.00, 2nd day 10.00-17.00, 24 hour information line: 0171 649 1885

Exhibition Centres

Human Resources Development

13/4/99   EARLS COURT OLYMPIA
15/4/99   Tel: 0171 385 1200

Olympia National Hall. Organiser: Touchstone Exhibitions Ltd.

Exhibition Centres

75th Birthday Gala Concert

14/4/99   ROYAL FESTIVAL HALL AND HAYWARD GALLERY
14/4/99   Tel: 0171 960 4242

Sir Neville Marriner's 75th Birthday Gala is celebrated in masterworks from three centuries. Mozart composed the D major Symphony (K385) for the same Haffner family for whom he had previously composed the serenade. This time, instead of marriage, the celebration was the enoblement of Siegmund Haffner the younger, and the resulting work, first performed in 1783, remains one of the most energetic and exciting of Mozart's symphonies. Britten's Serenade comprises a series of inspired settings of night poems by writers such as Tennyson, Blake and Keats. Evocatively scored for string orchestra, the songs are unified by the inclusion of a French horn, whose solo epilogue is one of the most magical and thrilling moments in music. The concert concludes with Mendelssohn's sparkling score to Shakespeare's immortal fairy frolic, A Midsummer Night's Dream. The overture was written when the composer was a mere 17 years old, the rest of the incidental music following 17 years later. Incredibly, Mendelssohn succeeded in recapturing the spirit of the original overture, uniting the whole through cunning thematic references. Performance Time: 19.30. Ticket Prices: £30.00 (dest), £24.00 (cfg), £18.00 (blu), £14.50 (hv), £10.00 (jm), £5.00 (aknor).

Concessions: Westminster Rescard 10% discount on single tickets. Standby concessions available (£6.00) for students, OAPs and the unemployed. All concessions are subject to availability. Telephone credit card booking: £1.00 handling charge applies when booking through the RFH Box Office

Arts & Entertainment

Stanley Gibbons Publications - Stamp '99

15/4/99 WEMBLEY CONFERENCE AND EXHIBITION CENTRE

17/4/99 Tel: 0181 902 8833

A public show aimed at serious collectors, dealers, enthusiasts and children in the stamp collection world. Halls 2&3

Exhibition Centres

David Bailey:

15/4/99 BARBICAN ART GALLERY

27/6/99 Tel: 0171 588 9023 24hr info

Birth of the Cool. An exhibition of early photographs by Britain's best known photographer, alongside recent work from the 90s

Art Galleries

Kandinsky

15/4/99 ROYAL ACADEMY OF ARTS

27/6/99 Tel: 0171 300 8000

Although Wassily Kandinsky (1866-1944) is one of the most important and influential painters of the twentieth century, this will be the first major exhibition of his work ever held in this country. The exhibition will focus on his works on paper and will include over 100 watercolours and drawings as well as a number of outstanding prints.

Art Galleries

The Beautiful South

17/4/99 WEMBLEY CONFERENCE AND EXHIBITION CENTRE

18/4/99 Tel: 0181 902 8833

Plus special guests Barenaked Ladies. Peformances 17 & 18 April at 19.30. Tickets £18.50

Exhibition Centres

Firing Day

18/4/99 TILBURY FORT

18/4/99 Tel: 01375 858489

The Garrison. Normal admission prices apply.

Forts

Thames Barrier Operation Scheme

19/4/99 THAMES BARRIER VISITORS CENTRE

19/4/99 Tel: 0181 305 4188

See the Thames Barrier in operation this Wednesday approximate closure times 10.00-12.30

The Unusual

John Falconer - Images of India

20/4/99 BRITISH LIBRARY

20/4/99 Tel: 0171 412 7332

The British Library's Oriental and India Office Collections holds the world's largest archive of historical photographs from South Asia: a unique visual record of the architecture, peoples, landscape and history of the subcontinent from the 1850's to the early 20th-century. This material has been the subject of a detailed cataloguing project over the last five years. John Falconer introduces some of its riches. Time: 13.30

Museum- Library

The Victorian Garden

20/4/99 MUSEUM OF GARDEN HISTORY

20/4/99 Tel: 0171 401 8865

Chronology of Gardening Day with Caroline Holmes. Tickets £40.00 commences 11.00-16.00

Museum- Gardening

Helmetica

20/4/99 JILL GEORGE GALLERY LTD

21/5/99 Tel: 0171 439 7319

Exhibition based on ELBA by Duncan Bullen

Art Galleries

Anniversary of the Queen's Birthday

21/4/99 HORSE GUARDS

21/4/99 Tel: 0891 505452

41 Gun Royal Salute fired by The King's Troop Royal Horse Artillery in Hyde Park at 12.00 and 62 Gun Royal Salute fired the the Honourable Artillery Company at the Tower of London at 13.00 hours to mark the Anniversary of the Queen's Birthday, free public access

Historic Buildings

Proposals and Consultations

21/4/99 BANKSIDE GALLERY

25/4/99 Tel: 0171 928 7521

Unveiling proposals for the refurbishment of the Gallery with particular emphasis on consultation with the local community

Art Galleries

West Country Gardens with a Classical Theme

21/4/99 MUSEUM OF GARDEN HISTORY

6/5/99 Tel: 0171 401 8865

An exhibition by Hilary Adair

Museum- Gardening

William Kentridge

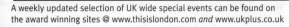

21/4/99
30/5/99
SERPENTINE GALLERY
Tel: 0171 298 1515
The first major survey in the UK of video projections and associated drawings by this distinguished South African artist. William Kentridge works with an unusually broad spectrum of media from charcoal and wall drawings, etchings and animated film, to theatre and opera. He explores, with wit and insight, history, the relationship between human desire and moral responsibility

Art Galleries

Barker Brown Ltd - BBC Fashion Week Live 1999

22/4/99
25/4/99
WEMBLEY CONFERENCE AND EXHIBITION CENTRE
Tel: 0181 902 8833
This event will cover all aspects of a busy 90s lifestyle, with areas devoted to beauty, fitness, health and aspirational design products in addition to fashion and shopping. The Arena will be transformed into a 4,000 seat fashion theatre, with an additional 2,000 seat designer theatre house in the Grand Hall in which visitors will be able to preview the latest rends in fashion. There is also the chance for visitors to preview and purchase the hottest new looks from over 200 top designers. Thur 10.30-20.30, Fri-Sun 09.00-18.30. Halls CC & Arena, Admission £15.00 (+£1.00 booking fee)

Exhibition Centres

London International Dive Show

24/4/99
25/4/99
EARLS COURT OLYMPIA
Tel: 0171 385 1200
Olympia Grand Hall. Organiser: The Dive Show Ltd.

Exhibition Centres

Open Art Exhibition

24/4/99
23/5/99
HALL PLACE
Tel: 01322 526574 x204
The Arts Council of Bexley's Open art exhibition.

Historic Houses & Gardens

Scots Guards Regimental Rememberance Service

25/4/99
25/4/99
HORSE GUARDS
Tel: 0891 505452
In the Guards Chapel, Wellington Barracks at 13.00 and march to the Guards Memorial on Horse Guards Parade at 13.40

Historic Buildings

Plant & Produce Sale

25/4/99
25/4/99
MUSEUM OF FULHAM PALACE
Tel: 0171 736 3233
Unusual plants, books and home-made produce for sale. Teas. Time: 11.00-16.00. Cost: £0.50

Historic Houses & Gardens

This War Without An Enemy

25/4/99
25/4/99
NATIONAL ARMY MUSEUM
Tel: 0171 730 0717
A day of special events focusing on the experience of soldering during the Civil Wars of Britain and including talks, readings from contemporary accounts, re-enactment, film, demonstrations with model soldiers and the opportunity to handle artefacts relating to the period. Admission Free

Museum- Military

Kite Day

25/4/99
25/4/99
OSTERLEY PARK
Tel: 0181 568 7714
Kite making and flying for beginners using recycled materials. Learn to make a basic kite and, wind permitting, fly it in the park! Suitable for all ages and abilities. Basic material free. Usual car parking charges apply

Historic Houses

Breakfast with the Birds

25/4/99
25/4/99
OSTERLEY PARK
Tel: 0181 568 7714
An early morning guided walk to hear the dawn chorus in Osterley Park followed by a continental breakfast. Meet in the Stableyard at 04.30, for 04.45. No dogs please. Advance booking essential A£8.00 C£4.00 incl breakfast

Historic Houses

International Accessories Show

25/4/99
28/4/99
EARLS COURT OLYMPIA
Tel: 0171 385 1200
Olympia 2. Organiser: M&S Management Services.

Exhibition Centres

RHS Flower Show

27/4/99
28/4/99
RHS ROYAL HORTICULTURAL HALLS
Tel: 0171 834 4333
Open 1st day 10.30-19.00, 2nd day 10.00-17.00, 24 hour information line: 0171 649 1885

Exhibition Centres

Customer Service & Support '99

27/4/99
29/4/99
EARLS COURT OLYMPIA
Tel: 0171 385 1200
Olympia 2. Organiser: Leonardo International Ltd.

Exhibition Centres

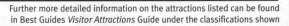

Further more detailed information on the attractions listed can be found in Best Guides *Visitor Attractions* Guide under the classifications shown

Massacre! - English Civil War Crimes
29/4/99 NATIONAL ARMY MUSEUM
29/4/99 Tel: 0171 730 0717
Commences:13.15, duration: 30mins. A lunchtime talk marking the 400th Anniversary of Cromwell's birth. Talks are free and no tickets are required. As the subjects of the talks may be altered at short notice, visitors coming for a particular talk are advised to call the Museum on 0171 730 0717 x 2210 to check the programme
Museum- Military

The Wedding Entertainer
29/4/99 THE JEWISH MUSEUM
29/4/99 Tel: 0171 284 1997
Jacob Stern, international badchan (wedding entertainer), talks about the many weddings he has attended and the ways in which he entertains the bride and groom and their guests. Admission: £4.00 (Museum Friends £3.00) including admission to the Museum Galleries. Please book in advance. Time: 14.00.
Museum- Religious

Gary Barlow
29/4/99 WEMBLEY CONFERENCE AND EXHIBITION CENTRE
29/4/99 Tel: 0181 902 8833
And guests. At 19.30. Tickets: £15.00 & £17.50
Exhibition Centres

The Cosmopolitan Show
29/4/99 EARLS COURT OLYMPIA
3/5/99 Tel: 0171 385 1200
Earls Court 2. Organiser: The National Magazine Company.
Exhibition Centres

New Art for a New Era
29/4/99 BARBICAN ART GALLERY
27/6/99 Tel: 0171 588 9023 24hr info
Part of the Barbican's St. Petersberg Festival - an exhibition of modern art from the State Russian Museum
Art Galleries

Canon Photography Gallery
29/4/99 VICTORIA AND ALBERT MUSEUM
1/8/99 Tel: 0171 938 8441
Silver and Syrup Selections: From the history of photography. Rediscoveries: Clementina, Lady Hawarden
Museum- Art

Festival for Life
1/5/99 FESTIVAL FOR LIFE 1999
2/5/99 Tel: 01992 850357
Over 90 exhibitors offering a wide range of complimentary therapies, including shiatsu, aromatherapy, reiki and osteopathy, along with stalls selling books, pottery, jewellery and tarot cards. Demonstrations of T'ai Chi, belly dancing and Yoga, live music etc. Disabled access to main exhibition. No access to psychics or to attend lectures. £3.50 per day
Festivals

Family History Fair
1/5/99 RHS ROYAL HORTICULTURAL HALLS
2/5/99 Tel: 0171 834 4333
An annual consumer event organised by the Society of Genealogists relating to family history tracing and records. Call for further details
Exhibition Centres

Bluebells and Broomsticks
1/5/99 KEW GARDENS ROYAL BOTANIC GARDENS
3/5/99 Tel: 0181 940 1171
Begin May in a delightful way, the sights and scents of the Bluebells will have you in awe. Woodland and conservation skills demonstrated in the Bluebell Wood
Gardens- Botanical

Crafts and Countryside Come to Town
1/5/99 MORDEN HALL PARK
3/5/99 Tel: 0181 648 1845
A Robin Hood Theme for 1999. Come to the Crafts and Countryside Fayre for those unusual gifts, please telephone 0181 648 1845 for further information
Gardens

Spring Concert Series
1/5/99 HORNIMAN MUSEUM AND GARDENS
31/5/99 Tel: 0181 699 1872
A wealth of music brought to you for FREE, covering classical and contemporary music
Museums

Prints and Drawing Exhibitions
1/5/99 BRITISH MUSEUM
1/9/99 Tel: 0171 636 1555
The popular print in tradition in Britain 1530-1930 and Castiglione in context in room 90, catalogue available, dates are provisional please check before visiting
Museums

Jewish Magic and Mysticism
1/5/99 THE JEWISH MUSEUM
1/9/99 Tel: 0171 284 1997
Exhibition exploring Jewish traditions of magic and mysticism from ancient times to the present
Museum- Religious

Shakespeare's Globe Theatre Season

1/5/99 30/9/99	**SHAKESPEARE'S GLOBE** Tel: 0171 902 1500 The season starts here, exact dates to be confirmed. Call for further information *Historic Buildings*

Tea

2/5/99
3/5/99
CHISWICK HOUSE
Tel: 0181 995 0508
Tea with Hogarth's Heroes. Normal admission prices apply
Historic Houses & Gardens

May Day 1740s

2/5/99
3/5/99
MARBLE HILL HOUSE
Tel: 0181 892 5115
18th century drama with Beaux Stratagems. Normal admission prices apply
Historic Houses

Spring at Syon

2/5/99
3/5/99
SYON HOUSE
Tel: 0181 560 0883
The national Association of Flower Arrangement Societies (NAFAS) celebrate Spring with flower displays in Syon House
Historic Houses & Gardens

Racing from Kempton

3/5/99
3/5/99
KEMPTON PARK RACECOURSE
Tel: 01932 782292
Bank Holiday Racing with the Jubilee Handicap. For further details including race times and ticket prices please contact venue direct
Racecourses

1760s Living History

3/5/99
3/5/99
RANGER'S HOUSE
Tel: 0181 853 0035
18th-century history seen through the eyes of Hoi Polloi. A£2.50 C£1.30 Concessions£1.90
Historic Houses & Gardens

The Spectacle of Life

3/5/99
29/11/99
TATE GALLERY
Tel: 0171 887 8000
Matisse, Braque, Léger and Beckman. Brings together major works for four European modern masters. The works, which include Beckmann's Carnival 1922 and Léger's The Acrobat and his Partner 1948, reflect the artists' varied responses to modernity and the threat of spiritual dislocation. Admission Free
Art Galleries

Upstairs and Downstairs:

4/5/99
5/4/99
SYON HOUSE
Tel: 0181 560 0883
And in My Lady's Chamber. Life and work of Syon House servants in the 1830s
Historic Houses & Gardens

Firm Impressions

5/5/99
31/5/99
BANKSIDE GALLERY
Tel: 0171 928 7521
Featured artist: Jennier Dickson RA RE. The annual show of the Royal Society of Painter-Printmakers spotlights the work of Jennifer Dickson, whose extraordinary etchings reveal an artist transfixed by the beauty of the past. Her feeling for the classical age makes her work atmospheric and otherwordly.
Art Galleries

Glenn Brown

5/5/99
13/6/99
JERWOOD SPACE
Tel: 0171 654 0171
This exhibition brings together a significant body of this artist's work including painting, sculpture and photography. Glenn Brown was shortlisted for the Jerwood Painting Prize in 1996.
Arts & Entertainment

Annual Inspection

6/5/99
6/5/99
HORSE GUARDS
Tel: 0891 505452
Major General's Annual Inspection of the Household Cavalry Mounted Regiment in Hyde Park at 10.00, free public access
Historic Buildings

Roundhead and Cavalier - Myths of the Civil War

6/5/99
6/5/99
NATIONAL ARMY MUSEUM
Tel: 0171 730 0717
Commences:13.15, duration: 30mins. A lunchtime talk marking the 400th Anniversary of Cromwell's birth. Talks are free and no tickets are required. As the subjects of the talks may be altered at short notice, visitors coming for a particular talk are advised to call the Museum on 0171 730 0717 x 2210 to check the programme
Museum- Military

Royal Society of Portrait Painters

6/5/99
24/5/99
MALL GALLERIES
Tel: 0171 930 6844
The Annual Exhibition by members of the Royal Society including many important recent commissions
Art Galleries

The Golf Show

7/5/99 9/5/99	*Historic Buildings* **EARLS COURT OLYMPIA** Tel: 0171 385 1200 Olympia 2. Organiser: Europa Exhibitions Ltd. *Exhibition Centres*

Business Expo '99

8/5/99 – 9/5/99 **WEMBLEY CONFERENCE AND EXHIBITION CENTRE**
Tel: 0181 902 8833
A public exhibition for visitors wishing to start up a new business. Sat 10.00-18.00 Sun 10.00-16.00. Hall 3. Admission £6.00 pre-booked
Exhibition Centres

His Holiness the Dalai Lama

8/5/99 – 10/5/99 **WEMBLEY CONFERENCE AND EXHIBITION CENTRE**
Tel: 0181 902 8833
Teachings by the Dalia Lama, Transforming the Mind. Tickets range in price, call for details
Exhibition Centres

Orpington Sketch Club

8/5/99 – 15/5/99 **BROMLEY MUSEUM AND PRIORY GARDENS**
Tel: 01689 873826
Contact Brian Wren 0181 658 7390 for further information
Museums

Contemporary Photography - Rich Living

8/5/99 – 4/7/99 **ORLEANS HOUSE GALLERY**
Tel: 0181 892 0221
Images created by photographer Stephen Gill, examine eight historic properties in Richmond Borough including Hampton Court Palace, Marble Hill House and David Garrick's Villa
Art Galleries

Antique and Collectors Fair

9/5/99 – 9/5/99 **ALEXANDRA PALACE**
Tel: 0181 365 2121
Great Hall. London's largest Antiques Fair with over 700 stands plus furniture selling wide range of quality items from 18th century onwards. Established for over 25 years. Times: Public 11.30-17.00, Trade 10.00. Admission: A£3.00 (Accompanied)C£Free Trade£5.00 (with business card). Organiser: Pig & Whistle Promotions 0181 883 7061
Historic Buildings

Old Comrades

9/5/99 – 9/5/99 **HORSE GUARDS**
Tel: 0891 505452
Combined Cavalry Old Comrades Parade and Memorial Service at 11.00 at the Cavalry Memorial in Hyde Park

Remembrance Service

9/5/99 – 9/5/99 **HORSE GUARDS**
Tel: 0891 505452
Coldstream Guards Regimental Remembrance Service in the Guards Chapel, Wellington Barracks at 14.00 and march to the Guards Memorial on Horse Guards Parade at 14.40
Historic Buildings

Photographica '99

9/5/99 – 9/5/99 **RHS ROYAL HORTICULTURAL HALLS**
Tel: 0171 834 4333
An annual consumer collectors fair run by the Photographic Collectors Club of Great Britain covering all aspects of photographic equipment and photography.
Exhibition Centres

Art Now: Doris Salcedo

11/5/99 – 18/7/99 **TATE GALLERY**
Tel: 0171 887 8000
Supported by The Penny McCall Foundation, in-kind support from Delfina, London
Art Galleries

Oliver Cromwell, Warts and All

13/5/99 – 13/5/99 **NATIONAL ARMY MUSEUM**
Tel: 0171 730 0717
Commences:13.15, duration: 30mins. A lunchtime talk marking the 400th Anniversary of Cromwell's birth. Talks are free and no tickets are required. As the subjects of the talks may be altered at short notice, visitors coming for a particular talk are advised to call the Museum on 0171 730 0717 x 2210 to check the programme
Museum- Military

Words and Songs

13/5/99 – 13/5/99 **THE LONDON CANAL MUSEUM**
Tel: 0171 713 0836
"Words and Songs - an Anthology of the River Thames", by Chris Elmers, Director, Museum in Docklands. Call for further details
Museum- Canal

England v Sri Lanka 1999 Cricket World Cup

14/5/99 – 14/5/99 **CRICKET WORLD CUP CARNIVAL 1999**
Tel: 0870 606 1999 (nat rates)
At Lord's Cricket Ground, tickets £24.00, £36.00 & £60.00. Call 0870 606 1999 (calls charged at National Rate) Lines open from 09.30-17.30 Mon-Fri. Tickets also available from your First Class County Office
Carnivals

A weekly updated selection of UK wide special events can be found on the award winning sites @ www.thisislondon.com *and* www.ukplus.co.uk

India v South Africa 1999 Cricket World Cup

15/5/99
15/5/99
CRICKET WORLD CUP CARNIVAL 1999
Tel: 0870 606 1999 (nat rates)
At Hove Cricket Ground, tickets £18.00.
Call 0870 606 1999 (calls charged at National Rate) Lines open from 09.30-17.30 Mon-Fri. Tickets also available from your First Class County Office

Carnivals

Zimbabwe v Kenya 1999 Cricket World Cup

15/5/99
15/5/99
CRICKET WORLD CUP CARNIVAL 1999
Tel: 0870 606 1999 (nat rates)
At Taunton Cricket Ground, tickets £14.00. Call 0870 606 1999 (calls charged at National Rate) Lines open from 09.30-17.30 Mon-Fri. Tickets also available from your First Class County Office

Carnivals

Exercise Executive Stretch

15/5/99
16/5/99
HORSE GUARDS
Tel: 0891 505452
The National Employers Liaison Committee's awareness weekend for civilian managers organised by the Territorial Army on Pirbright ranges. Call 0171 414 5515

Historic Buildings

Visitors Trail

15/5/99
23/5/99
APSLEY HOUSE, THE WELLINGTON MUSEUM
Tel: 0171 499 5676
As part of National Museums Week Apsley House will be offering a trail for visitors, the first ever, as part of CLMGG travel and exploration theme for the week. The trail will be fun and there will be a small prize for the first three correct answers to be drawn from a hat.

Historic Houses

Museums Week

15/5/99
23/5/99
GRANT MUSEUM OF ZOOLOGY AND COMPARATIVE ANATOMY
Tel: 0171 504 2647
You are invited to attend a special demonstration of zoological museum relating to some major, global conservation issues. The theme of this special demonstration is conservation awareness. It will aim to educate visitors about some of the major environmental issues we are currently faced with. This event is in the planning stages and therefore details cannot be confirmed. Further information will be available

from mid February, call 0171 504 2647

Museums

Kyushu Ceramics

15/5/99
15/9/99
BRITISH MUSEUM
Tel: 0171 636 1555
A loan exhibition from the Kyushu Ceramic Association in rooms 92-94, catalogue tbc, dates are provisional please check before visiting

Museums

Australia v Scotland 1999 Cricket World Cup

16/5/99
16/5/99
CRICKET WORLD CUP CARNIVAL 1999
Tel: 0870 606 1999 (nat rates)
At Worcester Cricket Ground, tickets £24.00. Call 0870 606 1999 (calls charged at National Rate) Lines open from 09.30-17.30 Mon-Fri. Tickets also available from your First Class County Office

Carnivals

West Indies v Pakistan 1999 Cricket World Cup

16/5/99
16/5/99
CRICKET WORLD CUP CARNIVAL 1999
Tel: 0870 606 1999 (nat rates)
At Bristol Cricket Ground, tickets £24.00. Call 0870 606 1999 (calls charged at National Rate) Lines open from 09.30-17.30 Mon-Fri. Tickets also available from your First Class County Office

Carnivals

Sunday Racing

16/5/99
16/5/99
KEMPTON PARK RACECOURSE
Tel: 01932 782292
For further details including race times and ticket prices please contact venue direct

Racecourses

Firing Day

16/5/99
16/5/99
TILBURY FORT
Tel: 01375 858489
The Garrison. Normal admission prices apply.

Forts

New Zealand v Bangladesh 1999 Cricket World Cup

17/5/99
17/5/99
CRICKET WORLD CUP CARNIVAL 1999
Tel: 0870 606 1999 (nat rates)
At Chelmsford Cricket Ground, tickets £16.00. Call 0870 606 1999 (calls charged at National Rate) Lines open from 09.30-17.30 Mon-Fri. Tickets also available from your First Class County Office

Carnivals

Rememberance Day Service

17/5/99	**HORSE GUARDS**
17/5/99	Tel: 0891 505452

Grenadier Guards Rememberance Day
Service in the Guards Chapel, Wellington
Barracks at 15.00. This will be followed
by a march to the Guards Memorial on
Horse Guards to lay a wreath

Historic Buildings

	Boyzone
17/5/99	**WEMBLEY CONFERENCE AND EXHIBITION CENTRE**
17/5/99	Tel: 0181 902 8833

Plus special guests. Performance 17 May
at 19.30. Tickets: £18.50

Exhibition Centres

	Museum's Week
17/5/99	**GUNNERSBURY PARK MUSEUM**
23/5/99	Tel: 0181 992 1612

To be announced

Museum- Social History

	Exhibition: Food for Thought
17/5/99	**BROMLEY MUSEUM AND PRIORY GARDENS**
28/7/99	Tel: 01689 873826

For further information please contact Dr
Alan Tyler, Curator or Melanie Parker,
Assistant Curator, at the Museum on
01689 873826

Museums

	England v Kenya 1999 Cricket World Cup
18/5/99	**CRICKET WORLD CUP CARNIVAL 1999**
18/5/99	Tel: 0870 606 1999 (nat rates)

At Canterbury Cricket Ground, tickets
£28.00. Call 0870 606 1999 (calls
charged at National Rate) Lines open
from 09.30-17.30 Mon-Fri. Tickets also
available from your First Class County
Office

Carnivals

	Sri Lanka v South Africa 1999 Cricket World Cup
19/5/99	**CRICKET WORLD CUP CARNIVAL 1999**
19/5/99	Tel: 0870 606 1999 (nat rates)

At Northampton Cricket Ground, tickets
£24.00. Call 0870 606 1999 (calls
charged at National Rate) Lines open
from 09.30-17.30 Mon-Fri. Tickets also
available from your First Class County
Office

Carnivals

	India v Zimbabwe 1999 Cricket World Cup
19/5/99	**CRICKET WORLD CUP CARNIVAL 1999**
19/5/99	Tel: 0870 606 1999 (nat rates)

At Leicester Cricket Ground, tickets
£16.00. Call 0870 606 1999 (calls
charged at National Rate) Lines open

from 09.30-17.30 Mon-Fri. Tickets also
available from your First Class County
Office

Carnivals

	Free Admission Day
20/5/99	**APSLEY HOUSE, THE WELLINGTON MUSEUM**
20/5/99	Tel: 0171 499 5676

Apsley House will be offering free admission to the museum to celebrate
National Museums Week.

Historic Houses

	Australia v New Zealand 1999 Cricket World Cup
20/5/99	**CRICKET WORLD CUP CARNIVAL 1999**
20/5/99	Tel: 0870 606 1999 (nat rates)

At Cardiff Cricket Ground, tickets £24.00.
Call 0870 606 1999 (calls charged at
National Rate) Lines open from 09.30-
17.30 Mon-Fri. Tickets also available
from your First Class County Office

Carnivals

	Pakistan v Scotland 1999 Cricket World Cup
20/5/99	**CRICKET WORLD CUP CARNIVAL 1999**
20/5/99	Tel: 0870 606 1999 (nat rates)

At Chester-le-Street Cricket Ground, tickets £216.00. Call 0870 606 1999 (calls
charged at National Rate) Lines open
from 09.30-17.30 Mon-Fri. Tickets also
available from your First Class County
Office

Carnivals

	Oliver's Army - Cromwell, Fairfax and the New Model Army
20/5/99	**NATIONAL ARMY MUSEUM**
20/5/99	Tel: 0171 730 0717

Commences:13.15, duration: 30mins. A
lunchtime talk marking the 400th
Anniversary of Cromwell's birth. Talks
are free and no tickets are required. As
the subjects of the talks may be altered
at short notice, visitors coming for a particular talk are advised to call the
Museum on 0171 730 0717 x 2210 to
check the programme

Museum- Military

	West Indies vv Bangladesh 1999 Cricket World Cup
21/5/99	**CRICKET WORLD CUP CARNIVAL 1999**
21/5/99	Tel: 0870 606 1999 (nat rates)

At Dublin Cricket Ground, tickets £16.00.
Call 0870 606 1999 (calls charged at
National Rate) Lines open from 09.30-
17.30 Mon-Fri. Tickets also available
from your First Class County Office

Carnivals

A weekly updated selection of UK wide special events can be found on
the award winning sites @ www.thisislondon.com *and* www.ukplus.co.uk

Mind, Body, Spirit Festival

21/5/99 RHS ROYAL HORTICULTURAL HALLS

31/5/99 Tel: 0171 834 4333

Comprehensive exhibition of natural, healthy lifestyles, complementary therapies, personal growth and spiritual development. Also continuous lectures, workshops and performances. Open Sat-Mon 10.00-19.00, Tue-Fri 11.00-18.00. (1998 prices for guidance only) A£4.00 Concessions£2.50 other dates A£8.00 Concessions£5.00 under 15's £Free. Bookings on 0171 938 3788

Exhibition Centres

Raphael and his Circle

21/5/99 THE QUEEN'S GALLERY

10/10/99 Tel: 0171 839 1377

Raphael, was arguably the single most influential painter in the history of western art. In his short career, he developed principals of composition, types of figure drawing and systems of workshop collaboration that set the standards for much of the next four centuries. The drawings by Raphael and his circle in the Royal library provide an overview of this remarkable exhibition. The evolution begins with the drawings of the artists who formed his early style - his father Giovanni Santi and his principal teacher Perugino. From there we follow the course of Raphael's career in twenty five drawings, from an early study of heads for the Vatican Coronation of the Virgin, through drawings for Holy families, the Vatican Stanze and the Sistine tapestries, to the sheets produced in his studio in the last years of his life. The exhibition then examines the drawings of Raphael's assistants, Gianfrancesco Penni, Giulio Romano, Perino Del Vaga and Polodoro da Caravaggio - how their styles were formed in Raphael's workshop, and how they developed his idiom in highly individual ways after the master's death in 1520, spreading radically differing interpretations of Raphael's style throughout Italy over the next three decades. The exhibition will be accompanied by a complete catalogue written by Martin Clayton, assistant Curator in the Print Room, with all exhibits reproduced in colour

Art Galleries

England v South African 1999 Cricket World Cup

Cricket World Cup Carnival 1999

22/5/99 CRICKET WORLD CUP CARNIVAL 1999

22/5/99 Tel: 0870 606 1999 (nat rates)

At The Oval Cricket Ground, tickets £24.00, £36.00 & £60.00. Call 0870 606 1999 (calls charged at National Rate) Lines open from 09.30-17.30 Mon-Fri. Tickets also available from your First Class County Office

Carnivals

Zimbabwe v Sri Lanka 1999 Cricket World Cup

22/5/99 CRICKET WORLD CUP CARNIVAL 1999

22/5/99 Tel: 0870 606 1999 (nat rates)

At Worcester Cricket Ground, tickets £20.00. Call 0870 606 1999 (calls charged at National Rate) Lines open from 09.30-17.30 Mon-Fri. Tickets also available from your First Class County Office

Carnivals

Ring and Brymer Achilles Stakes

22/5/99 KEMPTON PARK RACECOURSE

22/5/99 Tel: 01932 782292

For further details including race times and ticket prices please contact venue direct

Racecourses

Australian Wine Tasting

22/5/99 RHS ROYAL HORTICULTURAL HALLS

22/5/99 Tel: 0171 834 4333

An annual wine tasting event to sample the best in Australian wines. Run by the Australian Wine Club, call for further details

Exhibition Centres

Kenya v India 1999 Cricket World Cup

23/5/99 CRICKET WORLD CUP CARNIVAL 1999

23/5/99 Tel: 0870 606 1999 (nat rates)

At Bristol Cricket Ground, tickets £14.00. Call 0870 606 1999 (calls charged at National Rate) Lines open from 09.30-17.30 Mon-Fri. Tickets also available from your First Class County Office

Carnivals

Australia v Pakistan 1999 Cricket World Cup

23/5/99 CRICKET WORLD CUP CARNIVAL 1999

23/5/99 Tel: 0870 606 1999 (nat rates)

At Headingly Cricket Ground, tickets £18.00, £24.00 & £30.00. Call 0870 606 1999 (calls charged at National Rate) Lines open from 09.30-17.30 Mon-Fri. Tickets also available from your First Class County Office

Carnivals

Festival of Artist Bears

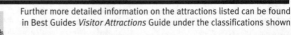

23/5/99
23/5/99

FESTIVAL OF ARTIST BEARS
Tel: 01273 697974
Venue: Kensington Town Hall, Hornton Street, London. Over 100 stands showing hand made artist bears, many one-offs, limited editions and show specials. Suppliers of bear making components and fabrics. Opportunity to meet leading bear makers from the UK and around the world. Time: 12.00-16.30. Ticket Prices: A£4.00 C(0-16)£2.00 Family Ticket (A2+C2)£10.00. Tickets available from: Hugglets Publishing: 01273 697974 - credit cards accepted

Festivals

West Indies v New Zealand 1999 Cricket World Cup

24/5/99
24/5/99

CRICKET WORLD CUP CARNIVAL 1999
Tel: 0870 606 1999 (nat rates)
At Southampton Cricket Ground, tickets £18.00. Call 0870 606 1999 (calls charged at National Rate) Lines open from 09.30-17.30 Mon-Fri. Tickets also available from your First Class County Office

Carnivals

Scotland v Bangladesh 1999 Cricket World Cup

24/5/99
24/5/99

CRICKET WORLD CUP CARNIVAL 1999
Tel: 0870 606 1999 (nat rates)
At Edinburgh Cricket Ground, tickets £16.00. Call 0870 606 1999 (calls charged at National Rate) Lines open from 09.30-17.30 Mon-Fri. Tickets also available from your First Class County Office

Carnivals

Exhibition: The Flowering of Botanical Art

24/5/99
28/5/99

CHELSEA PHYSIC GARDEN
Tel: 0171 352 5646
Open 12.00-17.00. Special Chelsea Flower Show Exhibition

Gardens- Botanical

England v Zimbabwe 1999 Cricket World Cup

25/5/99
25/5/99

CRICKET WORLD CUP CARNIVAL 1999
Tel: 0870 606 1999 (nat rates)
At Trent Bridge Cricket Ground, tickets £24.00, £36.00 & £60.00. Call 0870 606 1999 (calls charged at National Rate) Lines open from 09.30-17.30 Mon-Fri. Tickets also available from your First Class County Office

Carnivals

Painting Exhibition

25/5/99
18/6/99

JILL GEORGE GALLERY LTD
Tel: 0171 439 7319
Small paintings by Rod Judkins

Art Galleries

Sri Lanka v India 1999 Cricket World Cup

26/5/99
26/5/99

CRICKET WORLD CUP CARNIVAL 1999
Tel: 0870 606 1999 (nat rates)
At Taunton Cricket Ground, tickets £18.00. Call 0870 606 1999 (calls charged at National Rate) Lines open from 09.30-17.30 Mon-Fri. Tickets also available from your First Class County Office

Carnivals

South Africa v Kenya 1999 Cricket World Cup

26/5/99
26/5/99

CRICKET WORLD CUP CARNIVAL 1999
Tel: 0870 606 1999 (nat rates)
At Amsterdam Cricket Ground, Holland, tickets £16.00. Call 0870 606 1999 (calls charged at National Rate) Lines open from 09.30-17.30 Mon-Fri. Tickets also available from your First Class County Office

Carnivals

Australia v Bangladesh 1999 Cricket World Cup

27/5/99
27/5/99

CRICKET WORLD CUP CARNIVAL 1999
Tel: 0870 606 1999 (nat rates)
At Chester-le-Street Cricket Ground, tickets £20.00. Call 0870 606 1999 (calls charged at National Rate) Lines open from 09.30-17.30 Mon-Fri. Tickets also available from your First Class County Office

Carnivals

West Indies v Scotland 1999 Cricket World Cup

27/5/99
27/5/99

CRICKET WORLD CUP CARNIVAL 1999
Tel: 0870 606 1999 (nat rates)
At Leicester Cricket Ground, tickets £20.00. Call 0870 606 1999 (calls charged at National Rate) Lines open from 09.30-17.30 Mon-Fri. Tickets also available from your First Class County Office

Carnivals

Chelsea Flower Show

27/5/99
28/5/99

LONDON TOURIST BOARD
Tel: 0171 932 2000
Venue: The Royal Hospital, Chelsea, London SW3. Dazzling the senses, a bewitching blend of the beautiful and the practical. Chelsea is the world's best loved and most prestigious flower show. It combines inspirational show gardens

by the world's leading designers, every conceivable bloom from specialist nurseries, top gardening products and a range of conservation, education and science displays. Chelsea is the very best opportunity to plan and order for the gardening year. Companion with blind visitor or wheelchair user admitted free. Children 5+ only. Guide dogs admitted. No tickets will be sold at the gate. Public booking on 0171 344 4343. No group discounts. Coach parking available in Battersea Park, also paid car parking & free shuttle service. Free of charge shuttle bus to ground available from BR: Victoria, call: 0171 413 3306. Tube: Sloane Square 10 mins walk.

Tourist Information Centres

Spring Bank Holiday Fun Fair
27/5/99 **ALEXANDRA PALACE**
6/6/99 Tel: 0181 365 2121
Traditional family fun fair held on the boating lake car park. Dodgems, waltzers and many other rides, stalls, sideshows, kiddies rides, candy floss etc. Weekends & Bank Holiday 12.00-22.00, Weekdays 12.00-20.00 (special reduced price on all rides for Tuesday). Organiser: Fun Fair Amusements, Mobile No: 0860 310970

Historic Buildings

New Zealaand v Pakistan 1999 Cricket World Cup
28/5/99 **CRICKET WORLD CUP CARNIVAL 1999**
28/5/99 Tel: 0870 606 1999 (nat rates)
At Derby Cricket Ground, tickets £18.00. Call 0870 606 1999 (calls charged at National Rate) Lines open from 09.30-17.30 Mon-Fri. Tickets also available from your First Class County Office

Carnivals

England v India 1999 Cricket World Cup
29/5/99 **CRICKET WORLD CUP CARNIVAL 1999**
29/5/99 Tel: 0870 606 1999 (nat rates)
At Edgbaston Cricket Ground, tickets £24.00, £36.00 & £60.00. Call 0870 606 1999 (calls charged at National Rate) Lines open from 09.30-17.30 Mon-Fri. Tickets also available from your First Class County Office

Carnivals

Zimbabwe v South Africa 1999 Cricket World Cup
29/5/99 **CRICKET WORLD CUP CARNIVAL 1999**
29/5/99 Tel: 0870 606 1999 (nat rates)
At Chelmsford Cricket Ground, tickets

£20.00. Call 0870 606 1999 (calls charged at National Rate) Lines open from 09.30-17.30 Mon-Fri. Tickets also available from your First Class County Office

Carnivals

Trooping the Colour First Rehearsal
29/5/99 **HORSE GUARDS**
29/5/99 Tel: 0891 505452
The Major General's Review. Trooping the Colour ceremony by the Massed Bands and Troops of the Household Division. The Major General commanding the Household Division takes the salute. Starts at 10.40 from Buckingham Palace arriving at Horse Guards Parade at 11.00. Applications for tickets accepted until end Feb each year £Free. If it is too late to obtain tickets for this event, but you may wish to watch along the route. Admission £Free. Tube: Westminster

Historic Buildings

Heron Stakes
29/5/99 **KEMPTON PARK RACECOURSE**
29/5/99 Tel: 01932 782292
For further details including race times and ticket prices please contact venue direct

Racecourses

Sculpture Exhibition
29/5/99 **HALL PLACE**
11/7/99 Tel: 01322 526574 x204
Belinda Rush Jansen - a sculptor with a difference. Life-size wirework figures.

Historic Houses & Gardens

Sugar and Spice, and all things nice
29/5/99 **SYON HOUSE**
30/8/99 Tel: 0181 560 0883
Demonstrations of confectionery making and sugarwork from historic Syon House recipes

Historic Houses & Gardens

The King's Court
30/5/99 **CHAPTER HOUSE AND PYX CHAMBER OF WESTMINSTER ABBEY**
30/5/99 Tel: 0171 222 5897
Meet members of Henry III's court. Find out about life in the 13th century from court to country, learn about ecclesiastical architecture, medieval faith, pilgrimages and shrines. From 12.00. Normal admission price

Abbeys

West Indies v Australia 199 Cricket World Cup

Further more detailed information on the attractions listed can be found in Best Guides *Visitor Attractions* Guide under the classifications shown

30/5/99 30/5/99	**CRICKET WORLD CUP CARNIVAL 1999** Tel: 0870 606 1999 (nat rates) At Old Trafford Cricket Ground, tickets £18.00, £24.00 & £30.00. Call 0870 606 1999 (calls charged at National Rate) Lines open from 09.30-17.30 Mon-Fri. Tickets also available from your First Class County Office

Carnivals

30/5/99 30/5/99	**Sri Lanka v Kenya 1999 Cricket World Cup** **CRICKET WORLD CUP CARNIVAL 1999** Tel: 0870 606 1999 (nat rates) At Southampton Cricket Ground, tickets £14.00. Call 0870 606 1999 (calls charged at National Rate) Lines open from 09.30-17.30 Mon-Fri. Tickets also available from your First Class County Office

Carnivals

30/5/99 31/5/99	**Afro Hair & Beauty '99** **ALEXANDRA PALACE** Tel: 0181 365 2121 Great Hall & West Hall. The latest hair and beauty ideas for black women, including fashion shows. This year sees the launch of a bridal suite and natural hair and beauty village. Times: Sun & Mon 10.00-19.00. Admission: A£10.00 C&OAPs£6.00, Advance tickets £8.00. Organiser: Hawker Consumer Publications Ltd 0171 498 1795

Historic Buildings

30/5/99 31/5/99	**The Soprano in Pink** **MARBLE HILL HOUSE** Tel: 0181 892 5115 Rhiannon Gayle. Delightful 17th and 18th century song and spinet music, with gossip and talks about Georgian fashions. Normal admission prices apply

Historic Houses

30/5/99 31/5/99	**Ducal Desserts** **SYON HOUSE** Tel: 0181 560 0883 Historical desserts, ices and jelly making including banqueting displays in Syon House

Historic Houses & Gardens

30/5/99 29/8/99	**Grove Shows '99** **ALEXANDRA PALACE** Tel: 0181 365 2121 Now in their 15th year the ever popular Grove Shows begin on 30 May for 14 weeks through to 29 Aug - every Sunday 15.00-17.00, Admission Free. Children's shows begin on the 29 July through to 26 Aug for 5 weeks - every Thursday

14.00-15.00, Admission £0.50 entrance by donation

Historic Buildings

31/5/99 31/5/99	**Pakistan v Bangladash 199 Cricket World Cup** **CRICKET WORLD CUP CARNIVAL 1999** Tel: 0870 606 1999 (nat rates) At Northampton Cricket Ground, tickets £16.00. Call 0870 606 1999 (calls charged at National Rate) Lines open from 09.30-17.30 Mon-Fri. Tickets also available from your First Class County Office

Carnivals

31/5/99 31/5/99	**Scotland v New Zealand 1999 Cricket World Cup** **CRICKET WORLD CUP CARNIVAL 1999** Tel: 0870 606 1999 (nat rates) At Edinburgh Cricket Ground, tickets £16.00. Call 0870 606 1999 (calls charged at National Rate) Lines open from 09.30-17.30 Mon-Fri. Tickets also available from your First Class County Office

Carnivals

31/5/99 31/5/99	**Freightliners Farm Open Day** **FREIGHTLINERS FARM** Tel: 0171 609 0467 Sheep shearing, pony and donkey rides, bouncy castle, spinning and weaving and lots of other activities

Farms

1/6/99 1/7/99	**Hornimania** **HORNIMAN MUSEUM AND GARDENS** Tel: 0181 699 1872 A free festival of world music and culture, with food, children's activities, beer tent and craft fair. Actual dates to be confirmed. Call for further details

Museums

1/6/99 1/10/99	**Cracking Codes** **BRITISH MUSEUM** Tel: 0171 636 1555 The Rosetta Stone and Decipherment in room 28, admission charged, catalogue available, dates are provisional please check before visiting

Museums

1/6/99 31/10/99	**Thames Tour of the Puppet Theatre Barge** **PUPPET THEATRE BARGE** Tel: 0171 249 6876 Box Office Including Abingdon, Henley, Marlow, Cliveden & Richmond. Programme to be announced. Call the Box Office for details 0836 202745 (open June-Oct only)

Boat Trips

Hitchcock - From Leytonstone to Hollywood

1/6/99
10/1/00

VESTRY HOUSE MUSEUM

Tel: 0181 509 1917

Celebrating the centenary of Hitchcock in Leytonstone, 13 Aug 1899, and his work

Museum- Local History

Anniversary of The Queen's Cornonation

2/6/99
2/6/99

HORSE GUARDS

Tel: 0891 505452

41 Gun Royal Salute fired by The King's Troop Royal Horse Artillery in Hyde Park at 12.00 and 62 Gun Royal Salute fired the Honourable Artillery Company at the Tower of London at 13.00 hours to mark the Anniversary of The Queen's Cornonation, free public access

Historic Buildings

Beating Retreat - Massed Bands of the Household Division

2/6/99
3/6/99

HORSE GUARDS

Tel: 0891 505452

The Massed Band of the Household Division occupy the unique position in the ceremonial scene and have a world-wide reputation for their musical excel-lence and versatility. Besides providing marching and mounted bands for The Queen's Birthday Parade and other State Occasions, they provide a string orches-tras for State Banquets and Investitures at Buckingham Palace and dance and concert bands for engagements through-out the country. All seven bands fre-quently undertake tours abroad and broadcast on television and radio. The beating of sounding of the Retreat has its' origins in the 16th century when it was possibly the same ceremony as Tattoo, "ye retrete to beate att 9 att night and take it from ye garde." In 1727, "half and hour before the setting of the sun Drummers and Post-Guards are to go upon the ramparts and beat a Retreat to give notice to those without the gates are to be shut. The Drummers will not take more than quarter of an hour to beat Retreat." The modern method of Beating Retreat is not unlike the 18th century procedure. Nowadays the ceremony, usually at sunset, denotes the end of a working day and heralds the mounting of the Guard. Seats (all reserved seats) £10.00, £8.00

& £5.00, party rates 10+ 10% reduction. Tickets 0171 414 2271 from 1st March or from Household Division Funds, Horse Guards, Whitehall, London SW1A 2AX. Guards Bookshop, Wellington Barracks, Birdcage Walk, London SW1E 6HQ (09.00-15.00 daily)

Historic Buildings

The Summer Olympia Fine Art & Antiques Fair

3/6/99
13/6/99

EARLS COURT OLYMPIA

Tel: 0171 385 1200

Olympia Grand Hall. Held at the height of the summer season, this fair attracts serious collectors, private buyers and treasure seekers from around the world. The fair has an unrivalled mix of fine art and antiques from the executive and expensive to the genuinely affordable. Opening Times: 3 June 11.00-21.00, 4 June 11.00-20.00, 5-6 June 11.00-19.00, 7 June CLOSED, 8-11 June 11.00-20.00, 12 June 11.00-19.00, 13 June 11.00-17.00. Pre-booking is advisable. For further information please contact P&O Events, tel: 0171 370 8212

Exhibition Centres

Group A - 2 v Group B - 2 1999 Cricket World Cup

4/6/99
4/6/99

CRICKET WORLD CUP CARNIVAL 1999

Tel: 0870 606 1999 (nat rates)

At The Oval Cricket Ground, tickets £24.00, £36.00 & £60.00. Call 0870 606 1999 (calls charged at National Rate) Lines open from 09.30-17.30 Mon-Fri. Tickets also available from your First Class County Office

Carnivals

Bright Now!

5/6/99
5/6/99

ALEXANDRA PALACE

Tel: 0181 365 2121

West Hall. Meditation / Chanting / Singing in the afternoon. Party with great live music in the evening (bands to be announced). Times: 12.00-24.00. Admission: £26.00. Organiser: CAER SIDI 01993 883475

Historic Buildings

Group A - 1 v Group B - 1 1999 Cricket World Cup

5/6/99
5/6/99

CRICKET WORLD CUP CARNIVAL 1999

Tel: 0870 606 1999 (nat rates)

At Trent Bridge Cricket Ground, tickets £24.00, £36.00 & £60.00. Call 0870 606 1999 (calls charged at National Rate) Lines open from 09.30-17.30 Mon-Fri. Tickets also available from your First

Further more detailed information on the attractions listed can be found in Best Guides *Visitor Attractions* Guide under the classifications shown

Class County Office

Carnivals

Trooping of the Colour Practice
HORSE GUARDS

5/6/99
5/6/99
Tel: 0891 505452

The Colonel's Review. Trooping the Colour ceremony by the Massed Bands and Troops of the Household Division. The Colonel takes the salute. Starts at 10.40 from Buckingham Palace arriving at Horse Guards Parade at 11.00. Applications for tickets accepted until end Feb each year £7.50. If it is too late to obtain tickets for this event, but you may wish to watch along the route. Admission £Free. Tube: Westminster

Historic Buildings

Family Activities
ROYAL AIR FORCE MUSEUM

5/6/99
6/6/99
Tel: 0181 205 2266

Inside and out the Museum plenty of activities based on the theme of Flight, including parachute displays and aircraft simulators to 'fly'

Museum- Aviation

Children's Summer Fun Fair
ALEXANDRA PALACE

5/6/99
12/6/99
Tel: 0181 365 2121

Small family fun fair held on the boating lake car park, with a selection of rides and stalls themed for children and parents. Weekends only up to 18 July 12.00-19.00. From Monday 19 July - 12 September daily 12.00-19.00. Organiser: Fun Fair Amusements, Mobile: 0860 310970

Historic Buildings

Group A - 3 v Group B - 3 1999 Cricket World Cup
CRICKET WORLD CUP CARNIVAL 1999

6/6/99
6/6/99
Tel: 0870 606 1999 (nat rates)

At Headingly Bridge Cricket Ground, tickets £24.00, £36.00 & £60.00. Call 0870 606 1999 (calls charged at National Rate) Lines open from 09.30-17.30 Mon-Fri. Tickets also available from your First Class County Office

Carnivals

Fun Day
VAUXHALL CITY FARM

6/6/99
6/6/99
Tel: 0171 582 4204

Stalls, side shows, demonstrations, gymkana, refreshments, along a theme with prizes for best fancy dress

Farms

Royal Academy 230th Summer Exhibition

7/6/99
22/8/99
ROYAL ACADEMY OF ARTS
Tel: 0171 300 8000

The 'Summer Exhibition,' where internationally renowned artists exhibit alongside aspiring artists, is unique in the arts calendar. The galleries are eye-catching, full of colour and vitality with around 1,200 works on show. Sculpture from the exhibition is exhibited in the elegant Courtyard in front of Burlington House. Most of the paintings, sculpture, prints and drawings are for sale with prices starting from around £50. Visitors purchasing their tickets after 18.00 can enjoy live music and a free glass of Pimms in the open-air Courtyard Café, before or after visiting the exhibition. Free admission for disabled and parents with children 0-5. Pre booking is advisable, wheelchairs may be booked in advance on 0171 439 7438

Art Galleries

Group A - 2 v Group B - 1 1999 Cricket World Cup
CRICKET WORLD CUP CARNIVAL 1999

8/6/99
8/6/99
Tel: 0870 606 1999 (nat rates)

At Old Trafford Cricket Ground, tickets £24.00, £36.00 & £60.00. Call 0870 606 1999 (calls charged at National Rate) Lines open from 09.30-17.30 Mon-Fri. Tickets also available from your First Class County Office

Carnivals

Intrade Exhibition
EARLS COURT OLYMPIA

8/6/99
10/6/99
Tel: 0171 385 1200

Olympia 2. Organiser: Hemming Group Ltd.

Exhibition Centres

Group A - 3 v Grouup B - 2 1999 Cricket World Cup
CRICKET WORLD CUP CARNIVAL 1999

9/6/99
9/6/99
Tel: 0870 606 1999 (nat rates)

At Lord's Cricket Ground, tickets £24.00, £36.00 & £60.00. Call 0870 606 1999 (calls charged at National Rate) Lines open from 09.30-17.30 Mon-Fri. Tickets also available from your First Class County Office

Carnivals

Evening Racing
KEMPTON PARK RACECOURSE

9/6/99
9/6/99
Tel: 01932 782292

For further details including race times and ticket prices please contact venue direct

Racecourses

Open College Of the Arts
9/6/99 BANKSIDE GALLERY
12/6/99 Tel: 0171 928 7521
Degree show, call for details
Art Galleries

Nichole Farhi Designer Clothing Sale
9/6/99 RHS ROYAL HORTICULTURAL HALLS
12/6/99 Tel: 0171 834 4333
Designer garments at high street prices,
open to the public, call for further
details
Exhibition Centres

Spitalfields Festival
9/6/99 SPITALFIELDS FESTIVAL 1999
30/6/99 Tel: 0171 377 0287
Recitals, ensembles, choirs of St Johns
College, Cambridge and Winchester
Cathedral, vocal, festival bands, readings, lectures, education and community
work. Full access for disabled and lift for
wheelchairs. Helpers for partially sight-
ed. A£3.00-£25.00. Also free events.
Groups 20% discount. £2.00 off top
bands for ES40s & OAPs. Tickets available from Festival Box Office Hotline:
0171 377 1362
Festivals

Rembrandt Self Portraits
9/6/99 NATIONAL GALLERY
5/9/99 Tel: 0171 839 3321
Sainsbury Room. Admission Charge.
Further information will appear when
available
Art Galleries

**Group A - 1 v Group B - 3 1999 Cricket
World Cup**
10/6/99 CRICKET WORLD CUP CARNIVAL 1999
10/6/99 Tel: 0870 606 1999 (nat rates)
At Edgbaston Cricket Ground, tickets
£24.00, £36.00 & £60.00. Call 0870 606
1999 (calls charged at National Rate)
Lines open from 09.30-17.30 Mon-Fri.
Tickets also available from your First
Class County Office
Carnivals

**Anniversary of the Birthday of The
Duke of Edinburgh**
10/6/99 HORSE GUARDS
10/6/99 Tel: 0891 505452
41 Gun Salute fired by The King's
Troop Royal Horse Artillery in Hyde Park
at 12.00 and 62 Gun Royal Salute fired
the the Honourable Artillery Company at
the Tower of London at 13.00 hours to
mark the Anniversary of the Birthday of
The Duke of Edinburgh, free public
access

Historic Buildings
**"The Regent's Canal" by Alan
Faulkner**
10/6/99 THE LONDON CANAL MUSEUM
10/6/99 Tel: 0171 713 0836
Alan Faulkner, author of a new book on
the Regent's Canal. Commences 19.30,
call for further details
Museum- Canal

**Group A - 3 v Group B - 1 1999 Cricket
World Cup**
11/6/99 CRICKET WORLD CUP CARNIVAL 1999
11/6/99 Tel: 0870 606 1999 (nat rates)
At The Oval Cricket Ground, tickets
£24.00, £36.00 & £60.00. Call 0870 606
1999 (calls charged at National Rate)
Lines open from 09.30-17.30 Mon-Fri.
Tickets also available from your First
Class County Office
Carnivals

**Group A - 2 v Group B - 3 1999 Cricket
World Cup**
12/6/99 CRICKET WORLD CUP CARNIVAL 1999
12/6/99 Tel: 0870 606 1999 (nat rates)
At Trent Bridge Cricket Ground, tickets
£24.00, £36.00 & £60.00. Call 0870 606
1999 (calls charged at National Rate)
Lines open from 09.30-17.30 Mon-Fri.
Tickets also available from your First
Class County Office
Carnivals

**The Queen's Birthday Parade -
Trooping the Colour**
12/6/99 HORSE GUARDS
12/6/99 Tel: 0891 505452
At 11.00 on Horse Guards Parade. Colour
trooped by 1st Battalion Coldstream
Guards - Applications for tickets accept-
ed until end Feb each year £14.50. If it is
too late to obtain tickets for this event,
but you may wish to watch along the
route. Admission £Free. Tube:
Westminster. ALSO 41 Gun Royal Salute
fired by Te King's Troop Royal Horse
Artillery to Green Park as 12.00 and 62
Gun Royal Salute fired by the
Honourable Artillery Company at the
Tower of London at 13.00 to mark The
Queen's Official Birthday, free public
access
Historic Buildings

**Group A - 1 v Group B - 2 1999 Cricket
World Cup**
13/6/99 CRICKET WORLD CUP CARNIVAL 1999
13/6/99 Tel: 0870 606 1999 (nat rates)
At Headingly Cricket Ground, tickets
£24.00, £36.00 & £60.00. Call 0870 606

Further more detailed information on the attractions listed can be found
in Best Guides *Visitor Attractions* Guide under the classifications shown

1999 (calls charged at National Rate) Lines open from 09.30-17.30 Mon-Fri. Tickets also available from your First Class County Office

Carnivals

National Gardens Scheme Open Day
13/6/99 OSTERLEY PARK
13/6/99 Tel: 0181 568 7714
A chance to see areas of the garden not normally open to visitors and to meet the gardeners, 11.00-16.00. Admission to Walled Garden: A£1.00 C£Free. Normal parking and House admission

Historic Houses

Stoke Newing Midsummer Festival
13/6/99 STOKE NEWINGTON MIDSUMMER FESTIVAL 1999
27/6/99 Tel: 0171 923 1599
Music, theatre, comedy, dance, live art and poetry. Contact Arts Line: 0171 388 2227 for disability information

Festivals

New English Arts Club
15/6/99 BANKSIDE GALLERY
4/7/99 Tel: 0171 928 7521
Provisional. The first exhibition by the NEAC under their new President Ken Howard

Art Galleries

1999 Cricket World Cup 1st Semi-Final
16/6/99 CRICKET WORLD CUP CARNIVAL 1999
16/6/99 Tel: 0870 606 1999 (nat rates)
At Old Trafford Cricket Ground, tickets £30.00, £40.00 & £65.00. Call 0870 606 1999 (calls charged at National Rate) Lines open from 09.30-17.30 Mon-Fri. Tickets also available from your First Class County Office

Carnivals

Business Intelligence
16/6/99 EARLS COURT OLYMPIA
17/6/99 Tel: 0171 385 1200
Olympia 2. Organiser: Business Intelligence Ltd.

Exhibition Centres

1999 Cricket World Cup 2nd Semi-Final
17/6/99 CRICKET WORLD CUP CARNIVAL 1999
17/6/99 Tel: 0870 606 1999 (nat rates)
At Edgbaston Cricket Ground, tickets £30.00, £40.00 & £65.00. Call 0870 606 1999 (calls charged at National Rate) Lines open from 09.30-17.30 Mon-Fri. Tickets also available from your First Class County Office

Carnivals

Verner Panton

Design Museum
17/6/99 DESIGN MUSEUM
10/10/99 Tel: 0171 403 6933
Often dubbed 'The Madman of Danish Design', Verner Panton was one of the most controversial figures in twentieth-century design. Producing furniture, interiors and architecture, Panton's work is dominated by his groundbreaking use of psychedelic colours and experimental forms. This exhibition, his last project, is sensuous and stimulating, challenging, delightful and fun, and reveals a major international creative talent

Museums

Free Admission Day
18/6/99 APSLEY HOUSE, THE WELLINGTON MUSEUM
18/6/99 Tel: 0171 499 5676
Waterloo Day. Apsley House will be offering free admission to the museum to celebrate National Museums Week.

Historic Houses

The Evening Standard Hot Tickets Theme World Experience Show '99
18/6/99 ALEXANDRA PALACE
20/6/99 Tel: 0181 365 2121
A show for all the family featuring theme parks, visitor attractions and fun days out! Times: Fri & Sun 10.00-18.00, Sat 10.00-20.00. Admission: A£5.00 C£3.00. Organiser: Hamlyn Events 0181 451 6385

Historic Buildings

Open-Air Theatre
18/6/99 MORDEN HALL PARK
20/6/99 Tel: 0181 648 1845
The Taming of the Shrew. Performed by the popular maqama Theatre Company at 19.30. Price: A£7.00 Concessions£5.00.

Gardens

1999 Cricket World Cup Final
20/6/99 CRICKET WORLD CUP CARNIVAL 1999
20/6/99 Tel: 0870 606 1999 (nat rates)
At Lord's Cricket Ground, tickets £40.00, £70.00 & £100.00. Call 0870 606 1999 (calls charged at National Rate) Lines open from 09.30-17.30 Mon-Fri. Tickets also available from your First Class County Office

Carnivals

Firing Day
20/6/99 TILBURY FORT
20/6/99 Tel: 01375 858489
The Garrison. Normal admission prices apply.

Forts

RHS Flower Show

22/6/99 23/6/99	**RHS Royal Horticultural Halls** Tel: 0171 834 4333 Open 1st day 11.00-19.00, 2nd day 10.00-17.00, 24 hour information line: 0171 649 1885 *Exhibition Centres*

City of London Festival

22/6/99 15/7/99	**City of London Festival 1999** Tel: 0171 377 0540 Over 160 events. Shakespearean drama, orchestral concerts, recitals, operas, chamber music, jazz, masterclasses, dance, free open air events, theatre, Hayden string quartet series, performances from all around the world *Festivals*

Prize Winning Exhibitor

22/6/99 23/7/99	**Jill George Gallery Ltd** Tel: 0171 439 7319 Paintings by Thomas Watson, prize winner of National Portrait competition *Art Galleries*

Gala Evening

23/6/99 23/6/99	**Kempton Park Racecourse** Tel: 01932 782292 Racing from Kempton. For further details including race times and ticket prices please contact venue direct *Racecourses*

The In-Store Marketing Show

23/6/99 25/6/99	**Earls Court Olympia** Tel: 0171 385 1200 Olympia 2. Organiser: Centaur Exhibitions Ltd. *Exhibition Centres*

Directions 1999

23/6/99 25/6/99	**Wembley Conference and Exhibition Centre** Tel: 0181 902 8833 The largest school leaver and high education fair in the UK. A careers exhibition for school leavers. Exhibitors will be from commerical organisations, public sector departments and voluntary organisations offering detailed advice on careers. Jobs may be offered to suitable applicants on leaving school and graduating from University. Hall 2 *Exhibition Centres*

The Gere Collection

23/6/99 30/8/99	**National Gallery** Tel: 0171 839 3321 Sunley Room. Admission Free. Further information will appear when available *Art Galleries*

End of Summer Term Degree Show

24/6/99	**City and Guilds of London Art**

27/6/99	**School 1999** Tel: 0171 735 2306/735 5210 A show held at the end of the Summer Term Thursday-Sunday, admission free 10.00-18.45 *Festivals*

The Daily Telegraph House & Garden Fair '99

24/6/99 27/6/99	**Earls Court Olympia** Tel: 0171 385 1200 Olympia Grand & National Halls. Exclusive interiors and gardening fair, with stylish products for the home and garden on show and on sale from leading companies and designers, as well as designer roomsets, feature gardens, demonstrations and tastings. Opening Times: 24-26 June 10.00-18.00, 27 June 10.00-17.00. For further information please contact National Events Ltd, tel: 0171 453 5340 *Exhibition Centres*

All Saints

25/6/99 25/6/99	**Wembley Conference and Exhibition Centre** Tel: 0181 902 8833 Plus special guests. This is an extra performance due to public demand as Thur 24 is SOLD OUT. Performance: 25 June at 19.30 Tickets: £17.50 *Exhibition Centres*

B P Portrait Award

25/6/99 26/9/99	**National Portrait Gallery** Tel: 0171 306 0055 Annual award for young portrait painters *Art Galleries*

Cyprus Wine Festival

26/6/99 27/6/99	**Alexandra Palace** Tel: 0181 365 2121 Cyprus Wine Festival is organised by Parikiaki Greek Newspaper, the purpose of the event is to promote Cypriot products, especially the wine and to bring the Cypriot Community together. Times: 11.00-21.00. Admission: A£3.00 C(under 12)£Free OAPs£2.00. Organiser: Parikiaki Haraavki (UK) Ltd 0171 272 6777 *Historic Buildings*

Forest Festival

27/6/99 27/6/99	**Queen Elizabeth's Hunting Lodge** Tel: 0181 529 6681 Tudor re-enactments and crafts, medieval entertainments plus forestry demonstrations and wildlife displays *Historic Buildings*

Turner's Rivers of France: The Seine

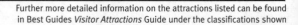

Further more detailed information on the attractions listed can be found in Best Guides *Visitor Attractions* Guide under the classifications shown

29/6/99
3/10/99 TATE GALLERY
Tel: 0171 887 8000
This will bring together works that led to the finished set of views along the Seine which were published in two volumes in the mid 1850s. Sketches in watercolour and gouaches on blue paper from the Turner Bequest will be re-united with the finished paintings, some of which were separates from the main group. The exhibition will ens with a series of view of Paris. Admission Free

Art Galleries

Tomorrow's World 1999
30/6/99 EARLS COURT OLYMPIA
4/7/99 Tel: 0171 385 1200
Earls Court 1. Organiser: Haymarket Exhibitions Ltd.

Exhibition Centres

Holiday Fun Days
1/7/99 OSTERLEY PARK
31/8/99 Tel: 0181 568 7714
Special days for the school holidays between 10.00-15.00. Please telephone for programme: 0181 568 4178

Historic Houses

TES Children's Bookfair
2/7/99 RHS ROYAL HORTICULTURAL HALLS
4/7/99 Tel: 0171 834 4333
This is a new event featuring books on every subject just for kids. Tickets £5 tel 0171 352 9017 for pre registration.

Exhibition Centres

Croydon Summer Festival Event
4/7/99 CROYDON CLOCKTOWER
4/7/99 Tel: 0181 253 1030
Croydon Carnival Parade: North End - Lloyd Park

Arts & Entertainment

Croydon Summer Festival 1999
4/7/99 CROYDON CLOCKTOWER
19/7/99 Tel: 0181 253 1030
A riot of fun at Croydon Clocktower, North End, Queens Gardens, Lloyd Park and other venues around Croydon, Croydon Summer Festival incorporates The Croydon Jazz Festival, the Folk Music Festival - Music in the Gardens, The Street Theatre Festival, The Croydon Film Festival and The Croydon Arts Festival. Opening with Croydon's Carnival Weekend and closing with the Croydon Mela, Croydon Summer Festival is a two week feast of culture not to be missed!

Arts & Entertainment

Croydon Summer Festival Event
5/7/99 CROYDON CLOCKTOWER
5/7/99 Tel: 0181 253 1030
Croydon Carnival International Music Day Carnival   Lloyd Park

Arts & Entertainment

Croydon Summer Festival Event
6/7/99 CROYDON CLOCKTOWER
6/7/99 Tel: 0181 253 1030
Steve Williamson; Jazz Festival at the Clocktower

Arts & Entertainment

Croydon Summer Festival Event
7/7/99 CROYDON CLOCKTOWER
7/7/99 Tel: 0181 253 1030
Jean Toussaint: Jazz Festival at the Clocktower. Windrush Film Festival: Film Festival at the Clocktower

Arts & Entertainment

Croydon Summer Festival Event
8/7/99 CROYDON CLOCKTOWER
8/7/99 Tel: 0181 253 1030
Frog Island and Big Chief: Jazz Festival at North End. Dan Knight: Jazz Festival at the Clocktower

Arts & Entertainment

The Canals of Birmingham
8/7/99 THE LONDON CANAL MUSEUM
8/7/99 Tel: 0171 713 0836
By Arthur Farrand-Radley MBE, Vice President, IWA London. Call for further details

Museum- Canal

Croydon Summer Festival Event
9/7/99 CROYDON CLOCKTOWER
9/7/99 Tel: 0181 253 1030
Mervyn Africa: Jazz Festival at North End. John Mayer: Jazz Festival at the Clocktower

Arts & Entertainment

Croydon Summer Festival Event
10/7/99 CROYDON CLOCKTOWER
10/7/99 Tel: 0181 253 1030
Wade Austin and The Tube: Jazz Festival at North End. Tommy Smith: Jazz Festival at the Clocktower

Arts & Entertainment

The Fleadh 1999
10/7/99 THE FLEADH 1999
10/7/99 Tel: 0181 963 0940
London's longest running outdoor festival - 10 years. A feast of musical entertainment. Please call for times and prices.

Festivals

A weekly updated selection of UK wide special events can be found on the award winning sites @ www.thisislondon.com *and* www.ukplus.co.uk

20th Century Fine Art - Cynthia Pell (1933-1977) A Retrospective
10/7/99
5/9/99
ORLEANS HOUSE GALLERY
Tel: 0181 892 0221
In this exhibition organised in collaboration with the 'Museum of Women's Art', we bring together the seminal work of srtist Cynthia Pell for the first time since her death
Art Galleries

House of Cards
10/7/99
12/9/99
BEXLEY MUSEUM
Tel: 01322 526574
The history of playing cards and games of chance
Museum- Local History

Croydon Summer Festival Event
11/7/99
11/7/99
CROYDON CLOCKTOWER
Tel: 0181 253 1030
Louisiana Joy Makers and Tony Woods: Jazz Festival at North End. J-Life: Jazz Festival at the Clocktower

Arts & Entertainment

Osterley Day
11/7/99
11/7/99
OSTERLEY PARK
Tel: 0181 568 7714
Local artists and musicians display and perform their work around the park, plus children's games, displays, dancing, stalls, a poetry trail and much more. A great day out for all the family. Admissoin Free (includes free parking and free admission tot he Park)
Historic Houses

Firing Day
11/7/99
11/7/99
TILBURY FORT
Tel: 01375 858489
The Garrison. Normal admission prices apply.
Forts

Summer Exhibition: Rainforests for Health
11/7/99
5/9/99
CHELSEA PHYSIC GARDEN
Tel: 0171 352 5646
Exhibition opening during normal garden opening times
Gardens- Botanical

Croydon Summer Festival Event
12/7/99
12/7/99
CROYDON CLOCKTOWER
Tel: 0181 253 1030
Mistura: Jazz Festival at the Clocktower. Windrush Film Festival: Film Festival at the Clocktower
Arts & Entertainment

Croydon Summer Festival Event

13/7/99
13/7/99
CROYDON CLOCKTOWER
Tel: 0181 253 1030
Best of Croydon 100: Film Festival at the Clocktower. The Journey: Arts Festival at the Clocktower
Arts & Entertainment

Croydon Summer Festival Event
14/7/99
14/7/99
CROYDON CLOCKTOWER
Tel: 0181 253 1030
Life With the Lid On: Arts Festival at the Clocktower. Best of Croydon 100: Film Festival at the Clocktower
Arts & Entertainment

Evening Racing
14/7/99
14/7/99
KEMPTON PARK RACECOURSE
Tel: 01932 782292
Racing from Kempton. For further details including race times and ticket prices please contact venue direct
Racecourses

Children's Open Air Theatre
14/7/99
14/7/99
OSTERLEY PARK
Tel: 0181 568 7714
The Water Babies by Charles Kingsley presented by Illyria. Illyria's fantastical new production of Kingsley's classic story takes us on a journey down river to the seas and the Other End of Nowhere, where we meet the Water Babies and the magical creatures of the Deep. Bring a rug, chair and a picnic for this open air performance in the Park. Commences: 18.00 gates open 17.00. Tickets in advance: A£8.00 C£6.00 Family Ticket £28.00. Tickets on the Gate: All £10.00
Historic Houses

Music and Arts Festival
15/7/99
15/7/99
CROYDON CLOCKTOWER
Tel: 0181 253 1030
Saffron Summerfield and Band of Two, Music in the Gardens, venue Queens Gardens. Estudio Macuba, Arts Festival, venue the Clocktower
Arts & Entertainment

Watercolour 21
15/7/99
15/8/99
BANKSIDE GALLERY
Tel: 0171 928 7521
The Challenge for Watercolour in the Twenty-First Century. Successful submissions to the RWS new Open painting competition selected by Eileen Hogam, Martin Gayford, the Daily Telegraph and Catherine Lampert. The exhibition features a curated section with works by Michael Andrews, Edward Burra, Callum Innes, Anish Kapoor, David Hockney, Sir Howard Hodgkin, Richard Long, Andy

Further more detailed information on the attractions listed can be found in Best Guides *Visitor Attractions* Guide under the classifications shown

Goldsworthy, Lubaina Himid, Bridget Riley.

Art Galleries

Abracadabra: International Contemporary Art

15/7/99
26/9/99
TATE GALLERY
Tel: 0171 887 8000

Presenting the work of sixteen international artists (paintings, drawings and sculpture along with text, video, sound and installation works) whose work reflects a new spirit in contemporary art. Often playful or surreal, their work deals in fantasy and transformation, taking ordinary things and making them extraordinary. Exciting, poetic, disturbing and extravagant, this new art aims to establish new lines of communication with its audience, and in many of the works, the element of humour it used to support a more serious message. A£5.00 Concessions£3.00

Art Galleries

Arts, Music, Film and Workshop

16/7/99
16/7/99
CROYDON CLOCKTOWER
Tel: 0181 253 1030

Weird and Wonderful, Street Theatre Festival, venue: North End. Walking the Witch, Music in the Gardens, venue: Queens Gardens. Banerjee Sisters, Arts Festival, venue: Clocktower. Windrush Film Festival, venue: Clocktower. Find Yourself Workshop venue: Clocktower

Arts & Entertainment

Arts, Street Theatre and Music

17/7/99
17/7/99
CROYDON CLOCKTOWER
Tel: 0181 253 1030

Circus, Street Theatre Festival, venue: North End. The Flying Chaucers, Music in the Gardens, venue: Queens Gardens. Short Stories, Arts Festival, venue: Clocktower

Arts & Entertainment

Shakespeare In The Park

17/7/99
17/7/99
OSTERLEY PARK
Tel: 0181 568 7714

Twelfth Night. Illyria's lively presentation of one of Shkespeare's best loved comedies. Enjoy this comic tale of romance, poetry and lust. Bring seating and a picnic to enjoy this open air performance. Commences 19.00, Gates open 18.00. Ticketsin advance: A£9.00 C£5.00 Family Ticket £25.00. All tickets on the gate £10.00

Historic Houses

Elizabeth I and the Spanish Armada

17/7/99
18/7/99
TILBURY FORT
Tel: 01375 858489

Performed by the Bills and Bows Group, a Tudor re-enactment. A£3.00 C£1.50 Concessions£2.30

Forts

The American West Exhibition

17/7/99
5/9/99
HALL PLACE
Tel: 01322 526574 X204

Paintings by Albert R. Tilburne, as well as sculptures and cowboy and Indian artefacts.

Historic Houses & Gardens

Arts, Music and Street Theatre

18/7/99
18/7/99
CROYDON CLOCKTOWER
Tel: 0181 253 1030

Family Fun, Street Theatre Festival, venue: North End. Fun in the Sun, Music in the Gardens, venue: Queens Gardens. Dead Match, Arts Festival, venue: Clocktower. Kingdom of the Birds, Arts Festival, venue: Stanley Halls

Arts & Entertainment

Arts, Film & Croydon Mela

19/7/99
19/7/99
CROYDON CLOCKTOWER
Tel: 0181 253 1030

Medici String Quartet, Arts Festival, venue: Clocktower. Best of Croydon 100, Film Festival, venue: Clocktower. Capital Nights, Arts Festival, venue: Warehouse. Croydon Mela, Mela, venue: Lloyd Park

Arts & Entertainment

Summer Jazz Festival

20/7/99
24/7/99
KEW GARDENS ROYAL BOTANIC GARDENS
Tel: 0181 940 1171

A summer celebration of a Century of popular music before the start of the new millennium. Artists are not confirmed until late Jan, call for details nearer the time

Gardens- Botanical

The Royal Tournament

20/7/99
2/8/99
HORSE GUARDS
Tel: 0891 505452

Taking place at Earls Court Exhibition Centre. The final performance will be the matinee of Mon 2 Aug, all details on 0171 799 2323

Historic Buildings

Much Ado About Nothing

21/7/99
21/7/99
CHISWICK HOUSE
Tel: 0181 995 0508

Shakespeare in the park. Theatre set-up perform in the afternoon. Normal admission prices apply

Historic Houses & Gardens

Society of Wildlife Artists Annual Exhibition

22/7/99
6/8/99
MALL GALLERIES
Tel: 0171 930 6844
An exhibition of work in a variety of media depicting wildlife subjects.
Art Galleries

Exhibition: Pottery in Fulham

22/7/99
26/9/99
MUSEUM OF FULHAM PALACE
Tel: 0171 736 3233
Pottery by Martin Brothers, Fulham Pottery and Des Morgan. Admission: £1.00 Concessions£0.50
Historic Houses & Gardens

The Soprano in Pink

24/7/99
25/7/99
CHISWICK HOUSE
Tel: 0181 995 0508
Delightful 17th and 18th century song and spinet music, with gossip and talks about Georgian fashions with Rhiannon Gayle. From 12.00. Normal admission price
Historic Houses & Gardens

The King's Court

25/7/99
CHAPTER HOUSE AND PYX CHAMBER OF WESTMINSTER ABBEY
25/7/99
Tel: 0171 222 5897
Meet members of Henry III's court. Find out about life in the 13th century from court to country, learn about ecclesiastical architecture, medieval faith, pilgrimages and shrines. From 12.00. Normal admission price
Abbeys

Young Archaeologists Day

25/7/99
25/7/99
CROFTON ROMAN VILLA
Tel: 01689 873826
Activities about the Roman Villa, especially for 6-11 year olds. Time: 10.00-13.00 & 14.00-17.00. Cost: £0.80/£0.40
Roman Villas

Exhibition: From the Cradle to the Grave

31/7/99
6/10/99
BROMLEY MUSEUM AND PRIORY GARDENS
Tel: 01689 873826
For further information please contact Dr Alan Tyler, Curator or Melanie Parker, Assistant Curator, at the Museum on 01689 873826
Museums

Poetry Readings

1/8/99
1/8/99
RANGER'S HOUSE
Tel: 0181 853 0035
17th-century poetry read by Poesia. A£2.50 C£1.30 Concessions£1.90
Historic Houses & Gardens

Autumn Concert Series

1/8/99
31/8/99
HORNIMAN MUSEUM AND GARDENS
Tel: 0181 699 1872
A lively mixture of music through the ages. All concerts are FREE
Museums

Summer Fun For Children

1/8/99
31/8/99
HORNIMAN MUSEUM AND GARDENS
Tel: 0181 699 1872
Children's activities and entertainment throughout the summer, prices vary, however, many activities are Free
Museums

Windsor Castle Guard

1/8/99
30/4/00
HORSE GUARDS
Tel: 0891 505452
Guard Mounting will take place at Windsor Castle at 11.00 on alternate days from Aug-April. There will be NO Guard Mounting in very wet weather or on certain Ceremonial Days.
Historic Buildings

The Queen's Guards

1/8/99
30/4/00
HORSE GUARDS
Tel: 0891 505452
Guard Mounting at Buckingham Palace will take place at 13.00 on alternate days from Aug-April. There will be NO Guard Mounting in very wet weather or on certain Ceremonial Days.
Historic Buildings

Art Now 19

3/8/99
10/10/99
TATE GALLERY
Tel: 0171 887 8000
Simon Callery. The Art Now programme is supported by the Patrons of New Art and Hereford Salon
Art Galleries

Anniversary of the Birthday of Queen Elizabeth, The Queen Mother

4/8/99
4/8/99
HORSE GUARDS
Tel: 0891 505452
41 Gun Royal Salute fired by The King's Troop Royal Horse Artillery in Hyde Park at 12.00 and 62 Gun Royal Salute fired the the Honourable Artillery Company at the Tower of London at 13.00 hours to mark the Anniversary of the Birthday of Queen Elizabeth, The Queen Mother, free public access
Historic Buildings

Irish Night

4/8/99
4/8/99
KEMPTON PARK RACECOURSE
Tel: 01932 782292
Racing with an Irish Theme. For further details including race times and ticket prices please contact venue direct
Racecourses

Further more detailed information on the attractions listed can be found in Best Guides *Visitor Attractions* Guide under the classifications shown

Children's Activities

5/8/99
26/8/99
MUSEUM OF FULHAM PALACE
Tel: 0171 736 3233
Every Thursday, 14.00-16.00. £2.00 per child.

Historic Houses & Gardens

Traditional Song

7/8/99
7/8/99
MARBLE HILL HOUSE
Tel: 0181 892 5115
The Dunns. A family of musicians performing delightful unaccompanied song. Normal admission prices apply

Historic Houses

Big Band Concert with Fireworks

7/8/99
7/8/99
OSTERLEY PARK
Tel: 0181 568 7714
The 1940's come alive again to the sounds of the John Watson Orchestra and special guests in this stunning tribute to Glenn Miller and the Big Swing Bands. Bring a rug/seating and a picnic, dance the night away. Dress: 1940s optional. Fabulous fireworks finale 19.30. Commences 19.30, Gates open 17.30. Tickets: A£13.50 C£6.00 Family £30.00

Historic Houses

Medieval Monastic Entertainers

7/8/99
8/8/99
CHAPTER HOUSE AND PYX CHAMBER OF WESTMINSTER ABBEY
Tel: 0171 222 5897
Try your hand at calligraphy or authentic period games as this popular duo take a light-hearted look at monastic customs, crafts and lifestyles. Learn about food preparation, herbs and spices in cooking and medicine, the mechanics of building and lifting and many other skills. From 12.00. A£2.50 C£1.30 Concessions£1.90. EH Members £Free

Abbeys

Traditional Song

8/8/99
8/8/99
CHISWICK HOUSE
Tel: 0181 995 0508
The Dunn family perform delightful unaccompanied song. From 12.00. Normal admission price

Historic Houses & Gardens

RHS Flower Show

10/8/99
11/8/99
RHS ROYAL HORTICULTURAL HALLS
Tel: 0171 834 4333
Open 1st day 11.00-19.00, 2nd day 10.00-17.00, 24 hour information line: 0171 649 1885

Exhibition Centres

18th Century Dance

15/8/99
15/8/99
RANGER'S HOUSE
Tel: 0181 853 0035
18th century revelries with costumed dancers. From 12.00. Normal admission price

Historic Houses & Gardens

Meet the Romans

16/8/99
17/8/99
CROFTON ROMAN VILLA
Tel: 01689 873826
Fun and activities with Secundus (a Roman Soldier) and his sister, Agrippina. Suitable for ages 6-12. Time: 10.00 & 14.00. Cost: £2.50 per child. Bookings on 01869 873826

Roman Villas

Evening Racing

18/8/99
18/8/99
KEMPTON PARK RACECOURSE
Tel: 01932 782292
A night at the races. For further details including race times and ticket prices please contact venue direct

Racecourses

Children's Open Air Theatre

21/8/99
21/8/99
OSTERLEY PARK
Tel: 0181 568 7714
Openwide present a new play from the favourite children's tale The Pied Piper. Bring a picnic and a rug/seating for this open air performance, commences 14.00. Tickets: All£10.00

Historic Houses

The Global City Festival

22/8/99
22/8/99
ALEXANDRA PALACE
Tel: 0181 365 2121
For further information please contact the organiser: Global Partnership Association 0171 924 0974

Historic Buildings

Sunday Racing

22/8/99
22/8/99
KEMPTON PARK RACECOURSE
Tel: 01932 782292
For further details including race times and ticket prices please contact venue direct

Racecourses

Summer Fair

26/8/99
19/9/99
BANKSIDE GALLERY
Tel: 0171 928 7521
Looking goods and feeling fine with a free admission, drop-in-and-bye-one show of works on paper

Art Galleries

The Military Vehicle Rally

28/8/99
30/8/99
TILBURY FORT
Tel: 01375 858489
The Essex Classic Military Vehicle Trust. Stalls, static displays, classic vehicles

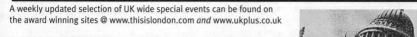

A weekly updated selection of UK wide special events can be found on the award winning sites @ www.thisislondon.com *and* www.ukplus.co.uk

from WWII to the present day. Driving displays and firing of the 25 pounder gun. Now the 3rd largest show of it's kind in Britain. From 12.00. A£5.00 C£2.50 Concessions£3.80. EH Members Free

Forts

Festival For Life
29/8/99 FESTIVAL FOR LIFE 1999
30/8/99 Tel: 01992 850357
Over 90 exhibitors offering a wide range of complimentary therapies, including shiatsu, aromatherapy, reiki and osteopathy, along with stalls selling books, pottery, jewellery and tarot cards. Demonstrations of T'ai Chi, belly dancing and Yoga, live music etc. Disabled access to main exhibition. No access to psychics or to attend lectures. £3.50 per day

Festivals

Past Pleasures
29/8/99 MARBLE HILL HOUSE
30/8/99 Tel: 0181 892 5115
Pleasures of the 18th-century. Normal admission prices apply

Historic Houses

The Soprano in Pink
29/8/99 RANGER'S HOUSE
30/8/99 Tel: 0181 853 0035
Delightful 17th and 18th century song and spinet music, with gossip and talks about Georgian fashions with Rhiannon Gayle. From 12.00. Normal admission price

Historic Houses & Gardens

Wembley Antiques and Collectors Antiques Fair
30/8/99 WEMBLEY CONFERENCE AND EXHIBITION CENTRE
30/8/99 Tel: 0181 902 8833
Antiques fair open to the trade and the public displaying antiques, collectibles plus an area specifically for antique furniture. Hall 3. Admission £2.75 on the door

Exhibition Centres

The Picture Postcard Show 1999
1/9/99 RHS ROYAL HORTICULTURAL HALLS
4/9/99 Tel: 0171 834 4333
An annual consumer fair for postcard collectors worldwide. Call for further details

Exhibition Centres

Opening Of Shakespeare's Globe Exhibition

Shakespeare's Globe
1/9/99 SHAKESPEARE'S GLOBE
30/9/99 Tel: 0171 902 1500
Exact date to be confirmed. New ground-breaking exhibition opens beneath the Globe Theatre.

Historic Buildings

Prints and Drawings Exhibitions
1/9/99 BRITISH MUSEUM
1/12/99 Tel: 0171 636 1555
Landscape drawings by Van Dyck and his Contemporaries, catalogue avialable, and Gifts from the National Art Collections Funds to the Department of Prints and Drawings, both in room 90, dates are provisional please check before visiting

Museums

Mary Beale
1/9/99 GEFFRYE MUSEUM
1/1/00 Tel: 0171 739 9893
An exhibition exploring the work of 17th century artist Mary Beale, call for further details

Museum- Interiors

Mind Body Spirit Festival
2/9/99 ALEXANDRA PALACE
5/9/99 Tel: 0181 365 2121
For further information please contact the organiser: New Life Promotions Limited 0171 938 3788

Historic Buildings

Toys for the Boys '99
3/9/99 WEMBLEY CONFERENCE AND EXHIBITION CENTRE
5/9/99 Tel: 0181 902 8833
A lifestyle event for males aged between 18-35 providing a showcase for the connecting indutries of lad culture. Exhibitors will include the following industries: travel, computer, music, Wheels for the Boys, gadgets, and Sport for the Boys, amongst others. Hall 1

Exhibition Centres

1760s Living History
5/9/99 CHISWICK HOUSE
5/9/99 Tel: 0181 995 0508
18th-century living history told by Hoi Polloi. Normal admission prices apply

Historic Houses & Gardens

Sirenia Stakes
8/9/99 KEMPTON PARK RACECOURSE
8/9/99 Tel: 01932 782292
For further details including race times and ticket prices please contact venue direct

Racecourses

Second World War Special Events

Further more detailed information on the attractions listed can be found in Best Guides *Visitor Attractions* Guide under the classifications shown

Weekend
11/9/99 NATIONAL ARMY MUSEUM
12/9/99 Tel: 0171 730 0717
The popular mix of re-enactment, talks and film continues with a look at the Second World War
Museum- Military

Armed Forces Weekend
11/9/99 ROYAL AIR FORCE MUSEUM
12/9/99 Tel: 0181 205 2266
Enjoy a military vehicle rally and meet some of the men and women of today's regular and reserve armed forces. Assault courses to try, abseil walls to climb and lots to see and do
Museum- Aviation

Gardening Exhibition
11/9/99 HALL PLACE
10/10/99 Tel: 01322 526574 x204
An exhibition to complement the Bexley Garden Festival on 4/5 September.
Historic Houses & Gardens

Craft Show - Cultural Connections
11/9/99 ORLEANS HOUSE GALLERY
31/10/99 Tel: 0181 892 0221
Incorporating a major education project, the project displays responses to the lives of Lord Leighton and Sir Richard Burton through the work of three contemporary artists
Art Galleries

Firing Day
12/9/99 TILBURY FORT
12/9/99 Tel: 01375 858489
The Garrison. Normal admission prices apply.
Forts

RHS Great Autumn Show
14/9/99 RHS ROYAL HORTICULTURAL HALLS
15/9/99 Tel: 0171 834 4333
Open 1st day 10.00-19.00, 2nd day 10.00-17.00, 24 hour information line: 0171 649 1885
Exhibition Centres

The National Self Build Homes Show
16/9/99 ALEXANDRA PALACE
19/9/99 Tel: 0181 365 2121
For further information please contact the organiser: Inside Communications 0171 837 8727
Historic Buildings

Anthony Van Dyck
16/9/99 ROYAL ACADEMY OF ARTS
16/12/99 Tel: 0171 300 8000
1999 is the four hundredth anniversary of the birth of Anthony Van Dyck. The Royal Academy and the City of Antwerp are organising the largest ever retrospective of the artist's work. Comprising more than 80 works from Van Dyck's entire career. Key works from all over the world and from Britain's most prestigious collections will be brought together.
Art Galleries

Live Crafts Show
17/9/99 OSTERLEY PARK
19/9/99 Tel: 0181 568 7714
Up to 150 carefully selected craft makers and artists from all over Britain offer original contemporary and traditional crafts. Demonstrations include blacksmith, bee keeping, raku firing and more. Live music and children's entertainment. All NT members free admission of Friday only. Pay at the gate. Commences 10.00-17.00. Tickets: A£3.50 C£1.00 Family Ticket £8.00
Historic Houses

Erith Theatre Group's 50th Anniversary Exhibition
18/9/99 HALL PLACE
3/10/99 Tel: 01322 526574 x204
Posters, set models, and memorabilia from the past 50 years of the Erith Theatre Group.
Historic Houses & Gardens

Spelthorne Stakes
20/9/99 KEMPTON PARK RACECOURSE
20/9/99 Tel: 01932 782292
For further details including race times and ticket prices please contact venue direct
Racecourses

Van Dyck at The Wallace Collection
23/9/99 THE WALLACE COLLECTION
15/12/99 Tel: 0171 935 0687
To celebrate the 400th Anniversary of the artists birth, there will be a special display of Van Dycks paintings in the collection
Art Galleries

Sir John Soane RA
25/9/99 ROYAL ACADEMY OF ARTS
12/12/99 Tel: 0171 300 8000
120 drawings and up to 40 models will demonstrate Soane's distinctive handling of space and style. Projects included in the exhibition will be the Bank of England, Lincoln's Inn Fields and Chelsea Barracks. Organised by the Royal Academy of Arts and Sir John Soane's Museum, London, the exhibition will tour venues in America and Canada.

Held in the Weston Rooms and Galleries 1 & 2.

Art Galleries

Alexandra Palace Antique & Collectors Fair

26/9/99 ALEXANDRA PALACE
26/9/99 Tel: 0181 365 2121
For further information please contact the organiser: Pig & Whistle Promotions 0181 883 7061

Historic Buildings

Joseph Beuys:

30/9/99 BARBICAN ART GALLERY
12/12/99 Tel: 0171 588 9023 24hr info
Multiples. An exhibition of multiples by one of the most important figures of 20th century art

Art Galleries

Royal Watercolour Society Autumn Exhibition

1/10/99 BANKSIDE GALLERY
31/10/99 Tel: 0171 928 7521
Featured artist: John Newbury. Most of his paintings are complete in an hour and a half! and have a quality with a contemporary perspective.

Art Galleries

Reserve Collection Store

1/10/99 LONDON TRANSPORT MUSEUM
31/10/99 Tel: 0171 836 8557/565 7299
NEW, NEW opening this month the Depot - the museums's new reserve collection store, call for details

Museum- Transport

Burmese Lacquer

1/10/99 BRITISH MUSEUM
15/12/99 Tel: 0171 636 1555
In rooms 92-94, catalogue available, dates are provisional please check before visiting

Museums

Design Process

1/10/99 DESIGN MUSEUM
1/2/00 Tel: 0171 403 6933
Dates to be confirmed. Have you ever wondered how Concorde, the Titanic or even a pair of jeans made it off the drawing board? Using 100 designs to investigate the working methods of designers - from brief to concepts, working drawings and models to completion, this exciting exhibition goes behind the scenes to reveal how the great, and the not-so-great designs of the twentieth century were conceived

Museums

Portrait of a Century

NATIONAL PORTRAIT GALLERY

1/10/99 Tel: 0171 306 0055
1/2/00 This exhibition will celebrate the century through portraits of significant social, cultural, political and celebrity figures. Provisional dates

Art Galleries

Israel Zangwill and the Wanderers of Kilburn

1/10/99 THE JEWISH MUSEUM
1/2/00 Tel: 0171 284 1997
Exhibition on the distinguished writer and activist known as 'the Jewish Dickens' and other prominent figures

Museum- Religious

RHS Flower Show

5/10/99 RHS ROYAL HORTICULTURAL HALLS
6/10/99 Tel: 0171 834 4333
Open 1st day 11.00-19.00, 2nd day 10.00-17.00, 24 hour information line: 0171 649 1885

Exhibition Centres

John Hoyland RA

6/10/99 ROYAL ACADEMY OF ARTS
31/10/99 Tel: 0171 300 8000
John Hoyland RA is one of Britain's most distinctive contemporary artists. During the early 1960's he was associated with Situation, a group of British artists who concentrated on the fundamental elements of painting; shape, form colour and scale. His non- figurative, large scale canvases have developed over the following two decades with a growing emphasis on the richness of the surface and sensuous use of colour and application of paint. This exhibition of over 20 paintings will provide a concise survey of Hoyland's vision and development. Held in the Sackler Wing.

Art Galleries

Exhibition: What is a Museum?

8/10/99 BROMLEY MUSEUM AND PRIORY GARDENS
20/10/99 Tel: 01689 873826
For further information please contact Dr Alan Tyler, Curator or Melanie Parker, Assistant Curator, at the Museum on 01689 873826

Museums

The Knitting & Stitching Show

14/10/99 ALEXANDRA PALACE
17/10/99 Tel: 0181 365 2121
For further information please contact the organiser: Creative Exhibitions 0181 690 8888

Historic Buildings

A Grand Design: The Art of the Victoria

& Albert Museum

14/10/99 VICTORIA AND ALBERT MUSEUM
16/1/00 Tel: 0171 938 8441

A fascinating exhibition, celebrating the painting, sculpture, design, fashion and decorative arts spanning 2000 years

Museum- Art

Charisma Gold Cup

16/10/99 KEMPTON PARK RACECOURSE
16/10/99 Tel: 01932 782292

For further details including race times and ticket prices please contact venue direct

Racecourses

The London Wedding Fair

16/10/99 RHS ROYAL HORTICULTURAL HALLS
17/10/99 Tel: 0171 834 4333

An simply wonderful consumer fair, ideal for all those planning to marry in the new Millennium. Just about everything you'd want all under one roof. Call for further details

Exhibition Centres

Shell Poster & Valentine Exhibition

16/10/99 HALL PLACE
6/11/99 Tel: 01322 526574 x204

Shell Posters from the Twenties and Thirties and Shell Valentines form the Shell Art Collection.

Historic Houses & Gardens

Firing Day

17/10/99 TILBURY FORT
17/10/99 Tel: 01375 858489

The Garrison. Normal admission prices apply.

Forts

Exhibition: Orpington Sketch Club

22/10/99 BROMLEY MUSEUM AND PRIORY GARDENS
31/10/99 Tel: 01689 873826

Contact Brian Wren on 0181 658 7390 for further information

Museums

Faces of the Century

22/10/99 NATIONAL PORTRAIT GALLERY
30/1/00 Tel: 0171 306 0055

Major millennium exhibition of images from the 20th century selected by a distinguished panel

Art Galleries

Children's Workshops

27/10/99 MUSEUM OF FULHAM PALACE
29/10/99 Tel: 0171 736 3233

Half term activities for children to keep them busy. Time: 14.00-16.00. Cost: £2.00 per child

Historic Houses & Gardens

London International Stamp and Cover

Fair

28/10/99 RHS ROYAL HORTICULTURAL HALLS
31/10/99 Tel: 0171 834 4333

A consumer show with a wide range of dealers selling stamps and postal history. Call for further details

Exhibition Centres

Medieval Monastic Life

30/10/99 CHAPTER HOUSE AND PYX CHAMBER OF
31/10/99 WESTMINSTER ABBEY

Tel: 0171 222 5897

Try your hand at calligraphy or authentic period games as this popular duo take a light-hearted look at monastic customs, crafts and lifestyles. Learn about food preparation, herbs and spices in cooking and medicine, the mechanics of building and lifting and many other skills. From 12.00. A£2.50 C£1.30 Concessions£1.90. EH Members £Free

Abbeys

Halloween - Beaux Stratagems

30/10/99 MARBLE HILL HOUSE
31/10/99 Tel: 0181 892 5115

Make a Hallowe'en mask and join Lady Suffolk's footman for a tour of the Marble Hill House. Learn about Hallowe'en traditions and listen to ghostly tales! From 12.00. Normal admission price

Historic Houses

London Bach Festival

30/10/99 LONDON BACH FESTIVAL 1999
13/11/99 Tel: 01883 717372

The London Bach Festival was founded in 1990 to develop, extend and foster the purpose of the London Bach Society. Programme available from 1 September 1999.

Festivals

RHS Flower Show

2/11/99 RHS ROYAL HORTICULTURAL HALLS
3/11/99 Tel: 0171 834 4333

Open 1st day 11.00-19.00, 2nd day 10.00-17.00, 24 hour information line: 0171 649 1885

Exhibition Centres

Gunpowder Plot Chase

3/11/99 KEMPTON PARK RACECOURSE
3/11/99 Tel: 01932 782292

For further details including race times and ticket prices please contact venue direct

Racecourses

Putting the House to Bed

4/11/99	**OSTERLEY PARK**
5/11/99	Tel: 0181 568 7714

Discover what goes on behind the scenes in winter at Osterley Park House as staff put the house to 'bed'. Commences 10.00-12.30. Tickets: A£12.00 C£6.00, includes tea and biscuits

Historic Houses

The Art of Bloomsbury

4/11/99	TATE GALLERY
30/1/00	Tel: 0171 887 8000

Roger Fry (1866-1934), Vanessa Bell (1879-1961) and Duncan Grant (1885-1978). The lives of the various artists, writers and intellectuals associated with Bloomsbury have been the subject of almost obsessive biographical attention in recent decades, but there has never been a comprehensive exhibition in Britain of Bloomsbury art. This celebratory new show, curated by Richard Shone, seeks to redress the balance, and will focus on the paintings of the Bloomsbury artists, together with their contribution to the Omega Workshops (1913-19), the firm they established for design and interior decoration. A£6.00 Concessions£4.00

Art Galleries

20th Century History - 2000 Aspirations:

6/11/99	ORLEANS HOUSE GALLERY
8/1/00	Tel: 0181 892 0221

Artefacts of Rememberance from the 20th Century. Using everyday objects and the tales that relate to them, the exhibiton will look at people's personal histories of this century and their aspirations for the next

Art Galleries

Cancer Relief Macmillan Fund Christmas Market

9/11/99	RHS ROYAL HORTICULTURAL HALLS
9/11/99	Tel: 0171 834 4333

A delightful consumer show with plenty of ideas for Christmas presents. To raise money for cancer relief, call for further details

Exhibition Centres

Eiilnee Hogan RWS

10/11/99	BANKSIDE GALLERY
28/11/98	Tel: 0171 928 7521

Emeritus Professor of The London Institute, curator and selector of Watercolour 21, ileen Hogan shows the full range of her work on a one person exhibition. Noted for the use of structure, shadow and light in her watercolours, Eileen Hogan also has her own imprint in the Burntwood Press.

Art Galleries

Exhibition: National Inventory of War Memorials

10/11/99	BROMLEY MUSEUM AND PRIORY GARDENS
11/12/99	Tel: 01689 873826

A touring display by the Imperial War Museum. For further information please contact Dr Alan Tyler, Curator or Melanie Parker, Assistant Curator, at the Museum on 01689 873826

Museums

Healing Arts Festival

11/11/99	RHS ROYAL HORTICULTURAL HALLS
14/11/99	Tel: 0171 834 4333

An alternative medicine and healing consumer festival with demonstrations, presentation and speakers. Call for further details

Exhibition Centres

Sight Savers International Exhibition

13/11/99	HALL PLACE
11/12/99	Tel: 01322 526574 x204

Tom Stoddart's black and white photographs taken in India for the largest UK charity.

Historic Houses & Gardens

Limber Hill Chase

17/11/99	KEMPTON PARK RACECOURSE
17/11/99	Tel: 01932 782292

For further details including race times and ticket prices please contact venue direct

Racecourses

Homes and Gardens Grand Christmas Sale

18/11/99	RHS ROYAL HORTICULTURAL HALLS
20/11/99	Tel: 0171 834 4333

A consumer show with many unusual and exciting gifts for sale, ideal for Christmas, call for further details

Exhibition Centres

Boer War Special Events Weekend

20/11/99	NATIONAL ARMY MUSEUM
21/11/99	Tel: 0171 730 0717

One hundred years after the start of the Boer War this special events weekend runs in conjunction with a new Exhibition on the British Army in South Africa

Museum- Military

Antique & Collectors Fair

Further more detailed information on the attractions listed can be found in Best Guides *Visitor Attractions* Guide under the classifications shown

21/11/99	ALEXANDRA PALACE
21/11/99	Tel: 0181 365 2121

For further information please contact the organiser: Pig & Whistle Promotions 0181 883 7061

Historic Buildings

"Across the Black Waters" - Indian soldiers and the First World War

23/11/99	NATIONAL ARMY MUSEUM
27/11/99	Tel: 0171 730 0717

Adapted from Mulk Raj Anand's novel, this play depicts the experiences of an Indian soldier in the trenches of the Western Front. More than 1 million Indian soldiers fought in the First World War and over 62,000 of them died. The play also includes material drawn from letters sent home by Indian servicemen and folk music from both the Punjab and England. Performances at 11.00am and 13.30, Monday 23 to Friday 27 November 1998. Tickets priced at £2.00, available from the National Army Museum Education Department. Please telephone 0171 730 0717 ext 2228 for reservations.

Museum- Military

Dolls House Fair and Teddy Bear Fair 'The Event of '99'

27/11/99	ALEXANDRA PALACE
28/11/99	Tel: 0181 365 2121

For further information please contact the organiser: EMF Publishing 01903 244900

Historic Buildings

Christmas Craft Fair

27/11/99	SUTTON HOUSE
28/11/99	Tel: 0181 986 2264

On 40 stalls throughout Sutton House, local craftspeople will display and sell a wide variety and range of work

Historic Houses

Japanese Clocks, Zodiac and Calendar Prints

1/12/99	BRITISH MUSEUM
1/3/00	Tel: 0171 636 1555

In rooms 92-94, catalogue details tbc, dates are provisional please check before visiting

Museums

Prints and Drawings Exhibitions

1/12/99	BRITISH MUSEUM
1/4/00	Tel: 0171 636 1555

The Apocalypse and the Western Pictorial Tradition in room 90, catalogue available, dates are provisional please check before visiting

Museums

Divine Rule

1/12/99	BRITISH MUSEUM
1/5/00	Tel: 0171 636 1555

In room 29, admission charged, catalogue available, dates are provisional please check before visiting

Museums

Christmas Craft Fair & The Festive Table

3/12/99	ALEXANDRA PALACE
5/12/99	Tel: 0181 365 2121

For further information please contact the organiser: Marathon Event Management Limited 01273 833884

Historic Buildings

International Festival of Chocolate

3/12/99	RHS ROYAL HORTICULTURAL HALLS
5/12/99	Tel: 0171 834 4333

This choc-lovers' paradise will include a non-stop programme of mouthwatering tastings and recipe demos, a chocolate-tasting tunnel, and the opportunity to sample and buy chocolate products from around the world. Ticket price: (1998 prices for guidance only) £7.50 on the day, £5.00 in advance. Call the ticket hotline on 01634 296005 for more information

Exhibition Centres

Light Fantastic

4/12/99	BANKSIDE GALLERY
30/1/00	Tel: 0171 928 7521

The mid-winter festival and the dawn of the new millennium celebtraed in prints by Members of the RWS and the RSofPP. Artists are always concerned with the use of light in their pictures, at this dark time of the year we can offer you illumination from works that range from glow to dazzle.

Art Galleries

International Model Show and Model Engineering Exhibition

8/12/99	ALEXANDRA PALACE
12/12/99	Tel: 0181 365 2121

For further information please contact the organiser: Nexus Special Interests Limited 01442 266551

Historic Buildings

RHS Christmas Show

14/12/99	RHS ROYAL HORTICULTURAL HALLS
15/12/99	Tel: 0171 834 4333

Open 1st day 11.00-19.00, 2nd day 10.00-17.00, 24 hour information line: 0171 649 1885

Exhibition Centres

A weekly updated selection of UK wide special events can be found on the award winning sites @ www.thisislondon.com *and* www.ukplus.co.uk

Exhibition: Special Millennium Exhibition

15/12/99 BROMLEY MUSEUM AND PRIORY GARDENS
17/3/00 Tel: 01689 873826
For further information please contact Dr Alan Tyler, Curator or Melanie Parker, Assistant Curator, at the Museum on 01689 873826

Museums

A Chronical of the Century Exhibition

18/12/99 HALL PLACE
15/1/00 Tel: 01322 526574 x204
A collection of photographs covering events in Bexley during the last century.

Historic Houses & Gardens

Peter Pan Swimming Race

25/12/99 HYDE PARK
25/12/99 Tel:
A 100-yard swimming race for the Peter Pan Cup always held on Christmas Day. Race meets 08.30 for 09.00 start. Admission free

Parks

Bank Holiday Racing

27/12/99 KEMPTON PARK RACECOURSE
28/12/99 Tel: 01932 782292
Monday is the King George VI Chase. Tuesday is the Christmas Hurdle. For further details including race times and ticket prices please contact race venue direct

Racecourses

Millennium Firework Display

31/12/99 BATTERSEA PARK CHILDREN'S ZOO
31/12/99 Tel: 0181 871 7540
Provisional date. Firework display to welcome in the Millennium. A family extravaganza featuring street theatre, children's entertainment and music. Held in Battersea Park, commences 20.00-00.30. For further details call 0181 871 7532

Zoos

Millennium Countdown: New Year's Eve Celebrations

31/12/99 ROYAL OBSERVATORY GREENWICH
31/12/99 Tel: 0181 858 4422
A rich mixture of live musical performance, pageant and spectacular displays, admission by tickets only - on sale Summer 1999

Observatories

The Dome Opens

31/12/99 THE DOME
31/12/00 Tel: 0870 603 2000 info line
Described as "The biggest, most thrilling, most entertaining, most thought-provoking experience anywhere

on the planet in the year 2000." It will be the world's largest millennial celebration throughout the year 2000, designed to entertain, educate and inspire the nation. The opening on 31/12/99, performed by the Queen, is by invitation only. The Dome will be open to the public from 1/1/2000.

Millennium Project

London Parade

1/1/00 PARLIAMENT SQUARE
1/1/00 Tel:
Parliament Square, SW1 to Berkeley Square W1. London American-style extravaganza of 7000 musicians, dancers, acrobats, cheerleaders, clowns and floats will twirl, march and drum their way to Berkeley Square via Whitehall, Trafalgar Square, Lower Regent Street and Piccadilly. The Lord Mayor of Westminster will lead the procession. Starts at 12.00 arriving at Berkeley Square at 15.00. Admission free. Tube: Westminster

Scenic

Exhibition: Orpington Photographic Society

20/3/00 BROMLEY MUSEUM AND PRIORY GARDENS
25/3/00 Tel: 01689 873826
Contact Miss Pettigrew on 01689 857313 for further information

Museums

The Thames Festival

27/5/00 GREENWICH TOURIST INFORMATION CENTRE
30/5/00 Tel: 0181 858 6376
This is a free programme of arts, sports and river -themed events on the river and its banks, between Westminster Bridge and Southwark Cathedral. Events will include fireworks, theatrical shows, sculpture, art exhibitions, riverside entertainment, children's treasure hunt and a River Pageant and Torch-lit procession.

Tourist Information Centres

Prints and Drawings Exhibitions

1/6/00 BRITISH MUSEUM
1/9/00 Tel: 0171 636 1555
Landmarks in Print Collecting: Connoisseurs and Donors at the British Museum, catalogue should be available AND A 'Polite' Recreation: Amateurs and Drawing Masters in British Art 1680-1880, catalogue details tbc, dates are provisional please call before making a special visit

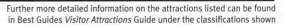

Further more detailed information on the attractions listed can be found in Best Guides *Visitor Attractions* Guide under the classifications shown

	Museums
	Buckminster Fuller
1/6/00	**DESIGN MUSEUM**
1/10/00	Tel: 0171 403 6933
	Dates to be confirmed. The pioneering American architect and designer of cars, domes and homes for sustainable living
	Museums
	Prints and Drawings Exhibitions
1/10/00	**BRITISH MUSEUM**
1/12/00	Tel: 0171 636 1555
	Emilian Drawings, catalogue avialable, AND selection from the Permanent Collection, catalogue details tbc, in room 90, dates are provisional please call before making a special visit
	Museums
	Luis Barragan
1/10/00	**DESIGN MUSEUM**
1/2/01	Tel: 0171 403 6933
	Dates to be confirmed. The celebrated architect whose work has stretched far beyond his native Mexico. This will be the first British exhibition of his work
	Museums
	Inaugural Exhibition
1/11/00	**BRITISH MUSEUM**
30/11/00	Tel: 0171 636 1555
	In the Great Court Gallery, dates are provisional please call before making a special visit
	Museums
	Prints and Drawings Exhibition
1/12/00	**BRITISH MUSEUM**
1/3/01	Tel: 0171 636 1555
	Rembrandt the Printmaker in room 90, catalogue available, dates are provisional please call before making a special visit
	Museums
	Prints and Drawings Exhibition
1/6/01	**BRITISH MUSEUM**
1/9/01	Tel: 0171 636 1555
	Recent Acquisitions 1996-2001, in room 90, catalogue tbc, dates are provisional please call before making a special visit
	Museums
	Exhibition for Japan Festival
1/9/01	**BRITISH MUSEUM**
1/12/01	Tel: 0171 636 1555
	In rooms 92-94, full details not yet available, dates are provisional please call before making a special visit
	Museums
	Prints and Drawings Exhibition

1/10/01	**BRITISH MUSEUM**
1/11/01	Tel: 0171 636 1555
	Italian 16th century Printmaking, catalogue available, AND The Prints of S W Hayter, both in room 90, dates are provisional please call before making a special visit
	Museums

North West England

Including:
Lancashire
Greater Manchester
Cheshire
Merseyside

Spring at the Walled Garden
6/3/99
6/3/99
NORTON PRIORY MUSEUM AND GARDENS
Tel: 01928 569895
An opportunity to find out about the garden from our Head Gardener from 14:30-15:30.
Gardens

The UK's Premier Travel Show
6/3/99
7/3/99
G-MEX CENTRE
Tel: 0161 834 2700
Over 200 specialist travel exhibitors. Over 130 FREE travel talks. Excellent value flights. Travel writing and photography workshops. Specialist equipment and health advice. Job opportunities abroad. Cyber Café. Women & Travel Seminar. One-stop travel vaccination clinic. Climbing wall and Hang Gliding simulator. Passport competition. Entry from £5.00
Exhibition Centres

Cheshire County Antiques Fair
12/3/99
14/3/99
ARLEY HALL AND GARDENS
Tel: 01565 777353
A quality antique fair, datelined 1890 with quality additions to 1920. Times: Fri 12.00-18.00, Sat & Sun 11.00-17.00. Admission charged
Historic Houses & Gardens

Mothering Sunday Carvery and Cruise
14/3/99
14/3/99
MERSEY FERRIES LTD
Tel: 0151 630 1030
Let your mum put her feet up for a change! Bring her along to Woodside Restaurant for a well-deserved carvery meal to celebrate her special day. Meals are served between 15.30-18.30 with the cruises operating between 10.00-18.00. Tickets A£8.50 C£4.50, advanced booking is necessary call 0151 330 1456
Boat Trips

Mother's Day Discount
14/3/99
14/3/99
SOUTHPORT ZOO AND CONSERVATION TRUST
Tel: 01704 538102
Entrance to the Zoo FREE to mums accompanied by a child age 2-13years
Zoos- Conservation

Artistic Alphabets
20/3/99
20/3/99
GALLERY OF COSTUME
Tel: 0161 224 5217
Explore the decorative potential of lettering in embroidery in this workshop with Sylvia Wood. Tickets £14/£10 booking essential on 0161 224 5217
Museum- Costume

Spring Shopping Weekend

20/3/99
21/3/99
NORTON PRIORY MUSEUM AND GARDENS
Tel: 01928 569895
With new lines and special seasonal offers.
Gardens

Picasso and Printmaking in Paris
20/3/99
8/5/99
WARRINGTON MUSEUM AND ART GALLERY
Tel: 01925 442392/442398
A touring exhibition from the Hayward Gallery with prints from Picasson, Matisse, Braque and Miro
Museums

Bird Trail
27/3/99
27/3/99
NORTON PRIORY MUSEUM AND GARDENS
Tel: 01928 569895
A family activity at the Museum from 14:00-16:00.
Gardens

Signs and Sounds for Spring
27/3/99
11/4/99
NORTON PRIORY MUSEUM AND GARDENS
Tel: 01928 569895
A quiz for Easter.
Gardens

Easter Eggsplorers
27/3/99
11/4/99
WWT MARTIN MERE
Tel: 01704 895181
Easter egg hunt and egg activities, call for times
Waterfowl Parks

John Park
27/3/99
26/6/99
HARRIS MUSEUM AND ART GALLERY
Tel: 01772 258248
Landscape painting by John Park and fellow St. Ives artists
Art Galleries

Violent Incident
27/3/99
1/3/00
TATE GALLERY LIVERPOOL
Tel: 0151 709 3223/709 0507
Throughout the modern period, avant-garde artists have used drastic measures to break with tradition and an element of violence has become a liberating artistic tool. The display includes the 'action painters' in America and Europe who left traces of the act of painting in their work: figurative artists who have used the human body as a site for distortion and mutilation; and video art of the 1980s in which violent events and performances are recorded. Francis Bacon, Rebecca Horn, Roy Lichtenstein, Bruce Nauman, Cornelia Parker and Antoni Tapiès are some of the artists included in this display.
Art Galleries

The Touchy Feely Squashy Show

30/3/99	**LIVERPOOL MUSEUM**
30/6/99	Tel: 0151 478 4399

For details on this exhibition, please call the venue direct.

Museums

Reptile Encounter Days

1/4/99	**SOUTHPORT ZOO AND CONSERVATION TRUST**
30/9/99	Tel: 01704 538102

All you ever wanted to know about reptiles and the opportunity to handle a live snake - meet in our Reptile House, call for dates and times so you don't miss out

Zoos- Conservation

Meet the Keeper Days

1/4/99	**SOUTHPORT ZOO AND CONSERVATION TRUST**
30/9/99	Tel: 01704 538102

Anytime - anywhere - meet one of our animal keepers - find out more about their work

Zoos- Conservation

Clash of the Tuscans (BRSCC)

2/4/99	**OULTON PARK**
2/4/99	Tel: 01829 760301

TVR Tuscans, Irish Puntos, Caterham Graduates, Formula Ford 1600s, Classic 1600s. Full Circuit, Grade-C. On the Gate: £10.00-£28.00. In Advance: Non £8.00-£25.00, Club £7.00-£22.00. Two Day Pass: Non £11.00-£30.00, Club £10.00-£27.00. Three Day Pass: Non £32.00, Club £29.00, Qualifying: £5.00-£14.00. C£Free. Programme £Free-£5.00. Seating (BH): £Free-£8.00. Group Tickets: Non £90.00-£95.00, Club £80.00-£85.00. Season Ticket Inc. of Club Membership: £160.00. You can buy your tickets for any of the 1999 events in advance any time up to 4 days before an event and make a saving, Tel: 0870 60 60 611

Motor Racing Circuit

Medieval Re-Enactments

2/4/99	**PECKFORTON CASTLE**
12/9/99	Tel: 01829 260930

Weather permitting. Friday: 2 Apr; Every Sunday from 4 Apr-12 Sept & Bank Hol Mondays. Two shows daily at 13.30 & 15.30. Normal admission charges apply.

Castles

Easter Saturday Springtime Festival Dance 1999

3/4/99	**EASTER SATURDAY SPRINGTIME FESTIVAL**

DANCE 1999

3/4/99	Tel: 01706 878778

Every Easter Saturday, no matter what the weather, the Britannia Coconutters accompanied by members of Stacksteads Brass Band dance their way through the streets following a tradition that takes them from boundary to boundary of the town of Bacup. Starting at 09.00 at the Travellers Rest Public House on the A671 Rochdale to Bacup road, culminating in an exhibition of their dances in the town centre amongst throngs of people that have gathered creating a festive atmosphere at approx. 13.00-14.00. It is also tradition they dance inside every public house en-route and the landlord reciprocates with a free beverage for the team to keep them going, finally ending at 18.00-19.00 with a dance at the old folks bungalows at the boundary on the A681 Bacup to Rawtenstall road. Admission Free

Festivals

The National Collection of Quinces

3/4/99	**NORTON PRIORY MUSEUM AND GARDENS**
3/4/99	Tel: 01928 569895

Find out from our Head Gardener about this special fruit collection at the Walled Garden at 14:30.

Gardens

Easter Flower Festival

3/4/99	**TATTON PARK**
5/4/99	Tel: 01625 534400

Circus, family show, craft hall, fairground rides, pottery fun, Victorian household recreation, hog bending contest, pancake race and lots more. 10.30-16.30. A£4.50 C£2.50 (guide only based on 1998 prices). Tickets available from 01625 534400 or at the gate

Country Parks

Easter Bunny Cruises

4/4/99	**MERSEY FERRIES LTD**
4/4/99	Tel: 0151 630 1030

All day long the Easter Bunny will be hiding clues on board the boat, find them and win an Easter Egg

Boat Trips

Hares and Eggs!

5/4/99	**NORTON PRIORY MUSEUM AND GARDENS**
5/4/99	Tel: 01928 569895

Games and quizzes for the family from 12.00-16.00. Free admission for children with entries for the decorated egg competition.

Gardens

Further more detailed information on the attractions listed can be found in Best Guides *Visitor Attractions* Guide under the classifications shown

Clubmans Motorcycles (CHESHIRE ACU)
OULTON PARK
5/4/99
5/4/99
Tel: 01829 760301
All classes of national solo motorcycles and sidecars. Full Circuit, Grade-D. On the Gate: £10.00-£28.00. In Advance: Non £8.00-£25.00, Club £7.00-£22.00. Two Day Pass: Non £11.00-£30.00, Club £10.00-£27.00. Three Day Pass: Non £32.00, Club £29.00. Qualifying: £5.00-£14.00. C£Free. Programme £Free-£5.00. Seating (BH): £Free-£8.00. Group Tickets: Non £90.00-£95.00, Club £80.00-£85.00. Season Ticket Inc. of Club Membership: £160.00. You can buy your tickets for any of the 1999 events in advance any time up to 4 days before an event and make a saving, Tel: 0870 60 60 611

Motor Racing Circuit

The Martell Grand National Festival
AINTREE RACECOURSE
8/4/99
10/4/99
Tel: 0151 523 2600
The world famous Grand National Festival is the host to the country's best national hunt horses - an event no other sporting occasion can match. Cost: from £6.00

Racecourses

Rare and Unusual Plant Fair
ARLEY HALL AND GARDENS
11/4/99
11/4/99
Tel: 01565 777353
A one day specialist event bringing together over 30 specialist nurseries from across the country, exhibiting and selling a wide range of garden plants. Time: 10.00-16.00. Admission: £2.50

Historic Houses & Gardens

In the Ice House
NORTON PRIORY MUSEUM AND GARDENS
17/4/99
17/4/99
Tel: 01928 569895
A family activity led by our Ranger at the Walled Garden at 14:30.

Gardens

Historic Touring Cars (BARC)
OULTON PARK
17/4/99
17/4/99
Tel: 01829 760301
Classic Saloon & Historic Touring Car, National 250cc Kart, Champion of Oulton - FFord 1600, Sport & Saloon Car, Post Historic Touring Car, Group 1 Touring Car, Modified Production Saloon. Island Circuit, Grade-D. On the Gate: £10.00-£28.00. In Advance: Non £8.00-£25.00, Club £7.00-£22.00. Two Day Pass: Non £11.00-£30.00, Club £10.00-£27.00.

Three Day Pass: Non £32.00, Club £29.00. Qualifying: £5.00-£14.00. C£Free. Programme £Free-£5.00. Seating (BH): £Free-£8.00. Group Tickets: Non £90.00-£95.00, Club £80.00-£85.00. Season Ticket Inc. of Club Membership: £160.00. You can buy your tickets for any of the 1999 events in advance any time up to 4 days before an event and make a saving, Tel: 0870 60 60 611

Motor Racing Circuit

Quilters' Guild Heritage Collection
HARRIS MUSEUM AND ART GALLERY
17/4/99
26/6/99
Tel: 01772 258248
Celebration of Guild's 25th anniversary including quilts never before displayed

Art Galleries

MCN British Superbike Championship (MCRCB)
OULTON PARK
24/4/99
25/4/99
Tel: 01829 760301
British Superbike x 2, British 125cc, British 250cc, British 600cc plus support. Full Circuit, Grade-B. On the Gate: £10.00-£28.00. In Advance: Non £8.00-£25.00, Club £7.00-£22.00. Two Day Pass: Non £11.00-£30.00, Club £10.00-£27.00. Three Day Pass: Non £32.00, Club £29.00. Qualifying: £5.00-£14.00. C£Free. Programme £Free-£5.00. Seating (BH): £Free-£8.00. Group Tickets: Non £90.00-£95.00, Club £80.00-£85.00. Season Ticket Inc. of Club Membership: £160.00. You can buy your tickets for any of the 1999 events in advance any time up to 4 days before an event and make a saving, Tel: 0870 60 60 611

Motor Racing Circuit

Creating from Scratch
WALKER ART GALLERY
30/4/99
13/6/99
Tel: 0151 478 4199
For the first time, the Walker Art gallery brings together the unique and intricate work of Merseyside's most distinguished potter, Julia Carter Preston. Her hall-mark has been the use of the Sgraffito technique of decoration. Much of her recent work will be for sale.

Art Galleries

Van Dyck
WALKER ART GALLERY
30/4/99
18/7/99
Tel: 0151 478 4199
This year 1999 is the 400th anniversary of the birth of Van Dyck, one of Europe's finest portrait painters. To celebrate the

year, the Royal Collection is lending to the Walker Art Gallery, Van Dyck's portrait The Five Eldest Children of Charles I. The most impressive of Van Dyck's of Charles I's children, it was commissioned by the King for the Breakfast Chamber of his apartments at Whitehall Palace. The painting will be on display at the Walker during the spring and summer as this year's Masterpiece loan and will be shown ONLY at the Walker.

Art Galleries

Rare and Unusual Trees

1/5/99   NORTON PRIORY MUSEUM AND GARDENS
1/5/99   Tel: 01928 569895

A guided walk led by our Head Gardener for National Blossom Day at the Walled Garden at 14:30.

Gardens

Photographic Competition

1/5/99   WWT MARTIN MERE
3/5/99   Tel: 01704 895181

Natural history photographic competition, visitors are asked to choose the best photograph from an exhibition by the local photographers. Prizes will be awarded to the winning exhibitor and to the first nominee of the winning picture drawn from the box

Waterfowl Parks

Tantalising Trees

1/5/99   NORTON PRIORY MUSEUM AND GARDENS
9/5/99   Tel: 01928 569895

A quiz for all the family.

Gardens

Streets Ahead 1999

1/5/99   STREETS AHEAD 1999
31/5/99   Tel: 0161 224 0020

A Month of magic in a jam-packed outdoor festival of street entertainment - theatre, music, dance, circus, spectacular big shows, stunning fireworks and special events, renowned for its party-like atmosphere. All events are FREE and for all ages. Highlights of 1999 include street festivals, colourful parades, 1200 samba drummers, American and European shows, a finale of fire and the x.trax showcase.

Festivals

Manchester Ship Canal Cruises

1/5/99   MERSEY FERRIES LTD
26/9/99   Tel: 0151 630 1030

6 hour cruises along the Manchester Ship Canal with live commentary relating to the history and present day of the canal will compliment your day. Full bar

and servery service will be available throughout the cruise. You choose your starting point from which to travel from and you will be returned there by bus to collect your vehicle. Parking information will be sent to you with your tickets. Timetable: 1 & 15 May departs Pier Head, Liverpool at 11.00, 2 & 16 May departs Salford Quays 10.00. 19 June departs Pier Head, Liverpool at 13.00, 20 June departs Salford Quays 12.00. 3 July departs Pier Head, Liverpool at 12.00, 4 July departs Salford Quays 11.00. 7 Aug departs Pier Head, Liverpool at 10.00, 8 Aug departs Salford Quays 13.00. 11 Sept departs Pier Head, Liverpool at 10.30, 12 Sept departs Salford Quays 10.00. 25 Sept departs Pier Head, Liverpool at 10.30, 26 Sept departs Salford Quays 09.30. Prices: A£22.00 per person with discounts of 10% for groups of 20+ and a reduction of £1.00 per person for those not wishing to use our transport following the cruise. Tickets will be on sale from Monday 1st February 1999, call 0151 630 1030

Boat Trips

Victor Pasmore

1/5/99   TATE GALLERY LIVERPOOL
1/3/00   Tel: 0151 709 3223/709 0507

This display will pay tribute to the British artist Victor Pasmore who died earlier this year. It will include a selection of prints and archive material from the Tate Collection, as well as loans from regional galleries. The display will provide an overview of Pasmore's diverse output from his early work and involvement with the Euston Road School, through his shift to Constructivism in the early 1950s, to his late, more organic abstractions.

Art Galleries

Medieval Combat

2/5/99   BEESTON CASTLE
3/5/99   Tel: 01829 260464

Harlech Medieval Society, knights combat, archery, have a go archery and games, from 12.00. A£3.50 C£1.80 Concessions£2.60

Castles

Oulton Park Gold Cup for GTs & Cheshire Formula 3 (BRDC)

2/5/99   OULTON PARK
3/5/99   Tel: 01829 760301

British GT Championship, British Formula 3 Championship, National

Saloon Cup, MGF Cup, Supersports 200, Marcos Mantis Challenge, Porsche Cup, Mini Miglias, Mini Se7ens. Full Circuit, Grade-B. On the Gate: £10.00-£28.00. In Advance: Non £8.00-£25.00, Club £7.00-£22.00. Two Day Pass: Non £11.00-£30.00, Club £10.00-£27.00. Three Day Pass: Non £32.00, Club £29.00. Qualifying: £5.00-£14.00. C£Free. Programme £Free-£5.00. Seating (BH): £Free-£8.00. Group Tickets: Non £90.00-£95.00, Club £80.00-£85.00. Season Ticket Inc. of Club Membership: £160.00. You can buy your tickets for any of the 1999 events in advance any time up to 4 days before an event and make a saving, Tel: 0870 60 60 611

Motor Racing Circuit

The May Day Craft Show
2/5/99
3/5/99
TATTON PARK
Tel: 01625 534400
An Aladdin's cave of ideas to enchance your home with crafts, fashion demonstrations and entertainment

Country Parks

May Day Monday
3/5/99
3/5/99
NORTON PRIORY MUSEUM AND GARDENS
Tel: 01928 569895
Activities and puzzles for all the family from 12.00-16.00.

Gardens

Millennium Trees
9/5/99
9/5/99
NORTON PRIORY MUSEUM AND GARDENS
Tel: 01928 569895
Join our Rangers for ESSO Walk in the Woods Day starting at 14.30 at the Museum and 15.30 at the Walled Garden.

Gardens

Ladies Evening Race Meeting
14/5/99
14/5/99
AINTREE RACECOURSE
Tel: 0151 523 2600
Aintree comes alive for a lively Friday evening. Top quality horse racing with additional entertainment i.e. fashion shows, best dress competitions, etc. Cost: from £6.00

Racecourses

Clubmans Bikes (BMCRC)
15/5/99
15/5/99
OULTON PARK
Tel: 01829 760301
All classes of national solo motorcycles and sidecars. Full Circuit, Grade-D. On the Gate: £10.00-£28.00. In Advance: Non £8.00-£25.00, Club £7.00-£22.00. Two Day Pass: Non £11.00-£30.00, Club £10.00-£27.00. Three Day Pass: Non

£32.00, Club £29.00. Qualifying: £5.00-£14.00. C£Free. Programme £Free-£5.00. Seating (BH): £Free-£8.00. Group Tickets: Non £90.00-£95.00, Club £80.00-£85.00. Season Ticket Inc. of Club Membership: £160.00. You can buy your tickets for any of the 1999 events in advance any time up to 4 days before an event and make a saving, Tel: 0870 60 60 611

Motor Racing Circuit

Ellie Williams
15/5/99
16/5/99
NORTON PRIORY MUSEUM AND GARDENS
Tel: 01928 569895
Meet Ellie, a local artist, who will be working in the Walled Garden from 14.00-16.00.

Gardens

Canon's Conundrum
15/5/99
23/5/99
NORTON PRIORY MUSEUM AND GARDENS
Tel: 01928 569895
A special quiz for Museum's Week and Adult Learner's Week.

Gardens

Hanging Basket Workshop
19/5/99
2/6/99
STAPELEY WATER GARDENS
Tel: 01270 623868
To be held on: 19 May, 26 May & 2 June from 17.00-20.00. Free compost, fertilizer and a Nemesia 'Confetti' plant when you make your hanging basket here with us at our workshop

Gardens

National 3000 Race Day (BRSCC)
22/5/99
22/5/99
OULTON PARK
Tel: 01829 760301
National 3000s, TVR Tuscans, Caterham Superlights, Caterham Roadsports, Formula Renaults, Formula Ford 1600s. Full Circuit, Grade-C. On the Gate: £10.00-£28.00. In Advance: Non £8.00-£25.00, Club £7.00-£22.00. Two Day Pass: Non £11.00-£30.00, Club £10.00-£27.00. Three Day Pass: Non £32.00, Club £29.00. Qualifying: £5.00-£14.00. C£Free. Programme £Free-£5.00. Seating (BH): £Free-£8.00. Group Tickets: Non £90.00-£95.00, Club £80.00-£85.00. Season Ticket Inc. of Club Membership: £160.00. You can buy your tickets for any of the 1999 events in advance any time up to 4 days before an event and make a saving, Tel: 0870 60 60 611

Motor Racing Circuit

Myles Birket Foster

22/5/99
21/7/99
WARRINGTON MUSEUM AND ART GALLERY
Tel: 01925 442392/442398
A touring exhibition of watercolours and
book illustrations to celebrate the centenary of the artists' death

Museums

24/5/99
6/6/99
Friend or Foe
NORTON PRIORY MUSEUM AND GARDENS
Tel: 01928 569895
A quiz about insects.

Gardens

26/5/99
26/5/99
Guided Walk around Salford Quays
SALFORD QUAYS HERITAGE CENTRE
Tel: 0161 876 5359
Starting at 19.30 from the Centre, the
walk lasts approximately 1-1.5 hours, followed by an opportunity to visit the
exhibition area. Cost: £1.00, pre-booking
essential. This walk will also take place
on Wednesday 14 July & Sunday 17
October at 11.00

Heritage Centres

29/5/99
6/6/99
Downy Duckling Days
WWT MARTIN MERE
Tel: 01704 895181
The time of year for fluffy ducklings,
goslings and cygnets in the waterfowl
gardens, ahhh

Waterfowl Parks

30/5/99
30/5/99
Guided Walk
WEAVER'S TRIANGLE VISITOR CENTRE
Tel: 01282 452403
Guided walk through Weavers Triangle.
Duration: 1 hour. Meet at Visitor Centre
at 14.15

Museum- Local History

30/5/99
31/5/99
Countryside Fayre
ARROWE COUNTRY PARK
Tel: 0151 678 4200
Two days of countryside activities and
events offering something for all the
family at Arrowe Country Park including
displays, country crafts and trade
stands. Commences: 10.00-17.00

Country Parks

30/5/99
31/5/99
Norman Knights
BEESTON CASTLE
Tel: 01829 260464
Medieval re-enactment performed by
Conquest. A£3.50 C£1.80
Concessions£2.60

Castles

30/5/99
31/5/99
**Autotrader British Touring Car
Championship (TOCA)**
OULTON PARK
Tel: 01829 760301
Touring Cars x 2, Formula Ford, Ford

Fiestas, Formula Renault, Renault
Spiders, Formula Vauxhall Jnr, Vauxhall
Vectras. Fosters Circuit, Grade-A. On the
Gate: £10.00-£28.00. In Advance: Non
£8.00-£25.00, Club £7.00-£22.00. Two
Day Pass: Non £11.00-£30.00, Club
£10.00-£27.00. Three Day Pass: Non
£32.00, Club £29.00. Qualifying: £5.00-
£14.00. C£Free. Programme £Free-£5.00.
Seating (BH): £Free-£8.00. Group
Tickets: Non £90.00-£95.00, Club
£80.00-£85.00. Season Ticket Inc. of
Club Membership: £160.00. You can buy
your tickets for any of the 1999 events in
advance any time up to 4 days before an
event and make a saving, Tel: 0870 60
60 611

Motor Racing Circuit

30/5/99
6/6/99
Downham Market Festival 1999
DOWNHAM MARKET FESTIVAL 1999
Tel: 01366 382963
Eight days of festival fun for all the family. An exceptional variety of entertainment and activities that will keep you
coming back for more. Why not spend
the week in Donwham Market and make
sure you get to see and do everything!

Festivals

31/5/99
31/5/99
Insects - friend or foe?
NORTON PRIORY MUSEUM AND GARDENS
Tel: 01928 569895
Activities and games for all the family
around the theme of Insects. Time:
12.00-16.00

Gardens

5/6/99
5/6/99
National Gardens Scheme
ARLEY HALL AND GARDENS
Tel: 01565 777353
Admission: normal admission applies.
Time: 10.00-17.00

Historic Houses & Gardens

5/6/99
6/6/99
The Woman's Touch
TATTON PARK
Tel: 01625 534400
Contemporary patchwork and quilt mak-
ing demonstrations, sales, traders and
books

Country Parks

5/6/99
30/8/99
The Froehlich Collection
TATE GALLERY LIVERPOOL
Tel: 0151 709 3223/709 0507
Widely regarded as one of the finest pri-
vate collections of contemporary art in
the world, the Collection of the Froehlich
Foundation focuses on the work of ten
artists from the USA and nine from
Germany and traces many of the most

notable developments in art for the past four decades. This exhibition will include work by Richard Artschwager, Bruce Nauman, Andy Warhol, Georg Baselitz, Joseph Beuys and Sigmar Polke. Admission A£3.00 Concessions£2.00 Family Ticket £6.00

Art Galleries

Cheshire County Antiques Fair

11/6/99 ARLEY HALL AND GARDENS
13/6/99 Tel: 01565 777353

A quality antique fair, datelined 1890 with quality additions to 1920. Times: Fri 12.00-18.00, Sat & Sun 11.00-17.00. Admission charged

Historic Houses & Gardens

750 M/C Motorsport Magic (750 M/C)

12/6/99 OULTON PARK
12/6/99 Tel: 01829 760301

Hot Hatch, Stock Hatch, 750 Formula, Clubsport 2000, Formula 4, Formula Vee, Kit Cars, Roadsports, Caterham A & B, Caterham C & D. Fosters Circuit, Grade-D. On the Gate: £10.00-£28.00. In Advance: Non £8.00-£25.00, Club £7.00-£22.00. Two Day Pass: Non £11.00-£30.00, Club £10.00-£27.00. Three Day Pass: Non £32.00, Club £29.00. Qualifying: £5.00-£14.00. C£Free. Programme £Free-£5.00. Seating (BH): £Free-£8.00. Group Tickets: Non £90.00-£95.00, Club £80.00-£85.00. Season Ticket Inc. of Club Membership: £160.00. You can buy your tickets for any of the 1999 events in advance any time up to 4 days before an event and make a saving, Tel: 0870 60 60 611

Motor Racing Circuit

Garden Festival

12/6/99 NESS BOTANIC GARDENS
13/6/99 Tel: 0151 353 0123

A busy programme with something of interest for everyone, including children; gardening, plants, crafts, fine foods, lectures, demonstrations and music. For times, prices and booking information please call the venue

Gardens- Botanical

Walk: The Herb Garden

13/6/99 NORTON PRIORY MUSEUM AND GARDENS
13/6/99 Tel: 01928 569895

A guided walk at the Walled Garden at 14.30.

Gardens

Guided Walk

13/6/99 WEAVER'S TRIANGLE VISITOR CENTRE
13/6/99 Tel: 01282 452403

Guided walk through Weavers Triangle. Duration: 1 hour. Meet at Visitor Centre at 14.15

Museum- Local History

Wave 1999

19/6/99 MERSEY FERRIES LTD
19/6/99 Tel: 0151 630 1030

A family fun day out with entertainment to suit all ages and tastes. Call for further details

Boat Trips

Protecting Ponds

19/6/99 NORTON PRIORY MUSEUM AND GARDENS
19/6/99 Tel: 01928 569895

A family activity at the Museum at 14.30 with our Ranger

Gardens

Midsummer National 3000 (BRSCC)

19/6/99 OULTON PARK
19/6/99 Tel: 01829 760301

National 3000s, Mini Miglias, Mini se7ens, Tomcat/Vento Challenge, Formula Ford 1600s, Classic Formula Ford 2000s. Island Circuit, Grade-C. On the Gate: £10.00-£28.00. In Advance: Non £8.00-£25.00, Club £7.00-£22.00. Two Day Pass: Non £11.00-£30.00, Club £10.00-£27.00. Three Day Pass: Non £32.00, Club £29.00. Qualifying: £5.00-£14.00. C£Free. Programme £Free-£5.00. Seating (BH): £Free-£8.00. Group Tickets: Non £90.00-£95.00, Club £80.00-£85.00. Season Ticket Inc. of Club Membership: £160.00. You can buy your tickets for any of the 1999 events in advance any time up to 4 days before an event and make a saving, Tel: 0870 60 60 611

Motor Racing Circuit

Ellie Williams

19/6/99 NORTON PRIORY MUSEUM AND GARDENS
20/6/99 Tel: 01928 569895

Meet Ellie, a local artist, who will be working in the Walled Garden from 14.00-16.00

Gardens

Medieval Fair

19/6/99 TATTON PARK
20/6/99 Tel: 01625 534400

Living history re-enactments, combat displays, craft demonstrations and more!

Country Parks

Father's Day Discount

20/6/99 SOUTHPORT ZOO AND CONSERVATION

20/6/99	**TRUST** Tel: 01704 538102 Entrance to the Zoo FREE to dads when accompanied by a child age 2-13years *Zoos- Conservation*

The Cheshire Show

22/6/99 23/6/99	**TABLEY HOUSE** Tel: 01565 750151 County Agricultural Show on Tabley Showground *Historic Houses*

Evening Outdoor Concert

26/6/99 26/6/99	**NESS BOTANIC GARDENS** Tel: 0151 353 0123 Bring your own chairs and a picnic; enjoy beautiful music in a wonderful setting. For times, prices and booking information please call the venue *Gardens- Botanical*

Healthy Herbs

26/6/99 26/6/99	**NORTON PRIORY MUSEUM AND GARDENS** Tel: 01928 569895 A family activity at the Walled Garden at 14.30 led by our Ranger *Gardens*

Endurance Bikes (KRC)

26/6/99 26/6/99	**OULTON PARK** Tel: 01829 760301 6 Hour Endurance Bike Series. Full Circuit, Grade-D. On the Gate: £10.00-£28.00. In Advance: Non £8.00-£25.00, Club £7.00-£22.00. Two Day Pass: Non £11.00-£30.00, Club £10.00-£27.00. Three Day Pass: Non £32.00, Club £29.00. Qualifying: £5.00-£14.00. C£Free. Programme £Free-£5.00. Seating (BH): £Free-£8.00. Group Tickets: Non £90.00-£95.00, Club £80.00-£85.00. Season Ticket Inc. of Club Membership: £160.00. You can buy your tickets for any of the 1999 events in advance any time up to 4 days before an event and make a saving, Tel: 0870 60 60 611 *Motor Racing Circuit*

The Arley Garden Festival

26/6/99 27/6/99	**ARLEY HALL AND GARDENS** Tel: 01565 777353 A high quality garden event featuring specialist nurseries, garden related accessories, garden designers and celebrity gardeners' question time. Time: 10.00-17.00 both days. Admission: A£6.00 Family Ticket £14.00 OAPs£5.00 *Historic Houses & Gardens*

Open Air Theatre

1/7/99 2/7/99	**BRAMALL HALL** Tel: 0161 485 3708 Shakespeare's 'Twelfth Night' will be performed in the beautiful grounds of Bramall Hall, bring a rug and picnic, call for times and prices *Stately Homes*

Liverpool Cathedral Festival

2/7/99 18/7/99	**LIVERPOOL CATHEDRAL** Tel: 0151 709 6271 A variety of musical events including choral concerts, organ recitals and a Barber Shop evening. Time: various. Ticket Prices: various *Cathedrals*

Henri Cartier-Bresson

2/7/99 22/8/99	**WALKER ART GALLERY** Tel: 0151 478 4199 Portraits: Tete a Tate. The first ever exhibition by the famous French photographer to be held in the country. Selected by Cartier-Bresson himself, the exhibition contains many of his acknowledged masterworks, portraits of French artists and intellectuals such as Matisse, Colette, Jean Paul Satre and Simone de Beauvoir, as well as many less well-known but equally striking images. *Art Galleries*

"Francis House Charity Concert"

3/7/99 3/7/99	**ARLEY HALL AND GARDENS** Tel: 01565 777353 A night to remember! Music by Trafford Youth Concert Band. Guest stars "The Bootleg Beatles" followed by the ever popular Last Night of the Proms with the Camerata Concert Orchestra. Firework displays by Dragonfire. Admission charged. Please contact Judy Bailey, 01625 583453 for further information *Historic Houses & Gardens*

Cross the Mersey

3/7/99 3/7/99	**NORTON PRIORY MUSEUM AND GARDENS** Tel: 01928 569895 A family activity making model boats at the Museum at 14.30 with our Ranger *Gardens*

Clubmans Bikes (NEW ERA)

3/7/99 3/7/99	**OULTON PARK** Tel: 01829 760301 All classes of national solo motorcycles and sidecars. Full Circuit, Grade-D. On the Gate: £10.00-£28.00. In Advance: Non £8.00-£25.00, Club £7.00-£22.00. Two Day Pass: Non £11.00-£30.00, Club £10.00-£27.00. Three Day Pass: Non £32.00, Club £29.00. Qualifying: £5.00-

£14.00. C£Free. Programme £Free-£5.00. Seating (BH): £Free-£8.00. Group Tickets: Non £90.00-£95.00, Club £80.00-£85.00. Season Ticket Inc. of Club Membership: £160.00. You can buy your tickets for any of the 1999 events in advance any time up to 4 days before an event and make a saving, Tel: 0870 60 60 611

Motor Racing Circuit

Green Fayre
3/7/99   ARROWE COUNTRY PARK
4/7/99   Tel: 0151 678 4200
Two days of green entertainment for all the family at Arrowe Country Park

Country Parks

Nantwich & District Fuchsia & Geranium Society
4/7/99   STAPELEY WATER GARDENS
4/7/99   Tel: 01270 623868
11th Annual Nantwich and district geranium show

Gardens

Evening Jazz along the Canal Cruise
9/7/99   MERSEY FERRIES LTD
10/7/99 Tel: 0151 630 1030
6 hour cruises along the Manchester Ship Canal with live commentary relating to the history and present day of the canal will compliment your day. Full bar and servery service will be available throughout the cruise. You choose your starting point from which to travel from and you will be returned there by bus to collect your vehicle. Parking information will be sent to you with your tickets. Timetable: 9 July departs Pier Head, Liverpool at 16.30, 10 July departs Salford Quays 16.00. Prices: A£22.00 per person with discounts of 10% for groups of 20+ and a reduction of £1.00 per person for those not wishing to use our transport following the cruise. Tickets will be on sale from Monday 1st February 1999, call 0151 630 1030

Boat Trips

Dragonflies at Norton
10/7/99 NORTON PRIORY MUSEUM AND GARDENS
10/7/99 Tel: 01928 569895
A family activity with our Ranger at the Museum at 14.30

Gardens

Classic Bike Race Day (CRMC)
10/7/99 OULTON PARK
10/7/99 Tel: 01829 760301
All classes of national solo motorcycles and sidecars. Full Circuit, Grade-D. On

the Gate: £10.00-£28.00. In Advance: Non £8.00-£25.00, Club £7.00-£22.00. Two Day Pass: Non £11.00-£30.00, Club £10.00-£27.00. Three Day Pass: Non £32.00, Club £29.00. Qualifying: £5.00-£14.00. C£Free. Programme £Free-£5.00. Seating (BH): £Free-£8.00. Group Tickets: Non £90.00-£95.00, Club £80.00-£85.00. Season Ticket Inc. of Club Membership: £160.00. You can buy your tickets for any of the 1999 events in advance any time up to 4 days before an event and make a saving, Tel: 0870 60 60 611

Motor Racing Circuit

Summer Shopping Weekend
10/7/99 NORTON PRIORY MUSEUM AND GARDENS
11/7/99 Tel: 01928 569895
Shopping at the Museum with ideas for holiday reading and activities.

Gardens

Handmade in India / Draped and the Shaped
10/7/99 HARRIS MUSEUM AND ART GALLERY
11/9/99 Tel: 01772 258248
Two complementary exhibitions offering varied Indian crafts and Pakistani textiles

Art Galleries

Brass in the Gardens
11/7/99 ARLEY HALL AND GARDENS
11/7/99 Tel: 01565 777353
A wonderful evening of Brass by the Brighouse & Rastrick Brass band, held in the beautiful Walled garden. Bring a picnic. Walled gardens open from 18.00. Admission charge. For further information please contact Goff Richards 01925 601112

Historic Houses & Gardens

Manchester International Caribbean Carnival 1999
11/7/99 MANCHESTER INTERNATIONAL CARIBBEAN CARNIVAL 1999
11/7/99 Tel: 0161 226 0486
With the help of the Moss Side and Hulme Business Federation, Carnival in Manchester is being dramatically re-organised. A dynamic 5 year business plan is developing the Carnival up to the Commonwealth Games Carnival in 2002, taking it from a small local event to one that the city of Manchester and the North West region can be proud of. Carnival is a multi-faceted entity, appealing to many different constituents and offering multiple benefits. Above all,

Carnival brings people together, bringing down social barriers, suspending divisions and celebrating unity in diversity. Time: 12.00-21.00. Admission Free but donations welcome

Carnivals

Open-Air Theatre - As You Like It
15/7/99 LITTLE MORETON HALL
24/7/99 Tel: 01260 272018
Will be held on: 15, 16, 17, 22 & 23 July, starting at 20.00, grounds open from 19.00 for picnics. Marquee if wet. Tickets: £10.00 to include wine.

Historic Houses

Saddleworth Folk and Roots Festival
16/7/99 SADDLEWORTH FOLK AND ROOTS FESTIVAL 1999
18/7/99 Tel: 01457 870391
Come to our second festival in the beautiful surroundings of Saddleworth which offers attractions for all to enjoy. Picturesque camping site, concerts, sessions, dance displays, children's entertainment, ceilidh and superb guests who include Vin Garbutt and Clive Gregson. A£18.00 C£10.00 OAPs£15.00

Festivals

MCN British Superbike Championship (MCRCB)
17/7/99 OULTON PARK
18/7/99 Tel: 01829 760301
British Superbike x 2, British 125cc, British 250cc, British 600cc plus support. Full Circuit, Grade-B. On the Gate: £10.00-£28.00. In Advance: Non £8.00-£25.00. Club £7.00-£22.00. Two Day Pass: Non £11.00-£30.00, Club £10.00-£27.00. Three Day Pass: Non £32.00, Club £29.00. Qualifying: £5.00-£14.00. C£Free. Programme £Free-£5.00. Seating (BH): £Free-£8.00. Group Tickets: Non £90.00-£95.00, Club £80.00-£85.00. Season Ticket Inc. of Club Membership: £160.00. You can buy your tickets for any of the 1999 events in advance any time up to 4 days before an event and make a saving, Tel: 0870 60 60 611

Motor Racing Circuit

Engaging
17/7/99 NORTON PRIORY MUSEUM AND GARDENS
24/7/99 Tel: 01928 569895
Contemporary art quiz, events and activities for Gallery Week.

Gardens

Fleetwood Tram Sunday Festival 1999

18/7/99 FLEETWOOD TRAM SUNDAY FESTIVAL 1999
18/7/99 Tel: 01253 876525
A great family day out. Several vintage trams and tram rides. Transport of all descriptions, bands, buskers, entertainers of all types with children's fun fair and rides.

Festivals

Royal Horticultural Flower Show
22/7/99 TATTON PARK
25/7/99 Tel: 01625 534400
A spectacular new event takes place presented by the organisers of the world famous Chelsea Flower Show, and will present visitors with a host of horticultural delights. Call for details

Country Parks

Championship Race Day (BRSCC)
24/7/99 OULTON PARK
24/7/99 Tel: 01829 760301
Formula 600s, Formula Ford 1600s, XR2 Challenge, XR3 Challenge, Alfas, Auto Italia. Fosters Circuit, Grade-D. On the Gate: £10.00-£28.00. In Advance: Non £8.00-£25.00, Club £7.00-£22.00. Two Day Pass: Non £11.00-£30.00, Club £10.00-£27.00. Three Day Pass: Non £32.00, Club £29.00. Qualifying: £5.00-£14.00. C£Free. Programme £Free-£5.00. Seating (BH): £Free-£8.00. Group Tickets: Non £90.00-£95.00, Club £80.00-£85.00. Season Ticket Inc. of Club Membership: £160.00. You can buy your tickets for any of the 1999 events in advance any time up to 4 days before an event and make a saving, Tel: 0870 60 60 611

Motor Racing Circuit

St Christopher's Day
25/7/99 NORTON PRIORY MUSEUM AND GARDENS
25/7/99 Tel: 01928 569895
An event to celebrate the return of the 600 year old statue of St Christopher to Norton Priory. Please call for further information.

Gardens

Medieval Country Craft Fayre
30/7/99 TABLEY HOUSE
1/8/99 Tel: 01565 750151
An exciting three days ahead. Entertainment for all the family. A£3.00-£5.00 C(5-15)£1.00 OAPs£2.00-£3.00 Commences 10.00-18.00

Historic Houses

Hallé Firework and Light Concert

Further more detailed information on the attractions listed can be found in Best Guides *Visitor Attractions* Guide under the classifications shown

31/7/99 31/7/99	**TATTON PARK** Tel: 01625 534400

With the Hallé Orchestra, a night of unforgettable midsummer magic. Over 1000 large scale fireworks and lighting effects choreographed to favourite classical compositions, 20.15, grounds open 18.00. Call for further details on 01625 534400

Country Parks

Ellie Williams

31/7/99 1/8/99	**NORTON PRIORY MUSEUM AND GARDENS** Tel: 01928 569895

Meet Ellie, a local artist, who will be working in the Walled Garden from 14.00-16.00.

Gardens

Brouhaha International Street Theatre Festival 1999

31/7/99 8/8/99	**BROUHAHA INTERNATIONAL STREET THEATRE FESTIVAL 1999** Tel: 0151 709 3334

Merseyside's annual free street theatre festival features international and local companies performing on the streets of Liverpool City Centre and in venues and locations across Merseyside.

Festivals

What's in the Woods?

31/7/99 5/9/99	**NORTON PRIORY MUSEUM AND GARDENS** Tel: 01928 569895

A quiz for all the family.

Gardens

Travellers' Tales

3/8/99 31/8/99	**NORTON PRIORY MUSEUM AND GARDENS** Tel: 01928 569895

Every Tuesday throughout August, story telling and mask-making for the National Year of Reading at the Museum at 14.30.

Gardens

Make your own St. Christopher

4/8/99 25/8/99	**NORTON PRIORY MUSEUM AND GARDENS** Tel: 01928 569895

Every Wednesday help us with ours - family workshops at the Museum at 14.30.

Gardens

Pilgrims' Badges

5/8/99 26/8/99	**NORTON PRIORY MUSEUM AND GARDENS** Tel: 01928 569895

Every Thursday a family activity at the Museum at 14.30.

Gardens

The Squishy, Squashy, Touchy, Crawly Show

5/8/99 18/9/99	**WARRINGTON MUSEUM AND ART GALLERY** Tel: 01925 442392/442398

Interactive sculptures by Jan Niepojadlo, call for further details

Museums

Eurocar Battle of Oulton Park (BRSCC)

7/8/99 7/8/99	**OULTON PARK** Tel: 01829 760301

Eurocar V6 & V8 Championships, Pick-Ups, Legends. Fosters Circuit, Grade-C. On the Gate: £10.00-£28.00. In Advance: Non £8.00-£25.00, Club £7.00-£22.00. Two Day Pass: Non £11.00-£30.00, Club £10.00-£27.00. Three Day Pass: Non £32.00, Club £29.00. Qualifying: £5.00-£14.00. C£Free. Programme £Free-£5.00. Seating (BH): £Free-£8.00. Group Tickets: Non £90.00-£95.00, Club £80.00-£85.00. Season Ticket Inc. of Club Membership: £160.00. You can buy your tickets for any of the 1999 events in advance any time up to 4 days before an event and make a saving, Tel: 0870 60 60 611

Motor Racing Circuit

Fuchsia Show

8/8/99 8/8/99	**STAPELEY WATER GARDENS** Tel: 01270 623868

11th Annual Nantwich and district show

Gardens

Midweek Manchester Ship Canal Cruise

11/8/99 12/8/99	**MERSEY FERRIES LTD** Tel: 0151 630 1030

6 hour cruises along the Manchester Ship Canal with live commentary relating to the history and present day of the canal will compliment your day. Full bar and servery service will be available throughout the cruise. You choose your starting point from which to travel from and you will be returned there by bus to collect your vehicle. Parking information will be sent to you with your tickets. Timetable: 11 Aug departs Pier Head, Liverpool at 11.00, 12 Aug departs Salford Quays 10.00. Prices: A£22.00 per person with discounts of 10% for groups of 20+ and a reduction of £1.00 per person for those not wishing to use our transport following the cruise. Tickets will be on sale from Monday 1st February 1999, call 0151 630 1030

Boat Trips

Championship Cars (BARC)

| 14/8/99 | **OULTON PARK** | *Motor Racing Circuit* |

14/8/99 Tel: 01829 760301
Classic Formula Ford 2000s, Formula
Ford 1600s, Formula Saloons,
Westfields, MGs, 250 Gearbox Karts.
Island Circuit, Grade-D. On the Gate:
£10.00-£28.00. In Advance: Non £8.00-
£25.00, Club £7.00-£22.00. Two Day
Pass: Non £11.00-£30.00, Club £10.00-
£27.00. Three Day Pass: Non £32.00,
Club £29.00. Qualifying: £5.00-£14.00.
C£Free. Programme £Free-£5.00.
Seating (BH): £Free-£8.00. Group
Tickets: Non £90.00-£95.00, Club
£80.00-£85.00. Season Ticket Inc. of
Club Membership: £160.00. You can buy
your tickets for any of the 1999 events in
advance any time up to 4 days before an
event and make a saving, Tel: 0870 60
60 611

Motor Racing Circuit
Medieval Fair

15/8/99 **TATTON PARK**
16/8/99 Tel: 01625 534400
Living History re-enactments combat displays, craft demonstrations and entertainment

Country Parks
Boredom Buster

17/8/99 **TATTON PARK**
20/8/99 Tel: 01625 534400
Activities for children to include harness
cleaning, horse grooming, egg collecting
and chicken feeding. Call 01625 534431
for further details

Country Parks
Mighty MGs (MGCC)

21/8/99 **OULTON PARK**
21/8/99 Tel: 01829 760301
Thoroughbred Sports Cars, International
BCV8, Midget Challenge, Metro
Challenge, MG Phoenix, ACE MG
Cockshoot, MGF Trophy. Fosters Circuit,
Grade-D. On the Gate: £10.00-£28.00. In
Advance: Non £8.00-£25.00, Club £7.00-
£22.00. Two Day Pass: Non £11.00-
£30.00, Club £10.00-£27.00. Three Day
Pass: Non £32.00, Club £29.00.
Qualifying: £5.00-£14.00. C£Free.
Programme £Free-£5.00. Seating (BH):
£Free-£8.00. Group Tickets: Non £90.00-
£95.00, Club £80.00-£85.00. Season
Ticket Inc. of Club Membership: £160.00.
You can buy your tickets for any of the
1999 events in advance any time up to 4
days before an event and make a saving,
Tel: 0870 60 60 611

St Christopher

30/8/99 **NORTON PRIORY MUSEUM AND GARDENS**
30/8/99 Tel: 01928 569895
Activities and games for all the family
based on the Norton Priory St
Christopher

Gardens
Bank Holiday Car Races (BRSCC)

30/8/99 **OULTON PARK**
30/8/99 Tel: 01829 760301
Porsche 924s, Fiats, BMWs, Formula
Ford 1600s, XR2 Challenge, XR3
Challenge. Fosters Circuit, Grade-D. On
the Gate: £10.00-£28.00. In Advance:
Non £8.00-£25.00, Club £7.00-£22.00.
Two Day Pass: Non £11.00-£30.00, Club
£10.00-£27.00. Three Day Pass: Non
£32.00, Club £29.00. Qualifying: £5.00-
£14.00. C£Free. Programme £Free-£5.00.
Seating (BH): £Free-£8.00. Group
Tickets: Non £90.00-£95.00, Club
£80.00-£85.00. Season Ticket Inc. of
Club Membership: £160.00. You can buy
your tickets for any of the 1999 events in
advance any time up to 4 days before an
event and make a saving, Tel: 0870 60
60 611

Motor Racing Circuit
Saint Monday Festival

30/8/99 **WEAVER'S TRIANGLE VISITOR CENTRE**
30/8/99 Tel: 01282 452403
Charity stalls, entertainment, refreshments. Time: 11.00-16.00

Museum- Local History
The People's Palace

31/8/99 **HARRIS MUSEUM AND ART GALLERY**
31/12/99 Tel: 01772 258248
The history of Preston's well loved Town
Hall, destroyed by fire in 1947

Art Galleries
Liverpool Biennial of Contemporary Art

1/9/99 **LIVERPOOL TOURIST INFORMATION CENTRE**
1/9/99 Tel: 0151 708 8838
To open in September 1999 it is the
United Kingdom and Ireland's first ever
international contemporary art Biennial
and will take place throughout the city
of Liverpool's many arts, architectural
and cultural sites, including Tate Gallery
Liverpool, Bluecoat Gallery. Open Eye
Gallery, Walker Art Gallery, the Tea
Factory and other venues.

Tourist Information Centres
Flyde Folk Festival 1999

Further more detailed information on the attractions listed can be found
in Best Guides *Visitor Attractions* Guide under the classifications shown

3/9/99 5/9/99	**FLYDE FOLK FESTIVAL 1999** Tel: 01253 872317 A feast of traditional and contemporary folk music, song and dance. With over 130 events staged in the luxurious Marine Hall on Fleetwood Promenade, and 17 other venues over three days. Now in it's 27th year. Times:10.00-24.00. Prices: Sessions from: £9.50. Full weekend £32.50 C(11-14) half price C(0-11)£Free *Festivals*

Cheshire Cats (JCC)

4/9/99 4/9/99	**OULTON PARK** Tel: 01829 760301 Jaguar XK Saloon x 2, Sports Racing & GT Championship, Jaguar Challenge, Sports & Saloon, MG Cockshoot, Sports Car Race, Allcomers Race, JCC Centurian Challenge. Full Circuit, Grade-D. On the Gate: £10.00-£28.00. In Advance: Non £8.00-£25.00, Club £7.00-£22.00. Two Day Pass: Non £11.00-£30.00, Club £10.00-£27.00. Three Day Pass: Non £32.00, Club £29.00. Qualifying: £5.00-£14.00. C£Free. Programme £Free-£5.00. Seating (BH): £Free-£8.00. Group Tickets: Non £90.00-£95.00, Club £80.00-£85.00. Season Ticket Inc. of Club Membership: £160.00. You can buy your tickets for any of the 1999 events in advance any time up to 4 days before an event and make a saving, Tel: 0870 60 60 611 *Motor Racing Circuit*

The Arley Bridal Fair

11/9/99 11/9/99	**ARLEY HALL AND GARDENS** Tel: 01565 777353 For further information please contact Amanda Acton 01565 733267. This date has not yet been confirmed *Historic Houses & Gardens*

Heritage Open Day

11/9/99 11/9/99	**WEAVER'S TRIANGLE VISITOR CENTRE** Tel: 01282 452403 Guided walk as contribution to Open Day. Meet at Visitor Centre at 14.15 *Museum- Local History*

Open Weekend

11/9/99 12/9/99	**NORTON PRIORY MUSEUM AND GARDENS** Tel: 01928 569895 Special activities for all the family run by Merseyside Archaeological Society for Heritage Open Days. Free entry. *Gardens*

Autotrader British Touring Car Championship (BTCC)

11/9/99 12/9/99	**OULTON PARK** Tel: 01829 760301 Touring Cars x 2, Formula Ford, Ford Fiestas, Formula Renault, Renault Spiders, Formula Vauxhall Jnr, Vauxhall Vectras. Island Circuit, Grade-A. On the Gate: £10.00-£28.00. In Advance: Non £8.00-£25.00, Club £7.00-£22.00. Two Day Pass: Non £11.00-£30.00, Club £10.00-£27.00. Three Day Pass: Non £32.00, Club £29.00. Qualifying: £5.00-£14.00. C£Free. Programme £Free-£5.00. Seating (BH): £Free-£8.00. Group Tickets: Non £90.00-£95.00, Club £80.00-£85.00. Season Ticket Inc. of Club Membership: £160.00. You can buy your tickets for any of the 1999 events in advance any time up to 4 days before an event and make a saving, Tel: 0870 60 60 611 *Motor Racing Circuit*

Aston Martin Race Day (AMOC)

18/9/99 18/9/99	**OULTON PARK** Tel: 01829 760301 Intermarque, Post War Astons, Anglo-American, Porsche Classic, Pre War Sports/Feltham/50's Sports, Porsche v Ferrari Challenge, Flemings. Full Circuit, Grade-D. On the Gate: £10.00-£28.00. In Advance: Non £8.00-£25.00, Club £7.00-£22.00. Two Day Pass: Non £11.00-£30.00, Club £10.00-£27.00. Three Day Pass: Non £32.00, Club £29.00. Qualifying: £5.00-£14.00. C£Free. Programme £Free-£5.00. Seating (BH): £Free-£8.00. Group Tickets: Non £90.00-£95.00, Club £80.00-£85.00. Season Ticket Inc. of Club Membership: £160.00. You can buy your tickets for any of the 1999 events in advance any time up to 4 days before an event and make a saving, Tel: 0870 60 60 611 *Motor Racing Circuit*

Wood Weekend: A Wood Exhibition

18/9/99 19/9/99	**TATTON PARK** Tel: 01625 534400 A wood and tree fair. See touch and learn about natures renewable gift. Demonstrations, displays, products for sale *Country Parks*

Norton Priory Horticultural Show

19/9/99 19/9/99	**NORTON PRIORY MUSEUM AND GARDENS** Tel: 01928 569895 Vegetables, fruit, flowers, domestic produce and free-to-enter Children's Section *Gardens*

The John Moores Liverpool Exhibition 21

24/9/99
9/1/00
WALKER ART GALLERY
Tel: 0151 478 4199
Part of the Living Biennial of Contemporary Arts. Britain's biggest and nest national open exhibition for contemporary art, selected by a jury of experts, comes of age in 1999. Founded in 1957 by Sir John Moores, of Littlewoods Pools fame, the John Moores Liverpool Exhibition has been held every two years since and has a consistent track record for spotting rising talent. In 1999, for the first time, the John Moores will be part of a wider visual clecbration with the launch in Liverpool of the UK's first international biennial of contemporary art.

Art Galleries

Formula Palmer Audi Race Day (BARC)

25/9/99
25/9/99
OULTON PARK
Tel: 01829 760301
Formula Palmer Audi, Porsche Cup, Ginettas, 2CVs, Caterham Superlights, Caterham Roadsports, Celebrity Race. Full Circuit, Grade-C. On the Gate: £10.00-£28.00. In Advance: Non £8.00-£25.00, Club £7.00-£22.00. Two Day Pass: Non £11.00-£30.00, Club £10.00-£27.00. Three Day Pass: Non £32.00, Club £29.00. Qualifying: £5.00-£14.00. C£Free. Programme £Free-£5.00. Seating (BH): £Free-£8.00. Season Ticket Inc. of Club Membership: £160.00. You can buy your tickets for any of the 1999 events in advance any time up to 4 days before an event and make a saving, Tel: 0870 60 60 611

Motor Racing Circuit

The 1999 Liverpool Biennial of Contemporary Art: Trace

25/9/99
7/11/99
TATE GALLERY LIVERPOOL
Tel: 0151 709 3223/709 0507
The 1999 Liverpool Biennial of Contemporary Art is a major new international visual arts event which will take place across the city with a programme of exhibitions and projects. Entitled: TRACE, the first Liverpool Biennial will explore place, memory, materiality and mapping. Tate Gallery Liverpool will host a contemporary group exhibition of both existing and newly commissioned works which will examine and illuminate the theme. Admission price to be confirmed

Art Galleries

Clubmans Bikes (CHESHIRE ACU)

2/10/99
2/10/99
OULTON PARK
Tel: 01829 760301
All classes of national solo motorcycles and sidecars. Full Circuit, Grade-D. On the Gate: £10.00-£28.00. In Advance: Non £8.00-£25.00, Club £7.00-£22.00. Two Day Pass: Non £11.00-£30.00, Club £10.00-£27.00. Three Day Pass: Non £32.00, Club £29.00. Qualifying: £5.00-£14.00. C£Free. Programme £Free-£5.00. Seating (BH): £Free-£8.00. Group Tickets: Non £90.00-£95.00, Club £80.00-£85.00. Season Ticket Inc. of Club Membership: £160.00. You can buy your tickets for any of the 1999 events in advance any time up to 4 days before an event and make a saving, Tel: 0870 60 60 611

Motor Racing Circuit

The Autumn Cheshire Antiques Fair

8/10/99
10/10/99
ARLEY HALL AND GARDENS
Tel: 01565 777353
A quality antique fair, datelined 1890 with quality additions to 1920. Times: Fri 12.00-18.00, Sat & Sun 11.00-17.00. Admission charged

Historic Houses & Gardens

Autumn Spectacular (BRSCC)

9/10/99
9/10/99
OULTON PARK
Tel: 01829 760301
Sports Palmer Audi, Formula Renault, Formula Ford 1600s, XR2 Challenge, XR3 Challenge. Island Circuit, Grade-D. On the Gate: £10.00-£28.00. In Advance: Non £8.00-£25.00, Club £7.00-£22.00. Two Day Pass: Non £11.00-£30.00, Club £10.00-£27.00. Three Day Pass: Non £32.00, Club £29.00. Qualifying: £5.00-£14.00. C£Free. Programme £Free-£5.00. Seating (BH): £Free-£8.00. Group Tickets: Non £90.00-£95.00, Club £80.00-£85.00. Season Ticket Inc. of Club Membership: £160.00. You can buy your tickets for any of the 1999 events in advance any time up to 4 days before an event and make a saving, Tel: 0870 60 60 611

Motor Racing Circuit

Seed Gathering Day

10/10/99
10/10/99
NORTON PRIORY MUSEUM AND GARDENS
Tel: 01928 569895
Join in our trees-for-the-millennium project and help grow 2,000 oaks for Halton as part of the Family Learning Weekend.

Gardens

Crewe and District Cage Bird Society
10/10/99 STAPELEY WATER GARDENS
10/10/99 Tel: 01270 623868
Bird show. All day

Gardens

Finding Fungi
16/10/99 NORTON PRIORY MUSEUM AND GARDENS
16/10/99 Tel: 01928 569895
Join our Ranger for a search through the Museum grounds at 14.30

Gardens

Apple Day
21/10/99 NORTON PRIORY MUSEUM AND GARDENS
21/10/99 Tel: 01928 569895
A free apple for everyone visiting the Walled Garden today!

Gardens

Art Exhibition
22/10/99 ARLEY HALL AND GARDENS
24/10/99 Tel: 01565 777353
Please contact Geoffrey key for further information

Historic Houses & Gardens

Fruit and Nuts
23/10/99 NORTON PRIORY MUSEUM AND GARDENS
31/10/99 Tel: 01928 569895
A seasonal quiz for all the family.

Gardens

A Celebration of Orchards
24/10/99 NORTON PRIORY MUSEUM AND GARDENS
24/10/99 Tel: 01928 569895
A family fun day with plenty of activities on Apple Day

Gardens

Ossie Clark - A Dazzling Decade 1967-1077
25/10/99 WARRINGTON MUSEUM AND ART GALLERY
1/1/00 Tel: 01925 442392/442398
A stunning collection of costumes from one of the nations most creative post-war fashion designers

Museums

Churchtown Country Show
26/10/99 MEOLS HALL
27/10/99 Tel: 01704 228326
Arena entertainment: Horse Show & Jumping, Family Pet Show, Gun Dogs, Sight Hounds Display, Lurcher, Terrer and Ferret Show and Racing. Fly Fishing, Open Air Rifle Competition - prizes. Rural Crafts and Handicraft, Floral Art and much much more. Gates open 10.30. (98 prices for guide only): A£3.00 C(0-12)£1.00. Call for further details

Historic Houses

The Great Norton Priory Plant Sale

30/10/99 NORTON PRIORY MUSEUM AND GARDENS
30/10/99 Tel: 01928 569895
End of season bargains for the serious gardener at our Walled Garden 14.00-16.00.

Gardens

Christmas Crafts at Arley
30/10/99 ARLEY HALL AND GARDENS
31/10/99 Tel: 01565 777353
70 exhibitors from all over the county with a selection of the finest examples of British Craftsmanship. Time: 10.00-17.00 both days. Admission: £1.50, concessions

Historic Houses & Gardens

Fantastic Fireworks Cruise
5/11/99 MERSEY FERRIES LTD
5/11/99 Tel: 0151 630 1030
Come aboard Mersey Ferries Fantastic Fireworks Cruise for the best view of the spectacular Liverpool City Council fireworks display off the Albert Dock, call for details

Boat Trips

Bonfire and Grand Firework Display
6/11/99 MEOLS HALL
6/11/99 Tel: 01704 228326
Presented by Millennium Pyrotechnics with side shows, fairground, barbecue. Gates open at 17.00, display approximately at 19.30. A£2.00 C£1.00. Pedestrians via the main gate, free car parking - Moss Lane entrance.

Historic Houses

Holsten Bier Fest
16/11/99 G-MEX CENTRE
6/12/99 Tel: 0161 834 2700
It's back again, and it's bigger than ever! Come along and boogie to 70s, 80s & 90s music every night. 16 Nov: Fast Freddie & The Fabulous Fingertips; 17 & 26 Nov: The F.B.I. Band; 18 Nov & 4 Dec: The Real ABBA Gold; 19 Nov: Vinyl Kutz; 20 Nov: Cheeky Monkees; 21 Nov: Queen B; 22 Nov: Gidea Park; 23 Nov: The Sounds of the Bee Gees; 24 Nov: The Blues Brothers Experience; 25 Nov: The New Recruits; 27 Nov: Wham/Duran; 28 Nov: Blurasis; 29 Nov & 6 Dec: Ballroom Blitz; 30 Nov: Borstal Boys; 1 Dec: Time Warp; 2 Dec: Platform Four; 3 Dec: Sunday Girl; 5 Dec: Bucks Fizz. Book today on: 0161 930 8888. Ticket Prices: Thur-Sat Evenings: £6.00, Sun-Wed Evenings: £4.00. Times: Mon-Wed: 19.00-23.00; Thur-Sat: 19.00-24.00; Sun: 19.00-22.30.

Exhibition Centres

Tree Dressing Celebration
20/11/99 NORTON PRIORY MUSEUM AND GARDENS
20/11/99 Tel: 01928 569895
Help our Ranger make environmentally friendly decorations at the Museum at 14.00.

Gardens

North West Bird Fair
20/11/99 WWT MARTIN MERE
21/11/99 Tel: 01704 895181
Stalls and exhibits, full programme of workshops and talks. See 1000's of wild ducks, geese and swans. Swan feeding times at 15.00 & 17.00

Waterfowl Parks

Family Fun Day
21/11/99 AINTREE RACECOURSE
21/11/99 Tel: 0151 523 2600
Aintree's first ever Sunday raceday ensures that all of the family will be entertained. Various sideshows and entertainers promise a great day out. Cost: from £6.00

Racecourses

National Tree Week
24/11/99 NORTON PRIORY MUSEUM AND GARDENS
5/12/99 Tel: 01928 569895
Special activities running.

Gardens

Christmas at the Priory
1/12/99 NORTON PRIORY MUSEUM AND GARDENS
17/12/99 Tel: 01928 569895
Victorian events for schools in the 800 year old priory storage range; please telephone for details. Enjoy the decorations and peaceful surroundings, and relax over tea and homemade cakes.

Gardens

Christmas in the Mansion
4/12/99 TATTON PARK
19/12/99 Tel: 01625 534400
Magnificent weekends in the Christmas Mansion. Special weekends each with their own themes, call for details

Country Parks

Winter Words
4/12/99 NORTON PRIORY MUSEUM AND GARDENS
9/1/00 Tel: 01928 569895
A quiz for children.

Gardens

Advent Carol Service
5/12/99 NORTON PRIORY MUSEUM AND GARDENS
5/12/99 Tel: 01928 569895
In the 800 year old priory storage range at 16.00; please book as numbers are limited.

Gardens

Winter Shopping Weekend
11/12/99 NORTON PRIORY MUSEUM AND GARDENS
12/12/99 Tel: 01928 569895
Ideas for last minute Christmas presents.

Gardens

Victorian Christmas
11/12/99 WEAVER'S TRIANGLE VISITOR CENTRE
12/12/99 Tel: 01282 452403
Santa visits by boat (weather permitting). Staff in Victorian costume in Victorian surroundings. Time: 14.00-16.00

Museum- Local History

Yuletide Magic
12/12/99 BRAMALL HALL
12/12/99 Tel: 0161 485 3708
Festive Open Days with Santa and entertainment. Also to be held on Sunday 19 Dec

Stately Homes

Christmas Concerts
13/12/99 TATTON PARK
17/12/99 Tel: 01625 534400
A staged pageant of Christmas music for orchestra and choir, including readings and carols. Mulled wine reception and candlelit tour of the Mansion

Country Parks

Adrian Henri
1/1/00 WALKER ART GALLERY
1/5/00 Tel: 0151 478 4199
Further details on the exhibition will be nearer the time

Art Galleries

String Quartets of the 20th Century
13/1/00 MANCHESTER QUARTET FEST 2000
16/1/00 Tel: 01625 530140
RNCM Manchester Quartet Fest celebrate String Quartets of the 20th century. Tickets available from Box Office: 0161 907 5278/5279

Festivals

Constable's Clouds
1/5/00 WALKER ART GALLERY
1/7/00 Tel: 0151 478 4199
Further details on this exhibition will be available nearer the time

Art Galleries

Death in Victorian And Edwardian Art
1/9/00 WALKER ART GALLERY
1/12/00 Tel: 0151 478 4199
Further details will be available nearer the time

Art Galleries

George Romney 1734-1802

Further more detailed information on the attractions listed can be found in Best Guides *Visitor Attractions* Guide under the classifications shown

1/1/02 1/6/02	**WALKER ART GALLERY** Tel: 0151 478 4199 Further details on this exhibition will be available nearer the time <div align="right">*Art Galleries*</div>
	Liverpool Pre-Raphaelites
1/7/02 1/9/02	**WALKER ART GALLERY** Tel: 0151 478 4199 Further details on this exhibition will be available nearer the time <div align="right">*Art Galleries*</div>

Northern England

Including:
Cumbria
Northumbria
Isle of Man

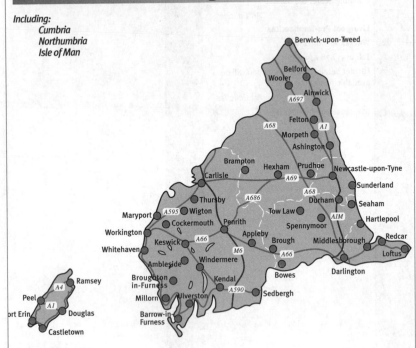

National Hunt Racing
1/3/99
1/3/99
NEWCASTLE RACECOURSE
Tel: 0191 236 2020
Enjoy a special day at Newcastle's historic racecourse. First Race 14.20, Last Race 16.55

Racecourses

Exhibition: Portrait of the Artist
1/3/99
11/4/99
ABBOT HALL ART GALLERY
Tel: 01539 722464
Portrait prints, including works by Rembrandt, Augustus John and Pierre Bonnard.

Art Galleries

Exhibitions: Tony Bevan
1/3/99
11/4/99
ABBOT HALL ART GALLERY
Tel: 01539 722464
New work by this leading British contemporary artist.

Art Galleries

Print Room Exhibition
2/3/99
14/3/99
DURHAM LIGHT INFANTRY MUSEUM AND DURHAM ART GALLERY
Tel: 0191 384 2214
Exhibition by Martin Fearnley

Museums

The People Show
12/3/99
1/4/99
UNIVERSITY GALLERY
Tel: 0191 227 4424
The People Show is an art competition and exhibition organised by The Journal newspaper and Cravens Advertising, to celebrate the creative talent of the many gifted amateur and professional artists living in the North East region. The theme of the competition is about people. Entries can include portraits, self-portraits, life studies and narrative or figure compositions in any recognised medium. This can include paintings, drawings, watercolours, prints, ceramics, sculpture or photography

Art Galleries

Durham Young Musicians
20/3/99
20/3/99
DURHAM LIGHT INFANTRY MUSEUM AND DURHAM ART GALLERY
Tel: 0191 384 2214
Helen Bruce and Kirsten Stuart - soprano and violin. Performance Time: 14.00. Tickets: £2.00 on the door

Museums

National Hunt Racing
20/3/99
20/3/99
NEWCASTLE RACECOURSE
Tel: 0191 236 2020
Enjoy a special day at Newcastle's historic racecourse. First Race 14.00, Last Race 16.35

Decorated Blankets
20/3/99
25/4/99
DURHAM LIGHT INFANTRY MUSEUM AND DURHAM ART GALLERY
Tel: 0191 384 2214
This exhibition will draw together the DLI Museum and Durham Art Gallery. Textile artist, Soraya Smithson has created pieces of work based on medals worn by specific individuals. These include the famous, the fictional, the unknown and the personal. The subjects range from Lord Mountbatten, Corporal Jones from Dad's Army to her own father. The exhibition will also include a piece commissioned by Durham Art Gallery featuring the medals of Colonel Annand from the DLI Regiment

Museums

Wildlife Photographer of the Year
20/3/99
25/4/99
DURHAM LIGHT INFANTRY MUSEUM AND DURHAM ART GALLERY
Tel: 0191 384 2214
An exhibition of the winning and commended photographs from the BG Wildlife Photographer of the Year Competition organised by BBC Wildlife Magazine and the Natural History Museum. The aim of the competition is to find the best wildlife pictures taken by photographers world-wide, and to emphasise through the work of such photographers, the beauty, wonder and importance of the natural world

Museums

Wedding Fayre
21/3/99
21/3/99
ORMESBY HALL
Tel: 01642 324188
Exhibits from cakes to cars, bouquets to bridal wear and lots more for your perfect wedding day. Civil wedding ceremonies now available at Ormesby Hall. Shop/tearoom open. Time: 12.00-16.00. Cost: 1.00.

Historic Houses & Gardens

National Hunt Racing
22/3/99
22/3/99
NEWCASTLE RACECOURSE
Tel: 0191 236 2020
Enjoy a special day at Newcastle's historic racecourse. First Race 14.00, Last Race 17.05

Racecourses

Artist blows up Belsay!
26/3/99
31/5/99
BELSAY HALL
Tel: 01661 881636
Artist, Maddi Nicholson blows up Belsay! Normal admission prices apply

---

A weekly updated selection of UK wide special events can be found on the award winning sites @ www.thisislondon.com *and* www.ukplus.co.uk

Castles

Ceilidh with "Coffee Bridge"

27/3/99   DURHAM LIGHT INFANTRY MUSEUM AND DURHAM ART GALLERY

27/3/99   Tel: 0191 384 2214

In association with Darwin Brewery. Time: 20.00-22.45. Licensed Bar. Tickets: £2.00-£3.00 on the door

Museums

House Open Day

27/3/99   ORMESBY HALL

27/3/99   Tel: 01642 324188

Come and view this spectacular house.

Historic Houses & Gardens

BRDA Rallycross First Round

28/3/99   CROFT CIRCUIT

28/3/99   Tel: 01325 721815

Take the rough with the smooth and see action-packed racing with grunt and grit!!

Motor Racing Circuit

Lambing Time

28/3/99   HALL HILL FARM

18/4/99   Tel: 01388 730300

A wonderful time of the year, lambs are springing up all over the Farm

Farm Parks

First Mixed Meeting

30/3/99   NEWCASTLE RACECOURSE

30/3/99   Tel: 0191 236 2020

Flat and National Hunt Racing. First Race 14.15, Last Race 17.00

Racecourses

Exhibition: "Funny Ha! Ha!" by Andy Hollingworth

30/3/99   THE BEACON

6/6/99   Tel: 01946 592302

This photographic exhibition has emerged from Hollingworth's life-long love of comedy and comedians. It represents a marvellous cross section of the different movements in British comedy over the last 40 years, and captures rare moments with many top comedians such as, Frank Carson, Harry Secombe, Ken Dodd, Bruce Forsyth, Victoria Wood, Jasper Carrot, Jo Brand, Alexei Sayle, and many more. It starts with the music halls, moves on to the 'golden age' of radio comedy, stars of the "Carry on Films", stand-up comedians made famous by television in the 1970's, the "new wave" comedians centred around the "Young Ones" and "Comic Strip" Series of the early 1980's, plus those representing the resurgence of stand up and "club" comedy. The exhibition also

reminds us of those who are now absent, which include: Frankie Howerd, Les Dawson, Eric Morecambe and Tommy Cooper. The exhibition features a unique photograph of Beryl Reid, Andy Hollingworth was the last person to photograph her before her death, this piece is now owned by The National Portrait Gallery, London

Museum- Local History

Easter Treasure Hunt

2/4/99   CURRAGHS WILDLIFE PARK

5/4/99   Tel: 01624 897323

Look for hidden objects in the Park and win yourself a prize

Wildlife Parks

National Hunt Racing

3/4/99   CARLISLE RACECOURSE

5/4/99   Tel: 01228 522973

Bank Holiday racing on Easter Sat & Mon with free creche and children's entertainer

Racecourses

Exhibition

3/4/99   GRIZEDALE SOCIETY - SCULPTURE TRAILS AND GALLERY

30/4/99   Tel: 01229 860291

By Artist in Residence: 1998 - Ian Walton

Art Gallery- Open Air

Music in the Hall

4/4/99   ORMESBY HALL

4/4/99   Tel: 01642 324188

First Sunday in every month, come and enjoy music in the hall. Program varies, ring for details. Time: 14.00-17.00.

Historic Houses & Gardens

Napoleonic Redcoats

4/4/99   CARLISLE CASTLE

5/4/99   Tel: 01228 591922

68th Display Team and 33rd Foot Light infantry drills, tactics and musket firing. From 12.00. A£3.00 C£1.50 Concessions£2.30

Castles

Medieval Music

4/4/99   LANERCOST PRIORY

5/4/99   Tel: 016977 3030

Misericcordia. Lively medieval music played by a costume duo. From 12.00. A£3.00 C£1.50 Concessions£2.30

Priory

Easter Monday

5/4/99   NEWCASTLE RACECOURSE

5/4/99   Tel: 0191 236 2020

Bank Holiday Meeting. First Race 14.25, last race 17.35

Racecourses

Further more detailed information on the attractions listed can be found in Best Guides *Visitor Attractions* Guide under the classifications shown

Easter Eggstravaganza
5/4/99 ORMESBY HALL
5/4/99 Tel: 01642 324188
Egg decorating competition. Bring your own decorated egg or have great fun decorating an egg at the Hall. Prizes for different age groups. Easter bonnet competition. Easter trail around the Hall and Gardens with prizes for all!! Time: 14.00-16.00.
Historic Houses & Gardens

John Davies Exhibition
14/4/99 UNIVERSITY GALLERY
21/5/99 Tel: 0191 227 4424
An exhibition displaying the sculptures and drawings of John Davies
Art Galleries

Club Motorcycles New Era
17/4/99 CROFT CIRCUIT
18/4/99 Tel: 01325 721815
Club Motorcycling new era. Fast paced action with something for all two wheel fans. Sat A£5.00 C£2.00 Sun £9.00 Weekend £12.00
Motor Racing Circuit

North East Birdwatching Festival
17/4/99 WILDFOWL AND WETLANDS TRUST WASHINGTON
18/4/99 Tel: 0191 416 5454
Pit your wits in the Bird Brain of Northumbria Quiz, browse among the many stalls of wildlife merchandise.
Wildlife Trusts

Trusty's Birthday
18/4/99 ORMESBY HALL
18/4/99 Tel: 01642 324188
Guest appearance from Trusty himself to blow out the candles on his cake. Old fashion party games. Prize for all winners. Time: 14.00-16.00.
Historic Houses & Gardens

Art & the Historic Environment
19/4/99 PRUDHOE CASTLE
2/5/99 Tel: 01661 833459
Please call for further information. A£1.80 C£0.90 Concessions£1.40
Castles

Exhibition: Maria Chevska
20/4/99 ABBOT HALL ART GALLERY
6/6/99 Tel: 01539 722464
Beautiful abstract paintings exploring the links between the spoken and written word.
Art Galleries

Exhibition: Edward Hughes - Pottery

ABBOT HALL ART GALLERY
20/4/99
6/6/99 Tel: 01539 722464
New pottery by this highly acclaimed Cumbrian-based maker, which will then tour to Japan.
Art Galleries

Flat Racing at Carlisle
23/4/99 CARLISLE RACECOURSE
10/6/99 Tel: 01228 522973
Racing on 23 Apr, 7 May, 10 June
Racecourses

Victorian Day & Teachers Free Day
25/4/99 ORMESBY HALL
25/4/99 Tel: 01642 324188
Try your hand at possing, mangling, baking bread whilst experiencing life in the Victorian kitchen and laundry. Enjoy Victorian games and pastimes. Teachers have the opportunity to find out about our education programme.
Historic Houses & Gardens

Garden Tour
29/4/99 ORMESBY HALL
29/4/99 Tel: 01642 324188
Tour Ormesby Hall's garden with the Gardener in Charge on the last Thursday of every month. Lots of expert tips to be learnt. Time: 14.30.
Historic Houses & Gardens

Racing at Redcar
29/4/99 REDCAR RACECOURSE
1/11/99 Tel: 01642 484068
Race meetings every month. Please call for further information
Racecourses

The Teesdale Thrash
30/4/99 BARNARD CASTLE
3/5/99 Tel: 01833 638212
Come along to this Folk Dancing and Morris Dancing Festival which will be held at various venues within the Castle. There will be a parade, street dancing, craft fair, circus-style entertainment for children, singaround sessions, ceilidh, folk club, bouncy castles, evening folk concert, workshops, dance parade, dancing at Bowes Museum. From 20.00 on 30th-12.00 on 3rd. Ceilidh/Concert: A£5.00 C£2.50, Workshops £1.00. For further information please contact Roy Tranter 01833 638288
Castles

Pookie and the Animal Shelf
1/5/99 DURHAM LIGHT INFANTRY MUSEUM AND

DURHAM ART GALLERY
13/6/99 Tel: 0191 384 2214
Original artwork for children's books,
plus photographs and sets created for
the television series by Ivy Wallace.
From the Collins Gallery, Glasgow
Museums

Folk Songs
2/5/99 BRINKBURN PRIORY
2/5/99 Tel: 01665 570628
Northumbrian folk songs performed by
Ann Wilkinson
Priory

Music in the Hall
2/5/99 ORMESBY HALL
2/5/99 Tel: 01642 324188
First Sunday in every month, come and
enjoy music in the hall. Program varies,
ring for details. Time: 14.00-17.00.
Historic Houses & Gardens

Medieval Living History - Rosa Mundi
2/5/99 AYDON CASTLE
3/5/99 Tel: 01434 632450
Visit a 15th century household with
retainers, servants and soldiers as
Easter and the end of Lent are celebrat-
ed with raucous games. From 12.00.
A£3.00 C£1.50 Concessions£2.30
English Heritage Members Free
Historic Houses

Legends of King Arthur
2/5/99 BARNARD CASTLE
3/5/99 Tel: 01833 638212
Labyrinth Productions. Magical stories
about King Arthur, with Guinevere,
Lancelot, Merlin, the Black Knight and
the evil Morgan Le Fay. From 14.30.
A£3.50 C£1.80 Concessions£2.60
Castles

The Bard's Best Bits
2/5/99 BELSAY HALL
3/5/99 Tel: 01661 881636
Once again this hugely entertaining
group comprehensively demolish
Shakespeare! See the best bits from
Julius Caesar, Romeo and Juliet and A
Midsummer Night's Dream. Don't miss
it! A£3.80 C£1.90 Concessions£2.90
Castles

Past Pleasures
2/5/99 CHESTERS ROMAN FORT
3/5/99 Tel: 01434 681379
Come sample 17-century pleasures of
the past with John Clayton. A£2.80
C£1.40 Concessions£2.10
Roman Forts

DDMC Club Cars

CROFT CIRCUIT
2/5/99
3/5/99 Tel: 01325 721815
Club racing at it's best watch as a Skoda
takes on and beats an MG!!
Motor Racing Circuit

Medieval War Battle
2/5/99 TYNEMOUTH CASTLE
3/5/99 Tel: 0191 257 1090
Escafield Medieval Society. Living
History encampment, with a battle
between union and. A£3.50 C£1.80
Concessions£2.60 English Heritage
Members Free
Priory

Have-a-go-Archery
2/5/99 WARKWORTH CASTLE AND HERMITAGE
3/5/99 Tel: 01665 711423
Arrowflight. 14th century archers introduce visitors to the art of archery.
A£2.50 C£1.30 Concessions£1.90
Castles

May Day
3/5/99 NEWCASTLE RACECOURSE
3/5/99 Tel: 0191 236 2020
Bank Holiday Meeting. first race 14.30,
last race 17.05
Racecourses

Beatrix Potter Day
3/5/99 ORMESBY HALL
3/5/99 Tel: 01642 324188
Fun for all ages with Beatrix Potter's
favourite characters. Storytelling,
games, colouring competition and mystery guest.
Historic Houses & Gardens

Tinemouth May Day Festival
3/5/99 WINDOW ON THE WORLD INTERNATIONAL
MUSIC FESTIVAL 1999
3/5/99 Tel: 0191 200 5415
In a beautiful renovated Victorian
Station, crafts, exhibitions and street
entertainment for all the family
Festivals

Dog Agility Festival
8/5/99 NORTH OF ENGLAND OPEN-AIR MUSEUM
9/5/99 Tel: 01207 231811
Watch 400 of the country's top agility
dogs in action against the clock.
Featuring jumps, see-saws, tunnels and
more. For further information please
contact Jacki Winstanley 01207 231811
Museum- Social History

World of Interiors
13/5/99 BELSAY HALL
13/5/99 Tel: 01661 881636
With various performers. Normal admission prices apply

Further more detailed information on the attractions listed can be found
in Best Guides *Visitor Attractions* Guide under the classifications shown

Castles

Fell Pony Society Stallion Show

15/5/99   DALEMAIN HISTORIC HOUSE AND
GARDENS

15/5/99   Tel: 017684 86450

The Fell Pony Society's premier display of registered stallions and young colts from all over Britain in the heart of this ancient Native Breed's homeland. Further information from 01670 76117

Historic Houses & Gardens

The Knight's Templar

15/5/99   MOUNT GRACE PRIORY

16/5/99   Tel: 01609 883494

Medieval re-enactment by The Troop. A£3.50 C£1.80 Concessions£2.50

Priory

Spring Garden Show & Quality Craft Fair

15/5/99   ORMESBY HALL

16/5/99   Tel: 01642 324188

Marquees and outside stalls featuring a wide selection of growers of plants, specialist growers, garden accessories and ornaments, displays and advice. Garden tours. Large craft fair with a massive range of quality crafts and gifts. Children's activities and entertainment. Floral Art Competition throughout the mansion. 10.00-17.00

Historic Houses & Gardens

Ballads & Bayonets - 47th Hautbois

15/5/99   RICHMOND CASTLE

16/5/99   Tel: 01748 822493

Lively music, British redcoats, drill, musket firing, encampment and a fascinating comparison between a soldier of 1778 and 1998. From 12.00. A£3.50 C£1.80 Concessions£2.60

Castles

Windermere Model Boat Rally

15/5/99   WINDERMERE STEAMBOAT MUSEUM

16/5/99   Tel: 015394 45565

Rally of model boats from all over the country, judging and competitions, call for further details

Museum- Ships/Boat

Museums Week

15/5/99   THE CUMBERLAND TOY AND MODEL MUSEUM

23/5/99   Tel: 01900 827606

Something special for all children this week, try our Children's Travel Quiz

Museum- Toy

North West Driving Club

16/5/99   DALEMAIN HISTORIC HOUSE AND
GARDENS

16/5/99   Tel: 017684 86450

One day horse driving trials held in The Park at Dalemain. Further information from 01539 726503

Historic Houses & Gardens

Spring Plant Fair

16/5/99   SOUTER LIGHTHOUSE

16/5/99   Tel: 0191 529 3161

Sale of volunteer grown plants of all types, commences 11.00. Attractive prices

Lighthouses

Jennings Keswick Jazz Festival

21/5/99   JENNINGS KESWICK JAZZ FESTIVAL 1999

23/5/99   Tel: 01900 602122 Box Office

More than 80 separate events of non-stop traditional jazz featuring Britain's leading bands and guests from the USA and Europe. Colourful New Orleans-style street parade on the Saturday morning and a morning jazz service and an early evening 'Songs of Praise.' Time: 12.00-23.00 daily. Ticket Prices: Fri: £12.50, Sat £19.50, Sun £13.00. Tickets available from: 01900 602122. Continuous jazz bus services links all venues and are free to ticket holders. Please telephone 01900 602122 for further information

Festivals

The Grizedale International Piano Festival

21/5/99   THE GRIZEDALE INTERNATIONAL PIANO FESTIVAL

23/5/99   Tel: 01229 860291

Venue: Grizedale Forest Park. In the daytime there are over 80 site-related sculptures on many miles of forest track. All forest walks are freely available. In the evening the very best piano music from around the world - 22 May: Katya Apekisheva (Israel), 23 May: artist to be announced, 24 May: Christof Berner (Austria). Times: Daytime: Gallery in Forest 10.00-16.00, Evening: performance starts at 20.00. Ticket Prices: A£12.00 C£8.00. Special Series Ticket £32.00. Free admission to the Gallery in Forest

CLOSED FOR GOOD

Garden Tour

23/5/99   BELSAY HALL

23/5/99   Tel: 01661 881636

The first in a season of tours at 19.00 with Paul Harrigan (Head Gardener) and/or expert guides around Belsay's beautiful and unusual gardens. Tickets are strictly limited to 40 and pre-booking is essential. Please call for details

Castles

Coniston Water Festival 1999

23/5/99 CONISTON WATER FESTIVAL 1999
31/5/99 Tel: 01539 441707
Sailing, fell running, bowling, tennis, cricket, pony trekking, lake cruises, mountain biking. Various exhibitions. Price: Various. Some events are free.

Festivals

Art in Collaboration 1999

24/5/99 PRUDHOE CASTLE
11/6/99 Tel: 01661 833459
Title to be confirmed. A£1.80 C£0.90 Concessions£1.40

Castles

Bank Holiday Racing

26/5/99 CARTMEL RACECOURSE
31/5/99 Tel: 01539 536340
Enjoy a truly unique atmosphere with National Hunt Racing at Cartmel on 26, 29, 31 May. Plenty of refreshment and catering facilities to suit all tastes, with a large fairground and market stalls in the Course Enclosure

Racecourses

Window on the World - FRINGE - International Music Festival

26/5/99 WINDOW ON THE WORLD INTERNATIONAL MUSIC FESTIVAL 1999
6/6/99 Tel: 0191 200 5415
World, Jazz, Pop, Folk Music. Street Theatre. Children's entertainment, exhibitions, boat trips, craft-market, funfair, workshops, details programme available.

Festivals

Flat Meeting

27/5/99 NEWCASTLE RACECOURSE
27/5/99 Tel: 0191 236 2020
Enjoy a special day at Newcastle's historic racecourse. First Race 14.20, Last Race 16.50

Racecourses

Diverse Landscapes

28/5/99 UNIVERSITY GALLERY
2/7/99 Tel: 0191 227 4424
Exhibtion of the works of Angela Hughes and Paul Gallagher

Art Galleries

Window on the World Outdoors International Music Festival

29/5/99 WINDOW ON THE WORLD INTERNATIONAL MUSIC FESTIVAL 1999
31/5/99 Tel: 0191 200 5415
Celebrate International music on the

working Quayside, 4 stages, 2 street arenas, markets, fair, exhibitions and street theatre

Festivals

Downy Duckling Days

29/5/99 WILDFOWL AND WETLANDS TRUST WASHINGTON
25/7/99 Tel: 0191 416 5454
Visit the nursery to see ducklings and goslings take their first wobbly steps. Also, children's activities.

Wildlife Trusts

Brass Band Music

30/5/99 BRINKBURN PRIORY
30/5/99 Tel: 01665 570628
Performed by the Phoenix Brass Band. Normal admission prices apply

Priory

Roman Festival

30/5/99 CORBRIDGE ROMAN SITE
30/5/99 Tel: 01434 632349
Sample recipes, try your hand at mosaic making and meet Roman Soldiers of the 1st and 3rd centuries. From 12.00. A£4.00 C£2.00 Concessions£3.00 English Heritage Members Free

Archaeological Sites

Ford RS Owners Club Rally

30/5/99 DALEMAIN HISTORIC HOUSE AND GARDENS
30/5/99 Tel: 017684 86450
Well established and popular Rally. Concourse displays, trade stands and family attractions. Further information from 01539 728469

Historic Houses & Gardens

Vintage & Classic Motorcycle Show & Sprint

30/5/99 ORMESBY HALL
30/5/99 Tel: 01642 324188
Teedside's premier mototcycle event. Witness the exhilaration of vintage and classic machines from the last 80 years speeding through the park in a hotly contested speed competition. Visit the static display of motorcycles exhibited in a competition to be the best in their class. Apply to Ormesby Hall for competitors entrance forms.
Commemorative brass plaques for all entrants to the static competition. Entrance price includes entrance to the Hall, Gardens, Model Railway layouts and exhibition. 11.00-17.00.

Historic Houses & Gardens

The Bard's Best Bits

30/5/99 31/5/99	**BARNARD CASTLE** Tel: 01833 638212 Once again this hugely entertaining group comprehensively demolish Shakespeare! See the best bits from Julius Caesar, Romeo and Juliet and A Midsummer Night's Dream. Don't miss it! A£3.50 C£1.80 Concessions£2.60 *Castles*

Medieval Combat

30/5/99 31/5/99	**CARLISLE CASTLE** Tel: 01228 591922 The Escafeld Medieval Society. Exciting 13th century tournament, mime, juggling and dance from 12.00. A£3.50 C£1.80 Concessions£2.60 *Castles*

Sheep Shearing

30/5/99 31/5/99	**HALL HILL FARM** Tel: 01388 730300 Spend Bank Holiday see our sheep losing their winter coats *Farm Parks*

Have-a-go Archery

30/5/99 31/5/99	**MOUNT GRACE PRIORY** Tel: 01609 883494 14th century archers introduce visitors to the art of archery, from 12.00. A£2.80 C£1.40 Concessions£2.10 English Heritage Members Free *Priory*

Medieval Living History

30/5/99 31/5/99	**NORHAM CASTLE** Tel: 01289 382329 Rosa Mundi. Life in a 15th century household, from 12.00. A£3.00 C£1.50 Concessions£2.30 English Heritage Members Free *Castles*

More Skulduggery!

30/5/99 31/5/99	**WARKWORTH CASTLE AND HERMITAGE** Tel: 01665 711423 Silly tales of secret maps, buried treasure and famous pirates. From 12.00. A£2.50 C£1.30 Concessions£1.90 English Heritage Members Free *Castles*

Vintage Motorcycle Rally

31/5/99 31/5/99	**BELSAY HALL** Tel: 01661 881636 An excellent car show with various performers. Normal admission prices apply *Castles*

Traditional Music

31/5/99 31/5/99	**BRINKBURN PRIORY** Tel: 01665 570628 Performed by Robin Dunn & Sue Morgan *Priory*

Roman Festival

31/5/99 31/5/99	**CHESTERS ROMAN FORT** Tel: 01434 681379 Sample recipes, try your hand at mosaic making and meet Roman Soldiers of the 1st and 3rd centuries, from 12.00. A£4.00 C£2.00 Concessions£3.00 *Roman Forts*

Scottish Pipe Band Association

31/5/99 31/5/99	**RICHMOND CASTLE** Tel: 01748 822493 Royal Scottish Pipe Band Association, from 12.00. Enjoy the skirl of the pipes as top bands compete in this annual competition. A£3.00 C£1.50 Concessions£2.30 *Castles*

Family Entertainers

1/6/99 3/6/99	**WARKWORTH CASTLE AND HERMITAGE** Tel: 01665 711423 Games, have-a-go archery, costumes for children to try on and talks on weaponry. A£3.00 C£1.50 Concessions£2.30 *Castles*

Flat Racing

2/6/99 2/6/99	**NEWCASTLE RACECOURSE** Tel: 0191 236 2020 Enjoy a special day at Newcastle's historic racecourse. First Race 14.20, Last Race 16.55 *Racecourses*

Bat Watch

4/6/99 4/6/99	**BELSAY HALL** Tel: 01661 881636 Come and watch these fabulous creatures with Dr. Veronica Howard. Normal admission prices apply *Castles*

Holker Garden Festival

4/6/99 6/6/99	**HOLKER HALL AND GARDENS** Tel: 015395 58328 Holker's eighth Garden Festival promising to be the friendliest and finest horticultural event in the Summer calendar. Attractions include: Horticultural Marquee, Festival Gardens, Society Displays, Floral Art, Large Sales Marquee containing Horticultural sundries, crafts and fine foods. Times of Opening: Fri & Sat 10.00-18.00, Sun 10.00-17.30. Gate Price A£7.00, C£3.00, OAPs£5.50. Advance Ticket Price A£6.00, C(0-12)Free C(12-16)£2.50

OAPs£5.00. Advance tickets available from the Show Office or from Tourist Information Centres within the area. Please call Holker Hall for further information

Historic Houses & Gardens

Garden Tour
5/6/99 BELSAY HALL
5/6/99 Tel: 01661 881636
Paul Harrigan (Head Gardener) shows you around Belsay Hall gardens. Normal admission prices apply

Castles

Cantabile
5/6/99 BRINKBURN PRIORY
5/6/99 Tel: 01665 570628
A musical performance with various performers

Priory

Medieval Entertainers - Heuristics
5/6/99 BARNARD CASTLE
6/6/99 Tel: 01833 638212
Games, squire-training and talks on weaponry and armour. Also, try your hand at spinning, weaving and calligraphy and learn about herbal medicine. From 12.00. A£3.00 C£1.50 Concessions£2.30

Castles

The TFM Tuscan Parade & TVR Championship Weekend
5/6/99 CROFT CIRCUIT
6/6/99 Tel: 01325 721815
TVR Tuscans, Mini Se7en, Mini Miglia, Porsche 924, Protons, Alfa Romeo, Formula 600 & Croft Saloon and Sports Car. Sat A£6.00, Sun A£11.00 (£9.00 in advance if purchased before 26 July), Weekend Ticket A£15.00, C£2.00

Motor Racing Circuit

Model Railway Day
6/6/99 ORMESBY HALL
6/6/99 Tel: 01642 324188
A special Model Railway day for model enthusiasts. Special demonstrations of modelling techniques and layout construction. Trade stalls and expert advice on all aspects of modelling. Four demonstration layouts featuring amazing Corfe Castle Layout, Pilmoor and Braferton Junction (used to be near Northallerton) and a children's 'hands-on' layout with Thomas and his friends. Shop and tearoom open from 10.00. Time: 10.00-17.00.

Historic Houses & Gardens

Exhibition: "Reflections: Historic

Views of Whitehaven Harbour"
8/6/99 THE BEACON
1/8/99 Tel: 01946 592302
A stunning exhibition produced from the Museums Collection of paintings of Whitehaven Harbour. This exhibition will chart the development of the harbour and provide a rare opportunity to view some of The Beacon's 700 paintings. The paintings on display span from the early 18th century to the 20th century, and will include the famous "Birds eye view of Whitehaven" by Mathias Read, 1736. Other artists on display include: Edward Lyon, Leonard Roope, Robert Salmon, John Bousfield, Frank Waddington and George Nelson. This exhibition will be taking place during Whitehaven's spectacular Festival of the Sea. The Festival is planned for late June and will see the arrival of square rigged sailing ships and various other maritime attractions

Museum- Local History

Medieval Entertainers
12/6/99 NORHAM CASTLE
13/6/99 Tel: 01289 382329
Games, squire-training and talks on weaponry and armour. Also, try your hand at spinning, weaving and calligraphy and learn about herbal medicine. A£3.00 C£1.50 Concessions£2.30

Castles

Legends of King Arthur
12/6/99 PRUDHOE CASTLE
13/6/99 Tel: 01661 833459
Labyrinth Productions. Magical stories about King Arthur, with Guinevere, Lancelot, Merlin, the Black Knight and the evil Morgan Le Fay. A£3.00 C£1.50 Concessions£2.30

Castles

NCCPG Plant Sale
13/6/99 BELSAY HALL
13/6/99 Tel: 01661 881636
Various participants. Stock up on a huge variety of interesting and unusual plants. Normal admission prices apply

Castles

Choral Concert
13/6/99 BRINKBURN PRIORY
13/6/99 Tel: 01665 570628
Performed by the Alnwick Choral Society

Priory

Dalemain Garden Enthusiast's Plant Day
13/6/99 DALEMAIN HISTORIC HOUSE AND

GARDENS

13/6/99   Tel: 017684 86450

Stock up on classic English plants including the much loved familiar perennials, old fashioned roses and rarer and more unusual plants. Further information from 017684 86450

Historic Houses & Gardens

Canine Capers

13/6/99   ORMESBY HALL

13/6/99   Tel: 01642 324188

A fun dog show for all the family including 'Fido'! Enter your family pet in the 'dog that ate the sausages the fastest' or 'the dog who looks the most like it's owner'. There are special 'doggy' prizes in each competition with consolation prizes for others. Enjoy the antics and skills of the Cleveland Dog Agility Group. Why not pamper your dog with our 'Dog Beautician'. 14.00-16.30.

Historic Houses & Gardens

Exhibition: Queen Victoria's Travels and Family

15/6/99   ABBOT HALL ART GALLERY

19/9/99   Tel: 01539 722464

A touring exhibition of watercolours from Windsor Castle, commissioned by Queen Victoria as souvenirs of royal visits in Britain and abroad.

Art Galleries

Exhibition: 20th-Century Works from the Abbot Hall Collection

15/6/99   ABBOT HALL ART GALLERY

31/10/99   Tel: 01539 722464

A small exhibition of paintings from the permanent collection. The show will also include recent acquisitions by Ben Nicholson, Frank Auerbach, Alison Wilding and Bridget Riley.

Art Galleries

Mananan International Festival of Music and the Arts 1999

18/6/99   MANANAN INTERNATIONAL FESTIVAL OF MUSIC AND THE ARTS 1999

3/7/99   Tel: 01624 835858

Over the years the Mananan Festival has expanded from a few days to two full weeks. It has become one of the best of the small festivals, known all over the world, and internationally favous artists ask to take part. Classical music, opera and ballet, jazz, theatre, films, lectures, Indian Music, art exhibitions and mixed media presentations have been included in the programme together with special events for children.

Festivals

Medieval Monastic Entertainers

19/6/99   BRINKBURN PRIORY

20/6/99   Tel: 01665 570628

Heuristics. Try your hand at calligraphy or authentic period games as this popular duo take a lighthearted look at monastic customs, crafts and lifestyles. Learn about food preparation, herbs and spices in cooking and medicine, the mechanics of building, lifting and many other skills. Part of Cistercian 900. A£3.00 C£1.50 Concessions£2.30

Priory

Have-a-go-Archery

19/6/99   BROUGHAM CASTLE

20/6/99   Tel: 01768 862488

Arrowflight. 14th century archers introduce visitors to the art of archery. A£2.50 C£1.30 Concessions£1.90

Castles

The Lion, the Witch and the Wardrobe

19/6/99   LINDISFARNE PRIORY

20/6/99   Tel: 01289 389200

A classic children's tale performed by Labyrinth Productions. A£3.50 C£1.80 Concessions£2.60

Priory

Medieval Living History

19/6/99   RICHMOND CASTLE

20/6/99   Tel: 01748 822493

Various performers. A small 15th century military encampment, drill, archery, ,mumming plays and dancing, plus courtly music. A£3.50 C£1.80 Concessions£2.60

Castles

Contemporary Glasswork

19/6/99   DURHAM LIGHT INFANTRY MUSEUM AND DURHAM ART GALLERY

1/8/99   Tel: 0191 384 2214

Please telephone for further information

Museums

Guild of Glass Engravers

19/6/99   DURHAM LIGHT INFANTRY MUSEUM AND DURHAM ART GALLERY

1/8/99   Tel: 0191 384 2214

New work from members of the Northern Branch of the GGE

Museums

Music Treat

20/6/99   CURRAGHS WILDLIFE PARK

20/6/99   Tel: 01624 897323

Dance and Folk music all day in the Park

Wildlife Parks

Carlisle Bell and Cumberland Plate

23/6/99 24/6/99	**CARLISLE RACECOURSE** Tel: 01228 522973 Flat Racing at 14.00

Racecourses

EBF Condition Stakes

24/6/99 24/6/99	**NEWCASTLE RACECOURSE** Tel: 0191 236 2020 Flat Racing at Newcastle. First race 14.20, last race 16.50

Racecourses

Northern Rock Gosforth Park Cup

25/6/99 25/6/99	**NEWCASTLE RACECOURSE** Tel: 0191 236 2020 Evening Race meeting at Newcastle's historic racecourse. First Race 19.00, Last Race 21.30

Racecourses

Raby Classical Concert

25/6/99 25/6/99	**RABY CASTLE** Tel: 01833 660202 Outdoor classical concert with fireworks in aid of South Durham Hospice

Castles

The Newcastle Brown Ale Northumberland Plate

26/6/99 26/6/99	**NEWCASTLE RACECOURSE** Tel: 0191 236 2020 Enjoy a special day at Newcastle's historic racecourse. First Race 14.10, Last Race 17.20

Racecourses

Falconry

26/6/99 27/6/99	**CARLISLE CASTLE** Tel: 01228 591922 Medieval costumed falconer flying birds of prey. A£3.50 C£1.80 Concessions£2.60

Castles

1660s Living History

26/6/99 27/6/99	**MOUNT GRACE PRIORY** Tel: 01609 883494 17th-century re-enactment by The Siege Group. A£3.50 C£1.80 Concessions£2.50

Priory

Whitehaven Maritime Festival

26/6/99 27/6/99	**WHITEHAVEN MARITIME FESTIVAL** Tel: 0117 9276614 Tall ships and small ships. Exhibitions. Live music, street entertainment, food and drink

Festivals

Longbow Shooting Competition

27/6/99 27/6/99	**BELSAY HALL** Tel: 01661 881636 The Ponteland Archers. Have-a-go archery, exhibition and longbow competition, from 10.00

Castles

Last Night of The Leighton Proms

2/7/99 2/7/99	**LEIGHTON HALL** Tel: 01524 734474 A nationally acclaimed evening of classical music and pyrotechnics, call for further details. The following info is for guide lines only: Proms concerts tend to sell out early: please reserve tickets in good time, especially group bookings. Tickets A£16.50 C(5-18)£9.00. Ticket Hotline: 01625 56 00 00

Historic Houses

Open-Air Concert: The Music of the Night

2/7/99 2/7/99	**ORMESBY HALL** Tel: 01642 324188 This spectacular outdoor concert featuring hits of some of the world's greatest musicals. Four stars direct from London's West End, Sarah Ryan (Christine - Phantom), Alistair Robins (Marius - Les Miserables), Garth Bardsley (Raoul - Phantom) and Ria Jones (Grizabella - Cats) bring you great hits from Phantom of the Opera, Les Miserable, Miss Saigon, Westside Story, Guys and Dolls and many more of your favourites from the West End shows concluding with a spectacular fireworks finale live to the finale of the show! Grounds open 18.00. Support band from 19.00. Bring picnics, chairs/rugs. Ticket Prices: A£15.00 C(under 14)£7.00. Group discounts: buy 15 tickets get one free. Ample free parking close to concert area.

Historic Houses & Gardens

60s Spectacular

3/7/99 3/7/99	**ORMESBY HALL** Tel: 01642 324188 Relive the swinging 60s/early 70s at this super concert featuring the original stars of the hits. The entertainment kicks off with hits such as 'The Crying Game', 'Mama' and 'Little Things' by Dave Berry and the Cruisers. Followed by all time favourites Mike Penders Searchers. Remember hits like 'Sweets for my Sweet', 'Sugar and Spice', 'Don't throw your love Away', 'Needles and Pins' plus many more. The finale of the evening are the fabulous Billy Lewis's Drifters! A fantastic fireworks finale concludes the evening. Grounds open 18.00. Show starts at 19.30. Bring picnics, rugs/chairs. Ticket Prices: A£15.00 C(under 14)£7.00. Group discounts: buy

15 get one free. Ample free parking close to concert area.

Historic Houses & Gardens

Inspiration to Paint in Watercolour

3/7/99
4/7/99
BELSAY HALL
Tel: 01661 881636
An art demonstration by Susan Edwards. Normal admission prices apply

Castles

The Siege of Carlise Castle, 1645

3/7/99
4/7/99
CARLISLE CASTLE
Tel: 01228 591922
The second Civil War, July 1645. Scots soldiers of the ill-fated invasion of England hold the castle for King Charles I. Living history, musket, pike and cannon drill from 12.00. A£4.00 C£2.00 Concessions£3.00

Castles

Border Reivers!

3/7/99
4/7/99
CHESTERS ROMAN FORT
Tel: 01434 681379
Exciting equestrian skills-at-arms of the dreaded Borders Reivers, from 12.00. A£4.00 C£2.00 Concessions£3.00 English Heritage Members Free

Roman Forts

The Auto Trader RAC British Touring Car Championship

3/7/99
4/7/99
CROFT CIRCUIT
Tel: 01325 721815
The Auto Trader RAC Touring Cars, Formula Ford, Ford Fiesta, Formula Renault, Renault Spider, Vauchall Vectra, Formula Vauxhall Junior. Fri A£5.00, Sat A£10.00, Sun A£18.00 (£15.00 in advance if purchased before 7 June), Weekend Ticket A£28.00 (£25.00 in advance if purchased before 7 June), C£3.00

Motor Racing Circuit

Flat Meetings

3/7/99
16/7/99
CARLISLE RACECOURSE
Tel: 01228 522973
Evening meeting at 18.40 on 3 July, 14.15 start on 16 July

Racecourses

American Independence Day Celebrations

4/7/99
4/7/99
WASHINGTON OLD HALL
Tel: 0191 416 6879
Raising of the Stars and Stripes and various presentations and displays from local groups. Refreshments and stalls, free admission

Historic Buildings

Calligraphy Group

5/7/99
24/7/99
PRUDHOE CASTLE
Tel: 01661 833459
A£1.80 C£0.90 Concessions£1.40. Please call for further information

Castles

Amble Sea Fayre Festival '99

10/7/99
11/7/99
AMBLE SEA FAYRE FESTIVAL '99
Tel: 01665 712929
Festival celebrating many aspects of fishing / sea faring heritage including water sports, travelling theatre, craft stalls, angling competition, boat races and cookery competitions with celebrity chef. Time: 11.00-17.00. Admission free except entrance to Cookery Demonstration: A£2.50 C£2.50 (if seat taken)

Festivals

One Man Band Shebang 1999

10/7/99
11/7/99
ONE MAN BAND SHEBANG 1999
Tel: 01524 582803
Venue: Morecambe Bay Arena & Promenade Gardens. A celebration of musical co-ordination arriving from across the globe. Admission Free

Festivals

The Power of the Normans

10/7/99
11/7/99
RICHMOND CASTLE
Tel: 01748 822493
Medieval group The Troop & the Conquest. A£3.50 C£1.80 Concessions£2.60

Castles

Flat Racing

12/7/99
12/7/99
NEWCASTLE RACECOURSE
Tel: 0191 236 2020
Enjoy a special day at Newcastle's historic racecourse. First Race 14.15, Last Race 16.45

Racecourses

Inspiration to Paint in Watercolour

12/7/99
16/7/99
BELSAY HALL
Tel: 01661 881636
An art demonstration by Susan Edwards. Normal admission prices apply

Castles

Brampton Live '99

16/7/99
18/7/99
BRAMPTON LIVE '99
Tel: 01228 534664
Wide range of Roots music and dance by top performers from all over the world. Various dance, song and instrumental workshops. Creative activities for children.

Festivals

Early Music Festival

16/7/99	**BRINKBURN PRIORY**
18/7/99	Tel: 01665 570628
	Performed by the Northern Sinfonia & Gabrielli

Priory

Medieval Monastic Entertainers

16/7/99	**LINDISFARNE PRIORY**
18/7/99	Tel: 01289 389200

Heuristics. Try your hand at calligraphy or authentic period games as this popular duo take a lighthearted look at monastic customs, crafts and lifestyles. Learn about food preparation, herbs and spices in cooking and medicine, the mechanics of building, lifting and many other skills. Part of Cistercian 900. A£3.00 C£1.50 Concessions£2.30

Priory

Rothbury Traditional Music Festival 1999

16/7/99	**ROTHBURY TRADITIONAL MUSIC FESTIVAL 1999**
18/7/99	Tel: 01669 620718

The annual gathering of musicians, singers and dancers in Northumberland's Coquet Valley. Dances, ceilidhas, sing-arounds, workshops, pub sessions, outdoor displays (including puppets, dancers, mummers). Concerts, also 19 competitions for Fiddle, Accordian, Ceilidh Bands, Pipes, tradiitional singing, flute, recorder, drums, and much more.

Festivals

22 x 22 Annual Summer Exhibition of Small Scale Works

16/7/99	**UNIVERSITY GALLERY**
13/8/99	Tel: 0191 227 4424

Exhibtion of small scale works. Entry forms and deadline for fees is 11 June

Art Galleries

Jazz in the Garden

17/7/99	**ORMESBY HALL**
17/7/99	Tel: 01642 324188

Enjoy an evening of Traditional Jazz in the gardens. Accomplished musicians The Tyne Valley Stompers will enliven the night with memorable jazz. Grounds open at 16.30. Bring picnics, rugs/chairs. Wine bar. Limited tickets available £10.00.

Historic Houses & Gardens

13th Great Annual Dalemain Rainbow Craft Fair

17/7/99	**DALEMAIN HISTORIC HOUSE AND**

GARDENS

18/7/99	Tel: 017684 86450

Even bigger marquees featuring visiting craftspeople from all over Britain with displays, demonstrations and goods for sale. Something for all the family. Further information from 017684 86450

Historic Houses & Gardens

Dalemain Rainbow Craft Fair

17/7/99	**DALEMAIN HISTORIC HOUSE AND**
	GARDENS
18/7/99	Tel: 017684 86450

Visiting craftspeople from all over the country with displays, demonstrations and goods for sale. Bigger this year with larger marquees

Historic Houses & Gardens

Summer Breeze 1999

17/7/99	**SUMMER BREEZE 1999**
18/7/99	Tel: 01524 582803

A weekend of cool grooves on the Bay. Admission Free

Festivals

Quilt Exhibition

17/7/99	**BELSAY HALL**
25/7/99	Tel: 01661 881636

Beatiful quilts on display from the Quilter's Guild. Normal admission prices apply

Castles

Artistic Treat

18/7/99	**CURRAGHS WILDLIFE PARK**
18/7/99	Tel: 01624 897323

Art work on display in the Park

Wildlife Parks

Family Fun Day

18/7/99	**SOUTER LIGHTHOUSE**
18/7/99	Tel: 0191 529 3161

Day of free family entertainment and activities, commences 11.00

Lighthouses

Steamboat Rally

20/7/99	**WINDERMERE STEAMBOAT MUSEUM**
20/7/99	Tel: 015394 45565

Rally of The Steamboat Association of Great Britain. Beautiful historic boats with crew in period costume. Call for further details

Museum- Ships/Boat

Early Music Festival

23/7/99	**BRINKBURN PRIORY**
25/7/99	Tel: 01665 570628

Performed by the Northern Sinfonia & Gabrielli

Priory

Beeswing Ladies Day

| 24/7/99 | NEWCASTLE RACECOURSE |
| 24/7/99 | Tel: 0191 236 2020 |

Enjoy a special day at Newcastle's historic racecourse. First Race 14.10, Last Race 16.55

Racecourses

Medieval Falconry

| 24/7/99 | FURNESS ABBEY |
| 25/7/99 | Tel: 01229 823420 |

Raphael Falconry Bird of Prey display from 12.00. A£3.00 C£1.50 Concessions£2.30

Abbeys

Have-a-go-Archery

| 24/7/99 | MOUNT GRACE PRIORY |
| 25/7/99 | Tel: 01609 883494 |

Whitby Company of Archers introduce visitors to the art of archery, from 12.00. A£3.00 C£1.50 Concessions£2.30 English Heritage Members Free

Priory

Peripatetic Promenaders 1999

| 24/7/99 | PERIPATETIC PROMENADERS 1999 |
| 25/7/99 | Tel: 01524 582803 |

A Weird and wonderful, sometimes wild and always wacky weekend. Admission charge - please call for details 01524 582803

Festivals

Medieval Living History

| 24/7/99 | WARKWORTH CASTLE AND HERMITAGE |
| 25/7/99 | Tel: 01665 711423 |

15th century military and domestic life, with crafts, men-at-arms and period games. A£3.00 C£1.50 Concessions£2.30

Castles

Teddy Bears' Picnic

| 25/7/99 | BELSAY HALL |
| 25/7/99 | Tel: 01661 881636 |

Various performers. Magicians, face painting, balloons and lots of clowning about. Bring a teddy to get in! From 12.00. A£2.90 C£1.50 Concessions£2.20 English Heritage Members Free

Castles

Family Entertainments

| 27/7/99 | CARLISLE CASTLE |
| 29/7/99 | Tel: 01228 591922 |

Labyrinth Productions. Have a go archery, juggling and face painting from 12.00. A£3.00 C£1.50 Concessions£2.30

Castles

Flower Festival

| 30/7/99 | BRINKBURN PRIORY |
| 1/8/99 | Tel: 01665 570628 |

A NAFAS flower show. Please call for further information

Priory

10th Annual British Classic Boat Rally

| 31/7/99 | WINDERMERE STEAMBOAT MUSEUM |
| 31/7/99 | Tel: 015394 45565 |

Rally of beautiful and historic motor boats from Britain and Europe, call for further details

Museum- Ships/Boat

More Skulduggery!

| 31/7/99 | BERWICK UPON TWEED BARRACKS |
| 1/8/99 | Tel: 01289 304493 |

Silly tales of secret maps, buried treasure and famous pirates. A£3.00 C£1.50 Concessions£2.30

Museum- Military

The Bard & the Blade

| 31/7/99 | CARLISLE CASTLE |
| 1/8/99 | Tel: 01228 591922 |

Dramatic duels and dialogue from some of Shakespare's most famous plays. Performed by LK Productions. A£3.50 C£1.80 Concessions£2.60

Castles

Medieval Music

| 31/7/99 | LINDISFARNE PRIORY |
| 1/8/99 | Tel: 01289 389200 |

Enjoy melodies and dance tunes dating back to the 12th century with Peter Bull

Priory

Viking Living History

| 31/7/99 | PRUDHOE CASTLE |
| 1/8/99 | Tel: 01661 833459 |

Saxon/Viking re-enactment of Viking history with Anmod Dracon. A£3.00C£1.50 Concessions£2.30

Castles

Streetbands Festival 1999

| 31/7/99 | STREETBANDS FESTIVAL 1999 |
| 1/8/99 | Tel: 01524 582803 |

Various venues around Lancaster & Morecambe. Music to make you want to dance. Music to make you want to laugh. Music to listen to and be amazed. Admission Free.

Festivals

The Wordsworth Summer Conference

| 31/7/99 | THE WORDSWORTH SUMMER CONFERENCE 1999 |
| 13/8/99 | Tel: 01539 435003 |

Talks and discussions about books, authors, artists and collectors. Take part in practical workshops and surgeries on printing, book binding and restoring works of art

Festivals

Northumbrian Heritage

31/7/99	PRUDHOE CASTLE
22/8/99	Tel: 01661 833459

A£1.80 C£0.90 Concessions£1.40. Please call for further information

Castles

Festival & Forest Open Day

1/8/99	KIELDER CASTLE FOREST PARK CENTRE
1/8/99	Tel: 01434 250209/220242

Kielder's event of the year. A not-to-be-missed day out with entertainments and activities all day long at Kielder Castle. On the agenda will be circus-theatre shows, falconry, crafts, live music, children's activities and a whole lot more. All this plus trips to see a working forest in action. Time: 10.00-17.00. Prices: A£2.50 C&Concessions£2.50

Forest Visitor Centres

Classic Car Rally

1/8/99	LEIGHTON HALL
1/8/99	Tel: 01524 734474

Up to 500 classic cars on display. Bring your own classic car and join in!

Historic Houses

Eurofest '99

1/8/99	WINDOW ON THE WORLD INTERNATIONAL MUSIC FESTIVAL 1999
31/8/99	Tel: 0191 200 5415

Outdoor events with music and theatre in Whitley Bay town centre and on the links. Further details available on 0191 200 5164

Festivals

Ladies Evening

2/8/99	CARLISLE RACECOURSE
2/8/99	Tel: 01228 522973

Evening Meeting starting at 18.20

Racecourses

Hotspur at Warkworth Castle

3/8/99	WARKWORTH CASTLE AND HERMITAGE
7/8/99	Tel: 01665 711423

Performed by the 1939 Theatre Company. A£8.00 C&Concessions£6.00

Castles

Exhibition: "Coast to Coast" by Ken Watts

3/8/99	THE BEACON
26/9/99	Tel: 01946 592302

Ken Watts was born in London in 1932 and has lived and worked in Tyneside since the 1950's. Over the last six years he has painted full time and won several awards for his work. This exhibition will comprise of oil paintings and drawings which lie along the "C2C" Cycle Route from Whitehaven to Sunderland and Tynemouth. The works will feature views of the towns, harbours, industrial and agricultural landscapes along the way

Museum- Local History

Flat Racing

4/8/99	NEWCASTLE RACECOURSE
4/8/99	Tel: 0191 236 2020

Enjoy a special day at Newcastle's historic racecourse. First Race 14.30, Last Race 17.00

Racecourses

Shakespeare in The Garden

6/8/99	LEIGHTON HALL
7/8/99	Tel: 01524 734474

Leighton Hall's beautiful gardens play host to a performance of Shakespeare's Taming of the Shrew. Please reserve tickets in good time, call for details

Historic Houses

Civil War Living History

7/8/99	AYDON CASTLE
8/8/99	Tel: 01434 632450

Performed by Winchester's Social Living History Group. A£3.00 C£1.50 Concessions£2.30

Historic Houses

Past Pleasures

7/8/99	CHESTERS ROMAN FORT
8/8/99	Tel: 01434 681379

Come sample 17-century pleasures of the past with John Clayton. A£2.80 C£1.40 Concessions£2.10

Roman Forts

Festival of Light and Water 1999

7/8/99	FESTIVAL OF LIGHT AND WATER 1999
8/8/99	Tel: 01524 582803

A spectacular weekend of music and action-packed performances with a breath-taking firework finale. Admission Free

Festivals

More Skulduggery!

7/8/99	MOUNT GRACE PRIORY
8/8/99	Tel: 01609 883494

Silly tales of secret maps, buried treasure and famous pirates. From 12.00. A£3.00 C£1.50 Concessions£2.30 English Heritage Members Free

Priory

Alnwick International Dance and Music Festival 1999

7/8/99	ALNWICK INTERNATIONAL MUSIC AND DANCE FESTIVAL 1999
17/8/99	Tel: 01665 602682

This Festival has been running since 1976. Entertainers visit the event from all over the world and perform daily in the Market Place against a backdrop of

Further more detailed information on the attractions listed can be found in Best Guides *Visitor Attractions* Guide under the classifications shown

an ancient Northumbrian market town. Traditional costumes are worn by all dance groups and provide a colourful and changing spectacle during performances. Evening events are held in the Playhouse and the Northumberland Hall.

Festivals

Changing Pages

7/8/99 DURHAM LIGHT INFANTRY MUSEUM AND DURHAM ART GALLERY

19/9/99 Tel: 0191 384 2214

An exhibition of novelty and pop-up books organised by the Collins Gallery, Glasgow

Museums

A Medieval Tournament

8/8/99 BELSAY HALL

8/8/99 Tel: 01661 881636

Nottingham Jousters. Armoured knights fight for supremacy in a colourful tourney

Castles

Garden Tour

8/8/99 BELSAY HALL

8/8/99 Tel: 01661 881636

Paul Harrigan (Head Gardener) shows you around Belsay Hall gardens. Normal admission prices apply

Castles

Animal Olympics

8/8/99 CURRAGHS WILDLIFE PARK

8/8/99 Tel: 01624 897323

What is going on in the Park today, come along and find out

Wildlife Parks

Family Entertainers

10/8/99 WARKWORTH CASTLE AND HERMITAGE

12/8/99 Tel: 01665 711423

Games, have-a-go archery, costumes for children to try on and talks on weaponry. A£3.00 C£1.50 Concessions£2.30

Castles

Proms in the Park

14/8/99 ORMESBY HALL

14/8/99 Tel: 01642 324188

Following the sell out success of the 1998 Proms, Teesside's outdoor classical spectacular returns for 1999. An unforgettable evening of popular classics with soloist performers Susanah Clarke and Graeme Kennedy. Firework and laser finale. Gates open at 17.00. Advance tickets from £16.00 from Ormesby Hall Box Office 01642 316060. Information line 01642 866880.

Historic Houses & Gardens

Northumberland Fuschia Society Show

14/8/99 BELSAY HALL

15/8/99 Tel: 01661 881636

Various exhibitors. Large exhibition of beautiful fuchsias in the Hall from 10.00. A£3.60 C£1.80 Concessions£2.70 English Heritage Members Free

Castles

Out of Africa - A Festival of Music and Dance 1999

14/8/99 OUT OF AFRICA - A FESTIVAL OF MUSIC AND DANCE 1999

17/8/99 Tel: 01524 582803

Various venues around Lancaster & Morecambe. Four days of pure spectacle. The sights, sounds and dances of Africa bring venues in Morecambe and Lancaster alive. Don't miss the Fiesta Fireworks on Sunday! Admission charge - please call for details: 01524 582803

Festivals

Northumberland Pipes

15/8/99 BRINKBURN PRIORY

15/8/99 Tel: 01665 570628

A musical session with Ann Sessons. Please call for further information

Priory

Edward Weston 1886-1958

17/8/99 UNIVERSITY GALLERY

10/9/99 Tel: 0191 227 4424

The American photographer Edward Weston is one of the masters of modernist photography. His reputation continued to grow since his death, and recent decades have seen a dramatic re-evaluation of his work, as well as world record values at auction for his vintage prints

Art Galleries

Jungle Book

19/8/99 ORMESBY HALL

21/8/99 Tel: 01642 324188

Wonderful children's theatre production of Rudyard Kipling's story of the Man Cub 'Mowgli', his companions and their adventures in the jungle as performed by the English Playtour Theatre. Gardens open 18.00. Performance concludes 21.30. Bring picnics, chairs/rugs. Ice cream and snacks available. Please note this is a promenade performance and involves some movement of the audience lead by the actors, so please wear sensible shoes. Ticket Prices: A£8.00 C(under 14)£4.00 Concessions£7.00. No group discounts available.

Historic Houses & Gardens

Flat Racing

20/8/99	**NEWCASTLE RACECOURSE**
20/8/99	Tel: 0191 236 2020

Enjoy a special day at Newcastle's historic racecourse. First Race 17.45, Last Race 20.15

Racecourses

Annual Flower Show

21/8/99	**WARKWORTH CASTLE AND HERMITAGE**
21/8/99	Tel: 01665 711423

Beautiful flowers contributed by various participants

Castles

Medieval Surgeon

21/8/99	**AYDON CASTLE**
22/8/99	Tel: 01434 632450

A fascinating and gruesome insight into 13th century medical care with presentations about cause, effect and treatment of wounds and everyday ailments. A£3.00 C£1.50 Concessions£2.30

Historic Houses

The Aston Martin Owners' Club Historic Weekend

21/8/99	**CROFT CIRCUIT**
22/8/99	Tel: 01325 721815

If you're a fan of Ferraris, Adore Astons, are Mad about MG's of just Prefer Porsches than Croft is definitely the destination for you this weekend. Sat A£6.00, Sun A£11.00, Weekend Ticket A£15.00, C£2.00

Motor Racing Circuit

Medieval Monastic Entertainers

21/8/99	**FURNESS ABBEY**
22/8/99	Tel: 01229 823420

Games, squire-training and talks on weaponry and armour. Also, try your hand at spinning, weaving and calligraphy and learn about herbal medicine. A£3.00 C£1.50 Concessions£2.30

Abbeys

The History Man

21/8/99	**NORHAM CASTLE**
22/8/99	Tel: 01289 382329

Enjoy unusual guided tours with Brian McNerney, presenter of the BBC's popular History Man programmes. But be warned, his enthusiasm is notoriously contagious... and there is no antidote! Performing without costumes, props or even a safety net, he brings the past to life before your very eyes! A£2.50 C£1.30 Concessions£1.90

Castles

Organ Recital

22/8/99	**BRINKBURN PRIORY**
22/8/99	Tel: 01665 570628

Recited by Alan Gidney. Please call for further information

Priory

Grasmere Lakeland Sports and Show

22/8/99	**GRASMERE LAKELAND SPORTS AND SHOW**
22/8/99	Tel: 015394 32127

Cumberland and Westmorland wrestling, hound trails, mountain bike races, fell and guides races, displays of sheep handling, falconry, 1st Dragoon Cavalry, dog show, crafts, antiques, trade stands, band competitions and tug-of-war. Events commence at 10.00. Admission A£5.00 C£2.00

Festivals

Family Day

25/8/99	**CARLISLE RACECOURSE**
25/8/99	Tel: 01228 522973

Fun for all the family with free creche and children's entertainer. First Flat race at 14.20

Racecourses

Isle of Man International Jazz Festival '99

27/8/99	**ISLE OF MAN INTERNATIONAL JAZZ FESTIVAL '99**
29/8/99	Tel: 01624 622530/861095

Traditional to mainstream jazz. Evening events in the Villa Marina, Promenade Douglas. Daytime open air events at Douglas, Pel, Laxey and Castletown. Artists include Chicago Teddy Bears Jazz Band, West Jesmond Rhythm Kings, Gary Potter Trio, Tommy Burton, Roy Williams, Nic Dawson and Alan Barnes: Times: evening events 20.00-24.00. Prices: A£26.00. Groups rates available. Rover Tickets all 3 nights

Festivals

Worldbeat Weekend 1999

27/8/99	**WORLDBEAT WEEKEND 1999**
29/8/99	Tel: 01524 582803

A celebration of global culture - a pure carnival weekend in Morecambe. Admission charge - please call for details 01524 582803

Festivals

Choral Concert

28/8/99	**BRINKBURN PRIORY**
28/8/99	Tel: 01665 570628

Performed by the Fitzsimons Choir. Please call for further information

Priory

Wildlife Fayre

| 28/8/99 | CURRAGHS WILDLIFE PARK |
| 28/8/99 | Tel: 01624 897323 |

So much to see and buy, call for further details

Wildlife Parks

Music From the Movies

| 28/8/99 | LEIGHTON HALL |
| 28/8/99 | Tel: 01524 734474 |

A Bank Holiday treat from the organisers of Last Night of the Leighton Proms, please call for booking and ticket information

Historic Houses

Rosecarpe Flower Show

| 28/8/99 | BELSAY HALL |
| 30/8/99 | Tel: 01661 881636 |

The Rose, Carnation and Sweet Pea Society. Beautiful blooms on show. Also inlcudes the Gladioli Society Show and a Vegetable selection, from 10.00 (from 12.00 on Saturday). A£3.60 C£1.80 Concessions£2.70 English Heritage Members Free

Castles

Bank Holiday Racing

| 28/8/99 | CARTMEL RACECOURSE |
| 30/8/99 | Tel: 01539 536340 |

Enjoy a truly unique atmosphere with National Hunt Racing at Cartmel on 28 & 30 Aug. Plenty of refreshment and catering facilities to suit all tastes, with a large fairground and market stalls in the Course Enclosure

Racecourses

The History Man

| 29/8/99 | CORBRIDGE ROMAN SITE |
| 29/8/99 | Tel: 01434 632349 |

Enjoy unusual guided tours with the presenter of the BBC's popular History Man programmes. But be warned, his enthusiasm is notoriously contagious...and there is no antidote! Performing without costumes, props or even a safety net, he brings the past to life before your very eyes! From 12.00. A£2.80 C£1.40 Concessions£2.10 English Heritage Members Free

Archaelogical Sites

The Cumbrian Classic Car Show

| 29/8/99 | DALEMAIN HISTORIC HOUSE AND GARDENS |
| 29/8/99 | Tel: 017684 86450 |

Enjoy a family day out in beautiful surroundings. Concourse displays, competitions, trade stands and family attractions. Further information from 01900 825642

Historic Houses & Gardens

Civil War Surgeon

| 29/8/99 | CARLISLE CASTLE |
| 30/8/99 | Tel: 01228 591922 |

Listen to presentations about gruesome 17th century surgery, see the implements used and meet the leeches who were used as an important medical aid. A£3.00 C£1.50 Concessions£2.30

Castles

Teddy Bears Picnic

| 29/8/99 | HALL HILL FARM |
| 30/8/99 | Tel: 01388 730300 |

Spend the Bank Holiday Weekend enjoy tea with the teddies, bring yours along too...

Farm Parks

Teddy Bear's Picnic, Transport Festival & Craft Show

| 29/8/99 | ORMESBY HALL |
| 30/8/99 | Tel: 01642 324188 |

Teddy Bear's Picnic is on Sunday and Transport Festival on Monday with the Craft Show running both days. 5th Annual Vintage Classic Car Show also featuring motorcycles, static engines, commercial vehicles, owners clubs and kit cars, autojumble. Entries compete for special prizes in each class. Entry forms for show available from Ormesby Hall. Please enclose a S.A.E. All entries receive a commemorative brass plaque. Other attractions include Helicopter rides, Armed Forces displays, Longbow Archery and children's entertainment. 11.00-17.00.

Historic Houses & Gardens

Medieval Jousting Spectacular

| 29/8/99 | TYNEMOUTH CASTLE |
| 30/8/99 | Tel: 0191 257 1090 |

Discover the secrets of the tourney, as the jousting area resounds to the sounds of the battle, clash of steel and thunder of horses hooves as the mighty knights charge at full tilt. A£4.00 C£2.00 Concessions£3.00

Priory

Medieval Combat

| 29/8/99 | WARKWORTH CASTLE AND HERMITAGE |
| 30/8/99 | Tel: 01665 711423 |

Escafield Medieval Society. 13th century knights in combat, archery contest, have-a-go archery and games. A£3.50 C£1.80 Concessions£2.60

Castles

The History Man

CHESTERS ROMAN FORT

30/8/99
30/8/99

Tel: 01434 681379

Enjoy unusual guided tours with the presenter of the BBC's popular History Man
programmes. But be warned, his enthusiasm is notoriously contagious… and
there is no antidote! Performing without
costumes, props or even a safety net, he
brings the past to life before your very
eyes! From 12.00. A£2.80 C£1.40
Concessions£2.10

Roman Forts

**The Newcastle Exhibition Ale Blaydon
Races**

30/8/99
30/8/99

NEWCASTLE RACECOURSE

Tel: 0191 236 2020

Flat Racing. First Race 14.10, last race
17.15

Racecourses

The Berwick Military Tattoo

4/9/99
5/9/99

BERWICK UPON TWEED BARRACKS

Tel: 01289 304493

Various performers, military bands,
pipes and drums and other displays,
20.00. Please telephone for details and
advance tickets

Museum- Military

**The F3 & GT Championship Race
Meeting**

4/9/99
5/9/99

CROFT CIRCUIT

Tel: 01325 721815

BRDC GT's, British Formula 3, Formula
Palmer Audi, National Saloon Cars, MGF
Cup, Supersport 200, Formula Vauxhall,
Marcos Mantis Challenge & Croft Saloon
and Sports Car. Sat A£6.00, Sun
A£12.00, Weekend Ticket A£16.00,
C£2.00

Motor Racing Circuit

Medieval Music

4/9/99
5/9/99

LANERCOST PRIORY

Tel: 016977 3030

Enjoy melodies and dance tunes dating
back to the 12th century. Normal admission prices apply

Priory

Medieval Monk

4/9/99
5/9/99

MOUNT GRACE PRIORY

Tel: 01609 883494

The Ringwoods of History. A£3.00
C£1.50 Concessions£2.30

Priory

Medieval Music

4/9/99
5/9/99

WARKWORTH CASTLE AND HERMITAGE

Tel: 01665 711423

Enjoy melodies and dance tunes dating
back to the 12th century. A£3.00 C£1.50

Concessions£2.30

Castles

Choral Concert

5/9/99
5/9/99

BRINKBURN PRIORY

Tel: 01665 570628

Performed by the St. Paul's Church Choir.
Please call for further information

Priory

Medieval Living History & Music

11/9/99
12/9/99

CARLISLE CASTLE

Tel: 01228 591922

York City Levy / Galloway Concort. 15th
century military encampment, drill,
archery and dancing plus courtly music
from the era, from 12.00. A£3.50 C£1.80
Concessions£2.50

Castles

Rainbow Craft Fair

11/9/99
12/9/99

LEIGHTON HALL

Tel: 01524 734474

One of the Country's biggest craft fairs
visits Leighton Hall, do not miss it!

Historic Houses

Pre-War Austin Club Car Rally

12/9/99
12/9/99

BELSAY HALL

Tel: 01661 881636

Various participants. A wide variety of
vintage and veteran cars on display and
chance to talk to owners about their
vehicles. A£3.60 C£1.80
Concessions£2.70 English Heritage
Members Free

Castles

National Hunt Meeting

18/9/99
18/9/99

CARLISLE RACECOURSE

Tel: 01228 522973

Free creche and children's entertainer.
First race 14.05

Racecourses

17th Century Garrison

18/9/99
19/9/99

RICHMOND CASTLE

Tel: 01748 822493

17th-century re-enactment by The
English Civil War Society. A£3.50 C£1.80
Concessions£2.60

Castles

Saxon/Viking Battle

18/9/99
19/9/99

TYNEMOUTH CASTLE

Tel: 0191 257 1090

A battle re-enactment performed by
Regia Anglorum. A£3.50 C£1.80
Concessions£2.50

Priory

**Exhibition: Watercolours from the
Permanent Collection**

| 18/9/99 | **ABBOT HALL ART GALLERY** |
| 31/10/99 | Tel: 01539 722464 |

An exhibition including works by John Ruskin, Edward Lear and John Robert Cozens.

Art Galleries

Heritage Gala 1999

| 19/9/99 | HERITAGE GALA 1999 |
| 19/9/99 | Tel: 01524 582803 |

Various sites along Morecambe Promenade. Incorporating the Bradford to Morecambe historic vehicle run. A fun packed day with aerobatics and static displays plus the very best of street theatre. Admission Free

Festivals

Sunday Funday

| 19/9/99 | NEWCASTLE RACECOURSE |
| 19/9/99 | Tel: 0191 236 2020 |

Fun for all the family. First Race 14.05, last race 15.40

Racecourses

Northumbria Lacemakers

| 20/9/99 | PRUDHOE CASTLE |
| 3/10/99 | Tel: 01661 833459 |

An exhibition of beautiful lace. A£1.80 C£0.90 Concessions£1.40

Castles

Exhibition: "Whitehaven News Cartoons,1989-1999" by Trevor Green

| 28/9/99 | THE BEACON |
| 14/11/99 | Tel: 01946 592302 |

Artist and illustrator Trevor Green has been drawing for the Whitehaven News for 30 years, this selection is from over 500 produced in the last 10 years. Often thought provoking, invariably funny, the exhibition reflects Trevor's off-beat view of many aspects of local and national life during the last decade

Museum- Local History

Exhibition: Callum Innes

| 28/9/99 | ABBOT HALL ART GALLERY |
| 24/12/99 | Tel: 01539 722464 |

New work by the Scottish abstract artist Callum Innes made specially for the galleries at Abbot Hall.

Art Galleries

Flat Racing

| 29/9/99 | NEWCASTLE RACECOURSE |
| 29/9/99 | Tel: 0191 236 2020 |

Enjoy a special day at Newcastle's historic racecourse. First Race 14.00, last race 17.00

Racecourses

Choral Concert

| 2/10/99 | **BRINKBURN PRIORY** |
| 2/10/99 | Tel: 01665 570628 |

Performed by the Berwick Male Voice Choir. Please call for further information

Priory

Garden Tour

| 3/10/99 | BELSAY HALL |
| 3/10/99 | Tel: 01661 881636 |

Paul Harrigan (Head Gardener) shows you around Belsay Hall gardens. Normal admission prices apply

Castles

National Hunt Racing

| 8/10/99 | CARLISLE RACECOURSE |
| 30/12/99 | Tel: 01228 522973 |

Meetings on 8 & 23 Oct, 8 & 25 Nov, 30 Dec

Racecourses

Medieval Monastic Entertainers

| 16/10/99 | MOUNT GRACE PRIORY |
| 17/10/99 | Tel: 01609 883494 |

Games, squire-training and talks on weaponry and armour. Also, try your hand at spinning, weaving and calligraphy and learn about herbal medicine. From 12.00. A£3.00 C£1.50 Concessions£2.30 English Heritage Members Free

Priory

BRDA Rallycross - Final Round

| 17/10/99 | CROFT CIRCUIT |
| 17/10/99 | Tel: 01325 721815 |

Take the rough with the smooth and see action-packed racing with grunt and grit!!

Motor Racing Circuit

Flat Racing

| 20/10/99 | NEWCASTLE RACECOURSE |
| 20/10/99 | Tel: 0191 236 2020 |

Enjoy a special day at Newcastle's historic racecourse. First Race 14.00, Last Race 16.40

Racecourses

Lancaster LitFest '99

| 20/10/99 | LANCASTER LITFEST '99 |
| 24/10/99 | Tel: 01524 62166 |

Various venues. Events include readings, performances, workshops, cabaret sessions and exhibitions. You can experience every type of writing from humorous to serious, accessible to challenging, and the premieres of specially commissioned works. Events take place at various venues around the historic city, and visitors are guaranteed a warm and friendly welcome. LitFest '99 includes the launch of the anthology of winning

pieces from our annual poetry competition. We also provide a year-round development service for writers, including a monthly performance cabaret events. Times: 12.00-24.00. Prices: Some venues free to £6.50

Festivals

National Trust Book Fair

23/10/99 SOUTER LIGHTHOUSE
24/10/99 Tel: 0191 529 3161
Book sale

Lighthouses

Halloween Nightwatchers

29/10/99 WILDFOWL AND WETLANDS TRUST WASHINGTON
31/10/99 Tel: 0191 416 5454
Join our famous nightwaters walk and take part in lots of ghostly activities.

Wildlife Trusts

Halloween Haunts

31/10/99 ORMESBY HALL
31/10/99 Tel: 01642 324188
Scary fun with storytelling, crafts, traditional games etc. Wear your best Halloween outfit and bring your lanterns for the competitions. 14.00-16.30.

Historic Houses & Gardens

Exhibition: Ruskin Pottery

6/11/99 ABBOT HALL ART GALLERY
24/12/99 Tel: 01539 722464
A touring exhibition of over 70 rare pieces made at the Ruskin Pottery from the turn of the century.

Art Galleries

Barbour Billy Bow

12/11/99 NEWCASTLE RACECOURSE
12/11/99 Tel: 0191 236 2020
National Hunt Racing. First Race 12.55, Last Race 15.45

Racecourses

Exhibition: "A Woman's Place is in the Home? Victorian Women in Whitehaven"

16/11/99 THE BEACON
9/1/00 Tel: 01946 592302
This in-house exhibition will examine the myths and realities of women's lives in Whitehaven in the Victorian era. What was the woman's proper role in society and was it really all that bad! Various areas of life will be looked at which include: prostitution, middle-class domesticity, child-rearing, women in factories, mines and "below stairs" in other women's kitchens. Individual characters such as Sal Madge will be highlighted and many items from The Beacon's

reserve collection will be on display for example, clothing, personal belongings and historic photographs

Museum- Local History

Christmas Gift Fair

20/11/99 BELSAY HALL
21/11/99 Tel: 01661 881636
Various participants. Beat the Christmas shopping rush! A wide variety of crafts and unusual gifts for sale, 10.00-16.00. A£2.70 C£Free Concessions£1.80 English Heritage Members Free

Castles

National Hunt Racing

22/11/99 NEWCASTLE RACECOURSE
22/11/99 Tel: 0191 236 2020
Enjoy a special day at Newcastle's historic racecourse. First Race 13.00, Last Race 15.30

Racecourses

Newcastle Building Society Fighting Fifth Hurdle

27/11/99 NEWCASTLE RACECOURSE
27/11/99 Tel: 0191 236 2020
National Hunt Racing. First race 12.20, Last race 15.30

Racecourses

Tyndale Artists Network Christmas Show

27/11/99 PRUDHOE CASTLE
28/11/99 Tel: 01661 833459
A wonderful time to be had by all. Please call for further information. A£1.80 C£0.90 Concessions£1.40

Castles

Christmas Lunches

29/11/99 WILDFOWL AND WETLANDS TRUST WASHINGTON
22/12/99 Tel: 0191 416 5454
Treat yourself to Christmas lunch. Excellent food in beautiful surroundings.

Wildlife Trusts

Santa Specials

1/12/99 TANFIELD RAILWAY
1/12/99 Tel: 0191 388 7545
Join Santa on Tanfield Railway and add a touch of steam to your Christmas. Booking is essential £5.00 per head, call for details

Railways Steam/Light

Tyndale Artists Network Christmas Show

4/12/99 PRUDHOE CASTLE
5/12/99 Tel: 01661 833459
A wonderful time to be had by all. Please call for further information. A£1.80 C£0.90 Concessions£1.40

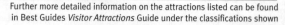

Further more detailed information on the attractions listed can be found in Best Guides *Visitor Attractions* Guide under the classifications shown

Castles

Christmas Carols at the Hall

11/12/99 ORMESBY HALL
11/12/99 Tel: 01642 324188
Mulled wine, mince pies to accompany an evening of traditional Christmas carols sung by a local choir.

Historic Houses & Gardens

Christmas at Belsay

12/12/99 BELSAY HALL
12/12/99 Tel: 01661 881636
Various participants. Magician, children's games, entertainments and carol singing at this traditional annual event, 12.00-16.00. A£3.60 C£1.80 Concessions£2.70 English Heritage Members Free

Castles

National Hunt Racing

13/12/99 NEWCASTLE RACECOURSE
13/12/99 Tel: 0191 236 2020
Enjoy a special day at Newcastle's historic racecourse. First Race 12.50, Last Race 15.30

Racecourses

Old Year

22/12/99 NEWCASTLE RACECOURSE
22/12/99 Tel: 0191 236 2020
National Hunt Racing. Enjoy a special day at Newcastle's historic racecourse. First Race 12.25, Last Race 15.25

Racecourses

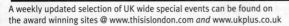

Scotland

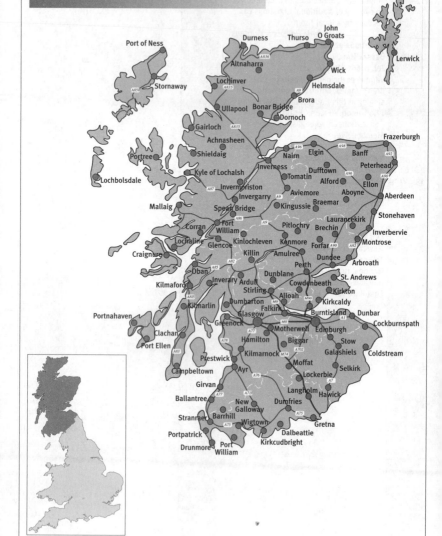

Exhibition: Roots
1/3/99 STRANRAER MUSEUM
10/4/99 Tel: 01776 705088
An African experience in Scotland
Museums

Alba Adventure Company present "A Scottish Clansman"
3/3/99 EDINBURGH CASTLE
4/3/99 Tel: 0131 225 9846
A costumed Scottish Clansman will describe the clothing worn at the time, as well as providing a weaponry demonstration. 10.00-16.00.
Included in price of admission to the Castle
Castles

Race Meeting
5/3/99 KELSO RACECOURSE
5/3/99 Tel: 01668 281611
First Race Time: 14.20. Race time is provisional
Racecourses

Alba Adventure Company present "A Scottish Clansman"
10/3/99 EDINBURGH CASTLE
11/3/99 Tel: 0131 225 9846
A costumed Scottish Clansman will describe the clothing worn at the time, as well as providing a weaponry demonstration. 10.00-16.00.
Included in price of admission to the Castle
Castles

Lloyds Bowmaker Scottish Motorcycle Show
13/3/99 KNOCKHILL RACING CIRCUIT
14/3/99 Tel: 01383 723337
Ingliston Royal Highland Showground. See what's new in the motorcycle scene in 1999 at this mega show. Visit the Knockhill stand and find out the latest information on Race Events. Bike Track Days and the Honda Ron Haslam Race School. £1.00 Prize Draw to win a £5,000 Honda at the Knockhill Stand.
Motor Racing Circuit

Alba Adventure Company present "A Scottish Clansman"
17/3/99 EDINBURGH CASTLE
18/3/99 Tel: 0131 225 9846
A costumed Scottish Clansman will describe the clothing worn at the time, as well as providing a weaponry demonstration. 10.00-16.00.
Included in price of admission to the Castle
Castles

Animal Architecture
20/3/99 HUNTERIAN MUSEUM
27/6/99 Tel: 0141 330 4221
As part of Glasgow's City of Architecture 1999, the wondrous constructions of the animal kingdom
Museum- Science

Motorcycle Owners Track Day
21/3/99 KNOCKHILL RACING CIRCUIT
21/3/99 Tel: 01383 723337
See what you and your bike can do on the famous Superbike Circuit. £6.00.
Motor Racing Circuit

Alba Adventure Company present "A Scottish Clansman"
24/3/99 EDINBURGH CASTLE
25/3/99 Tel: 0131 225 9846
A costumed Scottish Clansman will describe the clothing worn at the time, as well as providing a weaponry demonstration. 10.00-16.00.
Included in price of admission to the Castle
Castles

Race Meeting
26/3/99 KELSO RACECOURSE
26/3/99 Tel: 01668 281611
First Race Time: 13.40. Race time is provisional
Racecourses

Scottish Championship Motorcycle Racing
28/3/99 KNOCKHILL RACING CIRCUIT
28/3/99 Tel: 01383 723337
Featuring 2 rounds of the 160mph Regal 600 series. Supersport 250, Supersport 600, Sidecars, 125GP and support classes. £10.00.
Motor Racing Circuit

Racing at Hamilton
29/3/99 HAMILTON PARK RACECOURSE
29/3/99 Tel: 01698 283806
Enjoy a day at the races. Club Enclosure £12.00 Public Enclosure £7.00 C(0-16)£Free OAPS&Students£4.00. Group discount rates available
Racecourses

Alba Adventure Company present "A Scottish Clansman"
31/3/99 EDINBURGH CASTLE
1/4/99 Tel: 0131 225 9846
A costumed Scottish Clansman will describe the clothing worn at the time, as well as providing a weaponry demonstration. 10.00-16.00.
Included in price of admission to the Castle

Castles

Weekends and Bank Holidays

1/4/99   HIGHLAND WILDLIFE PARK
31/10/99   Tel: 01540 651270

Join in the fun at special animal themed events every weekend Apr-Oct with talks, trails, face-painting, quizzes and much more! Please call for further information

Wildlife Parks

Easter Activity Day

2/4/99   HEATHERSLAW LIGHT RAILWAY COMPANY
2/4/99   Tel: 01890 820244/820317

Egg decorating and Easter bonnet making. Usual stalls and refreshments. Time: 10.30-16.00. Venue: Etal Village Hall.

Railways Steam/Light

Easter Eggcitement

2/4/99   THE ALMOND VALLEY HERITAGE CENTRE
2/4/99   Tel: 01506 414957

Meet baby lambs, chicks and many other new arrivals on the farm. Hunt for easter eggs, follow the springtime trail, and make a wonderful easter bonnet

Museums

Fun Gemstone Panning

2/4/99   CREETOWN GEM ROCK MUSEUM
16/4/99   Tel: 01671 820357/820554

A chance to learn how to pan. Fun and exciting for all the family.

Museum- Jewellery

Celtic Easter Fair

3/4/99   ARCHAEOLINK PREHISTORY PARK
4/4/99   Tel: 01464 851500

An exciting array of displays will be on offer at this opening event. Activities and displays will take place throughout Easter weekend

The Unusual

Easter Events

3/4/99   HIGHLAND WILDLIFE PARK
5/4/99   Tel: 01540 651270

It's Easter time at the Highland Wildlife Park - with face-painting, Easter chicks, trails and lots more!

Wildlife Parks

Edinburgh International Science Festival '99

3/4/99   EDINBURGH INTERNATIONAL SCIENCE FESTIVAL '99
18/4/99   Tel: 0131 220 3977

To be held at 35 venues in Edinburgh. Edinburgh International Science Festival is the world's first and largest public celebration of science and technology. Every year over 150,000 people of all ages descend on Edinburgh to enjoy a massive programme of shows, workshops, exhibitions, talks, walks and tours which entertain and explain! For a copy of the official programme please call 0131 473 2070 or see our website. Times: 10.00-20.00 daily. Prices: various, some free

Festivals

Egg Painting

4/4/99   ALFORD VALLEY RAILWAY
4/4/99   Tel: 019755 62811

Have fun painting your favourite design on an egg, winner every train trip!

Railways Steam/Light

Vintage Tractor Rally

4/4/99   CULZEAN CASTLE AND COUNTRY PARK
4/4/99   Tel: 01655 760274/269

Passing through Culzean Country Park between mid morning and noon

Castles

Garden Walks

4/4/99   EDZELL CASTLE
4/4/99   Tel: 01356 648631

David Jamieson, Edzell Castle's gardener, gives a talk on the history and general layout of the Castle garden. 14.00-16.00. Included in price of admission to the Castle

Castles

Gaddgedlar Historical Re-Enactment Society

4/4/99   STIRLING CASTLE AND ARGYLL'S LODGING
4/4/99   Tel: 01786 450000

Gaddgedlar will transport you back to the turbulent years of Scotland's War of Independence, where you will have the opportunity to see the arms and armoury of the period. Highlights will include a longbow and combat display, culminating in a medieval tournament. Visitors will be able to view the camp between 12.00-16.00 with shows at 13.30 and 15.00. Included in price of admission to the Castle

Castles

Easter Egg Hunt

4/4/99   TRAQUAIR HOUSE
4/4/99   Tel: 01896 830323/830785

Over 2000 mini eggs hidden in the Traquair Maze, for under 10's only

Historic Houses & Gardens

Day at the Races

10/4/99   HAMILTON PARK RACECOURSE
10/4/99   Tel: 01698 283806

Have a flutter at the races. Club

Enclosure £12.00 Public Enclosure £7.00
C(0-16)£Free OAPS&Students£4.00.
Group discount rates available
Racecourses

Best of Scottish Race Day
11/4/99 KNOCKHILL RACING CIRCUIT
11/4/99 Tel: 01383 723337
The first combined Championship Race
Day with the best of two and four wheel
action. See the fabulous Regal 600
Series one minute and the extremely
competitive Waverley Press XR2's the
next in this full day of action together
with PDS Sports and Saloon cars and
Anglo-Scottish Starcup featuring Sierra
Cosworths. £6.00.
Motor Racing Circuit

Race Meeting
12/4/99 KELSO RACECOURSE
12/4/99 Tel: 01668 281611
First Race Time: 14.00. Race time is provisional
Racecourses

Pictures from an Exhibition
17/4/99 STRANRAER MUSEUM
8/5/99 Tel: 01776 705088
Paintings, prints and drawings from the
Museum's collections.
Museums

Spring Fair
18/4/99 ALFORD VALLEY RAILWAY
18/4/99 Tel: 019755 62811
Barbecue, small side shows, bouncy castle, 12.00- 16.00. Held at Houghton Park
Station
Railways Steam/Light

Hot-Hatch Owners Track Day
18/4/99 KNOCKHILL RACING CIRCUIT
18/4/99 Tel: 01383 723337
Bring along your Hot-Hatch and try it on
the famous Touring Car Circuit. Track
action all day from 09.30. Paddock displays and Sound Off Competition. £6.00.
Motor Racing Circuit

Festival Meeting
21/4/99 PERTH RACECOURSE
23/4/99 Tel: 01738 551597
Have you won the Lottery yet! Racing is
a better bet! 21-22 Apr racing starts at
14.20, 23 Apr first race 14.15
Racecourses

Family Fun Run
25/4/99 CULZEAN CASTLE AND COUNTRY PARK
25/4/99 Tel: 01655 760274/269
Band at 13.00, run starts at 14.00. 6
scenic miles around Country Park.
Entries in by 20/4/99

Castles

Motorcycle Owners Track Day
25/4/99 KNOCKHILL RACING CIRCUIT
25/4/99 Tel: 01383 723337
See what you and your bike can do on
the famous Superbike Circuit. £6.00.
Motor Racing Circuit

Evening Race Meeting
28/4/99 KELSO RACECOURSE
28/4/99 Tel: 01668 281611
First Race Time: 17.45. Race time is provisional
Racecourses

Hirsel May Fair
1/5/99 HIRSEL COUNTRY PARK
3/5/99 Tel: 01890 882834
A family day out with live entertainment,
music and over 30 craft stalls. Hot and
cold food available
Historic Houses & Gardens

Hirsel May Fair
1/5/99 THE HIRSEL GROUNDS AND DUNDOCK
WOOD
3/5/99 Tel: 01890 882834/882965
A family day out with live entertainment,
music and over 30 craft stalls. Hot and
cold food available
Country Parks

Exhibition
1/5/99 CITY ART CENTRE
1/7/99 Tel: 0131 529 3993
An exhibition on the Scottish Parliament.
Art Galleries

'Locale'
1/5/99 CITY ART CENTRE
1/7/99 Tel: 0131 529 3993
Contemporary art in Edinburgh. A major
exhibition of work by Edinburgh based
artists.
Art Galleries

The Romans
1/5/99 CALLENDER HOUSE
29/8/99 Tel: 01324 503770
A celebration of the Roman Occupation
of the area, and the building of Rome's
most northern frontier, the Antonine
Wall, call for further information
Historic Houses

Day at the Races
2/5/99 HAMILTON PARK RACECOURSE
2/5/99 Tel: 01698 283806
Enjoy a day at the races. Club Enclosure
£12.00 Public Enclosure £7.00 C(0-
16)£Free OAPS&Students£4.00. Group
discount rates available
Racecourses

Day at the Races

| 6/5/99 | **HAMILTON PARK RACECOURSE** |
| 6/5/99 | Tel: 01698 283806 |

Enjoy a day at the races. Club Enclosure £12.00 Public Enclosure £7.00 C(0-16)£Free OAPS&Students£4.00. Group discount rates available

Racecourses

	George Penman Jazzmen
7/5/99	PEEBLES JAZZ FESTIVAL 1999
7/5/99	Tel:

Supported by Festival Band Ex-Servicemen's Club. Time: 19.00-24.00. Tickets: A£6.00, £4.00 if purchased before 7 May. A great start to a great weekend!

Festivals

	Honestas Marching Band
8/5/99	PEEBLES JAZZ FESTIVAL 1999
8/5/99	Tel:

Meet at Tontine Hotel at 10.00. Don't't forget your brollies, ladies!

Festivals

	On and Off the Wall
8/5/99	CITY ART CENTRE
19/6/99	Tel: 0131 529 3993

Contemporary textile art from members of the '62 Group'.

Art Galleries

	Children's Mega Party
9/5/99	GRAMPIAN TRANSPORT MUSEUM
9/5/99	Tel: 01975 562292

Games, competitions, magicians, vintage vehicle rides. Free entry for children

Museum- Transport

	Scottish Championship Motorcycle Racing
9/5/99	KNOCKHILL RACING CIRCUIT
9/5/99	Tel: 01383 723337

Featuring 2 rounds of the 160mph Regal 600 series. Supersport 250, Supersport 600, Sidecars, 125GP and support classes. £10.00.

Motor Racing Circuit

	Big Softies Day
10/5/99	THE ALMOND VALLEY HERITAGE CENTRE
10/5/99	Tel: 01506 414957

Bring along your soft toys and join in a special party for younger visitors. There will be stories, games, kite flying, and the chance for your teddy to go parachuting...!

Museums

	Spring Meeting
12/5/99	PERTH RACECOURSE
13/5/99	Tel: 01738 551597

Have you won the Lottery yet? Racing is a better bet! 12 May is an evening meeting starting at 18.10, 13 May racing starts at 14.25

Racecourses

	Evening at the Races
14/5/99	HAMILTON PARK RACECOURSE
14/5/99	Tel: 01698 283806

Enjoy an evening at the races. Club Enclosure £12.00 Public Enclosure £7.00 C(0-16)£Free OAPS&Students£4.00. Group discount rates available

Racecourses

	Eurocars 'Days of Thunder' Race Day
15/5/99	KNOCKHILL RACING CIRCUIT
16/5/99	Tel: 01383 723337

An action packed 20 race programme starting at 09.00 starring the awesome V8 & V6 Eurocars, the amazing USA-style Racing Pick-up Trucks and the incredible Legend mini-racers. Full supporting programme including Beetle Cup, Waverley Press XR2 Championship and Karts. A fantastic days racing. £10.00.

Motor Racing Circuit

	Homes of Football
15/5/99	STRANRAER MUSEUM
26/6/99	Tel: 01776 705088

Stuart Clarke's evocative football photographs plus a look at the story of football in Wigtownshire.

Museums

	Race Meeting
19/5/99	KELSO RACECOURSE
19/5/99	Tel: 01668 281611

First Race Time: 14.00. Race time is provisional

Racecourses

	Perth Festival of the Arts 1999
20/5/99	PERTH FESTIVAL OF THE ARTS 1999
30/5/99	Tel: 01738 472706 Box Office

An annual festival in May including Opera, Classical music, folk, drama, jazz and art exhibitions. Full programme and booking forms available from mid March from the above address

Festivals

	British Gold Panning Championships and Mineral Fair
22/5/99	THE MUSEUM OF LEAD MINING
23/5/99	Tel: 01659 74387

Panning Championships open to veterans and novices. Adults and Children's sections. 10.00-17.00. Panning Demonstrations available

Museum- Mining

Commerical Vehicle Show

23/5/99
23/5/99
GRAMPIAN TRANSPORT MUSEUM
Tel: 01975 562292
A day devoted to ancient and modern
utility vehicles of all types: P.S.V. Lorries,
Horse Drawn Steam and Municipal.
Time: 11.00-16.30. Cost: A£3.50 C£1.00
OAPs£2.50

Museum- Transport

23/5/99
23/5/99
Hot-Hatch Owners Track Day
KNOCKHILL RACING CIRCUIT
Tel: 01383 723337
Bring along your Hot-Hatch and try it on
the famous Touring Car Circuit. Track
action all day from 09.30. Paddock displays and Sound Off Competition. £6.00.

Motor Racing Circuit

24/5/99
24/5/99
Day at the Races
HAMILTON PARK RACECOURSE
Tel: 01698 283806
Enjoy a day at the races. Club Enclosure
£12.00 Public Enclosure £7.00 C(0-
16)£Free OAPS&Students£4.00. Group
discount rates available

Racecourses

29/5/99
29/5/99
Atholl Highlanders Annual Parade
BLAIR CASTLE
Tel: 01796 481207
Annual Parade of the Atholl Higlanders'.
One hour parade and inspection of the
Atholl Highlanders and their Pipe Band.

Castles

29/5/99
30/5/99
Loch Fyne Sea Food Fair
LOCH FYNE SEA FOOD FAIR 1999
Tel: 01499 600217
Annual Sea Food Fair - feast of West
Coast Sea Food along with specially
selected wines and beers, live music,
cooking demonstrations and children's
entertainment. 12.00-23.00 each day

Festivals- Food

29/5/99
30/5/99
Traquair Scottish Beer Festival
TRAQUAIR HOUSE
Tel: 01896 830323/830785
A festival to celebrate Scottish Beer.
Featuring cask ales from every Scottish
independent brewery with live jazz,
good food, tasting competitions and
family entertainment

Historic Houses & Gardens

30/5/99
30/5/99
Blair Castle Highland Games
BLAIR CASTLE
Tel: 01796 481207
March-on by Atholl Highlanders, tradi-
tional Highland Games events including
Tossing the Caber, Tug-of-war, etc. Trade
Stands, Stalls and Refreshments. Call
01796 481 355 for further information

Castles

Doune & Dunblane Fling
30/5/99
30/5/99
DOUNE CASTLE
Tel: 0131 668 8600
This tremendously popular event, now in
its 5th year, is presented as part of the
Doune & Dunblane Fling (29-31 May) in
association with Historic Scotland. The
event is particularly suited to all members of the family, combining activities
such as music, song, drama, children's
games and storytelling. The afternoon
shows the wealth of talent in the area
and will also include special
guests.13.30 onwards. Included in price
of admission to the Castle

Castles

Best of Scottish Race Day
30/5/99
30/5/99
KNOCKHILL RACING CIRCUIT
Tel: 01383 723337
The first combined Championship Race
Day with the best of two and four wheel
action. See the fabulous Regal 600
Series one minute and the extremely
competitive Waverley Press XR2's the
next in this full day of action together
with PDS Sports and Saloon cars and
Anglo-Scottish Starcup featuring Sierra
Cosworths. £6.00.

Motor Racing Circuit

Arbroath Quatrocentenary
1/6/99
23/11/99
ARBROATH MUSEUM
Tel: 01241 875598
Celebration of Arbroath receiving its
Charter 400 years ago

Museum- Local History

Sporting Extravaganza
3/6/99
4/6/99
PERTH RACECOURSE
Tel: 01738 551597
Great place, Great buzz, Come and enjoy
the party! 3 June racing starts at 14.20, 4
June racing from 18.50

Racecourses

Special Gardens Weekend
5/6/99
6/6/99
CAWDOR CASTLE
Tel: 01667 404615
Guided tours of Cawdor Gardens by
Head Gardener and guided "Bluebell
Walks" in Cawdor big wood by Estate
Ranger - included in normal cost of
admission

Castles

Jessie M King Anniversary Exhibition
5/6/99
17/7/99
TOLBOOTH ART CENTRE
Tel: 01557 331556
A special exhibition to make the 50th

anniversary of the death of Jessie M King, one of Kirkcudbright's most celebrated artists

Art Galleries

Scottish Championship Motorcycle Racing Day

6/6/99 KNOCKHILL RACING CIRCUIT
6/6/99 Tel: 01383 723337
Featuring 2 rounds of the 160mph Regal 600 series. Supersport 250, Supersport 600, Sidecars, 125GP and support classes. £10.00.

Motor Racing Circuit

Historic Motoring Extravaganza

6/6/99 MELLERSTAIN HOUSE
6/6/99 Tel: 01573 410225
Historic car show organised by the Borders Vintage Automobile Club

Historic Houses

Evening at the Races

9/6/99 HAMILTON PARK RACECOURSE
9/6/99 Tel: 01698 283806
Spend a fun evening at the races. Club Enclosure £12.00 Public Enclosure £7.00 C(0-16)£Free OAPS&Students£4.00. Group discount rates available

Racecourses

Clan Donald Lands Trust Sheep Dog Trials

12/6/99 CLAN DONALD VISITOR CENTRE
12/6/99 Tel: 01471 844305/844227
Held at Ostaig, Sleat. All day event

Castles

Garden Walks

13/6/99 EDZELL CASTLE
13/6/99 Tel: 01356 648631
David Jamieson, Edzell Castle's gardener, gives a talk on the history and general layout of the Castle garden. 14.00-16.00. Included in price of admission to the Castle

Castles

Edinburgh Bird of Prey Centre

14/6/99 STIRLING CASTLE AND ARGYLL'S LODGING
28/6/99 Tel: 01786 450000
14th, 17th, 21st, 24th & 28th June. A selection of birds will be on show, ranging from owls, hawks, buzzards and falcons. In addition, some members of the public may have the opportunity to hold the birds. There will also be two spectacular flying displays from the beauty of the owls to the majesty of the falcons. 14.00-17.00. Flying displays at 14.30 and 15.30.
Included in price of admission to the Castle

Castles

Day at the Races

16/6/99 HAMILTON PARK RACECOURSE
16/6/99 Tel: 01698 283806
Enjoy a day at the races. Club Enclosure £12.00 Public Enclosure £7.00 C(0-16)£Free OAPS&Students£4.00. Group discount rates available

Racecourses

Donald MacDonald

18/6/99 CLAN DONALD VISITOR CENTRE
18/6/99 Tel: 01471 844305/844227
Memorial Quaich. 4 of Scotland's top pipers compete

Castles

Carrick 800 Battle Re-Enactment "Robert the Bruce and his Carrick Spears"

20/6/99 CROSSRAGUEL ABBEY
20/6/99 Tel: 01655 883113
Return to the camp of King Robert Bruce at Glentrool in 1307. Witness the training of his Carrick Spearmen, the use of sword, bow and battle axe. Learn of the King's progress to win his country's freedom and cheer on his men against the troops of the Earl of Pembroke as the English attempt to take the camp by surprise. Don't miss this exciting display! The group will be at the Castle from 13.30 with the main show starting at 14.30. Included in price of admission to the Castle

Abbeys

Find a Clue

20/6/99 ETAL CASTLE
20/6/99 Tel: 01890 820332
A regional event. Please call for further information

Castles

Evening Race Meeting

23/6/99 HAMILTON PARK RACECOURSE
23/6/99 Tel: 01698 283806
Spend an evening at Hamilton Park; horseracing is not only for the dedicated 'form follower', its a great social occasion for those who enjoy a small flutter and for those who are happy to just enjoy the event with family and friends . Club Enclosure £12.00 Public Enclosure £7.00 C(0-16)£Free OAPS&Students£4.00. Group discount rates available

Racecourses

Grampian Classic Sprint

Further more detailed information on the attractions listed can be found in Best Guides *Visitor Attractions* Guide under the classifications shown

27/6/99	**GRAMPIAN TRANSPORT MUSEUM**
27/6/99	Tel: 01975 562292

A half-mile sprint run under RAC regulations for classic cars - a unique speed spectacle. Time: 11.00-16.30. Cost: A£3.30 C£1.00 OAPs£2.50

Museum- Transport

Best of Scottish Race Day

27/6/99	**KNOCKHILL RACING CIRCUIT**
27/6/99	Tel: 01383 723337

The first combined Championship Race Day with the best of two and four wheel action. See the fabulous Regal 600 Series one minute and the extremely competitive Waverley Press XR2's the next in this full day of action together with PDS Sports and Saloon cars and Anglo-Scottish Starcup featuring Sierra Cosworths. £6.00.

Motor Racing Circuit

Scottish Storytelling Centre present Story Castle

27/6/99	**STIRLING CASTLE AND ARGYLL'S LODGING**
27/6/99	Tel: 01786 450000

"Tales in the kitchen", "stories in the court", "upstairs and downstairs" and "in the King's chamber." Experience the delights of Stirling Castle through the stories and songs of Scotland - for Kings and commoners, Queens and cooks, chiefs and chiels. 13.00-16.00. Included in price of admission to the Castle

Castles

Astounding Discoveries

28/6/99	**THE ALMOND VALLEY HERITAGE CENTRE**
13/8/99	Tel: 01506 414957

Weekdays from 28 June-13 Aug. Keep the kids amused over the summer holidays, and make something interesting to take home with you. There's a different craft, experiment or activity going on every week: please phone for details

Museums

Race Meeting

29/6/99	**HAMILTON PARK RACECOURSE**
29/6/99	Tel: 01698 283806

Spend an day at Hamilton Park; horseracing is not only for the dedicated 'form follower', its a great social occasion for those who enjoy a small flutter and for those who are happy to just enjoy the event with family and friends . Club Enclosure £12.00 Public Enclosure £7.00 C(0-16)£Free OAPS&Students£4.00. Group discount rates available

Racecourses

Edinburgh Bird of Prey Centre

1/7/99	**STIRLING CASTLE AND ARGYLL'S LODGING**
29/7/99	Tel: 01786 450000

1st, 5th, 8th, 12th, 15th, 19th, 22nd, 26th & 29th July. A selection of birds will be on show, ranging from owls, hawks, buzzards and falcons. In addition, some members of the public may have the opportunity to hold the birds. There will also be two spectacular flying displays from the beauty of the owls to the majesty of the falcons. 14.00-17.00. Flying displays at 14.30 and 15.30. Included in price of admission to the Castle

Castles

'Line'

1/7/99	**CITY ART CENTRE**
1/9/99	Tel: 0131 529 3993

Exhibition exploring ideas and process in the work of selected artists for whom drawing is a central of definable element of their work.

Art Galleries

Hot-Hatch Festival Weekend

3/7/99	**KNOCKHILL RACING CIRCUIT**
4/7/99	Tel: 01383 723337

A unique party weekend with action and activities and track time on Sat & Sun. Live music, Stunt Drivers, Beer Tent, mega Weekend Sound-Off and celebrities. £8.00.

Motor Racing Circuit

The Tinkler-Gypsies

3/7/99	**STRANRAER MUSEUM**
4/9/99	Tel: 01776 705088

Gypsy life in Dumfries and Galloway during the 18th and 19th centuries.

Museums

Art Exhibition

3/7/99	**CITY ART CENTRE**
25/9/99	Tel: 0131 529 3993

An exhibition of art from the City of Edinburgh Collection.

Art Galleries

An Infinite Storm of Beauty

3/7/99	**CITY ART CENTRE**
25/9/99	Tel: 0131 529 3993

Exhibition on the life and achievements of John Muir, Herald of the World Conservation Movement - marking the 150th anniversary of his emigration from Scotland to the U.S.A.

Art Galleries

Forres Archers

| 4/7/99 | **BALVENIE CASTLE** |
| 4/7/99 | Tel: 01340 820121 |

The Forres Archers will provide a demonstration of this most ancient of sports. Visitors will also have the opportunity to try their hand. 14.30-16.30. Included in price of admission to the Fort.

Castles

Sheepdog Competition

| 4/7/99 | **CULZEAN CASTLE AND COUNTRY PARK** |
| 4/7/99 | Tel: 01655 760274/269 |

Judged by Peter Hetherington. Young handlers compete for individual and team cups.

Castles

Bella Anderson & Charles Coutts

| 4/7/99 | **SPYNIE PALACE** |
| 4/7/99 | Tel: 01343 546358 |

Come along and enjoy a performance of traditional fiddle music. 14.30. Included in price of admission to the Palace

Palaces

National Archery Tournament

| 6/7/99 | **CLAN DONALD VISITOR CENTRE** |
| 10/7/99 | Tel: 01471 844305/844227 |

In the grounds of Armadale Castle. Free with entrance ticket

Castles

Race Meeting

| 9/7/99 | **HAMILTON PARK RACECOURSE** |
| 9/7/99 | Tel: 01698 283806 |

Spend an evening at Hamilton Park; horseracing is not only for the dedicated 'form follower', its a great social occasion for those who enjoy a small flutter and for those who are happy to just enjoy the event with family and friends . Club Enclosure £12.00 Public Enclosure £7.00 C(0-16)£Free OAPS&Students£4.00. Group discount rates available

Racecourses

Scottish Hill Rally

| 9/7/99 | **KNOCKHILL RACING CIRCUIT** |
| 9/7/99 | Tel: 01383 723337 |

Return of these incredible off-road machines. £5.00.

Motor Racing Circuit

Drumlanrig Castle Horse Driving Trials

| 9/7/99 | **DRUMLANRIG CASTLE GARDENS AND COUNTRY PARK** |
| 11/7/99 | Tel: 01848 330248/331682/331555 |

Premier carriage driving trials including dressage (Friday), cross country (Saturday) and cone driving (Sunday).

Year after year, this major event attracts competitors such as the Duke of Edinburgh. Also main ring attractions, trade stands, craft tent and children's fair. 08.00-17.30

Castles

Knockhill/BMF Motorcycle Festival

| 10/7/99 | **KNOCKHILL RACING CIRCUIT** |
| 11/7/99 | Tel: 01383 723337 |

Once again the motorcyclists weekend with Beer Tent, Camping, Bands, Trade Stands and Personalities, Track Riding Sessions both days. £7.00.

Motor Racing Circuit

Carrick 800 Battle Re-enactment

| 11/7/99 | **CULZEAN CASTLE AND COUNTRY PARK** |
| 11/7/99 | Tel: 01655 760274/269 |

Viking and Medieval Scottish Footsoldiers. 14.30 in Fountain Court

Castles

Garden Walks

| 11/7/99 | **EDZELL CASTLE** |
| 11/7/99 | Tel: 01356 648631 |

David Jamieson, Edzell Castle's gardener, gives a talk on the history and general layout of the Castle garden. 14.00-16.00. Included in price of admission to the Castle

Castles

Harness Racing

| 11/7/99 | **PERTH RACECOURSE** |
| 11/7/99 | Tel: 01738 551597 |

Racing from 14.00, meeting to be confirmed,

Racecourses

Forres Archers

| 11/7/99 | **SPYNIE PALACE** |
| 11/7/99 | Tel: 01343 546358 |

The Forres Archers will provide a demonstration of this most ancient of sports. Visitors will also have the opportunity to try their hand. 14.30-16.30. Included in price of admission to the Fort

Palaces

Saundersfoot in Bloom Flower Festival 1999

| 13/7/99 | **SAUNDERSFOOT IN BLOOM FLOWER FESTIVAL 1999** |
| 17/7/99 | Tel: 01834 812880 |

Community event with 34 organisations taking part. Very colourful and artistic, certainly worth a visit. Admission Free but donations welcome. Time: 10.00-20.00, last admission: 19.45

Festivals

Evening Race Meeting

Further more detailed information on the attractions listed can be found in Best Guides *Visitor Attractions* Guide under the classifications shown

16/7/99 16/7/99	**HAMILTON PARK RACECOURSE** Tel: 01698 283806 Spend an evening at Hamilton Park; horseracing is not only for the dedicated 'form follower', its a great social occasion for those who enjoy a small flutter and for those who are happy to just enjoy the event with family and friends . Club Enclosure £12.00 Public Enclosure £7.00 C(0-16)£Free OAPS&Students£4.00. Group discount rates available *Racecourses*

Stonehaven Folk Festival 1999

16/7/99 **STONEHAVEN FOLK FESTIVAL 1999**
18/7/99 Tel: 0159 763519
Weekend festival of traditional and contemporary music based aroun three Concerts in the Town Hall, plus ceilidh, workshops, sessions and Children's concert; Aqua Ceilidh in the Open Air Pool, 1999 Paper and Comb World Championships. 1999 guests include Alastair Fraser, Andy M Stewart and Gerry O'Beirne.
Festivals

3D/2D Craft Fair

17/7/99 **CULZEAN CASTLE AND COUNTRY PARK**
18/7/99 Tel: 01655 760274/269
Lots of unusual gifts to buy or look at. 10.30-17.30 in the Events Field
Castles

Redcoats at Corgarff Castle 1749

18/7/99 **CORGARFF CASTLE**
18/7/99 Tel: 01975 651640
His Majesty's 36th Regiment of Foote will garrison the stronghold of Corgarff Castle. Experience 18th century military life with a company of Redcoats as they undertake guard duty, drill and cook whilst maintaining discipline in the surrounding area. 10.00-16.00. Included in price of admission to the Castle
Castles

Gaddgedlar Historical Re-Enactment Society

18/7/99 **DUNSTAFFNAGE CASTLE AND CHAPEL**
18/7/99 Tel: 01631 562465
Gaddgedlar will transport you back to the turbulent years of Scotland's War of Independence, where you will have the opportunity to see the arms and armoury of the period. Highlights will include a longbow and combat display, culminating in a medieval tournament. Visitors will be able to view the camp between 12.00-16.00 with shows at

13.30 & 15.00. Included in price of admission to the Castle
Castles

Bella Anderson & Charles Coutts

18/7/99 **TOLQUHON CASTLE**
18/7/99 Tel: 01651 851286
Come along and enjoy a performance of traditional fiddle music. 14.30. Included in price of admission to the Castle.
Castles

Alford Cavalcade

19/7/99 **GRAMPIAN TRANSPORT MUSEUM**
19/7/99 Tel: 01975 562292
One of Scotland's largest vehicle shows. Over 200 entries, trade stands, arena acts. A really great family day out
Museum- Transport

Knockhill 25th Anniversary Race Meeting

24/7/99 **KNOCKHILL RACING CIRCUIT**
25/7/99 Tel: 01383 723337
Join in the celebration of the 25th year of Knockhill in this mega spectacular race day featuring the awesome TVR Tuscans, MGF Championship, Supersport 200, Mini Se7en, Mini Miglia, Porsche Cup and Porsche Classic Cup. It is intended that celebrities who have featured over the years will be present to add to the exceitement and glamour of this special event. £15.00.
Motor Racing Circuit

Scotland's Riches

24/7/99 **CITY ART CENTRE**
2/10/99 Tel: 0131 529 3993
Spectacular display of Scottish art from Scottish public collections.
Art Galleries

Roman & Celtic Day

25/7/99 **ARCHAEOLINK PREHISTORY PARK**
25/7/99 Tel: 01464 851500
This event promises to be a thrilling experience for all the family - realistic combat and fighting displays
The Unusual

Strathearn Music Festival 1999

28/7/99 **STRATHEARN MUSIC FESTIVAL 1999**
2/8/99 Tel: 01764 652578
Diverse musical festival encompassing brass, jazz, folk, blues, opera, cajun, traditional - something for all tastes and ages in a mixture of indoor and outdoor venues. These dates are provisional, it is not certain that the Festival will be held, call nearer the time
Festivals

Evening Race Meeting

31/7/99
31/7/99

HAMILTON PARK RACECOURSE
Tel: 01698 283806

Great racing, and great fun is promised at Hamilton Park. Club Enclosure £12.00 Public Enclosure £7.00 C(0-16)£Free OAPS&Students£4.00. Group discount rates available

Racecourses

Classic Vehicle Show

1/8/99
1/8/99

CULZEAN CASTLE AND COUNTRY PARK
Tel: 01655 760274/269

500 Classic vehicles of all types. 10.00-17.00 in the Events Field.

Castles

Extravaganza

1/8/99
1/8/99

FORT GEORGE
Tel: 01667 462777

Historic Scotland will once again provide an array of entertainment to cater for all tastes. Combat and weaponry displays, falconry, living history and archery are only some of the activities that will feature throughout the afternoon. All included in the normal admission price to the Fort!
12.00-16.00

Forts

Insects

1/8/99
1/9/99

HUNTERIAN MUSEUM
Tel: 0141 330 4221

In the Zoology Museum. A historical collection of insects at the University of Glasgow

Museum- Science

Edinburgh Bird of Prey Centre

2/8/99
30/8/99

STIRLING CASTLE AND ARGYLL'S LODGING
Tel: 01786 450000

2nd, 5th, 9th, 12th, 16th, 19th, 23rd, 26th & 30th August. A selection of birds will be on show, ranging from owls, hawks, buzzards and falcons. In addition, some members of the public may have the opportunity to hold the birds. There will also be two spectacular flying displays from the beauty of the owls to the majesty of the falcons.
14.00-17.00. Flying displays at 14.30 and 15.30.
Included in price of admission to the Castle

Castles

MCN British Superbike Championship

7/8/99
8/8/99

KNOCKHILL RACING CIRCUIT
Tel: 01383 723337

Saturday: See the stars do battle in

qualifying plus support action from 250GP and Supersport 600, £8.00.
Sunday: A must for motorcycle race enthusiasts with Britain's premier and biggest televised championship. See works riders on 180mph Superbike machines from all the leading manufacturers. Full race action from 09.00. Meet the stars in a paddock walk-about. Trade and Merchandise stands. £20.00.

Motor Racing Circuit

Traquair Fair

7/8/99
8/8/99

TRAQUAIR HOUSE
Tel: 01896 830323/830785

A superb family weekend with over 30 acts each day including theatre shows, children's shows, workshop, dance, music, storytelling, magic, street theatre, complimentary medicine and the delicious fair ale, brewed at Traquair! Not to be missed

Historic Houses & Gardens

Falconry Day

8/8/99
8/8/99

CULZEAN CASTLE AND COUNTRY PARK
Tel: 01655 760274/269

These beautiful birds of prey will amaze you with their agility and power. 10.30-17.00 in the Events Field

Castles

Garden Walks

8/8/99
8/8/99

EDZELL CASTLE
Tel: 01356 648631

David Jamieson, Edzell Castle's gardener, gives a talk on the history and general layout of the Castle garden. 14.00-16.00. Included in price of admission to the Castle

Castles

Eco Marathon

8/8/99
8/8/99

GRAMPIAN TRANSPORT MUSEUM
Tel: 01975 562292

A look at transport of the future - specially constructed economy and ecologically friendly vehicles competing in an "Economy Marathon" on the museum's sprint circuit. Time: 11.00-16.30. Cost: A£3.50 C£1.00 OAPs£2.50

Museum- Transport

Family Funday

8/8/99
8/8/99

THE ALMOND VALLEY HERITAGE CENTRE
Tel: 01506 414957

The highlight of the summer... A festival of music, madness, mischief and making things, climaxing in our famous plastic duck race

Museums

Evening Racing

11/8/99	**HAMILTON PARK RACECOURSE**
11/8/99	Tel: 01698 283806

Spend an evening at Hamilton Park; horseracing is not only for the dedicated 'form follower', its a great social occasion for those who enjoy a small flutter and for those who are happy to just enjoy the event with family and friends . Club Enclosure £12.00 Public Enclosure £7.00 C(0-16)£Free OAPS&Students£4.00. Group discount rates available

Racecourses

Commission of Array

14/8/99	**CAERLAVEROCK CASTLE**
15/8/99	Tel: 01387 770244

From the time of Wallace and Bruce (1290-1325), knights clash again over disputed land. The population is called to arms and the Castle is alive again with the sights and sounds of the 13th century. The Scottish Knights defend the people, while others fight for land or money. A soldiers camp just outside the Castle walls holds the arms and armour of the period, men at arms practice their sword skills, while squires prepare the knights for battle. Come along and examine the weapons, visit the camp and be ruled over by medieval warlords. The programme starts at 13.00 with a major clash of arms at 15.00 (both days). Tickets (1 day) Adults £3, Reduced £2, Children £1. Reductions for Friends of Historic Scotland. Available at site on each day. Price includes entry to the Castle

Castles

Medieval Entertainers

14/8/99	**ETAL CASTLE**
15/8/99	Tel: 01890 820332

Games, squire training and talks on weaponry and armour plus spinning and herbal medicine. A£3.00 C£1.50 Concessions£2.30 English Heritage Members Free. Please telephone for times

Castles

Auto Trader British Touring Car Championship

14/8/99	**KNOCKHILL RACING CIRCUIT**
15/8/99	Tel: 01383 723337

Saturday: Touring cars do battle for grid positions in two 1 hour qualifying sessions plus support races, £10.00. Sunday: Racing from 09.30 featuring 2 rounds of this world famous championship. Starring CLELAND, LESLIE, MENU and many more with cars from leading manufacturers inc. Volvo, Vauxhall, Honda, Nissan, Ford. Lunch time driver parade and autograph session, £25.00.

Motor Racing Circuit

Hawick Summer Festival

14/8/99	**HAWICK SUMMER FESTIVAL 1999**
29/8/99	Tel: 01450 375263

This is an action packed two week event with something for all the family. Our watchword is Welcome! Various venues, please call for further information

Festivals

Traditional Storytelling - Sea Stories and Fishy Tales

15/8/99	**ARBROATH ABBEY**
15/8/99	Tel: 01241 878756

In association with the Scottish Storytelling Centre. 12.00 & 13.00. Included in price of admission to the Abbey

Abbeys

Forres Archers

15/8/99	**BALVENIE CASTLE**
15/8/99	Tel: 01340 820121

The Forres Archers will provide a demonstration of this most ancient of sports. Visitors will also have the opportunity to try their hand. 14.30-16.30. Included in price of admission to the Fort.

Castles

Festival of Scottish Music and Dance

15/8/99	**CULZEAN CASTLE AND COUNTRY PARK**
15/8/99	Tel: 01655 760274/269

12.30-16.30 in the Fountain Court

Castles

Clan Heritage Society

15/8/99	**SPYNIE PALACE**
15/8/99	Tel: 01343 546358

Members of the Clan Heritage Society will give a talk on the history of the Clans, as well as performing a combat and weaponry display. 14.30 and 15.30. Included in price of admission to the Palace

Palaces

Seafest

15/8/99	**ARBROATH MUSEUM**
16/8/99	Tel: 01241 875598

Celebration of Arbroath's maritime culture and traditions

Museum- Local History

Summer Holiday Meeting
20/8/99 PERTH RACECOURSE
21/8/99 Tel: 01738 551597
Great Place, Great Buzz, Come and Enjoy the Party. 20 Aug racing from 14.25, 21 Aug racing starts at 14.05

Racecourses

Glen Varigill Ferrari/Porsche Owners Track
21/8/99 KNOCKHILL RACING CIRCUIT
21/8/99 Tel: 01383 723337
See millions of pounds worth of Supercars being put through their paces on track. £8.00.

Motor Racing Circuit

Bella Anderson & Charles Coutts
22/8/99 CORGARFF CASTLE
22/8/99 Tel: 01975 651640
Come along and enjoy a performance of traditional fiddle music. 14.30. Included in price of admission to the Castle

Castles

Clan Heritage Society
22/8/99 HUNTLY CASTLE
22/8/99 Tel: 01466 793191
Members of the Clan Heritage Society will give a talk on the history of the Clans, as well as performing a combat and weaponry display. 14.30 & 15.30. Included in price of admission to the Castle

Castles

Hot-Hatch Owners Track Day
22/8/99 KNOCKHILL RACING CIRCUIT
22/8/99 Tel: 01383 723337
Bring along your Hot-Hatch and try it on the famous Touring Car Circuit. Track action all day from 09.30. Paddock displays and Sound Off Competition. £6.00.

Motor Racing Circuit

Forres Archers
22/8/99 SPYNIE PALACE
22/8/99 Tel: 01343 546358
The Forres Archers will provide a demonstration of this most ancient of sports. Visitors will also have the opportunity to try their hand. 14.30-16.30. Included in price of admission to the Fort

Palaces

Race Meeting
24/8/99 HAMILTON PARK RACECOURSE
24/9/99 Tel: 01698 283806
Enjoy a day at the races. Club Enclosure £12.00 Public Enclosure £7.00 C(0-16)£Free OAPS&Students£4.00. Group discount rates available

Racecourses

Bowmore Blair Castle Horse Trials
26/8/99 BLAIR CASTLE
29/8/99 Tel: 01796 481207
International Equestrian three day event. Dressage, Show Jumping and Cross Country all around Blair Castle. Stands, Stalls, Refreshments. Conact the Horse Trials Office for further information 01796 481 543

Castles

Railway Shuntabout
28/8/99 THE ALMOND VALLEY HERITAGE CENTRE
29/8/99 Tel: 01506 414957
A weekend of special trains on the narrow-gauge railway, and the chance for some of our more unusual engines to trundle along the line....!

Museums

Geology Week
28/8/99 HUNTERIAN MUSEUM
4/9/99 Tel: 0141 330 4221
Talks, Tours, bring your own rocks and fossils to be identified, call for further details

Museum- Science

Ancient Craft Fair
29/8/99 ARCHAEOLINK PREHISTORY PARK
29/8/99 Tel: 01464 851500
Craftsmen and women carry out ancient skills and traditions dating back thousands of years

The Unusual

Scottish Championship Motorcycle Racing
29/8/99 KNOCKHILL RACING CIRCUIT
29/8/99 Tel: 01383 723337
Featuring 2 rounds of the 160mph Regal 600 Series, Supersport 250, Supersport 600, Sidecars, 125GP and support classes. £10.00.

Motor Racing Circuit

Edinburgh Bird of Prey Centre
2/9/99 STIRLING CASTLE AND ARGYLL'S LODGING
16/9/99 Tel: 01786 450000
2nd, 6th, 9th, 13th & 16th September. A selection of birds will be on show, ranging from owls, hawks, buzzards and falcons. In addition, some members of the public may have the opportunity to hold the birds. There will also be two spectacular flying displays from the beauty of the owls to the majesty of the falcons. 14.00-17.00. Flying displays at 14.30 and 15.30.
Included in price of admission to the Castle

Castles

Braemar Gathering 1999
BRAEMAR GATHERING 1999
4/9/99
4/9/99
Tel: 013397 55377
The programme includes: Highland Dancing, Piping, Tossing the Caber, Putting the Stone, Throwing the Hammer, Sprinting, Long Leap, Inter-Services Tug of War and Relay Race. All Competitions are held under the Society's Regulations. On the Day: A£5.00 C(0-14)£1.00. Advanced booking for Grandstand tickets(£Not known), Uncovered stand tickets(£10.00) and Ringside seat tickets(£8.00) are available from February 1999 by postal applications only to: The Booking Secretary, B.R.H.S, Coilacreich, Ballater, Aberdeenshire, AB35 5UH, please include a stamped addressed envelope with your remittance. Overseas booking must include the equivalent of £5.00 handling charge

Festivals

Grampian Motorcycle Convention
5/9/99
5/9/99
GRAMPIAN TRANSPORT MUSEUM
Tel: 01975 562292
Dedicated to all forms of motorcycling: classic racers, arena trials, trade show, Moped Marathon, stunts and parades
Museum- Transport

Yesterday's Harvest
5/9/99
5/9/99
THE ALMOND VALLEY HERITAGE CENTRE
Tel: 01506 414957
Some of the museum's old farm machinery is dusted off to bring in the harvest. Join in the tattie howkin, help stack a stook, and roll around in a haystack
Museums

Race Meeting
6/9/99
6/9/99
HAMILTON PARK RACECOURSE
Tel: 01698 283806
Day at the Races. Club Enclosure £12.00 Public Enclosure £7.00 C(0-16)£Free OAPS&Students£4.00. Group discount rates available
Racecourses

Borders Festival of Jazz and Blues 1999
10/9/99
BORDERS FESTIVAL OF JAZZ AND BLUES 1999
12/9/99
Tel: 01450 377278
To be held at various venues in Hawick. This is a weekend Jazz Festival in the beautiful Scottish Border Country. At present all events are in Hawick. Over 30 events with 20+ bands, in good venues

add to the jazz weekend with a few days of golf, fishing, walking, cycling. Great country for them all. Please call for times and prices.
Festivals

Traquair Needlework Fair
11/9/99
12/9/99
TRAQUAIR HOUSE
Tel: 01896 830323/830785
Classes, workshops, demonstrations, needlework goods for sale and exhibitions of contemporary and historical needlework
Historic Houses & Gardens

The Bronze Age
11/9/99
30/10/99
STRANRAER MUSEUM
Tel: 01776 705088
A touring exhibition on the British Bronze Age including material from South-West Scotland.
Museums

Motorcycle Owners Track Day
12/9/99
12/9/99
KNOCKHILL RACING CIRCUIT
Tel: 01383 723337
See what you and your bike can do on the famous Superbike Circuit. £6.00.
Motor Racing Circuit

Extravaganza
12/9/99
12/9/99
STIRLING CASTLE AND ARGYLL'S LODGING
Tel: 01786 450000
See one of Scotland's grandest castles come alive with a huge selection of entertainment for all the family in one of the most popular events in the calendar. The Clann, the top fight display team, will build an authentic living history camp, as well as providing a spectacular fighting performance. Other activities will include music and song, storytelling, drama, comedy and lots more! 12.30-16.30. Included in price of admission to the Castle
Castles

Creetown Country & Western Music Festival
17/9/99
19/9/99
CREETOWN GEM ROCK MUSEUM
Tel: 01671 820357/820554
Best of type of music festival in South Scotland. 15 top bands, great fun for all the family. Sideshows, market etc.
Museum- Jewellery

Country & Western Themed Weekend
17/9/99
19/9/99
CREETOWN GEM ROCK MUSEUM
Tel: 01671 820357/820554
To coincide with the Creetown Country & Western Music Festival.
Museum- Jewellery

County Living In The Borders

18/9/99
19/9/99

KAILZIE

Tel: 01721 720007

A window on the way of life in the Borders. Many displays from agriculture, horticulture, cookery, sporting activities, fun slides for children. A real family day out!

Gardens

Scottish Superprix Race Week

18/9/99
19/9/99

KNOCKHILL RACING CIRCUIT

Tel: 01383 723337

One of the biggest meetings ever staged in Scotland, starring the 180mph UK Formula 3000 Single Seaters, Caterham 7's, Alfa Romeo, BRSCC XR2, BRSCC XR3, F600 and Mighty Mini's. See budding Formula 1 stars race an outright lap record speeds in the fastest ever race championship at Knockhill. A special prize to be awarded for the fastest ever official lap. £15.00.

Motor Racing Circuit

Horse Trials

19/9/99
19/9/99

CULZEAN CASTLE AND COUNTRY PARK

Tel: 01655 760274/269

Novice and pre-novice trials. Organised by British Horse Society.

Castles

Garden Walks

19/9/99
19/9/99

EDZELL CASTLE

Tel: 01356 648631

David Jamieson, Edzell Castle's gardener, gives a talk on the history and general layout of the Castle garden. 14.00-16.00. Included in price of admission to the Castle

Castles

Scottish Festival

19/9/99
19/9/99

THE MUSEUM OF LEAD MINING

Tel: 01659 74387

Display of country dancing, Pipe Band, Traditional Scottish Music Band and Scottish Fare in the Tea Room, 12.30-16.30

Museum- Mining

Glorious Finale Meeting

22/9/99
23/9/99

PERTH RACECOURSE

Tel: 01738 551597

Have you won the lottery Yet? Racing is a better bet! Racing from 14.10

Racecourses

Eurocars 'Days of Thunder' Race

25/9/99
26/9/99

KNOCKHILL RACING CIRCUIT

Tel: 01383 723337

An action packed 20 race programme starting at 09.00 starring the awesome

V8 and V6 Eurocars, the amazing USA-style Racing Pic-up Trucks and the incredible Legend Mini-Racers. Full supporting programme including Beetle Cup, Waverley Press XR2 Championship, PDS Sports and Saloon Cars, Anglo-Scottish Starcup and Karts. £10.00.

Motor Racing Circuit

Alford Auction and Autojumble

26/9/99
26/9/99

GRAMPIAN TRANSPORT MUSEUM

Tel: 01975 562292

Major autojumble and sale of vehicles and automobilia

Museum- Transport

Race Meetings

27/9/99
27/9/99

HAMILTON PARK RACECOURSE

Tel: 01698 283806

Last meeting of the season. Club Enclosure £12.00 Public Enclosure £7.00 C(0-16)£Free OAPS&Students£4.00. Group discount rates available

Racecourses

The King's Head: Charles I, King & Martyr

1/10/99
31/3/00

PALACE OF HOLYROODHOUSE

Tel: 0131 556 7371

Between October and April the Palace gardens are closed and a special exhibition from the Royal Collection is mounted in the Palace. This exhibition of portraits of Charles I marks the 350th anniversary of the death of the King. The exhibits range from exquisite miniatures by Isaac Oliver to full-length oil paintings by Daniel Mytens and from engravings of the young Prince Charles to memorial medals and rings produced after his execution

Palaces

Jock Taylor Memorial Trophy Meeting

3/10/99
3/10/99

KNOCKHILL RACING CIRCUIT

Tel: 01383 723337

Scotland's final motorcycle championship meeting featuring sidecar race in memory of a past world champion. Full Scottish Championship classes plus support races including the final of Regal 600 series. £10.00.

Motor Racing Circuit

Special Needlework and Lace Exhibition

8/10/99
17/10/99

BLAIR CASTLE

Tel: 01796 481207

Annual Exhibition of the Castles work and Lace Collection. One of th finest Needlework exhibitions in the country, most of which is attributed to lady

Evelyn Stewart Murray (1868-1940). In all over 120 pieces of lace and embroidery. No extra charge for this event.

Castles

Scottish Championship Motor Racing
10/10/99 KNOCKHILL RACING CIRCUIT
10/10/99 Tel: 01383 723337
Featuring Waverley Press XR2 Championship, Anglo-Scottish Starcup, finals of the Northern Irish Formula Ford Championship and Metro Challenge. £10.00.

Motor Racing Circuit

Monuments and Money
10/10/99 HUNTERIAN MUSEUM
24/12/99 Tel: 0141 330 4221
Monuments and buildings depicted on coins as part of Glasgow, City of Architecture 1999

Museum- Science

Spooky Happenings
14/10/99 THE ALMOND VALLEY HERITAGE CENTRE
31/10/99 Tel: 01506 414957
14-25 & 31 October. Strange goings on in some of the darkest corners of the old mill. Follow the cryptic clues and encounter ghoulish surprises in a quest for the ghost of the white lady, then make masks and scary lanterns. Further horrors await at a special Halloween day on the 31st

Museums

Glenfiddich World Piping Championships
30/10/99 BLAIR CASTLE
30/10/99 Tel: 01796 481207
Annual International Piping Championships. Please contact Mrs L. Maxwell 01698 843 843 for further information

Castles

Halloween - Myths and Legends
31/10/99 ARCHAEOLINK PREHISTORY PARK
31/10/99 Tel: 01464 851500
The superstition of north-east Scotland revealed

The Unusual

Halloween Horror
31/10/99 THE MUSEUM OF LEAD MINING
31/10/99 Tel: 01659 74387
Haunted Tours with the Ghost of 'Tom Bell,' Horror stories in our Miners' Cottages, 12.00-16.00. Gruesome menu in our tea room. Fancy dress judging 15.00, Face Painter 12.30-14.00. Hunt the severed finger 12.30

Museum- Mining

Craft Fair for Christmas
6/11/99 HIRSEL COUNTRY PARK
7/11/99 Tel: 01890 882834
Over 30 visiting and local craft stalls selling original Christmas gifts. Hot and cold food available. Why not look for that exclusive but elusive Christmas gift here

Historic Houses & Gardens

Crafts for Christmas Fair
6/11/99 THE HIRSEL GROUNDS AND DUNDOCK WOOD
7/11/99 Tel: 01890 882834/882965
Over 30 visiting and local craft stalls selling original Christmas gifts. Hot and cold food available

Country Parks

Motorcycle Owners Track Day
7/11/99 KNOCKHILL RACING CIRCUIT
7/11/99 Tel: 01383 723337
See what you and your bike can do on the famous Superbike Circuit. £6.00.

Motor Racing Circuit

National Photographic Society
7/11/99 STRANRAER MUSEUM
20/11/99 Tel: 01776 705088
The Society's annual exhibition and the chance to see some of the best in contemporary photography.

Museums

A Century of Childhood
12/11/99 HAWICK MUSEUM AND SCOTT GALLERY
14/2/00 Tel: 01450 373457
Millennium Exhibition. Opening times: Mon-Fri 13.00-16.00, Sun 14.00-16.00

Museum- Local History

Hot-Hatch Owners Track Day
14/11/99 KNOCKHILL RACING CIRCUIT
14/11/99 Tel: 01383 723337
Bring along your Hot-Hatch and try it on the famous Touring Car Circuit. Track action all day from 09.30. Paddock displays and Sound Off Competition. £6.00.

Motor Racing Circuit

Christmas at Callendar House
30/11/99 CALLENDER HOUSE
1/1/00 Tel: 01324 503770
A celebration of Christmas past, spit roasting goose and seasonal recipes prepared in our working Georgian kitchen. Traditional tree and carols in the Hall

Historic Houses

Santa Specials
3/12/99 ALFORD VALLEY RAILWAY
11/12/99 Tel: 019755 62811
Children and Adults alike will enjoy this

Christmas treat, take a trip on the steam train, visit Santa's Grotto in the Station, munch of mince pies and warm yourself with hot drinks. Trains run 3-4 Dec and 10-11 Dec from 10.00. Fri reserved bookings for playgroups and schools. Sat trains for all

Railways Steam/Light

National Hunt Racing

15/12/99 MUSSELBURGH RACECOURSE

15/12/99 Tel: 0131 665 2859

Whether you're a horse racing enthusiast or a novice you are promised a day of colour, action and excitement here at Musselburgh. First Race at 12.45. Admission Club Badge £12.00 Grandstand £6.00 C(o-16)£Free Concessions £3.00

Racecourses

Edinburgh's Millennium Hogmanay

29/12/99 EDINBURGH & SCOTLAND INFORMATION CENTRE

1/1/00 Tel: 0131 557 1700

Five day extravaganza starting on Dec 27th the highlight will be the New Year's Eve Virgin and McEwan's Street Party incorporating the Bank of Scotland Fireworks. For information write to P O Box 1-2000 Edinburgh EH1 1XB or call 0131 557 3990. Tickets will be available from 5th May 99 onwards.

Tourist Information Centres

Glasgow's Hogmanay

31/12/99 GLASGOW TOURIST INFORMATION CENTRE

1/1/00 Tel: 0141 204 4400

Put some Mardi Gras into your Hogmanay celebrations this year and Come Dancing In The Streets - Glasgow style. The fun zone extends over George Square and The Merchant City with six free party stages and street performances offering something for everyone. Disco sensation on the Main Stage 22.00-00.45 with midnight fireworks in the sky. BBC Radio 1 Dance Party in Merchant City 21.00-00.45 with some of the best dance anthems of the year. Outrageous good fun on Virginia Street on the Pink Stage from Glasgow's vibrant gay scene. Entertainment also on the Smirnoff Stage in Bell Street, the Hip-Hop Stage in Albion Street, Fruitmarket in Albion Street (ticketed venue) ticket centre: 0141 287 5511, and Blackfriars St Candleriggs Street Performances outside The Stratdui and Bar 91. Info Line: 0141 553 1937

Tourist Information Centres

Hirsel May Fair

6/5/00 THE HIRSEL GROUNDS AND DUNDOCK WOOD

8/5/00 Tel: 01890 882834/882965

A family day out with live entertainment, music and over 30 craft stalls. Hot and cold food available

Country Parks

Crafts for Christmas Fair

4/11/00 THE HIRSEL GROUNDS AND DUNDOCK WOOD

5/11/00 Tel: 01890 882834/882965

Over 30 visiting and local craft stalls selling original Christmas gifts. Hot and cold food available

Country Parks

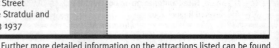

Further more detailed information on the attractions listed can be found in Best Guides *Visitor Attractions* Guide under the classifications shown

South East England

Including:
Surrey
East and West Sussex
Kent

A Response to the Environment: Landscape after Turner

1/3/99
21/3/99

HASTINGS MUSEUM AND ART GALLERY

Tel: 01424 781155

This is an open submission which is open to all art societies in the 1066 area which are properly constituted and run by a committee. The selection committee will be: Caroline Collier, Director of the De La Warr Pavillion; Lesley Cornish, Former Visual Arts Officer for Hastings Museum and Art Gallery; Eric Money, Rye Art Gallery. Turner in 1066 Country which was held last summer at Hastings Museum and Art Gallery, signalled the opening of a new season of work. The emphasis will be on the way in which artists have responded to the local environment and the histories that underpin their work. Stephen Turner, who was artist-in-residence during the Turner exhibition is giving a talk and will be opening the exhibition is giving a talk and will be opening the exhibition. There has also been a major re-hang of our collection. This display has been chosen to reflect our changing relationship with landscape.

Museums

Demonstration: Rose Pruning

3/3/99
3/3/99

RHS GARDEN WISLEY

Tel: 01483 224234

Watch Dean Peckett demonstrate his rose pruning skills at 14.00. This demonstration will also take place on: Sun 21st at 10.30. Cost: Members £5.00, non-members £10.00. To book tickets send a cheque made payable to RHS, enclosing a SAE and including your membership number (if applicable) and day time telephone number to the Administration Department at RHS Garden, Wisley, Woking GU23 6QB. We are sorry but we cannot accept telephone bookings. Please note that all events may be subject to cancellation due to insufficient ticket sales

Gardens

Classic/Vintage Practice Day

6/3/99
6/3/99

LYDDEN INTERNATIONAL MOTOR RACING CIRCUIT

Tel: 01304 830557

For further details including times and ticket prices please contact venue direct

Motor Racing Circuit

Toy Collectors Fair

6/3/99
6/3/99

SANDOWN EXHIBITION CENTRE

Tel: 01372 467540

Opening Times: 10.30-16.00. A£3.50 OAPs£1.00. Please call 01604 770025 for further information

Exhibition Centres

Roman Clay Workshop

6/3/99
6/3/99

THE WHITE CLIFFS EXPERIENCE

Tel: 01304 214566/210101

Make your own Roman style masks with our resident experts.

Interactive

Garden Crafts

6/3/99
14/3/99

RHS GARDEN WISLEY

Tel: 01483 224234

Wisley hosts Garden Crafts for a third year with live demonstrations by practising craftsmen taking place in the Demonstration Shed. These include wheelbarrow making, rake and basket making, trug making, pot throwing, wood turning and furniture making. There will also be an informative display of old garden tools

Gardens

Arts and Crafts 1999

6/3/99
20/3/99

TUNBRIDGE WELLS MUSEUM AND ART GALLERY

Tel: 01892 526121/554171

Annual arts and crafts show by local residents

Museums

£1.00 Day (BMCRC)

7/3/99
7/3/99

BRANDS HATCH

Tel: 0171 344 4444Ticketmaster

All classes of solo motorcycles and side-cars plus trade stands, track displays and demonstrations. Indy Circuit. Admission £1.00

Motor Racing Circuit

Walk at Wisley

7/3/99
7/3/99

RHS GARDEN WISLEY

Tel: 01483 224234

See the winter-flowering heathers with Andy Collins at 10.30. Cost: Members £5.00, non-members £10.00. To book tickets send a cheque made payable to RHS, enclosing a SAE and including your membership number (if applicable) and day time telephone number to the Administration Department at RHS Garden, Wisley, Woking GU23 6QB. We are sorry but we cannot accept telephone bookings. Please note that all events may be subject to cancellation due to insufficient ticket sales

Gardens

Steeplechase Meeting
8/3/99 FONTWELL PARK RACECOURSE
8/3/99 Tel: 01243 543335
Celebrate 75 years of racing at Fontwell Park. Daily Member £13.00 Tattersalls £9.00 Silver Ring £5.00 OAPs£2.50 C(0-16)£Free. Advance group rates available
Racecourses

Lecture: Local Suffragettes
9/3/99 GUILDFORD MUSEUM
9/3/99 Tel: 01483 444750
As part of the Women's Festival, Guildford Museum have organised this lecture. Tickets: £5.00 to include a glass of wine.
Museum- Local History

Getting Started in the Greenhouse Tickets
10/3/99 RHS GARDEN WISLEY
10/3/99 Tel: 01483 224234
Led by the Superintendent of the Glass Department, Nick Morgan, this day will concentrate on various aspects of growing plants in greenhouses. Time: 10.00-16.00. Cost: members £40.00, non-members £45.00
Gardens

Demonstration: Practical Gardening Skills
10/3/99 RHS GARDEN WISLEY
10/3/99 Tel: 01483 224234
Watch Bernard Boardman demonstration his practical gardening skills at 14.00. This demonstration will also take place on: Sun 14th at 10.30. Cost: Members £5.00, non-members £10.00. To book tickets send a cheque made payable to RHS, enclosing a SAE and including your membership number (if applicable) and day time telephone number to the Administration Department at RHS Garden, Wisley, Woking GU23 6QB. We are sorry but we cannot accept telephone bookings. Please note that all events may be subject to cancellation due to insufficient ticket sales
Gardens

Horse and Hound Grand Military Gold Cup
12/3/99 SANDOWN PARK RACECOURSE
13/3/99 Tel: 01372 463072
Friday is the Horse and Hound Grand Military Gold Cup and Saturday is the Sunderlands Imperial Cup. For further details including times and ticket prices please contact venue direct
Racecourses

Science Education & Technology Week
12/3/99 GUILDFORD MUSEUM
20/3/99 Tel: 01483 444750
Please contact the Museum for further information.
Museum- Local History

Lydden Car Practice
13/3/99 LYDDEN INTERNATIONAL MOTOR RACING CIRCUIT
14/3/99 Tel: 01304 830557
Car practice on Saturday, BARC Sprint on Sunday. For further details including times and ticket prices please contact venue direct
Motor Racing Circuit

Techology Weekend
13/3/99 PAINSHILL LANDSCAPE GARDEN
14/3/99 Tel: 01932 868113/864674
Fascinating technological features of Painshill brought to life. Demonstrations based around 30 feet diameter Bramah Wheel and Animal Engine
Gardens

Special Camellia Days
15/3/99 BORDE HILL GARDEN
30/3/99 Tel: 01444 450326
57th Anniversary of Camellia 'Donation' created at Borde Hill Garden. Also the chance to view the other 33 varieties of Camellia on show within the gardens. On various days there will be talks and tours by Camellia specialists, call for further details
Gardens

The Defence of Sussex 1502-1980
17/3/99 HASTINGS MUSEUM AND ART GALLERY
17/3/99 Tel: 01424 781155
From castles to nuclear bunkers, a history of the defence of the county. A joint meeting with Hastings Area Archaeological Research Group. Speaker: Martin brown, Assistant County Archaeologist for East Sussex. Time: 19.30.
Museums

Meet the Gardener
17/3/99 PAINSHILL LANDSCAPE GARDEN
31/3/99 Tel: 01932 868113/864674
Three days only: 17, 24 & 31 March. Behind the scenes look at running and development of 18th century landscape, including looking at 18th century methods of plant management
Gardens

World of Property

19/3/99 21/3/99	**SANDOWN EXHIBITION CENTRE**

19/3/99
21/3/99 **SANDOWN EXHIBITION CENTRE**
Tel: 01372 467540
Fri & Sat 10.30-17.30, Sun 10.30-17.00.
Price A£2.50. Please call 0181 542 9088
for further information
Exhibition Centres

Junior Museum Club: Sweet Wrapper Fabric
20/3/99
20/3/99 **HASTINGS MUSEUM AND ART GALLERY**
Tel: 01424 781155
Start saving those brightly coloured
sweet wrappers and use them to create
unusual fabric constructions. Two separate workshops run by Anne Valler for
the East Sussex Branch of the Young
Textiles Group of the Embroiderer's
Guild. Other day to be held on: Saturday
10th April. £2.00
Museums

BMCRC Practice Day
20/3/99
20/3/99 **LYDDEN INTERNATIONAL MOTOR RACING CIRCUIT**
Tel: 01304 830557
For further details including times and
ticket prices please contact venue direct
Motor Racing Circuit

The Fossil Roadshow
20/3/99
21/3/99 **DOVER MUSEUM**
Tel: 01304 201066
Geology experts identify your fossils and
rocks and answer any geology queries.
Plus a chance to handle fossils from the
museum collection. 10.00-17.00
Museum- Local History

Technology Weekend
20/3/99
21/3/99 **PAINSHILL LANDSCAPE GARDEN**
Tel: 01932 868113/864674
Fascinating technological features of
Painshill brought to life. Demonstrations
based around 30 feet diameter Bramah
Wheel and Animal Engine
Gardens

Racing Ahead Race Day (BRSCC)
21/3/99
21/3/99 **BRANDS HATCH**
Tel: 0171 344 4444Ticketmaster
Formula 600, Formula Saloons, Kent
Championship Forumula Fords,
Westfields, Fiats, Alfas, Auto Italia. Indy
Circuit, Grade-D. On the Gate: £10.00-
£28.00. In Advance: Non £8.00-£25.00,
Club £7.00-£22.00. Two Day Pass: Non
£11.00-£30.00, Club £10.00-£27.00.
Three Day Pass: Non £32.00, Club
£29.00, Qualifying: £5.00-£14.00.
C£Free. Programme £Free-£5.00.
Seating (BH): £Free-£8.00. South Bank:
£2.00-£5.00. Group Tickets: Non £90.00-

£95.00, Club £80.00-£85.00. Season
Ticket Inc. of Club Membership:
£200.00. You can buy your tickets for
any of the 1999 events in advance any
time up to 4 days before an event and
make a saving, Tel: 0870 60 60 611
Motor Racing Circuit

Walk at Wisley
21/3/99
21/3/99 **RHS GARDEN WISLEY**
Tel: 01483 224234
Come and walk around Wisley to see the
spring flowers with David Hutchins at
10.30. This walk will also take place on:
Wed 21st April at 10.30. Cost: Members
£5.00, non-members £10.00. To book
tickets send a cheque made payable to
RHS, enclosing a SAE and including your
membership number (if applicable) and
day time telephone number to the
Administration Department at RHS
Garden, Wisley, Woking GU23 6QB. We
are sorry but we cannot accept telephone bookings. Please note that all
events may be subject to cancellation
due to insufficient ticket sales
Gardens

Steeplechase Meeting
23/3/99
23/3/99 **FONTWELL PARK RACECOURSE**
Tel: 01243 543335
Celebrate 75 years of racing at Fontwell
Park. Daily Member £13.00 Tattersalls
£9.00 Silver Ring £5.00 OAPs£2.50 C(o-
16)£Free. Advance group rates available
Racecourses

Classic Car Auction
23/3/99
23/3/99 **SANDOWN EXHIBITION CENTRE**
Tel: 01372 467540
Opening times and prices to be
announced. Please call 01954 232332
for further information
Exhibition Centres

Flower Arranging Demonstration
24/3/99
24/3/99 **RHS GARDEN WISLEY**
Tel: 01483 224234
'Springtime delights' with Gill Cubitt.
Time: 10.00-12.30. Cost: members
£18.00, non-members £23.00
Gardens

Garden Design Weekends
25/3/99
28/3/99 **RHS GARDEN WISLEY**
Tel: 01483 224234
Father and son teams, Robin and Robin
Templar Williams run a garden design
consultancy. They have worked on
designs in Europe, USA, Japan and the
Far East as well as the UK. Robin has
been awarded several gold medals at

Further more detailed information on the attractions listed can be found
in Best Guides *Visitor Attractions* Guide under the classifications shown

the Chelsea and Hampton Court Flower Shows for his designs. Time: Thur 25 (18.30-20.30), Fri 26-Sun 28 (09.00-16.30). Cost: £185.00. This weekend will be repeated: 11-14 Nov

Gardens

The Society of Limners

26/3/99 TUNBRIDGE WELLS MUSEUM AND ART GALLERY

14/4/99 Tel: 01892 526121/554171

Members' miniature paintings, calligraphy, and silhouettes

Museums

Whitstable Model Railway Exhibition

27/3/99 CHUFFA TRAINS MUSEUM

27/3/99 Tel: 01227 277339

Venue: United Reform Church, Middle Hall, Whitstable. Trade and preservation stands, working layouts. Refreshments, disabled access. Ample car parking. Doors Open: 10.00-17.00. A£1.75 C£1.00 Family Ticket (A2+C3)£4.50

Museum- Steam

MCN British Superbike Chammpionship (MCRCB)

27/3/99 BRANDS HATCH

28/3/99 Tel: 0171 344 4444Ticketmaster

British Superbike x 2, British 125cc, British 250cc, British 600cc plus support. Indy Circuit, Grade-B. On the Gate: £10.00-£28.00. In Advance: Non £8.00-£25.00, Club £7.00-£22.00. Two Day Pass: Non £11.00-£30.00, Club £10.00-£27.00. Three Day Pass: Non £32.00, Club £29.00. Qualifying: £5.00-£14.00. C£Free. Programme £Free-£5.00. Seating (BH): £Free-£8.00. South Bank: £2.00-£5.00. Group Tickets: Non £90.00-£95.00, Club £80.00-£85.00. Season Ticket Inc. of Club Membership: £200.00. You can buy your tickets for any of the 1999 events in advance any time up to 4 days before an event and make a saving, Tel: 0870 60 60 611

Motor Racing Circuit

Car Practice

27/3/99 LYDDEN INTERNATIONAL MOTOR RACING CIRCUIT

28/3/99 Tel: 01304 830557

Car Practice on Saturday, Grass Track on Sunday. For further details including times and ticket prices please contact venue direct

Motor Racing Circuit

Armada!

27/3/99 PENSHURST PLACE AND GARDENS
28/3/99 Tel: 01892 870307

Penshurst Place in 1588 as it prepares for the Spanish invasion, 12.00-16.00

Historic Houses

Art Full Boxes: Group Show by New Fibre Arts

27/3/99 HASTINGS MUSEUM AND ART GALLERY
9/5/99 Tel: 01424 781155

The participating artists, all members of New Fibre Art, an international exhibiting group, look identical brown boxes, normally viewed as 'packaging' and let their imagination take flight. The exhibit may be the box, the contents, or the box and contents. These transformed boxes span the whole spectrum of fibre art.

Museums

The Homes of Football

27/3/99 THE WHITE CLIFFS EXPERIENCE
4/7/99 Tel: 01304 214566/210101

Stuart Clarke's National Touring Exhibition in Dover Museum.

Interactive

Volksworld

28/3/99 SANDOWN EXHIBITION CENTRE
29/3/99 Tel: 01372 467540

Opening Times: Sat 10.00-18.00, Sun 10.00-17.00 Prices to be announced

Exhibition Centres

Stitch & Paper Workshop & Art in Boxes

29/3/99 HASTINGS MUSEUM AND ART GALLERY
29/3/99 Tel: 01424 781155

A two-part session. Come to one or both workshops. Ideal for those who wish to teach new techniques. Suitable for adults and young people 12+. Led by Cas Holmes. Morning - Stitch & Paper (10.30-13.00): Experiment with ways of transforming the surface of paper - staining, crumpling, oiling and stitch used as line or mark. Bring decorative waste papers and found ephemera. Afternoon - Art in Boxes (14.00-16.30): Create your own art work in a box. Please bring a shoe box (or similar) as well as found ephernera and decorative paper. Admission: £3.00 per session.

Museums

Loseley Park Farms Children's' Holiday Activity Days

29/3/99 LOSELEY PARK
16/4/99 Tel: 01483 304440

Excluding Sat, Sun and Public Holidays. Fun filled days on the farm. Commences 09.30-16.00. Call 01483 304440 for booking details

Historic Houses & Gardens

Artist in Residence

29/3/99 PALLANT HOUSE GALLERY
16/5/99 Tel: 01243 774557

Wendy Ramshaw, plus The Wilson Bequest. Details of residency to be confirmed. Paintings from the private collection of Professor Wilson

Art Galleries

Royal Artillery Gold Cup

30/3/99 SANDOWN PARK RACECOURSE
30/3/99 Tel: 01372 463072

For further details including race times and ticket prices please contact venue direct

Racecourses

A Walk in the Woods

1/4/99 WALMER CASTLE
1/4/99 Tel: 01304 364288

Take a walk with Richard Squires your guide. A£4.50 C£3.40 Concessions£3.40

Castles

Eggcellent Eggs Family Quiz

1/4/99 THE WHITE CLIFFS EXPERIENCE
12/4/99 Tel: 01304 214566/210101

A family themed Easter quiz.

Interactive

Easter Egg Trail

2/4/99 SHEFFIELD PARK GARDEN
2/4/99 Tel: 01825 790231

Starting on Good Friday and carries on until all the eggs are found! £1.00.

Gardens

Easter Bunny Hunt

2/4/99 BIDDENDEN VINEYARDS
5/4/99 Tel: 01580 291726

Easter Bunny Hunt on Easter Sun 11.00-16.00. Bring the children and enjoy a leisurely stroll around Kent's oldest vineyard and help your children spot our Easter Bunnies, then back to the winery for a tasting a piece of Easter Cake. Chocolate Bunnies for the children. Meet the owls from Hawkhurst Bird Sanctuary. The shop is open for cider and wine by the bottle or case. Apple juice available for drivers and children. Opening Times: Good Fri, Easter Sun & Bank Hol Mon 11.00-17.00, Easter Sat 10.00-17.00. Easter Bunny Hunt £1.20, Star Trek competition £2.50

Vineyards

Medieval Weekend with the Paladins of Chivalry

2/4/99 BODIAM CASTLE
5/4/99 Tel: 01580 830436

A weekend of demonstrations of medieval life from cooking to dressing a knight, have-a-go archery and authentic dance. In the castle and grounds. Normal admission prices apply, to car park and castle.

Historic Buildings

Medway Craft Show

2/4/99 COBHAM HALL
5/4/99 Tel: 01474 823371

Now firmly established as one of the area's largest Craft Shows, Cobham Hall is the magnificent setting for some of the finest Craftsmen in the Country to blend superbly with demonstrations, exciting arena entertainment and plenty for the children to see. A£3.50 OAPs£2.50 C£2.00

Historic Houses & Gardens

Drusillas Easter Egg Hunt

2/4/99 DRUSILLAS PARK
5/4/99 Tel: 01323 870234

Treasure hunt style event

Zoos

Easter Weekend

2/4/99 HEVER CASTLE AND GARDENS
5/4/99 Tel: 01732 865224

Children's Easter Egg Trail and local brass bands around the grounds. Event included in the Gardens only ticket

Castles

Easter Egg Hunt

2/4/99 PARADISE FAMILY LEISURE PARK
5/4/99 Tel: 01273 616006

Great fun for all the family, get painting and win a prize, hunt for the egg (before it melts!!)

Theme Parks

MG Magic (MGCC)

3/4/99 BRANDS HATCH
3/4/99 Tel: 0171 344 4444Ticketmaster

Thoroughbred Sports Cars, International BCV8, Midget Challenge, Metro Challenge, MG Phoenix, ACE MG Cockshoot, MGF Trophy. Indy Circuit, Grade-D. On the Gate: £10.00-£28.00. In Advance: Non £8.00-£25.00, Club £7.00-£22.00. Two Day Pass: Non £11.00-£30.00, Club £10.00-£27.00. Three Day Pass: Non £32.00, Club £29.00. Qualifying: £5.00-£14.00. C£Free. Programme £Free-£5.00. Seating (BH): £Free-£8.00. South Bank: £2.00-£5.00. Group Tickets: Non £90.00-£95.00, Club £80.00-£85.00. Season Ticket Inc. of

Club Membership: £200.00. You can buy your tickets for any of the 1999 events in advance any time up to 4 days before an event and make a saving, Tel: 0870 60 60 611

Motor Racing Circuit

Easter Egg Hunt
3/4/99 CLAREMONT LANDSCAPE GARDEN
3/4/99 Tel: 01372 467806
Celebrate Easter in traditional style by joining on of our six Easter Egg Hunts, an array of competitions, egg-rolling and trials to lead participants to a deliciously edible goal. A charged entrance fee will raise money for urgent conservation work at the property. Call for further details

Gardens

Easter Egg Hunt
3/4/99 LULLINGSTONE ROMAN VILLA
3/4/99 Tel: 01732 778000
They're here, there, everywhere, but can you find them? A£3.00 C£1.50 Concessions£2.30

Archaeological Sites

Easter Egg Hunt
3/4/99 ST AUGUSTINE'S ABBEY
3/4/99 Tel: 01227 767345
They're here, there, everywhere, but can you find them? A£3.00 C£1.50 Concessions£2.30

Abbeys

Easter Egg Hunt Activities
3/4/99 WALMER CASTLE
3/4/99 Tel: 01304 364288
A fun day for children & adults. A£4.50 C£2.30 Concessions£3.40

Castles

Children's Entertainment
3/4/99 DOVER CASTLE AND SECOND WORLD WAR TUNNELS
5/4/99 Tel: 01304 201628/202754
Siege tactics for children. Crew Of Patches. A£6.90 C£3.50 Concessions£5.20

Castles

A Celebration of Easter
3/4/99 LEEDS CASTLE
5/4/99 Tel: 01622 765400
Puppet shows, egg painting, face painting, mask making, maypole dancing, kite flying, an Easter Garden, a circus workshop and a fun Tea Tent make this long weekend a real Easter Celebration

Castles

Easter Egg Hunt

3/4/99 **PETWORTH HOUSE AND PARK**
5/4/99 Tel: 01798 342207/343929
Brighten up the Easter weekend and chase after some craftily hidden Easter Eggs. 12.00-16.00. C£1.50, turn up at the car park for the Treasure Trail leading to an edible prize!

Historic Houses & Gardens

Craft Fayre
3/4/99 SANDOWN EXHIBITION CENTRE
5/4/99 Tel: 01372 467540
10.00-18.00. Prices to be announced. Please call 01344 874787 for further information

Exhibition Centres

Easter Gift, Food and Craft Fayre
3/4/99 SANDOWN PARK RACECOURSE
5/4/99 Tel: 01372 463072
Up to 225 skilled crafts people. Quality crafts created by experts from all over the country. Call for further detalis

Racecourses

The Sports of Kings
3/4/99 HAMPTON COURT PALACE AND GARDENS
11/4/99 Tel: 0181 781 9500
Presentations from costumed guides, and a chance to participate in some of the games and pastimes enjoyed by courtiers throughout the ages, including skittles, sword play, and board games.

Royal Palace

Eggstravaganza
3/4/99 PAINSHILL LANDSCAPE GARDEN
18/4/99 Tel: 01932 868113/864674
Exciting new trail searching for different shapes and designs, answering questions and drawing. Children use the shapes they have discovered to complete egg design

Gardens

Car Boot Sale
4/4/99 RURAL LIFE CENTRE
4/4/99 Tel: 01252 792300/795571
09.00-13.00, £5.00 per car to sell. Buyers admitted to sale free

Museums

Easter Egg Extravaganza
4/4/99 RURAL LIFE CENTRE
4/4/99 Tel: 01252 792300/795571
Miller's Art Animals and rides on the Old Kiln Light Railway and much more. Time: 11.00-18.00. Cost: A£3.00 C£1.50 OAPs£2.50 Groups 30+ 10% discount

Museums

Garden Tour

4/4/99 4/4/99	**WALMER CASTLE** Tel: 01304 364288 Past, Present and Future with Richard Squires, your guide. A£4.50 C£2.30 Concessions£3.40 *Castles*

Easter Special for Children

4/4/99 5/4/99	**BORDE HILL GARDEN** Tel: 01444 450326 Easter Sunday and Monday at Borde Hill Gardens can be a treat for the kids and a rest for the parents, plenty to see and do, call for further details *Gardens*

The King's Shilling

4/4/99 5/4/99	**DEAL CASTLE** Tel: 01304 372762 18th-century. British Marines, 1777. A£3.00 C£1.50 Concessions£2.30 *Castles*

Easter Eggstravagansa

4/4/99 5/4/99	**GROOMBRIDGE PLACE GARDENS** Tel: 01892 863999 *Gardens*

Easter at Penshurst Place

4/4/99 5/4/99	**PENSHURST PLACE AND GARDENS** Tel: 01892 870307 Trailer Rides, Easter stories and free Easter Eggs for children *Historic Houses*

Easter Bunny Hunt and Crafts Fair

4/4/99 5/4/99	**SOUTH OF ENGLAND RARE BREEDS** **CENTRE** Tel: 01233 861493 Look for the 'bunnies' around the farm, join in the fun. Puppet show *Farm- Rare Breeds*

Easter Fun

4/4/99 5/4/99	**THE HOP FARM COUNTRY PARK** Tel: 01622 871577 Fun and entertainment for all the family both days with egg decorating, Easter Parade and clown workshop activities. Prices on application. Time: 10.00-18.00. *Museum- Agricultural*

Easter Treats

4/4/99 5/4/99	**THE WHITE CLIFFS EXPERIENCE** Tel: 01304 214566/210101 Roman and Ration book sweets for the family to sample. *Interactive*

Easter Boss Formula (BRSCC)

5/4/99 5/4/99	**BRANDS HATCH** Tel: 0171 344 4444Ticketmaster British Open Single Seaters (70's/80's Formula 1 Cars), Kent Championship

Formula Fords, XR2 Challenge, XR3
Challenge, Porsche 924s. Indy Circuit,
Grade-C. On the Gate: £10.00-£28.00. In
Advance: Non £8.00-£25.00, Club £7.00-
£22.00. Two Day Pass: Non £11.00-
£30.00, Club £10.00-£27.00. Three Day
Pass: Non £32.00, Club £29.00.
Qualifying: £5.00-£14.00. C£Free.
Programme £Free-£5.00. Seating (BH):
£Free-£8.00. South Bank: £2.00-£5.00.
Group Tickets: Non £90.00-£95.00, Club
£80.00-£85.00. Season Ticket Inc. of
Club Membership: £200.00. You can buy
your tickets for any of the 1999 events in
advance any time up to 4 days before an
event and make a saving, Tel: 0870 60
60 611

Motor Racing Circuit

Alternative Power Day

5/4/99 5/4/99	**BROOKLANDS MUSEUM** Tel: 01932 857381 Wind; Sun; Pedal; Steam; Electric - not a petrol engine in sight *Museum- Motor*

BRDA Rallycross

5/4/99 5/4/99	**LYDDEN INTERNATIONAL MOTOR RACING** **CIRCUIT** Tel: 01304 830557 For further details including times and ticket prices please contact venue direct *Motor Racing Circuit*

Water Gardens Specialist Day Tickets

8/4/99 8/4/99	**RHS GARDEN WISLEY** Tel: 01483 224234 Come and find out more about con- structing a pond suitable for your gar- den as well as how to maintain and stock it. Time: 10.30-16.30. Cost: mem- bers £40.00, non-members £45.00 *Gardens*

The Great Dinosaur Hunt

9/4/99 12/4/99	**PARADISE FAMILY LEISURE PARK** Tel: 01273 616006 Track down the dinosaurs - you may think it's easy but it won't be - and you could win a prize! *Theme Parks*

Kentish Gallery Choice

9/4/99 16/5/99	**MAIDSTONE MUSEUM AND ART GALLERY** Tel: 01622 754497 Selected by members of the Bentlif Trust, this exhibition represents a per- sonal choice from our collections, works by painters with local connections, like Albert Goodwin are to be displayed *Museums*

The Remarkable Tales of Ambrose

Gwinnett
10/4/99 DEAL CASTLE
11/4/99 Tel: 01304 372762
Crew Of Patches. A£3.00 C£1.50
Concessions£2.30

Castles

SEMSEC Car Races
10/4/99 LYDDEN INTERNATIONAL MOTOR RACING CIRCUIT
11/4/99 Tel: 01304 830557
For further details including times and ticket prices please contact venue direct

Motor Racing Circuit

Photographic Workshop Weekend
10/4/99 RHS GARDEN WISLEY
11/4/99 Tel: 01483 224234
Beginners level. This two-day workshop led by specialist RHS staff with an invited guest photographer will teach participants the techniques used in photographing plants and gardens in the spring. Time: 10.00-17.00. Cost: members £70.00, non-members £75.00

Gardens

Parrot Show
11/4/99 SANDOWN EXHIBITION CENTRE
5/4/99 Tel: 01372 467540
Held by The Parrot Society. 10.00-17.00
A£5.00 C£Free

Exhibition Centres

Clubmans Motorcycles (NEW ERA)
11/4/99 BRANDS HATCH
11/4/99 Tel: 0171 344 4444Ticketmaster
All classes of national solo motorcycles and sidecars. Indy Circuit, Grade-D. On the Gate: £10.00-£28.00. In Advance: Non £8.00-£25.00, Club £7.00-£22.00. Two Day Pass: Non £11.00-£30.00, Club £10.00-£27.00. Three Day Pass: Non £32.00, Club £29.00. Qualifying: £5.00-£14.00. C£Free. Programme £Free-£5.00. Seating (BH): £Free-£8.00. South Bank: £2.00-£5.00. Group Tickets: Non £90.00-£95.00, Club £80.00-£85.00. Season Ticket Inc. of Club Membership: £200.00. You can buy your tickets for any of the 1999 events in advance any time up to 4 days before an event and make a saving, Tel: 0870 60 60 611

Motor Racing Circuit

Walk at Wisley
11/4/99 RHS GARDEN WISLEY
11/4/99 Tel: 01483 224234
Come and walk around Wisley and see the rock garden, alpine meadow and alpine house with your guide Allan Robbinson at 10.30. This walk will also

take place on: Wed 14th at 10.30. Cost: Members £5.00, non-members £10.00. To book tickets send a cheque made payable to RHS, enclosing a SAE and including your membership number (if applicable) and day time telephone number to the Administration Department at RHS Garden, Wisley, Woking GU23 6QB. We are sorry but we cannot accept telephone bookings. Please note that all events may be subject to cancellation due to insufficient ticket sales

Gardens

Garden Tour
11/4/99 WALMER CASTLE
11/4/99 Tel: 01304 364288
Past, Present and Future with Richard Squires, your guide. A£4.50 C£2.30
Concessions£3.40

Castles

Plantsman's Days Tickets
13/4/99 RHS GARDEN WISLEY
30/9/99 Tel: 01483 224234
Join our special guest horticulturists who, through illustrated talks and guided walks round Wisley will impart their knowledge and enthusiasm for plants. These days will be held on: Tue 13 Apr, Fri 7 May, Fri 2 July, Mon 6 & Thur 30 Sept, 10.00-16.30. Cost: members £40.00, non-members £45.00

Gardens

Container Gardening Tickets
15/4/99 RHS GARDEN WISLEY
15/4/99 Tel: 01483 224234
Specialist RHS staff will show you how to use a variety of containers to create beautiful displays. In addition to plants traditionally associated with container gardening, participants will gain ideas for using fruit, vegetables and alpine plants. Time: 10.00-16.00. Cost: members £40.00, non-members £45.00

Gardens

17/4/99 SANDOWN EXHIBITION CENTRE
17/4/99 Tel: 01372 467540

Exhibition Centres

The Ninth Annual Garden Festival
17/4/99 BORDE HILL GARDEN
18/4/99 Tel: 01444 450326
A festival with a range of specialist nurseries, collectable plants, crafts, fine foods and wine. A Floral Pavilion with Floral Art Competition. Gardener's

Question Time and lectures, garden tours. 10.00-17.00 both days. Normal admission prices apply

Gardens

Clubman Cars (750 M/C)

17/4/99   BRANDS HATCH

18/4/99   Tel: 0171 344 4444Ticketmaster
750 Formula, Sports 2000s, Formula 4, Formula Vee x2, Kitcars, Caterhams x2, Radicals x2. Indy Circuit, Grade-D. On the Gate: £10.00-£28.00. In Advance: Non £8.00-£25.00, Club £7.00-£22.00. Two Day Pass: Non £11.00-£30.00, Club £10.00-£27.00. Three Day Pass: Non £32.00, Club £29.00. Qualifying: £5.00-£14.00. C£Free. Programme £Free-£5.00. Seating (BH): £Free-£8.00. South Bank: £2.00-£5.00. Group Tickets: Non £90.00-£95.00, Club £80.00-£85.00. Season Ticket Inc. of Club Membership: £200.00. You can buy your tickets for any of the 1999 events in advance any time up to 4 days before an event and make a saving, Tel: 0870 60 60 611

Motor Racing Circuit

The Remarkable Tales of Ambrose Gwinnett

17/4/99   DEAL CASTLE

18/4/99   Tel: 01304 372762
Crew Of Patches. A£3.00 C£1.50 Concessions£2.30

Castles

Greenhouse Weekend

17/4/99   LEEDS CASTLE

18/4/99   Tel: 01622 765400
Meet the plantsmen over this weekend and find out, how, why, what & where...

Castles

Children's Entertainment

17/4/99   LULLINGSTONE ROMAN VILLA

18/4/99   Tel: 01732 778000
Roman Siege tactics for children. Entertainers: Crew Of Patches. A£2.50 C£2.00 Concessions£1.90

Archaeological Sites

BMCRC Motorcycles/Sidecars

17/4/99   LYDDEN INTERNATIONAL MOTOR RACING CIRCUIT

18/4/99   Tel: 01304 830557
For further details including times and ticket prices please contact venue direct

Motor Racing Circuit

Silk Painting Workshop

17/4/99   RHS GARDEN WISLEY

18/4/99   Tel: 01483 224234
Learn the beautiful art of painting directly onto silk during a relaxed two-day

workshop. time: 10.00-16.30 both days. Cost: members £45.00, non-members £50.00. This workshop will be repeated: 16-17 Feb

Gardens

Grow '99

17/4/99   SANDOWN EXHIBITION CENTRE

18/4/99   Tel: 01372 467540
Opening Times14.00 Admission £3.00

Exhibition Centres

The Varied Works of a Jobbing Artist

17/4/99   TUNBRIDGE WELLS MUSEUM AND ART GALLERY

1/5/99   Tel: 01892 526121/554171
By Barbarann Lang

Museums

The South East Arts Collection

17/4/99   CHERTSEY MUSEUM

19/6/99   Tel: 01932 565764
A selection of works from the Region's outstanding fine art and craft collections

Museum- Local History

Antiques Fair

20/4/99   SANDOWN EXHIBITION CENTRE

20/4/99   Tel: 01372 467540
Opening times 14.00-18.00. Admission: £3.00. Please call 0171 249 4050 for further information

Exhibition Centres

Spring Meeting

21/4/99   EPSOM RACECOURSE

21/4/99   Tel: 01372 726311
For further details including race times and ticket prices please contact venue direct

Racecourses

Flower Arranging Demonstration

21/4/99   RHS GARDEN WISLEY

21/4/99   Tel: 01483 224234
'It's a good life' with Anna Sparks. Time: 10.00-12.30. Cost: members £18.00, non-members £23.00

Gardens

Steeplechase Meeting

22/4/99   FONTWELL PARK RACECOURSE

22/4/99   Tel: 01243 543335
Celebrate 75 years of racing at Fontwell Park. Daily Member £13.00 Tattersalls £9.00 Silver Ring £5.00 OAPs£2.50 C(o-16)£Free. Advance group rates available

Racecourses

Garden Tour - Bird Walk

22/4/99   SHEFFIELD PARK GARDEN

22/4/99   Tel: 01825 790231
Led by the gardeners, and limited to 30 per walk, maximum. To see the gardens through the eyes of the people who

know it best, book early. Time: 07.00.
Cost: £5.00.

Gardens

Botanical Art Weekend
22/4/99 RHS GARDEN WISLEY
25/4/99 Tel: 01483 224234
(Beginners Course). Pauline Dean is a
practising botanical artist working in a
freelance capacity for horticultural publications. Pauline began her painting
career in 1984 and has won five RHS
Gold Medals. She has designed three
Winter Flower RHS collectors' plates and
the 1996 Chelsea Flower Show Plate.
Pauline has tutored the Wisley botanical
art courses for eight years. Times: Thur
22nd (18.00-21.00), Fri 23 & Sat 24
(09.00-18.00), Sun 25 (09.00-16.30).
Cost: £185.00

Gardens

Why We Work Our Woodlands
23/4/99 SCOTNEY CASTLE GARDEN
23/4/99 Tel: 01892 891081
Commences 14.00. A Themed tour
around the working estate, showing the
work of the forestry team, from planting
to the production of timber products
used on National Trust properties - such
as gates, wattle fencing, seats. Two and
a half - three hours, about 3 miles. Tours
does not include the Garden. £3.50,
must be pre-booked on 01892 891001 or
write to The Box Office, The National
Trust, Scotney Castle, Lamberhurst, Kent
TN3 8JN

Gardens

The Sandown Mile
23/4/99 SANDOWN PARK RACECOURSE
24/4/99 Tel: 01372 463072
Friday is the Sandown Milw and
Saturday is the Whitbread Gold
Cup/Thresher Classic Trial. For further
details including race times and ticket
prices please contact venue direct

Racecourses

Cubs Challenge Days
24/4/99 DRUSILLAS PARK
24/4/99 Tel: 01323 870234
Please call for further information. Also
to be held on: 22 May & 9 Oct

Zoos

Visit to Petworth House
24/4/99 HASTINGS MUSEUM AND ART GALLERY
24/4/99 Tel: 01424 781155
Following the highly successful Turner in
1066 Country Exhibition, visit Petworth
to see the many works he painted there.

Details from the Museum Office.

Museums

Kent Formula 3 Cup (BARC)
24/4/99 BRANDS HATCH
25/4/99 Tel: 0171 344 4444Ticketmaster
British Formula 3, Formula Palmer Audi,
Supersports 200, BMW Challenge,
Classic Porsche, Ginettas, Gilera
Scooters, 250 Gearbox Karts. Indy
Circuit, Grade-C. On the Gate: £10.00-
£28.00. In Advance: Non £8.00-£25.00,
Club £7.00-£22.00. Two Day Pass: Non
£11.00-£30.00, Club £10.00-£27.00.
Three Day Pass: Non £32.00, Club
£29.00. Qualifying: £5.00-£14.00.
C£Free. Programme £Free-£5.00.
Seating (BH): £Free-£8.00. South Bank:
£2.00-£5.00. Group Tickets: Non £90.00-
£95.00, Club £80.00-£85.00. Season
Ticket Inc. of Club Membership:
£200.00. You can buy your tickets for
any of the 1999 events in advance any
time up to 4 days before an event and
make a saving, Tel: 0870 60 60 611

Motor Racing Circuit

**The Remarkable Tales of Ambrose
Gwinnett**
24/4/99 DEAL CASTLE
25/4/99 Tel: 01304 372762
Crew Of Patches. A£3.00 C£1.50
Concessions£2.30

Castles

MMK Sprint
24/4/99 LYDDEN INTERNATIONAL MOTOR RACING
CIRCUIT
25/4/99 Tel: 01304 830557
For further details including times and
ticket prices please contact venue direct

Motor Racing Circuit

Walk at Wisley
25/4/99 RHS GARDEN WISLEY
25/4/99 Tel: 01483 224234
Come and see Wisley's birds with your
guide David Elliott at 09.30. This walk
will also take place on: Sun 16th May at
09.30. Cost: Members £5.00, non-members £10.00. To book tickets send a
cheque made payable to RHS, enclosing
a SAE and including your membership
number (if applicable) and day time telephone number to the Administration
Department at RHS Garden, Wisley,
Woking GU23 6QB. We are sorry but we
cannot accept telephone bookings.
Please note that all events may be subject to cancellation due to insufficient
ticket sales

Gardens

Designer Clothes Sale

26/4/99 CLANDON PARK

26/4/99 Tel: 01483 222482

Admission: £1.00 on the door, no need to book

Historic Houses & Gardens

From Dust to Digital

26/4/99 HASTINGS MUSEUM AND ART GALLERY

26/4/99 Tel: 01424 781155

Jane Flannis from Lighthouse will introduce the Events Coasts Commissions, and the collaboration with Brighton Museum and Art Gallery. This lecture coincides with the first of the digital projects opening at the De La Warr Pavillion, Bexhill - Maximum Cube by Anna Heinrich and Leon Palmer. Time: 19.30. Cost: A£3.00 Concessions£2.00.

Museums

Alpine Specialist Day Tickets

27/4/99 RHS GARDEN WISLEY

27/4/99 Tel: 01483 224234

Consisting of practical demonstrations and illustrated talks, this day will cater for anyone interested in finding out more about growing alpines. Time: 10.00-16.00. Cost: members £40.00, non-members £45.00

Gardens

Sold: The Art of Selling

27/4/99 HORSHAM MUSEUM

19/6/99 Tel: 01403 254959

A display of 200 years of selling, from posters to packaging and advertising material. To tie in with Arts Fanfare

Museum- Local History

Demonstration: The Mixed Border

28/4/99 RHS GARDEN WISLEY

28/4/99 Tel: 01483 224234

Come and let David Jewell give you some good advice on mixed borders at 14.00. This demonstration will also take place on: Wed 15th September at 14.00. Cost: Members £5.00, non-members £10.00. To book tickets send a cheque made payable to RHS, enclosing a SAE and including your membership number (if applicable) and day time telephone number to the Administration Department at RHS Garden, Wisley, Woking GU23 6QB. We are sorry but we cannot accept telephone bookings. Please note that all events may be subject to cancellation due to insufficient ticket sales

Gardens

Walk at Wisley

28/4/99 RHS GARDEN WISLEY

28/4/99 Tel: 01483 224234

Come and let your Guide, Colin Crosbie show you the trees, shrubs and herbaceous perennials at Wisley at 10.30. Cost: Members £5.00, non-members £10.00. To book tickets send a cheque made payable to RHS, enclosing a SAE and including your membership number (if applicable) and day time telephone number to the Administration Department at RHS Garden, Wisley, Woking GU23 6QB. We are sorry but we cannot accept telephone bookings. Please note that all events may be subject to cancellation due to insufficient ticket sales

Gardens

Race Meeting

29/4/99 BRIGHTON RACECOURSE

29/4/99 Tel: 01273 603580

Racing from Brighton between 12.00 and18.00. Admission A£4.00-£12.00 C£Free

Racecourses

Philharmonia Orchestra at The Dome Theatre

BRIGHTON FESTIVAL 1999

1/5/99 Tel: 01273 292951

1/5/99

Conductor - Vladimir Ashkenazy, Piano - Arcadi Volodos. Rachmaninov: Three Etudes Tableaux. Piano Concerto No. 3, Symphony No. 2. Sponsored by American Express, call venue to book

Festivals

Children's Parade

1/5/99 BRIGHTON FESTIVAL 1999

1/5/99 Tel: 01273 292951

Madeira Drive to Pavilion Gardens, theme of 'Tunes and Tales' commences 11.30

Festivals

Beaver Challenge Day

1/5/99 DRUSILLAS PARK

1/5/99 Tel: 01323 870234

Please call for further information. Also held on: 19 & 26 June, 10 July, 18 Sept, 2 & 16 Oct

Zoos

Junior Museum Club: Art in Boxes

1/5/99 HASTINGS MUSEUM AND ART GALLERY

1/5/99 Tel: 01424 781155

Using the exhibition Art Full Boxes as stimulation create your own fantasy world in a box. Bring a shoe box (or similar), decorative waste papers found ephernera. Led by Cas Holmes. £2.00.

Museums

Rye Mayor Making Ceremony
1/5/99 THE STORY OF RYE
1/5/99 Tel: 01797 226696
Procession of Mayors culminating in the
election of the new Mayor in full regalia.
Including throwing of hot pennies to the
poor!

Heritage Centres

Bexhill 100 Festival of Motoring 1999
1/5/99 BEXHILL 100 FESTIVAL OF MOTORING
1999
2/5/99 Tel: 01424 730564
This unique Festival celebrates Bexhill-
on-Sea as the birthplace of British Motor
Racing in 1902 and takes place on the
May Bank Holiday Weekend each year,
displaying hundreds of veteran, vintage,
classic, custom, racing, American and
military vehicles on Bexhill's elegant
Edwardian seafront, the original track. It
is now one of the largest, most popular
family events in the South of England
with stands, shops, stalls, funfair, aerobatics, kid's rides, marching bands, an
entertainment marquee and yachts bobbing out at sea - something for everyone. There is a Classic Vehicle Town
Parade on Saturday with street entertainment and in the evening a fireworks
display. The Festival itself is on Sunday
and Monday. Come and enjoy this wonderful celebration of Motor Racing
History. From 10:00. Admission Free.

Festivals

Bentley Spring Fair
1/5/99 BENTLEY WILDFOWL AND MOTOR MUSEUM
3/5/99 Tel: 01825 840573
Please telephone for details

Waterfowl Parks

**Live the Legend of The Ballads of
Robin Hood**
1/5/99 BODIAM CASTLE
3/5/99 Tel: 01580 830436
Witness the story of Robin Hood as it
unfolds within and around Bodiam
Castle as he is outlawed, how he fights
Little John, shoots at the silver arrow
contect. See a medieval encampment
and try your hand at shooting a bow. In
the castle and grounds. Normal admission charges apply, to car park and castle.

Historic Buildings

May Day Music and Dance

1/5/99 **HEVER CASTLE AND GARDENS**
3/5/99 Tel: 01732 865224
A weekend of traditional dance featuring
local Morris Dancing sides. Event included in the Gardens only ticket

Castles

Bonsai Weekend
1/5/99 LEONARDSLEE GARDENS
3/5/99 Tel: 01403 891212
Demonstrations and advice on the growing of Bonsai

Gardens

**The Pleasures of Peace: Craft, art and
design in Britain 1939 - 1968**
1/5/99 BRIGHTON FESTIVAL 1999
20/6/99 Tel: 01273 292951
At the Brighton Museum and Art Gallery.
Organised by Sainsbury Centre,
University of East Anglia, Curator - Tania
Harrod

Festivals

Aston Martin Races (AMOC)
2/5/99 BRANDS HATCH
2/5/99 Tel: 0171 344 4444Ticketmaster
MGCC Anglia Phoenix Championship, TR
Register Championship, TWMC
Championship, MGCC BCV8, Ferrari v
Porsche Challenge, Pre-War
Sportscars/Felthams/suitable 50's
sports, Jaguars, Enduro Part 1. Indy
Circuit, Grade-D. On the Gate: £10.00-
£28.00. In Advance: Non £8.00-£25.00,
Club £7.00-£22.00. Two Day Pass: Non
£11.00-£30.00, Club £10.00-£27.00.
Three Day Pass: Non £32.00, Club
£29.00. Qualifying: £5.00-£14.00.
C£Free. Programme £Free-£5.00.
Seating (BH): £Free-£8.00. South Bank:
£2.00-£5.00. Group Tickets: Non £90.00-
£95.00, Club £80.00-£85.00. Season
Ticket Inc. of Club Membership:
£200.00. You can buy your tickets for
any of the 1999 events in advance any
time up to 4 days before an event and
make a saving, Tel: 0870 60 60 611

Motor Racing Circuit

**Hagen Quartet at the Glyndebourne
Opera House**
2/5/99 BRIGHTON FESTIVAL 1999
2/5/99 Tel: 01273 292951
Haydn Quartet No. 5 op. 76 Weber
Quartet 1905 Beethoven Quartet op.
132. 2 May at 3pm, call venue to book

Festivals

Car Boot Sale

2/5/99	**RURAL LIFE CENTRE**
2/5/99	Tel: 01252 792300/795571
	09.00-13.00, £5.00 per car to sell.
	Buyers admitted to sale free

Museums

Tudor Re-enactment

2/5/99	**DOVER CASTLE AND SECOND WORLD WAR TUNNELS**
3/5/99	Tel: 01304 201628/202754
	Henry VIII and the Mary Rose. Group: Bills & Bows. A£6.90 C£3.50 Concessions£5.20

Castles

Reptile Rendezvous

2/5/99	**DRUSILLAS PARK**
3/5/99	Tel: 01323 870234
	East Sussex Reptile & Amphibian Society in the marquee. Reptiles on show and special talks given

Zoos

Robin Hood Revisits Groombridge with his Medieval Fair

2/5/99	**GROOMBRIDGE PLACE GARDENS**
3/5/99	Tel: 01892 863999

Gardens

May Day Celebrations

2/5/99	**MUSEUM OF KENT LIFE**
3/5/99	Tel: 01622 763936
	Traditional May Day celebrations include: crowning of the Cobtree May Queen, Morris and country dancing, Jack-in-the-Green and talks about May Day customs and symbols.

Museum- Local History

The Power of the Normans

2/5/99	**PEVENSEY CASTLE**
3/5/99	Tel: 01323 762604
	Conquest and the Troop. A£4.00 C£2.00 Concessions£3.00. Please call for further information

Castles

Easter Chicken Hunt

2/5/99	**MUSEUM OF KENT LIFE**
5/5/99	Tel: 01622 763936
	Children can hunt the wooden chickens hidden around the museum and win a prize. Also egg colouring and other seasonal activities.

Museum- Local History

Aston Martin Races (AMOC)

3/5/99	**BRANDS HATCH**
3/5/99	Tel: 0171 344 4444Ticketmaster
	Ferrari Maranello, Intermarque, Anglo-American, Formula Junior, Flemings, Morgans, Porsche Classic, Austin Healeys, Enduro Part II, Post War

Astons. Indy Circuit, Grade-D. On the Gate: £10.00-£28.00. In Advance: Non £8.00-£25.00, Club £7.00-£22.00. Two Day Pass: Non £11.00-£30.00, Club £10.00-£27.00. Three Day Pass: Non £32.00, Club £29.00. Qualifying: £5.00-£14.00. C£Free. Programme £Free-£5.00. Seating (BH): £Free-£8.00. South Bank: £2.00-£5.00. Group Tickets: Non £90.00-£95.00, Club £80.00-£85.00. Season Ticket Inc. of Club Membership: £200.00. You can buy your tickets for any of the 1999 events in advance any time up to 4 days before an event and make a saving, Tel: 0870 60 60 611

Motor Racing Circuit

'May-Day' - Emergency Vehicle Gathering

3/5/99	**BROOKLANDS MUSEUM**
3/5/99	Tel: 01932 857381
	All manner of vintage and classic emergency vehicles with demonstrations, ambulances, recovery vehicles, fire engines, breakdown truck, AA/RAC roadside assistance vehicles, military emergency rigs, airport crash tenders etc

Museum- Motor

Bank Holiday Steeplechase Meeting

3/5/99	**FONTWELL PARK RACECOURSE**
3/5/99	Tel: 01243 543335
	Bank Holiday fun for all the family. Children's entertainment and face painting. Daily Member £13.00 Tattersalls £9.00 Silver Ring £5.00 OAPs£2.50 C(0-16)£Free. Advance group rates available

Racecourses

BRSCC F/Ford/Saloons

3/5/99	**LYDDEN INTERNATIONAL MOTOR RACING CIRCUIT**
3/5/99	Tel: 01304 830557
	For further details including times and ticket prices please contact venue direct

Motor Racing Circuit

Absolute Zero at the Corn Exchange

3/5/99	**BRIGHTON FESTIVAL 1999**
8/5/99	Tel: 01273 292951
	Performance piece, ice sculptures and dance. Walter Bailey/Charlie Morrissey. Sponsored by Birds Eye Walls, call for further details

Festivals

Race Meeting

4/5/99	**BRIGHTON RACECOURSE**
4/5/99	Tel: 01273 603580
	Racing from Brighton between 12.00 and18.00. Admission A£4.00-£12.00

C£Free

Racecourses

Maly Theatre of St Petersburg at the Theatre Royal

4/5/99
8/5/99

BRIGHTON FESTIVAL 1999

Tel: 01273 292951

Shakespeare - The Winters Tale, directed by Declan Donnellan. 4-8 May at 7.45pm, call for further details

Festivals

Fairy Tales

5/5/99
6/5/99

WALMER CASTLE

Tel: 01304 364288

Fairy tales from the Enchanted Garden with Crew of Patches. A£4.50 C£2.30 Concessions£3.40

Castles

Streets Of Brighton 1999

6/5/99

NATIONAL STREET ARTS FESTIVALS FOR 1999

9/5/99

Tel: 01273 821588

To kick off the summer season of street art events, Zap Productions will be staging another innovative range of acts. Expect up to 100,000 spectators and more exciting work from acts such as last year's Stickleback Plasticus. A continuation of the work started by Lino Hellings with students from the University of Brighton plus more collaborations with the Viva Citè and Fête dans la Ville festival in France

Festivals

London Symphony Orchestra at The Dome Theatre

7/5/99
7/5/99

BRIGHTON FESTIVAL 1999

Tel: 01273 292951

Conductor - Christopher Eschenbach, Soloist - Midori
Bruch Violin Concerto No 1, Mahler Symphony No5, 7 May at 8pm, call venue to book

Festivals

Pottery Sale

7/5/99
9/5/99

DODDINGTON PLACE GARDENS

Tel: 01795 886101

Sale of handmade terracotta garden pots made by Whichford Pottery.

Gardens

Rainbow Challenge Day

8/5/99
8/5/99

DRUSILLAS PARK

Tel: 01323 870234

Please call for further information. Also held on: 17 July & 23 Oct

Zoos

National Council For the Conservation of Plants and Gardens

8/5/99
8/5/99

MILLAIS RHODODENDRONS

Tel: 01252 792698

Surrey Group. Rare plant sale. Invited Specialist Nurseries showing and selling rare plants within the garden

Gardens

Music

8/5/99
9/5/99

DEAL CASTLE

Tel: 01304 372762

17-century music performed by Captain Generall's Musick. A£3.50 C£1.80 Concessions£2.60

Castles

Surrey Advertiser Motor Show

8/5/99
9/5/99

LOSELEY PARK

Tel: 01483 304440

Stands displaying and selling new cars and hands-on 4x4

Historic Houses & Gardens

CMCC Classic Motorcycles

8/5/99

LYDDEN INTERNATIONAL MOTOR RACING CIRCUIT

9/5/99

Tel: 01304 830557

For further details including times and ticket prices please contact venue direct

Motor Racing Circuit

Sandown Model Symposium

8/5/99
9/5/99

SANDOWN EXHIBITION CENTRE

Tel: 01372 467540

Opening times and further details to be announced

Exhibition Centres

Duel to the Death!

8/5/99
9/5/99

WALMER CASTLE

Tel: 01304 364288

A Napoleonic duel to the death performed by The Duelling Association. A£4.50 C£2.30 Concessions£3.40

Castles

Barbarella: Dolls and Doll Imagery

8/5/99

TUNBRIDGE WELLS MUSEUM AND ART GALLERY

1/6/99

Tel: 01892 526121/554171

The doll as a craft-made object, its position in a social context, and its use in art

Museums

Children's Animal Fair

9/5/99
9/5/99

BORDE HILL GARDEN

Tel: 01444 450326

Wide selection of animals including penguins, meerkats, snakes, ferret racing, rare rabbits and chickens. There will be a craft and gift marquee, children's entertainers, along with donkey and tractor rides, trout fishing and children's adventure playground. 10.00-17.00.

Gardens

	The British National 3000 Race Day (BRSCC)
9/5/99	BRANDS HATCH
9/5/99	Tel: 0171 344 4444Ticketmaster
	National 3000s, TVR Tuscans, Tomcat/Vento Challenge, Mighty Minis. Indy Circuit, Grade-C. On the Gate: £10.00-£28.00. In Advance: Non £8.00-£25.00, Club £7.00-£22.00. Two Day Pass: Non £11.00-£30.00, Club £10.00-£27.00. Three Day Pass: Non £32.00, Club £29.00. Qualifying: £5.00-£14.00. C£Free. Programme £Free-£5.00. Seating (BH): £Free-£8.00. South Bank: £2.00-£5.00. Group Tickets: Non £90.00-£95.00, Club £80.00-£85.00. Season Ticket Inc. of Club Membership: £200.00. You can buy your tickets for any of the 1999 events in advance any time up to 4 days before an event and make a saving, Tel: 0870 60 60 611
	Motor Racing Circuit

	Street of Brighton (street theatre)
9/5/99	BRIGHTON FESTIVAL 1999
9/5/99	Tel: 01273 292951
	Street Music Day. All day long the streets of Brighton will be alive to the sound of world music
	Festivals

	Plant Sale
9/5/99	DODDINGTON PLACE GARDENS
9/5/99	Tel: 01795 886101
	Lots of bulbs and plants for sale organised by the Hardy Plant Society.
	Gardens

	Garden Design Course
10/5/99	BORDE HILL GARDEN
14/5/99	Tel: 01444 450326
	Robin Williams and associate shows you how to transform your garden in this week long course at Borde Hill, call for further details
	Gardens

	City of Birmingham Touring Opera at the Corn Exchange
11/5/99	BRIGHTON FESTIVAL 1999
11/5/99	Tel: 01273 292951
	Smetana The Two Widows. 11 May at 7.45pm, call venue to book
	Festivals

	Classic Car Auction
11/5/99	SANDOWN EXHIBITION CENTRE
11/5/99	Tel: 01372 467540
	Viewing: 10.30 Auction: 14.00. Please call 01954 232332 for further information
	Exhibition Centres

	Moscow State Circus
11/5/99	BRIGHTON FESTIVAL 1999
23/5/99	Tel: 01273 292951
	in Preston Park, call for further details
	Festivals

	Garden Tour - The Judas Tree
12/5/99	ALFRISTON CLERGY HOUSE
12/5/99	Tel: 01323 870001
	Led by the gardeners, and limited to 30 per walk, maximum. To see the gardens through the eyes of the people who know it best, book early. Time: 18.30. Cost: £5.00.
	Historic Houses

	Race Meeting
12/5/99	BRIGHTON RACECOURSE
12/5/99	Tel: 01273 603580
	Racing from Brighton between 12.00 and18.00. Admission A£4.00-£12.00 C£Free
	Racecourses

	Flower Arranging Demonstration
12/5/99	RHS GARDEN WISLEY
12/5/99	Tel: 01483 224234
	'Spare time, past times' with Eleanor Brown. Time: 10.00-12.30. Cost: members £18.00, non-members £23.00
	Gardens

	Festival Opera at the Theatre Royal
13/5/99	BRIGHTON FESTIVAL 1999
15/5/99	Tel: 01273 292951
	Britten The Turn of The Screw. 13 & 15 May at 7.30pm, call venue to book
	Festivals

	Red Earth - Fire Sounding
13/5/99	BRIGHTON FESTIVAL 1999
16/5/99	Tel: 01273 292951
	at outdoor performance held at the Gardner Arts Centre
	Festivals

	Kim Itoh & the Glorious Future at the Corn Exchange
14/5/99	BRIGHTON FESTIVAL 1999
16/5/99	Tel: 01273 292951
	Dead and Alive and 3SEX. 14-16 May at 8pm, call for booking details
	Festivals

	Brownie Challenge Day
15/5/99	DRUSILLAS PARK
15/5/99	Tel: 01323 870234
	Please call for further information. Also to be held on: 12 June, 3 July, 11 & 25 Sept
	Zoos

	Apex Track Day
15/5/99	LYDDEN INTERNATIONAL MOTOR RACING

Circuit

15/5/99 Tel: 01304 830557
For further details including times and
ticket prices please contact venue direct
Motor Racing Circuit

**Autotrader British Touring Car
Championship (TOCA)**

15/5/99 **Brands Hatch**
16/5/99 Tel: 0171 344 4444Ticketmaster
Touring Cars x 2, Formula Ford, Ford
Fiestas, Formula Renault, Renault
Spiders, Formula Vauxhall Jnr, Vauxhall
Vectras. Indy Circuit, Grade-A. On the
Gate: £10.00-£28.00. In Advance: Non
£8.00-£25.00, Club £7.00-£22.00. Two
Day Pass: Non £11.00-£30.00, Club
£10.00-£27.00. Three Day Pass: Non
£32.00, Club £29.00. Qualifying: £5.00-
£14.00. C£Free. Programme £Free-£5.00.
Seating (BH): £Free-£8.00. South Bank:
£2.00-£5.00. Group Tickets: Non £90.00-
£95.00, Club £80.00-£85.00. Season
Ticket Inc. of Club Membership:
£200.00. You can buy your tickets for
any of the 1999 events in advance any
time up to 4 days before an event and
make a saving, Tel: 0870 60 60 611
Motor Racing Circuit

Albuhera Day

15/5/99 **Dover Castle and Second World War
Tunnels**
16/5/99 Tel: 01304 201628/202754
Multi-period with various performers.
A£6.90 C£3.50 Concessions£5.20
Castles

A Festival of English Food and Wine

15/5/99 **Leeds Castle**
16/5/99 Tel: 01622 765400
From coastline to countryside, all that is
best in the way of produce from the
south east of England is gathered
together at the Castle. Samplings, fascinating talks on food and wine related
topics, celebrity cooking demonstrations, puppet shows and Morris Dancing
offer something for groups of all ages at
this family event
Castles

Medieval Monastic Entertainers

15/5/99 **St Augustine's Abbey**
16/5/99 Tel: 01227 767345
Heuristics. Try your hand at calligraphy
or authentic period games as this popular duo take a lighthearted look at
monastic customs, crafts and lifestyles.
Learn about food preparation, herbs and
spices in cooking and medicine, the

mechanics of building, lifting and many
other skills. Part of Cistercian 900.
A£3.00 C£1.50 Concessions£2.30
Abbeys

Fairy Tales

15/5/99 **Walmer Castle**
16/5/99 Tel: 01304 364288
Tales from the Enchanted Garden, Crew
Of Patches. A£4.50 C£2.30
Concessions£3.40
Castles

Museum's Week

15/5/99 **Guildford Museum**
23/5/99 Tel: 01483 444750
The theme for this week will be
'Treasures, Food and Travel'
Museum- Local History

**City of Birmingham Symphony
Orchestra at The Dome Theatre**

16/5/99 **Brighton Festival 1999**
16/5/99 Tel: 01273 292951
Conductor - Paavo Berglund, Soloist -
Lief Ove Andsnes. Tippett Concerto for
Double String Orchestra Schumann
Piano Concerto Mendelssohn Symphony
No 3. 16 May at 3pm call venue to book
Festivals

Mackerel Fair

16/5/99 **Brighton Festival 1999**
16/5/99 Tel: 01273 292951
at the Fishing Museum, call for further
details
Festivals

Dieppe Market

16/5/99 **Brighton Festival 1999**
16/5/99 Tel: 01273 292951
held in Bartholomew Square from 09.00-
14.00
Festivals

Spring Plant Fair

16/5/99 **Claremont Landscape Garden**
16/5/99 Tel: 01372 467806
Sale of donated plants. Non National
Trust Members A£3.00 C£1.50
Gardens

Spring Plant Fair

16/5/99 **Petworth House and Park**
16/5/99 Tel: 01798 342207/343929
Delight for garden lovers come and
search for your Spring plants 11.00-16.00
Admission to grounds only £1.00
Historic Houses & Gardens

Steam and Diesel Gala

16/5/99 **Romney Hythe and Dymchurch
Railway**
16/5/99 Tel: 01797 362353/363256
All available enquiries in operation.

Trade Stands, Model Exhibition, lots of trains all day

Railways

Celebration 2000: Ancient Britons & Romans

16/5/99   RURAL LIFE CENTRE

16/5/99   Tel: 01252 792300/795571

A day of fun - chariot race, "archaeological dig", make Roman lamps and pots, listen to the Celtic storytellers. Come dressed as Roman or Celt - prizes! 11.00-17.30. Cost: A£3.00 C£1.50 OAPs£2.50 Groups 30+ 10% discount

Museums

Sdasa Chorale at the Theatre Royal

17/5/99   BRIGHTON FESTIVAL 1999

17/5/99   Tel: 01273 292951

South African and English vocal music. Sponsored by KPMG. Call for further details

Festivals

Classical Opera Company at the Theatre Royal

18/5/99   BRIGHTON FESTIVAL 1999

18/5/99   Tel: 01273 292951

La Finta Semplice, call for further details

Festivals

Bluebells on top of the World

18/5/99   EMMETTS GARDEN

18/5/99   Tel: 01732 868381/750367

19.00. A guided tour of this attractive hill-top garden, with Head Gardener, allow 2 hours, £6.00, must be pre-booked on 01892 891001 or write to The Box Office, The National Trust, Scotney Castle, Lamberhurst, Kent TN3 8JN

Gardens

Christian Resources Exhibition

18/5/99   SANDOWN EXHIBITION CENTRE

21/5/99   Tel: 01372 467540

Opening times 10.00-17.00

Exhibition Centres

Royal Shakespeare Company at the Moulsecoomb Leisure Centre

18/5/99   BRIGHTON FESTIVAL 1999

22/5/99   Tel: 01273 292951

Sponsored by American Express , call for further details

Festivals

English Festival Opera at the Theatre Royal

19/5/99   BRIGHTON FESTIVAL 1999

19/5/99   Tel: 01273 292951

Conductor - Christopher Eschenbach, Soloist - Midori
Bruch Violin Concerto No 1 Mahler Symphony No5, call venue to book

Festivals

Insects in Amber

19/5/99   HASTINGS MUSEUM AND ART GALLERY

19/5/99   Tel: 01424 781155

An overview of these fascinating time-capsules with their fossilised inclusions. A joint meeting with Hastings & District Geological Society. Speaker: Andrew Ross, Curator of fossil Arthropods, Natural History Museum, London. Time: 19.30.

Museums

Tilford Bach Festival 1999

20/5/99   TILFORD BACH FESTIVAL 1999

22/5/99   Tel: 01252 782167

The provisional programme for 1999 is : 20 May The Guildhall String ensemble making a return after their outstanding performance in 1997. 21 May A Baroque Chamber Music group. 22 May London Handel Orchestra conducted by Denys Darlow which will include two Bach Cantatas plus other music by Bach and his contemporaries.

Festivals

Garden Tour - Rhododendrons

21/5/99   SHEFFIELD PARK GARDEN

21/5/99   Tel: 01825 790231

Led by the gardeners, and limited to 30 per walk, maximum. To see the gardens through the eyes of the people who know it best, book early. Time: 18.30. Cost: £6.00.

Gardens

Nederlands Dans Theater 2 at the Theatre Royal

21/5/99   BRIGHTON FESTIVAL 1999

22/5/99   Tel: 01273 292951

Sponsored by Van den Bergh Foods Ltd. 21-22 May at 7.45pm call for further details

Festivals

BARC F/Ford and Saloons

22/5/99   LYDDEN INTERNATIONAL MOTOR RACING CIRCUIT

23/5/99   Tel: 01304 830557

For further details including times and ticket prices please contact venue direct

Motor Racing Circuit

Medieval Monastic Entertainers

22/5/99   ST AUGUSTINE'S ABBEY

23/5/99   Tel: 01227 767345

Heuristics. Try your hand at calligraphy or authentic period games as this popular duo take a lighthearted look at monastic customs, crafts and lifestyles. Learn about food preparation, herbs and

Further more detailed information on the attractions listed can be found in Best Guides *Visitor Attractions* Guide under the classifications shown

spices in cooking and medicine, the mechanics of building, lifting and many other skills. Part of Cistercian 900. A£3.00 C£1.50 Concessions£2.30

Abbeys

Edwardian Weekend
22/5/99 WALMER CASTLE
23/5/99 Tel: 01304 364288
Hogarth's Heroes present an Edwardian weekend. A£4.50 C£2.30 Concessions£3.40

Castles

Microhenge: Where did we go Yesterday
22/5/99 HASTINGS MUSEUM AND ART GALLERY
4/7/99 Tel: 01424 781155
Simon Poulter creates a virtual 'ancient' monument. This is a new multi-media and digital art project which ahs been specially commissioned to celebrate John Logie Baird's first TV transmission in Hastings in 1923. Simon Poulter's virtual monumental museum will offer the visitor all sorts of information. There will be walk-throughs of the monument and an opportunity to have your picture taken at Microhenge. Find out how information is stored on you, the visitor, and access the Microhenge website from both within and outside the Museum. www.microhenge.com

Museums

Bruckner Symphony Orchestra at the The Dome Theatre
23/5/99 BRIGHTON FESTIVAL 1999
23/5/99 Tel: 01273 292951
Conductor - Martin Sieghart, Soloist - Raphael Oleg with Brighton Festival Chorus. Wagner Tannhauser Overture Mozart Violin Concerto no 4 K218. Bruckner Four Motets. Bruckner Te Deum. 23 May at 8pm call venue to book

Festivals

Digital Art and New Curatorship
25/5/99 HASTINGS MUSEUM AND ART GALLERY
25/5/99 Tel: 01424 781155
Simon Poulter will discuss the background to his work Microhenge. This will incorporate issues relating to site specific practice and new technology. He will also talk about devising digital work for gallery and non-gallery spaces and issues of curatorship which emerge from this. Time: 19.30. Cost: A£3.00 Concessions£2.00.

Museums

Garden Tour -Rhododendrons
25/5/99 SCOTNEY CASTLE GARDEN
25/5/99 Tel: 01892 891081
Led by the gardeners, and limited to 30 per walk, maximum. To see the gardens through the eyes of the people who know it best, book early. Time: 14.00. Cost: £6.00.

Gardens

Racing from Brighton
28/5/99 BRIGHTON RACECOURSE
28/5/99 Tel: 01273 603580
Racing from Brighton between 12.00 and18.00. Admission A£4.00-£12.00 C£Free

Racecourses

Inspirit
28/5/99 MAIDSTONE MUSEUM AND ART GALLERY
27/6/99 Tel: 01622 754497
A winning selection from an open submission of visual art currently being produced in Kent, Sussex and Surrey includes painting, photography, printmaking, sculpture and installation

Museums

Toy Collectors' fair
29/5/99 SANDOWN EXHIBITION CENTRE
29/5/99 Tel: 01372 467540
Opening Times 10.30-16.00, Prices A£3.50 C£1.00 OAPs£3.00

Exhibition Centres

Real Ale Festival
29/5/99 SOUTH OF ENGLAND RARE BREEDS CENTRE
29/5/99 Tel: 01233 861493
CAMRA fun this festival. Jazz band, magician and puppets, Morris dancing, barbecue, pub games, kiddies funfair. Transport from Ashford, Tenterden

Farm- Rare Breeds

Pavement Picasso
29/5/99 THE WHITE CLIFFS EXPERIENCE
29/5/99 Tel: 01304 214566/210101
A pavement chalking competition for the children. Free to enter. Prizes for all entries.

Interactive

Merrie England Weekend
29/5/99 HEVER CASTLE AND GARDENS
31/5/99 Tel: 01732 865224
A weekend of archery and foot combat demonstrations, medieval music and dance and medieval stalls. Event included in the Gardens only ticket

Castles

Gothic Tower Restoration

29/5/99 31/5/99	**PAINSHILL LANDSCAPE GARDEN** Tel: 01932 868113/864674 Find out how the gothic tower and other follies have been restored. Children will be captivated by storytelling in the tower *Gardens*

Craft Festival

29/5/99
31/5/99
PETWORTH HOUSE AND PARK
Tel: 01798 342207/343929
All things crafty with stalls and displays in the marquees in Petwork Park. A£3.50 C(0-5)£Free C(5-16)£2.00, (these are 98 prices and for guidance only) call for further details
Historic Houses & Gardens

K M Chatham Navy Days

29/5/99
31/5/99
THE HISTORIC DOCKYARD, CHATHAM
Tel: 01634 823800
Naval tradition and family fun combine when vessels from around the world are opened to the public along with air displays, bands and fun fairs
Museum- Maritime

Official Opening of Pet Centre

29/5/99
6/6/99
DRUSILLAS PARK
Tel: 01323 870234
A Celebrity will open the centre. Southern FM. Volunteers. Dog Obedience Display
Zoos

Flower Power

29/5/99
6/6/99
HAMPTON COURT PALACE AND GARDENS
Tel: 0181 781 9500
The significance of flowers at court in the 17th century; paper flower making workshops for children. Other events to be confirmed
Royal Palace

Teddy Bear Reunion

29/5/99
6/6/99
PARADISE FAMILY LEISURE PARK
Tel: 01273 616006
Hunt down the Bears! Help our little furry friends find each other and enjoy a beary reunion
Theme Parks

Echoes of an Era

29/5/99
6/6/99
THE WHITE CLIFFS EXPERIENCE
Tel: 01304 214566/210101
Historically based family quiz.
Interactive

Longbow Warfare

29/5/99
30/8/99
HEVER CASTLE AND GARDENS
Tel: 01732 865224
The Company of 1415 will demonstrate the use of the Longbow as a military weapon on 29-31 May, 25 July, 1, 8, 15, 22, 29 & 30 Aug. Event included in the

Gardens only ticket
Castles

Napoleonic Battle Spectacular

30/5/99
31/5/99
BATTLE ABBEY
Tel: 01424 773792
Hundreds of brightly uniformed infantry, cavalry and artillery of 1808 from all over Europe. A£6.00 C£3.00 Concessions£4.50
Battlefields

Awaiting the Armada

30/5/99
31/5/99
DEAL CASTLE
Tel: 01304 372762
Tudor re-enactment performed by Bills & Bows. A£4.00 C£2.00 Concessions£3.00
Castles

World War II Living History

30/5/99
31/5/99
DOVER CASTLE AND SECOND WORLD WAR TUNNELS
Tel: 01304 201628/202754
What was it like living in amidst World War II? The Garrison tell you. A£6.90 C£3.50 Concessions£5.20
Castles

Spring Garden Fair and Flower Festival

30/5/99
31/5/99
FINCHCOCKS
Tel: 01580 211702
Fair in the gardens, marquee, music in the House; special events planned all weekend long, call for further details
Museum- Music

Bank Holiday Family Fun

30/5/99
31/5/99
GROOMBRIDGE PLACE GARDENS
Tel: 01892 863999
Gardens

End of Empire

30/5/99
31/5/99
LULLINGSTONE ROMAN VILLA
Tel: 01732 778000
Performers: End of the Roman Age Society. A£3.00 C£1.50 Concessions£2.30
Archaelogical Sites

Family Fun Weekend

30/5/99
31/5/99
MUSEUM OF KENT LIFE
Tel: 01622 763936
Fun for all the family. Enjoy races for children, circus workshops, various displays and other participation events.
Museum- Local History

Piggy Picnics and Crafts Fair

30/5/99
31/5/99
SOUTH OF ENGLAND RARE BREEDS CENTRE
Tel: 01233 861493
Lots of porky fun! Pig obstacle course, Piggy bathtime, Piglet racing, Piggy poetry competition and a puppet show

Farm- Rare Breeds

Medieval Archery Competition
31/5/99 BODIAM CASTLE
31/5/99 Tel: 01580 830436
The annual longbow competition with archers in period costume. Free admission to the event field.

Historic Buildings

Eurocar Bank Holiday Spectacular
31/5/99 BRANDS HATCH
31/5/99 Tel: 0171 344 4444Ticketmaster
Eurocar V6 & V8 Championships, Pick-Ups, Legends, Kent Championship Formula Fords, Gilera Scooters. Indy Circuit, Grade-D. On the Gate: £10.00-£28.00. In Advance: Non £8.00-£25.00, Club £7.00-£22.00. Two Day Pass: Non £11.00-£30.00, Club £10.00-£27.00. Three Day Pass: Non £32.00, Club £29.00. Qualifying: £5.00-£14.00. C£Free. Programme £Free-£5.00. Seating (BH): £Free-£8.00. South Bank: £2.00-£5.00. Group Tickets: Non £90.00-£95.00, Club £80.00-£85.00. Season Ticket Inc. of Club Membership: £200.00. You can buy your tickets for any of the 1999 events in advance any time up to 4 days before an event and make a saving, Tel: 0870 60 60 611

Motor Racing Circuit

Bank Holiday Steeplechase Meeting
31/5/99 FONTWELL PARK RACECOURSE
31/5/99 Tel: 01243 543335
Bank Holiday entertainment for all the family with face painting and bouncy castle for children. Daily Member £13.00 Tattersalls £9.00 Silver Ring £5.00 OAPs£2.50 C(0-16)£Free. Advance group rates available

Racecourses

Tripleprint Temple Stakes and Bonusprint Henry II Stakes
31/5/99 SANDOWN PARK RACECOURSE
31/5/99 Tel: 01372 463072
Bank Holiday racing. For further details including race times and ticket prices please contact venue direct

Racecourses

Family Maze and Garden Week
31/5/99 LEEDS CASTLE
6/6/99 Tel: 01622 765400
Come along and soak up the atmosphere of Leeds Castle

Castles

Brigadier Gerard Stakes and National Stakes

1/6/99 SANDOWN PARK RACECOURSE
1/6/99 Tel: 01372 463072
For further details including race times and ticket prices please contact venue direct

Racecourses

Loseley Park Farms Children's' Holiday Activity Days
1/6/99 LOSELEY PARK
4/6/99 Tel: 01483 304440
Fun filled days on the farm. Commences 09.30-16.00. Call 01483 304440 for booking details

Historic Houses & Gardens

Music Festival
1/6/99 HAMPTON COURT PALACE AND GARDENS
30/6/99 Tel: 0181 781 9500
Dates for 1999 to be confirmed. Since its inception in 1993, the Hampton Court Palace Festival has played host to some of the world's greatest performers, including José Carreras, Vanessa Mae, Montserrat Caballé, Yehudi Menuhin and Kiri Te Kanawa. The Festival combines world class performers with the beauty of one of Europe's greatest palaces. For further information contact Jamie Jeeves on 0181 747 9977

Royal Palace

Corpus Christi Carpet of Flowers and Floral Festival 1999
2/6/99 CORPUS CHRISTI CARPET OF FLOWERS AND FLORAL FESTIVAL 1999
3/6/99 Tel: 01903 882297
The Carpet of Flowers, the only one of its kind in the British Isles, was instigated by His Grace Henry, 15th Duke of Norfolk shortly after the Cathedral was built. The Carpet is now 93 feet long and is totally made up of fresh flowers and greenery. Each year sees a newly designed carpet and every year the ladies of the parish excel themselves in their creative artistry. The Feast Day Mass will be celebrated at 17.30 in the Cathedral by The Right Reverend Cormac Murphy-O'Connor, Bishop of Arundel and Brighton. This will be followed at 18.30 by a Procession of the Blessed Sacrament, down the Carpet of Flowers, to the quadrangle of Arundel Castle where Benediction will be given by the Bishop. Times: Wed 09.30-21.00, Thur 10.30-17.30

Festivals

Leeds Castle Flower Festival

3/6/99	**LEEDS CASTLE**
6/6/99	Tel: 01622 765400
	Simply wonderful blooms, aromas and colours

Castles

Racing from Epsom

4/6/99	**EPSOM RACECOURSE**
4/6/99	Tel: 01372 726311
	Vodafone Oaks, Vodafone coronation Cup, Vodafone Derby. For further details including race times and ticket prices please contact venue direct

Racecourses

Live Crafts

4/6/99	**LOSELEY PARK**
6/6/99	Tel: 01483 304440
	Stalls selling and demonstrating Arts and Crafts

Historic Houses & Gardens

Flowers of the Fin de Siecle

4/6/99	**PALLANT HOUSE GALLERY**
5/9/99	Tel: 01243 774557
	Major exhibition of fine and applied art from Northern Europe, illustrating the symbolic use of flower imagery at the turn of the century

Art Galleries

Visit to Pevensey and Westham

5/6/99	**HASTINGS MUSEUM AND ART GALLERY**
5/6/99	Tel: 01424 781155
	A walk around these two villages. View the Castle and the Norman Church, and visit The Mint House and The Court Hall. Guide: Brian Purdey. Details from Museum Office.

Museums

Biggin Hill International Air Fair 1999

5/6/99	**BIGGIN HILL INTERNATIONAL AIR FAIR 1999**
6/6/99	Tel: 01959 540959
	World famous 7 hour international flying display with top teams and pilots. Unique mixture of modern, military, vintage and civilian aircraft. Very popular with families as well as enthusiasts. Disabled facilities and privileged viewing area. Gates open 08.00, flying commences 11.00-18.00 each day. PRICES TBC: Advance tickets: A£10.00 C(5-15)£4.00 Family Ticket (Car+5 people)£20.00. Car Park £Free. Gate Prices: A£12.50 C(5-15)£4.50 Family Ticket (Car+5 people)£25.00. Car Park £Free

Airports

Faversham Secret Gardens

5/6/99	**FLEUR DE LYS HERITAGE CENTRE**
6/6/99	Tel: 01795 534542
	15 Private gardens open to public. Admission to all by programme, with detailed notes. £3.50

Heritage Centres

SEMSEC F/Ford and Saloons

5/6/99	**LYDDEN INTERNATIONAL MOTOR RACING CIRCUIT**
6/6/99	Tel: 01304 830557
	For further details including times and ticket prices please contact venue direct

Motor Racing Circuit

Jazz & Hot Air Balloon Festival

5/6/99	**THE HOP FARM COUNTRY PARK**
6/6/99	Tel: 01622 871577
	Two of the most pleasurable sights, hot air balloons taking gracefully to the sky to the lively strains of JAZZ! Both days 10.00-18.00

Museum- Agricultural

Fairy Tales

5/6/99	**WALMER CASTLE**
6/6/99	Tel: 01304 364288
	Fairy tales from the Enchanted Garden with Crew of Patches. A£4.50 C£2.30 Concessions£3.40

Castles

Tunbridge Wells & Environs

5/6/99	**TUNBRIDGE WELLS MUSEUM AND ART GALLERY**
19/6/99	Tel: 01892 526121/554171
	Captured in oil, pastel, and water-colour by John Leech

Museums

Historic Raceday (HSCC)

6/6/99	**BRANDS HATCH**
6/6/99	Tel: 0171 344 4444Ticketmaster
	Racing for all clases of Historic and Classic cars. Indy Circuit, Grade-D. On the Gate: £10.00-£28.00. In Advance: Non £8.00-£25.00, Club £7.00-£22.00. Two Day Pass: Non £11.00-£30.00, Club £10.00-£27.00. Three Day Pass: Non £32.00, Club £29.00. Qualifying: £5.00-£14.00. C£Free. Programme £Free-£5.00. Seating (BH): £Free-£8.00. South Bank: £2.00-£5.00. Group Tickets: Non £90.00-£95.00, Club £80.00-£85.00. Season Ticket Inc. of Club Membership: £200.00. You can buy your tickets for any of the 1999 events in advance any time up to 4 days before an event and make a saving, Tel: 0870 60 60 611

Motor Racing Circuit

London to Brighton Classic Car Run

6/6/99 6/6/99	**GROOMBRIDGE PLACE GARDENS** Tel: 01892 863999

Gardens

Heavy Horse Day
6/6/99 **HEAVY HORSE DAY 1999**
6/6/99 Tel: 01227 742690
See the Gentle Giants parade in Memorial Park and along the sea front. Other rural attractions on site! Admission Free. 10.00-15.00

Festivals

Walk at Wisley
6/6/99 **RHS GARDEN WISLEY**
6/6/99 Tel: 01483 224234
Come and have a summer stroll in the garden with your Guide Colin Crosbie at 10.30. This walk will also take place on: Wed 9th at 10.30. Cost: Members £5.00, non-members £10.00. To book tickets send a cheque made payable to RHS, enclosing a SAE and including your membership number (if applicable) and day time telephone number to the Administration Department at RHS Garden, Wisley, Woking GU23 6QB. We are sorry but we cannot accept telephone bookings. Please note that all events may be subject to cancellation due to insufficient ticket sales

Gardens

Car Boot Sale
6/6/99 **RURAL LIFE CENTRE**
6/6/99 Tel: 01252 792300/795571
09.00-13.00, £5.00 per car to sell. Buyers admitted to sale free

Museums

Hampton Court Flower Festival
6/6/99 **HAMPTON COURT PALACE AND GARDENS**
11/6/99 Tel: 0181 781 9500
The annual show returns to Hampton Court Palace

Royal Palace

British Sportscar Day
7/6/99 **BROOKLANDS MUSEUM**
6/6/99 Tel: 01932 857381
A special tribute to the post-war launch of such great sports cars as the XK120

Museum- Motor

Growing Vegetables Tickets
9/6/99 **RHS GARDEN WISLEY**
9/6/99 Tel: 01483 224234
Jim England, Superintendent of the Trials Department is responsible for the superb selection of quality vegetables grown at Wisley. During this Specialist Day he shares with participants the

secrets of his success. Time: 10.00-16.00. Cost: members £40.00, non-members £45.00

Gardens

Demonstration: Summer Treatment of Grapes: indoors and out
9/6/99 **RHS GARDEN WISLEY**
9/6/99 Tel: 01483 224234
Come and watch Ron Gilkerson and Jim Arbury's deomonstration at 10.30. The winter treatment of grapes demonstration will take place on: Wed 24th Nov at 10.30. Cost: Members £5.00, non-members £10.00. To book tickets send a cheque made payable to RHS, enclosing a SAE and including your membership number (if applicable) and day time telephone number to the Administration Department at RHS Garden, Wisley, Woking GU23 6QB. We are sorry but we cannot accept telephone bookings. Please note that all events may be subject to cancellation due to insufficient ticket sales

Gardens

Garden Tour - Flora and Fauna
10/6/99 **IGHTHAM MOTE**
10/6/99 Tel: 01732 811145
18.30. A guided walk with the warden, of the woodland and farmland surrounding Ightham Mote. Allow 2 hours. Tickets £6.00. 30 persons per walk, best to pre-book on 01892 891001 or write to The Box Office, The National Trust, Scotney Castle, Lamberhurst, Kent TN3 8JN

Historic Houses

SBJ Group Day
11/6/99 **SANDOWN PARK RACECOURSE**
12/6/99 Tel: 01372 463072
Friday is SBJ Group Day and Saturday is Johnstone Douglas Stakes. For further details including race times and ticket prices please contact venue direct

Racecourses

Battle Festival 1999
11/6/99 **BATTLE FESTIVAL 1999**
27/6/99 Tel: 01424 844641
Battle Festival, now in its 39th year, is a well established annual event with a long tradition of high quality artistic productions. Features of the 1999 Festival include a wide range of programme appealing to all tastes and interests, with Arts and Crafts, Dance Jamboree, Street Theatre, Town Walks, Horticultural and Parent and Toddler events. A Shakespeare production amongst the

Abbey ruins, Recitals, Sussex Concert Orchestra and a talk by Robert Hardy reflecting the Festival theme 'War and Roses.' For a full Brochure of events and booking facilities contact the Battle TIC on 01424 773721 from 15th March 99 onwards.

Festivals

Painshill Promenade
12/6/99 PAINSHILL LANDSCAPE GARDEN
12/6/99 Tel: 01932 868113/864674
TBC

Gardens

Saturday Night Jazz
12/6/99 POLESDEN LACEY
12/6/99 Tel: 01372 458203/452048
Welcoming back the Mardi Gras Joymakers, the Alan Gretsy/Brian White Ragtime Band, the legendary Temperance Seven and Johnny Maes and his Blues Band, complete with fireworks finale. Time: 20.00. Cost: £14.00, £28.00 Premium Tickets.

Historic Houses & Gardens

Clubmans Bikes (BMCRC)
12/6/99 BRANDS HATCH
13/6/99 Tel: 0171 344 4444Ticketmaster
Champion of Brands Hatch, all classes of solo motorcycles and sidecars, on the fulll Grand Prix Circuit. Grade-D. On the Gate: £10.00-£28.00. In Advance: Non £8.00-£25.00. Club £7.00-£22.00. Two Day Pass: Non £11.00-£30.00, Club £10.00-£27.00. Three Day Pass: Non £32.00, Club £29.00. Qualifying: £5.00-£14.00. C£Free. Programme £Free-£5.00. Seating (BH): £Free-£8.00. South Bank: £2.00-£5.00. Group Tickets: Non £90.00-£95.00, Club £80.00-£85.00. Season Ticket Inc. of Club Membership: £200.00. You can buy your tickets for any of the 1999 events in advance any time up to 4 days before an event and make a saving, Tel: 0870 60 60 611

Motor Racing Circuit

Soldiers of George III
12/6/99 DOVER CASTLE AND SECOND WORLD WAR TUNNELS
13/6/99 Tel: 01304 201628/202754
Re-enactment of 18th-century by the Association of Crown Forces. A£6.90 C£3.50 Concessions£5.20

Castles

18th Century Wedding & History Fair
12/6/99 GROOMBRIDGE PLACE GARDENS
13/6/99 Tel: 01892 863999

Gardens

Track Day and Eurocars
12/6/99 LYDDEN INTERNATIONAL MOTOR RACING CIRCUIT
13/6/99 Tel: 01304 830557
Apex Track Day on Saturday, BRSCC Eurocars on Sunday. For further details including times and ticket prices please contact venue direct

Motor Racing Circuit

Model Railway Exhibition
12/6/99 THE HISTORIC DOCKYARD, CHATHAM
13/6/99 Tel: 01634 823800
A great favourite with families as well as enthusiasts. A world in miniature with over two dozen superb layouts and exhibits from all over England. Also specialist traders and demonstrations.

Museum- Maritime

Direct Line Insurance International Ladies Tennis Championships
12/6/99 DIRECT LINE INSURANCE INTERNATIONAL LADIES TENNIS CHAMPIONSHIPS
19/6/99 Tel: 01323 736373
Tennis has been played here for over 100 years and is the setting for this traditional pre-Wimbledon Ladies Championships and features many of the world's top women players.

Festivals

East Preston Festival Week 1999
12/6/99 EAST PRESTON FESTIVAL WEEK 1999
20/6/99 Tel: 01903 771161
A village festival from Sat 12 June to Sun 20 June. Over 65 events to suit all ages including: sporting events, model railways, Grand Festival Fete, Festival Queen Contest, Carnival Procession, Art and Flowers Exhibition, Antiques and Collectors Market, Open Gardens Day, Quizzes and much more.

Festivals

London Mozart Players with Julian Lloyd Webber
13/6/99 POLESDEN LACEY
13/6/99 Tel: 01372 458203/452048
The world-renowned London Mozart Players make their first appearance at Polesden Lacey. A programme crammed with popular orchestral classics, culminating in Handel's Fireworks Music. Time: 20.00

Historic Houses & Gardens

Sunday Morning Family Concert
13/6/99 POLESDEN LACEY
13/6/99 Tel: 01372 458203/452048
Musical Director Jonathan Butcher

brings the lawns of Polesden Lacey an energy guaranteed to make the Surrey Hills alive with the sound of music! This year's highlight will be 'The Young Person's Guide to the Orchestra' narrated by Ian Lavender - famous for his role in Dad's Army. Gates open 09.30 for 11.00 start. Cost: A£8.00 C£5.00

Historic Houses & Gardens

Rainbow Ride

13/6/99 SOUTH OF ENGLAND RARE BREEDS CENTRE
13/6/99 Tel: 01233 861493
Sponsored cycle ride around Romney Marsh, raising funds for learning disabled adults

Farm- Rare Breeds

Afternoon Racing

14/6/99 BRIGHTON RACECOURSE
14/6/99 Tel: 01273 603580
Racing from Brighton between 12.00 and18.00. Admission A£4.00-£12.00 C£Free

Racecourses

Landscape as Art Tours

15/6/99 PAINSHILL LANDSCAPE GARDEN
20/6/99 Tel: 01932 868113/864674
A look at Italian influences and the garden as a work of art, embracing poetry, painting and gardening

Gardens

Garden Tour - Judas Tree & Roses

16/6/99 ALFRISTON CLERGY HOUSE
16/6/99 Tel: 01323 870001
Led by the gardeners, and limited to 30 per walk, maximum. To see the gardens through the eyes of the people who know it best, book early. Time: 18.30. Cost: £5.00.

Historic Houses

As You Like It

16/6/99 POLESDEN LACEY
19/6/99 Tel: 01372 458203/452048
Polesden Lacey is the perfect backdrop for this delightful comedy of romance, humour, disguise, jealously, music and magic. Time: 20.00. Sat matinee 14.30. Prices: Wed eve & Sat mat: £10.00, grass £8.00; Thur & Fri: £12.00, grass £8.00; Sat eve: £15.00, grass £12.00.

Historic Houses & Gardens

Outdoor Shakespeare

16/6/99 MOUNT EPHRAIM GARDENS
26/6/99 Tel: 01227 751496
Outdoor production of Two Gentlemen of Verona. Picnic in garden before performance

Gardens- Botanical

Medieval Minstrels on the Road to Santiago de Compostela

17/6/99 QUEBEC HOUSE
17/6/99 Tel: 01892 890651
Dr Mary Remnant brings to life the pilgrimage route from Paris to Spain with medieval instruments on colour slides. 15.00 - £10.00, 19.30 - £12.00, must be pre-booked on 01892 891001 or write to The Box Office, The National Trust, Scotney Castle, Lamberhurst, Kent TN3 8JN

Historic Houses

Environmental Education Fair

17/6/99 SOUTH OF ENGLAND RARE BREEDS CENTRE
17/6/99 Tel: 01233 861493
A day of fun and learning with plenty of hands-on activities for Primary School children. Over 1,000 children visited in 1998 - don't choose today for a quiet day out!

Farm- Rare Breeds

Botanical Art Weekend

17/6/99 RHS GARDEN WISLEY
20/6/99 Tel: 01483 224234
(Advanced Course). Pauline Dean is a practising botanical artist working in a freelance capacity for horticultural publications. Pauline began her painting career in 1984 and has won five RHS Gold Medals. She has designed three Winter Flower RHS collectors' plates and the 1996 Chelsea Flower Show Plate. Pauline has tutored the Wisley botanical art courses for eight years. Times: Thur 17th (18.00-21.00), Fri 18 & Sat 19 (09.00-18.00), Sun 20 (09.00-16.30). Cost: £185.00

Gardens

A Mid Summer Night's Dream

18/6/99 BORDE HILL GARDEN
20/6/99 Tel: 01444 450326
Set in Borde Hill's Parkland, Shakespeare comes alive with this production by Robert Williamson and his professional touring company. Call for further details

Gardens

Arab Horse Racing Society Meeting

19/6/99 BRIGHTON RACECOURSE
19/6/99 Tel: 01273 603580
Evening racing from Brighton

Racecourses

Music, Memories and Moonlight with the Herb Miller Orchestra

19/6/99 19/6/99	**CHARTWELL** Tel: 01732 866368 infoline Dress up and get 'in the mood' and dance the night away, or just enjoy the wonderful music of the 1940s Big Band sound. Bring picnics and seating. Commences 19.30. Tickets £17.50, must be pre-booked on 01892 891001 or write to The Box Office, The National Trust, Scotney Castle, Lamberhurst, Kent TN3 8JN

Historic Houses

Wildflower Walk

19/6/99 19/6/99	**WALMER CASTLE** Tel: 01304 364288 Take a walk in a Kentish Wildflower meadow with your guide, Richard Squires. A£4.50 C£2.30 Concessions£3.40

Castles

Rose Weekend

19/6/99 20/6/99	**BORDE HILL GARDEN** Tel: 01444 450326 In celebration of the 4th anniversary of the Rose Garden designed by Robin Williams. Lectures on roses, advice stand on the care of roses, floral displays, tours, plants sales, craft and gift stands. Call for further details

Gardens

Midsummer GT Weekend (BRDC/BRSCC)

19/6/99 20/6/99	**BRANDS HATCH** Tel: 0171 344 4444Ticketmaster British GT Championship, British Formula 3, Formula Palmer Audi, Caterham Road Sport, Caterham Superlight, MGF Cup, Marcos Mantis, Formula Ford 1600, National Saloon Car Championship, Super Sport 200. Grand Prix Circuit, Grade-B. On the Gate: £10.00-£28.00. In Advance: Non £8.00-£25.00, Club £7.00-£22.00. Two Day Pass: Non £11.00-£30.00, Club £10.00-£27.00. Three Day Pass: Non £32.00, Club £29.00. Qualifying: £5.00-£14.00. C£Free. Programme £Free-£5.00. Seating (BH): £Free-£8.00. South Bank: £2.00-£5.00. Group Tickets: Non £90.00-£95.00, Club £80.00-£85.00. Season Ticket Inc. of Club Membership: £200.00. You can buy your tickets for any of the 1999 events in advance any time up to 4 days before an event and make a saving, Tel: 0870 60 60 611

Motor Racing Circuit

Twelfth Night

19/6/99 20/6/99	**IGHTHAM MOTE** Tel: 01732 811145 19 June: 18.30 for 19.30, 20 June 18.00-19.00. Presented by Illyria, a sparkling comedy laced with a soupcon of romance, a touch of poetry, and huge great dollops of seething lust! Tickets £9.00, must be pre-booked on 01892 891001 or write to The Box Office, The National Trust, Scotney Castle, Lamberhurst, Kent TN3 8JN

Historic Houses

Children's Entertainment

19/6/99 20/6/99	**LULLINGSTONE ROMAN VILLA** Tel: 01732 778000 Roman Siege tactics for children. Entertainers: Crew Of Patches. A£2.50 C£2.00 Concessions£1.90

Archaeological Sites

Victorian Redcoats

19/6/99 20/6/99	**PEVENSEY CASTLE** Tel: 01323 762604 Victorian re-enactment by The Diehard Company. A£3.50 C£1.80 Concessions£2.60

Castles

Broadstairs Dickens Festival 1999

19/6/99 26/6/99	**BROADSTAIRS DICKENS FESTIVAL 1999** Tel: 01843 601364 Over 70 events, both Free and Ticketed, during the 8 Day Festival, including: Opening Parade followed by; Opening Ceremony with Entertainment, Victorian Cricket Match, Duels, Melodramas, Festival Play, (Dickens' Oliver Twist), Victorian Bazaar, A Childrens' Day with local schools participating. Victorian Music Hall. Local Male Voice Choir, Victorian Garden Party, Victorian Sea Bathing, Talks, Street Entertainment, Victorian Collectors' Fair, Victorian Songs of Praise, Morning Coffee with the Dickensians present, Musical Entertainments.

Festivals

Midsummer Hot-Air Balloon Classic

20/6/99 20/6/99	**GROOMBRIDGE PLACE GARDENS** Tel: 01892 863999

Gardens

National Gardens Scheme

20/6/99 20/6/99	**LULLINGSTONE CASTLE** Tel: 01322 862114 Locally grown flowers and plants for sale. Proceeds donated to National Gardens Scheme Trust.

Castles

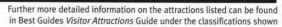

Further more detailed information on the attractions listed can be found in Best Guides *Visitor Attractions* Guide under the classifications shown

BARC F/Ford and Saloons

20/6/99
20/6/99

LYDDEN INTERNATIONAL MOTOR RACING CIRCUIT

Tel: 01304 830557

For further details including times and ticket prices please contact venue direct

Motor Racing Circuit

Think Wood

20/6/99
20/6/99

RURAL LIFE CENTRE

Tel: 01252 792300/795571

Discover the importance of timber; woodland crafts, tree walk talks in the arboretum, bug hunts with the rangers and "Toys for Free". Train rides and Miller's Ark Animals. Time: 11.00-18.00. Cost: A£3.00 C£1.50 OAPs£2.50 Groups 30+ 10% discount

Museums

The Garden of England Motorcycle Show

20/6/99
20/6/99

THE HOP FARM COUNTRY PARK

Tel: 01622 871577

In partnership with the British Motorcyclist Federations 130,000 members. Prices on application.

Museum- Agricultural

Jazz & Strawberries

20/6/99
20/6/99

WALMER CASTLE

Tel: 01304 364288

What could be nicer? A lazy June afternoon listening to Jazz and munching on strawberries, ahhh! A£5.50 C£3.30 Concessions£4.40

Castles

Summer Festival '99

20/6/99
29/8/99

HEVER CASTLE AND GARDENS

Tel: 01732 865224

To be held at The Hever Lakeside Theatre. Since it started in the early eighties, the Lakeside Theatre has become one of the most popular outdoor venues in the south east, attracting many thousands every summer, many of whom return year after year. Situated in the magnificent Italian Garden of Hever Castle overlooking the lake, it offers an ideal setting for a pre-show picnic with family and friends. The tiered and covered seating makes for an unusually intimate auditorium to enjoy the superb programme of music, opera and drama which comprises the Summer Festival: as well as a high degree of protection against inclement weather, which has only twice interrupted proceedings since the festival began. Picnics from 18.30. Prices: A£10.50-£15.50. Groups rates

10+ 10% discount

Castles

History of Buchanan Hospital

21/6/99
21/6/99

HASTINGS MUSEUM AND ART GALLERY

Tel: 01424 781155

An illustrated talk tracing the history of the Buchanan from Cottage Hospital to Maternity Hospital. Speaker: Carol Stace, Midwifery Manager, Conquest Hospital. Time: 19.30.

Museums

Antiques Fair

22/6/99
22/6/99

SANDOWN EXHIBITION CENTRE

Tel: 01372 467540

Opening times 14.00. A£3.00. Please contact 0171 249 4050 for further information

Exhibition Centres

Demonstration: Pruning of Shrubs

23/6/99
23/6/99

RHS GARDEN WISLEY

Tel: 01483 224234

Come and watch Bernard Boardman prune his shrubs at 14.00. This demonstration will also take place on: Sun 27th at 10.30. Cost: Members £5.00, nonmembers £10.00. To book tickets send a cheque made payable to RHS, enclosing a SAE and including your membership number (if applicable) and day time telephone number to the Administration Department at RHS Garden, Wisley, Woking GU23 6QB. We are sorry but we cannot accept telephone bookings. Please note that all events may be subject to cancellation due to insufficient ticket sales

Gardens

The Importance of Being Earnest

23/6/99
26/6/99

POLESDEN LACEY

Tel: 01372 458203/452048

Oscar Wilde said of his play thus: "The first act is ingenuous, the second is beautiful and the third astonishingly clever. Exquisitely trivial, a delicate bubble of fancy." Time: 20.00. Sat matinee 14.30. Prices: Wed eve & Sat mat: £10.00, grass £8.00; Thur & Fri: £12.00, grass £8.00; Sat eve: £15.00, grass £12.00.

Historic Houses & Gardens

Microhenge and Intervention

24/6/99
24/6/99

HASTINGS MUSEUM AND ART GALLERY

Tel: 01424 781155

Simon Poulter will talk about the conceptual basis and underlying themes of Microhenge. This will include an appraisal of interventionist work produced since 1995. He will also discuss interdisciplinary and cross-media approaches to experimental art arising out of new technological practice. The talk will be provocative and wide-ranging, opening up a discussion around media ownership. Time: 19.30. Cost: A£3.00 Concessions£2.00.

Museums

Gardening for Wheelchair Users Tickets

24/6/99 RHS GARDEN WISLEY
24/6/99 Tel: 01483 224234
Find out more about garden design and special tools and equipment to help wheelchair-using gardeners. Time: 10.00-16.30. Cost: members £30.00, non-members £35.00

Gardens

The Dodd Family of Tunbridge Wells Artists

24/6/99 TUNBRIDGE WELLS MUSEUM AND ART
19/7/99 GALLERY
Tel: 01892 526121/554171
Works by Charles Tattershall Dodd Snr., Jnr., and Joseph Josiah Dodd from the Museum's reserve collections

Museums

Midsummer Event

25/6/99 HASTINGS MUSEUM AND ART GALLERY
25/6/99 Tel: 01424 781155
A musical evening on the theme of the sea. Bring a picnic and enjoy a balmy summer evening in the Museum grounds. Further details available later.

Museums

Open Air Concert

25/6/99 PETWORTH HOUSE AND PARK
27/6/99 Tel: 01798 342207/343929
Friday: Friday Night Fever; Saturday: Petworth Proms; Sunday: Swing in the Park. Gates open from 18.30 for picnics show commences 20.00. Bookings before end of April 1999: A£10.00 C£5.00. 1 May-25 June: A£11.00 C£6.00. On the night: A£12.00 C£7.00. Groups: 10+ 10% discount, Coach bookings: 30+ 12% discount. Credit Card booking from 2 March 99: 01372 451596/457223. NB: Prices are from 98 for guidance only call for 99 prices

Historic Houses & Gardens

Midsummers Evening Walk

26/6/99 EMMETTS GARDEN
26/6/99 Tel: 01732 868381/750367
A guided tour of the estate surrounding Scotney Castle Garden looking at

aspects of the working history of the estate. Time: 17.00. Cost: £10.00. This tour does not include the garden, must be pre-booked on 01892 891001 or write to The Box Office, The National Trust, Scotney Castle, Lamberhurst, Kent TN3 8JN

Gardens

The 21st Anniversary Leeds Castle Open Air Concert

26/6/99 LEEDS CASTLE
26/6/99 Tel: 01622 765400
The first of two celebratory open air summer night classical music concerts, with the 1812, cannons and fireworks, as the triumphant finale. Gates open at 16.00. Entertainment from 17.30. Concert begins at 20.00. Advance ticket sales only from Box Office. Group rates available

Castles

The Petworth Proms

26/6/99 PETWORTH HOUSE AND PARK
26/6/99 Tel: 01798 342207/343929
Presenting a choral extravaganza with all your favourites - from the Hallelujah Chorus and Zadock the Priest to the Grand March from Aida and the Chorus of the Hewbrew Slaves... The Royal Philharmonic Orchestra together with the London Philharmonic Choir and brought into line by Neville Creed, bring you another Night at the Proms, in the delightful surroundings of this landscaped park with floodlit house. Gates open from 18.30 for picnics show commences 20.00. Bookings before end of April 1999: A£18.00 C£10.00. 1 May-26 June: A£16.00 C£6.00. On the night: A£17.00 C£7.00. Groups: 10+ 10% discount, Coach bookings: 30+ 12% discount. Credit Card booking from 2 March 98: 01372 451596/457223

Historic Houses & Gardens

Crawley Folk Festival 1999

26/6/99 CRAWLEY FOLK FESTIVAL 1999
27/6/99 Tel: 01293 553636 Box Office
A two-day spectacular featuring performances from top British and Irsh bands and American music, plus dance groups, stalls, workshops, food, bars, camping facilities and free parking. Plus concerts Friday and Saturday featuring top named bands. Full programme available from the end of May 1999.

Festivals

Civil War Garrison

26/6/99 27/6/99	**DEAL CASTLE** Tel: 01304 372762 The life and times during the Civil War - the castle occupiers fear attack. The English Civil War Society. A£3.50 C£1.80 Concessions£2.60

Castles

Groombridge Place Gardens First Annual Gardening Show

26/6/99 27/6/99	GROOMBRIDGE PLACE GARDENS Tel: 01892 863999

Gardens

Gardeners' Weekend

26/6/99 27/6/99	HEVER CASTLE AND GARDENS Tel: 01732 865224 Highlights include a Gardeners' Question Time with BBC Radio Kent and seminars for amateur gardeners. Event included in the Gardens only ticket

Castles

West Sussex Country Craft Fair

26/6/99 27/6/99	LEONARDSLEE GARDENS Tel: 01403 891212 10th year of this Craft Fair with stalls and demonstrations. Please call for further information.

Gardens

Roman Soldiers

26/6/99 27/6/99	LULLINGSTONE ROMAN VILLA Tel: 01732 778000 Milites Litores Saxonici. A£3.00 C£1.50 Concessions£2.30

Archaelogical Sites

BMCRC Motorcycles and Sidecars

26/6/99 27/6/99	LYDDEN INTERNATIONAL MOTOR RACING CIRCUIT Tel: 01304 830557 For further details including times and ticket prices please contact venue direct

Motor Racing Circuit

Wellington

26/6/99 27/6/99	WALMER CASTLE Tel: 01304 364288 18-century entertainment performed by Past Pleasures. A£4.50 C£2.30 Concesssions£3.40

Castles

Swing in the Park

27/6/99 27/6/99	PETWORTH HOUSE AND PARK Tel: 01798 342207/343929 For all you jivin', jazzin' swingers out there... a top bill awaits you! Including Swing is Here, Again, Plus The Jiving Lindy Hoppers. Fireworks Finale. Gates open at 18.30 for picnics. Performance starts at 20.00.

Historic Houses & Gardens

Victorian Fair

27/6/99 27/6/99	SHEFFIELD PARK GARDEN Tel: 01825 790231 Demonstrations of traditional skills, family entertainment - a great day out for the family in the setting of a wonderful landscaped agarden. Normal admission applies.

Gardens

Classic Car Rally and Autojumble

27/6/99 27/6/99	SOUTH OF ENGLAND RARE BREEDS CENTRE Tel: 01233 861493 Lots of cars with character, plus stalls selling automobilia, books and 'bits'

Farm- Rare Breeds

Garden Tour

27/6/99 27/6/99	WALMER CASTLE Tel: 01304 364288 Past, Present and Future with Richard Squires, your guide. A£4.50 C£2.30 Concessions£3.40

Castles

Herb Days Tickets

28/6/99 28/6/99	RHS GARDEN WISLEY Tel: 01483 224234 Cultivating Herbs. This day looks at growing herbs and includes a guided tour of Wisley's herb garden. Time: 10.30-16.30. Cost: members £40.00, non-members £45.00

Gardens

Herb Days Tickets

28/6/99 28/6/99	RHS GARDEN WISLEY Tel: 01483 224234 Culinary herbs. Spend the day learning about cultivating herbs and their many culinary uses. Time: 10.30-16.30. Cost: members £15.00, non-members £20.00

Gardens

Classic Car Fair

29/6/99 29/6/99	SANDOWN EXHIBITION CENTRE Tel: 01372 467540 Please call 01943 232332 for further information

Exhibition Centres

Afternoon Racing

30/6/99 30/6/99	BRIGHTON RACECOURSE Tel: 01273 603580 Racing from Brighton between 12.00 and18.00. Admission A£4.00-£12.00 C£Free

Racecourses

Evening Racing

30/6/99 30/6/99	EPSOM RACECOURSE Tel: 01372 726311 For further details including race times and ticket prices please contact venue direct *Racecourses*

Flower Arranging Demonstration

30/6/99 30/6/99	RHS GARDEN WISLEY Tel: 01483 224234 'Summer splendour' with Fred Wilkinson. Time: 10.00-12.30. Cost: members £18.00, non-members £23.00 *Gardens*

Fiddler on the Roof

30/6/99 3/7/99	POLESDEN LACEY Tel: 01372 458203/452048 The classic musical telling the story of a Russian/Jewish family trapped in the throes of political and military unrest. Time: 20.00, Sat matinee 14.30. Prices: Wed eve & Sat mat: £11.00, grass £9.00; Thur & Fri: £13.00/£11.00, grass £9.00; Sat eve: £16.00/£13.00, grass £11.00. *Historic Houses & Gardens*

Streets of the North 1999

1/7/99 31/8/99	NATIONAL STREET ARTS FESTIVALS FOR 1999 Tel: 01273 821588 Coming to streets of Chester-le-Street, Barrow-in-Furness, Darlington, Leeds, Sheffield and Stockton (venues and dates still to be confirmed). The second year of Streets of the North promises visitors the very best in street art. It's the artform of the 21st century and it's all FREE. Full details and brochure will be available from beginning of June 1999 by calling 01273 821588 *Festivals*

Streets of the South 1999

1/7/99 30/9/99	NATIONAL STREET ARTS FESTIVALS FOR 1999 Tel: 01273 821588 Coming to streets of Canterbury, Gillingham, King's Hill, Slough, Eastbourne, Crowborough, Heathfield, Hailsham and Uckfield (venues and dates still to be confirmed). Streets of the South is now in its 4th year. Alongside the events runs and education programme, with pubic workshops and community performances. Street Art is accessible to all and it's all FREE. Full details and brochure will be available from beginning of June 1999 by calling 01273 821588 *Festivals*

The Walter Trout Blues Band & Hank Wangford and The Lost Cowboys

2/7/99 2/7/99	HATCHLANDS PARK Tel: 01483 222482 One of the open air concerts in the Hatchlands Hat Trick. Doors open 18.30 for 19.00 performance. Walter Trout (ex John Mayall's Bluesbreakers) regarded by many as one of the greatest guitarists in the world shows off his distinct inventive style. Support band Hank Wangford and The Lost Cowboys epitomise the "cool" side of country music. Ticket Prices: £12.50, Two nights £22.50, Three nights £34.00 *Historic Houses*

Racing from Sandown Park

2/7/99 3/7/99	SANDOWN PARK RACECOURSE Tel: 01372 463072 Friday is Hong Kong Day and Saturday is Coral-Eclipse Stakes. For further details including race times and ticket prices please contact venue direct *Racecourses*

Special Events Day

3/7/99 3/7/99	GUILDFORD MUSEUM Tel: 01483 444750 The Museum will celebrate the 'First Millennium' this year for their special events day. *Museum- Local History*

Humphrey Lyttleton & Helen Shapiro with the Humprey Lyttleton Band

3/7/99 3/7/99	HATCHLANDS PARK Tel: 01483 222482 One of the open air concerts in the Hatchlands Hat Trick. Doors open 18.30 for 19.30 performance. What a combination! They bring you the latest version of their hit show which includes numbers like: 'Someone to watch over me,' 'Bad Penny Blues,' 'Walking Back to Happiness,' 'Caravan,' 'Java Jive' and many more. Book early for this musical treat from two legendary figures. Ticket Prices: £12.50, Two nights £22.50, Three nights £34.00 *Historic Houses*

Music at the Mote - Music of the Night

3/7/99 3/7/99	IGHTHAM MOTE Tel: 01732 811145 18.00 for 19.30. Four lead singers from the West End bring you the best from the shows (Crazy For You, Chicago, Guys and Dolls, Phantom of the Opera, Buddy etc.) in the delightful setting of Ightham Mote. The moated manor house will be

Further more detailed information on the attractions listed can be found in Best Guides *Visitor Attractions* Guide under the classifications shown

open before the concert and guests can picnic on the lawn both before and during the performance. Bring picnics and seating. Dress in appropriate style - characters from your favourite musical, Tickets £15.00, must be pre-booked on 01892 891001 or write to The Box Office, The National Trust, Scotney Castle, Lamberhurst, Kent TN3 8JN

Historic Houses

The 21st Anniversary Leeds Castle Open Air Concert

3/7/99
3/7/99

LEEDS CASTLE

Tel: 01622 765400

The second of two celebratory open air summer night classical music concerts, with the 1812, cannons and fireworks, as the triumphant finale. Gates open at 16.00. Entertainment from 17.30. Concert begins at 20.00. Advance ticket sales only from Box Office. Group rates available

Castles

BHTA Borde Hill Horse Trials

3/7/99
4/7/99

BORDE HILL GARDEN

Tel: 01444 450326

Seventh Borde Hill Horse Trials held in Borde Hill's heritage parkland. There will be cross-country, show jumping and dressage from local and international riders. 10.00-17.00.

Gardens

FIA International Historic Superprix (HSCC)

3/7/99
4/7/99

BRANDS HATCH

Tel: 0171 344 4444Ticketmaster

Thoroughbred Formula 1 x 2, Historic Racing Saloons, Derek Ball Trophy, Historic / 70's Road Sport, Classic F3, Classic Racing Cars, MG / TR Challenge, Dutch Alfa, Thundersports, Classic Ford, 3 Hour Endurance. Grand Prix Circuit, Grade-C. On the Gate: £10.00-£28.00. In Advance: Non £8.00-£25.00, Club £7.00-£22.00. Two Day Pass: Non £11.00-£30.00, Club £10.00-£27.00. Three Day Pass: Non £32.00, Club £29.00. Qualifying: £5.00-£14.00. C£free. Programme £Free-£5.00. Seating (BH): £Free-£8.00. South Bank: £2.00-£5.00. Group Tickets: Non £90.00-£95.00, Club £80.00-£85.00. Season Ticket Inc. of Club Membership: £200.00. You can buy your tickets for any of the 1999 events in advance any time up to 4 days before an event and make a saving, Tel: 0870 60 60 611

Motor Racing Circuit

Royal Harbour Ramsgate

3/7/99
4/7/99

MARITIME MUSEUM

Tel: 01843 587765

Ships, Steam and Vintage Festival, details from Maritime Museum

Museum- Maritime

Ships Open Weekend

3/7/99
4/7/99

MARITIME MUSEUM

Tel: 01843 587765

Maritime spectacular with water-borne and shore based activities including steam/vintage festival

Museum- Maritime

Garden Tour

3/7/99
4/7/99

WALMER CASTLE

Tel: 01304 364288

Past, Present and Future with Richard Squires, your guide. A£4.50 C£2.30 Concessions£3.40

Castles

The Runnymede Art Collection

3/7/99
11/9/99

CHERTSEY MUSEUM

Tel: 01932 565764

A selection of recently restored watercolours, including works by John and Edward Hassell and Frank Galsworthy

Museum- Local History

Hot Rods and Custom Show

4/7/99
4/7/99

BENTLEY WILDFOWL AND MOTOR MUSEUM

Tel: 01825 840573

Please telephone for details

Waterfowl Parks

Music of the Night

4/7/99
4/7/99

HATCHLANDS PARK

Tel: 01483 222482

One of the open air concerts in the Hatchlands Hat Trick. Doors open 18.30 for 19.30 performance. Contains fast-moving, originally written medleys of songs from the world's greatest musicals (Phantom Of The Opera, Les Miserables, Crazy For You, Miss Saigon, West Side Story and many more), featuring four star performers from London's West End Shows including the leading lady form the West End production of Phantom. This exciting show has played to acclaim to packed audiences at other National Trust venues and has successfully toured the world. Ticket Prices: £12.50, Two nights £22.50, Three nights £34.00

Historic Houses

Polesden Fair

4/7/99
4/7/99

POLESDEN LACEY

Tel: 01372 458203/452048

With folk dance teams, fairground area,

Punch and Judy, storytelling and more
11.00-17.00. Tickets: £4.00, members
£3.00, non-members £5.00 at the gate,
Children free

Historic Houses & Gardens

Miller Magic

4/7/99
4/7/99
POLESDEN LACEY
Tel: 01372 458203/452048
Celebrating American Independence Day
at Polesden Lacey, we are delighted to
welcome the Herb Miller Orchester,
directed by John Miller for an hour or
two of big band swing in the unforgettable style of Glen Miller played as only
the Miller Band know how. Time: 20.00.
Cost: £12.00

Historic Houses & Gardens

Punch and Judy Day

4/7/99
4/7/99
PUNCH AND JUDY DAY 1999
Tel: 01227 742690
Where's the baby? An opportunity to see
a number of Punch and Judy shows performing in continuous traditional manner along Herne Bay sea front.
Admission Free. 11.00-16.00

Festivals

Friends of Thomas the Tank

4/7/99
ROMNEY HYTHE AND DYMCHURCH
RAILWAY

4/7/99
Tel: 01797 362353/363256
Fat Controller, Henry, Gordon,
Troublesome Trucks and clowns, Punch
and Judy, Magicians etc make a great
day of family fun

Railways

Car Boot Sale

4/7/99
4/7/99
RURAL LIFE CENTRE
Tel: 01252 792300/795571
09.00-13.00, £5.00 per car to sell.
Buyers admitted to sale free

Museums

The Look: The Fashion of the 20th Century

6/7/99
28/8/99
HORSHAM MUSEUM
Tel: 01403 254959
One hundred years of fashion including
hats, costume shoes and designs

Museum- Local History

Evening Racing

7/7/99
7/7/99
EPSOM RACECOURSE
Tel: 01372 726311
For further details including race times
and ticket prices please contact venue
direct

Racecourses

Another View of Ightham

7/7/99
7/7/99
IGHTHAM MOTE
Tel: 01732 811145
A walk around the woodland and farmland surrounding Ightham Mote. Time:
14.00. Cost: £3.50. Restricted numbers
so must be pre-booked.

Historic Houses

Royal International Horse Show

7/7/99
HICKSTEAD SHOWGROUND (ALL ENGLAND JUMPING COURSE)

11/7/99
Tel: 01273 834315
The Royal International Horse Show will
again stage the extremely popular
Eventing Grand Prix, where some of the
world's top showjumpers take on the
world's top event riders. Also included in
it's busy schedule is the British Nations
Cup, the British Grand Prix, the King
George V Gold Cup and the Queen
Elizabeth II Cup. Gates Open: 08.30,
Closure: 17.30/18.00. Tickets: A£5.00-
£20.00 C(5-14)&OAPs£2.00-£15.00
Family Ticket (A2+C2&Car Pass)£15.00-
£34.00. Car Parking: £3.00-£4.00

Showgrounds

Rallye Entene Cordiale 1999

8/7/99
11/7/99
RALLYE ENTENE CORDIALE 1999
Tel: 01323 415442
Cross Channel Regatta, fleet sail into
harbour take part in a range of fun water
activities before the boats set sail from
Sovereign Harbour to Le Treport Marina
in Northern France. Grand firework
finale. Admission Free.

Festivals

Opera in the Garden with Opera Brava

8/7/99
11/7/99
SCOTNEY CASTLE GARDEN
Tel: 01892 891081
8 & 10 July - Don Giovanni - Opera
Brava's new production this year, one of
the most frequently praised of operas
with its unique blend of the irresistibly
comic and the tragically serious; 9 July -
Carmen - Back for one last performance,
this colourful, innovative production is
vibrant with energy and passion and has
thrilled audiences on its previous
appearances; 11 July Gala Concert - A pot
pourri of opera's most inspiring music - a
slecetion of well-known arias, duets,
trios and ensembles, ranging from
Mozart to Gershwin, 18.30 for 19.30.
Bring your picnics and seating and enjoy
an evening of beautiful music in the
romantic setting of Scotney Castle,
Tickets £20.00, must be pre-booked on
01892 891001 or write to The Box Office,

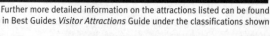

Further more detailed information on the attractions listed can be found
in Best Guides *Visitor Attractions* Guide under the classifications shown

The National Trust, Scotney Castle, Lamberhurst, Kent TN3 8JN

Gardens

Open Air Concert - Peter Pan
8/7/99
17/7/99
LULLINGSTONE CASTLE
Tel: 01322 862114
Performances on: July 8th, 11th, 14th & 17th only. Bring picnics and rugs/chairs. Please contact venue for further information.

Castles

Jazz Nights in the Garden
9/7/99
10/7/99
NYMANS GARDEN
Tel: 01444 400321
Our unique formula returns to thrill you. Bring a picnic and enjoy music at various atmospheric spots in these beautiful gardens during the first part of your evening. Then, take a seat on the main lawn by the floodlit ruins for the big band sound and let the heady feeling of nostalgia transport you away. Early booking advisable! Gates open 18.30 for picnics. Performance at 19.30. Tickets: £12.00, available from the Box Office at Poleden Lacey, 01372 455052

Gardens

Summer Ball
10/7/99
10/7/99
BORDE HILL GARDEN
Tel: 01444 450326
Borde Hill's prestigious Summer Ball to be held on the South Lawn within a marquee. Dinner will be served during the evening and our guests will be able to dance the night away to the UK's foremost dance band, The Bark Blues. Call for further information

Gardens

Clubmans Bikes (NEW ERA)
10/7/99
10/7/99
BRANDS HATCH
Tel: 0171 344 4444Ticketmaster
All classes of national solo motorcycles and sidecars. Indy Circuit, Grade-D. On the Gate: £10.00-£28.00. In Advance: Non £8.00-£25.00, Club £7.00-£22.00. Two Day Pass: Non £11.00-£30.00, Club £10.00-£27.00. Three Day Pass: Non £32.00, Club £29.00. Qualifying: £5.00-£14.00. C£Free. Programme £Free-£5.00. Seating (BH): £Free-£8.00. South Bank: £2.00-£5.00. Group Tickets: Non £90.00-£95.00, Club £80.00-£85.00. Season Ticket Inc. of Club Membership: £200.00. You can buy your tickets for any of the 1999 events in advance any time up to 4 days before an event and make a saving, Tel: 0870 60 60 611

Motor Racing Circuit

Jousting
10/7/99
11/7/99
BATTLE ABBEY
Tel: 01424 773792
Discover the secrets of the tourney, as the jousting area resounds to the sounds of the battle, clash of steel and thunder of horses hooves as the mighty knights charge at full tilt. A£6.00 C£3.00 Concessions£4.50

Battlefields

Esher Model Flying Club
10/7/99
11/7/99
BROOKLANDS MUSEUM
Tel: 01932 857381
A two day extravaganza with realistic display of model aicraft and special effects

Museum- Motor

Tudor Weekend
10/7/99
11/7/99
DEAL CASTLE
Tel: 01304 372762
Various performers dressed in Tudor costume re-enacting Tudor life. A£3.50 C£1.80 Concessions£2.50

Castles

SEMSEC F/Ford and Saloons
10/7/99
11/7/99
LYDDEN INTERNATIONAL MOTOR RACING CIRCUIT
Tel: 01304 830557
For further details including times and ticket prices please contact venue direct

Motor Racing Circuit

The Water Babies
11/7/99
11/7/99
BODIAM CASTLE
Tel: 01580 830436
Following their nationwide success last year with Alice in Wonderland, the Illyria team return with an even more fantastical production. With excitement, surprises and a range of characters from a snobbish salmon to a jobsworth truncheon (and another lobster!), Charles Kingley's classic for children is an unforgettable adventure! A£8.00 C£4.00, must be pre-booked on 01892 891001 or write to The Box Office, The National Trust, Scotney Castle, Lamberhurst, Kent TN3 8JN

Historic Buildings

Clubmans Bikes (BMCRC)
11/7/99
11/7/99
BRANDS HATCH
Tel: 0171 344 4444Ticketmaster
Champion of Brands Hatch, all classes of national solo motorcycles and sidecars. Indy Circuit, Grade-D. On the Gate: £10.00-£28.00. In Advance: Non £8.00-£25.00, Club £7.00-£22.00. Two Day

Pass: Non £11.00-£30.00, Club £10.00-£27.00. Three Day Pass: Non £32.00, Club £29.00. Qualifying: £5.00-£14.00. C£Free. Programme £Free-£5.00. Seating (BH): £Free-£8.00. South Bank: £2.00-£5.00. Group Tickets: Non £90.00-£95.00, Club £80.00-£85.00. Season Ticket Inc. of Club Membership: £200.00. You can buy your tickets for any of the 1999 events in advance any time up to 4 days before an event and make a saving, Tel: 0870 60 60 611

Motor Racing Circuit

Historic Commercial Vehicle Gathering

11/7/99　MUSEUM OF KENT LIFE
11/7/99　Tel: 01622 763936

A fantastic display of beautifully restored Historic Commercial Vehicles.

Museum- Local History

International Sheep Shearing Contest

11/7/99　SOUTH OF ENGLAND RARE BREEDS CENTRE

11/7/99　Tel: 01233 861493

Champion shearers from Australia, New Zealand, Ireland and United Kingdom compete for the Romney Shears Trophy. Wool craft demonstrations. Dates to be confirmed

Farm- Rare Breeds

Afternoon Racing

12/7/99　BRIGHTON RACECOURSE
12/7/99　Tel: 01273 603580

Racing from Brighton between 12.00 and18.00. Admission A£4.00-£12.00 C£Free

Racecourses

Heathland and Heathers

12/7/99　RHS GARDEN WISLEY
12/7/99　Tel: 01483 224234

This afternoon looks at the history behind the heathland in an illustrated talk and then a guided walk with Andy Collins, responsible for the heather collection at Wisley. Time: 14.00-16.00. Cost: members £15.00, non-members £20.00

Gardens

Afternoon Racing

13/7/99　BRIGHTON RACECOURSE
13/7/99　Tel: 01273 603580

Racing from Brighton between 12.00 and18.00. Admission A£4.00-£12.00 C£Free

Racecourses

Demonstration: Pruning of Fruit Trees and Bushes

14/7/99　RHS GARDEN WISLEY
14/7/99　Tel: 01483 224234

Come and watch Charlie Day and Jim Arbury show you how to purne your fruit trees and bushes at 10.30. This demonstration will also take place on: Sun 18th at 10.30 & Wed 17th, Fri 19th & Sun 21st November at 10.30. Cost: Members £5.00, non-members £10.00. To book tickets send a cheque made payable to RHS, enclosing a SAE and including your membership number (if applicable) and day time telephone number to the Administration Department at RHS Garden, Wisley, Woking GU23 6QB. We are sorry but we cannot accept telephone bookings. Please note that all events may be subject to cancellation due to insufficient ticket sales

Gardens

Fete Champêtre

14/7/99　CLAREMONT LANDSCAPE GARDEN
17/7/99　Tel: 01372 467806

The Big Top comes to Claremont and with it all the fun of the fair. In a pageant of spectacular acts, bright lights, sawdust and grease paint, feel yourself flying through the air alongside our acrobats and trapeze artists. (Prices are for guideline only, those quoted were for 98) Wed/Thur A£14.00 C£7.00 Fri/Sat A£18.00 C£12.00 10% discount on bookings of 10+ on Wed and Thur only. 19.00-23.00. Call 01372 451596/457223 for details

Gardens

Hedges and Screens Tickets

15/7/99　RHS GARDEN WISLEY
15/7/99　Tel: 01483 224234

This day will be led by David Jewell, Superintendent of the Floral Ornamental Department at Wisley. It will focus on hedges and screens in use at Wisley, cover choice of materials and give advice on their placement and maintenance. Time: 10.00-16.00. Cost: members £40.00, non-members £45.00

Gardens

Kent County Show 1999

15/7/99　KENT COUNTY SHOWGROUND
17/7/99　Tel: 01622 630975

Kent's premier agricultural show featuring over 500 trade stands, livestock, equestrian events, demonstrations and other related attractions. (guide prices based on 1998 entrance fees) A£9.00 C£4.50 Family Ticket £25.00. Cheaper if

Further more detailed information on the attractions listed can be found in Best Guides *Visitor Attractions* Guide under the classifications shown

pre paid 01622 630975

Showgrounds

Garden Pests and Diseases Tickets
16/7/99 RHS GARDEN WISLEY
16/7/99 Tel: 01483 224234
Through illustrated talks and practical
demonstration, Chris Prior, Head of Plant
Pest and Disease Science and Andrew
Halstead, Senior Entomologist at Wisley
take you through the steps of identifying
and dealing with garden pests and diseases. Time: 10.00-16.00. Cost: members £40.00, non-members £45.00

Gardens

**Natural History Photographic
Exhibition**
16/7/99 MAIDSTONE MUSEUM AND ART GALLERY
5/9/99 Tel: 01622 754497
This exhibition shows one hundred photographs taken by some of Kent's natural history enthusiasts. Open to amateur
and professionals - get your cameras
ready for action now!

Museums

Classic Car Fair
17/7/99 SANDOWN EXHIBITION CENTRE
17/7/99 Tel: 01372 467540
Opening times and prices to be
announced. Please call for further information

Exhibition Centres

**The Remarkable Tales of Ambrose
Gwinnett**
17/7/99 DEAL CASTLE
18/7/99 Tel: 01304 372762
Crew Of Patches. A£3.00 C£1.50
Concessions£2.30

Castles

Tudor Players
17/7/99 DOVER CASTLE AND SECOND WORLD WAR
TUNNELS
18/7/99 Tel: 01304 201628/202754
Performed by the Melford Hys Companie
a Tudor re-enactment. A£6.90 C£3.50
Concessions£5.20

Castles

750 Saloon Cars
17/7/99 LYDDEN INTERNATIONAL MOTOR RACING
CIRCUIT
18/7/99 Tel: 01304 830557
For further details including times and
ticket prices please contact venue direct

Motor Racing Circuit

Grand Tour
17/7/99 PAINSHILL LANDSCAPE GARDEN
18/7/99 Tel: 01932 868113/864674
Find out how the Grand Tour influenced

Painshill with characters in costume,
costumes on display and guided tours to
special features

Gardens

Teddy Bear's Picnic
17/7/99 ST AUGUSTINE'S ABBEY
18/7/99 Tel: 01227 767345
Various performers. Magicians, face
painting, balloons and lots of clowning
about. Bring a teddy to get in!

Abbeys

Children's Toy Exhibition
17/7/99 THE WHITE CLIFFS EXPERIENCE
7/11/99 Tel: 01304 214566/210101
An exhibition of toys in Dover Museum.

Interactive

Vintage Transport Rally
18/7/99 BENTLEY WILDFOWL AND MOTOR MUSEUM
18/7/99 Tel: 01825 840573
A large display of vintage vehicles will
be on view for you to take a closer look
at. Normal admission price and opening
hours apply

Waterfowl Parks

Championsip Cars (BRSCC)
18/7/99 BRANDS HATCH
18/7/99 Tel: 0171 344 4444Ticketmaster
Formula Renaults, Porsche Classics, Kent
Championship Formula Fords. Indy
Circuit, Grade-D. On the Gate: £10.00-
£28.00. In Advance: Non £8.00-£25.00,
Club £7.00-£22.00. Two Day Pass: Non
£11.00-£30.00, Club £10.00-£27.00.
Three Day Pass: Non £32.00, Club
£29.00. Qualifying: £5.00-£14.00.
C£Free. Programme £Free-£5.00.
Seating (BH): £Free-£8.00. South Bank:
£2.00-£5.00. Group Tickets: Non £90.00-
£95.00, Club £80.00-£85.00. Season
Ticket Inc. of Club Membership:
£200.00. You can buy your tickets for
any of the 1999 events in advance any
time up to 4 days before an event and
make a saving, Tel: 0870 60 60 611

Motor Racing Circuit

Sunday Concert
18/7/99 CLAREMONT LANDSCAPE GARDEN
18/7/99 Tel: 01372 467806
Last year it was the return of the 70s...
what is in store for you for 99? call for
details. Gates open at 19.00 for picnics.
Concert starts at 19.30. (98 prices for
guideline only) A£10.00 C£5.00 10% discount on bookings of 10+. Call 01372
451596/457223

Gardens

Walk at Wisley

18/7/99	**RHS GARDEN WISLEY**
18/7/99	Tel: 01483 224234

Come and see the beautiful summer borders at Wisley with your Guide David Hoodless. This walk will also take place on: Wed 21st at 10.30. Cost: Members £5.00, non-members £10.00. To book tickets send a cheque made payable to RHS, enclosing a SAE and including your membership number (if applicable) and day time telephone number to the Administration Department at RHS Garden, Wisley, Woking GU23 6QB. We are sorry but we cannot accept telephone bookings. Please note that all events may be subject to cancellation due to insufficient ticket sales

Gardens

Celebrities

18/7/99	**SMALLHYTHE PLACE**
18/7/99	Tel: 01580 762334

Timothy West and Prunella Scales welcome you to Smallhythe Place for a special viewing followed by a chance to hear their anecdotes and reminiscences.

Museums

Garden Tour - Bat Walk

19/7/99	**SHEFFIELD PARK GARDEN**
19/7/99	Tel: 01825 790231

Led by the gardeners, and limited to 30 per walk, maximum. To see the gardens through the eyes of the people who know it best, book early. Time: 20.30. Cost: £6.00.

Gardens

Plant Propagation for Beginners and Beyone Tickets

20/7/99	**RHS GARDEN WISLEY**
20/7/99	Tel: 01483 224234

This day will be led by David Hide, Senior Supervisor in the Research and Propagation Department at Wisley. It will consist of practical demonstrations where participants can learn the skills and techniques used in the art of Propagation. Time: 10.00-16.00. Cost: members £40.00, non-members £45.00

Gardens

Classic Car Auction

20/7/99	**SANDOWN EXHIBITION CENTRE**
20/7/99	Tel: 01372 467540

Opening times and prices to be announced. Please call for further information

Exhibition Centres

The Petworth Festival 1999

20/7/99	**THE PETWORTH FESTIVAL 1999**
28/7/99	Tel: 01798 343906

The Festival opens with an ecumenical service in St Mary's Parish Church on 20th July. The majority of events will be held in the three local churches, St Mary's, the United Reformed Church and the Roman Catholic Church of The Sacred Heart and in Petworth House. The programme has not yet been finalised but it is expected will include poetry reading, young musician winners, chamber ensemble, wind quartet art lecture, harpists and candle lit choral music (indoors). Courtyard Theatre and a Square Dance. Ticket Prices: A£5.00-£15.00 C(0-14)£Free. Tickets will be available from the Tourist Information Centre in Petworth: 01798 343523 from 1/6/99. At various times lunchtimes and evenings.

Festivals

Flower Arranging Demonstration

21/7/99	**RHS GARDEN WISLEY**
21/7/99	Tel: 01483 224234

'Flowers to charm and delight' with Keren Dean Taylor. Time: 10.00-12.30. Cost: members £18.00, non-members £23.00

Gardens

Racing from Sandown Park

21/7/99	**SANDOWN PARK RACECOURSE**
22/7/99	Tel: 01372 463072

Wednesday is Harpers and Queen Evening and Thursday is Milcars Star Stakes. For further details including race times and ticket prices please contact venue direct

Racecourses

Sea, Sand & Seagulls

21/7/99	**THE WHITE CLIFFS EXPERIENCE**
5/9/99	Tel: 01304 214566/210101

Holiday quiz for the family with a summer theme.

Interactive

Afternoon Racing

22/7/99	**BRIGHTON RACECOURSE**
22/7/99	Tel: 01273 603580

Racing from Brighton between 12.00 and18.00. Admission A£4.00-£12.00 C£Free

Racecourses

Kent Beer Festival '99

22/7/99	**KENT BEER FESTIVAL '99**
24/7/99	Tel: 01227 463478

This is the 25th Kent Beer Festival and will feature special brewed "Silver" beers as well as the usual range of over 100 real ales from home and abroad. The festival is held in a huge barn in a farmyard. There are food stalls, souvenir glasses and entertainment and local real ciders are available. The festival is run by volunteer members of the Campaign for Real Ale (CAMRA). The CAMRA shops offer special membership rates as well as a variety of real ale souvenirs. Times: 22nd: 18.30-23.00, 23rd: 12.00-16.00 & 18.30-23.00, 24th: 11.30-16.30 & 18.30-23.00. Prices: 22nd: A£2.00, CAMRA members Free, 23rd: Lunchtime free, evening A£4.00 in advance, 24th: A£2.00 (the session (free after 21.00). C£Free

Festivals

Great Gardening Show
23/7/99   LOSELEY PARK
25/7/99   Tel: 01483 304440
Show gardens, demonstrations, plants and garden accessories for sale

Historic Houses & Gardens

War & Peace Military Show
23/7/99   THE HOP FARM COUNTRY PARK
25/7/99   Tel: 01622 871577
Static and arena displays of wartime/peacetime memorabilia. Both days 10.00-18.00

Museum- Agricultural

Buddy Holly and the Cricketers
24/7/99   BODIAM CASTLE
24/7/99   Tel: 01580 830436
Join stars from hit West End musicals 'Buddy' and 'Lennon' for a fast, furious and funny rock 'n' roller coaster of a show! Hear all Buddy Holly's greatest hits live on stage. The wonderful setting of Bodiam Castle, specially floodlit for the evening, is the backdrop to this concert. The evening ends with a spectacular fireworks display. Time: 19.30. Tickets: £12.00.

Historic Buildings

Apex Track Day
24/7/99   LYDDEN INTERNATIONAL MOTOR RACING CIRCUIT
24/7/99   Tel: 01304 830557
For further details including times and ticket prices please contact venue direct

Motor Racing Circuit

Prom Evening
24/7/99   MOUNT EPHRAIM GARDENS
24/7/99   Tel: 01227 751496
Spectacular classical music concert with fireworks by Royal Philarmonic

Orchestra

Gardens- Botanical

Teddy Bears' Picnic
24/7/99   NYMANS GARDEN
24/7/99   Tel: 01444 400321
Bring your teddy bears to enjoy old-fashioned fun - all ages (of teddies and owners!). Bring a picnic. 11.00-17.00. Normal admission charges. Additional charge on the day.

Gardens

Theatre
24/7/99   DOVER CASTLE AND SECOND WORLD WAR TUNNELS
25/7/99   Tel: 01304 201628/202754
Drama by Crew of Patches. A£6.90 C£3.50 Concessions£5.20

Castles

Faversham Secret Gardens
24/7/99   FLEUR DE LYS HERITAGE CENTRE
25/7/99   Tel: 01795 534542
15 Private gardens open to public. Admission to all by programme, with detailed notes. £3.50

Heritage Centres

The Living Heritage Craft Fair
24/7/99   GROOMBRIDGE PLACE GARDENS
25/7/99   Tel: 01892 863999

Gardens

Elizabethan Entertainment
24/7/99   PENSHURST PLACE AND GARDENS
25/7/99   Tel: 01892 870307
Also on 31 July & 1 Aug. Two weekends of Elizabethan revels including, jugglers, jesters, music, dance and side shows

Historic Houses

The Lion, the Witch, and the Wardrobe
24/7/99   PEVENSEY CASTLE
25/7/99   Tel: 01323 762604
A children's classic performed by Labyrinth Productions. A£3.50 C£1.50 Concessions£2.60

Castles

Whitstable Oyster Festival '99
24/7/99   WHITSTABLE OYSTER FESTIVAL '99
1/8/99   Tel: 01227 265666
Various venues. A showcase of family events, theatre and art. This family festival celebrates Whitstable's heritage and links with the sea. Traditional, unpretentious events encompassing the warmth, charm and character of this small friendly town. Please call 01227 265666 for further information on events

Festivals

Käthe Kollwitz - Artist of the People

| 24/7/99 | **TUNBRIDGE WELLS MUSEUM AND ART GALLERY** |
| 21/8/99 | Tel: 01892 526121/554171 |

German Romantic and Expressionist prints reflecting motherhood, emancipation, and political struggle

Museums

Jousting Tournaments

| 24/7/99 | **HEVER CASTLE AND GARDENS** |
| 28/8/99 | Tel: 01732 865224 |

The Knights of Royal England will present traditional jousting tournaments on July 24 & 31, Aug 7, 14, 21 & 28. Event included in the Garden only ticket

Castles

Classic Car Show & Country Fair

| 25/7/99 | **BATTLE ABBEY** |
| 25/7/99 | Tel: 01424 773792 |

See those beautiful old cars and pick up those unusual gifts. The Rotary Club

Battlefields

Vintage Car Rally

| 25/7/99 | **DODDINGTON PLACE GARDENS** |
| 25/7/99 | Tel: 01795 886101 |

An interesting day for the whole family with lots of vintage vehicles on display.

Gardens

Rustic Sunday

| 25/7/99 | **RURAL LIFE CENTRE** |
| 25/7/99 | Tel: 01252 792300/795571 |

Lace making, wood cleaving and turning walking sticks, Patchwork, Morris dancers, Spinning, Weaving, Basket making, Pottery, Accordions, Handbells, Steam powered rides on the light railway. Refreshments available including lunches and teas. Come and enjoy a real family day out. Time: 11.00-18.00. Cost: A£4.00 C£1.00 OAPs£3.50

Museums

Antique Textiles Fair

| 25/7/99 | **SANDOWN EXHIBITION CENTRE** |
| 25/7/99 | Tel: 01372 467540 |

Please call venue for further information

Exhibition Centres

Gardens fit for a Queen

| 25/7/99 | **WALMER CASTLE** |
| 25/7/99 | Tel: 01304 364288 |

Beautiful garden tour with Richard Squires. A£4.50 C£2.30 Concessions£3.40

Castles

The Attics and Gardens of Ightham Mote

| 26/7/99 | **IGHTHAM MOTE** |
| 26/7/99 | Tel: 01732 811145 |

10.30. Guided tour of the house, with the experts explaining aspects of history and the conservation work, £8.00, must be pre-booked on 01892 891001 or write to The Box Office, The National Trust, Scotney Castle, Lamberhurst, Kent TN3 8JN

Historic Houses

Loseley Park Farms Children's' Holiday Activity Days

| 26/7/99 | **LOSELEY PARK** |
| 3/9/99 | Tel: 01483 304440 |

Excluding Sat, Sun and Public Holidays. Fun filled days on the farm. Commences 09.30-16.00. Call 01483 304440 for booking details

Historic Houses & Gardens

Julian Ford Birds of Prey Display

| 28/7/99 | **DRUSILLAS PARK** |
| 28/7/99 | Tel: 01323 870234 |

Fabulous display of these majestic birds with talks and small flying displays included. Also to be held on: 4, 11, 18 & 25 Aug

Zoos

Evening Racing

| 28/7/99 | **EPSOM RACECOURSE** |
| 28/7/99 | Tel: 01372 726311 |

For further details including race times and ticket prices please contact venue direct

Racecourses

Children's Open Day

| 29/7/99 | **MARITIME MUSEUM** |
| 29/7/99 | Tel: 01843 587765 |

Fun day for all the family with displays, activities, demonstrations and competitions

Museum- Maritime

Medway Flower Festival & Craft Show

| 29/7/99 | **COBHAM HALL** |
| 30/7/99 | Tel: 01474 823371 |

Call venue for further information. House open 13.00-16.00

Historic Houses & Gardens

Open-Air Theatre - Othello

| 29/7/99 | **SMALLHYTHE PLACE** |
| 1/8/99 | Tel: 01580 762334 |

Presented by The Summer Theatre Company in the garden. Bring chairs. Gates open 18.30 for picnickers. Please note: can be booked only at Smallhythe.

Museums

Clowns Day

| 30/7/99 | **DRUSILLAS PARK** |
| 30/7/99 | Tel: 01323 870234 |

Three fantastic clowns with workshops, walk abouts and shows throughout the day

Zoos

FIM World Superbike (MCRCB)
30/7/99 **BRANDS HATCH**
1/8/99 Tel: 0171 344 4444Ticketmaster
Featuring two rounds of the World
Superbike Championship and a host of
support races. Grand Prix Circuit, Grade-
AA. On the Gate: £10.00-£28.00. In
Advance: Non £8.00-£25.00, Club £7.00-
£22.00. Two Day Pass: Non £11.00-
£30.00, Club £10.00-£27.00. Three Day
Pass: Non £32.00, Club £29.00.
Qualifying: £5.00-£14.00. C£Free.
Programme £Free-£5.00. Seating (BH):
£Free-£8.00. South Bank: £2.00-£5.00.
Group Tickets: Non £90.00-£95.00, Club
£80.00-£85.00. Season Ticket Inc. of
Club Membership: £200.00. You can buy
your tickets for any of the 1999 events in
advance any time up to 4 days before an
event and make a saving, Tel: 0870 60
60 611

Motor Racing Circuit

First Night of the Sunflower Prom
31/7/99 **GROOMBRIDGE PLACE GARDENS**
31/7/99 Tel: 01892 863999

Gardens

Archery Tournament
31/7/99 **DOVER CASTLE AND SECOND WORLD WAR**
TUNNELS
1/8/99 Tel: 01304 201628/202754
The Medieval Siege Society, a medieval
archery tournament. A£6.90 C£3.50
Concessions£5.20

Castles

Historical Interpretation
31/7/99 **FARNHAM CASTLE KEEP**
1/8/99 Tel: 01252 713393
The Life of a Knight and Medieval Lady.
Normal admission prices apply

Castles

VMCC Vintage Motorcycles
31/7/99 **LYDDEN INTERNATIONAL MOTOR RACING**
CIRCUIT
1/8/99 Tel: 01304 830557
For further details including times and
ticket prices contact venue direct

Motor Racing Circuit

Siege of 1399
31/7/99 **PEVENSEY CASTLE**
1/8/99 Tel: 01323 762604
Various performers re-enact the 1399
Siege of Pevensey Castle. £3.00 C£1.50
Concessions£2.30

Castles

Family Entertainers
31/7/99 **ST AUGUSTINE'S ABBEY**
1/8/99 Tel: 01227 767345
Games, have-a-go archery, costumes for
children to try on and talks on weaponry.
A£3.00 C£1.50 Concessions£2.30

Abbeys

Roman Food Tasting
31/7/99 **THE WHITE CLIFFS EXPERIENCE**
1/8/99 Tel: 01304 214566/210101
Sample food and drink enjoyed by the
Romans including spiced wine apicius.

Interactive

Fairy Tales
31/7/99 **WALMER CASTLE**
1/8/99 Tel: 01304 364288
Fairy tales from the Enchanted Garden
with Crew of Patches. A£4.50 C£2.30
Concessions£3.40

Castles

Family Fortnight
31/7/99 **RHS GARDEN WISLEY**
15/8/99 Tel: 01483 224234
A fortnight of family fun provides children with educational and garden based
activities to do when they visit Wisley in
the school holidays. There will be storytelling, art and sculpture workshops,
flower arranging classes, creepy crawly
lectures and competitions. There will be
a selection of children's books on show
in the Reading Room, the opportunity to
buy games, books and toys in the Gift
Shop and the chance to pot up a plant in
the Plant Centre

Gardens

Car Boot Sale
1/8/99 **RURAL LIFE CENTRE**
1/8/99 Tel: 01252 792300/795571
09.00-13.00, £5.00 per car to sell.
Buyers admitted to sale free

Museums

Children's Sundays at Borde Hill
1/8/99 **BORDE HILL GARDEN**
29/8/99 Tel: 01444 450326
Every Sunday during August will mean
great fun for the children as we are holding plenty of fun activities in the parkland, call for further details

Gardens

Children's Activities in the Garden
1/8/99 **CLAREMONT LANDSCAPE GARDEN**
31/8/99 Tel: 01372 467806
Trusty's Trials: plenty of educational fun
for children 6-10 years, actual dates to
be confirmed 11.00-13.00. Book in
advance on 01372 469421. Tickets(98

prices): £2.00 members child, £3.50
non-members child.

Gardens

Streets of the East Midlands 1999
NATIONAL STREET ARTS FESTIVALS FOR
1999

1/8/99

31/8/99 Tel: 01273 821588
Coming to streets of Nottingham,
Leicester and Coalville (venues and
dates still to be confirmed). Welcome to
the fourth year of the Streets of the East
Midlands, which is just on of a series of
FREE festivals developed with funding
from the Arts Counci of England, through
the National Lottery. What is more, it's
all FREE. Full details and brochure will
be available from beginning of July 1999
by calling 01273 821588

Festivals

Streetfeast 1999
NATIONAL STREET ARTS FESTIVALS FOR
1999

1/8/99

31/8/99 Tel: 01273 821588
Coming to streets of Wolverhampton,
Walsall and Bromsgrove (venues and
dates still to be confirmed). Streetfeast
in is its fifth year and during 1998 joined
the National Streets Arts Fstival in celebrating this rapidly developing art form.
With an exciting programme of performance from established UK artists,
Streetfeast will be a vibrant display of
the very best in street theatre and it's all
FREE. Full details and brochure will be
available from beginning of July 1999 by
calling 01273 821588

Festivals

Streets of the South West 1999
NATIONAL STREET ARTS FESTIVALS FOR
1999

1/8/99

31/8/99 Tel: 01273 821588
Coming to streets of Sidmouth,
Teignmouth, Newton Abbot, Plymouth
and Bristol (venues and dates still to be
confirmed). The Streets of the South
West celebrates it's 5th year with our
most exciting programme of street art
yet. Dance, music, comedy, theatre, circus, sculpture - all of the highest quality
an the most spectacular energy - all at
the cutting edge of art and entertainment. All this and more and it's all FREE.
Full details and brochure will be available from beginning of July 1999 by calling 01273 821588

Festivals

Sci-Fi Adventure

1/8/99
31/8/99

PARADISE FAMILY LEISURE PARK
Tel: 01273 616006
Flying saucers have landed in the park
and unloaded aliens, can you spot
them?

Theme Parks

Standen at Play

2/8/99
2/8/99

STANDEN
Tel: 01342 323029
A full programme of activities and enter-
tainment for all the family

Historic Houses

Rainforest Experience

3/8/99
3/8/99

DRUSILLAS PARK
Tel: 01323 870234
Discover the secrets of the Rainforest in
our half hour sessions throughout the
day. Also to be held on: 17 & 26 Aug

Zoos

Garden Tour

4/8/99
4/8/99

WALMER CASTLE
Tel: 01304 364288
Past, Present and Future with Richard
Squires, your guide. A£4.50 C£2.30
Concessions£3.40

Castles

Afternoon Racing

4/8/99
5/8/99

BRIGHTON RACECOURSE
Tel: 01273 603580
Racing from Brighton between 12.00
and18.00. Admission A£4.00-£12.00
C£Free

Racecourses

Medieval Calligraphy & Spinning

4/8/99
5/8/99

PEVENSEY CASTLE
Tel: 01323 762604
Step back in time to the 15th century
and see how a 'clerk of minor orders'
went about his business! Authentic calligraphy, illuminating book making skills
are demonstrated, plus the use of an
unusual spindle wheel. A£3.00 C£1.50
Concessions£2.30

Castles

Charlie the Clown

5/8/99
5/8/99

DRUSILLAS PARK
Tel: 01323 870234
Charlie is back by popular demand on
his walk abouts with his trolley of tricks.
Also to be held on: 12, 19, 23 Aug, 1 Sept

Zoos

Open-Air Theatre - Othello

5/8/99
7/8/99

SMALLHYTHE PLACE
Tel: 01580 762334
Presented by The Summer Theatre
Company in the garden. Bring chairs.
Gates open 18.30 for picnickers. Please

Further more detailed information on the attractions listed can be found
in Best Guides *Visitor Attractions* Guide under the classifications shown

note: can be booked only at Smallhythe.

Museums

Jam Jar Jollities

6/8/99   CHARTWELL

18/8/99   Tel: 01732 866368 infoline

An entertaining afternoon on the estate. Commences 14.00. Tickets: £3.50. Very popular, must be pre-booked on 01892 891001 or write to The Box Office, The National Trust, Scotney Castle, Lamberhurst, Kent TN3 8JN

Historic Houses

Last Night of the Proms with Fireworks

7/8/99   BATEMAN'S

7/8/99   Tel: 01435 882302

Enjoy superb music in the setting of the beautiful Dudwell Valley, alongside Bateman's. Programme includes music by Tchaikovsky, Walton, John Williams plus the traditional "last night of the proms" finale with fireworks. Tickets £14.00, must be pre-booked on 01892 891001 or write to The Box Office, The National Trust, Scotney Castle, Lamberhurst, Kent TN3 8JN

Historic Houses

Herne Bay Festival

7/8/99   HERNE BAY FESTIVAL 1999

7/8/99   Tel: 01227 742690

Two weeks of family fun, almost all events are free. Herne Bay carnival on 14 Aug and Regatta on 15 Aug

Festivals

SEMSEC F/Ford and Saloons

7/8/99   LYDDEN INTERNATIONAL MOTOR RACING CIRCUIT

7/8/99   Tel: 01304 830557

For further details including times and ticket prices please contact venue direct

Motor Racing Circuit

Roman Interpretation

7/8/99   PEVENSEY CASTLE

7/8/99   Tel: 01323 762604

A Roman and his British Wife. A£3.00 C£1.50 Concessions£2.30

Castles

Classic Motorcycle Weekend (CRMC)

7/8/99   BRANDS HATCH

8/8/99   Tel: 0171 344 4444Ticketmaster

All classes of classic motorcycle and sidecars. Indy Circuit, Grade-D. On the Gate: £10.00-£28.00. In Advance: Non £8.00-£25.00, Club £7.00-£22.00. Two Day Pass: Non £11.00-£30.00, Club £10.00-£27.00. Three Day Pass: Non £32.00, Club £29.00. Qualifying: £5.00-

£14.00. C£Free. Programme £Free-£5.00. Seating (BH): £Free-£8.00. South Bank: £2.00-£5.00. Group Tickets: Non £90.00-£95.00, Club £80.00-£85.00. Season Ticket Inc. of Club Membership: £200.00. You can buy your tickets for any of the 1999 events in advance any time up to 4 days before an event and make a saving, Tel: 0870 60 60 611

Motor Racing Circuit

Medway Craft Show and Flower Festival

7/8/99   COBHAM HALL

8/8/99   Tel: 01474 823371

This event combines all aspects of the garden, from competitions and society displays, to trade, beautiful Crafts and lively question and answer areas where even the most difficult of problems may be answered. Open daily 10.00-18.00. A£4.00 OAPs£3.00 C£2.00

Historic Houses & Gardens

Theatre

7/8/99   DOVER CASTLE AND SECOND WORLD WAR TUNNELS

8/8/99   Tel: 01304 201628/202754

Drama performed by Crew Of Patches. Normal admission prices apply

Castles

Woodland and Traditional Craft Weekend

7/8/99   MUSEUM OF KENT LIFE

8/8/99   Tel: 01622 763936

See a wide range of traditional and woodland crafts being demonstrated - basket making, hurdle making, pole lathe turning, lead casting and many more. Also products for sale.

Museum- Local History

Steam Rally

7/8/99   PAINSHILL LANDSCAPE GARDEN

8/8/99   Tel: 01932 868113/864674

TBC

Gardens

Rye Medieval Festival 1999

7/8/99   RYE MEDIEVAL FESTIVAL 1999

8/8/99   Tel: 01797 226696

A grand procession of knights and ladies will parade through the streets; there will be medieval music and dancing, a medieval street market, juggling convention, medieval battles, medieval crafts, living history, street theatre, longbow tournament, children's pottery, vikings, pillory and falconry. For further information on the above number.

Festivals

Rye Medieval Festival and Longbow Tournament
7/8/99
8/8/99
THE STORY OF RYE
Tel: 01797 226696
Battles, tournaments, free dramatic entertainment for all the family
Heritage Centres

The Lion, the Witch, and the Wardrobe
7/8/99
8/8/99
WALMER CASTLE
Tel: 01304 364288
A wonderful children's classic performed by Labyrinth Productions. A£5.00 C£2.50 Concessions£3.50
Castles

The Searchers & Abba Gold
8/8/99
8/8/99
BATEMAN'S
Tel: 01435 882302
Relive the golden years of the sixties and seventies with these two bands. Abba Gold pay tribute to Abba, and The Searchers, who return by popular demand will be swinging back to the Sixties. A show for the young at heart! The concert will end with a spectacular fireworks display. Tickets: £12.00, must be pre-booked on 01892 891001 or write to The Box Office, The National Trust, Scotney Castle, Lamberhurst, Kent TN3 8JN
Historic Houses

Fuchsia Fanfare '99
8/8/99
8/8/99
BORDE HILL GARDEN
Tel: 01444 450326
Fuchsia displays from over 20 specialist Fuchsia societies in the garden making use of the myriad of natural features that are available. There will be a marquee with Fuchsia stands, craft stands and information tables, with talks given throughout the weekend.
Gardens

Arab Horse Racing Society Meeting
8/8/99
8/8/99
BRIGHTON RACECOURSE
Tel: 01273 603580
Afternoon meeting with racing 12.00-18.00
Racecourses

Wings, Wheels & Steam '99
8/8/99
8/8/99
GROOMBRIDGE PLACE GARDENS
Tel: 01892 863999
Gardens

Open Air Concert and Fireworks
8/8/99
8/8/99
LOSELEY PARK
Tel: 01483 304440
An evening of classical music performed by the Performing Art Symphony

Orchestra, call for further details and how to book
Historic Houses & Gardens

Historical Interpretation
8/8/99
8/8/99
PEVENSEY CASTLE
Tel: 01323 762604
Home Front 1940's. A£3.00 C£1.50 Concessions£2.30
Castles

Teddy Bear's Picnic
9/8/99
9/8/99
SHEFFIELD PARK GARDEN
Tel: 01825 790231
Bring your teddy and a picnic and meet Trusty the Hedgehog. Face-painting, story-telling etc. A£3.00 C£1.50 Teddies £Free!
Gardens

Family Fun Day
11/8/99
11/8/99
IGHTHAM MOTE
Tel: 01732 811145
Ightham presents a day for all. Come along and be entertained, call for further details
Historic Houses

Flower Arranging Demonstration
11/8/99
11/8/99
RHS GARDEN WISLEY
Tel: 01483 224234
'My world of flowers' with John Chennell. Time: 10.00-12.30. Cost: members £18.00, non-members £23.00
Gardens

Walk at Wisley
11/8/99
11/8/99
RHS GARDEN WISLEY
Tel: 01483 224234
Come and see our drought resistant plants with Dean Peckett at 10.30. Cost: Members £5.00, non-members £10.00. To book tickets send a cheque made payable to RHS, enclosing a SAE and including your membership number (if applicable) and day time telephone number to the Administration Department at RHS Garden, Wisley, Woking GU23 6QB. We are sorry but we cannot accept telephone bookings. Please note that all events may be subject to cancellation due to insufficient ticket sales
Gardens

Countryside Capers
11/8/99
11/8/99
SISSINGHURST CASTLE GARDEN
Tel: 01580 712850 infoline
In the grounds surrounding the garden. Time: 14.00. Cost: £3.50.
Gardens

Garden Tour

11/8/99 11/8/99	**WALMER CASTLE** Tel: 01304 364288 Past, Present and Future with Richard Squires, your guide. A£4.50 C£2.30 Concessions£3.40 *Castles*

Children's Fun Day

11/8/99 12/8/99	**BATTLE ABBEY** Tel: 01424 773792 Everything to entertain your children with various performers. A£4.50 C£2.80 Concessions£3.60 *Battlefields*

Racing from Sandown

11/8/99 12/8/99	**SANDOWN PARK RACECOURSE** Tel: 01372 463072 Wednesday is Elmbridge Evening, Thursday is Flat Racing. For further details including race times and ticket prices please contact venue direct *Racecourses*

A Midsummer's Nights Dream

11/8/99 14/8/99	**WALMER CASTLE** Tel: 01304 364288 A drama by Crew Of Patches. £5.00 per person *Castles*

The Order of St John 900th Anniversary Evening Racing

13/8/99 13/8/99	**EPSOM RACECOURSE** Tel: 01372 726311 For further details including race times and ticket prices please contact venue direct *Racecourses*

The Blues Band

14/8/99 14/8/99	**EMMETTS GARDEN** Tel: 01732 868381/750367 Time: 19.30. Featuring Paul Jones, Tom McGuinness, Dave kelly, Gary Fletcher and Rob Townsend, will be returning to this beautiful hill top garden, by invitation after last year's wonderful debut concert. Bring picnics and seating to enjoy the view and the blues! Tickets £12.00, must be pre-booked on 01892 891001 or write to The Box Office, The National Trust, Scotney Castle, Lamberhurst, Kent TN3 8JN *Gardens*

Toy Collectors' Fair

14/8/99 14/8/99	**SANDOWN EXHIBITION CENTRE** Tel: 01372 467540 Opening Times: 10.30-16.00. Prices A£3.50 C£1.00 OAPS£3.00 *Exhibition Centres*

Festival of 1000 Bikes (VMCC)

14/8/99 15/8/99	**BRANDS HATCH** Tel: 0171 344 4444Ticketmaster Classic and Vintage motorcycle displays, trade stands, glass track racing, memorabilia and fair. Indy Circuit, Grade-D. On the Gate: £10.00-£28.00. In Advance: Non £8.00-£25.00, Club £7.00-£22.00. Two Day Pass: Non £11.00-£30.00, Club £10.00-£27.00. Three Day Pass: Non £32.00, Club £29.00. Qualifying: £5.00-£14.00. C£Free. Programme £Free-£5.00. Seating (BH): £Free-£8.00. South Bank: £2.00-£5.00. Group Tickets: Non £90.00-£95.00, Club £80.00-£85.00. Season Ticket Inc. of Club Membership: £200.00. You can buy your tickets for any of the 1999 events in advance any time up to 4 days before an event and make a saving, Tel: 0870 60 60 611 *Motor Racing Circuit*

Theatre

14/8/99 15/8/99	**DOVER CASTLE AND SECOND WORLD WAR TUNNELS** Tel: 01304 201628/202754 Drama performed by Crew Of Patches. Normal admission prices apply *Castles*

Detling Transport & Country Festival 1999

14/8/99 15/8/99	**KENT COUNTY SHOWGROUND** Tel: 01622 630975 Steam engines, vintage and classic tractors, motorcycles, military and commercial vehicles, buses and coaches. Rural crafts, guest appearance by Fred Dibnah. Call for further information *Showgrounds*

Sheepdog Demonstrations

14/8/99 15/8/99	**PEVENSEY CASTLE** Tel: 01323 762604 Enjoyable demonstrations of sheepdogs, sheep and geese with Will Gray. A£3.50 C£1.80 Concessions£2.50 *Castles*

Food & Drink from the 1940s

14/8/99 15/8/99	**THE WHITE CLIFFS EXPERIENCE** Tel: 01304 214566/210101 Ration book fare from the 1940s in Coopers the Bakers and the Dover Arms. *Interactive*

The Bard and the Blade

14/8/99 15/8/99	**WALMER CASTLE** Tel: 01304 364288 Dramatic duels and dialogue from some of Shakespeare's most famous plays. A£4.50 C£2.30 Concessions£3.40 *Castles*

Twelfth Night

15/8/99
15/8/99

BODIAM CASTLE
Tel: 01580 830436
Presented by Illyria. A sparkling comedy laced with a soupcon of romance, a touch of poetry, and huge great dollops of seething lust! Tickets £9.00, must be pre-booked on 01892 891001 or write to The Box Office, The National Trust, Scotney Castle, Lamberhurst, Kent TN3 8JN

Historic Buildings

Children's Fun Day

15/8/99
15/8/99

FARNHAM CASTLE KEEP
Tel: 01252 713393
A wonderful and unique day out for children of all ages. Theatre and puppet shows, storytelling, arts and crafts workshops and themed activities. Normal admission prices apply

Castles

Rural Writers Remembered

15/8/99
15/8/99

RURAL LIFE CENTRE
Tel: 01252 792300/795571
Our literary heritage - the countryside as seen through the eyes of local writers of the past. 11.00-17.30

Museums

Afternoon Racing

17/8/99
18/8/99

BRIGHTON RACECOURSE
Tel: 01273 603580
Racing from Brighton between 12.00 and 18.00. Admission A£4.00-£12.00 C£Free

Racecourses

Garden Tour

18/8/99
18/8/99

WALMER CASTLE
Tel: 01304 364288
Past, Present and Future with Richard Squires, your guide. A£4.50 C£2.30 Concessions£3.40

Castles

Racing from Sandown Park

20/8/99
21/8/99

SANDOWN PARK RACECOURSE
Tel: 01372 463072
Friday is Solario Stakes and Saturday is Variety Club Day. For further details including race times and ticket prices please contact venue direct

Racecourses

Children's Open Day

21/8/99
21/8/99

MARITIME MUSEUM
Tel: 01843 587765
Fun day for all the family with displays, activities, demonstrations and competitions

Museum- Maritime

Craft Fair

21/8/99
21/8/99

NYMANS GARDEN
Tel: 01444 400321
A selection of hand-made items from craft workers around Sussex and beyond. Lots of unusual gifts, kits for doing your own craftwork at home plus original and creative ideas. Normal admission charges apply.

Gardens

Jousting

21/8/99
22/8/99

BATTLE ABBEY
Tel: 01424 773792
Discover the secrets of the tourney, as the jousting area resounds to the sounds of the battle, clash of steel and thunder of horses hooves as the mighty knights charge at full tilt. A£6.00 C£3.00 Concessions£4.50

Battlefields

Roman Soldiers

21/8/99
22/8/99

DEAL CASTLE
Tel: 01304 372762
Legio XIII. A£3.00 C£1.50 Concessions£2.30

Castles

Theatre

21/8/99
22/8/99

DOVER CASTLE AND SECOND WORLD WAR TUNNELS
Tel: 01304 201628/202754
Drama performed by Crew Of Patches. Normal admission prices apply

Castles

Track Day and F/Ford and Saloons

21/8/99
22/8/99

LYDDEN INTERNATIONAL MOTOR RACING CIRCUIT
Tel: 01304 830557
Track Day on Saturday, F/Ford and Saloons on Sunday. For further details including times and ticket prices please contact venue direct

Motor Racing Circuit

Children's Fun Day

21/8/99
22/8/99

PEVENSEY CASTLE
Tel: 01323 762604
Lots of fun entertainment's for children with various performers. A£3.00 C£1.50 Concessions£2.30

Castles

Medieval Music

21/8/99
22/8/99

ST AUGUSTINE'S ABBEY
Tel: 01227 767345
Enjoy melodies and dance tunes dating back to the 12th century. A£3.00 C£1.50 Concessions£2.30

Abbeys

Teddy Bear Trail

Further more detailed information on the attractions listed can be found in Best Guides *Visitor Attractions* Guide under the classifications shown

21/8/99 – 30/8/99 | PAINSHILL LANDSCAPE GARDEN
Tel: 01932 868113/864674
Search for teddy characters around the magical landscape. Find the hidden answer and answer a competition to win a prize bear. Colouring competition
Gardens

Rolls Royce Rally
22/8/99 – 22/8/99 | BENTLEY WILDFOWL AND MOTOR MUSEUM
Tel: 01825 840573
Please telephone for details
Waterfowl Parks

Midsummer Boss Formula (BRSCC)
22/8/99 – 22/8/99 | BRANDS HATCH
Tel: 0171 344 4444Ticketmaster
British Open Single Seaters (70's/80's Formula 1 Cars), Super Coupé Cup, Ford Si, Ford Saloon Car Challenge, Honda Superchance, Super Road Saloons. Indy Circuit, Grade-C. On the Gate: £10.00-£28.00. In Advance: Non £8.00-£25.00, Club £7.00-£22.00. Two Day Pass: Non £11.00-£30.00, Club £10.00-£27.00. Three Day Pass: Non £32.00, Club £29.00. Qualifying: £5.00-£14.00. C£Free. Programme £Free-£5.00. Seating (BH): £Free-£8.00. South Bank: £2.00-£5.00. Group Tickets: Non £90.00-£95.00, Club £80.00-£85.00. Season Ticket Inc. of Club Membership: £200.00. You can buy your tickets for any of the 1999 events in advance any time up to 4 days before an event and make a saving, Tel: 0870 60 60 611
Motor Racing Circuit

Celebrities
22/8/99 – 22/8/99 | SMALLHYTHE PLACE
Tel: 01580 762234
Sir Donald Sinden welcomes you to Smallhythe Place for this second viewing followed by a chance to hear his anecdotes and reminiscences.
Museums

9th Annual Rare Breeds Show and Country Fair
22/8/99 – 22/8/99 | SOUTH OF ENGLAND RARE BREEDS CENTRE
Tel: 01233 861493
Livestock Show of cattle and sheep. Country craft displays, demonstrations. Arena shows. Pig parade. Birds of Prey. Stationary engines. Kent produce
Farm- Rare Breeds

Afternoon Racing
23/8/99 – 23/8/99 | BRIGHTON RACECOURSE
Tel: 01273 603580
Racing from Brighton between 12.00 and 18.00. Admission A£4.00-£12.00 C£Free
Racecourses

Attics and Gardens of Ightham Mote
23/8/99 – 23/8/99 | IGHTHAM MOTE
Tel: 01732 811145
10.30. Guided tour of the house, with the experts explaining aspects of history and the conservation work, £8.00, must be pre-booked on 01892 891001 or write to The Box Office, The National Trust, Scotney Castle, Lamberhurst, Kent TN3 8JN
Historic Houses

Countryside Capers
25/8/99 – 25/8/99 | SISSINGHURST CASTLE GARDEN
Tel: 01580 712850 infoline
In the grounds surrounding the garden. Time: 14.00. Cost: £3.50.
Gardens

Garden Tour
25/8/99 – 25/8/99 | WALMER CASTLE
Tel: 01304 364288
Past, Present and Future with Richard Squires, your guide. A£4.50 C£2.30 Concessions£3.40
Castles

The European Show Jumping Championship and British Jumping Derby
25/8/99 – 30/8/99 | HICKSTEAD SHOWGROUND (ALL ENGLAND JUMPING COURSE)
Tel: 01273 834315
This year the immensely popular British Jumping Derby meeting takes on even greater dimensions by hosting the European Showjumping Championships. With European team and individual titles to be decided and the challenge of Hickstead's permanent obstacles to be met in the Peugeot Derby, the meeting's capacity crowds can anticipate the season's greatest feast of thrills. Gates Open: 08.30, Closure: 17.30/18.00. Tickets: A£8.00-£20.00 C(5-14)&OAPs£4.00-£15.00 Family Ticket (A2+C2&Car Pass)£20.00-£34.00. Car Parking: £3.00-£4.00
Showgrounds

The Ashton Bequest of Victorian Oil Paintings
25/8/99 – 8/9/99 | TUNBRIDGE WELLS MUSEUM AND ART GALLERY
Tel: 01892 526121/554171
A second showing this year of this popular collection
Museums

Textiles

27/8/99
5/9/99

BENTLEY WILDFOWL AND MOTOR MUSEUM
Tel: 01825 840573
Please telephone for details

Waterfowl Parks

The National Schools & Pony Clubs Showjumping Championships

28/8/99
28/8/99

HICKSTEAD SHOWGROUND (ALL ENGLAND JUMPING COURSE)
Tel: 01273 834315
Please call the venue for details.
Information was not confirmed at time of publication.

Showgrounds

Noel Coward Weekend

28/8/99
29/8/99

WALMER CASTLE
Tel: 01304 364288
Performed by Crew Of Patches. A£5.50
C£3.30 Concessions£4.40

Castles

Herstmonceux Castle Medieval Festival

28/8/99
30/8/99

HERSTMONCEUX CASTLE MEDIEVAL FESTIVAL 1999
Tel: 01273 723249
On August Bank Holiday weekend Herstmonceux Castle near Hailsham in East Sussex will again be host to the Medieval Festival. This Event, now in it's fifth year will be Britain's largest three day celebration of the colourful Middle ages and will attract over five hundred Medievalists from throughout the United Kingdom.

Festivals

The Beauty of the Romans

28/8/99
30/8/99

THE WHITE CLIFFS EXPERIENCE
Tel: 01304 214566/210101
Lotions and potions for a beautiful outlook - Roman style. Also hair and make-up.

Interactive

Robin Hood Craft Fayre

28/8/99
30/8/99

WAKEHURST PLACE
Tel: 01444 894066
A family fun day with crafts and entertainment for all 10.00-18.00. Tickets:
£3.50, £2.50 and £1.00 at the gate.
Contact Four Seasons (Events) Ltd on
01344 874787 for details

Gardens- Botanical

18th Century Gala

28/8/99
31/8/99

FINCHCOCKS
Tel: 01580 211702
Concerts, Dancing, 18th century costume, call for further details

Museum- Music

Autotrader British Touring Car Championship (TOCA)

29/8/99
30/8/99

BRANDS HATCH
Tel: 0171 344 4444Ticketmaster
Touring cars x2, Formula Ford, Ford Fiestas, Formula Renault, Renault Spiders, Formula Vauxhall Junior, Vauxhall Vectras. Indy Circuit, Grade-A. On the Gate: £10.00-£28.00. In Advance: Non £8.00-£25.00, Club £7.00-£22.00. Two Day Pass: Non £11.00-£30.00, Club £10.00-£27.00. Three Day Pass: Non £32.00, Club £29.00. Qualifying: £5.00-£14.00. C£Free. Programme £Free-£5.00. Seating (BH): £Free-£8.00. South Bank: £2.00-£5.00. Group Tickets: Non £90.00-£95.00, Club £80.00-£85.00. Season Ticket Inc. of Club Membership: £200.00. You can buy your tickets for any of the 1999 events in advance any time up to 4 days before an event and make a saving, Tel: 0870 60 60 611

Motor Racing Circuit

Legends of King Arthur

29/8/99
30/8/99

DOVER CASTLE AND SECOND WORLD WAR TUNNELS
Tel: 01304 201628/202754
Labyrinth Productions. Magical stories about King Arthur, with Guinevere, Lancelot, Merlin, the Black Knight and the evil Morgan Le Fay. Normal admission prices apply

Castles

Classic Transport Extravaganza

29/8/99
30/8/99

SOUTH OF ENGLAND RARE BREEDS CENTRE
Tel: 01233 861493
Large show of vehicles, military, commercial, private - with arena events and funfair. Special admission prices: A£4.00
C£2.00 OAPs£3.00

Farm- Rare Breeds

Bank Holiday

30/8/99
30/8/99

EPSOM RACECOURSE
Tel: 01372 726311
Moet and Chandon Silver Magnum National. For further details including race times and ticket prices please contact venue direct

Racecourses

The Great Vine

30/8/99
30/8/99

HAMPTON COURT PALACE AND GARDENS
Tel: 0181 781 9500
Harvesting the grapes from the Great Vine

Royal Palace

BRDA Rallycross

30/8/99	**LYDDEN INTERNATIONAL MOTOR RACING CIRCUIT**
30/8/99	Tel: 01304 830557

For further details including times and ticket prices please contact venue direct

Motor Racing Circuit

August Bank Holiday Event

30/8/99	**MUSEUM OF KENT LIFE**
30/8/99	Tel: 01622 763936

Collectors Roadshow. Bring along an old collectable that you've always wanted to know more about.

Museum- Local History

Garden Tour

30/8/99	**WALMER CASTLE**
30/8/99	Tel: 01304 364288

Past, Present and Future with Richard Squires, your guide. A£4.50 C£2.30 Concessions£3.40

Castles

Mister Scarecrow Family Fun

30/8/99	**GROOMBRIDGE PLACE GARDENS**
31/8/99	Tel: 01892 863999

Gardens

Race Meeting

1/9/99	**BRIGHTON RACECOURSE**
1/9/99	Tel: 01273 603580

Racing from Brighton between 12.00 and18.00. Admission A£4.00-£12.00 C£Free

Racecourses

Racing from Epsom

3/9/99	**EPSOM RACECOURSE**
4/9/99	Tel: 01372 726311

Friday is H&V News Day, Saturday is Grosvenor Casinos September Stakes. For further details including race times and ticket prices please contact venue direct

Racecourses

Britain Prepares for Rationing

3/9/99	**THE WHITE CLIFFS EXPERIENCE**
5/9/99	Tel: 01304 214566/210101

Chamberlain advised that Britain is at war from 3rd September 1939. Visitors are given the opportunity to sample wartime rationing.

Interactive

CAMRA Maidstone Beer Festival

4/9/99	**MUSEUM OF KENT LIFE**
4/9/99	Tel: 01622 763936

Over 100 different real ales on tap, plus music, food and other entertainment.

Museum- Local History

Shepway Wings & Wheels

4/9/99	**SHEPWAY FESTIVAL 1999**
4/9/99	Tel: 01303 852321

Men and machines gather together to provide a showcase of motoring and aviation exhibits, on and off the ground. The day's programme includes a Special 10th Anniversary Festival Meet of historic cars and motorcycles.

Festivals

National 3000 Race Day (BRSCC)

4/9/99	**BRANDS HATCH**
5/9/99	Tel: 0171 344 4444Ticketmaster

National 3000s, Formula Palmer Audi x 2, Classic Touring Cars, Caterham Superlights, Caterham Roadsports, Tomcat/Vento Challenge and Mighty Minis. Indy Circuit, Grade-C. On the Gate: £10.00-£28.00. In Advance: Non £8.00-£25.00, Club £7.00-£22.00. Two Day Pass: Non £11.00-£30.00, Club £10.00-£27.00. Three Day Pass: Non £32.00, Club £29.00. Qualifying: £5.00-£14.00. C£Free. Programme £Free-£5.00. Seating (BH): £Free-£8.00. South Bank: £2.00-£5.00. Group Tickets: Non £90.00-£95.00, Club £80.00-£85.00. Season Ticket Inc. of Club Membership: £200.00. You can buy your tickets for any of the 1999 events in advance any time up to 4 days before an event and make a saving, Tel: 0870 60 60 611

Motor Racing Circuit

History Fair, Riichard the Lionheart Home from the Crusade

4/9/99	**GROOMBRIDGE PLACE GARDENS**
5/9/99	Tel: 01892 863999

Gardens

Hop Picking Festival

4/9/99	**MUSEUM OF KENT LIFE**
5/9/99	Tel: 01622 763936

Help with the harvest. Visitors are invited to join in hand-harvesting the hops, see the oast fired up and working, Pearly Kings and Queens, crafts and much more.

Museum- Local History

Friends of Thomas The Tank Engine

4/9/99	**ROMNEY HYTHE AND DYMCHURCH RAILWAY**
5/9/99	Tel: 01797 362353/363256

Fat Controller, Henry, Gordon, Troublesome Trucks and clowns, Punch and Judy, Magicians etc make a great day of family fun

Railways

Shepway Model Transport Exhibition

| 4/9/99
5/9/99 | **Shepway Festival 1999**
Tel: 01303 852321
A mixed exhibition, displaying the finest
scale models in the country.
Festivals |

Rye Festivall

| 4/9/99
18/9/99 | **The Story of Rye**
Tel: 01797 226696
A literary and theatrical festival
Heritage Centres |

Rye Festival

| 4/9/99
19/9/99 | **Rye Festival 1999**
Tel: 01797 222552
Music for all tastes: classical through to
world music and jazz, blues, folk and the
mighty Wurlitzer. A wealth of literary and
drama events plus visual art exhibitons,
workshops, walks, tours and special
events for children, all providing a stimu-
lating insight into this ancient Cinque
Port.
Festivals |

Arab Horse Racing Society Meeting

| 5/9/99
5/9/99 | **Brighton Racecourse**
Tel: 01273 603580
Racing from Brighton between 12.00
and18.00
Racecourses |

MG Owners Rally 1999

| 5/9/99
5/9/99 | **M G Owners Rally 1999**
Tel: 01323 415442
An event featuring over 300 of the clas-
sic marque including magna's, Tickford's,
MGB's, GT's to the present RVB's. Shows
& displays. Admission Free.
Festivals |

Car Boot Sale

| 5/9/99
5/9/99 | **Rural Life Centre**
Tel: 01252 792300/795571
09.00-13.00, £5.00 per car to sell.
Buyers admitted to sale free
Museums |

Shepway Airshow

| 5/9/99
5/9/99 | **Shepway Festival 1999**
Tel: 01303 852321
The 10th Anniversary of this much
acclaimed Airshow features the cream of
Europe's top display teams and solo per-
formers. Spectacular viewing is guaran-
teed from Folkestone's unique cliff-top
venue.
Festivals |

Garden Tour

| 5/9/99
5/9/99 | **Walmer Castle**
Tel: 01304 364288
Past, Present and Future with Richard
Squires, your guide. A£4.50 C£2.30 |

Concessions£3.40
Castles

A Century for a Century

| 6/9/99
9/10/99 | **Horsham Museum**
Tel: 01403 254959
One hundred images of Horsham over
100 years
Museum- Local History |

Flower Arranging Demonstration

| 8/9/99
8/9/99 | **RHS Garden Wisley**
Tel: 01483 224234
'September splendour' with Anne Blunt.
Time: 10.00-12.30. Cost: members
£18.00, non-members £23.00
Gardens |

Historic Scotney

| 9/9/99
9/9/99 | **Scotney Castle Garden**
Tel: 01892 891081
A tour showing the working history of
the estate, to include the working hop
farm. Commences: 14.00. Two and a half
- three hours. £3.50, must be pre-
booked on 01892 891001 or write to The
Box Office, The National Trust, Scotney
Castle, Lamberhurst, Kent TN3 8JN
Gardens |

Patchwork and Quilting Exhibition

| 10/9/99
12/9/99 | **Hever Castle and Gardens**
Tel: 01732 865224
A magnificent display of patchwork
quilts and wall hangings in the grounds
of Hever Castle. Event included in the
Grounds only ticket
Castles |

Finchcocks Music Festival

| 10/9/99
26/9/99 | **Finchcocks**
Tel: 01580 211702
Each weekend of September there will
be a series of concerts played on period
instruments in the Musical Museum.
Concerts Fri, Sat & Sun 20.00, also 14.30
Sat
Museum- Music |

Championship Bikes (NEW ERA)

| 11/9/99
12/9/99 | **Brands Hatch**
Tel: 0171 344 4444Ticketmaster
All classes of national solo motorcycles
and sidecars. Indy Circuit, Grade-D. On
the Gate: £10.00-£28.00. In Advance:
Non £8.00-£25.00, Club £7.00-£22.00.
Two Day Pass: Non £11.00-£30.00, Club
£10.00-£27.00. Three Day Pass: Non
£32.00, Club £29.00. Qualifying: £5.00-
£14.00. C£Free. Programme £Free-£5.00.
Seating (BH): £Free-£8.00. South Bank:
£2.00-£5.00. Group Tickets: Non £90.00-
£95.00, Club £80.00-£85.00. Season |

Further more detailed information on the attractions listed can be found
in Best Guides *Visitor Attractions* Guide under the classifications shown

Ticket Inc. of Club Membership:
£200.00. You can buy your tickets for
any of the 1999 events in advance any
time up to 4 days before an event and
make a saving, Tel: 0870 60 60 611

Motor Racing Circuit

Medieval Archery

11/9/99 DOVER CASTLE AND SECOND WORLD WAR
TUNNELS

12/9/99 Tel: 01304 201628/202754
Displays of skilled archery, weaponry
and combat, plus shooting of a 14th century ballista. Mounted archer, knight and
have-a-go archery. Normal admission
prices apply

Castles

Reptile Weekend

11/9/99 DRUSILLAS PARK

12/9/99 Tel: 01323 870234
East Sussex Reptile & Amphibian
Society will be in the marquee. Reptiles
on show and special talks given

Zoos

Civil War LH

11/9/99 FARNHAM CASTLE KEEP

12/9/99 Tel: 01252 713393
SK - Col. Sam Jones Greencoats. A£3.00
C£1.50 Concessions£2.30

Castles

**The Great Leeds Castle Balloon and
Vintage Car Weekend**

11/9/99 LEEDS CASTLE

12/9/99 Tel: 01622 765400
The skies above the Castle are filled with
hot air balloons of all shapes and sizes.
Gates open at 06.00 each morning.
Flights leave early morning and early
evening (weather permitting). Tethered
displays, Tiger Moth aerobatics, vintage
car and bicycle parade, exhibitions and
champagne!

Castles

BRSCC F/Ford and Saloons

11/9/99 LYDDEN INTERNATIONAL MOTOR RACING
CIRCUIT

12/9/99 Tel: 01304 830557
For further details including times and
ticket prices please contact venue direct

Motor Racing Circuit

A Life's Work

11/9/99 TUNBRIDGE WELLS MUSEUM AND ART
GALLERY

24/9/99 Tel: 01892 526121/554171
A retrospective exhibition of the topographical work of the late Patricia Helm

Museums

Rare Plants Fair

12/9/99 BORDE HILL GARDEN

12/9/99 Tel: 01444 450326
A feast for plant hunters - specialist
nurseries selling unusual plants

Gardens

Sandown Futurity Stakes

15/9/99 SANDOWN PARK RACECOURSE

15/9/99 Tel: 01372 463072
For further details including race times
and ticket prices please contact venue
direct

Racecourses

**MCN British Superbike Championship
(MCRCB)**

18/9/99 BRANDS HATCH

19/9/99 Tel: 0171 344 4444Ticketmaster
British Superbike x 2, British 125cc,
British 250cc, British 600cc plus support. Grand Prix Circuit, Grade-B. On the
Gate: £10.00-£28.00. In Advance: Non
£8.00-£25.00, Club £7.00-£22.00. Two
Day Pass: Non £11.00-£30.00, Club
£10.00-£27.00. Three Day Pass: Non
£32.00, Club £29.00. Qualifying: £5.00-
£14.00. C£Free. Programme £Free-£5.00.
Seating (BH): £Free-£8.00. South Bank:
£2.00-£5.00. Group Tickets: Non £90.00-
£95.00, Club £80.00-£85.00. Season
Ticket Inc. of Club Membership:
£200.00. You can buy your tickets for
any of the 1999 events in advance any
time up to 4 days before an event and
make a saving, Tel: 0870 60 60 611

Motor Racing Circuit

Country Crafts

18/9/99 PAINSHILL LANDSCAPE GARDEN

19/9/99 Tel: 01932 868113/864674
See our Jacobs sheep up close and
watch their fleeces transformed with
spinning demonstrations. Country craft
stalls and other demonstrations
throughout the weekend

Gardens

Photographic Workshop Weekend

18/9/99 RHS GARDEN WISLEY

19/9/99 Tel: 01483 224234
Intermediate level. This workshop is
aimed at those with some experience of
photography and will cover aspects of
taking photographs of plants and gardens. Time: 10.00-17.00. Cost: members
£70.00, non-members £75.00

Gardens

Fairy Tales

18/9/99 WALMER CASTLE

19/9/99 Tel: 01304 364288
Tales from the Enchanted Garden, Crew

Of Patches. A£4.50 C£2.30
Concessions£3.40

Castles

MG Car Club Autumn Gathering (South East Centre)

19/9/99 GROOMBRIDGE PLACE GARDENS
19/9/99 Tel: 01892 863999

Gardens

SEMSEC F/Ford and Saloons

19/9/99 LYDDEN INTERNATIONAL MOTOR RACING CIRCUIT
19/9/99 Tel: 01304 830557
For further details including times and ticket prices please contact venue direct

Motor Racing Circuit

Steam, Wind & Water

19/9/99 RURAL LIFE CENTRE
19/9/99 Tel: 01252 792300/795571
A day of celebrating restoration of the Centre's wind pump, plus special attractions on the Old Kiln Light Railway. Time: 11.00-18.00. Cost: A£3.00 C£1.50 OAPs£2.50 Group rates 30+ 10% discount

Museums

Attics and Gardens of Ightham Mote

20/9/99 IGHTHAM MOTE
20/9/99 Tel: 01732 811145
10.30. Guided tour of the house, with the experts explaining aspects of history and the conservation work, £8.00, must be pre-booked on 01892 891001 or write to The Box Office, The National Trust, Scotney Castle, Lamberhurst, Kent TN3 8JN

Historic Houses

Demonstration: Lawn Maintenance

22/9/99 RHS GARDEN WISLEY
22/9/99 Tel: 01483 224234
Come and watch Greg Arthur demonstrate how to maintain your lawns and keep them looking beautiful at 14.00. This demonstration will also take place on: Sun 26th at 10.30. Cost: Members £5.00, non-members £10.00. To book tickets send a cheque made payable to RHS, enclosing a SAE and including your membership number (if applicable) and day time telephone number to the Administration Department at RHS Garden, Wisley, Woking GU23 6QB. We are sorry but we cannot accept telephone bookings. Please note that all events may be subject to cancellation due to insufficient ticket sales

Gardens

Botanical Art Weekend

23/9/99 RHS GARDEN WISLEY
26/9/99 Tel: 01483 224234
(Intermediate Course). Pauline Dean is a practising botanical artist working in a freelance capacity for horticultural publications. Pauline began her painting career in 1984 and has won five RHS Gold Medals. She has designed three Winter Flower RHS collectors' plates and the 1996 Chelsea Flower Show Plate. Pauline has tutored the Wisley botanical art courses for eight years. Times: Thur 23rd (18.00-21.00), Fri 24 & Sat 25 (09.00-18.00), Sun 26 (09.00-16.30). Cost: £185.00

Gardens

Woodworking Show

24/9/99 SANDOWN EXHIBITION CENTRE
26/9/99 Tel: 01372 467540
Opening Times 10.30-17.30. Prices to be announced

Exhibition Centres

Tunbridge Ware Symposium

25/9/99 TUNBRIDGE WELLS MUSEUM AND ART GALLERY
25/9/99 Tel: 01892 526121/554171
A day of lectures and discussion on the craft and industry of Tunbridge ware

Museums

SEMSEC/BARC F/Ford and Saloons

25/9/99 LYDDEN INTERNATIONAL MOTOR RACING CIRCUIT
26/9/99 Tel: 01304 830557
For further details including times and ticket prices please contact venue direct

Motor Racing Circuit

Chiddingly Festival 1999

25/9/99 CHIDDINGLY FESTIVAL 1999
3/10/99 Tel: 01825 872338
Chiddingly Festival is a small mixed rural Arts Festival extending over two weeks. Celebrating it's 21st anniversary in 1999, this small rural community, and award winning Festival, have attracted artists from all over the world. Providing a platform where both amateur and professionals can share their talent and abilities the Festival has managed, with the help of its sponsors, to come in within budget each year. Do join us in celebrating the Festival's 21st birthday.

Festivals

Ralph Steadman - Animal Farm

25/9/99 CHERTSEY MUSEUM
20/11/99 Tel: 01932 565764
Steadman's unique illustrations to

George Orwell's cautionary classic. A touring exhibiton from Kent County Council Arts & Libraries

Museum- Local History

Autocavan VW-Audi Swapfest 1999

26/9/99 AUTOCAVAN VW-AUDI SWAPFEST 1999

26/9/99 Tel: 01252 346810

A great day out for all motor enthusiasts! Sunday 26th September sees the return of the hugely successful Autocavan Swapfest. Last year VW enthusiasts flocked from around the country to enjoy the inaugural event and this year's show promises to be even better. Attractions include thousands of new and used parts for sale, Show 'n' Shine, race and custom car display, competitions, a prize draw and on-site refreshments.

Festivals

Championship Cars (BRSCC)

26/9/99 BRANDS HATCH

26/9/99 Tel: 0171 344 4444Ticketmaster

MGFs, Mini Miglias, Mini se7ens, K Sports, Kent Championship Formula Fords. Indy Circuit, Grade-D. On the Gate: £10.00-£28.00. In Advance: Non £8.00-£25.00, Club £7.00-£22.00. Two Day Pass: Non £11.00-£30.00, Club £10.00-£27.00. Three Day Pass: Non £32.00, Club £29.00. Qualifying: £5.00-£14.00. C£Free. Programme £Free-£5.00. Seating (BH): £Free-£8.00. South Bank: £2.00-£5.00. Group Tickets: Non £90.00-£95.00, Club £80.00-£85.00. Season Ticket Inc. of Club Membership: £200.00. You can buy your tickets for any of the 1999 events in advance any time up to 4 days before an event and make a saving, Tel: 0870 60 60 611

Motor Racing Circuit

Mystery n' Intrigue in The Enchanted Forest

26/9/99 GROOMBRIDGE PLACE GARDENS

26/9/99 Tel: 01892 863999

Gardens

Dexter Calf Show

26/9/99 SOUTH OF ENGLAND RARE BREEDS CENTRE

26/9/99 Tel: 01233 861493

Young stock show off these small, hardy cattle

Farm- Rare Breeds

Race Meeting

29/9/99 BRIGHTON RACECOURSE

29/9/99 Tel: 01273 603580

Racing from Brighton between 12.00 and18.00. Admission A£4.00-£12.00 C£Free

Racecourses

Out of the Dust

29/9/99 TUNBRIDGE WELLS MUSEUM AND ART GALLERY

13/10/99 Tel: 01892 526121/554171

Pencil and pen streetscenes, portraits, and topographical views by John Fagg

Museums

Flat Racing

2/10/99 SANDOWN PARK RACECOURSE

2/10/99 Tel: 01372 463072

For further details including race times and ticket prices please contact venue direct

Racecourses

MG Magic (MGCC)

2/10/99 BRANDS HATCH

3/10/99 Tel: 0171 344 4444Ticketmaster

Programme to be confirmed. Indy Circuit, Grade-D. On the Gate: £10.00-£28.00. In Advance: Non £8.00-£25.00, Club £7.00-£22.00. Two Day Pass: Non £11.00-£30.00, Club £10.00-£27.00. Three Day Pass: Non £32.00, Club £29.00. Qualifying: £5.00-£14.00. C£Free. Programme £Free-£5.00. Seating (BH): £Free-£8.00. South Bank: £2.00-£5.00. Group Tickets: Non £90.00-£95.00, Club £80.00-£85.00. Season Ticket Inc. of Club Membership: £200.00. You can buy your tickets for any of the 1999 events in advance any time up to 4 days before an event and make a saving, Tel: 0870 60 60 611

Motor Racing Circuit

The Anglo-Boer War

2/10/99 ROYAL ENGINEERS MUSEUM

2/5/02 Tel: 01634 406397

A changing exhibition to mark the centenary of the Boer War 1899-1902

Museum- Military

Car Boot Sale

3/10/99 RURAL LIFE CENTRE

3/10/99 Tel: 01252 792300/795571

09.00-13.00, £5.00 per car to sell. Buyers admitted to sale free

Museums

Harvest Home

3/10/99 RURAL LIFE CENTRE

3/10/99 Tel: 01252 792300/795571

This traditional ceremony with corn dollies, the produce of the countryside and

A weekly updated selection of UK wide special events can be found on the award winning sites @ www.thisislondon.com *and* www.ukplus.co.uk

a harvest festival in the chapel brings our open season to a close. Time: 11.00-18.00. Cost: A£3.00 C£1.50 OAPs£2.50 Group rates 30+ 10% discount

Museums

Witches, Wizards and Warlocks

3/10/99 THE WHITE CLIFFS EXPERIENCE
31/10/99 Tel: 01304 214566/210101
Holiday fun quiz for the family with a Halloween theme.

Interactive

Race Meeting

4/10/99 BRIGHTON RACECOURSE
4/10/99 Tel: 01273 603580
Racing from Brighton between 12.00 and18.00. Admission A£4.00-£12.00 C£Free

Racecourses

Garden Tour - Fungus Walk

4/10/99 SHEFFIELD PARK GARDEN
4/10/99 Tel: 01825 790231
Led by the gardeners, and limited to 30 per walk, maximum. To see the gardens through the eyes of the people who know it best, book early. Time: 14.30. Cost: £6.00.

Gardens

Autumn Colours

5/10/99 SCOTNEY CASTLE GARDEN
5/10/99 Tel: 01892 891081
14.00. A guided tour of the romantic garden, with its glorious autumn colour, by the Head Gardener, £6.00, must be pre-booked on 01892 891001 or write to The Box Office, The National Trust, Scotney Castle, Lamberhurst, Kent TN3 8JN

Gardens

Walk with the Warden - Secret Sissinghurst

7/10/99 SISSINGHURST CASTLE GARDEN
7/10/99 Tel: 01580 712850 infoline
14.00. A guided tour of the woodland and lakes which surround this famous garden. The garden is not included in the tour, £3.50, must be pre-booked on 01892 891001 or write to The Box Office, The National Trust, Scotney Castle, Lamberhurst, Kent TN3 8JN

Gardens

Cowardy Custard

7/10/99 CLANDON PARK
8/10/99 Tel: 01483 222482
The Life and Music of Noel Coward presented by Quazar Productions, celebrating the centenary year of Noel Coward. Doors open at 19.00 for 19.30 start. Tickets: £10.00 from 01372 451596

Historic Houses & Gardens

Finchcocks Fair

8/10/99 FINCHCOCKS
10/10/99 Tel: 01580 211702
Crafts, gifts in the House, Marquee in the Gardens, call for further details

Museum- Music

Clubmans Bikes (NEW ERA)

9/10/99 BRANDS HATCH
9/10/99 Tel: 0171 344 4444Ticketmaster
All classes of national solo motorcycles and sidecars. Indy Circuit, Grade-D. On the Gate: £10.00-£28.00. In Advance: Non £8.00-£25.00, Club £7.00-£22.00. Two Day Pass: Non £11.00-£30.00, Club £10.00-£27.00. Three Day Pass: Non £32.00, Club £29.00. Qualifying: £5.00-£14.00. C£Free. Programme £Free-£5.00. Seating (BH): £Free-£8.00. South Bank: £2.00-£5.00. Group Tickets: Non £90.00-£95.00, Club £80.00-£85.00. Season Ticket Inc. of Club Membership: £200.00. You can buy your tickets for any of the 1999 events in advance any time up to 4 days before an event and make a saving, Tel: 0870 60 60 611

Motor Racing Circuit

SEMSEC/BARC F/Ford and Saloons

9/10/99 LYDDEN INTERNATIONAL MOTOR RACING CIRCUIT
9/10/99 Tel: 01304 830557
For further details including times and ticket prices please contact venue direct

Motor Racing Circuit

Apple and Cider Festival

9/10/99 MUSEUM OF KENT LIFE
10/10/99 Tel: 01622 763936
A weekend celebrating apples. Taste and buy as many unusual varieties, see an antique apple crusher and press in operation, sample many Kent produced real ciders.

Museum- Local History

Champion of Brands Hatch Finals (BMCRC)

10/10/99 BRANDS HATCH
10/10/99 Tel: 0171 344 4444Ticketmaster
All classes of national solo motorcycles and sidecars. Indy Circuit, Grade-D. On the Gate: £10.00-£28.00. In Advance: Non £8.00-£25.00, Club £7.00-£22.00. Two Day Pass: Non £11.00-£30.00, Club £10.00-£27.00. Three Day Pass: Non £32.00, Club £29.00. Qualifying: £5.00-£14.00. C£Free. Programme £Free-£5.00. Seating (BH): £Free-£8.00. South Bank: £2.00-£5.00. Group Tickets: Non £90.00-

£95.00, Club £80.00-£85.00. Season Ticket Inc. of Club Membership: £200.00. You can buy your tickets for any of the 1999 events in advance any time up to 4 days before an event and make a saving, Tel: 0870 60 60 611

Motor Racing Circuit

The Autumn Hot-Air Balloon Classic
10/10/99 GROOMBRIDGE PLACE GARDENS
10/10/99 Tel: 01892 863999

Gardens

Walk at Wisley
10/10/99 RHS GARDEN WISLEY
10/10/99 Tel: 01483 224234
Let Jim Gardiner walk you around Wisley to see the beautiful autumn colours at 10.30. This walk will also take place on: Wed 13th at 10.30. Cost: Members £5.00, non-members £10.00. To book tickets send a cheque made payable to RHS, enclosing a SAE and including your membership number (if applicable) and day time telephone number to the Administration Department at RHS Garden, Wisley, Woking GU23 6QB. We are sorry but we cannot accept telephone bookings. Please note that all events may be subject to cancellation due to insufficient ticket sales

Gardens

Botanical Art Weekend
14/10/99 RHS GARDEN WISLEY
17/10/99 Tel: 01483 224234
(Advanced Course). Pauline Dean is a practising botanical artist working in a freelance capacity in horticultural publications. Pauline began her painting career in 1984 and has won five RHS Gold Medals. She has designed three Winter Flower RHS collectors' plates and the 1996 Chelsea Flower Show Plate. Pauline has tutored the Wisley botanical art courses for eight years. Times: Thur 14th (18.00-21.00), Fri 15 & Sat 16 (09.00-18.00), Sun 17 (09.00-16.30). Cost: £185.00

Gardens

1066 Living History and Skirmish
16/10/99 BATTLE ABBEY
17/10/99 Tel: 01424 773792
Normans and Saxons, combat and skills-at-arms from the Battle of Hastings, 1066. A£5.00 C£2.50 Concessions£3.80

Battlefields

RSPB - Focus on Wildlife

16/10/99 CLAREMONT LANDSCAPE GARDEN
17/10/99 Tel: 01372 467806
A whole weekend based around the work of the RSPB, call for further information 01372 467806

Gardens

Deal 300
16/10/99 DEAL CASTLE
17/10/99 Tel: 01304 372762
Crew Of Patches. £1.00 per person

Castles

Monson Road Life Workshop
16/10/99 TUNBRIDGE WELLS MUSEUM AND ART GALLERY
30/10/99 Tel: 01892 526121/554171
Drawings and paintings of the human figure from Monson Road artists

Museums

Europcup Formula Ford Final (BRSCC)
17/10/99 BRANDS HATCH
17/10/99 Tel: 0171 344 4444Ticketmaster
Support programme to be confirmed. Indy Circuit, Grade-D. On the Gate: £10.00-£28.00. In Advance: Non £8.00-£25.00, Club £7.00-£22.00. Two Day Pass: Non £11.00-£30.00, Club £10.00-£27.00. Three Day Pass: Non £32.00, Club £29.00. Qualifying: £5.00-£14.00. C£Free. Programme £Free-£5.00. Seating (BH): £Free-£8.00. South Bank: £2.00-£5.00. Group Tickets: Non £90.00-£95.00, Club £80.00-£85.00. Season Ticket Inc. of Club Membership: £200.00. You can buy your tickets for any of the 1999 events in advance any time up to 4 days before an event and make a saving, Tel: 0870 60 60 611

Motor Racing Circuit

Triumph show
17/10/99 SANDOWN EXHIBITION CENTRE
17/10/99 Tel: 01372 467540
Please contact 0121 745 5256 for further information

Exhibition Centres

Garden Tour - Autumn Colour
18/10/99 SHEFFIELD PARK GARDEN
18/10/99 Tel: 01825 790231
Led by the gardeners, and limited to 30 per walk, maximum. To see the gardens through the eyes of the people who know it best, book early. Time: 14.00. Cost: £6.00.

Gardens

Apple Days
18/10/99 RHS GARDEN WISLEY
21/10/99 Tel: 01483 224234
Come and enjoy a programme of demon-

strations, lectures and walks in celebration of Britain's favourite fruit, the versatile apple

Gardens

Autumn Colours
19/10/99 EMMETTS GARDEN
19/10/99 Tel: 01732 868381/750367
14.00. A tour with the Head Gardener, looking at the garden in its "autumn glory", £6.00, must be pre-booked on 01892 891001 or write to The Box Office, The National Trust, Scotney Castle, Lamberhurst, Kent TN3 8JN

Gardens

Flower Arranging Workshop
20/10/99 RHS GARDEN WISLEY
20/10/99 Tel: 01483 224234
'Now what can I do with these' with Monica Trigg. Time: 10.00-15.30. Cost: members £25.00, non-members £30.00

Gardens

Autumn Gold - A Festival of Flowers and Produce
20/10/99 LEEDS CASTLE
24/10/99 Tel: 01622 765400
Glorious displays of flowers and fruits throughout the Castle. (Castle ticket purchase necessary to view the festival)

Castles

Race Meeting
21/10/99 BRIGHTON RACECOURSE
21/10/99 Tel: 01273 603580
Racing from Brighton between 12.00 and 18.00. Admission A£4.00-£12.00 C£Free

Racecourses

Autumn Activity Quest
21/10/99 PAINSHILL LANDSCAPE GARDEN
31/10/99 Tel: 01932 868113/864674
Follow a discovery sheet to find as many different leaf shapes as you can and collect them. Colour your favourite leaf shape to add to the Painshill Tree

Gardens

Formula Ford Festival & World Cup (BRSCC)
23/10/99 BRANDS HATCH
24/10/99 Tel: 0171 344 4444 Ticketmaster
Zetec Formula Ford drivers from championships all over the world compete to win the most coveted title of the year. Indy Circuit, Grade-C. On the Gate: £10.00-£28.00. In Advance: Non £8.00-£25.00, Club £7.00-£22.00. Two Day Pass: Non £11.00-£30.00, Club £10.00-£27.00. Three Day Pass: Non £32.00, Club £29.00. Qualifying: £5.00-£14.00.

C£Free. Programme £Free-£5.00. Seating (BH): £Free-£8.00. South Bank: £2.00-£5.00. Group Tickets: Non £90.00-£95.00, Club £80.00-£85.00. Season Ticket Inc. of Club Membership: £200.00. You can buy your tickets for any of the 1999 events in advance any time up to 4 days before an event and make a saving, Tel: 0870 60 60 611

Motor Racing Circuit

The Living Heritage Craft Fair
23/10/99 GROOMBRIDGE PLACE GARDENS
24/10/99 Tel: 01892 863999

Gardens

Photographic Workshop Weekend
23/10/99 RHS GARDEN WISLEY
24/10/99 Tel: 01483 224234
Beginners level. A workshop aimed at beginners who would enjoy taking photographs of Wisley in the autumn. Time: 10.00-17.00. Cost: members £70.00, non-members £75.00

Gardens

Craft Fayre
23/10/99 SANDOWN EXHIBITION CENTRE
24/10/99 Tel: 01372 467540
Opening Times: 10.00-18.00. Please contact 01344 874787 for further information

Exhibition Centres

Pre Christmas Craft and Gift Fayre
23/10/99 SANDOWN PARK RACECOURSE
24/10/99 Tel: 01372 463072
Speciality quality gifts for the Christmas season including entertainment. Commences 10.00-18.00, tickets: A£3.00-£5.00 C(5-15)£1.00 OAPs£2.00-£3.00. Commences 10.00-18.00

Racecourses

Celebrity Connections Festival 1999
23/10/99 CELEBRITY CONNECTIONS FESTIVAL 1999
29/10/99 Tel: 01843 868718
Celebrity Connections is a mixed Festival with something for everyone. The week applauds famous people who have lived in or visited Broadstairs or St. Peter's, with talks, walks, concerts, film, theatre, music, children's clubs etc. From Annette Mills and Muffin the Mule, to John Buchan or Sir Malcolm Sargeant, many famous people have graced our lovely town, and the Town Council proudly showcases a choice of celebrities each year.

Festivals

Boo's Haunted Cottage

Further more detailed information on the attractions listed can be found in Best Guides *Visitor Attractions* Guide under the classifications shown

23/10/99
31/10/99 DRUSILLAS PARK
Tel: 01323 870234
Winifred Witch will be waiting for those of you who are brave enough to enter
Zoos

Autumn Half Term
23/10/99 HAMPTON COURT PALACE AND GARDENS
31/10/99 Tel: 0181 781 9500
Charles I, captured by Roundhead soldiers in 1647 is imprisoned at Hampton Court Palace. Secretly the King and his supporters plan a bid for freedom, but how can he outwit Cromwell's New Model Army and make his escpae? A series of tours and activities for adults and children recall the dramatic events leading up to the trial and execution of Charles I.
Royal Palace

Ghost and Ghouls Week
23/10/99 PARADISE FAMILY LEISURE PARK
31/10/99 Tel: 01273 616006
Everything spooky, ghoulie and scary! Great fun for all
Theme Parks

Half Term
23/10/99 SOUTH OF ENGLAND RARE BREEDS CENTRE
31/10/99 Tel: 01233 861493
Half Term - Half Price offer. Children's competition. Dates to be confirmed
Farm- Rare Breeds

BRDA Rallycross
24/10/99 LYDDEN INTERNATIONAL MOTOR RACING CIRCUIT
24/10/99 Tel: 01304 830557
For further details including times and ticket prices please contact venue direct
Motor Racing Circuit

Designer Clothes Sale
25/10/99 CLANDON PARK
25/10/99 Tel: 01483 222482
Time: 10.30-20.00. Please call for further information
Historic Houses & Gardens

Half Term Fun - Nature Week
25/10/99 LEEDS CASTLE
29/10/99 Tel: 01622 765400
Nature fun for children with plenty of activities to keep little hands busy. Please telephone for details
Castles

Demonstration: Soil Management for Gardeners
27/10/99 RHS GARDEN WISLEY
27/10/99 Tel: 01483 224234
Come and watch Jon Pickering demonstrate soil management for all you budding gardeners at 14.00. Cost: Members £5.00, non-members £10.00. To book tickets send a cheque made payable to RHS, enclosing a SAE and including your membership number (if applicable) and day time telephone number to the Administration Department at RHS Garden, Wisley, Woking GU23 6QB. We are sorry but we cannot accept telephone bookings. Please note that all events may be subject to cancellation due to insufficient ticket sales
Gardens

Horsham Town Centre Festival 1999
28/10/99 HORSHAM TOWN CENTRE FESTIVAL 1999
30/10/99 Tel: 01403 215265
Three days of fantastic festival fun. Live music, dance spectacular, Battle of the Bands, Street entertainment and old time stree fayre with steam engines, carousel, big wheel and chair-o-planes.
Festivals

Mathilda the Forgetful Witche
28/10/99 DEAL CASTLE
31/10/99 Tel: 01304 372762
Told by Crew Of Patches. A£3.00 C£1.50 Concessions£2.30
Castles

Race Meeting
29/10/99 BRIGHTON RACECOURSE
29/10/99 Tel: 01273 603580
Racing from Brighton between 12.00 and18.00. Admission A£4.00-£12.00 C£Free
Racecourses

Grass Track
30/10/99 LYDDEN INTERNATIONAL MOTOR RACING CIRCUIT
30/10/99 Tel: 01304 830557
For further details including times and ticket prices please contact venue direct
Motor Racing Circuit

Hallowe'en Adventure in The Enchanted Forest
31/10/99 GROOMBRIDGE PLACE GARDENS
31/10/99 Tel: 01892 863999

Gardens

Lantern Lit Tours
1/11/99 HAMPTON COURT PALACE AND GARDENS
31/12/99 Tel: 0181 781 9500
Exact dates to be confirmed. Join a costumed guide and discover the palace as the Tudors would have seen it - by lantern light
Royal Palace

Everything but the Kitchen Sink: The Handbag and its Contents

2/11/99
31/12/99 HORSHAM MUSEUM

Tel: 01403 254959

To include gloves, powder compacts, lipsticks, cigarette lighters, mirrors and the smoking gun for the femme fatale. This exhibition will be held in the Georgian Room

Museum- Local History

Walk at Wisley

3/11/99
3/11/99 RHS GARDEN WISLEY

Tel: 01483 224234

Come and see the charm of Wisley under glass with Nick Morgan at 10.30. Cost: Members £5.00, non-members £10.00. To book tickets send a cheque made payable to RHS, enclosing a SAE and including your membership number (if applicable) and day time telephone number to the Administration Department at RHS Garden, Wisley, Woking GU23 6QB. We are sorry but we cannot accept telephone bookings. Please note that all events may be subject to cancellation due to insufficient ticket sales

Gardens

Vision of the Future

5/11/99
6/12/99 TUNBRIDGE WELLS MUSEUM AND ART GALLERY

Tel: 01892 526121/554171

Exploring Agenda 21's aims to promote a brighter future enviomentally, economically, and socially

Museums

Fireworks '99

6/11/99
6/11/99 GROOMBRIDGE PLACE GARDENS

Tel: 01892 863999

Gardens

Grand Firework Spectacular

6/11/99
6/11/99 LEEDS CASTLE

Tel: 01622 765400

Spectacular and safe, the biggest display in the South East is reflected in the Castle Moat. Gates open at 17.00. Entertainment from 18.00. Display starts at 19.30. Prices to be confirmed. Advance ticket sales from Box Office. Tickets also available on the night

Castles

Bonfire Night Family Party

6/11/99
6/11/99 MUSEUM OF KENT LIFE

Tel: 01622 763936

A traditional bonfire night. Bring along a carved pumpkin for the competition,

enjoy a roaring bonfire and spectacular firework display. Food and drink available.

Museum- Local History

Jet Stationery Day

6/11/99
6/11/99 SANDOWN PARK RACECOURSE

Tel: 01372 463072

For further details including race times and ticket prices please contact venue direct

Racecourses

Winter Series - Class of 2000 (BARC)

7/11/99
7/11/99 BRANDS HATCH

Tel: 0171 344 4444Ticketmaster

Programme to be confirmed. Indy Circuit, Grade-D. On the Gate: £10.00-£28.00. In Advance: Non £8.00-£25.00, Club £7.00-£22.00. Two Day Pass: Non £11.00-£30.00, Club £10.00-£27.00. Three Day Pass: Non £32.00, Club £29.00. Qualifying: £5.00-£14.00. C£Free. Programme £Free-£5.00. Seating (BH): £Free-£8.00. South Bank: £2.00-£5.00. Group Tickets: Non £90.00-£95.00, Club £80.00-£85.00. Season Ticket Inc. of Club Membership: £200.00. You can buy your tickets for any of the 1999 events in advance any time up to 4 days before an event and make a saving, Tel: 0870 60 60 611

Motor Racing Circuit

Old Time Music Hall

12/11/99
12/11/99 CLANDON PARK

Tel: 01483 222482

They're back! Following their sell-out triumph last year, the Old Tyme Music Hall returns with an all-new programme to enthral and entertain. Your master of ceremonies will introduce a perfect procession of parlour performers - all assembled for your delectation and delight. Come suitably attired and will full lungs to join in the evening's fun. Tickets from £15.00 from 01372 451596

Historic Houses & Gardens

Loseley Christmas Fair

12/11/99
14/11/99 LOSELEY PARK

Tel: 01483 304440

Stalls selling fine wines and food, silver, silks and paintings

Historic Houses & Gardens

Artist in Residence

12/11/99
1/1/00 PALLANT HOUSE GALLERY

Tel: 01243 774557

plus Kathie Kollwitz: Artist of the People. Details of residency to be confirmed. A National Touring Exhibition of the graphic work of Kathe Kollwitz, communicating powerful social messages about capitalism and war

Art Galleries

Toy Collectors' Fair

13/11/99 SANDOWN EXHIBITION CENTRE

13/11/99 Tel: 01372 467540

10.30-16.00. A£3.50 C£1.00 OAPs£3.00. Please contact 01604 770025 for further information

Exhibition Centres

Santa's Here

13/11/99 PARADISE FAMILY LEISURE PARK

31/12/99 Tel: 01273 616006

He's here, he's jolly, he's got his big sack. Come and visit santa during the Christmas Holidays, call for details

Theme Parks

Winter Series - Class of 2000 (BARC)

14/11/99 BRANDS HATCH

14/11/99 Tel: 0171 344 4444Ticketmaster

Programme to be confirmed. Indy Circuit, Grade-D. On the Gate: £10.00-£28.00. In Advance: Non £8.00-£25.00, Club £7.00-£22.00. Two Day Pass: Non £11.00-£30.00, Club £10.00-£27.00. Three Day Pass: Non £32.00, Club £29.00. Qualifying: £5.00-£14.00. C£Free. Programme £Free-£5.00. Seating (BH): £Free-£8.00. South Bank: £2.00-£5.00. Group Tickets: Non £90.00-£95.00, Club £80.00-£85.00. Season Ticket Inc. of Club Membership: £200.00. You can buy your tickets for any of the 1999 events in advance any time up to 4 days before an event and make a saving, Tel: 0870 60 60 611

Motor Racing Circuit

Santa's Christmas Cottage

20/11/99 DRUSILLAS PARK

21/11/99 Tel: 01323 870234

Come and visit Santa and his elves at work. Also to be held on: 27-28 Nov, 4-5 & 11-23 Dec

Zoos

Christmas Gift Market

20/11/99 SOUTH OF ENGLAND RARE BREEDS CENTRE

21/11/99 Tel: 01233 861493

Indoor Craft stalls and Outdoor Winter Market. Hot chestnuts, mulled wine. Dutch organ music, Handbells on Sunday. Tombola, raffle. £0.50 entry, farm admission not necessary. Santa's Stable - extra charge to meet Santa and receive a gift

Farm- Rare Breeds

Christmas at Wisley

20/11/99 RHS GARDEN WISLEY

28/11/99 Tel: 01483 224234

With plants and gardens as the starting point, Christmas at Wisley sets the scene for this enchanting time of year. There will be a series of illustrated lectures, demonstrations and workshops inspired by the festive season which will give participants new skills and ideas to take away with them

Gardens

Winter Championship Finals (BRSCC)

21/11/99 BRANDS HATCH

21/11/99 Tel: 0171 344 4444Ticketmaster

Winter GT, Winter Saloons, Winter Formula Ford, Winter Formula First, Winter Minis, Winter Fiestas. Indy Circuit, Grade-D. On the Gate: £10.00-£28.00. In Advance: Non £8.00-£25.00, Club £7.00-£22.00. Two Day Pass: Non £11.00-£30.00, Club £10.00-£27.00. Three Day Pass: Non £32.00, Club £29.00. Qualifying: £5.00-£14.00. C£Free. Programme £Free-£5.00. Seating (BH): £Free-£8.00. South Bank: £2.00-£5.00. Group Tickets: Non £90.00-£95.00, Club £80.00-£85.00. Season Ticket Inc. of Club Membership: £200.00. You can buy your tickets for any of the 1999 events in advance any time up to 4 days before an event and make a saving, Tel: 0870 60 60 611

Motor Racing Circuit

Flower Arranging Demonstration

24/11/99 RHS GARDEN WISLEY

24/11/99 Tel: 01483 224234

'Flowers for the festive season' with Robert Barlow. Time: 10.00-12.30. Cost: members £18.00, non-members £23.00

Gardens

Demonstration: Festive Plants

24/11/99 RHS GARDEN WISLEY

24/11/99 Tel: 01483 224234

Come and watch Nick Morgan demonstrate arrangements for festive plants at 10.30. Cost: Members £5.00, non-members £10.00. To book tickets send a cheque made payable to RHS, enclosing a SAE and including your membership number (if applicable) and day time telephone number to the Administration Department at RHS Garden, Wisley, Woking GU23 6QB. We are sorry but we cannot accept telephone bookings. Please note that all events may be subject to cancellation due to insufficient

	ticket sales
	Gardens

Live Crafts

26/11/99	LOSELEY PARK
28/11/99	Tel: 01483 304440

Stalls selling and demonstrating British Arts and Crafts

Historic Houses & Gardens

Military Book Fair

28/11/99	ROYAL ENGINEERS MUSEUM
28/11/99	Tel: 01634 406397

Up to 50 dealers with books, medals and militaria

Museum- Military

Cool Yule Mini Show and Spares

28/11/99	SANDOWN EXHIBITION CENTRE
28/11/99	Tel: 01372 467540

Opening times and prices to be announced. Please call for further information

Exhibition Centres

Antiques Fair

30/11/99	SANDOWN EXHIBITION CENTRE
30/11/99	Tel: 01372 467540

Opening times 14.00, Prices A£3.00

Exhibition Centres

Antiques Fair

30/11/99	SANDOWN EXHIBITION CENTRE
30/11/99	Tel: 01372 467540

Admission 14.00-16.30. Please contact 0171 249 4050 for further information

Exhibition Centres

Tudor Christmas Celebrations

1/12/99	HAMPTON COURT PALACE AND GARDENS
31/12/99	Tel: 0181 781 9500

Exact dates to be confirmed. Re-enactment of a Tudor style Christmas, with feasting and merriment

Royal Palace

Racing from Sandown Park

3/12/99	SANDOWN PARK RACECOURSE
4/12/99	Tel: 01372 463072

Friday is Bovis Crowngap Winter Hurdle, Saturday is William Hill Handicap and Mitsubishi Shogun Tingle Creek Trophy. For further details including race times and ticket prices please contact race venue direct

Racecourses

1940s Christmas

4/12/99	THE WHITE CLIFFS EXPERIENCE
5/12/99	Tel: 01304 214566/210101

Prepare for a 1940s Christmas making Christmas cards and decorating during wartime rationing.

Interactive

Music & Readings

10/12/99	HATCHLANDS PARK
11/12/99	Tel: 01483 222482

Music and readings for the Christmas season with Ayres and Graces. Please call for further information

Historic Houses

Santa Specials

11/12/99	RURAL LIFE CENTRE
12/12/99	Tel: 01252 792300/795571

Ride on the Old Kiln Light Railway and visit Santa in his grotto. Send an SAE for booking form. Time: 11.00-17.00. Cost: A£2.00 C£5.00

Museums

2000 Interpreted

11/12/99	TUNBRIDGE WELLS MUSEUM AND ART GALLERY
11/1/00	Tel: 01892 526121/554171

Artists and craftsmen selected by the Museum Curator explore the millennium theme

Museums

Christmas Carols

12/12/99	KNOLE
12/12/99	Tel: 01732 450608 infoline

15.00. Sing along with the Kemsing Singers, £10.00, must be pre-booked on 01892 891001 or write to The Box Office, The National Trust, Scotney Castle, Lamberhurst, Kent TN3 8JN

Country Estates

Carols in the Barn

12/12/99	SOUTH OF ENGLAND RARE BREEDS CENTRE
19/12/99	Tel: 01233 861493

Traditional music in a traditional setting. Wrap up warmly and make this your start of the Christmas season. Mulled wine, mince pies in The Granary. Farm admission not necessary. A charity collection is taken

Farm- Rare Breeds

Christmas at the Castle

13/12/99	LEEDS CASTLE
24/12/99	Tel: 01622 765400

Festive fun and merriment- no extra charge

Castles

Carols at Clandon

17/12/99	CLANDON PARK
18/12/99	Tel: 01483 222482

Two family carol concerts with a surprise appearance from Santa (each child receives a small gift), tickets include biscuits, squash and tea in interval. Time: 15.00 each day

Historic Houses & Gardens

Further more detailed information on the attractions listed can be found in Best Guides *Visitor Attractions* Guide under the classifications shown

Santa Specials

18/12/99 RURAL LIFE CENTRE
19/12/99 Tel: 01252 792300/795571

Ride on the Old Kiln Light Railway and visit Santa in his grotto. Send an SAE for booking form. Time: 11.00-17.00. Cost: A£2.00 C£5.00

Museums

Christmas Carols

19/12/99 KNOLE
19/12/99 Tel: 01732 450608 infoline

15.00. Sing along with the Kemsing Singers, £10.00, must be pre-booked on 01892 891001 or write to The Box Office, The National Trust, Scotney Castle, Lamberhurst, Kent TN3 8JN

Country Estates

What Does Santa Do After Christmas?

27/12/99 DRUSILLAS PARK
9/1/00 Tel: 01323 870234

Come along and you might just see Santa relaxing in his secret Drusillas hide away

Zoos

Biggin Hill International Air Fair 2000

3/6/00 BIGGIN HILL INTERNATIONAL AIR FAIR 1999
4/6/00 Tel: 01959 540959

World famous 7 hour international flying display with top teams and pilots. Unique mixture of modern, military, vintage and civilian aircraft. Very popular with families as well as enthusiasts. Disabled facilities and privileged viewing area. Times and prices to be confirmed

Airports

Kent County Show 2000

13/7/00 KENT COUNTY SHOWGROUND
15/7/00 Tel: 01622 630975

Kent's premier agricultural show featuring over 500 trade stands, livestock, equestrian events, demonstrations and other related attractions. Cheaper if pre paid 01622 630975

Showgrounds

Detling Transport and Country Festival 2000

12/8/00 KENT COUNTY SHOWGROUND
13/8/00 Tel: 01622 630975

Steam engines, vintage and classic tractors, motorcycles, military and commercial vehicles, buses and coaches. Rural crafts. Call for further information (dates to be confirmed)

Showgrounds

Battle of Britain Open Day

17/9/00 BIGGIN HILL INTERNATIONAL AIR FAIR 1999
Tel: 01959 540959

Special event held at Biggin Hill to celebrate the 60th Anniversary of the Battle of Britain, more information available by calling 01959 572277

Airports

A weekly updated selection of UK wide special events can be found on the award winning sites @ www.thisislondon.com *and* www.ukplus.co.uk

Southern England

Including:
- *Channel Islands*
- *Oxfordshire*
- *Buckinghamshire*
- *Berkshire*
- *Hampshire*
- *East Dorset*

Channel Islands

Recent Acquisitions

2/3/99 ASHMOLEAN MUSEUM OF ART AND ARCHAEOLOGY
30/5/99 Tel: 01865 278000 / 278015
The Department of Western Art, Eldon Gallery. British Drawings and Watercolours of the 18th and 19th Centuries. The collection of British watercolours has had a number of notable additions in recent months, particularly from the bequest of Arthur David Murray, which includes works by J.M.W. Turner, Bonington and Lear.

Museum- Art

Buddhist Art from Tibet

3/3/99 ASHMOLEAN MUSEUM OF ART AND ARCHAEOLOGY
2/5/99 Tel: 01865 278000 / 278015
The Department of Eastern Art, Eric North Room. The E.M. Scratton Collection. Mr E.M. Scratton's extensive collection of Tibetan Buddhist art, formed in the 1950's and 60's, has been on loan to the Museum for many years but for reasons of space only small parts of it have been displayed at one time. The collection is notable for its rich and diverse representation of the arts of thangka (scroll) painting, bronze-casting, metalwork and ivory and bone carving.

Museum- Art

Friends of Thomas

5/3/99 DIDCOT RAILWAY CENTRE
7/3/99 Tel: 01235 817200
See 'Thomas', the children's favourite steam engine and his Great Western friends

Railways Steam/Light

Junior Workshop: Seed Sowing & Soft Cuttings

13/3/99 ENGLEFIELD HOUSE GARDEN
13/3/99 Tel: 0118 930 2221
Children will learn how to sow a tray of seeds, pick our seedlings and take soft tip cuttings. Suitable for ages 6-12 years. Time: 10.00-12.00. Cost: £7.50, includes a tray of pricked out seedlings and 12 potted rooted cuttings from our specialist range of bedding and basket plants.

Gardens

Adult Workshop: Seed Sowing and Soft Tip Cuttings

20/3/99 ENGLEFIELD HOUSE GARDEN
20/3/99 Tel: 0118 930 2221
You will learn how to sow a tray of seeds, pick our seedlings and take soft tip cuttings. Time: 10.00-12.00. Cost: £10.00, includes a tray of pricked out seedlings and 12 potted rooted cuttings from our specialist range of bedding and basket plants.

Gardens

Centenary of the Sinking of the 'Stella'

24/3/99 GUERNSEY MUSEUM AND ART GALLERY
4/7/99 Tel: 01481 726518
A commemoration of the Channel Islands worst maritime tragedy

Museum- Local History

The Stella - the Titanic of the Channel Islands

24/3/99 GUERNSEY MUSEUM AND ART GALLERY
24/10/99 Tel: 01481 726518
This centenary exhibition explores the history of this disaster with artefacts recovered from the wreck and on special days storytellers recount the passengers harrowing tales. Accompanying video and film

Museum- Local History

Guided Tour: Spring in the Park

25/3/99 STAUNTON COUNTRY PARK
25/3/99 Tel: 01705 453405
A guided walk to view spring wildlife, flora and fauna within the country park. Meet at the main car park at 10.30. Suitable for accompanied children. Normal admission rates apply.

Country Parks

40th Anniversary Celebrations

26/3/99 JERSEY ZOOLOGICAL PARK
26/3/99 Tel: 01534 864666
Also the opening of First Impressions. BBC Natural Photography Exhibtion, various special events planned for the whole day and running into the weekend, come along and join in the fun!

Zoos

Bird Show

27/3/99 WATERFOWL SANCTUARY AND CHILDREN'S FARM
27/3/99 Tel: 01608 730252
By the Banbury Bird Keepers Club to celebrate the 10th anniversary of the sanctuary. Starts at 14.00

Waterfowl Parks

Holiday Activities for Children

27/3/99 STAUNTON COUNTRY PARK
11/4/99 Tel: 01705 453405
Twice weekly (demand depending) from 10.00-13.30. Nature walk (2 miles - 3 hours) to identify flowers, insects and wildlife. Conservation games and activi-

ties. Meet at Shop entrance. Minimum of 6 to maximum of 12 children per day. Advance bookings only. Suitable for accompanied children 6-10 years. £2.00 per child

Country Parks

Stella Anniversary Day
30/3/99　GUERNSEY MUSEUM AND ART GALLERY
30/3/99　Tel: 01481 726518
Please call for further information

Museum- Local History

From Cozens to Palmer
30/3/99　ASHMOLEAN MUSEUM OF ART AND
27/6/99　ARCHAEOLOGY
Tel: 01865 278000 / 278015
The Department of Western Art, McAlpine Gallery: 30th March 27th June 1999 From Cozens to Palmer: Exhibition Watercolours from the Permanent Collections An exhibition to mark the completion of a programme of conservation and remounting of the outsize watercolours in the Museum's collections. It also draws attention to the importance of the "exhibition watercolour" as a feature of 19th Century British art at a time when watercolourists were attempting to rival contemporary painters in oil by creating large, ambitious, eye-catching works for exhibition.

Museum- Art

Gosport Easter Festival '99
1/4/99　GOSPORT EASTER FESTIVAL '99
5/4/99　Tel: 01329 231942 Box Office
The Fareham & Gosport Easter Folk Festival is one of the biggest folk festivals in Britain. Over 300 top musicians from across the globe will take part in a series of concerts, workshops, dance displays and sessions. This indoor festival is highly regarded for the high quality of entertainment and the warm, friendly family atmosphere. Artists booked to appear include Fairport Convention, The Dylan Project, Oyster Band, Frances Black (Ireland), Edward II, Show of Hands and many top-class performers from abroad. Prices: Day Tickets: £6.00 Evening Tickets: £10.00-£12.50 Weekend Season Tickets: £45.00 C(under 16)£Free

Festivals

Giant Cluedo Game
1/4/99　APPULDURCOMBE HOUSE
10/4/99　Tel: 01983 852484
Giant Cluedo Game. 10.00-16.00. Normal

prices plus £1.00 per detective

Historical Remains

Changing of the Guard
1/4/99　WINDSOR CASTLE
30/6/99　Tel: 01753 831118
The ceremony takes place Mon-Sat at 11.00

Castles

Kingston Lacy Easter Egg Hunt
2/4/99　KINGSTON LACY
2/4/99　Tel: 01202 883402
Have fun hunting for those hidden eggs, £1.00 per child. 10.00-12.00

Historic Houses

Easter Eggs-tra!
2/4/99　MARWELL ZOOLOGICAL PARK
5/4/99　Tel: 01962 777407
Easter egg hunt. Egg decorating. Make your own Easter Bonnet or enter the egg and spoon race

Zoos

Great Easter Egg Hunt
3/4/99　LA HOUGUE BIE MUSEUM
3/4/99　Tel: 01534 853823
Sponsored by checkers Superstore a family day with plenty of activities and games for all ages.

Museums

Musical Entertainment in the Manor House
3/4/99　COGGES MANOR FARM MUSEUM
5/4/99　Tel: 01993 772602
Parlour Singers on Saturday, Morris Dancers on Sunday and Baking in the Bread Oven on Monday. For further details including times and prices please call venue direct

Museum- Farms

Easter Egg Hunt
4/4/99　APPULDURCOMBE HOUSE
4/4/99　Tel: 01983 852484
Over 3,000 easter eggs to be found in 11 acres of grounds at Appuldrucombe House, 10.00-16.00

Historical Remains

Swallow's & Amazons Easter Trail
4/4/99　BROWNSEA ISLAND
4/4/99　Tel: 01202 707744
Fancy dress. Normal admission charges apply. 10.30-14.30.

Scenic

A Stour Valley Ramble
4/4/99　KINGSTON LACY
4/4/99　Tel: 01202 883402
Ramble starts at 10.00. A£2.50 C£1.00. Call 01202 882705 for meeting point

Further more detailed information on the attractions listed can be found in Best Guides *Visitor Attractions* Guide under the classifications shown

Historic Houses

Easter Fun Day

4/4/99
4/4/99

STAUNTON COUNTRY PARK

Tel: 01705 453405

Fun on the Farm for everyone, including children's entertainer, animal activities plus games, quizzes and competitions. Normal admission rates apply. 10.00-17.00.

Country Parks

Easter Egg Hunt

4/4/99
4/4/99

THE VYNE

Tel: 01256 881337

Fun for all the children as they search around the lovely grounds of The Vyne for clues that will lead to a chocolate prize for every participant. 11.00-14.00

Historic Houses

Easter Fun Weekend

4/4/99
5/4/99

BUCKINGHAMSHIRE RAILWAY CENTRE

Tel: 01296 655450

The circus comes to the railway. See jugglers, fire eaters, clowns and stilt walkers performing all around the station

Museum- Transport

Viking Battle

4/4/99
5/4/99

PORTCHESTER CASTLE

Tel: 01705 378291

The Vikings. 11th century encampment, living history, from 12.00, displays and a savage battle between Saxons and Vikings. A£4.00 C£2.00 Concessions£3.00

Castles

Easter Egg Specials

4/4/99
5/4/99

SWANAGE RAILWAY

Tel: 01929 425800

A free hand-made Swanage Railway Easter Egg for every child on the train this weekend

Railways

Traditional Food Fair

4/4/99

5/4/99

WEALD AND DOWNLAND OPEN AIR MUSEUM

Tel: 01243 811348

Further details available on 01243 811348

Museum- Social History

Easter Egg Trail

5/4/99
5/4/99

ASHRIDGE ESTATE

Tel: 01442 851227

Family fun hunting for Easter Eggs on the Spring Wildlife Trail. Time: 12.00-16.00. All tickets £1.50, pay on the day at the Ashridge Monument Visitor Centre

Country Estates

Boatjumble

11/4/99
11/4/99

BEAULIEU

Tel: 01590 612345

The event will boast nearly 1,000 stalls stacked high with every conceivable item connected with boating, and is Europe's biggest sale of boating bits. Starts at 10.00. Booking Office: 01590 612345

Museums

Patchwork and Quilting Demonstration

11/4/99
11/4/99

COGGES MANOR FARM MUSEUM

Tel: 01993 772602

For further details including times and prices please call venue direct

Museum- Farms

Garden Tour

11/4/99
11/4/99

OSBORNE HOUSE

Tel: 01983 200022

A seasonal garden tour of Osborne Garden with the Head Gardener. A£3.50 C£1.80 Concessions£2.60

Historic Houses & Gardens

Decoupage Day - Belinda Ballantine

15/4/99
15/4/99

ENGLEFIELD HOUSE GARDEN

Tel: 0118 930 2221

Belinda will have a selection of letter racks and hankie boxes on which to practise the art of decoupage. There will also be a choice from a selection of black and white prints, Belinda's own hand painted and printed designs and a wide range of borders, and flower designs for decoration. All materials and tools will be provided. Time: 10.00-16.00. Cost: £50.00, includes coffee and lunch.

Gardens

Organic Gardening Talks

18/4/99
18/4/99

COGGES MANOR FARM MUSEUM

Tel: 01993 772602

Talks at 13.30 and 15.00, for further details please call venue direct

Museum- Farms

Anna Gaskell

18/4/99
27/6/99

MUSEUM OF MODERN ART OXFORD

Tel: 01865 722733

An American born artist shows photographs in her first solo museum show

Museum- Art

Open Day

21/4/99
21/4/99

EXBURY GARDENS

Tel: 01703 891203

All proceeds will go to the British Red Cross on this special Open Day

Gardens

Up With The Lark
24/4/99 KINGSTON LACY
24/4/99 Tel: 01202 883402
05.30 start, A£8.00, C£7.00 to include a
cooked breakfast. Please call 01202
883402 for meeting point
Historic Houses

Wycombe Arts Festival
24/4/99 WYCOMBE ARTS FESTIVAL
22/5/99 Tel: 01494 523697
Held at various venues in and around
High Wycombe. Includes concerts, organ
recitals, variety showtime, poetry readings, theatre, open art exhibition, festival antiques fair, photography exhibition, comedy, toy theatre (puppets),
musicals (Hello Dolly), jazz café, children's choir and Mayor-making ceremony. Time: various. Ticket Prices:
Admission free but some events £3.00-
£10.00. Tickets from Festival Box Office:
01494 512000
Festivals

Guided Tours of the Manor House
25/4/99 COGGES MANOR FARM MUSEUM
25/4/99 Tel: 01993 772602
Tours at 14.00 and 15.30. For further
details please call venue direct

Museum- Farms
Reading CAMRA Beer Festival
29/4/99 READING CAMRA BEER FESTIVAL
2/5/99 Tel: 0118 959 0407
Real ales to sample and enjoy. Outside
events include belly dancers, local
bands, Morris men and on Friday
evening an R & B band. Bouncy castles
and children's areas during lunchtime
sessions. Held in various venues:
Hobgoblin Public House, Broad Street;
Hop Leaf, Southampton Street; Horse
and Jockey, Castle Street; Bottoms Up.
Children are not allowed into the marquee. Ticket Prices: A£2.00-£4.00. Free
admission Sunday. Tickets available by
post, please tel: 0118 959 0407. Time:
Thur, Fri & Sat: 16.30-23.00, also Fri &
Sat: 11.00-15.00, Sun: 12.00-16.00
Festivals

Jersey Jazz Festival
30/4/99 JERSEY JAZZ FESTIVAL 1999
3/5/99 Tel: 01534 873767
Held at various venues around St. Helier.
US Tenor Sax star Harry Allen, a tribute
to Burt Bacharach starring Claire Martin
- a recent winner of the UK Jazz Singer
Award and "Salute to Sinatra" starring

Louis Hoover and Pete Cater Big Band.
Browse around the VAT free shops of St
Helier. Explore the varied list of attrac-
tions on the beautiful and varied list of
attractions on the beautiful island of
Jersey. Ticket Prices: Afternoon: £Free.
Evening: various. 3 day pass: £39.00.
Lunch: £13.00. Tickets available from
Arts Centre Box Office: 01534 873767
Festivals

Paintings from our Collection
30/4/99 GUERNSEY MUSEUM AND ART GALLERY
31/7/99 Tel: 01481 726518
An exhibition of paintings from Guernsey
Museum's Art collection displayed in the
Rona Cole Art Gallery
Museum- Local History

Beale Park Model Boat Festival
1/5/99 BEALE PARK
2/5/99 Tel: 0118 984 5172
Widely considered by modellers to be
the best model boat show in the country,
this festival makes great use of the variety of waters at Beale Park, includes
demonstrations, competitions and many
trade stands. Normal admission prices
(inclusive of park), 10.00-18.00 daily
Wildlife Parks

Children's Weekend
1/5/99 APPULDURCOMBE HOUSE
3/5/99 Tel: 01983 852484
Each day the 'Great Smarty Hunt,' side
shows, special entertainment, music
workshop, teddy bears picnic (inside if
wet)!
Historical Remains

Oxfordshire Craft Fair
1/5/99 BLENHEIM PALACE
3/5/99 Tel: 01993 811325

Stately Homes
Mapole Dancing
1/5/99 COGGES MANOR FARM MUSEUM
3/5/99 Tel: 01993 772602
Events planned include Maypole
Dancing on Saturday, Folk Singing on
Sunday, Baking in the Bread Oven and
Corn Dolly Making on Monday. For fur-
ther details including times and prices
please call venue direct

Museum- Farms
**Hampshire's Beautiful Garden and
Craft Festival**
1/5/99 EXBURY GARDENS
3/5/99 Tel: 01703 891203
A superb Festival for craft and garden

lovers alike, come along, there's plenty to see and do over this three day event
Gardens

Poole Cockle Festival
1/5/99
3/5/99
POOLE COCKLE FESTIVAL
Tel: 01202 682247
The festival is taking place in and around the licensed premises of Poole Old Town. The seaport of Poole is the largest natural harbour in the world, boasting some 32 pubs, clubs and wine bars all within a 20 minute circular walk! with music (folk, blues, rock and country) in old Town pubs. Civil War displays, Witness displays, diving demonstrations using hard hat equipment, maypole and folk dancing and children's entertainment. Time: 09.00-24.00. Prices: Admission Free except for occasional guest acts
Festivals

Environmental Festival
1/5/99
15/5/99
HAMPTONNE COUNTRY LIFE MUSEUM
Tel: 01534 863955
Sponsored by Jersey Electricity - two weeks free access to the rural heart of Jersey.
Museum- Country

Occupation Memories
1/5/99
31/5/99
CASTLE CORNET
Tel: 01481 721657
Local residents share their memories of the German occupation of Guernsey with opportunities to hear Guernsey French and taste wartime recipes such as parsnip coffee!
Castles

Babes in the Park
2/5/99
2/5/99
KINGSTON LACY
Tel: 01202 883402
Performances at 10.00, 11.30, 13.30, 15.00 and 16.30. Please call 01202 882705 for further information
Historic Houses

Variety Club Dog Show
2/5/99
3/5/99
BROADLANDS
Tel: 01794 505010
Please call for further information
Historic Houses

Miniature Railway Gala
2/5/99
3/5/99
BUCKINGHAMSHIRE RAILWAY CENTRE
Tel: 01296 655450
Take a free ride on the newly extended miniature railway. Children's magic show and fairground
Museum- Transport

The Siege of 1643

2/5/99
3/5/99
CORFE CASTLE
Tel: 01929 481294
The English Civil War Society aim to accurately portray the events of and leading up to the first siege of Corfe Castle. Normal admission charges apply
Castles

Bird of Prey Demonstrations
2/5/99
3/5/99
COTSWOLD WILDLIFE PARK
Tel: 01993 823006
See the Birds of Prey in flight. Approximately 13.00 and 15.30 weather permitting
Zoos

Medieval Re-enactment
2/5/99
3/5/99
PORTCHESTER CASTLE
Tel: 01705 378291
Preparing for War, 1483 by The White Company. A£4.00 C£2.00 Concessions£3.00
Castles

May Fayre and Country Fair
3/5/99
3/5/99
MAY FAYRE AND COUNTRY FAIR 1999
Tel: 01344 423147
Venue: Wokingham Town Centre. The Town Centre is closed but some shops open and old pubs put on special food for example, Pig Road and Grills. Town Hall will be used for art exhibition and flower display. Street market, maypole, Scottish and morris dancing, youth jazz service scene, jugglers, mime artists, funfair, country fair, farm animals, craft demo, steam train, games etc. Time: 10.00-17.00. Admission Free
Festivals

Birds of Prey Demonstrations
4/5/99
5/4/99
COTSWOLD WILDLIFE PARK
Tel: 01993 823006
See the Birds of Prey in flight. Approximately 13.00 and 15.30 weather permitting
Zoos

Charity Open Day
5/5/99
5/5/99
EXBURY GARDENS
Tel: 01703 891203
The garden is open today to assist the great work carried out by the National Gardens Scheme
Gardens

Workshop: Introduction to Woodland Birds
8/5/99
8/5/99
ASHRIDGE ESTATE
Tel: 01442 851227
Identification, song, behaviour and ecology of birds. Bring a packed lunch. Time: 08.30-15.00. Cost: £20.00

Country Estates

Hanging Basket Workshop

8/5/99 ENGLEFIELD HOUSE GARDEN

8/5/99 Tel: 0118 930 2221

Following a demonstration on the principles and methods of making and maintaining a basket, you will have the opportunity to choose and plant your own. This will be left with us to grow and will be ready for collection in 1 month's time. Further demonstrations will be given on how to create simple baskets using imagination and flair. Time: 10.00-12.00. Cost: £18.45, includes 12" basket. £23.00, includes 23" basket.

Gardens

The Saville Garden May Plant Fair

8/5/99 THE SAVILL GARDEN - WINDSOR GREAT PARK

8/5/99 Tel: 01753 847518

Many small specialist nurseries offering a wide range of unusual plants

Gardens

Spring Autojumble and Classic Car Show

8/5/99 BEAULIEU

9/5/99 Tel: 01590 612345

500 stalls plus over 200 classic cars to make this a great day out for anyone. The stalls display everything for the car enthusiast from car manuals to car models. Start: 10.00

Museums

Hurdle Maker

8/5/99 COGGES MANOR FARM MUSEUM

9/5/99 Tel: 01993 772602

Activities include Hurdle Maker and on Sunday the Poultry Club Annual show. For further details including times and prices please call venue direct

Museum- Farms

Secrets of the Woodland

8/5/99 KINGSTON LACY

9/5/99 Tel: 01202 883402

An insight into the habitat of the Woodland. For times and prices please call 01202 882705

Historic Houses

Newbury Spring Festival

8/5/99 NEWBURY SPRING FESTIVAL

22/5/99 Tel: 01635 528766

Orchestral concerts, recitals, chamber music, jazz, film, children's events. Art exhibitions and lectures. Events held in and around Newbury including Parish churches, county houses and hotels. For

further information please contact Bronwen Sutton, tel 01635 32421. Some venues have limited wheelchair access, please telephone first. Ticket Prices: Various. Tickets from The Administrator 01635 528766

Festivals

Garden Tour

9/5/99 OSBORNE HOUSE

9/5/99 Tel: 01983 200022

A seasonal garden tour of Osborne Garden with the Head Gardener. A£3.50 C£1.80 Concessions£2.60

Historic Houses & Gardens

Hanging Basket Workshop

15/5/99 ENGLEFIELD HOUSE GARDEN

15/5/99 Tel: 0118 930 2221

Following a demonstration on the principles and methods of making and maintaining a basket, you will have the opportunity to choose and plant your own. This will be left with us to grow and will be ready for collection in 1 month's time. Further demonstrations will be given on how to create simple baskets using imagination and flair. Time: 10.00-12.00. Cost: £18.45, includes 12" basket. £23.00, includes 23" basket.

Gardens

Havant Arts Festival Finale

15/5/99 STAUNTON COUNTRY PARK

15/5/99 Tel: 01705 453405

Climax of local community's "Nine days in May," Finale to a week of art activities within the borough. Large bonfire and fireworks planned. Situated in Leigh Park Gardens. Admission Free. Suitable for all the family. From 12.00 and into the evening.

Country Parks

Joint Transport Weekend with Oxford Bus Museum

15/5/99 COGGES MANOR FARM MUSEUM

16/5/99 Tel: 01993 772602

FREE bus service between museum sites. For further details including times and prices please call venue direct

Museum- Farms

Country Gardening Festival

15/5/99 LULWORTH CASTLE

16/5/99 Tel: 01929 400352

Castles

Garden Show

15/5/99 OSBORNE HOUSE

16/5/99 Tel: 01983 200022

Further more detailed information on the attractions listed can be found in Best Guides *Visitor Attractions* Guide under the classifications shown

The Isle of Wight County Press Garden Show with leading UK nurseries. A&Concessions£5.00 C£Free

Historic Houses & Gardens

Out of the Wood Show
15/5/99 WEALD AND DOWNLAND OPEN AIR MUSEUM
16/5/99 Tel: 01243 811348
Further details available on 01243 811348

Museum- Social History

Jersey International Food Festival 1999
15/5/99 JERSEY INTERNATIONAL FOOD FESTIVAL 1999
23/5/99 Tel: 01534 500700
Various venues in St. Helier. A beach barbeque at Grouville, a wine harvesters supper, an evening of wines and foods of the world at the Jersey Pottery, a breakfast competition and a 'pudding evening' are just some of the events taking place during the festival. A week long celebration featuring events in unusual settings. This annual gastronomic event gives the visitors the chance to taste the very best local produce and sample the cooking skills of top Jersey Chefs. 'Fusion Food' is the integration of Eastern and Western culinary styles and has become a trend in our ever shrinking culinary world. The 1999 Festival hopes to play host to this and the organisers hope to invite chefs from England, Germany and possibly Hong Kong to demonstrate their skills in this particular style. The highlight of this week has become a major event in the Jersey Calendar. Around 10,000 people seize the opportunity to sample food and wine in an informal atmosphere which is enhanced by musicians and street entertainers. The 1999 Fair will be staged at St Helier at the start of the Festival and will coincide with the official opening on Sunday 16th May.

Festivals

Museums Week
15/5/99 THE KING'S ROYAL HUSSARS MUSEUM IN WINCHESTER
23/5/99 Tel: 01962 828539
Extra displays and access to areas not usually open to the public

Museum- Regimental

Museums Week
15/5/99 CASTLE CORNET
24/5/99 Tel: 01481 721657

Tickets are 2 for the price of 1 to celebrate Museums Week. Local residents share memories of the German occupation in the Amherst Room

Castles

Museums Week
15/5/99 FORT GREY SHIPWRECK MUSEUM
24/5/99 Tel: 01481 726518
Tickets are 2 for the price of 1 to celebrate Museums Week and Fort Grey is brought to life with nineteenth century characters and a variety of performances

Museum- Ships/Boat

Museums Week
15/5/99 GUERNSEY MUSEUM AND ART GALLERY
24/5/99 Tel: 01481 726518
Tickets are 2 for the price of 1 to celebrate Museums Week and storytellers bring to life the centenary exhibition of "Stella - the Titanic of the Channel Islands"

Museum- Local History

Porsche Club Owners Day
16/5/99 BASILDON PARK
16/5/99 Tel: 0118 984 3040
Thames and Chilterns owners club meet to talk Porsche and display their cars including 30 competition cars. Open to all visitors at no extra charge. Time: 11.00-17.00.

Historic Houses

Brian Moses - Writer's Trail
16/5/99 FORT GREY SHIPWRECK MUSEUM
16/5/99 Tel: 01481 726518
Children's poet Brian Moses brings his own style of poetry to Fort Grey

Museum- Ships/Boat

Spring Plant Fair
16/5/99 KINGSTON LACY
16/5/99 Tel: 01202 883402
For further details including times and prices please call venue direct

Historic Houses

Spring Plant Fair
16/5/99 THE VYNE
16/5/99 Tel: 01256 881337
Wide range of plants and garden related items for sale. Proceeds towards continued restoration of the Gardens at The Vyne. Normal admission arrangements. Starting at 11.00

Historic Houses

Goodwood Meetings
18/5/99 GOODWOOD RACECOURSE
20/5/99 Tel: 01243 755022
The three day May meeting features the Derby and Oaks Trials with pointers

towards the winners of the year's Classic races. Racing from 14.10 approximately

Racecourses

Sheep Shearing

23/5/99 COGGES MANOR FARM MUSEUM
23/5/99 Tel: 01993 772602
Shearing our flock of Oxford Down and Cotswold Sheep. For further details including times and prices please call venue direct

Museum- Farms

In the Kitchen Garden - Jez Taylor

25/5/99 ENGLEFIELD HOUSE GARDEN
25/5/99 Tel: 0118 930 2221
Jez will take you on a walk through his organic vegetable smallholding and offer advice and information on all-year-round production. The evening will finish with a visit to the walled kitchen garden at Englefield. Numbers limited. Please meet in Englefield Garden Centre Car Park. Time: 19.00-21.00. Cost: £7.50.

Gardens

The Exbury Gardens Event

28/5/99 EXBURY GARDENS
31/5/99 Tel: 01703 891203
Arts and Craft, Food and Wine Festival. A fun day for all the family with much to see and do

Gardens

Lively Entertainment at the Manor

29/5/99 COGGES MANOR FARM MUSEUM
31/5/99 Tel: 01993 772602
Activities include Spinning demonstration on Saturday, Solstice Bards with storytelling, poetry and song on Sunday and Morris Dancing on Monday. For further details including times and prices please call venue direct

Museum- Farms

Holiday Activities for Children

29/5/99 STAUNTON COUNTRY PARK
6/6/99 Tel: 01705 453405
Twice weekly (demand depending) from 10.00-13.30. Nature walk (2 miles - 3 hours) to identify flowers, insects and wildlife. Conservation games and activities. Meet at Shop entrance. Minimum of 6 to maximum of 12 children per day. Advance bookings only. Suitable for accompanied children 6-10 years. £2.00 per child

Country Parks

Workshop: General Wildlife

30/5/99 ASHRIDGE ESTATE
30/5/99 Tel: 01442 851227
Focusing on the Glis Glis (doormouse)

and other animals. Time: 14.30-17.00. Cost: £15.00

Country Estates

Countryside Day

30/5/99 STAUNTON COUNTRY PARK
30/5/99 Tel: 01705 453405
Countryside activities and crafts. Learn how to tow a tractor. Environmental and conservational games and activities. Suitable for all the family. Normal admission rates apply. 10.00-17.00

Country Parks

Country Fair

30/5/99 BROADLANDS
31/5/99 Tel: 01794 505010
Spectacular arena entertainments such as falconry, gun dogs, shire horses and sheepdog handling, children's entertainment and a large quality craft show

Historic Houses

Birds of Prey Demonstrations

30/5/99 COTSWOLD WILDLIFE PARK
31/5/99 Tel: 01993 823006
See the Birds of Prey in flight. Approximately 13.00 and 15.30 weather permitting

Zoos

Ballads & Bayonets

30/5/99 FORT BROCKHURST
31/5/99 Tel: 01705 581059
Lively music, British redcoats, drill, musket firing, encampment and a fascinating comparison between a soldier of 1778 and 1998. A£3.00 C£1.50 Concessions£2.30

Forts

Legends of King Arthur

30/5/99 PORTCHESTER CASTLE
31/5/99 Tel: 01705 378291
Labyrinth Productions. Magical stories about King Arthur, with Guinevere, Lancelot, Merlin, the Black Knight and the evil Morgan Le Fay. A£3.50 C£1.80 Concessions£2.60

Castles

Neolithic Week

30/5/99 LA HOUGUE BIE MUSEUM
5/6/99 Tel: 01534 853823
This will give young and old alike the chance to help create a dug-out canoe, watch skilled craftsmen build a curragh, and learn about life in prehistoric times

Museums

A Week of Monkey Business

30/5/99 MARWELL ZOOLOGICAL PARK
6/6/99 Tel: 01962 777407
Primate awareness, monkey mask-mak-

ing, monkey games, monkey fund-raising, and monkey talks

Zoos

Bus Rally
31/5/99 BUCKINGHAMSHIRE RAILWAY CENTRE
31/5/99 Tel: 01296 655450
Up to 25 veteran buses will visit for a spectacular rally. Children's magic show and fairground organ

Museum- Transport

Corfe Castle Village May Fair
31/5/99 CORFE CASTLE
31/5/99 Tel: 01929 481294
Come along and enjoy all the fun of the May Fair. No extra charge

Castles

Summer Exhibition
31/5/99 STANLEY SPENCER GALLERY
31/10/99 Tel: 01628 520890 (info line)
Self-portraits and portraits by Sir Stanley Spencer

Art Galleries

New Exhibition
1/6/99 ROYAL ELECTRICAL AND MECHANICAL ENGINEERS (REME) MUSEUM OF TECHNOLOGY
31/7/99 Tel: 0118 976 3567
The new Vehicle Display Hall opens this year (above dates are provisional), further information will be made available from beginning of June 99 onwards, please call for fuller details

Museum- Military

Badger Brewery Raceday
2/6/99 GOODWOOD RACECOURSE
2/6/99 Tel: 01243 755022
Great racing, great value and great fun is on offer at Goodwood today with the first race at 14.10

Racecourses

Festival Art Exhibition
4/6/99 BISHOP WALTHAM FESTIVAL 1999
13/4/99 Tel: 01489 893197
In the Palace Farm House. Open 10.00-18.00, except Sun day 13 10.00-16.00. Admission £Free

Festivals

Evening Race Meeting
4/6/99 GOODWOOD RACECOURSE
4/6/99 Tel: 01243 755022
As well as racing there are lots of extras including live music and barbecues - come and party the night away! First race at18.30

Racecourses

Fireworks Fantasia with English Sinfonia

MOTTISFONT ABBEY GARDEN
4/6/99
4/6/99 Tel: 01794 340757
Works from Handel, Mozart, Vivaldi and others in the wonderful setting of Mottisfont Abbey with spectacular fireworks finale. Time: 19.30. Cost: 15.00

Historic Houses & Gardens

Country Time at The Vyne
4/6/99 THE VYNE
4/6/99 Tel: 01256 881337
A new event! The Vyne goes Country & Western. Gates open at 18.30 for picnics for 19.30 start. Cost: £8.00

Historic Houses

Children's Craft Activity
4/6/99 COGGES MANOR FARM MUSEUM
6/6/99 Tel: 01993 772602
Activities include Children's Craft Activity (pre-booking essential) on Friday, book binding and repair advice with Bookbinder on Saturday and Coloured Sheep Breeders Wool and Fleece event on Sunday. For further details including times and prices please call venue direct

Museum- Farms

Festival Week
4/6/99 BISHOP'S WALTHAM PALACE
13/6/99 Tel: 01489 892460
It's festival week at Bishop's Waltham with various performers. A£2.00 C£1.00 Concessions£1.50

Historical Remains

Children's Open-Air Theatre
5/6/99 BASILDON PARK
5/6/99 Tel: 0118 984 3040
'Alice in Wonderland' presented by Troubador Theatre. A new and imaginative production of Lewis Carroll's classic suitable for boys and girls of all ages. Gates open at 18.00, theatre starts 18.30. Price: A£8.00 C£6.00 Family Ticket £28.00.

Historic Houses

Folk Night with Shebeen
5/6/99 BISHOP WALTHAM FESTIVAL 1999
5/6/99 Tel: 01489 893197
In Palace grounds at 19.30 tickets all £2.50. Booking Office opens 1 March 1999, Access/Visa sales via Bath Travel Tel: 01489 896428 Fax: 01489 896160

Festivals

La Traviata
5/6/99 MOTTISFONT ABBEY GARDEN
5/6/99 Tel: 01794 340757
Music at Winchester brings this wonderful work by Verdi to the picturesque setting of Mottisfont Abbey. Gates open at

	18.30 for picnics, performance starts at 19.30. Cost: £20.00

Historic Houses & Gardens

Jazz at The Vyne

5/6/99 · THE VYNE

5/6/99 · Tel: 01256 881337

What better setting than on the lawns between a fine Tudor house and the lake to swing to two very well-respected jazz bands The Mike Daniels Delta Jazzmen & The Alan Gresty/Brian White Ragtimers Jazz Band. As ever, a popular event - so book early. Time: 19.30. Cost: 10.00

Historic Houses

Exploring Space

5/6/99 · WYCOMBE LOCAL HISTORY AND CHAIR MUSEUM

17/7/99 · Tel: 01494 421895

Touring exhibition using interactive displays to explore astronomy

Museum- Local History

Tea and Trumpets

6/6/99 · APPULDURCOMBE HOUSE

6/6/99 · Tel: 01983 852484

Bring a chair or rug. Teas available but you're welcome to bring a picnic and enjoy a varied programme of popular music with Island Bands

Historical Remains

1940's

6/6/99 · BARTON MANOR GARDENS AND VINEYARDS

6/6/99 · Tel: 01983 292835

A chance to reflect on the grace and elegance of the 1940's. A special day to meet staff and volunteers of the Hospice and to enjoy the tranquility of the grounds. Light refreshments will be on sale. The shop will be open to sell goods, jewellery, toiletries, Barton Manor wine and Island gifts, etc. in support of the Earl Mountbatten Hospice and each day will have a theme. Dressing up is encouraged but optional.

Historic Houses & Gardens

Gilbert and Sullivan

6/6/99 · BISHOP WALTHAM FESTIVAL 1999

6/6/99 · Tel: 01489 893197

In Palace grounds, a variety of musical greats from Gilbert and Sullivan from 19.00. Tickets all £3.50. Booking Office opens 1 March 1999, Access/Visa sales via Bath Travel Tel: 01489 896428 Fax: 01489 896160

Festivals

Snake Awareness Days

6/6/99 · COTSWOLD WILDLIFE PARK

6/6/99 · Tel: 01993 823006

Come and meet a snake and receive expert advice from their keeper 14.00-17.00 approximately weather permitting

Zoos

Family Event - Alice

6/6/99 · HUGHENDEN MANOR

6/6/99 · Tel: 01494 532580

This exciting new production of Alice is full of fun and adventures in Wonderland. Bring a picnic and a rug. Gates open at 17.30 for 18.00 start. A£8.00 C£5.00 Family Ticket £26.00

Historic Houses

Heavy Horse Summer Spectacular

6/6/99 · WEALD AND DOWNLAND OPEN AIR MUSEUM

6/6/99 · Tel: 01243 811348

Further details available on 01243 811348

Museum- Social History

Bournemouth Sinfonietta Concert

7/7/99 · BISHOP WALTHAM FESTIVAL 1999

7/7/99 · Tel: 01489 893197

Venue: palace Grounds commences 20.00. Conductor: Richard Studt; Horn Soloist: Richard Berry. Planned programme includes: Mozart Symphony No. 33 in Bb, K319, Mozart Horn Concerto No. 1 in D, Larsson Cencertino for Horn, Strauss R Sextet from Capriccio, Haydn Symphony No. 59 in A (Feuer). Fireworks Finale. Grounds open 17.30. Tickets: A£13.00 C&OAPs£10.50, earlybirds A£10.50 C&OAPs£8.00. 10% discount for groups of 10+. Chairs booked in advance £2.00. Booking Office opens 1 March 1999, Access/Visa sales via Bath Travel Tel: 01489 896428 Fax: 01489 896160

Festivals

Jazz at the Palace

8/6/99 · BISHOP WALTHAM FESTIVAL 1999

8/6/99 · Tel: 01489 893197

In Palace grounds. Commences 19.00. Tickets all £3.50. Booking Office opens 1 March 1999, Access/Visa sales via Bath Travel Tel: 01489 896428 Fax: 01489 896160

Festivals

In the Kitchen Garden - Jez Taylor

8/6/99 · ENGLEFIELD HOUSE GARDEN

8/6/99 · Tel: 0118 930 2221

Jez will take you on a walk through his organic vegetable smallholding and offer advice and information on all-year-round production. The evening will finish with a visit to the walled kitchen garden at

Englefield. Numbers limited. Please meet in Englefield Garden Centre Car Park. Time: 19.00-21.00. Cost: £7.50.

Gardens

Winchester Young Voices
11/6/99 Bishop Waltham Festival 1999
11/6/99 Tel: 01489 893197
Concert in St Peter's Church. Tickets A£4.00 C&OAPs£3.00. Booking Office opens 1 March 1999, Access/Visa sales via Bath Travel Tel: 01489 896428 Fax: 01489 896160

Festivals

Evening Race Meeting
11/6/99 Goodwood Racecourse
11/6/99 Tel: 01243 755022
As well as racing there are lots of extras including live music and barbecues - come and party the night away! First race at18.30

Racecourses

Thomas the Tank Engine Day
11/6/99 Buckinghamshire Railway Centre
13/6/99 Tel: 01296 655450
Meet the Fat Controller and take a ride with Thomas. Children's magic show, Punch and Judy and "Thomas" video theatre

Museum- Transport

Wimborne Folk Festival 1999
11/6/99 Wimborne Folk Festival 1999
13/6/99 Tel: 01202 743465
Traditional Music and Dance.including over 70 Dance teams from U K and Europe. Processions. Huge Craft Market. Concerts. Ceilidh's. Workshops. Childrens Entertainment including Street Theatre, Face Painting and Musical Workshops. Start Procession 20.00 11th June-till late. Main Festival Procession 14.30 12th June-till late. Market 13th June 10.30-17.30. Concert till late.

Festivals

Last Night of the Proms with Firework Finale
12/6/99 Blenheim Palace
12/6/99 Tel: 01993 811325
Proms Concerts have now established themselves firmly in the outdoor concert calendar, giving many of the audience a chance to return to a favourite venue for one final concert before the end of the summer. After last year's brilliant success, Jayne Carpenter once again leads the audience in the singing of 'Jerusalem' and 'Rule Britannia'. Rousing, singing, waving flags, terrific

atmosphere and stunning fireworks all add up to a breathtaking finale, as the orchestra plays 'Land of Hope and Glory'. Proms concerts tend to sell out early: please reserve tickets in good time, especially group bookings. Tickets A£16.50 C(5-18)£9.00, these are 1998 prices an increase may be applicable. Ticket Hotline: 01625 56 00 00

Stately Homes

Queen's Birthday Celebration
12/6/99 Castle Cornet
12/6/99 Tel: 01481 721657
All the Guernsey Museum Service sites are open free today and a 21 gun salute will be fired from Castle Cornet accompanied by the Guernsey Concert Band

Castles

The Queen's Birthday Celebration
12/6/99 Fort Grey Shipwreck Museum
12/6/99 Tel: 01481 726518
All Guernsey Museums Service sites offer free entry today and Fort Grey will come alive with visitors from the nineteenth century

Museum- Ships/Boat

The Queen's Birthday Celebration
12/6/99 Guernsey Museum and Art Gallery
12/6/99 Tel: 01481 726518
All Guernsey Museum Service sites offer free entry today and Guernsey Museum is visited by characters from Victorian times

Museum- Local History

In Celebration of Wildflowers
12/6/99 Kingston Lacy
12/6/99 Tel: 01202 883402
Admire the beauty of our wildflowers.19.30 start A£1.50 C£1.00

Historic Houses

Open Air Concert
12/6/99 Lulworth Castle
12/6/99 Tel: 01929 400352
Bournemouth Orchestras lead open air concert and fireworks

Castles

The Taming of the Shrew
12/6/99 Bishop Waltham Festival 1999
13/6/99 Tel: 01489 893197
Sat 12 June performance at 19.00, Sunday 13 June performances at 15.00 and 19.00. Tickets A£6.50 C&OAPs£5.50, early birds ticket A5.00 C&OAPs£4.00. Booking Office opens 1 March 1999, Access/Visa sales via Bath Travel Tel: 01489 896428 Fax: 01489 896160

Chair Caning and Rush Seating Demonstration

12/6/99
13/6/99
COGGES MANOR FARM MUSEUM
Tel: 01993 772602
For further details including times and prices please call venue direct
Museum- Farms

Living Heritage Craft Show

12/6/99
13/6/99
HUGHENDEN MANOR
Tel: 01494 532580
Nationally selected artists, designers and craftsmen will be exhibiting, demonstrating and selling their crafts and skills. See Britain's only mobile Glass Blowing team at work, wander around the demonstration areas or just relax in the catering marquee listening to gentle strains of jazz. Time: 10.00-18.00.
A£3.00 C£1.50 OAPs£2.50 NT members 10% discount
Historic Houses

Country Craft Fair

13/6/99
13/6/99
APPULDURCOMBE HOUSE
Tel: 01983 852484
Lots of wonderful stalls with wonderful gifts
Historical Remains

Garden Tour

13/6/99
13/6/99
OSBORNE HOUSE
Tel: 01983 200022
A seasonal garden tour of Osborne Garden with the Head Gardener. A£3.50 C£1.80 Concessions£2.60
Historic Houses & Gardens

Echoes from the Past "Tudor Re-enactment"

14/6/99
24/6/99
CASTLE CORNET
Tel: 01481 721657
Characters including 'Adele de la Mare', the Cook and 'Thomas Knowles' the Cartographer evoke the everyday life of Castle Cornet in early Tudor Times
Castles

The Total Exclipse of the Sun Exhibition

14/6/99
19/9/99
GUERNSEY MUSEUM AND ART GALLERY
Tel: 01481 726518
Working title only. This summer sees the total eclipse of the sun, our exhibition will help you understand how and why
Museum- Local History

Classical Candlelight Concert - 'Arietta'

15/6/99
15/6/99
BASILDON PARK
Tel: 0118 984 3040
The first in our series of three candle-light concerts this year. 'Arietta', a flute and harp duo play 'in the round' in the Garden room. The programme will include Bizet, CPE Bach and Faure. Followed by a 2 course dinner also by candlelight. Black tie please. Doors open at 18.30, concert starts at 19.00. Price: £40.00, limited tickets so booking advisable.
Historic Houses

Royal Ascot Race Meeting

15/6/99
18/6/99
ASCOT RACECOURSE
Tel: 01344 622211
Royal Ascot in June is an international occasion of Fashion and Style and the four days of racing are the finest anywhere in the world. Britain's most popular race meeting welcomes over 230,000 people annually. The highlight each day is the Royal Procession at 14.00. There is nothing quite like it in the social calendar, an atmospheric cocktail of priceless horses and the most extraordinary fashion parade in the world. Please book early to avoid disappointment. Please telephone 01344 878555 for a hospitality brochure
Racecourses

A Taste of Tudor

18/6/99
18/6/99
CASTLE CORNET
Tel: 01481 721657
An evening of music, dance and sumptuous tasting in the Castle, whilest "Echoes from the Past" recreate early Tudor life around you
Castles

Evening Racing

18/6/99
18/6/99
GOODWOOD RACECOURSE
Tel: 01243 755022
As well as racing there are lots of extras including live music and barbecues - come and party the night away! First race at18.40
Racecourses

Goodwood Festival of Speed

18/6/99
20/6/99
GOODWOOD HOUSE
Tel: 01243 755000
This three day Festival is the ultimate garden party for motor racing enthusiasts. Friday 18th is Enthusiasts Day, Saturday 19th is Family Day and Sunday 20th is billed as The Greatest Show on Earth! Entry is by advanced ticket only.
Historic Houses

Goodwood Festival Of Speed

18/6/99
20/6/99
GOODWOOD MOTOR RACING CIRCUIT
Tel: 01243 755055

Further more detailed information on the attractions listed can be found in Best Guides *Visitor Attractions* Guide under the classifications shown

There is no other event in the world like the Goodwood Festival of Speed. It is quite simply, the greatest gathering of motor racing machinery on the planet, attracting stars and cars to Goodwood Park from every corner of motor racing's Hall of Fame. The Festival is much more than an historic motor sport event - it is a happening, a high point of the English sporting summer and a social occasion not to be missed. This is the closest you'll get to the stunning speed of Formula 1 and the super stars who race them. This year the Festival celebrates a millennium of horsepower and traces the story of the car from Year One to F1.

Festivals

Midsummer Festival of Traditional Crafts

19/6/99 CORFE CASTLE
20/6/99 Tel: 01929 481294
Experience the atmosphere of a working Castle and see Dorset craftsmen demonstrating their skills. No extra charge.

Castles

Gardening on the Wild Side

19/6/99 MARWELL ZOOLOGICAL PARK
20/6/99 Tel: 01962 777407
Advice on how to make your garden a wildlife haven. BBC Radio Solent's popular 'Topsoil' programme will be broadcast from the park on Sunday

Zoos

Celebrating Ancient Trees

20/6/99 ASHRIDGE ESTATE
20/6/99 Tel: 01442 851227
Two workshops led by leading environmental artist Creeping Toad. Workshop A: Sculpture, lanterns. Workshop B: Forest puppets. Time: 11.00-13.00 & 14.00-16.00. Suitable for ages 7+. One session £5.00, both sessions £8.00, accompanying adults £Free

Country Estates

The Tree Cathedral Annual Service

20/6/99 ASHRIDGE ESTATE
20/6/99 Tel: 01442 851227
Ecumenical service for all the family at the Whipsnade Tree Cathedral. Bring a rug or seating. Time: 15.00-16.00. Donation

Country Estates

Corn Dolly Making

20/6/99 COGGES MANOR FARM MUSEUM
20/6/99 Tel: 01993 772602
For further details including times and prices please call venue direct

Museum- Farms

Triumph Roadster Club Rally

20/6/99 COTSWOLD WILDLIFE PARK
20/6/99 Tel: 01993 823006
Rally starts at 10.00

Zoos

Echoes from the Past

20/6/99 FORT GREY SHIPWRECK MUSEUM
20/6/99 Tel: 01481 726518
Nineteenth century characters recount the loss of HMS Boreas on the Hanois Reef in 1807 with the loss of 127 men. Also on 24 June

Museum- Ships/Boat

Open Air Theatre Festival

23/6/99 CLIVEDEN
4/7/99   Tel: 01628 605069
The celebrated Cliveden Festival features two of Shakespeare's best-loved comedies. Following last year's success the Maidenhead Players present A Midsummer Night's Dream (23-27 June). In the second week the renowned Webber Douglas Academy return with The Merchant of Venice (30 June-4 July). The performances are set against the backdrop of Cliveden's magical gardens. Rakes seating is provided. Early booking is advised. Commences Evening Performances: 18.00 for 19.30. Matinee Performances: 12.00 noon. Tickets: Wed & Thur £10.00, Fri Sat & Sun £12.50, Sat matinee £8.50

Historic Houses

Evening Meeting

25/6/99 GOODWOOD RACECOURSE
25/6/99 Tel: 01243 755022
As well as racing there are lots of extras including live music and barbecues - come and party the night away! First race at18.40

Racecourses

Workshop: Wildlife of the Ivinghoe Hills

26/6/99 ASHRIDGE ESTATE
26/6/99 Tel: 01442 851227
Investigating wildlife including wildflowers, butterflies and birds. Time: 09.00-12.30. Cost: £15.00

Country Estates

Open Air Concert with Fireworks - Symphony Under the Stars

26/6/99 WEST WYCOMBE PARK
26/6/99 Tel: 01494 524411
Open air music and fireworks return to West Wycombe for a night of opera classics presented by Richard Baker and

starring members of the English National Opera. Bring a picnic to enjoy in the Park's elegant surroundings. Commences 17.00 for 20.00. Tickets: £18.00 C£12.00

Historic Houses

Motor Cycle World
26/6/99 BEAULIEU
27/6/99 Tel: 01590 612345
Top stars, leading bike manufactures, stunt riders plus much more to see and do. This great event will feature leading stunt riders plus numerous top name riders. British Superbike machines to vintage Japanese Motorcycles will be on display as well as an Old and Classic Bike Show. Plus numerous trade stands to . Starts at 10.00. Advance tickets can be purchased from the Booking Office

Museums

Pictures of Summer
26/6/99 HAMPTONNE COUNTRY LIFE MUSEUM
27/6/99 Tel: 01534 863955
Art Master classes enjoy professional tuition in a beautiful setting.

Museum- Country

Jeersey Festival Rose Show
26/6/99 SAMARES MANOR
27/6/99 Tel: 01534 870551
A two day event incorporating Rose and floral displays, plenty of entertainment for all the family

Historic Houses & Gardens

The Garden Event
26/6/99 WEST DEAN GARDENS
27/6/99 Tel: 01243 818210/811301
Sundials to Salvias. The best specialist nurseries from around the south-east selling all types of rare and unusual plants. Also garden sundries, locally produced food and drink, flower arranging demonstrations and displays of garden and rural skills. Guided tours of the gardens with the head gardeners. All set in the 35 acre gardens which feature the walled kitchen gardens and pleasure gardens as well as a 45 acre arboretum

Gardens

A Day of Music
27/6/99 BROWNSEA ISLAND
27/6/99 Tel: 01202 707744
Children with a musical instrument gain FREE entry. 11.00-15.00

Scenic

Victorian Clothes Talks
27/6/99 COGGES MANOR FARM MUSEUM
27/6/99 Tel: 01993 772602

Talks at 13.30 and 15.00. For further details please call venue direct

Museum- Farms

Sunday Fun Day
27/6/99 GOODWOOD RACECOURSE
27/6/99 Tel: 01243 755022
Bring the family to share the thrills and spills of the Sport of Kings! Racing from14.10

Racecourses

Classical Candlelight Concert - 'Fiori Musicali'
29/6/99 BASILDON PARK
29/6/99 Tel: 0118 984 3040
The second of our candlelight concerts featuring 'Fiori Musicali'. This specialist group comprising harpsichord, violin, flute and cello will perform 'in the round' works by Telemann, Bach and others. Followed by a 2 course dinner also by candlelight. Black tie please. Doors open at 18.30, concert starts at 19.00. Price: £40.00, limited tickets so booking advisable.

Historic Houses

Table Decorations with a Difference - Maureen Roke
29/6/99 ENGLEFIELD HOUSE GARDEN
29/6/99 Tel: 0118 930 2221
The day will start with a demonstration of ways to make an imaginative arrangement using fresh flowers, fruit and herbs. Some materials for you to make your own will be available free of charge and there will be a selection for sale. Please meet at Englefield Garden Centre. Time: 19.00-21.00. Cost: £13.00.

Gardens

A Ride Through the Countryside
30/6/99 KINGSTON LACY
30/6/99 Tel: 01202 883402
A fun evening is planned, £12.00 to include Bangers and Mash supper. Meet at 18.45

Historic Houses

Outdoor Play "The Scarlet Pimpernel"
2/7/99 APPULDURCOMBE HOUSE
4/7/99 Tel: 01983 852484
Lots of action and special effects. Fri & Sat (evening), Sun (matinee)

Historical Remains

The Pergola Open Air Theatre
2/7/99 WEST DEAN GARDENS
18/7/99 Tel: 01243 818210/811301
Programme to be announced. Please call for further information

Gardens

Water Colours with Pamela Grayburn
3/7/99
3/7/99   ENGLEFIELD HOUSE GARDEN
Tel: 0118 930 2221
Pamela Grayburn has lived and travelled extensively in Africa and Europe. She is known for her expert use of light and sinade which brings an unusual cepia and life to her watercolours. She will give advice on selecting subjects in a large garden or landscape. What to bring - paint, brushes, water-colour paper, water jar, tissues/paper towels, folding chair, hat, picnic lunch. Time: 10.00-15.00. Cost: 15.50, including coffee.
Gardens

Jazz Concert
3/7/99
3/7/99   UPTON HOUSE
Tel: 01295 670266
Picnic concert at 19.30, lay back, enjoy the food and listen to the music. £8.00, for tickets please send a cheque payable to 'National Trust (Enterprises)' and s.a.e. to the property
Historic Houses & Gardens

Victorian Laundry Demonstration
3/7/99
4/7/99   COGGES MANOR FARM MUSEUM
Tel: 01993 772602
Laundry Display on Saturday and Harness Maker on Sunday. For further details including times and prices please call venue direct
Museum- Farms

American Civil War Battle & Garrison
3/7/99
4/7/99   FORT BROCKHURST
Tel: 01705 581059
Spectacular actions as Union and Confederate soldiers clash, with infantry and artillery and living history encampments. A£4.00 C£2.00 Concessions£3.00
Forts

Medieval Living History
3/7/99
4/7/99   PORTCHESTER CASTLE
Tel: 01705 378291
15th century military and domestic life, with crafts, men-at-arms and period games. A£3.50 C£1.80 Concessions£2.60
Castles

Workshop: Badgers
4/7/99
4/7/99   ASHRIDGE ESTATE
Tel: 01442 851227
Examine the habitat and life of badgers, including a badger watch (seeing badgers is not guaranteed). Time: 18.30-22.00. Cost: £15.00
Country Estates

American Independence Day
4/7/99
4/7/99   BARTON MANOR GARDENS AND VINEYARDS
Tel: 01983 292835
Help us to celebrate the 4th July, plenty of themed entertainment and the opportunity to meet the staff of the Hospice who work so hard all year round. Light refreshments will be on sale. The shop will be open to sell goods, jewellery, toiletries, Barton Manor wine and Island gifts, etc. in support of the Earl Mountbatten Hospice and each day will have a theme. Dressing up is encouraged but optional.
Historic Houses & Gardens

Snake Awareness Days
4/7/99
4/7/99   COTSWOLD WILDLIFE PARK
Tel: 01993 823006
Come and meet a snake and receive expert advice from their keeper 14.00-17.00 approximately weather permitting
Zoos

Wycantores Singers at Kingston Lacy
4/7/99
4/7/99   KINGSTON LACY
Tel: 01202 883402
For further details including times please call venue direct. No extra charge
Historic Houses

Lulworth 'Classic' Car Event
4/7/99
4/7/99   LULWORTH CASTLE
Tel: 01929 400352

Castles

Children's Open-Air Theatre
6/7/99
6/7/99   BASILDON PARK
Tel: 0118 984 3040
'The Water Babies' - Charles Kingsley's classic story presented by Illyria, at 18.30, gates open 18.00. A£8.00 C£6.00 Family Ticket £28.00
Historic Houses

Family Event - The Water Babies
7/7/99
7/7/99   HUGHENDEN MANOR
Tel: 01494 532580
When Tom is transformed into a Water Baby he must make a dangerous journey to the Other End of Nowhere. Bring a picnic and a rug. Gates open at 17.30 for 18.00 start. A£8.00 C£5.00 Family Ticket £26.00
Historic Houses

The Art of Pebble Mosaics
8/7/99
8/7/99   ENGLEFIELD HOUSE GARDEN
Tel: 0118 930 2221
There is a strong tradition of cobbling in Britain, but it is rarely seen in decorative

form. The day will start by showing slides of some examples of pebble mosaic from around the world including some of her own designs. Students will have the opportunity to create a design and mosaic on an afternoon workshop. Some materials will be provided and more will be for sale. Please bring folding chair and hat. Time: 10.00-16.00. Cost: £50.00.

Gardens

Through the Mists of Time
8/7/99
8/7/99
KINGSTON LACY
Tel: 01202 883402
A£2.00 C£0.50. Starts 14.00. Please call 01202 882705 for further information on this event

Historic Houses

Hi There! 1999
8/7/99
18/7/99
HI THERE! 1999
Tel: 01705 468409
Various venues on Hayling Island. A celebration of art, blues, celtic, circus, classical, community arts, folk, indie-pop, jazz, kite-making, literature, rock, the internet world, and more - to tickle your cultural tastebuds! Tickets available in person: Hayling Library, Elm Grove, Hayling Island or Hayling Bookshop, Mengham, Hayling Island. By post: 45 St. Leonard's Avenue, Hayling Island, PO11 9BN, cheques made payable to 'Hi-Peractive'.

Festivals

Music in the Park
9/7/99
9/7/99
KINGSTON LACY
Tel: 01202 883402
Presenting the show 'Music of the Night' with major stars bringing the top West End shows to life at Kingston Lacy. Advance Tickets: A£13.00 C£6.50. On the gate: A£15.00 C£7.00. Gates open 17.30, performance starts at 19.30

Historic Houses

Music in the Park
9/7/99
10/7/99
KINGSTON LACY
Tel: 01202 883402
Presenting the show 'Music of the Night' with major stars bringing the top West End shows to life at Kingston Lacy. Fireworks Finale on Saturday. Gates open at 17.30 for 19.30 start both days. Prices: A£13.00 C£6.50 in advance, A£15.00 C£7.00 on the gate. Special Offer: buy for both nights and save £6.00, Double ticket £20.00

Historic Houses

Popular Classics with Fireworks
9/7/99
10/7/99
THE VYNE
Tel: 01256 881337
The Riverside Sinfonia returns to The Vyne with an enchanting programme of popular classics, on the lawns in front of the house. Friday concert sponsored by Bradford & Bingley Building Society. Gates open at 18.30 for picnics for 20.00 start. Cost: £13.00

Historic Houses

Palace House Prom
10/7/99
10/7/99
BEAULIEU
Tel: 01590 612345
Enjoy a superb evening of classical music and choreographed fireworks all in a setting which is hard to rival in the New Forest - The Palace House Prom at Beaulieu. Held on the lawns of Lord Montagu's family home, the Bournemouth Symphony Orchestra will be playing a diverse, exciting and memorable programme including Vaughan Williams, Strauss and Elgar's Pomp and Circumstance. Gates open from 18.30. Advance tickets can be purchased from the booking office

Museums

Music in the Park
10/7/99
10/7/99
KINGSTON LACY
Tel: 01202 883402
Presenting 'Last Night of the Proms' performed by the English National Orchestra with all your favourite popular pieces with a firework finale. Advance Tickets: A£13.00 C£6.50. Tickets on the gate: A£15.00 C£7.00. Buy for the two nights and save £6.00, double ticket £20.00. Gates open 17.30, performance at 19.30

Historic Houses

Living Heritage Craft Show
10/7/99
11/7/99
ASHRIDGE ESTATE
Tel: 01442 851227
In keeping with the countryside aspect of the Ashridge Estate, the Craft Show will include Gundogs, Shire Horses and Ferret Displays and rural Craftsmen such as Bodgers, Hurdle Makers and general coppice skills. Time 10.00-18.00. Cost: A£4.00 C£2.00 OAPs£3.00, pay at gate. NT members £0.50 discount

Country Estates

Morris Dancing
10/7/99
11/7/99
COGGES MANOR FARM MUSEUM
Tel: 01993 772602
Booking bind and repairs advice on

Saturday, and Morris Dancing on
Sunday. For further details including
times and prices please call venue direct

Museum- Farms

Annual Classic Vehicle Rally

10/7/99 SWANAGE RAILWAY

11/7/99 Tel: 01929 425800

Over 300 classic and vintage vehicles on
display all weekend

Railways

Garden Tour

11/7/99 OSBORNE HOUSE

11/7/99 Tel: 01983 200022

A seasonal garden tour of Osborne
Garden with the Head Gardener. A£3.50
C£1.80 Concessions£2.60

Historic Houses & Gardens

Alfred Hitchcock

11/7/99 MUSEUM OF MODERN ART OXFORD

3/10/99 Tel: 01865 722733

A challenging and innovative exhibition
to mark the 100th anniversary of
Hitchcock's birth

Museum- Art

Jousting

12/7/99 CARISBROOKE CASTLE

12/7/99 Tel: 01983 522107

Discover the secrets of the tourney, as
the jousting area resounds to the
sounds of the battle, clash of steel and
thunder of horses hooves as the mighty
knights charge at full tilt

Castles

Guided Tour

12/7/99 FLYING FLOWERS

12/7/99 Tel: 01534 866000

Flying Flowers guided tour with Adrienne
at 14.00-16.00

Gardens

Jersey Floral Festival

12/7/99 FLYING FLOWERS

17/7/99 Tel: 01534 866000

Garden celebrities will be giving talks
and demonstrations throughout the
Island

Gardens

The Jersey Garden Festival 1999

12/7/99 JERSEY GARDEN FESTIVAL 1999

18/7/99 Tel: 01534 500700

Various venues. Jersey's popular week
long Floral Festival celebrates gardening
and flowers in the company of some of
the UK's top celebrity gardeners. The
Island looks at its very best during the
Festival as it coincides with the annual
Garden Awards Scheme when private

gardeners and businesses have their
finest floral displays on show. Guided
walks, demonstrations in attractive and
unusual settings, and tours of private
open gardens are just some of the activities that take place. Jersey Tourism is
delighted to welcome the Society of
Floral Painters to Jersey for the 1999
Festival, where they will be exhibiting
their floral paintings in the members
room of the Societe Jersiaise. The public
will be able to take part in workshops
and enjoy demonstrations hosted by
members of the guild.

Festivals

Guernsey Teddies Summer Holiday

12/7/99 CASTLE CORNET

31/8/99 Tel: 01481 721657

Guernsey Teddies' friends and relations
can be found in Castle Cornet this summer. Come and join in the Nat West Coin
Hunt and other activities

Castles

Classical Candlelight Concert

13/7/99 BASILDON PARK

13/7/99 Tel: 0118 984 3040

After last year's stunning concert the
Delme String Quartet return to conclude
our season of Garden Room concerts.
The programme will include Haydn,
Dvorjak and Hummel and will be fol-
lowed by a 2 course candlelight dinner.
Black tie please. Doors open at 18.30,
Concert starts 19.00. Ticket: £40.00, lim-
ited tickets so booking advisable.

Historic Houses

Rotary Band Concert

14/7/99 CLIVEDEN

14/7/99 Tel: 01628 605069

The Rotary Club of Slough present a special Band Concert featuring the prestigious Band of the Royal Marines and the
London Welsh Male Voice Choir. Enjoy a
family and friends picnic on the magnificent parterre and evening strolls overlooking the Rover Thames. Beating
Retreat and fireworks will provide a
spectacular finale. Space is limited and
entry is by ticket only. Commences 17.00
for 19.00. Tickets: A£14.00 C£8.00

Historic Houses

Eclipse '99 Exhibition

15/7/99 GUERNSEY MUSEUM AND ART GALLERY

26/9/99 Tel: 01481 726518

An exhibition charting the history of
'eclipse watching' to celebrate the first
total eclipse of the sun in the Channel

Islands for over 1000 years!

Museum- Local History

Music of the Movies

16/7/99 BROADLANDS
16/7/99 Tel: 01794 505010
Enjoy the music of the famous movies with a firework finale

Historic Houses

Raku Work And Solstice Bards

17/7/99 COGGES MANOR FARM MUSEUM
18/7/99 Tel: 01993 772602
Raku Work on Saturday and storytelling, poetry and song on Sunday. For further details including times and prices please call venue direct

Museum- Farms

Birds of Prey Demonstrations

17/7/99 COTSWOLD WILDLIFE PARK
18/7/99 Tel: 01993 823006
See the Birds of Prey in flight. Approximately 13.00 and 15.30 weather permitting

Zoos

Children's Open Air Theatre

20/7/99 CLIVEDEN
20/7/99 Tel: 01628 605069
The Water Babies presented by Illyria. After their success with Peter Pan last year, Illyria return with The Water Babies. Join young Tom on his adventures as a Water Baby in a world full of magical creatures of the deep. Suitable for boys and girls of all ages. Commences: Matinee 14.30 for 15.00. Evening 18.00 for 18.30. Tickets: A£8.00 C£5.00 Family Ticket £26.00

Historic Houses

Workshop: Bats

21/7/99 ASHRIDGE ESTATE
21/7/99 Tel: 01442 851227
Identification, ecology and habitat of bats, including a visit to a bat roost. Time: 19.00-22.00. Cost: £15.00

Country Estates

Dog Show

22/7/99 APPULDURCOMBE HOUSE
22/7/99 Tel: 01983 852484
Beautiful dogs strutting their stuff for one and all

Historical Remains

Southern Cathedrals Festival

22/7/99 WINCHESTER CATHEDRAL
24/7/99 Tel: 01962 853137
Festival of music and worship with the combined cathedral choirs of Winchester, Salisbury and Chichester

Cathedrals

The Light Fantastic - Glow-worm Hunt

23/7/99 KINGSTON LACY
23/7/99 Tel: 01202 883402
Moonlit hunt for glowworms around the hill-fort. A£2.00 C£0.50

Historic Houses

Craft Fayre

23/7/99 THE VYNE
25/7/99 Tel: 01256 881337
Craft Fayre held in the parkland at The Vyne with up to 225 skilled crafts people. Quality crafts created by experts from all over the country.

Historic Houses

Open Air theatre - A Midsummer Night's Dream

23/7/99 BROWNSEA ISLAND
6/8/99 Tel: 01202 707744
This event will be held on: 23, 26, 28 & 30 July & 2, 4 & 6 Aug at 19.00. Tickets for this event only available through B.O.A.T on 01202 690952 (ansaphone)

Scenic

Holiday Activities for Children

23/7/99 STAUNTON COUNTRY PARK
5/9/99 Tel: 01705 453405
Twice weekly (demand depending) from 10.00-13.30. Nature walk (2 miles - 3 hours) to identify flowers, insects and wildlife. Conservation games and activities. Meet at Shop entrance. Minimum of 6 to maximum of 12 children per day. Advance bookings only. Suitable for accompanied children 6-10 years. £2.00 per child

Country Parks

De Beers Diamond Day

24/7/99 ASCOT RACECOURSE
24/7/99 Tel: 01344 622211
One of the most prestigious and sparkling race days.

Racecourses

Birds of Prey Demonstrations

24/7/99 COTSWOLD WILDLIFE PARK
25/7/99 Tel: 01993 823006
See the Birds of Prey in flight. Approximately 13.00 and 15.30 weather permitting

Zoos

Medieval Living History

24/7/99 MEDIEVAL MERCHANT'S HOUSE
25/7/99 Tel: 01703 221503
15th century military and domestic life, with crafts, men-at-arms and period games. Gylda Cinque Portuum. A£3.00 C£1.50 Concessions£2.30

Historic Houses

Further more detailed information on the attractions listed can be found in Best Guides *Visitor Attractions* Guide under the classifications shown

Alice by Lewis Carroll
25/7/99 ASHRIDGE ESTATE
25/7/99 Tel: 01442 851227
Fun and frolics with Alice and her friends
in the enchanting world of Wonderland
presented by Troubador Theatre
Company. Bring a picnic and a rug.
Gates open at 17.30 for 18.00 start.
Tickets: A£8.00 C£5.00 Family Ticket
£26.00

Country Estates

Buckler's Hard Fun Day
25/7/99 BUCKLER'S HARD VILLAGE AND MARITIME
MUSEUM
25/7/99 Tel: 01590 616203
See the 18th century village brought to
life with roving players, military skills
and stalls from yesteryear

Museum- Maritime

**Reptiles from the Cotswold Wildlife
Park**
25/7/99 COGGES MANOR FARM MUSEUM
25/7/99 Tel: 01993 772602
Meet the reptiles at 14.00-16.30. For further details including times and prices
please call venue direct

Museum- Farms

**Oxfordshire Beekeeping Association
Field Day**
25/7/99 COTSWOLD WILDLIFE PARK
25/7/99 Tel: 01993 823006
Field Day, please contact the Wildlife
Park for further information

Zoos

Children's Fun Day
25/7/99 KINGSTON LACY
25/7/99 Tel: 01202 883402
Bring the family to Kingston Lacy for a
fun day. Small charge for some rides,
11.00-16.00

Historic Houses

Tropicana
25/7/99 STAUNTON COUNTRY PARK
25/7/99 Tel: 01705 453405
A tropical party with the tropical
glasshouses at their best. World music
and food; workshops for all ages. If you
like Womad - you'll like this

Country Parks

Rare and Traditional Breeds Show
25/7/99 WEALD AND DOWNLAND OPEN AIR
MUSEUM
25/7/99 Tel: 01243 811348
Further details available on 01243
811348

Museum- Social History

Exhibition

JERSEY MUSEUM
26/7/99 JERSEY MUSEUM
8/8/99 Tel: 01534 633300
An exhibition from 'Pictures of Summer'
Master Classes.

Museums

July Festival Meeting
27/7/99 GOODWOOD RACECOURSE
31/7/99 Tel: 01243 755022
One of the major events of the racing
calendar, featuring five days of absolute-
ly top class racing. Early booking recom-
mended with admission discount if
booked before 1 June: Gordon Enclosure
£17.00 Groups 20+ £15.00 Public
Enclosure £6.00 Groups 20+ £5.00 After
1 June: Gordon Enclosure £20.00 Public
Enclosure £7.00 Groups 20+ £5.00.
Racing from 14.15

Racecourses

Animal Farm
28/7/99 COGGES MANOR FARM MUSEUM
28/7/99 Tel: 01993 772602
Children's Craft and Drama Workshop.
Pre-booking essential. For further details
including times and prices please call
venue direct

Museum- Farms

Mottistone Jazz Open Air Concert
30/7/99 MOTTISTONE MANOR GARDEN
31/7/99 Tel: 01983 741302
Open air concerts. Picnic. Dance under
the stars. 1920 Dress. Gates open 18.30
for picnics. Concert starts at 19.30-
23.00. Admission £10.00 Fri, £11.00 Sat.
Please telephone 01983 741020 for further information

Gardens

Live Crafts Show
30/7/99 BASILDON PARK
1/8/99 Tel: 0118 984 3040
Up to 150 carefully selected craft makers
and artists from all over Britain offer
original, contemporary and traditional
crafts. Demonstrations include blacksmith, bee-keeping, raku firing and
more. Live music and children's entertainment. All NT members £Free on
Friday only. Pay at the gate. Commences
10.00-17.00. A£3.50 C£1.00 OAPs£3.00

Historic Houses

Medieval Craft Show
30/7/99 BROADLANDS
1/8/99 Tel: 01794 505010
Complementing the thousands of unique
craft ideas on display will be demonstrating craftsmen in period dress, jousting, jesters and many other medieval

attractions

Historic Houses

Toy Weekend

30/7/99
1/8/99

COGGES MANOR FARM MUSEUM

Tel: 01993 772602

Children's craft activities on Friday, pre-booking essential followed by Toy weekend. For further details including times and prices please call venue direct

Museum- Farms

Birds of Prey Demonstrations

31/7/99
31/7/99

COTSWOLD WILDLIFE PARK

Tel: 01993 823006

See the Birds of Prey in flight. Approximately 13.00 and 15.30 weather permitting

Zoos

Music in the Air

31/7/99
31/7/99

MUSEUM OF ARMY FLYING

Tel: 01980 674421

Open air classical music and flying extravaganza featuring the London Philharmonic Youth Orchestra with aerial displays by aircraft, balloons, gliders, freefall display teams and the amazing Blue Eagles

Museum- Aviation

The Waterbabies

31/7/99
31/7/99

THE VYNE

Tel: 01256 881337

Outdoor theatre for children by the company: Illyria

Historic Houses

Skandia Life Cowes Week 1999

31/7/99
7/8/99

SKANDIA LIFE COWES WEEK 1999

Tel: 01983 295744

An international yacht racing regatta run over eight days based at Cowes on the Isle of Wight. Racing takes place in the Solent, the area of water between the Isle of Wight and the mainland with the majority of races starting adjacent to the Royal Yacht Squadron from a mile long starting line (free public viewing). Approximately 30 different classes of yachts compete daily from 10.15 with the duration of races from 3 to 6 hours. Social events include fireworks display at 20.30 on 6 August, public entertainment, bands, shows, disco's, childrens entertainment etc.

Festivals

Grand Plant and Produce Sale & Antiques Fair

1/8/99

BARTON MANOR GARDENS AND VINEYARDS

1/8/99

Tel: 01983 292835

Wear your gardening clothes and be ready for planting your purchases on your return home! Light refreshments will be on sale. Also, "the largest Antiques and Collectors fair on the Island now at Barton Manor". The shop will be open to sell goods, jewellery, toiletries, Barton Manor wine and Island gifts, etc. in support of the Earl Mountbatten Hospice Development Fund and each day will have a theme. Dressing up is encouraged but optional.

Historic Houses & Gardens

Birds of Prey Demonstrations

1/8/99
1/8/99

COTSWOLD WILDLIFE PARK

Tel: 01993 823006

See the Birds of Prey in flight. Approximately 13.00 and 15.30 weather permitting

Zoos

Snake Awareness Days

1/8/99
1/8/99

COTSWOLD WILDLIFE PARK

Tel: 01993 823006

Come and meet a snake and receive expert advice from their keeper 14.00-17.00 approximately weather permitting

Zoos

Victorian Garden Party

1/8/99
1/8/99

STAUNTON COUNTRY PARK

Tel: 01705 453405

Traditional gardens activities including Victorian clothing competition, games and activities. Suitable for all the family. Fancy dress welcomed. Normal admission rates apply. Discounted rates for those in Victorian dress. 10.00-17.00

Country Parks

Children's Fun Day

1/8/99
1/8/99

WOLVESEY CASTLE

Tel: 01962 854766

Everything to entertain the children, and parents! A£2.50 C£1.30 Concessions£1.90

Castles

The Pete Allen Jazz Band

6/8/99
6/8/99

HUGHENDEN MANOR

Tel: 01494 532580

From the early jazz sounds of Louis Armstrong to Dixieland and New Orleans Jazz, this entertaining show of light-hearted humour and lively jazz songs is a great night out. Bring a picnic and a rug. Gates open at 18.00 for a 19.00 start. A£12.00 C£8.00

Historic Houses

A Traditional Ale and Jazz Evening with a Firework Finale

Further more detailed information on the attractions listed can be found in Best Guides *Visitor Attractions* Guide under the classifications shown

6/8/99 6/8/99	**KINGSTON LACY** Tel: 01202 883402 Entertainment by Monty Sunshine and Kenny Ball and his Jazzmen, supported by The Stour Valley Stompers. Advance tickets: A£12.00 C£6.00. On the gate A£14.00 C£7.00

Historic Houses

A Traditional Ale & Jazz Evening with Fireworks Finale

6/8/99 6/8/99	**KINGSTON LACY** Tel: 01202 883402 With Monty Sunshine and Kenny Ball and his Jazzmen, supported by The Stour Valley Stompers. Gates open at 17.30 for 20.00 start. A£12.00 C£6.00 in advance, A£14.00 C£7.00 on the gate

Historic Houses

Country Fair

6/8/99 8/8/99	**HAMPTONNE COUNTRY LIFE MUSEUM** Tel: 01534 863955 A combination of all the fun of a country fair with the serious issues of the environmental behind it. Great fun for all the family

Museum- Country

The Runnymede Pageant

6/8/99 8/8/99	**RUNNYMEDE** Tel: 01784 432891 Craft and entertainment for all the family 10.00-18.00. Tickets £3.50, £2.50 and £1.00 at the gate. Contact Four Seasons (Events) Ltd on 01344 874787 for details

Country Parks

Last Night At The Proms

7/8/99 7/8/99	**BROADLANDS** Tel: 01794 505010 With spectacular firework finale, this is everyone's favourite music including "Land of Hope and Glory"

Historic Houses

The Best of Gilbert & Sullivan

7/8/99 7/8/99	**HUGHENDEN MANOR** Tel: 01494 532580 Hilarious scenes, quick costume changes and great singing combine in Hatstand's lively performance of more than 25 extracts from all the great G&S operas. A wonderful evening for newcomers and opera buffs and what better setting to listen to these Victorian masters than the Victorian Hughenden Manor! Bring a picnic and a rug. Gates open at 18.00 for 19.00 start. A£12.00 C£8.00

Historic Houses

By the Light of the Silvery Moon

7/8/99 7/8/99	**KINGSTON LACY** Tel: 01202 883402 Musical evening with barbecue. A£7.00 C£5.00 to include BBQ. Starts at 19.00

Historic Houses

Vintage Tractors and Falconry Display

7/8/99 8/8/99	**COGGES MANOR FARM MUSEUM** Tel: 01993 772602 Vintage Tractors on Saturday and Falconry Display on Sunday. For further details including times and prices please call venue direct

Museum- Farms

Birds of Prey Demonstrations

7/8/99 8/8/99	**COTSWOLD WILDLIFE PARK** Tel: 01993 823006 See the Birds of Prey in flight. Approximately 13.00 and 15.30 weather permitting

Zoos

Lulworth Horse Trials and Country Fair

7/8/99 8/8/99	**LULWORTH CASTLE** Tel: 01929 400352

Castles

Children's Story Trail

8/8/99 8/8/99	**ASHRIDGE ESTATE** Tel: 01442 851227 Listen to environmental stories and join in with the adventures. Time: 14.00-15.30 & 16.00-17.30. All tickets £5.00

Country Estates

Fairthorpe Sports Car Specials Day

8/8/99 8/8/99	**COTSWOLD WILDLIFE PARK** Tel: 01993 823006 The events starts at 10.00, please contact the Wildlife Park for further information

Zoos

Garden Tour

8/8/99 8/8/99	**OSBORNE HOUSE** Tel: 01983 200022 A seasonal garden tour of Osborne Garden with the Head Gardener. A£3.50 C£1.80 Concessions£2.60

Historic Houses & Gardens

Opera - Cosi Fan tutti

10/8/99 14/8/99	**BROWNSEA ISLAND** Tel: 01202 707744 Presented by Opera Del Mar. Sung in English. 19.30 daily and Saturday matinee at 14.00. Cost: £15.00 to include ferry

Scenic

Eclipse Day

11/8/99 11/8/99	**GUERNSEY MUSEUM AND ART GALLERY** Tel: 01481 726518

Please call for further information

Museum- Local History

The Swinging 60's: Open Air Concert for Fireworks

13/8/99 BASILDON PARK

13/8/99 Tel: 0118 984 3040

Sounds of the 60's with The Bruvvers, The Ludwig Beatles again and The Tremeloes. Dress up, bring a picnic and prepare to swing the night away in this fabulous setting. Fireworks bring the evening to a spectacular close. Car Park and gates open 17.30 for start at 19.00. A£13.50 C£6.00 Family Ticket £34.00.

Historic Houses

The Magic of Opera - Don Giovanni

13/8/99 CLIVEDEN

13/8/99 Tel: 01628 605069

Irresistibly comic, yet tragically serious, Mozart's Don Giovanni provides a thrilling night of high drama. Gates open at 18.00 for 19.30 start. All tickets £22.00. Early booking is advised.

Historic Houses

Twlfth Night

13/8/99 THE VYNE

14/8/99 Tel: 01256 881337

The outdoor theatre company, Illyria, play Shakespeare on two nights

Historic Houses

Medieval Countryside and Craft Fair

13/8/99 KINGSTON LACY

15/8/99 Tel: 01202 883402

Four Season Medieval Craft Fair. A display of traditional crafts including entertainment with stilt walkers, Punch & Judy and Strolling Minstrels. Commences 10.00-18.00, Tickets: A£3.00-£5.00 C(5-15)£1.00 OAPs£2.00-£3.00. Commences 10.00-18.00

Historic Houses

Annual Jazz Concert with Fireworks

14/8/99 BASILDON PARK

14/8/99 Tel: 0118 984 3040

A repeat of last year's concert featuring West Jesmond Rhythm Kings and the Pete Allen Jazz Band play 1920s New Orleans jazz. The evening concludes with spectacular fireworks. Sponsored by Thames Water. Bring a picnic and seating to start at 19.00. A£13.50 C£6.00 Family Ticket £34.00

Historic Houses

The Magic of Opera - Opera Gala

14/8/99 CLIVEDEN

14/8/99 Tel: 01628 605069

A wonderful music medley of opera

highlights ranging from Mozart to Gershwin and everything in between. Bring a picnic and seating for these stylish evenings of summer entertainment. Gates open at 18.00 for 19.30 start. All tickets £22.00. Early booking is advised.

Historic Houses

Medieval Craft Show

14/8/99 BEALE PARK

15/8/99 Tel: 0118 984 5172

Over 100 nationally selected craftsmen demonstrating and selling their crafts and skills; twice daily jousting and falconry display, wandering minstrels and period singers

Wildlife Parks

Medieval Calligraphy & Spinning

14/8/99 BISHOP'S WALTHAM PALACE

15/8/99 Tel: 01489 892460

Step back in time to the 15th century and see how a 'clerk of minor orders' went about his business! Authentic calligraphy, illuminating book making skills are demonstrated, plus the use of an unusual spindle wheel. A£2.50 C£1.30 Concessions£1.90

Historical Remains

Hampshire Flower Show

14/8/99 BROADLANDS

15/8/99 Tel: 01794 505010

The complete gardening experience, combining major floral displays, associations, question and answer areas and competitions

Historic Houses

Birds of Prey Demonstrations

14/8/99 COTSWOLD WILDLIFE PARK

15/8/99 Tel: 01993 823006

See the Birds of Prey in flight. Approximately 13.00 and 15.30 weather permitting

Zoos

Children's Activity Weekend

14/8/99 WEALD AND DOWNLAND OPEN AIR MUSEUM

15/8/99 Tel: 01243 811348

Further details available on 01243 811348

Museum- Social History

Chilli Fiesta

14/8/99 WEST DEAN GARDENS

15/8/99 Tel: 01243 818210/811301

'Natures Napalm' - a calorific celebration of peppers with a punch!

Gardens

Open-Air Concert - The Water Babies

15/8/99 ASHRIDGE ESTATE

Further more detailed information on the attractions listed can be found in Best Guides *Visitor Attractions* Guide under the classifications shown

15/8/99 Tel: 01442 851227
Presented by Illyria. Join Tom on his adventures as a Water Baby in this fantastical new production. Bring a picnic and a rug. Gates open at 17.30 for 18.00 start. Price: A£8.00 C£5.00 Family Ticket £26.00

Country Estates

Model Wheelwrights

15/8/99 COGGES MANOR FARM MUSEUM
15/8/99 Tel: 01993 772602
For further details including times and prices please call venue direct

Museum- Farms

Family Wildlife Workshop

18/8/99 ASHRIDGE ESTATE
18/8/99 Tel: 01442 851227
Time: 14.00-15.00. Cost: £5.00 per child, accompanying adults £Free

Country Estates

Birds of Prey Demonstrations

21/8/99 COTSWOLD WILDLIFE PARK
22/8/99 Tel: 01993 823006
See the Birds of Prey in flight. Approximately 13.00 and 15.30 weather permitting

Zoos

Downs Steam Show 1999

21/8/99 DOWNS STEAM SHOW 1999
22/8/99 Tel: 01243 641284
A working event for traction engines, one of the major steam events in the south. With timber sawing and hauling, road rolling and a vintage fair, plus a range of vintage machinery, models and rural bygones, the event and the Museum present a superb day out.

Festivals

Isle of Wight Garlic Festival 1999

21/8/99 ISLE OF WIGHT GARLIC FESTIVAL 1999
22/8/99 Tel: 01983 853411
The Isle of Wight Garlic Festival is the largest event of its kind on the Island with two days of varied family entertainment, including a Children's Fun Zone, spectacular arena events, live music throughout the day, huge variety of foods, locally grown garlic, live music throughout the day, fun fair, arts and crafts marquee's, over 250 stallholders and more. This event has raised hundreds of pounds for Island Charities over the past 14 years. Time: 10.00-18.00. Prices: A£5.00 C£2.00 OAPs£4.00

Festivals

Children's Fun Day

22/8/99 BISHOP'S WALTHAM PALACE

22/8/99 Tel: 01489 892460
Everything to entertain the children and parents. A£2.50 C£1.30 Concessions£1.90

Historical Remains

Sealed Knot

22/8/99 COGGES MANOR FARM MUSEUM
22/8/99 Tel: 01993 772602
For further details including times and prices please call venue direct

Museum- Farms

Wild Flowers of Badbury Rings

22/8/99 KINGSTON LACY
22/8/99 Tel: 01202 883402
Meet at Badbury Rings at 14.00. A£2.00 C£1.00

Historic Houses

Family Wildlife Workshop

25/8/99 ASHRIDGE ESTATE
25/8/99 Tel: 01442 851227
Time: 14.00-15.00. Cost: £5.00 per child, accompanying adults £Free

Country Estates

Medieval Calligraphy & Spinning

25/8/99 WOLVESEY CASTLE
26/8/99 Tel: 01962 854766
Step back in time to the 15th century and see how a 'clerk of minor orders' went about his business! Authentic calligraphy, illuminating book making skills are demonstrated, plus the use of an unusual spindle wheel. A£2.50 C£1.30 Concessions£1.90

Castles

Jousting

26/8/99 CARISBROOKE CASTLE
26/8/99 Tel: 01983 522107
Discover the secrets of the tourney, as the jousting area resounds to the sounds of the battle, clash of steel and thunder of horses hooves as the mighty knights charge at full tilt

Castles

Opera al Fresco - Golden Moments from Opera

27/8/99 BASILDON PARK
27/8/99 Tel: 0118 984 3040
Hilarious scenes and heart rending arias from the world's favourite operas, presented by Hatstand opera. Quick costume changes and informal presentation combine with top-notch singing for a great evening. Hatstand perform on the East Lawn behind the house. Bring a picnic and something to sit on. Black tie please. Car Park opens at 18.30, doors open at 19.00. Price: £20.00, limited

tickets so booking advisable.

Historic Houses

Brownsea Proms
27/8/99 BROWNSEA ISLAND
28/8/99 Tel: 01202 707744
Presented by South Coast Opera. 19.30
and Saturday matinee 14.30. Cost:
£13.00 to include ferry. All tickets £7.00
including ferry.

Scenic

Towersey Village Festival 1999
27/8/99 TOWERSEY VILLAGE FESTIVAL 1999
30/8/99 Tel: 01296 433669
A feast of Bank Holiday entertainment,
spectacular international shows, non-
stop children's entertainment, walka-
bout circus performers, craft fair and
market, hot and cold food and drink.
Major headline acts to be announced
with a focus on Folk/Roots music,
including open air concerts, international dance shows and much more.

Festivals

The Best of Gilbert and Sullivan
28/8/99 BASILDON PARK
28/8/99 Tel: 0118 984 3040
Basildon Park and the village of
Basildon join forces to bring you over 25
extracts from all the Savoy opera, including The Mikado, Pirates of Penzance and
HMS Pinafore, plus surprises from
Iolanthe and Utopia Ltd. Hatstand perform on the East Lawn behind the
house. Bring a picnic and something to
sit on. 50% of the profit from this event
will go to the Basildon Village Hall
Appeal. Black tie please. Car Park opens
at 18.30, doors open at 19.00. Price: All
tickets £20.00.

Historic Houses

The Saville Garden August Plant Fair
28/8/99 THE SAVILL GARDEN - WINDSOR GREAT
        PARK
28/8/99 Tel: 01753 847518
Many small specialist nurseries offering
a wide range of unusual plants

Gardens

Oxfordshire Craft Fair
28/8/99 BLENHEIM PALACE
30/8/99 Tel: 01993 811325

Stately Homes

Magic Toy Man
28/8/99 COGGES MANOR FARM MUSEUM
30/8/99 Tel: 01993 772602
Storyteller visits on Monday, also baking
in the bread oven in the Manor House.

For further details including times and
prices please call venue direct

Museum- Farms

Birds of Prey Demonstrations
28/8/99 COTSWOLD WILDLIFE PARK
30/8/99 Tel: 01993 823006
See the Birds of Prey in flight.
Approximately 13.00 and 15.30 weather
permitting

Zoos

Reading 1999
28/8/99 READING 1999
30/8/99 Tel: 0181 963 0940 (info)
A feast of rock and pop.

Festivals

Exhibition: Wildlife and Ashridge
28/8/99 ASHRIDGE ESTATE
2/9/99 Tel: 01442 851227
Ashridge Monument Visitor Centre. Little
Gaddesdon Art Society. Time: 14.00-
17.00. Admission Free.

Country Estates

Bank Holiday Meeting
28/8/99 GOODWOOD RACECOURSE
29/9/99 Tel: 01243 755022
The August Bank Holiday Meeting is all
about relaxation with entertainment for
all the family. Racing from 14.15

Racecourses

Classic Cars Weekend
29/8/99 BUCKINGHAMSHIRE RAILWAY CENTRE
30/8/99 Tel: 01296 655450
Rover car rally on Sunday with 250 veteran and vintage cars, motorbikes and
lorries on show on Monday

Museum- Transport

The Lion, the Witch, and the Wardrobe
29/8/99 CARISBROOKE CASTLE
30/8/99 Tel: 01983 522107
A children's classic from Narnia performed by Labyrinth Productions.
A£4.50 C£2.30 Concessions£3.40

Castles

Napoleonic
29/8/99 PORTCHESTER CASTLE
30/8/99 Tel: 01705 378291
Prisoners at Portchester, the Historical
Maritime Society. A£3.50 C£1.80
Concessions£2.60

Castles

**Patchwork and Quilting
Demonstration**
4/9/99 COGGES MANOR FARM MUSEUM
5/9/99 Tel: 01993 772602
Craft demonstrations on Saturday,
Guided Tours at 14.00 and 15.30 on
Sunday. For further details please call

Further more detailed information on the attractions listed can be found
in Best Guides *Visitor Attractions* Guide under the classifications shown

venue direct

Museum- Farms

Birds of Prey Demonstrations

4/9/99 COTSWOLD WILDLIFE PARK

5/9/99 Tel: 01993 823006

See the Birds of Prey in flight. Approximately 13.00 and 15.30 weather permitting

Zoos

Appuldurcombe Antique Fair

5/9/99 APPULDURCOMBE HOUSE

5/9/99 Tel: 01983 852484

Large antiques fair with numerous stalls selling 'all-sorts' or antiques and collectables

Historical Remains

Jazz Day

5/9/99 BARTON MANOR GARDENS AND VINEYARDS

5/9/99 Tel: 01983 292835

A day to enjoy listening to jazz whilst wearing your 1920s/30s clothes. Light refreshments will be on sale. The shop will be open to sell goods, jewellery, toiletries, Barton Manor wine and Island gifts, etc. in support of the Earl Mountbatten Hospice and each day will have a theme. Dressing up is encouraged but optional.

Historic Houses & Gardens

Snake Awareness Days

5/9/99 COTSWOLD WILDLIFE PARK

5/9/99 Tel: 01993 823006

Come and meet a snake and receive expert advice from their keeper 14.00-17.00 approximately weather permitting

Zoos

Children's Deer Watch

8/9/99 ASHRIDGE ESTATE

8/9/99 Tel: 01442 851227

Suitable for ages 7+. Time: 18.30-20.00. Tickets: £5.00 per child, accompanying adults £Free

Country Estates

Belnheim International Horse Trials

9/9/99 BLENHEIM PALACE

12/9/99 Tel: 01993 811325

Stately Homes

Racing at Goodwood

10/9/99 GOODWOOD RACECOURSE

11/9/99 Tel: 01243 755022

Top class racing is promised with the Schroder Investment Management Stakes and Select Stakes. Racing from 14.10

Racecourses

Romsey Show

11/9/99 BROADLANDS

11/9/99 Tel: 01794 505010

One of the largest agricultural events in the south

Historic Houses

Autojumble and Automart

11/9/99 BEAULIEU

12/9/99 Tel: 01590 612345

Over 1500 stalls for everything connected with motoring and motorcycling plus more than 100 cars in the automart, undoubtedly Europe's biggest autojumble event. Admission also includes entry into the National Motor Museum, Palace house and Abbey and Exhibition of monastic life.. Events starts at 10.00

Museums

Friends of Thomas the Tank Engine

11/9/99 BUCKINGHAMSHIRE RAILWAY CENTRE

12/9/99 Tel: 01296 655450

Take a ride with Thomas on his branch line train and meet the Fat Controller. Punch and Judy show and Thomas video theatre

Museum- Transport

Edwardian Craft Show

11/9/99 CLIVEDEN

12/9/99 Tel: 01628 605069

Living Heritage hosts a unique Edwardian-themed craft show with demonstrations, music and traditional amusements. Set in the lovely grounds of the Cliveden Estate there's something for everyone to enjoy. Time: 10.00-17.30. A£4.00 C£2.00 OAPs£3.00 NT members £0.50 discount

Historic Houses

Corn Dolly Weekend

11/9/99 COGGES MANOR FARM MUSEUM

12/9/99 Tel: 01993 772602

For further details including times and prices please call venue direct

Museum- Farms

Archaeology Weekend

11/9/99 CORFE CASTLE

12/9/99 Tel: 01929 481294

Part of the National Archaeology days coordinated by the Council for British Archaeology. Various hands-on activities and guided tours of the Castle and Boar Mill. No extra charge

Castles

Victorian History

11/9/99 FORT BROCKHURST

12/9/99 Tel: 01705 581059

Victorian Quack Medicine Seller. The

Ringwoods of History. A£2.00 C£1.00 Concessions£1.50

Forts

People and Places of the Past

11/9/99 KINGSTON LACY
12/9/99 Tel: 01202 883402

An insight into people and places of the past. 14.00 start. A£2.00 C£1.00

Historic Houses

Annual Steam Galla

11/9/99 SWANAGE RAILWAY
12/9/99 Tel: 01929 425800

All our locos in steam, plus vintage traction rally

Railways

Exhibition: Ashridge Women's Institute

11/9/99 ASHRIDGE ESTATE
16/9/99 Tel: 01442 851227

Ashridge Monument Visitor Centre. Craft exhibition. Time: 14.00-17.00. Normal entry fee

Country Estates

Garden Tour

12/9/99 OSBORNE HOUSE
12/9/99 Tel: 01983 200022

A seasonal garden tour of Osborne Garden with the Head Gardener. A£3.50 C£1.80 Concessions£2.60

Historic Houses & Gardens

Hardy Plant Propagation

16/9/99 ENGLEFIELD HOUSE GARDEN
16/9/99 Tel: 0118 930 2221

Students will learn how to propagate after finding suitable herbaceous perennials and semi-ripe and hard wood cuttings from a specialist range of plants in Englefield House Garden. Time: 13.30-15.00. Cost: £13.00, includes 2 potted herbaceous perennials and 2 rooted hard wood cuttings.

Gardens

International Floral Design Show and Competition

16/9/99 LULWORTH CASTLE
19/9/99 Tel: 01929 400352

Castles

Goodwood Motor Circuit Meeting

17/9/99 GOODWOOD HOUSE
19/9/99 Tel: 01243 755000

One of the highlights of the sporting year. This classic circuit, the spiritual home of British Racing Green, hosts it's second major meeting. See the famous marques of Maserati, Ferrari, BRM, Cooper and Lotus-and many of their original drivers. The new banking provides spectators with thrilling views. Fri 17th is practice day, Sat 18th practice and race day, Sun 19th The Big Day! A£35+ extra for grandstand seats, Children free.

Historic Houses

Goodwood Motor Circuit Race Meeting

17/9/99 GOODWOOD MOTOR RACING CIRCUIT
19/9/99 Tel: 01243 755055

Lord March will bring the world's greatest racing cars back to this classic racing circuit, many of the greatest drivers of all times being reunited with the cars they raced in the 1950s and 60s . Spectators are encouraged to wear 1950s dress as Goodwood becomes a time capsule for three days of spectacular entertainment. Spitfires and Hurricanes will revive the spirit of the Battle of Britain. Goodwood in September is a chance to forget the modern world and revel in the revival of the glory days of British Racing Green.

Festivals

Guernsey Lily International Amateur Film and Video Festival

17/9/99 GUERNSEY LILY INTERNATIONAL AMATEUR
19/9/99 FILM AND VIDEO FESTIVAL 1999
Tel: 01481 38147

Venue: Peninsula Hotel, Les Dicqs Vale. Screening of successful films followed by presentation of awards and dinner, films and talks. The Festival is considered to be one of the most prestigious. Events on morning, afternoon and evenings. To stay in the Peninsula Hotel: A£28.00 B&B Double/Twin room; Single room: supplement of £8.00 per night. Entry fees for competitions £5.00. Tickets available from: Peninsula Hotel: 01481 48706

Festivals

The Grand Dorset Expedition

18/9/99 KINGSTON LACY
18/9/99 Tel: 01202 883402

Hear fascinating tales of ancient history and folklore. 10.00 start. Bring picnic and drinks. A£2.50 C£1.00. Please call 01202 882705 for meeting point

Historic Houses

Medieval Entertainment

18/9/99 BISHOP'S WALTHAM PALACE
19/9/99 Tel: 01489 892460

Fighting knights, dancing, stories, children's games and juggling. A£3.50 C£1.80 Concessions£2.60

Historical Remains

Steam Threshing Weekend

18/9/99
19/9/99
COGGES MANOR FARM MUSEUM
Tel: 01993 772602
Brill Vintage Small Engine Preservation Society Show. For further details including times and prices please call venue direct

Museum- Farms

National Heritage Weekend

18/9/99
19/9/99
THE KING'S ROYAL HUSSARS MUSEUM IN WINCHESTER
Tel: 01962 828539
Open 10.00-17.00 Sat & Sun with areas not usually open to the public plus extra items on display and handling exhibits

Museum- Regimental

Workshops: Deer

19/9/99
19/9/99
ASHRIDGE ESTATE
Tel: 01442 851227
An introduction to Ashridge's fallow and Muntjac deer, including deer watching. Time: 16.30-19.30. Cost: £15.00

Country Estates

Racing at Goodwood

22/9/99
23/9/99
GOODWOOD RACECOURSE
Tel: 01243 755022
Last weekend of racing bringing the season to a close in style. Racing from 14.00

Racecourses

15th-Century Living History Weekend

23/9/99
24/9/99
CORFE CASTLE
Tel: 01929 481294
Set in the period when Richard, Duke of Gloucester, later to be Richard III was Constable of the Castle. No extra charge.

Castles

Ascot Festival

25/9/99
26/9/99
ASCOT RACECOURSE
Tel: 01344 622211
Combines high quality horseracing with entertainment for the whole family. Flat Meeting. First Race 14.00, Members Enclosure £15.00, Grandstand & Paddock £10.00, Silver Ring £5.00

Racecourses

Craft Demonstrations

25/9/99
26/9/99
COGGES MANOR FARM MUSEUM
Tel: 01993 772602
Painting on Silk demonstration on Saturday and jam and pickle making in the Victorian kitchen on Sunday. For further details including times and prices please call venue direct

Museum- Farms

Looking Ahead to Winter - Maureen Roke

28/9/99
28/9/99
ENGLEFIELD HOUSE GARDEN
Tel: 0118 930 2221
More imaginative ideas for decorating your home for the winter months with fresh and dried flowers. Some materials will be available free of charge and there will be a selection for sale. Please meet at Englefield Garden Centre. Time: 19.00-21.00. Cost: £13.00.

Gardens

Jersey Festival of World Music

30/9/99
4/10/99
JERSEY FESTIVAL OF WORLD MUSIC
Tel: 01534 607860
Held at various venues around the Island. A mix of dances, concerts, informal sessions and family events. 1999 will be the 24th consecutive year of the Festival. From humble beginnings, (it started as a folk festival) it is now an integral part of the Island's cultural calendar and is recognised in Europe and further afield as a festival of very high quality. Festival pass A£25.00, OAPs&Students£15.00 C(under 14)£Free. Tickets available from: Jersey Arts Centre, Phillips Street, St Helier 01534 873767

Festivals

Friends of Thomas

1/10/99
3/10/99
DIDCOT RAILWAY CENTRE
Tel: 01235 817200
See 'Thomas', the children's favourite steam engine and his Great Western friends

Railways Steam/Light

Harvest Home

3/10/99
3/10/99
COGGES MANOR FARM MUSEUM
Tel: 01993 772602
For further details including times and prices please call venue direct

Museum- Farms

Fruits of the Autumn

3/10/99
KINGSTON LACY
Tel: 01202 883402
Walk to discover nature's autumn harvest. A£2.00 C£1.00. 14.00 start

Historic Houses

Gardening in the Autumn

6/10/99
6/10/99
KINGSTON LACY
Tel: 01202 883402
Event starts at 11.00. For further details please call venue direct

Historic Houses

Bulbs (Adults)

9/10/99
9/10/99
ENGLEFIELD HOUSE GARDEN
Tel: 0118 930 2221
The day will include planting a container

of mixed bulbs and seasonal bedding for a spring display and learning how to propagate bulbs including twin scaling. Time: 10.00-12.00. Cost: 15.00.

Gardens

Victorian Entertainment

9/10/99　FORT BROCKHURST

10/10/99　Tel: 01705 581059

Goodbye Dolly Gray by The Diehard Company. A£3.00 C£1.50 Concessions£2.30

Forts

Garden Tour

10/10/99　OSBORNE HOUSE

10/10/99　Tel: 01983 200022

A seasonal garden tour of Osborne Garden with the Head Gardener. A£3.50 C£1.80 Concessions£2.60

Historic Houses & Gardens

Bulbs (Children)

16/10/99　ENGLEFIELD HOUSE GARDEN

16/10/99　Tel: 0118 930 2221

The day will include planting a container of mixed bulbs and seasonal bedding for a spring display and learning how to propagate bulbs including twin scaling. Time: 10.00-12.00. Cost: 10.00.

Gardens

Guided Tour

17/10/99　COGGES MANOR FARM MUSEUM

17/10/99　Tel: 01993 772602

Guided tour of the Manor House at 14.30. For further details please call venue direct

Museum- Farms

What's Happening in the Park

17/10/99　KINGSTON LACY

17/10/99　Tel: 01202 883402

Event starts at 11.00. For further details including times and prices please call venue direct

Historic Houses

Apple Day

17/10/99　WEST DEAN GARDENS

17/10/99　Tel: 01243 818210/811301

Over 100 varieties of apples. Apple cookery demonstrations. Guided tours of the Walled Garden. Apple Games and 'Apple Bobbing'. Apple dishes served in the restaurant

Gardens

Michelangelo Pistoletto

17/10/99　MUSEUM OF MODERN ART OXFORD

2/1/00　Tel: 01865 722733

'The Shifting Perspective'. Founder of Italian Arte Povera, this major exhibition brings his work to Great Britain

Museum- Art

Friends of Thomas the Tank Engine Weekend

23/10/99　SWANAGE RAILWAY

24/10/99　Tel: 01929 425800

He's Back. Everyone's favourite little engine, come along a see Thomas on our Branch Line!

Railways

Autumn Countryside Collection

23/10/99　WEALD AND DOWNLAND OPEN AIR MUSEUM

24/10/99　Tel: 01243 811348

Further details available on 01243 811348

Museum- Social History

Half Term Activities

23/10/99　COGGES MANOR FARM MUSEUM

31/10/99　Tel: 01993 772602

The venue is open through Half Term (not Monday) with daily demonstrations

Museum- Farms

Giant Cleudo Game

24/10/99　APPULDURCOMBE HOUSE

31/10/99　Tel: 01983 852484

Giant Cluedo Game. 10.00-16.00. Normal prices plus £1.00 per detective

Historical Remains

Hallowe'en Thriller

29/10/99　STAUNTON COUNTRY PARK

31/10/99　Tel: 01705 453405

Largest special event of its kind in the country! Theatrical thriller with a twist, with actors and actress's from the Ashcroft Theatre, Fareham. Suitable for accompanied children from 5 years, and all the family. Tickets from £5.00. Advance bookings only available from 1 Oct.

Country Parks

Halloween Ghosts

30/10/99　APPULDURCOMBE HOUSE

30/10/99　Tel: 01983 852484

A s-s-spooooky day at Appuldurcombe House, come if you dare!

Historical Remains

Spooks and Sparks

30/10/99　BEAULIEU

30/10/99　Tel: 01590 612345

There will be ghostly goings on, tricks and treats for children, old-time fairground rides, two great bonfires plus a grand fireworks spectacular set to ghostly music. Gates open 15.00

Museums

Cider Making

30/10/99　HAMPTONNE COUNTRY LIFE MUSEUM

31/10/99 Tel: 01534 863955
Follow the traditional process of apple crushing and pressing, using Elégant the horse, to make a most delicious end result
Museum- Country

Schools Art and Craft Exhibition
3/11/99 GUERNSEY MUSEUM AND ART GALLERY
9/1/00 Tel: 01481 726518
See art and craft carefully produced by the local school children
Museum- Local History

Artspace 1999
4/11/99 GUERNSEY MUSEUM AND ART GALLERY
31/1/00 Tel: 01481 726518
Student Art and Design. The finest examples of paintings, pastels, textiles, sculptures and ceramics from the Island's artists of the future
Museum- Local History

Fireworks Party
6/11/99 BEALE PARK
6/11/99 Tel: 0118 984 5172
Massive bonfire, funfair, stalls, BBQ and other hot food, music, two bars and wonderful fireworks over the lake. 18.00-23.00. A£3.00 C£2.00
Wildlife Parks

Falling Leaves
7/11/99 KINGSTON LACY
7/11/99 Tel: 01202 883402
An afternoon strolling through woodland at 14.00. A£2.00 C£0.50
Historic Houses

Christmas Craft Show
13/11/99 BROADLANDS
14/11/99 Tel: 01794 505010
Enjoy hundreds of unique ideas in floored and heated marquees with plenty of Christmas flavour
Historic Houses

Christmas Craft Show
20/11/99 BEALE PARK
21/11/99 Tel: 0118 984 5172
Local craftspeople demonstrating and selling. Come along to buy that extra special Christmas gift. Please telephone for times
Wildlife Parks

Advent Weekend
4/12/99 COGGES MANOR FARM MUSEUM
5/12/99 Tel: 01993 772602
Traditional preparations for a Victorian Christmas. 11.00-16.00
Museum- Farms

Santa's Magic Steaming
4/12/99 BUCKINGHAMSHIRE RAILWAY CENTRE

19/12/99 Tel: 01296 655450
Ride on Santa's own steam train. Presents for the children and seasonal refreshments for adults with a children's magic show
Museum- Transport

Thomas Santa Special
10/12/99 DIDCOT RAILWAY CENTRE
12/12/99 Tel: 01235 817200
Thomas Santa Special: Let Thomas take you to see Santa in his Grotto, advanced booking essential
Railways Steam/Light

Christmas Event
18/12/99 STAUNTON COUNTRY PARK
19/12/99 Tel: 01705 453405
Father Christmas, carol singers, games and activities. Suitable for all the family. Reduced admission rates.
Country Parks

The End is Nigh
29/12/99 KINGSTON LACY
29/12/99 Tel: 01202 883402
For times and prices of this event please call 01202 882705
Historic Houses

Millennium Steamings
31/12/99 DIDCOT RAILWAY CENTRE
3/1/00 Tel: 01235 817200
Great Western Railway steam trains celebrate the new millennium
Railways Steam/Light

Korean War 50th Anniversary Exhibition
1/7/00 ROYAL ELECTRICAL AND MECHANICAL ENGINEERS (REME) MUSEUM OF TECHNOLOGY
31/12/00 Tel: 0118 976 3567
Exhibition detailing REME's involvement in the Korean War
Museum- Military

Wales

Saint David's Day Celebration
CELTICA

1/3/99
1/3/99 Tel: 01654 702702
Please telephone for further information
Exhibition Centres

St David's Day
NATIONAL MUSEUM AND GALLERY
CARDIFF

1/3/99
1/3/99 Tel: 01222 397951
Celebrations include free entry, traditional music and dancing
Museums

Open Day
PENRHYN CASTLE

1/3/99
1/3/99 Tel: 01248 353084
St David's Day opening. 12.00-16.00.
Grounds open day free to all - come and enjoy the spring bulbs. Tea room open
Castles

Exhibition: Christian & David Lloyd
TALIESIN ARTS CENTRE

1/3/99
27/3/99 Tel: 01792 296883 Box Office
Father and son compare notes with their first joint exhibition. David's abstracts balance colour and form to produce dynamic compositions while Christian tackles the themes of Swansea Bay, mythical trees and the Ship of Fools.
Arts & Entertainment

Theatre: Penelope Flowers
TALIESIN ARTS CENTRE

3/3/99
3/3/99 Tel: 01792 296883 Box Office
Penelope Flowers celebrates the theatre culture and community of Swansea and it's surrounding areas. We present the work of two of Swansea's emerging theatre artists making work about the textures of Swansea. Mandy Connell - "Who Needs Manhattan?" Just returned from manhattan, Welsh cabaret artist Sylvia is dejected. New York wasn't what she hoped for. The Chrysler, Empire State, Times Square all meant nothing. Retracing her childhood in the local supermarket, Sylvia finds inspiration. Asda, the Half Way Inn and Randolf's Florists provide the glamour she craves.....dead Penelope "A Map For The Pursuit of Happiness". Stella Far is a secretary. She is thirty seven years old, nearly thirty eight. Stella has a boyfriend and a flat, but she's bored. And you know what? Some of life's most interesting developments happen along when you're bored. Time: 19.30. Tickets: £4.00 & £2.00 discounts, Penelope Flowers Card 10% discount.

Arts & Entertainment

Jump Meetings at Chepstow
CHEPSTOW RACECOURSE

3/3/99
24/3/99 Tel: 01291 622260
Racing on 3,13 & 24 Mar. Please call for further information
Racecourses

World Music: Harp & Soul
TALIESIN ARTS CENTRE

4/3/99
4/3/99 Tel: 01792 296883 Box Office
A unique opportunity to hear some of the world's top harp players in a seamless evening of entertainment. From China comes Cui Jun Zhi; from Scotland, Mary Macmaster, known to many from the harp duo Sileas, playing with fellow Scot, Corrina Hewat; Triple Harper, Llio Rydderch, a key link in the unbroken tradition of Welsh harp playing; Laoise Kelly, one of the most in-demand harpers in Ireland and finally the dynamic and jazzy Kristen Nogues from Brittany. The music will charm, delight, soothe and excite, showing the range and versatility of this beautiful instrument. Time: 19.30. Tickets: £8.00, £5.50 discounts.
Arts & Entertainment

Modern Theatre: Rising Tide presented by Steel Wasp
TALIESIN ARTS CENTRE

5/3/99
5/3/99 Tel: 01792 296883 Box Office
Behind the doors of a Welsh city, stranded individuals hurtle through lives of quiet desperation. Behind their eyes they live out fantasies of disturbing passion. Unlikely relationships form, painfully funny experiences are shared and lurking beneath the daily rituals is the need "to be someone". Time: 19.30. Tickets: £6.00, £4.00 discounts. Buy a ticket for both this and 'East From the Gantry' and save money! 2 for £10.00, £7.00 discounts.
Arts & Entertainment

Modern Theatre: East from the Gantry by Ed Thomas
TALIESIN ARTS CENTRE

6/3/99
6/3/99 Tel: 01792 296883 Box Office
Bella met Ronnie by phoning him up at random. Trampas called himself Trampas after a character from "the Virginian". Bella met Trampas on a derelict hill, Ronnie shot a cat dead. In a world of drunkenness and memories we discover a "play of possibilities where anything can happen". The play is staged using

three actors, three ladders and a hundred umbrellas - and enormous physical energy. Time: 19.30. Tickets: £6.00, £4.00 discounts. Buy a ticket for both this and 'Rising Tide' and save money! 2 for £10.00, £7.00 discounts.

Arts & Entertainment

18th Century Derby Porcelain

6/3/99
25/4/99

GLYNN VIVIAN ART GALLERY
Tel: 01792 655006
In Room 1. Charles Norman Collection Touring Exhibition. Products of the 'Golden Age' at the Derby Factory (from about 1775 to 1805), which are universally acknowledged as masterpieces of ceramic production

Art Galleries

Signs of Spring

7/3/99
7/3/99

ERDDIG HALL
Tel: 01978 313333 / 355314
Walk with the Warden. 12.00-14.00, £1.00 per person.

Historic Houses & Gardens

Guides in the Hides

7/3/99
28/3/99

WWT LLANELLI
Tel: 01554 741087
Every Sunday, 14.00-16.00. An expert will be at hand to help you with bird identification and enhance your enjoyment of the spectacular wildlife of the marsh.

Bird Centres

Follow a Feed

7/3/99
26/9/99

WWT LLANELLI
Tel: 01554 741087
Every Sunday, 16.00. Join one of our wardens on the Sunday afternoon feed, and learn more about the birds and how WWT cares for them.

Bird Centres

Lunch Time Talk: A Single Currency

10/3/99
10/3/99

NATIONAL MUSEUM AND GALLERY CARDIFF
Tel: 01222 397951
British Imperial Currency. Please telephone for further information

Museums

New Dance: Fist, a Docks Drama

12/3/99
12/3/99

TALIESIN ARTS CENTRE
Tel: 01792 296883 Box Office
R.I.P.E. The distinctive R.I.P.E trio: Marc Rees, Sean Tuan John and John Rowley bring their first major collaboration to Swansea after a sell-out run at Chapter. Together with German composer Hendrik Lorenzen, R.I.P.E weave live action, pre-recorded material and a dynamic sound score in a powerful inter-disciplinary performance that's been described as a common, clever and cynical comedy. Based on the bizarre encounter that took place in Cardiff Docks in 1956 between Kingsley Amis and Francis Bacon. "Fist" punches you in the face and drags you bound, gagged but smiling into the sordid world of sailors, sex, stilettos, violence and eight seconds of silence. Time: 20.00. Tickets: £7.50, £5.00 discounts.

Arts & Entertainment

Daffodil Walk

13/3/99
14/3/99

CHIRK CASTLE
Tel: 01691 777701
Subject to weather conditions. Garden and tearoom open. 12.00-16.00. A£1.00 C£0.50 (inc. NT members).

Castles

National Garden Scheme

14/3/99
14/3/99

ERDDIG HALL
Tel: 01978 313333 / 355314
Walks with the Head Gardener at 13.00 & 14.00. A£2.00 C£Free

Historic Houses & Gardens

Mothering Sunday

14/3/99
14/3/99

PENRHYN CASTLE
Tel: 01248 353084
Come and enjoy a walk around the Garden and a special tea in the Tea Room (tea served: 14.00-17.00), opening: 13.00-17.00

Castles

Moorhens - an illustrated talk

14/3/99
14/3/99

WWT LLANELLI
Tel: 01554 741087
A common but little studied bird whose habits have been the focus of study at WWT Llanelli by PhD student Dan Forman. His findings are intriguing! Time: 14.00. Cost: £2.00.

Bird Centres

Designer Clothes Sale

19/3/99
19/3/99

CHIRK CASTLE
Tel: 01691 777701
Ladies daywear, jewellery, evening wear, leather goods plus children's clothes and toys. Designer labels include casual clothes from Versace, Armani, Ralph Lauren; coats, suits and separates from Fendi, Mansfield, Guy Laroche, Yarrell, Mondi, Ara and Basler. 11.00-16.00. £1.00 entry.

Castles

Modern Theatre: the Hydrographer's Daughter

Further more detailed information on the attractions listed can be found in Best Guides *Visitor Attractions* Guide under the classifications shown

19/3/99
19/3/99

TALIESIN ARTS CENTRE
Tel: 01792 296883 Box Office

A Solo performance by Vanya Constant. The haunting began with my father's last words: "Well, well, my darling, it makes you wonder. It's funny isn't it. All your life, your work and then it all comes to this." The performance has been created from her father's diaries, letters and photographs; archival and published material relating to the changing role of the South Wales Ports 1950-1980; film documentary and video interviews of people living in the ports today relating their experience. Time: 19.30. Tickets: £5.00, £3.50 discounts.

Arts & Entertainment

Daffodil Walk

20/3/99
20/3/99

CHIRK CASTLE
Tel: 01691 777701

Garden and tearoom open. 12.00-16.00. A£1.00 C£0.50 (inc. NT members). Subject to weather conditions.

Castles

Sadwrn Siarad

20/3/99
20/3/99

MUSEUM OF WELSH LIFE
Tel: 01222 573500

Please call for further information

Museum- Social History

Designer Clothes Sale

20/3/99
20/3/99

PENRHYN CASTLE
Tel: 01248 353084

Ladies daywear, jewellery, evening wear, leather goods plus childrens clothes and toys. Labels include Versace, Armani, Raplh Lauren. A£1.00, tea room and shop open. 11.00-16.00

Castles

Peter Bailey: Celebration Dance and other works

20/3/99
3/5/99

BRECKNOCK MUSEUM
Tel: 01874 624121

This Welsh sculptor's work wittily embraces literary, political and other themes

Museum- Local History

Syzygy, Philip Mead and Alan Rogers

20/3/99
9/5/99

GLYNN VIVIAN ART GALLERY
Tel: 01792 655006

In the Main Gallery. Springing from their joint experiences as artists-in-residence in Rajestan, this exhibition shows the work of two leading South Wales based artists

Art Galleries

Painting Days with Janet Bligh

20/3/99
11/12/99

WWT LLANELLI
Tel: 01554 741087

Expert tuition in inspiring surroundings. Painting Days are held throughout the year on Saturdays, 10.00-16.30, starting on January 16th. The day includes a talk, a demonstration and a look at examples of the work of well known artists, followed by a chance to practice and produce a work of art. 'The Challenge of Water Colour' is the theme for the year with a different focus on techniques each session. The sessions will be held on the following dates: Mar 20; Apr 17; May 1, 22; June 12; July 3, 24; Sept 4, 18; Oct 2, 23; Nov 13; 27, Dec 11. Cost: £15.00 (Members £12.50), booking essential. Please contact the Centre for a leaflet giving full details of all sessions.

Bird Centres

National Garden Scheme

21/3/99
21/3/99

CHIRK CASTLE
Tel: 01691 777701

Open Day where the admission you pay goes to local charities. 11.00-17.00 A£1.50 C£0.75 including NT Members

Castles

Daffodil Day and Daffodil Walks

27/3/99
27/3/99

LLANERCHAERON
Tel: 01545 570200

A chance to see the extensive daffodil collection in the walled gardens and naturalised throughout the estate. Proceeds from the walks to the National Gardens Scheme. Walks 12.00-13.00 and 14.30-15.30. Normal admission price plus £1.00 per walk

Historic Houses & Gardens

Modern Music: Conga Line in Hell

27/3/99
27/3/99

TALIESIN ARTS CENTRE
Tel: 01792 296883 Box Office

Charlie Barber and Band return to Taliesin with a colourful concert of Latin-American rhythms and dance music. The festive atmosphere kicks off with Charlie Barber's Samba-Round which brings together traditional Spanish street music with drumming from Brazilian carnival. Also in the programme is a brand new work from Swansea-born Paula Gardiner, the Band's finest bass player and an established musician and composer on the national jazz circuit. The evening also includes the extraordinary music of Uruguayan composer Miguel del Aguila, as well as the master of the Argentinian tango Aster Piazzolla and

Mexican composers Arturo Marquez and Javier Alvarez. Time: 19.30. Tickets: £7.50, £5.00 discounts.

Arts & Entertainment

Demonstration

28/3/99 ERDDIG HALL
28/3/99 Tel: 01978 313333 / 355314
Tom Hanson, Wood Carver and Stick Maker. 11.00-16.00.

Historic Houses & Gardens

Daffodil Day

28/3/99 LLANERCHAERON
28/3/99 Tel: 01545 570200
A chance to see the extensive daffodil collection in the walled gardens and naturalised throughout the estate.

Historic Houses & Gardens

Art Exhibition

28/3/99 PENRHYN CASTLE
24/4/99 Tel: 01248 353084
Shelley Hocknell exhibition in the Stableblock Gallery 12.00-17.00

Castles

Craft Exhibition

1/4/99 ST DAVIDS CATHEDRAL
10/4/99 Tel: 01437 720199
Local craftsmen exhibiting their work - wood turning, weaving, jewellery with demonstrations

Cathedrals

Pax Romana

1/4/99 ROMAN LEGIONARY MUSEUM
18/4/99 Tel: 01633 423134
The Roman Empire covered an enormous area, but did everyone speak the same language? What goods were traded? Discover some facts about the Empire and follow Marcus the Pearl Merchant's quest

Museum- Roman

Easter Egg Trail

2/4/99 ERDDIG HALL
5/4/99 Tel: 01978 313333 / 355314
Come and hunt the Easter Eggs in the gardens. 12.00-16.00. Normal admission + £1.00 to take part.

Historic Houses & Gardens

Photographic Exhibition

2/4/99 PENRHYN CASTLE
5/4/99 Tel: 01248 353084
Ken Morton Photographic exhibition in the Brushing Room, 12.00-17.00

Castles

Easter Eggstravaganza

2/4/99 COLBY WOODLAND GARDEN
9/4/99 Tel: 01834 811885
Eggstra special Woodland trail with a

prize for every child. Make your own ornamental Easter Egg. Normal admission. NT Members Free.

Gardens

Easter Eggsplorers

2/4/99 WWT LLANELLI
18/4/99 Tel: 01554 741087
Easter holiday activities, including the Great Egg Trail, for you to have fun finding out about eggs.

Bird Centres

Women Artists and Pembrokeshire

2/4/99 TENBY MUSEUM AND ART GALLERY
31/12/99 Tel: 01834 842809
Highlighting the changing times, lives and works of women artists over the last two hundred years.

Museum- Local History

Daffodil Day

3/4/99 LLANERCHAERON
3/4/99 Tel: 01545 570200
A chance to see the extensive daffodil collection in the walled gardens and naturalised throughout the estate.

Historic Houses & Gardens

Easter Fun Day

3/4/99 PENRHYN CASTLE
3/4/99 Tel: 01248 353084
With Easter Egg trails around the Castle and grounds, competitions and Mr Bimbamboozle, magic and puppets. An Easter Bonnet competition! Lots of prizes. 12.00-16.00

Castles

Easter Egg Trail

3/4/99 POWIS CASTLE AND GARDEN
3/4/99 Tel: 01938 554338
Follow the trail around the garden and collect your prize egg. Normal admission prices plus £1.00 charge for the Easter Egg Trail. Sponsored as part of the Barclays Country Focus Initiative. 12.00-15.30.

Castles

Easter Egg Hunt

4/4/99 ABERDULAIS FALLS
4/4/99 Tel: 01639 636674
Bring the children along for a fun day with egg hunt and quiz.

Waterfalls

Easter Egg Hunt

4/4/99 DINEFWR PARK
4/4/99 Tel: 01558 823902
Quiz trail in the park with a prize for all. 14.00-16.00. £1.00. Supported by Barclays under its Barclays CountryFocus Initiative.

Further more detailed information on the attractions listed can be found in Best Guides *Visitor Attractions* Guide under the classifications shown

Parks

Easter Egstravaganza
4/4/99
4/4/99
PLAS NEWYDD
Tel: 01248 714795
Chocolate Filled Family Fun Day! Bring a decorated egg competition - judging 15.00. Egg races, face-painting, quiz trails and activities with Trusty the Hedgehog. 12.00-14.00. Usual admission + optional activity bag £1.50.

Historic Houses & Gardens

Easter Egg Trail
4/4/99
5/4/99
CHIRK CASTLE
Tel: 01691 777701
Come along and see how many of our Eggs you can find

Castles

Operamint Performance
4/4/99
5/4/99
MUSEUM OF WELSH LIFE
Tel: 01222 573500
Please call for further information

Museum- Social History

Daffodil Day
5/4/99
5/4/99
LLANERCHAERON
Tel: 01545 570200
A chance to see the extensive daffodil collection in the walled gardens and naturalised throughout the estate.

Historic Houses & Gardens

Jump Meetings
5/4/99
20/4/99
CHEPSTOW RACECOURSE
Tel: 01291 622260
Race meetings on 5 & 20 Apr

Racecourses

Art Exhibition
7/4/99
12/4/99
PENRHYN CASTLE
Tel: 01248 353084
Ray Keates and Alan Beattie paintings exhibition. Artists in Residence. Brushing Room, 12.00-17.00

Castles

Garden Demonstration
8/4/99
8/4/99
POWIS CASTLE AND GARDEN
Tel: 01938 554338
Rose pruning and training demonstrated by the Gardeners at Powis. Normal admission prices. 14.00-16.00.

Castles

Exhibition & Demonstrations
10/4/99
11/4/99
ERDDIG HALL
Tel: 01978 313333 / 355314
By Chester Wood Turners, 11.00-16.00

Historic Houses & Gardens

10km Road Race
11/4/99
11/4/99
CHIRK CASTLE
Tel: 01691 777701
Phew, would you rather enter or watch?

Starts 10.30

Castles

Victorian Childhood Experience
11/4/99
11/4/99
PENRHYN CASTLE
Tel: 01248 353084
A laundry without gadgets, a schoolroom without computers, and toys without batteries. How did those Victorians cope? Come and find out - lots of hands-on Victorian fun. 12.00-16.00

Castles

Wetland Craft Day
11/4/99
11/4/99
WWT LLANELLI
Tel: 01554 741087
Your chance to try a range of crafts, including basket making, hurdle making, well dressing and making a miniature coracle. You can even try sailing in a real coracle.

Bird Centres

Bank Holiday Craft Demonstrations
13/4/99
13/4/99
BRECKNOCK MUSEUM
Tel: 01874 624121
Phil Davies - walking stick carving, call for further details

Museum- Local History

A Walk with the Gardener
13/4/99
13/4/99
PLAS NEWYDD
Tel: 01248 714795
The Spring flowers and shrubs are at their best; flowering cherries, daffodils, magnolia and rhododendron. A good time to see the Camellia Dell. Time: 14.00. Admission + £2.50 (inc. members).

Historic Houses & Gardens

Megamessy Art Sessions
13/4/99
16/4/99
WWT LLANELLI
Tel: 01554 741087
For 6-13 year olds. Time: 10.00-12.00 & 13.30-15.30. Cost: £2.50 per session. Booking essential.

Bird Centres

Woodturners
14/4/99
19/4/99
PENRHYN CASTLE
Tel: 01248 353084
Gwynedd Woodturners with a display of the group's products on sale in the Brushing Room, 12.00-17.00

Castles

Course: Gate Making
17/4/99
18/4/99
ERDDIG HALL
Tel: 01978 313333 / 355314
Two day course. 10.00-16.30 each day. £15.00 for course + £90.00 to purchase gate. Please book in advance.

Historic Houses & Gardens

Trusty the Hedgehog
18/4/99 ERDDIG HALL
18/4/99 Tel: 01978 313333 / 355314
Fancy Dress and Kite Making Day. 14.00-16.30

Historic Houses & Gardens

Star Party
23/4/99 WWT LLANELLI
23/4/99 Tel: 01554 741087
Come and star gaze! Telescopes to see the stars; talks and experiments to find out about the stars and the moon, and why they are important to birds. Time: 18.00-21.00. Cost: £2.00. Booking essential.

Bird Centres

Art Exhibition
23/4/99 PENRHYN CASTLE
3/5/99 Tel: 01248 353084
By Mr B F Blackburn - Artist in Residence in the Brushing Room, 12.00-17.00

Castles

The Oppe Collection
24/4/99 NATIONAL MUSEUM AND GALLERY
CARDIFF
20/6/99 Tel: 01222 397951
Organised by the Tate Gallery, one hundred of the finest water-colours in the Oppe Collection including masterpieces by Bonnington, Constable, Cotman and Cozens, as well as major works by the Welsh artists Richard Wilson, Thomas Jones and John Downman

Museums

Demonstration
25/4/99 ERDDIG HALL
25/4/99 Tel: 01978 313333 / 355314
Jim Heath, wood carver, 11.00-17.00

Historic Houses & Gardens

Federation of Art Socities - North Wales Group
28/4/99 PENRHYN CASTLE
31/5/99 Tel: 01248 353084
An annual exhibition in the Stableblock Gallery, 11.00-17.00

Castles

May Day Celebration
1/5/99 CELTICA
1/5/99 Tel: 01654 702702
Please telephone for further information

Exhibition Centres

Garden Tour
1/5/99 ERDDIG HALL
1/5/99 Tel: 01978 313333 / 355314
Led by Head Gardener. Ivy collection. 13.00 & 15.00. Normal admission + £2.00 per person.

Historic Houses & Gardens

Morris Dancing
1/5/99 PENRHYN CASTLE
1/5/99 Tel: 01248 353084
Eryri Morris Dancers - enjoy the fun and join in, 14.00-16.00

Castles

Vintage Military Weeknd
1/5/99 LLANGOLLEN STATION PLC
2/5/99 Tel: 01978 860951/860979
Advance in good order to Llangollen for a thrilling day at the front with military vehicles troops, steam trains and a 'Glen Miller' style dance band

Railways Steam/Light

Steam Gala
1/5/99 FFESTINIOG RAILWAY
3/5/99 Tel: 01766 512340
Plans are afoot for a major event at the railway for the 1st,2nd,3rd May 1999. Plans include a major Art exhibition featuring a well known international railway artist, a large narrow gauge model railway exhibition, a grande calvacde of all the FR loco's, the inaugural run of Taliesin and just to add to the fun an 'it's a knockout' for steam loco crews. Watch this space for more information. Further details of the event can be obtained from the Marketing Department, Harbour Station, Porthmadog, Gwynedd, LL49 9NF. Telephone 01766 512340.

Railways Steam/Light

May Fair - Living History Theme
1/5/99 MUSEUM OF WELSH LIFE
3/5/99 Tel: 01222 573500
Please call for further information

Museum- Social History

Powys Wood '99 Festival
1/5/99 POWIS CASTLE AND GARDEN
3/5/99 Tel: 01938 554338
Demonstrations by craftspeople working in wood in the Orangery in the Garden. Normal admission prices. 12.00-16.00.

Castles

Bank Holiday Weekend
1/5/99 WWT LLANELLI
3/5/99 Tel: 01554 741087
Bank holiday fun and games, including pond dipping for young and old to enjoy trying to net pond minibeasts.

Bird Centres

Medieval Dinefwr
2/5/99 DINEFWR PARK
2/5/99 Tel: 01558 823902
A guided walk along the medieval trackways and ancient woodlands of Dinefwr

Park. 14.00-16.00. Normal admission prices.

Parks

Musical Afternoon

2/5/99 ERDDIG HALL
2/5/99 Tel: 01978 313333 / 355314

Celtic and Folk music, performed by Foxes Bark. 14.00-16.30

Historic Houses & Gardens

Stepping Into Spring Family Fun Day

2/5/99 PLAS NEWYDD
2/5/99 Tel: 01248 714795

A celebration of Spring. Seed planting, face-painting, quiz trails and activities with Trusty the Hedgehog. Spring dancing with Dawnswyr Môn. Young Musicians Platform by the Anglesey Music Trust. Time: 12.00-16.00. Usual admission + optional activity bag £1.50.

Historic Houses & Gardens

Spring Plant Fair

2/5/99 POWIS CASTLE AND GARDEN
2/5/99 Tel: 01938 554338

An opportunity to buy interesting and unusual plants from specialist nurseries and meet the Gardeners at Powis. Normal admission prices. 11.00-16.00.

Castles

Photographic Exhibition

3/5/99 ABERDULAIS FALLS
3/5/99 Tel: 01639 636674

A photographic exhibition for month of May Conservation and Industry at Aberdulais Falls.

Waterfalls

Bank Holiday Craft Demonstrations

4/5/99 BRECKNOCK MUSEUM
4/5/99 Tel: 01874 624121

Phil Jeremiah - lovespoon carving

Museum- Local History

Young National Trust Theatre

4/5/99 CHIRK CASTLE
14/5/99 Tel: 01691 777701

With a production entitles The Wonder of the World set in 1855 and written by Matthew Townsend, call for details

Castles

Anglesey in Black and White

5/5/99 PENRHYN CASTLE
10/5/99 Tel: 01248 353084

An exhibition of black and white photographs of Anglesey by Ernie Greenwood in the Brushing Room, 12.00-17.00

Castles

Racing from Chepstow

5/5/99 CHEPSTOW RACECOURSE
31/5/99 Tel: 01291 622260

Jump Meeting 5 May, Evening Flat Meeting 19 May, Flat Meeting on 31 May

Racecourses

Meet the Gardener Tour

6/5/99 PLAS YN RHIW
6/5/99 Tel: 01758 780219

Lasts approximately 1 hour. Starts at 14.00. Normal admission + £1.00 (inc. members). Numbers limited so booking advisable.

Historic Houses & Gardens

National Gardens Scheme Open Day

7/5/99 PLAS NEWYDD
7/5/99 Tel: 01248 714795

A special opening of the garden to raise funds for the National Gardens Scheme. The heady scent of azaleas and magnolias at their peak. Also a good time for rhododendron, camellias and wild flowers particularly bluebells along the Woodland Walk. Time: 11.00-16.00. Admission: £2.20 (inc. NT members). Take a walk with the Gardener at 14.00. Admission: £2.50 (inc. NT members). Please Note: The House will NOT be open today.

Historic Houses & Gardens

National Garden Scheme Open Day

8/5/99 COLBY WOODLAND GARDEN
8/5/99 Tel: 01834 811885

All proceeds are donated to local charities.

Gardens

National Mills Weekend

8/5/99 ABERDULAIS FALLS
9/5/99 Tel: 01639 636674

Featuring famous artists at the Falls.

Waterfalls

Inagaki, Cox & Furuta

8/5/99 BRECKNOCK MUSEUM
13/6/99 Tel: 01874 624121

Major exhibition by Japanese & Japanese influenced artists: Tumike Inagaki, Richard Cox and Hideo Furuta. Exhibition jointly with Theatr ,Brycheiniog, Brewn

Museum- Local History

Victorian Life

9/5/99 ERDDIG HALL
9/5/99 Tel: 01978 313333 / 355314

Domestic life of Victorian Erddig. 12.00-16.00. A day of education for all ages.

Historic Houses & Gardens

National Gardens Scheme Open Day

11/5/99 11/5/99	**PLAS NEWYDD** Tel: 01248 714795 A special opening of the garden to raise funds for the National Gardens Scheme. The heady scent of azaleas and magnolias at their peak. Also a good time for rhododendron, camellias and wild flowers particularly bluebells along the Woodland Walk. Time: 11.00-16.00. Admission: £2.20 (inc. NT members). Take a walk with the Gardener at 14.00. Admission: £2.50 (inc. NT members). Please Note: The House will NOT be open today. *Historic Houses & Gardens*

Llangollen International Jazz Festival 1999

12/5/99 14/5/99	**LLANGOLLEN INTERNATIONAL JAZZ FESTIVAL 1999** Tel: 0151 339 3367 The 13th annual Jazz Festival with forty sessions of continuous jazz music of all styles from Trad to Mainstream and from Modern to Contemporary in seven venues in Llangollen over three days. A must for all Jazz enthusiasts. *Festivals*

Local Landscapes

12/5/99 17/5/99	**PENRHYN CASTLE** Tel: 01248 353084 Come and enjoy a display of local landscapes painted by Eirlys Hughes in the Brusing Room, 12.00-17.00 *Castles*

Garden Demonstration

13/5/99 13/5/99	**POWIS CASTLE AND GARDEN** Tel: 01938 554338 The care of herbaceous borders demonstrated by the Gardeners at Powis. Normal admission prices. 14.00-16.00. *Castles*

Family Fun Day

15/5/99 15/5/99	**COLBY WOODLAND GARDEN** Tel: 01834 811885 Rupert the Bear visits Colby. Try the teddy trail and win a prize. Puppet show, prize for best dressed/most loved/biggest and smallest teddies. *Gardens*

1999 National Annual Meeting of Stickmakers

15/5/99 15/5/99	**PLAS NEWYDD** Tel: 01248 714795 The North Wales Stickmakers are the hosts this year at Plas Newydd. Exhibitions and demonstrations of the traditional skills of stick-dressing.

Normal admission prices apply.
Historic Houses & Gardens

Take 4 - New Perspective on British Quilt Art

15/5/99 11/7/99	**GLYNN VIVIAN ART GALLERY** Tel: 01792 655006 In the Main Gallery. A major exhibition of textile art, bringing together the work of Jo Budd, Pauline Burbidge, Dinah Prentice and Michele Walker. *Art Galleries*

Spring Plant Fair

16/5/99 16/5/99	**ABERDULAIS FALLS** Tel: 01639 636674 Locally grown spring flowers and plants for sale. *Waterfalls*

Spring Plant Fair

16/5/99 16/5/99	**COLBY WOODLAND GARDEN** Tel: 01834 811885 Bargain buys grown by volunteers. Normal admission. NT Members Free. *Gardens*

Spring Plant Fair

16/5/99 16/5/99	**DINEFWR PARK** Tel: 01558 823902 Sale of plants grown by volunteers, local gardening clubs and centres. All proceeds will be used towards the refurbishment of the Victorian Garden. 11.00-16.00. £1.00 - Plant Fair only, otherwise normal admission charges apply. *Parks*

Spring Plant Fair

16/5/99 16/5/99	**ERDDIG HALL** Tel: 01978 313333 / 355314 Come and buy all your beautiful spring bulbs and flowers. 11.00-17.00. £1.00 *Historic Houses & Gardens*

Spring Plant Fair

16/5/99 16/5/99	**LLANERCHAERON** Tel: 01545 570200 Extensive sale of quality plants grown by dedicated and highly experienced volunteers. 11.00-17.00. Normal admission price *Historic Houses & Gardens*

Spring Plant Fair and Guided Garden Walk

16/5/99 16/5/99	**PLAS NEWYDD** Tel: 01248 714795 Sale of plants grown and donated by volunteers. Additional stalls selling books, plants and garden products. Seed planting for children. Proceeds from this event go towards maintaining the gardens at Plas Newydd. Time:

11.00-16.00. There will also be a guided garden walk at 14.00, £2.50.

Historic Houses & Gardens

Painting and Drawing Workshop
18/5/99 CHIRK CASTLE
18/5/99 Tel: 01691 777701
Landscape painting and drawing. A day painting and drawing within the magnificent ground of Chirk Castle under the expert guidance of art tutor Mr. Leslie Jones. 09.30-16.30, £8.00. Booking essential

Castles

Antiques Valuation Day
18/5/99 PLAS NEWYDD
18/5/99 Tel: 01248 714795
With Phillips International Valuers and Auctioneers. Specialists in Ceramics and Glass, Silver and Jewellery, Pictures, Collectors items and Works of Art will value any four items for £5.00. Time: 11.00-16.00. Normal admission prices apply.

Historic Houses & Gardens

Course: Landscape in Watercolour
20/5/99 DINEFWR PARK
20/5/99 Tel: 01558 823902
One day painting course for adults. Booking essential. £8.00 per person.

Parks

Llantilio Crossenny Festival 1999
20/5/99 LLANTILIO CROSSENNY FESTIVAL
20/5/99 Tel: 01873 856928 Box Office
A Performance by:- Tubalaté. Formed in 1991 Tubalaté was the first tuba-euphonium ensemble to graduate and gain the Professional Performance Diploma from the Royal Northern College of Music. Their concerts contain a variety of musical styles from 16th century Lute Dances to light popular classics and contemporary repertoire specially commissioned by Tubalaté. Each member of the group is a well-established soloist and performs regularly with the county's leading orchestras and brass bands. The group recently performed at Buckingham Palace as part of Prince Charles' 50th birthday celebrations. Peter Walton (Euphonium), Ian Anstee and Ryan Breen (Tubas) and John Powell (Euphonium)

Festivals

Art Exhibition
20/5/99 PENRHYN CASTLE
31/5/99 Tel: 01248 353084
Conwy Valley Art Society Exhibition in

the Brushing Room, 12.00-17.00

Castles

Meet the Gardener Tour
21/5/99 POWIS CASTLE AND GARDEN
21/5/99 Tel: 01938 554338
Atmospheric 2-2.5 hour evening tour of the world famous Garden at Powis. Time: 19.00. Tickets: £11.00 to include a drink. Please book in advance.

Castles

A Performance of:- Hansel and Gretel
21/5/99 LLANTILIO CROSSENNY FESTIVAL
22/5/99 Tel: 01873 856928 Box Office
By Humperdink. Given by The London Opera Players with asistance from children from Cross Ash and Raglan Schools

Festivals

Grand Piano Classics
22/5/99 PLAS NEWYDD
22/5/99 Tel: 01248 714795
Nina Vinogradova-Biek plays Grand Piano. Following the success of her previous concerts, Nina returns to Plas Newydd to perform a new programme of Grand Piano Classics. Time: 19.30. Tickets: £10.00 to include glass of wine.

Historic Houses & Gardens

Art Salutes The Boat
22/5/99 GLYNN VIVIAN ART GALLERY
4/7/99 Tel: 01792 655006
In Room 1. Victoria Art Gallery, Bath, touring exhibition. An exhibition exploring the theme of boats through the work of artists including Alfred Wallis and Graham Rich

Art Galleries

Puppetry
23/5/99 ERDDIG HALL
23/5/99 Tel: 01978 313333 / 355314
Indian Puppets and storytelling, 14.00-16.00

Historic Houses & Gardens

Orchestral Concert
23/5/99 LLANTILIO CROSSENNY FESTIVAL
23/5/99 Tel: 01873 856928 Box Office
An orchestral concert given by the Festival Orchestra Charles Farncombe, Conductor.
Programme: Handel, The Arrival of the Queen of Sheba. Mozart, Concerto for Flute and Harp K299, Soloists Eddie Beckett and Skaila Kanga. Sans Seans, Duet for Violin and Harp, Soloists Rolfe Wilson and Skaila Kanga. Haydn, The Farewell Symphony

Festivals

Round and Round the Garden Family

Fun Day
23/5/99 PLAS NEWYDD
23/5/99 Tel: 01248 714795
Meet 'Rupert the Bear'. Bring A bear and enter the Teddy Competition with prizes. Judging at 15.00. Bring a picnic and join in the Teddy Bears Picnic.' Story-telling, Free activity sheets, Face-painting, Garden quiz trail, House Quiz Trail. Time: 12.00-16.00. Normal admission price applies + optional activity bag £1.50.

Historic Houses & Gardens

Bank Holiday Craft Demonstrations
25/5/99 BRECKNOCK MUSEUM
25/5/99 Tel: 01874 624121
Morag Colquhoun - greenwood crafts

Museum- Local History

National Gardens Scheme Open Day
26/5/99 POWIS CASTLE AND GARDEN
26/5/99 Tel: 01938 554338
Garden tours for charity. Time: 11.00-18.00. Normal admission prices apply.

Castles

Craft Exhibition
27/5/99 ST DAVIDS CATHEDRAL
26/6/99 Tel: 01437 720199
Local craftsmen exhibiting their work, glass etching, weaving, fabric printing with demonstrations

Cathedrals

The Way It Was, Spring Steam Gala
29/5/99 LLANGOLLEN STATION PLC
31/5/99 Tel: 01978 860951/860979
A megamix of steam with visiting engines of types not seen here for 30 years! and a packed timetable

Railways Steam/Light

Return of the Romans
29/5/99 ROMAN LEGIONARY MUSEUM
6/6/99 Tel: 01633 423134
Your chance to ask a Roman soldier questions like what did they eat? How long were they in the army for? And exactly what did they wear under their tunics?

Museum- Roman

St Davids Cathedral Festival
29/5/99 ST DAVIDS CATHEDRAL
6/6/99 Tel: 01437 720199
This special anniversary festival offers a feast of classical music in the superb ambience and acoustic of St David's Cathedral, Wales' National Shrine. An ideal opportunity to enjoy by day the pleasures of the Pembrokeshire Coast National Park and its magnificent spring flowers, with music making in the evening by some of the world's top musicians, and a selling exhibition by the Pembrokeshire Craftsmens' Circle in the adjacent St Mary's Hall. Artistes include: BBC NOW, Alun Hoddinott, Bernard Roberts, Brodsky Quartet, Robert Plane, Fine Arts Brass Ensemble, Holst Singers, John Stuart Anderson, Vireai, St David's Cathedral Choir, Charivari Agréable, Festival Chorus and Orchestra and Geraint Bowen

Cathedrals

Duckling Days - Half-Term Activities
29/5/99 WWT LLANELLI
6/6/99 Tel: 01554 741087
Get really close to ducklings! Look behind the scenes with special tours of the hatchery and duckery. Plus activities and trail to find out how tough life can be for a duckling.

Bird Centres

Annual Coast Path Walk 1999
29/5/99 PEMBROKESHIRE COAST NATIONAL PARK
11/6/99 Tel: 01437 764636
Offering walkers a chance to complete the full 299km National Trail on 14 consecutive days with the back-up of experienced guides and pre-arranged transport. Organised by the Pembrokeshire Coast National Park Authority and costs £120.00 per person. The walk will cover around 12-14 miles a day in the company of experienced guides and includes outward coach transport from daily meeting points. Walkers who complete the route receive a personalised certificate and commemorative badge. The price of the walk does not include accommodation, but details of places to stay are available in the National Park's 1999 edition Coast Path accommodation guide priced at £2.33 including postage. For further information or to make a booking (£30.00 deposit required) please contact David Matthews at the Pembrokeshire Coast National Park Authority on 01437 775293.

National Parks

Scavenger Hunt
30/5/99 DINEFWR PARK
30/5/99 Tel: 01558 823902
Collect the weird and wonderful from around Dinefwr Park. For children and adults alike. £0.50 per person otherwise normal admission prices apply.

Parks

Park Race

30/5/99 30/5/99	**ERDDIG HALL** Tel: 01978 313333 / 355314 Erddig 10km Park Race starting at 10.30 *Historic Houses & Gardens*

Children Victorian Extravaganza

30/5/99 30/5/99	**LLANERCHAERON** Tel: 01545 570200 An opportunity for children to try their hand at Threshing, Basket Weaving, Candle Making, Victorian Toys, Stone Cobbling and many more Victorian activities. 12.30-16.30. Normal admission price *Historic Houses & Gardens*

Kite Flying Fun Day

30/5/99 30/5/99	**PENRHYN CASTLE** Tel: 01248 353084 What a site to fly your own kite! Bring along your kite, or design and colour in your own in our competitions and lots more! 12.00-16.00 *Castles*

Forest Fair

30/5/99 31/5/99	**MUSEUM OF WELSH LIFE** Tel: 01222 573500 Please call for further information *Museum- Social History*

Model Steam and Railway Day

31/5/99 31/5/99	**ABERDULAIS FALLS** Tel: 01639 636674 Model trains and ships with working layouts and demonstrations. National Trust shop, audio tours, teas and refreshments by the Friends of Aberdulais Falls. 11.00-18.00. *Waterfalls*

Fete and Gala in Cyfartha Park

31/5/99	**CYFARTHFA CASTLE MUSEUM AND ART GALLERY** Tel: 01685 723112 A day of fun for all the family. *Museums*

National Garden Scheme Open Day

1/6/99 1/6/99	**CHIRK CASTLE** Tel: 01691 777701 Open Day where the admission you pay goes to local charities. 11.00-17.00 A£1.50 C£0.75 including NT Members *Castles*

Diesel Gala Weekend

1/6/99 30/6/99	**LLANGOLLEN STATION PLC** Tel: 01978 860951/860979 Dates to be confirmed. A fine collection of vintage internal-combustion-engined motive power it let loose on the railway for the weekend *Railways Steam/Light*

Art Exhibition

2/6/99 28/6/99	**PENRHYN CASTLE** Tel: 01248 353084 Kay Rees-Davies is back at Penrhyn with her Exhibition of Botanic Art. Artist in Residence, Brushing Room 12.00-17.00 *Castles*

Rupert Bear Visit

3/6/99 3/6/99	**COLBY WOODLAND GARDEN** Tel: 01834 811885 Rupert the Bear invites you to a teddies day out. Games and magic in the meadow, teddy trail and best dressed teddy competition. Normal admission. NT Members and teddies Free. *Gardens*

Magic and Puppets

3/6/99 3/6/99	**PENRHYN CASTLE** Tel: 01248 353084 Mr Bimbamboozle entertains children and adults! delightfully with magic and puppets, 12.00-16.00 *Castles*

Discovery Zone (Smelly Schools)

4/6/99 5/9/99	**NATIONAL MUSEUM AND GALLERY CARDIFF** Tel: 01222 397951 50 years of museum's School Service *Museums*

Horrible Histories

4/6/99 5/9/99	**NATIONAL MUSEUM AND GALLERY CARDIFF** Tel: 01222 397951 An exhibition with a difference, working in partnership with best selling author of the books of the same name, Terry Deary on his first ever exhibition. Visitors of all ages are guaranteed fun, fun and more fun in this hands-on, interactive exhibition which looks at the 'horribles' of the last millennium by using cartoons and illustrations, quizzes and games, replicas and real objects *Museums*

Badger Watch

5/6/99 5/6/99	**DINEFWR PARK** Tel: 01558 823902 Watch the badgers of Dinefwr Park in their natural habitat. £1.00 per person. Time: 19.15. Places are limited so please book. *Parks*

Exhibition

5/6/99 16/6/99	**ERDDIG HALL** Tel: 01978 313333 / 355314 Sat, Sun, Mon, Tue, & Wed only. Exhibition by the North Wales Society of

Botanical and fine Watercolour Artists.
11.00-17.00

Historic Houses & Gardens

Picnic Day

6/6/99 PLAS NEWYDD

6/6/99 Tel: 01248 714795

Bring a picnic and relax in the gardens on the banks of the Menai Strait and enjoy the lively and colourful Eryri Morris Dancers (12.00-14.00) followed by music performed by the Menai Bridge Band (14.00-16.00). Traditional garden games and activities for children with Trusty the Hedgehog (some with small charge).

Historic Houses & Gardens

Paradise Garden

7/6/99 PENRHYN CASTLE

30/8/99 Tel: 01248 353084

Daily except Tuesdays. A Fine Art Exhibition specially for Penrhyn by the national Museuma dn Galleries of Wales. It depicts Botanic Art and its influence on Science through the Centuries. Stableblock Gallery, 11.00-17.00

Castles

Children's Fun Day

9/6/99 ERDDIG HALL

9/6/99 Tel: 01978 313333 / 355314

Fun in the Country Park at 10.00-14.30. £1.00 per child

Historic Houses & Gardens

Meet the Gardener Tour

9/6/99 PLAS YN RHIW

9/6/99 Tel: 01758 780219

Lasts approximately 1 hour. Starts at 14.00. Normal admission + £1.00 (inc. members). Numbers limited so booking advisable.

Historic Houses & Gardens

Open Air Theatre

10/6/99 ERDDIG HALL

10/6/99 Tel: 01978 313333 / 355314

Illyria perform Twelfth Night in the Park at 19.30. Cost: A£7.0 C£5.00

Historic Houses & Gardens

Flat Meetings

11/6/99 CHEPSTOW RACECOURSE

29/6/99 Tel: 01291 622260

Evening Meeting on 11 June, Flat Meeting on 29 June

Racecourses

Miners Gala - Mining and Education

12/6/99 MUSEUM OF WELSH LIFE

12/6/99 Tel: 01222 573500

Please call for further information

Museum- Social History

National Garden Day

12/6/99 PENRHYN CASTLE

12/6/99 Tel: 01248 353084

All proceeds from today will go to local Charities, 11.00-17.00

Castles

Medieval Weekend

12/6/99 CALDICOT CASTLE AND COUNTRY PARK

13/6/99 Tel: 01291 420241

Medieval market and battles over weekend

Castles

Specialist Plant Fair

13/6/99 COLBY WOODLAND GARDEN

13/6/99 Tel: 01834 811885

Nurserymen from all over the region exhibit their unusual shrubs and plants in the meadow at Colby. Normal admission. NT Members Free.

Gardens

Pirates Ahoy! Family Fun Day

13/6/99 PLAS NEWYDD

13/6/99 Tel: 01248 714795

Look out! Pirates have landed at Plas Newydd! Piratical story-walks, face-painting, treasure trails and activities. 12.00-16.00. Normal admission prices apply + optional activity bag £1.50. Free admission to children dressed as pirates!

Historic Houses & Gardens

Poetryfest

13/6/99 ABERYSTWYTH ARTS CENTRE

26/6/99 Tel: 01970 623232

International poetry festival. Residential courses also available. Please telephone for details

Art Galleries

A Walk with the Gardener

15/6/99 PLAS NEWYDD

15/6/99 Tel: 01248 714795

A last opportunity to catch the Azaleas. A variety of wild flowers, Terrace Garden and various summer shrubs. Time: 14.00. Admission + £2.50.

Historic Houses & Gardens

Meet the Gardener Tour

18/6/99 POWIS CASTLE AND GARDEN

18/6/99 Tel: 01938 554338

Atmospheric 2-2.5 hour evening tour of the world famous Garden at Powis. 19.00. Tickets £11.00 to include a drink, please book in advance

Castles

Gwyl Ifan 1999

18/6/99 20/6/99	**GWYL IFAN 1999**

Tel: 01222 563989

The 23rd celebration of Gwyl Ifan, the midsummer festival of Welsh folk dancing. This year will include massed dancing, raising the Summer Pole, grand procession and guest teams from foreign climes! Held in various venues throughout Cardiff and district at various times

Festivals

Badger Watch
19/6/99 **DINEFWR PARK**
19/6/99 Tel: 01558 823902
Watch the badgers of Dinefwr Park in their natural habitat. £1.00 per person. Time: 19.15. Places are limited so please book.

Parks

Archaeology Experience
19/6/99 **ABERDULAIS FALLS**
20/6/99 Tel: 01639 636674
With quiz trail 'digs' for children of all ages.

Waterfalls

Craft Show
19/6/99 **ERDDIG HALL**
20/6/99 Tel: 01978 313333 / 355314
Eastern Events. 11.00-18.00. A£3.00 C(under 14)£Free C(14+)£1.50 OAPs£2.50 NT members £1.50 Members' children (14-17) £0.75

Historic Houses & Gardens

Art Exhibition
19/6/99 **ERDDIG HALL**
30/6/99 Tel: 01978 313333 / 355314
North Wales Federation of Artists. 11.00-17.00

Historic Houses & Gardens

Shirley Jones Retrospective Show: Artist books from the Red Hen Press
19/6/99 **BRECKNOCK MUSEUM**
25/7/99 Tel: 01874 624121
Major exhibition of artists books and prints by this internationally celebrated figure

Museum- Local History

Father's Day Frolics
20/6/99 **PLAS NEWYDD**
20/6/99 Tel: 01248 714795
To celebrate Fathers Day enjoy the lively performance by the Eryri Morris Dancers (participation welcome!) Then treat him to lunch at the Tearoom. Complete the day with the Anglesey Harmony Barbershop Club before tea with a free treat for every Dad! Normal admission prices apply.

Historic Houses & Gardens

Gwyl Criccieth Festival '99
22/6/99 **GWYL CRICCIETH FESTIVAL '99**
27/6/99 Tel: 01766 522778/522680
Venue: Various. star-studded Festival this year features an Opera Box production of a Gilbert and Sullivan evening with Dame Hilda Brackett, the North Wales Orchestra with soloist Rhys Meirion, the Rhos Male Voice choir and Shân Cothi, and a fun evening with the Temperance Seven. Together with recitals, walks, a lecture by Rabbi Julia Neuberger and Children's Events, Gwyl Criccieth Festival promises to be a week of fun and entertainment not to be missed. Prices: from A£3.00-£12.00 C£1.50-6.00

Festivals

Summer Evening Stroll
23/6/99 **WWT LLANELLI**
23/6/99 Tel: 01554 741087
A special Cheese and Wine evening. Come and meet the staff and find out what goes on behind the scenes. Visit the duckery; learn about bird counts and other research; visit the Swannery and find out how it is progressing. Time: 18.00-21.00. Cost: £5.00, booking essential.

Bird Centres

Badger Watch
26/6/99 **DINEFWR PARK**
26/6/99 Tel: 01558 823902
Watch the badgers of Dinefwr Park in their natural habitat. £1.00 per person. Time: 19.15. Places are limited so please book.

Parks

Stadium Opening Ceremony
26/6/99 **MILLENNIUM STADIUM**
26/6/99 Tel: 01222 232661
Wales v South Africa

Sports Grounds

Antiques
30/6/99 **PENRHYN CASTLE**
12/7/99 Tel: 01248 353084
Donald Taylor brings antiques to our Brushing Room. Come and browse. 11.00-17.00

Castles

Heritage Festival
1/7/99 **CYFARTHFA CASTLE MUSEUM AND ART GALLERY**
4/7/99 Tel: 01685 723112
Municipal outdoor event. A celebration of Merthyr Tydfil's unique historical and

cultural past.

Museums

North Wales Bluegrass Music Festival 1999

2/7/99 NORTH WALES BLUEGRASS MUSIC FESTIVAL 1999

4/7/99 Tel: 01492 580454

Two top American Bluegrass bands, Czech Republic band, and twenty-five of the Best of British and Old Time Bands play throughout the weekend. Eight concerts, 10 workshops from complete novices to advanced on all instruments - banjo, dobro, guitar, fiddle, double bass, mandolin etc. Dance workshops and displays of Appalachian clog and flat footing. Marquees on 7 acre festival site in Bodlondeb Park with food and bars. In it's 11th year. The site overlooks the harbour and river of Conwy, a wonderful setting for this marvellous feast of Bluegrass music.

Festivals

Badger Watch

3/7/99 DINEFWR PARK

3/7/99 Tel: 01558 823902

Watch the badgers of Dinefwr Park in their natural habitat. £1.00 per person. Time: 19.15. Places are limited so please book.

Parks

International Rugby Match

3/7/99 MILLENNIUM STADIUM

3/7/99 Tel: 01222 232661

Wales v France

Sports Grounds

Morris Dancing

3/7/99 PENRHYN CASTLE

3/7/99 Tel: 01248 353084

Eryri Morris Dancers - enjoy the fun and join in, 14.00-16.00

Castles

Gwyl Plant - Children's Festival

3/7/99 MUSEUM OF WELSH LIFE

4/7/99 Tel: 01222 573500

Please call for further information

Museum- Social History

Flat Meetings

3/7/99 CHEPSTOW RACECOURSE

23/7/99 Tel: 01291 622260

Meeting on 3 July, Evening Meetings 9 & 23 July

Racecourses

Greenwood Exhibition & Activities

3/7/99 CALDICOT CASTLE AND COUNTRY PARK

1/10/99 Tel: 01291 420241

Display and demonstrations of green-

wood product manufacture - furniture, hurdles, utensils etc

Castles

Young Musicians Platform

4/7/99 DINEFWR PARK

4/7/99 Tel: 01558 823902

Young, talented, local musicians will be performing in the Library at Newton House. 14.00-16.00

Parks

BDA Carriage Driving

4/7/99 DINEFWR PARK

4/7/99 Tel: 01558 823902

The BDA will be holding a carriage driving competition through the grounds of Dinefwr Park. Time trials, Orienteering and much more! From 11.00 onwards. Normal admission charges apply.

Parks

Traditional Music

4/7/99 ERDDIG HALL

4/7/99 Tel: 01978 313333 / 355314

Music by Fools Jig, 12.00-16.00

Historic Houses & Gardens

Llagollen International Musical Eisteddfod

6/7/99 LLANGOLLEN INTERNATIONAL MUSICAL EISTEDDFOD 1999

7/7/99 Tel: 01978 860236

Six magical days of music, song and dance from around the world, catering for all ages and tastes. Competitions representing over 45 Nations in colourful National costumes compete in daily competitions. Gala evening concerts with world renowned artists including Kiri Te Kanawa. Prices from A£3.00 C&OAPs£1.50 Family Ticket £12.00. Discounted group rates available

Festivals

Piano Recital

7/7/99 PENRHYN CASTLE

7/7/99 Tel: 01248 353084

Performed in the Grand Hall by Vivienne Hooson. 14.00-16.00

Castles

Meet the Gardener Tour

7/7/99 PLAS YN RHIW

7/7/99 Tel: 01758 780219

Lasts approximately 1 hour. Starts at 14.00. Normal admission + £1.00 (inc. members). Numbers limited so booking advisable.

Historic Houses & Gardens

Open-Air Concert

Further more detailed information on the attractions listed can be found in Best Guides *Visitor Attractions* Guide under the classifications shown

9/7/99	**ABERDULAIS FALLS**
9/7/99	Tel: 01639 636674

Featuring the Bryncoch Male Voice Choir.
Tickets: £3.00, refreshments included.
NT shop open.

Waterfalls

Fete

10/7/99	**LLANERCHAERON**
10/7/99	Tel: 01545 570200

Ceredigion Association of National Trust
Members' Annual Fete. Prices and times
to be agreed

Historic Houses & Gardens

Piano Recital

10/7/99	**PENRHYN CASTLE**
10/7/99	Tel: 01248 353084

Performed in the Grand Hall by Vivienne
Hooson. 14.00-16.00

Castles

Mid Wales Festival of Transport

10/7/99	**MID WALES FESTIVAL OF TRANSPORT 1999**
11/7/99	Tel: 01938 553680

Wales premier motoring event with up to
100 exhibitors. 10.00-17.00, A£3.50
C£Free

Festivals

Mid Wales Festival of Transport 1999

10/7/99	**MID WALES FESTIVAL OF TRANSPORT 1999**
11/7/99	Tel: 01938 553680

A superb family event with lots of attractions. Lots of rare and historic vehicles
including WW1 military vehicles and
guns. Time: 10.00-17.00. Price: A3.50
C(0-16)£Free

Festivals

Art Exhibition

10/7/99	**ERDDIG HALL**
21/7/99	Tel: 01978 313333 / 355314

Wrexham Art Group Exhibition, 11.00-
17.00

Historic Houses & Gardens

The Gilbert Collection

10/7/99	**NATIONAL MUSEUM AND GALLERY CARDIFF**
12/9/99	Tel: 01222 397951

Forty magnificent pieces of silver-gilt
selected from the Gilbert Collection, one
of the most important collections of
works of art ever to have been given to
Britain

Museums

Heritage Regained

10/7/99	**NATIONAL MUSEUM AND GALLERY**

	CARDIFF
12/9/99	Tel: 01222 397951

Silver from the Gilbert Collection, once
part of the most important collections of
works of art ever to have been given to
Britain and was formed in California over
the past thirty years by English-born real
estate developer Arthur Gilbert. The
munificent gift to the nation, at the time
worth an estimated £75million, was
announced in 1996 and, as a result of
substantial grant from the Heritage
Lottery Fund, it is hoped that it will be
permanently on display at Somerset
House in London by the end of the century.

Museums

Young Musicians Platform

11/7/99	**DINEFWR PARK**
11/7/99	Tel: 01558 823902

Young, talented, local musicians will be
performing in the Library at Newton
House. 14.00-16.00.

Parks

Demonstration

11/7/99	**ERDDIG HALL**
11/7/99	Tel: 01978 313333 / 355314

Ted Bruce, Basket Maker, 12.00-17.00

Historic Houses & Gardens

Open Evening

12/7/99	**ABERDULAIS FALLS**
12/7/99	Tel: 01639 636674

Guided tours, video presentation. NT
shop open and refreshments.

Waterfalls

Evening Walk with the Gardener

13/7/99	**PLAS NEWYDD**
13/7/99	Tel: 01248 714795

The beginning of the massed
hydrangeas of which Plas Newydd has
700. Orchids in the Arboretum, and
splendid hot borders in the Terrace
Garden. Time: 19.00. Cost: £3.50 (inc. NT
members).

Historic Houses & Gardens

Musicfest

13/7/99	**ABERYSTWYTH ARTS CENTRE**
30/7/99	Tel: 01970 623232

Major music festival concentrating on
music of this century. Summer School
and nightly festival concert programme

Art Galleries

Piano Recital

14/7/99	**PENRHYN CASTLE**
14/7/99	Tel: 01248 353084

Performed in the Grand Hall by Vivienne
Hooson. 14.00-16.00.

Castles

Wood Carving
14/7/99 PENRHYN CASTLE
19/7/99 Tel: 01248 353084
Anthony Griffiths; an exhibition with demonstrations of delicate wood carving specialising in Love Spoons, 11.00-17.00

Castles

Paradise Garden Fun Day
15/7/99 PENRHYN CASTLE
15/7/99 Tel: 01248 353084
Plants go Potty at Penrhyn for this fun afternoon based on botanical art and plants in science. Come and paint and pot some plants! Competition and prizes. 12.00-16.00

Castles

Meet the Gardener Tour
16/7/99 POWIS CASTLE AND GARDEN
16/7/99 Tel: 01938 554338
Atmospheric 2-2.5 hour evening tour of the world famous Garden at Powis. 19.00. Tickets £11.00 to include a drink, please book in advance

Castles

Piano Recital
17/7/99 PENRHYN CASTLE
17/7/99 Tel: 01248 353084
Performed in the Grand Hall by Vivienne Hooson. 14.00-16.00

Castles

Gower Festival '99
17/7/99 GOWER FESTIVAL '99
30/7/99 Tel: 01792 391132
Various churches. The Gower Festival is a very special blend of beautiful churches, wonderful music and summer evenings. Mostly evening concerts from 19.30. Prices: A£8.00-£10.00 C£4.00-£5.00, please tel: 01792 475715

Festivals

Josef Koudelka
17/7/99 GLYNN VIVIAN ART GALLERY
26/9/99 Tel: 01792 655006
In the Main Gallery. An exhibition showcasing the recent work in Wales of one of the great 20th century photographers, Magnum member Josef Koudelka

Art Galleries

Young Musicians Platform
18/7/99 DINEFWR PARK
18/7/99 Tel: 01558 823902
Young, talented, local musicians will be performing at the Library at Newton House, 14.00-16.00

Parks

Harp Recital

18/7/99 ERDDIG HALL
18/7/99 Tel: 01978 313333 / 355314
Tim Morgan plays harp, 14.00-16.00

Historic Houses & Gardens

Grenadier a Cheval de la Guard
18/7/99 PLAS NEWYDD
18/7/99 Tel: 01248 714795
Re-enactors portray soldiers of Napoleon's elite horse guards during the period 1805-1815. An insight in to the life and times of cavalrymen who carried the French flag on the battlefields of Europe during the Napoleonic Wars. 11.00-17.00, usual admission

Historic Houses & Gardens

Alice in Wonderland Family Fun Day
20/7/99 PLAS NEWYDD
20/7/99 Tel: 01248 714795
With Mr Bimbamboozle. Bring your own tea party! Shows of puppetry and magic, face-painting, quiz trails and activities. Come as a character and enter costume competition with prizes! 12.00-16.00 Usual admission + optional activity bag £1.50

Historic Houses & Gardens

Craftsworkers Exhibition
21/7/99 PENRHYN CASTLE
26/7/99 Tel: 01248 353084
Gwynedd and Clwyd Craftsworkers Guild displaying and selling their goods daily in the Brushing Room, 11.00-17.00

Castles

Everyman Open-Air Theatre
21/7/99 MUSEUM OF WELSH LIFE
31/7/99 Tel: 01222 573500
Please call for further information

Museum- Social History

Teddy Bears Fun Day
22/7/99 PENRHYN CASTLE
22/7/99 Tel: 01248 353084
Bring your Teddy for an afternoon of competitions and fun. Best Dressed Teddy competition, treaure trails and lots more, 12.00-16.00

Castles

Young Environmentalists
22/7/99 DINEFWR PARK
25/7/99 Tel: 01558 823902
Our Education Officer will offer a programme of activities for the budding environmentalist. £1.00 per session. 10.00-12.00 and 13.30-15.30. Normal admission charges

Parks

Celtic Music in the Meadow

Further more detailed information on the attractions listed can be found in Best Guides *Visitor Attractions* Guide under the classifications shown

Colby Woodland Garden
23/7/99
23/7/99
Tel: 01834 811885
Dance the night away or sit and be serenaded under the stars. Bring your own seating and picnic supper for a night to remembers. A£5.00 C£2.50.
Gardens

Archery
23/7/99
23/7/99
Penrhyn Castle
Tel: 01248 353084
Come and have a go with the experts, 12.00-16.00
Castles

Exhibition & Demonstration
24/7/99
4/8/99
Erddig Hall
Tel: 01978 313333 / 355314
By Gresford Quilters Group. 11.00-17.00.
Historic Houses & Gardens

Waterways, Waterwise
24/7/99
31/8/99
WWT Llanelli
Tel: 01554 741087
We don't like it when it falls from the sky, but come and find out about water by trying the exciting hands-on activities in the new Millennium Discover Centre. Plus outdoor activities.
Bird Centres

Specialist Plant Fair
25/7/99
25/7/99
Colby Woodland Garden
Tel: 01834 811885
Nurserymen from all over the region exhibit their unusual shrubs and plants in the meadow at Colby. Normal admission. NT Members Free.
Gardens

Young Musicians Platform
25/7/99
25/7/99
Dinefwr Park
Tel: 01558 823902
Young, talented, local musicians will be performing at the Library at Newton House, 14.00-16.00
Parks

Archery
25/7/99
25/7/99
Penrhyn Castle
Tel: 01248 353084
Come and have a go with the experts, 12.00-16.00
Castles

Old Bangers!
25/7/99
25/7/99
Penrhyn Castle
Tel: 01248 353084
Vintage and Classic Cars on display all day. Come and view and talk to the owners.
Castles

Talking Roman

Roman Legionary Museum
26/7/99
31/7/99
Tel: 01633 423134
A programme of talks for adults, with artefacts to handle and storytelling for children
Museum- Roman

All the Fun of the Annual Summer Fair
27/7/99
27/7/99
Plas Newydd
Tel: 01248 714795
Organised by the Menai Association. A variety of traditional stalls and games. 11.00-16.00. Usual admission
Historic Houses & Gardens

A Midsummer Night's Dream
27/7/99
29/7/99
Caerphilly Castle
Tel: 01222 883143
Performed in the magnificent setting of Caerphilly Castle, this classic Shakespeare will be performed over 3 nights.
Castles

Exhibition
28/7/99
2/8/99
Penrhyn Castle
Tel: 01248 353084
Margaret Stevens and the Penrhyn Group with a colourful exhibition in the Brushing Room, 11.00-17.00.
Castles

Treasure Island Fun Day
29/7/99
29/7/99
Penrhyn Castle
Tel: 01248 353084
Pirates at Penryhn! Treasure trails around the Castle and grounds, competitions, prizes - and watch out for those pirates! 12.00-16.00.
Castles

Archery
30/7/99
30/7/99
Penrhyn Castle
Tel: 01248 353084
Come and have a go with the experts. 12.00-16.00.
Castles

Fun on Fridays
30/7/99
27/8/99
WWT Llanelli
Tel: 01554 741087
Every Friday. Discover more about the fascinating world of water through activities and games. For 7-13 year olds. Time: 10.30-12.30. Cost: £2.50 per session.
Bird Centres

Garden Tour - Sweet Peas
31/7/99
31/7/99
Erddig Hall
Tel: 01978 313333 / 355314
Tour with the Head Gardener at 13.00 & 15.00. Normal admission + £2.00 per person.

Historic Houses & Gardens

Open-Air Theatre - Twelfth Night

31/7/99   POWIS CASTLE AND GARDEN

31/7/99   Tel: 01938 554338

Shakespeare in the garden. Illyria perform 'Twelfth Night'. Bring your picnic, garden chairs and rug. Time: 19.30. Please book in advance. A£7.50 C£5.00 Family Ticket (A2+C2)£20.00.

Castles

Elizabethan Life at Chirk Castle

31/7/99   CHIRK CASTLE

1/8/99   Tel: 01691 777701

The Education Department opens its doors for a taste of life at the Castle during Elizabethan times. 12.00-16.00

Castles

Friends of Thomas the Tank Engine

31/7/99   LLANGOLLEN STATION PLC

1/8/99   Tel: 01978 860951/860979

Thomas the Tank Engine visits all his friends at Llangollen whilst the Fat Controller tries to keep order

Railways Steam/Light

Archery

1/8/99   PENRHYN CASTLE

1/8/99   Tel: 01248 353084

Come and have a go with the experts, 12.00-16.00

Castles

Brecon Jazz Festival Exhibition

1/8/99   BRECKNOCK MUSEUM

5/9/99   Tel: 01874 624121

Jazz drawings by Valerie Ganz and Jazzy ceramics from The South Wales Potters

Museum- Local History

Mosaic Workshops

2/8/99   ROMAN LEGIONARY MUSEUM

6/8/99   Tel: 01633 423134

Both children and adults can turn their hand to this most spectacular of Roman arts, and make a mosaic to take away

Museum- Roman

King's Week

2/8/99   LLANCAIACH FAWR MANOR

8/8/99   Tel: 01443 412248

Annual celebrations at the country's leading Living History Museum. Normal admission charges apply.

Museum- Living History

Open-Air Theatre - The Water Babies

3/8/99   PLAS NEWYDD

3/8/99   Tel: 01248 714795

Performed by Illyria. Bring a picnic and a chair or rug and enjoy the performance in the stunning setting of the garden on the banks of the Menai Strait with the

back drop of the beautiful mountains of Snowdonia. Garden open from 17.30, performance starts 18.30. A£7.50 C£5.00 Family Ticket (A2+C2)£20.00.

Historic Houses & Gardens

Piano Recital

4/8/99   PENRHYN CASTLE

4/8/99   Tel: 01248 353084

Performed in the Grand Hall by Vivienne Hooson. 14.00-16.00

Castles

Open Air Theatre Shakespeare

4/8/99   PLAS NEWYDD

4/8/99   Tel: 01248 714795

Twefth Night performed by Illyria. Bring your own 'tea party' and a chair or rug. Performance starts at 19.30 unless otherwise stated, grounds open from 18.00. Audience numbers are limited so please book in advance to avoid disappointment. A£7.50 C(3-17)£5.00 Family(A2+C2)£20.00.

Historic Houses & Gardens

Exhibition

4/8/99   PENRHYN CASTLE

9/8/99   Tel: 01248 353084

An art exhibition by Steven Jones, artist in residence, in the Brushing Room. 12.00-17.00.

Castles

Puppets Fun Day

5/8/99   PENRHYN CASTLE

5/8/99   Tel: 01248 353084

Make your own puppets, colouring competitions, puppet demonstration and a Punch and Judy show - all under the expert eye of puppeteer Mr Bimbamboozle. 12.00-16.00.

Castles

Flat Meetings

5/8/99   CHEPSTOW RACECOURSE

30/8/99   Tel: 01291 622260

Meeting on 5 Aug and Bank Holiday Mon 30 Aug

Racecourses

Teddy Bears Picnic

6/8/99   DINEFWR PARK

6/8/99   Tel: 01558 823902

Family Fun for everyone! Free entry to all Teddy Bears bringing the human! 14.00-16.00

Parks

Archery

6/8/99   PENRHYN CASTLE

6/8/99   Tel: 01248 353084

Come and have a go with the experts. 12.00-16.00.

Castles

Big Weekend
6/8/99 NATIONAL MUSEUM AND GALLERY
        CARDIFF
8/8/99 Tel: 01222 397951
Special promotion weekend, the museum's contribution to the Cardiff Summer Festival. Discounted entry, children's events and museum trails

Museums

Piano Recital
7/8/99 PENRHYN CASTLE
7/8/99 Tel: 01248 353084
Performed in the Grand Hall by Vivienne Hooson. 14.00-16.00

Castles

The Enchanted Garden
7/8/99 POWIS CASTLE AND GARDEN
7/8/99 Tel: 01938 554338
Fun for all the family in the Garden at Powis. Normal admission prices. Small additional charge for some activities. 12.00-16.00

Castles

Erddig Gala Weekend
7/8/99 ERDDIG HALL
8/8/99 Tel: 01978 313333 / 355314
Open air concert. Fully costumed opera. Proms evening with Firework Finale. Time: 19.00. Cost: A£16.00 C£8.00.

Historic Houses & Gardens

Archery
8/8/99 PENRHYN CASTLE
8/8/99 Tel: 01248 353084
Come and have a go with the experts. 12.00-16.00.

Castles

Myths and Legends Family Fun Day
8/8/99 PLAS NEWYDD
8/8/99 Tel: 01248 714795
Meet Sit Lupin of Pipwithers - a 9ft tall Knight in full armour! Sit Lupin has lost his horse and so must be carried on the heads of his unfaithful peasants, Bleare and Bloutte who mutter - and occasionally revolt! Puppet show, story-walks, quiz trails, face-painting and activities. 12.00-16.00. Usual admission + optional activity bag £1.50

Historic Houses & Gardens

Treasure Hunt
9/8/99   ROMAN LEGIONARY MUSEUM
15/8/99 Tel: 01633 423134
Flavius has been murdered! Become a Roman detective, follow the clues to try and solve the case, and maybe end up with the treasure!

Museum- Roman

An Evening Walk with the Gardener
10/8/99 PLAS NEWYDD
10/8/99 Tel: 01248 714795
The beginning of the massed hydrangeas of which Plas Newydd has 700. Orchids in the Arboretum, and splendid hot borders in the Terrace Garden. 19.00, A£2.50 (incl NT members)

Historic Houses & Gardens

Piano Recital
11/8/99 PENRHYN CASTLE
11/8/99 Tel: 01248 353084
Performed in the Grand Hall by Vivienne Hooson. 14.00-16.00

Castles

Art Exhibition
11/8/99 PENRHYN CASTLE
23/8/99 Tel: 01248 353084
Hilary Leigh, a local artist with a colourful exhibition of her work. Artist in Residence in the Brushing Room, 11.00-17.00.

Castles

Dolls & Trains Day
12/8/99 PENRHYN CASTLE
12/8/99 Tel: 01248 353084
Bring your doll or train for a Dollies and Trains Parade and Best Dressed / Decorated Competitions, Castle and Gardens treasure trails and lots of prizes to win. Ride the miniature train! 12.00-16.00.

Castles

Piano Recital
14/8/99 PENRHYN CASTLE
14/8/99 Tel: 01248 353084
Performed in the Grand Hall by Vivienne Hooson. 14.00-16.00

Castles

The Fleece to Garment
14/8/99 PLAS NEWYDD
14/8/99 Tel: 01248 714795
North Wales Guides of Spinners, Weaver and Dyers Annual Competition. With an unwashed fleece, teams compete to spin, knit and sew a garment in 4 hours! 11.00-16.00. Usual admission

Historic Houses & Gardens

The Bala Lake Society Celebrations
14/8/99 BALA LAKE RAILWAY
15/8/99 Tel: 01678 540666
Special weekend planned celebrating 25 years of the Society. Visiting trains and engines are amongst the attractions

Railways Steam/Light

Archery
15/8/99
15/8/99 PENRHYN CASTLE
Tel: 01248 353084
Come and have a go with the experts.
12.00-16.00.

Castles

MG Rally
15/8/99
15/8/99 PLAS NEWYDD
Tel: 01248 714795
As part of the Snowdon Rally a visit to
Plas Newydd gives the opportunity to
view the cars and talk to the participants. From midday. Usual admission

Historic Houses & Gardens

Theatre Production - The Young
National Trust Theatre
15/8/99
21/8/99 DINEFWR PARK
Tel: 01558 823902
Performances by the YNTT telling the
tale of Dizzy Spells and her friend
Dormouse in their battle against pollu-
tion. A£1.00 C£0.50.

Parks

Mr Bimbamboozle
16/8/99
16/8/99 PENRHYN CASTLE
Tel: 01248 353084
Entertainment for children and adults!
Delightful magic and puppets. 12.00-
16.00.

Castles

Tadius and Giaus
16/8/99
20/8/99 ROMAN LEGIONARY MUSEUM
Tel: 01633 423134
Meet Giaus, one of the armies grumpiest
soldiers, and Tadius his room mate.
Listen and learn as a new recruit, as they
explain army life

Museum- Roman

National Garden Scheme Day
19/8/99
19/8/99 ERDDIG HALL
Tel: 01978 313333 / 355314
Walks with the Head Gardener at 13.00
& 14.00. A£2.00 C£Free.

Historic Houses & Gardens

Mystery Family Fun Day
19/8/99
19/8/99 PENRHYN CASTLE
Tel: 01248 353084
Follow the clues to find the villain. Lots
to do and lots of prizes! Meet Sherlock
Holmes and Dr Watson. 12.00-16.00.

Castles

Merthyr Tydfil County Borough Show
20/8/99
20/8/99 CYFARTHFA CASTLE MUSEUM AND ART
GALLERY
Tel: 01685 723112
Game Fayre type event. 'The Show of
Shows'.

Museums

Piano Recital
21/8/99
21/8/99 PENRHYN CASTLE
Tel: 01248 353084
Performed in the Grand Hall by Vivienne
Hooson. 14.00-16.00

Castles

Open Air Jazz Concert with Firework
Finale
21/8/99
21/8/99 PLAS NEWYDD
Tel: 01248 714795
Featuring The Temperance Seven, supported by Dr Jazz. Bring a picnic and
something to sit on, bar and food available. A£15.00 C£7.50 on the door,
£12.50 C£6.50 in advance. Garden open
17.00. Performance commences 19.00

Historic Houses & Gardens

Coracle Races
21/8/99
21/8/99 THE NATIONAL CORACLE CENTRE
Tel: 01239 710507
Coracle Races at Cilgerran at 14.00

Visitor Centres

Fiddlesticks
22/8/99 ERDDIG HALL
Tel: 01978 313333 / 355314
Entertainment for the whole family with
circus skills. Time: 14.00-16.30

Historic Houses & Gardens

Teddy Bears' Picnic
22/8/99 ERDDIG HALL
Tel: 01978 313333 / 355314
Circus skills, face painting, demonstrations and workshops. 14.00-16.30

Historic Houses & Gardens

National Gardens Scheme Open Day
22/8/99 LLANERCHAERON
Tel: 01545 570200
Also plant sale. 11.00-17.00. A£2.00
C£Free. All proceeds to the National
Gardens Scheme

Historic Houses & Gardens

Archery
22/8/99
22/8/99 PENRHYN CASTLE
Tel: 01248 353084
Come and have a go with the experts.
12.00-16.00.

Castles

Piano Recital
25/8/99
25/8/99 PENRHYN CASTLE
Tel: 01248 353084
Performed in the Grand Hall by Vivienne
Hooson. 14.00-16.00

Castles

Elizabethan Life at Chirk Castle

25/8/99 26/8/99	**CHIRK CASTLE** Tel: 01691 777701 The Education Department opens its doors for a taste of life at the Castle during Elizabethan times. 12.00-16.00. *Castles*
25/8/99 6/9/99	**Exhibition** **PENRHYN CASTLE** Tel: 01248 353084 Bill Swann with his amazing exhibition of his own art in glass. Artist in Residence. Come and see him in the Brushing Room, 12.00-17.00. *Castles*
26/8/99 26/8/99	**Peter Rabbit Visit** **COLBY WOODLAND GARDEN** Tel: 01834 811885 Peter Rabbit visits Colby for fun and games in the meadow. Competition for Puppet show with prize for everyone. Normal admission. NT Members Free. *Gardens*
26/8/99 26/8/99	**Open Air Theatre - Water Babies** **ERDDIG HALL** Tel: 01978 313333 / 355314 Performed by Illyria. Bring your own 'tea party' and a chair or rug. Performances at 14.30 & 19.30, gardens open one hour before. Audience numbers are limited so please book in advance to avoid disappointment. A£7.50 C(3-17)£5.00 Family(A2+C2)£20.00. *Historic Houses & Gardens*
26/8/99 26/8/99	**Medieval Madness Fun Day** **PENRHYN CASTLE** Tel: 01248 353084 Archery, treasure trails, Soak the Serf in the Stocks, and lots more! Watch the Jester doesn't get you! 12.00-16.00. *Castles*
27/8/99 27/8/99	**Performing Arts Open Air Concert** **CHIRK CASTLE** Tel: 01691 777701 Music from the Movies, with firework finale. Tickets: A£17.00 C£10.00. Ticket Hotline: 01625 560000 *Castles*
27/8/99 27/8/99	**International Rugby Match** **MILLENNIUM STADIUM** Tel: 01222 232661 Wales v Canada *Sports Grounds*
27/8/99 10/9/99	**Exhibition** **ABERDULAIS FALLS** Tel: 01639 636674 An art exhibition by local artists. *Waterfalls*

28/8/99 28/8/99	**Country Day** **ERDDIG HALL** Tel: 01978 313333 / 355314 Get away from it all and spend a quiet day in the countryside. Time: 10.00-16.00. £1.00 *Historic Houses & Gardens*
28/8/99 28/8/99	**Morris Dancing** **PENRHYN CASTLE** Tel: 01248 353084 Eryri Morris Dance Group perform. Enjoy the fun and join in! 14.00-16.00. *Castles*
28/8/99 28/8/99	**The Water Babies** **POWIS CASTLE AND GARDEN** Tel: 01938 554338 Open Air Performance in the Garden. Illyria perform The Water Babies. Bring your picnic, garden chairs and rug. 18.30. Please book in advance. A£7.50 C£5.00 Family Ticket (A2+C2)£20.00 *Castles*
28/8/99 15/9/99	**Art Exhibition** **ERDDIG HALL** Tel: 01978 313333 / 355314 Held on Sat, Sun, Mon, Tue & Wed only. Welsh Landscape Painters. 11.00-17.00. *Historic Houses & Gardens*
28/8/99 28/9/99	**Art Exhibition** **PENRHYN CASTLE** Tel: 01248 353084 North Wales Botanic and Watercolour Artists with their annual exhibition shown in the Stableblock Gallery. 11.00-17.00. *Castles*
29/8/99 29/8/99	**Archery** **PENRHYN CASTLE** Tel: 01248 353084 Come and have a go with the experts. 12.00-16.00. *Castles*
29/8/99 29/8/99	**Clown Around with James the Juggler!** **PLAS NEWYDD** Tel: 01248 714795 Family fun day. Circus skills workshop - come and have a go! Face-painting, quiz trail and activities (small extra charge for some activities). 12.00-16.00. Normal admission prices apply. *Historic Houses & Gardens*
29/8/99 30/8/99	**Bank Holiday Craft Festival** **WWT LLANELLI** Tel: 01554 741087 Discover a new skill - try making a willow ring or basket, add flowers to the well dressing, help to make a hurdle, make

(or ride in) a coracle and more. At the same time, discover how important wetlands are.

Bird Centres

Arts and Crafts Day
30/8/99 ABERDULAIS FALLS
30/8/99 Tel: 01639 636674
Demonstrations of weaving, lace making, woodturning, jewellery, dried flowers, calligraphy. Time: 11.00-18.00.

Waterfalls

3D at Dinefwr
30/8/99 DINEFWR PARK
30/8/99 Tel: 01558 823902
Dragonflies, Dipping and Damselflies at Dinefwrs Park's mill pond, trail through the Bog Wood. Safari Snacks. £1.00. 14.00-16.00

Parks

Fruit, Veg and Herb Day
30/8/99 LLANERCHAERON
30/8/99 Tel: 01545 570200
Guided tours of extensive walled gardens plus produce sales. 11.00-17.00. Normal admission prices

Historic Houses & Gardens

Meet the Gardener Tour
3/9/99 POWIS CASTLE AND GARDEN
3/9/99 Tel: 01938 554338
Atmospheric 2-2.5 hour evening tour of the world famous Garden at Powis. 19.00. Tickets £11.00 to include a drink, please book in advance

Castles

Country Day
4/9/99 ERDDIG HALL
4/9/99 Tel: 01978 313333 / 355314
Get away from it all and spend a quiet day in the countryside. Time: 10.00-16.00. £1.00

Historic Houses & Gardens

Barmouth Arts Festival 1999
5/9/99 BARMOUTH ARTS FESTIVAL 1999
12/9/99 Tel: 01341 280392
Annual Arts Festival in its 25th year, with a variety of vocal and instrumental music, jazz, brass, literary lunch, art and craft exhibitions.

Festivals

Exhibition
8/9/99 PENRHYN CASTLE
13/9/99 Tel: 01248 353084
Gwynedd Woodturners Exhibition in the Brushing Room. 12.00-17.00.

Castles

Meeting at Chepstow

9/9/99 CHEPSTOW RACECOURSE
9/9/99 Tel: 01291 622260
Flat meeting from the premier racecourse in Wales

Racecourses

Craft Exhibition
10/9/99 ST DAVIDS CATHEDRAL
29/9/99 Tel: 01437 720199
Local craftsmen exhibiting their work, photographs, dried flower pictures, pottery with demonstrations

Cathedrals

Medieval Weekend
11/9/99 CALDICOT CASTLE AND COUNTRY PARK
12/9/99 Tel: 01291 420241
Medieval market and battles over the weekend

Castles

Woodland & Wildlife Family Fun Day
11/9/99 PLAS NEWYDD
12/9/99 Tel: 01248 714795
A fun day for all ages. Quiz trails, face-painting and activities with Trusty the Hedgehog. Guided Fungus Foray at 14.30 - bring a container. Wood turning and the chance to have a go! Stick making, water divining, hurdle making, charcoal burning and more. Time: 11.00-16.00. Normal admission prices apply (small extra charge for some activities).

Historic Houses & Gardens

Hilda Carline
11/9/99 GLYNN VIVIAN ART GALLERY
7/11/99 Tel: 01792 655006
In Room 1. The first exhibition ever to be devoted to the work of Hilda Carline, Stanley Spencer's first wife, giving a comprehensive presentation of her artistic career

Art Galleries

Brecknock Museum Exhibitions
11/9/99 BRECKNOCK MUSEUM
16/11/99 Tel: 01874 624121
'Field': Recent drawings by Susan Milne

Museum- Local History

Exhibition
15/9/99 PENRHYN CASTLE
27/9/99 Tel: 01248 353084
Christine Rodger with her first Exhibition at Penrhyn. Artist in Residence in the Brushing Room, 12.00-17.00.

Castles

Garden Demonstration
16/9/99 POWIS CASTLE AND GARDEN
16/9/99 Tel: 01938 554338
The care of hedges demonstrated by the Gardeners at Powis. Normal admission

prices. 14.00-16.00

Castles

Welsh Comic Postcards
16/9/99 BRECKNOCK MUSEUM
16/11/99 Tel: 01874 624121
Please call for further information

Museum- Local History

Gwyl Glyndwr
17/9/99 CELTICA
19/9/99 Tel: 01654 702702
Medieval festival in Machynlleth. Hog Roast on Friday evening, a Medieval Market on Saturday. Archery demonstrations, Medieval re-enactment by the White Company on the lawn outside Celtica all weekend

Exhibition Centres

Tenby Arts Festival
17/9/99 TENBY ARTS FESTIVAL 1999
25/9/99 Tel: 01834 842974
Tenby Arts Festival takes place in the historic walled town of Tenby. It includes classical music, jazz, drama, poetry, talks and celtic exploration. It is nine days of activity and fun for all ages using local, National and International artists. The festival adds a vibrant dimension to the increasing number of visitors who choose festival week for their holiday.

Festivals

Wood Turning Demonstrations
18/9/99 ERDDIG HALL
19/9/99 Tel: 01978 313333 / 355314
Demonstrated by Chester Wood Turners, 11.00-16.00.

Historic Houses & Gardens

Transport Extravaganza '99
18/9/99 LLANGOLLEN STATION PLC
19/9/99 Tel: 01978 860951/860979
Over 500 vintage bikes, cars, lorries, buses, farm machinery, traction engines and craft displays join the railway's own steam fleet for a massive weekend bonanza! Don't miss it

Railways Steam/Light

Art Exhibition
20/9/99 ERDDIG HALL
3/10/99 Tel: 01978 313333 / 355314
White Peacock by Maggie Humphrey, 11.00-17.00.

Historic Houses & Gardens

Harvest Festival
25/9/99 MUSEUM OF WELSH LIFE
26/9/99 Tel: 01222 573500
Please call for further information

Museum- Social History

Country House Technology
26/9/99 DINEFWR PARK
26/9/99 Tel: 01558 823902
A guided walk through Dinefwr Park, exploring the ingenious methods of water transportation used in bygone days. Time: 14.00-16.00.

Parks

Demonstration
26/9/99 ERDDIG HALL
26/9/99 Tel: 01978 313333 / 355314
Basket making demonstrated by Molly Rathbone, 12.00-17.00

Historic Houses & Gardens

Rugby World Cup
1/10/99 MILLENNIUM STADIUM
1/10/99 Tel: 01222 232661
Opening Ceremony Match

Sports Grounds

Tydfil Arts Festival
1/10/99 TYDFIL ARTS FESTIVAL '99
30/10/99 Tel: 01685 389995
Various venues. With limited resources and maximum co-operation, we are building a new tradition of local events using talent from throughout the community. The festival celebrates local talent, but it also introduces opportunity to enjoy the work of new performers. We are delighted to welcome artists sharing their creative gifts and experience with us. Most venues are suitable for wheelchairs, please telephone first. Most venues are admission free

Festivals

Development of Erddig's Garden
2/10/99 ERDDIG HALL
2/10/99 Tel: 01978 313333 / 355314
Garden tour with Head Gardener, 13.00 & 15.00. Normal admission + £2.00 per person.

Historic Houses & Gardens

Jump Meetings
2/10/99 CHEPSTOW RACECOURSE
20/10/99 Tel: 01291 622260
Meetings from the premier racecourse in Wales on 2 & 20 Oct

Racecourses

Swansea Festival of Music and the Arts 1999
2/10/99 SWANSEA FESTIVAL OF MUSIC AND THE ARTS 1999
22/10/99 Tel: 01792 205318
The 1999 Swansea Festival of Music and the Arts focuses on France. Concerts by the BBC National Orchestra of Wales and the City of Birmingham Symphony

Orchestra include music by Berlioz, Debussy, Ravel, Poulenc and Messiaen. The Festival also features opera, theatre, dance and art exhibitions reflecting the French theme and young people's workshops. Set at the gateway to the beautiful Gower Peninsula, Swansea, with its many shops, maritime quarter and leisure facilites, it s an ideal palce to enjoy the arts.

Festivals

Harp Recital

3/10/99 CHIRK CASTLE
3/10/99 Tel: 01691 777701
Dylan Cernyw play harp in the Chapel throughout the afternoon

Castles

World Birdwatch

3/10/99 WWT LLANELLI
3/10/99 Tel: 01554 741087
Join thousands of people all over the world in a massive birdwatch. Activities start with an early morning Wader Walk, followed by breakfast. Time: 07.00. Cost: £6.00, Members £4.00. Later in the day at 14.00, 'An Introduction to Birdwatching' - a talk for all ages, followed by birdwatching in the grounds.

Bird Centres

Guides in the Hides

3/10/99 WWT LLANELLI
19/12/99 Tel: 01554 741087
Every Sunday, 14.00-16.00. An expert will be at hand to help you with bird identification and enhance your enjoyment of the spectacular wildlife of the marsh.

Bird Centres

Garden Demonstration

7/10/99 POWIS CASTLE AND GARDEN
7/10/99 Tel: 01938 554338
Propagating techniques and overwintering of plants demonstrated by the Gardeners at Powis. Normal admission prices.

Castles

Designer Clothes Sale

8/10/99 CHIRK CASTLE
8/10/99 Tel: 01691 777701
Ladies daywear, jewellery, evening wear, leather goods plus childrens clothes and toys. Designer labels include casual clothes from Versace, Armani, Ralph Lauren. £1.00 entry, 11.00-16.00

Castles

Apple Festival

9/10/99 ERDDIG HALL
10/10/99 Tel: 01978 313333 / 355314
A weekend of apple bobbing, cider tasting, apple recipes and much more! 11.00-17.00. Normal admission prices.

Historic Houses & Gardens

John Bonner: A Designer's Life

9/10/99 NATIONAL MUSEUM AND GALLERY CARDIFF
2/1/00 Tel: 01222 397951
A unique record of the life of an Arts and Crafts designer and maker, illustrating the quality and range of work in jewellery and metalwork, stained, glass, architecture, sculpture and other media

Museums

David Hockney

9/10/99 NATIONAL MUSEUM AND GALLERY CARDIFF
5/1/00 Tel: 01222 397951
Photographs that inspired his painting alongside finished works

Museums

Harp Recital

10/10/99 CHIRK CASTLE
10/10/99 Tel: 01691 777701
Dylan Cernyw play harp in the Chapel throughout the afternoon

Castles

Victorian Childhood Experience

10/10/99 PENRHYN CASTLE
10/10/99 Tel: 01248 353084
A laundry without gadgets, a schoolroom without computers, and toys without batteries. How did those Victorians cope? Come and find out - lots of hands-on Victorian fun. 12.00-16.00.

Castles

A Walk with the Gardener

12/10/99 PLAS NEWYDD
12/10/99 Tel: 01248 714795
Autumn colour. Last walk of the season at 14.00. Admission + £2.50.

Historic Houses & Gardens

Rugby World Cup

15/10/99 MILLENNIUM STADIUM
15/10/99 Tel: 01222 232661
date to be confirmed (but during October 99) Quarter Finals

Sports Grounds

Harp Recital

17/10/99 CHIRK CASTLE
17/10/99 Tel: 01691 777701
Dylan Cernyw play harp in the Chapel throughout the afternoon

Castles

Fungus Foray

Further more detailed information on the attractions listed can be found in Best Guides *Visitor Attractions* Guide under the classifications shown

17/10/99	**DINEFWR PARK**
17/10/99	Tel: 01558 823902

A guided walk through the ancient woodland of Dinefwr Park to view the rare fungi of the Site of Special Scientific Interest. Booking essential. 14.00-16.00

Parks

Demonstration

17/10/99	**ERDDIG HALL**
17/10/99	Tel: 01978 313333 / 355314

Wood carving demonstrated by Jim Heath, 11.00-17.00.

Historic Houses & Gardens

Exhibition

20/10/99	**PENRHYN CASTLE**
31/10/99	Tel: 01248 353084

Ray Keats and Alan Beattie paintings exhibition. Artists in Residence in the Brushing Room. 12.00-17.00.

Castles

Make a Difference Day

23/10/99	**DINEFWR PARK**
23/10/99	Tel: 01558 823902

Welcoming new volunteers to the Park who are interested in contributing to a programme of tree care. Please bring suitable outdoor clothing. 13.00-16.00

Parks

Friends of Thomas the Tank Engine

23/10/99	**LLANGOLLEN STATION PLC**
24/10/99	Tel: 01978 860951/860979

Thomas the Tank Engine visits all his friends at Llangollen whilst the Fat Controller tries to keep order

Railways Steam/Light

Muddy Matters - Half-Term Activities

23/10/99	**WWT LLANELLI**
31/10/99	Tel: 01554 741087

It's messy, it can be fun, but does mud matter? Come and try our activities to help you decide the answer to this question.

Bird Centres

Harp Recital

24/10/99	**CHIRK CASTLE**
24/10/99	Tel: 01691 777701

Dylan Cernyw play harp in the Chapel throughout the afternoon

Castles

Domestic Life of Victorian Erddig

24/10/99	**ERDDIG HALL**
24/10/99	Tel: 01978 313333 / 355314

A day of education and fun for everyone. 12.00-16.00

Historic Houses & Gardens

Trusty's October Half-Term Holiday Fun

24/10/99	**PLAS NEWYDD**
24/10/99	Tel: 01248 714795

Family Fun Day. 'A Masquerade' - Come with a home-made mask - prizes for the best! Competition judged at 15.00. Mask-making, quiz trails and face-painting. Followed by 'An Afternoon with The Storyteller' Story-walks and enter 'Tell Trusty a Story' writing competition. 12.00-16.00. Normal admission prices apply + small extra charge for some activities.

Historic Houses & Gardens

Science Week for Children

25/10/99	**ABERDULAIS FALLS**
29/10/99	Tel: 01639 636674

Quizzes, experiments with water and electricity. Computer displays.

Waterfalls

Trusty's October Half-Term Holiday Fun

26/10/99	**PLAS NEWYDD**
26/10/99	Tel: 01248 714795

Family Fun Day. Kite workshop - come and make a kite and fly it on the banks of the Menai Strait. 12.00-16.00. Normal admission prices apply + small extra charge for some activities.

Historic Houses & Gardens

Megamessy Art Sessions

26/10/99	**WWT LLANELLI**
29/10/99	Tel: 01554 741087

For 6-13 year olds. Time: 10.00-12.00 & 13.30-15.30. Cost: £2.50 per session, booking essential.

Bird Centres

Mr Bimbamboozle

28/10/99	**PENRHYN CASTLE**
28/10/99	Tel: 01248 353084

Entertainment for children and adults! Delightful magic and puppets. 12.00-16.00.

Castles

Meet the White Park Cattle

29/10/99	**DINEFWR PARK**
29/10/99	Tel: 01558 823902

A guided walk through the parkland to see this rare, ancient and endangered breed

Parks

Craft Fair

29/10/99	**PENRHYN CASTLE**
31/10/99	Tel: 01248 353084

Christmas Craft Fair in Stableblock Gallery. 11.00-17.00.

Castles

Gothic Horrors

| 30/10/99 | DINEFWR PARK |
| 30/10/99 | Tel: 01558 823902 |

Spooky tales of terror in the basement for young and old alike! 14.00-16.00

Parks

Hallowe'en

| 30/10/99 | MUSEUM OF WELSH LIFE |
| 30/10/99 | Tel: 01222 573500 |

Please call for further information

Museum- Social History

Friends of Thomas the Tank Engine

| 30/10/99 | LLANGOLLEN STATION PLC |
| 31/10/99 | Tel: 01978 860951/860979 |

Thomas the Tank Engine visits all his friends at Llangollen whilst the Fat Controller tries to keep order

Railways Steam/Light

Trusty's October Half-Term Holiday Fun

| 31/10/99 | PLAS NEWYDD |
| 31/10/99 | Tel: 01248 714795 |

Family Fun Day. Haunted Happenings! Spooky story-telling, apple bobbing, face-painting, quiz trails and activities. Bring a lantern - prizes for the best! Make a pumpkin lantern and string a conker! Guess the number of bricks LEGO competition - spooky prize for the nearest guess! 12.00-16.00. Normal admission applies + small extra charge for some activities.

Historic Houses & Gardens

Rugby World Cup

| 3/11/99 | MILLENNIUM STADIUM |
| 4/11/99 | Tel: 01222 232661 |

Third place play off

Sports Grounds

Fireworks Skyshow

| 5/11/99 | CYFARTHFA CASTLE MUSEUM AND ART GALLERY |
| 5/11/99 | Tel: 01685 723112 |

Spectacular professionally fired display, with the emphasis on safety as well as fun.

Museums

Christmas Craft Fair

| 5/11/99 | ABERYSTWYTH ARTS CENTRE |
| 23/11/99 | Tel: 01970 623232 |

Annual Christmas extravaganza! Over 80 stalls, open daily for 2 months

Art Galleries

Rugby World Cup Final

| 6/11/99 | MILLENNIUM STADIUM |
| 6/11/99 | Tel: 01222 232661 |

World Cup Final

Sports Grounds

Book Fair

| 6/11/99 | PLAS NEWYDD |
| 7/11/99 | Tel: 01248 714795 |

Sale of donated second hand and anti-quarian books. Come and browse for bargains and stock up with winter reading! 10.00-16.00. Admission £1.00 (inc. NT members). Please Note: The House will NOT be open.

Historic Houses & Gardens

Jump Meetings

| 6/11/99 | CHEPSTOW RACECOURSE |
| 24/11/99 | Tel: 01291 622260 |

Jump meetings from the premier race-course in Wales on 6 & 24 Nov

Racecourses

Designer Clothes Sale

| 13/11/99 | PENRHYN CASTLE |
| 13/11/99 | Tel: 01248 353084 |

Ladies daywear, jewellery, evening wear, leather goods plus children's clothes and toys. Designer labels include casual clothes from Versace, Armani, Ralph Lauren; coats, suits and separates from Fendi, Mansfield, Guy Laroche, Yarrell, Mondi, Ara and Basler. Time: 11.00-16.00. £1.00 entry.

Castles

Behind the Scenes Winter Conservation Tour

| 20/11/99 | POWIS CASTLE AND GARDEN |
| 21/11/99 | Tel: 01938 554338 |

A tour of the Castle. 1.5-2 hour tour of the Castle including demonstrations of the National Trust's housekeeping and conservation techniques. 11.00. Tickets £12.50 to include hot punch. Please book in advance.

Castles

The Museum of Welsh Life Eisteddfod

| 21/11/99 | MUSEUM OF WELSH LIFE |
| 20/11/99 | Tel: 01222 573500 |

Please call for further information

Museum- Social History

British Gas Wildlife Photographer of the Year

| 21/11/99 | BRECKNOCK MUSEUM |
| 30/1/00 | Tel: 01874 624121 |

The best entries to this international competition

Museum- Local History

Behind the Scenes Winter Conservation Tour

| 27/11/99 | POWIS CASTLE AND GARDEN |
| 28/11/99 | Tel: 01938 554338 |

A tour of the Castle. 1.5-2 hour tour of the Castle including demonstrations of the National Trust's housekeeping and conservation techniques. 11.00. Tickets £12.50 to include hot punch. Please book in advance.

Castles

Late Night Christmas Shopping

30/11/99 WWT LLANELLI
30/11/99 Tel: 01554 741087
FREE admission all day. Shop in a relaxed but festive atmosphere until 20.30. Watch the birds being fed by floodlight. Visit Father Christmas 16.00-17.00 & 18.00-19.00. Cost: £2.00 including gift.

Bird Centres

Santa's Grotto

4/12/99 LLECHWEDD SLATE CAVERNS
31/12/99 Tel: 01766 830306
Father Christmas in his spectacular underground Grotto. Trains running every 15 minutes. Apply for details and prices. Running every Weekend during December

Caverns

Carols and Illuminations

3/12/99 ABERDULAIS FALLS
3/12/99 Tel: 01639 636674
Christmas carols and tree illuminations. Refreshments available. Please call for further information.

Waterfalls

Carol Singing Evening

3/12/99 ERDDIG HALL
3/12/99 Tel: 01978 313333 / 355314
Carols in the Stableyard at 18.30. Donation on the night.

Historic Houses & Gardens

Children's Trail & Quiz

4/12/99 ABERDULAIS FALLS
5/12/99 Tel: 01639 636674
Trail with quiz and gift. Cost: A£Free C£2.00. Come and do your Christmas shopping. 10.00-16.00.

Waterfalls

Santa Weekend Specials

4/12/99 LLANGOLLEN STATION PLC
24/12/99 Tel: 01978 860951/860979
Santa will be on board every one of our 52 steam hauled trains giving presents to the children and seasonal refreshments to the adults. Santa Specials run: 4th & 5th Dec, 11th & 12th Dec, 18th-24th Dec. Call NOW for more details.

Railways Steam/Light

Alfred Janes

4/12/99 GLYNN VIVIAN ART GALLERY
30/1/00 Tel: 01792 655006
In the Main Gallery. This overdue major retrospective exhibition highlights the remarkable talent and breathtaking artistic craftmanship of the revered Swansea-born artist (b. 1911)

Art Galleries

Santa on a Sunday

5/12/99 WWT LLANELLI
19/12/99 Tel: 01554 741087
Every Sunday. Come and feed the birds with Santa at 14.00, then visit him in his grotto from 14.15-15.15. Cost: £2.00 including gift.

Bird Centres

Late Night Christmas Shopping

7/12/99 WWT LLANELLI
7/12/99 Tel: 01554 741087
FREE admission all day. Shop in a relaxed but festive atmosphere until 20.30. Watch the birds being fed by floodlight. Visit Father Christmas 16.00-17.00 & 18.00-19.00. Cost: £2.00 including gift.

Bird Centres

Christmas Tree

8/12/99 MUSEUM OF WELSH LIFE
11/12/99 Tel: 01222 573500
Please call for further information. 8-10 Dec18.00-21.00. 11 Dec 14.00-18.00

Museum- Social History

Children's Trail & Quiz

11/12/99 ABERDULAIS FALLS
12/12/99 Tel: 01639 636674
Trail with quiz and gift. Cost: A£Free C£2.00. Come and do your Christmas shopping. 10.00-16.00.

Waterfalls

Carols in the Courtyard

13/12/99 PLAS NEWYDD
13/12/99 Tel: 01248 714795
Further information from the Property. Time: 19.00.

Historic Houses & Gardens

Children's Trail & Quiz

18/12/99 ABERDULAIS FALLS
19/12/99 Tel: 01639 636674
Trail with quiz and gift. Cost: A£Free C£2.00. Come and do your Christmas shopping. 10.00-16.00.

Waterfalls

New Years Eve Millennium Celebration

31/12/99 MILLENNIUM STADIUM
31/12/99 Tel: 01222 232661
For more information please call the venue.

Sports Grounds

West Country

Including:
Bristol
Somerset
Wiltshire
West Dorset
Devon
Cornwall

Exhibition
1/3/99 DORSET COUNTY MUSEUM
1/3/99 Tel: 01305 262735
An exhibition of paintings and drawings
by Brian Busfield
Museums

Discovering Cabots Bristol
1/3/99 BRISTOL CITY MUSEUM AND ART GALLERY
26/4/99 Tel: 0117 922 3571
Major exhibition of what Bristol was like
in Cabot's time.
Museums

Erik Lessing-Magnum Photographer
1/3/99 FOX TALBOT MUSEUM OF PHOTOGRAPHY
31/5/99 Tel: 01249 730459/730141
A retrospective exhibition of the work of
this important European master photographer; images of the Hungarian revolution in the 1950s to the present time
Museum- Photographic

**Mendip Decorative & Fine Arts Society
Meeting**
2/3/99 ROYAL BATH AND WEST SHOWGROUND
2/3/99 Tel: 01749 822200
Westex Suite. Please call for details
Showgrounds

Travellers' Tale 6
3/3/99 DORSET COUNTY MUSEUM
3/3/99 Tel: 01305 262735
"Tokyo, Kyoto and a volcano by
Japanese train". Dr Tony Goodings. Time:
19.30
Museums

**Anne Desmet: Towers and
Transformations**
3/3/99 HOLBURNE MUSEUM AND CRAFTS STUDY
CENTRE
11/4/99 Tel: 01225 466669
Touring exhibition of one of the most
original talents in Contemporary British
print making
Museums

**A Respectable Trade? Bristol &
Transatlantic Slavery**
4/3/99 BRISTOL CITY MUSEUM AND ART GALLERY
1/9/99 Tel: 0117 922 3571
A major exhibition examining Bristol's
role in a trade that made fortunes for a
few and living hell for many. It follows
the slave trade route from Bristol to
Africa, the Caribbean and finally back to
Bristol. The exhibition looks at the workings of the trade, the people involved
and the myths that have grown up and
around it.
Museums

Archaeology Meeting

5/3/99 DORSET COUNTY MUSEUM
5/3/99 Tel: 01305 262735
"Forensic Archaeology - a new arena".
Dr Margaret Cox, Bournemouth
University. Time: 19.30
Museums

22nd Annual Antiques Fair
5/3/99 WILTON HOUSE
7/3/99 Tel: 01722 746729
Prestigious dateline fair held in the
Cloisters of Wilton House and 18th century Riding School
Historic Houses & Gardens

**Palmer Snell Vintage Motorcycle
Auction**
6/3/99 ROYAL BATH AND WEST SHOWGROUND
6/3/99 Tel: 01749 822200
A twice yearly event held in the Spring
and Autumn at the Showground since
1982, attracting buyers and sellers from
all over the Country. Over 100 motorcycles of all ages, shapes and sizes are
offered for sale, with an Autojumble
organised by the Somerset Section of
the Vintage Motorcycle Club. Starts
13.00
Showgrounds

Vintage Motorcycle Club Autojumble
6/3/99 ROYAL BATH AND WEST SHOWGROUND
6/3/99 Tel: 01749 822200
Over 300 stalls catering for veteran, vintage and classic motorcycles. run in conjunction with Palmer Snell classic motorcycle auction. Admission £1.00 or by catalogue for auction, 09.30-16.00
Showgrounds

Crafts Fair
6/3/99 LONGLEAT
7/3/99 Tel: 01985 844400
Ceramics, pottery, children's wear, working craft makers, food court, artists and
much more
Safari Parks

Hedgehog Weekend
6/3/99 SECRET WORLD-BADGER AND WILDLIFE
RESCUE CENTRE
7/3/99 Tel: 01278 783250
A chance to see everyone's favourite -
the hedgehog. Meet our winter visitors
who were too small to survive in the
wild, and are enjoying the hotel service
at Secret World until the spring comes!
Find out how to encourage hedgehog
into your garden and maybe, even draw
or make a model hedgehog in our special hedgehog room
Wildlife Rescue

Workshop: Introduction to Adobe Photoshop 5.0

6/3/99
7/3/99

THE ROYAL PHOTOGRAPHIC SOCIETY

Tel: 01225 462841

A workshop organised in conjunction with the City of Bath College. This is a hands on introductory workshop using Macs and taught by professionals. Places limited to 10 so that everyone has their own computer. Covers scanning and digital manipulation. Participants need to possess a basic knowledge of working with a computer. Tutor: Graham Morgan. Venue: City of Bath College. Time: 09.30-17.00 daily. Cost: £190.00 - lunch included.

Museum- Photographic

Sunday Funday - Return of the Sun

7/3/99
7/3/99

BRISTOL CITY MUSEUM AND ART GALLERY

Tel: 0117 922 3571

Free family activities on a topical theme. Visitors will also be shuttled between Bristol City Art Gallery and the Bristol Industrial Museum, on a vintage Loddeka bus.

Museums

Make your very own Mother's Day Card

7/3/99
7/3/99

CREALY PARK

Tel: 01395 233200

Make a Mother's Day card 11.00-15.00 in the shop

Country Parks

Walk: High Willhays & Yes Tor

7/3/99
7/3/99

DARTMOOR NATIONAL PARK

Tel: 01626 832093

4 hour guided walk starting from Meldon (car park on approach road to dam, by information board) at 10:45. More strenuous, longer route, steep sections likely, quicker pace. Suitable for reasonably fit walkers who want to stride out and enjoy the moor at a lively pace. Cost: A£3.50 C£0.75. FREE WALKS OFFER: arrive at a walk start point by bus and you may go on any walk completely free. Simply show the guide your bus ticket. No dogs allowed. Clothing: strong shoes, if dry, wellingtons or walking boots if wet. Good waterproofs and comfortable clothing. Snack or packed lunch. Please bring a hot drink and extra food.

National Parks

Bristol & District Canine Show

7/3/99
7/3/99

ROYAL BATH AND WEST SHOWGROUND

Tel: 01749 822200

Edmund Rack Pavillion. Please call for details

Showgrounds

Daffy Down Dilly Day

7/3/99
7/3/99

TREBAH GARDEN

Tel: 01326 250448

See the valley awash with 30,000 daffodils in their varying yellows, oranges and whites

Gardens

Walk: Spring Woodland Walk with NT

9/3/99
9/3/99

DARTMOOR NATIONAL PARK

Tel: 01626 832093

2 hour guided walk starting from Hembury Woods (National Trust car park) at 14:00. Average route and pace, may be some steep ground, suitable for anyone used to walking. Cost: A£2.00 C£0.75. FREE WALKS OFFER: arrive at a walk start point by bus and you may go on any walk completely free. Simply show the guide your bus ticket. No dogs allowed. Clothing: sensible shoes. Showerproof or waterproof jacket and comfortable clothing. Please bring a hot drink and extra food.

National Parks

People's Collections - Gemma Bradley's Smurfs

9/3/99
6/4/99

THE TIME MACHINE

Tel: 01934 621028

Opportunity for private individuals to show their collection

Museum- Local History

Lecture: Mapping for the British Geological Survey in Dorset

10/3/99
10/3/99

DORSET COUNTY MUSEUM

Tel: 01305 262735

Dr Ted Freshney, British Geological Survey, Exeter. Time: 19.30

Museums

Lacock Garden Tours

10/3/99

LACOCK ABBEY, FOX TALBOT MUSEUM AND VILLAGE

10/3/99

Tel: 01249 730227/730459

Tour and talk on the history of Lacock Gardens, 11.00 start, 1.5 hours. No extra charge but donations welcome

Historic Houses

Gardening the Past - Preserving the Future

10/3/99
10/3/99

STOURHEAD HOUSE GARDEN AND HOUSE

Tel: 01747 841152

A morning with the Garden Team looking at how the world-famous landscape

Garden is maintained, with some useful gardening tips. Meet at The Spread Eagle Inn at 10.30. £10.00 to include lunch

Historic Houses

Inset Session with Joy Gregory

10/3/99
10/3/99
THE ROYAL PHOTOGRAPHIC SOCIETY
Tel: 01225 462841

A session aimed at teachers to coincide with Joy Gregory's exhibition. 'Memory and Skin' on show at the RPS (see exhibition listing). Time: 16.30-18.30.

Museum- Photographic

Beautiful Beasts

10/3/99
7/11/99
THE AMERICAN MUSEUM IN BRITAIN
Tel: 01225 460503

An exhibition showing animals in American Art from pictures to weather-vanes

Museums

Wincanton Logistics Steeplechase

11/3/99
11/3/99
WINCANTON RACECOURSE
Tel: 01963 32344

Competitive National Hunt racing with the first race at 14.20. Admission: Club £14.00 Tattersalls £10.00 Course & Cars to Course £5.00 C(0-16)Free Students (with I.D) £5.00 in Tattersalls. Discount for pre-booked groups10+ in Club & Tattersalls

Racecourses

Ivano Rocca - Wine Buyer from Eldridge Pope

12/3/99
12/3/99
BARRINGTON COURT
Tel: 01460 241938

Lecture, lunch and wine tasting. 12.00. £15.00

Gardens

Early Shops in Dorset

12/3/99
12/3/99
DORSET COUNTY MUSEUM
Tel: 01305 262735

Dorset Industrial Archaeological Society. Bob Machin MA (Oxon), Social Historian. Time: 19.30

Museums

National Science Week

12/3/99
21/3/99
SCIENCE MUSEUM
Tel: 01793 814466

A week of science events for schools and families, this year's SET week revolves around the theme of agriculture and food. Learn about agriculture past and present; get to know the facts in the genetic foods debate; join in activities and drama. Opening times 10.00-17.00. Pre-booked school groups Mon-Fri; Families Day Sat

Museum- Science

Science, Engineering & Technology Week

12/3/99
21/3/99
THE HELICOPTER MUSEUM
Tel: 01934 635227

Many events going on during the special week which aims to explain how science, engineering and technology fits into our everyday lives

Museum- Aviation

The Issues

13/3/99
13/3/99
BRISTOL CITY MUSEUM AND ART GALLERY
Tel: 0117 922 3571

Be part of an audience putting questions to people who put the exhibition together. Three sessions are available: 10.30-12.00, 13.00-14.30 & 15.30-17.00.

Museums

Walk: Sticklepath to Hound Tor

13/3/99
13/3/99
DARTMOOR NATIONAL PARK
Tel: 01626 832093

4 hour guided walk starting from Sticklepath (car park in village behind Finch Foundry Museum) at 10:45. More strenuous, longer route, steep sections likely, quicker pace. Suitable for reasonably fit walkers who want to stride out and enjoy the moor at a lively pace. Cost: A£3.50 C£0.75. FREE WALKS OFFER: arrive at a walk start point by bus and you may go on any walk completely free. Simply show the guide your bus ticket. No dogs allowed. Clothing: strong shoes, if dry, wellingtons or walking boots if wet. Good waterproofs and comfortable clothing. Snack or packed lunch. Please bring a hot drink and extra food.

National Parks

Talk & Slide Show: Sun, Moon and Standing Stones

13/3/99
13/3/99
DARTMOOR NATIONAL PARK
Tel: 01626 832093

1 hour talk at the High Moorland Visitor Centre, Princetown starting at 14:30. Park in the main car park adjacent to the centre. Cost: A£2.00 C(under 14)£0.75.

National Parks

Talk: How Women Do Colour Better Than Men!

13/3/99
13/3/99
THE ROYAL PHOTOGRAPHIC SOCIETY
Tel: 01225 462841

An informal gallery talk on the 'Between Two Worlds' exhibition at the RPS by RPS Curator Pam Roberts. Pam will discuss aspects of photography by women between 1855 and 1939 with the emphasis on women's mastery of colour photography in the 1920s and 30s e.g. Olive Edis, Madame Yevonde and Rosalind Maingot. Time: 14.30. Cost: £3.00 - includes entry to exhibitions.

Museum- Photographic

Two-day Practical: It's a Small World

13/3/99
14/3/99 DORSET COUNTY MUSEUM
Tel: 01305 262735
For the layman on the use of the microscope in geology (Saturday) and natural history (Sunday)

Museums

Collective Fair

13/3/99
14/3/99 ROYAL BATH AND WEST SHOWGROUND
Tel: 01749 822200
Please call for details

Showgrounds

Mars Invades Britain

13/3/99
14/3/99 THE TIME MACHINE
Tel: 01934 621028
The Planetary Society's project 'Mars invades Britain' will be in the form of a display of the projected Pathfinder Lander and the Sojourner Rover vehicles. The vehicles will be displayed in the museum courtyard in a simulated Martian landscape. Exhibition from 10.30-16.30

Museum- Local History

The Homes of Football

13/3/99
24/4/99 ROYAL ALBERT MEMORIAL MUSEUM
Tel: 01392 265858
A collection of outstanding photographs which truly capture the passion of the games at all levels

Museum- Local History

The Art of Hilda Carline: Mrs Stanley Spencer

13/3/99
3/5/99 ROYAL ALBERT MEMORIAL MUSEUM
Tel: 01392 265858
First retrospective of the work of Stanley Spencer's first wife; oils, watercolours and pastels

Museum- Local History

Woodlands Falconry Displays

13/3/99
31/10/99 WOODLANDS LEISURE PARK
Tel: 01803 712598
Superb flying displays with Falconers Karen and Neil. Sundays and Thursdays 12.30-15.00, Friday & Saturday 14.30

Country Leisure Parks

Mothering Sunday

14/3/99
14/3/99 CREALY PARK
Tel: 01395 233200
A free gift for every Mother visitng Crealy and a piece of Simnel cake

Country Parks

Walk: Grim & Sort Leat & Pew Tor

14/3/99
14/3/99 DARTMOOR NATIONAL PARK
Tel: 01626 832093
3 hour guided walk starting from Pork Hill (car park on south side of B3357 between Tavistock and Merrivale) at 10:45. Average route and pace, may be some steep ground, suitable for anyone used to walking. Cost: A£3.00 C£0.75. FREE WALKS OFFER: arrive at a walk start point by bus and you may go on any walk completely free. Simply show the guide your bus ticket. No dogs allowed. Please bring a hot drink and extra food.

National Parks

Course: Back In Print - Darkroom Skills Refresher Course

14/3/99
14/3/99 THE ROYAL PHOTOGRAPHIC SOCIETY
Tel: 01225 462841
A practical one day course in black and white processing and printing for those who had some experience in the past but are feeling a little rusty! Tutor, Chris Baker will cover the basics of processing and printing skills and give guidance on current material costs. There are only 8 places available. Time: 10.00-17.00. Cost: £30.00.

Museum- Photographic

Mothers Day Treat

14/3/99
14/3/99 WOODLANDS LEISURE PARK
Tel: 01803 712598
Celebrate with a free cream tea for Mum accompanied by a child under 16 years

Country Leisure Parks

Helicopter Pleasure Flights

14/3/99
10/10/99 THE HELICOPTER MUSEUM
Tel: 01934 635227
Normally take place in conjunction with Open Cockpit Days and on additional days during the peak summer period July-Aug and Bank Holidays. Further details, including prices, Sight-Seeing Specials and Trial Lessons can be obtained from the Museum

Museum- Aviation

Open Cockpit Days

14/3/99
10/10/99 THE HELICOPTER MUSEUM
Tel: 01934 635227
The public are given access to selected Helicopters with an experienced guide to explain the cockpit operation and mechanical working, normal admission prices apply. 1999 dates are: 21 Mar, 11 Apr, 9 May, 13 June, 11 July, 15 Aug, 12

Sept and 10 Oct

Museum- Aviation

Natural History Meeting

16/3/99 DORSET COUNTY MUSEUM

16/3/99 Tel: 01305 262735

"Koalas and other Marsupials". Miss
Kate Hebditch. Time: 19.30

Museums

**Mid-Somerset Decorative & Fine Arts
Society Meeting**

16/3/99 ROYAL BATH AND WEST SHOWGROUND

16/3/99 Tel: 01749 822200

Westex Suite. Please call for details

Showgrounds

Musical Performance: Florilegium

17/3/99 DORSET COUNTY MUSEUM

17/3/99 Tel: 01305 262735

Dorset County Museum Music Society.
The Baroque Group. Time: 19.30

Museums

**Play: Beyond Paradise: The Wildlife of
a Gentleman**

18/3/99 DORSET COUNTY MUSEUM

18/3/99 Tel: 01305 262735

A one-man play about Charles Darwin.
Written by poet and playwright Sean
Street and performed at 19.30 by
christopher Robbie

Museums

**Life and Environments in Purbeck
Times**

19/3/99 DORSET COUNTY MUSEUM

22/3/99 Tel: 01305 262735

This international symposium sponsored
by the Palaeontological Association
focuses on Purbeck and its sequences of
stratigraphy, sedimentology, palaeob-
otany and invertebrate and vertebrate
life, placing Purbeck in a regional and
world context.

Museums

Channel 4's Time Team

20/3/99 BRISTOL CITY MUSEUM AND ART GALLERY

20/3/99 Tel: 0117 922 3571

Excavation of John Pinney's slave plantation. 11.30-14.30

Museums

Season Opener

20/3/99 CASTLE COMBE CIRCUIT

20/3/99 Tel: 01249 782417

Porsch 924's, Caterham Graduates plus
round 1 of the home championships -
HEAT FF1600, National Mobile
Windscreens Special GT's and the Pagid
Saloon Car Championship. A£8.00
C&OAPs Paddock £2.50. Practice 09.30-
12.00, racing from 13.30

Motor Racing Circuit

Weston Super Mare Canines

20/3/99 ROYAL BATH AND WEST SHOWGROUND

20/3/99 Tel: 01749 822200

Showering Pavillion. Please call for
details

Showgrounds

West Country Game Fair

20/3/99 ROYAL BATH AND WEST SHOWGROUND

21/3/99 Tel: 01749 822200

Please call for details

Showgrounds

**Workshop: Introduction To The Zone
System**

20/3/99 THE ROYAL PHOTOGRAPHIC SOCIETY

21/3/99 Tel: 01225 462841

A practical weekend workshop with
Harry Fearn ARPS designed to explain
simply how to use this system to
improve your exposure. Includes darkroom demonstration, outdoor practical
session and darkroom printing. There
are 8 places available. Time: 10.00-17.00
daily. Cost: £80.00.

Museum- Photographic

Wildlife Photographer of the Year

20/3/99 ROYAL CORNWALL MUSEUM

24/4/99 Tel: 01872 272205

A touring exhibiton of the 150 winning
and commended images

Museums

Ray Atkins and the Figure (1958-1998)

20/3/99 ROYAL CORNWALL MUSEUM

22/5/99 Tel: 01872 272205

A major retrospective exhibition of figurative work

Museums

Walk: Spring Equinox Stroll

21/3/99 DARTMOOR NATIONAL PARK

21/3/99 Tel: 01626 832093

1.5 hour stroll starting from Merrivale
('Four Winds,' large walled car park in
trees on south side of B3357 Two
Bridges - Tavistock road) at 06:30. Easy
route and pace, little steep ground.
Suitable for children and fairly slow
walkers. No dogs allowed. Clothing: sensible shoes. Showerproof or waterproof
jacket and comfortable clothing. Please
bring a hot drink and extra food.

National Parks

Walk: Belstone Tor & Irishman's Wall

21/3/99 DARTMOOR NATIONAL PARK

21/3/99 Tel: 01626 832093

4 hour guided walk starting from
Okehampton Youth Hostel (turn up
Station Road and follow signs to the

Youth Hostel) at 10:45. More strenuous, longer route, steep sections likely, quicker pace. Suitable for reasonably fit walkers who want to stride out and enjoy the moor at a lively pace. Cost: A£3.50 C£0.75. FREE WALKS OFFER: arrive at a walk start point by bus and you may go on any walk completely free. Simply show the guide your bus ticket. No dogs allowed. Clothing: strong shoes, if dry, wellingtons or walking boots if wet. Good waterproofs and comfortable clothing. Snack or packed lunch. Please bring a hot drink and extra food.

National Parks

SW Hounds

21/3/99 **ROYAL BATH AND WEST SHOWGROUND**

21/3/99 Tel: 01749 822200

Edmund Rack Pavillion. Please call for details

Showgrounds

Club Meeting

21/3/99 **THRUXTON MOTORING RACING CIRCUIT**

21/3/99 Tel: 01264 772696

BARC Formula Renault, BARC/BRSCC Classic Ford 1600, Sports, 1600, BARC Modified Production Saloons, BARC/CSCC Group 1 Touring Cars, BARC/CSCC Classic Saloons & Historic Touring Cars. A£10.00(£8.00) C£Free Paddock £Free Grandstand £4.00 - (in advance)

Motor Racing Circuit

the Buildings of Wiltshire

23/3/99 **STOURHEAD HOUSE GARDEN AND HOUSE**

23/3/99 Tel: 01747 841152

An illustrated talk by Chris Bubb at 11.00 at The Spead Eagle Inn. £10.00 to include lunch

Historic Houses

Locock Garden Tour

24/3/99 **LACOCK ABBEY, FOX TALBOT MUSEUM AND VILLAGE**

24/3/99 Tel: 01249 730227/730459

Tour and talk on the history of Lacock Gardens, 11.00 start, 1.5 hours. No extra charge but donations welcome

Historic Houses

South Western Broiler Conference

24/3/99 **ROYAL BATH AND WEST SHOWGROUND**

24/3/99 Tel: 01749 822200

Westex Suite. Please call for details

Showgrounds

Countryside Day

25/3/99 **WINCANTON RACECOURSE**

25/3/99 Tel: 01963 32344

Competitive National Hunt racing with the first race at 14.15. Admission: Club £14.00 Tattersalls £10.00 Course & Cars to Course £5.00 C(0-16)Free Students (with I.D) £5.00 in Tattersalls. Discount for pre-booked groups10+ in Club & Tattersalls

Racecourses

AGM

26/3/99 **DORSET COUNTY MUSEUM**

26/3/99 Tel: 01305 262735

Dorchester Association AGM followed by the Presidential Address and lecture. "The Moule Family of Fordington". Mrs Jill Pope. Time: 19.30

Museums

Lynton Jazz Weekend

26/3/99 **NICK HOLT'S MOST EXCELLENT JAZZ WEEKENDS 1999**

28/3/99 Tel: 01271 372064

Venue: Town Hall, Lynton. Jam session with Simon Banks on Saturday afternoon. Artists include: Chris Watford's Dallas Dandies, Boulevard Django, Papajars All Stars, Alice's Wonderland Band and more.

Festivals

Walk: Combeshead Tor - prehis & med

27/3/99 **DARTMOOR NATIONAL PARK**

27/3/99 Tel: 01626 832093

4 hour guided walk starting from Norsworthy (small car park at north east end of Burrator Reservoir) at 10:45. More strenuous, longer route, steep sections likely, quicker pace. Suitable for reasonably fit walkers who want to stride out and enjoy the moor at a lively pace. This start point provides interesting opportunities to see how man has made use of Dartmoor in the past. Cost: A£3.50 C£0.75. FREE WALKS OFFER: arrive at a walk start point by bus and you may go on any walk completely free. Simply show the guide your bus ticket. No dogs allowed. Clothing: strong shoes, if dry, wellingtons or walking boots if wet. Good waterproofs and comfortable clothing. Snack or packed lunch. Please bring a hot drink and extra food.

National Parks

Antique & Collectors Fair

27/3/99 **ROYAL BATH AND WEST SHOWGROUND**

28/3/99 Tel: 01749 822200

Westex Complex. Please call for details

Further more detailed information on the attractions listed can be found in Best Guides *Visitor Attractions* Guide under the classifications shown

Photo Forum

Showgrounds

27/3/99
28/3/99 THE ROYAL PHOTOGRAPHIC SOCIETY
Tel: 01225 462841

All spaces in the Octagon Galleries will be devoted once again to displays from all the major photographic manufacturers and distributors of equipment and materials in this major RPS fund raising event. This will be accompanied by a full programme of lectures, workshops and demonstrations bookable in advance (various prices). Details from Lorinda Coombes at the RPS. Time: Sat 12.00-18.00, Sun 10.00-17.00. Cost: £5.00 entry to be paid on the day.

Museum- Photographic

Easter Eggstravaganza

27/3/99 BREWERS QUAY AND THE TIMEWALK JOURNEY

11/4/99 Tel: 01305 777622 24hr 766880

An eggs-traspecial programme of family fun featuring entertainers, craft workshops, competitions and demonstrations

Family Attraction

Deja View and Some Things New

27/3/99 ROYAL ALBERT MEMORIAL MUSEUM

12/6/99 Tel: 01392 265858

Favourite works from the museum's Fine Art Collection, many of which were on show recently in galleries across the world. Also includes new acquisitions

Museum- Local History

2D 3D South

27/3/99 SALISBURY AND SOUTH WILTSHIRE MUSEUM

12/6/99 Tel: 01722 332151

Exhibition by artists from Southern England working to the highest level of contemporary art in paintings, prints and sculpture

Museums

Walk: Harford & Three Barrows

28/3/99 DARTMOOR NATIONAL PARK
28/3/99 Tel: 01626 832093

4 hour guided walk starting from Ivybridge (from B3213 turn into Erme Road by NatWest Bank, follow into Station Road and park under viaduct) at 10:45. Average route and pace, may be some steep ground, suitable for anyone used to walking. This walk guides you over the solitude of the open moor to long abandoned communities and industries. Cost: A£3.50 C£0.75. FREE WALKS OFFER: arrive at a walk start point by bus and you may go on any walk completely free. Simply show the guide your bus ticket. No dogs allowed. Clothing: strong shoes, if dry, wellingtons or walking boots if wet. Good waterproofs and comfortable clothing. Please bring a hot drink and extra food.

National Parks

Haynes Spring Classic

28/3/99 HAYNES MOTOR MUSEUM
28/3/99 Tel: 01963 440804

The tour for motorsport enthusiasts visiting five motorsport venues in one day, call for details

Museum- Motor

Be a Star Talent Competition

28/3/99 WOODLANDS LEISURE PARK
28/3/99 Tel: 01803 712598

£15.00 1st prize, £10.00 2nd Prize, £6.00 3rd Prize. For boys and girls.

Country Leisure Parks

Longleat's 50th Anniversary Celebration Day

29/3/99 LONGLEAT
29/3/99 Tel: 01985 844400

Tons of entertainment of the whole family.

Safari Parks

Exploratory Easter Event

29/3/99 EXPLORATORY HANDS-ON SCIENCE CENTRE

9/4/99 Tel: 0117 907 5000 info line

Celebrate the Exploratory's 10 years at Temple Meads. New exhibits and resurrected old favourites.

Science Centres

Talk & Slide Show: Flowers and Plants of Dartmoor

30/3/99 DARTMOOR NATIONAL PARK
30/3/99 Tel: 01626 832093

1 hour talk at the High Moorland Visitor Centre, Princetown starting at 14:30. Park in the main car park adjacent to the centre. Cost: A£2.00 C(under 14)£0.75.

National Parks

Walk: Leisurely river & hillside walk

31/3/99 DARTMOOR NATIONAL PARK
31/3/99 Tel: 01626 832093

2 hour guided walk starting at Newbridge (meet in car park by bridge, 4 miles west of Ashburton) at 14:00. Easy route and pace, little steep ground. Suitable for children and fairly slow walkers. Cost: A£2.00 C£0.75. FREE WALKS OFFER: arrive at a walk start point by bus and you may go on any walk completely free. Simply show the

guide your bus ticket. Clothing: sensible shoes. Showerproof or waterproof jacket and comfortable clothing. Please bring a hot drink and extra food.

National Parks

Easter Egg Hunt
1/4/99 TREBAH GARDEN
18/4/99 Tel: 01326 250448
Children's Easter fun. Follow the trail and claim your easter egg prize. No booking required

Gardens

Easter Extravaganza
1/4/99 WOODLANDS LEISURE PARK
18/4/99 Tel: 01803 712598
10 days of Easter fun. Including top daily entertainment, Easter Bunny Hunts, woodlands famous Easter Egg Hunt Easter Sunday and Monday with the Easter Bonnet Competition of Monday

Country Leisure Parks

School Holiday Entertainment
1/4/99 WOODLANDS LEISURE PARK
5/9/99 Tel: 01803 712598
Unique live entertainment at Woodlands, a fabulous programme every day.

Country Leisure Parks

Countryside Weekend
1/4/99 THE HAWK CONSERVANCY
30/9/99 Tel: 01264 773850
Each weekend during the season. Country crafts, tractor rides, gun dog displays, pond dipping etc, call for further details

Birds of Prey Centre

Archaeology Meeting
2/4/99 DORSET COUNTY MUSEUM
2/4/99 Tel: 01305 262735
"Another Dorchester Henge and its Context". Mr Peter Cox, AC Archaeology and Mr Peter Woodward. Time: 19.30

Museums

Easter Show
2/4/99 ATHELHAMPTON HOUSE AND GARDENS
5/4/99 Tel: 01305 848363
Demonstration, Exhibition and Sale of Contemporary and Traditional Arts and Crafts from Dorset Craft workers in marquee on the north west lawn. Birds of Prey Flying Display 2-3 April. Medieval Re-enactment, cooking, archery and combat 4-5 April. Time: 10.00-17.30. Prices: A£3.50 (House £1.45 extra), C£0.50 (House £1.00), Family Ticket £11.00 (fully inclusive), OAPs£3.50 (House £1.10 extra)

Historic Houses

Easter Egg Hunt
3/4/99 CASTLE DROGO
3/4/99 Tel: 01647 433306
In the Woodland Walk. This activity forms part of Barclays Country Focus - a programme to support the greater enjoyment of National Trust Countryside, 11.30, £1.50

Historic Houses & Gardens

Easter Bunny Day!
3/4/99 CREALY PARK
3/4/99 Tel: 01395 233200
Meet the rabbits and babies in the world of pets. Bunny Bonanza at 15.00 in the show ring

Country Parks

Easter Egg Hunt
3/4/99 DUNSTER CASTLE
3/4/99 Tel: 01643 821314/823004
Plenty of Easter Eggs to hunt for, keep a sharp look out and you just might spot some... No extra charge, 10.00-16.30

Castles

Easter Egg Hunt
3/4/99 LYDFORD GORGE
3/4/99 Tel: 01822 820441
Picnic area and orchard, 10.30, £1.50. This activity forms part of Barclays Country Focus - a programme to support the greater enjoyment of National Trust Countryside

Walks

All Night Dance Party
3/4/99 ROYAL BATH AND WEST SHOWGROUND
3/4/99 Tel: 01749 822200
Westex Complex. Please call for details

Showgrounds

Barn Owls Live
3/4/99 THE TIME MACHINE
3/4/99 Tel: 01934 621028
A display by the Barn Owl Conservation Trust. Come and find out why the barn owl is becoming an endangered species and what is being done about it. Meet some owls. Free to museum ticket holders. 10.30-16.00

Museum- Local History

Mini Easter Egg Hunt & Ballooning & Kite Flying Festival
3/4/99 LONGLEAT
5/4/99 Tel: 01985 844400
Look around Longleat for these small eggs - they are harder to find than you think! Take a look up to the skies for more entertainment with balloons and kites to please the eye.

Further more detailed information on the attractions listed can be found in Best Guides *Visitor Attractions* Guide under the classifications shown

Safari Parks

Easter Egg Trail
3/4/99 PRIOR PARK LANDSCAPE GARDENS
5/4/99 Tel: 01225 833422
Come and try to find these craftily hidden eggs. £1.00 per child

Gardens

Easter Egg Hunt
4/4/99 BARRINGTON COURT
4/4/99 Tel: 01460 241938
Find those missing eggs somewhere in Barrington Court. No extra charge. 11.00-15.00

Gardens

Sunday Funday - Origins and Roots
4/4/99 BRISTOL CITY MUSEUM AND ART GALLERY
4/4/99 Tel: 0117 922 3571
Free family activities. Everyone starts out from somewhere. Share you stories with ours.

Museums

British Superbike Championship
4/4/99 THRUXTON MOTORING RACING CIRCUIT
4/4/99 Tel: 01264 772696
Qualifying. A£7.00 C£Free Paddock £Free Grandstand £5.00(£4.00) - (in advance)

Motor Racing Circuit

The History Man
4/4/99 BERRY POMEROY CASTLE
5/4/99 Tel: 01803 866618
Enjoy unusual guided tours with Brian McNerney, presenter of the BBC's popular History Man programmes. But be warned, his enthusiasm is notoriously contagious... and there is not antidote! Performing without costumes, props or even a safety net, he brings the past to life before your very eyes! From 12.00. A£2.50 C£1.30 Concessions£1.90 English Heritage Members Free

Castles

Steam Up
4/4/99 COLD HARBOUR MILL WORKING WOOL MUSEUM
5/4/99 Tel: 01884 840960
Two giant mill engines 'in steam' - a 1910 Pollitt & Wizzell engine, 1867 Beam Engine and 1888 Lancashire Boilers in action. Time: 10.30-17.00

Museum- Industrial

Easter Egg Hunts
4/4/99 CREALY PARK
5/4/99 Tel: 01395 233200
Over ten thousand chocolate eggs have been hidden all around the Park. See how many you can find!

Country Parks

Easter Chick Hunt
4/4/99 DAIRY LAND FARM WORLD
5/4/99 Tel: 01872 510246 info: 510349
One for the whole family! Come on kids find the chicks - great Easter FUN

Animal Farms

Echoes from the Past
4/4/99 MUCHELNEY ABBEY
5/4/99 Tel: 01458 250664
Tales of a medieval rat catcher. A£2.00 C£1.00 Concessions£1.50

Abbeys

Easter Egg Hunt
4/4/99 PAIGNTON ZOO, ENVIRONMENTAL PARK
5/4/99 Tel: 01803 527936
Follow the trail around the Zoo to find 1000s of eggs in the Egg Mine

Zoos- Conservation

Stories & Mask Making
4/4/99 PENDENNIS CASTLE
5/4/99 Tel: 01326 316594
Michael & Wendy Dacre. Traditional folk tales, myths and legends, plus mask making. From 12.00. A£3.80 C£1.90 Concessions£2.90

Castles

Civil War Garrison
4/4/99 PORTLAND CASTLE
5/4/99 Tel: 01305 820539
The life and times during the Civil War - the castle occupiers fear attack. From 12.00. A£3.50 C£1.80 Concessions£2.60 English Heritage members Free

Castles

Easter Egg Treaure Hunt Quiz
4/4/99 WILTON HOUSE
5/4/99 Tel: 01722 746729
Twenty question quiz around the House and Visitor Centre for children with a boxed Easter Egg prize. Normal prices and times apply. Nominal charge for under 5's to participate

Historic Houses & Gardens

Easter Monday Raceday
5/4/99 CASTLE COMBE CIRCUIT
5/4/99 Tel: 01249 782417
Classic Porsche, Mighty Mini, Morgans plus round 2 of the National Mobile Winscreens, HEAT and Pagid Championships. Admission A£10.00 C&OAPS/Paddock £2.50 Practice from 08.30, racing from 13.30

Motor Racing Circuit

Dorchester Teddy Bear Fair

| 5/4/99 5/4/99 | **Dorchester Teddy Bear Fair 1999**
Tel: 01305 269741
Thousands of teddy bears on show and for sale from exhibitors from all over the country. Time: 10.00-16.30. Price: A£2.50 C£1.00 |

Festivals

| 5/4/99 5/4/99 | **Easter Eggsplosion**
Flambards Village Theme Park
Tel: 01326 564093 info line
Easter egg hunt for children with fancy dress competition |

Theme Parks

| 5/4/99 5/4/99 | **Easter Egg Hunt**
Lacock Abbey, Fox Talbot Museum and Village
Tel: 01249 730227/730459
Come and try to find these craftily hidden eggs at Laycock. From 11.00. £1.00 per child |

Historic Houses

| 5/4/99 5/4/99 | **British Superbike Championship**
Thruxton Motoring Racing Circuit
Tel: 01264 772696
Motor Cycle News British Superbikes (two rounds), British 250cc, British 125cc, British Supersports 600, National Supersports 600 Shoot Out.
A£15.00(£13.00) C£Free Paddock £4.00(£3.00) Grandstand £7.00(£6.00) - (in advance) |

Motor Racing Circuit

| 5/4/99 5/4/99 | **Bank Holiday Monday Racing**
Wincanton Racecourse
Tel: 01963 32344
Spend an enjoyable day at the races with the first race at 14.00. Admission: Club £14.00 Tattersalls £10.00 Course & Cars to Course £5.00 C(0-16)Free Students (with I.D) £5.00 in Tattersalls. Discount for pre-booked groups10+ in Club & Tattersalls |

Racecourses

| 6/4/99 6/4/99 | **Mendip Decorative & Fine Arts Society Meeting**
Royal Bath and West Showground
Tel: 01749 822200
Westex Suite. Please call for details |

Showgrounds

| 7/4/99 7/4/99 | **Lacock Garden Tours**
Lacock Abbey, Fox Talbot Museum and Village
Tel: 01249 730227/730459
Tour and talk on the history of Lacock Gardens,11.00 start, 1.5 hours. No extra charge but donations welcome |

Historic Houses

People's Collections - Nick Isles' Dolphins

| 7/4/99 11/5/99 | **The Time Machine**
Tel: 01934 621028
Opportunity for private individuals to show their collection |

Museum- Local History

Tall Trees and Tall Stories

| 8/4/99 8/4/99 | **Stourhead House Garden and House**
Tel: 01747 841152
Children aged 5-11 can learn from the Garden team how a tree works, how to measure its height, and many other facts about the extensive tree collection in the Garden. Meet at the Visitor Reception at 10.30. £3.50 |

Historic Houses

Storytelling

| 8/4/99 9/4/99 | **Castle Drogo**
Tel: 01647 433306
Storytelling for children around the castle with Steve Manning. 14.00. Normal admission prices. Booking advisable. Also on 19 Aug. |

Historic Houses & Gardens

Please Do Touch!

| 10/4/99 26/6/99 | **Devizes Museum**
Tel: 01380 727369
A "Touchy, Feely" exhibition encouraging people to come and handle objects from the museum collections of different ages, materials, textures, uses and sizes |

Museum- Archaeology

Open Doors

| 11/4/99 11/4/99 | **Blaise Castle House Museum**
Tel: 0117 950 6789
Craft demonstrations, plus butter making in the dairy. Don't miss the special openings of Blaise Castle and Stratford Mill. 10.00-16.00. |

Museums

Bridgwater & District Canine Show

| 11/4/99 11/4/99 | **Royal Bath and West Showground**
Tel: 01749 822200
Edmund Rack Pavillion. Please call for details |

Showgrounds

British Formula Three Championship

| 11/4/99 11/4/99 | **Thruxton Motoring Racing Circuit**
Tel: 01264 772696
British Formula Three, Formula Palmer Audi, MG F Cup, National Saloons, Classic Touring Cars. A£12.00 C£Free Paddock £4.00(£3.00) Grandstand £7.00(£6.00) - (in advance) |

Motor Racing Circuit

Garden Tour

14/4/99 14/4/99	**CASTLE DROGO** _Showgrounds_ Tel: 01647 433306 With Head Gardener Mick Little. Normal admission prices. 14.00. Booking advisable. _Historic Houses & Gardens_

Lecture: The Life and Times of Mary Anning (1799-1847) - A Bicentenary Tribute

14/4/99 14/4/99	**DORSET COUNTY MUSEUM** Tel: 01305 262735 Dr Hugh Torrens, Keele University. Time: 19.30 _Museums_

The Archaeology of the Stourhead Estate

15/4/99 15/4/99	**STOURHEAD HOUSE GARDEN AND HOUSE** Tel: 01747 841152 An illustrated talk by Ian Mays at 11.00 at The Spread Eagle Inn. £10.00 to include lunch _Historic Houses_

Lecture: The Stone Diaries: 4,000 Million Years of Evolution

16/4/99 16/4/99	**DORSET COUNTY MUSEUM** Tel: 01305 262735 Dr Richard Fortey, Merit Researcher in the Department of Palaeontology at the Natural History Museum and prize-winning author. Time: 19.30 _Museums_

Dorset Local History Group AGM and Lecture

17/4/99 17/4/99	**DORSET COUNTY MUSEUM** Tel: 01305 262735 "Learning from the Past: the Rebuilding of Blandford after the Great Fire of 1731". Dr Michael Turner. Time: 14.30 _Museums_

Bestseller

17/4/99 20/6/99	**THE TIME MACHINE** Tel: 01934 621028 Revisit the bestsellers and famous books of the century _Museum- Local History_

Looking at Landscapes

18/4/99 18/4/99	**PRIOR PARK LANDSCAPE GARDENS** Tel: 01225 833422 Walk led by Matthew Ward, Gardener in Charge at Prior Park. Walk starts at 14.00, lasting 2 hours. Admission £2.50 _Gardens_

Collectors' Toy Fair

18/4/99 18/4/99	**ROYAL BATH AND WEST SHOWGROUND** Tel: 01749 822200 Showering Pavillion. Please call for details

Natural History Meeting

20/4/99 20/4/99	**DORSET COUNTY MUSEUM** Tel: 01305 262735 "From Kimmeridge to Galapagos - the need for marine conservation management". Dr Ken Collins, Southampton Oceanography Centre. Time: 19.30 _Museums_

The Skills of the Stonemason

21/4/99 21/4/99	**CASTLE DROGO** Tel: 01647 433306 How Castle Drogo was built. A talk and tour by master stonemason, Wesley Key. Includes a short visit to the roof. 14.00. Booking advisable. Also held on 14 July & 8 Sept. _Historic Houses & Gardens_

Garden Tours

21/4/99 21/4/99	**LACOCK ABBEY, FOX TALBOT MUSEUM AND VILLAGE** Tel: 01249 730227/730459 Tour and talk on the history of Lacock Gardens, 11.00 start, 1.5 hours. No extra charge but donations welcome _Historic Houses_

Exhibition

21/4/99 18/7/99	**HOLBURNE MUSEUM AND CRAFTS STUDY CENTRE** Tel: 01225 466669 Outstanding miniatures from a private collection. A touring exhibition _Museums_

The 15th Southern Knitting & Needlecraft Exhibition

22/4/99 25/4/99	**ROYAL BATH AND WEST SHOWGROUND** Tel: 01749 822200 Westex Complex. Superb exhibition with some of the latest ideas and designs. 10.00-17.00 each day _Showgrounds_

Dorchester Association Members Evening

23/4/99 23/4/99	**DORSET COUNTY MUSEUM** Tel: 01305 262735 Time: 19.30 _Museums_

Wildlife on the Drogo Estate

24/4/99 24/4/99	**CASTLE DROGO** Tel: 01647 433306 A 2 hour walk. Booking advisable. Meet at visitor reception at 10.00. Dogs on leads welcome. Also, launch of Castle Drogo Children's Wildlife Painting and Poetry Competition. Also held on 26 July & 18 Aug. _Historic Houses & Gardens_

Teachers' Open Day

24/4/99   CREALY PARK

24/4/99   Tel: 01395 233200

Teachers are invited to join us for a free day out - with their families too - when we will prove that "Learning is part of the fun at Crealy!"

Country Parks

St. George's Day

24/4/99   FARLEIGH HUNGERFORD CASTLE

25/4/99   Tel: 01225 754026

Medieval Music and entertainment. A£3.50 C£1.80 Concessions£2.60

Castles

Medieval Jousting Spectacular

24/4/99   OLD SARUM CASTLE

25/4/99   Tel: 01722 335398

Discover the secrets of the tourney, as the jousting area resounds to the sounds of the battle, clash of steel and thunder of horses hooves as the mighty knights charge at full tilt. A£5.00 C£2.50 Concessions£3.80

Historical Remains

Badger Weekend

24/4/99   SECRET WORLD-BADGER AND WILDLIFE RESCUE CENTRE

25/4/99   Tel: 01278 783250

Pauline will be giving illustrated talks throughout the day. At 11.00 and 15.00 visitors will hear about the orphan badger cub rearing that is carried out at the centre and the individual characters that have lived in Pauline's kitchen! Members of the Badger Group will be on hand to explain how you can become more involved with badgers wherever you live in the country

Wildlife Rescue

Past Pleasures

24/4/99   STONEHENGE

25/4/99   Tel: 01980 624715 info line

Famous 17th century antiquarian John Aubrey explains his theories to a lady companion. Meet the gossiping pair and hear why he thought Stonehenge was built by the Druids. From 12.00. A£4.00 C£2.00 Concessions£3.00 English Heritage members Free

Ancient Monuments

Celebration of Shakespeare

24/4/99   WILTON HOUSE

25/4/99   Tel: 01722 746729

Reading in the house to celebrate the first performance of 'As You Like It' at Wilton House. Normal prices and times apply

Historic Houses & Gardens

National Gardens Scheme

25/4/99   CASTLE DROGO

25/4/99   Tel: 01647 433306

Come along and view the beautiful gardens at Castle Drogo. Also held on 16 June

Historic Houses & Gardens

Guided Walk - Birdsong

25/4/99   LYDFORD GORGE

25/4/99   Tel: 01822 820441

Expert identification of birdsong. Meet at the main entrance at 08.00

Walks

Fabulous Circus Day

25/4/99   WOODLANDS LEISURE PARK

25/4/99   Tel: 01803 712598

Workshops and circus fun with circus Bezercus. Faice-painting, competitions and prizes.

Country Leisure Parks

Young Musicians Concert

28/4/99   THE TIME MACHINE

28/4/99   Tel: 01934 621028

The best of North Somerset's young musicians present a programme of music in the charming setting of the museum courtyard. Admission by programme. Refreshments available in interval. A£2.50 C£Free Concessions£2.00. Doors open 19.00

Museum- Local History

Disappearing Dorset

30/4/99   DORSET COUNTY MUSEUM

30/4/99   Tel: 01305 262735

Dorset evening with Mr Geoffrey Poole. Time: 19.30

Museums

South West Custom & Classic Bike Show

30/4/99   ROYAL BATH AND WEST SHOWGROUND

2/5/99   Tel: 01749 822200

A weekend extravaganza for anyone with an interest in motorbikes. Exhibition of 250 Custom & Classic bikes, Trade Stands, bike jumble and a wide range of entertainment. Attractions include The Firebird Aerobatics Display and The Scott May Daredevil Show. Camping available on site. All enquiries 01749 823260

Showgrounds

Women of Style

30/4/99   MUSEUM OF COSTUME

5/11/00   Tel: 01225 477785

Fashionable women whose clothes form an important part of the museum's collection of 19th and 20th century fashion. The displays feature Mary Chamberlain, wife of the politician Joseph Chamberlain and Mary Curzon, first wife of Lord Curzon, Viceroy of India. Both were American beauties who dressed at the finest couture houses of their day. The stylish Ranee of Pudukottai was Australian-born and with her husband, and Indian Prince, spent much of the 1920s and 1930s living in the South of France. Martita Hunt, a well-known stage and screen actress and Dame Margot Fonteyn, the famous ballerina, both gave clothes to the Museum of Costume which illustrate the work of leading British and French designers from the 1940s to the 1960s

Museum- Costume

Norton Magna
BARRINGTON COURT

1/5/99
3/5/99

Tel: 01460 241938
The Somerset and Dorset Joint Railway model recreation in 1:43 scale. No extra charge, family discount

Gardens

Weymouth International Beach Kite Festival
WEYMOUTH INTERNATIONAL BEACH KITE FESTIVAL

1/5/99

3/5/99

Tel: 01305 772444
A packed programme of kite displays, international firework festival, stunts, kite stalls, fun fair, competitions, kite workshops, kite stall village (kit bits and pieces and lots of advice). 10.00-18.00. Admission Free

Festivals

Spring Flowers in the Cloisters
WILTON HOUSE

1/5/99
3/5/99

Tel: 01722 746729
A profusion of spring colour in the Cloisters. Normal House admission prices and times apply

Historic Houses & Gardens

Great May Day Weekend
WOODLANDS LEISURE PARK

1/5/99
3/5/99

Tel: 01803 712598
Happy Holiday Merriment. Top live entertainers every day providing good old fashioned fun

Country Leisure Parks

Loose Parts: A Simon Nicholson retrospective
HIGH CROSS HOUSE

1/5/99
27/6/99

Tel: 01803 864114
An opportunity to see the varied work of

one of the Hepworth Nicholson Triplets

Historic Houses

Chard Festival On Tour 1999
CHARD FESTIVAL OF WOMEN IN MUSIC ON TOUR 1999 & 2000

1/5/99

30/6/99

Tel: 01460 66115
Chard Festival promotes music by women for the enjoyment of everyone. The next biennial festival is 24-29 May 2000 and Chard Festival On Tour during May & June 1999. Full details are not yet available, please call Festival Office for brochure.

Festivals

As Dark as Light
TATE GALLERY ST IVES

1/5/99
1/11/99

Tel: 01736 796226
To coincide with the forthcoming Millennium and the Solar Eclipse in August 1999, 3 artists will be making new work for Tate St Ives. Yuko Shirdishi, Gia Edzveradze and Garry Fabian Miller, who all work in different media, will create work in response to the Solar Eclipse, which will be seen in its totality in W Cornwall.

Art Galleries

British Touring Car Championship
THRUXTON MOTORING RACING CIRCUIT

2/5/99
2/5/99

Tel: 01264 772696
Qualifying. A£8.00(£7.00) C£Free Paddock £4.00(£3.00) Grandstand £5.00 - (in advance)

Motor Racing Circuit

Medieval Entertainment
BERRY POMEROY CASTLE

2/5/99
3/5/99

Tel: 01803 866618
Fighting knights, dancing, stories, children's games and juggling. A£3.00 C£1.50 Concessions£2.30

Castles

Steam Up & Sheep & Country Fair
COLD HARBOUR MILL WORKING WOOL MUSEUM

2/5/99

3/5/99

Tel: 01884 840960
Two giant mill engines 'in steam' - a 1910 Pollitt & Wizzell engine, 1867 Beam Engine and 1888 Lancashire Boilers in action. Time: 10.30-17.00.

Museum- Industrial

May-Day Lost Toys Treasure Hunt!
CREALY PARK

2/5/99
3/5/99

Tel: 01395 233200
A free toy for every child when you find the counters hidden throughout the Park. Choose from the THOUSANDS of brilliant toys and take part in the most

famous of Crealy's fantastic Treasure Hunts!

Country Parks

Medieval Entertainment
2/5/99
3/5/99
FARLEIGH HUNGERFORD CASTLE

Tel: 01225 754026

Fighting knights, dancing, stories, children's games and juggling. A£4.00 C£2.00 Concessions£3.00

Castles

The Thunder of the Guns
2/5/99
3/5/99
PENDENNIS CASTLE

Tel: 01326 316594

Portsdown Artillery Volunteers. Firing of a selection of the castles guns, from Elizabethan to WWII. Visitors are advised to check details with venues closer to the event. A£3.80 C£1.90 Concessions£2.90 English Heritage Members Free

Castles

Tudor Music - Richard York
2/5/99
3/5/99
PORTLAND CASTLE

Tel: 01305 820539

Delightful 16th century style music played upon stringed instruments. From 12.00. A£2.50 C£1.30 Concessions£1.90 English Heritage members Free

Castles

Tudor Artillery
2/5/99
3/5/99
ST MAWES CASTLE

Tel: 01326 270 526

Lots of bangs from the Courteneye Household. A£3.00 C£1.50 Concessions£2.30

Castles

Storytelling
2/5/99
3/5/99
TINTAGEL CASTLE

Tel: 01840 770328

Rough Magic. Ancient tales to enjoy. From 12.00. A£2.80 C£1.40 Concessions£2.10 English Heritage members Free

Historical Remains

May Day Bank Holiday Car Races
3/5/99
3/5/99
CASTLE COMBE CIRCUIT

Tel: 01249 782417

ARP F3, Caterhams, Fiats and the thrid round of the Pagid, Heat and national Mobile Windscreens Championships. Admission A£10.00 C&OAPS/Paddock £2.50 Practice from 08.30, racing from 13.30

Motor Racing Circuit

Penalty Shoot Out Competition

3/5/99
3/5/99
FLAMBARDS VILLAGE THEME PARK

Tel: 01326 564093 info line

Boys and girls under 12 penalty shoot out at noon. Free admission if wearing team shirt

Theme Parks

British Touring Car Championship
3/5/99
3/5/99
THRUXTON MOTORING RACING CIRCUIT

Tel: 01264 772696

Auto Trader British Touring Cars, Formula Renault Sport, Formula Vauxhall Junior, Slick 50 Formula Ford, Renault Sport Spider, Vauxhall Vectra SRi V6, Ford Credit Fiesta. A£19.00(£15.00) C£Free Paddock £5.00(£4.00) Grandstand £9.00 - (in advance)

Motor Racing Circuit

National Hunt Racing
7/5/99
7/5/99
WINCANTON RACECOURSE

Tel: 01963 32344

Evening racing with first race at 17.55. Admission: Club £14.00 Tattersalls £10.00 Course & Cars to Course £5.00 C(0-16)Free Students (with I.D) £5.00 in Tattersalls. Discount for pre-booked groups10+ in Club & Tattersalls

Racecourses

Daphne du Maurier Festival
7/5/99
16/5/99
DAPHNE DU MAURIER FESTIVAL

Tel: 01726 77477 Box Office

Held around Fowey and surrounding areas. Celtic and folk music, art exhibitions, guided walks, street fayres, drama, comedy, day schools, camera clubs, orchestras and more. Most venues are not suitable for wheelchairs. Full list available on request from Festival Information Line: 01726 74324. Prices: Various. Some venues £Free. Booking Fee £1.00. Concessions for Children

Festivals

Family Field Outing
8/5/99
8/5/99
DORSET COUNTY MUSEUM

Tel: 01305 262735

A day out to look at the way geology affects the settlements, industries, environments and wildlife of two locations: Portland Bill and Portesham. Own transport. Leaders Richard Edmonds, Jurassic Coast Project Officer, Dorset County Council and Dr Mike Cosgrove, Chairman of DIGS.

Museums

Helston Flora Day

Further more detailed information on the attractions listed can be found in Best Guides *Visitor Attractions* Guide under the classifications shown

8/5/99 8/5/99	**HELSTON FLORA DAY 1999** Tel: 01326 572082 Continuous programme of dancing. Children's dance featuring over 1000 children dressed in white, the Hal-An-Tow pageant about the history of Helston. Early dance and evening dance. Thousands dance their way through the town in colourful costumes and top hats. First dance starts 07.00. Admission Free *Festivals*

Wildlife 1st Aid Course - Stage 1

8/5/99 SECRET WORLD-BADGER AND WILDLIFE

8/5/99 RESCUE CENTRE

Tel: 01278 783250

This is a full day covering first aid treatment for wildlife animals and birds. The aim is to create confidence when dealing with a situation involving wildlife. Capture, initial care, procedure and individual requirements are subjects covered during the day. There is also some practical work on bandaging, gavaging and injections. Start: 09.45 for 10.00. Finish: 16.00. Cost: £20.00. Lecturers: Pauline Kidner and a Vetinary Surgeon. Stage 1 will also be held on: 25 September & 17 October. These courses are held at the centre and can only be attended if booked in advance. The cost of each course is inclusive of tea and coffee throughout the day but does not include lunch. This can be booked separately for an extra £5.00 giving any special consideration with regards to diet. Those attending the course will have the chance to see the centre and its facilities during breaks. For information regarding accommodation near the centre, please telephone

Wildlife Rescue

Norton Magna

8/5/99 BARRINGTON COURT

9/5/99 Tel: 01460 241938

The Somerset and Dorset Joint Railway model recreation in 1:43 scale. No extra charge, family discount

Gardens

The History Man

8/5/99 DARTMOUTH CASTLE

9/5/99 Tel: 01803 833588

Enjoy unusual guided tours with Brian McNerney, presenter of the BBC's popular History Man programmes. But be warned, his enthusiasm is notoriously contagious... and there is no antidote! Performing without costumes, props or even a safety net, he brings the past to life before your very eyes! A£3.00 C£1.50 Concessions£2.30

Castles

Antique & Collectors Fair

8/5/99 ROYAL BATH AND WEST SHOWGROUND

9/5/99 Tel: 01749 822200

Westex Complex. Please call for details

Showgrounds

Swindon International Kite Festival

8/5/99 SCIENCE MUSEUM

9/5/99 Tel: 01793 814466

This ever popular event is back at Wroughton for another fun-filled year. Learn how to make and fly a kite: watch the experts in stunt kite flying location. Time: 10.00-17.00. Admission: A£3.00 C(5-16)£1.00 C(0-5)£Free

Museum- Science

Stories & Mask Making

8/5/99 STONEHENGE

9/5/99 Tel: 01980 624715 info line

Michael & Wendy Dacre. Traditional folk tales, myths and legends, plus mask making. A£4.00 C£2.00 Concessions£3.00 English Heritage members Free

Ancient Monuments

Tiverton Spring Festival

8/5/99 TIVERTON SPRING FESTIVAL 1999

16/5/99 Tel: 01884 258952

Operas, orchestral, street entertainment, drama, lectures, sports events, music and dancing, rock concerts, morris dancers, treasure hunts, exhibitions and much more. Tickets: available from: Tourist Information 01884 255827

Festivals

Exeter Arts Society

8/5/99 ROYAL ALBERT MEMORIAL MUSEUM

7/6/99 Tel: 01392 265858

Work encompassing a range of subject matter, styles and media by members of this local art society

Museum- Local History

The Druids

8/5/99 DEVIZES MUSEUM

28/8/99 Tel: 01380 727369

An exhibition exploring the history, beliefs and practises of the Druids, both past and present

Museum- Archaeology

Woodland Walk

9/5/99 CASTLE DROGO

9/5/99 Tel: 01647 433306

A 2.5 hour woodland and gorge walk. Wear stout shoes, dogs on leads welcome. Meet at visitor reception at 10.00

Historic Houses & Gardens

Woodland Bluebell Walk

9/5/99
9/5/99
STOURHEAD HOUSE GARDEN AND HOUSE
Tel: 01747 841152

A walk with the Estate Warden. Meet at 10.30 at Visitor Reception. A£3.50 C£Free.

Historic Houses

Jan Niedojadlo

10/5/99
12/6/99
ROYAL ALBERT MEMORIAL MUSEUM
Tel: 01392 265858

Huge and spectacular interactive sculptures made from recycled materials, can be touched, crawled inside and listened to.

Museum- Local History

The Life and Times of George III

10/5/99
5/9/99
BREWERS QUAY AND THE TIMEWALK JOURNEY
Tel: 01305 777622 24hr 766880

A fascinating portrait of one of Weymouth's most famous royal patrons set against the backcloth of significant changes in the structure of society, the industrial revolution and the on-going wars with both Bonaparte's Europe and the American colonies striving for their independence

Family Attraction

Evening Tour

11/5/99
11/5/99
CASTLE DROGO
Tel: 01647 433306

A tour of the Castle with dinner in the restaurant. An opportunity to "see behind the scenes". £10.95 inclusive. Booking essential. 19.00

Historic Houses & Gardens

Mendip Decorative & Fine Arts Society Meeting

11/5/99
11/5/99
ROYAL BATH AND WEST SHOWGROUND
Tel: 01749 822200

Westex Suite. Please call for details

Showgrounds

Sydenham Camera Club Photographic Exhibition

11/5/99
21/5/99
ADMIRAL BLAKE MUSEUM
Tel: 01278 456127

Annual exhibition of photographs by members of local society

Museum- Local History

Summer Special

12/5/99
12/5/99
SECRET WORLD-BADGER AND WILDLIFE RESCUE CENTRE
Tel: 01278 783250

A personal evening with Derek and Pauline at their home when they will tell

you about their work. A chance to see behind the scenes, catch the sight of the badgers at night and enjoy a buffet style meal with wine included, in the lovely farmhouse tearooms. Due to demand, bookings are required for limited numbers only. Cost: £20.00 per person (inclusive)

Wildlife Rescue

Lecture: Three Hundred Years of Dorset Geologists

14/5/99
14/5/99
DORSET COUNTY MUSEUM
Tel: 01305 262735

The history of geological science in Dorset. Dr Hugh Torrens, Keele University. Time: 19.30

Museums

Canterbury Tales

15/5/99
LACOCK ABBEY, FOX TALBOT MUSEUM AND VILLAGE
Tel: 01249 730227/730459

Presented by John Watts in the Grreat Hall. Doors open at 19.00 for 19.30 start. £12.50, to include a glass of wine and canapes.

Historic Houses

The Bard's Best Bits - Oddsocks Productions

15/5/99
16/5/99
FARLEIGH HUNGERFORD CASTLE
Tel: 01225 754026

Once again this hugely entertaining group comprehensively demolish Shakespeare! See the best bits from Julius Caesar, Romeo and Juliet and A Midsummer Night's Dream. Don't miss it! A£3.50 C£1.80 Concessions£2.60

Castles

The Tudor Kitchen

15/5/99
16/5/99
PENDENNIS CASTLE
Tel: 01326 316594

the Courteneye Household demonstrate how hard it was in a Tudor kitchen. A£3.80 1.90 Concessions£2.90

Castles

Wildlife Weekend

15/5/99
16/5/99
SECRET WORLD-BADGER AND WILDLIFE RESCUE CENTRE
Tel: 01278 783250

A unique chance to see behind the scenes. Guided tours of the hospital room, casualty pens and rehabilitation enclosures will be at 12.00 and 15.00. There will be a talk at 11.00 on wildlife care and first aid as well as introductions to the different creatures that come to our centre. An opportunity to see Sage, the Barn Owl, bats, dormice,

Further more detailed information on the attractions listed can be found in Best Guides *Visitor Attractions* Guide under the classifications shown

hedgehogs and even foxes too! Many other surprises in a wildlife bonanza

Wildlife Rescue

Stories & Mask Making
15/5/99 STONEHENGE
16/5/99 Tel: 01980 624715 info line
Michael & Wendy Dacre. Traditional folk tales, myths and legends, plus mask making. A£4.00 C£2.00 Concessions£3.00 English Heritage members Free

Ancient Monuments

Alice in Wonderland
15/5/99 WENLOCK PRIORY
16/5/99 Tel: 01952 727466
Labyrinth Productions. Follow Alice and White Rabbit as they go through Wonderland, meeting all manner of weird, wonderful and totally mad characters. A£3.50 C£1.80 Concessions£2.60

Priory

Museums Week
15/5/99 THE HELICOPTER MUSEUM
23/5/99 Tel: 01934 635227
Why not be part of the biggest annual museums promotion in the World by coming along to The Helicopter Museum, plenty of events planned to take you on flights of knowledge

Museum- Aviation

Museums Week
15/5/99 THE TIME MACHINE
23/5/99 Tel: 01934 621028
The themes for 1999 will be food, travel and treasures. There will also be links to the Year of Reading and Adult Learners' Week.

Museum- Local History

Spring Plant Fair
16/5/99 DUNSTER CASTLE
16/5/99 Tel: 01643 821314/823004
Large variety of plants. Fair starts at 10.00

Castles

Plant Fair
16/5/99 LYDFORD GORGE
16/5/99 Tel: 01822 820441
A plant fair for all those gardening enthusiasts. 10.30

Walks

Walk on the Wild Side
16/5/99 PRIOR PARK LANDSCAPE GARDENS
16/5/99 Tel: 01225 833422
Walk led by Alison Payne, Senior Recruiter at Prior Park. Walk starts at 14.00, lasting 2 hours. Admission £2.50

Gardens

Festival of Birds
16/5/99 ROYAL BATH AND WEST SHOWGROUND
16/5/99 Tel: 01749 822200
Showering Pavillion. Please call for details

Showgrounds

10th Birthday Party
16/5/99 WOODLANDS LEISURE PARK
16/5/99 Tel: 01803 712598
Free entry to £25.00 draw. Fun with our famous entertainers. Two free season tickets to the 1,989th customer to the party. Mammoth birthday cake. Surprises galore.

Country Leisure Parks

Mid-Somerset Decorative & Fine Arts Society Meeting
18/5/99 ROYAL BATH AND WEST SHOWGROUND
18/5/99 Tel: 01749 822200
Westex Suite. Please call for details

Showgrounds

Stourhead in the Evening
19/5/99 STOURHEAD HOUSE GARDEN AND HOUSE
19/5/99 Tel: 01747 841152
Join the Head Gardener for a walk in the Garden. Meet at 19.00 at Visitor Reception. Members £4.00, Non-members £8.00

Historic Houses

The Hunting of the Earl of Rone
21/5/99 THE HUNTING OF THE EARL OF RONE
24/5/99 Tel: 01271 882524
Villagers parade with Grenadiers and a de-ribboned Hobby Horse led by a Fool in a Smock. Spectacle includes drummers, musicians and a masked person in a sack cloth riding back to front on a donkey - Earl of Rone. He is regularly shot, revived and finally cast into the sea. Admission Free

Festivals

English Riveria Festival 1999
21/5/99 ENGLISH RIVERIA FESTIVAL 1999
5/6/99 Tel: 01895 632143
Provisional dates, call for details nearer the time. Modern ballroom, Latin American, disco, rock 'n' roll and sequence dancing.

Festivals

50th Bath International Music Festival '99
21/5/99 50TH BATH INTERNATIONAL MUSIC
FESTIVAL '99
6/6/99 Tel: 01225 463362
Various venues. Set in the magnificent surroundings of Britain's finest Roman city, Bath International Music Festival,

this year celebrating it's 50th anniversary, features the world's best music. Opening Night Celebrations and fireworks herald the beginning of the 17-day Festival, presenting classical and early music concerts in many of Bath's historic Georgian venues, as well as unique, weekend-long celebrations of contemporary European jazz, contemporary classical music and world music. Prices: Ticket prices vary from £6.00-£30.00. Concessionary and group rates available

Festivals

Exhibition: Mary Anning: Her Life, Times and Fossils

21/5/99
2/9/99

DORSET COUNTY MUSEUM

Tel: 01305 262735

An exhibition to mark the September bicentenary of her birth in 1799. With adult and children fossil-handling sessions in the school holidays.

Museums

Tudor Living History

22/5/99
23/5/99

FARLEIGH HUNGERFORD CASTLE

Tel: 01225 754026

Hungerford Household. A masque is rehersed for a family celebration and the servants plan a mummers' play. From 12.00. A£3.00 C£1.50 Concessions£2.30 English Heritage Members - Free

Castles

Alice in Wonderland

22/5/99
23/5/99

OLD WARDOUR CASTLE

Tel: 01747 870487

Labyrinth Productions. Follow Alice and White Rabbit as they go through Wonderland, meeting all manner of weird, wonderful and totally mad characters. A£3.50 C£1.80 Concessions£2.60

Castles

Brixham Heritage Festival

22/5/99
30/5/99

BRIXHAM HERITAGE FESTIVAL 1999

Tel: 01803 855262

Live music, car rally, classic boat rallies, children's entertainment, firework displays on the pier with synchronised music, photography exhibition. Punch and Judy shows, Scottish country dancing, Gloucestershire Youth Jazz Orchestra and barbecues. Time: 14.00-21.00 daily except firework displays which finish at 21.50. Prices vary

Festivals

Greening the Blasted Oak

22/5/99
6/6/99

WILTON HOUSE

Tel: 01722 746729

Grass work by Heather Ackroyd and Dan

Harvey. Salisbury Festival Project

Historic Houses & Gardens

Barbie Doll Picnic

23/5/99
23/5/99

WOODLANDS LEISURE PARK

Tel: 01803 712598

Free picnic to Barbie doll owners. Spangles the Clown. Barbie look alike competition.

Country Leisure Parks

Bat Walk

26/5/99
26/5/99

DUNSTER CASTLE

Tel: 01643 821314/823004

Come along and discover the world of bats. 20.30. A£3.00 C£1.50. Call the Box Office on 01643 821314

Castles

Attics and Cellar Tours

26/5/99
26/5/99

STOURHEAD HOUSE GARDEN AND HOUSE

Tel: 01747 841152

An upstairs-downstairs look behind the scenes at Stourhead House. Tours on intervals between 12.00—17.30. No additional charge with House ticket. £3.00 for tour only - no booking necessary

Historic Houses

Brynna Choir

29/5/99
29/5/99

MONTACUTE HOUSE

Tel: 01935 823289

Welsh Male Voice Choir in the Great Hall at 18.00 & 19.30. £5.00, no concessions and limited numbers

Historic Houses

Fun Days

29/5/99
31/5/99

CREALY PARK

Tel: 01395 233200

Fun Days with a different magic show at 15.00 each day

Country Parks

Spring Holiday Bonanza

29/5/99
6/6/99

WOODLANDS LEISURE PARK

Tel: 01803 712598

World famous live entertainers everyday.

Country Leisure Parks

Matisse Jazz

29/5/99
27/6/99

ROYAL CORNWALL MUSEUM

Tel: 01872 272205

Matisse's Jazz series, created in 1942 when the artist was aged 73

Museums

Weymouth Old Harbour 9th Annual Oyster Festival

30/5/99
30/5/99

BREWERS QUAY AND THE TIMEWALK JOURNEY

Tel: 01305 777622 24hr 766880

A unique fun-filled festival with live musical entertainment, competitions

and side-shows, plus oysters galore!
Family Attraction

Weymouth Oyster Festival

30/5/99 **WEYMOUTH OYSTER FESTIVAL**

30/5/99 Tel: 01305 785747

Oyster market, oyster displays and competitions. Full programme of live music, Shire horses, street entertainment, fancy dress, fair, face painting, oyster trail and challenge. Time: 10.00-16.00. Admission Free

Festivals

Storytelling - Old Fairweather

30/5/99 **BERRY POMEROY CASTLE**

31/5/99 Tel: 01803 866618

Enjoyable gossip, folklore and history. From 12.00. A£2.50 C£1.30 Concessions£1.90 English Heritage Members Free

Castles

Steam Up

30/5/99 **COLD HARBOUR MILL WORKING WOOL MUSEUM**

31/5/99 Tel: 01884 840960

Two giant mill engines 'in steam' - a 1910 Pollitt & Wizzell engine, 1867 Beam Engine and 1888 Lancashire Boilers in action. Time: 10.30-17.00

Museum- Industrial

Life in the Age of Chivalry

30/5/99 **FARLEIGH HUNGERFORD CASTLE**

31/5/99 Tel: 01225 754026

Ye Compaynye of Chevalrye. Weaponry, skills-at-arms, have-a-go archery, crafts and 14th century living history. From 12.00. A£3.00 C£1.50 Concessions£2.30 English Heritage Members - Free

Castles

World War Two Battle

30/5/99 **OLD SARUM CASTLE**

31/5/99 Tel: 01722 335398

WWII Living History Association re-enact World War II. A£4.00 C£2.00 Concessions£3.00

Historical Remains

Elizabethan Dance and Longbows

30/5/99 **PENDENNIS CASTLE**

31/5/99 Tel: 01326 316594

Dance and longbow demonstrations, come along and have a go. Visitors are advised to check details with venues closer to the event. From 12.00. A£3.80 C£1.90 Concessions£2.90 English Heritage Members Free

Castles

Restoration & Engineering Open Days

30/5/99 **THE HELICOPTER MUSEUM**

31/5/99 Tel: 01934 635227

Visitors are given the opportunity to tour our restoration workshops, have the mechanics of the helicopters and autogyros explained, discuss the work being undertaken by our Volunteer Staff and understand the problems of restoring old helicopters, normal admission prices apply

Museum- Aviation

Storytelling

30/5/99 **TINTAGEL CASTLE**

31/5/99 Tel: 01840 770328

Rough Magic. Ancient tales to enjoy. From 12.00. A£2.80 C£1.40 Concessions£2.10 English Heritage members Free

Historical Remains

Flower Festival

30/5/99 **ATHELHAMPTON HOUSE AND GARDENS**

3/6/99 Tel: 01305 848363

Fresh and dried flower arrangements in the House with special Garden displays. Organisers from Owermoigne floral group with collection for Dorset MRi Scanner Appeal, 10.00-17.30, A£4.95 C£1.50 OAPs£4.60 Family Ticket £11.00 Groups£3.95

Historic Houses

Baby Swans Hatching

30/5/99 **ABBOTSBURY SWANNERY**

30/6/99 Tel: 01305 871858/871130

Hundreds of baby swans smother the pathways. Over 120 nests, an average of six eggs in each nest, visitors can actually take photographs of eggs hatching

Waterfowl Parks

Spring Bank Holiday Raceday

31/5/99 **CASTLE COMBE CIRCUIT**

31/5/99 Tel: 01249 782417

Ferrar, Tomcat/Vento, Porsche OPen, Formula 600 plus round 4 of the National Mobile Wincscreens, HEAT and Pagid Championships. Admission A£10.00 C&OAPS/Paddock £2.50 Practice from 08.30, racing from 13.30

Motor Racing Circuit

Specialist Plant Sale

31/5/99 **MILTON LODGE GARDENS**

31/5/99 Tel: 01749 672168

If you are looking for something unusual for the garden come along between 10.00 & 16.00

Gardens

Half-Term Activities

| 31/5/99 | CASTLE DROGO |
| 4/6/99 | Tel: 01647 433306 |

Various activities for children. Normal admission prices.

Historic Houses & Gardens

Primate Week

| 31/5/99 | PAIGNTON ZOO, ENVIRONMENTAL PARK |
| 6/6/99 | Tel: 01803 527936 |

Come along and find out more about these fascinating animals

Zoos- Conservation

Children's Woodland Trail and Quiz

| 1/6/99 | LACOCK ABBEY, FOX TALBOT MUSEUM AND VILLAGE |
| 1/6/99 | Tel: 01249 730227/730459 |

Great fun for children, 11.00-13.00, no extra charge, call 01249 730227 for booking

Historic Houses

'South' Frank Hurley

| 1/6/99 | FOX TALBOT MUSEUM OF PHOTOGRAPHY |
| 31/8/99 | Tel: 01249 730459/730141 |

Frank Hurley with Ernest Shackleton on his remarkable expedition to the Antarctic

Museum- Photographic

Storytelling

| 2/6/99 | TOTNES CASTLE |
| 2/6/99 | Tel: 01803 864406 |

Dave Oliver. Enjoyable gossip, folklore and history. From 12.00. A£1.60 C£0.80 Concessions£1.20 English Heritage members Free

Castles

Mary Anning and Her Times: The Discovery of British Palaeontology 1820-1850

| 2/6/99 | DORSET COUNTY MUSEUM |
| 4/6/99 | Tel: 01305 262735 |

A symposium to be held at Lyme Regis with speakers including Sir Crispin Tickell, Stephen Jay Gould, Hugh Torrens and John Fowles. Details from the Philpot Museum at Lyme Regis.

Museums

The Royal Bath and West of England Show

| 2/6/99 | ROYAL BATH AND WEST SHOWGROUND |
| 5/6/99 | Tel: 01749 822200 |

It's Show time! The South and West's largest Agricultural Show with a wide range of attractions and exhibits. With over 1,000 tradestands the Bath and West has something for everyone. Main Ring Attractions include The Kings Troop Royal Horse Artillery, The Honda Imps, Falconry displays, Free Fall Parachutists, and Sheep dogs. Book early and save £'s on 01225 447770

Showgrounds

The Grand Tour

| 3/6/99 | STOURHEAD HOUSE GARDEN AND HOUSE |
| 3/6/99 | Tel: 01747 841152 |

A talk by Donald Hutchings with a tour of the picture collection in the House. 15.00. £7.00, to include afternoon tea.

Historic Houses

Heritage and Archaeology Workshop

| 3/6/99 | KENTS CAVERN SHOWCAVES |
| 5/6/99 | Tel: 01803 215136 |

Archaeology and heritage displays from around Torbay, artefacts from the British Museum, visitors can bring in artefacts for assessment by experts

Caverns

Garden Weekend

| 4/6/99 | SALISBURY AND SOUTH WILTSHIRE MUSEUM |
| 5/6/99 | Tel: 01722 332151 |

A weekend of gardening lectures and demonstrations by experts. Plants from specialist growers and garden gifts.

Museums

Longleat Horse Trials

| 4/6/99 | LONGLEAT |
| 6/6/99 | Tel: 01985 844400 |

Watch these beautiful creatures prance around for your enjoyment.

Safari Parks

Gala Opera

| 5/6/99 | DYRHAM PARK |
| 5/6/99 | Tel: 0117 937 2501 |

Presented by Opera Brava. Gates open at 18.00 for 19.30 start. Tickets: £15.00 in advance, £16.00 on the gate if available

Historic Houses

Annual Plant Sale

| 5/6/99 | FORDE ABBEY |
| 5/6/99 | Tel: 01460 221290 |

The Hardy Plant Society Annual Plant Sale at 10.30. The Abbey will also be open to the public from 12.00

Historic Houses & Gardens

Top Brass at Stourhead

| 5/6/99 | STOURHEAD HOUSE GARDEN AND HOUSE |
| 5/6/99 | Tel: 01747 841152 |

The band of the Royal Electrical and Mechanical Engineers play favourite music from films, stage musicals and opera on the Terrace of Stourhead House. Gates open at 18.00 for 19.00 start. A£8.00 C£6.00

Historic Houses

Further more detailed information on the attractions listed can be found in Best Guides *Visitor Attractions* Guide under the classifications shown

Creepy Crawlie Weekend
5/6/99 SECRET WORLD-BADGER AND WILDLIFE
RESCUE CENTRE
6/6/99 Tel: 01278 783250
Meet up with Field Detective, Francis
Farr-cox at 12.15 to scour the centre for
lurking spiders, hedge sweeping too - no
bug will be safe from his searching eyes!
At 15.15 each day, a chance to go pond
dipping to discover the creepy crawlies
that live in our pond. No stone left
unturned, this is an exciting weekend
especially for children - and those who
never grow up!
Wildlife Rescue

Club Meeting
6/6/99 THRUXTON MOTORING RACING CIRCUIT
6/6/99 Tel: 01264 772696
European BOSS Formula, Goodyear
Maranello Ferrari, BARC Westfield
Sportscars, URS Classic Ford 2000, BMW
Four Plus, Bell Security Guarding
Formula Saloons. A£12.00(£10.00)
C£Free Paddock £4.00(£3.00)
Grandstand £5.00 - (in advance)
Motor Racing Circuit

Stitching Extravaganza
9/6/99 LONGLEAT
11/6/99 Tel: 01985 844400
Demonstrations and goods for sale.
Safari Parks

Jazz in June
9/6/99 BREWERS QUAY AND THE TIMEWALK
JOURNEY
13/6/99 Tel: 01305 777622 24hr 766880
Five fabulous days of free jazz in character venues around Weymouth's picturesque Old Harbour, plus live outdoor
entertainment in Hope Street
Family Attraction

Devizes Festival 1999
10/6/99 DEVIZES FESTIVAL '99
26/6/99 Tel: 01380 728151
Devizes Festival aims to bring the people
of Devizes and the surrounding area during June each year a varied programme
of professional performances - folk,
blues, jazz, world, classical music; comedy, poetry, dance, talks, walks and
cycle rides, brewery tours, an art exhibition - all at keen prices. A small and
beautiful festival! Ask for a brochure on
01380 728151. Various times and prices
throughout various venues in Devizes.
Festivals

Lecture: Geology - Who Cares?

11/6/99 DORSET COUNTY MUSEUM
11/6/99 Tel: 01305 262735
The everyday and commercial advan-
tages of geological research; how rocks
affect our lives. Andrew Woollett,
Chairman, Reunion (Zinc) Mining plc.
Time: 19.30
Museums

Wessex Craft and Flower Fayre
11/6/99 WILTON HOUSE
13/6/99 Tel: 01722 746729
Craft exhibits in marquees, open air
demonstrations and flower fayre.
Organised by ICHF. Separate access and
admission charges apply. For further
information please call 01425 272711
Historic Houses & Gardens

**Fowlers Motorcycles Pro-Bike
National**
12/6/99 CASTLE COMBE CIRCUIT
12/6/99 Tel: 01249 782417
Round 5 of the Honda Super Club
Championship, 125 Grand Prix, 250
Grand Prix, Formula 400, Formula 600,
F2 Sidecars, ProBike Open, Sound of
Thunder and the MUZ Scorpion Super
Cup, plus the return of the popular
General Guarantee T.T. Riders
Association Parade. A£8.00
C&OAPs/Paddock £2.50 Practice 09.00-
12.00, Parades 12.15, Racing 13.00
Motor Racing Circuit

**Medieval Archery - The Wolfshead
Bowmen**
12/6/99 OLD WARDOUR CASTLE
13/6/99 Tel: 01747 870487
Displays of skilled archery, weaponry
and combat, plus shooting of a 14th century ballista. Mounted archer, knight and
have-a-go archery. A£3.00 C£1.50
Concessions£2.30
Castles

Pecorama Steam & Model Festival
12/6/99 PECORAMA
13/6/99 Tel: 01297 21542
Live steam engines in many forms, from
table top models to full size traction
engines, plus a fleet of locomotives on
the Beer Heights Light Railway
Railways Miniature

16th-Century Living History
12/6/99 PENDENNIS CASTLE
13/6/99 Tel: 01326 316594
Witness the life and times of a 16th-cen-
tury Garrison under the threat of invasion! Visitors are advised to check
details with venues closer to the event.

From 12.00. A£3.80 C£1.90 Concessions£2.90 English Heritage Members Free

Castles

Wiltshire Agriculture Preservation Society

12/6/99 13/6/99 SCIENCE MUSEUM

Tel: 01793 814466

From plough horses to steam tractors, see the reality behind the rustic idyll. A great day out for all the family, including ploughing competitions, working steam engines and traditional country fayre

Museum- Science

Military and Veterans Festival

12/6/99 18/6/99 MILITARY AND VETERANS FESTIVAL 1999

Tel: 01305 785747

Festival includes major parade with marching bands on 13 June, historic vehicles, Forces Music Hall, band concerts and international veterans rendezvous.

Festivals

The 4th Annual International Military & Veterans Festival

12/6/99 18/6/99 THE PAVILION COMPLEX

Tel: 01305 785747

The main feature of the Festival will be the Remembrance Service and Parade along Weymouth Seafront on Sunday 13 June in which over 1,800 veterans will march, together with 8 military marching bands. These will be followed by a Military Vehicle Convoy with over 70 military and historic vehicles. Free Band performances throughout the afternoon. The highly acclaimed FREE International Veterans Rendezvous takes place on the 2nd Wednesday morning in every month 10.00-12.00.

Arts & Entertainment

Bristol Volksfest 1999

13/6/99 13/6/99 BRISTOL VOLKSFEST 1999

Tel: 0117 955 9559

Local bands and DJs, community entertainers, cult fashion, surf wear, VW air-cooled motor show, trade stands, autojumble, Gladiator-style pugel stick fighting and a car cruise around Bristol.

Festivals

Toy & Train Collectors Fair

13/6/99 13/6/99 ROYAL BATH AND WEST SHOWGROUND

Tel: 01749 822200

300+ stalls, selling dolls & teddies, dinky, corgi, Meccano, model railways, lead figures, tin toys, science fiction toys and lots more. Refreshments available

Showgrounds

The Matchstick Fleet

13/6/99 20/6/99 NOTHE FORT

Tel: 01305 787243

Exhibition of astonishing fleet of 300 scale warships made only from matchsticks

Forts

Evening Garden Tour

15/6/99 15/6/99 CASTLE DROGO

Tel: 01647 433306

A tour around the garden with head gardener Mick Little. £10.95 to include dinner. Booking essential. 19.00

Historic Houses & Gardens

World War II Commemoration Events

15/6/99 15/6/99 NOTHE FORT

Tel: 01305 787243

Service and sing-a-long in the courtyard

Forts

Much Ado About Nothing

16/6/99 16/6/99 DUNSTER CASTLE

Tel: 01643 821314/823004

Theatre Set-up presentation. Performance starts at 19.30. Advance Tickets A£8.00 C£5.00, Tickets on the Gate: A£10.00 C£7.00

Castles

Bat Talk & Watch

16/6/99 16/6/99 LYDFORD GORGE

Tel: 01822 820441

Guided walk and talk for bat enthusiasts. 19.30

Walks

Garden Demonstration Day

17/6/99 17/6/99 MONTACUTE HOUSE

Tel: 01935 823289

Hardy Perennials in the Garden - Lawn Care & Garden Machinery. 12.00, 14.00 & 16.00. Garden entrance tickets from Reception Centre. A£2.90 C£1.30

Historic Houses

National Garden Scheme

17/6/99 17/6/99 MONTACUTE HOUSE

Tel: 01935 823289

For further details including times and prices please call venue direct

Historic Houses

Summer Special

18/6/99 18/6/99 SECRET WORLD-BADGER AND WILDLIFE RESCUE CENTRE

Tel: 01278 783250

A personal evening with Derek and Pauline at their home when they will tell you about their work. A chance to see behind the scenes, catch the sight of the badgers at night and enjoy a buffet style meal with wine included, in the lovely farmhouse tearooms. Due to demand, bookings are required for limited numbers only. Cost: £20.00 per person (inclusive)

Wildlife Rescue

Sturminster and Fiddleford
19/6/99 DORSET COUNTY MUSEUM
19/6/99 Tel: 01305 262735
Dorset Local History field meeting.
Leader: Mr L J Keen. Time: 10.00

Museums

Fire Sculpture plus Royal Philharmonic Concert Orchestra
19/6/99 LONGLEAT
19/6/99 Tel: 01985 844400
Sounds exciting! Please call for further information.

Safari Parks

A Civil War Surgeon - The Ringwoods of History
19/6/99 FARLEIGH HUNGERFORD CASTLE
20/6/99 Tel: 01225 754026
Rory McCready. Listen to presentations about gruesome 17th century surgery, see the implements used and meet the leeches who were used as an important medical aid. From 12.00. A£3.00 C£1.50 Concessions£2.30 English Heritage Members - Free

Castles

15th-Century Nuns
19/6/99 MUCHELNEY ABBEY
20/6/99 Tel: 01458 250664
The White Company. A£2.50 C£1.30 Concessions£1.90

Abbeys

Native American Weekend
19/6/99 THE AMERICAN MUSEUM IN BRITAIN
20/6/99 Tel: 01225 460503
Enjoy watching and taking part in native American dancing. Special exhibition

Museums

Arthurian Soldiers
19/6/99 TINTAGEL CASTLE
20/6/99 Tel: 01840 770328
Inner State Theatre. Confusion reigns in Camelot as King Arthur, Queen Guinevere and their pet dragon Pen search for Merlin and Sir Lancelot, from 12.00. A£2.80 C£1.40 C£2.10

Historical Remains

Polperro Festival
19/6/99 POLPERRO FESTIVAL 1999
27/6/99 Tel: 01503 272579
Art - music - choirs - poetry - street entertainment - Morrismen - the Second Polperro World Limerick Championship - all Public Houses have live music, varied tastes - Furry Dance and a variety of other events.

Festivals

Embroidery by Gertrude Hickson
19/6/99 SALISBURY AND SOUTH WILTSHIRE
7/8/99 MUSEUM
Tel: 01722 332151
Without any experience, Gertrude Hickson, aged 71, made dazzling, lively embroidery panels in the space of one year after her beloved husband died. A stunning exhibition.

Museums

Writing Arabic
19/6/99 ROYAL ALBERT MEMORIAL MUSEUM
28/8/99 Tel: 01392 265858
Examples of arabic script and writing tools. A British Museum exhibition

Museum- Local History

British Doll Association
19/6/99 SALISBURY AND SOUTH WILTSHIRE
25/9/99 MUSEUM
Tel: 01722 332151
Over 100 superb dolls designed, sculpted, painted and clothed by professional artists for their Association's annual exhibition

Museums

Off the Beaten Track
20/6/99 CASTLE DROGO
20/6/99 Tel: 01647 433306
A 4-5 hour walk occasionally strenuous. Wear stout shoes and waterproof clothing. Bring packed lunch. Dogs on leads welcome. Meet visitor reception at 10.00

Historic Houses & Gardens

Father's Day
20/6/99 CREALY PARK
20/6/99 Tel: 01395 233200
A free present for every Dad

Country Parks

Father's Day
20/6/99 DAIRY LAND FARM WORLD
20/6/99 Tel: 01872 510246 info: 510349
Free entry today all day for DADS! Save £5.20 go on bring him along he'll love it

Animal Farms

Ralph Allen's Vision
20/6/99 PRIOR PARK LANDSCAPE GARDENS
20/6/99 Tel: 01225 833422
Walk led by Paul Paulton, Warden at Prior Park. Walk starts at 14.00, lasting 2 hours. Admission £2.20

Gardens

Wildlife 1st Aid Course - Stage 2

20/6/99	SECRET WORLD-BADGER AND WILDLIFE RESCUE CENTRE
20/6/99	Tel: 01278 783250

Stage 2 is the follow up to the first course, with rehabilitators in mind who will hopefully contribute to the day and have the opportunity to exchange ideas. Further discussion of fluid therapy, more advanced care, ethics and final release will make this a very interesting day. Start: 09.45 for 10.00. Finish: 16.00. Cost: £20.00. Lecturers: Pauline Kidner, Colin Seddon (RSPCA), and a Vetinary Surgeon. Also to be held on: 27 November. These courses are held at the centre and can only be attended if booked in advance. The cost of each course is inclusive of tea and coffee throughout the day but does not include lunch. This can be booked separately for an extra £5.00 giving any special consideration with regards to diet. Those attending the course will have the chance to see the centre and its facilities during breaks. For information regarding accommodation near the centre, please telephone

Wildlife Rescue

Wilton and District Youth Band

20/6/99	WILTON HOUSE
20/6/99	Tel: 01722 746729

Event starts at 14.15. Please call venue direct for further information

Historic Houses & Gardens

Fathers Day

20/6/99	WOODLANDS LEISURE PARK
20/6/99	Tel: 01803 712598

Free BBQ Burger. Welly boot throwing competition. Medieval Battle.

Country Leisure Parks

Shakespeare at the Nothe

21/6/99	NOTHE FORT
26/6/99	Tel: 01305 787243

Daily performances of Midsummers Night Dream by Weymouth Drama Club . Enjoy a picnic on the ramparts from 18.00, curtain up at 19.30

Forts

Teddy Bears Picnic

23/6/99	WOODLANDS LEISURE PARK
23/6/99	Tel: 01803 712598

Free Picnic to Teddy owners under 14 years. Best Teddy Bear Mask competition, Storyteller, Most loved Teddy of the Decade

Country Leisure Parks

Taming of the Shrew

25/6/99	MONTACUTE HOUSE
25/6/99	Tel: 01935 823289

Presented by The Festival Players Theatre Company at 19.30. A£10.00 Concessions£8.00 in advance, £12.00 & £10.00 on the gate

Historic Houses

Glastonbury Festival of Contemporary Performing Arts 1999

25/6/99	GLASTONBURY FESTIVAL OF CONTEMPORARY PERFORMING ARTS 1999
27/6/99	Tel: 01749 890470

As always, the best in contemporary music from anywhere is the world on the seven main stages and numerous other smaller stages; theatre, dance and cabaret; circus and street theatre; two cinema screens - one outdoor; the Greenfields with their Green Politics and campaigners; alternative healing and diverse crafts, music and food. A wonderful selection of colourful market stalls and food outlets catering for every tastes imaginable. All this and plenty of surprises. Possibly the best entertainment in the world! Animals will NOT be admitted, please do not bring them.

Festivals

Summer Fete

26/6/99	CASTLE DROGO
26/6/99	Tel: 01647 433306

Fun and games for all the family. Normal admission prices. 10.30

Historic Houses & Gardens

Chew Valley Plant Sale

26/6/99	SHERBORNE GARDEN (PEAR TREE HOUSE)
26/6/99	Tel: 01761 241220

Organised by Mill House Plants. Various nurseries selling plants, with refreshments, 10.30-16.00

Gardens

Bristol on Water

26/6/99	BRISTOL ON WATER 1999
27/6/99	Tel: 0117 9276614

Canal and waterways vessels from around the country. Exhibitons, trade stands, craft fairs. Live music, street entertainment, funfair and firework display.

Festivals

Bristol on Water Weekend 1999

26/6/99	BRISTOL ON WATER WEEKEND
27/6/99	Tel: 0117 927 6614

Venue: Bristol Harbour. See the arrival of over 150 canal and waterways vessels from all over the country. Among the main attractions will be live music, a fun fair, some water based activities, street entertainment, a firework display, exhibitions, craft stalls and boat competitions. Admission Free

Festivals

English Civil War Living History
26/6/99 OLD WARDOUR CASTLE
27/6/99 Tel: 01747 870487
Living history during the Civil War re-enacted by The Wardour Garrison.
A£3.00 C£1.50 Concessions£2.30

Castles

1549 Rebellion
26/6/99 RESTORMEL CASTLE
27/6/99 Tel: 01208 872687
Tudor re-enactment by The Courteneye Household. A£3.00 C£1.50 Concessions£2.30

Castles

Try Drive '99
26/6/99 SCIENCE MUSEUM
27/6/99 Tel: 01793 814466
Ever wanted to drive a tank? Ever wondered how articulated lorries get round those corners? Find out how by doing it yourself! The Try Drive '99 is jointly run by the Wiltshire County Council Road Safety Division and ??.. Attractions include the !CB Digger Challenge, mini motorbikes, off-road karting, helicopter rides and vintage vehicles. An action packed day out. Time: 10.00-17.00

Museum- Science

Bluebell Sett Fun Weekend
26/6/99 SECRET WORLD-BADGER AND WILDLIFE RESCUE CENTRE
27/6/99 Tel: 01278 783250
A weekend with special events. Ferret racing, face painting, lots of fun and games besides the usual displays always given at Secret World. We shall be inviting our patrons - so there may be a few well known faces around!

Wildlife Rescue

Wilton Horse Trials
26/6/99 WILTON HOUSE
27/6/99 Tel: 01722 746729
Traditional country horse trial event across the River from Wilton House. Separate access and admission charges apply. For further information please call 01749 812994

Historic Houses & Gardens

Bath Abbey Flower Festival
26/6/99 BATH ABBEY
29/6/99 Tel: 01225 422462
Flower festival celebrating the miracles

as describe by St. John. Commences: 09.00-18.00. Admission by £2.00 donation. Sunday times will be disrupted by Services, please call for further details

Churches

Mosaic - A Living Art
26/6/99 ROYAL ALBERT MEMORIAL MUSEUM
4/9/99 Tel: 01392 265858
A large and dazzling show featuring work by 15 leading British and Italian artists

Museum- Local History

Crealy Bears 10th Birthday Party
27/6/99 CREALY PARK
27/6/99 Tel: 01395 233200
Games, Story-Telling, Picnic. The highlight of the year for your teddy! All teddies invited to join the party at 15.00

Country Parks

Radio and Computer Rally
27/6/99 LONGLEAT
27/6/99 Tel: 01985 844400
Please call for further information.

Safari Parks

Mevagissey Feast Week
27/6/99 MEVAGISSEY FEAST WEEK 1999
3/7/99 Tel: 01726 842920
Choral concerts, flower festival, traditional processions and dancing, live music events, water sports, gig racing, carnivals, village fete and firework display. An ancient festival celebrating the Feast of St. Peter, the Patron Saint of Mevagissey and Fishermen.

Festivals

Annual General Meeting
29/6/99 DORSET COUNTY MUSEUM
29/6/99 Tel: 01305 262735
DNH & AS. Time: 18.30

Museums

The Totnes Taborer - Strolling Medieval Musician
29/6/99 TOTNES CASTLE
29/6/99 Tel: 01803 864406
A costumed entertainer performing on pipes and drum throughout the day. From 11.00. A£1.60 C£0.80 Concessions£1.20 English Heritage members Free

Castles

Pecorama Millennium Garden
1/7/99 PECORAMA
31/7/99 Tel: 01297 21542
Actual date to be confirmed. The first phase opening during July, of the Pecorama Millennium Garden, a magical mix of traditional garden settings and

	original, innovative ideas
	Railways Miniature
	Dance in a Cold Climate
1/7/99	HIGH CROSS HOUSE
29/8/99	Tel: 01803 864114
	Exhibition which celebrates 20th century dance
	Historic Houses

An Evening with Jools Holland
2/7/99 DYRHAM PARK
2/7/99 Tel: 0117 937 2501
Featuring Jools Holland and his Rhythm and Blues Orchestra, to include support group. Gates open at 12.00 for 19.30 start. A£17.00 C£12.00 in advance, A£20.00 C£15.0 on the gate if available. Special Offer! Book before 31/3/99 and receive £0.50 off the advanced price. 10% off bookings of 10+ tickets
Historic Houses

Forts and Flora
2/7/99 STOURHEAD HOUSE GARDEN AND HOUSE
2/7/99 Tel: 01747 841152
An evening walk over Whitesheet Down. Meet at 18.30 at Whitesheet Hill car park. No charge
Historic Houses

Lyme Regis Jazz Festival 1999
2/7/99 LYME REGIS JAZZ FESTIVAL
4/7/99 Tel: 01297 445216
Featuring top UK and International jazz artists - traditional New Orleans Jazz. Umbrella Parade on Saturday at 11.00.
Festivals

Amesbury Carnival 1999
3/7/99 AMESBURY CARNIVAL 1999
3/7/99 Tel: 01980 622866
Join in the procession to Holders Field. At 13.00 the Arena Displays begin, among them kite flying, log sawing, dog handling/agility displays, the amazing Devizes 'Major Wreks' and of course all the Fun of the Fair.
Carnivals

Tribute Night
3/7/99 DYRHAM PARK
3/7/99 Tel: 0117 937 2501
Featuring 'Magic' a tribute to Freddie Mercury and Queen. To include support group. Gates open at 12.00 for 19.30 start. A£12.00 C£6.00 in advance, A£15.00 C£10.00 on the gate. Special Offer! Buy before 31/3/99 and receive £0.50 off the advanced price. 10% off bookings of 10+ tickets
Historic Houses

Falmouth Big Green Fair 1999

Falmouth Big Green Fair 1999
3/7/99
3/7/99 Tel: 01326 375158
Music (drumming, hurdy-gurdy, belly dancing and other exotica), green art exhibitions, vegan food stalls, local cider and ale, environmental stalls. Bouncy castles, workshops, complimentary healing tasters such as reflexology, massage etc. Due to some steep slopes and steps, access for disabled is slightly curtailed. However, help is available upon request.
Festivals

Glastonbury Anglican Pilgrimage
3/7/99 GLASTONBURY ABBEY
3/7/99 Tel: 01458 832267
Annual pilgrimage within the Abbey grounds
Abbeys

Longleat Proms Concert
3/7/99 LONGLEAT
3/7/99 Tel: 01985 844400
Longleat Proms Concert: Outdoor Proms Concert with spectacular fireworks. Bring a pcinic, flags, good voices and enjoy the lively atmosphere. Call for further information
Safari Parks

Summer Sensation Raceday
3/7/99 CASTLE COMBE CIRCUIT
4/7/99 Tel: 01249 782417
TVR, Porsche, Mini Se7en and Miglia, Auto Italia, Ford Saloons, XZR2 & XR3 plus the fifth round of the HEAT, National Mobile Windscreens and Pagid Championships. Admission Saturday A£5.00 C&OAPs/Paddock £Free. Practice from 08.30, racing from 13.30. Admission Sunday A£10.00 C&OAPs£2.50 Paddock £Free. Practice from 09.00, racing from 12.00
Motor Racing Circuit

Military Vehicle Rally
3/7/99 PENDENNIS CASTLE
4/7/99 Tel: 01326 316594
Rally of military vehicles of all ages. Visitors are advised to check details with venues closer to the event. From 12.00.
Castles

Truckfest South West
3/7/99 ROYAL BATH AND WEST SHOWGROUND
4/7/99 Tel: 01749 822200
Truckfest South West: The Star studded Truckfest spectacular - now in its 10th year at the Showground. Main arena action, T.V. Celebrities, trade stands and fun fair - lots to see and do for all the

Further more detailed information on the attractions listed can be found in Best Guides *Visitor Attractions* Guide under the classifications shown

family. All enquiries: 01775 768661
Showgrounds

Festival of Free Flight
3/7/99 SCIENCE MUSEUM
4/7/99 Tel: 01793 814466
Organised by the British Hang Gliding and Paragliding Association, this premier event in the free flight calendar encompasses all forms of free flight from parascenders to balloons. With activities for all the family, this is a spectacular display. Admission: A£5.00 C(0-14)£Free
Museum- Science

Independence Celebration
3/7/99 THE AMERICAN MUSEUM IN BRITAIN
4/7/99 Tel: 01225 460503
Special displays and campsite illustrate how British soldiers lived at the time of American Independence
Museums

Touring Exhibition - Our South West
3/7/99 ADMIRAL BLAKE MUSEUM
20/7/99 Tel: 01278 456127
Touring Exhibition by young people. Includes interactive display
Museum- Local History

Weston Retrospective
3/7/99 THE TIME MACHINE
22/8/99 Tel: 01934 621028
An exhibition of art, sculpture and video by Weston's John Butler
Museum- Local History

Bournemouth and Poole MG Owners' Club Car Rally
4/7/99 ATHELHAMPTON HOUSE AND GARDENS
4/7/99 Tel: 01305 848363
Display of MG cars of all ages with cars from all MG clubs in the south of England (region 10). £3.00 admission for arriving in an MG., in aid of local charity, 10.00-17.30, A£4.95 C£Free OAPs£4.60 Garden & MGs only: £3.50, House admission £1.50 extra
Historic Houses

Roman Catholic Pilgrimage
4/7/99 GLASTONBURY ABBEY
4/7/99 Tel: 01458 832267
Annual pilgrimage procession from the Tor to the Abbey
Abbeys

A Parcel of Rougues
4/7/99 RESTORMEL CASTLE
4/7/99 Tel: 01208 872687
Drama by the Miracle Theatre. A£3.00 C£1.50 Concessions£2.30
Castles

MacRobertson Girl's School Choir and

Orchestra
4/7/99 STOURHEAD HOUSE GARDEN AND HOUSE
4/7/99 Tel: 01747 841152
The girls from this Australian school perform in St Peter's Church, Stourton at 19.00
Historic Houses

Festival of Motorsport
4/7/99 THRUXTON MOTORING RACING CIRCUIT
4/7/99 Tel: 01264 772696
BTRA National Trucks, 250cc Gearbox Karts (double header), R&D Motorsport Austin Healey Club, Firestone MG Owners' Club, Porsche Classic, Gilera Scooters. A£10.00(£8.00) C£Free Paddock £4.00(£3.00) Grandstand £5.00 - (in advance)
Motor Racing Circuit

Wild West Day
4/7/99 WOODLANDS LEISURE PARK
4/7/99 Tel: 01803 712598
Tamar Valley Westerners, Line Dancers, Majorettes.
Country Leisure Parks

A Celebration of the Century
4/7/99 NEWQUAY 1900 WEEK - A CELEBRATION OF THE CENTURY
13/7/99 Tel: 01637 878735 Box Office
The first three days will be spent in the Victorian Era and will then progress on through the succeeding Era's ending with a final New Years Eve Party taking us into the 21st Century. In addition to the Victorian theme, events based around the 1920's (The Roaring Twenties), 1940's (British Bulldog Spirit), 1950's (Rock Around The Clock), 1960's (Newquay Flower Power Festival), 1970's (Flares and Squares), up to the present day will be included. There will be Processions, Carnivals, Evening concerts, Choirs and Bands, Old Time Music Hall, Markets and Craft Fairs, Children's Sports, Entertainment and Baby Show, Torchlight Procession and a Firework Display and many, many more events. This will be the most exciting, biggest and best event ever that Newquay has staged. For further details please call Mary Cook 01637 878735
Festivals

The Totnes Taborer - Strolling Medieval Musician
6/7/99 TOTNES CASTLE
6/7/99 Tel: 01803 864406
A costumed entertainer performing on pipes and drum throughout the day.

From 11.00. A£1.60 C£0.80
Concessions£1.20 English Heritage
members Free

Castles

Attics and Cellar Tours

7/7/99 STOURHEAD HOUSE GARDEN AND HOUSE

7/7/99 Tel: 01747 841152

An upstairs-downstairs look behind the
scenes at Stourhead House. Tours on
intervals between 12.00-17.30. No additional charge with House ticket. £3.00
for tour only - no booking necessary

Historic Houses

Mirace Play

7/7/99 GLASTONBURY ABBEY

10/7/99 Tel: 01458 832267

Evening performance of "Play of Arthur"
the last days of a king at 19.30

Abbeys

Twelfth Night

8/7/99 WENLOCK PRIORY

8/7/99 Tel: 01952 727466

Presented by Heartbreak Productions, a
sparkling comedy laced with a soupcon
of romance, a touch of poetry, and huge
great dollops of seething lust! A£8.00
C£4.00 Concessions£6.00

Priory

**Lecture: A Layered Vision: Artists and
Landscape**

9/7/99 DORSET COUNTY MUSEUM

9/7/99 Tel: 01305 262735

How does the mind of the artist interpret
ancient life and landforms? A display of
his work on paper to accompany lecture.
John Danvers, Master Director (Art and
Design), University of Plymouth. Time:
19.30

Museums

The Ceremony of the Keys

9/7/99 PORTLAND CASTLE

9/7/99 Tel: 01305 820539

Various participants. A£2.50 C£1.30
Concessions£1.90

Castles

Larmer Tree Music Festival

9/7/99 LARMER TREE MUSIC FESTIVAL 1999

11/7/99 Tel: 01722 415223

This unique folk roots and world music
event takes place at the Larmer Tree
Grounds, near Tollard Royal, on the
Wiltshire/Dorset border. There are 11
acres of Victorian Pleasure Gardens, full
of Eastern artifacts, pagodas, sunken
gardens, an incredible neo-classical
wooden stage, and various exotic birds
flying freely about the place. During the

weekend over 30 bands perform on 4
stages and children are kept entertained
in The Larmer Parler a venue for workshops, storytelling and fun! Free camping is available to all ticketholders.

Festivals

Ways with Words

9/7/99 WAYS WITH WORDS 1999

19/7/99 Tel: 01803 867311

Over 150 writers will be giving talks, lectures and readings and holding workshops and taking part in discussions.
Fiction, non-fiction and poetry are covered, plus special theme days on
Psychology and Science.
Accommodation possible on site in
beautiful medieval buildings. A£4.00

Festivals

Somerton Summer Arts Festival 1999

9/7/99 SOMERTON SUMMER ARTS FESTIVAL 1999

17/9/99 Tel: 01458 274148

A colourful and entertaining Summer
Festival for all the family including exhibitions and talks, markets and fairs,
sport and leisure, music and theatre.

Festivals

Medieval Dance Music

10/7/99 MUCHELNEY ABBEY

11/7/99 Tel: 01458 250664

Daughters of Elvin. Medieval music and
songs from the 11th to 16th centuries,
played on a variety of traditional instruments. From 12.00. A£3.00 C£1.50
Concessions£2.30 English Heritage
Members - Free

Abbeys

Civil War Garrison

10/7/99 PORTLAND CASTLE

11/7/99 Tel: 01305 820539

The life and times during the Civil War -
the castle occupiers fear attack. From
12.00. A£3.50 C£1.80 Concessions£2.60
English Heritage members Free

Castles

Antique & Collectors Fair

10/7/99 ROYAL BATH AND WEST SHOWGROUND

11/7/99 Tel: 01749 822200

The biggest and best in the West. Inside
and outside stands offering over 2 miles
of antiques to choose from

Showgrounds

The Story of Astronomy in Cornwall

10/7/99 ROYAL CORNWALL MUSEUM

11/9/99 Tel: 01872 272205

An exhibition to celebrate the total
eclipse of the sun in Cornwall

Museums

Wiltshire Castles Portrayed
10/7/99 DEVIZES MUSEUM
25/9/99 Tel: 01380 727369
An exhibition of paintings, both historic and contemporary of Wiltshire castles
Museum- Archaeology

Music in the Afternoon
11/7/99 CASTLE DROGO
11/7/99 Tel: 01647 433306
Jazz from the Twenties and Thirties with City Steam Jazz Band. Normal admission prices. 14.00-17.00. Also on 29 Aug.
Historic Houses & Gardens

Whitstone Community Ladies Choir
11/7/99 MONTACUTE HOUSE
11/7/99 Tel: 01935 823289
Delightful ladies with delightful voices, singing in the Long Gallery at 15.00. No extra charge
Historic Houses

Science Museum 'More in Store' Open Day
11/7/99 SCIENCE MUSEUM
11/7/99 Tel: 01793 814466
A chance to delve deep into the storage facilities behind the scenes as the Science Museum Wroughton opens the hangar doors. This is the only opportunity to see the objects in deep storage as all seven hangars are opened up to the public. A real adventure as you never know what you will find!
Museum- Science

A Parcel of Rougues
11/7/99 ST MAWES CASTLE
11/7/99 Tel: 01326 270 526
Drama by the Miracle Theatre. A£3.50 C£1.80 Concessions£2.60
Castles

Morris Dancing
11/7/99 STONEHENGE
11/7/99 Tel: 01980 624715 info line
The Sarum Morris Dancers perform 10.30-12.00. Traditional dances to enjoy. A£4.00 C£2.00 Concessions£3.00 English Heritage members Free
Ancient Monuments

Wilton and district Youth Band
11/7/99 WILTON HOUSE
11/7/99 Tel: 01722 746729
Event starts at 14.15. Please call venue for further information
Historic Houses & Gardens

Moonrock and Meteorites
12/7/99 DORSET COUNTY MUSEUM
19/7/99 Tel: 01305 262735
A display of samples by kind permission

of the Particle Physics and Astronomy Research Council.
Museums

The Totnes Taborer - Strolling Medieval Musician
13/7/99 TOTNES CASTLE
13/7/99 Tel: 01803 864406
A costumed entertainer performing on pipes and drum throughout the day. From 11.00. A£1.60 C£0.80 Concessions£1.20 English Heritage members Free
Castles

Planetarium Activities
13/7/99 DORSET COUNTY MUSEUM
18/7/99 Tel: 01305 262735
In the Victorian gallery
Museums

Musical Evening
14/7/99 DORSET COUNTY MUSEUM
14/7/99 Tel: 01305 262735
Dorset County Museum Music Society AGM, short programme of music and a celebratory party. Time: 19.15
Museums

Musical Theatre
14/7/99 TINTAGEL CASTLE
14/7/99 Tel: 01840 770328
Masquerade. A£2.80 C£1.40 Concessions£2.10
Historical Remains

Lecture: Britain's First Astronaut
16/7/99 DORSET COUNTY MUSEUM
16/7/99 Tel: 01305 262735
Helen Sharman OBE. This lecture is for schools.
Museums

Open Air Jazz
16/7/99 DUNSTER CASTLE
16/7/99 Tel: 01643 821314/823004
Theatre Set-up presentation. Performance starts at 19.30. Advance Tickets A£8.00 C£5.00, Tickets on the Gate: A£10.00 C£7.00
Castles

Hearts on Fire
17/7/99 GLASTONBURY ABBEY
17/7/99 Tel: 01458 832267
Christian 'pop' concert at 19.00 in the Abbey grounds
Abbeys

Jazz In The Park
17/7/99 LANHYDROCK
17/7/99 Tel: 01208 73320
Outdoor Jazz concert featuring Acker Bilk and his Paramount Jazz Band. Tel Bookings: 01208 74084/73320

Historic Houses

Open Air Concert
17/7/99
17/7/99
WILTON HOUSE
Tel: 01722 746729
An open air classical extravaganza featuring the Bournemouth Sinfonietta. For ticket information please call 01202 669925

Historic Houses & Gardens

Iron Age Living History
17/7/99
18/7/99
CHYSAUSTER ANCIENT VILLAGE
Tel: 0831 797934
The Silures. Iron Age warriors and villagers recreate everyday life. From 12.00. A£2.50 C£1.30 Concessions£1.90 English Heritage members Free

Historical Remains

Medieval Living History
17/7/99
18/7/99
CLEEVE ABBEY
Tel: 01984 640377
The Courteneye Household. 15th century military and domestic life, with crafts, men-at-arms and period games. A£3.00 C£1.50 Concessions£2.30

Abbeys

The Portable Planetarium
17/7/99
18/7/99
DORSET COUNTY MUSEUM
Tel: 01305 262735
A preview of the 1999 solar eclipse by Mizar and 4 Astronomy in a 35-place planetarium dome. Please send payment (A£1.00 C£0.50) and state preferred time of day between 10.30-16.00. Wheelchair access. (The total eclipse of the sun will be 11 August).

Museums

Elizabethan Dance & Longbows
17/7/99
18/7/99
MUCHELNEY ABBEY
Tel: 01458 250664
Renaissance Historical Dance. 14th century formal court and exuberant folk dances, with the chance to join in. Plus archery. From 12.00. A£3.00 C£1.50 Concessions£2.30 English Heritage Members - Free

Abbeys

A Warning to Country Folk
17/7/99
18/7/99
OLD SARUM CASTLE
Tel: 01722 335398
Sun Jester. A£2.50 C£1.30 Concessions£1.90

Historical Remains

Medieval Life
17/7/99
18/7/99
OLD WARDOUR CASTLE
Tel: 01747 870487
The Medieval Free Company. 15th century military and domestic life, with crafts,

children's games, archery, squire training and combat. A£3.00 C£1.50 Concessions£2.30

Castles

Elizabethan Dance
17/7/99
18/7/99
PORTLAND CASTLE
Tel: 01305 820539
Performed by Coranto. A£3.00 C£1.50 Concessions£2.30

Castles

National Homes and Living Show
17/7/99
18/7/99
ROYAL BATH AND WEST SHOWGROUND
Tel: 01749 822200
The National Homes and Living Show will be inspirational, aspirational and will provide ideas and information for the home and living environment. Decor, Interior Design, DIY, Furnishings, Kitchens, Bathrooms, Conservatories, Restoration, Household products and hardware, Mortgage advice, New Homes and products and services meet the profile. A show for all the family in a lively and interactive atmosphere designed to capture the imagination

Showgrounds

Tortoise and Turtle Weekend
17/7/99
18/7/99
SECRET WORLD-BADGER AND WILDLIFE RESCUE CENTRE
Tel: 01278 783250
The British Chelonia Group are with us for the weekend along with many different species of Tortoise and Turtles. Experienced members will be happy to discuss how to keep these creatures and to advise on any problems that you may have. Additional information will be available from our Red-eared Terrapin Education centre. An unusual opportunity to see these reptiles and to learn which end to feed!

Wildlife Rescue

Weymouth International Maritime Modelling Festival
17/7/99
18/7/99
THE PAVILION COMPLEX
Tel: 01305 785747
Featuring over 1,000 models up to 20ft in length. 50mph power boat racing, parades of Tall Ships, racing yachts, trawlers and steam boats.

Arts & Entertainment

The History Man
17/7/99
18/7/99
WENLOCK PRIORY
Tel: 01952 727466
Enjoy unusual guided tours with Brian McNerney, presenter of the BBC's popular History Man programmes. But be

warned, his enthusiasm is notoriously contagious... and there is no antidote! Performing without costumes, props or even a safety net, he brings the past to life before your very eyes! A£3.00 C£1.50 Concessions£2.30

Priory

Weymouth International Maritime Modelling

17/7/99
18/7/99

WEYMOUTH INTERNATIONAL MARITIME MODELLING
Tel: 01305 785747
Over 1,000 operational models and displays, battleships with live battles, Tall Ships, yacht racing, steam powered, electric speedboats, tug towing, novelty class displays and trawlers, trade stalls and workshops. 10.00-17.00 daily. Grand Illuminated night sail on 17 July at 21.30

Festivals

A Parcel of Rougues

18/7/99
18/7/99

BERRY POMEROY CASTLE
Tel: 01803 866618
Drama by The Miracle Theatre. A£3.50 C£1.80 Concessions£2.60

Castles

The Complete Works of Shakespeare

18/7/99

LACOCK ABBEY, FOX TALBOT MUSEUM AND VILLAGE
Tel: 01249 730227/730459
Presented by The Reduced Shakespeare Company. Gates open at 18.00 for 19.00 start on the South Lawn. Bring a picnic and a rug or chair. £12.50 in advance, £14.00 on the gate if available. Special Offer! Book for this and The Water Babies and receive a 10% discount.

Historic Houses

Tolpuddle Train Union Festival

18/7/99
18/7/99

TOLPUDDLE MARTYRS MUSEUM
Tel: 01305 848237
Free festival with live music and drama as well as the traditional march through the village, 11.30-16.30

Museum- Local History

South West Yo-Yo Championship

18/7/99
18/7/99

WOODLANDS LEISURE PARK
Tel: 01803 712598
With World Famous Richie of Team Yomega - Novice, advanced and Masters Classes - Excellent prizes.

Country Leisure Parks

Portraiture

19/7/99
21/11/99

ROYAL ALBERT MEMORIAL MUSEUM
Tel: 01392 265858
A selection of portraits through the ages from the Museum's Fine Art Collection

Museum- Local History

The Totnes Taborer - Strolling Medieval Musician

20/7/99
20/7/99

TOTNES CASTLE
Tel: 01803 864406
A costumed entertainer performing on pipes and drum throughout the day. From 11.00. A£1.60 C£0.80 Concessions£1.20 English Heritage members Free

Castles

The Tent of a Thousand Tales

21/7/99
21/7/99

TINTAGEL CASTLE
Tel: 01840 770328
Rough Magic. Legends and fables using masks and puppets. Bring a rug and picnic and enjoy the atmosphere of the legendary birthplace of King Arthur! 19.30-21.00. A£2.80 C£1.40 Concessions£2.10 English Heritage members Free

Historical Remains

Stourhead Fete Champetre

22/7/99
24/7/99

STOURHEAD HOUSE GARDEN AND HOUSE
Tel: 01747 841152
Open air themed extravaganza with fireworks "Stourhead celebrates with style the Belle Epoque 1890-1910. Dress in period costume and enjoy entertainment all around the Garden. Garden opens at 17.30. Thur A£15.00 C£9.00, Fri A£17.00 C£11.00, Sat A£20.00 C£14.00. Special Offer! £1.00 off prices shown if tickets ordered and paid for by 31/3/99

Historic Houses

Great Swan Round Up

23/7/99
24/7/99

ABBOTSBURY SWANNERY
Tel: 01305 871858/871130
Over 800 to 1,000 swans herded together for ringing, weighing, measuring and treatment only held once every other year. Not to be missed!

Waterfowl Parks

National Archaeology Days

24/7/99
24/7/99

THE TIME MACHINE
Tel: 01934 621028
These are organised nationally every year to promote archaeology. Please call the venue for details of events planned

Museum- Local History

Victorian Quack Medicine Seller

24/7/99
25/7/99

DARTMOUTH CASTLE
Tel: 01803 833588
The Ringwoods of History. A£3.00 C£1.50 Concessions£2.30

Castles

Soldiers of George III

24/7/99 25/7/99	**FARLEIGH HUNGERFORD CASTLE** Tel: 01225 754026 The Association of Crown Forces. Living history encampment, drill, musket firing. A£3.00 C£1.50 Concessions£2.30 *Castles*

Hot Air Balloon Night Glow

24/7/99 25/7/99	**LONGLEAT** Tel: 01985 844400 Balloon spectacular, orchestral music, fireworks - an evening to remember, call for further details *Safari Parks*

Shakespeare in the Park - Twelfth Night

24/7/99 25/7/99	**LYDIARD PARK** Tel: 01793 770401 Enjoy one of Shakespeare's finest come-dy's in the surroundings of Lydiard Park. Bring a picnic hamper and rugs *Historic Houses & Gardens*

17th-Century Dance

24/7/99 25/7/99	**OLD WARDOUR CASTLE** Tel: 01747 870487 Coranto perform 17th-century dance. A£3.00 C£1.50 Concessions£2.30 *Castles*

The King's Shilling

24/7/99 25/7/99	**PORTLAND CASTLE** Tel: 01305 820539 British Marines, 1777. A£2.50 C£1.30 Concessions£1.90 *Castles*

Medieval Dance & Longbows

24/7/99 25/7/99	**RESTORMEL CASTLE** Tel: 01208 872687 Renaissance Historical Dance. 14th cen-tury formal court and exuberant folk dances, with the chance to join in. Plus archery. From 12.00. A£3.00 C£1.50 Concessions£2.30 English Heritage members Free *Castles*

Medieval Calligraphy and Spinning

24/7/99 25/7/99	**WENLOCK PRIORY** Tel: 01952 727466 Step back in time to the 15th century and see how a 'clerk of minor orders' went about his business! Authentic cal-ligraphy, illuminating book making skills are demonstrated, plus the use of an unusual spindle wheel. From Noon. A£3.00 C£1.50 Concessions£2.30. EH Members Free *Priory*

Holiday Showtime

24/7/99 4/9/99	**WOODLANDS LEISURE PARK** Tel: 01803 712598 Enjoy Jugglers, Clowns, Punch & Judy, everyday. *Country Leisure Parks*

The Totnes Taborer - Strolling Medieval Musician

27/7/99 27/7/99	**TOTNES CASTLE** Tel: 01803 864406 A costumed entertainer performing on pipes and drum throughout the day. From 11.00. A£1.60 C£0.80 Concessions£1.20 English Heritage members Free *Castles*

Wildlife Face Paining and Mask Making

28/7/99 28/7/99	**CASTLE DROGO** Tel: 01647 433306 With Colin John. Normal admission prices. 11.00-16.00 *Historic Houses & Gardens*

The Tent of a Thousand Tales

28/7/99 28/7/99	**TINTAGEL CASTLE** Tel: 01840 770328 Rough Magic. Legends and fables using masks and puppets. Bring a rug and pic-nic and enjoy the atmosphere of the leg-endary birthplace of King Arthur! 19.30-21.00. A£2.80 C£1.40 Concessions£2.10 English Heritage members Free *Historical Remains*

Possum Fez Week 1999

28/7/99 1/8/99	**POSSUM FEZ WEEK 1999** Tel: 01305 871316 Village Crier competition, concerts, chil-dren's sports, model boat race, barn dance, Scarecrow Scrummidge, folk dancing, street fair, craft show, whist drive, dancing, street stalls, ending with "Songs of Praise" on Sunday in the gar-den of a public house. *Festivals*

Wildlife 1st Aid Course - Junior - Stage 1

29/7/99 29/7/99	**SECRET WORLD-BADGER AND WILDLIFE RESCUE CENTRE** Tel: 01278 783250 A special First Aid day aimed for children aged between 10-14 years. It will be a complete day from 10.00-16.00. The day will include tuition on wildlife care, as well as a chance to see behind the scenes. We recommend that the children bring packed lunches. Stage 1 also to be held on: 14 August. Cost: £5.00. These courses are held at the centre and can

Further more detailed information on the attractions listed can be found in Best Guides *Visitor Attractions* Guide under the classifications shown

only be attended if booked in advance. The cost of each course is inclusive of tea and coffee throughout the day but does not include lunch. This can be booked separately for an extra £5.00 giving any special consideration with regards to diet. Those attending the course will have the chance to see the centre and its facilities during breaks. For information regarding accommodation near the centre, please telephone

Wildlife Rescue

The Water Babies

29/7/99 LACOCK ABBEY, FOX TALBOT MUSEUM AND VILLAGE

30/7/99 Tel: 01249 730227/730459
Presented by Illyria. Gates open at 18.00 for 19.00 start on the South Lawn. Bring a picnic and a rug or chair. A£7.50 C£5.00 Family Ticket (A2+C2)£22.00, £2.00 extra on the gate if available. Special Offer! Book for this and The Complete Works of Shakespeare and receive a 10% discount.

Historic Houses

Weston-Super-Helidays (3 days)

30/7/99 THE HELICOPTER MUSEUM

1/8/99 Tel: 01934 635227
Takes place on the Sea Front at Weston-Super-Mare. The event includes the static display of military and civil helicopters and autogyros, pleasure flights, stalls and other entertainment along a 1.2km (3/4m) frontage. Entrance fee to be confirmed - all proceeds go to The Helicopter Museum Development Fund

Museum- Aviation

Sidmouth International Festival 1999

30/7/99 SIDMOUTH INTERNATIONAL FESTIVAL 1999

6/8/99 Tel: 01296 433669 Box Office
700 events over 8 days. International music and dance spectaculars, concerts, ceilidhs, workshops, processions, craft fair and children's festival.

Festivals

Christian Family Conference

30/7/99 ROYAL BATH AND WEST SHOWGROUND

21/8/99 Tel: 01749 822200
Please call for details as to which days they will be held

Showgrounds

British Touring Car Championship

31/7/99 THRUXTON MOTORING RACING CIRCUIT

31/7/99 Tel: 01264 772696
Qualifying. A£8.00(£7.00) C£Free
Paddock £4.00(£3.00) Grandstand £5.00

- (in advance)

Motor Racing Circuit

Stories & Mask Making

31/7/99 BERRY POMEROY CASTLE

1/8/99 Tel: 01803 866618
Michael & Wendy Dacre. Traditional folk tales, myths and legends, plus mask-making. From 12.00. A£2.20 C£1.10 Concessions£1.70 English Heritage Members Free

Castles

Medieval Monastic Entertainers

31/7/99 CLEEVE ABBEY

1/8/99 Tel: 01984 640377
Heuristics. Try your hand at calligraphy or authentic period games as this popular duo take a lighthearted look at monastic customs, crafts and lifestyles. Learn about food preparation, herbs and spices in cooking and medicine, the mechanics of building, lifting and many other skills. Part of Cistercian 900. A£3.00 C£1.50 Concessions£2.30

Abbeys

Medieval Cooking

31/7/99 MUCHELNEY ABBEY

1/8/99 Tel: 01458 250664
A mini-event. Come and sample the delights of medieval cookery. Historic Haute Cuisine. A£2.50 C£1.30 Concessions£1.90

Abbeys

Medieval Dance Music

31/7/99 OKEHAMPTON CASTLE

1/8/99 Tel: 01837 52844
The Daughters of Elvin perform historical music to your ears! A£3.00 C£1.50 Concessions£2.30

Romantic Ruin

History Fair

31/7/99 OLD SARUM CASTLE

1/8/99 Tel: 01722 335398
Various performers. Normal admission prices apply

Historical Remains

Wroughton Nostalgia Show

31/7/99 SCIENCE MUSEUM

1/8/99 Tel: 01793 814466
Now in its fifth successful year, the Nostalgia show gets bigger and better. Packed with classic vehicles, antique stalls and craft fairs as well as helicopter rides, entertainers and a band, this is a great summers day out with something for everyone

Museum- Science

Pirate Treasure Hunt

31/7/99 1/8/99	St Mawes Castle Tel: 01326 270 526 Oh Arh Jim Lad! Come hunt some trea- sure with me! *Castles*
31/7/99 1/8/99	**French and Indian Wars Re-enactment** The American Museum in Britain Tel: 01225 460503 Living history at its best. Visit campsites of both French and British troops and the Indian encampment *Museums*
1/8/99 2/8/99	**Victorian Festival** Nothe Fort Tel: 01305 787243 Recreation time at the Nothe *Forts*
1/8/99 21/8/99	**Christian Family Conferences** Royal Bath and West Showground Tel: 01749 822200 Please call for details as to which days they will be held *Showgrounds*
2/8/99 30/8/99	**FREE International Fireworks Festivals** The Pavilion Complex Tel: 01305 785747 Held in Weymouth bay on the 2,9,18,23 & 30 Aug. Famous highlight of the Weymouth summer season. Internationally themed & fired from a special floating pontoon. Spectacular views from the esplanade. *Arts & Entertainment*
2/8/99 30/8/99	**Weymouth International Fireworks Display** Weymouth International Firework Displays 1999 Tel: 01305 785747 Internationally famed fireworks fired from a special floating pontoon in Weymouth Bay. Spectacular views from Weymouth Esplanade *Festivals*
3/8/99 3/8/99	**Medieval Fun & Games - Elfic the Jester** Totnes Castle Tel: 01803 864406 Slapstick, tomfoolery, tricks, juggling and storytelling. From 11.00-16.30. A£1.60 C£0.80 Concessions£1.20 English Heritage members Free *Castles*
4/8/99 4/8/99	**Summer Woodland Walk** Castle Drogo Tel: 01647 433306 3 hour easy walk along the banks of the River Teign. Dogs on leads welcome.

	Meet at Fingle Bridge car park. Commences 10.00 *Historic Houses & Gardens*
4/8/99 4/8/99	**Bat Walk** Dunster Castle Tel: 01643 821314/823004 Come along and discover the world of bats. A£3.00 C£1.50. Limited spaces call the Box Office on 01643 821314 for tick- ets and times *Castles*
4/8/99 4/8/99	**The Tent of a Thousand Tales** Tintagel Castle Tel: 01840 770328 Rough Magic. Legends and fables using masks and puppets. Bring a rug and pic- nic and enjoy the atmosphere of the leg- endary birthplace of King Arthur! 19.30- 21.00. A£2.80 C£1.40 Concessions£2.10 English Heritage members Free *Historical Remains*
6/8/99 6/8/99	**La Boheme** Dyrham Park Tel: 0117 937 2501 Opera Project presents La Boheme. Gates open 18.00. Commences 19.30. Tickets £16.00 in advance, £18.00 on the gate. Call the Box Office on 01985 843601/2. Special Weekend offer! £25.00 if you book both La Boheme and La Cosi Fan Tutti. *Historic Houses*
7/8/99 7/8/99	**Classic Raceday** Castle Combe Circuit Tel: 01249 782417 Historic Road Sports, 70's Road Sports, Classic Sports Car, Historic Formula Ford, Classic Racing Cars. Classic Formula 3 and an invitation race, plus the sixth round of HEAT, National Mobile Windscreens Special GT's and Pagid Championships. A£8.00 C&OAPs/Paddock £2.50. Practice from 08.30, racing from 13.30 *Motor Racing Circuit*
7/8/99 7/8/99	**Tamba Day** Crealy Park Tel: 01395 233200 Free entry to twins and triplets *Country Parks*
7/8/99 7/8/99	**Cosi Fan Tutti** Dyrham Park Tel: 0117 937 2501 Opera Project presents Cosi Fan Tutti. Gates open 18.00. Commences 19.30. Tickets £16.00 in advance, £18.00 on the gate. Call the Box Office on 01985

Further more detailed information on the attractions listed can be found
in Best Guides *Visitor Attractions* Guide under the classifications shown

843601/2. Special Weekend offer! £25.00 if you book both La Boheme and La Cosi Fan Tutti.

Historic Houses

Bat Day 7/8/99
SECRET WORLD-BADGER AND WILDLIFE 7/8/99
RESCUE CENTRE
Tel: 01278 783250
See live bats in a flight cage and realise you don't have to be Dracula to like them! Come and meet these enchanting mammals. Bat specialists will be on hand to explain their complex lifestyle and their disappearing habitat! It will also be a fundraising day to help towards much needed bat rehabilitation facilities at Secret World

Wildlife Rescue

Shakespeare at Stourhead 7/8/99
STOURHEAD HOUSE GARDEN AND HOUSE 7/8/99
Tel: 01747 841152
Much Ado About Nothing presented by Theatre Set-up on the Terrace of Stourhead House. Gates open 18.00 for picnics prior to performance at 19.30. A£8.00 C£6.00

Historic Houses

Storytelling - Old Fairweather 7/8/99
BERRY POMEROY CASTLE 8/8/99
Tel: 01803 866618
Enjoyable gossip, folklore and history. From 12.00. A£2.50 C£1.30 Concessions£1.90 English Heritage Members Free

Castles

Medieval Dance and Longbows 7/8/99
FARLEIGH HUNGERFORD CASTLE 8/8/99
Tel: 01225 754026
Renaissance Historical Dance. 17th century formal court and exuberant folk dances, with the chance to join in. Plus archery. From 12.00. A£3.00 C£1.50 Concessions£2.30 English Heritage Members - Free

Castles

A Day with Trusty the Hedgehog 7/8/99
LACOCK ABBEY, FOX TALBOT MUSEUM AND 8/8/99
VILLAGE
Tel: 01249 730227/730459
Children's activities with a helping hand from Trusty. 13.00-16.00. No extra charge

Historic Houses

Medieval Living History 7/8/99
OKEHAMPTON CASTLE 8/8/99
Tel: 01837 52844
15th century military and domestic life, with crafts, men-at-arms and period

games. A£3.00 C£1.50 Concessions£2.30

Romantic Ruin

The Bard and the Blade 7/8/99
OLD SARUM CASTLE 8/8/99
Tel: 01722 335398
Dramatic duels and dialogue from some of Shakespeare's most famous plays. A£3.00 C£1.50 Concessions£2.30

Historical Remains

Medieval Music 7/8/99
OLD WARDOUR CASTLE 8/8/99
Tel: 01747 870487
Enjoy melodies and dance tunes dating back to the 12th century. A£3.00 C£1.50 Concessions£2.30

Castles

Jousting 7/8/99
PENDENNIS CASTLE 8/8/99
Tel: 01326 316594
Discover the secrets of the tourney, as the jousting area resounds to the sounds of the battle, clash of steel and thunder of horses hooves as the mighty knights charge at full tilt. A£5.00 C£2.50 Concessions£3.80

Castles

Have a go at Archery 7/8/99
WILTON HOUSE 8/8/99
Tel: 01722 746729
Local archery club provides an opportunity for visitors to try their hand at archery. Minimum grounds entry and normal opening hours apply

Historic Houses & Gardens

Eclipse Festival 7/8/99
N.E.D.D.I DONKEY SANCTUARY 14/8/99
Tel: 01208 841710
Camping available for "Eclipse Week" with Eclipse Information display, "Teddy Bears Picnic", Dog Show. Barbeque. Early bookings essential. All facilities. See the TOTAL eclipse with the donkeys

Animal Sanctuary

Teddy Bears Picnic 8/8/99
LAUNCESTON CASTLE 8/8/99
Tel: 01566 772365
Various performers. Magicians, face painting, balloons and lots of clowning about. Bring a teddy to get in! A£1.60 C£1.80 Concessions£1.20

Castles

Coombe Martin Carnival Week 1999 9/8/99
COOMBE MARTIN CARNIVAL WEEK 1999 16/8/99
Tel: 01271 882671
Procession on Wednesday evening with various events each day. The main street

is closed around the time of the procession but there are car parks in the village.

Carnivals

Medieval Fun & Games - Elfic the Jester

10/8/99 TOTNES CASTLE
10/8/99 Tel: 01803 864406

Slapstick, tomfoolery, tricks, juggling and storytelling. From 11.00-16.30. A£1.60 C£0.80 Concessions£1.20 English Heritage members Free

Castles

Cornwall Total Eclipse

11/8/99 CORNWALL ECLIPSE
11/8/99 Tel: 01872 274057/08706 081199

For 2.04 mins at 11.10am the Total Eclipse will be on view. It is only the 5th to be seen from England in the past Millennium. The central line of the eclipse is just north of Land's End, and exits over Falmouth Bay.

The Unusual

Total Eclipse at Flambards

11/8/99 FLAMBARDS VILLAGE THEME PARK
11/8/99 Tel: 01326 564093 info line

Total eclipse of the sun as seen from best viewing location at Flambards. Entertainment, showing big screen TV re-run

Theme Parks

Eclipse Event

11/8/99 NOTHE FORT
11/8/99 Tel: 01305 787243

Details to be announced to mark this spectacular event

Forts

Science Museum Eclipse Watch and Star Party

11/8/99 SCIENCE MUSEUM
11/8/99 Tel: 01793 814466

An all day event for all the family. Experts will be on hand to help you make the most of this fantastic experience. Workshops throughout the day and evening will be followed by a stargazing session with an expert astronomer. Special indoor planetaria and workshops make this an all weather day! 10.00-21.00

Museum- Science

Solar Eclipse

11/8/99 THE PAVILION COMPLEX
11/8/99 Tel: 01305 785747

Excellent viewing opportunities along the coast around Weymouth and Portland. You'll see nothing like this

again, as the next total eclipse will be in 2135AD. Weymouth plans to commemorate this 'Galactical Experience' with many activities including 'Parade of Sail,' Solar Eclipse Display and Competitions.

Arts & Entertainment

The Tent of a Thousand Tales

11/8/99 TINTAGEL CASTLE
11/8/99 Tel: 01840 770328

Rough Magic. Legends and fables using masks and puppets. Bring a rug and picnic and enjoy the atmosphere of the legendary birthplace of King Arthur! 19.00-21.00. A£2.80 C£1.40 Concessions£2.10 English Heritage members Free

Historical Remains

Total Eclipse of the Sun

11/8/99 TOTAL ECLIPSE OF THE SUN 1999
11/8/99 Tel: 01872 322000

The total eclipse will last on average a little over 2 minutes. The sudden darkness and drop in temperature has a marked effect on wildlife and the man-made environment such as street lighting etc. Partial Eclipse will begin at 09.57 in Falmouth, followed by Total Eclipse at 11.11, lasting until 11.13 and again followed by a partial eclipse until 12.32

Festivals

Total Eclipse Party of a Lifetime

11/8/99 WOODLANDS LEISURE PARK
11/8/99 Tel: 01803 712598

Continuous entertainment. Stalls, Jazz Band, Bar, Surprises. Fantastic Fireworks Display. Park open from 07.30-22.30.

Country Leisure Parks

Stourhead at DFawn

12/8/99 STOURHEAD HOUSE GARDEN AND HOUSE
12/8/99 Tel: 01747 841152

A Garden walk with the Assistant Head Gardener. Meet at 17.30 at Visitor Reception. Members £4.00 Non-members £8.00

Historic Houses

Glastonbury Abbey Classical Extravaganza 1999

13/8/99 GLASTONBURY ABBEY CLASSICAL
EXTRAVAGANZA 1999
14/8/99 Tel: 01749 834596 box office

The floodlit ruins of Glastonbury's medieval Abbey have provided the perfect backdrop for the last 3 classical extravaganzas. It is a setting so inspirational that the Royal Philharmonic Orchestra can't wait to return.

Further more detailed information on the attractions listed can be found in Best Guides *Visitor Attractions* Guide under the classifications shown

Festivals

Fireworks & Laser Symphony Concert
BOWOOD HOUSE AND GARDENS
4/8/99
4/8/99 Tel: 01249 812102
Fireworks & Laser concerts are an irresistible summer cocktail. The piquant mixture is a blend of some of the best classical music ever written spiced with your mouth-watering picnics in the park and the whole topped by a liberal sprinkling of spectacle. It is delectable, exciting, satisfying and fun. Included in the programme this year are 'Light Cavalry Overtures' 'Skaters' Waltz' and Borodin's breathtaking 'Polovtsian Dances'...all with magnificent fireworks, brilliant lasers and whirling water fountains. Book early. Group bookings, with a discount of up to 20% for all concerts, can be made by reserving now and confirming final numbers at a later date. Ticket Hotline: 01625 56 00 00

Historic Houses & Gardens

Outdoor Proms Concert
4/8/99 LONGLEAT
4/8/99 Tel: 01985 844400
Sit back on this balmy August afternoon and listen to the proms. Bring a chair or a rug and a picnic.

Safari Parks

Medieval Combat & Entertainment
4/8/99 TOTNES CASTLE
4/8/99 Tel: 01803 864406
Excalibur14th century life, knights in armour, music, dancing and tournament. From 14.30. A£2.50 C£1.20 Concessions£1.80 English Heritage members Free

Castles

The Lion, the Witch and the Wardrobe
4/8/99 FARLEIGH HUNGERFORD CASTLE
5/8/99 Tel: 01225 754026
Narnia awaits! A wonderful children's classic performed by Labyrinth Productions. A£3.50 C£1.80 Concessions£2.60

Castles

Montacycle Weekend
4/8/99 MONTACUTE HOUSE
5/8/99 Tel: 01935 823289
Bring your bicycles along. 11.00-17.30

Historic Houses

Children's Weekend
4/8/99 ST MAWES CASTLE
5/8/99 Tel: 01326 270 526
Entertainment for children and adults too! Various performers. Please call for further information

Castles

'Our National Shrine' - E.M. Forster in Wiltshire
14/8/99 SALISBURY AND SOUTH WILTSHIRE MUSEUM
25/9/99 Tel: 01722 332151
E.M. Forster was inspired by the Wiltshire countryside. This exhibition explores Forster's Wiltshire and the friends and relatives he knew there.

Museums

Paint the Garden Day
15/8/99 CASTLE DROGO
15/8/99 Tel: 01647 433306
Bring your easel and paints and enter the competition. Professional help available if needed. Normal admission prices. First Prize £50.00 worth of National Trust Books. 11.00

Historic Houses & Gardens

VJ Service of Commemoration
15/8/99 NOTHE FORT
15/8/99 Tel: 01305 787243
Commemoration events and World War II entertainment beginning at 19.30

Forts

Teddy Bears Picnic
15/8/99 PENDENNIS CASTLE
15/8/99 Tel: 01326 316594
Various performers. Magicians, face painting, balloons and lots of clowning about. Bring a teddy to get in! A£3.80 C£1.90 Concessions£2.90

Castles

Fowey Royal Regatta and Carnival
15/8/99 FOWEY ROYAL REGATTA AND CARNIVAL 1999
21/8/99 Tel: 01726 832133
Gig racing, male voice choir, children's entertainment, torchlight procession on river, great fun for all. Voluntary donation appreciated. C£Free

Festivals

The Matchstick Fleet
15/8/99 NOTHE FORT
22/8/99 Tel: 01305 787243
Exhibition of astonishing fleet of 300 scale warships made only from matchsticks

Forts

Medieval Fun & Games - Elfic the Jester
17/8/99 TOTNES CASTLE
17/8/99 Tel: 01803 864406
Slapstick, tomfoolery, tricks, juggling and storytelling. From 11.00-16.30.

A£1.60 C£0.80 Concessions£1.20 English Heritage members Free

Castles

Bat Walk

18/8/99 DUNSTER CASTLE

18/8/99 Tel: 01643 821314/823004
Come along and discover the world of bats. A£3.00 C£1.50. Limited spaces call the Box Office on 01643 821314 for tickets and times

Castles

Much Ado About Nothing

18/8/99 PENDENNIS CASTLE

18/8/99 Tel: 01326 316594
Shakespeare in the park. Theatre set-up perform in the afternoon

Castles

Attics and Cellar Tours

18/8/99 STOURHEAD HOUSE GARDEN AND HOUSE

18/8/99 Tel: 01747 841152
An upstairs-downstairs look behind the scenes at Stourhead House. Tours on intervals between 12.00—17.30. No additional charge with House ticket. £3.00 for tour only - no booking necessary

Historic Houses

Weymouth Carnival

18/8/99 THE PAVILION COMPLEX

18/8/99 Tel: 01305 785747
The Red Arrows, over 120 decorated float parade, aerobatic displays, beach events, parachute drops etc.

Arts & Entertainment

The Tent of a Thousand Tales

18/8/99 TINTAGEL CASTLE

18/8/99 Tel: 01840 770328
Rough Magic. Legends and fables using masks and puppets. Bring a rug and picnic and enjoy the atmosphere of the legendary birthplace of King Arthur! 19.30-21.00. A£2.80 C£1.40 Concessions£2.10 English Heritage members Free

Historical Remains

Cosi Fan Tutti

21/8/99 LACOCK ABBEY, FOX TALBOT MUSEUM AND VILLAGE

21/8/99 Tel: 01249 730227/730459
Presented by Opera Project. Gates open at 18.00 for 19.00. Bring a picnic and a rug or chair. £16.00 in advance, £18.00 on the gate if available.

Historic Houses

Mapperton Courtyard Fair

21/8/99 MAPPERTON GARDENS

21/8/99 Tel: 01308 862645
An annual and popular event with stalls,

crafts, children's competitions and teas, 14.00-17.00

Gardens

Storytelling - Old Fairweather

21/8/99 BERRY POMEROY CASTLE

22/8/99 Tel: 01803 866618
Enjoyable gossip, folklore and history. From 12.00. A£2.50 C£1.30 Concessions£1.90 English Heritage Members Free

Castles

18th-Century Dance

21/8/99 OLD WARDOUR CASTLE

22/8/99 Tel: 01747 870487
Performed by Coranto. A£3.00 C£1.50 Concessions£2.30

Castles

Tudor Living History

21/8/99 PORTLAND CASTLE

22/8/99 Tel: 01305 820539
Witness the life and times of a Tudor Garrison under the threat of invasion! Visitors are advised to check with the venue closer to the event. From 12.00. A£3.00 C£1.50 Concessions£2.30 English Heritage members Free

Castles

Elizabethan Dance & Longbows

21/8/99 ST MAWES CASTLE

22/8/99 Tel: 01326 270 526
Renaissance Historical Dance. 16th century formal court and exuberant folk dances, with the chance to join in if wished. Plus archery. From 12.00. A£3.00 C£1.50 Concessions£2.30 English Heritage Members Free

Castles

Children's Fun Weekend

21/8/99 WILTON HOUSE

22/8/99 Tel: 01722 746729
Bouncy castle, live entertainment, facepainting and competitions. Normal admission charges and opening hours apply

Historic Houses & Gardens

ECW Living History

21/8/99 DARTMOUTH CASTLE

25/8/99 Tel: 01803 833588
ECWS - Bevil Grenviles, 17th Century. A£3.50 C£1.80 Concessions£2.60

Castles

St Mary's Arts Festival

21/8/99 ST MARY'S ARTS FESTIVAL 1999

8/9/99 Tel: 01736 367659
Art Exhibition, Photograph Exhibition, Concerts and Organ Recitals

Festival

Family Meet-the-Stars Day
22/8/99 LONGLEAT
22/8/99 Tel: 01985 844400
Come and be star-struck!
Safari Parks

The Totnes Taborer - Strolling Medieval Musician
24/8/99 TOTNES CASTLE
24/8/99 Tel: 01803 864406
A costumed entertainer performing on pipes and drum throughout the day. From 11.00. A£1.60 C£0.80 Concessions£1.20 English Heritage members Free
Castles

Children's Treasure Hunt
27/8/99 CASTLE DROGO
27/8/99 Tel: 01647 433306
Solve the clues, win a prize. Normal admission prices. 11.00-16.00
Historic Houses & Gardens

Under the Table
27/8/99 STOURHEAD HOUSE GARDEN AND HOUSE
27/8/99 Tel: 01747 841152
An opportunity to discover more about Stourhead's fine furniture collection - a talk by Sonja Rogers, Stourhead Collections Manager. 15.00. £7.00 to include afternoon tea.
Historic Houses

Swan Fair
28/8/99 ABBOTSBURY SWANNERY
30/8/99 Tel: 01305 871858/871130
Crafts, rural pursuits, ferrett racing, rare breeds, shire horse and cart rides, sheep shearing, and of course who could forget over 600 swans?!
Waterfowl Parks

August Show
28/8/99 ATHELHAMPTON HOUSE AND GARDENS
30/8/99 Tel: 01305 848363
Demonstration, Exhibition and Sale of Contemporary and Traditional Arts & Crafts from Dorset craft workers in the marquee on the north west lawn. Other details on displays to be arranged. Time: 10.00-17.30, A£3.50 (House £1.45 extra), C£0.50 (House £1.00), Family Ticket £11.00 (fully inclusive), OAPs£3.50 (House £1.00 extra)
Historic Houses

Bude Jazz Festival
28/8/99 BUDE JAZZ FESTIVAL 1999
4/9/99 Tel: 01288 356360
200 jazz events in 8 days - all day, every day. 100 bands with leading jazz musicians from all over Britain. 20 different venues hosting jazz events. Four New Orleans style street parades, jazz services. In addition there are 5 late evening 'Festival Extra' events. £11.50 per day, full week £52.50
Festivals

Art from Hildesheim
28/8/99 THE TIME MACHINE
10/10/99 Tel: 01934 621028
An exhibition of art from Hildesheim
Museum- Local History

Medieval Music
29/8/99 BERRY POMEROY CASTLE
30/8/99 Tel: 01803 866618
Enjoy melodies and dance tunes dating back to the 12th century. A£3.00 C£1.50 Concessions£2.30
Castles

Steam Up
29/8/99 COLD HARBOUR MILL WORKING WOOL MUSEUM
30/8/99 Tel: 01884 840960
Two giant mill engines 'in steam' - a 1910 Pollitt & Wizzell engine, 1867 Beam Engine and 1888 Lancashire Boilers in action. Time: 10.30-17.00
Museum- Industrial

Adventure Sports Special
29/8/99 CREALY PARK
30/8/99 Tel: 01395 233200
Free canoeing; free abseiling and free archery
Country Parks

Medieval Life
29/8/99 FARLEIGH HUNGERFORD CASTLE
30/8/99 Tel: 01225 754026
The Medieval Free Company. 15th century military and domestic life, with crafts, children's games, archery, squire training and combat. From 12.00. A£3.00 C£1.50 Concessions£2.30 English Heritage Members - Free
Castles

Stories & Mask Making
29/8/99 MUCHELNEY ABBEY
30/8/99 Tel: 01458 250664
Michael & Wendy Dacre. Traditional folk tales, myths and legends, plus mask making. A£2.00 C£1.50 Concessions£1.75
Abbeys

Viking Battle
29/8/99 OLD SARUM CASTLE
30/8/99 Tel: 01722 335398
The Viking Troops re-enact a Saxon/Viking battle before your very eyes! A£4.00 C£2.00 Concessions£3.00

Historical Remains

Firewpower!

29/8/99 PENDENNIS CASTLE
30/8/99 Tel: 01326 316594
The Courteneye Household, Tudor life.
A£3.80 C£1.90 Concessions£2.90

Castles

Medieval Dance Music

29/8/99 RESTORMEL CASTLE
30/8/99 Tel: 01208 872687
Daughters of Elivn. Lively historical
music. From 12.00. A£2.50 C£1.30
Concessions£1.90 English Heritage
members Free

Castles

Restoration & Engineering Weekend

29/8/99 THE HELICOPTER MUSEUM
30/8/99 Tel: 01934 635227
Visitors are given the opportunity to tour
our restoration workshops, have the
mechanics of the helicopters and autogyros explained, discuss the work being
undertaken by our Volunteer Staff and
understand the problems of restoring
old helicopters, normal admission prices
apply

Museum- Aviation

Storytelling

29/8/99 TINTAGEL CASTLE
30/8/99 Tel: 01840 770328
Rough Magic. Ancient tales to enjoy.
From 12.00. A£2.80 C£1.40
Concessions£2.10 English Heritage
members Free

Historical Remains

Medieval Family Entertainers

29/8/99 WENLOCK PRIORY
30/8/99 Tel: 01952 727466
Try your hand at calligraphy or authentic
period games as this popular duo take a
light-hearted look at monastic customs,
crafts and lifestyles. Learn about food
preparation, herbs and spice in cooking
and medicine, the mechanics of building
and lifting and many other skills. A£3.00
C£1.50 Concessions£2.30

Priory

LUX Traffic Controls Raceday

30/8/99 CASTLE COMBE CIRCUIT
30/8/99 Tel: 01249 782417
MGF, Group N, Classic FF2000, Flemings,
MGBV8, Classic Formula Ford plus round
7 of the National Mobile Windscreens
Special GT, Pagid and HEAT
Championships. A£10.00
C&OAPs/Paddock £2.50. Practice from
08.30, racing from 13.30

Motor Racing Circuit

Children's Woodland Trail and Quiz

31/8/99 LACOCK ABBEY, FOX TALBOT MUSEUM AND
VILLAGE
31/8/99 Tel: 01249 730227/730459
Great fun for children, 11.00-13.00, no
extra charge, call 01249 730227 for
booking

Historic Houses

British Touring Car Championship

31/8/99 THRUXTON MOTORING RACING CIRCUIT
31/8/99 Tel: 01264 772696
Auto Trader British Touring Cars, Formula
Renault Sport, Formula Vauxhall Junior,
Slick 50 Formula Ford, Renault Sport
Spider, Vauxhall Vectra SRi V6, Ford
Credit Fiesta. A£19.00(£15.00) C£Free
Paddock £5.00(£4.00) Grandstand £9.00
- (in advance)

Motor Racing Circuit

**Medieval Fun & Games - Elfic the
Jester**

31/8/99 TOTNES CASTLE
31/8/99 Tel: 01803 864406
Slapstick, tomfoolery, tricks, juggling
and storytelling. From 11.00-16.30.
A£1.60 C£0.80 Concessions£1.20 English
Heritage members Free

Castles

Edmund Dewaal at Dartington

1/9/99 HIGH CROSS HOUSE
29/10/99 Tel: 01803 864114
Eminent Potter Dewaal shows his work
with his favourites from the important
collection of the Dartington Hall Trust

Historic Houses

Dawlish Folk Festival 1999

3/9/99 DAWLISH FOLK FESTIVAL 1999
5/9/99 Tel: 01626 778071
Concerts with Ian Carr, Karen Tweed,
Jimmy Crowley, Old Rope String Band.
Dances with the Committee Band, Tango
Band, and Racing Demon. Concerts in
pubs, singalong sessions, workshops
etc. Dawlish Obby Oss Procession and
lots more. Prices: A£18.00 C£9.00
Concessions£15.00. Tickets available
from 01626 778071

Festivals

The National Amateur Garden Show

3/9/99 ROYAL BATH AND WEST SHOWGROUND
5/9/99 Tel: 01749 822200
An Annual Event for the seasoned gardener or newcomer. The show ill appeal
to both flower and vegetable gardeners.
Featuring 100's of tradestands, festive
gardens and practical hands-on opportu-

nities for all, including the young. A special day out for all the family. The event is organised in conjunction with Amateur Gardening Magazine, Mon-Fri 09.00-17.00

Showgrounds

UFO Laser & Firework Show
4/9/99 LONGLEAT
4/9/99 Tel: 01985 844400
A spectacular sight for all.

Safari Parks

The Blues Band
4/9/99 NOTHE FORT
4/9/99 Tel: 01305 787243
Music in the courtyard. Please call for further information

Forts

Music from the age of Henry VIII
4/9/99 DARTMOUTH CASTLE
5/9/99 Tel: 01803 833588
Enjoy melodies and dance tunes dating back to the the times of Henry VIII. A£3.00 C£1.50 Concessions£2.30

Castles

The History Man
4/9/99 OLD SARUM CASTLE
5/9/99 Tel: 01722 335398
Enjoy unusual guided tours with Brian McNerney, presenter of the BBC's popular History Man programmes. But be warned, his enthusiasm is notoriously contagious... and there is no antidote! Performing without costumes, props or even a safety net, he brings the past to life before your very eyes! A£3.00 C£1.50 Concessions£2.30

Historical Remains

St. Ives September Festival 1999
6/9/99 ST. IVES SEPTEMBER FESTIVAL 1999
18/9/99 Tel: 01736 796888
Music, poetry, exhibitions, folk, jazz, world music. Outdoor pursuits such as walking, beaches, cliffs swimming.

Festivals

The Totnes Taborer - Strolling Medieval Musician
7/9/99 TOTNES CASTLE
7/9/99 Tel: 01803 864406
A costumed entertainer performing on pipes and drum throughout the day. From 11.00. A£1.60 C£0.80 Concessions£1.20 English Heritage members Free

Castles

A Master of Mexican Photography

10/9/99 **FOX TALBOT MUSEUM OF PHOTOGRAPHY**
31/10/99 Tel: 01249 730459/730141
Details to be announced; please call the Museum nearer the date, thank you

Museum- Photographic

Eurocar Racing Extravaganza
11/9/99 CASTLE COMBE CIRCUIT
12/9/99 Tel: 01249 782417
The Eurocar package returns to Castle Coombe once again. Saturday: TVR, Ferrari, AMOC Intermarque, Anglo American Challenge, Formula Renault, HEAT FF1600. Admission A£5.00 C&OAPs/Paddock £Free. Practice from 08.30, racing from 14.00. Sunday: Eurocars, National Mobile Windscreens, Special GT, Pagid Saloons and final round of the HEAT FF1600 Championship. . Admission A£10.00 C&OAPs/Paddock £2.50. Practice from 09.00, racing from 12.00

Motor Racing Circuit

Medieval Music
11/9/99 FARLEIGH HUNGERFORD CASTLE
12/9/99 Tel: 01225 754026
Lammas. Medieval music and songs from the 11th to 16th centuries, played on a variety of traditional instruments. From 12.00. A£3.00 C£1.50 Concessions£2.30 English Heritage Members - Free

Castles

Legends of King Arthur
11/9/99 OKEHAMPTON CASTLE
12/9/99 Tel: 01837 52844
Labyrinth Productions. Magical stories about King Arthur, with Guinevere, Lancelot, Merlin, the Black Knight and the evil Morgan Le Fay. A£3.50 C£1.80 Concessions£2.60

Romantic Ruin

Edwardian
11/9/99 OLD SARUM CASTLE
12/9/99 Tel: 01722 335398
Hogarth's Heroes. A£3.00 C£1.50 Concessions£2.30

Historical Remains

Countryside Cavalcade
11/9/99 ROYAL BATH AND WEST SHOWGROUND
12/9/99 Tel: 01749 822200
The all-family Heavy Horse Show depicting a full range of countryside activities past and present. Rural pursuits and pastimes, traditions and entertainments for everyone from 5-95 years

Showgrounds

Sold in Devizes

| 11/9/99 | **DEVIZES MUSEUM** |
| 31/12/99 | Tel: 01380 727369 |

An exhibition showing goods from and photos of Devizes shops and trades of yesteryear in association with the Devizes Local History Group

Museum- Archaeology

Off The Beaten Track

| 12/9/99 | **PRIOR PARK LANDSCAPE GARDENS** |
| 12/9/99 | Tel: 01225 833422 |

Walk led by Jim Parry, Volunteer Coordinator for Prior Park. Walk starts at 14.00, lasting 2 hours. Admission £2.50

Gardens

Science Museum Conservation Open Day

| 12/9/99 | **SCIENCE MUSEUM** |
| 12/9/99 | Tel: 01793 814466 |

See conservation in action in this fascinating look at the work of the Science Museum Wroughton. As a centre of excellence in the conservation of large objects in the national collections, you can talk to our experts, see how we prepare objects for display and bring in your own scientific curiosities for identification, advice or to see if you can fox the experts. 10.00-17.00

Museum- Science

Powerbike International

| 12/9/99 | **THRUXTON MOTORING RACING CIRCUIT** |
| 12/9/99 | Tel: 01264 772696 |

British Powerbikes, British Sports Production, Aprilia RS250, Aprilia RS125, Honda Hornets, Honda Hornets Stars of Tomorrow. A£13.00(£11.00) C£Free Paddock £4.00(£3.00) Grandstand £5.00 - (in advance)

Motor Racing Circuit

Wilton and District Youth Band

| 12/9/99 | **WILTON HOUSE** |
| 12/9/99 | Tel: 01722 746729 |

Event starts at 14.15. Please call venue for further information

Historic Houses & Gardens

Pirates Day

| 12/9/99 | **WOODLANDS LEISURE PARK** |
| 12/9/99 | Tel: 01803 712598 |

Free ice cream to Pirates. Workshops, Competitions, Prizes.

Country Leisure Parks

Around the World in Eighty Minutes

| 14/9/99 | **STOURHEAD HOUSE GARDEN AND HOUSE** |
| 14/9/99 | Tel: 01747 841152 |

A talk by the Head Gardener on the tree collection in Stourhead Garden. 11.00 at The Spread Eagle Inn. £10.00 to include lunch

Historic Houses

Bath & West Motor Caravan Show

| 17/9/99 | **ROYAL BATH AND WEST SHOWGROUND** |
| 19/9/99 | Tel: 01749 822200 |

One of the largest shows of its kind anywhere in the World, held at the Showground annually, attracting up to 25,000 people. The biggest selection of new and used motor caravans in one place plus hundreds of caravan/camping accessories

Showgrounds

English Civil War Living History

| 18/9/99 | **PORTLAND CASTLE** |
| 19/9/99 | Tel: 01305 820539 |

Living history during the Civil War re-enacted by The Wardour Garrison. A£3.00 C£1.50 Concessions£2.30

Castles

Care for the Wild World-Wide Weekend

| 18/9/99 | **SECRET WORLD-BADGER AND WILDLIFE RESCUE CENTRE** |
| 19/9/99 | Tel: 01278 783250 |

Care For The Wild International will be with us for the whole week-end with talks being given every day at 15.00 about many projects protecting elephants, tigers, rhinos and even orang-utans. Bernadette McArdle, who did the wonderful displays in the CFTW's Discovery Den at Secret World, will be here painting, together with a fantastic exhibition of completed works. A truly 'wild' week-end

Wildlife Rescue

Trebah Plant Sale Extravaganza

| 18/9/99 | **TREBAH GARDEN** |
| 19/9/99 | Tel: 01326 250448 |

A real treat for bargain hunters, unusual shrubs from our nursery. Free entry to garden

Gardens

From Script to Print to Hypertext

| 18/9/99 | **ROYAL ALBERT MEMORIAL MUSEUM** |
| 27/11/99 | Tel: 01392 265858 |

Two millennia of Devon's written heritage

Museum- Local History

Riverside Walk

| 19/9/99 | **CASTLE DROGO** |
| 19/9/99 | Tel: 01647 433306 |

A 2 hour walk along the banks of the River Teign. Meet Fingle Bridge car park. Dogs on leads welcome. 10.00

Historic Houses & Gardens

Falling Leaves Classic Tour

Further more detailed information on the attractions listed can be found in Best Guides *Visitor Attractions* Guide under the classifications shown

19/9/99 19/9/99	**HAYNES MOTOR MUSEUM** Tel: 01963 440804 One day tour through beautiful country-side and interesting venues, call for further details *Museum- Motor*

Antique & Collectors Fair

25/9/99 ROYAL BATH AND WEST SHOWGROUND
26/9/99 Tel: 01749 822200
The biggest and best in the West. Inside and outside stands offering over 2 miles of antiques to choose from
Showgrounds

Festival of Transport

25/9/99 SCIENCE MUSEUM
26/9/99 Tel: 01793 814466
An early autumn feast for transport lovers featuring buses, lorries, bikes, display driving, classic cars and vintage vehicles. Time: 10.00-17.00
Museum- Science

Past Pleasures

25/9/99 STONEHENGE
26/9/99 Tel: 01980 624715 info line
Famous 17th century antiquarian John Aubrey explains his theories to a lady companion. Meet the gossiping pair and hear why he thought Stonehenge was built by the Druids. From 12.00. A£4.00 C£2.00 Concessions£3.00 English Heritage members Free
Ancient Monuments

Early Bird

26/9/99 CREALY PARK
26/9/99 Tel: 01395 233200
Grandparents visit free when accompanied by grandchildren
Country Parks

Dinosaur Day

26/9/99 WOODLANDS LEISURE PARK
26/9/99 Tel: 01803 712598
Help make a giant Dinosaur. Workshops, competitions, prizes.
Country Leisure Parks

Formula Ford Carnival

2/10/99 CASTLE COMBE CIRCUIT
2/10/99 Tel: 01249 782417
Lots of Formula Ford action plus Classic Touring Cars, Radicals plus the final rounds of the National Mobile Windscreens Special GT and Pagid Saloons championships. Admission A£8.00 C&OAPs/Paddock £2.50. Practice from 08.30, racing from 13.30
Motor Racing Circuit

Medieval Monastic Entertainers

2/10/99 MUCHELNEY ABBEY
3/10/99 Tel: 01458 250664
Heuristics. Try your hand at calligraphy or authentic period games as this popular duo take a lighthearted look at monastic customs, crafts and lifestyles. Learn about food preparation, herbs and spices in cooking and medicine, the mechanics of building, lifting and many other skills. Part of Cistercian 900. A£3.00 C£1.50 Concessions£2.30 English Heritage Members - Free
Abbeys

Music - Hautbois

2/10/99 PORTLAND CASTLE
3/10/99 Tel: 01305 820539
Music of the Roundheads and Cavaliers. A£3.00 C£1.50 Concessions£2.30
Castles

Eeles Pottery: 50 Years a Potter

2/10/99 ROYAL CORNWALL MUSEUM
13/11/99 Tel: 01872 272205
A specially selected selling exhibiton
Museums

The Society of Wood Engravers

2/10/99 DEVIZES MUSEUM
27/11/99 Tel: 01380 727369
An exhibition of works by members of The Society of Wood Engravers
Museum- Archaeology

Conker Day

3/10/99 BARRINGTON COURT
3/10/99 Tel: 01460 241938
Soak them in vinegar, tie them on string and come and relive your childhood. 11.00-15.00. C£Free
Gardens

It's a Knockout Conker Contest

3/10/99 CREALY PARK
3/10/99 Tel: 01395 233200
With conkers provided and Rangers to help
Country Parks

Festival of Birds

3/10/99 ROYAL BATH AND WEST SHOWGROUND
3/10/99 Tel: 01749 822200
Please call for details
Showgrounds

South West Dairy Show

6/10/99 ROYAL BATH AND WEST SHOWGROUND
6/10/99 Tel: 01749 822200
The UK's largest Dairy event for farmers, with over 300 tradestands, 350 cattle and £16,000 prize money on offer. Bringing new ideas and innovations to the Dairy industry with the latest equipment and advice, plus the supreme

Cattle Championships and the results of the South West Dairy Farmer of the Year Awards

Showgrounds

Vintage Motorcycle club Autojumble

9/10/99 ROYAL BATH AND WEST SHOWGROUND
9/10/99 Tel: 01749 822200

Over 300 stalls catering for veteran, vintage and classic motorcycles. run in conjunction with Palmer Snell classic motorcycle auction

Showgrounds

Palmer Snell Vintage Motorcycle Auction

9/10/99 ROYAL BATH AND WEST SHOWGROUND
9/10/99 Tel: 01749 822200

A twice yearly event held in the Spring and Autumn at the Showground since 1982, attracting buyers and sellers from all over the Country. Over 100 motorcycles of all ages, shapes and sizes are offered for sale, with an Autojumble organised by the Somerset Section of the Vintage Motorcycle Club

Showgrounds

Family Activity Morning

9/10/99 STOURHEAD HOUSE GARDEN AND HOUSE
9/10/99 Tel: 01747 841152

Kite Flying on Whitesheet Down. This is a family event, no unaccompanied children please. Meet at Whitesheet Hill car park at 10.30. No charge.

Historic Houses

Maskmaking & Storytelling

9/10/99 PENDENNIS CASTLE
10/10/99 Tel: 01326 316594

Michael & Wendy Dacre. Traditional folk tales, myths and legends, plus mask making. From 12.00. A£3.80 C£1.90 Concessions£2.90

Castles

Food and Drink Weekend

9/10/99 WILTON HOUSE
10/10/99 Tel: 01722 746729

Come along and sample the variety of food and drink produced locally in Wessex

Historic Houses & Gardens

Bristol Sound '99

9/10/99 BRISTOL SOUND '99
16/10/99 Tel:

A music festival taking place in a network of venues in Bristol. To incorporate all types of music, a music industry base and a free seminar programme.

Festivals

Toy & Train Collectors Fair

10/10/99 ROYAL BATH AND WEST SHOWGROUND
10/10/99 Tel: 01749 822200

300+ stalls, selling dolls & teddies, dinky, corgy, Meccano, model railways, lead figures, tin toys, science fiction toys and lots more. Refreshments available

Showgrounds

Weymouth Beach Motocross Championships

10/10/99 THE PAVILION COMPLEX
10/10/99 Tel: 01305 785747

Over 300 top riders compete on a specially designed assault course. Spectacular free viewing from Weymouth Esplanade.

Arts & Entertainment

Kareoke Fun

10/10/99 WOODLANDS LEISURE PARK
10/10/99 Tel: 01803 712598

Great prizes for boys and girls.

Country Leisure Parks

Lowender Peran

13/10/99 LOWENDER PERAN 1999
17/10/99 Tel: 01872 553413

Venue: Ponshere Hotel, Perranporth. Ceilidhs, Celtic dance spectacular, concerts, dance displays, pipers, storytelling, poetry reading, singers session, dance workshops, children's sessions. Also Celtic craft market, costumed pageant through streets, guided historical walk. Prices: Season Ticket A£24.00 Accompanied C(under 13)£Free. Tickets available from Gerald Morris 01872 553413

Festivals

Great Western Octoberfest

14/10/99 BREWERS QUAY AND THE TIMEWALK JOURNEY
17/10/99 Tel: 01305 777622 24hr 766880

Four days of great entertainment, with the opportunity to sample over 100 Real Ales! Sponsored by the South West region of The Society of Independent Brewers

Family Attraction

Apple Weekend

16/10/99 MONTACUTE HOUSE
17/10/99 Tel: 01935 823289

For further details including times and prices please call venue direct

Historic Houses

British Formula Three Championship Final

17/10/99 THRUXTON MOTORING RACING CIRCUIT
17/10/99 Tel: 01264 772696

British Formula Three, Formula Palmer

Audi (double header), Bridgestone Ginetta, Flemings Thoroughbred Sports, Porsche Cup. A£12.00(£10.00) C£Free Paddock £4.00(£3.00) Grandstand £5.00 - (in advance)

Motor Racing Circuit

Handicrafts Weekend

18/10/99 WILTON HOUSE
19/10/99 Tel: 01722 746729
Demonstrations and exhibitions in the Cloisters/Visitors Centre. Normal inclusive House admission charges and times apply

Historic Houses & Gardens

Lifeboat

20/10/99 BREWERS QUAY AND THE TIMEWALK JOURNEY
31/10/99 Tel: 01305 777622 24hr 766880
Commemorating the 175th Anniversary of the Royal National Lifeboat Institute and the 130th Anniversary of the Weymouth Lifeboat Station, this unique exhibition pays tribute to the brave volunteers who have risked their lives to save others, both in peace and war

Family Attraction

History in the Planting - Great Trees at Stourhead

21/10/99 STOURHEAD HOUSE GARDEN AND HOUSE
21/10/99 Tel: 01747 841152
A Garden walk with the Head Gardener. Meet 10.30 at Visitor Reception. Members £4.00 Non-Members £8.00

Historic Houses

Ghost, Ghouls and Witches Activity Day

23/10/99 DUNSTER CASTLE
23/10/99 Tel: 01643 821314/823004
Plenty of magical, mystical and horrible things to do for the children, 11.00-15.30. No extra charge.

Castles

Spooks!

23/10/99 STOURHEAD HOUSE GARDEN AND HOUSE
23/10/99 Tel: 01747 841152
Children's activity afternoon, followed by a spooky tea! 14.00-17.30. £6.00

Historic Houses

Family Entertainers - Labyrinth Productions

23/10/99 FARLEIGH HUNGERFORD CASTLE
24/10/99 Tel: 01225 754026
Games, have-a-go archery, costumes for children to try on and talks on weaponry. A£3.00 C£1.50 Concessions£2.30

Castles

Tudor Warfare

23/10/99 PORTLAND CASTLE
24/10/99 Tel: 01305 820539
Group: History Matters. A£3.00 C£1.50 Concessions£2.30

Castles

Hallowe'en Spooktacular

23/10/99 BREWERS QUAY AND THE TIMEWALK JOURNEY
31/10/99 Tel: 01305 777622 24hr 766880
Week-long programme of entertainment for all ghosties, ghoulies and long-legged beasties of all ages

Family Attraction

Halloween Horror Trail

23/10/99 TREBAH GARDEN
31/10/99 Tel: 01326 250448
An exciting new trail to entertain and amuse children under 16, with certificate and prize

Gardens

Disco

24/10/99 WOODLANDS LEISURE PARK
24/10/99 Tel: 01803 712598
Best Disco Gear competition - Great prizes. 16.00.

Country Leisure Parks

Halloween Magic Lantern Days

25/10/99 CREALY PARK
31/10/99 Tel: 01395 233200
Held throughout the half term. Make your own Halloween Magic Lantern with one of our pumpkins and take it home afterwards! Lighting-up ceremony every afternoon by the Crealy Witch. Pumpkins just £1.50

Country Parks

Digging up the Past

25/10/99 THE TIME MACHINE
5/12/99 Tel: 01934 621028
With its many interactive things for you to do, this exhibition takes a fun look at what archaeologists dig up from the past

Museum- Local History

Children's Autumn Woodland Trail

26/10/99 LACOCK ABBEY, FOX TALBOT MUSEUM AND VILLAGE
26/10/99 Tel: 01249 730227/730459
11.00 start, lasting 2 hours. No extra charge

Historic Houses

Family G.g.g.host Tour

28/10/99 DUNSTER CASTLE
29/10/99 Tel: 01643 821314/823004
Want to be SPOOKED? Have your spine TINGLE, and get GOOSEBUMPS on your GOOSEBUMPS? Then this is for

yooooou! From 20.00. No extra charge

Castles

Spooky Halloween Spectacular

29/10/99 LONGLEAT

29/10/99 Tel: 01985 844400

Come along if you dare!

Safari Parks

Special Halloween Tours

29/10/99 MONTACUTE HOUSE

30/10/99 Tel: 01935 823289

A spoooooky tour of Montacute House to discover it's past. C-c-come if you d-d-d-dare! A£6.00 C£4.00, no under 10's

Historic Houses

Halloween Activities

30/10/99 BARRINGTON COURT

30/10/99 Tel: 01460 241938

Activities for the whole family, 11.00-15.00. Children in costume gain FREE admission. Halloween supper in Strode House Restaurant, please call 01460 241244 for reservations and information

Gardens

End of Season Firework Show

30/10/99 FLAMBARDS VILLAGE THEME PARK

30/10/99 Tel: 01326 564093 info line

Firework extravaganza. Admission by ticket only to park from noon onwards, plus fairy dress competition

Theme Parks

Halloween Spooktacular

30/10/99 WOODLANDS LEISURE PARK

30/10/99 Tel: 01803 712598

Pumpkin choosing from the Pumpkin Patch, Woodlands' weirdest costume wearer competition, treat for dressed up dudes, pumpkin lantern procession to Haunted Lake led by the Witch of the Woods, Spook Hunt

Country Leisure Parks

NFBG Badger Weekend

30/10/99 SECRET WORLD-BADGER AND WILDLIFE RESCUE CENTRE

31/10/99 Tel: 01278 783250

This special weekend is being held to promote National Badger Day. All funds raised will go towards supporting The National Federation of Badger Groups. Mini talks will be held throughout the day including face painting. Meet Mr Fox and Mr Badger for a special walk at 12.15 and 15.15 to meet all the animals that a badger finds on his evening forays! And, of course, you will see real badgers!

Wildlife Rescue

The History Man

30/10/99 TINTAGEL CASTLE

31/10/99 Tel: 01840 770328

Enjoy unusual guided tours with Brian McNerney, presenter of the BBC's popular History Man programmes. But be warned, his enthusiasm is notoriously contagious... and there is no antidote! Performing without costumes, props or even a safety net, he brings the past to life before your very eyes! A£2.80 C£1.40 Concessions£2.10

Historical Remains

Witch's Halloween Party

31/10/99 CREALY PARK

31/10/99 Tel: 01395 233200

Starting at 15.00 with Apple Bobbing, Fancy Dress, Magic Corners - lots of games and prizes to be won! Join the spooky train ride to see magic on the Dragonfly lake

Country Parks

Halloween Fun and Games

31/10/99 DAIRY LAND FARM WORLD

31/10/99 Tel: 01872 510246 info: 510349

For further details including times and prices please call venue direct

Animal Farms

Taste of the West in Montacute Restaurant

31/10/99 MONTACUTE HOUSE

31/10/99 Tel: 01935 823289

Please call 01935 826294 for reservations

Historic Houses

Weymouth Guy Fawkes Celebrations

5/11/99 THE PAVILION COMPLEX

5/11/99 Tel: 01305 785747

Weymouth Beach. Giant beach bonfire, Free firework festival, fun fair and attractions.

Arts & Entertainment

Woodlands Famous Fireworks Festival

6/11/99 WOODLANDS LEISURE PARK

6/11/99 Tel: 01803 712598

Dracula's Castle Bonfire, Spangles the Clown, Benco the Master Juggler, Stalls, Jazz Band, Bar. Firework spectacular by Firemagic of Bristol. 17.30-20.00.

Country Leisure Parks

Crafts Fair

6/11/99 LONGLEAT

7/11/99 Tel: 01985 844400

Meet the makers, see them at work and purchase some of the finest examples of British art, craft, fashion and design for Christmas

Safari Parks

Further more detailed information on the attractions listed can be found in Best Guides *Visitor Attractions* Guide under the classifications shown

Axminster Tool & Machinery Exhibition
12/11/99
14/11/99
ROYAL BATH AND WEST SHOWGROUND
Tel: 01749 822200
Featuring hand tools, power tools, woodworking and light engineering machinery plus wood turning equipment for both the enthusiast and the trade, together with displays and demonstrations
Showgrounds

Autumn Colour Walk
14/11/99
14/11/99
STOURHEAD HOUSE GARDEN AND HOUSE
Tel: 01747 841152
A walk with the Estate Warden through the magnificent woodlands of the Stourhead Estate. Meet 10.30 at Visitor Reception. Tickets A£3.50 C£Free
Historic Houses

Christmas Festival
15/11/99
24/12/99
BREWERS QUAY AND THE TIMEWALK JOURNEY
Tel: 01305 777622 24hr 766880
Six week festival celebrating the sights, sounds and tastes of a traditional Christmas including Santa in his fairytale grotto, tempting tastings, craft demonstrations, carol singing and much more
Family Attraction

Antique & Collectors Fair
20/11/99
21/11/99
ROYAL BATH AND WEST SHOWGROUND
Tel: 01749 822200
The biggest and best in the West. Inside and outside stands offering over 2 miles of antiques to choose from
Showgrounds

Beef & Sheep South West
25/11/99
25/11/99
ROYAL BATH AND WEST SHOWGROUND
Tel: 01749 822200
The Smithfield of the South West! A specialist farming event for the livestock producer. Run in conjunction with Yeovil Fatstock Society, with over 140 tradestands, livestock classes, auction, carcase displays, seminars and demonstrations covering "Beef from the Dairy Herd"
Showgrounds

The 20th Century Community Show
27/11/99
25/3/00
SALISBURY AND SOUTH WILTSHIRE MUSEUM
Tel: 01722 332151
A community exhibition celebrating the last 100 years using the memories, culture, art, souvenirs - and experience of local people. Events for all ages
Museums

Crafts for Christmas
3/12/99
5/12/99
ROYAL BATH AND WEST SHOWGROUND
Tel: 01749 822200
When your Christmas list has to be tackled seriously, this Show has to be the answer! Between 180 and 200 craftsmen gathered under one roof with a wealth of unusual handmade ideas, including food and drink!
Showgrounds

Father Christmas Visits
4/12/99
4/12/99
DUNSTER CASTLE
Tel: 01643 821314/823004
It's that time once again when we all want to curl up and let Christmas pass us by... but the children DON'T, so why not visit Santa, 11.00-16.00. Call Box Office on 01985 843601/2
Castles

Christmas comes to Woodlands
4/12/99
19/12/99
WOODLANDS LEISURE PARK
Tel: 01803 712598
See Father Christmas in his grotto at the weekends. Christmas Stocking Hunt. Discover the Treat Trial
Country Leisure Parks

Devizes Past and Present
4/12/99
31/12/99
DEVIZES MUSEUM
Tel: 01380 727369
A photographic exhibition of the Devizes Local History Group depicting changes in Devizes over the last century
Museum- Archaeology

Toy & Train Collectors Fair
5/12/99
5/12/99
ROYAL BATH AND WEST SHOWGROUND
Tel: 01749 822200
300+ stalls, selling dolls & teddies, dinky, corgi, Meccano, model railways, lead figures, tin toys, science fiction toys and lots more. Refreshments available. A£2.00 C&OAPs£1.00
Showgrounds

Santa's Grotto
8/12/99
23/12/99
DAIRY LAND FARM WORLD
Tel: 01872 510246 info: 510349
Tell Santa what you'd like for Christmas, you too Mums and Dads!
Animal Farms

Weymouth Victorian Shownight
9/12/99
9/12/99
THE PAVILION COMPLEX
Tel: 01305 785747
Weymouth Town Centre. Weymouth erupts into a frenzy of Victorian nostalgia. Late night shopping extravaganza. Christmas lights, brass bands, choirs, musicians, period costume and street theatre, children's fun fair, 30ft fair-

ground organ and visit from Santa Claus.

Arts & Entertainment

Christmas Piano Recital by Katie Brooks

11/12/99 DUNSTER CASTLE

11/12/99 Tel: 01643 821314/823004

Please call 01643 821314 for further information

Castles

Special Christmas Weekend

11/12/99 SECRET WORLD-BADGER AND WILDLIFE RESCUE CENTRE

12/12/99 Tel: 01278 783250

Father Christmas comes to Secret World! Children have the chance to see the mammals that usually sleep all through the winter and miss Christmas altogether! Father Christmas arrives at 12.00 and 15.00. You will find him in his grotto listening to children's wishes for Christmas Day - he will even have a present for you! No age limit on who can go and see Santa - just a weight limit as to who can sit on his knee!

Wildlife Rescue

Father Christmas Visits Crealy

11/12/99 CREALY PARK

23/12/99 Tel: 01395 233200

Meet Father Christmas in his grotto every afternoon. Tell him your wishes and receive a present. Just £1.00 per child

Country Parks

Santa's Workshop

11/12/99 KENTS CAVERN SHOWCAVES

24/12/99 Tel: 01803 215136

Enter a magical world of make believe... guided by an elf helper, you are taken into part of the cave system on a tour of Santa's workshop. See where and how your presents are made, boxed, wrapped and tested before being loaded onto the sleigh..and "WHO KNOWS WHEN OR WHERE FATHER CHRISTMAS MIGHT APPEAR?"! Dec 11, 12, 20, 21, 22, 23 & 24. Visits start half hourly throughout the day. Booking essential, A£1.50 C£2.10. Schools & playgroups on other days please call for details and bookings.

Caverns

Henri Cartier Bresson

11/12/99 ROYAL ALBERT MEMORIAL MUSEUM

29/1/00 Tel: 01392 265858

120 photographs by one of the 20th century's most admired and imitated photographers

Museum- Local History

Winter Walk

12/12/99 STOURHEAD HOUSE GARDEN AND HOUSE

12/12/99 Tel: 01747 841152

A walk with the Estate Warden taking in some of the less familiar parts of the Estate. Mulled wine and mince pies will be served at the end of the walk. Meet 10.30 at Visitor Reception. Tickets: A£4.00 C£Free

Historic Houses

Millennium Art for the Future

12/12/99 THE TIME MACHINE

31/1/00 Tel: 01934 621028

Display of Art for the Future

Museum- Local History

Christmas Shopping and Music

17/12/99 STOURHEAD HOUSE GARDEN AND HOUSE

17/12/99 Tel: 01747 841152

Enjoy selecting gifts at the National Trust Shop and the craft stalls in the courtyard. With music in St Peter's Church, Stourton.

Historic Houses

Special Christmas Weekend

18/12/99 SECRET WORLD-BADGER AND WILDLIFE RESCUE CENTRE

19/12/99 Tel: 01278 783250

Father Christmas comes to Secret World! Children have the chance to see the mammals that usually sleep all through the winter and miss Christmas altogether! Father Christmas arrives at 12.00 and 15.00. You will find him in his grotto listening to children's wishes for Christmas Day - he will even have a present for you! No age limit on who can go and see Santa - just a weight limit as to who can sit on his knee!Please see 11-12 Dec entry for details

Wildlife Rescue

Shortest Day Train Ride

21/12/99 CREALY PARK

21/12/99 Tel: 01395 233200

A Christmas special with Crealy Bear and Father Christmas at sunset!

Country Parks

Christmas Santa Trail

22/12/99 TREBAH GARDEN

22/12/99 Tel: 01326 250448

Our annual Santa trail around the garden ending at Santa's grotto to receive a gift

Gardens

Haynes Boxing Day Treasure Hunt

| 26/12/99 | **HAYNES MOTOR MUSEUM** |
| 26/12/99 | Tel: 01963 440804 |

Open to all cars, bikes and other forms of transport. Blow away the Christmas Blues, call for further details

Museum- Motor

Christmas River Walk

| 28/12/99 | **LACOCK ABBEY, FOX TALBOT MUSEUM AND VILLAGE** |
| 28/12/99 | Tel: 01249 730227/730459 |

Meet at Red Lion car park. 11.00 start, lasting 2 hours

Historic Houses

Pecorama Steam and Model Festival

| 10/6/00 | **PECORAMA** |
| 11/6/00 | Tel: 01297 21542 |

A two day festival of live steam with exhibits ranging from miniature locomotives to full size vintage traction engines

Railways Miniature

Textiles 2000

| 1/7/00 | **SALISBURY AND SOUTH WILTSHIRE MUSEUM** |
| 21/10/00 | Tel: 01722 332151 |

Embroidery, quilting, lace, knitting, weaving and all textile arts based on themes of Salisbury and South Wiltshire - past and future

Museums

Official Opening: Peco Millennium Garden

| 23/7/00 | **PECORAMA** |
| 23/7/00 | Tel: 01297 21542 |

The opening of a new attraction at Pecorama - The Peco Millennium Garden - featuring innovative gardening ideas in an intriguing landscaped setting

Railways Miniature

Yorkshire

Including:
Humberside

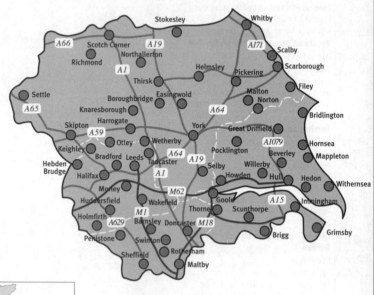

Neil Diamond

2/3/99 SHEFFIELD ARENA
2/3/99 Tel: 0114 256 5656

America's top solo artiste, Neil Diamond has personally arranged for the concert to be 'in the round', saying 'I'm not willing to give up the closeness to the audience that the in-the-round stage provides. This staging brings everyone 50% closer to me and gives me the freedom to really move around'. Tickets £30.00 Box Office 0114 256 56 56

Arts & Entertainment

Holiday On Ice presents Evolution

4/3/99 SHEFFIELD ARENA
7/3/99 Tel: 0114 256 5656

With special guest star Robin Cousins. Please call for further information

Arts & Entertainment

Bradford Film Festival

5/3/99 NATIONAL MUSEUM OF PHOTOGRAPHY
20/3/99 FILM AND TELEVISION (MUSEUM IN EXILE)
Tel: 01274 202030

Film Festival taking place at the Pictureville Cinema, please call for further information

Museum- Communications

Science Week

12/3/99 CLIFFE CASTLE MUSEUM AND GALLERY
21/3/99 Tel: 01535 618230
SET99

Museum- Art

Friends of Thomas the Tannk Engine

13/3/99 ELSECAR - THE POWERHOUSE
14/3/99 Tel: 01226 740203

Meet 'Thomas' and 'Sir Topham Hatt, The Fat Controller' open 10.00-17.00. A£2.00 C£1.00

Museum- Science

Science Week SET99 - Movers and Shakers

15/3/99 ELSECAR - THE POWERHOUSE
21/3/99 Tel: 01226 740203

The Science of the Circus Workshops, Rocket Making, plus "Sleepover for Science" for a whole night of scientific exploration

Museum- Science

The Hull Charter

20/3/99 FERENS ART GALLERY
11/4/99 Tel: 01482 613902

(Dates to be confirmed). As part of the Hull 700 anniversary celebrations the city's Royal Charter will be on display at the Ferens. This will be a unique opportunity to see this historic document. Related pictures from the gallery's permanent collection will also be on show as well as information about the Charter and a Modern English translation. Live performances of medieval music will mark the opening of the display on the 20 March.

Art Galleries

Hull Silver Exhibition

20/3/99 FERENS ART GALLERY
30/5/99 Tel: 01482 613902

A selection of some of the best pieces of silver from collections in the City. The focus will be on Hull silver but striking examples of early British silver from other makers will also be included. This exhibition celebrates Hull 700 and Hull's silver collections and will provide accessible information about the history of Hull silver and its makers.

Art Galleries

Wedding Fair with Marriage in Mind

21/3/99 NOSTELL PRIORY
21/3/99 Tel: 01924 863892

Fashion Show, Photographs, Florists, Vehicle Hire - all that is needed to plan that very important day

Stately Homes

Fun for Easter Time

27/3/99 NATIONAL RAILWAY MUSEUM
11/4/99 Tel: 01904 621261

There's a variety of activities for you to enjoy over the Easter period, be it a short ride behind one of our steam engines or interactive fun with Play Train. And on certain days you can even enjoy one of our Gallery Tours or perhaps a taste of the theatre with Platform 4 - our resident theatre company

Museums

Literature Comes to Life

27/3/99 EUREKA! THE MUSEUM FOR CHILDREN
25/4/99 Tel: 01422 330069

Popular characters from children's books come to life as children take part in storytelling, trails and interactive activities. This will be held on weekends and holidays

Museums

Art Exhibition

27/3/99 NUNNINGTON HALL
28/4/99 Tel: 01439 748283

John Ives - North York Moores and Beyond

Historic Houses

Northern Potters Exhibition

27/3/99 6/6/99	**CLIFFE CASTLE MUSEUM AND GALLERY** Tel: 01535 618230 Stunning items from clay. Events and activities too *Museum- Art*

The Riddlesden Riddle

2/4/99
4/4/99   EAST RIDDLESDEN HALL
Tel: 01535 607075
Self-guided quiz for children aged 4-11
Historic Houses & Gardens

Harrogate International Youth Music Festival '99

2/4/99
9/4/99   HARROGATE INTERNATIONAL YOUTH
MUSIC FESTIVAL '99
Tel: 01306 744360
The Harrogate International Youth Music Festival is celebrating it's 27th year in 1999. Musicians, singers and dancers from around the world come together to perform in venues in the Harrogate district. Venues from the prestigious Harrogate International Centre to the beautiful Ripon Cathedral hold performances throughout the festival week, as well as many different community venues in the district play host to performances from the young festival participants. An exciting week to sample music and dance from around the world.
Prices: A£4.00 C&Concessions£2.50.
Group rates & School parties £3.00
Festivals

Heritage Regained

2/4/99
20/6/99   TEMPLE NEWSAM HOUSE AND PARK
Tel: 0113 264 7321/264 5535
Silver from the Gilbert Collection, once part of the most important collections of works of art ever to have been given to Britain and was formed in California over the past thirty years by English-born real estate developer Arthur Gilbert. The munificent gift to the nation, at the time worth an estimated £75million, was announced in 1996 and, as a result of substantial grant from the Heritage Lottery Fund, it is hoped that it will be permanently on display at Somerset House in London by the end of the century.
Historic Houses & Gardens

Easter Egg Hunt

3/4/99
3/4/99   BRIMHAM ROCKS
Tel: 01423 780688
Fun day planned with the Easter Egg Hunt between 11.00-16.00. Small admission charge
Scenic

Living Heritage Craft Fair

3/4/99
5/4/99   NOSTELL PRIORY
Tel: 01924 863892
A tented village with arena entertainment, ongoing demonstrations, and children's attractions
Stately Homes

Easter Egg Hunt

4/4/99
5/4/99   BRODSWORTH HALL
Tel: 01302 722598
See if you can find these craftily hidden Easter Eggs, please telephone 01302 722598 for further information
Historic Houses

Medieval Music

4/4/99
5/4/99   HELMSLEY CASTLE
Tel: 01439 770442
Enjoy melodies and dance tunes dating back to the 12th century. A£2.50 C£1.30 Concessions£1.90
Castles

Easter Egg Hunt

4/4/99
5/4/99   NUNNINGTON HALL
Tel: 01439 748283
£1.00 per person - normal admission applies
Historic Houses

Easter Egg Hunt

4/4/99
5/4/99   RIEVAULX TERRACE AND TEMPLES
Tel: 01439 748283
£1.00 per person during normal opening hours
Historic Buildings

The Snitchity-Titch Show

5/4/99
5/4/99   EAST RIDDLESDEN HALL
Tel: 01535 607075
Puppet Show by Ronnie Le Drew. Snitchity-Titch saves up his pocket money to buy a boat and off he goes for an adventure. Who does he meet on his travels? Show at 12.30 and 15.00 in the Airedale Barn. Suitable for all the family
Historic Houses & Gardens

Elsecar Easter Country Fayre

5/4/99
5/4/99   ELSECAR - THE POWERHOUSE
Tel: 01226 740203
Meet all types of animals and birds, plus treasure hunts, rides and giant balloon release. 10.00-17.00. Call for further details
Museum- Science

Fountains Handicap

7/4/99
7/4/99   RIPON RACES
Tel: 01765 602156
First Race Time: 14.20
Racecourses

Garden Walk

Further more detailed information on the attractions listed can be found in Best Guides *Visitor Attractions* Guide under the classifications shown

9/4/99	**NUNNINGTON HALL**
9/4/99	Tel: 01439 748283

£2.00 per person inc NT Members - normal admission applies. Starts at 14.00

Historic Houses

Meat Loaf

10/4/99	SHEFFIELD ARENA
11/4/99	Tel: 0114 256 5656

With sell out shows at the Arena in 1993, 1994 and 1996 already under his sizeable belt, Meat Loaf will return to Sheffield Arena following the release of his 'Very best Of' album. 'The Very Best Of' showcases the highlights of Meat Loaf's chart topping career, including hits like 'Dead Ringer For Love,' 'Bat Out Of Hell,' 'You Took The Words Right Out Of My Mouth' and 'I Would Do Anything For Love'. Tickets are now on sale from the Box Office priced £25.00 and £22.50, 0114 256 56 56

Arts & Entertainment

The Floating World in Miniature

10/4/99	YORK CITY ART GALLERY
16/5/99	Tel: 01904 551861

Netsuke, Okimono and miniature carvings from Japan

Art Galleries

James Last & His Orchestra

12/4/99	SHEFFIELD ARENA
12/4/99	Tel: 0114 256 5656

James Last & His Orchestra will make their debut at Sheffield Arena, where they promise something for fans of all kinds of music. Tickets priced at £20 & £25. Box Office 0114 256 56 56

Arts & Entertainment

Lecture

13/4/99	TEMPLE NEWSAM HOUSE AND PARK
13/4/99	Tel: 0113 264 7321/264 5535

Paul de Lamerie: Triumph of the Rococo, 14.00, Anthony Wells-Cole.

Historic Houses & Gardens

Racing Meetings

14/4/99	BEVERLEY RACECOURSE
21/9/99	Tel: 01482 867488

Racing from Beverley on 14 & 22 Apr, 8 & 25 May, 2, 9 & 22 June, 2-3, 13, 19 & 27 July, 11-12, 28-29 Aug, 15 & 21 Sept

Racecourses

Cocked Hat 'Cock of the North' Handicap

15/4/99	RIPON RACES
15/4/99	Tel: 01765 602156

First Race Time: 14.10

Racecourses

Friends of Thomas the Tank Engine

17/4/99	MIDDLETON RAILWAY LEEDS
18/4/99	Tel: 0113 271 0320

Come one and all and see Thomas chuffing his way along the branch line

Railways Steam/Light

Streetfighters '99 - The Ultimate Performance Bike Show

17/4/99	SHEFFIELD ARENA
18/4/99	Tel: 0114 256 5656

Ticket Prices: In Advance A£6.50 C£3.50, On The Door A£8.00 C£4.50. Please call for further information

Arts & Entertainment

Liz Rideal

17/4/99	FERENS ART GALLERY
13/6/99	Tel: 01482 613902

Recent work by innovative British photographer exploring the possibilities of the abstract and formal portrait from which the actual human presence has disappeared. A selection of restrospective work will also be shown. The artist has made extensive use of the 'photobooth' as a means of creating photographs.

Art Galleries

Historic Stitches

18/4/99	EAST RIDDLESDEN HALL
18/4/99	Tel: 01535 607075

A presentation at 09.30 by Maeve Greenwood, a member of the embroidery and Textile Tutor's Association. Looking at the historic background to the intricate design, colour and stitchery of stumpwork - raised embroidery. £15.00. Booking essential through the property

Historic Houses & Gardens

Vintage Trains

18/4/99	KEIGHLEY AND WORTH VALLEY RAILWAY
18/4/99	Tel: 01535 645214/647777

Enjoy a journey in historic wood-bodies compartment coaches hauled by a Victorian steam locomotive. L&NWR Coal Tank No. 1054 or Well Tank Bellerophon will be used to haul these trains whenever possible

Railways Steam/Light

Pulmonaria Day

18/4/99	STILLINGFLEET LODGE
18/4/99	Tel: 01904 728506

Conducted tours round the National Collection of Pulmonaria

Gardens

Family Silver

| 18/4/99 | **TEMPLE NEWSAM HOUSE AND PARK** |
| 18/4/99 | Tel: 0113 264 7321/264 5535 |

A chance for the family to make up their own "silver" objects using silver foil and card using genuine silver objects from the Leeds collections as inspiration. 14.00-16.00.

Historic Houses & Gardens

Spring Watercolour Masterclass

| 20/4/99 | **EAST RIDDLESDEN HALL** |
| 20/4/99 | Tel: 01535 607075 |

Masterclass with artist in residence from Channel 4's Watercolour Challenge, Granville D Clarke, YWS and FRSA. Discover the artistic delights of Riddlesden Hall with this popular artist. Limited places available. All abilities welcome. Booking essential, please contact East Riddlesden Hall

Historic Houses & Gardens

Gary Barlow

| 21/4/99 | **SHEFFIELD ARENA** |
| 21/4/99 | Tel: 0114 256 5656 |

Ticket Prices: £17.50, £15.00. Please call for further information

Arts & Entertainment

Creative Stitches and Pastimes

| 23/4/99 | **SHEFFIELD ARENA** |
| 25/4/99 | Tel: 0114 256 5656 |

Tickets available on 01425 277988

Arts & Entertainment

C. B. Hutchinson Memorial Cup

| 24/4/99 | **RIPON RACES** |
| 24/4/99 | Tel: 01765 602156 |

First Race Time: 14.05

Racecourses

Friends of Thomas the Tank Engine

| 24/4/99 | **MIDDLETON RAILWAY LEEDS** |
| 25/4/99 | Tel: 0113 271 0320 |

Come along one and all and see Thomas chuffing his way along the branch line

Railways Steam/Light

A Look at 17th Century Life

| 25/4/99 | **EAST RIDDLESDEN HALL** |
| 25/4/99 | Tel: 01535 607075 |

A Costumed tour of the Hall takes place every fourth Sunday throughout the season and Sun-Tue & Thur from mid July-end of Aug excluding Bank Hol Mon and Sun in Sept. Also a tour for children at 14.00

Historic Houses & Gardens

B B King with special guests John Mayall and the Bluesbreakers

| 26/4/99 | **SHEFFIELD ARENA** |
| 26/4/99 | Tel: 0114 256 5656 |

Red hot Blues sizzles into town when long reigning monarch of the Blues guitar B B King plays Sheffield Arena with special guests John Mayall and The Bluesbreakers. Riley B King was born on a Missippippi cotton plantation in 1925 and started recording in the 1940's. He has released over 50 albums, many of which are considered Blues classics, like the 1965 definitive live blues album 'Live At The Regal' and the 1976 collaboration with Bobby "Blue" Bland, 'Together For The First Time'. B B King developed his unique guitar style from time spent with Blues legends including Bukka White, Blind Lemon Jefferson and T-Bone Walker creating techniques that have become the model for generations of rock guitarists including Eric Clapton, George Harrison and Jeff Beck. With seven Grammy awards, past tours with the Rolling Stones and U2, lifetime achievement awards from the Grammys and the Songwriters' Hall of Fame and a recently completed album featuring among others Tracy Chapman, The Rolling Stones, Van Morrison, Dave Gilmore and Eric Clapton, B B King truly is a living legend. Ticket Prices: £23.50 from the Sheffield Arena Box Office 0114 256 56 56

Arts & Entertainment

Lecture

| 27/4/99 | **TEMPLE NEWSAM HOUSE AND PARK** |
| 27/4/99 | Tel: 0113 264 7321/264 5535 |

The Regency Goldsmiths: Patrons and Craftsmen with a Common Purpose, 14.00, James Lomax.

Historic Houses & Gardens

The Beautiful South

| 27/4/99 | **SHEFFIELD ARENA** |
| 28/4/99 | Tel: 0114 256 5656 |

Ticket Prices: £18.50. Please call for further information

Arts & Entertainment

Pets, Pets, Pets

| 1/5/99 | **HAREWOOD HOUSE AND BIRD GARDEN** |
| 3/5/99 | Tel: 0113 288 6331 |

The popular Pet Rescue (Channel Four) returns with Pet Shows, events and accessory trade stands, call for more details

Historic Houses & Gardens

Enthusiasts' Weekend

| 1/5/99 | **KEIGHLEY AND WORTH VALLEY RAILWAY** |
| 3/5/99 | Tel: 01535 645214/647777 |

Gala steam event including visiting engines, on-train meals, freight trains,

Further more detailed information on the attractions listed can be found in Best Guides *Visitor Attractions* Guide under the classifications shown

vintage trains and transport

Railways Steam/Light

Exhibition

1/5/99 NUNNINGTON HALL

16/5/99 Tel: 01439 748283

Please telephone for further information

Historic Houses

Cannon Hill Capers

1/5/99 CANNON HALL

31/5/99 Tel: 01226 790270

The Final event of the Barnsley Children's Festival. A carnival atmosphere with lots of fun things to do. Actual date not finalised, please call for details

Museums

Ingenious Inventions

1/5/99 EUREKA! THE MUSEUM FOR CHILDREN

5/9/99 Tel: 01422 330069

Children can join the Eureka! Academy of inventors and use some of the World of Invention's weird and wonderful creations as inspiration for their own original masterpiece

Museums

Indoor Classic Car Show

2/5/99 ELSECAR - THE POWERHOUSE

3/5/99 Tel: 01226 740203

Classic Cars from every decade hosted inside Elsecar's "Building 21", commences 10.00-17.00, call for further details

Museum- Science

Napoleonic Redcoats

2/5/99 PICKERING CASTLE

3/5/99 Tel: 01751 474989

68th Display Team and 33rd Foot Light infantry drills, tactics and musket firing. From 12.00. A£3.00 C£1.50 Concessions£2.30

Castles

A Tapestry of Music

3/5/99 EAST RIDDLESDEN HALL

3/5/99 Tel: 01535 607075

An afternoon of music and song, 13.00-16.00. Peter Bull will entertain you with music from the time of the English Civil War with sounds from the hurdy gurdy, lute, dulcimer, recorder and flute. Fiona-Katie Roberts will play fast and rhythmical traditional music on the Triple Harp and the Pinsuti choir will sing madrigals in the garden

Historic Houses & Gardens

May Festival

3/5/99 KELHAM ISLAND MUSEUM

3/5/99 Tel: 0114 272 2106

Folk festival to celebrate the coming of summer with folk music, song and dance

Museum- Industrial

Lecture

4/5/99 TEMPLE NEWSAM HOUSE AND PARK

4/5/99 Tel: 0113 264 7321/264 5535

A Silversmith Speaks, 14.00, Christopher Phillipson.

Historic Houses & Gardens

Royalty and Silver 1714-1837

7/5/99 TEMPLE NEWSAM HOUSE AND PARK

7/5/99 Tel: 0113 264 7321/264 5535

Many of the works of art in the exhibition were formerly the property of royalty: they can be considered as expressions of power or of taste. The six lectures will explore the role of silver in the workings of government and monarch in the Georgian period. Further information from Marilyn Moreland, School of Continuing Education, University of Leeds, LS2 9JT, 0113 233 3220

Historic Houses & Gardens

Medieval Music & Monastic Entertainers

8/5/99 BYLAND ABBEY

9/5/99 Tel: 01347 868614

Enjoy melodies and dance tunes dating back to the 12th century. A£3.00 C£1.50 Concessions£2.30

Abbeys

Yorkshire Photographic Union

8/5/99 LEEDS CITY ART GALLERY

20/6/99 Tel: 0113 247 8248

1999 sees the centenary of the body which operates on behalf of all the region's long-established photographic societies and camera clubs. An important event in the amateur photography world.

Art Galleries

Creatures of the Black Lagoon

9/5/99 LONGSHAW ESTATE

9/5/99 Tel: 01433 631757

Pond dipping with National Trust Warden. For families

National Parks

Spring Plant Fair

9/5/99 NEWBY HALL AND GARDENS

9/5/99 Tel: 01423 322583

Buy your spring plants today

Historic Houses & Gardens

Racing from York

| 11/5/99 | YORK RACECOURSE |
| 9/10/99 | Tel: 01904 620911 |

Race days: 11-13 May, 11-12 June, 9-10 July, 17-19 Aug, 1-2 Sept, 6-7 Oct, 9 Oct. Please call for further information

Racecourses

Valuation Day

| 12/5/99 | EAST RIDDLESDEN HALL |
| 12/5/99 | Tel: 01535 607075 |

Dig out those treasures from your attic and drawers and see what they are worth. A valuation day with experts from Bonhams. In the Airedale Barn. 11.00-15.00, last admission 14.45. £2.00 first item, £1.00 subsequent items

Historic Houses & Gardens

Spring Flower Walk

| 12/5/99 | RIEVAULX TERRACE AND TEMPLES |
| 12/5/99 | Tel: 01439 748283 |

Come along and look at the beautiful spring flowers at 14.00. £2.00 per person inc NT Members - Normal admission applies

Historic Buildings

The Best Disco in Town

| 13/5/99 | SHEFFIELD ARENA |
| 13/5/99 | Tel: 0114 256 5656 |

Featuring K C & The Sunshine Band, Tavares, Sister Sledge, Rose Royce, The Three Degrees, Odyssey, The Real Thing. It will be the first time that such prominent artistes from the 70's have performed together on the same bill - all will be performing their greatest hits with full backing musicians, with the show running like one major disco party. Since the beginning of their careers, these artistes have between them sold over a staggering 250 million records worldwide, received in excess of 5000 gold, silver and platinum discs, and received numerous awards including various Grammys. Ticket Prices: £25.00 from Box Office 0114 256 56 56

Arts & Entertainment

Boyzone

| 14/5/99 | SHEFFIELD ARENA |
| 15/5/99 | Tel: 0114 256 5656 |

Boyzone are here at Sheffield Arena as part of 'The Hits' tour. Since they first burst into the charts in 1994 with 'Love Me For A Reason', Boyzone have sole in excess of 5 million albums, enjoyed twelve Top Five singles - including four Number Ones - and sold out tours throughout the world. They have long since outgrown their flimsy boy band

image and are rightly enjoying an upsurge in musical respect, recently picking up the prestigious Ivor Novello Award for The Best Original Song on a Film Soundtrack for 'Picture of You'. Ticket Prices: £17.50 from Box Office 0114 256 56 56

Arts & Entertainment

Silversmith in Residence

| 15/5/99 | TEMPLE NEWSAM HOUSE AND PARK |
| 15/5/99 | Tel: 0113 264 7321/264 5535 |

Christopher Phillipson, well known silversmith and jeweller from Knaresborough, will have a temporary studio adjacent to the exhibition where he will show some of his current work in progress and discuss his approach to design and craftsmanship. 10.30-12.30 & 14.00-16.00.

Historic Houses & Gardens

Mason's Pottery Exhibition

| 15/5/99 | CLIFTON PARK MUSEUM |
| 1/8/99 | Tel: 01709 823635 |

An exhibition organised with the Mason's Collectors Society of some of the finest examples of Mason's pottery

Museums

Wildflower Walk

| 16/5/99 | LONGSHAW ESTATE |
| 16/5/99 | Tel: 01433 631757 |

Led by National Trust Wardens. Meet outside Visitor Centre at 13.30. No dogs please

National Parks

Nostell Priory Plant Fair

| 16/5/99 | NOSTELL PRIORY |
| 16/5/99 | Tel: 01924 863892 |

Plants of all varieties for sale

Stately Homes

Plant Sale

| 16/5/99 | NUNNINGTON HALL |
| 16/5/99 | Tel: 01439 748283 |

Buy your plants and accessories at this plant sale 12.30-17.00

Historic Houses

Family Fun Day

| 16/5/99 | RIPON RACES |
| 16/5/99 | Tel: 01765 602156 |

First Race Time: 14.15

Racecourses

Spring Flower Walk

| 19/5/99 | RIEVAULX TERRACE AND TEMPLES |
| 19/5/99 | Tel: 01439 748283 |

Come along and look at the beautiful spring flowers at 14.00. £2.00 per person inc NT Members - Normal admission applies

Historic Buildings

Embroidery Exhibition
19/5/99 NUNNINGTON HALL
31/5/99 Tel: 01439 748283
Please telephone for further information

Historic Houses

Les Miserables
21/5/99 SHEFFIELD ARENA
19/6/99 Tel: 0114 256 5656
Box Office 0114 256 56 56

Arts & Entertainment

Railways of the World
22/5/99 NATIONAL RAILWAY MUSEUM
6/9/99 Tel: 01904 621261
Photographs by Colin Garratt

Museums

A Look at 17th Century Life
23/5/99 EAST RIDDLESDEN HALL
23/5/99 Tel: 01535 607075
Costumed tour of Hall with a tour for
children at 14.00

Historic Houses & Gardens

Flights of Fancy
23/5/99 EAST RIDDLESDEN HALL
23/5/99 Tel: 01535 607075
Diane Bates will give a humourous presentation at 09.30 about her collection
of machine embroidered bodices, as
seen here in 1998. £10.00 per person.
Booking essential through the property

Historic Houses & Gardens

Vintage Trains
23/5/99 KEIGHLEY AND WORTH VALLEY RAILWAY
23/5/99 Tel: 01535 645214/647777
Enjoy a journey in historic wood-bodies
compartment coaches hauled by a
Victorian steam locomotive. L&NWR Coal
Tank No. 1054 or Well Tank Bellerophon
will be used to haul these trains whenever possible

Railways Steam/Light

The Ripon Festival Evening
26/5/99 RIPON RACES
26/5/99 Tel: 01765 602156
First Race Time: 18.40

Racecourses

**Beverley and East Riding Early Music
Festival '99**
27/5/99 BEVERLEY AND EAST RIDING EARLY MUSIC
FESTIVAL '99
31/5/99 Tel: 01904 645738
Various venues. This charming Festival
celebrates the rich architectural heritage
of East Yorkshire with concerts in
Beverley Minster and some of England's
finest medieval churches. Guest artists
in 1999 include the extraordinary

American vocal ensemble Anonymous 4.
Ring for details of the Festival hotel
package at the Beverley Arms Hotel and
enjoy a musical tour of the region with
associated walks, illustrated talks and
opportunities to explore the countryside. Please call for prices

Festivals

Garden Walk
28/5/99 NUNNINGTON HALL
28/5/99 Tel: 01439 748283
£2.00 per person inc NT Members -
Normal Admission applies. Starts at
14.00

Historic Houses

Childrens Weekend
29/5/99 CASTLE HOWARD
31/5/99 Tel: 01653 648444
Bring the children along for a fun-filled
weekend

Castles

Enid Blyton Family Fun Event
29/5/99 ELSECAR - THE POWERHOUSE
31/5/99 Tel: 01226 740203
Meet 'Noddy and Big Ears', join the
'Famous Five' on a Mystery Train, and
make you wish aboard the 'Wishing
Chair'. Great day out for all the family,
call for further details

Museum- Science

Bank Holiday Craft Festival
29/5/99 HAREWOOD HOUSE AND BIRD GARDEN
31/5/99 Tel: 0113 288 6331
One of the largest craft festival returns
to Harewood bringing the cream of
British Craftspoeple and Artists to exhibit their latest works, call for further
details

Historic Houses & Gardens

Steam Threshing Weekend
29/5/99 MAJOR BRIDGE PARK
31/5/99 Tel: 01430 860992
Victorian Spectacular with steam
engines, fair organs, shire horses, working demonstrations. From 10.00-18.00.
A£1.50 C(accompanied)Free OAPs£1.00

Farm Parks

Red Wyvern Society Re-enactment
29/5/99 SKIPTON CASTLE
31/5/99 Tel: 01756 792442
Life a Skipton Castle in the 15th century,
call venue for further details

Castles

The Artist and the Pre-Raphaelite
29/5/99 YORK CITY ART GALLERY
11/7/99 Tel: 01904 551861
Including other Victorian paintings

Art Galleries

World's Greatest Showman
ROYAL ARMOURIES MUSEUM
29/5/99
5/9/99
Tel: 0990 106666 gen info
A major block-buster exhibition devoted
to one of the world's greatest showmen.
The exhibition is drawn from a range of
public and private collections in the USA
and includes material seldom seen in
public.

Museum- Military

Rydale Spring Fair
NUNNINGTON HALL
30/5/99
30/5/99
Tel: 01439 748283
Come and have fun at the Rydale Spring
Fair 12.30-17.00, £1.50 admission for Fair

Historic Houses

The Bilsdale Silver Band
RIEVAULX ABBEY
30/5/99
30/5/99
Tel: 01439 798228
Plainsong, chants and music from the
5th to the 16th century as part of
Cistercian 900, 14.00-16.00. A£3.00
C£1.50 Concessions£2.30 English
Heritage Members Free

Abbeys

Medieval Siege
HELMSLEY CASTLE
30/5/99
31/5/99
Tel: 01439 770442
Re-enactment by Livery & Maintenance.
A£4.00 C£2.00 Concessions£3.00

Castles

Medieval Entertainment
MIDDLEHAM CASTLE
30/5/99
31/5/99
Tel: 01969 623899
Fighting knights, dancing, stories, chil-
dren's games and juggling. A£4.00
C£2.00 Concessions£3.00

Castles

Viking Battle
SCARBOROUGH CASTLE
30/5/99
31/5/99
Tel: 01723 372451
Re-enactment of a Viking Battle per-
formed by The Vikings. A£4.00 C£2.00
Concessions£3.00

Historical Remains

Art Exhibition
NUNNINGTON HALL
1/6/99
13/6/99
Tel: 01439 748283
By local artist, Dianne Smith

Historic Houses

Victorian Music and Dance
BRODSWORTH HALL
5/6/99
6/6/99
Tel: 01302 722598
Performed by Hautbois, Arbeau Dancers.
A£3.50 C£1.80 Concessions£2.60

Historic Houses

Friends of Thomas the Tank Engine
KEIGHLEY AND WORTH VALLEY RAILWAY
5/6/99
6/6/99
Tel: 01535 645214/647777
Park you car at Marsh Lane Oxenhope,
ride on Bertie and Bulgy to Oxenhope
Station, the travel by train to meet
Thomas, Percy, Diesel, Duck, Annie and
Clarabel and other friends at Ingrow and
Keighley

Railways Steam/Light

The History Man
RIEVAULX ABBEY
5/6/99
6/6/99
Tel: 01439 798228
Enjoy unusual guided tours with Brian
McNerney, presenter of the BBC's popular History Man programmes. But be
warned, his enthusiasm is notoriously
contagious... and there is no antidote!
Performing without costumes, props or
even a safety net, he brings the past to
life before your very eyes! A£3.00 C£1.50
Concessions£2.30

Abbeys

Postman Pat
MIDDLETON RAILWAY LEEDS
6/6/99
6/6/99
Tel: 0113 271 0320
Middleton Colliery Railway delivers
Postman Pat to the station to meet all
his little fans

Railways Steam/Light

**Medieval Music on the Terrace by
Peter Bull**
RIEVAULX TERRACE AND TEMPLES
6/6/99
6/6/99
Tel: 01439 748283
Performances at 14.00, 15.00 & 16.00.
Normal admission. Bring a picnic

Historic Buildings

A Ramble around Riddlesden
EAST RIDDLESDEN HALL
9/6/99
9/6/99
Tel: 01535 607075
The House Steward will lead you on a
circular walk to look at local sites and
the Murgatroyd family connection with
Riddlesden. Moderate walk. 13.30. £3.30
per head including NT members. Age
14+. Limited spaces available. Booking
essential through the property

Historic Houses & Gardens

Bramham International Horse Trials
BRAMHAM PARK
10/6/99
13/6/99
Tel: 01937 844265
Horse Trials and Yorkshire Country Fair

Historic Houses & Gardens

**Obadiah Ringwood - 17th Century
Soldier**

12/6/99 13/6/99	**CLIFFORD'S TOWER**

Tel: 01904 646940

Ralph Needham. Master Ringrood relates his early years spent as a soldier in both armies during the English Civil war when he first learnt his trade as a surgeon. From 12.00. A£1.80 C£0.90 Concessions£1.40 English Heritage Members Free

Keeps

A Medieval Murder Mystery

12/6/99 **MIDDLEHAM CASTLE**
13/6/99 Tel: 01969 623899

Performed by Knights in Battle. A£3.00 C£1.50 Concessions£2.30

Castles

Rainbow Craft Fair

12/6/99 **NEWBY HALL AND GARDENS**
13/6/99 Tel: 01423 322583

Plenty to see and do for the whole family

Historic Houses & Gardens

Ingrow Yard Brake Van Trips

13/6/99 **KEIGHLEY AND WORTH VALLEY RAILWAY**
13/6/99 Tel: 01535 645214/647777

Travel in a rare Southern Railway brake van hauled by L&NWR Coal Tank locomotive No. 1054 built in 1888 and still going strong. This locomotive operates by courtesy of the National Trust

Railways Steam/Light

Hebden Bridge Arts Festival

13/6/99 **HEBDEN BRIDGE ARTS FESTIVAL 1999**
11/7/99 Tel: 01422 842395

Hebden Bridge Arts Festival runs for a full month in June and July every summer. There are exhibitions throughout the festival and events every night. The festival includes: Fine arts, all types of music, drama, dance, textiles, photography, street entertainment, spoken word, film, children's events and workshops. Further information available from Hebden Bridge Tourist Information Centre

Festivals

Garden Tour

14/6/99 **EAST RIDDLESDEN HALL**
14/6/99 Tel: 01535 607075

A tour with the gardener at 14.00. Explore the wonderful herb and herbaceous borders

Historic Houses & Gardens

Exhibition and Demonstrations

15/6/99 **NUNNINGTON HALL**
27/6/99 Tel: 01439 748283

Rags and rugs by Ebor Rag Ruggers

Historic Houses

Garden Walk

16/6/99 **NUNNINGTON HALL**
16/6/99 Tel: 01439 748283

Join the gardener for a stroll around the magnificent gardens at Nunnington Hall - 19.00. £5.00 including glass of wine - booking essential

Historic Houses

Mid-Summer Evening Meeting

16/6/99 **RIPON RACES**
16/6/99 Tel: 01765 602156

First Race Time: 19.00

Racecourses

Flower Festival

16/6/99 **CASTLE HOWARD**
20/6/99 Tel: 01653 648444

Bloomin' marvellous in bloomin' June

Castles

City of Ripon Handicap

17/6/99 **RIPON RACES**
17/6/99 Tel: 01765 602156

First Race Time: 14.10

Racecourses

Jazz At Harlow Garr

18/6/99 **HARLOW CARR BOTANICAL GARDENS**
18/6/99 Tel: 01423 565418

Enjoy the tranquil 68 acres with the sound of jazz. Bring picnics, tables and chairs! Performance Time: 19.00-22.00

Gardens- Botanical

Beverley and East Riding Folk Festival 1999

18/6/99 **BEVERLEY AND EAST RIDING FOLK**
　　　　FESTIVAL 1999
20/6/99 Tel: 01377 217662

The festival takes place in the historic market town of Beverley and presents leading international music, song and dance artists in the fields of folk, roots and world music. It also present a Comedy Club along with writers and poets in it new expanding programme. The events are suitable for people of all ages and interests with an opportunity for participation as well as passive enjoyment.

Festivals

Outdoor Concert

19/6/99 **NUNNINGTON HALL**
19/6/99 Tel: 01439 748283

Evening of Nostalgia performed by The York Concert Band playing Glen Miller, Sinatra, Rock & Roll Explosion, Beatles and Gershwin. Tickets: A£10.00 C£5.00 Family Ticket £25.00. Performance starts at 19.00. Grounds open 18.00. Bring a picnic

Historic Houses

Plant Fair/Craft Fair
19/6/99 CASTLE HOWARD
20/6/99 Tel: 01653 648444
For all those gardening enthusiasts

Castles

Viking Battle
19/6/99 WHITBY ABBEY
20/6/99 Tel: 01947 603568
The Vikings. 11th century encampment,
living history, from 12.00, displays and a
savage battle between Saxons and
Vikings at 15.00. A£3.00 C£1.50
Concessions£2.30English Heritage
Members Free

Abbeys

Indoor Classic Bike Show
20/6/99 ELSECAR - THE POWERHOUSE
20/6/99 Tel: 01226 740203
Classic Bikes, entertainment, and rides
aboard the Elsecar Steam Railway, especially for Father's Day

Museum- Science

All Saints
21/6/99 SHEFFIELD ARENA
21/6/99 Tel: 0114 256 5656
Chart topping pop divas All Saints have
established themselves as one of the
UK's most successful pop acts. A new
full state of the art production promises
a great show. Tickets £17.50

Arts & Entertainment

Open-Air Shakespeare - Twelfth Night
24/6/99 FOUNTAINS ABBEY AND STUDLEY ROYAL
WATER GARDEN
26/6/99 Tel: 01765 608888
Performance by Illyria in the Abbey
Cloister. Refreshments on sale. A£9.00
C£6.50. Grounds open 18.00 for 19.30
start

Abbeys

Bradford Festival 1999
25/6/99 BRADFORD FESTIVAL 1999
18/7/99 Tel: 01274 309199
Artists from around rhe world join with
multicultural local talent, for 24 days of
colourful summer fun, music, dance and
street theatre. The main events are free.
Café Bradford is the city centre focus,
with food and drinks and entertainment
in a continental atmosphere, Bradford
Mela has over 150,000 visitors annually,
The Carnival Parade, with thousands of
colourful participants, The Finale Day
party in the park, ending with spectacular fireworks.

Festivals

**Great Dutch Paintings from The
National Gallery**
25/6/99 LEEDS CITY ART GALLERY
29/8/99 Tel: 0113 247 8248
20 major,17th century Dutch paintings
from National Gallery including Verner,
Rembrandt & Hobbema

Art Galleries

Outdoor Concert
26/6/99 CASTLE HOWARD
26/6/99 Tel: 01653 648444
Lots of fresh air and great music

Castles

Jazz in the Garden
26/6/99 EAST RIDDLESDEN HALL
26/6/99 Tel: 01535 607075
An evening of jazz with the Yorkshire
Post Jazz Band. Bring a picnic and rugs.
18.30 for 19.00. Tickets £10.00, call
01765 609999

Historic Houses & Gardens

History of Longshaw Walk
26/6/99 LONGSHAW ESTATE
26/6/99 Tel: 01433 631757
Meet: 14.00, outside Visitor Centre

National Parks

**Abbey National 150th Anniversary
Celebration**
26/6/99 HAREWOOD HOUSE AND BIRD GARDEN
27/6/99 Tel: 0113 288 6331
An innovative and interactive exhibition
showing the past, present and future of
Abbey national, together with a host of
entertainment for all ages, call for further details

Historic Houses & Gardens

Medieval Entertainers
26/6/99 HELMSLEY CASTLE
27/6/99 Tel: 01439 770442
Games, squire-training and talks on
weaponry and armour. Also, try your
hand at spinning, weaving and calligraphy and learn about herbal medicine.
A£3.00 C£1.50 Concessions£2.30

Castles

Discover Nature Wonders
27/6/99 RIEVAULX TERRACE AND TEMPLES
27/6/99 Tel: 01439 748283
Sensory awareness activity day for the
whole family with an 11.00 start. Please
wear suitable footwear and clothing and
bring a packed lunch. Booking essential.
Family Ticket(A2+C2)£13.00 Individual
price including admission fee to house
£8.00

Historic Buildings

Further more detailed information on the attractions listed can be found
in Best Guides *Visitor Attractions* Guide under the classifications shown

Lincolnshire Heritage Day
27/6/99 SANDTOFT TRANSPORT MUSEUM
27/6/99 Tel: 01724 711391 24hr info
Please call for further information
Museum- Transport

Art Exhibition
29/6/99 NUNNINGTON HALL
28/7/99 Tel: 01439 748283
By local artist Jim Wright
Historic Houses

Michael Pinsky: Transparent Room
1/7/99 LEEDS CITY ART GALLERY
1/8/99 Tel: 0113 247 8248
A young Scottish artist who works with
photography and new technology, uses
video projection to create a 3-D space,
transforming real space in a "x-ray" of
the space beyond the walls, floor and
ceiling of the gallery.
Art Galleries

Cleckheaton Folk Festival 1999
2/7/99 CLECKHEATON FOLK FESTIVAL 1999
4/7/99 Tel: 01924 404346
Come along and enjoy this value for
money, friendly weekend folk festival.
The guests list has something for all
tastes including: Bayou Gumbo,
Blackstone Edge, Chris Sherburn and
Deny Bartley, Dave Burland, Derek
Brimstone, Edna Kenny, Jez Lowe and
the Bad Pennies, Ray Fisher, Roy Bailey,
Tom McConville and Pauline Cato and
many more. Concerts, ceilidh, workshops, meets, singarounds, music sessions, dancers, street parade, craft fair
etc. Times: Fri 19.00-24.00, Sat 10.00-
24.00, Sun 10.00-22.00. Prices: Advance
weekend ticket: £14.00 to 1/4/99,
£19.00 to 24/6/99 or £24.00 after
24/6/99
Festivals

York Early Music Festival '99
2/7/99 YORK EARLY MUSIC FESTIVAL '99
11/7/99 Tel: 01904 658338
Guest artists will include the American
renaissance wind band Piffaro making
their UK debut, the South African
Chorale working with the early music
vocal specialists I Fagionlini, the Tibetan
Monks accompanying the Dali Lama
when he comes to Britain next summer
and the Italian ensemble Mala Punica
also making their UK debut. Highlights
will include a spectacular Venetian
extravaganza in York Minster on the
opening night and a performance of
Purcell's Kings Arthur by the Gabrieli

Consort and Players. Please call for
prices
Festivals

Tercentenary Day
3/7/99 CASTLE HOWARD
3/7/99 Tel: 01653 648444
Celebrating 300 years of Castle Howard
Castles

The Imperial Roman Army
3/7/99 ALDBOROUGH ROMAN TOWN AND
MUSEUM
4/7/99 Tel: 01423 322768
With the Ermine St. Guard/Troop. Price:
A£4.00 C£2.00 Concessions£3.00
Museum- Roman

Richard III at Home
3/7/99 MIDDLEHAM CASTLE
4/7/99 Tel: 01969 623899
Buckingham's Retinue. Meet the king as
he relaxes at his childhood home. Plus
military displays and music. From 12.00.
A£3.50 C£1.80 Concessions£2.50
English Heritage Members Free
Castles

Alice in Wonderland
3/7/99 PICKERING CASTLE
4/7/99 Tel: 01751 474989
Labyrinth Productions. Follow Alice and
White Rabbit as they go through
Wonderland, meeting all manner of
weird, wonderful and totally mad characters. A£3.50 C£1.50 Concessions£2.60
Castles

Have-a-go-Archery
3/7/99 WHITBY ABBEY
4/7/99 Tel: 01947 603568
Whitby Company of Archers. 14th century archers introduce visitors to the art of
archery. A£1.70 C£0.90
Concessions£1.30
Abbeys

Third Evening Meeting
5/7/99 RIPON RACES
5/7/99 Tel: 01765 602156
First Race Time: 19.00
Racecourses

Music by Moonlight - Miller Magic
9/7/99 FOUNTAINS ABBEY AND STUDLEY ROYAL
WATER GARDEN
10/7/99 Tel: 01765 608888
The music of Glen Miller and Cole Porter
performed by the Herb Miller and the
Chris Allen Orchestras with fireworks
finale. Sponsored by Bradford & Bingley
Building Society. Fri 18.00 for 18.30, Sat
17.30 for 18.00. Tickets: Fri £17.50, Sat
£19.00

Abbeys

Discover Natures Wonders

10/7/99 NUNNINGTON HALL

10/7/99 Tel: 01439 748283

Sensory awareness activity day for the whole family. 11.00 start, suitable footwear and clothing - bring packed lunch - booking essential. Family Ticket(A2+C2)£15.00, individuals price £9.00 includes admission fee to house

Historic Houses

Medieval Monastic Entertainers

10/7/99 WHITBY ABBEY

11/7/99 Tel: 01947 603568

Heuristics. Try your hand at calligraphy or authentic period games as this popular duo take a lighthearted look at monastic customs, crafts and lifestyles. Learn about food preparation, herbs and spices in cooking and medicine, the mechanics of building, lifting and many other skills. Part of Cistercian 900. A£1.70 C£0.90 Concessions£1.30 English Heritage Members - Free

Abbeys

Ingrow Yard Brake Van Trips

11/7/99 KEIGHLEY AND WORTH VALLEY RAILWAY

11/7/99 Tel: 01535 645214/647777

Travel in a rare Southern Railway brake van hauled by L&NWR Coal Tank locomotive No. 1054 built in 1888 and still going strong. This locomotive operates by courtesy of the National Trust

Railways Steam/Light

A Look at 17th Century Life

12/7/99 EAST RIDDLESDEN HALL

31/8/99 Tel: 01535 607075

Costumed tours take place every Sun, Mon, Tue & Thur from 12 July to 30 Aug. A tour for children at 14.00 each day

Historic Houses & Gardens

Summer Wildflower Walk

14/7/99 RIEVAULX TERRACE AND TEMPLES

14/7/99 Tel: 01439 748283

Walk starts at 14.00. £2.00 Inc NT Members - normal admission applies

Historic Buildings

Outdoor Concert

17/7/99 CASTLE HOWARD

17/7/99 Tel: 01653 648444

'Single Star' Event, bring along a picnic, firework finale

Castles

Institute of Journalists Royal Charter Meeting

17/7/99 RIPON RACES

17/7/99 Tel: 01765 602156

First Race Time: 14.35

Racecourses

Stories & Mask Making

17/7/99 CLIFFORD'S TOWER

18/7/99 Tel: 01904 646940

Michael & Wendy Dacre. Traditional folk tales, myths and legends, plus mask making. From 12.00. A£1.80 C£0.90 Concessions£1.40

Keeps

Arthurian Antics

17/7/99 HELMSLEY CASTLE

18/7/99 Tel: 01439 770442

Inner State Theatre. Confusion reigns in Camelot as King Arthur, Queen Guinevere and their pet dragon Pen search for Merlin and Sir Lancelot, from 12.00. A£3.00 C£1.50 Concessions£2.30

Castles

Have-a-go Archery

17/7/99 MIDDLEHAM CASTLE

18/7/99 Tel: 01969 623899

Arrowflight, from 12.00. 14th century archers introduce visitors to the art of archery. A£2.50 C£1.30 Concessions£1.90

Castles

Nostell Priory Country Fair

17/7/99 NOSTELL PRIORY

18/7/99 Tel: 01924 863892

A fair steeped in tradition. Value for money fun for all the family. Music, merriment and country pursuits

Stately Homes

Viking Living History

17/7/99 ROCHE ABBEY

18/7/99 Tel: 01709 812739

See Viking history re-enacted by Anmod Dracon. A£3.00 C£1.50 Concessions£2.30

Abbeys

Historic Vehicle Rally

18/7/99 NEWBY HALL AND GARDENS

18/7/99 Tel: 01423 322583

North East Club for pre-war Austins, an excellent day planned at this popular Historic Vehicle Rally

Historic Houses & Gardens

Outdoor Music Afternoon

18/7/99 NUNNINGTON HALL

18/7/99 Tel: 01439 748283

Performed by the Mowbray Singers 14.00-16.00

Historic Houses

Summer Wildflower Walk

Further more detailed information on the attractions listed can be found in Best Guides *Visitor Attractions* Guide under the classifications shown

21/7/99 21/7/99	**RIEVAULX TERRACE AND TEMPLES** Tel: 01439 748283 Walk starts at 14.00. £2.00 inc NT Members - normal admission applies *Historic Buildings*

Harrogate International Festival 1999

22/7/99 7/8/99	**HARROGATE INTERNATIONAL FESTIVAL 1999** Tel: 01423 562303 The 34th Harrogate International Festival, brings a feast of world class entertainment to this beautiful spa town. Enjoy the cream of Jazz and Blues, Fringe, Classical, Dance and Open Air events with rare performances by internationally renowned artists. Call the Festival office to join our FREE mailing list (details published in May). *Festivals*

Open-Air Opera - The Barber of Seville

24/7/99 24/7/99	**FOUNTAINS ABBEY AND STUDLEY ROYAL WATER GARDEN** Tel: 01765 608888 Based on Beaumarchais's play, Rossini's comic masterpiece of 1816 remains as sparklingly fresh as ever in Opera. Grounds open 18.00 for 19.30 start *Abbeys*

Shakespeare - Henry V by Oddsocks Theatre Co

24/7/99 24/7/99	**NUNNINGTON HALL** Tel: 01439 748283 Performed in their own inimitable whacky and irreverent style. Great summer outing for all the family bring a picnic. A£10.00 C£5.00 Family Ticket(A2+C2)£25.00. Performance starts at 19.00, grounds open from 18.00 *Historic Houses*

Elsecar Garden Lover's Weekend

24/7/99 25/7/99	**ELSECAR - THE POWERHOUSE** Tel: 01226 740203 Displays, societies, Garden Centre, and Nurseries, with everything for your garden, plus bands and refreshments *Museum- Science*

Family Entertainers

24/7/99 25/7/99	**HELMSLEY CASTLE** Tel: 01439 770442 Games, have-a-go archery, costumes for children to try on and talks on weaponry. A£3.50 C£1.50 Concessions£2.60 *Castles*

More Skulduggery!

24/7/99 25/7/99	**MIDDLEHAM CASTLE** Tel: 01969 623899 Silly tales of secret maps, buried trea-

sure and famous pirates. From 12.00.
A£3.00 C£1.50 Concessions£2.30
Castles

Medieval Living History

24/7/99 25/7/99	**PICKERING CASTLE** Tel: 01751 474989 15th century military and domestic life, with crafts, men-at-arms and period games with The Lincoln Castle Garrison. A£3.50 C£1.80 Concessions£2.60 *Castles*

Jousting

24/7/99 25/7/99	**SCARBOROUGH CASTLE** Tel: 01723 372451 Discover the secrets of the tourney, as the jousting area resounds to the sounds of the battle, clash of steel and thunder of horses hooves as the mighty knights charge at full tilt. A£4.00 C£2.00 Concessions£3.00 *Historical Remains*

Music Afternoon

25/7/99 25/7/99	**RIEVAULX TERRACE AND TEMPLES** Tel: 01439 748283 The Mowbray Singers perform 14.00-16.00. Bring a picnic *Historic Buildings*

Sandtoft Gathering and Sale of Axholme Festival of Transport

25/7/99 25/7/99	**SANDTOFT TRANSPORT MUSEUM** Tel: 01724 711391 24hr info Including 30th Anniversary celebrations. Preview Saturday (Evening Running) 24 July 12.00-late. Gathering Day Sunday 25 July 10.00-18.00 *Museum- Transport*

Woodland Furniture Workshop

28/7/99 28/7/99	**RIEVAULX TERRACE AND TEMPLES** Tel: 01439 748283 Starts at 11.00. Cost: £5.00 *Historic Buildings*

Life In The Garden

30/7/99 30/7/99	**HARLOW CARR BOTANICAL GARDENS** Tel: 01423 565418 A fascinating art exhibition covering several subjects *Gardens- Botanical*

Garden Walk

30/7/99 30/7/99	**NUNNINGTON HALL** Tel: 01439 748283 £2.00 per person - inc NT Members - Normal Admission applies - 14.00 *Historic Houses*

The CLA Game Fair

30/7/99 1/8/99	**HAREWOOD HOUSE AND BIRD GARDEN** Tel: 0113 288 6331 Europe's greatest countryside event

attracts both enthusiasts and public in general - hundreds of stands, events together with 'have-a-go' country pursuits. Call for further information

Historic Houses & Gardens

Last Night At The Proms
31/7/99
31/7/99 NOSTELL PRIORY
Tel: 01924 863892
A spectacular outdoor concert with firework finale with the London Gala Orchestra and soloist Beryl Korman

Stately Homes

Diesel Weekend
31/7/99
1/8/99 KEIGHLEY AND WORTH VALLEY RAILWAY
Tel: 01535 645214/647777
An array of post-war diesel locomotives visiting the Worth Valley; a repeat of last year's amazing success

Railways Steam/Light

Legends of King Arthur
31/7/99
1/8/99 WHITBY ABBEY
Tel: 01947 603568
Labyrinth Productions. Magical stories about King Arthur, with Guinevere, Lancelot, Merlin, the Black Knight and the evil Morgan Le Fay. A£2.50 C£1.30 Concessions£1.90

Abbeys

Exhibition
31/7/99
31/8/99 NUNNINGTON HALL
Tel: 01439 748283
By members of the British Toymakers Guild

Historic Houses

Outdoor Music Afternoon
1/8/99
1/8/99 NUNNINGTON HALL
Tel: 01439 748283
By members of the York Concert Band 14.00-16.00

Historic Houses

Dizzy Spells and Wicked Wheelies
1/8/99
5/8/99 EAST RIDDLESDEN HALL
Tel: 01535 607075
The Young National Trust Theatre presents a fun enviornmental theatre where you can meet a witch and her dormouse, Nike the Tyke on a Bike, a horde of mini-beasts and many more. Show at 14.00 and 15.30. A£3.00 C£2.00. Box office 01765 609999. Separate charge for House

Historic Houses & Gardens

Ripon's Centenery Celebration Day
2/8/99
2/8/99 RIPON RACES
Tel: 01765 602156
First Race Time: 14.15

Racecourses

Troubadour Theatre present 'Alice in Wonderland'
6/8/99
6/8/99 LONGSHAW ESTATE
Tel: 01433 631757
Performance starts: 18.30. Bring rugs and picnics

National Parks

The Revels - A Venetian Masquerade
7/8/99 FOUNTAINS ABBEY AND STUDLEY ROYAL WATER GARDEN
7/8/99 Tel: 01765 608888
Nothing is what it appears in Studley Royal Water Garden! Come dressed in mask and costume to a Venice Carnival promenade. Entertainment includes comedy, music, acrobatics, street performers, magic and illusion with spectacular illuminations and fireworks. A£13.00 C£6.50 Family Ticket (A2+C2)£35.00. Food and drink on sale. Event starts at 17.30

Abbeys

Model Engineering Gala
7/8/99
8/8/99 ELSECAR - THE POWERHOUSE
Tel: 01226 740203
Model railways, boats, planes, cars, and many displays from societies from around the country

Museum- Science

Croquet on the Lawn
7/8/99
8/8/99 LONGSHAW ESTATE
Tel: 01433 631757
Cost: £1.00 per person, refundable deposit of £10.00. Time: 11.00-16.00

National Parks

Have-a-go Archery
7/8/99
8/8/99 ROCHE ABBEY
Tel: 01709 812739
Arrowflight, from 12.00. 14th century archers introduce visitors to the art of archery. A£2.50 C£1.30 Concessions£1.90

Abbeys

Have-a-go-Archery
7/8/99
8/8/99 WHITBY ABBEY
Tel: 01947 603568
Whitby Company of Archers. 14th century archers introduce visitors to the art of archery. A£1.70 C£0.90 Concessions£1.30

Abbeys

Ingrow Yard Brake Van Trips
8/8/99
8/8/99 KEIGHLEY AND WORTH VALLEY RAILWAY
Tel: 01535 645214/647777
Travel in a rare Southern Railway brake van hauled by L&NWR Coal Tank locomotive No. 1054 built in 1888 and still going

Further more detailed information on the attractions listed can be found in Best Guides *Visitor Attractions* Guide under the classifications shown

strong. This locomotive operates by
courtesy of the National Trust

Railways Steam/Light

Medieval Monastic Entertainers

10/8/99 RIEVAULX ABBEY
12/8/99 Tel: 01439 798228

Games, squire-training and talks on
weaponry and armour. Also, try your
hand at spinning, weaving and calligraphy and learn about herbal medicine.
A£3.50 C£1.80 Concessions£2.60

Abbeys

Animal Antics

11/8/99 EAST RIDDLESDEN HALL
11/8/99 Tel: 01535 607075

Storytelling in the garden and a visit by
Trusty the Hedgehog. 14.00-16.00.
Suitable for children ages 3-9

Historic Houses & Gardens

Discover Natures Wonders

11/8/99 RIEVAULX TERRACE AND TEMPLES
11/8/99 Tel: 01439 748283

Sensory awareness activity day for the
whole family. Starts at 11.00, please
wear suitable footwear and clothing and
bring a packed lunch. Booking essential.
Family Ticket(A2+C2)£13.00, individuals
£8.00 includes admission fee to house

Historic Buildings

Special Railway Days

11/8/99 SANDTOFT TRANSPORT MUSEUM
18/8/99 Tel: 01724 711391 24hr info

Special Railway Days including motor-
bus tour, Wednesday 11 and 18 August,
12.00-16.00

Museum- Transport

**"William Hill Great St. Wilfrid
Handicap" Day**

14/8/99 RIPON RACES
14/8/99 Tel: 01765 602156

First Race Time: 14.20

Racecourses

**Wynndebagge the Piper - Paul
Saunders**

14/8/99 MIDDLEHAM CASTLE
15/8/99 Tel: 01969 623899

Lively medieval music played on the
English pipes and a chance to learn pop-
ular period dances, from 12.00. A£2.50
C£1.30 Concessions£1.90 English
Heritage Members Free

Castles

Legends of King Arthur

14/8/99 SCARBOROUGH CASTLE
15/8/99 Tel: 01723 372451

Labyrinth Productions. Magical stories
about King Arthur, with Guinevere,

Lancelot, Merlin, the Black Knight and
the evil Morgan Le Fay. From 14.30.
A£3.50 C£1.80 Concessions£2.60

Historical Remains

The Pits

14/8/99 CLIFTON PARK MUSEUM
21/11/99 Tel: 01709 823635

An exhibition celebrating the mining heritage of the Rotherham area

Museums

Medieval Monastic Entertainers

17/8/99 KIRKHAM PRIORY
19/8/99 Tel: 01653 618768

Heuristics. Try your hand at calligraphy
or authentic period games as this popular duo take a lighthearted look at
monastic customs, crafts and lifestyles.
Learn about food preparation, herbs and
spices in cooking and medicine, the
mechanics of building, lifting and many
other skills. Part of Cistercian 900.
A£2.50 C£1.30 Concessions£1.90 English
Heritage Members - Free

Priory

An Ant's Eye View

18/8/99 EAST RIDDLESDEN HALL
18/8/99 Tel: 01535 607075

Children's activities in the garden, 14.00-
16.00. Suitable for children 4-9 years

Historic Houses & Gardens

Family Day

18/8/99 HARLOW CARR BOTANICAL GARDENS
18/8/99 Tel: 01423 565418

Special day for all the family with
quizzes, trails, games etc

Gardens- Botanical

Garden Walk

18/8/99 NUNNINGTON HALL
18/8/99 Tel: 01439 748283

Join the gardener for a stroll around the
magnificent gardens at Nunnington Hall
- 19.00 - £5.00 including glass of wine -
booking essential

Historic Houses

Open Air Theatre

20/8/99 BRIMHAM ROCKS
22/8/99 Tel: 01423 780688

Illyria presents Water Babies, an exciting
dramatisation of Charles Kingsley's
immortal story. Grounds open at 18.00
for performance at 19.00. Fri/Sat A£9.00
C£6.50; Sun A£8.00 C£6.00.
Refreshments on sale.

Scenic

**Last Night of the Proms Outdoor
Concert**

21/8/99 21/8/99	**Castle Howard** Tel: 01653 648444 Brilliant atmospheric concert in the fresh air with spectacular firework finale *Castles*

Race Meeting

21/8/99 **Ripon Races**
21/8/99 Tel: 01765 602156
First Race Time: 14.20

Racecourses

The Bard and the Blade

21/8/99 **Brodsworth Hall**
22/8/99 Tel: 01302 722598
Dramatic duels and dialogue from some
of Shakespeare's most famous plays.
A£3.50 C£1.80 Concessions£2.60

Historic Houses

Traditional Song

21/8/99 **Middleham Castle**
22/8/99 Tel: 01969 623899
The Dunns. A family of musicians per-
forming delightful unaccompanied song.
From 12.00. A£3.00 C£1.50
Concessions£2.30

Castles

A Victorian Cricket Weekend

21/8/99 **Scarborough Castle**
22/8/99 Tel: 01723 372451
Come along for a lazy afternoon and lis-
ten to the sound of leather on willow.
With various performers. A£3.00 C£1.30
Concessions£2.30

Historical Remains

Childrens Weekend

28/8/99 **Castle Howard**
30/8/99 Tel: 01653 648444
A weekend especially for the children
and grown-ups, special attractions in the
house and grounds

Castles

Aire Valley YFC Country Show

29/8/99 **East Riddlesden Hall**
29/8/99 Tel: 01535 607075
Sheep and cattle, crafts, dog agility, pet
show, heavy horses, brass band, children's activities and much more. On the
field. £1.00 admission or admission by
House ticket. 13.00-17.00

Historic Houses & Gardens

The Art of Hilda Carline

29/8/99 **York City Art Gallery**
29/8/99 Tel: 01904 551861
Mrs Stanley Spencer

Art Galleries

Have-a-go Archery

Helmsley Castle

29/8/99 **Helmsley Castle**
30/8/99 Tel: 01439 770442
Arrowflight. 14th century archers introduce visitors to the art of archery. From
12.00. A£2.50 C£1.30 Concessions£1.90
English Heritage Members Free

Castles

Medieval Entertainers

29/8/99 **Middleham Castle**
30/8/99 Tel: 01969 623899
Games, squire-training and talks on
weaponry and armour. Also, try your
hand at spinning, weaving and calligraphy and learn about herbal medicine.
A£3.00 C£1.50 Concessions£2.30

Castles

Medieval Murder Mystery

29/8/99 **Roche Abbey**
30/8/99 Tel: 01709 812739
Knights in Battle, from 12.00. A "who-
dunit" that enfolds as suspicion
between two opposing factions grow...
A£3.00 C£1.50 Concessions£2.30

Abbeys

European Weekend

29/8/99 **Sandtoft Transport Museum**
30/8/99 Tel: 01724 711391 24hr info
Display and operation of trolleybuses
and motorbuses from Europe. The museum has three trolleybuses from Europe.
The most recent one added to the collection is the unique trolleybus from
Portugal. Visiting trolleybus and buses
are being invited but if you own a vintage or classic car originating from
Europe this could be the event to bring it
along to

Museum- Transport

World War II Battle

29/8/99 **Scarborough Castle**
30/8/99 Tel: 01723 372451
Re-enacted by The WWII Living History
Association. A£4.00 C£2.00
Concessions£3.00

Historical Remains

Circus Skills

30/8/99 **East Riddlesden Hall**
30/8/99 Tel: 01535 607075
Learn to juggle and stilt walk. Join in the
magic of the Curious Eyebrows family
show at 15.00. Fun starts 12.00-16.00.
Suitable for children ages 4-13

Historic Houses & Gardens

Bank Holiday Meeting

30/8/99 **Ripon Races**
30/8/99 Tel: 01765 602156
First Race Time: 14.25

Further more detailed information on the attractions listed can be found in Best Guides *Visitor Attractions* Guide under the classifications shown

Racecourses

Race Meeting
31/8/99   **RIPON RACES**
31/8/99   Tel: 01765 602156
First Race Time: 14.30

Racecourses

The Yorkshire "Open"
1/9/99   **LEEDS CITY ART GALLERY**
1/10/99   Tel: 0113 247 8248
Open to anyone living and working in the region to submit their paintings, watercolours, drawings, photographs for consideration by a panel of selectors. The resulting exhibition sees up-and-coming as well as established professional artists alongside amateur talent.

Art Galleries

Exhibition
3/9/99   **NUNNINGTON HALL**
30/9/99   Tel: 01439 748283
Etchings and Watercolours by Richard Keeton

Historic Houses

War of the Worlds
4/9/99   **CASTLE HOWARD**
4/9/99   Tel: 01653 648444
Outdoor laser and firework spectacular

Castles

Elsecar Vintage Weekend
4/9/99   **ELSECAR - THE POWERHOUSE**
5/9/99   Tel: 01226 740203
Vehicles from a bygone age including cars, motorcycles, engines, trains, aircraft and memorabilia, plus entertainment for all the family. Commences 10.00 17.00 call for further information

Museum- Science

Rainbow Craft Fair
4/9/99   **NEWBY HALL AND GARDENS**
5/9/99   Tel: 01423 322583
Crafts galore, come and see specialists in their craft demonstrating and selling a wide range of crafts

Historic Houses & Gardens

Medieval Monastic Entertainers
4/9/99   **RIEVAULX ABBEY**
5/9/99   Tel: 01439 798228
Games, squire-training and talks on weaponry and armour. Also, try your hand at spinning, weaving and calligraphy and learn about herbal medicine. A£3.50 C£1.80 Concessions£2.60

Abbeys

Sowerby Bridge Rushbearing Festival 1999
4/9/99   **SOWERBY BRIDGE RUSHBEARING**

FESTIVAL 1999
5/9/99   Tel: 01422 836316
The focal point of this festival is the 16ft high, two-wheeled thatched rushcart, pulled by sixty local men dressed in panama hats, white shirts, black trousers and clogs. They are accompanied by music and teams of Morris dancers. The colourful procession is an unforgettable spectacle as it winds it way down from the village of Warley on the Saturday, through Sowerby Bridge and up the hill to Sowerby. On Sunday, after a Rushbearing service at St. Peter's Church, Sowerby, the procession continues to Ripponden via hilltop villages. The total distance covered is about 9 miles. All of the churches provide refreshments. Including barbecues with live music, school galas, Victorian craft/charity market, street entertainers, brass bands, country dancing, boat trips, a duck race and a canoe demonstration and various exhibitions. Most of the entertainment is free.

Festivals

Textillia III
4/9/99   **EAST RIDDLESDEN HALL**
12/9/99   Tel: 01535 607075
An exhibition of creative textile art by this talented group of ex-textile students in the Airedale Barn. 14.00 each Sunday a presentation on the history of needlework. Held 4,5,6,7,8,11,12 Sept

Historic Houses & Gardens

Music Afternoon
5/9/99   **RIEVAULX TERRACE AND TEMPLES**
5/9/99   Tel: 01439 748283
Performed by members of the York Concert Band. 14.00-16.00. Please bring a picnic

Historic Buildings

Discover Natures Wonders
11/9/99   **NUNNINGTON HALL**
11/9/99   Tel: 01439 748283
Sensory awareness activity day for the whole family - 11.00 start, suitable footwear and clothing - bring packed lunch - booking essential. Family Ticket(A2+C2)£15.00, Individuals £9.00 includes admission fee to house

Historic Houses

The Lion, the Witch, and the Wardrobe
11/9/99   **BRODSWORTH HALL**
12/9/99   Tel: 01302 722598
A children's classic performed by Labyrinth Productions. A£3.50 £1.80

Concessions£2.60

Historic Houses

Redcoats of George III
11/9/99 HELMSLEY CASTLE
12/9/99 Tel: 01439 770442
The 47th Foot. Living history encampment, drill, musket firing and a fascinating comparison between the uniform, weaponry and conditions of a British Soldier from 1778 and 1998, presented by this award-winning small group.
A£3.00 C£1.50 Concessions£2.30

Castles

Monastic Entertainers and 16th Century Music
11/9/99 ROCHE ABBEY
12/9/99 Tel: 01709 812739
Hautbois and Heuristics, from 12.00.
A£3.00 C£1.50 Concessions£2.30

Abbeys

King Charles I
11/9/99 YORK CITY ART GALLERY
17/10/99 Tel: 01904 551861
Portraits of the Martyr King

Art Galleries

Railart 99
11/9/99 NATIONAL RAILWAY MUSEUM
28/11/99 Tel: 01904 621261
Paintings by the Guild of Railway Artists

Museums

The Bilsdale Silver Band
12/9/99 RIEVAULX ABBEY
12/9/99 Tel: 01439 798228
Plainsong, chants and music from the 5th to the 16th century as part of Cistercian 900, 14.00-16.00. A£3.00 C£1.50 Concessions£2.30 English Heritage Members Free

Abbeys

York Festival of Food and Drink 1999
17/9/99 YORK FESTIVAL OF FOOD AND DRINK 1999
26/9/99 Tel: 01904 554430
The UK's largest, liveliest and tastiest city wide festival of food and drink returns with the City's treets once again being filled with a unique concoction of tastes, aromas and sounds from all over the world.

Festivals

Friends of Thomas The Tank Engine
18/9/99 KEIGHLEY AND WORTH VALLEY RAILWAY
19/9/99 Tel: 01535 645214/647777
Park you car at Marsh Lane Oxenhope, ride on Bertie and Bulgy to Oxenhope Station, the travel by train to meet Thomas, Percy, Diesel, Duck, Annie and Clarabel and other friends at Ingrow and

Keighley

Railways Steam/Light

Viking Living History
18/9/99 WHITBY ABBEY
19/9/99 Tel: 01947 603568
Saxon/Viking re-enactment performed by Anmod Dracon. A£1.70 C£0.90 Concessions£1.30

Abbeys

Scarborough Angling Festival
18/9/99 SCARBOROUGH ANGLING FESTIVAL 1999
26/9/99 Tel: 01723 507034
Sea-boat, freshwater fishing plus England Codingling Championships, guaranteed cash prizes £4,500, 55 silver cups and trophies plus many other prizes. A£3.50-£5.00, C£1.50-£3.00

Festivals

Pear Day
19/9/99 CANNON HALL
19/9/99 Tel: 01226 790270
A day of fruitful enlightenment with pear and culinary experts in the walled garden

Museums

Garden Walk
24/9/99 NUNNINGTON HALL
24/9/99 Tel: 01439 748283
£2.00 per person inc NT Members - Normal Admission applies. Starts at 14.00

Historic Houses

Lord Montagu's Regiment
25/9/99 EAST RIDDLESDEN HALL
26/9/99 Tel: 01535 607075
A living history re-enactment group will present scenes from the 17th century. As you walk through the house and garden you will experience a glimpse of domestic life, crafts, games, music, costume and armour

Historic Houses & Gardens

Living Heritage Craft Fair
25/9/99 NOSTELL PRIORY
26/9/99 Tel: 01924 863892
A tented village with arena entertainment, ongoing demonstrations, and children's attractions

Stately Homes

September Craft Fair
26/9/99 KELHAM ISLAND MUSEUM
26/9/99 Tel: 0114 272 2106
Many stalls offering a variety of quality gifts and crafts

Museum- Industrial

Elizabethan Gems

Further more detailed information on the attractions listed can be found in Best Guides *Visitor Attractions* Guide under the classifications shown

| 26/9/99 | **NUNNINGTON HALL** |
| 26/9/99 | Tel: 01439 748283 |

Peter Bull 14.00,15.00 & 16.00

Historic Houses

Ilkley Literature Festival 1999

| 1/10/99 | **ILKLEY LITERATURE FESTIVAL** |
| 31/10/99 | Tel: 01943 601210 |

Final dates have not been confirmed, please call for further details and festival programme. Ilkley Literature Festival is the largest festival in the North and presents a wide variety of events from readings to plays.

Festivals

Out of the Forest

| 2/10/99 | **EAST RIDDLESDEN HALL** |
| 3/10/99 | Tel: 01535 607075 |

A working display of woodcraft and furniture by creative woodworkers. Demonstrations, sales and advice. In the magnificent 17th century oak framed Airedale Barn

Historic Houses & Gardens

Friends of Thomas the Tank Engine

| 2/10/99 | **NATIONAL RAILWAY MUSEUM** |
| 5/10/99 | Tel: 01904 621261 |

Friends of Thomas the Tank Engine are making a very special visit to the Museum to give free rides. Children's activities and competitions make this event a must for Thomas fans everywhere. To find out more, call our Thomas 24 hour recorded information line on 01904 686282. Rides are free with admission

Museums

Exhibition

| 2/10/99 | **NUNNINGTON HALL** |
| 30/10/99 | Tel: 01439 748283 |

Découpage & Limited Prints by Joyce and Keith Henderson

Historic Houses

Vintage Locomotives Weekend

| 9/10/99 | **KEIGHLEY AND WORTH VALLEY RAILWAY** |
| 10/10/99 | Tel: 01535 645214/647777 |

Festival of Victorian Steam Engines and old fashioned carriages

Railways Steam/Light

East Midlands Doll Fair

| 10/10/99 | **NOSTELL PRIORY** |
| 10/10/99 | Tel: 01924 863892 |

A wonderful Doll Fair with dolls houses and teddies - 'a miniature wonderland.' Top quality collectors, artists and craftspeople bring old and soft dolls, doll-shouse dolls, miniatures, teddy bears, dollcraft materials, kits, magazines and

juvenilia. Refreshments available

Stately Homes

Apple Week

| 20/10/99 | **NUNNINGTON HALL** |
| 24/10/99 | Tel: 01439 748283 |

Display of apples plus delicious apple recipes in the tea room - during normal opening times

Historic Houses

Friends of Thomas The Tank Engine

| 23/10/99 | **ELSECAR - THE POWERHOUSE** |
| 24/10/99 | Tel: 01226 740203 |

Meet 'Thomas' and 'Sir Topham Hatt, The Fat Controller' open 10.00-17.00. A£2.00 C£1.00

Museum- Science

Music of the Normans and Plantagenesta

| 23/10/99 | **HELMSLEY CASTLE** |
| 24/10/99 | Tel: 01439 770442 |

12th and 13th century music to enjoy, with (safe) archery game for children, from 12.00. A£3.00 C£1.50 Concessions£2.30

Castles

A Look at 17th Century Life

| 24/10/99 | **EAST RIDDLESDEN HALL** |
| 24/10/99 | Tel: 01535 607075 |

A Costumed tour of the Hall takes place every fourth Sunday throughout the season and Sun-Tue & Thur from mid July-end of Aug excluding Bank Hol Mon and Sun in Sept. Also a tour for children at 14.00

Historic Houses & Gardens

Yorkshire Day

| 24/10/99 | **SANDTOFT TRANSPORT MUSEUM** |
| 24/10/99 | Tel: 01724 711391 24hr info |

Please call for further information

Museum- Transport

Autumn Antics

| 27/10/99 | **EAST RIDDLESDEN HALL** |
| 27/10/99 | Tel: 01535 607075 |

Mask Making 14.00-16.00. Suitable for children aged 4-9

Historic Houses & Gardens

Hallowe'en Steamings

| 31/10/99 | **ELSECAR - THE POWERHOUSE** |
| 31/10/99 | Tel: 01226 740203 |

Spooky fun aboard the Earl Fitzwilliam Steam Train, plus gruesome games, and fearsome fun. Trains 16.00-21.00. Booking essential, call for details

Museum- Science

Festival fo Crafts

6/11/99
7/11/99
EAST RIDDLESDEN HALL
Tel: 01535 607075
A wonderful selection of handmade crafts will be on sale in the Airdale Barn. £1.00 entry. Wheelchair access
Historic Houses & Gardens

Friends of Thomas the Tank Engine
6/11/99
7/11/99
MIDDLETON RAILWAY LEEDS
Tel: 0113 271 0320
Come along one and all and see Thomas chuffing his way along the branch line
Railways Steam/Light

Friends of Thomas the Tank Engine
13/11/99
14/11/99
MIDDLETON RAILWAY LEEDS
Tel: 0113 271 0320
Come along one and all and see Thomas chuffing his way along the branch line
Railways Steam/Light

Rydale Craft Fair
20/11/99
21/11/99
NUNNINGTON HALL
Tel: 01439 748283
10.30-15.30. £1.00 inc NT Members all proceeds to the National Trust
Historic Houses

BT Family Days - Edwardian Christmas Festival
27/11/99
28/11/99
NATIONAL RAILWAY MUSEUM
Tel: 01904 621261
Come and enjoy the atmosphere at the NRM as costumed characters recreate the excitement and nostalgia of the Edwardian era. To make the day extra special, Santa and his helpers will be dropping in with gifts for children. Come dressed in Edwardian costume and get free admission!
Museums

Santa Specials 1999
27/11/99
19/12/99
KEIGHLEY AND WORTH VALLEY RAILWAY
Tel: 01535 645214/647777
Santa Specials 1999: 27 & 28 Nov, Sat 4 & Sun 5 Dec, Sat 11 & Sun 12 Dec, Sat 18 & Sun 19 Dec. Britain's original and still the best! Our Santa Special trains remain as popular as ever! 1 hour steam-hauled journey on the Line. On-board entertainment and seasonally decorated stations. Visit from Santa and his team of elves and pixies with a quality present for children. Advance booking is essential. Santa Special Fares 99 (based on 98 prices and for reference only) A&C(4 years & over)£8.00. C(3 years & under)no seat reserved £4.00. Early booking is essential! Departure Times From Oxenhope 10.45, 11.55, 13.05, 14.15, 15.25. From Haworth 10.25, 11.35,

12.45, 13.55, 15.05. From Keighley 11.15, 12.25, 13.35, 14.45. Bookings open on the 1 Sept 1998, please call 01535 645214 with your credit card details from this date. Don't forget - a diesel multiple unit service also operates on the line on dates of Santa Special operation. See the Railway's seasonally decorated stations even if Santa Special trains are fully booked! Prices and times are based on 1998 schedule, please call venue in Sept 99 for times and prices
Railways Steam/Light

Christmas Concert
4/12/99
4/12/99
NUNNINGTON HALL
Tel: 01439 748283
Sing we Noel by the St Gregory's Minster Choir - 19.00. £9.50 inc Mulled wine and mince pies
Historic Houses

Victorian Christmas Market
4/12/99
5/12/99
KELHAM ISLAND MUSEUM
Tel: 0114 272 2106
Over 50 stalls with traditional gifts and crafts. Daily demonstrations, traditional music and dance and Christmas entertainment
Museum- Industrial

Santa Special
4/12/99
5/12/99
MIDDLETON RAILWAY LEEDS
Tel: 0113 271 0320
Get on board with Father Christmas, call station for timetable and prices
Railways Steam/Light

Christmas Fair
4/12/99
11/12/99
EAST RIDDLESDEN HALL
Tel: 01535 607075
Gifts galore for Christmas, mulled wine, mince pies, music, carols and crafts in the Airedale Barn. Free admission. Carol singing around the tree at 15.00 each Sunday. Fair held 4&5 and 11&12 Dec 11.00-16.30
Historic Houses & Gardens

Santa on the Steam Train
4/12/99
21/12/99
ELSECAR - THE POWERHOUSE
Tel: 01226 740203
Meet Father Christmas aboard the Elsecar Steam Railway. Presents and refreshments for all. Trains run weekends and pre-Christmas week. Booking essential, call for details
Museum- Science

Elsecar Christmas Fayre
11/12/99
12/12/99
ELSECAR - THE POWERHOUSE
Tel: 01226 740203
Crafts galore, plus festive entertainment

and refreshments, and a chances to visit Father Christmas aboard the Steam Railway. 11.00-18.00

Museum- Science

Santa Specials
11/12/99 MIDDLETON RAILWAY LEEDS
12/12/99 Tel: 0113 271 0320
Ho Ho Ho, Santa steams in to meet children arriving at the Middleton Colliery Railway. Call for timetables and prices

Railways Steam/Light

A Fascinating Hands-On Exhibition
11/12/99 EUREKA! THE MUSEUM FOR CHILDREN
31/12/99 Tel: 01422 330069
Children can use their own creativity and originality. This exhibition TBC

Museums

Bilsdale Silver Band
12/12/99 RIEVAULX ABBEY
12/12/99 Tel: 01439 798228
Plainsong, chants and music from the 5th to the 16th century as part of Cistercian 900, 14.00-16.00. A£3.00 C£1.50 Concessions£2.30 English Heritage Members Free

Abbeys

Santa Special
12/12/99 SANDTOFT TRANSPORT MUSEUM
19/12/99 Tel: 01724 711391 24hr info
Sunday's 12 & 19 December 11.00-17.00. Take a Train and Trolleybus ride to see Santa in his Grotto. Presents, Hot Drinks, Soft Drinks, Mince Pies, Live Christmas Music, Souvenir Shop

Museum- Transport

Santa Specials
18/12/99 MIDDLETON RAILWAY LEEDS
19/12/99 Tel: 0113 271 0320
All aboard for a Father Christmas special. Call for timetables and prices

Railways Steam/Light

York Millennium Mystery Plays 2000
22/6/00 YORK MILLENNIUM MYSTERY PLAYS 2000
22/7/00 Tel: 01904 635444
For the first time ever, the York Millennium Mystery Plays will take place in York Minster. Tickets will go on sale to group operators from Jan 1999. Please advise us at the earliest opportunity if you intend to place a group booking. There will be a facility for tickets to be ordered online or by telephone in the New Year. Tickets will go on sale to individuals in Spring 2000.

Festivals